世界职业技术教育发展大会
WORLD VOCATIONAL AND TECHNICAL EDUCATION DEVELOPMENT CONFERENCE



# 2022年 世界职业技术教育发展大会成果汇编

## （上册）

世界职业技术教育发展大会组委会

# Compilation of Achievements of World Vocational and Technical Education Development Conference 2022

（Volume I）

Organizing Committee of World Vocational and Technical Education Development Conference

中国教育出版传媒集团
高等教育出版社·北京

**图书在版编目（C I P）数据**

2022年世界职业技术教育发展大会成果汇编 ：全3册/世界职业技术教育发展大会组委会编. -- 北京 ：高等教育出版社，2023.6

ISBN 978-7-04-060676-8

Ⅰ. ①2… Ⅱ. ①世… Ⅲ. ①职业技术教育－世界－文集 Ⅳ. ①G71-53

中国国家版本馆CIP数据核字(2023)第104511号

策划编辑 贾瑞武　　责任编辑 董梦也　于海宁　　封面设计 赵　阳　　责任绘图 邓　超
版式设计 赵　阳　　责任校对 刘娟娟　　责任印制 赵义民

出版发行 高等教育出版社
社　　址 北京市西城区德外大街4号
邮政编码 100120
印　　刷 北京盛通印刷股份有限公司
开　　本 787mm×1092mm 1/16
本册印张 10.25
本册字数 190千字
购书热线 010-58581118
咨询电话 400-810-0598

网　　址 http://www.hep.edu.cn
http://www.hep.com.cn
网上订购 http://www.hepmall.com.cn
http://www.hepmall.com
http://www.hepmall.cn

版　　次 2023年6月第1版
印　　次 2023年6月第1次印刷
总 定 价 260.00元

本书如有缺页、倒页、脱页等质量问题，请到所购图书销售部门联系调换

物 料 号 60676-00

世界职业技术教育发展大会
World Vocational and Technical
Education Development Conference
中国·天津 TIANJIN·CHINA
世界职业技术教育发展大会
WORLD VOCATIONAL AND TECHNICAL
EDUCATION DEVELOPMENT CONFERENCE

世界职业技术教育发展大会
World Vocational and Technical
Education Development Conference
中国·天津 TIANJIN·CHINA

世界职业技术教育发展大会
World Vocational and Technical Education Development Conference
中国·天津 TIANJIN·CHINA

互动留言区

# 前言

为落实习近平主席在第七十六届联合国大会上提出的全球发展倡议，经国务院同意，教育部、中国联合国教科文组织全国委员会和天津市人民政府于2022年8月19日至20日共同举办了首届世界职业技术教育发展大会（以下简称大会）。在本届大会上，习近平主席向大会致贺信，孙春兰副总理发表视频致辞，来自123个国家和地区、17个国际组织的700余位国内外代表围绕“后疫情时代职业技术教育发展：新变化、新方式、新技能”这一主题进行了充分而有效的讨论，分享了各国发展职业教育的实践经验，取得了一系列重要会议成果。

本届大会是首次由中国政府举办的世界性、高规格的职业教育领域盛会，大会的成功举办具有“立示范、推发展”的里程碑意义。跳出教育看教育，教育与产业界、企业界和经济社会深度交融，是本届大会的最大特点和基本共识。各国教育部部长和国际组织负责人，以及相关专家学者重点介绍了所在国家或组织在推动职业教育发展方面的战略、政策、项目、平台等经验，提出了希望进一步加强职业教育国际合作交流的意愿和建议。经过讨论，各国与会嘉宾一致认为，在世界百年未有之大变局和新型冠状病毒感染疫情全球大流行交织叠加背景下，职业教育是促进公平全纳、服务每位公民特别是弱势群体人生出彩的重要通道，是提升产业效能、促进就业创业的重要途径，以职业教育促进经济复苏是各国的重要共识，携手推动全球职业教育高质量发展、助力建设后疫情时代美好世界，是摆在世界各国教育界面前的一个重大课题。大会的主题充分反映了时代发展趋势，与全球经济社会发展和职业教育未来发展重点，以及联合国倡导的可持续发展议程高度契合、紧密相关。大会搭建了崭新的世界职业教育发展公共平台，在提供高质量职业技术教育与培训产品供给、赋能劳动者就业创业、提升参与当地和全球社区事务能力、促进全民终身学习、促进人的全面发展和获得感，助力实现全球绿色经济发展和社会可持续发展等方面开展了丰富和深入的探讨。会议还提出了许多可供继续研究的问题。为便于大会成果总结和进一步交流，在各方的共同支持下，世界职业技术教育发展大会组委会对大会有关资料进行了整理并汇编成册，涉及中文、英语、法语、西班牙语、俄语、塔吉克语、日语、德语、泰语等 9 种语言。汇编共分三册，上册为开幕式、主论坛、闭幕式，收录了习近平主席贺信、孙春兰副总理视频致辞、重要嘉宾演讲稿、《天津倡议》、筹建世界职业技术教育发展联盟的倡议和创设国际职教大奖的倡议等内容；中册收录了围绕数字化赋能、产教融合、绿色技术、技能与减贫、促进公平、终身学习、科学与工程教育等主题研讨的十四个平行论坛部分嘉宾演讲稿；下册收录了本届大会及同期活动综述、主要媒体报道，以及由北京大学教育经济研究所哈巍教授牵头研制的《国际视野与中国国情——2022 年世界职业技术教育发展报告》，附录包含了参会国家（地区）和十四个平行论坛发言嘉宾名单详表，以供读者查阅。

本汇编力求全面客观地反映世界各国职业教育发展的共同关切，展示各国为推进职业教育发展进行的实践探索，以期为后疫情时代职业教育功能定位、职责使命和发展方向提供借鉴和参考。收录的成果具有三个鲜明特征：一是广泛性和代表性，从各国和各地区嘉宾代表的发言中遴选了部分具有代表性的发言文稿，既包括发达国家，也包括广大发展中国家，所进行的对话具有广泛的代表性和示范价值；二是时代性和实践性，嘉宾发言稿主要围绕后疫情时代各国职业教育发展所面临的共同问题，思考破解之道，力求完整呈现所做的探索和努力；三是前瞻性和引领性，通过研究具体问题，提炼出共性问题，探讨提出未来发展方向的建议。

职业教育是未来研究、创造和技术创新、实现高水平开放的重要来源，职业教育的国际化，已成为不可逆转的时代潮流。本次大会提供了落实全球发展倡议的经验，达成了后疫情时代全球职业教育发展普遍共识，搭建了国际职业教育交流合作崭新平台和机制，是中国职业教育不断融入世界服务大局的一个缩影。未来，中国愿进一步学习借鉴国际先进的职业教育发展经验，也愿与各国共享改革发展成果，以更加开放的姿态和自觉的担当，为建设更高水平的现代职业教育、助力建设人类命运共同体作出积极贡献。期待中外各方加强务实合作，共同推进联合国 2030 年可持续发展议程的落实，为构建人类命运共同体注入“技能力量”。

希望通过本书的出版，为中外从事职业教育相关工作的研究者、实践者了解中国职业教育发展成果及全球职业教育发展方向提供借鉴。本书的编辑出版得到各有关单位、中外发言嘉宾、高等教育出版社的大力支持和帮助，组委会成员单位、各平行论坛协助组织单位付出了辛勤努力，在此一并表示衷心感谢。由于时间仓促，疏漏难免，请广大读者提出宝贵意见。

世界职业技术教育发展大会组委会

2022 年 12 月 5 日

# Preface

To implement the Global Development Initiative put forward by President Xi Jinping at the 76th Session of the United Nations General Assembly, the Ministry of Education of China, the Chinese National Commission for UNESCO and the Tianjin Municipal People's Government jointly organized the first World Vocational and Technical Education Development Conference (hereinafter referred to as WVTEDC) from August 19 to 20, 2022, with the consent of the State Council. President Xi Jinping sent a congratulatory letter to the Conference, Vice Premier Sun Chunlan delivered a video speech, and more than 700 domestic and foreign delegates from 123 countries and regions and 17 international organizations had a thorough and productive discussion on the theme of "Vocational and Technical Education Development in the Post-pandemic Era—New Changes, New Ways and New Skills", sharing practical experiences of developing vocational education in various countries, and achieving a series of significant outcomes.

WVTEDC is the first world-class, high-profile event organized by the Chinese government concerning vocational education, marking the milestone of setting an example and promoting further progress. The broader view to look into education, and the deep integration of education with industries, enterprises and the economy and society are the most important feature and basic consensus of the Conference. Ministers of Education and heads of international organizations, as well as relevant experts and scholars, introduced the experiences on strategies, policies, projects and platforms of their countries and organizations in promoting the development of vocational education, and put forward their wishes and suggestions to further strengthen international cooperation and exchange in this field. After discussion, the delegates agreed that in the context of the world's profound changes unseen in a century and the global pandemic, vocational education is an important access to promote fairness and inclusiveness for every citizen, especially the disadvantaged groups, to excel in life, and is an essential way to enhance industrial efficiency and promote employment and entrepreneurship. To promote economic recovery by means of vocational education has been an important consensus of all countries. It is a major issue faced by education circles around the world to jointly promote the high-quality development of global vocational education so as to help build a better world in the post-pandemic era. The theme of WVTEDC was fully in line with the theme of the times, and was highly consistent with and closely related to global economic and social development and the future development priorities of vocational education, as well as the *United Nations 2030 Agenda for Sustainable Development*. The Conference served as a new public platform for the development of vocational education around the world. In-depth discussions were carried out on providing high-quality vocational and technical education and training products, empowering workers to find jobs and start businesses, enhancing their ability to participate in local and global community affairs, promoting lifelong learning for all, fostering all-round human development and sense of fulfillment, and helping to achieve global green economic development and sustainable social development. Many questions were raised for continuous research. In order to facilitate the implementation of achievements and further exchange, with the joint support of all parties, the Organizing Committee of World Vocational and Technical Education Development Conference compiled the materials related to the Conference, covering nine languages, including Chinese, English, French, Spanish, Russian, Tajik, Japanese, German and Thai. The compilation is divided into three volumes. Volume I includes the opening ceremony, the keynote session and the closing ceremony, containing the congratulatory letter from President Xi Jinping, the video speech from Vice Premier Sun Chunlan, the speeches by important guests, the Tianjin Initiative, the initiative to establish the World TVET league and the initiative to establish the International TVET Prize. Volume II contains the selected speeches delivered at the 14 parallel sessions on the themes of digital empowerment, integration of industry and education, green technology, skills and poverty reduction, promotion of equity, lifelong learning, science and engineering education, etc. Volume III contains the introduction to WVTEDC and the parallel activities, major media digests and the *Global Vision and China's Reality—World Vocational and Technical Education Development Report 2022*, led by Professor Ha Wei from the Institute of Economics of Education, Peking University. The appendices include the lists of countries (regions) participated and speakers of 14 parallel sessions for readers' reference.

The Compilation aims to comprehensively and objectively reflect the common concerns of vocational education development in various countries around the world and present the practical explorations conducted by these countries to promote the development of vocational education, with a view to providing a reference for the functions, responsibilities and directions of vocational education in the post-pandemic era. The achievements included in the Compilation have three distinctive features: Firstly, they are extensive and representative; the speeches are selected from those delivered by delegates from various countries and regions, including the discussions from both developed countries and developing countries, which are extensively representative and of exemplary value. Secondly, they are contemporary and practical; the speeches of the delegates mainly focus on the common problems faced by all the countries regarding the development of vocational education in the post-pandemic era, and reflect on the practical approach and endeavour to present the exploration and efforts having been made. Thirdly, they are forward-looking and groundbreaking; by studying specific issues, they distil common problems, discuss and put forward proposals for the direction of future development.

Vocational education is an important source for future research, creativity and technological innovation, and high-level opening-up, and its internationalization has become an irreversible trend of the times. The Conference provided experience in implementing the Global Development Initiative, reached a general consensus on global vocational education development in the post-pandemic era, and built a brand new platform and mechanism for international vocational education exchange and cooperation, which illustrates the continuous integration of China's vocational education into the world service. In the future, China is not only willing to further learn from the international advanced experience of vocational education development, but also willing to share the fruits of reform and development with other countries, and make positive contributions to building a higher level of modern vocational education and helping to build a community with a shared future of mankind with a more open attitude and conscious commitment. It is expected that all parties in China and abroad will strengthen practical cooperation, jointly promote the implementation of the *United Nations 2030 Agenda for Sustainable Development*, and inject "skill power" in building a community with a shared future for mankind.

It is hoped that the publication of this Compilation will provide a reference for researchers and practitioners engaged in vocational education-related work in China and abroad to learn about the achievements of China's vocational education development and the direction of global vocational education development. This book is edited and published with the support and help of all relevant units, speakers, and the Higher Education Press. The members of the Organizing Committee and the co-organizers of the parallel sessions have also made great efforts. We would like to express our sincere thanks to them all. Due to the shortage of time, imperfections are inevitable, and we sincerely appreciate the readers' valuable comments.

Organizing Committee of World Vocational and
Technical Education Development Conference
December 5, 2022

## 怀进鹏
Huai Jinpeng

中华人民共和国教育部部长
Minister of Education of the People's Republic of China

跳出教育看教育，教育与产业界、企业界和经济社会深度交融，是这次职业教育大会最大的特色，也是我们本届大会的基本共识。

It is the most prominent feature and basic consensus of this conference that we consider education beyond education circles and pay attention to the deep integration of education with industrial circles, enterprises, economy and society.

## 夏泽翰
Shahbaz Khan

联合国教科文组织驻华代表处主任
Director of the UNESCO Beijing Office

中国作为一个负责任的大国，为努力解决后疫情时代全球职业技术教育与培训的新问题召开了此次大会。

This Conference is a part of China's responses as a responsible great nation trying to support tackling the emerging global TVET issues in a post-pandemic era.

注：精选发言排名不分先后。

## 罗伯特·詹金斯
**Robert Jenkins**

联合国儿童基金会教育及青少年发展全球负责人
Director of Education and Adolescent Development of UNICEF

热烈祝贺中国政府举办首届世界职业技术教育发展大会，彰显了中国对培养技术技能人才的有力承诺。

Let me congratulate the Chinese government for hosting the first World Vocational and Technical Education Development Conference, demonstrating a strong commitment to skills development.

## 穆费里亚特·卡米勒
**Muferihat kamil**

埃塞俄比亚劳动与技能部部长
Ethiopia's Minister of FDRE Ministry of Labor and Skills

我希望这次会议能够像一盏明灯一样照亮前方的路，帮助我们应对重重挑战。同时也希望我们能够充分利用这次机会，进一步巩固迄今为止我们在职业技术教育与培训方面取得的成就。

I hope that the conference which shades light on new ways of overcoming those challenges also takes advantage of the opportunities to build on our achievements so far in TVET.

## 恩赫阿木格朗
**Enkh-Amgalan**

蒙古国教育科学部部长
Minister of Education and Science of Mongolia

本次世界职业技术教育发展大会至关重要。

Today's World Vocational and Technical Education Development Conference is very crucial.

## 诺莱妮·艾哈迈德
Noraini Ahmad

马来西亚高等教育部部长
Minister of Higher Education of Malaysia

在培养相关行业的合格劳动力，实现国家的社会和经济目标方面，职业技术教育与培训的教育体系具有巨大的潜力。

The TVET education track has tremendous potential in producing a competent workforce in related industries to meet the social and economic objectives of the country.

## 古德勒克·奥皮亚
Goodluck Opiah

尼日利亚教育部国务部长
Minister of State for Education of Nigeria

这是一次具有历史意义的盛会。

This is a historic event.

## 拉纳·坦维尔·侯赛因
Rana Tanveer Hussain

巴基斯坦联邦教育与职业培训部部长
Minister of Federal Education and Professional Training of Pakistan

此次会议将成为两国共同通过“一带一路”和中巴经济走廊实现地区繁荣目标的一个重要倡议和里程碑。

This conference will prove to be a significant initiative and a major milestone towards the mutual resolve of both nations to attain the objectives of regional prosperity through the BRI and CPEC.

**陈振声**
**Chan Chun Sing**

新加坡教育部部长
Minister for Education of Singapore

本次大会主题是“后疫情时代职业技术教育发展：新变化、新方式、新技能”。这一主题对我们这代人而言相当贴切。

The theme of today’s conference, ‘Vocational and Technical Education Development in the Post-pandemic Era—New Changes, New Ways and New Skills’, is an apt one for our generation.

**安黛文**
**Ann Derwin**

爱尔兰驻华大使
Irish Ambassador to China

与中国一样，爱尔兰致力于通过提供高质量、更方便、更灵活的教育和培训计划，提高公民的社会参与水平，推动实现全民充分社会参与这个目标。

Like China, Ireland is committed to increasing levels of inclusion through the provision of high quality, more accessible and flexible education and training programmes and supports with the aim of enabling every citizen to participate fully in society.

**赵厚麟**
**Zhao Houlin**

国际电信联盟秘书长
Secretary-General of the International Telecommunication Union

中国政府发起并主办了这一次职业技术教育发展国际会议，意义重大。

The Chinese government proposes and organizes this World Vocational and Technical Education Development Conference, which is of great importance.

### 科菲·恩盖桑
**Koffi N'Guessan**

科特迪瓦技术教育、职业培训与学习部部长
Minister of Côte d'Ivoire Ministry of Technical Education, Vocational Training and Apprenticeship (METFPA)

通过全球范围内的经验交流与分享，本次论坛将有利于勾画后疫情时代职业教育的发展趋势。

Ces réflexions à l'échelle mondiale, contribueront à décrire l'évolution post-pandémique de l'enseignement professionnel, notamment grâce au partage d'expériences.

### 阿道夫·姆肯达
**Adolf Mkenda**

坦桑尼亚教育、科学和技术部部长
Minister of Education, Science and Technology, Tanzania

这次会议将激发中国和坦桑尼亚之间以及非洲和中国之间在技术和职业培训领域更深入的合作。

This conference will inspire even deeper cooperation between China and Tanzania and between Africa and China on matters of technical and vocational training.

### 柯马凯
**Michael Crook**

中国工合国际委员会主席、北京培黎职业学院理事
Chairman of International Committee for the Promotion of Chinese Industrial Cooperatives, Member of the Board of Beijing Bailie University

让我们大家发扬工合精神，“努力干、一起干”，积极开展国际民间友好往来，积极参与推进“一带一路”建设，为践行构建人类命运共同体历史使命作出新的贡献。

Let us all carry forward the spirit of "working hard, and working together", carry out international people-to-people friendly exchanges, participate in the construction of the "Belt and Road" initiative actively, and make new contributions to the historic mission of building a community with a shared future for mankind!

# 目录

## 开幕式



## 主论坛

## 闭幕式

# Contents

## Opening Ceremony



## Keynote Session

# Closing Ceremony

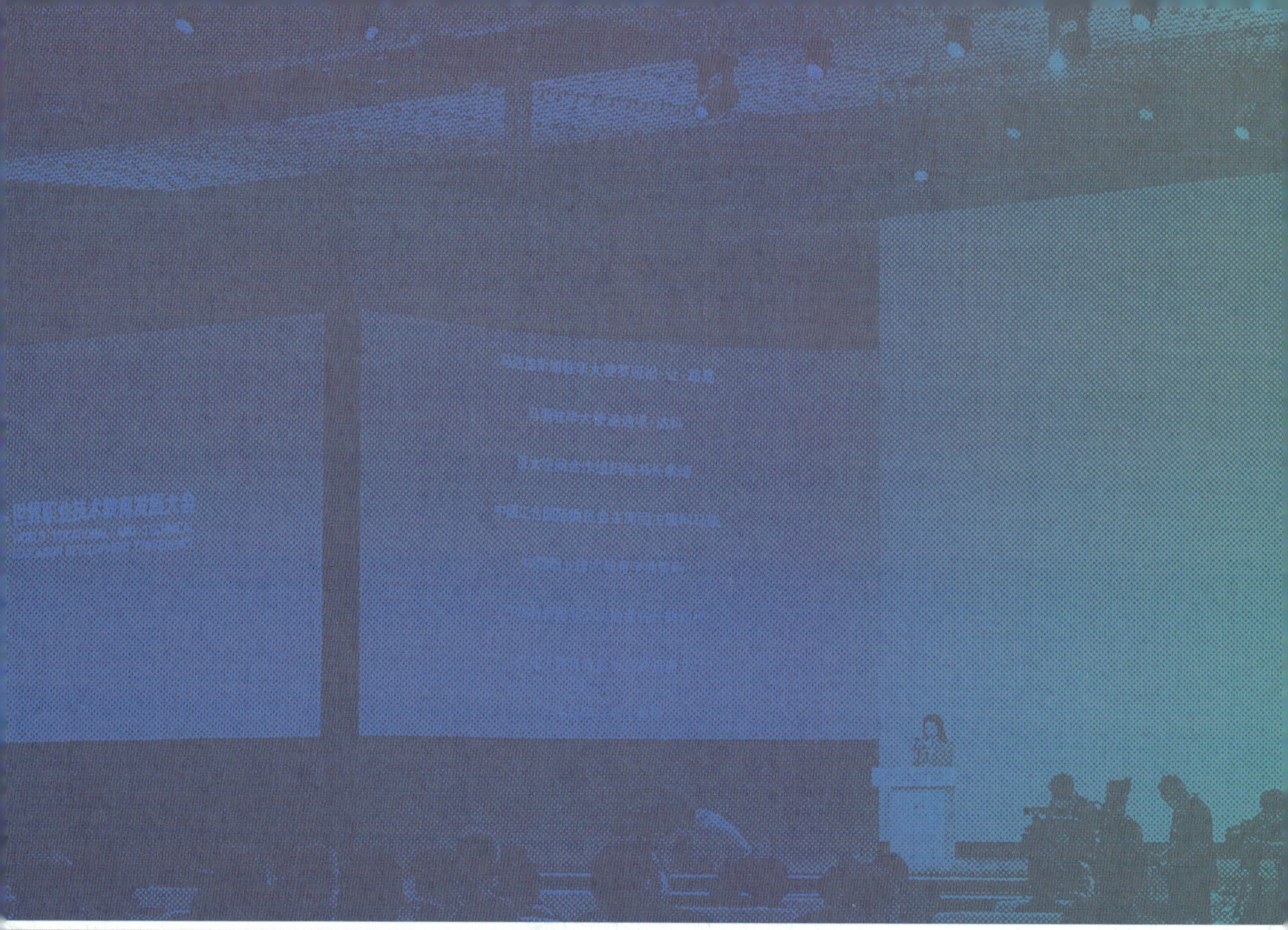

# 开幕式

# Opening Ceremony

# 一

# 习近平向世界职业技术教育发展大会致贺信

新华社北京8月19日电　8月19日，国家主席习近平向世界职业技术教育发展大会致贺信。

习近平指出，职业教育与经济社会发展紧密相连，对促进就业创业、助力经济社会发展、增进人民福祉具有重要意义。中国积极推动职业教育高质量发展，支持中外职业教育交流合作。中方愿同世界各国一道，加强互学互鉴、共建共享，携手落实全球发展倡议，为加快落实联合国2030年可持续发展议程贡献力量。

世界职业技术教育发展大会当日在天津开幕，主题为“后疫情时代职业技术教育发展：新变化、新方式、新技能”，由教育部、天津市人民政府共同主办。

# I. Xi Jinping Extends Congratulations to World Vocational and Technical Education Development Conference

BEIJING, Aug. 19 (Xinhua)—Chinese President Xi Jinping on Friday sent a congratulatory letter to the World Vocational and Technical Education Development Conference.

In his letter, Xi Jinping pointed out that vocational education is closely linked with economic and social development, and has great significance for promoting employment and entrepreneurship, boosting economic and social development, and improving people's well-being.

China, he said, actively pushes forward the high-quality development of vocational education, and supports exchanges and cooperation in vocational education with other countries. The Chinese side stands ready to work with other countries in the world to strengthen mutual learning, joint contribution and shared benefits, join hands to implement the Global Development Initiative, and contribute to accelerating the implementation of the UN 2030 Agenda for Sustainable Development, Xi added.

With the theme of "Vocational and Technical Education Development in the Post-pandemic Era—New Changes, New Ways and New Skills," the conference, co-hosted by the Chinese Ministry of Education and the Tianjin municipal government, opened on Friday in Tianjin.

# 二

# 世界职业技术教育发展大会召开<br>孙春兰宣读习近平主席贺信并<br>发表视频致辞

新华社天津8月19日电　世界职业技术教育发展大会19日在天津开幕，中共中央政治局委员、国务院副总理孙春兰宣读习近平主席贺信并发表视频致辞。

孙春兰指出，习近平主席的贺信，深刻阐述了职业教育对促进经济发展和民生改善的重要作用，为深化职业教育国际交流与合作增添了信心和动力。中国政府高度重视职业教育，坚持职业教育的类型定位，深化职教改革，建成世界规模最大的职教体系，既为高质量发展提供了重要支撑，也能够满足不同学生的成长需要，拓宽职业发展前景，让每个人都有人生出彩的机会。中国愿与国际社会一道，搭建多层次、宽领域的合作平台，加大对发展中国家特别是非洲国家职业教育支持力度，推动各国人民共享职业教育发展成果。

举办世界职业技术教育发展大会是全球发展高层对话会成果清单的重要内容，本次大会以“后疫情时代职业技术教育发展：新变化、新方式、新技能”为主题，有关国际组织负责人、各国教育部长、驻华使节等线上线下深入交流研讨。

# Ⅱ. World Vocational and Technical Education Development Conference Opening, Sun Chunlan Reading the Congratulatory Letter from President Xi Jinping and Delivering a Video Speech

TIANJIN, Aug. 19 (Xinhua)—World Vocational and Technical Education Development Conference opened on August 19th in Tianjin. Sun Chunlan, member of the Political Bureau of the CPC Central Committee and Vice Premier of the State Council, read a congratulatory letter from President Xi Jinping and delivered a video speech.

Sun Chunlan pointed out that the congratulatory letter from President Xi Jinping profoundly elaborated on the important role of vocational education in promoting economic development and improving people's livelihood, adding confidence and impetus to deepening international exchanges and cooperation in vocational education. The Chinese government attaches great importance to vocational education, adheres to the typical orientation of vocational education, deepens the reform of vocational education, and builds the world's largest vocational education system, which not only provides important support for high-quality development, but also can meet the growing needs of different students, broaden the career development prospects, and give everyone a chance to make a difference in life. China is willing to work with the international community to build a multi-level and wide-ranging cooperation platform, increase support for vocational education in developing countries, especially in Africa, and promote people around the world to share the achievements of vocational education development.

Holding World Vocational and Technical Education Development Conference is an important part of the list of achievements of High-level Dialogue on Global Development. With the theme of "Vocational and Technical Education Development in the Post-pandemic Era—New Changes, New Ways and New Skills, " the conference provides an avenue of online and offline in-depth exchanges and discussions among the heads of relevant international organizations, heads of education ministries of various countries, and ambassadors in China.

# 三

## 天津市委书记致辞

李鸿忠

世界职业技术教育发展大会19日在天津开幕。天津市委书记李鸿忠致欢迎辞。他说，要深入学习贯彻习近平主席贺信精神，以举办此次大会为契机，树立科学的职教理念，坚持立德树人，坚持以用立业，坚持提质培优，深度参与国际职业技术教育交流合作，对接产业和技术发展需求，推动产教融合、工学结合，努力把职业教育打造成为与普通教育并行贯通的开放式教育、培养能力的实践教育、面向市场的就业教育、服务全民的终身教育，以优异成绩迎接党的二十大胜利召开。

来源：天津日报（节选） 2022年8月20日

# 四

## 联合国教科文组织执行局主席致辞

塔玛拉·拉斯托瓦克·西亚马什维利
Tamara Rastovac Siamashvili

尊敬的中华人民共和国国务院副总理孙春兰女士，尊敬的中华人民共和国教育部部长怀进鹏先生，尊敬的阁下，与会来宾，女士们、先生们，很荣幸能够在后疫情时代世界职业技术教育发展大会开幕式上致辞。

2022 年 4 月 8 日是具有划时代意义的一天，这天联合国教科文组织执行局在其第 214 届会议上通过了“联合国教科文组织职业技术教育和培训新方案(2022—2029 年)”。该方案制定时充分考虑国际趋势，包括后疫情时代如何走上复苏之路。我们生活在一个全球化和不确定的时代，各种主要趋势正在改变我们的教育系统。

疫情前，我们就能感受经济、科技、环境、人口方面的变化，疫情更加速其转变。经济的快速数字化彻底转变了劳动力市场，市场所需技能也不同往常。联合国教科文组织报告显示，具有职业技术教育和培训背景的求职者在找工作时障碍重重，因为经济发展所需的技能改变，求职者的优势不再突出。正因为如此，此次会议将重点关注数字赋能、绿色科技、教育与行业深度融合、技能培养、减贫、促进平等和终生学习等话题。

女士们，先生们，此次疫情严重影响了职业技术教育与培训学生的学业，网上学习使他们无法正常进行技能培训，毕竟很大一部分能给他们提供实习机会的私企被迫关停。此次全球性健康危机使不同社会经济群体和城郊间的差距进一步加大，数字鸿沟愈发明显。2020 年 4 月，联合国教科文组织指出，因学校关停，全球 15 亿学生中有一半因经济和技术原因无法进行线上学习，大部分受影响学生来自发展中国家。

职业技术教育与培训机会不均等也导致了些许问题，数据显示，发展中国家招生人数明显低于高收入国家。另外，性别、社会经济背景差异也影响了职业教育学生组成。

女士们，先生们，职业技术教育与培训课程内容须符合当下和未来劳动力市场的需求，这点也是当务之急。目前，劳动力市场供需不对等影响学生就业，也不利于行业发展，这是全球性问题。数字、绿色经济发展急需不同技能，职业技术教育与培训课程内容应紧贴新需求，提高课程灵活度。

最后，职业教育费用要比普通教育高，有效管理和资金支持对职业技术教育与培训教学至关重要。费用高主要是因为职业教育需购进必要设备器材，且培训由企业提供。这一点在加强管理和监管时需注意。

尊敬的与会来宾，女士们，先生们，以上就是我们所处的大环境，下面我要继续谈联合国教科文组织职业技术教育与培训新方案（2022—2029 年），此方案旨在支持改进技能培训，以提高就业率和个人生活质量。此方案有 3 个要点：一是培育个人学习、工作和生活所需技能是根本；二是培育包容可持续发展经济所需的技能是关键；三是培育构建包容和平社会的技能是宗旨。为促进此方案顺利开展，联合国教科文组织将充分利用自己职业教育方面的专业知识，充分调动各大机构、国际专家和位于德国波恩的联合国教科文组织职业技术教育与培训国际中心。

为实现以上目标，我们将继续推动各国把职业技术教育与培训和终生学习结合在一起，努力使职业技术教育和培训成为个人学习、工作和生活的康庄大道。因此，我们需合力对青壮年进行新技能培训，帮助他们解锁潜力，在社会、经济和环境的剧烈变化中游刃有余。

# Ⅳ. Welcome Remarks by the Chairperson of the Executive Board of UNESCO

Your Excellency Ms Sun Chunlan, Vice Premier of the People's Republic of China,
Your Excellency Mr Huai Jinpeng, Minister of Education of the People's Republic of China,
Excellencies,
Distinguished participants,
Ladies and gentlemen,

I am pleased to address this message to you today at the opening of the 2022 World Vocational and Technical Education Development Conference in the Post-pandemic Era.

The 8th of April 2022 marked a key milestone when UNESCO's Executive Board adopted, at its 214th session, the new UNESCO Strategy for Technical and Vocational Education and Training (TVET) for the period 2022 to 2029. The Strategy has been developed taking into consideration global trends, including the path to recovery in the post-pandemic era.

Indeed, we live in a globalized and uncertain era where various major trends are transforming our education systems. If the world was undergoing transformations in the economic, technological, environmental and demographic fronts before the pandemic, its impact has certainly accelerated these transitions. The rapid digitization of the economy has completely transformed the labour market and affected the skills supply. UNESCO reports have shown that people entering the work force with a TVET background face some difficulties as the evolution of the skills needed by the economy gradually makes their competencies obsolete. For this reason, topics such as digital empowerment, green technology, industry/education integration, skills development, poverty reduction, the promotion of equity and lifelong learning will be of great importance to this conference.

Ladies and gentlemen, the COVID-19 pandemic and its repercussions particularly disturbed the pedagogical continuity for TVET students as the move to online instruction hindered their access to practical skills training and the great majority of apprenticeships were disrupted by the closure of private firms. The global health crisis has also exacerbated the "digital divide" by widening gaps between socio-economic groups, as well as between urban and rural areas. In April 2020, UNESCO reported that half of the 1.5 billion students affected by school closures worldwide faced economic and technical barriers to online learning—most of them in developing countries.

Several challenges are due to access to TVET as statistics show that developing countries enroll fewer students than higher income countries. Furthermore, various and sometimes intersectional disparities related to gender and socio-economic background are clearly visible in the composition of the TVET student body.

Ladies and gentlemen, the alignment of TVET curricula with the current and future needs of the labour market should be another key priority. Indeed, the current lack of synergy between supply and demand in the labour market has a negative impact on TVET graduates, as well as industries. This challenge is global and illustrates why TVET curricula should be structured with agility around the emerging need for skills in relation to the digital and green economy.

Finally, effective governance and funding are essential as the pedagogical delivery of TVET is often more expensive than that of general education. These higher costs, mainly due to the fact that equipment is necessary and training is provided by firms, should be taken into consideration to foster adequate governance and regulatory structures.

Distinguished participants, ladies and gentlemen, having briefly recalled these current tendencies, allow me to come back to the new UNESCO Strategy for TVET (2022-2029) which aims to support and improve skills development to increase employment levels and improve individuals' quality of life. This Strategy has formulated three main priorities. Firstly, developing skills for all individuals to learn, work and live is fundamental. Secondly, developing skills for inclusive and sustainable economies has been set as a key line of action. Thirdly, we consider that skills development should be aimed at building inclusive and peaceful societies. It will lever key internal expertise of the organisation in the domain of TVET, and will mobilise its key institutes, its network of international experts and the work of the UNESCO-UNEVOC International Centre in Bonn, Germany.

With these goals in mind, we will continue to support countries to enhance the relevance of their technical and vocational education and training systems within a lifelong learning perspective and seek to strategically put forward TVET to be a pathway for individuals to learn, work and live.

We must reunite our collective efforts to equip youth and adults with new skills, helping them unlock their potential to successfully navigate the social, economic, and environmental transformations that the world is undergoing.

# 五

# 联合国儿童基金会教育及青少年发展全球负责人致辞

罗伯特 · 詹金斯
Robert Jenkins

首先，热烈祝贺中国政府举办首届世界职业技术教育发展大会，彰显了中国对培养技术技能人才的有力承诺。我是联合国儿童基金会教育及青少年发展全球负责人罗伯特 · 詹金斯。很荣幸在本次大会上致辞。

新型冠状病毒疫情暴发之前，全球已有 8.25 亿学龄儿童无法在 2030 年前掌握最基本的中等水平技能。很多儿童未能做好准备，应对成年后的个人、社会及经济生活方面的挑战。

新冠病毒疫情加剧了这场学习危机，目前，超过 1.36 亿的中学生无法参与远程学习，包括最为弱势的群体。青少年在发展关键技能时面临更多障碍，其影响将延续一生。这一代青少年未来的潜在收入损失可能高达 21 万亿美元。

当今世界经历着快速变化，气候变化、科技发展、人口流动、冲突和流行病正在迅速重塑社会，未来的工作格局日益不可预测，很多青年人日后可能会从事今日完全未知的工作。面临种种变化，年轻人掌握全方位技能变得更为关键。这包括会读会算等基础技能，也包括可迁移能力，或被称为核心能力、21 世纪技能，还有用来畅游数字世界的数字技能以及创业技能和职业技能。这些都有利于年轻人应对快速变化的未来。可迁移能力对于年轻人成长为终身学习者至关重要，使他们得以随时获得新知、放下旧规、温故知新，步入职场、高效工作、做出明智决策、积极参与社会生活，并支持他们进一步巩固和发展包括基础技能、数字技能和职业技能在内的其他技能。

在全球层面，联合国儿童基金会与 120 多个国家的政府、私营部门、社会团体及青年组织合作，规模化推进青少年核心能力发展，尤其关注最为弱势的青少年群体，直接影响 3 300 多万名儿童和青少年。通过开展政府合作，提升当地教育和技能发展水平，使更多学生受益。在中国，联合国儿童基金会有幸与教育部合作，将核心能力培养纳入职业技术教育与培训体系，共同开发基于中国国情的青少年核心能力框架和评估工具，将学生核心能力培养融入专业技能课程。同时强调基于循证，确保双方合作的经验可追溯、可测量、可推广，最终惠及千千万万的中国年轻人。

中国职业技术教育与培训发展迅猛，在帮助年轻人做好准备以应对持续变化之职场要求的进程中积累了诸多可供借鉴的宝贵经验。最新修订的《中华人民共和国职业教育法》旨在强调技能发展的重要性，提升职业教育的地位，深化产教融合、提供多元学习途径，充分彰显了中国政府对实现联合国可持续发展教育目标的坚定承诺，即确保全纳和公平的优质教育，让全民享有终身学习机会。

最后，我代表联合国儿童基金会呼吁各级教育部门：优先保证学业恢复，让每一个学生有学上、上好学；评估学生学业水平；补回因疫情落下的功课；关注心理健康，确保孩子能在良好的身心状态中学习。助力年轻人全方位发展技能，尤其是可迁移能力，更好地迎接未来的世界。全球携力，共享智慧，共同致力于终结学习危机。让我们的下一代真正学有所得，绽放精彩。

# V. Speech by the Director of Education and Adolescent Development of UNICEF

Let me begin with congratulating the Chinese government for hosting the first World Vocational and Technical Education Development Conference, demonstrating a strong commitment to skills development. My name is Robert Jenkins and I am the Director for Education and Adolescent Development at UNICEF. I am honored to provide opening session remarks for this important conference.

Prior to the COVID-19 pandemic, 825 million school-age children globally were not on track to acquire minimum secondary level skills by 2030, leaving too many children unprepared to navigate personal, social and economic challenges in adulthood.

The pandemic exacerbated this crisis. Now more than 136 million secondary level students are unable to access remote learning, including those who are most marginalized, creating even more obstacles for adolescents to develop critical skills for life. The repercussions will reverberate throughout this generation's lifetime with a potential lost income of $21 trillion.

We live in a rapidly changing world, with climate change, technology, migration, conflict and epidemics reshaping society ever more quickly. The future of work is growing more unpredictable and the jobs that many young people will have in the coming years may not even exist today. With these changes, the future of work makes it even more critical that young people develop a full range of skills. This includes foundational skills such as reading and math; transferable skills also known as life skills or 21st century skills. Let's not forget the digital skills to navigate the digital world and entrepreneurial and job-specific skills that will prepare young people for a rapidly changing future. Transferable skills are essential to support young people to become successful lifelong learners, who can learn, un-learn and relearn again, find and retain productive work; make wise decisions; and positively engage in their communities. They also support and reinforce the other types of skills—including foundational, digital, and vocational skills.

Globally UNICEF works with governments, private sector, civil society and youth organizations in over 120 countries to advance the life skills agenda at scale and with a focus on reaching the most marginalized, directly impacting over 33 million children and young people and many more through strengthening government programmes to ensure they provide quality skills development opportunities. In China, UNICEF is privileged to work in partnership with the Ministry of Education to integrate life skills into the TVET system. This includes development of a common context-specific life skills framework and assessment tools, integration of life skills into technical skills curriculum and a stronger emphasis on evidence-based approaches to make sure our experience is traceable, measurable and scalable to benefit millions of young people in China.

China has important experiences to share from this rapidly growing TVET sector and how it is evolving to ensure that future generations are ready to thrive in the changing workplace. The recent Vocational Education Law aims to emphasize the value of skills development, elevate the status of vocational education, enhance industry-education linkages and provide multiple learning pathways available for young people. All these speak to and demonstrate a strong government commitment to achieving SDG4, ensuring inclusive and quality education and promoting lifelong learning opportunities for all.

So at UNICEF, let me conclude by recommending the following for all levels of education to: Prioritize learning recovery; Reach and retain every child in education; Assess learning levels; Increase catch-up learning and Develop psychosocial health and well-being so every child is ready to learn. Let us support young people to develop a full range of skills, especially transferable skills, that better prepare young people for the world of the future. Let's work together to share best practice and join efforts to combat and end the learning crisis. So our future generation can genuinely learn and thrive!

# 六

# 关于创设国际职教大奖的倡议

中国教育国际交流协会会长　刘利民
Liu Limin, President of China Education Association for International Exchange

在新的发展时期、承载新的发展使命，职业教育已经从培养技术工人，发展为能力教育和终身学习；从传授技术技能，发展为创造生产价值、经济价值和社会价值。职业教育不仅大有可为，而且大有作为，需要得到更广泛的认同和更强有力的支持，发展成果和成功举措需要更为高效地宣传和推广。

为此，借助世界职业技术教育发展大会平台，我们提议创设国际职教大奖和职业教育奖励基金，持续改善职业教育在国际社会的价值度和认可度。职业教育是创造价值的教育，国际职教大奖要支持一批对经济社会进步和产业升级发展、增进人民福祉有突出贡献的典范，重点奖励在职业教育改革创新、技术技能人才培养、创造产业价值等方面做出重要成果的组织和个人。

衷心感谢中国银行对国际职教大奖的创设给予的大力支持。我们诚挚邀请世界各国从事职教实践和研究的院校、行业企业、研究机构和有识之士，参与设立并支持实施国际职教大奖。让职业精神得到弘扬，让职业教育得到尊重，让教育与产业更加融合，让职业教育创造的价值得到彰显。

各位同仁，让我们携起手来，以跨界互动、融合创新共同推动全球职业教育发展共赢!

## Ⅵ. Initiative to Establish the International TVET Prize

In the new development period and carrying a new development mission, vocational education has developed from training skilled workers to competency-based education and lifelong learning; from teaching technical skills to creating productive, economic and social values. Vocational education is not only promising, but also well worth being developed, and needs wider recognition and stronger support, whose achievements and successful initiatives need to be publicized and promoted more effectively.

Therefore, we'd like to take the opportunity of World Vocational and Technical Education Development Conference to propose establishing the International TVET Prize and a TVET Incentive Fund to continuously improve the value and recognition of vocational education internationally. Vocational education creates value. The International TVET Prize should support a number of exemplary models that have made outstanding contributions to economic and social progress, industrial upgrading and development, as well as promoting people's well-being, with a special focus on organizations and individuals who have great achievements in vocational education reform and innovation, technical and skilled personnel training, and creating industrial value.

We sincerely thank the Bank of China for its strong support to the establishment of the International TVET Prize. We sincerely invite institutions, industry associations, enterprises, research institutes and farsighted personages from all over the world who are engaged in TVET practice and research to participate in the establishment and support the prize. Let the spirit of professionalism be promoted, let vocational education be respected, let education and industry be more integrated, and let the value created by vocational education be manifested.

Let's join hands to promote the development of global vocational education with cross-border interaction, integration and innovation!

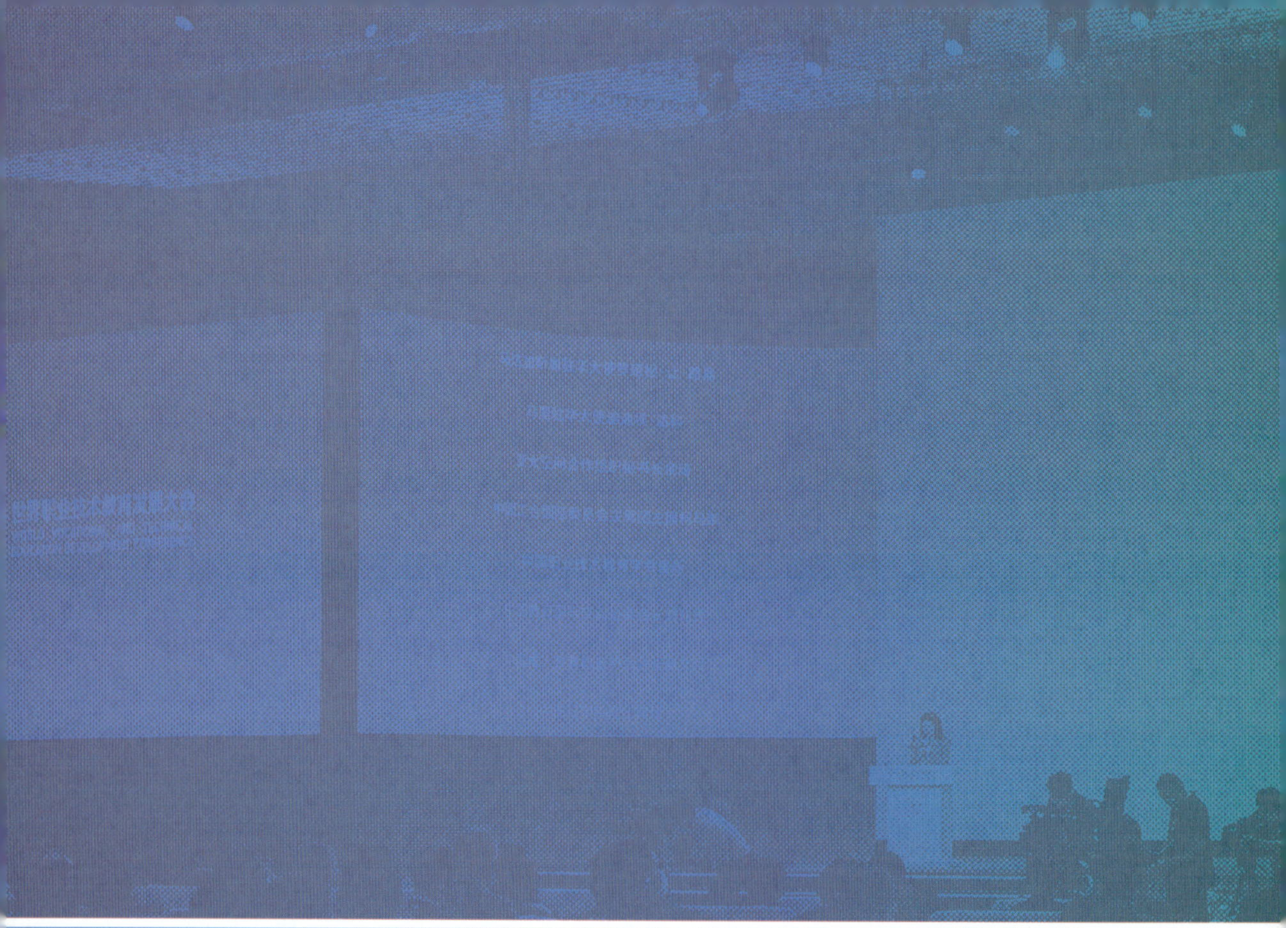

# 主论坛

# Keynote Session

# 一

# 中华人民共和国教育部部长主旨报告

## 携手推动全球职业教育高质量发展 助力建设后疫情时代美好世界

怀进鹏
Huai Jinpeng

中国古代伟大的思想家、教育家孔子曾说，有朋自远方来，不亦乐乎。今天，很高兴与大家相聚在中国工业重镇和现代职业教育改革创新示范区——天津，以“现场＋云端”的方式，共商全球职业教育改革发展大计。在此，我谨代表中华人民共和国教育部向各位嘉宾表示热烈的欢迎和诚挚的敬意！

女士们、先生们，朋友们！百年大计，教育为本。教育是人类传承文明、丰富知识技能、培养年轻一代、创造美好生活的根本途径。职业教育是教育的重要类型，是国民教育体系和人力资源开发的重要组成部分，肩负着培养多样化人才、传承并发展技术技能、促进就业创业的重要职责，在推动实现更加强劲、绿色、健康的全球发展中起着不可替代的独特作用。在百年变局和世纪疫情叠加并给全球经济发展和民生改善带来严峻挑战的大背景下，如何携手推动全球职业教育高质量发展、助力建设后疫情时代美好世界，成为摆在世界各国职业教育界面前的一个重大课题。我们由衷地期待各位嘉宾、各位朋友围绕这一课题深入研讨、集思广益、建言献策，为进一步深化各国职业教育交流合作凝聚新共识、绘制新蓝图、注入新动能！

女士们、先生们，朋友们！中国有 14 亿多人口，是世界上人口最多的发展中国家，中国式现代化是人口规模巨大的现代化。这就决定了我们必须不断加大投资于人的力度，努力办好人民满意的教育，加快实现从人力资源大国向人力资源强国、人才强国、教育强国的转变。

职业教育是与经济社会发展联系最为紧密的一类教育。中国始终高度重视职业教育。改革开放以来特别是近十年来，以习近平同志为核心的中共中央把职业教育摆在经济社会发展全局中更加突出的战略位置。习近平主席指出，在全面建设社会主义现代化国家新征程中，职业教育前途广阔、大有可为；要加快构建现代职业教育体系，大力推进产教融合，健全德技并修、工学结合的育人机制，培养更多高素质技术技能人才。在习近平主席的亲自关心支持下，我们立足中国国情，大力探索创新，走出了一条具有中国特色的职业教育发展道路。

一是有效支撑国家经济社会高质量发展。当前，全球经济发展模式和驱动力发生根本性转变，科技成为第一生产力，人才成为第一资源，创新成为第一动力。实现经济社会高质量发展，很关键的一点，就是通过发展职业教育，源源不断地培养和输送各类具备终身学习能力、适应科技革命和产业变革需要的高素质、创新型技术技能人才。中国现有职业院校超过 10 000 所，设置 1 300 余种专业和 12 余万个专业点，全面覆盖国民经济社会发展各领域、各行业。近十年来，中国职业教育累计为培养输送 6 100 多万高素质技术技能人才作出了贡献。实践充分证明，中国经济持续保持中高速增长，离不开职业教育的突出贡献。

二是不断满足人民群众对美好生活的追求。职业院校毕业生就业率连续保持高位稳定，受过高等教育的技能人才收入明显高于城乡居民人均可支配收入平均水平。职业院校毕业生成为中等收入群体的重要来源，“职教一人、富裕一家、带动一方”成为实现共同富裕的有效途径。近十年来，累计有 800 多万贫困家庭学生接受职业教育。实践充分证明，职业教育是阻断贫困代际传递、助力乡村振兴、促进共同富裕、帮助全体人民创造美好生活的有效途径。

三是持续畅通学生多样化成长成才的渠道。我们积极推进不同层次的职业教育发展和有效贯通，加快建设现代职业教育体系，中职的基础地位进一步巩固，专科高职的主体地位不断强化，职业本科教育稳步发展，为学生提供了多样化成长选择和多路径成才渠道。同时，职业院校面向企业职工、重点人群积极开展各类培训，年培训上亿人次。实践充分证明，职业教育是广大青年打开通往成功成才大门的重要途径，是让每个人都有人生出彩机会的重要基础。

四是积极服务构建全面开放新格局。中国已与 70 多个国家和国际组织建立了稳定联系，与 19 个国家和地区合作建成 20 余家鲁班工坊，在 40 多个国家和地区合作开设“中文 + 职业教育”特色项目。伴随越来越多中国企业和中国产品走向国际舞台，中国职业教育在助力建设开放型世界经济方面发挥着更大作用。实践充分证明，职业教育是各国人民加强交流合作、深化互学互鉴的重要载体，是人类社会跨越发展鸿沟、重振全球发展事业的重要力量。

会前，我们专门参观了职业院校技能大赛，看到不同国家、不同类型、不同院校的同学们在相互切磋，为竞赛、为技能做准备，也不断地形成他们的能力的培养、合作的交流和包容性的发展。期待这样的会议能使社会各界和国际友人共同研究思考不断提升职业教育的能力。

经过多年来的持续努力，中国建成了世界上最大规模的职业教育体系，构建了职业教育与普通教育协调发展的教育格局。中国的职业教育实现了从学校为主举办到多元参与办学、从规模扩张发展到高质量内涵发展的重要转变。

女士们、先生们，朋友们！当前，随着新一轮科技革命和产业变革的突飞猛进，以及新冠病毒疫情的深度影响，世界正在经历产业结构、经济结构与社会环境以及人口结构等的深刻调整与变化，各国职业教育不同程度地面临着一些共同挑战与发展机遇。劳动力市场与经济发展中技能人才需求大于供给、供需错配问题依然存在，职业能力培养与学术教育仍然不平衡，职业教育重理论轻实践、重知识轻能力的现象一定程度存在，传统对职业教育的认识观念与经济社会现代化发展仍有不适应，产教融合、终身学习与职业技能仍需加强。

站在新的历史起点上，实现职业教育转型发展，需要我们准确定位、主动求变，坚持创新、协调、绿色、开放、共享的新发展理念，推动教育界、产业界和经济社会发展各相关部门以及国际社会进一步加强合作交流，不断提高认识、转变观念，持续提高职业教育质量与发展能力。

第一，职业教育应当更好立足人的全面发展，坚持以人为本，提质增效。伴随产业结构和经济社会的新变化与高质量发展要求，职业教育已经不再是单一的学校教育和技能培训。它既是学历教育，也是能力教育，更是终身教育，是促进人的全面发展的重要途径。这决定了职业教育必须更好地服务人的全面发展，推动学生学会求知、学会做事、学会共处、学会做人，主动搭建学习与职场间的“旋转门”和终身学习的“充电站”，为人的职业可持续发展和一生幸福生活增值赋能。

第二，职业教育应当更好服务并融入经济社会发展，坚持以技能为先，深度融通。职业教育既涉及民生，更涉及国计，既需要解决劳动者就业问题，更需要解决国家战略和产业发展问题。从全球范围看，职业教育对当前经济振兴和更长时间的可持续发展都具有基础性的支撑作用，特别是对产业和区域发展都具有极其重要的支撑性。这决定了职业教育必须紧密对接产业发展、技术变革和劳动力市场变化，坚持走产教融合发展之路，加快构建现代职业教育体系，使职业教育更高质量、更有效地与产业、经济和社会协调发展。

第三，职业教育应当更好深化国际交流，以合作为要，互利共赢、包容发展。人类已经成为你中有我、我中有你的命运共同体，各国经济社会发展与民生福祉、利益高度融合，彼此相互依存。各国经济社会是在经济全球化背景下不断发展的，各国职业教育也需要加强合作，深度交流。应以更加开放的视野，共商、共建、助力消除贫困，增加就业、改善民生，提高技术技能，承担更多责任义务，为世界可持续发展做出应有贡献。

女士们、先生们，朋友们！教育是人类永恒的崇高事业。习近平主席在贺信中指出，职业教育与经济社会发展紧密相连，对促进就业创业、助力经济社会发展、增进人民福祉具有重要意义。孙春兰副总理在致辞中介绍了中国职业教育改革发展的经验和探索，发起了共创职业教育繁荣发展新局面的倡议。在中国，教育优先发展是国策，在国民经济社会发展中具有先导性、基础性和全局性作用。

我理解，一个国家的基础教育决定其传承文明、传承知识的广度，高等教育影响甚至决定其创新创造能力的高度，而职业教育与产教融合，影响甚至决定着区域和国家经济社会高质量发展的加速度。着力把职业教育摆在教育改革创新和经济社会发展中更加突出的位置，加快发展政府主导、社会参与、需求驱动，开放融合的现代职业教育，加快教育现代化，建设教育强国，办好人民满意的教育，是我们应尽职责。

我们将适应经济社会发展新要求，加快构建高质量发展的现代职业教育体系。主动融入国际发展趋势和潮流，立足中国国情、发展特色和已有基础，拓展和重构职业教育的时代内涵，加快完善“纵向贯通、横向融通”的现代职业教育体系，为接受职业教育的学生提供更为广阔的发展空间。一体化统筹设计技术技能人才培养体系，不断完善职业教育与各类教育相贯通的培养机制，为各行各业培养高素质的技术技能人才和生力军作出贡献。

我们将深化产教融合体制机制改革，形成教育与产业深度互动的新格局。我们将围绕区域行业和产业布局，与学校等主体建立多样化、立体化的产教融合平台体系，形成若干产教融合示范区。打造集人才培养、技术创新与转移、社会服务和文化传承于一体的产教融合发展新机制、新生态，不断完善投入和激励政策，形成政府搭台、社会广泛参与、互利共赢的创新发展新格局，不断推动实现职业教育与经济社会发展深度融合、人才供给与产业需求紧密对接，不断激发职业教育办学活力、办学动力、办学能力。

我们将整体提升职业院校办学能级，加强职业教育内涵建设和特色发展。在先进制造业、现代服务业和现代农业与战略新兴产业等领域、新业态吸纳产业界、科技与教育界专家及社会力量，把行业最新标准、企业高端技术、工艺方法及实际生产项目和产品引入职业教育教学中，探索构建一批示范性教育教学资源。深入实施国家教育数字化战略行动，大力推进职业教育数字化转型，以数字化、绿色化带动职业教育转型升级，发挥数字技术对教育高质量发展的叠加、倍增和放大作用。

我们将推动重构职业教育生态，营造崇尚劳动和技能、尊重和认可职业教育的社会氛围。加大对职业院校优秀师生、企业劳动模范和技能人才的宣传、奖励力度，在社会上形成“劳动光荣”的价值理念，切实提高一线技术技能人才的社会地位、经济收入和职业声望，鼓励广大青年走技能成才、技能报国之路，形成国家重视技能、社会崇尚技能、人人学习技能、人人拥有技能的社会风尚，打造学习型社会，终身学习社会。

女士们、先生们，朋友们！去年 9 月 21 日，习近平主席在第 76 届联合国大会上提出全球发展倡议，旨在共同推动全球发展面向平衡、协调、包容新阶段。召开世界职业技术教育发展大会，是对接联合国 2030 年可持续发展议程，落实全球发展倡议的一个重要的中国行动。基于此，本次大会期间还举办了首届世界职业院校技能大赛和世界职业教育产教融合博览会，并发起了创设国际职教大奖和筹建世界职业技术教育发展联盟的倡议。

面向未来，中国愿意以大会及相关活动的定期举办为契机，与各国携手打造职业教育国际交流合作新平台、新范式和新机制，共同推动世界职业教育高质量发展。

一是建立大会对话机制。我们将坚持“增进交流、深化合作、创新发展”的原则，每两年举办一次大会，聚焦全球趋势与热点，丰富大会形式，努力将大会打造成具有重要国际影响力的机制性会议，推动全球职业教育的共商、共建、共享。

二是建立大赛交流机制。我们将逐步扩大世界职业院校技能大赛赛项和参与国家、院校覆盖面，完善大赛标准和规则体系，将大赛打造成国际职业院校师生增进友谊、切磋技能、展示风采的重要平台。

三是建立联盟发展机制。我们将依托世界职业技术教育发展联盟，按照“全球性、非政府、非营利”的原则，构建国际职业教育的标准规则制订发布平台、交流合作平台、模式推广平台、发展创新研究平台。

四是建立展会合作机制。我们将推进产教融合主题展会模式创新，充分展示和交流世界各国产教融合先进经验、校企合作典型案例、产业发展新技术新趋势、新业态等诸多内容，将世界职业教育产教融合博览会打造成职业教育大型展览和世界一流的产教合作国际平台。

女士们、先生们、朋友们！海纳百川、相倚为强。我们生活在同一个地球家园，人类命运越来越紧密地联系在一起。让我们同心聚力、携手共进，推动全球职业教育高质量发展，共同建设更加幸福的家园、共同开创更加美好的未来。

# I. Keynote Speech by the Minister of Education of the People's Republic of China

### To Promote the High-quality Development of Global TVET through Cooperation, and Contribute to a Better World in the Post-pandemic Era

Confucius, the great philosopher and educator of ancient China, once said, "It is a pleasure to meet friends coming from afar!" Today, I am very delightful to meet all of you here in Tianjin, an important industrial city and also a model of modern TVET reform and innovation, via an "on-site+cloud" mode, and discuss the reform and development of global TVET. Here, on behalf of the Ministry of Education of the People's Republic of China, I'd like to extend our warm welcome and sincere respect to all of you.

Ladies and gentlemen, dear friends! Education is the foundation of national development in the long run. Education is the fundamental way to pass on our civilization, enrich our knowledge and skills, train our future generations, and create a better world. TVET is an important type of education, and an important part of the national education system and human resource development, which plays a major role in cultivating diversified talents, passing on and enhancing technical skills, and promoting employment and entrepreneurship. TVET also plays an irreplaceable and unique role in accelerating stronger, greener and healthier global development. In the context of changes unseen in a century and the pandemic, which have posed serious challenges to global economic growth and the improvement of livelihoods, how to promote the high-quality development of global TVET through cooperation, and contribute to a better world in the post-pandemic era has become a major issue for the TVET communities. We sincerely hope that all guests and friends will discuss this issue in depth, pool their wisdom and offer their suggestions, so as to forge a new consensus, draw a new blueprint and bring new dynamics to further deepen the exchange and cooperation in TVET among countries.

Ladies and gentlemen, dear friends! China is a developing country with a population of over 1.4 billion, which is the largest in the world. The modernization of

China is the modernization of a massive population. Therefore, we have to constantly increase our investment in talents, offer education that our people are satisfied with, and accelerate the transformation from a country with massive human resources to a country with strong human resources, competent talents and high-quality education.

TVET is the type of education most closely linked to economic and social development. China has always attached great importance to TVET. Since the Reform and Opening-up, especially in the past decade, the CPC Central Committee with Comrade Xi Jinping at its core has placed TVET in a more prominent strategic position in the overall economic and social development. President Xi pointed out that TVET has a promising future in the new journey of building a modern socialist country in all respects, and that it is necessary to speed up the development of a modern TVET system, vigorously promote the integration of industry and education, improve the education mechanism that combines moral, skills and work-based learning, and train more high-quality technical and skilled talents. With President Xi's care and support, we have explored and innovated a TVET path with Chinese characteristics based on China's national conditions.

Firstly, TVET effectively supports the high-quality economic and social development of the country. At present, the global economic development model and drivers are undergoing a fundamental change, with science and technology becoming the primary productivity, talents the primary resource and innovation the primary driver. One key driver of high-quality economic and social development is the development of TVET, which continuously trains and offers all kinds of high-quality, innovative technical and skilled talents with lifelong learning ability and adaptability to the needs of the technological revolution and industrial changes. Currently, there are over 10 000 TVET institutions in China, offering programs through over 120 000 course providers in more than 1 300 majors, which cover all areas and sectors of national economic and social development. In the past decade, TVET in China has trained more than 61 million highly qualified technical and skilled talents. It is proved that the sustained medium-to-high growth of the Chinese economy cannot be possible without the outstanding contribution of TVET.

Secondly, TVET continuously meets people's pursuit of a better life. The employment rate of TVET institution graduates has remained high and stable, and skilled talents who have received higher education earn significantly more than the average per capita disposable income of urban and rural residents. TVET institution graduates have become an important part of the middle-income class. "A person who has received TVET can support a well-off family and drives the development of an area". This has become an effective way to achieve common prosperity. In the decade, students from more than 8 million poor families have received TVET. Practice has fully proved that TVET is an effective way to prevent the intergenerational transmission of poverty, boost rural revitalization, promote common prosperity and help all people create a better life.

Thirdly, TVET continuously opens up channels for students to prosper in different ways. We actively promote the development and effective integration of TVET at different levels, accelerate the construction of a modern TVET system, further consolidate the fundamental position of secondary TVET, strengthen the main position of specialized and higher TVET, and steadily develop undergraduate TVET, providing students with diversified options and multiple pathways to achieve success. Meanwhile, TVET institutions are actively providing various types of training for enterprise employees and key communities, training hundreds of millions of people annually. Practice has demonstrated that TVET is an important way for young people to achieve success and prosper, and an important foundation for everyone to excel in life.

Fourthly, TVET actively serves to build a new model of comprehensive opening up. China has established stable ties with over 70 countries and international organizations, cooperated with 19 countries and regions to establish more than 20 Luban Workshops, and collaborated with more than 40 countries and regions to offer "Chinese + TVET" special programs. With an increasing number of Chinese enterprises and products going global, Chinese TVET is playing a greater role in contributing to an open world economy. As practice proves, TVET is an important vehicle for people from various countries to strengthen exchanges and cooperation, deepen mutual learning and appreciation, and also a critical driver for human society to narrow the development gap and revitalize the cause of global development.

Just before this conference, we visited the venue for World Vocational College Skills Competition, where we saw students from different countries and institutions and of different types communicating with each other, preparing for the competition and for their skills, and also continuously shaping their capacity building, cooperative exchanges and inclusive development. It is expected that conferences like this will enable domestic and international friends from all walks of life to think about how to continuously improve TVET.

After years of sustained efforts, China has established the largest TVET system in the world, and built an education structure in which TVET and general education develop in a coordinated manner. The main organizers of TVET in China have changed from colleges and schools to a plurality of participants, and the goal of TVET has been transformed from scale expansion to high-quality development.

Ladies and gentlemen, dear friends! At present, with the remarkable progress in the new round of technological revolution and industrial transformation as well as the in-depth impact of the COVID-19 pandemic, countries around the world are experiencing profound changes and adjustments in respective industrial structure, economic structure, social environment and demographic structure, etc. Hence,

TVET in different countries is facing some common challenges and development opportunities. There still exists the conflict between inadequate skilled talents and large demand in the labor market and for economic development as well as the mismatch of supply and demand. The imbalance between vocational capability development and academic education is still prominent. And to some extent, much more attention is paid to theory and knowledge than to practice and capability in TVET. The traditional cognitive beliefs of TVET are not in line with modern economic and social development. It is still required to strengthen the integration between industry and education, lifelong learning and vocational skill development.

Standing at a new historic starting point and focusing on the goal of TVET transformation and development, we need to determine our exact orientation, take the initiative to make changes, and adhere to the new development concept of innovation, coordination, green, openness and sharing. More efforts should be put into promoting further cooperation and exchanges among the education circles, industrial circles as well as different departments for economic and social development, which requires us to continuously deepen our understanding, transform the old mindset, and upgrade the quality and development capability of TVET.

First, TVET should be firmly based on the principles of better-serving people's all-around development, a people-first approach and quality and efficiency improvement. Along with the new changes and requirements on high-quality development in the industrial structure as well as economy and society, TVET is no longer a simple form of school education or skill training. Instead, it should be not only an academic education, but also a competency-based education, and more importantly, a lifelong education. It is an important way to promote people's all-around development, which determines that the underlying mission of TVET is to better serve the all-around development of people, and to promote students to learn to know, learn to do, learn to be and learn to live together. What's more, it should guide them to take the initiative to build the "revolving door" between study and work and the "recharging station" of lifelong learning so as to provide people with sustainable career development and a lifetime of happiness.

Secondly, TVET should better serve and integrate into the development of the economy and society, which should give priority to skills and seek deep integration with other aspects. TVET is not only about people's livelihoods, but also about national welfare. It not only offers solutions to difficult employment, but also national strategies and industrial development. Globally, TVET plays a fundamental role in current economic revitalization and sustainable development in the long run, especially in supporting industrial and regional development. In this case, TVET should be closely matched with industrial development, technological transformation and labor market changes. And we should firmly stick to the integrated development of industry and education and accelerate the development of a modern TVET system so as to make TVET develop in harmony with industry, economy and society in higher quality and more effective manner.

Thirdly, TVET should further deepen international exchanges and highlight cooperation to promote mutual benefits, win-win cooperation, and inclusive development. Today, countries are becoming a close-knit community of shared weal and woe in social development and people's well-being. In addition, as the world is facing an irresistible trend of economic globalization, we need to strengthen cooperation and in-depth exchanges in TVET. We should keep a broader vision to help eradicate poverty, increase employment, ameliorate people's livelihoods and improve technical skills with wide consultation and joint contributions. We should take on more responsibilities and make due contributions to the sustainable development of the world.

Ladies and gentlemen, dear friends! Education is an eternal and noble cause of human beings. President Xi Jinping pointed out in the congratulatory letter that TVET is closely related to economic and social development, which is of great significance in promoting employment and entrepreneurship, supporting economic and social development and enhancing people's well-being. Vice Premier Sun Chunlan's speech introduced the experience and exploration of TVET development and reform in China. She also proposed an initiative to break new ground for the prosperous development of TVET. In China, it's a national policy to give top priority to education, which occupies a pioneering, fundamental and leading position in national economic and social development.

In my opinion, basic education of a country determines the breadth of its inheritance of civilization and transfer of knowledge; Higher education influences and even determines a country's capability of innovation and creation; TVET and industry-education integration influence and even determine the acceleration of high-quality development of regional and even national economy and society. We should put TVET in a more prominent place in education reform and innovation as well as economic and social development, and accelerate to develop a modern vocational education system led by the government, driven by demands and featured by wide social participation. It's our responsibility to quicken the modernization of education, build China into a power of education and make our education meet people's needs.

We will adapt to the new requirements of economic and social development and propel to develop a modern vocational education system featuring high-quality development. We will take the initiative to join in the global development trend, take the condition of China as well as the characteristics of China's development and existing infrastructures into consideration, and expand and reconstruct the connotations of TVET in contemporary times. We will accelerate to improve an unobstructed modern TVET system that has further education channels horizontally and integrates with regular education vertically, offering a broader opportunity for development for students choosing TVET. We will coordinate the training system for technically skilled personnel, and gradually smooth the channels to integrate TEVT with all types of education so as to develop more and more highly qualified and technically skilled personnel and fresh blood for all walks of life.

We will deepen the reform of the institutional mechanism for industry-education integration and form a new pattern of in-depth interaction between education and industry. We will establish a diversified and 3D system of platforms for the integration of industry and education with schools and other entities and form a number of demonstration bases for industry-education integration based on regional industries and industrial layouts. We will create a new development mechanism and a new ecology for the integration of industry and education that combine talent cultivation, technological innovation and transfer, social services and cultural inheritance. We will keep improving investment and incentive policies and form a new development pattern of innovation and development in which government sets up the stage and the whole society participates for mutual interests and win-win cooperation. We will continuously promote the deep integration between TVET and economic and social development, and the precise match between talent supply and industrial demand so as to invigorate, stimulate and promote TVET.

We will enhance the overall capabilities of vocational institutions, and bring out the full potential and characteristics for the development of TVET. In some sectors and new business forms, such as the advanced manufacturing industry, modern service industry, modern agriculture and strategic emerging industries, we will gather the strengths of the industrial circles, the sci-tech community as well as the education circles and societal forces. We will introduce the latest industry standards, high-end technologies and techniques of enterprises as well as the actual projects and products into TVET, and try to develop a series of exemplary educational and teaching resources. We will further implement National Strategic Digital Education Action Plan, promote the digital transformation of TVET, boost digital and green TVET transformation and upgrading and bring into play the superimposing, multiplying and amplifying effects of digital technologies on high-quality development of education.

We will promote to reconstruct the ecology of TVET and create a social atmosphere that highlights labor and skills, and respects and recognizes TVET. We will strengthen the efforts to promote and award excellent teachers and students in vocational institutions, model workers and skilled talents in enterprises with the aim to form a sense of value in the society that labor is the most glorious, to actually improve the social status, economic returns and occupational prestige of first-line workers and skilled talents, to encourage the young people to harbor a dream of becoming a skilled talent and contribute to the country with their skills. All in all, we expect to form a social moral that the nation values skills, the society honors skills, everyone learns skills and everyone has skills, which makes a learning society and a lifelong learning society.

Ladies and gentlemen, dear friends! On September 21 last year, President Xi Jinping put forward the Global Development Initiative at the 76th General Assembly of the United Nations, which aimed to jointly promote the world to a new phase of balanced, coordinated and inclusive development. The World Vocational and Technical Education Development Conference is a response to the UN 2030 Agenda for Sustainable Development and an important action China has taken to implement the Global Development Initiative. On this basis, we also held the first World Vocational College Skills Competition and the World Expo on the Integration of Vocational Education with Industry during the conference and proposed to launch an International TVET Prize and establish the World TVET League.

Looking into the future, China is willing to take advantage of the conference and related events and join hands with other countries to build a new platform, a new paradigm and a new mechanism for international cooperation and exchange in TVET, and jointly promote the high-quality development of TVET around the world.

First, we will establish a conference-based dialogue mechanism. We will stick to the principle of "enhancing exchanges, deepening cooperation and innovating development". We will hold the conference every two years, focus on global trends and hot issues and enrich activities, working to make the conference a mechanism conference with significant global influence and promote extensive consultation, joint contribution and shared benefits of global TVET.

Second, we will establish a competition-based exchange mechanism. We will further expand the events of the World Vocational College Skills Competition and the scope of participating countries and institutions and improve the standards and rule system of the competition, making it an important platform for teachers and students from vocational institutions around the world to enhance friendship, learn from each other and present themselves.

Third, we will establish a league-based development mechanism. Based on the World TVET League and according to the principle of "global, non-government and non-profit", we will develop a platform for the promulgation and release of global TVET standards and regulations, a platform for communication and exchange, a platform for model promotion and a platform for research on development and innovation.

Fourth, we will establish an exhibition-based cooperation mechanism. We will promote an innovative exhibition model under the theme of industry-education integration and fully display the advanced experience of industry-education integration in different countries, classical cases of school-enterprise cooperation, new technologies, trends and business forms of industrial development. We aim to build the World Expo on the Integration of Vocational Education with Industry a grand exhibition for TVET and a world-class international platform for the cooperation between industry and education.

Ladies and gentlemen, dear friends! All rivers run into the sea and cooperation makes us stronger. As we live on the same Earth, our destiny is closely related. Let's join hands and make concerted efforts to drive the high-quality development of TVET, and work together to build a happier home and a better future.

# 二

# 阿根廷教育部部长发言

海梅 · 佩尔西克
Jaime Perczyk

在阿根廷，《国家教育法》规定教育和知识是一种公共利益，也是国家必须保障的一项个人与社会权利。因此，作为联邦制国家和民族国家的阿根廷以及阿根廷的各州、各省和布宜诺斯艾利斯自治市都有责任为全国人民提供全面的、长久的、优质的教育。

联合国教科文组织发布的全球性协定认为，职业技术教育不仅被视为普遍受教育权的一部分，而且被视为普遍工作权的一部分。协定也强调，职业技术教育在 2030 年可持续发展议程中对可持续发展、促进持续性经济增长与社会发展、环境保护以及消除贫困和饥饿等方面所起到的重要作用。

阿根廷教育体系面临的挑战之一是提升专业技术教育的质量及规模，因为这是社会发展和经济增长的一个重要因素。在我国各地方省市，职业技术教育影响着工作质量、生产力、经济质量和区域竞争力，职业技术教育在经济增长以及社会和人类发展方面具有突出的战略意义，这意味着要重视其社会和教育地位，确保国家统一的标准以及更新体制形式和干预策略。从这个意义上说，职业技术教育有助于促进对人权的包容与平等、性别平等和文化多样性的理解和尊重以及促进终身学习愿望的实现和能力的提升。

所有这一切对于社会经济参与都至关重要。职业技术教育的持续改进是一系列动态且复杂的过程，涉及社会多方参与、不同体制领域的优化。通过信息与通信技术、绿色技术以及教育和社会生产部门间的联系方式进行培训，是不断改善培训环境质量与职业技术教育体制条件策略所面临的挑战。这意味着要找到区域性和全球性的工具与机制，应当考虑教育机构和国家行政部门及其下属行政部门体制条件的多样性。根据社会对话框架中社会参与者的多样性及区域地方环境的差异性决定战略政策，做出正确决定。

# II. Speech by the Minister of Education of Argentina

En la Argentina, la ley de educación nacional dice que la educación y el conocimiento son un bien público y un derecho personal y social que debe garantizar el Estado. Es por eso que en nuestro caso como Estado federal, Estado nacional y también los estados nacionales, las provincias y la ciudad autónoma de Buenos Aires tienen la responsabilidad de proveer una educación integral, permanente y de calidad para todos los habitantes de la nación.

Acuerdos mundiales representados por la UNESCO reconocen que la educación técnico profesional se considera no solo parte del derecho universal a la educación, sino también como el derecho universal al trabajo. Se destaca su rol esencial en la Agenda 2030 para el desarrollo sostenible, para promover el crecimiento económico sostenido e inclusivo del desarrollo social, la protección medioambiental y la erradicación de la pobreza y el hambre.

Uno de los desafíos del sistema educativo argentino, entonces, es el de fortalecer la calidad y la masividad de la educación técnica profesional, porque es un factor clave para el desarrollo social y el crecimiento económico. De nuestro país en términos regionales y locales, la educación técnico profesional incide sobre la calidad del trabajo, la productividad, la calidad económica y la competitividad territorial. Destaca el carácter estratégico de la educación técnico profesional en términos del desarrollo social y humano del crecimiento económico. Implica valorar su estatus social y educativo, garantizar criterios de unidad nacional, así como también actualizar sus modelos institucionales y estrategias de intervención. En ese sentido, la educación técnico profesional contribuye a promover la comprensión y el respeto por los derechos humanos, la inclusión y la igualdad, la igualdad de género y la diversidad cultural, así como a impulsar el deseo y la capacidad de aprender a lo largo de toda la vida.

Y todo esto es esencial para la participación social y económica. El mejoramiento continuo de la educación técnico profesional se constituye en un conjunto de procesos dinámicos, y complejos en el que intervienen múltiples actores sociales y se vincula con el fortalecimiento de los diversos ámbitos institucionales. Entre los desafíos de la estrategia de mejorar continua de la calidad de los entornos formativos y las condiciones institucionales de la ETP están en la formación mediada por tecnologías de la información y la comunicación, las tecnologías verdes y las formas de vinculación entre educación y el sector socio productivo. Esto implica encontrar instrumentos y mecanismos de carácter regional y global que consideren la diversidad de las condiciones institucionales de las unidades educativas y de las administraciones nacionales y subnacionales. La multiplicidad de actores que participan en ellas en el marco del diálogo social, así como la heterogeneidad de los contextos regionales y locales que permiten orientar la definición de políticas estratégicas y la toma de decisiones adecuadas en esta materia.

# 三

## 巴西教育部部长发言

维克多·戈多伊
Victor Godoy

我们生活的世界瞬息万变，面临重重挑战，我们必须不断变革和创新来扫除影响教育发展的障碍。教育是我们必须尊重且需要不断加强的一项公民权利。如果不将此权利赋予每个人，使公民通过获得技能和能力来有所作为，社会和经济便无法进步。职业技术教育与培训是巴西政府的优先工作之一，它在培养年轻人就业和工作方面具有战略意义。目前，全国在校学生超过 380 万人。教育在未来的关键要素是教育与工作、科学和技术领域的结合。教育部认识到提供职业技术教育课程对国家经济发展的重要性，特别是在后疫情时代的背景下，教育部正设法制定能够在全社会范围内提供更多技术培训机会的教育政策。

根据经济合作与发展组织的数据，世界上许多国家在高中技术教育的招生方面表现突出。巴西也一直努力优先完成这方面的工作。到 2024 年，巴西国家教育计划的目标包括将中等职业技术教育的入学人数增至原来的三倍，并确保教育质量；作为公共政策的引导者，公立教育招生规模至少增加一半。

特别是在近三年以来，巴西不断完善了职业教育规范，更新了专门针对这种模式的国家课程指南，进一步加强了各级教育的课程设置。我们正在高中实施一种全新的模式，让学生有更多的自主性，使其有更多的时间学习基础知识，同时也能深入了解他们感兴趣的知识。从这个角度来看，将职业技术教育课程纳入必修课也将大大增加可行性。职业技术培训是高中学生发展的五条轨道中的一条。在这个轨道内，我们组织课程为该年龄段的学生提供技术教育。该模式通过不断扩展范围，让职业技术教育课程对于巴西年轻人来说更易获得，更具相关性和吸引力。我们一直在不断更新职业技术教育与培训的监管框架，建立了一个全新的架构来授权私立高等教育机构提供课程。这项措施制定的规则旨在优化教育机构提供技术课程的手续，仅在今年，批准数量就可能超过 100 万个招生名额。

在巴西各州和联邦地区，教育部下辖的 678 个公共单位组成了巴西联邦职业、科学和技术教育机构网络，其课程的多样性得到认可。到 2022 年该教育机构网络已经为超过 150 万注册学生提供了不少于 10 000 项课程选择。

这个教育机构网络除了努力提高地区在工作、文化和休闲方面的潜力外，还起到了联系民众和当地公司的作用。此外，它鼓励在学习过程中使用新技术，并使课程设置与生产部门的需求保持一致。

为了优化该网络，教育部在这些教育机构的整合和现代化进程中发挥了重要作用。在众多举措中，我们非常重视设备的采购和研究实验室的搭建，包括现代原型实验室。值得注意的是，在技术供需、职业资格、本科和研究生技术教育课程等领域，教育部已经开展了与本次会议重要议题直接相关的活动，包括培训数字化、绿色科技、产教融合和终身学习。这些建议旨在确保公民的教育质量，也有助于提高生产力和国家竞争力。我们也意识到职业技术教育面临许多挑战，这就是为什么在全球范围内与同行讨论这个话题很有必要的原因。只有这样，我们才能促进技术和技术解决方案的不断发展，以满足国内需求以及应对国内外日益激烈的竞争。

再次重申，巴西将坚定不移地与大家展开密切合作，扭转当前全球职业技术教育的局面。在未来，我们的首要任务是总结经验教训，并通过大量使用技术进行创新，改善学生的入学条件、学习条件和持续学习。

再次感谢大家，希望富有成果的讨论让我们的工作更具成效。

# Ⅲ. Speech by the Minister of Education of Brazil

Aware of how fast-changing the world we live in is and the challenges posed, there is a need to re-create and innovate to overcome the obstacles that directly affect education. Education is a human right that must be respected for the consolidation of citizenship. Achieving social and economic progress is not feasible without empowering every man and woman with the skills and capacities to operate positive changes. Technical and vocational education and training is one of the priorities of the Brazilian government. It is strategic in preparing young people for the exercise of professions and for the world of work. There are currently over 3 800 000 students enrolled across the country. The key element for the future of education is in the integration with the dimensions of work, science and technology. Recognizing the importance of offering Vocational and Technological Education courses for the nation's economic development, especially in the post-pandemic context, the Ministry of Education has sought to build educational policies that can guarantee an expansion in opportunities for technical training for the whole society.

On the international scene, according to data from the Organization for Economic Cooperation and Development (OECD), many countries stand out for the admission of students to high school technical courses. We are working to place Brazil in this prominent position as well. We have been striving to achieve, by 2024, the goal of the National Educational Plow, which is to triple enrollments in Technical Vocational Education at the secondary level, ensuring the quality of the offer, and at least 50% of expansion in the public segment, acting as an inducing agent of public policies.

Brazil has ensured the advancement of regulation for vocational education, especially in the last three years. We have updated the National Curriculum Guidelines specific to this modality, further strengthening courses offerings at all levels of education. We are implementing a new format for high school. With more autonomy and protagonism, students can have more time to learn the essentials and deepen the knowledge they are most interested in. From this perspective, the possibilities were expanded by including Vocational and Technological Education courses to complement the mandatory curriculum. Within the five trajectories available to students who enter high school, we have the path of technical and professional training. This option organizes the curriculum, enabling technical education for this age group. This measure aims to go far beyond offering expansion. It seeks to make Vocational and Technological Education courses more accessible, relevant and attractive to young Brazilians. We are in a constant process of updating the regulatory frameworks that govern TVET. We instituted a new structure for authorizing courses offered by Private Higher Education Institutions. This measure provides for rules aimed at optimizing and reducing bureaucracy in the process of enabling institutions to provide technical courses. For this year alone, the number of approvals may exceed more than one million seats.

In Brazil, under the Ministry of Education, we have 678 public units that compose the Federal Network of Professional, Scientific and Technological Education, present in all states and the Federal District. It is recognized for the diversity of courses, surpassing 10 000 options provided in 2022 for more than 1.5 million students enrolled.

This network of institution has a relevant role with the population and local companies, in addition to working to enhance each region's potential in terms of work, culture and leisure. Moreover, it encourages the use of new technologies in the learning process and the alignment of course offerings with the demands of the productive sectors.

In order to strengthen the Federal Network, the Ministry of Education has played a fundamental role in the consolidation and modernization of these educational institutions. Among the various actions, we highlight the acquisition of equipment and the structuring of laboratories for research, including modern prototyping laboratories. It is also worth noting that in the scope of the Ministry's actions aimed at technical accessing and offering, professional qualification, and undergraduate and graduate technical courses, we develop activities that are directly related to important themes that will be addressed in the conference—training digital, green technology, integration between industry and education and lifelong learning. These proposals seek to ensure the quality of education for citizens, also contributing to boosting productivity and national competitiveness. We are aware of many challenges involving Vocational and Technological Education, which is why debating this topic with peers at a global level is essential. Only in this way we will be able to stimulate the continuous development of technical and technological solutions that can meet internal demands and the growing flows of competitiveness on the national and international scene.

I reiterate, Brazil's unwavering in commitment to work closely with you to reverse the current Vocational and Technological Education scenario worldwide. For the time ahead, our priority is to recover the lessons learned and to innovate with the intensive use of technologies to improve the conditions of access, permanence and learning of students.

Thank you once again and I hope we have fruitful discussions and productive work.

# 四

# 埃塞俄比亚劳动与技能部部长发言

穆费里亚特 · 卡米勒
Muferihat Kamil

本次大会主题为“后疫情时代职业技术教育发展：新变化、新方式、新技能”，这一主题也是当今全球形势的真实写照，体现出了我们在疫情期间所取得的成就以及在技术革新方面的进步。

这些重大变化带来了大量的机会，也带来了新挑战。我希望这次会议能够像一盏明灯一样照亮前方的路，帮助我们应对重重挑战。同时也希望我们能够充分利用这次机会，进一步巩固迄今为止我们在职业技术教育与培训方面取得的成就。技术革新，特别是为我们带来了全新应用领域的高科技技术革命，包括人工智能、大数据、云计算和其他新兴领域的突破，能够提供更高效的服务，助力经济增长，从而影响我们的生活方式。

尽管许多和我们一样的南方国家正在努力追赶并适应这些新的成果，但有一点是毋庸置疑的：科技不再是一种奢侈品，而是能够帮助我们实现现代化转型的一个必要工具。无论是对于发展中国家，抑或是发达国家而言，都有着平等的相关性和重要性。那么，这一现状对职业技术教育与培训的发展意味着什么？换句话说，在这个技术革新的大环境下，职业技术教育与培训是否仍然有价值？是否仍然被需要？职业技术教育与培训领域应该如何进行重整与定位？我相信，这正是本次会议试图解决的问题。

各位嘉宾，女士们，先生们，为了实现职业技术教育与培训对个人、家庭、社会，乃至社会经济发展的价值，埃塞俄比亚政府制定了职业技术教育与培训计划，并为其提供法律、政策和体制框架。目前，本国建立职业技术教育与培训的目的，主要是为了鼓励公民自力更生、发挥创造力、提高工作技能水平，并能够对国家的可持续发展以及社会和经济发展作出贡献，从而改善社会公众的生活水平，特别是青年的生活水平。在减少贫困、走向繁荣的奋斗道路上，我们国家的青年人群也是中坚力量，发挥着巨大的作用。

各位嘉宾，女士们，先生们，数字化科技的发展正在改变全球的工作环境，并对贸易和各行各业的技术人员提出了新的要求，对于基于学院和公司的教学培训流程亦是如此。职业技术教育与培训和数字化技术与工作流程中变化的挑战、行业的发展以及依托于数字媒体的教与学息息相关。

考虑到这些发展，并为支持这一适应的过程，职业技术教育机构会为不同的目标群体提供灵活多样的培训项目。在这一发展进程中，埃塞俄比亚在与合作伙伴的合作过程中受益匪浅。当然，这也得益于中国和其他南方国家之间不断加强的经济联系，中国的公司正在努力扩大规模，吸纳越来越多的埃塞俄比亚雇员。

为了助力技能发展，考虑我们自身的国情，埃塞俄比亚从那些已经在培训和技能发展方面取得卓越成就的国家获取了宝贵的经验。众所周知，目前，中国在全球范围内设立了一个职业培训网络体系，叫作鲁班工坊，它是以中国古代发明家鲁班的名字来命名的。鲁班是中国古代擅长发明创造的能工巧匠，他的故事至今仍为人们所传颂。

2021 年，中国在埃塞俄比亚技术和职业培训学院开设了鲁班工坊，旨在提供高端技术技能培训，帮助大学生满足全球新兴市场的技能要求。该鲁班工坊由中国天津职业技术师范大学在中国教育部的指导下成立。它作为一个卓越的技术中心，横跨四个主要技术领域，即工业传感器技术、机电一体化技术、工业控制和机器人技术以及机械装备制造，这与埃塞俄比亚设定的职业技术教育与培训的目标相一致。同时，埃塞俄比亚职业技术教育与培训政策和战略也呼吁加大来自劳动力市场的投入，并希望业界相关方积极参与课程开发。

对于埃塞俄比亚来说，能在新时代与中国建立双边合作关系并在职业教育领域促成合作，这为本国所面临的一些难题提供了答案。正如在历次会议中商讨的那样，两国在促进职业技术教育与培训方面达成了合作。借此机会，我想表明，埃塞俄比亚强烈希望扩大在我国设立的鲁班工坊的规模，使其能覆盖本国的各个地区。

最后，让我们携手共进，通过分享交流经验，提升职业技术教育与培训机构的作用和价值。埃塞俄比亚已经做好了准备，继续与合作伙伴精诚合作，迎接新的趋势，发展新的技能，开拓新的道路！

# Ⅳ. Speech by Ethiopia's Minister of FDRE Ministry of Labor and Skills

The theme chosen for this conference, Vocational and Technical Education Development in the Post-pandemic Era—New Changes, New Ways and New Skills, is most fitting to the current global realities. It wrote about advancement we have made in innovation and technology during the pandemic.

These profound changes resulted in ample opportunities, and at the same time posed new challenges. I hope that the conference which shades light on new ways of overcoming those challenges also takes advantage of the opportunities to build on our achievements so far in TVET. Innovation in technology, particularly the high-tech revolution that resulted in unprecedented applications, including artificial intelligence, big data, cloud computing and other emerging breakthroughs, have impacted our way of life by contributing to efficient delivery of service and promoting economic growth.

Although many of us from the Global South are striving to catch up and embrace the new findings, one thing is certain: technology is not anymore a luxury, but an indispensable instrument in our transformation in modernization endeavor. It is as relevant and as important to us in the developing world as it is to the developed world. What does this imply for TVET in its development? In other words, in the case of immense innovation, will TVET remain useful and will still be in demand? And what kind of adaptation and orientation should be introduced in the sector? I believe this is what the conference intends to address.

Excellencies, ladies and gentlemen, in a strong will to realize the importance of TVET to individuals, households, society and to social economic development in general, the government of Ethiopia formulated a strategy on TVET and provides legislation, policy, institutional frameworks. The purpose in the establishment of the TVET in the current standing is to encourage citizens towards being self-reliant, creative and skillful and realize their contribution to the sustainable, social and economic development of the country, and hence to improve the livelihood of the society, especially the youth, the immense part in our national effort to reduce poverty and usher Ethiopia's prosperity.

Excellencies, ladies and gentlemen, increasing digitalization is changing the world of work and placing new demands for skilled workers in trade and industries in society as well as for college-based and company-based teaching & gaining training processes. TVET and digitalization are associated with changing challenges in work process, developments of industries and teaching and learning supported by digital media.

To take these developments into account, and to support the adaptation process, the technical vocational education institutions offer selected and flexible training for different target groups. In our effort to develop the sector, Ethiopia greatly benefited from cooperation with our partners, pertinent to this end as a component of a bigger effort to tighten the economic linkages between China and other Global South countries. Chinese companies are working going up-scaling in employing more and more Ethiopians.

In order to advance skills development, considering our own contexts, Ethiopia has taken necessary lessons from countries that have achieved excellence in training and skills development. Apparently, China is setting up a network of vocational colleagues around the world, which is called the Luban Workshop after Luban, a mythical figure referred to as an inventor, who is an exemplary role to date.

Accordingly, in 2021, China launched the Luban Workshop at the Technical and Vocational Training Institute in Ethiopia, with the aim of providing high-end technical skills training to help college students to meet the requirements of the emerging global market. The workshop was established by the Tianjin University of Technology and Education, under the guidance of the Ministry of Education of China. It serves as a center of excellence across four major areas, industrial sensor technology, mechatronics technology, industrial control and robotics technology, and machinery equipment manufacturing. This is in line with Ethiopia's goal for which it has set technical and vocational education and training. Concurrently, Ethiopia's technical and vocational education and training policy and strategy calls for improved input from the labor market, and active involvement of industry in development of curricula.

For Ethiopia to say the opportunity of bilateral ties in the new era with China, cooperation and vocational education provides answers to some of our challenges. It was for this reason that the two countries have pledged to cooperate in promoting technical and vocational education and training as provided in their successive agreements. I was to indicate that Ethiopia has a strong desire to expand the Luban Workshop in Ethiopia so that it also covers our regional states.

In conclusion, let's enhance our cooperation, learn from one another by sharing best practices and build the capacity of TVET institutions. Ethiopia is ready to continue to work with partners to meet the new trends, develop new skills and envision new ways.

# 五

# 韩国教育部副部长发言

张商允
Jang Sang-yoon

经历了两年半的新冠病毒疫情，我很高兴地看到日常生活得以慢慢恢复。同时，也很高兴参加这次会议，让我们共享全球职业教育发展的经验。毫无疑问，这场前所未有的流行疾病在多个领域引发了社会变革，包括人工智能、物联网、增强现实和虚拟现实在内的信息通信技术的使用已经深入我们的日常生活，这对数字化人才的需求越来越高。因此，为了实现飞跃，韩国政府已准备在半导体等尖端领域培养新人才，并努力构建符合未来需求的职业技术教育新模式。

韩国政府不仅在小学和中学教育阶段为学生提供多样化的成长途径，而且针对个人发展阶段提供政策支持，以帮助人们应对职场的最新变化。例如，就业前的中等教育阶段，高中（“大师高中”项目）能提供满足特定行业需求的职业教育，而在学徒制职业学校中，学生穿梭于学校和工作地点之间，能获得有效的职业培训。毕业生顺利就业后，政府会提供一系列的津贴和援助，包括帮助他们接受高等教育，以助其成长为有能力的社会成员。

为了给高中毕业生提供体面的就业机会，政府对雇用高中毕业生的企业给予奖励，并建立了连接中央政府、各地方政府和地方学校的就业支援体系，建立了紧密的青年就业支援基础配套体系。

在高等教育层面，政府发展涵盖合同化、专业化课程的多种职业教育模式，培养适应不同行业需求的个性化人才。在人工智能和未来汽车领域将设立专门职业学院，培养高技能技术人才。为此，还将设立“大师学院”，进一步发展涵盖初级到高级培训水平的课程体系。

在后疫情时代，我们将面临由信息通信技术和创新科学技术进步所带来的社会大变革，迎接“无接触”社会的出现，见证生物和智能技术的飞跃。韩国计划通过培养数字产业和新兴产业人才，提高国家竞争力，应对数字化转型。例如，政府将扩大专门从事软件工程、人工智能和半导体领域的“大师高中”项目，重组课程体系以培养能够促进未来数字化转型的高技能人才。

此外，韩国职业教育院校将与新引入的高等职业教育模式“大师学院”一道，为成年人学习者提供技能再培训机会。为积极应对新技术发展带来的社会变革，政府还将为职业高中和职业学院设立综合课程体系。

目前，韩国政府通过向亚洲、非洲等地传授开设“大师高中”和特殊高中时积累的经验，努力推进全球职业教育发展。值得关注的是，职业教育是对韩国发展作出巨大贡献的因素之一。如今，通过双边教育合作的形式与世界各国分享我们的经验，进一步推动职业教育的发展，确实是一个重要议程。

我希望本次会议围绕“后疫情时代职业技术教育发展：新变化、新方法、新技术”，能使我们分享各种政策和经验，为提供建设性的前进方向贡献智慧。

# V. Speech by the Vice Minister of Education of Republic of Korea

I'm glad to see that after two and a half years of COVID, we're starting to cautiously recover our daily life, and it's a great pleasure that this conference allows us to share the global experience of vocational education development. There's no doubt that the unprecedented pandemic has set off social changes on multiple fronts. Already, the use of ICT, including AI, IoT, AR and VR, has penetrated deeply into our everyday life, increasingly demanding for digital talent. That is why the government of Republic of Korea (ROK) is gearing up to develop new talent in leading-edge fields such as semi-conductors to take a leap forward, while striving to establish a new paradigm for vocational and technical education in line with what the future demands.

The ROK government has not only been providing diverse student growth pathways at the primary and secondary educational levels, but also pursuing policy-wise support corresponding to individual developmental stages to help respond to the latest changes in the workplace. For example, at the secondary educational level prior to employment, high schools (Meister High Schools) provide vocational education designed to meet specific industrial demands, along with apprenticeship-based vocational schools, where students shuttle between the school and work site for effective job training. And after the graduates successfully land a job, we further support them to grow into competent members of society by providing a range of allowances and assistance, including helping them to pursue higher education.

In order to give decent job opportunities for high school graduates, we offer incentives to companies that hire high school graduates, and have established employment support system connecting the central government, local governments and local schools altogether as part of a tight-knit infrastructure to support youth employment.

Moreover, at the higher education level, we've developed diverse types of vocational education models including contract-based curricula and specialized courses to cultivate tailored workforce that can meet various industrial demands. Specialized junior colleges in the fields of AI and futuristic automobiles will be fostered, for which highly-skilled technical workforce will be cultivated. To support, Meister Colleges are introduced to further develop the curricula which encompass elementary to advanced levels of training.

In the post-pandemic era, we'll face society-wide changes brought by technological advances of ICT and innovative scientific technologies with the emergence of a "no-contact" society, as well as the advancement of bio and smart technologies. ROK plans to respond to such digital transition by producing fully-equipped talent for digital and new industries to advance national competitiveness. For example, Meister High Schools that specialize on software engineering, AI and semi-conductors will be expanded, and their curricula will be reorganized to train highly-skilled workforce who can facilitate digital transition in the future.

Also, vocational education institutions will offer re-skilling opportunities to adult learners, along with Meister Colleges, a newly introduced model for higher vocational education. Moreover, integrated curricula for vocational high schools and junior colleges will be introduced to actively respond to social changes led by the development of new technologies.

Today, the ROK government is striving to strengthen vocational education around the world by transferring our extensive experience gained while operating Meister High Schools and Specialized High Schools to countries in Asia and Africa. It's noteworthy that vocational education is one of the factors that has immensely contributed to the development of ROK. Today, vocational education is further promoted by sharing our experience with countries around the world in the form of bilateral education cooperation, which is indeed an important agenda.

I hope this conference focusing on "Vocational and Technical Education Development in the Post-pandemic Era—New Changes, New Ways and New Skills" will allow us to share various policies and experiences, and offer us food for thought to present a constructive way forward.

# 六

# 马来西亚高等教育部部长发言

诺莱妮·艾哈迈德
Noraini Ahmad

首届世界职业技术教育发展大会的主办方精心组织了此次大会，我向你们表示由衷的祝贺。感谢中华人民共和国教育部、中国联合国教科文组织全国委员会、天津市人民政府，感谢你们邀请我在大会上发言。大会的主题是“后疫情时代职业技术教育发展：新变化、新方式、新技能”，我想对此发表一些看法。

首先，请允许我和大家分享马来西亚职业技术教育与培训方面的背景信息。迄今为止，在马来西亚有来自联邦部委、州技能中心和私立学校的 1 295 家机构提供职业技术教育与培训方面的课程。在培养相关行业的合格劳动力，实现国家的社会和经济目标方面，职业技术教育与培训的教育体系具有巨大的潜力。然而，对于希望在马来西亚接受高等教育的人来讲，职业技术教育与培训却不是他们的首选。此外，马来西亚的职业技术教育与培训由 11 个部委管理，在协调和监管方面遇到了不少挑战。

为应对这些挑战，实现职业技术教育与培训的目标，马来西亚内阁已批准在2020年底成立国家职业技术教育与培训理事会，即马来西亚职业技术教育与培训理事会。此举符合我国2021年到2025年的“第十二个发展计划”，也标志着马来西亚“2030年共享繁荣愿景”发展进程新阶段的开始。“第十二个发展计划”的增长目标要求是为满足经济增长的需求，培养高技能人才。根据该计划，截止到2025年，中学毕业生进入职业技术教育与培训体系的比例要达到55%。与此同时，“2030年共享繁荣愿景”的目标是截止到2030年，要有60%的中学毕业生进入职业技术教育与培训体系。

考虑到职业技术教育与培训对我国的重要性，马来西亚总理亲自担任马来西亚职业技术教育与培训理事会主席，而本人作为马来西亚高等教育部部长当选技术委员会主席。马来西亚职业技术教育与培训理事会列出了具有重大战略影响的多项举措，其中已成功实现的有：建立了职业技术教育与培训合作中心及政府—行业职业技术教育与培训协调机构。

政府—行业职业技术教育与培训协调机构的成员由12名代表不同行业的人士组成，来自汽车、航空航天和食品技术等领域。他们的职责包括就当前和未来行业所需的人才及马来西亚高等教育机构需要重点关注的技术为政府提供建议。

马来西亚职业技术教育与培训的项目之一是制定国家职业技术教育与培训品牌计划，目的是改变人们对这种教育类型的看法。计划包括设计马来西亚职业技术教育与培训的标志，标志象征着此领域所有机构同舟共济、团结一致。我们还选择了一个口号：“职业技术教育与培训：你的职业之选”，并将每年的6月2日定为全国职业技术教育与培训日。此外，马来西亚政府将为在公立高等教育机构接受职业技术教育与培训的来自40%最低收入群体的学生提供职业技术教育与培训奖学金计划。

必须承认，通过政府的各项举措，马来西亚的职业技术教育与培训计划已经取得了一定的成效。多年来，创新型的教学方法越来越多地被引入教育领域。例如，将包括人工智能在内的最新技术纳入职业技术教育与培训课程，以产出为导向的教育也越来越受到重视。

因此，现在我们以各地社区为单位，整合各类群体的终身学习计划，包括青年人、老年人、40%最低收入群体、残障人、土著群体以及单身母亲。我们还实施了一个名为“模块化PSH”的结构化终身学习计划，该计划用短期培训模块培训学员。此举有助于帮助社区提高其在职业技术教育与培训各个领域的技能和知识，并创造收入。截至 2022 年 6 月 30 日，已有超过 85 000 人参加了社区大学实施的 PSH 计划。社区感兴趣的五个领域为：餐饮和服务、计算机信息技术、商业与创业、图形与多媒体以及自我发展。

职业技术教育与培训本身具有其先进性，一方面我们希望这一点在未来有助于缩小毕业生的资质与实际工作需求之间的差距。另一方面，我们希望此举在未来发挥作用，让职业技术教育与培训课程成为有志于继续深造的学生的首选。

马来西亚与中国长期以来一直保持着和谐的双边关系，不论在教育还是行业伙伴关系方面皆是如此。马来西亚和中国的行业合作为许多职业技术教育与培训领域的学生和毕业生提供了宝贵的工作经验。马来西亚的职业技术教育与培训机构已经开始与中国的合作伙伴开展各种合作。我们期待马中两国政府机构和行业人士继续合作，不断提升两国职业技术教育与培训的水平。

最后，衷心希望本次大会能够为职业技术教育与培训的蓬勃发展提供更多的机会。

## VI. Speech by the Minister of Higher Education of Malaysia

Congratulations to the hosts of the first World Vocational and Technical Education Development Conference, for organizing this important event. Thank you to the Ministry of Education of the People's Republic of China, the National Commission of the People's Republic of China for UNESCO, and the Tianjin Municipal People's Government for inviting me to say a few words at this conference.

I am delighted to share with you some insights on the conference theme, "Vocational and Technical Education Development in the Post-pandemic Era—New Changes, New Ways and New Skills".

Allow me to begin by providing some background information on the scenario of Malaysia's Technical and Vocational Education and Training, known as TVET. To date, Malaysia has 1 295 institutions that offer TVET programs from federal ministries, state skills centers and private providers. The TVET education track has tremendous potential in producing a competent workforce in related industries to meet the social and economic objectives of the country. However, TVET has not been the first choice for those who wish to pursue their tertiary education in Malaysia. In addition, TVET is run by 11 ministries, causing challenges in terms of coordination and regulation.

To address these challenges, the cabinet of Malaysia has approved the formation of a National TVET Council, MTVET, at the end of 2020 to actualize the TVET agenda. This is in line with our 12th Malaysia Plan which spans from 2021 to 2025 and is also known as the beginning of a new phase in Malaysia's development journey of the Shared Prosperity Vision 2030. The growth targets of the 12th Malaysia Plan require the development of highly skilled talent to support the demands of a growing economy. Based on this plan, the target for intake of school leavers into TVET programs is set at 55% by 2025. At the same time, the Shared Prosperity Vision aims for 60% of school leavers to pursue TVET programs by 2030.

Considering the importance of TVET to the country, Malaysia's Prime Minister himself has been elected as the Chairman of the MTVET Council and I, as Malaysia's Minister of Higher Education have been elected as Chairman of the Technical Committee. MTVET outlines several initiatives that have a big and strategic impact.

Among those successfully achieved are the establishment of the TVET Collaboration Hub and the establishment of the Government-Industry TVET Coordination Body (GITC).

GITC members consist of 12 individuals representing different industry sectors ranging from automotive and aerospace to food technology. Their roles include advising the government on talent required by current and future industries, as well as the technologies that need focus in our higher education institutions (HEIs).

One of Malaysia's TVET agendas is to develop a National TVET Branding Plan that will change people's perception of TVET. One move in the plan is to introduce the TVET Malaysia logo which displays a symbol of togetherness of all TVET providers. We also chose the slogan "TVET, the Main Career Choice" and selected the 2nd of June as the National TVET Day. In addition, the Malaysian Government has agreed to implement a TVET Bursary Program for those from the bottom 40 (B40) income group who are studying in the TVET field at public HEIs.

It is important to acknowledge that through various government initiatives, the TVET programs in Malaysia have shown advancements. Over the years, there has been increased incorporation of innovative methods of teaching and learning such as the inclusion of the latest technologies including Artificial Intelligence in the TVET curriculum. There has also been an increased focus on Outcome Based Education.

As a result, we now see the integration of Lifelong Learning Programs targeting the local community involving the youth, the elderly, the B40 group, people with disabilities, indigenous groups and single mothers. A structured Lifelong Learning Program known as the Modular PSH which uses short-term training modules has been implemented. This helps communities to improve their skills and knowledge in various areas of TVET and aids them in generating income. As of the 30th of June 2022, more than 85 000 individuals participated in the PSH program implemented in community colleges. The five areas that are of interest to the community are: Catering and Serving, Computers and Information Technology, Business and Entrepreneurship, Graphics and Multimedia, and Self-Development.

We hope that the progressive nature of TVET will close the gap between the qualifications of our graduates and available jobs in the market. In turn, we hope this will make the TVET education track a preferred choice among those interested in furthering their studies.

Malaysia and China have long enjoyed harmonious bilateral ties—both in education and industrial partnership. The cooperation between the industries in Malaysia and China plays a major role in providing work experience to many TVET students and graduates. TVET institutions in Malaysia are already embarking on various collaboration efforts with our Chinese partners. We look forward to the continuous cooperation between the government agencies and the industry players in Malaysia and China to enhance TVET education in both countries.

On that note, I hope this conference will provide more opportunities for the dynamic development of TVET.

# 七

# 蒙古国教育科学部部长发言

恩赫阿木格朗
Enkh-Amgalan

目前，各国都在努力克服新冠病毒疫情给社会、经济各个领域带来的挑战，然而，我们还未找出最完美的解决方案，我希望各参会国能够分享应对新冠病毒疫情的有效措施与经验。根据有关应对措施的资料和不断变化的统计数据，现在我们可以确立未来的目标。最让人欣慰以及最重要的是，现在我们万众一心，共同寻求解决方案来应对面临的挑战。疫情之后，必须确定如何发展职业技术教育与培训，发现新的技能和方法，将损失转化为新的发展机会。所以，本次世界职业技术教育发展大会至关重要。

蒙古国目前有 76 个职业技术教育与培训机构，能够提供 200 多个专业的课程培训，有 50 000 名在校学生和 4 000 余名教职员工。毕业生在劳动力市场的就业率超过了 60%。但是，这一数字在新冠病毒疫情发生后下降了 10%。

正因如此，蒙古国政府采取了措施，防止职业技术教育与培训的学生人数减少。这是因为我们认为，在新冠病毒疫情之后，各个经济领域都将复苏并继续发展，因此，劳动力市场对技术工人的需求也将会随之大幅增加。

蒙古国政府也在此期间提出了“新复苏政策”，是国家“2050 年愿景”的第一阶段。希望在这一政策的支持下，蒙古国的经济平均增速能够保持在 6% 左右，人均国民收入翻倍，劳动力参与率达到 65%，预计边境城市的产能增加到 3 倍，能源行业的产能增加到 2 倍。

想要实现这些目标，最重要的是为劳动力市场准备好成熟的技术工人。今后，我们有必要利用不同的方法提高蒙古国职业教育部门教师的技能培训。在这个大环境下，在国际范围内定期组织在线教师培训是完全有可能的。

在此，我谨代表蒙古国政府和教育科学部，对组织本次会议的中华人民共和国教育部表示诚挚的感谢，让各国有机会相互交流，为解决后疫情时代教育行业出现的各种问题提出优质的方法策略。

# VII. Speech by the Minister of Education and Science of Mongolia

At present, all countries are trying to overcome the challenges brought by the pandemic in all areas of the society and economy, however, a perfect solution and an optimal way have not been fully discovered. I would like the participant countries to share their best practices of overcoming the pandemic. Based on all the information and changing statistics about these survival and coping measures, we can establish our future goals. The most delightful and vital thing is that we all stay and work together to seek solutions to the challenges faced. After the pandemic, it is necessary to determine how to develop the TVET sector, identify new skills and methods, and turn all loss into new opportunities for development. Therefore, today's World Vocational and Technical Education Development Conference is very crucial.

In Mongolia, currently we have 76 TVET institutions that provide training in more than 200 professions with approximately 50 000 students studying and 4 000 teachers and employees working. And the employment rate of the graduates in the labor market is more than 60%. This number decreased by 10% after the breakout of the pandemic. Due to this consequence, the government of Mongolia is following a strategy not to reduce the number of TVET students. This is related to our optimistic imagination that after COVID-19, all sectors of the economy will re-develop, and the demand for skilled workers will significantly increase in the labor market.

The government of Mongolia put forward a "New Recovery Policy", the first part of the country's Vision 2050 programme. It is expected that through the policy, Mongolia's economic growth will be maintained at an average of 6%. The national income per capita will double and the labor force participation rate will be 65%. It is estimated that the capacity of the border cities will increase by 3 times, and energy source will increase 2 times.

To implement all these goals, it is of utmost importance to prepare well-skilled workers for the labor market. In the future, it is necessary to pay special attention to improving the skills of the teaching staff in the Mongolian vocational education sector by using different methods. In this context, we have seen that it is possible to regularly organize online teacher training on an international scale.

On behalf of the government of Mongolia and the Ministry of Education and Science, I would like to express our sincere gratitude to the Ministry of Education of the People's Republic of China for organizing this event which brings an opportunity for countries to learn from each other. We find that this conference brought positive impact in solving thc problcms that have risen in our industry after the COVID-19 pandemic.

# 八

# 尼日利亚教育部
# 国务部长发言

古德勒克·奥皮亚
Goodluck Opiah

今天，我很荣幸出席由中华人民共和国教育部、中国联合国教科文组织全国委员会和天津市人民政府共同主办的首届世界职业技术教育发展大会，这是一次具有历史意义的盛会。全球正在应对动乱不安、气候变化和经济衰退，此次大会主题——“后疫情时代职业技术教育发展：新变化、新方式、新技能”恰逢其时。

新冠病毒疫情的到来迫使包括职业技术教育与培训在内的所有行业迫切吸收或加速将数字技术融入其实践。此外，以越来越多使用人工智能、云计算、机器人等新技术为特征的第四次工业革命迎来了一个新的经济颠覆时代，生活和就业所需的技能组合也发生了变化，数字技能处于突出地位。因此，迫切需要建立一个生态系统，实现职业技术教育与培训和技能发展的全球数字化转型。

新冠病毒疫情使包括尼日利亚在内的全球各国失学儿童现象进一步恶化。据联合国教科文组织估计，由于新冠病毒疫情对全球健康危机的共同影响，有 2 380 万儿童被迫辍学或被剥夺了上学的机会。现有数据表明，全世界有超过 12 亿人在疫情期间受到了学校停课的影响，其中就包括职业技术教育与培训的学生。

尼日利亚教育部部长阿达穆 · 阿达穆的指出，教学过程往往通过互联网、电视或广播远程进行，但包括职业技术教育与培训在内的课堂之外进行学习的程度往往受到电力供应、网络连接、设备或媒体学习平台的限制，教师和学生也存在准备不够充足的情况。

本届政府在总统穆罕默杜 · 布哈里的带领下，通过教育部门，特别是通过鼓励创业、职业和技术教育培训，为尼日利亚青年和毕业生创造就业机会和收入，提高全球竞争力，对尼日利亚的经济发展进行了重新定位，这是尼日利亚政府的一贯政策。针对如何通过政策和立法来重新定位职业技术教育与培训并制定新的方针，我们已经组织召开了各种会议、研修班和研讨会。例如我们不同教育水平的学生都学习编码编程和机器人方面的课程。

尼日利亚政府强调职业技术教育与培训的重要性，并将其列为国家教育部门计划的优先事项。这体现在以下几个方面：在全国各地建立了设备齐全的科技学院，成立卓越资源中心，推动创新和提升质量以及大规模的人力资源开发。此外，为了应对新冠病毒疫情，联邦教育部通过改革实践奠定了良好的基础，包括以下两方面。

一是组建由教育部门关键人员组成的指导小组，将新冠病毒疫情议定书纳入教育部门。这促进了各州教育部的有效协调，并推动了各州与教育部合作 / 协调的蓝图，以分享信息和经验。

二是通过迅速部署电子学习平台让学生继续上课。尼日利亚有 1 800 多个促进教学的教育网站，还有其他相关平台，并与电信服务提供商合作，为教育门户网站提供免费带宽。电视台和广播电台正在为偏远地区的学生提供教学平台，同时还制定了应急预案，避免新冠病毒或任何可能发生的大规模流行病在学校社区中（学生、教师和非教师身份的工作人员）的感染和传播。

在此，我代表尼日利亚教育部，对这一令人称赞的愿景感到高兴，并对中国为组织此次世界职业技术教育发展大会所做的努力表示感谢。此次盛会所带来的创新和重要贡献，将激发更多人用更好的方法来应对 21 世纪的挑战。

## Ⅷ. Speech by the Minister of State for Education of Nigeria

I am very pleased to join you today for this historic event of the first World Vocational and Technical Education Development Conference jointly organized by the Ministry of Education of the People's Republic of China, the National Commission of the People's Republic of China for UNESCO and the Tianjin Municipal People's Government. The theme of the conference— "Vocational and Technical Education Development in the Post-Pandemic Era—New Changes, New Ways and New Skills" is very appropriate at this time that the world is witnessing civil unrest, insecurity, climate change and economic recession.

The advent of COVID-19 has forced all industries, including Technical and Vocational Education Training (TVET), to urgently ingest or accelerate the integration of digitals into their practices. Furthermore, the Fourth Industrial Revolution (4IR), characterized by the increasing use of new technologies such as artificial intelligence, cloud computing, robotics, and many others, has ushered in a new era of economic disruption and a shift in the skill set required for life and employment, with digital skills in a prominent position. This therefore calls for urgent creation of an ecosystem that will enable global digital transformation of TVET and skills development.

The effect of the COVID-19 pandemic has further worsened the Out-of-School Children phenomenon globally, including Nigeria. UNESCO estimates that 23.8 million children have been forced to drop out of school or deprived of schooling as a result of the common impact of COVID-19 on the global health crisis. Available data indicates that more than 1.2 billion world-wide were affected by school closure amid COVID-19 including TVET students.

In Nigeria, on the directive of the Honourable Minister of Education, Adamu Adamu, teaching and learning was often done remotely through the Internet, television or radio but the degree to which learning can take place outside the classroom including TVET is often limited by access to electricity, Internet connectivity, devices or media learning platforms and even inadequate preparation of instructors and students.

The present administration of President Muhammadu Buhari has adopted and is re-positioning the economic development of Nigeria, through the education sector especially by embracing entrepreneurial, Technical and Vocational Education Training (TVET) for job creation, income generation and global competitiveness of Nigerian youths and graduates. This has remained a constant factor in Nigerian Government Policy. Conferences, seminars and workshops have been organized to chart a new course on how to reposition TVET through policy and legislative options. Our students at all levels of education receive lessons on coding, programming and robotics.

The Nigerian government places emphasis on the importance of Technical and Vocational Education and Training (TVET) and has prioritized it in the National Education Sector Plan. This is seen in the establishment of new well equipped Science and Technical Colleges across the country; establishment of Resource Centres of Excellence to promote innovations and improve quality; and massive human capacity development.

Furthermore, to tackle the challenges of Covid-19 pandemic, the Federal Ministry of Education has laid a good foundation through transforming practices including:

—the constitution of a steering task team made up of critical stakeholders in the education sector to domesticate the COVID-19 protocol in the education sector. This has resulted in the effective coordination and development of a blueprint for collaboration /coordination with States' Ministry of Education for information and experience sharing;

—rapid deployment of e-learning platforms for students to continue their lessons. Nigeria has over 1 800 education sites that promote teaching and learning. There are other associated platforms and collaboration with telecom service providers in offering free bandwidth to access educational portals. Television and radio stations are providing teaching platform to reach students in the remote location and this is also supported by development of contingency plan to ensure that the school community (learners, teaching and non-teaching staff) are protected from infection and transmission of COVID-19 or any pandemic that may occur.

At this juncture, ladies and gentlemen, may I state that the Ministry is happy with this laudable vision and wish to commend your efforts towards organizing this world conference on Vocational and Technical Education, a global issue that will afford many to learn better ways of tackling the challenges of the 21st century through innovative and critical contributions emanating from this conference.

# 九

# 巴基斯坦联邦教育与职业培训部部长发言

拉纳·坦维尔·侯赛因
Rana Tanveer Hussain

本次会议致力于应对后疫情时代不断变化的挑战，特别是与劳动力的技能发展有关的挑战。目前，全球对技能型劳动力的需求正在发生变化，从传统技能转向工业革命 4.0 的新兴未来型技能。

中国和巴基斯坦友谊源远流长，有着七十多年充满活力的合作历史和战略伙伴关系。巴基斯坦人民始终珍视与中国的友谊和外交关系，并为有这样一个伟大而真诚的朋友而感到无比自豪。近几十年来，中国已成为一个大国，中国在经济领域取得的发展，为包括巴基斯坦在内的所有国家提供了思路和经验。今天的巴基斯坦正面临着贫困和失业的挑战。我相信，在双方的共同努力下，中巴友谊将继续展现新的活力，巴基斯坦将从中受益，进入发展的新时代。

在全球范围内，职业技术教育及技能发展被认为是消除贫困，实现经济可持续发展，维护和平与繁荣、法律与秩序的关键。因此，对于巴基斯坦这样的发展中国家来说，技能发展不容忽视。巴基斯坦年轻人的人口数量世界排名第五，15—35岁年龄段的人口约占全国总人口的63%。职业技术教育与培训和技能发展是提高生产力和减少贫困的工具。任何国家的技能型劳动力和人均收入都密切相关。

巴基斯坦需要技能型劳动力，使本地产业和企业具有竞争力，从而提高生产力，促进出口。职业技术教育与培训和青年技能发展对于实现这些国家发展目标至关重要。因此，现在最需要的是投资于人才培养，在巴基斯坦创造更多的培训机会。运营本地产业至少需要100万高素质、技能型劳动力，包括专门建设中巴经济走廊和经济特区的技术工人。在联邦教育和职业培训部的指导下，国家职业技术培训委员会正在全力弥补巴基斯坦技术工人的供需差距。为满足本地就业市场的技能需求，特别是中巴经济走廊和国际就业市场，包括中国“一带一路”等充满活力的全球性倡议，我们推出了前瞻性、高科技、以信息技术为基础的尖端技术培训。

我很自豪地告诉大家，国家职业技术培训委员会为巴基斯坦人才培养作出了重要贡献。成千上万的巴基斯坦年轻人已经掌握了技术型实践技能，并在当地和海外就业，但仍有一大批非技术型工人需要更多的培训机会来满足他们的需求。

面对全球对技能型劳动力需求的不断变化，巴基斯坦政府已将重点转向高科技技能，以应对全球新兴需求。现在，巴基斯坦的年轻人正在接受新兴技术的培训，如人工智能、机器人技术、网络安全、大数据、物联网和其他新兴技术。联邦教育和职业培训部下属的国家职业技术培训委员会开发了一个强大的国家技能信息系统，并建立了全国技能青年就业交流平台和就业数据库门户网站，该数据库有超过47万名有技能、有证书的青年，最近还为青年提供了大约47万个工作岗位。巴基斯坦政府正在探索与其发展伙伴的合作，以促进巴基斯坦职业技术教育与培训的发展，并将中国视为该领域的先锋伙伴。

最后，我感谢中方对巴基斯坦教育和培训这一具体主题的密切关注。同时，我也期待两国通过交流项目、协作技能倡议、职教管理人员和教师的培训以及技术转让项目等外交关系，使巴基斯坦的青年群体具备新兴技能。我们希望此次会议将成为两国共同通过“一带一路”和中巴经济走廊实现地区繁荣目标的一个重要倡议和里程碑。

# IX. Speech by the Minister of Federal Education and Professional Training of Pakistan

This Conference is striving to address the evolving challenges in the post-pandemic era, particularly related to the skill development of workforce. At present, the demand for skilled labor force is globally evolving, with a shift from conventional skills to the emerging, futuristic skills of Industrial Revolution 4.0.

Both nations, the People's Republic of China and Pakistan are not only long lasting friends but also share the dynamic history of mutual cooperation and strategic partnership for more than 70 years. The people of Pakistan always cherish the friendship and diplomatic ties with the People's Republic of China and feel immense pride to have such a great and sincere friend. China has emerged as a major country in recent decades and the development made by China in economy is a source of inspiration for all the nations including Pakistan. Pakistan today is facing the challenges of poverty and unemployment. I'm confident that, with the joint diplomatic efforts of both sides, not only China-Pak friendship will continue to display new vigor but also Pakistan will reap the benefit to enter into the new era of development in coming years.

Technical and vocational education and skill development is globally perceived as the key to alleviating poverty, sustainable economic development, peace, prosperity and unrestraint law and order in any society. Foregoing, skill development cannot be ignored in case of a developing nation like Pakistan. A country having fifth largest young population in the world, comprising of around 63 percent of the whole population of the country in the age bracket of 15–35. Technical and Vocational Education and Training (TVET) and skill development is a tool for enhanced productivity and poverty reduction. There is a strong correlation between the skilled labor and per capita income of any state.

Pakistan needs skilled workforce to competitively enable our local industry and businesses, leading to enhanced productivity and export. TVET and youth skill development is crucial to the achievement of these national goals. Therefore, it is high need of time to invest in human resource development and create more training opportunities in Pakistan. At least one million quality skilled workforce is required to operate the local industry including purpose-built skilled workforce for China

Pakistan Economic Corridor (CPEC) and Special Economic Zones (SEZs). The National Vocational Technical Training Commission (NAVTTC) under the directions of Ministry of Federal Education and Professional Training is making all-out efforts to bridge the gap between demand and supply of skilled workforce in Pakistan. Skill trainings in futuristic, Hi-Tech, IT based cutting-edge technologies are being launched to address the skill needs of local job market especially CPEC and international job market including the dynamic global initiatives of China like the Belt and Road Initiative (BRI).

I am proud to share with you that the National Vocational and Technical Training Commission has made major contribution to Pakistan's national human resource development. Thousands of Pakistani youth have been equipped with technical hands-on skills and got employed locally as well as overseas, yet a big unskilled chunk needs to be catered by creating more training opportunities.

Realizing the globally changing demand of skilled workforce, Government of Pakistan has shifted the focus towards Hi-Tech skills to be able to cope with the emerging global demands. Today, the youth are being trained in emerging skills in Pakistan like: Artificial Intelligence, Robotics, Cyber Security, Big Data, Internet of Things (IoT) and other emerging skills. National Vocational Technical Training Commission under Ministry of Federal Education and Professional Training has developed one of its kind, a robust National Skills Information System (NSIS) and established National Employment Exchange Tool for Skilled Youth & Job Database Portal with databank of more than 470 000 skilled and certified youth and around 470 000 jobs have recently been made available for the youth. Government of Pakistan is exploring collaborative arrangements with its development partners for the uplift of TVET sector in Pakistan and perceives the People's Republic of China as a vanguard partner in this context.

In the end, I would extend my appreciation for my Chinese counterpart for keen interest for the specific subject of education and training in Pakistan. And also foresee to establish diplomatic ties for mutually equipping Pakistani youth bulge with emerging skills through exchange programs, collaborative skill initiatives, training of TVET administrators and trainers, and transfer of technology programs. We hope this conference will prove to be a significant initiative and a major milestone towards the mutual resolve of both nations to attain the objectives of regional prosperity through the BRI and CPEC.

# 十

## 俄罗斯教育部部长发言①

谢尔盖·克拉夫佐夫
Sergei Kravtsov

很高兴参加世界职业技术教育发展大会。本次活动聚集了来自世界各地直接影响青年人才培养和科研思想发展的各界人士，其中不乏学者、政府机构代表和来自大型企业、单位的人士。

我要指出的是，我国对中等职业教育体系一直高度重视。今年，我们将启动一个联邦专业项目，目的在于实现中等职业教育体系的全面现代化。该项目将建立一个培养具备现代前沿技能的高素质人才的专业模式。如今，俄罗斯正在建立全套生产技能的培训体系，许多工作均在进行当中，以确保毕业生能够投入到实际的生产工作中。

当然，诸如本次会议等相关活动都在为这个项目添砖加瓦，将为完善青年人才培养体系作出重大贡献，也将进一步促进教育领域的国际合作。

此外，根据总统令，10 月 2 日被确立为俄罗斯联邦的“中等职业教育日”。我相信，这样的倡议会得到其他国家的支持。

① 注：俄罗斯教育部提供讲稿和照片。

# X. Speech by the Minister of Education of Russia[1]

Очень рад присутствовать на Мировой профессионально–технической конференции по развитию технического образования. Это мероприятие объединило широкий круг участников из разных стран мира, в их числе: ученые, представители органов власти, крупных компаний, работодателей, те, кто напрямую влияет на подготовку молодых специалистов и развитие научной и исследовательской мысли.

Отмечу, что в нашей стране системе среднего профессионального образования уделяется самое серьезное внимание. Так, в этом году стартует Федеральный проект «Профессионалитет», нацеленный на ее комплексную модернизацию. Новая программа позволит выстроить отраслевую модель подготовки специалистов, обладающих высокой квалификацией и современными востребованными навыками. Сегодня в России создаются учебно-производственные комплексы, мастерские, многое делается для того, чтобы выпускники были готовы к работе на реальном производстве.

И, конечно, такие мероприятия, как нынешняя конференция, дополняют эту работу, вносят значимый вклад в совершенствование системы подготовки молодых кадров, содействуют укреплению международного сотрудничества в сфере образования.

Также Указом Президента 2 октября в Российской Федерации назначено как День среднего профессионального образования. Уверен, что такая инициатива может быть поддержана и в других странах мира.

① The speech and the photo are provided by the Ministry of Education of Russia.

# 十一

## 新加坡教育部部长发言①

后疫情时代的职业技术教育发展需聚焦三大重点：
“终生学习，学以致用”“通力合作，相辅相成”
“勇于创新，开拓未来”

陈振声
Chan Chun Sing

本次大会主题是“后疫情时代职业技术教育发展：新变化、新方式、新技能”。这一主题对我们这代人而言相当贴切。

未来有三大推动力将塑造教育的长期愿景。第一，科技的半衰期正在缩短，各种技能和知识也以前所未有的速度遭到淘汰；第二，全球互联互通程度不断提高，为所有人创造了更多机会，但也加剧了机会和结果不平等的问题；第三，随着各国变得更加相互依存，面对全球化的力量，我们需要在区域内加强协调，建立更好的合作。

---

① 注：陈振声部长于 2022 年 8 月在世界职业技术教育发展大会上的演讲。新加坡政府（通过新加坡教育部）拥有本演讲稿的版权，本汇编已获得他们的许可。

我们的职业教育机构需要与时俱进，不仅仅是被动地做出反应，而是主动地预测未来趋势，并积极做出调整，推进发展。各个机构需要通过以下三个“C”来创新求变：第一个C是Continual Learning，即“终生学习，学以致用”，让国人活到老学到老，并在生活中应用所学；第二个C是Connections and Collaboration，即“通力合作，相辅相成”，通过合作，大家取长补短，相得益彰；第三个C是Creation of New Solutions for Tomorrow's Challenges，即“勇于创新，开拓未来”，通过创新，给明日的挑战提出新的解决方案。

我先来说第一点，终生学习，学以致用（Continual Learning—Learning for Life; Learning Through Life）。从课程筹划、教员培训到学员教导直至毕业，教育机构一般需要花上数年时间。又鉴于所教授的技能有可能在学员毕业不久后便过时，教育机构需要改换这一传统运作模式。学无止境，在学校里预先学习再多知识都是不足够的。因此，我们需要摒弃“让国人在学生时期学会所有知识技能”这一思维模式，改而推动终身学习，培养国人于生活工作中学习以及终生持续学习的习惯。

转变需从教员开始，教员须掌握与行业息息相关的技能，才能教导并协助学习者应付瞬息万变的市场需求。教员也须具备合适的教学工具，用以丰富学习者的学习体验。更重要的是，教员还须抱有终生学习的正确心态，愿意为掌握各项所需技能而不断提升自己，接受再培训。

我们也需要克服信息不对称的问题，激发在职成年人对再培训和技能提升的兴趣。在新加坡推行的“技能创前程（SkillsFuture）”已经取得一些进展，但仍有许多工作待我们完成。第一，协助企业公司阐明对未来技能的需求；第二，将之汇总为各行业对新技能的需求；第三，启动技能教育机构来满足这些需求，这是我们当前的三个主要工作。只有这样，我们才能确保每个人都乐于终生学习，学以致用。但这绝非某一方凭一己之力就能做到的，教育机构需要和政府机构、行业协会以及企业公司展开合作，确认所需技能，并共同设计甚至共同教授适合在职成年人的短期、可堆叠课程。

这就引出了我要说的第二点，通力合作，相辅相成（Connections and Collaboration）。我们需和他人联系，才能合作无间。在这个互联程度越来越高、节奏越来越快、机会与结果不平等问题越来越严重的世界里，我们需要一个强大的联系网络，让我们能够保持团结、与时俱进。例如，东南亚教育部长组织和东盟通过推展区域计划和成立东盟技术和职业教育与培训理事会，在促进和鼓励区域内外的合作与交流方面发挥了重要的作用。

新加坡的教育机构也持续通过海外交流和实习计划，与世界各地建立或重建联系。例如，新加坡工艺教育学院就和深圳赛意法微电子有限公司达成了一项协议，让学员参与该公司的线上实习。这个例子也突显了学界与业界之间相互联系的重要性。当学员在职业教育机构学习的时候，他们必须能够在不受时间和学科限制的情况下，获得高质量的实习机会。同时，我们可将课堂嵌入工作场所，让学员得以利用职场中实际使用的工具，解决行业真实存在的问题，通过实践学习。

这里来到了我要说的最后一点，勇于创新，开拓未来（Creation of New Solutions for Tomorrow's Challenges）。教育不能仅关乎用现有的方案来解决眼下的问题。相反地，教育需要从海内外各机构行业汲取知识，甚至创造新知识，以便我们以新想法和方式迎接并解决未来的挑战。

设想有这样一个体制：前沿行业和行业协会与我们的职业教育机构合作成立"企业实验室"，或积极开展合作项目。在合作过程中，业界与教育机构不但共同设计具备前瞻性的课程，且一起应对未来的全球挑战，并为未来的市场提供新的产品和服务。

在新加坡，我们在理工学院里设立了创新中心和技术中心，让中小型企业和职业教育机构共同开发新点子和解决方案。我们欢迎来自中国和世界各地的与会者来新参观我们的高等院校，并相互分享交流最佳做法。那将有助于我们的业界、学员和劳动队伍更好地应对未来。

我们的教育制度必须不断创新。作为一个国家，我们在学习和创新方面可以更具韧性，并与来自不同文化和背景的人建立联系，加强协作，从而改善国人的生活。我们期待在本次大会上向各位学习。谢谢。

# XI. Speech by the Minister for Education of Singapore[①]

### Vocational and Technical Education Development in the Post-pandemic Era needs to focus on 3Cs: Continual Learning, Connections and Collaboration, and Creation of New Solutions for Tomorrow's Challenges

Thank you for inviting me to speak today. The theme of today's conference, 'Vocational and Technical Education Development in the Post-pandemic Era—New Changes, New Ways and New Skills', is an apt one for our generation.

We will experience three major forces that will shape the long-term vision of education: First, the half-life of technology is shrinking, and skills and knowledge are becoming obsolete faster than before. Second, a more connected world creates more opportunities for all, but also greater inequality of opportunities and outcomes. Third, as we become more interdependent, forces of globalisation will require us to build better coordination and collaboration within the region.

Our vocational institutions need to evolve, not just to respond and react; but to anticipate, adapt and advance. They need to innovate through these three 'C's: Continual Learning, where our students are learning for life and applying these lessons in life. Connections and Collaboration, where we collaborate to complement one another's strengths. Creation of New Solutions for Tomorrow's Challenges, to innovate so as to create solutions for the future.

Let me touch on my first point, Continual Learning—Learning for Life; Learning Through Life. The traditional way of preparing a course, training the trainers and finally graduating the students, which typically takes a few years, will need to change as skills taught may become obsolete not long after students graduate. No amount of prior learning in school will be adequate. Therefore, we need to shift our mindsets from frontloading education to Learning for Life; learning for the rest of our lives and

① Minister Chan Chun Sing's speech at the World Vocational and Technical Education Development Conference in August 2022. The Government of Singapore (c/o the Ministry of Education) owns the copyright to the speech and the speech had been reproduced with their permission.

learning through life.

This must start with our trainers. We must equip our trainers with the right industry-relevant skillset so they can in turn equip learners to meet the demands of a fast-evolving market. Trainers must also have the right teaching tools to enhance the learning experience for students. But more importantly, our trainers must have the right mindset for lifelong learning and be willing to upgrade and retrain themselves to acquire the right skills.

Next, we need to overcome the asymmetry of information and awaken the interests of the working adults in reskilling and upskilling. In Singapore, we have gone some way with the SkillsFuture Movement but more remains to be done. Three key areas that we need are to help companies articulate the demand for future skills, aggregate these into sectoral demand for new skills, and lastly to activate the supply of such future skills to meet these needs. Only then can we ensure individuals are interested in learning for life and learning through life.

But no party can do this alone. Our institutions need to partner with government agencies, industry associations and companies to identify skills in demand and co-create, and even co-teach short and stackable courses for working adults.

This brings me to my next point, Connections and Collaboration. We must be connectors to collaborate. In an inter-connected world that is becoming more fast-paced, with greater inequality of opportunities and outcomes, we will need a strong network of connections to keep us current and together. For example, SEAMEO and ASEAN play important roles in facilitating and encouraging collaborations and exchanges within the region and beyond, through regional programmes and the formation of the ASEAN TVET Council.

Our institutions in Singapore also continue to connect and reconnect with the world through their overseas exchange and internship programmes. For example, the Institute of Technical Education has an agreement with Shenzhen STS Microelectronics Co. Ltd, allowing students to participate in virtual internships. The example also shows the importance of the connection between academia and industry. As students go through our vocational institutions, they must have access to quality internships, without being constrained by time and subject of study. We can also bring our institutions into the workplace and allow students to learn by working with real-life tools to solve real-life industry problems.

This brings us to the final 'C', Creation of New Solutions for Tomorrow's Challenges. Education cannot be about solving today's problems with yesterday's or today's solutions only. Instead, education needs to draw out and even create knowledge from all institutions and industries together, not just locally but internationally, to pre-empt and solve tomorrow's challenges with new ideas and approaches.

Imagine a system where frontier industries and trade associations have 'corporate labs' or other active collaborations with our vocational institutions. In these collaborations, industry and institution co-create the curricula of tomorrow, tackle the global challenges of tomorrow, and produce new products and services for tomorrow's markets.

In Singapore, we set up Centres of Innovation and technology centres in our polytechnics, for our SMEs and vocational institutions to co-develop new ideas and solutions. We invite our Chinese and international participants to visit our IHLs and share best practices with one another. That will help make our industry, students and workforce more future ready.

Constant innovation to our education system is essential. As a nation, we can be more resilient learners and innovators, who make connections and collaborate with people of different cultures and backgrounds, to improve lives. We look forward to learning from your sharing and best practices in this conference. Thank you.

# 十二

## 委内瑞拉高等教育部部长发言

蒂比塞·卢萨纳
Tibisay Lucena

世界正面临着由新冠病毒疫情大流行带来的巨大挑战，最重要的是，人们需要在疫情传播和危及生命安全的风险压力下继续生活。发达国家开始进入“工业4.0”时代，以云计算、大数据、人工智能和区块链为代表的新一轮科技革命，引发了对高素质技术人才的需求。职业技术教育必须迅速应对这样的挑战。然而，这一趋势并没有在全球范围内均衡地反映出来。南北之间经济的差异，使欠发达国家在职业技术教育方面遭遇更多问题。如果说技术不能卓有成效，或者让这些欠发达国家沦为只能购买技术的消费者和只有依附他国才能不断获取技术的附属者，职业技术教育就没能完成培养高质量的高科技人员的任务。在这种情况下，政府和大学正在寻找摆脱依赖的方法，以转变生产关系、满足人民基本需求的新生产模式来谋求发展。

在我国，根据1999年的《委内瑞拉玻利瓦尔共和国宪法》规定，大学教育是一项公共利益，一项基本人权，也是国家的社会责任，无论在职业技术教育层面，还是在高等教育层面，大学教育都被认为是一种战略要素。目前的关键词是“衔接”和“地域”，即中等技术教育与大学教育之间的课程和学术衔接，以提高教育的质量，加强社会与地域的相关性。为实现这一目标而制定的大学政策赋予地方和区域特权，其基础是优先考虑国家需求的学术课程，大学教育的本土化以及在治理方面，大学、研究机构要与各国家和地方的需求相关联。大学教育的本土化是推进尼古拉斯·马杜罗总统提出的生产战略的关键，从而确保国家的优先项目。

最后，在委内瑞拉正在发展一种教育模式，在知识的产生和社会化的基础上，从宏观的角度谋划培训，以寻求解决社区、生产和职能部门具体问题的办法。

# XII. Speech by the Minister of University Education of Venezuela

El mundo se enfrenta a un enorme desafío, planteado por los cambios abruptos impuestos por la pandemia del Covid-19 y sobre todo por la necesidad de continuar con la vida en medio del riesgo que representa la posibilidad de contagio y la consecuente amenaza a la vida. En los países más desarrollados, esto ha impulsado una nueva ola de revolución científica y tecnológica representada por la computación en la nube, el big data, la IA y el blockchain en la era de la "Industria 4.0", causando a su vez que la demanda de personal técnico altamente calificado sea un desafío al cual la Formación Profesional y Técnica (FPT) debe responder con rapidez. Sin embargo, esta tendencia no se refleja de manera homogénea en el globo. Las diferencias económicas entre el Norte y el Sur, colocan a los países menos desarrollados ante otros desafíos para la Formación Profesional y Técnica, pues no se trata de formar técnicos calificados para tecnologías avanzadas si éstas no se pueden costear, o convertir a estos países en consumidores de tecnologías que no será posible sostener sin generar -al mismo tiempo- una alta dependencia tecnológica.

En medio de estas circunstancias, gobierno y universidades buscan vías para romper con la dependencia y desarrollar el país con un nuevo modelo productivo que transforme las relaciones de producción y que apunte a la satisfacción de las necesidades básicas de la población.

En nuestro país la educación universitaria es un bien público, un derecho humano fundamental y un deber social del Estado, establecido en la CRBV de 1999. Es considerada como un factor estratégico, tanto en el nivel de la educación técnica y profesional, como de la educación universitaria En los actuales momentos, las palabras clave son: "articulación" y "territorio", es decir, la vinculación curricular y académica de la educación media técnica con la formación universitaria, a fin de fortalecer tanto la calidad como la pertinencia social y territorial de la educación. Las políticas universitarias elaboradas para alcanzarlo privilegian lo local y territorial y se fundamentan en: una oferta académica con prioridad en las necesidades del país. la territorialización de la Educación Universitaria. la vinculación de instituciones e investigaciones universitarias con las necesidades locales, regionales o nacionales; y, por último, en materia de gobernanza La territorializacion de la educación universitaria es la clave para hacer avanzar en la estrategia productiva propuesta por el presidente Nicolás Maduro, y así asegurar las prioridades de la Republica.

Finalmente, en Venezuela, estamos desarrollando un modelo educativo que considera la formación con visión de integralidad, en un proceso de búsqueda de soluciones a problemas concretos de la comunidad, el sector productivo e institucional, basado en la generación y socialización del conocimiento.

# 十三

## 加纳驻华大使发言

温弗雷德·哈蒙德
Winfred Hammond

中非在后疫情时代职业技术教育发展“新变化、新方式、新技能”方面的合作都恰逢其时，因为现在全球经济正在努力应对新冠病毒疫情所带来的负面影响。

职业技术教育及其政策的总体目标是为经济的发展提供合格的、有竞争力的工人，并通过向所有社会群体提供一视同仁的培训机会，培养能够参与可持续发展和减少贫困的公民。

中国是非洲大陆最大的贸易合作伙伴，也是在非洲进行国外直接投资最多的国家。中国通过“一带一路”倡议和中非合作论坛的倡议，在非洲切实投入基础设施发展，包括铁路、港口、机场、医院、水资源、农业、公共卫生、教育、通信以及能源相关的基础设施方面。中国的投资对非洲的基建发展和经济增长起到了促进作用，但随着这些倡议而来的技术大量涌入暴露了非洲众多国家高技能人才不足的情况，这也要求我们将职业技术教育的改革制度化。例如，2012 年，中国公司在加纳阿图阿布建了一个天然气处理厂，需要在当地招募合格的氩弧焊工 / 气焊工。但是，却没有找到符合资质的工人。所以，该公司只好从中国带了 200 名工人乘机来到加纳履行合同。此外，中国资助的赞比亚和坦桑尼亚之间的铁路工程也遇到了当地技术工人不足的问题。许多非洲国家各行业都出现了劳动力受教育程度不足的情况，这是限制其进一步发展的主要因素。

知名国际研究机构的近期研究结果再一次证明，在非洲投资的中国公司为非洲的工人创造了大量的就业岗位。然而，这些就业岗位很多都是技能水平中等和较低的就业岗位，创造就业岗位的数量和本土化程度依国家和部门情况有所不同，但总的来说，中国在非洲创造就业岗位的贡献是非常突出。此外，中国公司也在帮助所在国工人培养相应的技能。看到中航国际成套设备有限公司在加纳等西非国家建设职业院校的相关升级项目，我们感到非常振奋。它充分体现了中非在职业技术教育发展上的努力和成果，但我们都知道，需要做的还有很多。

在新冠病毒疫情和其他全球性的挑战暴发前的过去十年，非洲因为迅速转型和外国投资经历了重要成长，这也扩大了更多技术技能的需求。新冠病毒疫情对劳动力市场和教育形势产生了非常不利的影响，在全球范围内，减缓病毒传播的方式包括关闭公共机构、学校及工作场所，和其他机构一样，职业技术教育机构也将课程转到了线上，确保学生继续接受教育和培训。职业技术教育需要动手实践的本质意味着教育机构将要面临将诸多挑战，比如将教学调整至线上模式，帮助师生做好应对环境变化的准备等。新冠病毒疫情造成的危机影响了劳动力市场，带来了不确定因素，同时也加剧了就业不足和不平等问题。此外，提升效率和增加利润的经济复苏的方式也常常导致失业率增长。疫情暴露出了职业技术教育机构和职业教育体系的问题，但因此产生的创新和实验的规模表明快速转变的可能性。只要我们同心协力，就能把挑战化为机遇。应对疫情包括防止辍学、挽救辍学者、彻底改变失学，另外，对工人进行再培训，加强他们在劳动市场的就业能力，使之适应或许已经发生结构性改变的劳动力市场。与此同时，全球很多职业技术教育系统仍然需要设法解决重要的结构差距，这些结构上的差距甚至在疫情前就持续削弱。

2020 年是全球遭遇新冠病毒疫情惊慌失措的一年，然而也是创造力集中的一年。随着经济体、学校和培训中心重新开放，我们迫切需要建立适应学生个人需求以及适应劳动力市场不断变化的技能需求的发展机制。数字技能、社会情感技能、高阶认知技能以及适应能力比任何时候都更加重要，而这为我们打开了一扇机会之窗，因为利益相关方认识到了职业技术教育结构性改变的潜力和必要性，从而实现更好的技能发展和更好的就业。

在第四次工业革命时期，许多人担心他们的工作被机器取代，给政府造成失业威胁和国内矛盾。但与此同时，也形成了更加紧密的公私合作，这其中蕴藏着巨大的机会，培养把职业技术教育有效转化成第四次工业革命所需的电子商务、数字治理、绿色经济技术、高端技术等的能力。

随着技术革命和科技创新，劳动力市场需求显著发展。我们必须迎接新的挑战，才能让我们提供的教育和职业需求相匹配。在这方面，一些国家必须要改变其教育制度，以满足国家、区域和国际市场关于职业技术教育的需求这样一种观点来培养青年。

由于世界面临着严重的威胁、挑战和不确定性，加强非洲与中国之间的合作非常必要。我们要利用 2021 年中非合作论坛议程中的创新和技术机会以及习近平主席 2021 年 11 月在达喀尔中非合作论坛会议上宣布的九项工程，这将有望实现 2030 年可持续发展目标和非洲的 2063 年议程——“我们想要的非洲”。请允许我重申，中非在教育方面的合作，特别是职业技术教育发展方面，必须在全球经济转型中占据中心的地位，尤其是在后疫情经济复苏时期的合作。

# XIII. Speech by Ghana's Ambassador to China

The timing of this conference, the choice of the theme and China-Africa cooperation on "Vocational and Technical Education Development in the Post-pandemic Era—New Changes, New Ways and New Skills", couldn't have been better, as global economies are still struggling to cope with the negative impact of the pandemic.

The overall objective of the Vocational and Technical Education, otherwise referred to as Technical and Vocational Education Training (TVET) policy, is to provide emerging and developed economies with qualified and competitive workers and to train citizens to participate in sustainable growth and poverty reduction by ensuring training opportunities to all social groups without discrimination.

China is the African continent's largest trading partner and source of foreign direct investment. Through the Belt and Road Initiative, and the Forum on China-Africa Cooperation (FOCAC) initiatives, China has invested tangibly in Africa's infrastructural development, including railways, ports, airports, hospitals, water, agriculture, sanitation, education, telecommunications and energy related infrastructures. These investments have helped spur infrastructure development and economic growth. However, the influx of technologies associated with these initiatives, exposed the lack of qualified advanced experts in many African countries, and calls for reforms to institutionalize TVET in Africa. For instance, the Chinese company that constructed the Atuabo gas processing plant in Ghana in 2012, needed qualified argon/acetylene welders. The reported unavailability of qualified local welders with the required skillset, compelled the Chinese construction company to import a plane load of 200 welders to Ghana to enable them execute the contract. I was informed yesterday by some Chinese friends of mine, that the Chinese-funded railway between Zambia and Tanzania, is facing many challenges due to unavailability of requisite local expertise. Industries in many African countries have identified the shortage of an adequately educated workforce as a major constraint to further growth and development.

Recent findings from reputable international research outfits strengthen existing evidence that Chinese firms investing in Africa contribute to substantial job creation for African workers. However, most of the jobs created are at the low- and semi-skilled levels. It was also found out that the numbers of jobs created and the extent to which they are localized vary according to country- and sector-specific characteristics, but overall, the contribution to job creation is considerable. In addition, Chinese companies are found to build the skills of host countries' workers and usually provide some forms of training to local workers (to varying degrees of formality). It is refreshing to note that the contribution of Chinese-built vocational institutions' upgrade projects in Ghana and other West African countries by AVIC-INTL Project Engineering Company, and it is a testament to China-Africa efforts at unearthing the development of vocational and technical education. But you will all agree with me that a lot more is needed.

Before the onset of the COVID-19 pandemic and other global challenges, the last decade or so, saw Africa experiencing a significant growth as a result of the rapid transformation and foreign investments which helped to boost the demand for greater technological skills.

The COVID-19 pandemic has adversely impacted the labour market and education landscape significantly. Around the world, measures to slow the spread of the virus included closing public institutions, schools and workplaces. Like many other institutions, TVET shifted to online learning to ensure that students continued to have access to education and training. However, the practical and hands-on nature of TVET meant that institutions faced challenges adapting teaching to online modes and equipping teachers and students to cope with the changing environment. The crisis has adversely impacted labour markets and led to deepening uncertainty, vulnerability of employment, and inequality. Furthermore, measures to improve efficiency and profitability in the economic recovery have often led to jobless growth. The pandemic exposed weaknesses in TVET institutions and systems, but the scale of innovation and experimentation also showed that rapid change is possible. Together, we can change challenges into opportunities. Responding to the pandemic involves preventing and remediating dropout and reversing learning losses as well as reskilling workers to strengthen their employability in a labor market that may have structurally changed. At the same time, many TVET systems worldwide still need to address important structural gaps that persistently weakened their performance even before the pandemic.

2020 was a year when the world was panic-stricken by the pandemic, but also one of intensive creativity. As economies, schools and training centers reopen, there is an urgent need for skills development mechanisms that are tailored both to students' individual needs and to the changing skill needs on the labor market, with digital skills, socioemotional skills, higher-order cognitive skills, and adaptability being valued more than ever. This opens a window of opportunity as stakeholders realize the potential and need for structural reforms of TVET for better skills development and better jobs.

In this era of the 4th Industrial revolution, many are scared of their jobs being taken over by machines, posing more threats of unemployment and civil conflicts to governments. But at the same time, tremendous opportunities exist for the formation of more intensive Public-Private-Partnerships to build the capacities required to effectively transform TVET towards e-commerce, digital governance, green economy technologies, high end technologies, etc. for the 4th Industrial Revolution.

With technical revolution and innovations in science and technology, labor market needs have significantly evolved. New challenges must be met in order to match the education proposed with vocational demands. In that regard, several countries must reform their education system, with a view to training the youth to meet national, regional or international market needs focusing on vocational and technical education.

Your Excellencies, Distinguished Ladies and Gentlemen, as the world is faced with serious threats, challenges and uncertainties, there is the need to strengthen the cooperation between Africa and China in taking advantage of innovations and technological opportunities enshrined in the FOCAC 2021 Agenda together with the nine programmes announced by President Xi Jinping at the Dakar Conference in November 2021. This gives hope towards achieving the Sustainable Development Goals 2030 and Africa's Agenda 2063, "the Africa we want". Let me reiterate that the implementation of a China-Africa Cooperation plan towards education, particularly, vocational and technical development must take centre stage in global economic transformation especially in this post COVID-19 economic recovery era.

# 十四

## 爱尔兰驻华大使发言

安黛文

Ann Derwin

在爱尔兰，继续教育和培训部门包括职业教育与培训以及成年人学习，无论学习者的年龄、能力或教育背景，他们都可以从中获益。

爱尔兰的每个社区都提供继续教育和培训，并为每个人提供了一条个人发展的通道，无论其之前受教育水平如何。

在爱尔兰，继续教育和培训基本上都是免费提供的，而且非常灵活。这类教育实用性强，聚焦行业。在许多情况下，这类教育结合课堂学习和实操培训、顶岗实习和工作经验。

众所周知，每个人想要从教育中获得的诉求都不同，有人把成年人读写能力或社区教育项目当成是实现个人独立的一个途径；有人则把它当作结交新朋友、学习新技能的途径，还有人将教育和培训视为求职或重返学业的手段。在爱尔兰，我们相信在教育和培训方面并没有一条唯一正确的途径。

与中国一样，爱尔兰致力于通过提供高质量、更方便、更灵活的教育和培训计划，提高公民的社会参与水平，推动实现全民充分社会参与这个目标。

我们还意识到，要将各个阶段的教育和培训与生机勃勃的 21 世纪的劳动力所需的技能相结合。

爱尔兰未来技能需求专家组找到了本国经济持续增长所需的技能，经济社会各方面的数字化转型加速，企业工作方式发生了翻天覆地的变化。要使这种转型成为爱尔兰经济和社会不断进步的积极力量，国民的继续教育和培训是关键因素。为满足现有和新兴技能的需求，爱尔兰实施了一系列创新举措，帮助提供解决方案，例如，我们的“技能网”网络和“跳板”平台。

我知道，中国的职业教育与培训领域正在开展许多令人振奋的工作，希望看到我们两国在这个重要领域开展进一步合作。

# XIV. Speech by Irish Ambassador to China

In Ireland, the Further Education and Training sector encompasses both vocational education and training and adult learning. I know the value it can bring to any individual, irrespective of their age, ability, or educational background.

Further Education and Training is available in every community in Ireland, and offers every individual, regardless of any previous level of education, a pathway to take them as far as they would like to go.

Further Education and Training provision in Ireland is largely free and very flexible. It is practical and industry focused; in many cases combining class-based learning with hands-on practical training, on-the-job learning and work experience.

As we all know, everyone has different desires as to what they hope to achieve from education. For some, it is regarded to be a road to independence through adult literacy or community education programmes and for some it is viewed as a way to engage with new people and to learn new skills. For others, education and training is a means to a job, or to return to study. In Ireland, we believe that there is no one 'right' pathway to education and training.

Like China, Ireland is committed to increasing levels of inclusion through the provision of high quality, more accessible and flexible education and training programmes and supports with the aim of enabling every citizen to participate fully in society.

We are also conscious of the need to align education and training at all stages with the skills that are needed in a dynamic 21st century workforce.

Ireland's Expert Group on Future Skills Needs identifies the skills required for the continued growth of our economy. Digital transformation across all aspects of the economy and society has accelerated, and the way enterprises work has changed forever. Further Education and Training of our people are critical elements in ensuring this transition continues to be a positive force in improving the Irish economy and society. Our SkillNet Network and Springboard platform are but some of the innovative initiatives Ireland has introduced to assist in providing solutions to meet existing and emerging skills needs.

I know that there is much exciting work being done in China in the area of vocational education and training and I am keen to see further cooperation between our two countries in this important sector.

# 十五

## 国际电信联盟秘书长发言

赵厚麟

Zhao Houlin

当前，世界正在努力从新冠病毒疫情的影响中恢复，经济复苏和可持续发展急需大量高水平技术技能人才。因此，加强世界职业技术教育领域的国际交流与合作十分重要。中国政府发起并主办了这一次世界职业技术教育发展大会，意义重大。

进入 21 世纪以来，以 5G、云计算、大数据、人工智能、区块链为代表的新一轮科技革命快速发展，深刻改变着人们的生活、工作和学习方式。原有的很多传统技能正在逐步失去用武之地，以数字经济为代表的各类新经济新业态兴起。持续两年多的新冠病毒疫情进一步凸显了新技术、新技能对保护人类生命健康和经济社会可持续发展的重要性。人类对新知识与新技能的需求比以往任何时候都强烈。此外，全世界仍然有 29 亿人没有连接上互联网，不同国家和人民之间存在着巨大的数字鸿沟，这使得实现联合国 2030 年可持续发展目标面临巨大挑战。为应对世界形势的新变化和产业变革的新需求，职业技术教育必须加快调整和变革，加快提升职业技术教育质量，扩大受益人群。同时，必须加强职业技术教育的国际合作。

国际电信联盟是负责信息通信技术的联合国专门机构，我们致力于连接所有人，让先进的信息通信技术惠及全人类。我们相信，信息通信技术可以推动各行各业的现代化和智能化，从而推动经济发展的方方面面。因此，国际社会需要大量不同层次的电信技术和技能人才，特别是以 5G 和人工智能为代表的现代通信技术应用、通信系统工程的安装与维护、卫星通信与导航技术、智能互联网技术等方面的人才。全球职业技术教育的普遍发展对于实现我们的目标至关重要。作为联合国专门机构，国际电信联盟非常愿意与职业技术教育系统加强合作。长期以来，国际电信联盟一直关注和推动当代信息通信技术在教育领域的应用，不断加强国际电信联盟与联合国教科文组织的紧密合作。从早期的远程教育到后来的校际互联，再到现在的线上教学、公益、医疗和农业等专业技能的培训，以及全生命周期的教育，包括对退休老人的数字技能培训等。国际电信联盟非常荣幸以指导委员会成员资格受邀参加联合国将于今年（2022 年）秋季举办的全球转变教育峰会。

本次会议关注全球职业技术教育的重要议题，如数字赋能、绿色技能、产教融合、促进公平和终身学习，中国在这些领域有很多成功经验可以与世界同行分享。大会邀请了来自世界各国的政府、国际组织、贸易协会、企业、研究团体和职业技术教育机构各方代表。中国也将能通过本次大会借鉴学习其他国家的经验。

我们相信，通过广泛深入的讨论，本次大会必将对全球职业技术教育合作与发展产生重要推动作用。我很高兴得知本次大会上将成立世界职业技术教育发展联盟。我相信这些努力都将为加快实现可持续发展目标提供新契机、作出新贡献。

# XV. Speech by the Secretary-General of the International Telecommunication Union

Currently, as the world is recovering from the COVID-19 pandemic, economic recovery and sustainable development urgently need a large number of talents mastering high-level technologies and skills. Therefore, it's of great significance to strengthen international exchange and cooperation in the field of world vocational and technical education. The Chinese government proposes and organizes this World Vocational and Technical Education Development Conference, which is of great importance.

Ladies and gentlemen. After entering the 21st century, a new round of technological reform, represented by 5G, cloud computing, big data, AI and blockchain, develops in a fast pace, and is bringing profound changes to our life, work and learning styles. Many traditional skills are gradually losing their importance, and various new economies and business types, which are presented by the digital economy, are emerging. Over the past two years, the COVID-19 pandemic has further emphasized the importance of new technologies and skills to the protection of people's life and health as well as sustainable economic and social development. Our needs for new knowledge and skills are stronger than ever. In addition, there are still 2.9 billion people who don't have access to the Internet worldwide. There are huge digital divides among different countries and their people, which brings tough challenges to the 2030 SDGs of the United Nations. To respond to the new changes in the global situation and the new needs from industrial reforms, vocational and technical education has to accelerate its adaptation and transformation, speed up the quality improvement of vocational education, and bring benefits to more people. Meanwhile, international cooperation in vocational education must be strengthened.

ITU is the specialized agency of the UN that is committed to ICT. We're dedicated to connecting all people, and bringing the benefits of advanced ICT to all people. We believe that ICT can promote the modern and intelligent development of various industries and sectors, thus advancing all aspects of economic development. Therefore, the international community needs a large number of talents at all levels, who master telecommunication technologies and skills, especially talents in the following aspects: application of modern communication technologies represented by 5G and AI, installation and maintenance of communication system projects, satellite communication and navigation technologies, and smart Internet. The general development of global vocational education is critical for the implementation of our intended goals. As a specialized agency of the UN, ITU is willing to strengthen our cooperation with the vocational education system. For a long time, ITU has paid attention to and promoted the application of modern ICTs in the field of education, and constantly intensified the close collaboration between ITU and UNESCO, which covers aspects from remote education in the early stage to the connection of schools, and then to the training of specialized skills in such fields as online teaching, public welfare, healthcare and agriculture, and the full-life-circle education, including training of digital skills provided to retirees. ITU is very honored to be invited to the Transforming Education Summit (TES) of the UN, which is scheduled to be held this autumn, as a member of the steering committee.

Ladies and gentlemen. This conference focuses on the important topics of global vocational and technical education, such as digital empowerment, green skills, the integration of industry and education, and the promotion of equity and lifelong learning. China has a lot of successful experience in these aspects to share with peers around the world. The conference invites representatives from governments, international organizations, trade associations, enterprises, research groups, and vocational and technical education institutions. China will also learn from the experience of other countries through this conference.

We believe that through extensive and in-depth discussions, this conference will strongly boost the cooperation and development of global vocational education. I am delighted to learn that the World TVET League will be established at this conference. I'd like to congratulate you on this. I believe that all these efforts of yours will provide new opportunities and make new contributions to the realization of SDGs.

# 十六

## 国际工程教育学协会主席发言

汉诺·霍尔茨
Hanno Hortsch

作为国际工程教育学协会的主席兼国际工程教育协会联盟主管能力建设的副主席，我谨向本次大会的召开表示衷心的祝贺，同时也对大会组织者制定的目标和愿景表达由衷的谢意，这些目标和愿景正是国际工程教育学协会和国际工程教育协会联盟一直以来不懈努力推动的。

我还要向大会转达国际工程教育协会联盟、国际工程教育学协会、全球工程学院院长委员会和德累斯顿工业大学对大会的祝贺，下面请允许我简要介绍一下这些组织。

国际工程教育协会联盟是一个由全球工程和技术协会组成的世界性组织，其与这些协会在技术教育领域有着共同的目标和愿景，这些协会由各个国家的区域性协会根据本国的实际条件实施管理工作。全球工程学院院长委员会是国际工程教育协会联盟的重要次级组织，为技术教育经验交流和技术教育国际标准提供了一个平台。

国际工程教育学协会则侧重技术教育在教学方面的工作。教育机构的教师或讲师是影响工程或专业教育与培训质量的关键因素。国际工程教育学协会与许多国际协会和机构共同合作，是唯一一家致力于技术教育教学工作的国际协会。

我的母校是德累斯顿工业大学。过去的二十多年以来，德累斯顿工业大学与中国的联系十分密切，合作形式多样，我们与中国国家留学基金管理委员会成功合作开展的活动就是很好的例子，我亲眼见证了中国经济的高速发展。

我想强调的是，近年来中国高等职业教育发展取得了卓越的成绩，职业技术教育与培训是高质量工程教育的重要基础。作为国际工程教育学协会主席兼国际工程教育协会联盟主管能力建设的副主席，我要向大家保证，我们愿意与中国继续携手合作，并进一步深化合作。衷心希望中国的职业技术教育和高等教育在未来取得更大的发展成就。

# XVI. Speech by the President of International Society for Engineering Pedagogy

As President of the International Society for Engineering Pedagogy (IGIP) and Vice President for Capacity Building of the International Federation of Engineering Education Societies (IFEES), I would like to congratulate you on initiating this important world conference, but also thank you for setting the goals and the visions the IGIP and IFEES sustainably promote.

Allow me to say a few words about the Societies IFEES, IGIP, GEDC and University of Technology Dresden, for whom I would like to convey the greetings for your conference.

The IFEES is a global society that represents an umbrella for all engineering and technical societies and agrees on common goals and visions of technical education with these societies, which are then implemented by the regional societies in the individual countries according to the conditions of these countries. An important sub-organization is the Global Engineering Deans Council (GEDC), which serves as a platform for the exchange of experiences as well as world standards for technical education.

The focus of the IGIP is particularly on the pedagogical aspect of technical education. The teacher or lecturer at the educational institutions is the key to excellent engineering or professional education and training. The IGIP is the only international society dedicated to this special task in association with many international societies and institutions.

I would also like to mention my alma mater, the TU Dresden, which has had very close and diverse connections to China for more than 20 years. One of the many good examples of this collaboration are the activities we do together with China Scholarship Council successfully carried out. In these 20 years I have been able to follow the rapid and successful development of the Chinese economy.

I would like to highlight China's excellent performance in the development of higher vocational education in recent years. Vocational education and training is a very important source of high quality engineering education. Both as President of IGIP and as Vice President of IFEES, I assure you that we would like to continue working with China and even deepen this cooperation. I wish China's technical vocational and higher education continue to develop well in the future.

# 十七

## 国际汽车工程师学会联合会主席发言

纳丁·雷克莱尔
Nadine Leclair

中国作为国际汽车工程师学会联合会成员，在这项重大事件上代表着我们的共同意愿，正如国际汽车工程师学会联合会代表着汽车工业的方向，各成员对与汽车相关的职业技术教育起着重要作用。自2018年以来，题为《FISITA移动工程2030》的移动工程专业白皮书已陆续出版三册。它得到了我们学术顾问委员会的认可，并汇集了学术界、工业界和专业学会的意见。

基于我们行业的三大革命性焦点，包括今天被认为是最亟待解决的能源、连通和智能三大主题，我们首先强调了技术范围和方法，以展示所需完成的重要且具有挑战性工作对年轻一代是多么激动人心。

首先，提出了非常深入的技术要求和跨学科的技能要求。在保持机械技能的同时，增加并理解电气电子系统的丰富知识，以便能够在跨职能团队中与同行协作，专精于前面提到的各项技术——能源、连通、软件和智能。

其次，是新的方法论。它是基于模型开发的系统工程及来自计算机领域，与软件、信号处理、数据智能相关的工作方法，以实现仿真、虚拟测试、虚拟原型制造、虚拟现实转变。这对博士和工程师来说是一个非常有吸引力的挑战。

从行业观点来看，我们通过调查确认，创新正在从系统集成、软件开发和连通、用户体验和机器学习之间的一系列合作中涌现出来，应用于新能源技术，自动驾驶和安全系统，以及全覆盖、无缝连接的移动体验。

新能源和全球连通正在改变客户体验，因此必须建立一个新的平台集群，以满足客户的需求，无论他们是城市居民，需要长途奔波或是身处农村环境中。

我们在白皮书中阐述了整个价值链的可持续性以及工程流程的挑战。我们还确定了连通优势及其与基础设施间的联系可以提高安全性和交通效率。大数据智能效果的影响和电子控制单元的进步，改变了活动方式及其位置（嵌入式或基于云的活动），通过一个全新的架构概念来改进活动。也就是以更短的响应时间，针对客户的需求，提出更高确定性的建议，改变生态系统中合作方式，同时考虑到循环经济。这是联合会即将出版的下一册白皮书的主要内容。

联合会教育委员会将非常乐意为各位的倡议作出贡献，同时也为其他行业的想法提供支持。

# XVII. Speech by the President of FISITA

China, as a member of the Fédération Internationale des Sociétés d'Ingénieurs des Technique de l'Automobile (FISITA), is representing us in this event. As they stand for auto industries, they play a big role for auto related vocational and technical education. Mobility engineering white paper, titled in our *FISITA Community 2030 Engineering Mobility* has been already published through a set of three chapters since 2018. It is endorsed by our academic advisory board and brings in academics, industrial companies and societies.

Based on three revolutions for our industry, energy—today considered as a prominent subject—connectivity and intelligence, we have highlighted both the technical scope and the methodologies in order to show how important and challenging the work to be performed is so motivating for young generation.

First, very deep technical and interdisciplinary skill requirements. Retain mechanical skills, add and understand the strong knowledge on electrical and electronic systems to be able to collaborate in cross-functional teams with peers specializing in the new previously-listed technologies—energy, connectivity, software and intelligence.

Second, new methodologies. System engineering with model-based development and those coming from the computer world related to software, signal processing and data intelligence, to transform simulation, virtual testing, virtual prototyping, virtual reality, which is a very attractive challenge for PhD's and engineers.

To argue from industrial view of point, we have confirmed through our survey that innovation is emerging from the basket of collaboration between system integration, software development and connectivity, user experience and machine learning, applied to new energy technologies, AD and security system, complete and seamless mobility experience.

New energies and global connectivity are transforming the customer experience. A new portfolio of platform must be built to meet customer demands, whatever they are, city dweller, for long distance transfer or in a rural context.

We have developed in our white paper the sustainability throughout a value chain and the challenges of the engineering process. We have also developed advantage of connectivity and interaction with infrastructure to improve safety and traffic validity.

The data intelligence effect and the progressions of the ECUs modify the activities and their location—embedded or cloud based—activities through a completely new concept of architecture. In this context, shorter lead time and uncertainty of the proposed answers to the needs of the customers change the way to collaborating in the ecosystem, taking into account the circular economy. This is the next chapter that FISITA will publish.

FISITA education committee will be very happy to contribute to your initiative, being also feeding on the thoughts of other industries.

# 十八

## 中国中车集团有限公司<br>董事长发言

孙永才
Sun Yongcai

本次大会的胜利召开，必将对中国乃至世界职业教育改革发展产生深远的影响。习近平总书记的重要指示，孙春兰副总理的重要讲话，为办好新时代职业教育指明了方向。

中国中车集团有限公司（以下简称中国中车）作为全球规模领先、品种齐全、技术一流的轨道交通装备企业，作为我国轨道交通装备行业唯一一家产业化集团，研制的以复兴号高速动车组为代表的系列化轨道交通装备产品，已达到世界先进水平，是一张亮丽的名片。中国中车始终坚决贯彻习近平总书记三次视察中车重要指示精神，紧紧依托管理、校企一体、人才、技术、资源、创新六大产教融合优势，持续深化产业链、创新链，与人才链、教育链有机衔接，积极构建中国中车特色职业教育体系，致力打造央企职业教育产教融合典范，为进一步探索职业教育改革创新之路，推动职业教育高质量发展，中国中车提出如下行动倡议。

注重发挥龙头企业重要办学主体作用，全力办好高质量职业教育。中国中车将充分发挥先进轨道交通装备引领作用，以建设职业教育培训中心、实训基地三位一体、产教融合基地为抓手，实施教育、培训师资人才、课程体系、实训基地、业务运营一体化管理机制，实现职业教育与培训的专业化管理、集约化运营。

注重发挥大国工匠人才优势，着力打造高水平、双师型教师队伍。中国中车将充分发挥以 9 名中华技能大奖获得者为代表的一大批高铁工匠人才优势，成立中国中车高铁工匠学院，发挥技术技能人才培养优势，积极推进“三教”改革，让企业技术人才、技能大师进校园，让企业培训技术、培训课程进课堂。

注重发挥行业企业实训资源优势，着力打造国家级公共实训基地。中国中车将带头践行技能强国战略，落实技能根基工程，以规范化、标准化为导向，全面评估现有 138 个实训基地，实现校企实训资源共享，以柔性化生产、智能化制造、数字化转型为基础，创新实训基地运营模式，建设开放共享的高水平、专业化产教融合实训基地。

注重推进产教深度融合，着力打造职业教育共融体。中国中车将发挥国家级产教融合型企业优势，加强顶层设计，建立学校 + 企业大学 + 行业企业，即 1+1+N 产教融合共同体，以企业大学为协作纽带，促进技术、人才、资源、文化深度融合，在政府、行业、企业和职业院校等四个主体领域中，组建先进轨道交通职业联盟，营造多元、开放、融合的办学格局。

注重培养高素质技术技能人才，有力支撑世界一流企业建设。中国中车将紧紧依托产融结合优势，萃取企业文化、安全管理、质量管理、精益管理等先进经验，融合职业标准、行业标准、岗位标准、人才标准，构建中国中车特色、双元育人模式，积极融入“一带一路”建设，建立与世界一流企业相适应的全球一体化职业教育模式，推进职业教育与产业发展同频共振，协同共进。

中国中车坚持以习近平新时代中国特色社会主义思想为指引，深入贯彻习近平总书记的重要指示精神和孙春兰副总理的重要讲话精神，贯彻落实全国职教大会和本次大会工作部署，聚焦国家产教融合型企业建设，创新实施灵活多样的育人模式和办学格局，努力打造引领改革、支撑发展、中车特色、世界水平的职业院校，为推动职业教育现代化贡献中国中车力量。

# 十九

## 珠海格力电器股份有限公司董事长发言

董明珠
Dong Mingzhu

今天很荣幸来到大会现场，我作为企业代表想在这里谈一点对教育的感受。格力电器股份有限公司（以下简称格力电器）是一个覆盖家电品类（空调、冰箱、洗衣机生活电器全品类）的制造企业，也是拥有智能装备、各类数控机床、机器人的制造企业，也是能够自主制造压缩机、电机电容等一系列关键部件的制造企业。格力电器始终坚定走自主创新、自主研发技术、自主制造的道路，经过30年的发展，已经从一个传统的制造企业发展成为一个智能制造企业。如今，格力电器有16个研究院，152个研究所，1 411个实验室，已拥有近16 000名研发人员，申请的专利技术已经超过10万项。

格力电器在发展的过程当中，也更加深刻领会到人才的重要性。格力电器在空调领域已经走在了世界的前列，在发展过程中，像中国中车集团一样，建立了很多专业化的标准，而格力电器的标准就是以人民美好生活为标准。虽然我们有国家标准，有国际标准，但只要是人们需要的消费品，我们都以最高标准满足他们的需求。所以格力电器一直在挑战中前行。我们认为创新是企业的灵魂，创新需要人才支撑，所以格力电器与很多高校都有了密切的结合和联系。格力电器在不断地培养人才的同时，更感受到人才再造的重要性，如何提高 8 万多名格力电器员工的能力和水平，同样给我们提出了新的要求和挑战。

在教育部的关心下，格力电器不仅和很多高校有合作，同时也建立了格力职业技术学院。这个学院的建设主要解决员工再升级问题。因为时代在变化，从过去传统的制造到今天的智能制造的转化，表明对人才的要求也有了更高的标准，所以不能只需要一个单一的、简单的操作工人，而是需要培养一个拥有智能技术的工人。虽然我们有 16 000 名研发人员，但是在生产制造过程中，也要培养出更多的实战人员。有了格力职业技术学院，加快了对人才再造的提升速率；同时我们也面向全国招生，希望格力职业技术学院不仅为格力电器的发展培养人才，也为中国乃至于世界培养人才，这就是我们的梦想。

格力电器如今拥有了庞大的制造体系支撑企业创新发展，企业的发展需要符合整个世界的发展，那就要不断地去创新。今天在会场听了很多专家、教授的发言，特别是教育界的前辈们，大家都谈了教育的重要性，我们同样也认为教育是根基，人才必须要受到良好的教育。因此格力电器建立了自己的研究院、职业技术学院，我们将不断地提升科学技术，紧跟世界的进步，适应时代的发展。在这个过程中，我们有了更好的生产基地和实操的平台，可以把实践教育和理论教育完美地结合起来。参与今天的大会，让我们感到自己身上肩负着一种使命和责任。作为中国的制造业，我们不仅要把中国的制造业做好，还应该帮助那些需要帮助的国家和企业。

今天，现场有一位部长分享了中国援助他们建了一些企业，但是他们没有人才的案例。所以我觉得我们不仅要把格力电器做好，还要承担一些社会责任。格力电器建立了自己的职业技术学院后，每年将拿出不少于 5 亿的资金投入到职业教育中，为继续深造的人才提供服务的同时，也为一些贫困地区需要帮助的人提供教育援助。

最后，格力电器未来的教育愿景和梦想是什么呢？按照习近平总书记实现人类命运共同体的理念，我们希望通过教育，能让人人都有尊严，人人都有工作，人人都有美好生活。

# 二十

# 德国比勒费尔德应用科学大学校长发言

## 德国应用科学大学学术教育与实践教育相结合的成功典范

施沃茵
Ingeborg Schramm-Wölk

今天，请允许我借此机会，向各位尊敬的参会者介绍“应用科学大学”——德国高等教育领域中的成功典范。作为比勒费尔德应用科学大学的校长，无论从专业角度还是个人角度，我多年来一直专注于应用科学大学的发展。

德国的应用科学大学如今愈发热门。第一所应用科学大学成立于约 50 年前。目前，德国有大约 40% 的学生就读于应用科学大学。德国共有 400 所高等教育机构，其中就有 200 多所应用科学大学，是德国研究领域的重要组成部分。

在德国任何地方，车程 1 小时范围内就会有一所应用科学大学。坐拥 421 个学区的，应用科学大学不仅是强有力的地区合作伙伴、驱动创新的中坚力量和中小型企业的问题解决者，还与社会、教育和卫生部门的机构合作，着重进行面向实践的研究。除此之外，我们在农村地区也有很强的影响力。

德国的经济实力很大一部分得益于其杰出的技术工人，这些技术工人大多接受过应用科学大学的教育和培训。我们是连接商业、社会和科学的桥梁，发挥着不可或缺的重要作用。

德国的应用科学大学在全球也具有很强的吸引力。目前，德国的应用科学大学共有 13.8 万名国际学生。此外，我们和世界各地的伙伴大学有许多国际合作项目，从学术交流、联合研究项目到双学位项目。

那么应用科学大学有什么特别之处呢?

应用科学大学是开展以科学和实践为导向的教育和研究的重要场所。近年来，德国学生人数的增加很大程度上也得益于应用科学大学提供的学习场所。因此，其他正在面临学生数量急剧增加的国家也可以参考这种模式。由于贴合实践、专业方向明确，应用科学大学对科学的社会渗透做出了重要贡献。与传统大学不同，这里超过一半的学生来自非学术家庭。应用科学大学在区域合作方面也至关重要。应用科学大学为当地用人以及培养、培训技术工人方面注入了强劲动力。此外，它们还是向经济领域传递知识和转化研究成果的重要合作伙伴。

比勒费尔德应用科学大学成立于 1971 年，是德国最早成立的应用科学大学之一。2021 年 9 月，学校建校 50 周年。我们有设计学院、工程与数学学院、社会科学学院、商学院和卫生学院等，分布在三个不同校区。比勒费尔德应用科学大学的课程选择范围广，包括 40 个学士项目和近 30 个硕士项目。学校还提供博士生项目，致力于提供丰富的知识、培养优秀的人才。我们现在拥有超过 10 000 名学生，是德国规模较大的应用科学大学之一。比勒费尔德应用科学大学的研究实力雄厚，各个研究重点在德国乃至全世界都是引人瞩目的。应用科学大学的研究工作首先注重实践，这就为研究成果的快速落地和向社会的转化提供了保证。

学校有多达 400 多家合作伙伴，而我们的成功要归功于就业安置方和大学之间的合作。值得一提的是，每个应用科学大学的教授都必须拥有多年的相关实践经验。在比勒费尔德应用科学大学，有 1 000 多名学生参加双元制项目，我们称之为“实践嵌入式”模式。在该模式中，合作伙伴选择学生，并提供工作岗位。有意向在比勒费尔德应用科学大学就读的学生直接向合作企业或机构提出申请，就读期间，学生按月获取报酬。这些毕业生拥有深厚的学术知识和丰富的实践经验，在就业市场上有良好的前景。

学校实践嵌入式项目的核心原则是以 3 个月为周期，学生穿梭于校园和为他们提供实践培训岗位的机构之间，更好地整合学术技能和工作相关的专业知识。应用科学大学的优势，尤其是实践嵌入式项目的优势是显而易见的：完美融合了知识转移和就业安置；让学生在运用学术知识的同时，不断获得基于实践的经验；学生能及时融入工作环境，工作安置伙伴能尽早保留熟练员工；为学业提供必要的资金保障。

德国应用科学大学的模式已经成功地传播到其他国家。在中国也有这样的模式，自 2004 年以来，著名的同济大学中德工程学院就将德国工程教育的基本要素融入中国高等教育体系之中。

目前，我们正计划在中国的海南省建立一所新型的、独立的、国际化的应用科学大学。它的学习模式将遵循“比勒费尔德模式”，这是一个创新项目。在海南省建校的许可已经获得批准，我们将在框架条件允许的情况下尽快开始开展教学活动。我相信这所新型的独立大学将为中国应用型学术教育的发展作出重要贡献。此外，这种独特的模式将帮助学生在学习之初就得到职业指导和实践经验。新大学将开设工程和经济类专业的学士和硕士学位课程，也会按照当地需求提供适合的课程。新大学计划容纳 12 000 名学生，并与当地伙伴和企业开展合作，以满足该地区对高素质专家和高管的需求。目前为止，已有超过 120 家海南省的企业表示有兴趣与即将成立的海南应用科学大学合作。我坚信这种模式会得到中国学生、学生家长、企业和社会的认可，正如同在德国获得的成就一样。希望下次会议上，我能向大家介绍这所大学的初步成果。

# XX. Speech by the President of Bielefeld University of Applied Sciences, Germany

### Excellent Academic Teaching Coupled with a Highly Practical and Business Orientation at Universities of Applied Sciences in Germany—A Successful Model

Please allow me to use this opportunity today to present to you, as exalted participants in this forum, the 'Universities of Applied Sciences', a highly successful model in the realm of higher education in Germany. As President of Bielefeld University of Applied Sciences, I have been professionally and personally involved with the development of the universities of applied sciences for many years.

Universities of Applied Sciences—so-called UAS—in Germany are more attractive than ever. The first UAS were established around 50 years ago. Around 40% of all students in Germany are currently enrolled at a UAS. With 400 higher education institutions in total, more than 200 UAS account for an important part of the German research landscape.

You will not find a single region in Germany that is not more than an hour's drive from a UAS. Comprising 421 locations, our institutions are strong regional partners, serving as a driver of innovation and a problem solver for small and medium enterprises (SMEs). We also cooperate with establishments in the social, education and health sectors, with a particular focus on application-oriented research. Not to forget, we also have a strong presence in our rural regions!

Germany owes its economic strength to its outstanding skilled workers, who are largely educated and trained by our UAS. We are an indispensable bridge between business, society and science.

Our institutions are also globally attractive. With 138 000 international students currently enrolled at UAS in Germany, these student numbers are a perfect example of this global attractiveness. Furthermore, there are many international cooperation projects with partner-universities all over the world, ranging from academic exchanges and joint research projects to joint or double degrees.

What is particularly special about universities of applied sciences?

UAS are important places for scientific and practice-oriented education and research. The increase in student numbers in Germany in recent years would hardly have been possible without the study places at the UAS. Therefore, this model can also serve as a model in other countries where student numbers are increasing sharply.

UAS make an important contribution to social permeability, due to their practical relevance and orientation towards clear professional fields. Unlike traditional universities, significantly more than half of the students here come from non-academic families.

UAS are also essential with regard to regional cooperation. They provide a fresh impetus for the people they employ and the skilled workers they educate and train. Moreover, they are a valued partner for the transfer of knowledge and research into the economy.

Founded in 1971, Bielefeld University of Applied Sciences (FH Bielefeld) was one of the first UAS to open in Germany. The university celebrated its 50th anniversary in September 2021. The faculties of 'Design', 'Engineering and Mathematics', 'Social Sciences', 'Business' and 'Health' are located at three different campuses throughout the region. Bielefeld University of Applied Sciences has an extensive course offering, comprising 40 Bachelor programmes and nearly 30 Master programmes. We strive to nurture knowledge and talent by providing PhD opportunities. With over 10 000 students, we are one of the larger UAS in Germany. Our research at Bielefeld UAS is strong, with various research focuses that are nationally and internationally visible. Research at UAS has, above all, the perspective of application orientation. This promises a rapid implementation of research results and their transfer into society.

An essential pillar of our success is the cooperation between work placement partners and the universities. We work together with over 400 partners. By the way, every professor at UAS must have several years of relevant practical experience. More than 1 000 students at Bielefeld UAS are enrolled in our dual-study programmes, which we call 'work-integrated'.

In our model, our corporate partners select their students and provide them with a work placement. For admission to Bielefeld UAS, prospective students apply directly to the chosen partner company or institution. During this time, they receive a monthly remuneration. Having attained profound academic knowledge and practical expertise, our graduates enjoy excellent prospects on the labour market and are highly employable.

The core principle of our work-integrated study programmes is the three-month cycle, during which students switch between university and their workplace-training provider, aiming to offer both academic skills and work-related expertise. The advantages of UAS, in particular work-integrated programmes, are evident: Optimal intertwining of knowledge transfer and work placements; Continuous practical-based experience whilst applying academic knowledge; Timely integration into the world of work for students and early retention of skilled workers for work placement partners; Securing necessary financial funds for study.

The German model of 'University of Applied Sciences' has already been successfully transferred to other countries. In China, too, the Sino-German College of Applied Sciences at the renowned Tongji University has been a flagship project for integrating essential elements of German engineering education into the Chinese higher education system since 2004.

We are currently planning to establish a new, independent, international UAS in the province of Hainan. Its study programmes will be developed following the so-called 'Bielefeld model'. The permission of founding the university in Hainan has already been granted and we will commence teaching as soon as the framework conditions allow us to do so. We are certain that this new, independent university will make a substantial contribution to broadening the perspective of application-oriented academic education in China. Furthermore, this unique model will enable students to receive career guidance and practical orientation from the very beginning of their studies. The university will offer Bachelor and Master programmes in the fields of 'Engineering' and 'Economics'. It will also be possible for the university to tailor its course offering to suit local needs. With a planned capacity for 12 000 students, the new university will meet future demand for highly qualified specialists and executives in the region, together with local partners and companies. Over 120 companies in Hainan have expressed their interest in cooperating with the future Hainan University of Applied Sciences. I am strongly convinced that this model will be recognised and appreciated by the students, their parents, and companies—i.e. by society—just like in Germany. I look forward to presenting the initial successes of the university to you at the next conference.

# 二十一

## 深圳职业技术学院党委书记发言

杨欣斌
Yang Xinbin

深圳职业技术学院成立于1993年，地处中国改革开放先锋城市——深圳。全校有招生专业86个，在校生33 000余人。习近平总书记指出“职业教育前景广阔、大有可为”。我们积极贯彻落实习近平总书记的重要指示，以当好中国职业教育创新发展的第一艘冲锋舟为己任，围绕产业所需、企业所急、市民所盼，锐意改革、先行先试交出了职业教育大有可为的深圳答卷。

一是服务学生成长成才，做技能成就精彩人生的践行者。学校紧紧围绕深圳战略新兴产业和支柱产业，优化专业布局，累积培养了16万余名毕业生，就业率始终保持在98%以上。每年，有16%的毕业生入职世界500强企业，就业质量稳居职业院校前列。学生毕业三年内创业率为12.7%，校友企业年盈利收入达到4 300亿元人民币，带动就业超过70余万人，年均培训企业员工12万人次，助力企业提升员工技术技能水平。学校探索形成的“九个共同”校企双主体育人模式被国内外职业院校广泛认可和借鉴，助力广大青年学子和企业员工演绎了技能成就精彩人生的动人故事。

二是服务高端产业转型，做中国制造、中国创造的支撑者。近年来，深圳涌现出一些世界一流创新型企业，为满足高端产业对高素质技能人才的需求，学校推动 14 个专业联合一批头部企业建成了 14 个特色企业，校企共同开发专业标准 81 个、特种标准 1 226 个，提升了人才培养的适应性。共同建设技术研发平台 25 个，攻克了一批关键核心技术，推动了源头创新，共同制定行业标准 106 个，提高了供需对接的精准性。携手民族企业走出去，为全球 13 个国家的 1 200 余名当地居民提供了岗位培训，通过模式创新、源头创新和服务创新，实现了对中国制造、中国创造的有力支撑。

三是服务职业教育改革，做数字化转型的引领者。学校积极拥抱数字经济浪潮，全面推动数字化转型。第一，推动专业数字化转型，基于“+ 数字”和“数字 +”，为全部专业进行数字化改造，打破学科壁垒，培养跨界人才。第二，加快特种数字化迭代，面对新职业、新场景开发数字化课程 2 003 种，将数字化的新知识、新技术和新技能融入人才培养全过程。第三，推进教学方法、手段革新，绘制学生的知识能力和行为数字化图谱，创设平台 + 资源 + 工具的智能教学化模式。第四，开发教师数字化能力培训模块，提升教师的数字化能力。

今年，学校获评联合国教科文组织职业技术教育数字化教席，是中国职业教育领域唯一的教席。在引领全球职业教育数字化转型方面开启了新的篇章。接下来，我们将积极践行会议倡议，落实好习近平总书记的重要指示，奋力当好中国职业教育创新发展的第一艘冲锋舟，与海内外同仁携手共创职业教育更加美好的未来。

# 闭幕式

# Closing Ceremony

# 一

# 联合国教科文组织驻华代表处主任致辞

夏泽翰
Shahbaz Khan

今天，我代表联合国教科文组织，很高兴也很荣幸在首届世界职业技术教育发展大会上致闭幕词。首先，请允许我向大会组织者、中华人民共和国教育部、中国联合国教科文组织全国委员会和天津市人民政府，对大会的圆满成功表示热烈祝贺。大会论坛水准极高，相关活动和讨论富有成果，我们深深地感受到东道主的热情好客。

很高兴来到天津，有机会聆听、见证职业技术教育与培训前沿领域的各界人士所发表的独到见解，彼此间的分享和交流，参会者包括政策制定者、职业技术教育工作者以及国际组织、行业协会、企业、学术界的研究人员。

职业技术教育与培训得到了越来越多的认可，可以有效地帮助年轻人，让他们有能力在知识经济和知识社会中从事生产性和可持续的工作。职业技术教育与培训、技能培训与联合国可持续发展目标的第 1、2、4、5、7、8、9、10、11、13 和 17 项目标全面挂钩。今天，全球化与技术正在成为教育改革的重要推动力。特别是在当前的宏观经济和金融环境下，职业技术教育与培训对社会经济发展、实现可持续发展目标、发展技能，社会繁荣、扶贫和不让任何一个人掉队方面都发挥着重要的作用。

可持续发展需要在各个层面采取全面、公平和长期的方法，不仅强调强劲的经济表现，还强调代内和代际公平、机会和质量。可持续发展需要在公共和私人决策中对社会、经济和环境目标进行整合和平衡考虑。全球职业技术教育与培训系统正在经历巨大的变化和改革，新冠病毒疫情扰乱了整个系统的发展，在这个背景下出现了许多新的议题，需要我们重新思考职业技术教育与培训的转型以及社会和经济中的各种相关因素，包括职业技术教育与培训的融资和治理，职业技术教育与培训提供者的多元化，标准驱动和能力为本的方法调整，职业技术教育与培训的效能与效率，绿色职业技术教育与培训促进可持续发展以及国际交流与合作等。许多问题迫切地需要我们的关注。我很高兴地看到本次会议做了巧妙的安排，让与会者能够就职业技术教育与培训的热点话题进行全面的讨论。

自 2015 年 5 月世界教育论坛上通过《仁川宣言》开始，联合国教科文组织作为联合国的专门教育机构受到委托，负责牵头《2030 年教育议程》并协调其合作伙伴。职业技术教育与培训是联合国教科文组织的首要战略重点，与联合国教科文组织全球职业技术教育与培训战略相一致。在一个强调社会、经济和环境因素之间联系的全球化世界中，未来的愿景是让职业技术教育与培训有机会为实现全球发展议程作出贡献。然而，当今我们面临的挑战使这项任务变得更加困难。新冠病毒疫情在全球范围内造成了严重的破坏，对我们生活和工作的方方面面产生了影响，现在是时候让我们去回顾、审视职业技术教育与培训在改革方面取得的进展，探索在全球范围内建立更具弹性的职业技术教育与培训系统的关键战略方向。我要为大会喝彩，为期两天的大会提供了一个平台，可以重新审视与技能发展相关的可持续发展目标，审视这些目标是否适应各个国家的国情以及职业技术教育与培训部门仍然存在的差距和挑战。

中国作为一个负责任的大国，为努力解决后疫情时代全球职业技术教育与培训的新问题召开了此次大会。我想借此机会重申，联合国教科文组织将继续全力支持各成员国职业技术教育与培训的转型，释放职业技术教育与培训的潜力，以满足个人、企业和社会的技能需求。正如一句中国谚语所说的，“众人拾柴火焰高”。女士们，先生们，在过去的两天里，我们齐心协力，共同审视、研究职业技术教育与培训系统更加大有可为的新方法，这是一个了不起的成果。各位参会者，请将在天津的收获带回您的国家，带到您的工作中，让我们一起努力，更好地履行职责，创造更大的影响、更强的协同效应、更高的合作效率，让每一位学习者充分释放自己的潜力。

# I. Speech by the Director of the UNESCO Beijing Office

On behalf of UNESCO, today I am pleased and honored to give the closing remarks at the first World Vocational and Technical Education Development Conference. First of all, please let me congratulate the Conference Organizers, the Chinese Ministry of Education, the Chinese National Commission for UNESCO and the Tianjin Municipal People's Government, on this successful Conference including the quality of the sessions, the useful activities and discussions, and the hospitality shown to all of us.

I am pleased to be here in Tianjin and witness the insightful contributions, sharing and exchanges regarding all the forefronts of technical and vocational education and training, widely participated by the policy makers, TVET practitioners, international organizations, trade associations, businesses, academia and research institutions.

TVET is increasingly recognized as an effective means of equipping and empowering young people to engage in productive and sustainable livelihoods in a knowledge economy and knowledge society. The TVET and skills training is comprehensively linked to the United Nations Sustainable Development Goals, of Goals 1, 2, 4, 5, 7, 8, 9, 10, 11, 13 & 17. Today, globalization and technology are becoming important drivers of education reforms. In the current macroeconomic and financial environment in particular, TVET is an effective programme to accelerate social-economic development, achieving SDGs, and empower people with skills that can contribute to prosperity, poverty alleviation and leaving no one behind.

Sustainable development requires a holistic, equitable and long-term approach at all levels. It emphasizes not just strong economic performance but intra-generational and intergenerational equity, access and quality. It rests on integration and a balanced consideration of social, economic and environmental goals and objectives in both public and private policy-making. At the time when the global TVET systems are undergoing tremendous changes and reforms, particularly facing the systematic disruption from the COVID-19 pandemic, there are many emerging topics that we need to rethink the transforming in TVET and all the relevant factors in society and economy: the financing and governance of TVET, the diversification of TVET providers, the adaptation of standard-driven and competency-based approaches, the effectiveness and efficiency in TVET trainings, the greening TVET for sustainable development, and international exchanges and cooperation…there are so many issues that requires our urgent attention. I'm pleased to see this Conference has smartly designed so the participants have been able to discuss over a comprehensive coverage of these burning points on TVET.

Through the Incheon Declaration adopted at the World Education Forum in May 2015, UNESCO, as the United Nations'specialized agency for education, was entrusted to lead and coordinate the Education 2030 Agenda with its partners. TVET is top strategic priority of UNESCO, aligned with the UNESCO Global TVET Strategy. In a globalized world underlined by linkages between social, economic and environmental factors, the vision is an opportunity for TVET to contribute to achieving the global development agenda. The task however is made more difficult by the challenges faced today. When the COVID-19 pandemic has caused major disruptions across the world and had an impact on every aspect of our life and of our work, it is timely to review progress toward TVET reforms and explore key strategic directions for building more resilient TVET systems worldwide. I applaud the two-day's conference that has provided a platform to revisit the SDG targets related to skills development, their alignment with the specific country contexts and the remaining gaps and challenges in the TVET sector.

This Conference is a part of China's responses as a responsible great nation trying to support tackling the emerging global TVET issues in a post-pandemic era. And I would like to take this opportunity to reiterate UNESCO's continuous full commitment in supporting the transforming of TVET in its Member States, to unleash the potential of TVET to meet skill needs of individuals, enterprises and societies. As the Chinese saying goes, "when everybody adds wood the flames rise high". Ladies and Gentlemen, again, it is a great achievement that we come together and worked together for the past two days reviewing and looking into the new ways for a more promising TVET system. Dear participants, please bring back what was discussed here in Tianjin to your work and your countries, and let us all work together, for the better delivery, greater impact, stronger synergies and up-scaled cooperation for greater efficiency to allow each and every learner to unleash their potential.

# 二

# 关于筹建世界职业技术教育发展联盟的倡议

中国教育国际交流协会会长　刘利民
Liu Limin, President of China Education Association for International Exchange

为落实全球发展高层对话会成果和本届大会成果，加强同世界各国职业教育的互鉴、互容、互通，拓展职业教育领域国际交流合作，形成更全方位、更宽领域、更多层次、更加主动的世界各国职业教育共同发展的局面，中国教育国际交流协会联合来自 36 个国家的 148 家职业院校、普通高校、研究机构、行业企业，共同发起筹建世界职业技术教育发展联盟的倡议。

在此，我谨代表联盟筹建的单位发出倡议，诚邀全球教育界、产业界和其他社会组织、有识之士一道，本着“自愿、平等、互利、共赢”为原则，协商组建世界职业技术教育发展联盟，共同构建全面、紧密、务实、包容的高质量全球伙伴关系，为促进各国职业教育共同应对挑战，加强沟通协作，扩大优质教育资源共享，助力全球经济复苏和产业振兴作出贡献，共同服务联合国 2030 可持续发展目标的实现。

各位同仁，让我们携起手来，共同创造职业教育更美好的未来！

## Ⅱ. Initiative to Establish World TVET League

In order to implement the results of the high-level dialogue on global development and the outcomes of this conference, strengthen mutual learning, inclusiveness and connectivity of vocational education with other countries in the world, expand international exchange and cooperation in the field of vocational education, and form a more comprehensive, broader, more multi-level and more proactive situation for the common development of vocational education around the world, China Education Association for International Exchange, together with 148 vocational colleges, universities, research institutions and industrial enterprises from 36 countries, has launched an initiative to prepare for the establishment of World TVET League.

Here, on behalf of the organizers of World TVET League, I would like to invite the global education, industry and other social organizations, as well as people with insight, to join together to form World TVET League based on the principles of "voluntariness, equality, mutual benefit and win-win", and to build a comprehensive, close, practical and inclusive global partnership of high quality. The purpose of setting up the league is to promote vocational education in all countries to jointly address challenges, strengthen communication and collaboration, expand the sharing of quality educational resources, contribute to global economic recovery and industrial revitalization, and jointly serve the achievement of the United Nations 2030 Sustainable Development Goals.

Let's join hands to create a better future for vocational education!

# 三

## 《天津倡议》

2022 年 8 月 19—20 日，世界职业技术教育发展大会在中国天津召开。来自 123 个国家（地区）的政府机构、国际组织、行业企业、学校、研究机构代表出席了大会，围绕“后疫情时代职业技术教育发展：新变化、新方式、新技能”的主题进行深入交流、广泛探讨。结合代表的观点、意见和建议，大会形成以下倡议。

我们认为，职业教育是创造价值的教育，可帮助人们获得技术技能，增强创新意识和能力，积极应对环境变化，是以能力为本位、需求为导向、贯穿人一生的教育，是提升产业效能、促进持久包容和可持续经济增长的重要力量，是促进充分和生产性就业、增进人民福祉、创造美好生活的重要途径。

我们秉持，公平全纳、有教无类、面向人人、质量优先的理念，为各类群体提供适宜的职业教育和培训，注重培养诚信敬业、精益求精、追求卓越、勇于创新的职业精神，注重培养可持续、可迁移的发展能力，促进人的全面可持续发展。

我们强调，职业教育要适应后疫情时代的特点和数字化变革需要，与终身教育相结合，与产业链条相契合，与经济社会高质量发展相融合。要进一步扩大高质量的技能人才供给，促进人才培养模式、评价方式、组织形式变革，提高职业教育适应性。要加快数字化转型，强化数字技能、绿色技能培养。

我们希望，政府、行业企业、学校和研究机构积极参与职业教育，不断创新合作形式，拓宽合作内容，建立产学研用深度合作机制，打造互利共赢的技术技能共同体，以科技创新、成果转化支撑引领产业发展与变革，以跨界互动、融合创新共同创造世界美好未来。

我们呼吁，各国政府加大对职业教育的支持和投入力度，提高劳动者的收入水平和社会地位，树立职业荣誉感、增强社会认同感，鼓励用双手创造美好生活；创设国际职教大奖，让职业精神得到弘扬，让职业教育得到尊重，让职业教育创造的价值得到奖励。

我们倡议，各国政府、国际组织、行业组织、企业界和教育界携起手来，加强互学互鉴和务实合作；组建世界职业技术教育发展联盟，构建全面、紧密、务实、包容的高质量伙伴关系，为实现联合国 2030 年可持续发展目标、构建人类命运共同体作出更大贡献。

# Ⅲ. Tianjin Initiative

The World Vocational and Technical Education Development Conference was held in Tianjin, China on 19–20 August 2022. Representatives of governments, international organizations, industries, enterprises, colleges and research institutes from 123 countries and regions attended the conference, and had extensive discussions and in-depth exchanges of views on the theme of "Vocational and Technical Education Development in the Post-pandemic Era—New Changes, New Ways and New Skills". Based on the views, opinions and suggestions of the representatives, the following initiative has come into being through the conference:

We believe that vocational education creates value. It helps people acquire skills and technologies, enhance innovation awareness and ability, and actively cope with environmental changes. It is a skills-oriented, demand-driven and lifelong education. Vocational education is a significant variant to increase industrial efficiency, promote lasting inclusiveness and advance sustainable economic development. It is also an important pathway to boost full and productive employment, improve people's wellbeing and create a better life.

We uphold that vocational education should be accessible to everyone without discrimination, shoulder the responsibility of promoting education equity and inclusiveness, and give priority to quality. We should provide suitable vocational education and training for all groups of people, to help them develop professionalism which focuses on integrity, dedication, improvement, excellence and innovation, and enhance sustainable and transferrable abilities, so as to promote sustainable all-round development of people.

We emphasize that vocational education should adapt to the post-pandemic era and digital transformation, integrate with lifelong education, industrial chains, and high-quality economic and social development. We should expand high-quality supply of skilled talents, promote the reform of the modes in talent training, assessment and organization, improve the adaptability of vocational education, accelerate digital transformation, and strengthen students' digital and green skills.

We hope that governments, industries, enterprises, colleges and research institutes may take active part in vocational education, innovate the collaboration modes, expand the collaboration scope, establish the industry-college-research-application collaboration mechanism, and build a mutually beneficial community focusing on skills and technologies, supporting and guiding industrial development and reform through innovation and transformation of technologies, and creating a better future for the world through cross-sector interaction, integration and innovation.

We appeal all countries to increase support and funding for vocational education, improve workers' income and social position, establish sense of professional honor, enhance sense of social recognition, and encourage citizens to create a better life with their own hands. We propose to establish International TVET Prize, promote professionalism, render vocational education respected and creation of value through vocational education awarded.

We advocate that governments, international organizations, industrial organizations and the business community join hands with the education community for mutual learning and practical cooperation. We suggest setting up World TVET League, and forging comprehensive, close, pragmatic, inclusive and quality partnerships, to contribute to achieving the UN Sustainable Development Goals and building a community with a shared future for mankind.

# 四

## 中华人民共和国教育部<br>部长总结讲话

怀进鹏
Huai Jinpeng

大家好！经过两天紧张而高效的交流和富有智慧的研讨，首届世界职业技术教育发展大会取得了丰硕的成果，即将落下帷幕。

本次大会以“后疫情时代职业技术教育发展：新变化、新方式、新技能”为主题，700 余位中外嘉宾线上线下参会，共同探讨未来世界职业教育的发展之路。中国国家主席习近平向大会发来贺信，深刻阐述了职业教育对促进就业创业、助力经济社会发展、增进人民福祉的重要意义，充分展现了中国愿同世界各国一道，加强互学互鉴、共建共享，携手落实全球发展倡议，为加快落实联合国 2030 年可持续发展议程贡献力量的责任担当，赢得了与会嘉宾的高度评价和热烈反响。

中国国务院副总理孙春兰致辞，她分享了中国政府大力推动职业教育改革发展的做法与经验，发起了各国共同应对挑战、共创职业教育繁荣发展新局面的倡议，得到了与会嘉宾的积极响应。大会期间，各国部长、国际组织负责人、驻华使节以及产业界、科技界、教育界专家代表们，以世界眼光、专业视角，围绕职业教育与经济社会发展深度融合、可持续发展进行了富有智慧的研讨，为推动全球职业教育高质量发展，助力经济社会协同发展建言献策。

我们交流了思想，聚焦世界发展面临的重要课题，围绕后疫情时代的不确定性和人民福祉，通过大会与平行论坛，进行了充分而有效地讨论，深化了我们对职业教育及其与经济社会发展重要关联性、协同性的理解和认识。

我们增进了了解，与会嘉宾结合各自实际、区域探索和本国经验以及经济社会发展的重要因素，深刻分析了职业教育所面临的重大问题，经济社会发展中的关切性，研究了相关领域的发展现状、共同的挑战以及服务人民福祉的重大议题，增进了各国的了解，各国对职业教育服务经济社会发展的典型做法，为进一步合作奠定了坚实的基础。

我们分享了实践，与会嘉宾介绍了所在国家、行业和国际组织推动职业教育与技能提升的战略设计、项目发展和实验平台，对推动全球职业教育高质量发展、可持续发展提出了具有探索性、经验性和多元化的启发和方法。各国、各界代表高度赞赏中国为推动世界职业教育发展作出的努力和贡献，认为本届大会的宗旨与全球经济社会发展和职业教育重点，特别是联合国倡导可持续发展议程相契合、紧密相关。同期举办的各项活动精彩纷呈，是一场高规格、高水平和高质量的大会。

女士们，先生们，朋友们！当前，世界百年之未有大变局与新冠病毒疫情全球大流行交织叠加，不确定性增强，不稳定性增加，经济社会转型加速加快，这些都对职业教育、科技发展以及劳动者就业和人民福祉以及所在国的经济社会发展产生了巨大而深刻的影响。因此，如何办好人民满意的教育，加快数字转型、绿色发展与技能提升，增强产教融合，服务终身学习和可持续性发展，共同应对人类共同的挑战，重振世界经济，共建美好家园，成为本次大会和各国嘉宾、国际组织共同关切和共同关注的重大议题，也是中国发起此次大会的初衷所在。在与会嘉宾的共同努力和支持下，大会取得圆满成功，达到预期成效。

第一，这次大会展现了创新成果。针对联合国教科文组织《技术与职业教育培训战略》，与会代表围绕数字化转型、可持续发展、终身学习等新议题，贡献了新观点、新实践。世界各国职业院校师生在大会期间同台竞技，展现了新技术和产教融合新成果，数百家单位通过云上博览会展示了各国、各行业职业教育与经济产业融合发展的新成果、新方法。可以说，这是一次富有新意的职教盛会，也为世界职业教育发展提出了新的思考、新的篇章和新的议题。

第二，这次大会促进了深度交融。跳出教育看教育，教育与产业界、企业界和经济社会深度交融，是这次职业教育大会最大的特色，也是我们本届大会的基本共识。本次大会聚焦产教融合，与会嘉宾不仅有来自教育界和科技界的专家代表，更有各国政府、机构和国际组织的充分共识。特别是来自企业界、经济界和社会多方力量，大家充分认识到职业教育对于经济社会发展的极端重要性，经济社会发展需要社会多个角色发挥重要作用，特别是政、产、学、研、用、经有效地结合。推动经济振兴，推动人民福祉振兴，提高教育质量是我们共同的努力方向，因此本次职业教育倡导与产业变革、技术革命、绿色发展、数字转型以及扶贫减贫形成了良性、有效的互动，本次大会是一次产学融合与国际合作交流的盛会。

第三，这次大会必将推动世界职业教育，特别是中国职业教育改革发展。习近平主席高度重视职业教育，专门发来贺信，指出职业教育与经济、社会紧密相连，助力经济社会发展，增进人民福祉，我们要加快构建中国现代职业教育体系，坚持推进职普融通、产教融合，把它作为我们职业教育与经济社会协同发展改革的重点。

会上，我们发布了《天津倡议》，提出了共同的价值认识、行业自律和发展方向，发布了筹建世界职业教育联盟、创设世界职业教育大奖的倡议，呼吁构建包容可持续发展的高质量伙伴关系，激励社会各界积极支持、理解和推动职业教育发展，以融合创新、跨界互动创造世界美好的未来。因此本次大会是一次职业教育改革发展与合作共赢的大会。通过构建大会交流合作机制，扩大利益汇合点，画出最大同心圆，着力构建共商、共建、共享的世界职业教育治理和发展新格局。

女士们，先生们，朋友们！ 2022 年是中国发展进程中极不平凡的一年，也是中国职业教育发展进程中极其重要的一年。今年，中国颁布了新修订的《中华人民共和国职业教育法》，为构建现代职业教育体系夯实了法制基础，参会嘉宾对此给予了高度肯定。今年，中国共产党将召开第二十次全国代表大会，对今后中国的发展将进行新的战略部署。中国职业教育也必将迎来改革发展新空间，也必将为构建人类命运共同体，促进全球经济社会可持续发展，增强国际之间的合作，高质量、高水平的交流作出新的更大贡献。

最后，我谨代表中华人民共和国教育部，向关心支持本次大会的各国政府、各国机构以及国际组织、驻华使馆、行业企业、经济界、教育界、科技界和社会各方、媒体朋友们表示衷心的感谢和敬意！大会的成功离不开组委会特别是天津市委市政府和各承办单位、国务院相关部门所作出的积极努力和大力支持，也离不开在疫情期间坚守岗位的各方面工作人员、翻译人员、志愿者的周到服务，特别是媒体朋友们，向社会宣传介绍职业教育的重要意义、社会价值、经济发展空间，我们对所有为本次大会、为职业教育、为经济社会发展做出努力和贡献的社会各界表示衷心的感谢！

现在，我宣布，世界职业技术教育发展大会闭幕！

祝各位身体健康、工作顺利、万事如意！

谢谢大家！

## Ⅳ. Concluding Remarks by the Minister of Education of the People's Republic of China

Good afternoon, everyone. After two days of intense and efficient exchange and resourceful workshops, the first World Vocational and Technical Education Development Conference is coming to an end with fruitful results.

This conference is under the theme of "Vocational and Technical Education Development in the Post-pandemic Era—New Changes, New Ways and New Skills". More than 700 guests from home and abroad attended the conference online and offline, discussing the future of world vocational and technical education. Chinese President Xi Jinping sent a congratulatory letter to the conference, in which President Xi profoundly expounded on the significance of vocational education for promoting employment and entrepreneurship, facilitating economic and social development and enhancing people's well-being. The letter fully demonstrated China's willingness to cooperate with other countries around the world, strengthen mutual learning and contribute to co-construction and sharing. China will join hands with countries around the world to implement global development initiative and make contributions to the 2030 Agenda for Sustainable Development. President Xi's letter won high praise and enthusiastic response from the participants.

Chinese Vice-Premier, Sun Chunlan delivered a speech, in which she shared the Chinese government's practices and experience in promoting vocational education reform and development. Vice-Premier Sun also launched an initiative that all countries should jointly address the challenges and break new ground for the prosperous development of vocational education, which received a positive response from the participants. During the conference, ministers from different countries, heads of international organizations, diplomatic envoys to China as well as experts and representatives from the industrial circles, scientific community and educational circles showed global perspectives and professional insights, conducting meaningful discussions on the deep integration and sustainable development of vocational education and economic and social progress. They provided advice on how to promote high-quality development of world vocational education and facilitate coordinated development of economy and society.

We have exchanged opinions. Focusing on important issues of world development, based on the uncertainties in the post-epidemic era and considering people's well-being, we had a full and effective discussion during the conference and the parallel forums, deepening our understanding of vocational education as well as its important relevance and synergy with economic and social development.

We have enhanced mutual understanding. Based on their own realities, regional explorations and local experience as well as their economic and social development, the participants profoundly analyzed the key problems facing vocational education, and concerns in economic and social development, and discussed key issues, such as the current situations in relevant fields, common challenges and how to meet people's requirements. In this way, each country has enhanced mutual understanding as well as typical practices to serve economic and social development with vocational education, which laid a solid foundation for further cooperation.

We have shared our practices. The participants respectively introduced their strategic designs, project developments and experimental platforms, combining with the realities in their countries, industries and international organizations, which provided some exploratory, empirical and diversified inspirations and approaches to the high-quality and sustainable development of global vocational education. Delegates from various countries and sectors spoke highly of China's efforts and contributions to promote the development of world vocational education. They thought that the objectives of the conference went perfectly with and were closely related to the global economic and social development and the priorities of vocational education, especially in accordance with the 2030 Agenda for Sustainable Development. A variety of fascinating events have been held during the conference, which can be said to be a high-profile, high-level and high-quality conference.

Ladies and gentlemen and our dear friends! At present, the world today is undergoing major changes unseen in a century and the widespread pandemic, which have brought about increasing instability and uncertainties. What's more, economic and social transformation is promoted at a faster pace. All of these have a great and profound impact on vocational education, scientific and technological development, employment and people's well-being as well as the economic and social development of each country. Therefore, it's not only of the common interests and concern of all participants from different countries and international organizations, but also the ultimate goal and original intention of the conference to explore how to make vocational education to people's satisfaction, how to quicken digital transformation, green development and skill upgrading, how to enhance the integration of education and industry, how to serve the demands of lifelong learning and sustainable development, how to meet the common challenges of mankind, how to reinvigorate world economy and build a better home. With the joint efforts and support of the participants, the conference concluded successfully with the expected results.

Firstly, innovative results are shown during the conference. Concerning "the

Technical and Vocational Education and Training Programme Strategy" developed by the United Nations, the participants provided a number of new ideas and practices based on digital transformation, sustainable development, lifelong learning and other new topics. Teachers and students from vocational institutions around the world competed during the conference, showing the new achievements of science and technology and the integration of industry and education. Via online exhibition platforms, hundreds of units exhibited new results and methods of integrating the development of vocational education, economy and industry in each country and industry. It can be said that this is an innovative grand gathering of vocational education, which brings about new thoughts, new chapters and new topics for world vocational education development.

Secondly, the conference facilitated deep integration. It is the most prominent feature and basic consensus of this conference that we consider education beyond education circles and pay attention to the deep integration of education with industrial circles, enterprises, economy and society. This conference focused on the integration of education and industry, attracting not only experts and representatives from educational circles and the scientific community, but also those from governments of different countries, institutions and international organizations. In particular, the conference received support from the business sector, economic circles and all walks of life, which shows that people have fully recognized the vital importance of vocational education for economic and social development. The development of the economy and society requires coordinated efforts from multiple groups, especially the effective collaboration of government, industry, academia, research institutions, application and economics. It's our common endeavor to promote an economic revival, enhance people's well-being and improve the quality of education. Hence, this conference carried forward a positive and effective interaction between vocational education and industrial transformation, technological revolution, green development, digital transformation and poverty alleviation and reduction, thus making this conference a grand gathering for industry-academia integration and international cooperation and exchange.

Thirdly, this conference will surely promote world vocational education development, especially the reform and development of China's vocational education. President Xi paid high attention to vocational education and especially sent a congratulatory letter in which he pointed out the close relationship between vocational education and economic and social development. In order to propel economic and social development and enhance people's well-being, we should speed up the development of China's modern vocational education system, firmly promote the integration of vocational education and general education and the integration between industry and education, regarding it as the key to the reform of coordinated development of vocational education and economic and social development.

At the conference, we released the "Tianjin Initiative", which put forward a common understanding of values, industrial self-discipline rules and orientation of development. We proposed to establish World TVET League and set up International TVET Prize. We call on people around the world to build a high-quality partnership featuring inclusive and sustainable development. We encouraged all walks of life to actively support, understand and promote the development of vocational education and create a better future with integrated innovation and cross-border interaction. For this reason, this conference marks the development of vocational education reform and win-win cooperation. By forming a mechanism for exchange and cooperation at this conference, we will expand the scope of common interests and devote ourselves to building a new pattern for world vocational education governance and development guided by the "golden principles" of extensive consultation, joint contribution and shared benefits.

Ladies and gentlemen and our dear friends! 2022 is a remarkable year in the development course of China, and also an extremely important year marking the development of China's vocational education. This year, China promulgated the newly revised "Vocational Education Law of the People's Republic of China", providing a solid legal foundation for building a modern vocational education system, which was highly appreciated by the participants. The Communist Party of China will convene its $20^{th}$ National Congress in 2022, making new strategic deployment of future development. China's vocational education will surely welcome a new phase of reform and development, which will further help build a community with a shared future for mankind, promote the sustainable development of the global economy and society, strengthen international cooperation and drive high-quality and high-level communication.

Lastly, on behalf of the Ministry of Education of the People's Republic of China, I would like to express my heartfelt thanks and respect to governments, institutions, international organizations, embassies, enterprises, the economic community, education circles, the scientific community, media friends and friends from all walks of life. Thanks for your support and concern. The success of the conference would not have been possible without the efforts and support of the organizing committee, especially the Tianjin Municipal Committee and Municipal People's Government as well as the organizing units and related departments of the State Council. Thanks also go to staff members, interpreters and volunteers who stuck to their posts during the outbreak of the epidemic and offered considerate services. In particular, we would like to thank our media friends, who actively promoted and introduced the importance and social value of vocational education as well as its benefits to economic and social development. We are grateful to all of you who have contributed to the conference, vocational education and economic and social development. Thank you for your efforts!

Now, I'd like to declare the closing of the World Vocational and Technical Education Development Conference!

Wish you all good health, success at work and all the best!

Thank you!

读者意见反馈

为收集对教材的意见建议，进一步完善教材编写并做好服务工作，读者可将对本教材的意见建议通过如下渠道反馈至我社。

咨询电话　400-810-0598

反馈邮箱　zz_dzyj@pub.hep.cn

通信地址　北京市朝阳区惠新东街4号富盛大厦1座
高等教育出版社总编辑办公室

邮政编码　100029

世界职业技术教育发展大会
WORLD VOCATIONAL AND TECHNICAL EDUCATION DEVELOPMENT CONFERENCE

# 2022年
# 世界职业技术教育发展大会成果汇编

（中册）

世界职业技术教育发展大会组委会

Compilation of Achievements of World Vocational and Technical Education Development Conference 2022 (Volume II)

Organizing Committee of World Vocational and Technical Education Development Conference

中国教育出版传媒集团
高等教育出版社·北京

**图书在版编目（C I P）数据**

2022年世界职业技术教育发展大会成果汇编 ： 全3册/
世界职业技术教育发展大会组委会编. -- 北京 ： 高等教
育出版社，2023.6
ISBN 978-7-04-060676-8

Ⅰ. ①2… Ⅱ. ①世… Ⅲ. ①职业技术教育－世界－
文集 Ⅳ. ①G71-53

中国国家版本馆CIP数据核字(2023)第104511号

策划编辑　贾瑞武　　责任编辑　董梦也　于海宁　　封面设计　赵　阳　　责任绘图　邓　超
版式设计　赵　阳　　责任校对　刘娟娟　　责任印制　赵义民

| | | | |
|---|---|---|---|
| 出版发行 | 高等教育出版社 | 网　　址 | http://www.hep.edu.cn |
| 社　　址 | 北京市西城区德外大街4号 | | http://www.hep.com.cn |
| 邮政编码 | 100120 | 网上订购 | http://www.hepmall.com.cn |
| 印　　刷 | 北京盛通印刷股份有限公司 | | http://www.hepmall.com |
| 开　　本 | 787mm×1092mm　1/16 | | http://www.hepmall.cn |
| 本册印张 | 40 | | |
| 本册字数 | 710千字 | 版　　次 | 2023年6月第1版 |
| 购书热线 | 010-58581118 | 印　　次 | 2023年6月第1次印刷 |
| 咨询电话 | 400-810-0598 | 总 定 价 | 260.00元 |

本书如有缺页、倒页、脱页等质量问题，请到所购图书销售部门联系调换

物 料 号　60676-001

## 大会主题

# 后疫情时代职业技术教育发展：新变化、新方式、新技能

# Vocational and Technical Education Development in the Post-pandemic Era — New Changes, New Ways and New Skills

### 数字化赋能 Digital Empowerment

- 职业教育数字化转型发展论坛 Digital Transformation of Vocational Education
- 人工智能+职业教育创新发展论坛 Artificial Intelligence Impacts on Innovation in Vocational Education

### 产教融合 Integration of Industry and Education

- 职业教育校企协同育人模式创新论坛 Innovation in Modes of Education Delivered Through Academia-Industry Collaboration
- 职业教育与产业转型发展论坛 Vocational Education and Industrial Restructuring

### 绿色技术 Green Technology

- 可持续发展背景下的全球绿色技能战略论坛 Green Skill Strategy for Sustainable Development
- 普通（学术）教育与职业教育协调发展论坛 Integration of Academic and Vocational Education

### 技能与减贫 Skills & Poverty Reduction

- 中非职业教育合作与发展论坛 China-Africa TVET Cooperation Forum
- “一带一路”合作与鲁班工坊建设发展论坛 “The Belt and Road Initiative” and Luban Workshop

### 促进公平 Promoting Equity

- 职业教育助推全球减贫进程论坛 Vocational Education for Poverty Reduction and Inclusive Growth
- 面向未来的职业教育课程变革论坛 Future-oriented Curriculum Reform in Vocational Education

### 终身学习 Lifelong Learning

- 技能重塑与终身学习论坛 Reskilling and Upskilling for Lifelong Learning
- 全球职业教育青年教师发展论坛 Teacher Professional Development in Vocational Education

### 科学与工程 Science & Engineering

- 职业院校科学教育发展论坛 Science Education Development in Vocational Education Institutions
- 职业院校工程教育发展论坛 Engineering Education Development in Vocational Education Institutions

# 目录

## 平行论坛嘉宾演讲文稿收录

## Contents

# Speeches at the Parallel Sessions

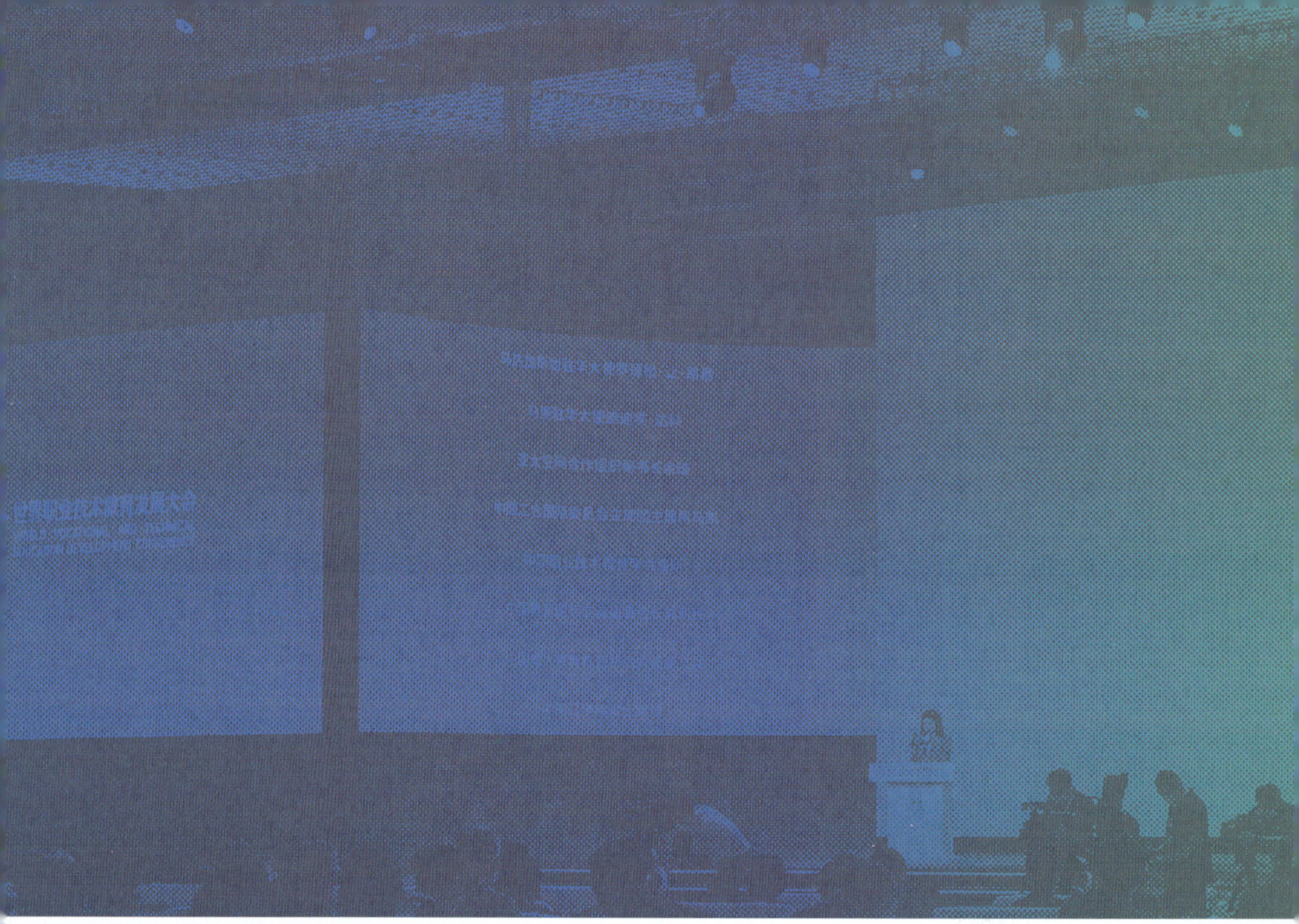

# 平行论坛嘉宾演讲文稿收录

# Speeches at the Parallel Sessions

# 一

# 人工智能+职业教育创新发展论坛

协助组织单位：中华人民共和国教育部高等学校科学研究发展中心

# I. Artificial Intelligence Impacts on Innovation in Vocational Education

Co-organizer: Center for Scientific Research and Development in Higher Education Institutes, Ministry of Education, P. R. China（CSRD）

02
富强
Fu Qiang

03
菲利普 · 波伦茨
Philipp Pohlenz

04
龚克
Gong Ke

05
田敏
Tian Min

06
马艳军
Ma Yanjun

**分享人工智能与信息化领域的前沿动态，研讨人工智能背景下的职业价值与职业素养，探索职业教育内容、方式、模式等方面的变革，共同谋划未来职业教育创新发展的策略与路径。**

The participants of this session share the cutting-edge updates in artificial intelligence (AI) and information technology, discuss the professional values and qualities in the context of AI, and explore the ways of transforming the content, ways and modes of VTE, and jointly planning the strategies and paths for the innovative development of VTE in the future.

## (一)

## 人工智能 + 职业教育创新发展论坛情况概述

中华人民共和国教育部高等学校科学研究发展中心项目主任　赵艳玲

作为世界职业技术教育发展大会的十四个平行论坛之一，由中华人民共和国教育部高等学校科学研究发展中心协助组织举办的人工智能 + 职业教育创新发展论坛于 2022 年 8 月 20 日下午在国家会展中心（天津）举行，北京师范大学教育学部教授赵志群负责主持。

论坛聚焦智能时代全球职业教育协同创新的主题，齐聚来自海内外职业教育、人工智能领域的12位专家学者分享人工智能与数字化领域的前沿动态，探讨智能化背景下职业教育内容、方式、模式等方面的变革，谋划未来职业教育创新发展的策略与路径，发言视角多元，内容精彩纷呈。

中华人民共和国教育部高等学校科学研究发展中心主任罗方述致欢迎辞。他指出，此次论坛是对习近平主席在国际人工智能与教育大会上提出推动人工智能和教育深度融合重要倡议的积极响应。作为与经济社会发展联系最为紧密的教育类型，职业教育的高质量创新发展必须顺应以人工智能等新技术为代表的更深层次、更广范围科技革命的挑战，必须适应更加开放的新发展格局，必须实现颠覆传统理念、课程体系和教育模式的革命性重塑。为此，他提出三点建议，一是以人为本，推动职业教育高质量发展；二是注重实效，促进人工智能与教育教学深度融合；三是合作共赢，构建智能职业教育命运共同体。并呼吁以本次论坛为契机，聚焦人工智能赋能职业教育发展的模式和路径，加速推进职业教育的数字化、智能化转型升级，为世界职业教育贡献中国智慧和中国方案。

中国新一代人工智能发展战略研究院执行院长龚克和联合国教科文组织教育信息技术研究所所长展涛作主题报告。龚克分析了教育数字化转型的原因，提出了数字化转型的内容和路径。他指出人工智能、大数据、物联网等新兴数字技术已经革命性地改变了生产和服务的范式，包括职业教育在内的整个教育系统应该适应数字化革命和可持续发展的双重转型。职业教育数字化转型的目标是培养具备数字伦理、科学知识、学习能力和创新能力的数字化时代合格公民和创新领袖。职业教育的数字化转型，即将数字化工具的普及与有效使用、数字化技术的通用化与专业化学习以及全民数字化素养的提高结合起来，创新教学模式、教学方案，提供培训和学习模式等。同时也指出了推动教育数字化转型的一些关键词：道德伦理、科学基础、跨学科、实践、教学相长。

展涛围绕联合国教科文组织在人工智能和职业技术教育方面的重要战略和关注重点，指出联合国教科文组织非常重视人工智能技术应用及在应用过程中所面临的一些新的问题和挑战，这些问题和挑战既包括人工智能技术广泛的应用是否会影响教育的以人为本、以学习者为中心以及个人隐私的保护、个人权利和自由发展，也包括能否有助于减少甚至最终消除数字鸿沟，还包括能否促进区域发展以及区域、地区的均衡发展等。为此，联合国教科文组织发布了《人工智能伦理问题建议书》和《北京宣言》两个重要文件。他还提到职业技术教育在联合国教科文组织教育规划中的特殊之处，既体现在《2030年教育议程》对职业技术教育的重视中，也体现在职业技术教育在联合国教科文组织整个发展规划中的独立性。同时他也指出了联合国教科文组织在人工智能和职业教育的结合点上的四个聚焦，即青年技能和创新能力的培养、弱势群体和性别平等、区域发展、多领域多伙伴的合作。

来自国内外的高等院校和行业企业专家也就人工智能与职业教育创新发展展开了研讨与实践经验分享。德国马格德堡大学人文社会科学与教育学院副院长菲利普·波伦茨、德国巴登−符腾堡双元制大学教授克里斯蒂安·李贝特、爱尔兰都柏林理工大学计算机科学学院院长保罗·多伊尔分别从后疫情时代教育数字化转型、人工智能引入职业教育与培训、人工智能赋能教育创新等视角分享人工智能赋能职业教育创新发展的背景与模式。

德国北黑森应用技术大学技术工程学院副院长本杰明·因登、新加坡工艺教育局商业及服务业学院副署长富强通过各自学校的实践案例分享了人工智能技术在教育中的应用路径。

南京信息职业技术学院校长田敏就高职培养人工智能应用人才的需求开展了分析，介绍了学校人工智能专业群建设与发展的情况，并分享了通过智能技术驱动其他专业升级的探索。

德国克诺尔轨道车辆系统有限公司工程与创新主管王福岗、百度集团 AI 技术生态总经理马艳军、国家职业教育虚拟仿真示范实训基地总经理项顺、深圳云天励飞技术股份有限公司副总裁郑文先分别分享了各自企业在智能化技术应用的实践与探索以及将人工智能技术融入人才培养的具体举措。

本次平行论坛为人工智能赋能职业教育创新发展搭建智慧分享、思想交锋的舞台，为推动全球职业教育的协同发展提供助力。

## i. Overview of the Session on Artificial Intelligence Impacts on Innovation in Vocational Education

**Zhao Yanling, Project Director of Center for Scientific Research and Development in Higher Education Institutes, Ministry of Education, P. R. China (CSRD)**

As one of the 14 parallel sessions of World Vocational and Technical Education Development Conference, the Session on Artificial Intelligence Impacts on Innovation in Vocational Education, organized by Center for Scientific Research and Development in Higher Education Institutes of the Ministry of Education, P. R. China (CSRD), was held at the National Convention and Exhibition Center (Tianjin) in the afternoon of August 20, 2022, presided over by Professor Zhao Zhiqun from the Faculty of Education of Beijing Normal University, China.

Focusing on the theme of collaborative innovation of global vocational education in the intelligent era, the session gathered 12 experts and scholars from the field of vocational education and artificial intelligence (AI) at home and abroad, with diverse perspectives and brilliant contents, to share the cutting-edge developments in the field of AI and information technology, explore the transformation of the content, ways, modes and other aspects of vocational education in the context of AI, plan future strategies and paths for the innovative development of vocational education.

Luo Fangshu, Director of Center for Scientific Research and Development in Higher Education Institutes of the Ministry of Education, P. R. China (CSRD), delivered a welcoming speech. He pointed out that the session was a positive response to the important initiative of President Xi Jinping to promote the deep integration of AI and education at the International Conference on Artificial Intelligence & Education. As the education type most closely related to economic and social development, the high-quality innovative development of vocational education must comply with the challenges of the deeper and broader scientific and technological revolution represented by new technologies such as AI, must adapt to the new development pattern that is more open, and must realize the revolutionary reconstruction that subverts traditional concepts, curriculum systems and education models. For this reason, he put forward three suggestions: first, be people-oriented, and promote the high-quality development of vocational education; second, pay attention to actual results, and promote the deep integration of AI and education and teaching; third, pursue win-win situations through cooperation, and build a community of shared future for intelligent vocational education. He also called for taking this session as an opportunity to focus on the development mode and path of vocational education empowered by AI, accelerate the digital and intelligent transformation and upgrading of vocational education, and contribute Chinese wisdom and Chinese approaches to world vocational education.

Gong Ke, Executive Director of the Chinese Institute of New Generation Artificial Intelligence Development Strategies (CINGAI), and Zhan Tao, Director of UNESCO Institute for Information Technologies in Education (IITE), delivered keynote reports. Gong Ke analyzed the reasons for the digital transformation of education, and proposed the content and path of the digital transformation. He pointed out that emerging digital technologies such as AI, big data and the Internet of Things have revolutionized the paradigm of production and service. The entire education system, including vocational education, should adapt to the dual transformation of digital revolution and sustainable development. The goal of the digital transformation of vocational education is to cultivate qualified citizens and innovation leaders with digital ethics, scientific knowledge, learning ability and innovation ability in the digital era. The digital transformation of vocational education is to combine the popularization and effective use of digital tools, the popularization and professional learning of digital technology, and the improvement of the digital literacy of all citizens, and to innovate the teaching mode, teaching scheme, provision of training and learning mode, etc. At the same time, he also pointed out some key words to promote the digital transformation of education: ethics, scientific basis, interdisciplinary approach, practice, and collaboration of teachers and students.

Zhan Tao focused on UNESCO's important strategies and priorities in AI and vocational and technical education (VTE). He pointed out that UNESCO attaches great importance to the application of AI technology and some new problems and challenges in the application process. These challenges include whether the widespread application of AI technology will affect people-oriented and learner-centered education, as well as the protection of personal privacy, personal rights and free development, whether it will help reduce or eventually eliminate the digital divide, as well as whether it will contribute to regional development and balanced regional and area development. To this end, UNESCO issued two important documents, namely, *Recommendation on the Ethics of Artificial Intelligence* and the *Beijing Declaration*. He also mentioned the particularity of VTE in the UNESCO education planning, which was reflected in the emphasis on VTE in the *2030 Education Agenda* and the independence of VTE in the overall development planning of UNESCO. At the same time, he pointed out four focuses of UNESCO on the combination of AI and vocational education, namely, the cultivation of young people's skills and innovation ability, vulnerable groups and gender equality, regional development, and the cooperation of multiple fields and partners.

Experts from higher education institutions and industrial enterprises at home and abroad also conducted discussions and shared practical experiences on the innovative development of AI and vocational education.

Philipp Pohlenz, Vice President of the Faculty of Humanities, Social Sciences and Education of Otto von Guericke University Magdeburg (OVGU) in Germany, Christian Liebelt, Professor of Baden-Wuerttemberg Cooperative State University in Germany, and Paul Doyle, Head of the School of Computer Science of Technological University Dublin in Ireland, shared the background and model of the innovative development of AI-empowered vocational education respectively from the perspective of post-pandemic digital transformation of education, the introduction of AI into vocational education and training, and AI-empowered innovative development of vocational education.

Benjamin Inden, Deputy Director of Technology Engineering Department of DIPLOMA University of Applied Sciences North Hesse in Germany, and Fu Qiang, Deputy Director of the School of Business & Services, Institute of Technical Education in Singapore, shared the application path of AI technology in education through the practice cases in their own school.

Tian Min, President of Nanjing Vocational College of Information Technology in China, analyzed the needs of training AI application talents in higher vocational education, introduced the construction and development of the school's AI specialty group, and shared the exploration of driving other specialties to upgrade through intelligent technology.

Wolfgang Paul Straube, Head of Engineering & Innovation of Knorr-Bremse Railway Vehicle Systems Co., Ltd. in Germany, Ma Yanjun, General Manager of Baidu AI Platform & Ecosystem of Baidu Inc. in China, Xiang Shun, General Manager of National Vocational Education Virtual Simulation Demonstration Training Base in China, and Zheng Wenxian, Vice President of Shenzhen Intellifusion Technologies Co., Ltd. in China, respectively shared their enterprises' practice and exploration in the application of intelligent technology, as well as specific measures to integrate AI technology into talent training.

This parallel session provides a platform to share wisdom and exchange ideas for AI-empowered innovative development of vocational education, as well as assistance for promoting the coordinated development of global vocational education.

## (二)

# 应用人工智能改善和加强教学
## ——新加坡视角

新加坡工艺教育局商业及服务业学院副署长　富　强

世界经济论坛发布的《2020未来就业报告》显示，到2025年，各行各业或将普遍应用人工智能等科学技术。根据首席信息官研究发布的2021年对企业董事会调查观点，公司和企业可以利用许多尖端变革性技术战胜新冠病毒疫情，变得更加强大。也就是说，对于各行各业来说，要从疫情中复苏，应用人工智能具有重要和深远的意义。

那么你可能会问，人工智能在教育中的应用如何呢？有许多人工智能在教育领域的应用都非常实用。比如，人工智能可以方便学生随时随地查阅学习资料，也可以把教师从烦冗重复的工作中解放出来。人工智能聊天机器人可以解答常见问题，它和人工智能助教还能帮助学生随时随地进行学习。更重要的是，人工智能可以根据学生能力适配定制化学习方案，实现个性化或基于个人水平的迭代。此类应用不胜枚举。

我想和大家分享新加坡工艺教育局的三个实践案例。在详细讨论这些案例之前，我先简单介绍一下新加坡工艺教育局的情况。新加坡工艺教育局是新加坡教育部下属政府公立学院，每年接收全国1/4的中学毕业生，为其提供两年到四年的职业技术教育，包括职业技能证书、学历文凭、继续教育和培训项目。目前，共有全日制学生约28 000人，年龄主要在17到19岁之间。

第一个案例是使用预测性人工智能数据分析，提高学生成才率。所有的教育机构都希望帮助学生取得成功，职业技术教育机构更是如此。主要的问题是如何尽早识别风险学生，从而迅速采取干预手段或提供针对性支持，帮助此类学生获得成功。

如果能在教学前期确定哪些学生风险较高，就可以尽早为其提供帮助。我们称其为“提升”或“上台阶”计划，使用监督性机器学习模型，为每位风险学生提供定向支持。基于机器学习算法，我们建立了风险学生评估模型，并用这个模型算出风险学生名单。提炼出干预对象列表后，我们会开展针对性的和量身定做的支持项目，帮助这些学生取得成功，即帮助他们进步，顺利完成学业。这就是这项计划所提供的解决方案，结果显示它非常有效，通过尽早识别风险学生，引入针对性干预措施，学生流失率有了明显的降低。

具体方法是使用 IBM SPSS 模型和微软 Power BI 创建后端引擎和建模，跟踪学校各学院 10 000 多名学生的记录。其中，加入了 40 个自变量，如学生的出勤率、人员和社会经济背景、课外活动、性格特征、考试成绩以及体能测试结果等。总之，在这个机器学习建模中，这 40 个自变量涵盖了学生校园生活的绝大多数方面。我们成功完成了 7 个模型，其中 70% 是训练数据，30% 是测试数据。最后优化选择的模型对这两项数据的应用分析准确率都相当高，均超过 90%。算法能帮助我们确定和挑选有风险的学生，我们就可以把这些学生挑出来，为他们提供针对性干预措施，即在第一学期结束后，也就是加入项目 6 个月之后，为他们提供帮助。这个方法取得了极大成功，达到了切实的帮助效果，有助于提高学生整体成功率。

第二个案例是使用人工智能聊天机器人，帮助实习生解决实际问题，了解实习生学习需求，助力他们顺利地完成实习生活。我们使用了名叫“拉里”的人工智能聊天机器人解答学生的常见问题，并提供学习数据分析，分析哪些方面存在问题，学生在哪类问题或任务上耗费的时间过多，从而更有效地帮助学生管理实习工作。

第三个案例是使用“noodlefactory.ai”人工智能评分和辅导软件。我们与该软件合作，帮助学生学习，帮助教职工开展工作。我们还利用该软件解决其中的问题。有两大关键点需要解决：一个是要减少教师花在给学生作业和模拟试卷打分上的时间，另一个是要全天候为学生提供帮助和建议，以实现个性化和自主学习。因为新冠病毒疫情暴发，只能转向线上教学，就更需要解决这个问题了。在新加坡，我们称这种教学模式为居家学习，虽然学生在听课，但我们不一定能完全掌握学生是否真正理解了课程内容、面临哪些问题，也不确定是否能够给学生提供单独的个性化帮助，这就是我们要解决的两个关键问题。

在人工智能评分器方面，教师会使用 noodlefactory.ai 在平台上设置模拟测评，利用人工智能引擎进行智能评分，并通过审核分数、向机器反馈审核结果，持续完善自动评分算法。

而在人工辅导方面，我们可以利用人工智能引擎，自动建立辅导知识库和辅导流程。基于学生的测评表现，关联辅导流程。如果学生某道问题回答错误，人工智能引擎会建议其就同一专题再接受一轮辅导。

我们来看教师如何向学生介绍这个特殊工具：“欢迎来到 noodlefactory.ai 平台。很高兴告诉各位，你们可以完成更多测评，得到即时反馈以及人工智能助教沃特的个性化辅导。通过测评，可以检测自己对某个专题的掌握程度，做得越多，考试就越有把握。

登录账户后，请在已选模块或专题中点击想测试的那个模块或专题，系统会提供一系列待做试题，包括多选题、开放题等。每完成一项测评，系统会进行打分，同时显示分数与标准答案。

如果认为评分有误，可以点击 ‘Send for review’（提交审核）。教师会收到提醒，审核答案；如确实有误，教师会订正分数。随后，系统会给学生发送通知，并更新分数。

（可以随时终止学习吗？）当然可以！如果需要休息，可以随时终止。但测评进度是无法保存的，所以请在终止前完成测评。结束时，请写下反馈，说明辅导的实用性。

（可以回顾历史辅导课程和模拟测评吗？）当然！点击 ‘Summary’（概览）标签，即可回顾已学习的专题、分数和反馈以及拓展学习资料链接。在回顾过程中，还可以使用书签功能，随时点亮重点内容和解释。如有需要，也可随时输入问题。

我们旨在使用沃特人工智能助教给大家提供最佳学习体验。祝各位学得开心！”

这的确是很美妙的体验，我们使用 noodlefactory.ai 平台在课堂上开展了一场行动研究计划。在 9 个月里，26 个班级的 24 位教师以沃特为辅助，讲授了 4 个模块。学生表现有了大幅改善，课堂参与更加积极，教师的效率也有了很大提升。

通过今天分享的三个案例，大家可以发现，人工智能可以为教学提供多方面的帮助。首先，通过采取针对性干预措施，可以帮助学生取得更大的成功；其次，可以使用人工智能聊天机器人帮助学生解决在实习时遇到的实际问题；最后，可以使用人工智能辅导、人工智能评分、人工智能平台为师生双方提供帮助。

## ii. Using AI Applications to Improve and Enhance Teaching & Learning
### —A Singapore Perspective

**Fu Qiang, Deputy Director of the School of Business & Services, Institute of Technical Education, Singapore**

Based upon *The Future of Jobs Report 2020* issued by the World Economic Forum, AI is one of the important technologies likely to be adopted by the year 2025. What's more, according to Board of Directors 2021, CIO Research, many top game-changing technologies can help the company emerge stronger from COVID-19. This means artificial intelligence can play an important role for all kinds of industries to emerge stronger from COVID-19.

How about AI applications in education? There are many applications we can benefit from by using AI in education. For instance, AI can help prepare learning resources that can be accessed anywhere anytime. AI will be able to take over tedious and repetitive tasks from teachers. AI chatbots can also help address frequently asked questions. AI chatbots and tutors can be made available to help students to learn anywhere anytime. And more importantly, learning can be tailored and adapted based upon learner's ability. It can be personalized or iterated at personal level. And there are many more applications of using AI in education.

I'm going to share three practice cases, adopted by Institute of Technical Education, Singapore. Before I dwell into the cases, I would like to have a brief introduction of our institution. We are a governmental institution under the Ministry of Education, Singapore. We provide 2-to-4-year vocational and technical education (VTE) to 1/4 of annual secondary school leavers. We have around 28 000 full-time students. They are typically at the age between 17 and 19. We offer vocational skill certificates, acdemic diplomas and continuous education and training programs.

The first case is using predictive AI data analytics to improve students' success rate. It's widely known and well recognized that all education institutions would like to help students be successful, which is especially true for VTE institutions. The major problem lies in how we can identify at-risk students early, so that interventions and targeted support can be provided or introduced to help them be successful.

If we know who the at-risk students are at the early stage of their study, we can help them early. This project, entitled "Step-Up", uses a supervised machine learning model to provide targeted support to every at-risk student. We create a list of students at risk, based upon the machine-learning algorithm. After extracting the intervention list, we perform targeted support and help them to be successful, I mean, to help them to step up, and help them to be able to complete their studies successfully. This is the solution provided through this project. It has turned out to be very effective, as our students' attrition rates were reduced, thanks to the early identification of at-risk students and targeted interventions introduced thereafter.

I'd like to share a bit more from a methodology perspective. We track more than 10 000 students' records. And it covers all different schools in our institute. We used IBM SPSS model and Microsoft Power BI to create the back-end engine and modeling. We threw in 40 independent variables here such as the students' attendance, their demographic and social economy background dataset, co-curricular activities, student profiling in terms of their personalities, exam results, fitness test results, among others. So all in all we cover most aspects of a student's life on campus through these 40 independent variables in this machine learning model. We complete 7 successful models, using 70% as training data and 30% as test data. We create very high accuracy rates. The training data and test data accuracy rates are both over 90%. The algorithm can actually help us to assign and pick up the individual student whoever is at risk. And we will be able to single them out to provide targeted interventions and help them after Term One, that is 6 months upon enrolment in our program. And indeed it is very successful and very helpful. It helps improve students' overall success rate.

The second case I'm going to share here is about using AI chatbots to help address internship students' situational problems, identifying their learning needs and trying to help them succeed in their internship journey. We have been using an AI chatbot named Larry to answer some of frequently asked questions by students and provide learning analytics to see what the problems are, and what types of questions or tasks students are spending too much time on. In doing so, we will be more efficient in helping students manage their internships or attachment.

The third one I'm going to share is on using AI-marking and AI-tutoring software by the name of noodlefactory.ai. Noodlefactory.ai is one of the partners we worked with to help our students and staff in learning and teaching. Indeed, it helps to address the issues here. There are two key pain points we are trying to address. The first one is that lecturers spend a lot of time in marking and grading students' homework and their mock test papers. Secondly, we are also trying to see how we are able to provide round-the-clock assistance and advice to students to achieve personalized and self-directed learning. This is especially needed due to COVID-19, when we had no choice but to move to online teaching and learning. In Singapore, we call it home-based learning. And while students are listening to the lecturers, we may or may not be able to fully identify how much they really understand, what the problems they're facing are, or whether we are able to help them individually in a personalized manner. So these are two key issues we are trying to address.

For AI-marking, lecturers use the noodlefactory.ai to set up mock assessment on the platform and use AI engine for auto marking and continuously improve the auto-marking algorithm through score review and feedback to the machine.

For AI-tutoring, we are able to use AI engine to automatically set up tutoring knowledge base and workflow. Therefore it links the tutoring workflow to how students perform in the assessments. If students cannot get certain questions right, AI engine will recommend them going through the tutoring for another round for the topic as well.

Let's see how the lecturers introduced this particular tool to their students:

*Welcome to noodlefactory. ai. We are excited to share that you can now complete more assessments, and get instant feedback and personalized tutoring with Walter, your AI tutor. With Walter, you can test your understanding of a particular topic by working on more assessments and better prepare yourself for the exams.*

*When you log in, choose the module of topic you want to be assessed on your chosen module or topic, and you will have a set of questions you need to work on. These include multiple choice and open-ended questions. Once you have completed each assessment, your answers will be scored, and the scores will be shown to you along with the ideal answer.*

*If you feel that you were incorrectly scored, you can choose to "Send for review", your lecturer will be notified and they will review your answers and correct the score if needed. You will then be notified and your score will be updated.*

*(Can I end the session anytime?) Definitely! If you need to take a break, you can end the session at any time. However, the assessment progress will not be saved, so we should complete the assessment before you end a session. At the end of the session, make sure you leave feedback on how helpful the session was.*

*(Can I review my past tutoring sessions and mock assessments?) Yes, you can! Head to the Summary tab to review the topics you have covered, your scores and feedback and the links to access additional learning resources. You may also use the bookmark tool to highlight important facts and explanations at any time during your session for review. You can choose to type a question whenever you need to.*

*With Walter, the AI tutor, we aim to give you the best learning experience. Happy learning!*

It is a very exciting experience. We conducted an action research project during our lectures using noodlefactory.ai. 24 lecturers used Walter for 9 months to teach 4 modules in 26 classes. You can see improvement in terms of student performance, the positive effect of student engagement as well as productivity of lecturers.

From the three cases I've shared, you can see, AI will be able to help lecturers in many ways. The first one is about how we help our students be more successful through targeted intervention. The second one is about how we use AI chatbots to help address our students' internship situational problems. And the last case is about how we use AI-marking, AI-tutoring, and the AI-powered platform to help both our students and lecturers.

## （三）

# 变是唯一的不变：人工智能时代对高等职业教育的新要求

## ——教育研究与发展的回应

德国马格德堡大学人文社会科学与教育学院副院长　菲利普·波伦茨

我们来思考这样一个问题：什么是现代世界变化的根本驱动力？答案是推动各行各业广泛应用数字技术的变革运动，也就是“工业 4.0”。在工业 4.0 时代，我们经历着怎样类型的变革？首先，网络物理系统问世，人机交互得到广泛应用。其次，基于数据的使用，所有流程的自动化水平都有所提升。自动化又与第三点也就是物联网相结合，让我们使用移动设备即可控制一系列工业生产流程。这些都要求我们对人工智能持开放心态。人工智能这项成果也将影响我们思考教育的方式以及未来教育服务的规划方向和形式。

为适应时代变化，需要进行人才开发。不仅要让人们了解技术创新相关知识，还要培养通用素质，以帮助人们适应变化，并实现自主发展，独立处理专业任务。

社会经济正在发生结构性变化，这对教育目标也产生了影响。要审视这个问题，最好通过案例来看。所以请大家跟随我的脚步，开启一场德国的示范区之旅，在那里，变革正在上演。这个示范区就是马格德堡，它坐落在德国首都柏林以西 100 多公里处，是我任职的大学——马格德堡大学的所在地。马格德堡位于德国腹地，曾是重型机械和土木工程中心，但是这座城市自 20 世纪 90 年代开始经历了一系列变化，包括去工业化，居民大量迁出，老龄化、出生率迅速下降等人口变化以及就业不足等。总而言之，与德国其他地区相比，马格德堡处于相当不利的局面。但这里还矗立着两所大学，在地理上是德国乃至欧洲的中心，拥有现代化基础设施，人口受教育水平良好。

这也促使世界领先的半导体产品制造商英特尔公司选址马格德堡，计划从

2023 年开始在此建设一家大型半导体工厂。2022 年 3 月，英特尔公司宣布在马格德堡新建超大晶圆厂。这是几十年来德国中部地区最大的投资项目。这座晶圆厂价值 170 亿欧元，对于马格德堡这样的地方来说，是笔巨大的资金。整个项目预计将为半导体和供应行业新增数千个就业岗位，并有望在未来 20 年吸引约 30 000 人来此定居。

当下，要为马格德堡市的工业环境注入新活力，我们需要强化各级劳动力的技能。为此，我们需要利用已有的资源。马格德堡大学设有工程学院，开设了一系列学科，提供最新科研技术。同时，我们还需要对教学做出改变。马格德堡大学和周边的应用技术大学已经结成合作伙伴，计划在人工智能领域开设一门全新的研究课程。此外，除了学士和硕士学位课程，还要把重点放在各级继续教育上，从而让整个地区都能从当地超大晶圆厂建设项目中获益。在未来，从长远来看，教师培训也要有所涉及，因为我们需要从学生的学习生涯开始就培养他们，为数字时代的新情况做好准备。不仅要培养学科以及内容相关的技能，开设研究课程，在变革的时代背景下，还要培养开放的心态，迎接变化，接纳新生产方式、新世界观，同样具有重要意义，如此才能树立健全的学术人格。不论是在大学的学习课程中，还是在专业人士继续教育课程中，这都是一项课程目标。

当然，工程学院的新研究项目会提供数学、工程以及计算机科学的基础知识，也会涉及由马格德堡大学周边合作伙伴主办的特定应用型专业课程。同时，还需要解决内容组合中的通用技能。这些将包括各行各业人工智能应用需要学习的人工智能道德伦理、云计算等。

总之，马格德堡这座中世纪城市正在走向数字化。这是一个巨大的机会，它对社会经济结构带来了深刻影响，这将在未来显现，也必将被人们接受并融入城市与居民生活。这是一个长期项目，教育、政治和文化活动等各个层面都将经历变革。作为教育工作者，我们必须确定在个人和系统层面需要做出哪些改变，并通过进一步完善教育系统，使其适应未来趋势，在即将到来的变革浪潮中保持可持续发展来作出回应。从政治意义上来说，重要的是要对社会变革持开放态度，不让任何一个人掉队。

## iii. Change Is the Only Constant: New Demands Towards Higher and Vocational Education in an Era of Artificial Intelligence

### —Responses of Educational Research and Development

**Philipp Pohlenz, Vice President of the Faculty of Humanities, Social Sciences and Education, Otto von Guericke University Magdeburg (OVGU), Germany**

If we ask ourselves, "What exactly is it that drives the change in our modern world?", the answer to it is the move toward the extensive use of digital technology in all kinds of industries, known as Industry 4.0. What types of change are we encountering at the moment or in the light of Industry 4.0? First of all, we see the introduction of cyber physical systems and an intensive use of man-machine interaction. Secondly, we see an increased level of automation of all processes which is based on the use of data. And this is combined, thirdly, with the Internet of Things, in which you can control a range of processes in industry production from your mobile devices, for instance, and all of these things altogether require us to develop an AI-friendly mindset. Artificial intelligence is a kind of development which will be impacting the way in which we think about education and how we plan and provide educational services in future times.

Human resources need to be developed in order to embrace the change. It's not only about supplying people with needed knowledge about technological innovation, but also about supplying them with generic competencies to adapt to the change and to independently develop themselves and process their professional tasks.

Structural change is happening and it is also having an impact on educational goals. The best possible way to look at these things is against an example. So please follow me on a journey to a German model region where change is happening right now. It's about Magdeburg, a city over a hundred kilometers west of the capital city of Berlin. And it's the city where my university is located. It is in the center of Germany. And it was once a center of heavy machinery and civil engineering. But it has seen de-industrialization, lots of emigration, demographic change (an ageing population and a rapid decline in the birth rate) and under-employment since the

1990s. In short, the region is encountering rather unfavorable conditions as compared to other regions in Germany. However, it accommodates two universities. It's centrally located in Germany and also Europe. And it has an up-to-date infrastructure and well-educated people.

This altogether inspired the Intel Corporation, a world-leading manufacturer of semi-conductor products, to found a branch in Magdeburg from 2023 on. A huge factory will be built in order to produce semi-conductors. Intel Corporation announced to open a Giga-Fab in Magdeburg back in March 2022. This will be the largest investment in decades in the region in central Germany. It will be worth 17 billion euros, which is a huge amount of money for a region like the one around Magdeburg. And this whole project is projected to attract thousands of new jobs in the semi-conductor and supplying industries and will produce an influx of about 30 000 new inhabitants over the next 20 years hopefully.

For the time being, in order to make the dream of a renovated industrial environment in the city of Magdeburg come true, we need to upskill the workforce at all levels. And for this purpose, we need to make use of what's already there. There are already Engineering Faculties at my university. They offer the latest technologies in scientific research in a range of disciplines. For teaching, we also have to change. There is already cooperation between the University of Magdeburg and the surrounding universities of Applied Sciences. We are about to launch a new study course in the field of artificial intelligence engineering. Besides Bachelor and Master Degree programs, we also attach importance to further education at all levels in order to make the whole region benefit from the project of building a Giga-Fab. And in the future, in the long run, one could also say that teacher training should be involved because we do need to train people from the beginning of their learning careers to get prepared for the new conditions in a digital era. It's not only about subject-related and content-related skills and study programs. It is also important to create a mindset that is open to change, new modes of production and new modes of thinking about the world in a transformative time. That makes a fully developed academic personality. It is also the learning target of all programs, be it study programs at a university or further education programs for professionals.

The new study program in Engineering provides, of course, basics in mathematics, engineering, and computer science, and also goes into specific application-oriented specializations which are being hosted by the surrounding partners of the university. This also requires to address rather generic skills in the portfolio of contents, which are going to range from artificial intelligence ethics to cloud computing for artificial intelligence applications of all kinds of industries.

To sum up, Magdeburg, a medieval city goes digital. It is a huge opportunity, with a deep impact on social and economic structures, which will be observable in future times and which will have to be embraced and incorporated into the life of the city and the inhabitants. It is a long-term project to embrace the change at all levels: educational, political and cultural activities will be involved. And it is necessary for us as educator to identify what change is needed at individual and system levels and to react to this by further developing education systems and making them fit for the future and sustainable for waves of change to come. And politically speaking, it is important to be open for the social dimension of the change and to leave no one behind.

# (四)

# 职业教育数字化转型：为什么，是什么，怎么做

中国新一代人工智能发展战略研究院执行院长　龚　克

请允许我用这一主题分享我对职业教育数字化转型的一些想法——为什么，是什么，怎么做。

中国一直高度重视职业教育。1996 年，首次通过了《中华人民共和国职业教育法》。2022 年年初，全国人民代表大会对该法进行了修订，并于 5 月起施行。该法规定职业教育是指为了培养高素质技术技能人才，使受教育者具备从事某种职业或者实现职业发展所需要的职业道德、科学文化与专业知识、技术技能等职业综合素质和行动能力而实施的教育，包括职业学校教育和职业培训。

中国大力发展职业教育，推进职业教育改革，提高职业教育质量，增强职业教育适应性，建立健全适应社会主义市场经济和社会发展需要、符合技能型专业人才成长规律的职业教育体系。近日，教育部在 5 月 24 日举行的新闻发布会上指出，中国已建成全世界规模最大的职业教育体系，中高职学校每年培养 1 000 万左右的高素质技术技能人才。然而，智能制造、养老托育等生活服务业却急需职业技能人才。

职业教育为什么需要进行数字化转型？今天，全世界都在谈论人类社会的两大转型，一是数字化转型，这是由人工智能、大数据、物联网等新兴数字技术驱动的转型。这些新兴的数字技术已经革命性地改变了生产和服务的范式，不仅对从业人员的知识和技能提出新的要求，而且提出更高的道德标准，促使包括职业教育在内的整体教育体系去适应这一历史性变化。世界经济论坛创始人克劳斯 · 施瓦布教授认为，“人工智能为商业生产过程创造了重要的可能性。以制造业为例，人工智能推动了机器人技术的应用，根据现有的数据集，避免了非必要的废料、时间和劳动

力的生产成本，从而提高了生产力、促进经济增长。”通过应用智能技术，我们可以看到智能制造、智能建筑、智慧交通、智能银行、智能生活的不同场景。这就是职业教育体系要进行的第一个转型。数字化转型还要促进第二个转型，就是将我们今天的世界转型为我们向往的可持续的未来世界，所以联合国《变革我们的世界：2030 年可持续发展议程》的主题是“变革我们的世界”。

当今世界，全球 29% 的人口难以获得安全饮用水，40% 的人口没有卫生设施，52% 的地区没有通过数字技术实现联通，600 多万儿童在 5 岁前死亡，到 2030 年将有 1 亿人因气候变化带来的影响而陷入贫困，8.4 亿人得不到电力供应，这就是现状。我们必须把当今的世界转变为一个光明的、更可持续发展的世界。我们所面临的最紧迫的危机是气候变化，它威胁到地球上人类的生存，现在我们称之为气候危机。根据最近联合国政府间气候变化专门委员会报告中的数据，可以看到自 18 世纪工业革命开始以来气温的变动情况，在很长一段时间气温平均上升是 0℃，但在过去的几十年里，气温明显升高。这就说明，近几十年的人类活动已经造成了地表温度的显著上升。联合国政府间气候变化专门委员会的报告拉响了全人类的“红色警报”，我们需要控制气候变化以适应和减缓这种影响，到 21 世纪末，将气温增长控制在 1.5℃以内。

这就是为什么联合国在经济、社会和环境三个维度制定了 17 个可持续发展目标。在这 17 个可持续发展目标中，目标 4 是专门针对教育设立的，要求到 2030 年，确保所有学习者获得促进可持续发展所需的知识和技能，还要求到 2030 年，大幅增加拥有技术技能、职业技能等相关才能的成年人人数，帮助他们就业、获得体面的工作和创业。

为了实现人类和地球的可持续发展，我们必须推动当今世界走向一个可持续的未来，也包括教育系统。这一转型和数字化转型是交织在一起的双重转型。可持续发展转型为数字化转型提供了方向，而数字化转型又为可持续发展转型提供了实现的手段。本质上来说，包括职业教育在内的教育体系转型也应该是数字化与可持续发展的双重转型。教育体系的双重转型应该成为全社会转型的基础和先导。

职业教育的数字化转型是什么？从转型的目的看，职业教育数字化转型是为数字化时代培养合格的公民和创新者，他们需要具备数字伦理，掌握科学知识，具备学习能力和创新能力；从教育内容看，我们不能只推出几门数字技术课程，而是要构建一个融合通用数字技术与专业数字技术、包含数字思维与方法论教学内容的教育体系，即要将数字思维和方法论融入所有阶段的课程体系中；从教育工具看，数字化工具，特别是人工智能工具，应该广泛有效地用于教学、学习、评价和服务，让教师和学生沉浸在数字化环境中，在做中学。

总之，数字化转型不仅包括校园内的数字技术工具的普及与有效使用、通用数字技术与专业数字技术的学习，还要与推动全民数字化素养的提高结合起来。为此，我们需要构建实体校园与虚拟校园相结合的数字化校园教学模式；制定通用内容与专业内容相结合的数字化教学方案；提供标准化与个性化相结合的数字技术培训；创新理论与实践相结合、教学与创作相结合、教师与学生相结合的数字技术学习模式。简而言之，职业教育的数字化是对教育体系进行的一场全面而深刻的改革。

如何推动职业教育和其他教育的数字化转型呢？我想提出一些关键词：道德伦理、科学基础、跨学科、实践、教学相长。

关于“科学基础”，我们历来重视培养学生的科学基础，为了学习快速发展变化的数字技术，扎实的科学基础更为重要。关于“跨学科”，我们看到数字化现在正在打破工业化形成的差异，所以教育也需要突破学科框架，这是基于传统工业化的，这样才能实现数字化转型。突破目前的学科教学体系是一项非常艰难的工作，但我们必须这样做，这是实现教育数字化转型的关键。关于“实践”，数字化不是一种理论，而是蓬勃发展的实践，因此包括职业教育在内的教育数字化转型，必须突出实践性。我所在的中国新一代人工智能发展战略研究院在过去几年对就业市场需求的调查研究表明，从事数字技术工作，特别是人工智能相关领域的就业市场特别重视实践经验，招聘要求中被提及最多的 50 个热词中，排名第一的是“实践经验”，这一方面表明就业市场对实践经验特别看重，另一方面，这也表明当前教育体系的不足之处在于缺乏实践训练。关于“教学相长”，数字化改变了人们获取知识的模式，师生共同协作学习和探究知识是未来数字化学习的一个非常重要的变化。最后，也是最重要的一点是“道德伦理”，数字化和可持续发展的双重变革，对人的综合素质提出了新的更高的要求，必须优先培养数字道德和伦理，以有道德的高素质人才确保数字化的伦理发展，造福人类和地球的可持续发展未来。

在此，请允许我介绍一下世界工程组织联合会所做的工作，我曾担任主席，现在依然是其中一员。我们与国际工程联盟开展了一个联合项目，国际工程联盟是一个涵盖七个国际工程教育和资质认定协议的合作组织，如华盛顿协议、悉尼协议和都柏林协议等，其中包含职业工程教育。我们的合作项目得到了联合国教科文组织的认可和支持，由国际工程教育协会联盟、国际咨询工程师联合会、国际女性工程师和科学家网络、联合国教科文组织国际工程教育中心共同参与，联合国教科文组织国际工程教育中心是联合国教科文组织设在中国的一个二类中心。我们合作修订了各类工程教育的毕业要求和职业能力基准框架，旨在提高工程师实现可持续发展目标的能力。该项目的首要目标是将不同类型的工程教育与可持续发展和数字化进程相适应。工程教育基准的更新有四个要点：第一，将必要的可持续发展知识和技能嵌入所有工程专业和各类工程教育课程，包括职业工程教育；第二，加强所有工程学习者的信息通信、数据技术和人工智能的相关技能，因为数字革命要求所有的工程师、技术专家、技术人员更好地掌握这些新兴的数字技术；第三，拓展跨界协作能力，即拓展跨越国界、跨越文化、跨越学科专业的协作能力；第四，很重要的一点，加强工程伦理教育，因为实现数字化进程和可持续发展对工程伦理提出了更高的要求。

最后总结一下。首先，在新兴数字技术推动社会经济转型的背景下，教育的数字化转型是必然的、深刻的、全面的。与社会经济转型一样，教育的数字化转型也应以可持续发展为导向，可持续发展是数字化转型的发展方向。其次，人工智能是第四次工业革命的主导力量，是当前数字化进程中的主导力量，目前人工智能正在赋能所有其他技术，包括制造业、建筑业、交通业等领域的技术。所以，在教育转型中应该更加重视人工智能的赋能作用。再次，教育的数字化转型不仅仅是利用数字化工具，教授几门数字化课程，而是要推动教育的范式转变，将数字素养与专业技能相结合，将学生培养的标准化与个性化相结合，将理论与实践相结合，将传承与创新相结合，师生合力，教学相长。最后，推动数字化转型，必须强调的关键词是：道德伦理、科学基础、跨学科、实践和教学相长。期待与大家进一步合作推动包括职业教育在内的教育系统的数字化转型，走向可持续发展的未来。

# iv. Digital Transformation in Vocational Education: Why, What, How

**Gong Ke, Executive Director of the Chinese Institute of New Generation Artificial Intelligence Development Strategies (CINGAI)**

Please allow me to use the following theme to share some of my ideas on digital transformation of vocational education: Why, What and How.

China has been attaching great importance to vocational education. *The Vocational Education Law of the People's Republic of China* was enacted in 1996 for the first time. And the law was recently revised by the People's Congress early this year, and has come into force in May. The Law stipulates that vocational education refers to the education carried out in order to cultivate high-quality technical and skilled personnel, so that the educated can have the professional ethics, scientific and cultural and professional knowledge, technical skills and other comprehensive professional qualities and action abilities required to engage in a certain occupation or achieve professional development, including vocational school education and vocational training.

The country has been vigorously developing vocational education, promoting the reform of vocational education, improving its quality, enhancing its adaptability and establishing and improving a vocational education system that meets the needs of the socialist market economy and social development and conforms to the growth law of skilled professionals. The Ministry of Education of the People's Republic of China held a Press Conference on May 24th, pointing out that China has built the world's largest vocational education system, training some 10 million skilled professionals every year. However, intelligent manufacturing, elderly care and other life service industries are in severe shortage of skilled professionals.

Why do we need digital transformation in vocational education? Today, the whole world is talking about two transformations of the human society. The first is digital transformation, which is driven by the emerging digital technologies, such as artificial intelligence, big data, Internet of Things, and so on. These emerging digital technologies have been revolutionarily changing the paradigm of production and services. It not only sets new requirements for the knowledge and skills of practitioners but also sets higher ethical standards, which urges the overall education system, including vocational education, to adapt to this historical change. Let me quote the words from Professor Klaus Schwab, the founder of the World Economic Forum. He said, "AI creates significant possibilities for the business production process. In manufacturing, for instance, AI drives the application of robotics, which avoids unnecessary production cost for material waste, time and labors according to available data set in turn for greater productivity and economic growth". Here you see different scenarios for intelligent manufacturing, intelligent construction, intelligent transportation, intelligent banking, intelligent life with the application of intelligent technology. So that's the first transformation the vocational education system has to go through. Digital transformation also contributes to the second transformation, which is to transform our world today into a sustainable world we aspire to. So the theme of the 2030 Agenda for Sustainable Development is Transforming Our World.

In today's world we see: 29% of the global population has no access to safe drinking water, 40% of the population does not have sanitation facilities, 52% of the regions is not digitally connected, and more than 6 million children die before the age of 5 100 million people will be pushed into poverty by 2030 due to climate impacts, and 840 million people will have no access to power supply. We have to transform today's world into a bright and more sustainable world. The most urgent crisis we are facing is climate change which threatens the survival of human beings on the earth. Now we call it climate crisis. According to the data in the recent report of Intergovermental Panel on Climate Change (IPCC), we can see the change of temperature since the beginning of the industrial revolution in the 18th century, during which the average rise was zero for a long time. However, there has been a significant growth of temperature in the last decades. It shows that human activities in recent decades have caused a significant rise in surface temperature. The IPCC report has sounded the "red alert" for all humankind. We need to control climate change to adapt to and mitigate this impact and keep the temperature growth within 1.5℃ by the end of this century.

That is why the United Nations has formulated 17 sustainable development goals in the three dimensions of economy, society and environment. Among the 17 sustainable development goals, Goal 4 is dedicated to education, which requires that by 2030, all learners should have the knowledge and skills needed to promote sustainable development. And it also requires that by 2030, the number of adults who have related talents, including technical skills and vocational skills, should be significantly increased so that they can obtain employment, decent jobs and entrepreneurship.

In order to realize the sustainable development of humankind and the earth, we must promote our world today to move toward a sustainable future, including the education system. The transformation of sustainable development and digital transformation are intertwined dual transformations. The former, I mean the transformation of sustainability provides the direction for digital transformation, and digital transformation provides the means for the transformation of sustainable development. In essence, the transformation of education system, including vocational education, should also be a dual transformation of digitalization and sustainable development. The dual transformation of the education system should be the basis and guide for the transformation of the whole society.

The next question is, what is digital transformation in vocational education? In view to the purpose of the transformation, the digital transformation of vocational education is to cultivate qualified citizens and innovators for the digital era. They need to have digital ethics, scientific knowledge, learning and innovation capability. In view to educational content, we should not only launch a few digital technology courses, but build an educational system that integrates general and professional digital technologies as well as digital thinking and methodology, that is, we should integrate digital thinking and methodology into the curriculum system at all stages. And in view to the tools of the transformation, digital tools, especially artificial intelligence tools, should be widely and effectively used for teaching, learning, evaluation and services, so that teachers and students can immerse themselves in the digital environment and learn by doing.

In a word, digital transformation should not only include the popularization and the effective use of digital tools on campus, and the study of general and professional digital technology, but also be combined with the improvement of digital literacy of all people. To that end, we need to build a digital campus teaching and learning mode that combines the physical campus and the virtual campus, formulate a digital teaching program that combines general content and specialized content, provide digital technology training that combines standardization and personalization, innovate the digital technology learning mode that combines theory and practice, teaching and creation and teachers and students. In short, the digital transformation of vocational education is a comprehensive and profound transformation of the education system.

Now, we come to the third question, how to advance digital transformation in vocational education or in other types of education. I think there are some keywords: morality and ethics, scientific basis, interdisciplinary approach, practice, collaboration of teachers and students.

As for scientific basis, we have always attached great importance to the cultivation of students' scientific basis. In order to learn the fast developing digital technology, a solid scientific basis is even more important. With regard to interdisciplinary approach, we can see that digitalization is now breaking the divisions formed by industrialization, so education which is based on traditional industrialization, also needs to break through the disciplinary framework, so that we can realize digital transformation. Breaking through the current disciplinary teaching system is a very difficult work, but we must do so because that's the key to realize digital transformation. As for practice, digitalization is not just a theory, but a booming practice. Therefore, the digitalization of education, including vocational education must highlight practicality. Research shows that the employment market engaged in digital technology work, especially in AI related fields, attaches particular importance to practical experience, according to the survey made by my institute in the past years. Among the 50 hot words frequently mentioned in the recruitment requirements, the first one is practical experience, which shows the job market pays special attention to practical experience. On the other hand, it also indicates the lack of practical training in the current education system. For collaboration of teachers and students, digitalization has changed the mode for acquiring knowledge, and the collaborative learning and exploring of knowledge jointly by teachers and students is a very important change of digital learning in the future. Finally, the most important is morality and ethics. The dual transformation of digitalization and sustainable development has put forward new and higher requirements for comprehensive qualities. The cultivation of digital morality and ethics must be prioritized, in order to ensure the ethical development of digitalization and to benefit humankind and the earth's sustainable future with moral and high-quality talents.

Here please allow me to introduce what have been done by the World Federation of Engineering Organizations in which I served as the president, and now I'm still a member. We have carried out a joint project with the International Engineering Alliance (IEA), which is a collaborative organization covering seven international engineering education and qualification accords, such as Washington Accord, Sydney Accord and Dublin Accord, including vocational engineering education. And this project has been recognized and supported by UNESCO and jointly participated by the International Federation of Engineering Education Societies (IFEES), Federation International Des Inginieurs Conseils (FIDIC), International Network of Women Engineers and Scientists (INWES), and International Center for Engineering Education (ICEE), a UNESCO secondary center based in China. We collaborated on the revison of Graduate Attributes and Professional Competencies (GAPC) for engineering education programs, which aims to improve the capability of engineers to achieve sustainable development goals. The primary goal of this project is to align different types of engineering education with sustainable development and digitalization. There are four main points for the update of the benchmark standards for engineering education. Firstly, to embed necessary knowledge and skills for sustainable development into the curriculum of all engineering professions and all types of engineering education, including vocational engineering education. Secondly, to strengthen skills related to information communication, data technology and artificial intelligence for all engineering learners, as the digital revolution requires all engineers, technologists and technicians to be better equipped with these emerging digital technologies. Thirdly, to expand cross-border collaboration capabilities, that is, to expand collaboration capabilities across borders, cultures and disciplines. Fourthly, a very important point, to enhance the education of engineering ethics, because the realization of digitalization and sustainable development sets higher requirements for engineering ethics.

Now, let me make some conclusion remarks. First, in the context of the social and economic transformation driven by the emerging digital technologies, the digital transformation of education is inevitable, profound and comprehensive. Like socio-economic transformation, the digital transformation of education should also be oriented to sustainable development, which is also the direction of digital transformation. Second, artificial intelligence is the leading force of the fourth industrial revolution, and the current process of digitalization. AI is now empowering all other technologies, including manufacturing, construction, transportation, and so forth. Therefore, more attention should be paid to the empowerment of AI in the transformation of education. Third, the digital transformation of education is not just about using digital tools and teaching a few digital courses, but about promoting a paradigm shift in education, which combines digital literacy with professional skills, standardization with personalization, theory with practice, inheritance with innovation, with joint and collective efforts of teachers and students to help each other forward. Finally, to promote digital transformation, there are some keywords: morality and ethics, scientific basis, interdisciplinary approach, practice and collaboration of teachers and students. I look forward to further collaboration with all of you to promote the digital transformation of the education system, including vocational education, toward a sustainable future.

# （五）

# 高职人工智能专业群建设的思考与实践

南京信息职业技术学院校长　田　敏

我是南京信息职业技术学院校长田敏，我报告的题目是《高职人工智能专业群建设的思考与实践》。在报告之前，我先把学校的一些基本情况和专业发展的历程给大家作简单的介绍。学校成立于 1953 年，是中华人民共和国成立后第一所培养无线电技术的中等专业学校，当时的校名叫南京无线电工业学校，服务新中国电子工业的发展，开设的主要专业是电子零件制造、电子器件制造和电子整机制造。进入 21 世纪，学校发展进入了第二个阶段。2002 年，学校升级为高等职业院校，随着信息时代的到来，学校培养的人才主要是为工业化和信息化以及“两化”融合服务。当时开设的专业主要是电子信息制造类专业群、计算机与软件类专业群以及信息服务类专业群。第三个阶段是到了 2019 年，学校成功入选国家“双高计划”B 档建设单位，人才培养服务数字经济与智能社会的发展，以人工智能为底色，构建了七大专业群，这就是学校的简单的发展历程。

下面从三个方面汇报我们在人工智能应用专业方面人才培养的情况：一是高职培养人工智能应用人才的需求分析，二是学校人工智能专业群的建设与发展情况，三是人工智能技术驱动学校其他专业升级的探索。

“十三五”期间，中国进入了人工智能发展的快车道。2017 年 7 月，国务院印发了《新一代人工智能发展规划》，将人工智能上升至国家战略。2018 年 4 月，教育部印发了《高等学校人工智能创新行动计划》，提出了完善人工智能领域的人才培养体系。“十四五”期间，人工智能市场需求进一步提升，需要进一步加快建设数字经济、数字社会、数字政府，以数字化转型驱动生产、生活方式和治理方式的变革。我们看到这几年物联网、大数据、云计算以及算法的技术升级，进一步推动了人工智能产业的加速发展。

人工智能产业化的特征有六个方面，即岗位细分、标准确定、应用明确、工具应用、人才分级、门槛降低。随着这几年人工智能技术的发展，其普及应用越来越广泛，比如人脸识别已广泛应用于机场、高铁，小区和家庭的门禁系统，商场里的刷脸支付已走入老百姓的生活当中，“有多少人工，就有多少智能”。人工智能应用人才需求量的快速加大，造就了许多岗位，如数据处理、运维与营销、应用咨询、解决方案设计、应用开发等。同时，人工智能产业对人才需求一方面是数量巨大，另外一方面也要求有不同的层次，既需要有最高级别的人工智能大师、研究员、教授，更需要有大量的人工智能产业的应用型人才。如果把高级人才，如博士、高级工程师的培养数量定为 1，那么对应的硕士、专业工程师的需求数量是 10，而对应的高职、应用型本科和高质量的实用人才的需求数量则高达 100，说明人工智能应用型人才的需求市场是非常广阔的。

下面谈一谈学校人工智能专业群的建设与发展情况。早在 2015 年，学校就启动了高职人工智能专业设置的研究和教材开发。2017 年，学校率先筹建了人工智能学院，完成了人工智能技术应用专业的设置预研。2019 年，由我校牵头成功申报了全国高职院校第一个人工智能类的专业——人工智能技术应用专业。这几年，我们依据人工智能的技术链，瞄准人工智能应用软件开发的相关岗位群，从数据治理、智能计算到应用开发，打造了一个人工智能的专业群，主要由大数据技术与应用、人工智能技术服务、移动应用开发和软件技术四个专业构成。

具体的做法，一是组织编写了系列教材，与华为、数据堂、新华三、科大讯飞等人工智能的龙头企业合作，先后开发了《人工智能技术应用导论》《机器学习案例驱动教程》《Python 数据处理技术》以及《深度学习 TensorFlow 案例驱动教程》等人工智能技术应用核心课程的系列教材，目前这些教材已被全国超过 100 多所院校采用。

二是建设产教融合平台，我们根据人工智能技术应用专业的岗位需求，制订了人工智能专业人才培养的规格、教学计划，同时构建了一个人工智能专业学院校内实训基地。在此基础上，我们与企业深度融合，政府、行业、学校、企业，共建、共用、共享人工智能的产教融合平台，集教育、培训、研发、生产于一体，主要有长三角人工智能产教联盟、人工智能技术展示体验中心、1+X 人工智能大数据培训认证中心、人工智能技能大师工作室。我们与新华三联合成立了智能产业学院，以生物工厂成立了大数据产业学院，还积极创建了人工智能系统创新应用研究院。

三是随着人工智能技术的不断发展和人工智能应用岗位的不断拓展，积极开发人工智能类新专业。最近，我们正在认真研究、积极准备申报人工智能数据工程专业，该专业主要为如下的岗位服务，即机器学习设计和生产数据集的系统化、工程化、流程化的组织与实施方法，包括数据设计、采集、处理、标注、质检与工具开发等流程。

除了建好人工智能应用本身的专业外，我们利用人工智能技术积极地驱动、赋能学校其他专业群的升级和改造。2019 年，学校以人工智能技术为核心，按照“AI+ 专业群”或“专业群 +AI”的思路，重组了学校的七大专业群，推进了全校专业的智能化升级改造。这七大专业群分别是人工智能专业群、智能制造专业群、智能交通专业群、电子信息专业群、数字商务专业群、数字创意专业群和网络与通信专业群，以人工智能为底色，这七个专业群分布在我校的七个二级学院，使得我校的专业群设置更加合理。

另外，我们还积极开展了人工智能通识教育，先后面向全校学生开设了人工智能与信息技术基础、人工智能应用素养等课程，在全校建设一个“人工智能展讯中心”，该中心的主要内容是通过各种多媒体、虚拟现实的方式介绍人工智能发展简史、人工智能基础概念与技术构成、人工智能典型应用场景、人工智能数据服务等，中心面向全校所有专业的学生开放，同时还面向中小学生开放，成为中小学生的人工智能体验中心，还要向社会开放，让这个中心成为普及人工智能知识、介绍人工智能最新发展和应用的科普基地。

同时，我们开发交叉课程，将智能技术融入各个专业群的顶层综合课程，助力复合型人才的培养。举全校之力建设共享型的实训基地，即 5G+ 智慧场景公共实训基地，打造智慧园区、智能交通、智慧供应链等应用场景，服务于学校网络与通信、人工智能、智能交通、智能制造、数字商务等多个专业群的人才培养。

以上就是我校在人工智能技术应用专业人才培养中做的一些尝试。本次论坛开幕之际，我们真诚地邀请兄弟院校、人工智能专家以及企业界专家来南京信息职业技术学院指导，大家共同探讨新时代人工智能应用型人才的培养。

# (六)

# 产教融合培育人工智能技术技能人才

百度集团 AI 技术生态总经理　马艳军

数字经济发展非常迅速，而人工智能为数字经济的发展提供了新动能。在数字经济发展过程中，积累了大量的数据，基于这些数据开展智能化应用是一个自然而然的事情。从“十四五”规划开始，我国非常重视人工智能与实体经济的结合，人工智能的发展与产业结合也越来越紧密。从现在的分析来看，人工智能与行业的结合，在不同的行业差别比较大。数字化水平比较高的行业，如通信、金融、智慧城市、智慧教育，乃至制造业，人工智能的渗透已经越来越深入，相应地就需要越来越多的人工智能人才。还有一些行业渗透得相对没那么深入，需要建设更多与产业结合的标杆，推动人工智能的应用和产业发展。

我们也做了很多关于人工智能人才分布的分析，目前来看，人工智能人才现在还是本科生、研究生偏多一些，职业人才未来会有非常大的增长空间，岗位类型也会非常多样化。这是因为现在人工智能与产业结合所需要的人才是多种多样的，如技术类的人才，即实用的技能岗；还有应用型人才，这类人才会占比很高，未来会需要得越来越多，因为产业有大量的需求。实体经济发展对人工智能人才的需求是多层次、多岗位、多方向的，所以职业技能人才的培养就显得越来越重要。

目前，伴随人工智能产业发展，人工智能的职业教育还面临一些挑战。第一，教学内容本身的体系性还不够，即职业教育中，人工智能教学内容本身体系性不是很强；第二，职业技能人才标准的制定和就业岗位之间的匹配没有非常明确的定义，我们最近也在持续研究；第三，教学的内容和最终的产业需求之间衔接不足，也就是我们常说的产教融合，即产业所需要的技能和真正教学中所教授的课程之间还需要更有效地对接起来。在这几个挑战之下，我们发现一定要培养比较多的应用实践型的人工智能人才。从学校的角度，可以通过综合素质培养形成技能基础，企业可以提供大量的实践资源，包括一些实际产业应用场景中的数据集以及一些实训工具和平台，来帮助学校培养人工智能人才，这就是产教融合的培养思路。

百度提出了培养500万人工智能人才的目标，相信其中很大比例是掌握人工智能技术的职业技能人才，所以我再分享一下百度在职业技能人才培养上的一些实践。首先，参与了国家标准的制定，即明确了掌握人工智能技术的职业技能人才应该具备哪些能力。现在这个阶段，标准的制定是非常重要的，需要有一些标准的指引。其次，百度建设了深度学习资源开放平台——飞桨，是我国首个自主研发、功能丰富、开源开放的产业级深度学习平台。前面提到的大量人工智能应用，像自然语言处理、计算机视觉等应用以及不同行业中大量的场景案例，都是基于这个平台建设和提供的。尤其是面向职业教育，我们提供了一个低门槛的人工智能开发平台“Easy DL”，它大幅减少了代码编写工作，甚至是不太需要写代码就能够开发人工智能应用，赋能职业教育人才的培养。

具体而言，整个培养方案分为三个部分。第一个部分是教学资源。作为企业方，我们提供了大量的数据集、产业实践项目案例，这些是企业平时在做应用落地时积累下来的内容；我们还提供了一些专业技术类的课程以及一些行业认知和项目类课程，因为不同的行业与人工智能结合的特点不同，所以还需要结合行业知识开展人才的培养。第二个部分，工具和平台非常重要，即提供了数据后，一定要有一个可以实践的地方。对于能够使用核心框架进行开发的学生，可以直接使用“飞桨”框架；而“Easy DL”则不太需要写代码，主要是上传数据，并按照相应流程操作就可以实现自动化人工智能应用开发。还有实训平台“AI Studio”，提供了免费的人工智能算力，方便教师教学和学生学习。教师上课的时候，学生登录该平台，在上面可以直接运行相关的人工智能任务。我们还提供一些硬件教具，支持学生完成一些具体的硬件部署任务，这些都属于工具和平台类。第三个部分也非常重要，就是在教学中的一系列运营服务，包括对专业课程的开发、师资培训、考试认证的组织、竞赛的组织、实习就业等多个方面。我们提供了一个完整的方案，目前为止已经在包括很多职业院校在内的300多所高校开设了学分课程，并且已经培训了3 900多位教师。“飞桨”从2018年开展师资培训，到现在为止已经组织了近30场培训，很多教师在参加这个师资培训之后回到学校开设了人工智能相关课程。

再具体介绍一下整个方案。首先，AI Studio实训平台汇聚了大量的技能相关课程，这些课程都可以免费看，有很多是视频，还有很多手把手教学的工具。平台上有 300 万个公开项目，是很多开发者自己贡献的场景，受到很多开发者的喜爱及点赞。所以平台上聚集了非常多的开发者，目前已注册有 160 多万名。他们既学习也贡献，这一点是非常重要的，可以把平台的热度拉得非常高，同时还有很多数据集，包括比赛等也在上面举办，大家学完了之后还能参加比赛，这个平台就形成了一个正向循环。

其次，人才培养方面，我们面向不同行业提供不同的实践类内容。因为不同的行业差别非常大，需要学习的内容差别也很大，所以我们面向行业，如智慧城市、制造业、交通等都提供不同类型的项目案例，这样学习起来就会更有针对性。再有就是一些行业认知类的内容，关于人工智能如何同这些行业相结合。当然也有一些专业技术类的课程，针对职业院校进行设计，对人工智能的一些技术，如机器学习、深度学习、视觉等领域都会提供课程内容。

刚才我也提到有一个非常适合职业院校使用的工具，就是零门槛的人工智能开发平台“Easy DL”，通过数据标注进行模型训练，然后结合特定场景就能完成部署落地。通过这个平台能够为职业教育提供基础保障，是一个非常典型的方便业务人员使用的实用平台，不需要写很多代码或掌握特别多的人工智能基础理论就能够使用，非常适用于职业教育。

到目前为止，百度已经与 100 余所高职院校达成了深度合作，支持相关的人工智能技能人才的培养。百度也发布了“大国智匠”人才培养计划，将与更多的职业院校进行深入的合作，为国家培养更多掌握人工智能技能的人才。

# 二
# 职业教育数字化转型发展论坛

协助组织单位：中国职业技术教育学会、中国电子学会

## II. Digital Transformation of Vocational Education

Co-organizers: The Chinese Society for Technical and Vocational Education (CSTVE), The Chinese Institute of Electronics (CIE)

02
鲁昕
Lu Xin

03
黄维
Huang Wei

04
葛道凯
Ge Daokai

05
陈达
Chen Da

06
许建领
Xu Jianling

07
王晖
Wang Hui

08
卢坤建
Lu Kunjian

09
汤兆武
Tang Zhaowu

10
王丹中
Wang Danzhong

11
张晓蕾
Zhang Xiaolei

12
刘积仁
Liu Jiren

13
韦青
Wei Qing

14
陈涛
Chen Tao

15
钟美华
Zhong Meihua

16
刘谦
Liu Qian

**应对数字化创新发展的机遇与挑战，探讨以数字化转型整体驱动职业教育教学模式和治理方式变革，增强技术技能人才数字化核心能力。**

This session focuses on utilizing digital transformation as a whole to drive the reform of teaching and governance modes of vocational education and enhance the core digital competencies of technical and skilled talents, in response to the opportunities and challenges of digital innovation development.

# （一）

# 职业教育数字化转型发展论坛情况概述

中国职业技术教育学会

2022 年 8 月 20 日上午，职业教育数字化转型发展论坛在国家会展中心（天津）线上线下同步举行。本论坛是世界职业技术教育发展大会的十四个平行论坛之一，由中国职业技术教育学会和中国电子学会协助组织，天津电子信息职业技术学院承办会务。本论坛邀请了来自中国、德国、英国、西班牙、马来西亚、文莱等国家的 21 位嘉宾，紧扣数字经济蓬勃发展的时代背景，瞄准新技术和产业变革，探讨职业教育数字化转型、智能化升级的新路径，着力培养适应经济社会发展需要的数字化技术技能人才，线上线下 1 000 余人参会。

### 1. 职业教育数字化转型的中国经验

中国职业技术教育学会会长鲁昕为论坛致辞并作总结。鲁昕在致辞中表示，习近平主席给大会的贺信，深刻阐述了职业教育对促进经济社会发展和改善民生的重要作用。学习领会习近平主席贺信精神，贯彻落实大会共识，要求职业教育必须以高质量发展为逻辑起点，以数字化转型为路径，形成产教互动新机制，重构改革发展新生态。鲁昕以“五五四”总结论坛成果，即论坛达成了要拥抱数字科技、适应数字技术、掌握数字技能、提高数字素养、增强数字能力的五个共识；明确了要树立适应新要求、重塑新内涵、构建新格局、提升新能级、重构新生态的五大愿景；提出了要建立对话合作、大赛交流、联盟发展、会展合作的四项工作机制。

中国科学院院士、西北工业大学学术委员会主任黄维结合自身经验，对开创全球职业教育合作新格局提出了三点建议：一是要提升全球职业教育创新资源配置能力，培育职业教育科技创新命运共同体；二是要形成凸显职业教育类型特色的现代治理体系，促进职业教育人才资源的全球有序流动；三是要建设合作平台连接全球创新资源，推进职业教育国际合作进程。

江苏省教育厅厅长葛道凯用“江苏范式”回答了职业教育数字转型的三个问题。为使优质教育教学资源覆盖面更广、惠及师生更多，江苏先后启动虚拟仿真实训基地、在线精品课程和数字教材等的全面共享。为加快建设覆盖所有学校的数字化基础设施，江苏建设了一批国家级、省级智慧校园以及示范校、样板校。为让更多的师生应用善用智慧平台和数字资源，江苏推动将职业教育数字资源建设和使用纳入学校高质量考核和教师教学评价。

浙江省教育厅职业教育与成人教育处处长陈达表示，浙江职业教育认真承担国家智慧教育平台试点省工作任务，积极构建职业教育大脑数字底座，建设应用型职业教育特色教学资源，打造职业教育特色服务场景应用，培育职业教育智慧试点示范校和示范案例。

### 2. 职业学校：建设数字专业，为本地培养人才

围绕职业学校如何开展数字化转型，浙江机电职业技术学院党委书记汤兆武、深圳职业技术学院校长许建领、深圳信息职业技术学院校长王晖、广东轻工职业技

术学院校长卢坤建、南京信息职业技术学院党委书记王丹中、北京信息职业技术学院副校长张晓蕾等 6 位嘉宾分享了他们的经验和观点。他们总结学校转型经验，形成了三点共识。

一是职业学校要服务区域经济发展。浙江机电职业技术学院将服务浙江省打造全球数字变革高地和全球先进制造业基地作为人才培养目标。深圳职业技术学院主动与政府部门、行业企业等成立深圳健康养老学院、机器人培训学院、社区旅游学院等，为广泛的市民数字化转型提供支撑。深圳信息职业技术学院针对深圳产业特点，提出了产教融合分层分类的“深信模式”，面向小微企业开展技术攻关，面向规模型企业建设订单班，面向头部企业建设现代产业学院。

二是职业学校要推进专业升级改造。深圳职业技术学院以专业群建设为抓手，成立了人工智能学院，设置了人工智能专业，开设了人工智能通识课程。广东轻工职业技术学院积极推进专业新基建，布局工业互联网 + 专业（群）建设，建设“虚拟工厂资源云”。南京信息职业技术学院构建了人工智能“同心圆”专业集群，围绕智能网络、智能技术、智能设备三大基础技术和智能制造、智能交通、数字商务、数字创意四大应用，组建七个专业群。

三是职业学校要转变人才培养模式。浙江机电职业技术学院重塑人才培养定位，以培养智能制造工程应用型人才为目标重建专业、重构课程、重组教师和重融实训基地等。深圳信息职业技术学院试点高等工程师学院，借鉴世界发达国家工程教育和“新工科”的成功经验，以产业解决方案（场景）为出发点和策源点，联合头部企业培养信息技术行业急需的复合型解决方案落地工程师。北京信息职业技术学院则聚焦教师数字素养建设，通过更新教师能力标准、开展数字素养培训，使职业院校教师尽快实现从教学观念到教学行为的数字化转型。

**3. 数字企业：适应数字经济，为学生创造价值**

东软集团股份有限公司董事长刘积仁探讨了数字经济时代职业教育变革的模式和路径。他认为，在未来，数字化将是所有行业的表现，所有的职业都将与数字化相关，数字技术教育将成为职业教育的基础教育。职业教育要以平台推动职业教育的同质发展，以大数据来精准度量职业教育的质量，以 TOPCARES 架构精准定义培养目标，以数字技术来保障培养目标的可靠实现，以创新的产教融合为学生创造价值，真正实现数字科技赋能职业教育变革。

微软（中国）有限公司首席技术官韦青基于数字时代的特征，分享了关于如何高效培养人才的思考。他认为，在数字时代，人类即将迈入以信息为主导的智能社会，但信息的强大功效尚未真正被大众理解，教育要培养符合时代特征并具有基本人类素养的人才，而信息获取、分析、判断、理解与使用能力是信息时代人才的基础能力之一。未来，由于信息技术赋能，虚拟与现实相结合的职业教育、泛在而又公平的职业教育将加速实现。

科大讯飞股份有限公司联合创始人、安徽信息工程学院董事长陈涛分享了“项目制”人才培养范式的观点和经验。他认为，数字技能人才应对变化的关键是要具备适应变化的能力；企业要想通过项目制达成目标，需要员工具备底层能力。安徽信息工程学院对标企业对人才底层能力的真实需要，提出“项目化教学”的项目目标、技术路径，探索了数字技能人才的“项目制教学”模式。

华为技术有限公司培训服务专家委员会主任钟美华分析了 5G 时代数字化人才的生态。他表示，5G 将为产业带来新动能和巨大影响力，泛行业生态、去中心平台化业务运营模式，呼唤泛行业数字化人才生态繁荣，企业需要重新思考数字化人才管理模式的转型。基于新基建，生态和垂直行业需要更多企业参与人才培养，相关学科和产学研需求也将蓬勃发展。华为构建了泛行业“人器业”数字化人才转型框架，致力于推进企业、行业、职业学校人才培养管理的共建、共创、共享的人才培养生态。

特许公认会计师公会中国教育事务总监蔡元文，广联达科技股份有限公司党委书记、董事、高级副总裁刘谦分别围绕会计和建筑行业数字化转型人才需求发言。

**4. 他山之石：应用数字技术，为从业者护好航**

深圳职业技术学院荣誉教授冯马丁，克兰菲尔德商学院物流采购供应链管理中心主任、英国教育科技协会专家迈克尔·布拉基斯，东南亚教育部长组织职业技术教育与培训区域中心电子学习教学设计和内容编辑师胡思莹，马来西亚奎斯特国际大学计算机和工程学院院长沈毅伟，西班牙机床技术学院董事伊克萨卡·埃古尔比德，德国海因策学院董事扬·海因策分别介绍了职业教育数字化转型的国别经验，探讨了不同国家和地区数字化转型的发展趋势和经验探索。

冯马丁分享了德国职业教育在“工业 4.0”背景下的转型经验。在德国职业教育的双元制下，学校为企业提供了有实战经验的人才，为学生和家长提供了大学学位，实现了双元职业培训和常规高等教育的完美结合。他建议，未来中国要增加应用型大学的数量，健全本科、硕士、博士贯通的职业教育体系，并通过完善法律让企业在职业教育中承担更多责任。

伊克萨卡·埃古尔比德表示，数字化转型过程中，学生和从业人员怎样学会技术是关键，而职业学校作为数字技术的主要培训中心要做行业的预言家，为行业从业者保驾护航。职业学校需要做到三点，一是实现学校管理的数字化，二是推进教学数字化转型，三是开发数字工厂。

# i. Overview of the Session on Digital Transformation of Vocational Education

The Chinese Society for Technical and Vocational Education

On the morning of August 20, 2022, the Session on Digital Transformation of Vocational Education was held simultaneously online and offline at the National Convention and Exhibition Center (Tianjin). As one of the 14 parallel sessions of World Vocational and Technical Education Development Conference, it was organized with the assistance of the Chinese Society for Technical and Vocational Education (CSTVE) and the Chinese Institute of Electronics (CIE), and Tianjin Electronic Information College undertook the meeting. The session invited 21 guests from China, Germany, UK, Spain, Malaysia, Brunei and other countries to closely follow the background of the booming development of digital economy, aimed at new technologies and industrial changes. They discussed the new path of the digital transformation and intelligent upgrading of vocational education, and focused on cultivating digital technical talents to meet the needs of economic and social development. More than 1 000 people participated online and offline.

## 1. China's Experience in the Digital Transformation of Vocational Education

Lu Xin, President of the Chinese Society for Technical and Vocational Education (CSTVE), delivered a speech and summarized the session. In her speech, Lu Xin said that President Xi Jinping's congratulatory letter to the conference elaborated on the important role of vocational education in promoting economic development and improving people's livelihood. To comprehend the spirit of President Xi Jinping's congratulatory letter and implement the consensus of the conference, vocational education should take high-quality development as its logical starting point, take digital transformation as the path, to form a new mechanism of industry-education interaction, and reconstruct a new ecology of reform and development. Lu Xin summarized the achievements of the session with "Five, Five, Four": the session reached five points of consensus—embrace digital technology, adapt to digital technology, master digital skills, improve digital literacy, and enhance digital capabilities; five visions—adapt to new requirements, reshape new connotations, build a new pattern, improve new levels, and reconstruct a new ecology; four working mechanisms—dialogue and cooperation, competition and exchange, alliance development, and exhibition cooperation.

Huang Wei, Academician of Chinese Academy of Sciences, Director of Academic Committee of Northwestern Polytechnical University, China, based on his own experience, put forward three suggestions for creating a new pattern of global vocational education cooperation. First, improve the ability to allocate innovative resources for global vocational education, and foster a community of shared future for scientific and technological innovation of vocational education. Second, form a modern governance system that highlights the characteristics of vocational education as one type of education, and promote the orderly global flow of vocational education talents. Third, build a cooperation platform to link global innovation resources, and promote the international cooperation process of vocational education.

Ge Daokai, Head of Jiangsu Education Department, China, answered three questions about the digital transformation of vocational education with "Jiangsu Paradigm". In order to expand the coverage of high-quality education and teaching resources and benefit more teachers and students, Jiangsu has launched a comprehensive sharing of virtual simulation training bases as well as online quality courses and digital textbooks. In order to speed up the construction of digital infrastructure covering all schools, Jiangsu has built a number of provincial and national smart campuses, demonstration schools and model schools. In order to enable more teachers and students to make good use of the smart platforms and digital resources, Jiangsu has pushed to include the construction and use of digital resources for vocational education in the high-quality assessment of schools and teachers' teaching evaluation.

Chen Da, Director of Vocational and Adult Education Division of Zhejiang Provincial Education Department, China, said that Zhejiang has seriously undertook the task of piloting a national smart education platform, actively built the digital base for vocational education brain, built and applied the teaching and learning resources with vocational education characteristics, created the application of service scenarios with vocational education characteristics, and cultivated wisdom pilot demonstration schools and demonstration cases for vocational education.

### 2. Building Digital Specialties and Cultivating Talents for the Region in Vocational Schools

Focusing on how vocational schools carry out digital transformation, six guests shared their experiences and views. They are: Tang Zhaowu, Secretary of CPC Committee of Zhejiang Institute of Mechanical and Electrical Engineering, China, Xu Jianling, President of Shenzhen Polytechnic, China, Wang Hui, President of Shenzhen

Institute of Information Technology, China, Lu Kunjian, President of Guangdong Industry Polytechnic, China, Wang Danzhong, Secretary of CPC Committee of Nanjing Vocational College of Information Technology, China, Zhang Xiaolei, Vice President of Beijing Information Technology College, China. They summarized their experience in school transformation and reached three points of consensus.

First, vocational schools should serve regional economic development. Zhejiang Institute of Mechanical and Electrical Engineering regards serving Zhejiang Province to build a global digital transformation highland and a global advanced manufacturing base as its talent cultivation goal. Shenzhen Polytechnic has taken the initiative to establish Shenzhen Elderly Healthcare College, Robot Training Institute, Community Tourism Institute, etc., with government departments and industrial enterprises to provide support for the digital transformation of citizens. In view of the characteristics of Shenzhen's industries, Shenzhen Institute of Information Technology has put forward Model of Shenzhen Institute of Information Technology with an integration of education and the industry in a hierarchical and categorical manner, to carry out technology research for small and micro enterprises, to build classes by order for large-scale enterprises, and to build modern industry colleges for leading enterprises.

Second, vocational schools should promote the upgrading and transformation of specialty groups. Taking the construction of specialty groups as a starting point, Shenzhen Polytechnic has established an AI college, set up an AI major and run a general course on AI. Guangdong Industry Polytechnic has actively promoted the construction of new professional infrastructure, laid out the construction of industrial Internet + specialities (groups), and built a "virtual factory resource cloud". Nanjing Vocational College of Information Technology has built a "concentric circle" speciality group of AI, and formed seven speciality groups on the three basic technologies of intelligent network, intelligent technology and intelligent equipment as well as the four applications of intelligent manufacturing, intelligent transportation, digital commerce and digital creativity.

Third, vocational schools should change the cultivation mode of talents. Zhejiang Institute of Mechanical and Electrical Engineering has reshaped the orientation of the cultivation of talents, rebuilt specialities, reconstructed the curriculum, reorganized teachers and re-integrated training bases, etc., with the aim to cultivate application-oriented talents of intelligent manufacturing engineering. Shenzhen Institute of Information Technology has piloted the College of Higher Engineers, drawn on the successful experience of engineering education and "new engineering" of the developed countries with advanced technologies and cooperated with leading enterprises to jointly cultivate urgently needed composite solution landing engineers in the information technology industry, taking industrial solutions (scenarios) as the starting point and policy source. Beijing Information Technology College has focused on the construction of teachers' digital literacy. By updating teachers' ability standards and carrying out digital literacy training, teachers in vocational colleges can realize the digital transformation from teaching concepts to teaching behaviors as soon as possible.

3. Adapting to Digital Economy and Creating Value for Students in Digital Enterprises

Liu Jiren, Chairman of Neusoft Corporation, China, discussed the mode and path of vocational education reform in the digital economy era. He believed that in the future, digitalization would be the expression of all industries, all occupations would be related to digitalization, and digital technology education would become the basic education of vocational education. Vocational education should promote the homogeneous development of vocational education with platforms, accurately measure the quality of vocational education with big data, accurately define the cultivation objectives with TOPCARES (each character representing an ability indicator) frame work, ensure the reliable realization of the cultivation objectives with digital technology, create value for students with the innovative integration of industries and education, and truly realize the transformation of digital technology-empowered vocational education.

Based on the characteristics of the digital era, Wei Qing, Chief Technology Officer of Microsoft (China) Co., Ltd. shared his thoughts on how to effectively cultivate talents. He believed that in the digital age, human beings are about to enter an intelligent society dominated by information, but the powerful effect of information has not yet been truly understood by the public. Education should cultivate talents who meet the characteristics of the times and have basic human qualities. The ability to obtain, analyze, judge, understand and use information is one of the basic abilities of talents in the information age. In the future, due to the empowerment of information technology, vocational education combining virtuality and reality, being ubiquitous and fair, will be accelerated.

Chen Tao, Co-founder of iFlytek Co., Ltd. and President of Anhui Institute of Information Technology, China, shared his views and experience of the "project-based" talent cultivation paradigm. He believed that the key for digital skilled talents to cope with changes is to have the ability to adapt to changes. If enterprises want to achieve their goals through the project-based system, employees' underlying ability is needed. To cater to the real needs of the enterprises for the underlying ability of talents, Anhui Institute of Information Technology has put forward the project objective and technical path of "project-based teaching", and explored the "project-based teaching" mode of digital skilled talents.

Zhong Meihua, Director of Learning Service Expert Committee of Huawei Technologies Co., Ltd., China, analyzed the ecology of digital talents in the 5G era. He said that 5G would bring new momentum and great influence to the industry. The business operation mode of the pan-industry ecosystem and decentralized platform calls for the ecological prosperity of pan-industry digital talents. Enterprises need to rethink the transformation of digital talent management mode. Based on the new infrastructure, the ecosystem and vertical industries need more enterprises to participate in talent training, and the needs for related disciplines and the cooperative education of Industry-University-Research will also boom vigorously. Huawei has built a digital talent transformation framework for the pan-industry "human-machinery-industry", and is committed to promoting the co-construction, co-creation and sharing of talent training ecology in talent training management of enterprises, industries and vocational schools.

Aileen Cai, Regional Head of Education of Association of Chartered Certified Accountants (ACCA), and Liu Qian, Secretary of CPC Committee, Director and Senior Vice President of Glodon Co., Ltd., China, respectively delivered special reports around the needs of digital transformation talents in the accounting and construction industries.

4. Stones from Other Mountains: Escorting Practitioners with Digital Technology

Martin Fleischer, Honorary Professor of Shenzhen Polytechnic, China, Michael Bourlakis, Director of the Center of Logistics, Procurement and Supply Chain Management of Cranfield School of Management and Expert of the Association of Education and Technology (AET) of UK, Foo Sze-yeng, E-learning Instructional Designer and Content Editor of Southeast Asian Ministers of Education Organization Regional Centre for Vocational and Technical Education and Training (SEAMEO VOCTECH), Yee Wai Sim, Dean of the Faculty of Computing and Engineering of Quest International University of Malaysia, Ixaka Egurbide, Managing Director of Machine Tool Institute, Spain, and Jan Heinze, Managing Director of Heinze Akademie, Germany, introduced their respective experience of the digital transformation of vocational education, and discussed the development trend and experience exploration of digital transformation in different countries and regions.

Martin Fleischer shared the transformation experience of German vocational education in the context of Industry 4.0. Under the dual system of German vocational education, schools provide enterprises with talents with real-world experience and students and parents with university degrees, achieving a perfect combination of dual vocational training and regular higher education. He suggested that in the future China should increase the number of application-oriented universities, improve the vocational education system with undergraduate, master and doctoral degrees through vocational education, and make enterprises bear more responsibilities in vocational education by improving the law.

Ixaka Egurbide said that in the process of digital transformation, how students and practitioners learn technology is the key, and vocational schools, as the main training center of digital technology, should be the prophet of the industry and escort industry practitioners. Vocational schools need to do three things: first, to realize the digitalization of school management; second, to promote the digital transformation of teaching and learning and third, to develop digital factories.

# （二）

# 欢迎辞

中国职业技术教育学会会长　鲁　昕

今天我们在这里举行职业教育数字化转型发展论坛，这个论坛作为世界职业技术教育发展大会的第一个平行论坛，足见它对整个论坛安排的意义和价值。

8 月 19 日，世界职业技术教育发展大会在天津隆重开幕，习近平总书记向大会致贺信，进一步强调了职业教育的地位和作用，进一步明确了职业教育在中国迈向社会主义现代化国家建设新征程当中的地位作用和历史意义。怀进鹏部长代表中华人民共和国教育部在大会作了主旨报告，我听了之后备受振奋。我的理解是，中国的职业教育在当今世界形势下开启了一个新的征程，翻开了一个新的篇章，迈上了一个新的起点，这个起点就是在公元 2022 年 8 月 19 号。

今天我们以“数字化转型”为命题讨论职业教育的新变化、新方式、新技能，用数字化转型的思路、理念、方法、路径研究新的变化、新的方式和新的技能，非常有意义。习近平总书记的贺信，进一步明确了职业教育和经济社会发展的联系，又进一步提升了职业教育对经济社会发展和建设人类命运共同体、落实联合国 2030 可持续发展议程的重要意义。

习近平总书记反复强调职业教育必须与经济社会发展紧密相连，一是促进就业创业，二是助力经济社会发展，三是增进人民福祉，这三大作用就是在当今世界条件下，在中国迈向现代化强国建设的过程中，职业教育新的历史定位和功能定位。习近平总书记的贺信为职业教育发展不断地提出了新的方向。总书记强调，中国积极推动职业教育高质量发展，支持中外职业教育交流合作。中方愿同世界各国一道，加强互学互鉴、共建共享，携手落实全球发展倡议，为加快落实联合国 2030 年可持续发展议程贡献力量。

在落实联合国 2030 可持续发展议程方面，中国的努力和贡献是有目共睹的，我们始终把可持续发展作为国家现代化进程的一个重要任务。中国的发展不仅仅是为了中国人民，中国也愿意和世界人民一道共同努力共建美好的地球家园。这充分彰显了中国政府的格局、中国政府的包容、中国政府的真诚和中国政府的善意。我们发展的目的非常明确，让人民得到幸福。那么在后疫情时代我们该如何发展呢？总书记又给出了方向，概括起来就是九个字：新变化、新方式、新技能。

第一个是新变化。当今世界百年未有之大变局和疫情交织叠加，这就是我们今天面临的形势。

第二个是新方式。由于科技进步，今天的发展方式发生了改变。尤其是在疫情后，我们见证了数字技术的加快发展。在这种背景下，不掌握数字技术，没有数字思维，我们无法适应新的变化。所以我们提出要进行数字化转型，中国职业技术教育学会（以下简称中国职教学会）为此已奋斗了近四年，从 2018 年起，中国职教学会第五届理事会就开始与职教同仁们共同推进数字化转型，邀请了一百多位院士参与我们的转型工作。

第三个是新技能。什么是新技能呢？就是数字素养。当前，传统的技能已经很不适应今天的数字经济，所以昨天二十多个国家和地区以及联合国等国际组织在演讲中反复强调一句话，就是“今天是数字经济时代”。数字技术快速发展也带来一个新的问题与挑战，就是如何实现高质量就业。我们常说，职业教育是以就业为导向的教育，但是也要以结果为导向。数字经济背景下必须掌握数字化技能，这就要求我们的教育必须要进行数字化转型。

怀进鹏部长就贯彻落实习近平总书记的贺信作了讲话，在此，我想谈四点感受，以帮助大家更加聚焦总书记提出的新变化、新方式、新技能。

一是新要求。建设高质量的现代教育体系，一定要把“高质量”这三个字作为一种思维范式，作为思考问题、设计方案的逻辑起点。职业教育不是补充教育，也不是低端教育，更不是淘汰教育，今天思考中国职业教育发展以及加强合作，一定要站在“高质量”的逻辑起点去进行。我们可以看到，发达国家和发展中国家都有鲁班工坊，但是发展中国家的鲁班工坊主要聚焦两个领域，第一个是基础设施，第二个是制造业，发达国家则聚焦对美好生活的向往，从英国等国家制作的糕点就可以看出。昨天，大会开幕式的暖场视频提到，职业教育使地球更加绿色，使生活更加美好，使制造更加智能。所以今天我们研究职业教育，就要以“高质量”为逻辑起点，一定要转变思维方式。

二是新机制。是产教互动的新机制，以前都强调“产教融合”，这次怀进鹏部长提出了“产教互动”，那么如何互动呢？就是要通过全要素互动，这里的“全要素”包括劳动、资本、土地、知识、技术、管理、数据七个要素，由过去的土地、劳动力、资本三要素增加到七要素。所以，今后再考虑职业教育办学机制、教学机制、教材机制，一定要明确一个逻辑定位——互动。这种互动应该是我中有你、你中有我，我们也应该用产教互动的思维来改造实训基地。由产教融合到产教互动，反映了产教双向之间的融合，融合是互动的前提，互动是为了更好地融合。

三是新内涵。怀进鹏部长指出，要提高职业教育办学能级，“能级”与“质量”相比，更加凸显力量和动力，前者是动态的，后者则是静态的，我们一定要把握怀进鹏部长讲话中的关键词，正如我们理解习近平总书记所强调职业教育的三大功能：促进就业创业、助力经济社会发展、增进人民福祉，在对经济社会发展的作用中，使用的是“助力”而非“支撑”，同样是为了凸显“助力”的能动性。所以，职业教育的内涵发展均需要提高能级。

四是新生态。要营造让社会尊重和认可的职业教育发展氛围。首先让社会尊重职业教育，其次让社会认可职业教育，改变社会对职业教育的刻板印象，纠正那种把职业教育视为低端教育、补充教育的误解。

世界职业技术教育发展大会的召开使得职业教育发展站到了新起点，中国职业教育将拥抱世界并携手世界共同前行。职业教育也开启了新的征程，努力让全社会、全世界都尊重和认可职业教育。在昨天 20 多个国家代表的讲话中，都提到了终身教育，职业教育是终身教育，绝不仅仅是一个阶段性教育。在此背景下，我们就是要终身学习，终身充实提升自我，要在快乐的劳动、快乐的奉献中度过一个让自己满意的人生，让周围所有人都羡慕的人生。

在论坛开幕之际，我们应该深刻理解习近平总书记对职业教育的新要求，深入思考怀进鹏部长落实总书记新要求的讲话，要站在新的思维起点思考职业教育，数字化转型正是我们思考、发展职业教育的重要路径之一。

谢谢大家！

# （三）

# 面向颠覆性技术创新体系<br>构建开创新时期职业教育国际合作新格局

中国科学院院士、西北工业大学学术委员会主任　黄　维

21 世纪以来，世界范围内职业教育进入“黄金时期”，制度体系逐步完善，投入持续增长，保障水平不断提高，职业教育在个人发展、经济增长和社会进步中发挥着越来越重要的作用。

随着经济全球化的不断发展，全球范围的教育和科技创新合作已成为世界教育和科技发展的重要推动力。与此同时，全球正处于新一轮科技革命和产业变革的关键节点。未来，包括中国在内的世界各主要经济体的长期繁荣，应该建立在高水平技术技能与高质量人力资源体系上。因此，发达的现代职业教育体系是基础。

2021 年以来，中国职业教育迎来了新的发展“窗口期”。习近平总书记对职业教育工作作出重要指示，全国职业教育大会胜利召开，中办、国办印发《关于推动现代职业教育高质量发展的意见》，《中华人民共和国职业教育法》修订工作取得重要进展……这些重大的利好信息，都预示着职业教育将肩负着更重大的历史使命。

目前，我国职业教育发展取得突破性进展，为经济社会发展提供了有力的人才支撑。中职毕业生就业率连续十年保持在 95% 以上，高职毕业生半年后就业率超过 90%；现代制造业、新兴产业新增从业人员 70% 以上来自职业院校。

随着全球教育治理体系的稳步推进，职业教育国际合作逐渐成为发展重点。这不仅是国家总体外交的组成部分，也是经济建设、社会发展、科技进步的重要支撑，是在新时期构建创新开放新格局的重要路径，是解决跨国、跨区域和涉及全人类共同利益难题的重要途径。坚持互利共赢的开放战略，全方位加强国际合作，深度参与国际职业教育的合作与竞争，不断提升统筹和综合运用国际、国内两种资源的能力，已经成为我国职业教育创新发展的重要内容。

当前，世界百年未有变局和世纪疫情叠加，深刻变化的外部环境对中国职业教育国际合作的发展提出了新的挑战。面对新形势，我们应该深化对教育及科技创新命运共同体的认识，以构建中国特色颠覆性技术创新体系为目标，主动提升教育和科技创新对外合作能力，以更加开放的姿态构建全方位、多领域、深层次的国际合作体系，为提高国家核心竞争力、增强国际话语权、规避产业风险做出新贡献。

当前，在“硅基材料 + 电子过程”基础上孕育形成的“微（纳）电子时代”已进入较低附加值的夕阳产业发展阶段，而以“碳基材料 + 光电过程”为基础形成的柔性电子这一关键根部技术引领的“柔性电子时代”将孕育具有超高产业附加值特征的巨型朝阳产业。

在此背景下，我们尤其需要在创新驱动发展战略的指引下，进行顶层设计、战略谋划、整体布局和超前部署，加快推进颠覆性技术体系创新的发展步伐，特别是要重点强化在 FAMISHED（柔性电子 +）领域，即柔性电子、人工智能、材料科学、泛物联网、空间科学、健康科学、能源科学和数据科学等领域的超前布局、政策倾斜和资源配置。

目前，柔性电子作为一种颠覆式科技创新的代表，国内正在逐步完善从职业教育到本科—硕士—博士全谱系的人才培养体系。二十多年来，我和团队一直致力于打造由中国引领的世界级“中国碳谷”，建设“柔性电子强国”。同时，作为亚太工程组织联合会的主席，我很欣慰地看到亚太地区、非洲和世界其他地区的工程职业技术领域的交流与合作不断加深，在过去几年我们有幸见证《非洲、亚洲和太平洋地区工程教育协议》的成功签署，也组织了多场高质量研讨会和职业教育培训等活动，正全力构建职业教育领域技术、数据、人才集聚发展、协同支撑的良好格局。

基于多年全球拓展工作的体悟，建议从以下三个方面开创全球职业教育合作新格局。

第一，提升全球职业教育创新资源配置能力，培育职业教育科技创新命运共同体。提升创新主体利用全球创新资源的能力，逐步建立国家产业系统与现代职业教育体系之间的互动与融合机制。在形成产教融合国家层面的体系与机制的基础上，建立区域层面产教融合的运行机制，依托组织载体建立产教融合的资源共享机制，加强信息沟通，实现资源有效配置，发挥市场创造力，促进产教双方实现更自主、自觉的合作，职业教育与产业界紧密互动、有效沟通。

第二，形成凸显职业教育类型特色的现代治理体系，促进职业教育人才资源的全球有序流动。不断完善治理框架与体系，强化各个治理主体之间的沟通与协调，以治理能力提升为目标，形成凸显职业教育类型特色的国际化现代治理体系。要特别重视优化创新、创业、营商环境，构建以战略科技人才、职业领军人才、青年科技人才和留学生为主的“梯次化”职业教育国际化人才队伍。努力营造制度环境、文化环境、保障环境，做到真心爱才、诚心待才、贴心育才、宽心容才，形成育才、识才、选才、用才的良好风尚。持续优化和创新人才科研、工作、居住、出入境等便利化措施，提高对各类人才的吸引力和凝聚力。同时，完善全球职业教育合作信息、资金、渠道、培训等中介服务平台，提升国际化人才培养的水平和能力，真正做到“聚天下英才而用之”。

第三，建设合作平台链接全球创新资源，推进职业教育国际合作进程。鼓励各类职业教育创新主体搭建中外合作平台，共建新型中外职业教育联合研发机构，打造全球合作创新高地，深度参与全球科技创新。以世界工程组织联合会、亚太工程组织联合会等一批国际重要学术组织为平台，面向“一带一路”建设中的重大创新需求，在先进制造、航空航天、信息通信、农业、交通运输等重点领域选择一批国际职业教育科技合作重大项目，加强联合研究，充分发挥教育和科技创新在“一带一路”产能合作中的重要作用。

职业教育是对未来的投资，它可以为个人、企业和社会带来收益。最后，希望世界各国关心职业教育的同事们、朋友们一道，以本次大会为契机，积极推进职业教育国际合作，推动全球职教界和产业界深度合作、共同发展，努力解决更多涉及全人类共同利益的难题。

# （四）

# 全力探索职业教育数字化转型的“江苏之路”

江苏省教育厅厅长　葛道凯

依托数字化重塑职业教育新生态、赋能职业教育新发展，形成职业教育的现代范式，恰逢其时、十分必要。围绕职业教育数字化转型，江苏先行先试、积极探索、系统推进，主要解决了三个问题。

第一个问题：如何使优质教育教学资源覆盖面更广、惠及师生更多。由于区域间职业教育水平存在差异，优质教育教学资源分布不均衡，需要搭建合适的平台实现资源共享。江苏在资源库、在线课程等优质资源建设方面具有良好的基础。今年4月，江苏被确定为国家智慧教育平台首批整省试点省份后，进一步全面加强职业教育数字资源建设。目前，江苏已择优遴选首批33所试点职业院校，先后启动虚拟仿真实训基地、在线精品课程和数字教材等资源建设，扩大了国家智慧教育平台的溢出效应和倍增效应。

第二个问题：如何加快建设覆盖所有学校的数字化基础设施。实现学校全覆盖，才能让每一个学生都能享受到公平、优质的教育，共享教育现代化的成果。江苏以智慧校园建设为抓手，不断推进职业院校校园数字化转型。省政府办公厅印发《关于推进智慧教育的实施意见》，将智慧校园建设纳入智慧江苏发展全局统筹谋划，省教育厅将智慧校园建设列为教育信息化重点工程，建设了一批国家级、省级智慧校园以及示范校、样板校。

第三个问题：如何让更多的师生使用智慧平台和数字资源。智慧教育平台和数字资源建好后，如何最大限度发挥数字化资源的作用至关重要。江苏以体制机制建设为保障，充分激发师生使用智慧教育平台和数字资源的动力。我省创新考核评价机制，推动将职业教育数字资源建设和使用纳入学校高质量考核和教师教学评价，引导各方参与职业教育数字化转型，推动更多师生使用数字资源。

同时，我们也认识到，推动职业教育数字化转型仍然面临诸多困难和挑战，主要表现在数字资源不够丰富、师生数字素养有待提升、体制机制保障亟待完善等三个方面。面向未来，我们将坚持“需求牵引、应用为王、示范引领、安全发展”的总要求，全力打造职业教育数字化转型的“江苏范式”。

### 1. 在丰富资源上拿出硬招，全力拓展职业教育数字化应用新场景

一是丰富数字教育资源。发挥江苏职业院校数量较多、水平较高的优势，继续推进各类资源建设。二是改革智慧教学模式。依托人工智能、大数据等新一代信息技术，打造智慧课堂、智慧学习、智慧考试等职业教育数字化典型应用场景。三是优化教学评价模式。通过大数据优化课堂教学对学生的评价、学校对教师的评价、行政管理部门对学校的评价，为学校治理决策提供依据。

### 2. 在提升素养上苦练内功，着力构建职业教育数字能力进阶新体系

一是提升数字化领导力。实施职业教育管理者数字素养提升工程，分层次、分类别、分阶段推进职业教育管理者全员培训。二是提升数字化教学创新能力。实施职业教育教师信息技术应用能力提升工程 2.0，开展教师人工智能、大数据等专项培训。三是提升数字化学习创新能力。推广数字化环境下的项目式、问题式、场景式等学习方式，培养学生多维素养，提升学生个性化和终身学习能力。

### 3. 在长效机制上主动作为，全面激活职业教育数字化转型新动能

一是制定职业教育数字化转型升级标准。为各级教育行政部门和职业院校数字化转型建设和评价提供指导。二是完善资源共建共享机制。规范优质职业教育资源建设的流程和标准，强化供需对接，做好资源应用的考核和评价。三是强化数字平台运维能力。开展职业院校数字化运维专业人员培训，不断提高运维质量。

职业教育数字化转型是一场深刻的时代变革，未来，希望我们对数字转型的探讨能够继续更广、更深入地推动下去，努力把习近平总书记对职业教育“大有可为”的殷切期待转化为职教战线“大有作为”的江苏实践。

# （五）

# 数字化转型与浙江职业教育模式变革

浙江省教育厅职业教育与成人教育处处长　陈　达

教育数字化既是时势所趋，也是现实需要。数字化转型是职业教育高质量发展的新机遇、新动力。浙江全面贯彻习近平总书记关于数字化变革和职业教育的重要论述，深入落实《中华人民共和国职业教育法》《国家职业教育改革实施方案》等法律法规和重要政策精神，协同推进全省数字化改革方略，积极探索实践数字化赋能职业教育路径，扎实推进职业教育数字化改革工作，努力为推动职业教育高质量发展、建设共同富裕示范区提供浙江样板。下面，分实践进展、思考体会和下一步思路三个方面，将浙江职业教育数字化改革工作向大家作报告。

**1. 浙江职业教育数字化改革的实践进展**

2021 年，浙江省委全面部署全省数字化改革工作。同年，省教育厅制定印发《浙江省教育领域数字化改革工作方案》，实施“教育魔方”工程，按照“综合集成、整体智治”原则和“教育大脑 + 智慧学校”思路，统筹推进数字技术与教育管理、教学实践的深度融合，推动数字教育新基建、新模式、新格局和新生态建设，不断提升教育现代化水平。职业教育数字化改革是教育数字化改革的重要内容。浙江省以支撑职业教育高质量发展为目标，按照“需求牵引、应用为王、成熟先上、技术保障”工作原则，积极构建“大脑 + 应用 + 服务 + 机制”的职业教育数字化深度融合浙江模式，自觉扛起推动现代职业教育提质培优、增值赋能的重大责任，深化提高效率、改善效果两大任务，拓宽增强大数据平台、推广特色应用、创新有效机制的发展路径，在行业发展、社会评价和政策要求相统一的原则下，努力开创数字化职业教育的新局面，培养更多适应数字时代需求的高素质技术技能人才、能工巧匠、大国工匠。

（1）构建职教大脑数字底座。“教育魔方”是浙江省教育厅依据教育公共服务行业特征，面向全省所有学校和教育部门设计开发的教育数据感知、共享和计算的基础支撑系统，贯通政务云和各级教育数据中心，并打通浙政钉、浙里办、浙教钉等各类终端，承载省级统建应用、区域学校自建应用等，为教育行政管理者、各级教育局、各类学校以及公众提供数字化教育服务。自 2021 年 11 月上线以来，“教育魔方”初步实现了业务应用一云支撑、教育数据一仓归集、信息安全一网统管、线上线下一码畅学、数据治理一屏呈现、创新应用一站可选，为教育领域高效管理、精准教学、泛在学习等创造了良好条件，为职业教育决策大脑系统和决策支持中心建设奠定了基础。

（2）建设与应用职教特色教学资源。组织职业院校教师基于全省网络学习个人空间建设共享专业教学资源，实现众智共享专业教学资源。组织名师集中开发“名师金课”“名师教研”等示范性优质课程资源，推动建设数字化、融媒体教材，实现名师共享优质示范资源。组织开展线上线下教学活动，实现共享教学生成性资源。组织校企合作开发前沿技术、技能培训等真实项目资源，实现共享企业前沿资源。继续面向量大面广的专业课分级遴选一批在线开放课程，创新政府购买优质教育资源服务机制，促进优质教育资源推广应用、优化与持续迭代。

（3）打造职教特色服务场景应用。打造双师型教师培养网络服务应用。通过创建“1+10+N”的名师和技能大师网络工作室的双师型教师培养模式，组建教学团队，发挥传帮带作用，将企业的新技术、新工艺、新规范及时纳入教学，将职业资格证书、职业技能等级证书内容及时融入教学，推广项目教学、案例教学、情景教学、工作过程导向教学，广泛应用线上线下混合教学，推动现代信息技术与职业教育深度融合。打造个性化网络学习服务应用。依托之江汇教育广场，构建了支撑全省一人一空间的职业教育教学的网络学习空间，提供空间服务、公共应用服务、数据分析服务，支持资源创建与共享、教学支持服务、学习交互服务、决策评估服务等公共应用服务。

（4）培育一批智慧试点示范院校与案例。通过国家、省级两级联动，开展智慧学校试点示范建设，加快虚拟仿真实训基地建设，启动省级职业学校信息化标杆学校建设试点，发挥基层首创精神，从环境、应用、治理等维度推进先行先试，探索形成可复制能推广的经验，发挥试点的典型引领、以点带面功效，培育形成智慧实训新型空间、教学模式创新、学校整体智治等一批高质量有特色的数字化改革案例和经验，引领示范全省职教数字化改革。

**2. 浙江深化职业教育数字化改革的思考**

数字化改革在本质上是一场技术革命，需要理念、方法、手段、机制同时到位，需要重大应用多跨协同。在先行先试的同时，对于如何深化职业教育数字化改革，浙江在且行且思，边实践边研究。

（1）要逐步发挥职教大脑的智治能效。建设职教“数字大脑”，构建人才立交桥课程体系建设、企业精准推荐、人才综合管理等应用，形成政、校、企间的数据互通和效率协同，服务精准管理决策、服务个体精准成长成才、服务校企深度合作，为职业教育高质量技术技能人才培养提供高效智能化服务。

（2）要开展多跨协同重要场景应用。厘清职业教育人才培养的多跨协同业务流程和业务需求，梳理技能人才培养过程中的问题清单和需求清单，绘制职业教育产教对接谱系图，通过开设数字化相关专业和专业数字化改造，实现职业教育和产业人才需求精准无缝对接，增强专业设置和课程体系与行业产业发展的适应性，为经济社会发展提供更强人才动力。

（3）打造名校名师名匠。推动名校、名师、名匠“上云”，形成学校网络共同体、教师网络共同体、校企网络共同体，共享优质教育资源，打造专业品牌和特色社会服务，全面提升学生数字化思维和适应社会变革的能力，增强职业教育吸引力，提升职业教育形象，形成“职业成才选职业学校、技能提升找职业学校”的社会氛围。

（4）加强理论应用研究与机制创新。加强政策、制度和机制创新，开展人才培养全过程中新技术、新模式研究，调动推动职业教育高质量发展的多元主体的动力和活力，重塑职业教育人才培养体系。创新信息技术产品购买服务方式，建立职教数据共享与流动机制，构建支撑职业教育高质量发展的数字生态环境。

### 3. 浙江推进职业教育数字化改革的下一步思路

浙江是国家智慧教育平台试点省，将以整省试点工作为契机，按照教育部和省委省政府要求，将职业教育数字化改革服务于提质培优，服务于职业教育高质量发展，一方面，健全数字化转型变革的推进机制，细化分工、建好台账，将责任传导到职教战线的“神经末梢”，把数字化转型变革的任务落细落小落地；另一方面，加强激励引导、强化制度保障，充分调动各方面积极性、主动性、创造性，扩大职业教育数字化转型变革的总体效应。不断推动信息技术成为破解职业教育难题的浙江解法，数字赋能技能人才培养，推动浙江省职业教育走出数字化改革先行先试的坚定步伐，让职业教育更加“有学头、有盼头、有奔头”，奋力打造与“重要窗口”、社会主义现代化先行省、共同富裕示范区建设相适应的全国职教高地。

# (六)

# 数字化时代高职院校人才培养模式转型

深圳职业技术学院校长　许建领

随着5G、云计算、大数据、人工智能与区块链为代表的数字技术的发展与应用，世界进入“数字化”发展的新阶段。2021年10月，习近平总书记在中共中央政治局第三十四次集体学习时强调，数字经济发展速度之快、辐射范围之广、影响程度之深前所未有，正在成为重组全球要素资源、重塑全球经济结构、改变全球竞争格局的关键力量。

## 1. 数字化时代呼唤高职院校人才培养模式转型

在数字经济时代，我国高职院校面向数字化的人才培养模式转型是其主动适应国家经济产业格局，为经济社会培养大批新型数字化能工巧匠、大国工匠的必经之路。习近平总书记强调，促进数字技术与实体经济深度融合，赋能传统产业转型升级，催生新产业新业态新模式，不断做强做优做大我国数字经济。现阶段我国严重缺乏既了解传统的行业技术、业务流程与发展需求，又能够掌握和应用数字技术的复合型人才，数据显示，当前我国数字化人才缺口达1 100万人左右。《“十四五”数字经济发展规划》提出，到2025年，数字经济核心产业增加值占GDP比重达到10%。数字经济高质量发展离不开一大批适应产业需求、具有扎实技术性的人才，这对职业教育人才的培养提出了更高的要求。数字经济时代，进行人才培养数字化模式的转型是高职院校主动适应国家的产业布局，为经济社会发展培养大批新型的数字化人工巧匠、大国工匠的必经之路。

## 2. 数字化时代高职院校人才培养模式转型发展的行动

以指导性专业目录为依托，加强素质人才的培养。教育部以《职业教育专业目录》修订优化为抓手，推动职业教育数字化转型。新版专业目录优化和加强5G、人工智能、大数据、云计算、物联网等领域相关专业设置，并且对所有的专业进行了全面的数字化改造。当前，已经有不少的高职院校加快数字化转型的步伐，与龙头企业共建了人工智能、大数据、云计算等学院，进行数字化产业及产业数字化专业群的布局，新开设了大数据技术等专业，部分教师采用多种新型数字化教学手段和方法，强调数字人才及能力培养，数字化职业教育育人生态初步成型。近年来，中国职业教育界积极地开展有关职业教育数字化转型的交流活动，一系列研讨会的召开，为明确高职院校人才培养模式数字化转型的方向、交流数字化人才培养实践及凝聚人才培养模式数字化转型共识发挥了积极作用。

**3. 数字化时代高职院校人才培养模式转型的案例**

深圳职业技术学院建校29年来，一直致力于中国职业教育的改革与发展，尤其是近年来，学校精准对接区域产业数字化发展的需求，建设了一批特色产业学院。同时以项目化课程建设和课程人工智能转型为重点，打造一批内容丰富、品质优良的数字化教学体系。深圳职业技术学院数字化转型有效地提升了人才培养工作的质量，毕业生近年来在世界500强、行业龙头知名企业的入职比例达到16%，今年毕业生的就业率已经超过了98.6%。在数字化转型实践中，我们总结了以下四点经验。

（1）加快人才培养组织方式的数字化转型。学校以专业群建设为抓手，设置人工智能相关专业，并且在全校进行了人工智能的通识教育。我们带动其他传统专业的转型升级，通过全方位改造专业教育生态，打造数字经济背景下全新的人才培养体系。

（2）基于校企深度合作的数字化人才培养综合实践。学校与世界500强和行业的龙头企业展开深度合作，创建数字化人才培养基地。企业的产品标准、技术标准、服务标准转化为人才认证标准，打通专业与职业的鸿沟。目前，我们与华为、比亚迪等企业合作开发认证的证书有十多种。深圳职业技术学院长期与华为公司展开深度合作，获得了国家教学成果奖的特等奖，全国首个华为5G+数字化人才产教融合基地落户深圳职业技术学院，双方共同规模化培养5G+数字化应用人才，为5G产业链、供应链企业提供人才支撑和治理支持。与腾讯联手共育符合产业互联网发展需求的复合型、应用型创新人才，与美团共建了数字生活学院，与比亚迪公司共同打造了师资共用、人才培育、产学共融、技术共研的教学合作模式，与西门子公司共建了中德智能制造数字化工程创新中心。

(3) 加快推动人才培养标准数字化转型。深圳职业技术学院实施“六融合”人才培养模式改革，以学生学习成效为导向，推进产教融合、职普融合、理实融合、教育与生活融合、技术与文化融合、现代信息技术与教学的深度融合。

(4) 建立数字型人才多元化的培养通道。深圳职业技术学院主动与一批政府部门、行业企业等合作，成立了深圳健康养老学院、机器人培训学院、社区旅游学院等一批行业和社区的培训学院，为市民生活的数字化转型提供支撑，为国家数字化战略的实施，提供人力资源基础。

# （七）

# 产教融合，分层分类推动专业建设改革创新

深圳信息职业技术学院校长　王　晖

站在数字经济大潮和数字化转型的背景之下，交流我们在分层分类产教融合，推动数字化人才培养方面的一些新的思考。

深圳信息职业技术学院由三所学校合并而成，2019 年，学校作为国家双高计划 B 档建设单位进入建设行列。在方向上，党建业务双融双促双发展，学校党委始终坚持“三同”办学理念，推动党的建设与学校事业发展深度融合，形成了“一示范、两标杆、四样板”的党建双创三级全优示范体系。两个“双高”专业群所在学院双双入选省级以上先进党组织，双双获得国家级职业教育教师教学创新团队。在师资上，获得众多国家级奖项。近五年内，学校在职在岗教师（教师团队）获得国家级奖励或荣誉八项，获得国家第一届职业技能大赛光电技术赛项金牌一项、全国先进工作者一人、全国优秀教师一人、全国职业院校信息化教学大赛一等奖一项、国家万人计划教学名师一人。在生源上，学生“进出口”态势良好，市外招生分数线连续三年超本科线，招生分数稳居省内同类院校前两名。2021 年毕业生就业平均起薪线比广东省高职院校毕业生平均值高出近 30%。其中，特色班毕业生月薪可超万元。学校被全国高校就业协会评为“2020 年全国高校毕业生就业创业工作典型案例学校”。

产教融合、校企合作是职业院校高质量发展的必由之路。党和国家对职业教育产教融合、校企合作作出系列重要指示批示，习近平总书记强调：职业教育前途广阔、大有可为。要坚持深化产教融合、校企合作。李克强总理作出批示：要瞄准技术变革和产业优化升级的方向，推进产教融合、校企合作，吸引更多青年接受职业技能教育，促进教育链、人才链与产业链、创新链有效衔接。孙春兰副总理在全国职业教育大会上指出：要健全多元办学格局，细化产教融合、校企合作政策。教育

部开展现代学徒制试点，支持校企联合招生，推进校企一体化育人，鼓励校企开设订单班，招生即招工，定向培养专业人才。各级教育行政部门将校企合作情况作为职业院校办学业绩和水平评价、工作目标考核的重要内容，督促职业院校深化产教融合、校企合作。

学校建设“四共四进”深信路径产教科融合新生态，共建优势专业与师资队伍，共研专业标准，共同开展技术攻关，共推实习就业与社会服务；推动产业教授进校园、产业资源进专业、产业先进技术进课程、产业实战项目进课堂。

学校试点高等工程师学院，借鉴世界先进国家工程教育和“新工科”的成功经验，围绕新一代信息技术、先进制造等战略新兴产业，以产业（场景）解决方案为出发点和策源点，联合头部企业深度开展产教科融合育人，以“厚实基础＋项目实践＋素质赋能”为特色，培养产业行业急需的复合型解决方案落地工程师（现场工程师），以适应产业快速升级需求。改革选拔方式、实施学分银行、设置长短学期、灵活考核方式、建立退出机制、专业交叉融合培养。深化校企合作，遴选链主企业，共同开发教材、共同实施教学、共同技术研发。试点工作分为三步走，一是专业群开设特色班，学校已经于 2021 年实施，开设 12 个班。二是个别试点、重点突破，2022 年软件学院＋腾讯，设立腾讯高等工程师学院，信通学院＋华为，设立华为 ICT 国际人才交流中心，智能制造学院＋汇川，设立汇川高等工程师学院；学校试点华为鲲鹏工程师培养体系，联合华为共同参与人才培养，建设了华南地区第一家鲲鹏产业学院，并在产业学院架构下开设鲲鹏班；学校联合华为建设全球唯一一家华为 ICT 国际人才交流中心，以考取华为 HCIE（华为认证 ICT 专家）专家级证书作为毕业条件。腾讯高等工程师学院设置腾飞班和腾实班，实行纵向贯通、横向融通培养模式，全校遴选生源，从大一入学学生到毕业生面向软件行业高端岗位和生态链复合型岗位，采取小班教学，动态淘汰，着力培养高水平应用型软件类工程师和复合型解决方案落地工程师。三是模式成熟后设立独立的高等工程师学院，统筹全校工程师人才培养。

# （八）

# 互联网 + 教育的变革：我们的实践探索

广东轻工职业技术学院校长　卢坤建

广东轻工职业技术学院历史原点是创建于 1933 年的广东省立第一职业学校，已有 89 年的职业教育办学历史，并曾先后于 1959—1963 年、1978—1983 年两段时期作为本科院校开办职业本科教育。近年来，学校响应国家新基建战略，加快推进教育新基建，构建高质量教育支撑体系，形成了发展的新动能、新起点。

**1. 提前布局——推进教育新基建**

随着产业的数字化快速转型，职业教育的一个重要主题是应用这一走向，推进互联网 + 教育的变革。国家新基建战略策应了产业数字化的要求，必然要求有效推进教育新基建：落实学校治校办学的数字化，快速推进专业（群）数字化赋能，这是推动职业教育高质量发展的必由之路。早在 2017 年、2018 年，学校顺势而为，乘势而上，提出了构建教育信息化高质量支撑体系的战略举措：构建学校统筹协调下专业（群）数字化赋能的体制机制，建设广轻智慧校园 3.0，打造广轻泛在教学与学习体系，在全国率先开启广轻新基建的进程。

**2. 三个重点——平台、体系、赋能**

重点之一，建设广轻智慧校园 3.0 平台。面向新技术、新理念、新机遇，自 2019 年至 2021 年，历时三年时间，基于中台技术一体化云上重构全域业务，建成了“广轻智慧校园 3.0 平台”，实现了业务融合、数据融通，推进了学校大数据治理的变革。以广东轻工业务为样板，标准先行，构建了以信息系统、数据资源、基础设施为基本要素的“广轻新基建”，有效解决了分散建设、重复建设、信息孤岛的问题。推进业财融合，依托平台深化内控管理，实现人财物全过程数字化监管，荣获全国审计先进集体。建成基于大数据平台的平安校园子平台，实现了校园安全动态预警和智能化、精准化的技防管控。总之，通过云上重构广东轻工，支撑起“三大一强”的学校治理模式，促进了新技术支持下的学校治理生态重塑。

重点之二，建设广轻泛在教学体系。此次大会上，黄维院士说了一句金句：“我们都是学生”。这实际上是对职业院校建设泛在教学体系使命的进一步界定。我们体系化建设智慧课室、教学中台、泛在学习平台和云教务平台，创新“互联网 + 教育”智慧教学模式，并形成广轻大学、网上党校、广轻社团等一批特色应用。规模化建设泛在同步智慧课室，实现校内多课室同步联动、跨校课堂同步共享、工业现场实景接入、企业大师远程授课，提高了课堂教学质量。创建了智慧教学空间，强化了师生互动，提升了教师能力，不断地充实了课程资源，推进了教学改革，提高了教学质量。

重点之三，推进专业群数字化赋能。此次会议怀部长发出了全面提升职教能级的号召，其中的核心就是对专业进行数字化赋能。这是一个深广的课题，早在2017 年，我们就敏锐地发现要进行有效的专业建设，就要实施专业建设的数字化协同，对专业（群）全面进行数字化赋能是专业建设的核心任务。2020 年，我们进一步依托工业互联网技术，布局工业互联网 + 专业群，基于教育部工业互联网虚拟仿真基地项目，建设了专业赋能数据中心，推动了“虚拟工厂资源云”建设，将虚实同步“虚拟工厂”引入了教学过程，服务了实践教学。

**3. 典型案例——云上重构数字广轻**

这几年，学校推进教育新基建，重构了数字广轻，形成了具有代表性的广轻案例。在实践探索中，打造了标准化、一体化、开放化、可扩展、可复制的高职信息化样板，学校入选教育部职教大脑第一批试点院校，联合中国工业互联网研究院、阿里云、科大讯飞等研制了多项团体标准，举办了新基建成果发布会，与多所院校开展互助、对口帮扶，共建高职教育大数据应用生态，重构了数字广轻。

尊敬的各位同仁，面对后疫情时代，“互联网 + 教育”变革方兴未艾，学校重构数字广轻、推进专业（群）数字化赋能的实践，仅仅是探索的开始。我们期待与各位同仁互学互鉴，共同努力，加快推进职业教育数字化转型升级，以教育信息化推动职业教育高质量发展！

# （九）

# 职业教育数字化转型与智能制造

浙江机电职业技术学院党委书记　汤兆武

非常荣幸就职业教育数字型转化与智能制造的主题向大家作交流汇报，主要谈三个问题。

### 1. 数字化转型赋能智能制造是时代的要求

从农业社会到工业社会再到数字化社会，是经济社会发展的一般规律。数字化经济是当前经济发展的主流形态。智能制造既是当前发展数字经济的主要路径，也是生产方式转型升级的主要形式。职业教育承担着为国民经济培养高素质技术技能人才的重任，在推进人的全面发展和经济社会转型发展中有着不可替代的作用。在数字时代更加需要发展适应新一轮科技革命和产业革命的职业教育。

### 2. 浙江机电职业技术学院的数字化转型实践与创新

学校主动对接新一代信息技术产业、高端装备等优势产业，五重举措（人才、专业、课程资源、教师团队、实训基地）开展数字化转型实践探索。近年来，浙江机电职业技术学院以补充为举措，初步探索一条职业技术教育数字化转型之路。

（1）人才培养定位重塑。伴随着数字经济的飞速发展，具有数字化素养的技术技能人才严重短缺。2020 年，学校推出了素质工匠的培养工程，以智能制造工程、应用型人才培养为定位，探索构建“数字化 +X”技术技能人才培养模式，全面推进各个专业的素质工匠的精准培养，为社会培养了大批具有数字化素养的高素质的技术技能人才。

（2）专业（群）重建。学校积极贯彻落实产业数字化、数字产业化的发展战略，践行产教互动、校企一体化的办学模式，重构智能制造技术、智能控制技术等七大智能制造相关专业群，将人才培养从传统制造向智能制造升级，人才素质从单一的技能型向技能型加数字化的复合，为制造业数字化转型提供了专业人才的支撑。

（3）模块化课程与教学资源重构。为了适应数字化产业的快速更新迭代，学校以人工智能+、数字化+为引领，搭建了通识课程+共享课程+专业核心课程+岗位方向课程的模块化课程体系，打通了教育学的“任督二脉”，实现了跨专业资源的共建共享。依托泛雅教学资源库，对接国家智慧职教资源平台，为学生提供了智能化的开放式的教学环境，实现了泛在学习。

（4）教师团队重组。教育、教师是关键，学校相继实施教授工程、博士工程、青蓝工程等六大工程，培养一批专兼结合“三人行”的师资队伍，通过承担一些重大攻关项目，提升教师队伍的科研实战能力。近年来，学校获评“全国黄大年式教师团队”两个，“全国教师教学创新团队”两个。

（5）实训基地重融。产教互动、工学结合是职业技术教育的本质要求。学校以“校企协同、三链融通、四化赋能”为构架，打造一流的创新实训基地，建有五位一体的校内实训基地30余个，与浙大中控、上海大众等头部企业建立了140余家紧密型的校外教学实训基地，实现了教、学、训为一体的人才闭环结构。

### 3. 系统性变革是数字化转型的必由之路

首先，教育的主体从职业院校转向有核无边。以人工智能为核心的新一代的信息技术将极大地突破职业教育的时空限制。一方面要加快建设一体化的智能化平台，使人工智能技术深度融入教育的全生命周期；另一方面要构建泛在科学的全民终身教育体系，放大职业教育在技能型社会建设、数字化社会建设当中的特殊贡献。其次，教学模式从统一标准走向个性化定制。数字化转型要主动迎合产业调整的快速化、学习需求个性化的新范式，通过数字化手段改进传统标准化的职业教育供给模式，尽快建立起标准化教学+个性化定制的新型教育体系，为职业教育变革提供新的业态、新的模式。最后，专业建设从跟跑产业走向领跑产业。跟跑产业是基本要求，领跑产业是职业教育的目标。要将大数据技术应用于对行业人才需求的预测、专业与区域产业发展匹配度分析等教育的各个环节，前瞻性的设置与未来产业息息相关的新兴产业，让数字化人才培养和技术服务领跑产业，为经济发展培育新动能。

# （十）

# 职业院校专业数字化转型的“南信实践”

南京信息职业技术学院党委书记　王丹中

“数字经济和实体经济深度融合”已经写入了中国“十四五”发展规划，为数字化技术技能人才培养和专业升级提供了战略指引。教育部于 2021 年颁布了《职业教育专业新目录》（2021 版），为职业学校专业数字化转型提供了具体的指导。下面我从五个方面介绍学院在专业数字化转型方面的一些探索。

第一项工作，是对接数字产业构建人工智能同心圆的专业集群。适应信息化发展向智能化发展趋势，围绕智能网络、智能技术和智能设备三大基础技术和制造、交通、商务、创意四大重点应用，对专业和专业群进行重构，形成了以人工智能为核心的专业集群。

第二项工作，是对接新职业升级人才培养的定位。认真研究数字化转型给行业职业带来的变化，细分行业、职业类别，找准高职院校人才培养的岗位群。

第三项工作，是对接新岗位重构专业群“平台 + 模块”课程体系。按照“底层共享、中层分立、高层互选、顶层综合”的原则，重构专业群“平台 + 模块”课程体系。这个平台包括四类，第一类是基础课程平台，在群间共享课程中加大了数字化通识课程教育。第二类是专业课程平台，把新技术、新工艺、新业态有机融入各专业课程中。第三类是专业拓展群平台，实现了数字化相关课程模块的互选，培养复合型人才和实现学生个性化发展。第四类是综合实训平台，助力学生整合并充分利用所学领域的知识，同时增加培养相关技能和态度等课程。贯穿这四类平台的是教学模式的改革，实施教师分工协作的模块化教学组织方式，信息技术和课堂教学深度融合，注重使用学生素质教学工具和终身学习意识的养成。

第四项工作，是对接新技能打造跨专业的共享实训基地。结合 5G 技术在智能产业中的典型运用，选择智慧园区、智能交通和智慧供应链等应用场景，构建“技术平台应用场景”的 5G 技术实训基地，服务于多个专业群的人才培养。建成了系列虚拟仿真课程资源，将线上平台虚拟仿真资源和教师课程混合打通，让虚拟资源真正帮助学生和教师解决学习和教学中的难点问题。基于综合实训平台，以完成“工程、研发及服务项目”为学习引擎，以“基础项目、岗位项目、企业项目”技能进阶为学习主线，构建了项目牵引技能进阶的实践课程体系。

第五项工作，是对接新素养提升教师素质和能力。围绕提升教师数字化生存和适应能力、教学研究能力、教育教学创新实践能力和专业发展终身学习能力，通过数字化培训，着力于把教师培养成为教学资源的开发者、学生学习活动的组织者、教学方法的创新者和职业发展终身学习者。

# （十一）

# 数字化时代教师职业能力提升

北京信息职业技术学院副校长　张晓蕾

非常荣幸能与大家共同讨论和交流职业教育数字化转型发展方面的热点问题。我发言的题目是“数字化时代教师职业能力提升”。教育数字化是我国教育事业的重要改革举措，这意味着教育理念的根本性变革，职业院校的教师正在尝试通过全过程教学大数据的采集、分析和应用，将传统经验性教学向以数据交互、信息评估为主的数字化教育转变，推动教育和学习活动突破时空局限，助力职业教育高质量发展。

## 1. 从信息化到数字化

在信息化时代，每所职业院校都在业务层面建设了教务系统、学工系统、人事系统、科研系统等诸多业务系统，将原本人工操作的线下业务流程迁移到线上，提高了管理的精细化程度和效率。在教育教学层面，学校建设以信息技术为基础的教学环境，如智慧教室、虚拟仿真实训环境等，搭建线上教学平台、教学资源库，教师依托这些平台和资源开展教学，大大提升了教学效果。各业务系统、教师信息化的教学过程、学生信息化的学习过程将产生大量数据，在数字化时代，打破学校各业务系统间的壁垒，对其产生的大数据进行分析、处理，并与人工智能、物联网等技术相结合，将形成学校的“教育大脑”，使教育教学产生根本性的变革，全面重塑学校的治理模式。

## 2. 数字化时代教师职业能力提升的路径

学院引入大数据、人工智能支持的“教师职业能力智能测评系统”，生成教师数字画像，以需求为导向精准推送培训资源，用数字化技术手段赋能教师，助力教师在职业能力方面持续提升。

教师职业能力智能测评系统充分整合学校各业务系统的数据，包括教务系统、人事管理系统、科研系统、学工系统等，开展全域数据采集、处理和展现，从数据采集到数据治理，再到数据价值挖掘与可视化呈现，让教师测评工作变得可描述、可对比、可分析、可跟踪。教师可以根据能力测评结果及教师画像及时发现自身的优势与不足，扬长补短，为职业生涯发展做好规划；学校可以针对岗位发展需求和在岗教师的能力素质现状定期组织培训。

智能测评系统根据教师数字画像分析得出教师职业发展需求，并向教师精准推送培训课程，供教师选择学习，同时收集教师的培训需求，经过智能建模，筛选、分析、综合形成适用于教师群体的共性需求，供学校决策者参考，作为开展教师定制化培训的依据。教师的职业能力培养不再是纯粹的经验判断，而是建立在科学的数据分析基础上的，为教师的成长发展奠定了坚实的基础。

### 3. 数字化时代教师应具备的数字素养

教育数字化转型涉及整个教育行业，作为职业院校的教师也亟待进行数字化升级。欧盟已经发布了关于教育工作者数字素养框架的研究报告，涵盖专业发展、数字资源、教与学、评估、增强学习者能力、提高学习者数字素养等 6 个领域的 22 种能力，但国内关于教师数字化素养的研究还不是很成熟。我们要持续跟进数字化教育技术的发展，深入研究教师数字素养框架，及时更新教师信息化教学能力标准，并优化更新培训课程体系，通过开展有针对性的培训提高教师的数字素养，使职业院校教师尽快实现从教学观念到教学行为、教学手段、教学模式的数字化转型。

# （十二）

# 数字经济与职业教育

东软集团股份有限公司董事长　刘积仁

当今世界，数字经济正在重塑全球经济格局，推动产业朝着数字化、智能化方向发展，数字经济已成为中国经济发展的核心动力。职业教育与经济社会的发展紧密相连，与产业、市场的距离最近。提高职业教育的适应性，促进职业教育的均衡发展和高质量发展，批量培养数字经济人才，是国家发展数字经济的重要基础。当前，职业教育正处于数字化转型的关键时期，我认为应该通过三种途径去应对职业教育面临的挑战和变革。

第一，数字技术教育应成为职业教育的基础教育。今天，数字化几乎已成为所有行业的外在表达，没有哪个行业不是以数字技术来驱动变革的行业。数字技术已经成为所有职业岗位在未来发展过程中十分依赖的一个基本知识和技能，所以职业教育应该把数字技术教育当作一个基础性的教育，在人才培养的各个环节，融入对学生数字素养和技能培养的相关内容。

第二，用数字技术推动职业教育的均衡发展。目前，我国已建成全世界规模最大的职业教育体系，全国职业院校共开设 12 余万个专业点，基本覆盖了国民经济的各个领域。不同的地理区域、不同的专业方向、不同的师资水平以及不同的产教融合深度及广度，使广大职业院校之间存在着较大的发展不均衡。我认为要通过教育科技的发展为职业教育赋能，构建智能、高效、规范的智慧教育平台，建设优质数字化教育教学资源，打造网络化、数字化、个性化、终身化的教育体系，积极探索数字教育的新机制、新模式、新形态，实现更科学、更高效、更精准的教学质量及学习效果评价，创造学生价值，实现职业教育的均衡发展。

第三，职业教育要与产业和市场更充分的对接融合。近年来，职业变化如此之快，新的职业不断涌现。与此同时，社会上对一些传统职业的需求在缩小，甚至一些职业在逐渐消失。随着数字经济的快速发展，当各行各业都在不断改变的时候，职业教育对技术革新、产业变革，对市场需求的洞察和认知就变得十分重要。如果说教育是创造学生的价值，任何一个教育机构在创造学生价值的过程中，最重要也是最高的选择就是如何理解未来社会对人才需求的结构、数量及人才的规格，并适时更新专业人才培养方案、教学内容和教学方法，使得职业院校的人才培养能更好地与时代同步、与产业对接。

东软集团是从大学里走出来的企业，依靠东北大学提供的人才支撑，从 3 个人发展到今天 2 万人的规模，主要得益于过去我们与东北大学人才培养的紧密融合。在这个融合的过程中，我们深刻地体会到教育赋予东软集团的强劲生命力。为了更好地回馈教育、回馈社会，我们依托产业背景，聚焦数字技术相关专业及健康医疗科技类专业，又创办了自己的大学。截至目前，在大连、成都、佛山建立的 3 所信息技术应用型大学在校生已超过 4.5 万人，累计为社会输送数字技术相关人才已超过 12 万人。

因为我们重视与产业、市场的紧密对接，重视在教学过程中采用特色教育方法论的引导，重视数字技术对教学实施和质量评价的支撑，使得 3 所大学的教师能够在一个标准的体系下完成混合式教学的全过程，更精准度量学生的学习过程，推动教育教学质量的不断提升。

我认为今天的职业教育迎来了发展的最好时期，应该随着数字技术的渗透和应用而发生根本性的变革。期望通过本次大会与更多的同仁互相学习、深入交流，在大家的共同努力下，共同开创职业教育美好的明天！

# （十三）

# 数智时代的职业教育

微软（中国）有限公司首席技术官　韦　青

“信息就是信息，它既不是能量也不是物质。”《控制论》一书的作者诺伯特·维纳在其书中指出，随着以电子计算机和通信技术为代表的现代科技的普及，信息将扮演与物质与能量同等重要的作用。农业社会的主要生产力要素是围绕着物质建立起来的；在工业社会，能量与机械成为新的生产力要素；而在后工业时代，也就是人们通常说的信息时代或者数智时代，人类即将迈入以信息为主导的智能社会。尽管信息化、数字化、智能化已经成为人们的口头禅，但是从我们在职场的经历与观察而言，信息的强大功效尚未能为大众所理解，例如，人们经常有对于信息化与数字化之间关系的不同解读以及对信息金字塔 D—I—K—W（数据—信息—知识—智能）的模糊理解。在此，我们会依据信息论的理论与大家简单分享信息在时代发展中所起到的关键作用。理解了信息时代的特征与信息的作用，就能更好地理解如何培养能够充分发挥信息力量的职业人才。

无论我们想培养何种职业人才，教育的首要目的是培养符合时代特征并具有基本人类素养的人才，而信息化时代需要的是能够理解信息与使用信息的人才。

数字时代的职业人士需要具备最基本的信息获取、分析、判断、理解与使用的能力。按照曾获得图灵奖和诺贝尔奖的经济学、管理学与人工智能科学专家司马贺（赫伯特·西蒙）的理论，在这个信息极度泛滥的年代，同时也是关注度极度缺乏以及真相极易丧失的年代，无论从事什么职业，都需要具备依据正确的信息作出正确决策的能力。获取真实和有价值的信息是跨职业、跨行业的职场必备技能。但是这种技能如同马歇尔·麦克卢汉在他的著作中指出，在信息被电子化之后，已经变成了需要经过专门的训练才可以获得的技能。因此，无论从事什么职业，在这个信息时代，每一个职业人士都需要重新培养对于信息理解的能力。

在工业时代，机器的机械能力已经逐步取代了人类的肌肉力量，而这一轮依赖数据、算力和算法的智能机器也将逐步减轻人类大脑的计算负担，按照信息金字塔D—I—K—W的描述，未来的职业人士不仅仅是要掌握基本的数字化信息技术，更重要的是以人类特有的智慧掌握应用智能机器的能力。如果以百年前电气化发展的路径作为参考，在电气化早期，职业能力关注点是围绕着电力的生成；当电力普及之后，全社会的发展重心就转移到如何利用电力来改造人类社会最基本的衣食住行的实现方式。目前，对于信息技术的关注和职业能力的培养，大多还局限在最基本的掌握信息技术能力的层面，但是随着信息技术慢慢普及之后，社会发展的关注点必然会回归人类社会最基本的衣食住行方式的转型与提高。这就需要职业能力的培养，从单纯的信息技术能力发展到使用信息技术改造人类社会的能力。这种职业能力需求的变化既微妙，又有本质的区别，它要求职业教育的关注点从教育学生拥有某种信息技术能力，转向教育学生如何利用这种技术能力来改造人类社会的基本形态。由于这种人类社会形态因信息技术而实现的改造是长期的，所以要求职业教育是终身的教育。如同百年前，人们对电一开始关注的只是发电和利用电的照明，经历了几十年发电的竞争之后，社会所需要的人才变成用电的人才，人类慢慢开始关注如何设计出用电驱动的冰箱、洗衣机、电视机等电器，直到如今非常热门的汽车电动化和智能化。因此，我们现在培养的人才是能够利用信息化技术对社会各个方面的形态进行彻底改造的人才，以最终进入一个智能的时代。

上述因信息技术的发展而对社会基本形态的改造，也会作用于职业教育的形式本身。未来的职业教育不仅是终身的职业教育，同时也是无时无刻不被信息技术赋能的虚拟与现实相结合的职业教育。教育的场所不再仅限于教室、实验室、车间、病房或者农田等物理性现场，未来的职业教育是虚拟与现实共存的无时无刻不在的职业教育，这意味着职业教育同时面临着内容与形式两方面的改造。

总而言之，在这个数智时代，职业教育首先是终身的，然后是需要回到第一性原理的，同时是无时无刻、随时随地都能够提供的泛在而又公平的和以“知行合一”方式实现的职业教育。

上述看似长远的职业教育愿景，将由于信息技术的快速进步与普及，成为现实，我们需要及早为此做好准备。

# （十四）

# 项目化教学在数字技能人才培养方面的思考与实践

科大讯飞股份有限公司联合创始人、安徽信息工程学院董事长　陈　涛

今天和大家分享如何用项目化教学的方式培养数字技能人才。

首先，我想刻画一下数字经济发展的三个特点。第一，技术正在日新月异地发展，这意味着教材中的成熟技术知识，待学生学到时可能已经过时或者是已经没有足够的新奇了。第二，数字场景应用的丰富度已经远远超过了我们的想象，包括像科大讯飞这种人工智能龙头企业也很难准确预测和规划下一步的应用场景热点。在这种情况下，企业该怎样规划数字技能人才和岗位成为关键问题。第三，我们现在培养出来的学生，他们就业的方向具有非常强的多样性，以科大讯飞为例，在智慧教育领域除了招聘研发工程师之外，还引进了很多师范类学生和教师，可能他们原先也没有规划过要进入科技型企业任职。因此，大家会发现数字经济发展的特点导致了技术手段不断更新迭代、应用场景不断丰富、学生就业方向更加多样化，职业教育面临着如何精准培养的问题。

在数字经济发展的时代，企业在招聘员工时，有着良好的职业技能或知识仅仅是“敲门砖”，我们更希望员工或者是学生具备能够应对变化的基本能力。因为无论是技术手段的变化还是应用场景的变化，只要能快速适应变化，那么对于社会、企业乃至其个人来说，都会带来正向的效果。那么变化的能力应当就是能力模型冰山之下的——正视问题、面对问题、解决问题等能力。

企业是把项目制引进到运营管理的体系中去，以项目的方式把企业的经营目标和活动进行分装，如销售项目管理、产品研发项目管理、交付项目管理等。因此，当员工需要进入项目的时候，我们会对其能力进行评估，评估结果如果有差距，就指定导师对其进行培训和培养。员工也拥有了进入到多个项目发展能力的机会，这

种即学即用、按需培养的方式就企业经营来说是最有效的。而不是像以前传统的方式一样，统一进行大规模人员培训，现在大规模培训主要是文化价值观和基本制度等方面。

安徽信息工程学院是经教育部、安徽省人民政府批准设立，由科大讯飞全资举办、安徽省教育厅主管的民办高校。自 2012 年科大讯飞主导办学以来进行了大胆的教育教学改革，把项目制这种企业经营和人才培养的方式引入学校的教育教学中，目前已经取得了良好的效果。项目制教学是在教育领域被大家谈论很多的话题，我们认为，项目制教学是教学手段的一次更新，比如会把原先课程的目标用项目化的方式进行分装之后，再以项目管理的方式来实现。但实际上从数字经济发展的角度来说，教育目标、教学目标和课程方式其实都会进行系统性的变化。只有意识到了这三个方面的变化，才能够用项目制的方式真正培养能够应对外界变化的人才。

因此，在数字技能人才项目化的培养过程中，我们认为要注意三个适应性的特点。如果项目制教学的这三个适应性特点没有展现出来，那么是无法实现前面所提的教学目标的。第一个是项目目标的适应性，不再维持几年不变的教育项目目标，而是这一次的目标是在之前的基础之上发展新的目标。第二个是技术路径的适应性，鼓励学生学习以及利用崭新、创新的方式去解决新的问题。第三个是教师成长的适应性，我们希望教师应该与时俱进。教师要从原先依托通用的培养体系去培养学生，变成是在培养体系中完成个人的职业目标，与学生共同成长。同时，还要用项目制的方式去培养学生的创新精神。

目前，我们正在和三十多所学院合作共建人工智能产业学院，把持续更新的人工智能技术打包成人工智能实验室，然后通过项目制教学的方式共同培养面向未来的、能够适应变化的数字技能人才。展望未来，我们也真切期盼能够立足于新发展阶段，坚持产教融合，通过“人工智能 +”和“项目 +”双轮驱动的方式，与更多的院校通力合作，为我国数字经济的发展贡献更多人才。

## （十五）

# 5G 时代呼唤泛行业数字化人才生态繁荣

华为技术有限公司培训服务专家委员会主任　钟美华

我非常荣幸代表华为公司与大家分享我们对 5G 时代泛行业数字化人才的理解。

5G 将构建一张满足人们、社区、经济和社会需求的网络，同时催生各行业业务创新，深入行业深度场景，催熟产业链，加速行业和社会的数字化转型。5G 具有社会性、行业性和系统性，本质是数字基础设施，与新兴数字技术和行业应用相结合，成为产业升级的催化剂、运营商和行业的撮合者，改变了行业的连接方式和推动组织能力的转变。与此同时，5G 跨界跨域运作、融合发展的特点，要求产业运营模式重新思考工作界面、优化业务价值流，将持续催生海量懂行业和数字化技术的复合型人才需求。5G 带来新的就业机会，5G 数字化人才的争夺加剧，急需新的人才管理模式和培养方式。

未来，运营商会将其信息与通信技术网络运营深度开放给行业企业，运营商与行业利用泛在平台连接渗透，并触及核心运作领域的开放，利用 5G 及相关技术共同对生产设施进行数字化改造。行业和运营商各自的平台通过 5G 网络连接，能够直接交互来创造新的技术、产品或服务，形成泛行业互联网。与消费互联网不同，行业互联网的价值链非常长，需要参与者共生、共创和共享，从而产生了新的运营模式，即“去中心平台化业务”。这一模式势必深刻改变社会和行业的运作管理方式和带来新的关键活动及其承担的职能角色。

未来，期望企业在 5G 泛行业生态中实现业务创新。跨行业、跨企业间的能力和技术差距是很大的，也意味着我们面临如何突破技术壁垒、跨越鸿沟，如何能让通用信息与通信技术和行业运营技术融合起来的问题，答案就是实现新的管理模式，需要在跨行业和跨企业的管理上实现创新，促进跨团队、跨组织、跨部门之间的融合。

对于技术人员和专家的能力画像，我们提出了一个梯子π模型，根据业务复杂性和网络专网等需求的灵活性，会带来更多的技术领域的跨域以及管理类、创新类等软能力的需求，从底层逻辑视角，看复合能力的整合，需要 DOICT（DT 数据技术、OT 运营技术、ZT 信息技术、CT 通信技术）的技术跨域的融合贯通能力和软能力的结构化整合，以形成支撑多样性的业务场景实现能力。

岗位角色变化：新技能需要新岗位，将传统角色分解、重组和扩展，加入新技能元素，成为复合型岗位角色。复合型岗位需要组织以新的方式来思考和设计其工作，需要重新诠释工作。因而在重新设计工作和岗位时，需要将人的工作特长与机器和平台结合起来，以支撑场景化应用落地。

人才类型变化：新技术为组织带来三类新复合型人才类型，需要业务与技术融合的技能，包括赋能型人才，负责对内对外的沟通、协调、推动和组织等职责。权威用户性人才，参与基于平台资产的业务能力设计与开发、集成与部署、组装与调测。专家型人才，规划平台资产能力，构建在平台上供调用，解决问题，创造价值。

举个例子，现在培养的技术专业人才，将来不一定就是成为技术工人，他也会走到前端做市场，这部分人群需求应被识别出来。同时，未来的数字化的转型，需要更多的专家把这个能力固化在数字化平台中。同时，我们也可以看到，在未来技术专业人才的能力需要跨领域、跨行业、跨企业之间进行互通，那我们职业教育培养的就不仅仅是技术工人。

数字孪生本质是数字显性化物理世界，5G、云、大数据、人工智能加速产业快速发展，在整个数字化转型的未来和生存空间里，大家可以看到从一个物理空间到一个数字空间，动态时代呼唤人才管理新哲学。数字化人才发展管理模式发生了变化，首先，由“人力资源量的规划”到“人才能力质的识别”的规划方式的转型。其次，“拥有人才”到“人才为我所用”的使用模式的转变。最后，“于经验的被动学习”到“基于知识系统的主动学习”的发展模式的转型。

数字化时代，组织发展与转型的策略为技术与组织能力兼顾，统筹识别环境、战略、结构和运营四维力量。

未来，基于数字化人才需求洞察，深度理解行业“人器业”数字化人才转型框架。从“人器业”看数字化转型意图动力、新业务模式对组织和人的能力要求、新技术对组织和人的能力要求。

未来，会有更多的不确定性的业务和需求，那就会对人才培养的方向产生一些思考，未来的学习者不仅仅是在校的学生，还有企业里大量的技能升级人员。同时，我们要考虑学习如何转化，我们的学习时间和空间如何与具体工作联系在一起，这也是从被动学习到主动学习的发展。

未来，5G 专业知识的受众将逐渐从设备商、集成开发商、运营商的网络技术维度，扩展到构筑“端 / 网 / 云 / 边”的运维运营能力；从产品和服务运营扩展到基于生态和行业的运营能力。基于新基建，生态和行业需要更多企业参与人才培养，具体体现在院校学科和产学研需求也将蓬勃发展。对此，提出两大举措助力 5G 未来人才培养。首先，华为希望贡献出自己的 5G 数字化使能的学习平台，把最核心的课程和师资、数字化学习平台以及数据运营经验交互分享给整个 5G 数字化生态；其次，面对运营商和行业人才数字化，将提供面向公众的专业认证、职业认证。未来，我们将共建一个数字化人才的生态，助力职业教育共建共赢共享。

# （十六）

# 人才为本建筑人才培养数字化转型正当时

广联达科技股份有限公司党委书记、董事、高级副总裁　刘　谦

数字经济浪潮奔涌向前，数字科技推动各行各业步入数字经济新时代，以数字化转型整体驱动生产方式、生活方式和治理方式的变革已是大势所趋。传统建筑产业面临着新的挑战与机遇，如何通过数字化实现行业高质量发展，已成为整个行业必须思考的重要课题。蓬勃发展的信息技术是破题关键，BIM（建筑信息模型）、云计算、大数据、物联网、人工智能、移动技术等为代表的新兴技术正与建筑产业深度融合，建筑产业转型升级大幕已经拉开。

从传统建筑产业的全要素、全过程、全参与方进行解构，再通过数字化、在线化、智能化进行重构，构建以新设计、新建造、新运维为代表的“三新”生产力，从而实现提质增效、降本节耗的产业转型升级目标，这将是未来建筑产业转型高质量发展的方向。

数字化是“十四五”期间建筑产业转型升级、实现绿色低碳发展的重要基础战略。中国建筑产业转型升级，最关键的不是数字化技术本身，而是借助数字化的技术手段，实现传统企业的管理升级和人才升级。以数字技术打造建筑产业数字化“人才基建”，是建筑产业高质量发展的基础，而完善现代教育体系，培养职业教育高素质人才是这一基础的重要组成部分。

职业教育肩负着培养多样人才、传承技术技能、促进就业创业的重要职责。2021 年，全国职业教育大会上，习近平总书记强调：“加快构建现代职业教育体系，培养更多高素质技术技能人才、能工巧匠、大国工匠。”这为实现职业教育提质增效指明了方向。

当前，行业最大的问题是人才供给与需求的不平衡，人才供给的数量及数字化能力质量均不能满足需求。落实到具体人才培养中，就需要学校适当扩大智能建

造、建筑信息化技术等专业的招生规模，明确专业培养目标，全方位培养技术研发、设计、施工、生产、管理等方面的建筑专业和数字技术专业的复合型人才。

在培养不同方向的数字建筑人才方面，要运用数字化工具与数字化平台以及快速迭代的应用场景，持续优化岗位能力，聚焦深化不同发展需要。其中，推动教育链、人才链、产业链、创新链“四链”融合是关键。在推动教育链、人才链发展时，同步构建行业生态体系；在打通产业链、创新链的同时，产业的新需求又会倒逼行业共同构建教育生态体系。未来，人才链的终极目标是“多快好省”的供给模式，即人才数量充足、质量有保障、供应及时、招聘成本低。

想要实现“四链”融合发展，以数字技术打造建筑产业数字化“人才基建”是必由之路，需要将课程内容、教学方式、工作现场、管理方式等各环节进行数字化。在人才供给侧，学校应充分利用数字化技术和手段，统筹做好专业安排、课程设置、教学设计以及教学质量把控，努力搭建起供给教学者与需求管理者沟通交流的桥梁。在需求方面，企业应将智慧工地的真实场景与高校实验室连接，将其变成线上真实的实训室，服务于教学实践与人才培养。

在打造建筑产业数字化“人才基建”的建设实践中，广联达携手政产学研等生态组织，紧跟产业政策、行业标准，围绕人、课、场、法、管五个纬度实践数字化教学；融合产业新设计、新建造、新运维的数字建筑新要求，打造贯穿“备、教、练、考、评”教学全流程的课程体系，并围绕“学、做、教、展、研”建设数字化综合实践中心、数字孪生实践中心、建筑工业化实践中心、人机协同实践中心等，全方位实现数字建筑人才培养。

建筑行业职业教育高素质人才培养是一项系统工程，当下的人才需求正从单一专业型转变为融合数字化的多元技能复合型人才。产业各方唯有通力合作，建立生态共赢融合发展的新范式，才能真正破解行业高素质职业人才短缺难题，更好地服务于建筑行业转型升级和高质量发展。

# 三

# 可持续发展背景下的全球绿色技能战略论坛

协助组织单位：中华人民共和国教育部职业教育发展中心

# Ⅲ. Green Skill Strategy for Sustainable Development

Co-organizer: Center for Vocational Education Development, Ministry of Education, P. R. China (CVED)

01
刘育锋
Liu Yufeng

02
彭斌柏
Peng Binbai

03
李昌徽
Changhee Lee

04
夏泽翰
Shahbaz Khan

05
孔海德
Harald Kumpfert

06
阿斯丽汗 · 阿利玟
Aslihan Arikan

07
玛格丽塔 · 帕夫洛娃
Magarita Parluva

08
菲尔 · 洛夫德
Phil Loveder

09
曾天山
Zeng Tianshan

10
辛秀兰
Xin Xiulan

11
梁克东
Liang Kedong

12
张萨萨
Zhang Sasa

13
刘宝民
Liu Baomin

**围绕全球可持续发展目标，确立绿色职教理念，分享绿色技能开发的国际经验，形成国际职业教育绿色发展的模式，倡导职业教育领域可持续发展行动。**

This session calls for the establishment of the concept of green VTE in line with the Global Sustainable Development Goals. The participants share experience in green skill development, work out the pattern of green development for global VTE, and encourage actions for sustainable development in VTE.

## (一)

# 可持续发展背景下的全球绿色技能战略论坛情况概述

中华人民共和国教育部职业教育发展中心研究员、联合国教科文组织高级项目专家　刘育锋

可持续发展背景下的全球绿色技能战略论坛于 2022 年 8 月 20 日下午成功举办。来自国际劳工组织、联合国开发计划署、联合国教科文组织、世界银行、澳大利亚、德国、土耳其、英国、中国的官员、专家、行业代表和院校代表，通过线上、线下方式参会。会议主题新颖，内容深入，既反映了国际社会发展总体趋势，又体现了我国职业教育改革发展的具体要求。会议围绕绿色技能开发的必要性、内

涵、类型、开发方法和实践经验等内容进行探索，达成了多方共识。

首届世界职业教育发展大会将“可持续发展背景下的全球绿色技能战略”作为十四个平行论坛之一，对于加深职业教育开发绿色技能重大意义的认识，明确绿色技能的内涵、类型、开发路径和开发方法，对于建立和加强国内外同行在绿色技能开发方面及案例合作伙伴关系，共同努力为职业教育更好地促进社会可持续发展具有重大意义。

#### 1. 绿色技能开发的诉求

发言嘉宾从资源不足与浪费、环境破坏、国际倡导与承诺、新环境标准引入以及客户选择偏好等方面，阐述了绿色技能的必要性。

（1）新技术、新职业和经济发展绿色转型。技术进步，新职业出现，旧职业消亡，经济发展方式转变，要求培育大量掌握绿色技能的人才。目前，经济发展方式不具可持续性。土耳其包装制造商协会秘书长阿斯丽汗·阿利坎介绍，新冠病毒疫情期间，全球电商快速增长导致严重的包装浪费问题。联合国教科文组织国际职业技术教育培训中心绿色技能开发项目助理贾科莫·博西奥同样认为当前的经济活动不具可持续性。

经济发展要向绿色转型，要求就职者掌握新技能。联合国教科文组织驻华代表处主任夏泽翰提出，向低碳、资源节约型经济转型需要系统性变革，不仅会带来新产品和新服务，还会带来生产流程和商业模式变革。联合国开发计划署驻华代表处常驻副代表乔展介绍，新冠病毒疫情后大批人员丢失工作。国际劳工组织中国和蒙古国局局长李昌徽介绍，未来全球绿色经济可能创造超过 1 亿个新绿色工作岗位，需要有足够的人才从事这些岗位工作。

绿色工作要求掌握专业性绿色技能。绿色工作有很多，新能源相关岗位是其中之一。英国汽车工业协会全球技能大使赫伯特·朗斯代尔介绍，新能源车正在发生深刻变化，需要培养更多高技能人才，教师是关键。澳大利亚国家职业教育研究中心执行经理菲尔·洛夫德也提出新能源产业发展对技能的要求。

经济绿色转型，大量绿色工作出现，要求人们掌握绿色技能，全面建设培养绿色技能的职业技术教育与培训体系。

（2）可持续发展议程及相关承诺。为推进可持续发展，2015 年联合国发布可持续发展议程，多国签署了巴黎协议，包括国际劳工组织在内的国际组织以及一些国家发布或签署了可持续发展相关协议或做出相关承诺，其中，绿色技能开发是重要内容。

中华人民共和国教育部职业教育发展中心副主任曾天山介绍了我国国家发展规划中提出的将绿色理念融入全方面全过程的要求。可持续发展是我国社会发展的理念、路径与目标。《中华人民共和国国民经济和社会发展“九五”计划和2010年远景目标纲要》提出“实施可持续发展战略”，“十五”到“十三五”国家发展规划提出“要提高我国持续发展能力”“建设资源节约型、环境友好型社会”目标，遵循绿色发展理念。《中华人民共和国国民经济和社会发展第十四个五年规划和2035年远景目标纲要》中则提出了更高要求，要“把新发展理念完整、准确、全面贯穿发展全过程和各领域，实现更高质量、更有效率、更加公平、更可持续、更为安全的发展”。

（3）环境标准引入行业。为促进可持续发展，很多行业都引入了环境标准。菲尔·洛夫德提出，为节约资源，在包括建筑和电力在内的行业，引入了新的环境标准，并进行了立法。

（4）客户选择和偏好。菲尔·洛夫德还提出，客户选择绿色产品的要求也是要求开发绿色技能的原因之一。

### 2. 绿色技能相关概念与类型

国际社会提出了不同的绿色技能内涵，对绿色技能也进行了不同的分类，但均包括环境保护和促进可持续发展方面所需要的知识、技能、价值和态度内容。

夏泽翰提到，绿色技能是生活、发展和支持可持续和资源节约型社会所需的知识、能力、价值观和态度。菲尔·洛夫德介绍了澳大利亚国家职业教育研究中心对绿色技能提出的定义：绿色技能是“劳动力在企业、行业和社区中促进和支持可持续社会、经济和环境结果而需要的技术技能、知识、价值和态度”。

在分析多种观点的基础上，教育部职业教育发展中心提出，绿色技能是可持续发展技能，它指劳动力支持并促进工商业和社区可持续的社会、经济发展和环境友好而需要的技术、知识、价值和态度。联合国教科文组织职业技术教育中心（香港）主任玛格丽塔·帕夫洛娃则介绍了绿色技能的第三种类型，即补充技能。

### 3. 绿色技能开发方法

绿色技能开发方法包括宏观、中观和微观层面，国际组织通过指导性文件制定、设置专门项目以及通过将绿色技能要素融入资格和课程标准等方式而开发绿色技能。

（1）发布指导或建议文件。制定并发布指导性文件是多个国际组织的共同做法。包括国际劳工组织、联合国教科文组织等国际组织均发布了绿色技能开发相关文件，为各国开发绿色技能提供咨询指导。

李昌徽提到，国际劳工组织 2022 年制定了《绿化技术与职业教育和培训及技能开发——实践指南》。国际劳工组织 2018 年发布的《绿色未来的职业技能——中国研究报告》，为我国的绿色技能开发提出了建议。

多年来，绿色技能均是联合国教科文组织和联合国教科文职业技术教育中心的重点倡导内容，贾科莫·博西奥介绍了绿色技能开发的五个维度，包括绿化校园、绿化课程和培训、绿化社区、绿化研究、绿化校园文化。

（2）执行绿色技能开发相关项目。设立专门项目或与有关机构合作执行项目，促进绿色技能开发。

国际劳工组织独立或与相关机构共同执行了多个绿色技能开发项目，如绿化技术与职教教育和培训及技能开发项目、南非能源技能项目等。世界银行执行了获得更好教育结果的制度方法的研究项目。联合国教科文组织职业技术教育中心将绿色技能作为工作重点，设立了绿色技能开发的专门项目。

曾天山介绍了教育部职业教育发展中心牵头执行的 APEC 项目“职业教育系统开发绿色技能”的成果，包括通过职业分析，基于经济、环境和社会三个要素，操作、技术和管理三个维度，开发出十二条通用性绿色技能内容。

（3）将绿色技能融入教学。绿色技能开发在实践中付诸实施，不同国家和地区有不同做法，但一般体现在专业设置、教学标准、课程内容等方面。

菲尔·洛夫德介绍了澳大利亚绿色技能开发的主要做法，培训包是澳大利亚教学标准开发的指导性文件，绿色技能内容是培训包所有专业所有层级的必要内容。

中国通过专业目录调整、教学标准改革，以促进绿色技能开发。2021 年新颁布的《职业教育专业目录》新增了很多新的绿色专业。中职和高职专业教学标准的教学目标中，均提出了环境保护内容。中国职业院校在实践过程中，也注重绿色技能开发工作，并形成了一定的特色，如梁克东校长介绍了金华职业技术学院通过开发活页式教材、打造多样式平台、开展浸润式活动进行绿色技能开发；辛秀兰副院长介绍了北京电子科技职业学院开发专业性绿色技能和通用性绿色技能的做法，并结合专业开展校园活动，降低教学污染，营造绿色学习氛围，培养学生绿色技能。张萨萨副院长则介绍了海南省技师学院立足海南生态立省省情，通过五育并举、产教融合、世赛引领、绿色校园的方式开发绿色技能的做法。玛格丽塔·帕夫洛娃将绿色技能研究成果落实到具体教学内容，如开发学生工作单、教师指南以及通用绿色模块。

（4）绿色技能开发的系统方法。联合国教科文组织总部政策与终身学习系统部主任博仁·沙克龙提出绿色技能开发要考虑五个维度和四个步骤。五个维度分别为：政策、课程、教学、认证以及监管和评估。四个步骤包括：与企业的合作、教学人员能力的提升、开发绿色技能框架并支持开发教育资源以及通过使用网络和平台共享。在职业教育机构层面，贾科莫·博西奥提到要系统开发绿色技能，包括绿色校园、绿色课程、绿色社区、绿色研究和绿色文化五个方面。

世界银行驻华代表处高级教育专家肖丽萍介绍了世界银行“促进绿色、韧性和包容性发展模式”，重点关注能源、农业、粮食、水、土地、交通、城市和制造系统的转型，用投资风险管理预防和应对气候变化、流行病、自然灾害、社会经济和金融冲击，促进包容，减少差异。

梳理论坛嘉宾发言可以得出如下结论。

（1）绿色技能开发是职业教育促进可持续发展的关键内容。绿色技能开发是实现联合国可持续发展议程 2030 目标的重要举措。需要开发专业性绿色技能，增进人们在绿色职业中的就业；需要开发通用性绿色技能，使所有人都具有节约资源、保护环境的意识和技能，并转化为行动，人人成为促进可持续社会发展的绿色公民。

（2）绿色技能开发是国际社会共同关注的重要热点问题。此次论坛，多个国家和国际组织都非常关注可持续发展和绿色技能开发内容。中国实施可持续发展战略，要求将绿色理念融入发展的全过程全方面。绿色技能开发，也须成为中国职业教育服务国家可持续发展战略的重要方面。

（3）一些国际组织和国家已经形成绿色技能开发成果。一些国际组织已经发布了绿色技能开发指南，将绿色技能开发与社会发展进行整体设计并形成了模式。一些国家将绿色技能内容融入教学标准和课程。中国通过研究也提出了绿色技能通用内容清单，一些院校在绿色技能开发方面进行了积极探索并形成了特色做法。

（4）在将来很长一段时间内，绿色技能依然是国际社会职业教育的重点内容。虽然取得了一定的成果，但总体说来，在绿色技能开发方面，还应进一步全方面全过程融入绿色理念，并系统性开发绿色技能，同时综合考虑经济、环境和社会要素对绿色技能开发的要求，形成对职业教育开发绿色技能的要求或激励机制。为激发职业教育服务可持续发展的潜力，更好地促进经济绿色转型，建议如下：系统开发，将绿色技能融入职业教育的全方面和全过程；形成机制，将绿色技能内容列入职业教育相关标准或指标；完善内容，将绿色技能通用清单融入所有专业；提升能力，开发职业教育教师绿色技能；服务社区，职业教育教师和学生成为绿色转型的促进者；加强国际合作与交流，互鉴互学，贡献中国方案。

职业教育开发绿色技能，既体现了国际社会职业教育的发展趋势，也彰显了中国职业教育改革的具体要求。有必要加大对职业教育开发绿色技能的支持力度，使职业教育为促进经济绿色转型进而促进可持续社会的发展作出更为积极的贡献。

# i. Overview of the Session on Green Skill Strategy for Sustainable Development

**Liu Yufeng, Researcher of Center for Vocational Education Development, Ministry of Education, P.R. China (CVED), Senior Programme Specialist UNESCO**

The Session on Green Skill Strategy for Sustainable Development ("the Session") was successfully held in the afternoon of August 20, 2022. Officials, experts, industry representatives and college representatives from Australia, Germany, Türkiye, the UK, and China as well as organizations such as the International Labour Organization (ILO), the United Nations Development Programme (UNDP), the United Nations Educational, Scientific and Cultural Organization (UNESCO), the World Bank, etc., attended the session online or offline. Featuring novel topics and in-depth content, the session revealed the overall development trend of the international community, and meanwhile reflected the specific demands that have to be met in the reform and development of vocational education in China. It ended with consensus among the attendants based on explorations into types of green skills and the necessity, implications, methods and know-how of green skill development.

The session, as one of the 14 parallel sessions under the 2022 World Vocational and Technical Education Development Conference, helps deepen people's awareness of how important it is to develop green skills in the vocational education community and gain insights into the implications and types of and ways to develop green skills. Building on that, the session will fuel the development and strengthening of Chinese and foreign stakeholders' partnerships and joint efforts of green skills development, and enable vocational education to better drive the sustainable development of society.

## 1. Demands for green skills development

The guest speakers addressed the necessity of green skills from the perspectives of resource shortage and waste, environmental damage, international initiatives and undertakings, and the introduction of new environmental standards and customer preferences.

(1) New technologies, new occupations and the green transformation of economic development models

Numerous talents with green skills are required amid technological progress, the emergence of new occupations, the disappearance of old occupations and the green transformation of economic development models. Current economic development models are unsustainable. The rapid growth of global e-commerce has led to serious problems of packaging waste during the ongoing COVID-19 pandemic, according to Aslihan Arikan, General Secretary of Turkish Packaging Manufacturers Association (ASD), Türkiye. The unsustainability of current economic activities was also mentioned by Giacomo Bosio, Assistant of Green Skills Project of UNEVOC (UNESCO International Centre for Technical and Vocational Education and Training).

The green transformation of economic development models requires workers to have new skills. The transformation into low-carbon, resource-efficient economic models, which entails systemic reform, will not only deliver new products and services, but also lead to reforms in production procedures and business models, said Shahbaz Khan, Director of the UNESCO Beijing Office. James George, UNDP Deputy Resident Representative in China, mentioned that numerous people lost their jobs after the outbreak of the COVID-19 pandemic. Changhee Lee, Director of ILO Country Office for China and Mongolia, stated that the global green economy may create more than 100 million new green jobs, for which sufficient talents must be trained.

Green jobs require professional green skills. New energy-related jobs are among the big pool of green jobs. Teachers hold the key to training more high-skilled personnel to adapt to the profound change New Energy Vehicles are undergoing, said Herbert Lonsdale, Global Skills Ambassador for the Institute of the Motor Industry (IMI), UK. Phil Loveder, Executive Manager of National Centre for Vocational Education Research (NCVER), Australia also described the requirements of the new energy industry for skills.

As a multitude of green jobs emerge amid the green transformation of economy, it is essential to fully build a TVET system that develops people's green skills.

(2) *2030 Agenda for Sustainable Development* and related undertakings

The United Nations (UN) published *2030 Agenda for Sustainable Development* as a means to fuel sustainable development, in 2015. Accordingly, many countries signed *Paris Agreement*, and international organizations like ILO and some countries signed agreements or gave undertakings concerning sustainable development. Green skills development plays an important part in such agreements and undertakings.

In his speech, Zeng Tianshan, Vice Director of Center for Vocational Education Development, Ministry of Education, P.R.China (CVED), introduced a requirement imposed in China's national development plans: the philosophy of green development must be followed throughout the whole process and across all aspects of development.

Sustainable development represents the philosophy, path and objective of social development in China. *Outline of the 9th Five-Year Plan for National Economic and Social Development and Vision 2010 of the People's Republic of China* stated that the country must "implement the sustainable development strategy" for the first time. Thereafter, the 10th, 11th, 12th and 13th Five-Year Plan called for improving the country's "capacity for continuous development", and set the goal of "building a resource-efficient environment-friendly society", to follow the philosophy of green development. Furthermore, higher requirements were imposed in *Outline of the 14th Five-Year Plan for National Economic and Social Development and Vision 2035 of the People's Republic of China*: the country must "ensure" the new development philosophy "is applied in full, in both letter and spirit, in every stage and aspect of development" to "achieve higher-quality development that is more efficient, equitable, sustainable, and secure".

(3) Introduction of environmental standards into industries

Many industries have introduced environmental standards to fuel sustainable development. To save resources, various industries including the construction and power industries have introduced new environmental standards and adopted legislation, said Phil Loveder.

(4) Customer choices and preferences

Customers' tendency to choose green products is also a factor that makes developing green skills a must-do, Phil Loveder added.

**2. Relevant concepts and types of green skills**

While different members of the international community have proposed different implications and types of green skills, it is agreed that green skills cover the knowledge, skills, values and attitudes necessary for environmental protection and sustainable development.

Green skills refer to the knowledge, abilities, values and attitudes needed to live in, develop and support a sustainable and resource-efficient society, said Shahbza Khan. In contrast, as Phil Loveder said, NCVER defines green skills as "the technological skills, knowledge, values and attitudes needed to fuel and support sustainable social, economic and environmental achievements across enterprises, industries and communities".

Based on an analysis of multiple viewpoints, CVED described green skills as sustainable development skills, which refer to the technologies, knowledge, values and attitudes laborers must have to support and promote sustainable socio-economic development and environmental friendliness in industrial and commercial enterprises and communities. In her speech, Margarita Pavlova, Director of the UNESCO-UNEVOC Centre (Hong Kong), introduced the third type of green skills, namely topping-up skills.

3. Methods for green skills development

Methods for green skills development include macro-level, meso-level and micro-level methods. International organizations develop green skills by preparing instructive documents, establishing special projects and integrating factors of green skills into qualification and curriculum standards.

(1) Issuing instructive or suggestive documents

Preparing and issuing instructive documents is an approach shared by multiple international organizations. For example, both ILO and UNESCO have issued documents concerning green skills development, as a way to instruct various countries to develop green skills.

As mentioned by Changhee Lee, ILO prepared *Greening TVET and Skills Development—A practical guidance tool* in 2022; *Skills for a Greener Future—China Report*, issued by ILO in 2018, provides suggestions on green skills development in China.

Green skills have been prioritized by UNESCO and UNESCO-UNEVOC in their advocating efforts for many years. As Giacomo Bosio said in his speech, green skills development covers five dimensions: green campuses, green curriculum and training, green communities, green studies, and green campus culture.

(2) Implementing green skills development projects

Establishing special projects or working with other organizations to implement projects is also a method for green skills development.

ILO has independently implemented or worked with other organizations to implement multiple green skills development projects, such as "Greening TVET and Skills Development" and "Skills for Energy in Southern Africa". The World Bank implemented a research project named "Systems Approach for Better Education Results (SABER)". Identifying green skills as a focus of its work, UNESCO-UNEVOC has established special projects of green skills development.

In his speech, Zeng Tianshan introduced the achievements of the APEC project named "Systematic Design of Green Skills Development in TVET". In this CVED-led project, based on economic, environmental and social factors, 12 general green skills were developed through occupational analysis across the dimensions of operation, technology and management.

(3) Integrating green skills into teaching activities

Green skills are developed in practice. Methods for green skills development vary with countries and regions, but generally relate to program provision, teaching standards and course content.

At the session, Phil Loveder introduced Australia's practices of green skills development. The country developed a training package that guides the definition of Australian teaching standards. Green skills are essential to all the programs and levels within the package.

China drives green skills development by adjusting speciality catalogs and reforming teaching standards. The new *Vocational Education Speciality Catalog* China issued in 2021 features many new green skills related majors. Environmental protection is covered by teaching objectives specified in secondary and higher vocational education standards. In practice, Chinese vocational colleges give priority to green skills development, and have shaped characteristic methods for this purpose. For example, as introduced by Liang Kedong (President of Jinhua Polytechnic, China), Xin Xiulan (Vice President of Beijing Polytechnic, China), Zhang Sasa (Vice President of Hainan Technician College, China) and Margarita Pavlova respectively: Jinhua Polytechnic developed green skills by editing loose-leaf textbooks, building diversified platforms and organizing immersive activities; building on the development of professional and general green skills, Beijing Polytechnic organizes program-specific activities within the campus to reduce pollutants produced in the course of teaching, foster an atmosphere of green learning and develop students' green skills; to develop green skills in line with the ecology-based development policy of Hainan, Hainan Technician College lays equal emphasis on moral, intelligent, physical, aesthetic and labor education, promotes integration between industry and education, brings into play the leading role of world-level contests, and builds green campuses; EdUHK integrates research achievements into teaching content, by developing student worksheets, guidelines for teachers and common green modules.

(4) Systematic methods for green skills development

Green skills development should encompass five dimensions (policy, course, teaching, certification, and supervision & assessment) and four steps (cooperation with enterprises, improvements in educators' ability, development of green skills frameworks & support for educational resource development, and use of the internet & platform sharing), said Borhene Chakroun, Director of the Division of Policies and Lifelong Learning Systems at UNESCO Headquarters. In particular, vocational education institutions should develop green skills in five aspects—green campuses, green curriculum, green communities, green studies, and green culture, in a systematic way, according to Giacomo Bosio.

Xiao Liping, Senior Education Specialist of the World Bank Office in Beijing introduced the World Bank's Green, Resilient, Inclusive Development (GRID) model. In the model, priority is given to the transformation of energy, agriculture, grains, water, land, transportation, cities and manufacturing systems; investment risk management serves as a means to prevent and address climate change, epidemics, natural disasters, socio-economic shocks and financial shocks; efforts are made to boost inclusion and reduce differences.

By systematizing the guests' speeches, it is concluded that:

(1) Green skills development holds the key to vocational education's role in promoting sustainable development.

Green skills development represents an important measure to achieve the goals under *2030 Agenda for Sustainable Development*. In this sense, it is essential to develop professional green skills to enable more people to take green jobs. Beyond that, general green skills must be developed to make everyone aware of the need to and enable everyone to save resources and protect the environment, and drive everyone to take actions in this regard. In this way, everyone may grow into a green citizen contributing to social sustainable development.

(2) Green skills development is a hotspot issue of common concern in the international community.

As revealed at the session, many countries and international organizations pay high attention to what sustainable development and green skills development cover. While implementing the sustainable development strategy, China emphasizes that the philosophy of green development must be followed throughout the whole process and across all aspects of development. Green skills development must play a key part in vocational education's role in serving sustainable development in China.

(3) Some international organizations and countries are bearing fruits of green skills development.

Some international organizations have issued green skills development guidelines where green skills development and social development are designed as a whole to shape a model. Some countries integrate green skills into teaching standards and curriculum. For instance, China has proposed a common list of green skills on the basis of research. Guided by the list, some Chinese colleges have shaped characteristic ways of green skills development through active explorations.

(4) In the foreseeable future, green skills will remain a focus of vocational education in the international community. While China has made achievements in green skills development, overall, vocational colleges need to further put in place the philosophy of green development throughout the whole process and across all aspects of the endeavor, so as to develop green skills in a systematic way. At the same time, we should take into full account economic, environmental and social factors' requirements for green skills development. In this context, requirements and incentives for vocational educators to develop green skills should be fulfilled. To tap into the potential of sustainable development in vocational education community and better fuel the green transformation of economy, suggestions are given as follows. Systematic development: Green skills should be integrated into the whole process and all aspects of vocational education; Mechanism shaping: Green skills should be included in vocational

education standards or indices; Content extension: The common list of green skills should be integrated into all programs; Ability improvement: Green skills should be developed among vocational educators; Community service: vocational educators and students should serve as promoters of the green transformation of economy; Enhanced international cooperation and communication: China should contribute Chinese approaches to green skills development to the international community, amid mutual learning.

Developing green skills in the vocational education community mirrors the development trend of vocational education in the international community while reflecting specific requirements of China's vocational education reform program. Given that, it is essential for China to provide more support for green skills development in the vocational education community, thereby enabling vocational education to be a stronger contributor to the green transformation of economy and socially sustainable development.

# (二)

# 欢迎辞

**中华人民共和国教育部职业教育发展中心主任　彭斌柏**

首先请允许我向线上、线下参加此次论坛的各位嘉宾表示诚挚欢迎！对论坛的顺利举办表示热烈祝贺！

生态环境是人类生存和发展的基本依托，直接影响文明兴衰和人类未来。生态兴则文明兴，生态衰则文明衰。历史和现实告诉我们，只有坚持绿色发展，才能实现永续发展，人类才会有一个更加美好的未来。

古代中国，具有丰富的环保思想、强烈的环保意识、自觉的环保实践。当代中国，作为一个负责任大国，高度重视生态文明建设。2012 年，生态文明建设首次被纳入中国特色社会主义总体布局；2015 年，中国提出新发展理念，其中之一就是“绿色发展”。

近几年，中国全面贯彻习近平生态文明思想，践行“绿水青山就是金山银山”的“两山”理论，坚定不移走生态优先、绿色发展之路，持续改善城乡环境，发展清洁生产。同时，积极参与全球环境治理，加强绿色基建、绿色能源、绿色金融等领域合作，完善“一带一路”绿色发展国际联盟、“一带一路”绿色投资原则等多边合作平台，积极打造“绿色丝绸之路”。

改善生态环境，实现绿色发展，很大程度上要落实到产业发展之中、体现在生产过程之中、融入日常生活之中，而职业教育则是与产业、生产、生活结合最紧、关系最近的一类教育。贯彻绿色发展理念，提高绿色发展技能，培养绿色发展人才，是现代职业教育的应有之义，责无旁贷。为此，我们倡议：

一是倡导绿色发展理念，助推绿色生活方式。中国有 1.1 万所职业院校，每年毕业生约 1 000 万人，专业几乎覆盖国民经济的各个领域和产业。在职业院校倡导绿色发展理念，打造绿色校园，让数以千万计的“职教人”成为绿色理念的践行者、宣传员，不断扩大绿色发展理念的影响。

二是培养绿色技能人才，助推产业绿色发展。按照绿色产业要求与标准培养绿色技能人才，是职业教育的使命和时代要求。要制定符合绿色发展理念、体现绿色发展要求的人才培养方案，培养更多具有推动绿色发展能力的技术技能人才，助推行业、产业、企业绿色发展。

三是加强国际交流合作，助推经验互鉴互学。我们同处一个“地球村”，彼此相依。在推动全球绿色发展这件大事上，谁也不能置身其外，需要共同携起手来。我们愿意搭建交流、合作的平台，分享各国成功做法和经验，相互学习、相互启发，共同为提高绿色技能做出职业教育的贡献。

# （三）

# 可持续发展的绿色技能战略

国际劳工组织中国和蒙古国局局长　李昌徽

国际劳工组织是联合国专门机构，通过制定国际劳工标准来推动社会正义、促进体面劳动。1969 年，国际劳工组织荣获诺贝尔和平奖。作为联合国唯一的三方机构，国际劳工组织将 187 个成员国的政府、雇主和工会代表汇聚在一起，共同协商制定劳工标准和劳工政策，并在全球实施技术合作项目，以促进在持久的和平、繁荣和发展中实现所有劳动者的体面劳动。

2015 年，国际劳工组织正式通过了《为全人类向可持续经济和社会实现公正转型的指导方针》，在全世界范围内明确指出如何成功向低碳经济转变，并提供了切实可行的政策建议。另外，它强调职业技能开发是重点政策领域之一，以促进向环境可持续、包容和公平的未来转变。2019 年，《国际劳工组织关于劳动世界的未来百年宣言》在国际劳工大会上通过，它指出提升人们技能的需求迫在眉睫，因此我们要让人们享有终身学习的机会，习得新技能。技能开发成为环境、经济和社会可持续性的关键政策领域。

关于绿色经济和绿色就业，国际劳工组织提供了一系列核心术语及定义。

绿色 / 绿色化经济：重新配置商业和基础设施，以获得更好的自然资源、人力和经济投资回报，同时减少温室气体排放，减少自然资源的开采和消耗，减少浪费，缩小社会不公平。

绿色工作：能够减少产业与企业对环境造成的负面影响，并最终达到可持续发展水平的工作。涵盖了在农业、工业、服务业和行政部门等领域有助于保护或修复环境质量并满足体面劳动标准的工作，还包含了减缓和适应气候变化的工作活动。

绿色工作技能：遵循相关环境法规和要求以遏制气候变化所必备的技能。

绿色未来中的工作：在向绿色转型的过程中，全球仅 2% 的工作岗位有消失的可能，但绿色经济有可能创造超过 1 亿个新工作岗位，而这取决于职业技能提升和再培训。

国际劳工组织致力于绿色未来的职业技能开发，包括知识研发、能力建设、项目实施与技术合作、提供政策建议。

2022 年，《让职业教育和技能开发更绿色环保——实用指南》发布，国际劳工组织基于《绿色未来的职业技能全球报告》中的分析发现、过往研究以及在不同成员国实施项目时积累的经验，开发了一套如何让职业教育和职业技能开发更绿色、环保的实用指南。该指南旨在为促进绿色职业教育和技能开发明确能力标准、设计课程和评估培训，对各国职业培训院校来说十分实用。2021 年，该指南在柬埔寨、加纳、菲律宾、泰国、赞比亚、津巴布韦等国家试用。

国际劳工组织在绿色技能开发方面的项目与合作如下。

绿色职业技术教育培训与技能发展项目：在柬埔寨、加纳、菲律宾、泰国、赞比亚和津巴布韦等六个国家试点使用国际劳工组织开发的《让职业教育和技能开发更绿色环保——实用指南》，预计明年将在更多国家进一步推广。

南部非洲能源技能项目：与南部非洲发展共同体和瑞典国际开发合作署开展可再生能源行业的公私发展合作、建立能源技能培训中心。

劳动力提升就业力技能发展项目：与欧盟合作，在赞比亚加强技能开发管理、优化培训设施、推动私营部门参与技能培训课程开发和工作导向型学习，促进绿色职业技能的主流化。

绿色企业创新发展项目：与津巴布韦和瑞典国际开发合作署合作，致力于绿色经济的能力课程开发和培训师培训。

加纳技能提升项目：与加纳职业教育从业者在绿色技能培训方面的能力提升、技能培训课程的绿色化开展合作。

绿色转型与人力资源升级的技能之路项目：与毛里求斯和联合国绿色经济行动合作伙伴关系网络合作，制定政策指导文件，用于在行业和国家层面进一步实施，助力实现 2030 年气候议程。

技能 21——为包容和可持续发展赋能项目：与孟加拉国和欧盟合作，实施绿色实践行动计划，在七个模范职业教育学院试点具体的技能绿化措施，修订能力标准和教材。

国际劳工组织长期以来和中国开展合作，总结在绿色技能开发方面取得的进步和面临的挑战，并向中国政府提供相关的技术建议。国际劳工组织在《绿色未来的职业技能——中国研究报告》中提出了政策建议：建立绿色工作或绿色技能的需求预测系统；在绿色技能规范方面加强政策协商、鼓励社会对话；在技能培训课程开发时融入相关绿色理念；鼓励私营部门加大对绿色技能开发的投入；建立完善的绿色技能评估体系和绿色职业资格标准；提升就业质量并使绿色就业潜力最大化。

## iii. Green Skill Strategy for Sustainable Development

**Changhee Lee, Director of International Labour Organization (ILO) Country Office for China and Mongolia**

The International Labour Organization (ILO) is a United Nations specialized agency whose mandate is to advance social justice and promote decent work through setting international labour standards. It is a Nobel Peace Prize winner in 1969. As the only tripartite UN agency, the ILO brings together governments, employers' and workers' representatives of 187 member States to set labour standards, develop policies and implement programs to promote decent work for all women and men in lasting peace, prosperity and progress.

In 2015, the ILO adopted the policy—Guidelines for a Just Transition towards Environmentally Sustainable Economies and Societies for All. These guidelines provide us a clear sense of direction, guidance, and practical framework at a global level to achieve a successful transition to a lower carbon economy. In particular, these guidelines stress the importance of skills development as one of the key policy areas in the transition for a future that's environmentally sustainable, inclusive, and just. In 2019, the *ILO Centenary Declaration for the Future of Work* was adopted. The Declaration points out that it's becoming more and more urgent investing in people's capability. Therefore it emphasizes the importance of enabling them to acquire new skills, throughout their entire life cycle. Skills development became the key policy area to address environmental, economic and social sustainability.

The ILO provided a series of core terms and definitions for green economy and green jobs:

Green/greening economy: The process of re-configuring businesses and infrastructure to deliver better returns on investments of natural, human and economic capital, while at the same time reducing greenhouse gas emissions, extracting and using fewer natural resources, creating less waste and reducing social disparities.

Green jobs: Jobs that reduce the environmental impact of enterprises and economic sectors, ultimately to levels that are sustainable. This definition covers work in agriculture, industry, services and administration that contributes to preserving or restoring the quality of the environment while also meeting the criteria for decent work. It also covers activities related both to mitigation of and adaptation to climate change.

Skills for green jobs: Skills necessary for adapting oneself to related envionmental regulation and requirements to curb climate change.

Work in a greener future: Only 2% of global jobs are at risk of disruption in the green transition, but the creation of over 100 million jobs is conditional on reskilling and upskilling.

The ILO makes great efforts to develop vocational skills for a greener future, including knowledge generation, capacity building, projects & partnerships and policy advice.

The ILO has developed a step-by-step guidance tool for greening TVET in 2022 and skills development, building on the recent findings from the ILO report "Skills for a Greener Future: A Global View", various earlier research and experience and lessons learnt from development cooperation projects in different Member States. Designed to set competency standards, curricula, training assessment to green vocational education and skills development, this practical guidance tool is very useful for vocational training and educational institutions among countries. In 2021, the tool was piloted in Cambodia, Ghana, the Philippines, Thailand, Zambia, Zimbabwe, etc.

ILO projects and partnerships on skills development for a greener future are as follows:

Greening TVET and Skills Development: in Cambodia, Ghana, the Philippines, Thailand, Zambia and Zimbabwe, "A practical guidance tool for greening TVET", including competency standards, curricula, training and assessment packages is to be piloted this year and further implemented in more countries next year.

Skills for Energy in Southern Africa (SESA): together with Southern African Development Community (SADC) and Swedish International Development Cooperation Agency (SIDA) to promote Public-Private Development Partnership (PPDP) on renewable energy sector; establish Centre of Excellence for energy training.

Skills Development for Increased Employability of Labour Force: together with Zambia and EU for Strengthening governance, upgrading training facilities, private sector engagement for curriculum development and Work-Based Learning as well as mainstreaming of skills for a green economy across all components.

Green enterPRIZE Innovation & Development: Zimbabwe and SIDA work for competency-based curricula and training of trainers for green economy.

SKILL-UP Ghana: Ghana's stakeholders on greener training practices promote capacity development for TVET and greening of training curricula.

Skills Roadmap for Green Transition and Advancing Human Capital: Mauritius and Partnership for Action on Green Economy (PAGE) develop policy-guidance documents for further implementation at sectoral and national levels to contribute to Climate Agenda by 2030.

Skills 21-Empowering citizens for inclusive and sustainable growth: Bangladesh and EU work together for implementation of action plans for green practices, piloting specific greening initiatives in seven model TVET institutes and revision of competency standards and learning materials.

The ILO has been collaborating with China to identify progress and challenges in green skills development and provide relevant technical advice. The ILO *Skills for a Greener Future—Country Study of China* made the following recommendations: Establish a system to identify and anticipate green jobs or green skills; Enhance policy coordination and encourage social dialogue in green skills provision; Incorporate green concepts in the development of skills training curricula; Encourage the private sector to invest more in green skills development; Set up a complete green skills evaluation system and green professional qualification standards; Improve the quality of jobs and maximize the green jobs potential.

## （四）

# 促进职业技术教育可持续发展技能

联合国教科文组织驻华代表处主任　夏泽翰

很荣幸向大家介绍联合国教科文组织关于职业技术教育与培训和绿色技能的一些想法。

首先，职业技术教育与培训和绿色技能对实现 17 项可持续发展目标至关重要。关于教育的第 4 项可持续发展目标对于职业技术教育与培训和绿色技能的素质教育来说非常关键。从更大范围来说，可持续发展目标涉及的所有领域都需要强有力的职业技术教育与培训技能和绿色技能。所以从这个角度来看，我们要研究每个具体的目标，尤其是 4.3、4.4、4.5、4.7，这些目标切实关注职业技术教育与培训的公平性和质量，也关注其他关联技能及性别不平等问题，例如，如何摆脱性别不平等、如何促进年轻人的可持续发展。在青年就业、入学率低、技术差异、两极分化的劳动力市场以及由于自动化和“工业 4.0”而面临风险的技术工作等方面，仍然存在着各种各样的挑战。

全球绿色发展需要新的技能，这也是联合国教科文组织可持续发展教育项目的重中之重。我们目前正在制定 2020—2030 年的新框架。2030 年可持续发展教育项目举足轻重，旨在推动可持续发展目标在政策领域的实现、改善学习和培训环境、提升教育工作者的能力、激励年轻人、与各方一道提供解决方案。从个人层面来说，要将个人技能转化为绿色技能；从社会层面来说，要向绿色社会转型；从技术层面来说，要推动技术进步并充分利用先进技术。从政府到青年再到全社会，各个层面都在共同努力。

数据显示，未来需要至少有 4.75 亿个新工作岗位，从这个角度来看，这是一个严峻的挑战。目前有 7 300 多万失业的年轻人，而日常开支只会让他们的生活更难。劳动力市场每年新增超过 4 000 万劳动力，他们需要培训。此外，还有 14.4 亿弱势就业群体。在失业率和劳动力市场就业率方面还存在性别不平等的问题。但有一个好消息：全球经济的绿色转型将提供 1 500 万~6 000 万个工作岗位。

联合国教科文组织在中国正在制定《2021—2025 年联合国可持续发展合作框架》，可持续发展目标需要指导。绿色技能的很多设想都与低碳排放有关，比如碳达峰和碳中和概念、生态文明概念、“十四五”乡村振兴计划、政府的 2035 年教育现代化计划、职业教育现代化、第 26 届联合国气候变化大会优先事项以及对绿色技能的需要。因此我们要在联合国系统内共同努力，推动可持续发展教育项目实现及职业技术教育与培训和绿色技能发展。需要注意的是，我们要了解学习者需要什么，要研究就业市场需要什么，技能再培训需要什么，技能提升需要什么，如何调动职业技术教育与培训组织和机构的积极性。

从 2021 年到 2023 年，联合国教科文组织国际职业技术教育培训中心正在开展战略行动，将应对气候变化纳入职业技术教育与培训技能的主流。

绿色技能是很重要的技能，我们需要积极的态度，研究所需要的通用技能，研究提高绿色技能所需的技术技能，研究如何通过技术催生新职业，研究实操技术、追踪监测技能。这个过程中，设计思维、创造性、适应性和弹性理念非常重要。因此改革教育体系需要一定的时间。

我还想强调的是，联合国教科文组织提出了职业技术教育与培训战略，包括六大支柱——经济复苏、技术变革、非正式化、人口转型（尤其关注青年膨胀）、社会和政治问题、教育和可持续发展（关注气候变化和生物多样性）。教育领域正在转型，今年 9 月将举办“教育转型峰会”，由联合国秘书长主持，会上也将探讨教育转型的诸多领域。

联合国教科文组织正以战略性的方式开展职业技术教育与培训和绿色技能的三大支柱工作，这是全球战略所需要的。第一个支柱是如何通过学习、工作和生活，通过终身学习，通过性别平等，将技能传授给个人；第二个支柱是旨在实现包容性和可持续经济发展的技能，包括需要哪些技能，如何通过科学、技术、工程和数学教育的发展提高技能，如何为教师提供支持，如何完善管理系统，如何向绿色经济转型；第三个支柱是通过绿色公民教育和全球公民教育实现和平与包容。因此联合国教科文组织的全球战略推动技能发展，促进包容性和可持续经济，不可避免地要考虑数字经济技能和绿色经济技能。要考虑如何通过“全球技能追踪器”来进行监测和评估技能，要调研技能培训、再培训、技能提升的文件以及绿色技能具体的全球分类和框架，这些对职业技术教育与培训绿色化的研究十分重要。

## iv. ESD+TVET Promoting Skills for Sustainable Development

**Shahbaz Khan, Director of the UNESCO Beijing Office**

It's an honor for me to present to you some of the ideas from UNESCO on TVET and green skills.

First of all, TVET and green skills are very important for the 17 Sustainable Development Goals. SDG No.4 on education is critical for quality education for TVET and for green skills. But all areas of SDGs need strong TVET skills and green skills. So in this regard, it's very important to note the different targets, especially target 4.3, 4.4, 4.5, 4.7, which are really looking into access and quality of TVET education, as well as the relevant skills and very importantly, gender disparities, such as how can we get rid of them, and how can we promote young people for sustainable development. There are still varying challenges in terms of youth employment, low student enrolment, technological disparities, polarized labor markets, and issues related to the skilled job which are at risk because of the automation and the Industrial 4.0.

With the green development, there are new skills needed. So that's where UNESCO program on Education for Sustainable Development is a critical program. We are now working on the new framework from 2020 to 2030. ESD for 2030 is a very important related program, contributing to SDGs in the area of policy, transforming learning and training environments, as well as building capacities of educators, mobilizing young people and providing solutions with a range of stakeholders. On individual level, there has been transformation into green skills; on societal level, transformation toward green societies; and on technological level, technological advancements and how can we take them on board. From the policy level, all the way to youth and communities are working together.

Statistics show that over 475 million new jobs are needed, where there are serious challenges from this point of view, for more than 73 million young people are currently unemployed and overheads only made it worse. There are more than 40 million new entrants to the labor market annually and we need to train them. At the same time the existing labor with 1.44 billion workers are vulnerable. There are also gender disparities in terms of unemployment, as well as in terms of participation into the labor markets. But there is one good news: more than 15 to 60 million jobs are needed towards transforming our economies to become greener.

UNECSO within China is working on the *United Nations Sustainable Development Cooperation Framework 2021-2025*. SDGs need direction. Ideas of green skills are related to low carbon emissions like the carbon peaking and carbon neutrality concept, ecological civilization concept, rural revitalization which links with the 14th 5-year-plan, the government's 2035 Education Modernization Plan and TVET Modernization Plan, the COP26 Priorities on climate change and the need for more green skills. So we are working together within the UN system for promoting the ESD and TVET for green skills. Very important to note here is that we need to look into what learners need. We need to look into what job markets need, what re-skilling is required, what up-skilling is required, and how we mobilize TVET organizations and institutions together.

From 2021 to 2023 UNESCO-UNEVOC system is working on strategic actions on mainstreaming climate change responses into TVET skills.

Greening skills are important skills, and we need positive attitudes, and we need to look into generic skills needed, as well as the technological skills which are needed for up-skilling toward the green skills, bringing new occupations through and getting technical, operational and monitoring skills. In this process, the idea of design thinking, creativity, adaptability and resilience is very important. So we need a period of time to transform education systems.

I would also like to highlight that, UNESCO pulls over TVET strategy with the six pillars from economic recovery, technological change, informality, demographic transition—especially focusing on the youth bulges, societal and political issues, as well as education and sustainable development—looking into climate change and biodiversity. Education is transforming. Transforming Education Summit in September, hosted by the UN Secretary General, will also be looking into many of these areas.

UNESCO is working in a very strategic way on three pillars for TVET and green skills which are needed through a global strategy. The first pillar is how we can bring the skills to individuals through learning, working, and living together, through lifelong learning, through gender equality. The second pillar is developing skills for inclusive and sustainable economies—what skills are needed, how those skills can be enhanced through STEM, how we can support the teachers, how we can reinforce the governance systems, as well as how we can transform towards green economies. And the third one is peace and inclusiveness realized with green citizenship and global citizenship education together. So global strategy to promote skills for inclusive and sustainable economies needs to look into digital and green economy skills. How do we look into monitoring and evaluation through a "global skills tracker" while looking into the documentation of skilling, re-skilling, up-skilling? And what should be the global taxonomy and framework for green skills? These are very important for us to look into the programs for greening TVET.

# （五）

# 德国双元制及绿色技能促进职业教育转型

欧盟商会东北分会主席、基艾弗姆（辽宁）教育科技有限公司董事长　孔海德

高素质的技术工人和工程技术专业人才历来被看作是德国经济发展的支柱，是“德国制造”产品的质量保障。职业教育在德国社会发展中承担着重要的角色，并形成了一套相对完备且不断调整的法规体系，保障了以双元制为主要特征的职业教育的长期稳定发展。

中国经济正在朝着创新发展转型，职业教育也面临着升级。我想与大家分享德国在职业教育方面的一些情况，希望能对中国职业教育的发展有所启示。我的报告内容主要包括三部分：德国如何从制度上设计并保障校企合作一体化；德国职业教育教师和企业内部培训师的双师培养制度；德国高素质技术技能人才纵向培养的层次。

第一部分，德国如何从制度上设计并保障校企合作一体化。根据德国《联邦职业教育法》的规定，德国职业教育包括四个阶段，分别是职业预备教育、职前教育、职业进修教育以及职业继续教育。而德国职业教育的主体是职前教育，属于十二年义务教育的范畴。也就是说，年轻人在完成最少九年的普通义务教育后，除非直接就读大学，都要接受职前教育。除了少量的全日制职业教育机构外，德国的职前教育基本上都采用双元制形式。在德国，每年约 60 万年轻人接受双元制职业教育，约占同龄人总数的 2/3。

联邦政府颁布的《职业教育条例》规定了培训企业如何设计和实施双元制职业教育在企业中的实践教学，它所提出的过程导向原则并不仅仅是对培训企业和职业学校的要求，课堂教学也必须贯彻这一原则。这样就从法律和制度上保证了校企合作体系的一体化运转。职业学校则依据各州制定的《框架教学计划》组织教学活动，该框架按照学习范围、学习目标、学习内容和学习时间来规范教学。职业学校

也必须以真实的企业过程为导向来设计教学，最大限度地与企业分享年度教学计划，创造交流和合作的机会。

职业学校和培训企业的教学不仅在时间上要相互协调，而且在有关职业教育的内容上也要相互补充。联邦政府的《职业教育条例》和各州的《框架教学计划》从法律上保障了这种协调一致。这就保证了年轻一代既能够掌握联邦范围内相对通行的职业能力，便于在全国流动就业，又能适应各具特色的当地社会生活，建立起家乡的归属感。

第二部分，德国职业教育教师和企业内部培训师的双师培养制度。如果说德国经济腾飞的秘密武器是德国双元制教育，那么制造这些秘密武器的就是德国高水平的职业教育师资队伍。

德国《联邦职业教育法》明确规定，只有具备相应品质和专业资质者，才能教育受教育者。专业资质合格者指的是具备传授教育内容必需的职业、职业教育学和劳动教育学的技能以及知识能力的人。

德国培养职业教育教师是一个非常严格的过程，由大学教育和见习期两阶段组成，专业教学法是必修课。准教师必须学习两门专业和一门专业教学法，最后通过两次国家考试才能拿到职业教师资格证书。第一阶段称为大学教育阶段，通常是 4.5—5 年，在综合性的大学或高等专科学校中进行，学生选择一个主修专业和一个辅修专业。第二阶段是预备教师 1.5—2 年的见习期。德国职业学校教师培养见习期在初始阶段主要是听课，对所学到的知识在研讨课上进行反思，并在指导教师陪同下授课。

德国职业教育双师的培养与其专业的发展密切相关。职业教育师资的资格具有两个实践性特征：一是作为职业教育教师的教学实践，体现在教学的具体组织与实施过程中；二是作为专业技术人员的生产实践，它存在于生产劳动的具体组织与实施过程中。职业教师的教学实践必须与不断变化的专业技术人员的职业实践相适应，从而保障高素质技术技能人才的持续培养。

德国职业学校教师每两年必须脱产进修，对他们平时的工作也已经形成了严格的考核与评价制度，这样不仅保证了教师队伍的质量，而且激励了教师的积极性。

第三部分，德国高素质技术技能人才纵向培养的层次。德国职业教育人才培养体系纵向可以分为三个不同层次，即初级职业教育、中级职业教育和高级职业教育。这三个层次的培养目标和主要区别：初级职业教育的培养目标是技术工人，主要特征是掌握某项基本技能或手艺，主要由双元制职业教育来完成；中级职业教育的培养目标是技术员或工长，主要特征在于它是由技术工人深造晋升而来；高级职业教育的培养目标是工程师，主要是解决复杂、不确定的高层次专业技术问题。

德国中级职业教育被定义为职业继续教育，衔接初级职业教育和高级职业教育。中级职业教育主要是针对已经有一定工作经验的技术工人，因此中级职业教育培养的技术员或工长也是企业职业结构中连接技术工人和工程师的纽带。

2013 年，德国联邦教育和研究部联合颁布的《德国国家资格框架》（Deutscher Qualifikationsrahmen，DQR）对德国的培训和教育体系定义了八个级别。DQR 中明确规定：通过职业教育途径获得的专业经济师和技术员资格定义为六级，与学士资格同级，即学术教育和职业技术教育的结业资格同级，这就在制度上明确了“技术员”的定位。

德国技术员的培养计划并没有采用职业学校的双元制模式，而是采用了类似学科体系的培养模式，确保了知识的系统性和实践应用性。

丰富的选修课实现了对技术员综合职业能力的培养；通过统一的州级毕业考试，确保了技术员培养的总体质量。这样，德国就从制度上保证了高素质技术技能人才的接续培养。

## v. German Dual-System and Promoting the Transformation of Vocational Education with the Green Technologies

**Harald Kumpfert, Chairman of Northeast Branch of European Chamber, General Manager of GfM (Liaoning) Education Technology Ltd., Co.**

Qualifizierte Facharbeiter und Ingenieure gelten seit jeher als Rückgrat der wirtschaftlichen Entwicklung Deutschlands und der Qualitätssicherung von Produkten „Made in Germany". Die Berufsbildung spielt eine wichtige Rolle in der Entwicklung der deutschen Gesellschaft und hat ein relativ vollständiges und ständig angepasstes Rechtssystem geformt, das die langfristige und stabile Entwicklung der Berufsbildung mit dem dualen System als Hauptmerkmal gewährleistet.

Chinas Wirtschaft wandelt sich in Richtung innovativer Entwicklung, und auch die Berufsbildung steht vor einem Upgrade. Ich möchte Ihnen einiges über die Situation der Berufsbildung in Deutschland erzählen und hoffe, Ihnen alle Anregungen für die Entwicklung der Berufsbildung in China zu geben. Mein Vortrtrag umfasst die folgenden drei Themengebiete: Wie gestaltet und gewährleistet Deutschland die Integration von betrieblicher Ausbildung und schulischer Berufsbildung; Die Ausbildung und Qualifikation der Berufslehrkräfte; Die vertikalen Ebenen der Ausbildung von Talenten im deutschen Berufsbildungssystem.

Kommen wir zum ersten Teil. Die berufliche Bildung in Deutschland umfasst nach dem Bundesberufsbildungsgesetz vier Perioden: die allgemeine Bildung, die berufsvorbereitende Bildung, die Berufsbildung und die kontinuierliche Berufsbildung. Das Hauptelement der deutschen Berufsbildung ist die Berufsvorbereitung, die zur Kategorie der zwölfjährigen Schulpflicht gehört. Das heißt, nach Absolvierung von mindestens neun Jahren allgemeiner Schulpflicht müssen Jugendliche eine berufsvorbereitende Ausbildung absolvieren, es sei denn, sie besuchen direkt die Universität. Bis auf wenige berufsbildende Vollzeiteinrichtungen folgt die Berufsvorbereitung in Deutschland grundsätzlich dem dualen System. In Deutschland beginnen jährlich ca. 600.000 junge Menschen eine duale Berufsausbildung, das sind etwa zwei Drittel der gleichen Altersgruppe.

Die von der Bundesregierung erlassene „Berufsbildungsordnung" legt fest, wie

Betriebe zur Gestaltung und Umsetzung der praktischen Lehre der dualen Berufsbildung in Betrieben ausgebildet werden; die darin vorgeschlagenen prozessorientierten Grundsätze sind nicht nur die Anforderungen an die Ausbildungsunternehmen und Berufsschulen. Auch der Unterricht sollte diesem Grundsatz folgen. Damit wird das intergrierte Kooperationssystem von Schule-Unternehmen rechtlich und institutionell gewährleistet. Berufsschulen hingegen organisieren den Unterricht nach dem von jedem Land formulierten „Rahmenlehrplan", dessen Struktur nach „Lernumfang, Lernzielen, Lerninhalten und Lernzeiten" geregelt ist. Berufsschulen müssen sich auch an realen Geschäftsprozessen orientieren, den Unterricht gestalten und den jährlichen Unterrichtsplan weitestgehend mit den Unternehmen teilen, um Möglichkeiten für Kommunikation und Zusammenarbeit zu schaffen.

Der Unterricht von Berufsschulen und Ausbildungsbetrieben sollte nicht nur zeitlich aufeinander abgestimmt sein, sondern sich auch inhaltlich berufsbildend ergänzen. Damit gewährleisten die „Berufsbildungsordnungen" des Bundes und die „Lehrrahmenpläne" der Länder diese Abstimmung rechtlich, die sicherstellt, dass die jüngere Generation nicht nur die im Bundesrahmen relativ weit verbreiteten beruflichen Kompetenzen beherrschen kann, sondern auch eine bundesweite mobile Beschäftigung ermöglicht. Die Schüler können sich auch an das einzigartige regionale Leben vor Ort anpassen und ein Zugehörigkeitsgefühl zu ihrer Heimatstadt kultivieren.

Als nächstes stelle ich den Ausbildungsmechanismus der qualifizierten Berufslehrervor. Wenn die deutsche duale Ausbildung die Geheimwaffe des wirtschaftlichen Aufschwungs Deutschlands ist, dann sind es Deutschlands hochrangige Berufspädagogen, die diese Geheimwaffen herstellen.

Das Bundesberufsbildungsgesetz schreibt eindeutig vor, dass nur Personen mit entsprechender Persönlichkeit und fachlicher Qualifikation Ausgebildete ausbilden können. Berufliche qualifizierte Lehrkräfte sind Personen, die über die zur Vermittlung von Bildungsinhalten erforderlichen Kompetenzen, Kenntnisse und Fähigkeiten der Berufs- und Arbeitspädagogik verfügen.

Die Ausbildung von Lehrkräften in der Berufspädagogik in Deutschland ist ein sehr strenger Prozess, der aus zwei Stufen der Hochschulausbildung und der Probezeit besteht, aber die Fachdidaktik ist ein Pflichtfach. „Angehende Lehrer" müssen zwei Hauptfächer und Berufspädagogik studieren und schließlich zwei nationale Prüfungen bestehen, um ein Lehrerqualifikationszertifikat zu erhalten. Die erste Stufe wird als Hochschulausbildungsstufe bezeichnet, die Semesterregel beträgt 4,5 bis 5 Jahre. Die universitäre Ausbildung findet an Gesamtuniversitäten oder Fachhochschulen statt. Die Studierenden wählen ein Haupt-und ein Nebenfach. Als Studienkolleg ist die zweite Stufe eine Probezeit von 1,5 bis 2 Jahren. In der Anfangsphase des Referendariats für Lehrkräfte an deutschen Berufsschulen hören sie hauptsächlich Vorlesungen, reflektieren ihre Erfahrungen in Vorlesungen und Seminaren, und unterrichten gemeinsam mit Ausbildern.

Die Ausbildung von dualen Lehrkräften in der dualen Berufsbildung ist eng mit der Berufsentwicklung verbunden. Die Berufsschullehrer-Qualifikation hat zwei praktische Merkmale: Zum einen ist die Lehrpraxis als Berufsschullehrer, die im konkreten Organisations-und Durchführungsprozess des Unterrichts besteht, zum anderen ist die Produktionspraxis als technisches Fachpersonal, die besteht in der spezifischen Organisation der Produktionsarbeit. Im Zuge der Umsetzung muss ihre Lehrpraxis an die sich ändernde Berufspraxis des Technik-und Fachpersonals angepasst werden, um die kontinuierliche Ausbildung von qualitativ hochwertigem Fachkompetenz zu realisieren.

Deutsche Berufsschullehrer müssen alle zwei Jahre eine Vollzeitausbildung absolvieren, und für ihre tägliche Arbeit wurde ein strenges Bewertungs-und Bewertungssystem entwickelt, das nicht nur die Qualität des Lehrpersonals sicherstellt, sondern auch die Begeisterung der Lehrer fördert.

Schließlich der dritte Teil, die vertikale Struktur des deutschen Berufsbildungssystems. Das deutsche Berufsbildungssystem lässt sich vertikal in drei unterschiedliche Ebenen unterteilen, nämlich: berufsbildende Grundbildung, mittlere berufsbildende Bildung und weiterführende berufsbildende Bildung. Die Ausbildungsziele und Hauptunterschiede zwischen den drei Niveaus sind wie folgt: Das Ausbildungsziel der beruflichen Grundbildung sind Facharbeiter, deren Hauptmerkmal die Beherrschung einer bestimmten Grundfertigkeit oder eines Handwerks ist. Das erfolgt durch die Dualausbildung. Das Ausbildungsziel der mittleren Berufsbildung sind Techniker oder Meister, deren Hauptmerkmal die Förderung durch Facharbeiter ist. Das Ausbildungsziel der höheren Berufsbildung sind Ingenieure und das Hauptmerkmal ist die Lösung komplexer und unsicherer beruflicher und technischer Probleme auf hohem Niveau.

Die mittlere berufliche Bildung wird in Deutschland als berufliche Weiterbildung definiert und verbindet die berufliche Grundbildung mit der beruflichen Weiterbildung. Da sich die mittlere Berufsbildung hauptsächlich an Facharbeiter richtet, die bereits über eine gewisse Berufserfahrung verfügen, sind die durch die mittlere Berufsbildung ausgebildeten Techniker oder Meister auch das Bindeglied zwischen Facharbeitern und Ingenieuren in der betrieblichen Berufsstruktur.

Der vom Bundesministerium für Bildung und Forschung gemeinsam erlassene Deutsche Qualifikationsrahmen (DQR) hat 2013 acht Niveaus für das nationale deutsche Bildungssystem definiert: Die Qualifikationen für Wirtschaftswissenschaftler und Techniker sind als Niveau 6 definiert, auf gleichem Niveau wie die Bachelor-Abschlüsse, d.h. die Abschlussqualifikationen für akademische Bildung und berufsbildende und technische Ausbildung sind auf gleichem Niveau, was auch die Positionierung von „Technikern“ im System verdeutlicht.

Der Ausbildungsplan der deutschen Techniker übernimmt nicht das duale Systemmodell der Berufsschulen, sondern ein dem Fachsystem ähnliches Ausbildungsmodell, das die systematische und praktische Anwendung des Wissens sicherstellt.

Die Wahlfächer des Fachhochschulen verwirklichen die Förderung umfassender Berufsfähigkeit, die Gesamtqualität der Technikerausbildung wird durch die einheitliche staatliche Abschlussprüfung garantiert, die die kontinuierliche Ausbildung hochwertiger und Fachkräfte sicherstellt.

## (六)

# 为环境可持续发展而制造

土耳其包装制造商协会秘书长　阿斯丽汗·阿利坎

今天我发言的主题是“为环境可持续发展而制造”。世界人口在增加，据估计到 2050 年，地球上将约有 90 亿人。我们生活在石油和天然气的时代，我们依赖这些资源。随着人口的增加，石油日产量也在增加。全球垃圾处理区资源有限，超过 900 亿吨原材料进入经济体系，大约 60% 的垃圾最终进入垃圾填埋场。

当前的经济模式可以用“获取—制造—处理”来概括。我们应该拥抱循环经济模式，简单来说就是“制造—利用—回收”。层次式废物管理方法列出了最有利到最不利的废物管理方案，减少废物、再利用和回收是最有利的选择，符合循环经济。大家认为消费者是否知道哪种包装系统对环境更好，或者环境因素对包装偏好和购买决策是否有影响呢？是或否都没关系。制造商、供应商和设计人员在设计时就应尽量减少对环境的影响。消费者应关心海洋垃圾和过度包装问题，正因如此，我们需要教育。包装保护性不足也是危险的，因为这会导致人们浪费食物。过度包装更没有好处，因为人们要节约资源。我们需要优化包装和产品设计，必须进行产品生命周期分析，同时不要忘记卫生方面的考虑，要在食物浪费和包装良好之间找到平衡点，实用为主，够用为度。不要忘了，塑料塑造了现代文明，在运动、住房、技术、交通和包装等很多领域都是如此。如果按行业来看塑料需求，可以说包装是最大的终端使用市场，占了总量的近 40%。不幸的是，由于环境问题，包装受到了很多负面宣传。其实包装是必要的，在解决废物填埋问题时，包装其实是解决方案的一部分，而非问题本身，但塑料包装污染环境确实是一个问题。例如，欧洲没有足够的能力回收包装废弃物中的聚烯烃，因此他们将这些废物出口到亚洲国家，很不幸，这些废物成为亚洲国家的问题。我们必须采取积极的行动，向循环经济迈出更进一步。由艾伦·麦克阿瑟基金会发起的“新塑料经济”倡议提出，要减少消费、使用可回收的物质、进一步做好资源回收，这在未来将非常重要。此外，还有气候变化问题。目前，全球排放总量的 55% 来自能源消耗，如汽车使用的燃料、日常生活使用的电力。其余 45% 来自产品的生产过程。为了在 2050 年实现零排放，我们必须将这 45% 转变为循环经济。目前这项任务还处于初级阶段，有太多的工作要做。资源回收被视为制造业的最后一道防线，对资源进行合理的回收利用，就能有效减少能源消耗、原材料使用和二氧化碳排放，回收包装也会减少二氧化碳的排放。《欧洲绿色协议》对于制造业非常重要，我们要遵循《欧洲绿色协议》的生产和出口目标及其完成进度，根据原材料效率和循环经济对生产线进行升级改造，当然还要计算产品的碳足迹。有一个很重要的机制是碳边界调节机制，它涉及原材料供应的所有操作，如纸张、玻璃、钢铁、铝、聚合物、石油产品和其他原材料。

2015 年，联合国制定了 17 个可持续发展目标，计划在 2030 年实现。例如，沃尔玛的目标是到 2035 年 100% 使用可再生能源；到 2040 年包括卡车在内的所有车辆实现电气化和零排放；保护至少 5 000 万英亩土地；恢复 100 万平方英里的海洋环境。另一个例子是可口可乐饮料公司，其目标是到 2030 年实现收集和回收卖出的每一个瓶子或罐子；在其瓶子或罐子中至少使用 50% 的回收材料；在所有可口可乐工厂使用 100% 可再生能源；成为碳中和的生产商。联合国和其他参与方在 1997 年签署了《京都议定书》，2015 年又签署了《巴黎气候协定》，为了实现所有这些目标，我们将进入可持续发展的时代，必须让消费者学会使用可持续产品，以更环保的方式生活；必须学会重新思考、重新设计、减少污染、重复使用和回收利用各项产品。疫情期间，我们在家里透过屏幕进行网购，可以说包装和物流将是未来的重点行业。同时，过度包装的问题依然存在，即电子商务在货物运输的不同阶段会有包装的叠加。由于电子商务的发展，包装浪费的问题随之出现。因此为了未来的可持续发展，我们必须重新思考、重新设计这些电商使用的材料。消费者都希望预期寿命能够延长，而延长预期寿命可以通过减少产品包装的浪费和污染来实现。让我们重新设计，正确使用包装，一起拯救共同的家园——地球。

## vi. Manufacturing for Environmental Sustainability

**Aslihan Arikan, General Secretary of Turkish Packaging Manufacturers Association (ASD), Türkiye**

Today I want to talk about manufacturing for environmental sustainability. World population increases as estimated, and in 2050 there will be about 9 billion people living on our planet. We live in the oil and natural gas era, and we are dependent on those resources. As population increases, the amount of oil produced every day also increases. The world has limited resources on disposal areas, so that more than 90 billion tons of raw materials enter the economic system. Around 60% of waste ends up in landfill.

The current economic model can be summarized as "take-make-dispose". We should embrace the circular economy model, which is simply defined as "make-use-recycle". Waste hierarchy sets out most favourable to least favourable options for waste management: reduction, reuse and recycling are the most favoured options, fitting the circular economy. Do you think that shoppers know which packaging systems are better for the environment? Or do environmental considerations have an impact on packaging preferences and purchase decision? Yes or no? It doesn't matter. Manufacturers, suppliers, and designers should design to minimize impact on the environment. Consumers are concerned about litter in the oceans and over-packaging issue, so we need education. Underpackaging is dangerous, because we might waste food. Overpackaging is not good for us too because we want to save resources. We need to optimize packaging and product design and perform life cycle analysis. And don't forget hygiene. We should trade off between food waste and packaging as little as possible, as much as necessary. Remember, plastic have shaped modern civilization, which is true in many applications such as sports, houses, technology, transport, and packaging. If looking at plastic demand by sector, we can say packaging is the biggest end-use market, having almost 40% share by volume. Unfortunately packaging receives much negative publicity because of environmental issues. There is a need for packaging. When landfill waste is considered, packaging is part of the solution, not the problem, but environmentally plastic packaging pollution is the problem. For example, Europe cannot have enough capacity to recycle the polyolefin in packaging waste. So European countries export those waste to Asian countries, which unfortunately will become the problem for Asian countries. We have to take a positive action for moving to a more circular economy. The "new plastics economy", instated by Ellen MacArthur foundation, shows reducing the matter of consumption, using recyclable material and recycling more will be very important in the future. Also, there is a climate change problem. 55% of the total current emissions of the world are from energy consumption, such as fuels in our cars and electricity we use every second. The remaining 45% is generated from making products. To reach zero emissions in 2050, we have to transfer these 45% to circular economy. It is at the beginning level and there is too much work to do. Recycling should be considered as the last line of defense for manufacturing industries. If we do recycling, we will reduce energy consumption, raw material usage and carbon dioxide emissions. If we recycle packaging, we will have less carbon dioxide emissions. *European Green Deal* is very important regarding manufacturing. We should follow the production and export targets and their progress regarding *European Green Deal* targets, convert production lines based on raw material efficiency and circular economy, and of course measure the carbon footprint of products. There is an important mechanism, which is carbon border adjustment mechanism. It is related to all supplying operations like paper, glass, steel, aluminum, polymers, petroleum products and other raw materials.

The United Nations sets its 17 sustainable development goals in 2015, and those goals are intended to be achieved by 2030. For instance, Walmart targets 100% renewable energy by 2035, electrifying and zeroing out emissions from all vehicles including trucks by 2040, protecting minimal 50 million acres of land, and restoring 1 million square miles of ocean. Another example is from Coca Cola beverage company. It is aiming to collect and recycle each bottle or can they sell by 2030, recycle at minimal 50% contents in all bottles globally, and use 100% renewable energy in all plants and be a carbon neutral production producer. United Nations and other consultants declared *Kyoto Protocol* in 1997 followed by the *Paris Climate Agreement* in 2015. Now we are going to the era of sustainability to reach all these goals. We have to empower consumers with the ability to lead their lives in a more environmentally positive way by using sustainable products. We have to rethink, redesign, reduce, reuse and recycle our products. During the pandemic, we stayed at home and did online shopping through small screens, so we can say packaging and logistics will be the key industries for the future. On the other hand, there is overpackaging, a mixture of different materials for shipment of goods in e-commerce. There is a package waste problem because of the growing e-commerce. Therefore we have to rethink and redesign those e-commerce materials for future sustainability. Consumers demand increase in life expectancy. Increasing life expectancy can be achieved by sustainable package products. Let us redesign and use them properly and let's save our planet together.

## （七）

# 面向未来的职业教育：可持续发展的绿色技能

联合国教科文组织职业技术教育中心（香港）主任　玛格丽塔·帕夫洛娃

在国际上，明确可持续发展的技能越来越重要。可持续发展议程始于 1980 年代，现在已有 17 个可持续发展目标。价值观念正在发挥非常重要的作用，因为它有助于我们采取具体行动，而这些行动是实施可持续发展议程所必需的。而且，中国在经济绿色发展、降低碳排放、关注循环经济方面有非常明确的政策。

职业技术教育与培训的作用在于支持劳动力市场的绿色重构，毕业生将更容易找到就业机会。学生是公民，因此需要确保他们接受可持续发展议程并努力执行。当然，职业技术教育与培训还可以支持绿色发展的区域和国际合作，通过技能发展及社区的绿色发展来支持政府政策的落实。

目前，联合国教科文组织有一项职业教育新战略。战略重点之一是为包容性和可持续经济培养技能。当我们谈论绿色经济和绿色技能时，可以看到有许多与此相关的定义。当我们考虑培养学生绿色技能的类型时，可以分为特定的绿色技能、补充技能和通用绿色技能。所有这一切的基础是对可持续发展的积极态度和心态。

几乎所有职业都需要“通用绿色技能”。人们会了解“绿化”的含义，理解自己可以做些什么来支持这一倡议。“补充技能”通常与实操中引入新绿色技术相关，大多数情况我们只需要将一些补充的技能纳入现有的培训项目或标准中。当我们谈论“特定技能”时，则涉及这个国家设立的新职业和新产业。这三种类型的技能培养可以通过正规的职业技术教育与培训，也可以通过工作场所和专业培养。

我们一直在与许多国家合作开发通用绿色技能的方法，几乎所有职业都需要通用绿色技能。我们设计了一个网站，在其中提供资源并解释如何培养学生通用绿色技能的方法。因此为了实现这一目标，我们确定了 20 个概念，主要关注环境领域以及环境、社会和经济领域之间的交集部分。因为当我们研究本地区如何落实可持续发展目标的报告时，这些就是需要付出更多努力的优先领域。我们还进行了案例研究，涉及 10 个不同的行业，我们向学生展示了这些行业的绿色环保情况，设计了通用绿色技能课程，如果教师教授酒店业、制造业或农业等产业相关的课程，可以使用这些案例研究作为主题。也就是说此案例研究有两种使用方式，一个是作为通用绿色技能课程的一部分，另一个是作为项目的主题。例如，在谈论第 9 个可持续发展目标时，教师要处理两个概念，即绿色技术和闭环经济。此外还有许多来自不同行业的案例研究，如建筑、可再生能源、废物管理。那么，每个培训包至少包含三个资源：第一个，案例研究的概念或描述；第二个，学生工作表，包含学生需要进行的各项活动，以帮助他们对案例概念的理解；第三个，教师指南，支持教师实施与这些案例研究概念相关的课程。

基于这个概念，我们设计了通用绿色技能教学模块，教学时长共 26 小时，其内容主要基于前文所述教学资源（概念和案例）。主题一涉及日常生活中的一般环境意识和原则。主题二是环境法律法规。主题三是地方性和全球性的紧迫问题。主题四与绿色工作场所有关：通用绿色技能的应用及其对职业 / 工作场所实践的影响。主题五是社会和经济影响。

最近，我们完成了联合国教科文组织国际职业技术教育培训中心的项目，该项目是关于通过课程和教学法实现可持续发展目标的能力建设。我们提供三个在线研讨会和一个网络研讨会，人们可以看到我们涵盖的主题。我们还设计了交互式课程，参与者需要做家庭作业并报告。我们还开发了具有情境性的资源。

关于项目前景的简短建议：需要考虑合作伙伴关系，如果想实现变革，需要与不同的利益相关者合作。在国家层面，制定与绿色人力资本相关的政策非常重要。在标准制定和课程开发层面，重要的是要囊括不同类型的新绿色职业技能，包括将绿色元素引入现有职业，开发和引入通用绿色技能模块，并在现有课程中引入可持续发展或绿色概念。帮助行业评估当前形势，进一步推动绿色发展，以确定合作伙伴和合作领域。在职业技术教育与培训院校层面，要积极采取行动，联合国教科文组织国际职业技术教育培训中心出版了《绿色职业技术教育与培训》一书，提出了体制发展的整体办法，深圳职业技术学院将其翻译成中文，目前该书有多种语言版本。

职业教育开发绿色技能的机制层面有五种可持续性方法：绿色校园、绿色课程、绿色研究、绿色机构文化以及绿色工作场所和社区。今天我的发言聚焦课程培训，但其他领域也非常重要。

## vii. Future Ready VTE: Green Skills for Sustainable Development

**Magarita Pavlova, Director of the UNESCO-UNEVOC Centre (Hong Kong)**

Identification of skills for sustainable development became more and more important internationally. Sustainable development agenda started from 1980s, and now we have 17 sustainable development goals. Values are playing a very important role because it feeds into our specific actions that are required to implement sustainable development agenda. And also it is very important that China has a very definite policy that relates to greening of economy and lowering the carbon emissions and also focusing on the circular economy.

The role of TVET is to support this green restructuring of the labour markets. So graduates will find employment opportunities easier. Students are citizens. So we need to ensure that they accept sustainable development agenda and put effort into its implementation. Of course TVET can support regional and international cooperation in the area of greening, support implementation of government policies through skills development and also greening of communities.

Currently UNESCO has a new strategy for vocational education. And one of the strategic priorities is developing skills for inclusive and sustainable economies. When we are talking about green economy and green skills, we can see that there are a number of definitions in relation to that. When we are thinking about the type of skills we need to develop in our students, we can classify them into specific green skills, topping-up skills and generic green skills. The foundation for all of that is positive attitude and mindset towards sustainability.

"Generic green skills" are required for almost all occupations. So people are aware of what do we mean by "greening" and what can they do to support this initiative. "Topping-up skills" are usually associated with the introduction of new green technologies in operational processes. And very often we just need to include a number of additional skills into our existing training programs or standards. When we're talking about 'specific skills', we're talking about new occupations, new industries that have been established in the country. So all of them can be developed by the formal TVET, as well as through workplace and also professional development.

We have been working with many countries in the region on developing the approaches: how to develop generic green skills. Generic green skills are required for almost all occupations. We designed a website where we are putting resources and explaining approaches how generic green skills can be developed in our students. So to achieve that, we identified 20 concepts which mainly focused on environmental areas and the intersections between environmental, social and economic areas. When we looked at the report of how sustainable development goals are implemented in our region, these are the priority areas where we need to put more effort. We also identified case studies. They relate to ten different industries. So we are showing students how greening is happening in these different industries. We designed this generic green course, and teachers can use these case studies as themes when teaching programmes in hotel industry, for example, or in manufacturing or in agriculture. So case studies can be used in two ways. One is as a part of generic green course and the other is as themes to be introduced into programmes. For example, there are two concepts you want to address when talking about the sustainable development goals: green technology and closed-loop economy. And also there are a number of case studies from different industries like construction, renewable energy and waste management. Each pack consists of at least three resources: The first one is a concept or description of the case study; The second one is a student worksheet where we put all activities that the students need to undertake to develop their understanding of the concept of the case; The third one is teacher guidelines that support teachers to implement the class that relates to these concepts of case study.

Based on this concept, we organised the model generic green module of 26 hours and it is based on the resources (the concepts and the case studies). Topic one relates to general environmental awareness and principles in daily life. The second topic is environmental laws and regulations. The next one is pressing local and global issues. Topic number four relates to greening workplaces: application and impact on occupation/workplace practice. The last topic is social and economic impact.

Recently we finalised the project for UNESCO-UNEVOC that was related to capacity building for addressing sustainable development goals through curriculum and pedagogy. We delivered three workshops online and one webinar. People can see the topics that we covered, and we also designed interactive courses. Participants need to do the homework and report on their homework. We also developed resources that are contextualized.

Short suggestions about how to move forward: Think about the partnership because if we want to achieve change, we really need to collaborate with different stakeholders. At the national level, it is important to have a policy that is related to green human capital. At the level of standards development and curriculum development, it is important to include different types of skills of new green occupations, including introduction of greening elements into existing occupations, as well as development and introduction of generic green skills module and addressing sustainable development or greening concept across existing courses. It is important to help industries to assess the current situation and put up further greener developments to identify partners and areas for collaboration. At the level of TVET institutions, it is possible to take actions and UNESCO-UNEVOC published the book: *Greening Technical and Vocational Education and Training*. It presents the holistic approach towards institutional development. Shenzhen Polytechnic translated this book into Chinese. Now it is available in a number of languages.

There are five sustainability approaches at the institutional level: greening of campus, curriculum, research, institutional culture, as well as workplace and community. Today I focused on curriculum training. But the other areas are also extremely important.

# （八）

# 绿色创新所需的技能

澳大利亚国家职业教育研究中心执行经理　菲尔·洛夫德

我将首先简要介绍绿色技能或可持续发展技能的一些定义，然后介绍绿色技能应用的经济和社会驱动因素，即在行业和社会中，哪些因素切实推动了绿色技能的提高，最后简要探讨一下职业教育和培训在绿色技能传授中的作用。

什么是绿色技能或可持续发展技能？国际上有很多定义，这是欧盟给出的定义：“环保技能是指在一个减少人类活动对环境影响的社会中，普通民众生活、发展和支持该社会所需的知识、能力、价值观和态度。通用的绿色技能包含在决策时，包括在选择工艺和技术时，综合考虑环境问题与其他问题（如性能和安全）的能力。”

是什么推动了环保意识和绿色技能的发展？有几个因素，首先，宏观层面上，围绕减少碳排放和应对气候变化有一系列国际目标和协议，如《巴黎气候协定》。当然，可持续性是联合国教科文组织可持续发展目标的一个关键要素。在国家和具体国情层面，通常还有对实现目标的渴望。以我的国家澳大利亚为例，我想指出的是，技能和培训往往是这些协议的组成部分，它们在帮助劳动力及普通民众向新的可持续的思维、工作和生活方式过渡等方面发挥着重要作用。

第二个因素是推动行业引入环境标准，结合环境和可持续发展法律法规的实践，尤其是在管道行业、电力技术和太阳能发电相关的建筑行业。这在更大范围上解决了人们对更大程度节约能源资源、引入和维持可持续方法的担忧。比如在立法改革方面，强制引入电器用水效率标签，这要求工人了解相关法律法规，了解产品设计，能够与客户和供应商谈判，这就要求培训系统做出相应回应。

第三个向绿色技能转变的一个非常重要的驱动因素是技术变革。技术创新产生了对绿色技能的需求。创新和新产品设计要求劳动力具备新的技能。在制造过程方面，新的可持续制造做法、减少浪费和增加再利用材料正在推动变革。例如，在管道和太阳能等行业，我们已经看到了技术的增量变化。这些技术的变化通常是由供应商开发的，比如太阳能发电领域的太阳能电池板公司要找到竞争优势，通常是通过组织流程创新来实现的，这导致公司通过提高采购效率降低成本，最终实现更可持续的做法。

最后一个因素是消费者的选择和偏好。即使在社会上，消费者也要求选择绿色产品，这些产品能提高能源效率，有助于保护环境、减少浪费，真正发挥作用。消费者在推动绿色可持续技术的发展中扮演着重要的角色，这将顺势产生培训需求。

绿色技能可以被纳入国家层面的正式框架，例如，新加坡技能框架提供了一个有趣的例子，即在其国家发布的框架中，所有六个级别的资格证书现在必须包括关于学习结果的说明，描述学习者应该如何在相关工作角色中发挥作用，与专注于创新和社会等方面的技能基础范围相对照。

除了我们期望从人们身上获得的技术技能，现在社会责任和创新能力都是国家和超国家层面需要考虑的重要能力。在澳大利亚，绿色技能和能力已经被纳入所有行业的培训方案中，已成为培训的组成部分。认识到绿色技能应纳入正式的职业技术教育课程是很重要的，绿色技能正被嵌入职业技术教育课程中，成为所有职业技术教育与培训学生跨学科和必修培训的一部分。此外，新形式的认证，如技能组合和微证书、行业徽章以及行业认可的证书也正在成为影响绿色技能的有益实践。

我们要在正式的评估过程中加入绿色技能，包括核心或特定任务的能力以及实用的、通用的或非正式的能力。当涉及新绿色技术的应用时，诸如销售商培训或由绿色技术供应商提供的教育培训也可以发挥作用，且可以确定这种能力如何匹配技能识别系统。这些培训可以发挥关键作用，帮助现有工人从传统的旧经济和衰落的产业中过渡到新的绿色产业环境或可持续型工作。培训，尤其是再培训，是确保工人特别是现有工人能够在新产业和更广泛的绿色经济中获得机会的关键因素。

职业技能培训在绿色技能议程中发挥着重要作用。提高政策制定者、职业技术教育培训人员、职业技术教育学生和行业部门员工对绿色技能的认识至关重要。我们要采取更广泛的方法学习绿色技能，为人们提供获得绿色技能的机会，包括非正式技能学习、销售商培训、在职培训和嵌入职业的特定职业教育与培训项目。提高教师群体的技能，使其提供可持续发展技能或绿色技能也是非常重要的。我们必须认识到，教师群体需要时间来跟上新的绿色理念，持续提高他们绿色技能的专业水平和信心是成功的关键。

# viii. Skills for Green Innovation

**Phil Loveder, Executive Manager of National Centre for Vocational Education Research (NCVER), Australia**

I'll briefly touch on firstly some definitions of green skills or skills for sustainability and then identify some economic and social drivers of green skills uptake—what are the things that are actually leading to increasing the green skills across the workplace and in the community, and then finish up with a quick exploration of VET's role in the delivery of green skills.

What are green skills or skills for sustainability? There are quite a few international definitions available. This one is from the European Union.

"Environmental awareness skills refer to the knowledge, abilities, values and attitudes [in the general population] needed to live in, develop and support a society which reduces the impact of human activity on the environment. These generic green skills include the capacity to include environmental concerns alongside others (such performance and safety) in taking decisions, including in the choice of processes and technologies."

What is driving this greater awareness and the move towards green skills? There are several factors. Firstly, at the macro level, there are a range of international goals and agreements around reducing carbon emissions and combating climate change, such as the *Paris Climate Agreement*. And of course sustainability is a key element of UNESCO sustainable development goals. With individual nations and their own contexts, there are usually also aspirations of targets. I'll detail one here and just for my own country's context. I want to make the point that skills and training are often aspects of these agreements and they play an important role in helping, for instance, transition in workforce and its people to new sustainable ways of thinking, working and living.

Another driver is moving industry to introduce environmental standards which incorporate environmental and sustainability code practice. We especially say this in industries such as plumbing, and construction industries in electric technology and in the solar powered generation. These address the concerns of a wider community for greater resources of energy conservation as well as the introduction and maintenance of sustainable methods. There are examples of legislative changes such as the mandatory introduction of things like water efficiency labeling for appliances which require workers to understand the relevant legislation of regulation and to be aware of product design and to be able to negotiate with customers and vendors. And the training system needs to reflect on this.

Thirdly, a really important driver of the move to green skills is technology change. Technology innovation drives the need for green skills. Innovations and new product designs are requiring that new skills are required in the workforce. Within the manufacturing process itself, new sustainable manufacturing practices and reducing waste and increased reuse materials is driving change. For instance, in industries such as plumbing and solar, we've seen incremental changes in technology. These changes to technology are usually developed by the suppliers. So for instance in solar generator, solar panel firms, for example, need to find a competitive edge and this is usually done through organizational process innovation, which results in things like cost reduction throughout sourcing efficiencies and ultimately leads to more sustainable practices.

Finally, there are customers' choices and preferences. Customers are demanding choice even in the community for green products which deliver on things such as energy efficiency and help to protect the environment, to reduce waste, and to actually make a difference. The consumers play an important role in driving the move towards green sustainable technologies. And ultimately this will have a flow-on effect to the need for training.

Green skills can be incorporated into things such as formal frameworks at the national level. For example, the Singapore skills framework provides an interesting example of how qualifications at all six levels of their national published framework must now include statements on learning outcomes describing how learners should function in the related job roles against the range of foundation of skills which focused on things like innovation and society.

In addition to the sort of technical skills that we expect from people, now social responsibility and the ability to innovate are both important competencies needed to be considered at the national and supra-national levels. In Australia, green skills and competencies have been integrated into all training packages in all industries. They are now accessible components of training. Recognizing that green skills should be integrated into formal VET curriculum is important. Green skills are being embedded into VET curriculum and becoming part of interdisciplinary and mandatory of training for all TVET students. Additionally, new forms of certifications such as skill-sets and micro-credentials, industry badges as well as industry-recognized certificates are also emerging as useful practices to impact green skills.

We should recognize green skills in the formal assessment process, including core or task-specific competencies as well as practical, generic or non-formal ones. When it comes to the adoption of new green technologies, things such as vendor training or education instruction which is provided by the suppliers of green technology has a role to play as well and can establish how this competency is fit into the border skills recognition system. They can play a crucial role in supporting the transition in the existing workers out of traditional old economy and declining industries into new environmentally friendly or sustainable jobs in new green industries. Training and especially retraining is an essential part of ensuring that workers, especially existing workers, are able to take up the opportunities available in new industries and the wider green economy.

VET plays a crucial role in the green skills agenda. Increasing the awareness of policy makers, VET trainers, VET students and employees in the industry sectors on green skills is essential. Adopting a broader approach to green skills is important, providing opportunities for people to acquire green skills from informal skills learning right through to vendor training, on-the-job training and specific VET programs that are embedded within occupations. The up-skilling of instructors and teachers to deliver skills for sustainability or green skills is very important. It has to be recognized that it can take time for instructors and lecturers to get up to speed with new green concepts. Supporting their ongoing professional development and confidence in teaching green skills is crucial to success.

# （九）

# 绿色技能开发的全球使命和中国方案

中华人民共和国教育部职业教育发展中心副主任　曾天山

## 1. 绿色发展推动全球可持续发展

（1）可持续发展与绿色发展。“可持续发展”在 2000 年 9 月联合国世纪峰会上被列为 21 世纪人类发展的基本模式，是指“既满足当代人的需求又不危害后代人满足其需求的发展”，要求发展经济、保护环境和资源的统一。

经济的快速发展往往伴随着生态环境遭受污染和破坏，人类历史上为此付出了巨大代价：20 世纪发生的比利时马斯河谷烟雾事件、美国洛杉矶光化学烟雾、英国伦敦烟雾、日本水俣病和骨痛病以及乌克兰切尔诺贝利核泄漏等，都在警醒人们环境污染给人类生存造成的恶劣影响。

可持续发展正是人类在深刻反思工业革命以来人与自然之间关系的思维转变。在可持续发展的理念下，“绿色”的概念融入“发展”之中，为经济社会发展提供了一种新型模式，衍生出的“绿色经济”“绿色制造”等倡议都是旨在实现发展的同时保护环境、节约能源。

（2）绿色发展是趋势。21 世纪初以来，国际社会制定和实施了千年发展目标和 2030 年可持续发展议程。倡导绿色发展已经成为许多国家的共识，是世界经济发展的主流趋势。绿色发展没有统一的制度或模式，各个国家依据本国国情制定适合其经济发展需求的政策和战略，不论处于哪种发展阶段，所有国家都可以通过更高效地利用自然资源和能源来提高生产力，通过政策优化来提升低碳环保的生产价值，通过对绿色技术、商品和服务的新兴需求创造新的市场和就业等，来实现绿色增长和更具包容性的发展。

绿色发展模式在保障人类经济和社会发展资源需求的同时，确保人类生存和发展所需的环境和生态基础，推动循环经济与低碳经济快速崛起，提高经济增长的质量和效益，是推进全球可持续发展的必然选择。

### 2. 绿色发展与绿色技能

（1）绿色发展对从业者的新要求。新要求：在绿色发展的模式下，经济社会发展会呈现出不同于以前的新特点，绿色转型既催生了大量以“低碳、环保、循环”为特征的绿色新兴职业，又对传统行业的思维和工作方式带来冲击。今天的从业者需要掌握促进经济社会和个人可持续发展的技能、知识、价值和态度，这就从社会和个体需求上对从业者绿色技能开发和培养提出了新要求。

规模需求：目前，绿色发展的重要瓶颈是绿色技能人才短缺，根据领英今年3月发布的《2022年全球绿色技能报告》，绿色人才在全球劳动力中占比正逐渐上升，由2015年的9.6%上升到2021年的13.3%，其增长率高达38.5%。报告指出，绿色人才的雇佣率高过非绿色人才，企业的招聘需求正在向绿色人才倾斜，但转入绿色和绿色化职位的人才数量太少，绿色人才将会供不应求。

质量需求：不仅是绿色经济产业规模发展需要大量绿色人才，更大的挑战往往在高技能领域。领英数据显示，2016年至2021年间，增长速度最快的前五大绿色职位分别是可持续发展经理（30%）、风力发电机技术人员（24%）、太阳能顾问（23%）、生态学家（22%）和环境健康与安全专家（20%）。这些岗位需要从业者可以批判性地在不同工作环境中、在转型后的资源条件下运用可持续发展相关的能力，将绿色的理念和行动创新地整合进日常工作中，最大限度地实现“低碳、环保、循环”的绿色转型。

（2）个体适应绿色发展。从个体发展角度而言，适应绿色发展的绿色技能是提升21世纪人类核心素养的关键技能，绿色技能能够帮助个体更好地适应未来经济社会的绿色发展和劳动力市场的新需求。绿色技能既是通用性技能，也是专业技能，既包括“最大限度地减少资源使用、提高能源和资源利用效率、减排、循环使用、保护自然环境”等，也是从事‘绿色工作’或‘绿色职业’所必须掌握的技术、知识、价值和态度”。

### 3. 中国开发绿色技能的方法路径

（1）中国绿色发展道路。在绿色发展模式导致成本上升的压力下，作为发展中国家，中国始终坚持立足国情实施可持续发展战略。党的十八大首次提出“推进生态文明建设，建设美丽中国”的战略任务，要构建“资源节约型、环境友好型社会”。党的十九大报告明确指出“建设生态文明是中华民族永续发展的千年大计”，要求要“实行最严格的生态环境保护制度，形成绿色发展方式和生活方式”。2021年提出的“双碳”战略更是反映了构建人类命运共同体和人与自然生命共同体的内在要求，也是人类可持续发展的客观需要。随着“双碳”目标上升至国家战略并纳入我国“十四五”规划当中，我国的绿色发展之路提升到新的高度，对绿色经济转型的需求也更为迫切。

（2）职业教育绿色技能开发经验。绿色发展已成为我国未来一段时期经济社会发展的主线之一。经济社会发展和劳动力市场的变化也会对教育产生倒逼效应，作为培养技术技能人才主体的职业教育，肩负着为实现绿色发展培养具有绿色人才的重要任务。为应对绿色发展对人才培养提出的新挑战，我国职业教育在开发绿色技能方面实施了多种形式的探索与尝试。

一是在顶层设计上发挥国家作为重大战略组织者的作用，以克服绿色发展与短期利益的冲突和传统发展模式的“路径依赖”。2016 年，教育部、人力资源和社会保障部、工业和信息化部联合印发的《制造业人才发展规划指南》在“提升制造业人才关键能力和素质”这一主要任务中专列“提升绿色制造的技术技能水平”，鼓励高等学校、职业学校根据绿色制造发展需要积极开设节能环保、清洁生产等相关学科专业；鼓励学校参与传统制造业绿色改造、参与绿色产品研发和相关标准制订等，并在重点工程和保障措施中做出了相应的政策制度安排。

二是在专业建设上进行“绿化”调整。我国于 2015 年就在“普通高等学校高等职业教育（专科）专业目录”中增补了“绿色”专业，如污染修复与生态工程技术、清洁生产与减排技术、资源综合利用与管理技术、安全健康与环保等，结合可持续发展、资源循环利用等绿色发展理念，挖掘绿色属性专业中的绿色技能纳入职教专业教学标准和人才培养目标。

对职业院校传统专业则是进行绿色转型和升级，融入可持续发展能力和低碳环保的绿色意识等绿色技能要素。2015 年，教育部职业教育发展中心（原教育部职业技术教育中心研究所）申请了亚太经济合作组织“职业教育与培训系统开发绿色技能”项目，通过“绿色技能通识教育”和“绿色技能专业教育”培养具备可持续发展意识、情感态度和绿色技能的技术型人才。项目校以专业为依托，从管理、技术、操作三个维度，围绕经济、社会、环境三个要素梳理分析具有代表性，能反映低碳环保、节能减排、安全健康等可持续发展理念的绿色技能点，归纳整理绿色技能内容，形成绿色技能清单并融入专业教学标准和人才培养目标中。

三是职业教育课程内容开发涵括绿色技能要点，包括“绿色环保”服务理念与安全意识、成本与效率意识、循环再利用和绿色操作习惯等。按照通识类课程、专业基础类课程和专业技能课程体系，融入通用和专业绿色技能，构建有层次、递进式的新型绿色课程体系。例如，唐山工业机械制造与自动化专业绿色技能课程体系，分别在通识类课程中融入“环保法和环境教育”，在专业基础类课程中融入“成本预算、生产效率和绿色设计”，在专业技能课程中融入“废品回收、冷却液回收、精益管理、环境保护、绿色制造”等内容以及相应的知识、技能和素质目标。

四是加强绿色师资队伍建设，主要是培养职业院校教师绿色意识和理念，加强与专业相关的绿色技能内容的了解以及在绿色技能相关教学和自身行为上体现绿色技能的要求。例如，浙江经济职业技术学院结合课程教学、实践教学和专业建设对教师进行绿色技能相关的各类培训，开展国际学术交流，帮助教师学习和了解绿色技能发展最新动态。

五是设置绿色技能相关的赛项，以赛促教。2019 年，我国全国职业院校技能大赛高职组设置了“水环境监测与治理技术”赛项，赛项围绕环保装备制造业发展需要，充分发挥技能大赛引领专业建设及课程改革的提升作用，促进高职学校水环境的监测与治理专业的建设及人才的培养进程，以提升学生综合职业能力和就业质量，满足社会对水环境监测和治理高素质技术技能型绿色人才的需求。

我国绿色技能开发、绿色人才培养仍然处于探索阶段，仍需要通过加强理论研究和试点实践形成符合人才成长规律和职业教育教学规律的、具有中国特色的绿色技能开发路径，为中国绿色经济转型提供通用型和专业型绿色人力资源支撑。

目前，新冠病毒疫情、气候变化、能源危机、粮食安全等，仍然是人类共同面临的全球性问题，推动绿色发展，关系人类前途和未来。加强生态文明建设，优化产业结构、能源结构，倡导绿色低碳的生产生活方式，是中国着眼长远、为实现可持续发展而做出的努力。开发绿色技能、培养绿色人才是促进经济社会绿色发展、人与自然生态和谐共处的重要着力点，也是职业教育服务人的可持续发展、经济社会的可持续发展以及生态环境可持续发展的价值所在。

# （十）

# 高职院校绿色技能的实践探索

## ——以北京电子科技职业学院为例

北京电子科技职业学院副院长　辛秀兰

北京电子科技职业学院建校于 1958 年，是国家首批独立设置的高职学院，是全国百所高职示范校之一，2019 年入选国家“双高计划”高水平学校建设单位（A 档）。

我从绿色技能的职教背景、实践探索和建设规划三个方面进行汇报。首先，介绍绿色技能的职教背景。绿色技能又称“可持续发展技能”，绿色技能既是通用性技能，又是专业技能。职业教育目标一般从知识目标、能力目标和素质目标三个维度描述，主要体现在从事“绿色工作”或“绿色职业”所必须掌握的技术、知识、价值和素质之中。2021 年，教育部启动了新一轮专业教学标准修订，明确指出每个专业要把绿色生产、环境保护、安全教育等内容融入培养规格要求。

其次，介绍我校绿色技能的实践探索。学校开设机电、航空、汽车、电信、生物、经管、艺术 7 个专业群共 32 个招生专业，实施全日制高职教育、中高职衔接培养等复合生源、多学制教育，建校以来已累计为社会培养高素质技能人才 10 万余名。学校绿色技能在多个专业覆盖面广，既开设环境工程技术等 5 个以绿色技能为专业技能的专业，也开设了新能源汽车、环境艺术设计等把绿色技能作为通用技能的专业。学校加强顶层设计，30 多个专业中，每个专业的培养规格都有安全环保能力要求，如新能源汽车专业的能力要求有环境保护，要求学生能正确处理装调与维修过程中出现的废液、废料等，确保生产环境安全及卫生；能按照 6S 要求对工作环境进行整理和规范，并具有节约意识。环境艺术设计专业对绿色技能的要求是遵照国家及行业安全要求，对设计、工程施工、材料等严格按照国家标准进行项目实施；学生要具有绿色环保意识、安全意识；具有勤俭节约精神；具有垃圾分类习惯等。

生物专业群承担了工业废水处理国家级教学资源库子项目，积累了食品工业废水、制药工业废水等丰富的教学资源。生物专业群不仅面向高职生，而且面向中小学生开展绿色技能培训，承办了7届市级以上环境保护类技能大赛，获得市级以上奖项20项，“变废为宝——厨余垃圾生物发酵应用创新”项目在全国“互联网+”大学生创新创业大赛中获奖。

汽车专业群应对行业变化，开设新能源汽车等“绿色”专业，为降低教学污染，升级实训环节，通过虚拟仿真和企业实践取代污染实训环节，并将企业规范、6S管理引入教学，营造绿色学习氛围，并通过垃圾分类等课余活动，强化绿色理念。

航空专业群广泛开展绿色技能宣传活动，增强学生绿色低碳意识，通过工具、耗材“三清点”等活动，将绿色发展理念落实在专业教学各环节中；专业群将绿色技能融入专业课，传统专业课程转型升级，建立了风光互补发电系统安装调试平台、智能微网发电系统安装调试平台等绿色平台，风光互补发电系统安装与调试赛项连续8年获全国一等奖。此外，还将绿色技能融入劳动课，实施绿色环保理念落实行动。

经管专业群承担北京市教育委员会开展的中德胡格教育模式改革项目，围绕环保主题将绿色技能纳入专业课程，其中一门课程主题是循环经济与绿色包装。通过全方位育人，将绿色技能与劳动技能、美育相结合，如学生将劳动技能课搜集的落叶制作成“花束”，装点美好生活，劳育、美育与绿色技能结合。

艺术专业群绿色技能通用技术的内容是节约资源、减少废物产生。课程着眼学生对材料认知、应用及环保创意，通过创意活动学习材料使用方法，了解新材料、新技术的应用，激发创新意识。例如，通过立体折纸方式面料改造、时装废料改造、抽线肌理面料改造、牛仔旧衣面料改造等方面，在专业教学过程中培养学生节约资源的意识。此外，艺术专业群发挥艺术特长，开展垃圾分类方面的宣传教育，通过校企合作，引进企业真实项目，进行垃圾分类图书、动画设计制作，宣传垃圾分类知识，树立环保理念，提高绿色技能。师生共同编写的图书《垃圾分类》获科学技术部颁发的“2019年全国优秀科普作品”和新闻出版总署评定的“2021年农家书屋重点出版物”。

最后，介绍绿色技能的建设规划。学校计划开发绿色技能教师用书、学生用书和教学资源及其配套电子化素材，在实践中不断完善和修订相关内容，并对材料进行电子化与双语化建设，方便在网络和国际上推行。基础模块计划开发5个单元、

12 个主题，包括水资源利用和可持续发展、废物资源化利用和绿色生产等；拓展模块是根据参研单位的专业设置，进行有针对性的拓展，完善绿色技能清单。我们计划在校内选取生物学院、汽车学院学生作为参与试点，配合教学资源，开发培训项目，验证理论的正确性和项目的有效性，推广研究成果。在校外计划与 5～10 所合作院校参与试点，开发拓展教学模块，并在合作院校开展教学试点，推广研究成果。

# （十一）

# 金华职院“三融三式”绿色教育的探索与实践

金华职业技术学院校长　梁克东

在世界绿色经济发展背景下，绿色技能成为绿色经济发展中的关键因素，绿色教育也成为国际职业教育发展的重要趋势。其一，“绿色发展”是推动我国经济社会发展的必然要求。党的十八大、十九大报告都相继提出要加快绿色发展，党的十九届五中全会提出“到 2035 年，广泛形成绿色生产生活方式，碳排放达峰后稳中有降，生态环境根本好转，美丽中国建设目标基本实现”，明确了我国经济社会发展的生态战略目标。其二，“绿色技能”是开发劳动力市场新增长的必然要求。《2022 年全球绿色技能报告》指出，绿色人才在全球劳动力中占比正逐渐上升，由 2015 年的 9.6% 上升到 2021 年的 13.3%，预计未来十年将产生超百万个职位。受新冠病毒疫情影响，未来职业资格将更加强调绿色技能和数字能力。其三，“绿色教育”是职业院校培养学生可持续发展能力的必然要求。我国的绿色技能人才培养工作的主体集中在职业院校，必须加强绿色教育，通过绿色技能开发使职业院校进一步更新办学理念，优化调整专业结构和课程体系、强化师资队伍建设、完善专业教学标准和人才培养方案，使绿色技能成为学生的基本素养。

作为教育部与联合国儿童基金会青少年“核心能力提升”项目《绿色技能（高职版）》培训材料开发项目牵头单位，金华职业技术学院积极发挥引领作用，把绿色发展理念融入教育教学与实践，以课程为核心，以基地为支撑，以文化为驱动，积极探索“三融三式”的绿色教育体系。

### 1. 融入课程，立足“三重”，开发“活页式”教材

学校积极适应“新技术、新产业、新业态、新模式”的经济形态，汇集全校名师组建教学团队，融合绿色通识类课程、绿色要素课程、专业课程，开发集“通用

性、专业性、实践性”于一体的活页式绿色教材。

通识绿色技能开发重在普适。面向全校学生，以认知性、人文性、态度性的通用绿色软技能为主，围绕“衣、食、住、行”四大主题，开发包含绿色家居、节能交通、垃圾分类等在内的 8 个绿色生态文明基础模块，培养学生绿色消费、绿色出行、低碳生活、循环利用等绿色理念。

专业绿色技能开发重在拓新。针对环境检测技术、建筑工程、新能源汽车、园林技术等具有明显绿色属性的专业，融入新的绿色知识和技术、要求和标准、操作程序和方式；针对管理服务、艺术设计类等传统专业，深挖专业绿色转型所必需的组织力、管理力、资源循环利用等技能点，呈现绿色技能的多样性。

绿色技能资源开发重在转化。将清洁生产服务、污染源普查、室内空气质量监测等绿色技术服务项目转化为教学案例，结合案例中的任务、目标、评价及效果，采用微视频等多种形式开发绿色技能资源包，实现课堂教学嵌入实践服务项目，让学生在真实工程环境中提升绿色技能。

**2. 融合基地，立足“绿色 +”，打造“多样式”平台**

学校不断扩展绿色教育载体，构建“绿色 +”平台，实现生产与学习融合、生活与绿色融合、绿色资源与教育资源融合。

“绿色 +”专业实践平台。充分挖掘校内实践基地绿色教育资源，满足学生自主性学习和专业实践需要。医药化工虚拟仿真实训中心实现无限制、无污染、无浪费、安全高效的循环操作；疫情期间同步推进在线实训平台建设，满足学生远程线上学习需求；对接“1+X”证书标准，新建装配式建筑智慧学习工场，为“岗课赛证”融通教学提供平台。

“绿色 +”社会培训平台。通过全国工业废水处理工技师培训基地，推进绿色人才一体化培训。每年与国家清洁生产中心联合开展资格培训，输送 500 余名专业技术人员；完成金华市大学生农村负责人、农村污水监管员等 5 000 人次绿色技能培训；为中国化工集团等中国 500 强企业提供清洁生产专题培训 14.8 万人次。

“绿色 +”公益服务平台。以浙江省生态文明教育基地为核心，依托专业性公司和引企入校企业，实现课堂教学嵌入服务项目，在真实工程环境中提升学生绿色技能。近 5 年，师生为 200 余家企业开展清洁生产审核、环保监测等服务 300 余项、安全咨询项目 900 余项，在第二次全国污染源普查中完成对 8 855 家企业的调查。

**3. 融育文化，立足“亮特实”，开展“浸润式”活动**

学校以文化赋能绿色发展，在丰富的校园活动浸润中厚植绿色文化。

做亮绿色育人品牌。积极培育“绿色制造科技节”“科技助农团”等绿色类活动品牌，打造绿色育人的“金名片”；成立“阿郎卫士”“绿之韵”“蔚蓝之青”等绿色类社团，开展环境保护、健康服务、职业安全等专项行动，其中，阿郎卫士社团被评为国家“双百双进”十佳团队、全国“一校一品”校园文化品牌。

做特绿色校园文化。以绿色文化怡情，在校园景观注入职教匠心，建有展现核心育人模式的“五位一体”雕塑，象征技术革命的工业雕塑群等；以绿色文化导行，聘请东阳木雕代表性传承人陆光正、婺州窑陶瓷烧制技艺非遗传承人陈新华等一批大师担任绿色技能社会导师，传递绿色理念、展示精湛匠艺、分享工匠情怀。

做实绿色宣传教育。以节能宣传周、世界无车日、世界环境日、世界地球日等为契机，定期开展节能、节水、垃圾分类、绿色出行等主题宣传、倡议活动。近年来，学校绿色荣誉不断，在生态文明、环境保护、节能减排等竞赛、评优评奖中共获得“国家级节约型公共机构”等国家级、省级奖项共 13 项。

“绿水青山就是金山银山”已经成为当代中国的发展共识，同时也在国际社会上得到了高度关注与期待。我理解，绿色是一个过程，而不是一次性的结果。绿色职业教育，需要世界各国职业院校一起行动起来！让我们携手努力，共同加快绿色技能开发，培养更多绿色人才，让绿色成为世界发展最动人的色彩！

# （十二）

# 积极探索绿色技能培养　助力自贸港可持续发展

海南省技师学院副院长　张萨萨

众所周知，如何携手共建绿色世界已经成为当前国际社会最重要的话题之一。绿色发展之路是我国可持续发展的必由之路。实现绿色发展关键取决于掌握“绿色”技能且拥有“绿色”行为的人。职业教育和技工教育是与经济社会结合最为紧密的教育形式之一，必然成为培养绿色技能人才的主要阵地。

国家重视绿色发展。党的十八大以来，在习近平生态文明思想的指引下，“绿水青山就是金山银山”的理念已经成为全党全社会的共识和行动。中国已经成为全球生态文明建设的重要参与者、贡献者和引领者。我国越来越重视绿色发展，绿色技能也将成为促进社会发展转型所必需的技能之一。

海南重视生态立省。海南省位于中国的最南端，自由贸易港和独一无二的生态环境是海南省最亮丽的名片。2018 年 4 月 13 日，习近平总书记在海南考察时强调:“要把保护生态环境作为海南发展的根本立足点，牢固树立绿水青山就是金山银山的理念，像对待生命一样对待这一片海上绿洲和这一汪湛蓝海水，努力在建设社会主义生态文明方面做出更大成绩。”近年来，海南一路逐绿前行、生态立省。现在的海南天更蓝、山更绿、水更清、生态更美好。

学院重视绿色技能。海南省技师学院创办于 1958 年，校园总面积约 35.53 公顷，目前分设海口府城和澄迈老城两个校区。学院先后被确认为国家中等职业教育改革发展示范建设学校、国家高技能人才培训基地、中国（海南）康养高技能人才培训基地、第 45、46 届世界技能大赛机电一体化、塑料模具工程、云计算项目等 3 个项目的中国集训基地。学院拥有 8 大专业系及公共基础教学部，共开设 25 个专业，现有学生 10 000 余人，在几代育人团队的努力下，学院办学成果显著。随着海南自由贸易港建设的不断推进，我院意识到绿色教育必将成为我国乃至世界职业教育发展的必然趋势，学院进行了绿色技能培育的探索行动，将绿色技能教育纳入专业人才培养方案之中，从通用绿色技能和绿色专业技能两方面入手，培养可持续发展的绿色技能人才。

首先，通用绿色技能培养。在面向全体学生的通用绿色技能培养方面，一是将绿色理念融入五育并举、产教融合、技能大赛和绿色校园建设之中，营造绿色氛围，在师生心中种下“绿色”种子。二是将绿色理念和绿色技能培养纳入教育教学和学生管理的全过程。与此同时，学院也培养了一批具备绿色教育理念、掌握绿色教学方法的师资队伍和班主任队伍。教师结合企业用人标准，从教学场所和工作站的清洁、节能设施设置、操作过程中的耗材使用、工具摆放、废料分类、循环利用等方面对学生进行综合培养。三是通过丰富多彩的绿色活动，让学生从被动接受绿色知识到主动践行绿色行为。志愿服务、海龟保护、海洋保护、垃圾分类知识竞赛、变废为宝手工作品制作比赛等活动已经成为学生们争相参加的绿色活动。例如，在学院开展的变废为宝手工作品制作比赛活动中，打坏的羽毛球被做成了白孔雀、废弃的电器元件被做成了小台灯和吸尘器、捡到的贝壳和吃完的果壳被做成了精美的艺术摆件。这样的活动不仅提升了学生节约资源、保护环境的意识，还培养了学生的动手能力和创新能力，学生们的作品得到了认可，他们备受鼓舞，增强了自信心。

其次，绿色专业技能开发。我院结合海南自由贸易港重点产业，设置环境保护系，建立新能源汽车高技能人才培训基地和可再生能源高技能人才实训基地。探索“四个融入”，即将绿色理念融入课堂教学、绿色技能融入实践教学、绿色技术融入教材开发、绿色标准融入教学评价。从课程标准、人才培养方案入手，开发活页式教材和相对应的教学资源包，培养具有绿色专业技能的人才。海南省是我国新能源汽车的主要推广地，我院在海南省新能源汽车高技能人才培训和技术推广方面作出了重要贡献。先后培养出新能源技术领域全国技术能手 2 名、国家级裁判 5 名、省级专业骨干教师 8 名、国赛一等奖教师 2 名。指导学生参加国家级比赛获一等奖 2 个、二等奖 6 个，参加行业赛事获一等奖 18 个。举办公益讲座培训 20 场次，培训鉴定 2 000 余人。新能源汽车教学团队完成省级课题 1 项，开发新能源教材 8 本，承办省级大赛 2 次。

在绿色专业人才的培养过程中，以职业岗位素养训练为重点，不断提升学生的可持续发展能力和就业竞争力。例如，2022 届毕业生所设计制作的新能源汽车交流充电桩综合实训系统，就是学生利用废旧的充电桩制作而成，节约了 80% 的成本，该系统可实现电桩组成、工作原理、参数调试、使用维护、故障诊断等实训内容。这些毕业作品将用于新一届学生的实习实训，更重要的是，毕业的学生将绿色环保及专业创新的理念传承了下去。

2022 年 6 月，我院被确定为教育部与联合国儿童基金会青少年“核心能力提升”项目《绿色技能（中职版）》培训材料开发牵头单位。我们将致力于推广、应用绿色理念，探索实践绿色技能人才培养新路径，践行绿色教育活动，培养可持续发展的绿色技能人才。同时，借助项目牵头单位优势，与兄弟院校一道，开展绿色师资培训、优秀案例征集、课程资源开发等项目，让绿色技能培养惠及更多学生。

学院将立足海南自由贸易港建设，积极探索具有国际视野和中国特色的绿色技能人才培养模式。依托“南南合作”、瑞士 GF 教育合作项目等国际合作交流平台，融入中国特色绿色技能，进行国际推广。

世界各国休戚与共，让我们共同为培养绿色技能人才而努力，相信在我们的不懈努力下，我们的学子一定会成为绿色技能的践行者、传播者和受益者。

# （十三）

# 总结词（摘录）

**中华人民共和国教育部职业教育发展中心副主任　刘宝民**

职业教育领域更应积极对接绿色经济社会发展潮流。在此，我们重申以下倡议。

一是建设绿色校园，用绿色智慧赋能学校建设。以培养满足绿色经济社会发展需要的绿色人才为目标，建立健全绿色学校创建制度、政策、标准体系，使师生养成绿色生活方式和良好习惯。加快培养绿色发展急需的技术技能人才，将职业院校打造成绿色低碳产业人才的培养高地。

二是坚持需求导向，为行业培养和输送合格的绿色技能人才。做好绿色职业培训与人才考评，发挥相关行业协会的优势和作用，将绿色技能培养延伸至产教融合全过程。制定和完善绿色职教相关课程和专业标准，形成较为完善的绿色职业从业者教育、培养和实践体系，提升人才培养质量，培养出具有绿色理念、绿色知识、绿色能力和绿色行为的新型技术技能型人才。

三是加强绿色职教和绿色技能的国际交流与合作。搭建绿色职教国际合作平台，积极学习借鉴绿色职教路径探索的国际先进理念和良好实践，充分利用已有实践成果，加快建立健全绿色人才培养体系，助力绿色低碳循环经济发展，为形成具有中国特色的绿色低碳发展道路提供人力资源保障。

在此，我们呼吁各国职教同仁携手，加强务实合作，以实际行动支持联合国2030可持续发展目标的实现。我们也将向世界分享中国绿色职教发展的成功经验，积极参与全球绿色转型，为后疫情时代的绿色复苏贡献中国职教方案。

# 四
# 全球职业教育青年教师发展论坛

协助组织单位：中华人民共和国教育部教师工作司、天津职业技术师范大学

# Ⅳ. Teacher Professional Development in Vocational Education

Co-organizers: Department of Teacher Education of Ministry of Education of the People's Republic of China, Tianjin University of Technology and Education

02
哲仁
Jarun Youbrum

03
史蒂文 · 罗兹
Steven Rhodes

04
韩士兰
Handiso Selamu Yisihak

05
任友群
Ren Youqun

06
张金刚
Zhang Jingang

07
袁振国
Yuan Zhenguo

08
黄维
Huang Wei

09
张建军
Zhang Jianjun

10
于立国
Yu Liguo

11
何辉
He Hui

12
米靖
Mi Jing

**围绕职业教育青年教师可持续专业化能力体系建设，探析职业教育教师发展的核心理念、能力体系和培养模式，研讨青年教师专业能力提升、发展路径等，形成全面提升职业教育教师专业能力的国际共识。**

This session focuses on the sustainable professional development of VTE faculty. The participants discuss the core concepts, capacity system, and training mode for the professional development of VTE faculty, especially the approaches to enhancing young faculty's professional capabilities, with a view to reaching global consensus on elevating professionalism of VTE faculty in an all-round way.

## （一）

## 全球职业教育青年教师发展论坛情况概述

天津职业技术师范大学　李文静

2022 年 8 月 20 日，首届世界职业技术教育发展大会平行论坛“全球职业教育青年教师发展论坛”在国家会展中心（天津）举行。该论坛由中华人民共和国教育部、中国联合国教科文组织全国委员会和天津市人民政府主办，中华人民共和国教育部教师工作司和天津职业技术师范大学协助组织，天津职业技术师范大学承办。会议采用线上线下相结合的形式，来自中国、瑞士、英国、泰国、埃塞俄比亚等国家教育管理部门和高等院校的 14 位演讲嘉宾，近百名国内外专家学者出席此次论坛。论坛由天津职业技术师范大学副校长吕景泉主持。

教师是发展职业教育的第一资源，是支撑新时代国家职业教育改革的关键力量。2022 年是中国“教育数字化元年”，数字化技术、数字化要素、数字化思维、数字化认知的发展正深刻影响着职业教育，伴随着后疫情时代的到来，对职业教育教师特别是青年教师的发展提出了新要求，职业教育青年教师的重要性日益凸显，肩负的使命责任越来越重。全球职业教育青年教师发展论坛，旨在围绕数字化赋能职业教育教师专业发展问题，研讨数字化转型过程中职业教育青年教师专业发展实践、专业能力提升、培养体系构建，推动职业院校教师队伍高质量发展。

论坛总共分为三个阶段，第一阶段是天津市人民政府副市长朱鹏，天津市政协副主席、天津中华职业教育社社务委员会主任李文海致欢迎辞。朱鹏指出，长期以来，天津市高度重视职业教育教师工作，特别是职业教育青年教师发展工作。天津职业技术师范大学作为中国最早的以培养职业教育师资为主要任务的普通本科师范院校，在职业教育教师发展上进行了有效探索，培养了我国首批“双师型”博士职业教育教师和“双师型”留学博士职业教育教师，取得了卓越成绩。青年教师是职业教育的未来，在人类阔步迈进数字化时代的背景下，首届世界职业技术教育发展大会专门举办“全球职业教育青年教师发展论坛”，汇聚全球专家学者之智慧，探索职业教育青年教师发展，对于促进职业教育在数字化时代的发展具有重要意义。李文海在致辞中表示，职业教育青年教师是数字化时代、绿色技能时代和全球化格局下职业教育发展的骨干力量。职业教育教师教育应着力培养职业教育青年教师新发展理念、国际化视野、数字素养和绿色技能。

论坛的第二阶段由中华人民共和国教育部教师工作司司长任友群作题为“中国职业教育教师队伍建设的经验与展望”的主旨报告。任友群从重视思想政治和师德师风建设、完善制度设计和治理体系、推进教师专业发展、提高职业教育教师岗位吸引力四个方面总结中国职业教育教师队伍建设的经验，提出按照“创新制度、完善体系、加快补充、提质赋能”的总体思路，进一步充实数量、优化结构、规范管理、加强保障，建设一支高素质双师型的教师队伍，全面推进职业教育教师工作高质量发展，服务支撑新时代职业教育高质量发展，为世界贡献中国职业教育师资建设模式。

论坛的第三阶段是嘉宾演讲报告，该阶段涵盖“职业教育教师专业发展的创新实践”“产业数字化转型与职业教育青年教师专业能力建设”“全球职业教育青年教师培养体系发展”三个研讨专题，为如何加强青年教师培养分享交流经验，为培养高素质的职业教育教师贡献智慧。

在“职业教育教师专业发展的创新实践”专题中，天津职业技术师范大学党委书记张金刚表示，在新技术、新业态、新模式的发展背景下，职业教育教师不仅要具备专业知识和技能，更需要具有持续学习能力、团队协作能力和创新能力，职业教育教师教育创新发展要与时俱进，并建立完善的标准体系。北京师范大学教育学部部长朱旭东提出从顶层设计上深化，进一步提升职业教育教师教育学科建设，这样才能不断提升职业教育教师质量。华东师范大学教育学部主任袁振国从职业教育教师来源的开放性、培养的专业性、标准的多样性等方面对如何建设一支高质量的职业教育教师队伍提出建议。泰国央拷镇行政管理机构理事会主席哲仁讲述泰国鲁班工坊作为世界上第一所鲁班工坊，泰国大城技术学院将工程实践创新项目应用在教育教学及工程科学系统思维的应用中，他还介绍，在工程实践项目中，师生学会了学习、应用和创新。

在“产业数字化转型与职业教育青年教师专业能力建设”专题中，中国科学院院士、西北工业大学学术委员会主任黄维提出，让数字化赋能职业教育，按照数字化要求，完善人才培养方案，搭建学科专业平台，健全课程教学体系，构建基于数字技术的职业教育教师职前培养体系和在职培训体系。天津职业技术师范大学鲁班工坊国际发展研究中心外籍专家、埃塞俄比亚联邦职业技术培训学院机器人研发工程师韩士兰具体阐释工程实践创新项目教学模式在职业技术教育与培训领域的实施和应用。唐山工业职业技术学院党委副书记、院长张建军认为数字化背景下教师应该具备6种能力，包括数字化教学的设计能力、数字化教学的实施能力、数字化教学资源的开发能力、数字化的评价能力、数字化技术能力和对未来行业的预测能力。河北石油职业技术大学校长于立国提出职业教育双师型教师队伍建设的问题，介绍学校“双师”队伍建设的实践做法。

在“全球职业教育青年教师培养体系发展”专题中，瑞士联邦职业教育与培训学院国际事务部主任埃里克·斯沃斯指出，在瑞士主要是以专业情境为主的教学特色，主要的教育和培训必须要基于专业背景，学生需要建立核心素养，素养的基础是教学内容和教学评价。英国尼斯港塔尔伯特学院全球营运副校长史蒂文·罗兹讲述英国职业教育教师教育与培训的经验做法。浙江建设职业技术学院校长何辉认为，要打造一支高素质、充满活力、教学能力强、行业有影响的青年教师队伍，需要聚焦提质增效，蹄疾步稳地实施教师队伍培养的“一四五六”战略。天津职业技术师范大学职业教育学院院长米靖以天津职业技术师范大学为例，介绍职业教育青年教师培养的三方面思路，一是从“双师型”到“工匠之师”，提出了明确的职业教育教师专业化发展目标；二是逐渐形成了“本硕博一体化”的青年职业教育教师专业化发展的路径；三是形成了基于跨学科、符合职业教育自身规律和职业教育教师成长发展需求而构建的教育学和工学相结合的青年教师专业化发展的模式。

数字化是实现职业教育现代化的重要抓手，是推动职业教育深化改革的重要途径。平行论坛集聚全球智慧，瞄准前沿，聚焦问题，共议挑战，共商良策，达成共识，集中反映了全球职业教育青年教师发展的最新前沿动态。论坛针对数字化背景下全球职业教育青年教师发展提出了诸多新思路，首先，坚持靶向发力，瞄准科学技术变革和产业优化升级方向，按照数字时代的新思维、新要求、新标准，优化职业教育教师培养与培训体系，增强在职业教育领域的适应性。其次，坚持育人为本，通过数字化引领教育理念变革、思想变革、方法变革、实践变革，推动职业师范教育办学模式、教育形式、教学方式和人才培养的数字化转型，培育具有数字化思维和能力的高质量职业教育教师。最后，坚持教学改革核心，加快技术更迭和升级，联通校内教学和管理等应用系统，构建一体化的智慧服务平台，使信息技术和智能技术深度融入学校教育教学和管理的全过程，通过数字教育实践与管理运用，提升职业教育教师的数字素养与实践能力。

在数字化时代，以数字技术作为手段赋能职业教育教师发展、以数字化支撑职业教育青年教师培养培训体系构建已成为必然趋势。全球化视角下，开展职业技术教育数字化理论研究、开发职业教育数字资源库建设、建设职业教育智慧课堂和虚拟实训系统、建立职业教育青年教师数字化素养标准体系，对于探索数字化时代职业教育青年教师培养创新模式，推动全球职业教育青年教师能力发展与培养体系构建具有重要意义。数字化在职业教育青年教师培养中的深度运用与融合，将为全球职业教育青年教师发展注入强劲动力和创新活力。

## i. Overview of the Session on Teacher Professional Development in Vocational Education

**Li Wenjing, Tianjin University of Technology and Education**

On August 20, 2022, "Teacher Professional Development in Vocational Education", a parallel session of the first World Vocational and Technical Education Development Conference, was held at the National Convention and Exhibition Center (Tianjin). The Session was organized by the Ministry of Education of the People's Republic of China, National Commission of the People's Republic of China for UNESCO and Tianjin Municipal People's Government, with the assistance of the Department of Teacher Education of the Ministry of Education and Tianjin University of Technology and Education, and was hosted by Tianjin University of Technology and Education. The session was held online and offline, with 14 guest speakers from education administrations and higher education institutions in China, Switzerland, the UK, Thailand and Ethiopia, and nearly 100 Chinese and international experts and scholars. The session was moderated by Lyu Jingquan, Vice President of Tianjin University of Technology and Education, China.

Teachers are the primary resource for the development of vocational education, and the key force supporting the national vocational education reform in the new era. 2022 is "the first year of the digitalization of education" in China, and the development of digital technologies, elements, thinking and awareness is profoundly influencing vocational education. In the post-pandemic era, new requirements for the development of teachers, especially young teachers, in vocational education have been put forward. Young teachers in vocational education have become increasingly prominent, and their mission and responsibility are increasingly heavier. Focused on the digitally-empowered professional development of teachers in vocational education, the World Vocational and Technical Education Development Conference aims to discuss the practice of professional development, the improvement of professional qualities, and the establishment of a training system for teachers in vocational education in the process of digital transformation, and promote the high-quality development of the teachers in vocational education institutions.

The session consisted of three parts. The first part was the welcome speeches by Zhu Peng, Vice Mayor of Tianjin Municipal People's Government, and Li Wenhai, Vice Chairman of CPPCC Tianjin Committee and Director of Tianjin Affairs Committee of China Vocational Education Association. As Zhu Peng pointed out, Tianjin has long attached great importance to the work related to teachers in vocational education, especially the development of young teachers in vocational education; Tianjin University of Technology and Education, as the earliest normal university in China with the main task of training teachers for vocational education, has made effective exploration in the development of teachers in vocational education and trained the first batch of "dual certified" vocational education teachers with doctoral degrees and "dual certified" vocational education teachers with overseas doctoral degrees in China, obtaining outstanding achievements. Young teachers represent the future of vocational education. As we are striding into the digital era, the first World Vocational and Technical Education Development Conference held the Session on "Teacher Professional Development in Vocational Education", gathering the wisdom of global experts and scholars to explore the development of young teachers in vocational education, which is of great significance to the development of vocational education in the digital era. In his speech, Li Wenhai said that young teachers in vocational education are the backbone of vocational education development in the digital era, the era of green skills and the pattern of globalization. The training of teachers in vocational education should focus on the new development concepts, international vision, digital qualities and green skills of young teachers in vocational education.

In the second part, Ren Youqun, Director of the Department of Teacher Education of Ministry of Education of the People's Republic of China, delivered a keynote speech entitled "Experience and Prospects of the Construction of Vocational Education Teachers in China". He summarized the experience of training teachers in vocational education in China from four aspects: the importance of ideology, politics and the professional ethics of teachers; the improvement of system design and governance system; the promotion of teachers' professional development; and the enhancement of the attractiveness of vocational education faculty positions. In addition, he proposed to further increase the number of teachers, optimize the structure, regulate the management and strengthen the guarantee for teachers, build a team of high-quality "dual certified" teachers, comprehensively boost the high-quality development of work related to teachers in vocational education, serve to support the high-quality development of vocational education in the new era, and contribute the development model of Chinese vocational education teachers to the world while following the general idea of "innovative mechanism, improved system, accelerated supplement, and strengthened empowerment".

The third part was reports of guest speakers, which covered three topics:

"Innovative Practice of Professional Development of Vocational Education Teachers", "Industrial Digital Transformation and Professional Capacity Building of Young Teachers in Vocational Education" and "Development of Global Vocational Education Young Teachers Training System". The guest speakers shared experiences on how to strengthen the training of young teachers, and contributed their wisdom to the development of high-quality teachers in vocational education.

Under the topic of "Innovative Practice of Professional Development of Vocational Education Teachers", Zhang Jingang, Secretary of CPC Committee of Tianjin University of Technology and Education, China, revealed that in the context of emerging technologies, business types and modes, vocational education teachers are required to not only possess professional knowledge and skills, but also have the abilities of continuous learning, teamwork and innovation. The innovative development of education for teachers in vocational education should keep pace with the times and establish an improved standard system. Zhu Xudong, Director of the Faculty of Education of Beijing Normal University, China, proposed to deepen the top-level design and further enhance the development of disciplines for the education of teachers so as to continuously improve the quality of teachers in vocational education. Yuan Zhenguo, Director of the Faculty of Education, East China Normal University, put forward recommendations on how to build a team of high-quality teachers in vocational education from such aspects as openness of sources, professionalism of training and diversity of standards of teachers in vocational education. Jarun Youbrum, Chairman of Yangkhao Subdistrict Administrative Organization Council, Thailand, talked about the story of Thailand Luban Workshop as the first Luban Workshop in the world, the application of the Engineering Practice Innovation Program (EPIP) project in education and teaching by the Institute of Technology Ayutthaya of Thailand, and the application of systematic thinking of engineering science. He also introduced that in engineering practice projects, teachers and students learn to study, apply and innovate.

Under the topic of "Industrial Digital Transformation and Professional Capacity Building of Young Teachers in Vocational Education", Huang Wei, Academician of Chinese Academy of Sciences and Director of Academic Committee of Northwestern Polytechnic University, China, proposed to empower vocational education with digitalization, and follow the requirements of digitalization to improve talent training programs, establish disciplinary and professional platforms, improve curriculum teaching system, and build an orientation training system and in-service training system for teachers in vocational education. Handiso Selamu Yisihak, Researcher of Luban Workshop International Development Research Center of Tianjin University of Technology and Education and Robot R&D Engineer from Federal Democratic Republic of Ethiopia Technical and Vocational Training Institute, explained in detail the implementation and application of the EPIP teaching model in the field of vocational education and training. Zhang Jianjun, Deputy Secretary of CPC Committee and President of Tangshan Polytechnic College, China, pointed out that in the digital context teachers should be equipped with six competencies: the ability to design digital teaching, the ability to implement digital teaching, the ability to develop digital teaching resources, the ability to evaluate digitalization, the ability of digital technologies and the ability to forecast the future industries. Yu Liguo, President of Hebei Petroleum University of Technology, China, put forward the issue of building a team of "dual certified" teachers in vocational education and introduced the practical approach of his university.

Under the topic of "Development of Global Vocational Education Young Teachers Training System", Eric Swars, Head of International Affairs of the Swiss Federal University for Vocational Education and Training (SFUVET), pointed out that in Switzerland, teaching and learning are mainly featured by professional contexts, where the main education and training must be based on professional contexts, and students need to build core competencies, which is based on the content and assessment of teaching and learning. Steven Rhodes, Assistant Principal Worldwide Operations, Neath Port Talbot College and Coleg Powys (NPTC) Group of Colleges, UK, introduced the experience and practices of education and training for teachers in vocational education in the UK. He Hui, President of Zhejiang College of Construction, China, said that in order to build a high-quality and dynamic team of young teachers with strong teaching ability and influence in the industry, it is necessary to focus on improving quality and efficiency, and implement the "One, Four, Five, Six" strategy for teacher training in a fast and steady manner. Taking his own school as an example, Mi Jing, Dean of School of Vocational Education in Tianjin University of Technology and Education, China, introduced the idea of training young teachers in vocational education from three aspects: the first is the change from "dual certified teachers" to "artisan teachers", putting forward a clear goal of professional development for teachers in vocational education; the second is the formation of the path of professional development of young teachers in vocational education through the integration of undergraduate, postgraduate and doctoral programs; the third is the formation of a model of professional development of young teachers based on the interdisciplinary combination of pedagogy and engineering in accordance with the laws of vocational education and the needs of growth and development of teachers in vocational education.

Digitalization is an important tool to modernize vocational education, and an important way to promote the in-depth reform of vocational education. The session gathered global wisdom, aimed at the frontier, focused on key issues, discussed challenges and solutions, and reached a consensus, reflecting the latest frontier development of young teachers in global vocational education. The session proposed many new ideas for the development of young teachers in global vocational education in the context of digitalization. First, we need to insist on targeted efforts, follow the direction of scientific and technological transformations and industrial optimization and upgrading, optimize the development and training system of teachers in vocational education according to the new ideas, requirements and standards of the digital era, and enhance adaptability in the field of vocational education. Secondly, we need to insist on the fundamental purpose of training talents, lead the transformation of education concepts, ideology, methodology and practice through digitalization, and promote the digital transformation of vocational normal education mode, education form, teaching method and talent training, and train high-quality teachers in vocational education with digital thinking and abilities. Thirdly, we need to insist on the core of teaching reform, accelerate technological iteration and upgrading, connect internal teaching, management and other application systems, build an integrated intelligent service platform, deeply integrate information technology and intelligent technology into the whole process of school education and management, and enhance the digital competence and practical ability of teachers in vocational education through the use of digital education practice and management.

In the digital era, the inevitable trend is to use digital technologies as a means to empower the development of teachers in vocational education and support the establishment of a training system for young teachers in vocational education with digitalization. From the perspective of globalization, we need to carry out theoretical research on the digitalization of vocational and technical education, develop vocational education digital resource library, establish vocational education smart classrooms and virtual training systems, and build a digital competence standard system for young teachers in vocational education. All these efforts are of great significance for exploring the innovative mode of training young teachers in vocational education in the digital era and promoting the development of competence and training system for young teachers in global vocational education. We believe that the in-depth use and integration of digitalization in the training of young teachers in vocational education will inject strong momentum and vitality of innovation into the development of young teachers in global vocational education.

## (二)

# 中国教学模式在泰国鲁班工坊的运用与推广

泰国央拷镇行政管理机构理事会主席　哲　仁

泰国和中国是亲密友好的近邻，两国人民在历史悠久的交往中结下了“中泰一家亲”的深厚情谊。我有很多中国朋友，比如吕景泉校长，还有泰国鲁班工坊的老师们。我也很荣幸能够和我的中国朋友们一起，参与并见证了全球首家鲁班工坊的建设发展。

泰国鲁班工坊是世界上第一所鲁班工坊，由泰国大城技术学院和天津渤海职业技术学院合作创建。目前，开设了机电一体化技术、物联网技术、数控机床、新能源汽车技术、（高铁）动车组检修技术和（高铁）铁道信号自动控制，共 6 个国际专业。中国的院校给了我们很大的支持和帮助，提供了先进的教学设备，还带来了适合职业教育的工程实践创新项目教学模式。

在中国院校的帮助下，泰国学生掌握了先进的制造业技术，泰国教师学会了运用工程实践创新项目的先进教学方法。工程实践创新项目通过泰国鲁班工坊正影响着泰国职业院校的教学改革，这种教学模式改革促进通过实践或完成任务来解决生活中遇到的问题，给学生创造经验、生活技能、创意和创新。通过融合工程和实践的教学，强调学生将学过的知识和技术技能应用在实际生活当中，解决日常生活问题，并且应用在未来的工作与生活中。

工程实践创新项目教学模式是让职业院校教师真教真做，职业院校学生真学真练，是在教学生学知识和技能的过程中，注重培养学生的关键能力，注重全过程的整体教学。关键能力的培养，应该是项目式的，在一个一个的项目教学中，培养学生认知能力、独立思考、逻辑推理、信息加工、文字应用；培养学生合作能力、自我管理、与他人合作；培养学生创新能力，激发学生的好奇心、想象力和创新思维，鼓励学生勇于探索、大胆尝试、创新创造；培养学生职业能力，引导学生适应社会需求，爱岗敬业、精益求精，动手实践和解决问题。

每门课程、每项活动、每个环节都要力求注重过程，保证完整性和全面性，教师指导学生（团队）不停地在“做”一件一件完整的事情，在一件一件完整的事情上“教”，在一件一件完整的事情上“学”。

在工程实践创新项目教学模式下，对于职业教育教师来说，就是要为学生寻找、营造适合的工程目标和环境（真实世界、现实生活），在工程目标和环境下培养学生，实施教、学、做一体，教会学生学；对于学生来说，就是要了解工程，掌握工程技术、构造、流程、工艺，养成工程思维和工程素养，在教、学、做的工程实践项目中，学会学习、学会应用、学会创新。让整个职业院校因为“完整”和“真实”焕发新的活力。

这些年来，泰国大城技术学院将工程实践创新项目应用在教育、教学、办学方面，尤其是在泰国鲁班工坊建设的专业中。在日常教学中融入工程实践创新项目的教学理念，培养学生创新和动手能力，给学生提供到中国读书的机会。将工程实践创新项目应用在主要专业和鲁班工坊专业的教学中，将工程实践创新项目的专业建设推广到大城技术学院的其他专业，并与工程实践创新项目国际教育联盟的其他泰国院校一起，努力推广工程实践创新项目教学模式。

总而言之，工程实践创新项目是将工程科学系统化思维传达给参加项目的学生和教师，通过鲁班工坊作为学习基地，使主要专业和其他专业的办学成果明显变得更好，这也让教师团队提升了国际视野和互鉴交流能力、校企协同和组织实施能力、工程实践和环境营造能力，锻炼了一支专业知识与实践技能好、专业技术与信息化应用能力强、教学组织与协作方式灵活、职业道德与文化素养高的教师团队。

# ii. Application and Promotion of Chinese Teaching Model in Thailand Luban Workshop

**Jarun Youbrum, Chairman of Yangkhao Subdistrict Administrative Organization Council, Thailand**

**นายจรัล ยุบรัมย์ ประธานสภาองค์การบริหารส่วนตำบลยางขาว ประเทศไทย**

**การประยุกต์ใช้และส่งเสริมรูปแบบการสอนของประเทศจีนในลูปันเวิร์คช็อปประเทศไทย**

ผมมาจากประเทศไทย ไทยและจีนเป็นเพื่อนบ้านใกล้ชิดสนิทกัน มีประวัติศาสตร์ความสัมพันธ์อันยาวนาน จึงมีคำกล่าวที่ว่า"ไทย-จีน ใช่อื่นไกล พี่น้องกัน" ผมมีเพื่อนชาวจีนหลายท่าน เช่น ผอ หลูจิ่งฉวน และยังมีเหล่าครูในโครงการลูปันเวิร์คช็อปประเทศไทย ผมรู้สึกเป็นเกียรติอย่างยิ่งที่ได้มีส่วนร่วมและเป็นสักขีพยานในการก่อตั้งและพัฒนาลูปันเวิร์คช็อปแห่งแรกของโลกด้วยกันกับเพื่อนๆ ชาวจีน

ลูปันเวิร์คช็อปประเทศไทยเป็นลูปันเวิร์คช็อปแห่งแรกของโลก ก่อตั้งโดยความร่วมมือของวิทยาลัยเทคนิคพระนครศรีอยุธยาและวิทยาลัยเทคนิคและอาชีวศึกษาเทียนจินโป๋ห่าย ปัจจุบันเปิดสอนรวม 6 สาขาวิชานานาชาติ ได้แก่ สาขาเทคโนโลยีเมคคาทรอนิกส์ สาขาเทคโนโลยีอินเตอร์เน็ตออฟติง สาขาซีเอ็นซี สาขาเทคโนโลยียานยนต์พลังงานใหม่ สาขาเทคโนโลยีการบำรุงรักษา EMU (รถไฟความเร็วสูง) และสาขาการควบคุมอัตโนมัติสัญญาณรางเหล็ก (รถไฟความเร็วสูง) สถานศึกษาจีนได้ให้การสนับสนุนและความช่วยเหลือแก่พวกเราเป็นอย่างมาก จัดหาและสนับสนุนเครื่องจักรครุภัณฑ์ที่นำสมัย ทั้งยังนำรูปแบบการสอนEPIPที่เหมาะสมแก่การศึกษาอาชีวะมาสู่พวกเรา

ภายใต้ความช่วยเหลือของสถานศึกษาจีน นักศึกษาไทยจึงมีความชำนาญในเทคโนโลยีการผลิตที่ทันสมัย ครูไทยได้เรียนรู้และประยุกต์ใช้วิธีการสอนที่ทันสมัยอย่างEPIP EPIPมีอิทธิพลต่อการปฏิรูปการสอนของวิทยาลัยอาชีวศึกษาในประเทศไทยผ่านลูปันเวิร์คช็อปประเทศไทย รูปแบบการสอนนี้ส่งเสริมการเรียนรู้ผ่านการปฏิบัติจริงหรือทำใบงานที่มุ่งแก้ไขปัญหาที่พบเห็นในชีวิตจริง เพื่อเสริมสร้างประสบการณ์ ทักษะชีวิต ความคิดสร้างสรรค์ และนวัตกรรมแก่นักศึกษา โดยผ่านการบูรณาการการเรียนการสอนวิศวกรรมและการปฏิบัติจริง เน้นให้นักศึกษานำความรู้และทักษะเทคโนโลยีไปประยุกต์ใช้ในชีวิตจริงแก้ไขปัญหาในชีวิตประจำวัน ตลอดจนการประกอบอาชีพและดำรงชีวิตในอนาคต

รูปแบบการสอนEPIPเป็นการให้ครูผู้สอนในสถานศึกษาอาชีวะสอนจริงและทำจริง ให้นักศึกษาในสถานศึกษาอาชีวะเรียนจริงและฝึกฝนจริง ในกระบวนการสอนให้นักศึกษาเรียนรู้ทักษะและความรู้ ต้องเน้นการปลูกฝังความสามารถที่สำคัญ และใส่ใจการสอนโดยรวมของกระบวนการทั้งหมด การผลิตอบรมความสามารถหลักควรเป็นแบบโครงงาน ในการสอนโครงงานแต่ละชิ้นต้องพัฒนาความสามารถทางปัญญาของนักศึกษา การคิดอย่างอิสระ การใช้เหตุผลเชิงตรรกะ การประมวลผลข้อมูล และการใช้ภาษา ปลูกฝังให้นักศึกษามีความสามารถในการทำงานเป็นทีม การจัดการตนเอง และการร่วมมือกับผู้อื่น ปลูกฝังคว

ามสามารถในการสร้างสรรค์ของนักศึกษา กระตุ้นความอยากรู้อยากเห็น จินตนาการและความคิดเชิงนวัตกรรมของนักศึกษา กระตุ้นให้นักศึกษากล้าสำรวจ กล้าลอง และสร้างสรรค์สิ่งใหม่ๆ ปลูกฝังความสามารถทางวิชาชีพแก่นักศึกษา แนะนำนักศึกษาให้ปรับตัวเข้ากับความต้องการทางสังคม ทุ่มเทในการทำงาน มุ่งมั่นเพื่อความสมบูรณ์แบบ ฝึกฝนการปฏิบัติและการแก้ปัญหา

ทุกรายวิชา ทุกกิจกรรม และทุกขั้นตอน ควรมุ่งมั่นให้เห็นถึงความสมบูรณ์ กระบวนการ และความครอบคลุม ครูแนะนำนักศึกษา (ทีม) ให้ "ทำ" แต่ละสิ่งจนครบถ้วน "สอน" ในแต่ละสิ่งจนครบถ้วน "เรียน" ในแต่ละสิ่งจนครบถ้วน

ภายใต้รูปแบบการสอนEPIP สำหรับครูอาชีวะแล้วก็คือการค้นหา สร้างเป้าหมายและสภาพแวดล้อมทางวิศวกรรมที่เหมาะสม (ในโลกแห่งความจริง ในชีวิตจริง) ให้แก่นักศึกษา ปลูกฝังนักศึกษาภายใต้เป้าหมายและสภาพแวดล้อมของวิศวกรรม ดำเนินการสอนโดยรวม และสอนนักศึกษาให้เรียนรู้ สำหรับนักศึกษาแล้วก็คือการทำความเข้าใจวิศวกรรม เข้าใจเทคโนโลยีวิศวกรรม โครงสร้าง กระบวนการ งานฝีมือ วัฒนธรรม พัฒนาความคิดและความรู้ทางวิศวกรรม เรียนรู้ที่จะเรียนรู้ เรียนรู้การประยุกต์ใช้ เรียนรู้นวัตกรรมท่ามกลางการเรียนการสอนในโครงการปฏิบัติทางวิศวกรรม ทำให้สถานศึกษาอาชีวะทั้งวิทยาลัยกระปรี้กระเปร่าขึ้นด้วย "ความสมบูรณ์" และ "ความจริง"

หลายปีมานี้ วิทยาลัยเทคนิคพระนครศรีอยุธยาได้นำโครงการ EPIP มาประยุกต์ใช้ในการจัดการเรียนการสอน โดยเฉพาะอย่างยิ่งในสาขาวิชาภายใต้โครงการลูปันเวิร์คช็อปประเทศไทย เราหลอมรวมแนวคิดการสอนEPIPเข้าสู่การสอนในชีวิตประจำวัน อบรมนักศึกษาให้มีความสามารถในการปฏิบัติและนวัตกรรม มอบโอกาสให้นักศึกษามาศึกษาที่ประเทศจีน เรานำEPIPมาประยุกต์ใช้ในสาขาวิชาหลักและการสอนในสาขาภายใต้ลูปันเวิร์คช็อป ส่งเสริมEPIPสู่สาขาอื่นๆ ในวิทยาลัยเทคนิคพระนครศรีอยุธยา ทั้งยังร่วมมือกับสถานศึกษาในไทยแห่งอื่นๆ ที่เป็นสมาชิกพันธมิตรการศึกษานานาชาติEPIP ร่วมกันส่งเสริมรูปแบบการสอนEPIP

กล่าวโดยสรุปว่า โครงการ EPIP นั้น ได้นำการคิดที่เป็นระบบเชิงวิศวกรรมและวิทยาศาสตร์ส่งต่อให้แก่นักศึกษาและครูที่เข้าร่วมโครงการ ผลสัมฤทธิ์ในการจัดการเรียนการสอนในสาขาหลักและสาขาอื่นๆ นั้น ดีขึ้นอย่างเห็นได้ชัดโดยใช้ลูปันเวิร์คช็อปเป็นฐานการเรียนรู้ สิ่งนี้ทำให้ทีมครูของเราได้ยกระดับวิสัยทัศน์ให้เป็นสากล ยกระดับความสามารถในการเรียนรู้และการสื่อสารระหว่างกัน ความร่วมมือระหว่างสถานศึกษากับภาคบริษัทและความสามารถในการจัดการและปฏิบัติ ความสามารถในการปฏิบัติงานด้านวิศวกรรมและการสร้างสิ่งแวดล้อม ได้ฝึกอบรมทีมครูให้มีความรู้ในสาขาวิชาและทักษะการปฏิบัติที่ดี มีความสามารถประยุกต์ใช้ข้อมูลและเทคโนโลยีในสาขาอาชีพ มีความยืดหยุ่นในการจัดองค์การสอนและวิธีการทำงานร่วมกันและดำรงจรรยาบรรณอันดีในวิชาชีพ

# （三）

# 职业教育教师培训

英国尼斯港塔尔伯特学院全球营运副校长　史蒂文·罗兹

英国尼斯港塔尔伯特学院职教集团（以下简称 NPTC 职教集团）的培训计划旨在为中国的职业教育教师提供培训，此外，还提供一系列以“21 世纪技能”为重点的技术课程。“教师培训在职业教育体系改革和教育现代化方面都起着最重要的作用。”NPTC 职教集团的目标是培训出职业能力强的教师，掌握基于证据的协作教学技术。NPTC 职教集团的课程不仅向教师介绍有效学习和教学的概念和原则，也介绍作为一名教师应承担的职责。

课程通过反思、审查、评估和规划，确保可持续的专业发展。课程介绍了一个经验丰富的教师所应扮演的角色和承担的责任、管理学生的规划技能和技巧、教学和学习环境、基于个人能力和团队合作的方法、行为准则和组织文化。

课程结构与学习和教学周期相对应，包括确定需求、教育规划、管理学习以及知识评估与评价。鼓励和支持教师培养自己的职业技能，加强对教学方法的理解。NPTC 职教集团开发了广泛的技能和能力课程，可以应用于不同的环境。但课程的重点落在学员作为该领域学科教师的个人和专业发展。

NPTC 职教集团为职业教育领域的教师、培训师等在终身学习领域提供高质量的课程已有三十多年的经验。在英国乃至国际的教育培训机构，该项目都当属前沿、高质量的课程。课程理念聚焦成年人，课程教学、学习内容都吸取了历年学员的专业经验，在鼓励个人学习方法的同时，课程也认识到小组和团队合作在启发专业经验、发展技能和专业知识方面的价值。

2012 年开始，NPTC 职教集团正式与中国职业教育界合作，在重庆启动了支持教学和职业技能发展的“工作站”项目，并为 36 所职业院校联盟中的教师提供服务。这个项目在疫情暴发之前都是在英国面对面授课进行的。该项目极具影响力，但要求与英国教师一同工作的中国职业教育教师有较高的英语水平。其实这个项目本身是很划算的，但旅行和住宿等费用导致这个项目的成本变得很高。

为了克服费用和语言障碍，2018 年，NPTC 职教集团推出了一个旗舰项目——中英职业教育卓越中心，这是一个以学生为中心的循证学习服务项目，为参与者提供专业和标准化的职业教育体系。这种教学模式为大多数发达国家所接受。最初，这是一个由 NPTC 职教集团的专家在中国提供面对面教师培训的项目。教师培训为期一年，英国专家每年来华教学 3 次，每次提供为期 10 天的强化培训。在中国的教师则通过课堂教学进行实际应用，并不断通过国内交流来评估自己的学习成果。

中英职业教育卓越中心项目有助于中国职业教育体系发展，培养高质量的教学团队，为毕业生提供技术技能培训，推动就业和教育进步，提升中国高校的国际影响力和竞争力，NPTC 职教集团使职业教育与培训系统能够可持续运行。中英职业教育卓越中心在英国设立总部，并在北京设立了中国办事处，负责发展英国优质职业院校与中国职业院校之间的合作关系。中英职业教育卓越中心旨在支持中国经济发展政策的实施，促进教学技术走向国际化并提高国际标准认可的技能水平，帮助高技能人力资源供应链服务关键的出口倡议，如中国的“一带一路”倡议，充分发挥毕业生对中国社会和经济发展的整体贡献。尽管中英职业教育卓越中心采用了英国继续教育部门采用的标准和方法，然而，它聚焦于培养适应中国特色的毕业生的就业能力。

由于新冠病毒疫情暴发，NPTC 职教集团发起一项活动，包括基于数字化建设等，继续向中国职业院校提供卓越的培训。NPTC 职教集团迅速为在上海合作学院学习的中国学生开发了在线“学生成长记录袋评价”。因此尽管有疫情的冲击，21 名学生仍于 2020 年 7 月完成了课程并获得了证书，学生进入课程的下一个阶段。2021 年，来自上海和哈尔滨的数百名中国学生报名参加了 NPTC 职教集团项目，这些课程都是在中国学习的，由中国老师采用中文授课。此外，通过在线会议，NPTC 职教集团已经制定了 5 个课程开发项目，并计划制定更多的项目。

NPTC 职教集团在技术职业教育和培训领域为教育和工业部门提供支持。NPTC 职教集团在职业教育领域已有九十多年的经验，使用的方法是本地化和情境化运用，旨在满足学生和雇主的需求。集团擅长处理学生事务，为即将工作和学徒前的学生制定职业教育项目，如汽车初级学徒等。这些项目强调将理论元素嵌入实际手工技能课程，辅之以额外的可迁移式就业技能。这样可以满足雇主需求，增强学生毕业后利用所学专业就业的机会，还会对职业教育领域内有特殊教育需求的个人提供支持。

NPTC 职教集团在提高和重塑现有技术人员的技能方面拥有丰富的经验，不仅开设满足特定需求的课程，同时，还确保获得资格和课程符合教学标准。这些课程由认证机构合作伙伴认可和监管，符合英国和全球标准。NPTC 职教集团通过创建在线支持和混合学习课程开展培训，如电动汽车驾驶培训项目提供质量保证、教师培训和课程开发 / 规划。这些课程旨在支持疫情时期的培训，师生能够继续保持互动，但预计疫情之后，我们会需要新的技术学习方法。

我们提倡混合的教学方法，让学生从电子学习资源和定向自学时间中受益，使得学生在工程、绿色技术和建筑领域的职业资格方面拥有丰富的经验。例如，我们通过多个国际认证机构提供组合式能力培训项目，如英国 IMI 集团、英国伦敦城市行业协会以及 NPTC 职教集团。

## iii. Vocational Teacher Training

**Steven Rhodes, Assistant Principal Worldwide Operations, Neath Port Talbot College and Coleg Powys (NPTC) Group of Colleges, UK**

NPTC Group of Colleges training offer is to provide training for vocational teachers in China, and additionally, a range of technical programmes with a focus on 21st Century Skills. 'Teacher Training is the single most important function in supporting the transformation and modernisation of any vocational education system'. NPTC Group of Colleges' objective is to train vocationally competent lecturers in the evidence-based collaborative teaching techniques. These programmes introduce candidates to the concepts and principles which underpin effective learning and teaching and what it means to be a teacher or trainer.

The Programmes use reflection, review, evaluation and planning to ensure ongoing professional development. Roles and responsibilities of an experienced practitioner, planning skills and techniques for managing learners, the teaching and learning environment, individual and team-based approaches, codes of practice and organisational cultures are introduced.

The course structure corresponds to the learning and teaching cycle and includes identifying needs, planning for education, managing learning, and assessing and evaluating knowledge. Lecturers will be encouraged and supported in developing their skills and understanding of teaching pedagogy. Like all education courses, NPTC Group's college programmes develop an extensive range of skills and aptitudes that can be applied in many different settings. However, the focus is on the student's personal and professional development as subject lecturers in this sector.

NPTC Group has over 30 years of experience delivering high-quality programmes for teachers, tutors, trainers, lecturers, and instructors in the Lifelong Learning sector. The programme maintains contemporary, cutting-edge quality and high status among training and education providers locally, across the UK and internationally. Our philosophy is firmly located within the notion of adults as learners, where instruction, learning and content draw on the professional experiences of our respected course members. Whilst encouraging individual learning approaches, the course programmes also recognise the value of group and teamwork in interrogating professional experience and developing skills and expertise.

NPTC Group of Colleges began working formally with the vocational sector in China in 2012—when the'Workstations' project to support the development of teaching and vocational skills was launched in Chongqing—and was offered to teachers within the consortium of 36 vocational colleges. This programme, which is face-to-face and delivered in the UK, and has run successfully until the pandemic. Whilst it is a very impactful programme, vocational teachers from China who worked along our UK teachers needed to be able to speak English to a high standard. The programme, which in itself was cost-effective, became expensive with travel and accommodation costs, plus the teachers from China were away from their colleges and classes for long periods.

To overcome the barriers of cost and language, in 2018, NPTC Group of Colleges launched their flagship programme—The Centre of Excellence for British Vocational Education in China (CEBVEC), a service programme offering participants a professional and standardised vocational education system of delivery based on evidence-based student-centred learning. This practice is accepted in most developed countries. This was initially designed as a face-to-face programme where the teacher training was delivered in China by experts from NPTC Group of Colleges. The teacher training element was a one year programme which consisted of three visits per year from the UK experts who would deliver 10 days of intense training. The teachers in China would implement their learning through practical application with their classes and evaluate their own learning with ongoing support between the in-country visits.

The CEBVEC programme contributes towards vocational education system development for secondary and higher vocational colleges in China and the applied undergraduate colleges, produce high-quality teaching teams, deliver graduates with technical skills training, employment, and education progression, and boost Chinese colleges and universities in enhanced international influence and competitiveness. NPTC Group of Colleges enables TVET systems to work sustainably and cohesively. CEBVEC has set up its headquarters in the UK and has a China office based in Beijing, responsible for developing partnerships between high-quality vocational colleges in the UK and China's secondary, higher vocational and application-oriented undergraduate colleges. CEBVEC is designed to support the progression of China's economic development policies, internationalising teaching techniques and improving the skill levels as recognised at international standards, for Highly Skilled Human Resource Supply Chains to support key export initiatives, e.g. China's 'Belt and Road Initiative' (BRI) and in the graduate's overall contribution to Chinese social and economic development. CEBVEC takes the standards and methodology adopted in the United Kingdom's Further Education sector. However, it encourages local Chinese characteristics in the focus of its outcome and employability of graduates.

As the COVID-19 pandemic broke in the Spring of 2020, the NPTC Group of Colleges launched its 'Supporting our colleagues in China campaign'. This campaign involved rapid digitalisation in continuing to deliver outstanding training to its Chinese vocational college clients. The NPTC Group of Colleges quickly developed an online 'External Portfolio Assessment' for Chinese students studying at its partner college in Shanghai. As a result, 21 students completed their programme and obtained their certificates in July 2020, despite the pandemic. Allowing students to progress to the next level of their programme. Hundreds of students in China enrolled on NPTC Group of Colleges programmes in 2021 from Colleges in Shanghai and Harbin. These programmes are studied in China, in Chinese and delivered by their Chinese Teachers. In addition, through online conferencing, the NPTC Group of Colleges has produced five Curriculum Development projects, with more planned.

NPTC Group of Colleges is offering to support the Educational and Industrial Sectors within Technical Vocational Education and Training. It has over 90 years of experience in the TVET sector. NPTC Group's approach is to localise and contextualise delivery, designed to meet the needs of students and employers. The College is an expert in dealing with students and developing TVET programmes intended for work-ready and pre-apprenticeship models, for example, the Automotive Junior Apprenticeship. These programmes emphasise embedding the theoretical element to the practical hand skills sessions, with additional transportable employability skills. It is a clear path to meet the needs of employers that have and will enhance students' prospects of graduating into employment within their chosen discipline; this would also incorporate supporting individuals within TVET with Special Education Needs (SEND).

NPTC Group has experience in upskilling and reskilling existing technical staff by creating courses of duration that meet a particular need, also ensuring qualifications and programmes meet the appropriate standard of quality assurance and pedagogies. These qualifications/programmes are recognised/regulated certificated programmes that meet the needs of UK/Global standards by our awarding body partners. NPTC Group of Colleges understands the importance of delivery by creating online support and blended learning programmes. For example, Automotive EV Ready Training Programme provides quality assurance, teacher training and curriculum development/mapping. These programmes are designed to support the delivery during these difficult times, to continue the interaction and support until travel can safely continue, though we envisage the new technological approaches to learning will continue to be in demand in the future, well after the pandemic.

We promote a blended approach to teaching and learning, allowing students to benefit from electronic learning resources and periods of directed self-study. They have extensive experience in delivering a variety of qualifications based on students' existing skills and made relevant to the vocational pathway that students follow within engineering, green technology and construction; for example, a portfolio of capabilities is offered across a wide range of International Awarding Bodies, such as the IMI, City & Guilds, and NPTC Group of Colleges Certificates.

# （四）

# 工程实践创新项目（EPIP）教学模式在职业教育领域的实施与应用

天津职业技术师范大学鲁班工坊国际发展研究中心外籍专家、
埃塞俄比亚联邦职业技术培训学院机器人研发工程师　韩士兰

今天我演讲的主题是“工程实践创新项目（EPIP）教学模式在职业教育领域的实施与应用”，将描述如何在重点行业领域实施工程实践创新项目教学模式。

国内外对教学模式概念的理解并不完全一致。在中国，可归纳为三种类型。第一种教学模式是“在教学实践中形成的设计和组织的教学理论的简化表达形式”，这就是“理论”。第二种教学模式是“在一定教学思想或理论指导下建立的各类教学活动的基本结构或框架”，称为“结构理论”。第三种教学模式是“在一定教学理念的指导下，为完成拟议的教学任务建立的相对固定的教学程序及其实施方法策略体系”，可以称之为“程序理论”。

基于工程实践创新项目的教学实践和理论研究，创始人认为，把握教学模式应注意：模式不是方法，教学模式与教学方法不属于同一层次；模式不是一个计划，教学计划是一个外在的表达，这不足以揭示所包含的教学思想；模式不是一种理论，至少不仅仅是教育理论，它还包含程序、结构、方法、策略等。

教学模式远比教育理论适用。教学模式应该是开展教育教学活动的一整套方法体系。它是在一定的教育理念、教学理念和教学理论指导下建立起来的一种相对稳定的教育教学活动的策略、方法、结构框架和活动程序。教学模式是教育理论的具体化和教学实践的系统化。

工程实践创新项目是中国职业教育话语系统下的一种教学模式。它以中国职业教育的现实为研究起点，体现继承性和民族性的立场和主张，具有主体性和独创性的理论观点，突出系统性和专业性的实践特征，构建了办学思想、专业建设模式、课程结构体系和策略以及具有中国特色的方法体系和标志性品牌概念，形成了职业教育的工程实践创新项目教育理论、工程实践创新项目专业理论和工程实践创新项目课程理论。工程实践创新项目是结合中国技能型人才培养实际建立的一种教学模式，是一种以实际工程为背景，以工程实践为指导，以能力培养为目标，以工程项目为指挥的技能型人才培养教学模式，它不仅是中国职业教育理论发展成果的具体化，也是中国职业教育实践改革经验的系统化。

工程实践创新项目的核心概念有：五观、四元、三谛、两核、一宗。

五观即达观、宏观、中观、微观和纳观。工程实践创新项目主要有三个层级，即所谓的三观：宏观、中观和微观，对应工程实践创新项目教育理论、工程实践创新项目专业理论、工程实践创新项目课程理论。如果再进行细分，拓展应用层级，那么可以说还有两个层级或两观，即更大的宏观，称为“达观”或“宇观”，更小的微观，称为“纳观”。

四元即工程实践创新项目是工程、实践、创新、项目 4 个元素的有机组合，即工程化、实践性、创新型、项目式。

三谛即名谛、实谛、合谛。

两核即真实的培训系统、完整的培训体系。

一宗即知识、技能与实践的统一（知行合一）。

由来自中国、美国、泰国、埃塞俄比亚等 8 个国家 20 多个研究所的 37 位知名专家学者发起了“工程实践创新项目国际教育联盟”，成立 5 年以来，该联盟与许多国家的教育部门、大学、职业学校和企业合作搭建国际研究和交流平台，在两个培训中心（职业教育和鲁班工坊）推动工程实践创新项目教学模式的研究、实践、推广和发展。此外，鲁班工坊的建设也取得了显著成果，完善国际专业标准和教师培训，开发国家级竞赛设备和教学资源。越来越多的国内外职业学校接受了工程实践创新项目的理念，应用工程实践创新项目教学模式，出现了“联盟效应”，即集群效应。它来自工程实践创新项目教学模式提供的整体教学解决方案，即“五个层次、四个维度、三个真实本质、两个基础和一个目标”，以解决“教师如何教学、学生如何学习”的普遍问题。

基于职业教育工程实践创新项目教学模式的鲁班工坊国际主要骨干教师实践培训开始于 2020 年。天津职业技术师范大学为埃塞俄比亚职业技术培训学院选派的 3 名博士和 4 名硕士提供了基于工程实践创新项目教学模式的一级和二级鲁班工坊骨干教师培训。

工程实践创新项目的“工程化”是指职业教育要让学生学会解决“真实”的问题和“实际”的问题，使学生能够在真实世界和现实生活中得心应手地工作和生活。为“真实”教，用真实的工程教；依“真实”学，在真实工程上学；凭“真实”考，借真实工程来考。

职业教育经过深入梳理、广泛吸收中国本土教育理念，形成了自己的特色办学模式、教学模式、话语系统、研究结果。工程实践创新项目是在中国职业教育实践和理论研究的基础上，围绕职业教育的教学模式，汲取中国古代和现代教育思想，借鉴国际先进职业教育经验而创立的。工程实践创新项目是一种技术技能人才培养的教学模式，具有以实际工程为背景和基础，以工程实践为导向和贯穿，以能力培养为目标和归依，强化实践创新和项目统领的特色。

# iv. Engineering Practice Innovation Project (EPIP) Teaching Model Implementation and Application in Technical and Vocational Education and Training (TVET) Sector

**Handiso Selamu Yisihak, Researcher of Luban Workshop International Development Research Center of Tianjin University of Technology and Education, Robot R&D Engineer from Federal Democratic Republic of Ethiopia Technical and Vocational Training Institute**

The topic that I present to you for discussion today is Engineering Practice Innovation Project (EPIP) Teaching Model Implementation and Application in Technical and Vocational Education and Training (TVET) Sector. I will also try to describe how we implement EPIP teaching model in the priority industry sector.

The understanding of the concept of teaching mode is not completely consistent at home and abroad. In China, it can be summarized into three types. The first is that the teaching model is "a theory of designing and organizing teaching formed in teaching practice, which is expressed in a simplified form", which is called "Basic Theory". The second is that the teaching mode is "the basic structure or framework of various types of teaching activities established under the guidance of certain teaching ideas or theories", which is called "Structure Theory". Third, the teaching mode is "a relatively fixed teaching procedure and its implementation method strategy system established under the guidance of certain teaching ideas to complete the proposed teaching tasks", which can be called "Procedure Theory".

Based on the teaching practice and theoretical research of EPIP, the founders of EPIP believe that to grasp the teaching mode, we should pay attention to: The mode is not a method, and the teaching mode and teaching method do not belong to the same level; The model is not a plan, the teaching plan is an external expression, which is not enough to reveal the teaching thought contained; The mode is not a theory, at least not just educational theory, but also contains procedures, structures, methods, strategies, etc.

The teaching mode is far more applicable than educational theory. The teaching mode should be a complete set of methodology systems for carrying out educational and teaching activities. It is a relatively stable strategy, method, structural framework, and activity procedure of educational and teaching activities established under the guidance of certain educational ideas, teaching ideas, and teaching theories. It is the concretization of educational theory and the systematization of teaching practice.

EPIP is a teaching model under the discourse system of Chinese vocational education. It takes the reality of China's vocational education as the research starting point, reflects the position and proposition of inheritance and nationality, has the theoretical viewpoint of subjectivity and originality, highlights the systematic and professional practical characteristics, constructs the school running thought, professional construction mode, curriculum structure system, strategy, and method system and logo brand concept with Chinese characteristics, and forms the EPIP education theory, EPIP specialty theory and EPIP curriculum theory of vocational education. EPIP is a teaching mode established in combination with China's reality of technical skill talent training. It is a teaching mode of technical skill talent training with actual engineering as the background, engineering practice as the guidance, ability training as the goal, and engineering projects as the command. It is not only the concretization of the theoretical development achievements of China's vocational education but also the systematization of the reform experience in the practice of China's vocational education.

The core concepts of EPIP are: Five Views, Four Elements, Three Noble Truths, Two Cores and One Lineage.

"Five Views" of EPIP means Philosophic, Macro, Medium, Micro, and Nano views. EPIP mainly has three levels, namely the so-called three views: Macro, Medium, and Micro views, corresponding to EPIP Education Theory, EPIP Specialty Theory, and EPIP Curriculum Theory. With further subdivision expanding onto the application level, it can be said to have two levels, or two views, namely: The Larger Macro level, called "Philosophy" or "Yu (Universe) View", and The Smaller Micro level, called "Nano View".

Four Elements means that EPIP is a combination of four elements: Engineering, Practice, Innovation, and Project. Namely, there is Engineering, Practicality, Innovation Activates, and Project.

Three Noble Truths means the realm of Name, the realm of Reality and the realm of Unity.

Two Cores means the training system is Factual/True; and the training system is Complete system.

One Purpose means the unity of knowledge/Skills and practice.

International research and exchange platform took shape 5 years ago since the establishment of the Alliance EPIP International Education, which was initiated by 37 renowned experts and scholars from over 20 institutes in more than 8 countries, including China, United States, Thailand, Ethiopia, etc. Mainly in the form of annual conferences, EPIP AIE works with education authorities, universities, vocational schools, and enterprises in many countries to push forward the research, practice, promotion, and development of the EPIP Teaching Model in both training centers (Vocational Education and Luban Workshop). Also, remarkable results have been achieved in the construction of Luban Workshops for international professional standards and teacher training, as well as development of equipment for national competitions and teaching resources. An increasing number of vocational schools at home and abroad have accepted the concept of EPIP and started to apply the EPIP teaching model, an "Alliance Effect", i.e., a cluster effect, has occurred. It comes from the overall teaching solution provided by the EPIP teaching model, namely "Five Levels, Four Dimensions, Three True Essences, Two Bases and One Goal", to solve the universal problem of "how teachers teach and how students study".

International Major Backbone Teachers Practical Training based on EPIP Teaching Model for Vocational Education and Luban Workshop Training Centers started in 2020. Tianjin University of Technology and Education (TUTE) conducted advanced certificate level one and two training for three PhDs and four Masters from Ethiopian Technical and Vocational Institute, who will be the major and backbone teachers based on EPIP Teaching Model for Vocational Education sector and Luban Workshop centers.

The "engineering" of EPIP means that vocational education should enable students to learn and solve "real" and "practical" problems. Students can work and live comfortably in the real world and real life. For "real" teaching, with real engineering teaching; Learn from "reality" and study real engineering; With the "real" test, borrow real engineering to test.

Vocational education has been deeply sorting out and extensively absorbing Chinese local educational ideas, forming its unique school-running mode, teaching mode, discourse system, and research results. EPIP is founded based on China's vocational education practice and theoretical research, centering on the teaching mode of vocational education, absorbing ancient and modern Chinese educational thoughts, and drawing lessons from advanced international vocational education experience. EPIP is a teaching model of training technical talents with practical engineering as the background and foundation, engineering practice as the guidance and penetration, ability training as the goal and dependence, strengthening practical innovation and project command.

# （五）

# 中国职业教育教师队伍建设的经验与展望

中华人民共和国教育部教师工作司司长　任友群

欢迎参加世界职业技术教育发展大会平行论坛之“全球职业教育青年教师发展论坛”，很高兴能有这样的机会跟大家交流学习。下面，我围绕“中国职业教育教师队伍建设的经验与展望”这个主题，与大家进行探讨。

**1. 中国职业教育教师队伍建设的经验**

教育是国之大计、党之大计，教师是立教之本、兴教之源，教师是办好教育的根本依靠。有高质量的职业教育教师，才会有高质量的职业教育。党的十八大以来，以习近平同志为核心的党中央对职业教育特别是职业教育教师队伍建设作出了一系列重大决策部署，职业教育教师队伍建设取得长足进步。

（1）高度重视思想政治和师德师风建设。坚持和加强党对教师工作的全面领导，充分发挥思想政治在职业教育师资队伍建设中的引领作用，以习近平新时代中国特色社会主义思想为广大教师赋能，提高教师思想政治修养和理论素养。坚持师德师风第一标准，认真学习习近平总书记关于职业教育工作的重要指示，深入学习习近平总书记关于师德师风的重要论述，扎实推进师德师风常态化建设，全面落实新时代教师行为准则。

（2）逐步完善制度设计和治理体系。2018 年，中共中央、国务院印发《关于全面深化新时代教师队伍建设改革的意见》。2019 年，国务院印发《国家职业教育改革实施方案》，教育部等四部门印发《深化新时代职业教育“双师型”教师队伍建设改革实施方案》，对职业教育教师工作进行了全面部署。今年新修订的《中华人民共和国职业教育法》也正式实施了。可以说，职业教育教师队伍建设的各项制度在逐步健全，治理体系基本确立。

（3）持续推进教师专业发展。启动实施国家职业教育教师素质提高计划，建立起了“国家示范引领、省级统筹实施、市县联动保障、校本特色研修”的四级培训体系。启动实施职业教育教师教学创新团队培育项目，分两批建设364个国家级团队，示范带动500余个省级团队，教师团队能力素质全面加强。今年，重点开展职业教育教师队伍能力提升行动，启动实施“职教国培”示范项目，着力打造一批能够发挥高端引领和示范带动作用的培训项目，不断提升教师队伍能力素质。

（4）不断提高职业教育教师岗位吸引力。教育部不断加大对职业教育教师表彰力度，在全国模范教师、全国优秀教师、全国教书育人楷模、国家级教学成果奖、“万人计划”教学名师等表彰项目中，均按照同等比例专设职业教育教师奖项。通过一系列激励举措，不断激发教师专业发展动力，增强教师职业认同，提高职业教育教师岗位吸引力。

**2. 新时代中国职业教育教师队伍的建设展望**

（1）进一步强化职业教育教师思想政治和师德师风建设引领作用。从“十四五”到2035年，是职业教育教师队伍建设进一步提质赋能、决战决胜的关键时期。强化教师思想政治和师德师风建设，是职业教育教师队伍建设的首要任务，是落实立德树人根本任务的关键。要坚定不移地贯彻落实习近平总书记关于教育的重要论述，坚守为党育人、为国育才的初心使命，引导广大教师以德立身、以德立学、以德施教，培养造就一大批热爱职业教育的“四有”好教师，当好学生成长成才的“四个引路人”，成为学生为学、为事、为人的“大先生”。

（2）进一步强化职业教育教师队伍建设的制度供给。我国人口红利已进入中后期，推动高质量发展的动力将由人口红利逐渐转换为教育红利。推进现代职业教育高质量发展，正是发挥教育红利的关键举措。要以打造高素质“双师型”职业教育师资为着力点，坚持实践探索和模式创新，推进体系完善和政策改革，特别是围绕职业教育教师发展标准、能力要求、培养机构、培训体系等方面，加大制度供给力度，为打造高质量职业教育教师队伍提供源源不断的制度动能。

（3）进一步强化职业教育教师队伍的类型特色。职业教育是跨界融合的教育，职业学校教师的培养和发展有独特的规律，需要进一步增强职业教育教师培养的“开放性、集成性和协同性”，吸引优质教育机构和企业资源进入到职业教育教师培养培训中，构建开放多元、高效协同的职业教育教师培养培训体系。在培养模式、评价标准、管理制度、资格准入等方面突显职业教育教师的类型特色。鼓励支持高水平工科大学参与职业教育师资培养，建立健全高等学校、职业学校与行业企业联合培养双师型教师的机制。

（4）进一步强化职业教育教师的地位和待遇保障。大力提升职业教育师资的职业吸引力，着力建立吸引社会各界顶尖技术技能人才进入职业院校任教的多元通道，把真正有志于职业教育的优秀人才吸引到职业教育事业中来。将职业教育教师队伍建设与人力资源强国建设相结合，采取更加有力的措施，做好待遇保障和权益维护，大力提升职业教育教师的政治地位、社会地位、职业地位，形成职业教育名师、技术技能大师脱颖而出的良好社会氛围。

各位来宾，习近平总书记指出，“教师不能只做传授书本知识的教书匠，而要成为塑造学生品格、品行、品味的‘大先生’。”青年教师应发挥自身优势，以“大先生”为目标追求，不断创新培养教育的方法，培育一代代新生力量，做好学生的引路人。下一步，我们将扎根中国大地，与世界各国在职业教育师资建设方面进行充分交流，按照“创新制度、完善体系、加快补充、提质赋能”的总体思路，进一步充实数量、优化结构、规范管理、加强保障，建设一支高素质双师型的教师队伍，全面推进职教教师工作高质量发展，为世界贡献中国职业教育师资建设模式。

# （六）

# 后疫情时代中国职教教师教育体系的创新发展

天津职业技术师范大学党委书记　张金刚

当前，中国职业教育正向高质量发展新阶段迈进，中国政府颁布系列政策文件提出要“加快构建现代职业教育体系”，而现代职业教育体系构建的主体支撑及重要保障即为职业教育教师教育体系建设。

## 1. 依靠创新赋能重申后疫情时代中国职业教育教师教育目标

后疫情时代，中国职业教育教师教育目标的实现必须依靠数字化等技术创新和终身学习等理念创新。新冠病毒疫情的暴发给“双师型”教师实践教学能力培养这一目标带来了巨大挑战，尽管可以通过搭建情景化线上平台、改革教学模式等方式破解这一难题，但最为根本的是要转变职业教育教师教育观念。新技术、新业态、新模式发展背景下，技术技能型人才不仅要具备专业知识和技能，更需要具备持续的学习能力、团队协作能力和创新能力，这也就对职业教育教师教育提出新的要求和挑战。后疫情时代，中国职业教育教师教育体系的创新发展应明确以“双师型”为核心的职业教师教育目标，将终身发展理念贯穿于职业教育教师的职业生涯和职业发展机制之中，在提升专业理论和实践素养高基础上，更加注重“互联网 +”技术的应用，突出创新、协作和终身学习等意识的培养和行为实践，使职业教育教师成长的各个阶段都能在“学术性”“职业性”“师范性”等方面得到培养、培训和提高，形成连续性的职业教育教师教育目标体系。

## 2. 通过要素细分完善后疫情时代中国职业教育教师教育标准

中国职业教育教师教育标准经历了从缺失到建立的跨越式发展，今后要通过要素和环节的细分不断实现标准的完善。教育部印发的《中等职业学校教师专业标准

(试行)》《中等职业教育专业师范生教师职业能力标准（试行)》等文件，对中等职业教育专业师范生应具有的教师职业能力进行了具象化、全新式、标准化描述。特别是为应对未来教育的不确定性，教师职业能力标准中提出“中等职业教育专业师范生应具备信息素养，主动适应信息化、人工智能等新技术变革，积极有效开展教育教学的意识”。同时，标准中也更加注重中职师范生自主发展能力的培养及工匠精神的培育。后疫情时代，未来职业教育教师教育创新发展仍需要与时俱进，加强相关要素标准建设，建立完善的标准体系。不只是职业教育教师教育课程标准、教学能力标准、师范生实习实践标准，还要进一步推动职业教育教师资格标准、教师准入标准、教师职称标准等的建立与完善。

**3. 从横向纵向重构后疫情时代中国职业教育教师教育模式**

后疫情时代，中国职业教育教师教育模式的发展既需要纵向的不断深化，也需要实现横向的不断扩展。中国为提升职业教育教师教育过程质量，在培养主体、培养模式等方面做出政策探索与实践努力。在培养主体上，形成了以职业技术师范院校为主体，高水平工科大学等职业技术师范教育新兴力量为辅助，健全普通高等学校与地方政府、职业院校、行业企业联合培养教师机制的新型培养格局。在培养模式上，历经“学科＋师范”为主导的培养模式，分段培养、分流培养的创新人才培养模式，继而到21世纪形成横纵贯通的培养体系。

天津职业技术师范大学积极创新模式，形成本硕博全层次职业教育师资培养体系，培养出我国首批“双师型”本科、硕士和博士，两次荣获国家级教学成果一等奖，形成了中国职业教育教师教育的特色与重要模式之一。后疫情时代，必须提高职业教育师资培养过程的针对性和实效性，我们也将继续探索纵向上本硕博多层次培养并存，横向上涵盖全日制、非全日制、联合培养、特需培养等不同种类多样化的职业教育教师教育培养格局，为中国职业教育教师教育的可持续发展奠定基础。

**4. 用“三化”扩展后疫情时代中国职业教育教师教育角色**

针对疫情带来的教育教学的变化，必须实现职业教育教师角色的扩展。后疫情时代，中国职业教育教师教育角色必须做到“三化”，即育人目标的全面化、教育过程的双重化和教育主体的双师化。其一是育人目标的全面化，育人目标应向国际21世纪教育委员会提出的四大教育支柱靠拢，即“学会认知、学会做事、学会共同生活、学会生存”。其二是教育过程的双重化，既重视“教”更重视“育”，既重视课堂教育更重视自主学习，既重视教师主导更重视学生主体作用的发挥。其三是教育主体的双师化，这里的“双师”是指教学授课将在网上进行，教师担任网络授课任务，学生既接受教师的教学又要靠主体自觉借助人工智能设备等实现自主教育，平台、设备等成为“双师”教学的物质基础与前提。

**5. 以一体化变革后疫情时代中国职业教育教师教育管理**

后疫情时代，职业教育教师教育管理的变革体现为纵向上实现职前、职中、职后三位一体的技术性管理，横向上实现职业教育教师教育培养模式、课程建设、专业结构等的时代性管理，内容上实现职业教育教师教育质量管理、评估以及反馈等环节的序列化管理。后疫情时代，需完善国家职业教育教师管理服务信息化平台，为职业教育教师队伍建设提供信息化决策和便捷化服务支撑。利用多种技术和途径对职业教育教师的职前、职中、职后三个过程进行跟踪、管理和评估，及时掌握职业教育教师动态。设立相应的专家团队或第三方评估机构对职业教育教师教育管理进行研究、分析、评估并做出及时反馈，引导制定更为科学、全面、立体、多元的职业教育教师教育一体化管理，助推职业教育教师教育体系的创新发展。

# （七）

# 职业教师队伍建设的全球议题

华东师范大学教育学部主任　袁振国

职业教育的发展在全世界来讲具有很多共同的特点。中国职业教育正面临着迅速发展，也面临着巨大挑战，这是中国职业教育的双重特点。很长一段时间以来，职业教育的发展和普通教育相比较而言，在质量上有一种“二类教育”的现象，也就是说职业教育和普通教育还存在一定的办学质量差距。现在，在《国家职业教育改革实施方案》和新修订的《中华人民共和国职业教育法》中，都已经明确规定，职业教育是一种教育类型，具有和普通教育同等重要的地位。这就从根本上解决了职业教育的定位问题，从战略思想上明确了职业教育的发展方向和目标，有利于推动职业教育高质量发展。

作为一种类型教育，职业教育高质量发展的关键是要建设好一支高质量的、专业化的教师队伍。然而，如果职业教育教师队伍建设参照普通教育的话，那么类型发展这个目标是难以实现的。这就需要我们思考应该如何建设一支高质量的职业教师队伍，我认为可以从以下几个方面来探讨。第一，职业教育教师来源的开放性。第二，职业教育教师队伍培养的专业性，职业教育需要双师型教师队伍，相对于普通教育，其对教师的实践能力要求更高，需要不断提升师资队伍培养的专业性以服务技术技能人才培养质量的提升。第三，职业教育教师培养标准的多样性，职业教育的跨界性和强应用属性决定了职业教育师资培养的复杂性，也使得职业教育教师培养标准体系组成具有多元性。第四，职业教育教师的核心素养，作为职业教育教师队伍，其核心素养有自身的独特性。第五，职业教育教师证书的系统性。

第一，职业教育教师来源的开放性。要求要改变现在职业教育教师主要还是从学校单一机构培养的局面，使职业教育教师不仅由学校培养，而且从社会从企业从各个方面，根据职业教育的发展需要来确定合适的人群进行选拔和征用，通过多元途径充实师资队伍，确保职业教育教师来源的多样性。教师队伍的丰富多样性取决于来源的丰富多样性。当前，职业教育教师队伍可以从企业、从其他各方面借用引用和共同使用，但后者始终仅是一个补充。校企师资共享借用互派的情况有效落实，要求职业教育教师队伍培养培训体系变得更加灵活开放多元。开放的职业教育师资培养培训体系，不仅能够使教师队伍获得相关的知识和能力，而且能够满足组成体系多元主体的多样诉求。

第二，职业教育教师培养的专业性。在我国，职业教育教师的培养有专门的师范院校，在一些理工类普通大学中也有职业教育教师的培养。但当前对职业教育教师专业性的培养，相较于普通教师专业性的重视程度和研究程度来讲还存在较大的差距。社会的快速发展使得职业教育教师在能力要求、知识储备、工作特点、信息技术素养等方面呈现出新的特点，对职业教育教师的职业适应性提出了新的要求。社会向数字化智能化转型、各种各样新业态的出现、产业结构的变迁、社会生产方式的变化，给职业教育教师的培养带来了诸多挑战。这些挑战需要加强职业教育教师培养的更深入、更专业性的研究，以提高职业教育教师专业化水平。

第三，职业教育教师标准的多样性。职业教育教师队伍的培养不仅需要解决好标准的有无问题，还需要在有标准的基础上进一步提升标准的丰富性。职业教育和普通教育最大的不同就在于其跨界性和与产业系统联系的紧密性。一所职业院校通常会设置几十甚至上百个专业，如果基于单一的专业标准或者某一特定的规范去要求职业教育师资的培养，将会导致职业教育教师队伍的培养出现“缘木求鱼”的现象，这对于职业教育教师队伍的长期培养是不利的。职业教育教师队伍来源的多样性不等同于来源的随意性，需要在职业教育教师培养的过程中处理好职业教育教师队伍来源多样性和标准统一性的关系。内容形式的多样性和质量标准的统一性以及二者之间关系的复杂性，使得标准化多样性问题的研究成为一个非常值得探究的话题。

第四，职业教育教师核心素养的独特性。核心素养的培养是当前社会各方面比较重视的领域，不仅是职业教育教师队伍，全社会的每一个公民都应重视核心素养的培养，特别是批判性思维能力、学习能力、交往沟通能力、信息素养以及其他核心素养。除了核心素养的共性要求之外，对不同类型的职业、不同的人群，核心素养也有其特殊性要求和呈现。职业教育教师队伍作为这样一类群体，在他们的专业领域应该如何培养核心素养，并体现特定职业的特殊要求，此类相关的研究较少。众所周知，当前新的课程标准，普通教育在高中和义务教育阶段课程标准构思以核心素养为导向。相较于普通基础教育，职业教育的核心素养是什么？如何培养？核心素养明确之后职业教育教师如何有针对性地培养相关核心素养，都值得深入研究。

最后，职业教育教师职业证书的系统性。当前的证书系统是多样的，并且在不同时间周期会有不同程度的增减。因此需要诸多探索提升职业证书的系统性，以更好地服务职业教育教师队伍的成长。逐步探索和打造我国职业教育教师职业证书体系的认证标准、管理标准、管理系统，是加强职业教育教师队伍建设水平提升的一个很重要方面，也是全世界关注的共同话题，更是中国需要特别去突破，探索中国经验的一个重要的话题。

# （八）

# 数字化与职业教育教师发展

中国科学院院士、西北工业大学学术委员会主任　黄　维

当前，职业教育与经济社会发展呈现日益密切的联系，数字化、信息化的新时代背景下，资本市场的持续运作、国家政策的迭代红利，进一步催化新职业教育的发展。新职业教育赛道呈百花齐放态势，已经形成“职普融通、产教融合、校企合作、全球拓展”等新的特点。

数字化与职业教育教师发展的关系可以用三句话进行概括：第一，数字化是职业教育教师发展的新的时代背景；第二，数字化是职业教育教师发展的方向；第三，数字化是职业教育教师发展的重要途径。

## 1. 作为职业教育教师发展背景的数字化

当今的世界，数字技术逐步融入人类生产生活各个领域，推动人类社会向数字化转型。在经济领域，产业数字化和数字产业化方兴未艾，数字经济快速发展。2022 年 7 月，中国信息通信研究院在全球数字经济大会上发布了《全球数字经济白皮书（2022 年）》，2021 年全球 47 个国家数字经济同比增长 15.6%。其中，发展中国家 2021 年数字经济增速更是高达 22.3%。在数字政府建设上，根据《2020 年联合国电子政务调查报告》显示，联合国所有成员国包括最不发达国家的电子政务发展平均指数都在提升，其中指数处于“高”水平或者“非常高”水平的成员国高达 126 个，占联合国全部成员国的 65%。在数字社会建设上，以数字技术为支撑的智慧城市和智慧乡村建设如火如荼。可以说，人类社会已经迈入数字化时代。数字化时代要求人类社会的每一个人都应该向数字化方向发展，具有较高的数字素养。这是今天在论及职业教育教师发展时不得不考虑的时代背景。

### 2. 作为职业教育教师发展方向的数字化

数字经济、数字社会和数字政府的建设依赖于具有较高数字素养的各类人才，其中就包括具有较高数字素养的技术技能人才。因此在数字化时代，职业教育必须将培养学生的数字素养作为核心目标。这首先就要求教师具有足够的数字素养。同时，在数字化时代，职业教育本身也要向数字化转型。数字技术在职业教育领域的嵌入，使得线上线下混合式教学成为常态，使得个性化学习成为可能。职业教育教师需要具备在数字化环境中准备教学、实施教学、评价教学的能力。这要求职业教育教师提高数字素养，向数字化方向发展。与普通教育的教师不同，职业教育的教师应该向“双师型”教师方向发展。通俗地讲，所谓“双师型”教师指的就是既能做“教师”，又能当“技师”的教师。从这个角度看，在数字化时代，职业教育教师除了要发展成为“数字教师”之外，还应成为“数字技师”。

从职业教育教师教育的实际情况看，职业教育教师的数字化转型首先需要做的是明确职业教育教师应具备什么样的数字素养。在这方面，中国已经做出了初步的探索。2020 年，教育部在《职业院校数字校园规范》中提出了职业教育教师应具备的五个方面信息素养，即信息意识与态度、信息知识与技能、信息化应用与创新、信息化研究与发展、信息社会责任。2021 年，教育部在《中等职业教育专业师范生教师职业能力标准（试行）》中对中等职业教育师范生的数字素养做出了规定。当然，这些标准还需要职业技术师范教育机构将其落实在人才培养方案之中，才能对职业教育教师数字化转型真正发挥作用。

我们建议着力发展科技基础工具的数学科学、以信息科学为代表的应用科学、以生命科学为代表的前沿科学、以物质科学为代表的基础科学、与自然科学互补共进的艺术科学。它们的英文首写字母组合起来的单词“MILPA”为“农田”之意，寓意“夯实发展基础”。希望职业教育从现在开始，就着力打破内外部界限，探索科学间的交叉融合，通过跨学科知识生产模式，提升职业教育教师的全面素质。

### 3. 作为职业教育教师发展重要手段的数字化

在数字化时代，以数字技术作为手段赋能职业教育教师发展，培养职业教育教师的数字素养，将成为职业教育教师教育的新现实。为此，一要按照数字化要求，完善人才培养方案，搭建学科专业平台，健全课程教学体系，构建“数字技术 + 教师教育”的职业教育教师职前培养体系和在职培训体系。二要加强数字化环境建设。职业院校和职业技术师范院校要强化校园数字基础设施建设，打造师生、生生互动的云端数字化学习平台，建设融线上线下教学为一体的智慧教室和实训基地。三要建设数字化教育资源库。职业技术师范院校和职业院校机构要自主开发与外部引进相结合，根据专业特点引进数字化资源；与行业企业合作，共同开发数字化职业教育教师发展资源；依托国家职业教育智慧教育平台和国家高等教育智慧教育平台，推动资源共享，发挥资源效益。

# (九)

# 数字化背景下职教青年教师专业化发展的院校实践

唐山工业职业技术学院党委副书记、院长　张建军

大数据、云计算、虚拟现实、人工智能等新一代智能技术的快速发展持续推动教育数字化转型。青年一代职业教育教师需要具备胜任未来数字化教育所需的数字素养，同时产业数字化转型也对其专业化发展提出了新要求。传统职业教育教师更多注重师生之间面对面的直接交流和课堂教学数据的人工处理，而数字化时代背景下则更多的需要以智慧化教学环境、共享型网络教学平台和互动式数字化资源等作为教学媒介，教学全过程行为大数据分析也是建立在智能化工具支持基础上的精准画像多维度呈现。下面，结合唐山工业职业技术学院的工作实际，就青年教师专业化发展问题做一些讨论。

## 1. 数字化背景下职业教育教师专业化能力标准

传统的职业教育教师专业化能力体系包括教学能力、实践能力、技术创新和社会服务能力等多个方面，其中教育教学知识和企业实践经验是最重要的基础。在数字化背景下，传统经验性教学向以数据交互、信息评估为主的数字化教育转变，教育教学活动正在打破时空、环境、地域藩篱，因此职业教育教师的专业化能力也随之发生颠覆性变化，不仅要求在教学内容重构上要及时融入工业数字化应用场景下的新技术、新工艺、新方法，推动数字科技催动下企业融合型生产任务向职业教育课程复合型教学模块转化，同时也要能够在全新的智慧教学环境下开展基于多维互动教学和数据驱动精准教学，推动以学生为中心的课堂革命。

根据我校实践经验，数字时代职业教育教师专业化能力主要包括以下六个维度：一是数字化教学设计能力，能够根据新的教学环境和技术条件整体设计教学目

标和教学过程，实现线上与线下学习、虚拟与现实的融合；二是数字化教学实施能力，能够利用信息手段预测和发现学生学习中的各种问题，促进教师精准指导下的自主学习；三是数字化教学资源开发能力，能够根据产业新技术变化编制和修订人才培养方案、课程标准和数字教材；四是数字化教学评价能力，能够运用大数据手段检测学生学习目标达成程度，并深度剖析学习问题，促进个性化学习；五是数字化生产技术能力，能够分析解决智能制造中的技术问题，对企业职工开展新技术培训；六是能够预测未来职业新变化，优化调整教学目标。

2. 数字化背景下职业教育青年教师专业化能力发展途径

为主动适应职业教育教师专业化能力要求新趋势，职业学校一方面需要实时升级新教师录用标准，将数字素养作为一项重要依据指标；另一方面需要建立健全教师专业化能力成长保障与激励机制，为青年教师创设积极向上的发展环境。我校在促进青年教师专业化发展方面主要采取了以下措施。

（1）打造混合式教学标准驱动青年教师教学理念变革。学校充分发挥数字技术对教育高质量发展的放大、叠加、倍增作用，实施打造教师乐教、学生乐学“金课堂”行动计划，围绕数智融入开展“教师、学生、资源、管理、文化”等五大板块顶层设计，出台《线上线下混合式教学实施标准》《“线上 + 线下”混改试点课程认定标准》《“线上 + 线下”混改“金课”开发指南》《线上线下混合式课堂教学质量评价标准》等 10 余个教学文件，为青年教师建立课程开发、教学行为以及质量评价等维度的“可控化、可测化、可视化”数据标准，将用数字技术改造升级课堂行为嵌入青年教师“日常教学习惯”，推动青年教师主动适应数字化时代的职业教育思想和改革观念升级。

（2）构筑智慧型学习环境促使青年教师方法手段升级。学校开展“数字化 +”教育资源供给升级工程，重构教育新生态。建成一站式服务师生的唐工 E 厅，建立统一数据中心、统一门户中心、统一身份识别中心，有效破除信息孤岛，实现数据辅助决策和精准化管理，使业务系统应用成为青年教师日常工作内容；依托校本开发的大数据分析与决策系统、专业教学资源公共服务平台等，实施线上线下混合式教学全覆盖，使平台功能模块使用成为青年教师教学行为常态；建成集“远程巡检、在线维护、统一平台、集中管理、智能控制”功能于一体的高互动式智慧教室 200 余间，青年教师率先在课堂应用，探索覆盖教师授课、学生个性化学习、跨校园远程课堂等多场景、跨区域互动教学；打造国家示范性虚拟仿真实训基地、智能制造实训中心、工业物联网实训基地等平台，构筑智慧化、沉浸式、共享型实训教学场所，促使青年教师常态化开展虚拟仿真实训教学、在线仿真实训教学、虚实融合式实训教学。

（3）开展定制式递进培训助力青年教师数字素养提升。聚焦青年教师专业化成长，优化学校教师发展中心职能与运行方式，修订完善学校《教师发展标准》《教职工分类考核实施方案》，将信息化教学能力和数字素养作为青年教师重要评价指标；通过教工管理平台建立教师电子档案，全过程、多维度实时记录青年教师个人发展轨迹，实施专业化能力大数据动态跟踪，将数字化素养提升融入教师职前培养、入职培训和在职研修三个维度的全周期培训，按照“信息技术应用—数字资源开发—教学流程重塑—课程重构再造”的难度递进原则设计培训主题和培训模块，逐步提高青年教师信息化教学设计、组织实施以及评价反思等能力；引导青年教师对接个人发展目标实时开展自我诊改，利用“画像”排名激励教师靶向改进，持续提高青年教师业务水平和数字素养。

（4）搭建多元化成长平台引擎青年教师云智技术应用。一是依托国家协同创新中心、省级研发中心、企业诊所、技术创新团队等校内科研平台以及企业教师工作站、国家技能大师工作室等校外创新平台，选派青年教师结合学科背景和技术专长，针对高端装备智造、大数据在线状态监测、智慧运维与健康管理、数字化产品设计与三维虚拟建模、数字孪生与人工智能等重点领域开展项目研发、技术创新和成果转化，同时将科学研究最新成果、前沿数字技术向课程模块任务进行课堂转化落地。近三年，青年教师在技能大赛、创新创业大赛中获奖百余项，涌现出全国技术能手 4 名，荣获省级科技进步三等奖。

二是以学校立项的国家、省级专业（群）教学资源库、在线精品课程、数字化教材、虚拟仿真实训中心（基地）等重大建设项目为抓手，组建以青年教师为主要成员的项目建设团队，构建“老中青”梯队化协作共同体，实施“以老带新”，使青年教师全程参与到高互动式、体感式微课和三维动画等数字化资源的开发及平台教学运行中。近三年，青年教师数字化资源开发与应用能力大幅提升，原创资源近万条，参与建成 2 个国家专业教学资源库、6 个省级专业（群）教学资源库、31 门省级在线精品课程和 20 余部新形态教材，立项信息技术相关教改课题 60 余项。

三是充分发挥教学能力大赛引领教学改革的示范作用，建立“校—省—国家”三级递进参赛机制，实施青年教师校级参赛全覆盖，遴选优秀青年教师团队参加高级别比赛，促使青年教师提高课程数字化升级以及应用数字化改造课堂流程等能力。近三年，青年教师参加省级及以上职业院校教学能力大赛获奖 30 余项，年龄均不足 30 岁的学前教师团队荣获 2019 年全国职业院校教学能力大赛一等奖。

数字化背景下，职业教育青年教师专业化发展是一个长期的系统性工程，需要在系统科学指导下攻破关键性问题。一是强化系统规划。在明确教师专业化标准和专业化发展问题的基础上，合理调配优质资源，实现青年教师整体发展。二是提供制度保障。在新教师聘用、在职教师培养途径、绩效考核和职务晋升等方面，应有利于青年教师快速成长。三是建立退出机制。对经考核确实不能胜任教师岗位的教师，应进行转岗或辞退，形成青年教师发展的闭环路径。

# （十）

# 产教融合背景下的职业教育“双师”队伍建设

河北石油职业技术大学校长　于立国

2018 年，《中共中央国务院关于全面深化新时代教师队伍建设改革的意见》强调，“全面提高职业院校教师质量，建设一支高素质‘双师型’的教师队伍”。2019 年，《国家职业教育改革实施方案》提出“到 2022 年，‘双师型’教师占专业课教师总数超过一半”。同年，教育部等四部委印发了《深化新时代职业教育“双师型”教师队伍建设改革实施方案》，对新时代职业教育“双师型”教师队伍建设进行了系统全面部署，提出“建立具有鲜明特色的‘双师型’教师资格准入、聘用考核制度，教师职业发展通道畅通，待遇和保障机制更加完善，职业教育教师吸引力明显增强，基本建成一支师德高尚、技艺精湛、专兼结合、充满活力的高素质‘双师型’教师队伍”。

近年来，中国职业教育“双师型”教师队伍建设稳步推进，成效显著。根据教育部官方数据显示，截至 2021 年，全国职业学校“双师型”教师在专业课教师中的占比均超过 55%，其中高职专科和高职本科均为 59%，达到了占比过半的要求。面对建设高素质“双师型”教师队伍，加快推进职业教育现代化的高标准、高要求，我们仍然任重而道远。

## 1. 职业教育“双师型”教师队伍建设的问题

一是学校吸引力不足，人才引进不达标。《国家职业教育改革实施方案》要求，“从 2019 年起，职业院校、应用型本科高校相关专业教师原则上从具有 3 年以上企业工作经历并具有高职以上学历的人员中公开招聘”。但在实际工作中，相当数量的学校达不到这样的要求，新引进教师的主体还是“从校门到校门”的应届毕业生，对博士等高学历人才和企业的高技能人才吸引力不足。

二是缺乏基于职业教育的教师评价标准。《关于推动现代职业教育高质量发展的意见》规定，“完善职业教育教师资格认定制度，制定双师型教师标准，完善教师招聘、专业技术职务评聘和绩效考核标准”。但在具体落实的过程中，一方面，国家出台的一系列政策尚未明确“双师型”教师的标准，据统计，目前仅有北京、安徽、江西、福建、吉林、广西等省市结合当地实际，制定了省级层面的高职院校“双师型”教师评价认定办法；另一方面，院校内部的评价标准体系尚不健全，低学历、高技能的人才难以进入职业教育教师队伍。

三是教师企业实践锻炼效果不佳。《国家职业教育改革实施方案》提出，“职业院校、应用型本科高校教师每年至少 1 个月在企业或实训基地实训，落实教师 5 年一周期的全员轮训制度”。但实际情况是教师缺编严重，学校派不出来，也缺乏激励机制和有效的手段措施；教师存在应付心理，到企业多是“走走”“转转”“看看”，企业实践锻炼流于形式，不能深入。由于企业难以从教师实践锻炼中获得短期的、眼前的利益，因此接收职业院校教师的积极性不高。

**2. 河北石油职业技术大学“双师”队伍建设实践**

河北石油职业技术大学始于 1903 年创办于天津的“北洋工艺学堂”，是我国兴办最早的高等工业职业院校之一。学校于 1929 年更名为河北省立工业学院，首次举办本科教育。1960—1965 年更名为河北石油学院，第二次举办本科教育。2021 年合并转设为河北石油职业技术大学，再次回归本科办学序列。在河北省立工业学院时期，院长魏元光就指出：

“工业职业教育之教学方法，要使学生能手脑并用，不仅应授以基本理论，同时并须令其有实用技术，故为师者，于应有之学识外，并当有实际经验之技术，与夫以作为学之习惯，以身作则之精神”。

“欲期教育办有成效，需先有优良之师资。职业教育更当需要特殊适当之专门职业师资”。

“往者工业职业学校教师心理，鄙夷技艺，不屑动手，对于技术之训练，只重在教室讲授理论，虽有高深之学识，实则一遇实际工作，转惑茫然，似此情形，不但不能使学生得到切实指导，并影响学生心理，养成重理论而不重实际，能口说而不能动手之习惯，殊违职业教育之本旨”。

近年来，学校坚持打造高水平“双师型”教师队伍，将“双师”队伍建设摆在优先发展的重要位置，多措并举，成效显著。在中国高等教育学会发布的 2021 年

“全国高职院校教师教学发展指数”中，我校位列全国第 24 名。具体做法如下。

一是优化双师型教师结构——高学历与高技能人才并重。《本科层次职业教育专业设置管理办法（试行）》要求“具有博士研究生学位专任教师比例不低于15%”。为实现这一目标，我校克服所在城市经济欠发达等不利因素，加大人才引进力度，目前博士学位教师数量已接近 100 人。改革人才评价标准，将学历不达标的高技能人才与博士等高学历人才并列。制定《技能大师工作室运行管理办法》，建设 1 个国家级技能大师工作室和 7 个省级技能大师工作室，形成了“国家级—省级—校级”技能大师的完整梯队，实现在办专业技能大师全覆盖。

二是搭建校企共育双师桥梁——政行校企共建科研平台。与承德市高新区共建国家级众创空间，与河北省仪器仪表协会共建河北省仪器仪表产业技术研究院，与冀东油田公司共建河北省油田化学剂工程技术研究中心等 8 个省级、11 个市级科技创新平台。通过这些平台，政府和企业提供来自生产一线的真实问题和资金支持，教师与企业技术骨干共建团队开展项目攻关，并将企业的典型工作任务引入课堂。

三是在龙头企业建立高质量双师培养基地。学校在燕山石化、华北油田、辽河油田、冀东油田等行业企业，在万华化学、长城汽车等知名龙头企业建立高质量长期稳定教师培养基地。学校根据年度培养计划派遣专业教师到企业培训，既保证双师培养的高质量，又实现双师培养工作的可持续。

四是建立双师型教师培养机制——全脱产 + 累计。早在 1988 年，学校就出台文件明确提出“新分配到校任教的大学毕业生、研究生，原则上安排一年的实践锻炼”。2011 年，学校进一步明确“双师型”教师队伍建设目标，提出“全脱产 + 累计”的教师企业实践锻炼新机制，要求“各教学单位每学期派出到企业参加实践锻炼的专任教师不少于 2 人，教师企业实践锻炼每次必须以全脱产形式（不承担任何校内工作）参加连续不间断的企业实践锻炼半年以上”。同时要求未参加全脱产形式企业实践锻炼的教师“每年累计 1 个月参加企业实践锻炼”，在制度上保证了教师企业实践锻炼的质量和效果。10 年来，学校累计派遣 450 余名教师到企业参加全脱产形式实践锻炼，直接投入资金 3 000 余万元，是区域内派出人数最多、涉及工业门类最多的院校。“全脱产 + 累计”为人才培养提供了高质量“双师”队伍保障，更推动了人才培养的加速。

五是构建双师型教师激励体系——协议年薪制。学校出台了《协议年薪制实施方案》，鼓励教师在教学、科研、竞赛、社会服务等任意一领域“冒尖”，不必面面俱到，专攻一项也能获得满意的薪酬收入，实现待遇留人。打破了身份限制，比如学校引进的技能大师多数是工人，但也可以不受身份限制而根据业绩享受年薪制。“协议年薪制”的实施让教师服务企业的热情空前高涨，教师攻克 210 余项技术难题，包括 10 余项“卡脖子”技术难题。其中，具有自主知识产权的飞机红外 / 雷达综合隐身特性快速数值评估系统打破了国外对高效、高精度通用红外隐身性能计算模型等关键技术的封锁和垄断。

## （十一）

# 高等职业院校促进青年教师全面发展的实践与创新

浙江建设职业技术学院校长　何　辉

贯彻一个根本遵循。党的十八大以来，习近平总书记高度重视教师队伍建设，先后提出了“四个相统一”“‘经师’和‘人师’统一者”等要求，指出了教师队伍建设对教育事业发展的关键性作用。习近平总书记对教师队伍发展作出的系列重要论述，是新时代教师队伍建设的根本遵循。学校以习近平新时代中国特色社会主义思想为指引，确立青年教师培养思路。以培育青年教师素质优良师德师风为指引，以提升青年教师整体双师素质质量为基础，以引培专业领军和高层次青年人才为重点，以创新青年教师人才培养体制机制为抓手，通过“党建引领建团队、目标引领树示范、产教融合新模式、科教融合哺育人、书证融通促教改、营造氛围强人才”，打造一支高素质、高水平，充满活力，教学能力强、行业有影响的青年教师队伍。

树立四大价值导向。一是学生为本。把引导青年教师树立正确的教育价值观作为学校青年教师培养的核心任务，让青年教师对“培养什么人、怎样培养人、为谁培养人”根本问题形成正确价值导向，牢固树立以学生为本的思想理念，切实担起立德树人的任务使命。二是师德为先。把提高思想政治素养和职业道德水平摆在学校青年教师培养的首要位置，突出全员全方位全过程师德养成，促使青年教师用自己的实践诠释师德的内涵，演绎师德的践行，担起传播知识、传播思想、传播真理的历史使命，扛起塑造灵魂、塑造生命、塑造人才的时代重任。三是能力为重。把青年教师作为学校教师队伍的重要组成部分，把青年教师能力培养作为促进学校可持续高质量发展和提升人才培养质量的重大任务。突出青年教师“双师素质”教师个体成长和“双师型”教学团队建设相结合，提高青年教师教育教学能力和专业实践能力。四是终身学习。把青年教师长期成长发展规划作为学校建设发展的重要战略，积极引导青年教师树立终身学习理念，做新时代终身学习型教师，推动青年教师始终处于学习状态，聚焦行业创新发展趋势，站在科学技术知识前沿。

创新五大培养路径。一是定制职业生涯发展规划。对全体青年教师开展职业生涯规划培训，强化青年教师职业规划意识，推动青年教师确立职业发展目标，根据自身实际科学划分职业发展阶段，为职业生涯开好头起好步。二是建强国家双师培养基地。以建设管理“双师型”教师培养培训基地、土建类建筑信息模型技术双师型教师培养培训基地等两个国家级基地为依托，突出强化青年教师“双师素质”培养。三是创新教师团队培养机制。跨专业跨领域打造团队，打破校企青年人才归属壁垒；顶层设计团队管理机制，打破影响青年发展制度壁垒；交叉融合校企工作机制，打破校企合作松散脱节壁垒。形成青年教师团队培养新局面。四是实施校企双导师指导制。学校为每一名青年教师配置校内校外两名结对指导教师，精心选择品德高尚、治学严谨、具有人格魅力的校企领军人才作为青年教师成长导师。五是分类培养青年教师能力。依据青年教师学历、工作经历等差异，实施分层分类个性化、定制化培养，在青年教师的教学能力、科研能力、专业建设能力、实践应用能力和社会服务能力等不同方向实施特色培养。

聚力六大实践举措。举措一：聚力师德师风，实施青年教师师德行动计划。一是制订师德规范，不断增强教师的责任感和荣誉感；二是健全师德考核，将师德师风考核结果作为教师评价的第一标准，实行“一票否决”；三是树立师德典型，充分发挥立德树人、爱岗敬业等典型人物激励、导向、示范作用；四是加强师德监督，建立学校、教师、学生、家长“四方联动”评价监管平台。举措二：聚力分层分类，推进青年教师筑基培优工程。实施“双师型”青年教师筑基工程、“工匠型”双师提质培优工程、“领军型”人才引进培育工程、“创新型”教师团队培养工程等四大工程。推动拓才引智筑巢项目、校企协同共育项目、全程进阶培养项目、团队共同成长项目等四个项目。提高教师职业价值知识、专业科学知识、职业科学知识和教学科学知识。重树师德标杆，重塑教学理念，重构综合素质，重建能力结构。举措三：聚力双师双能，实施青年教师协同培养模式。一是“集团 +”协同培养，建好示范性职教集团，搭建青年教师培养平台，架起沟通交流桥梁；二是“产业 +”协同培养，建好产业合作学院，拓宽青年教师眼界视野，掌握产业发展资讯；三是“行业 +”协同培养，建好行业联合学院，提升青年教师专业能力，服务行业转型升级；四是“企业 +”协同培养，建好企业专业学院，加大青年教师一线锻炼，培养双师队伍素质；五是“院校 +”协同培养，建好中高一体学院，激发青年教师内生动力，深度参与教学改革。举措四：聚力双百工程，构建青年人才专兼发展共同体。通过建平台、设基地，实施百名青年教师下企业，百名企业师傅上讲台，实现结对补位、双挂互聘、共聘共育、资源共享，建成以青年人才为重点专兼结合专业发展共同体。举措五：聚力“三教”改革，提升青年教师教学核心能力。一是开展“五个一”教师活动，两周一次专兼职教师课堂展示，每月一次专业群专题研讨，每师定点联系一个企业，每师每年完成一个实际项目，每学期一次校企同步日；二是实施“五活”教学改革，不断提升青年教师教学能力，实现教学主体鲜活、教学内容鲜活、教学手段鲜活、教研活动鲜活、教学评价鲜活；三是推动“五化”教法创新，鼓励青年教师熟练掌握信息技术，实现教学个性化、方法多样化、资源生态化、评价多元化、手段智能化。举措六：聚力持续长效，完善青年教师培养资源保障。一是协同化项目推进，成立青年教师培养领导小组；二是精细化项目管理，制定《青年教师培养培训办法》《新教师培养实施办法》，制度建设保障运行；三是多元化投入激励，专项建设每个团队每年 18 万元经费，“双高”建设团队经费 170 万元；四是融合化发展环境，教师发展中心开设团队建设辅导室、研讨室，打造青年教师活动之家。

青年教师兴则学校兴，青年教师强则学校强。近年来，学校青年教师发展取得了长足的进步，青年教师的教学能力、科研能力、专业建设能力、实践应用能力和社会服务能力等五大能力水平显著提升，立项国家级职业教育教师教学创新团队 2 支，省级教师教学创新团队 1 支。下一步，学校将继续把对青年教师的培养放在首位，不断完善青年教师管理机制，营造青年教师成长环境，拓宽青年教师发展平台，搭建青年教师提升阶梯，逐步打造出了一支师德高尚、业务精良的青年教师队伍，为学校高质量发展打下坚实基础。

# （十二）

# 职业教育青年教师培养的中国模式

## ——以天津职业技术师范大学为例

天津职业技术师范大学职业教育学院院长　米　靖

长期以来，关于职业教育教师的培养是全球职业教育领域不断探索的一个重要议题。当前，世界各国都在积极地夯实支撑高质量职业教育发展的基础，力求确立职业教育教师的有效培养模式。众所周知，普通教育的教师培养和职业教育的教师培养有着明显的差异，但也有共同的规律，因此在实践过程中，我们探索形成了三个方面的基本思路和做法。第一是从“双师型”到“工匠之师”，提出了明确的职业教育教师专业化发展目标。第二是逐渐形成了“本硕博一体化”的青年职业教育教师专业化发展的路径。第三是形成了基于跨学科、符合职业教育自身规律和职业教育教师成长发展需求而构建起来的教育学和工学相结合的青年教师专业化发展模式。

首先，关于职业教育教师专业化发展的目标。我们知道，在中国职业教育的话语体系中，形成了具有中国特色的职业教育教师发展基本模式，即打造“双师型”教师。而在探索“双师型”教师专业发展的过程中，以天津职业技术师范大学为牵头单位，形成了两个重要的阶段性探索成果，并且两个成果分别都获得国家级教学成果奖。第一是形成了双证书体系下的一体化的职业教育师资的培养模式；第二是在本科学历教育层次基础上，探索了融合工程师和技师等职业技能体系的职业教育教师培养模式。在此背景下，我校逐步形成了以工匠之师为目的的职业教育教师培养话语体系。在新时代，职业教育要适应新的发展需求，面向新的制造业发展方向要求培养更多的大国工匠，为各行各业提供有力的人才支撑。学校提出了工匠之师的培育目标，事实上是与工匠精神的传承和工匠精神的孕育结合在一起。其实，工匠之师就是指既具有工匠精神，又有娴熟技能，同时又具有教育教学综合能力的职业教育教师。也就是说，要让青年职业教育教师既能讲解书本知识，又能传授职业技能；既要让他能够服务国家发展，还要具备一种修炼匠心、格物致知的工匠精神。我们也更希望职业院校的教师能够成为中国制造的卓越雕塑师。因此工匠之师既要传承职业技能的“道”，又要传承工匠精神的“道”，要将两种“道”融合在一起，而这种品质需要通过未来的教育教学来培养出更多的技术技能型人才。在此背景下，全面推动对工匠之师的研究，对工匠之师培育规律的把握就显得尤为重要。为了进一步推动此项研究工作，天津市也批准由天津职业技术师范大学成立职业教育工匠之师研究中心。当前，核心工作主要聚焦在教师的师德养成领域，并产出了一些重要的研究成果。习近平总书记勉励学校培养的面向中西部的教师，提出“潜心读书，精心育人”的要求和指示。实际上，我们也是在这个师德孕育的过程中，把这八个字蕴含到日常的教师培养中，形成工匠之师的关键性的内核。

其次，关于职业教育教师专业化发展的路径。在探索过程中，形成了工匠之师培育的基本架构，也就是形成了“本硕博一体化”的职业教育青年教师专业发展的路径。在整个全球职业教育教师培养过程中，都还没有形成非常明确的如同普通教育教师培养的成熟体系。可以说，全球范围内职业教育教师的培养体系依然处于不断探索、创新的阶段，而我们的探索是基于本科推进到硕士层次，不断进行到博士层次的路径。具体来说，在本科层次全面推进卓越教师的培养计划，形成了具有工程化、项目式、实践性的本科层次卓越青年教师的培育路径。在培育过程中，坚持工程实践创新的教育理念，即将工程实践创新与本科层次的职业教育师资培养密切融合，用工程实践创新的模式、理念、成果来检验本科层次的职业教育师资培育的质量。此外，在本科层次还推行了三导师制，即将高等院校的教师、中等职业学校的教师以及企业专家整合在一起，形成了“三位一体”的支撑本科层次青年职业教育教师培养的基本格局。同时，还进一步优化资源生成的基本环境，引入基于职业教育教师培养的高校、政府和职业院校合作的 UGS 协同育人模式。事实上，必须要将国家对职业教育教师培养的需求、职业院校青年教师补充的需求以及职业教育教师培养院校的教育教学改革需求整合在一起，形成相互联动、互相协同、彼此共同推进的融合模式。在硕士层次的职业教育教师的培养领域中，以天津职业技术师范大学牵头探索产生了“三导师三基地”的职教硕士教师培养的创新的模式。具体来说，就是构建起校内导师，职业院校导师与企业导师相融合，学校基地、职业院校基地、企业事业基地相协同的培养模式。“三导师三基地”的培养模式强化了硕士层次职业教育教师卓越教学能力，凸显了工程实践创新能力。目前，“三导师三基地”的培养模式获得了广泛的认可，如借鉴“三导师三基地”的模式，进一步结合相关专业特点，融合职业教育教师培养具体专业的要求而创新了诸多专业培养模式。例如，在工程教育专业人才培养过程中，将教师资格证书、职业资格证书、学历证书和硕士学位证书相融合，不断地推动书证融通的创新模式。将理论课程、实践课程与一线职业院校和企业的需求相结合，创新课程体系。我校博士层次的职业教育青年教师的培养项目是近十年以来我国推动形成的面向一线职业院校教师发展的重要计划。我校作为此项目的唯一试点单位，已经历经了十年探索博士层次职业院校高水平专业带头人和骨干教师的经验。通过十年的探索形成了成熟的培养一线教育教学博士层次专业带头人的中国职业教育师资的培养创新模式。在博士层次的培养过程中，首先是基于实践的需求来提升职业教育教师培养的标准。我校博士层次职业教育教师培养还吸引了诸多国外留学生进入到博士项目，课程考核合格并顺利通过答辩后授予其教育学博士学位。当前，我校已经有多位国际留学生顺利毕业，可以说我校创新的职业教育教师博士层次培养模式已经走向了世界很多国家，产生了较好的影响力。

再次，关于跨学科的职业教育教师培养。众所周知，职业教育教师的特殊性在于专业门类和种类多样化，职业院校的教师要面向多个产业、行业、企业与职业培养其所需的技术技能型人才。相较于基础教育而言，职业教育教师的培养更为复杂，面向的领域更为广泛。因此天津职业技术师范大学探索出一条跨学科的职业教育教师培养基本路径，即基于教育学和工学相结合，这个模式体现了职业教育教师既要掌握专业的理论知识和技术技能，又要成为懂得教育教学的卓越教师。我们形成院校内部不同工科专业和教育学学科的紧密融合格局，形成了面向职业院校不同专业需求的职业教育教师培养的新模式。在这个过程中，不仅是学科融合，更重要的还有课程开发、教师教育等一些基本的资源建设以及在实训、实习、实践环节等方面，都体现了教育学工学相结合、教育学工学相融合的模式，实际上有助于破解全球范围内职业教育教师培养过程中的适应性难题。

最后，我校坚持“学术型、专业性、师范性、职业性”相融合的“双师型”职业教育师资培养模式，对标本科专业类教学质量国家标准和职业技术师范专业认证标准，制定适应现代职业教育发展需要的职业教育师资培养目标、培养标准和培养方案，在职业教育教师培养中形成了可推广的模式，期望全球各国以及国内的各个院校相互沟通，取长补短，共同进步。

# 五

# 中非职业教育合作与发展论坛

协助组织单位：中国教育国际交流协会

# V. China-Africa TVET Cooperation Forum

Co-organizer: China Education Association for International Exchange (CEAIE)

01
王永利
Wang Yongli

02
刘利民
Liu Limin

03
阿道夫 · 姆肯达
Adolf Mkenda

04
扎哈 · 法勒
Jahou Faal

05
奥塞依 · 乌苏阿齐奥
Osei Wusu-Achaw

06
方军
Fang Jun

07
刘俊峰
Liu Junfeng

08
刘鸿武
Liu Hongwu

09
戴裕崴
Dai Yuwei

10
刘建超
Liu Jianchao

11
易俊
Yi Jun

**总结中非职业教育合作经验，推动人文交流与经济发展，积极探索新形势下的职业教育合作新模式，通过交流机制贡献智慧和力量，推动构建中非职业教育共同体。**

This session introduces the experience in China-Africa TVET cooperation, aiming to promote people-to-people exchanges and economic development. The participants explore new modes of international cooperation in the new context and efficient ways of building the China-Africa TVET community with shared interests through an exchange mechanism.

## (一)

## 中非职业教育合作与发展论坛情况概述

中国教育国际交流协会秘书长　王永利

2022 年 8 月 20 日，中非职业教育合作与发展论坛在首届世界职业技术教育发展大会期间成功举办。本次论坛由中国教育国际交流协会承办，天津轻工职业技术学院协办。作为世界职业技术教育发展大会的十四个平行论坛之一，论坛分享了中国和非洲各国职业教育助力经济社会发展的成功做法，介绍了中国职业教育助力减贫脱贫、夯实经济高速发展基础的最佳实践，探讨了将非洲巨大人口红利转化为发展红利的合作模式和行动策略，探讨了新技术革命背景下通过产教融合、创新创业、教学改革、教师能力提升等方式提高职业教育适应性、赋能未来劳动者、提升就业质量和生活福祉的有效路径。

中国和非洲历来是休戚与共的命运共同体，是合作共赢的利益共同体。习近平主席先后 9 次踏上非洲大陆，中国外交部部长连续 32 年开年首访非洲，这些都传递着中非关系的历久弥坚和构建更加紧密的命运共同体的强烈信号。在“一带一路”发展背景下，中非合作处于历史最佳时期。

非洲是最古老而又最年轻的大陆，巨大的人口红利将带动非洲经济快速发展，伴随而来的是对教育培训供给和质量不断增长的需求，提供高质量的职业教育与培训刻不容缓，中国日趋成熟的职业技能培训体系可以为非洲国家提供实践经验、分享成功路径、传递优质成果。中国正在积极落实向非洲青年提供职业技能培训的承诺，助力非洲国家将人口红利转化为发展优势。

2018 年 9 月，习近平主席在中非合作论坛北京峰会上提出，未来三年和今后一段时间重点实施“八大行动”，其中“能力建设行动”承诺将在非洲设立 10 个鲁班工坊，向非洲青年提供职业技能培训。截至今年，我国已在非洲 14 个国家建设完成 16 个鲁班工坊。2021 年 11 月，习近平主席出席中非合作论坛第八届部长级会议，提出重大合作倡议，中国将同非洲密切配合共同实施“九项工程”，其中包括“未来非洲—中非职业教育合作计划”，这再次体现了中国同非洲共享发展成果、共促民生改善，一起向未来的合作愿景。

中非职业教育合作与发展论坛上，中国教育国际交流协会会长刘利民，天津市人民政府副市长杨兵，坦桑尼亚教育、科学和技术部部长阿道夫・姆肯达致辞。中华人民共和国教育部国际合作与交流司副司长方军和中华人民共和国国家国际发展合作署地区二司司长刘俊峰分别作主旨报告。论坛由中国教育国际交流协会秘书长王永利主持，副秘书长余有根做总结发言。来自中国、坦桑尼亚、肯尼亚、加蓬、加纳、南非、埃塞俄比亚、塞内加尔、乌干达等国政府、院校、研究机构、行业企业代表 200 余人以线下和线上方式参会。

刘利民表示，中国与非洲是老朋友、真朋友、好朋友。长期以来，中国秉持真、实、亲、诚的理念，同非洲各国开展多领域务实合作。面向未来，希望与非洲朋友一道努力，全力提升中非职业教育合作质量，在更高水平上实现共享、共赢、共同发展，使中非合作成果更好惠及双方人民。

阿道夫・姆肯达表示，职业技术教育是经济社会发展和转型的重要推动力量。他介绍了坦桑尼亚在疫情后的职业教育和技能培训发展情况，期待在院校合作、人才培养、技能交流等方面与中国进一步加深合作，为坦桑尼亚经济与产业转型升级培养更多高素质技术技能人才。

杨兵表示，本次论坛是落实中非合作论坛第八届部长级会议成果的重要载体，意义非凡。天津是国家首个职业教育改革创新示范区，在教育部指导支持下，首创并率先推动实施鲁班工坊，为非洲青年插上“实干成就梦想”的理想翅膀。

方军以“中非职业教育合作现状与展望”为题作主旨报告。他表示中非合作的希望在青年，青年的希望在教育，双方比以往任何时候都需要在职业教育领域加强经验交流，增进合作互鉴，共育青年英才。双方为落实中非合作论坛“九项工程”中共同实施“未来非洲—中非职业教育合作计划”，初步构建了较有影响力的合作项目群，成为中非职业教育合作的新典范。展望未来，中国愿与非洲各国政府部门、教育机构一道，通过加强政策对话、深化产教融合、完善协同发展、推进数字转型，共同绘就中非职业教育合作美好蓝图。

刘俊峰围绕“加强中非职教发展合作，助力非洲可持续发展”作主旨报告。他指出职业教育是中国对非合作的重要组成部分，国家国际发展合作署作为中国对外援助和国际发展合作的主管部门，将以落实全球发展倡议为契机，为促进非洲发展提供力所能及的支持帮助。他建议双方职业教育合作紧密对接非洲发展需求，不断充实发展合作内涵，不断深化国际合作水平，期待中非职业教育合作结出更多硕果。

会议期间，天津轻工职业技术学院党委书记戴裕崴发布非洲职业教育研究中心研究成果《中非职业教育合作发展研究》，研究聚焦中国与南非、赞比亚、肯尼亚、乌干达、布基纳法索、埃及 6 个国家的职业教育合作案例。

论坛专题研讨由戴裕崴和中国社会科学院西亚非洲研究所高级研究员贺文萍主持，非洲技术与应用型大学和学院协会秘书长扎哈·法勒、浙江师范大学非洲研究院院长刘鸿武、天津职业技术师范大学副校长吕景泉、加蓬职业教育部总学监邦雅曼·穆瓦尼翁、埃塞俄比亚职业技术培训学院校长特舍里·博里查、成都航空职业技术学院校长刘建超，加纳库马西技术大学副校长奥塞依·乌苏阿齐奥，重庆工程职业技术学院党委书记易俊，围绕“贡献职教智慧，助力经济腾飞”和“职业教育创新发展，强技赋能 Z 世代”两个主题进行专题研讨，分享中国和非洲各国职业教育助力经济社会发展的成功做法，共同探讨职业教育助力经济发展与产业转型有效实施路径。

中非职业教育合作与发展论坛的成功举办总结了中非职业教育合作经验，进一步凝聚中非各国共识，统筹国内外职业教育资源，为中非职业教育合作明确了发展方向，增添了新的内涵，助力推动职业教育在全球产业发展与转型中发挥更加积极的作用，共同打造中非职业教育共同体。

# i. Overview of the China-Africa TVET Cooperation Forum

**Wang Yongli, Secretary-General of China Education Association for International Exchange（CEAIE）**

On August 20, 2022, the China-Africa TVET Cooperation Forum was successfully held during the First World Vocational and Technical Education Development Conference. The Forum was co-organized by China Education Association for International Exchange and assisted by Tianjin Light Industry Vocational Technical College. As one of the 14 parallel sessions of World Vocational and Technical Education Development Conference, the Forum shared the successful practices of vocational education in China and African countries in helping economic and social development, introduced the best practices of vocational education in China in helping poverty reduction and elimination and strengthening the foundation of high-speed economic development, discussed the cooperation models and action strategies for transforming Africa's huge demographic dividend into a development dividend, and discussed effective paths to improve the adaptability of vocational education, empower future workers, and enhance the quality of employment and well-being of life through industry-education integration, innovative entrepreneurship, teaching reform, and improvement of teachers' capacity in the context of the new technological revolution.

China and Africa have always been a community of a shared future and a community of win-win cooperation and mutual interests. President Xi Jinping has traveled to the African continent nine times, and Chinese Foreign Ministers have made their first visits to Africa at the beginning of the year for 32 consecutive years, all of which convey a strong signal of the long-standing relationship between China and Africa and the building of a closer community of destiny. In the context of "the Belt and Road Initiative", China-Africa cooperation is at its best ever.

Africa is an "oldest and youngest" continent, whose huge demographic dividend will drive its rapid economic development, accompanied by a growing demand for the supply and quality of education and training, so it is urgent to provide high-quality vocational education and training, and China's increasingly mature vocational skills training system can provide practical experience, share successful paths and deliver high-quality achievements for African countries. China is actively implementing its commitment to provide vocational skills training to African youth, helping African countries turn the demographic dividend into development advantages.

In September 2018, President Xi Jinping proposed at the Beijing Summit of the Forum on China-Africa Cooperation (FOCAC) to focus on the launch of "Eight Major Initiatives" in the next three years and beyond, among which the "Capacity Building Initiative" promised 10 Luban Workshops will be set up in Africa to provide vocational training for young Africans. As of this year, China has completed the construction of 16 Luban Workshops in 14 African countries. In November 2021, President Xi Jinping attended the 8th FOCAC ministerial conference and put forward a major cooperation initiative, in which China would work closely with Africa to jointly implement "Nine Programs", including the "Future of Africa—A project for China-Africa cooperation on vocational education", which once again reflects the vision of cooperation between China and Africa to share the fruits of development, improve people's livelihoods and work together towards the future.

At the China-Africa TVET Cooperation Forum, Liu Limin, President of China Education Association for International Exchange (CEAIE), Yang Bing, Vice Mayor of Tianjin Municipal People's Government, China, Adolf Mkenda, Minister of Education, Science and Technology of Tanzania, delivered speeches; Fang Jun, Deputy Director General of the Department of International Cooperation and Exchanges of the Ministry of Education, P.R. China, and Liu Junfeng, Director General of the Second Department of Regional Affairs of China International Development Cooperation Agency, delivered keynote reports; Wang Yongli, Secretary-General of China Education Association for International Exchange, chaired the Forum, and Deputy Secretary-General Yu Yougen made the concluding remarks. More than 200 representatives from governments, institutions, research institutes and industrial enterprises from China, Tanzania, Kenya, Gabon, Ghana, South Africa, Ethiopia, Senegal and Uganda attended the Forum online and offline.

Liu Limin stated that China and Africa are old friends, true friends and good friends. Over the years, China has been carrying out practical cooperation with African countries in many fields with a vision of sincerity, real results, affinity and good faith. Facing the future, we hope to work together with our African friends to improve the quality of China-Africa vocational education cooperation, achieve sharing, win-win and mutual development at a higher level, and make the fruits of China-Africa cooperation better benefit the people of both sides.

Adolf Mkenda stated that vocational and technical education is an important driving force for economic and social development and transformation. He introduced the development of vocational education and skills training in Tanzania after the epidemic, and looked forward to further deepening cooperation with China in institute cooperation, talent training and skills exchange to cultivate more high-quality technical skills talents for Tanzania's economic and industrial transformation and upgrading.

Yang Bing stated that this Forum is an important activity to implement the outcomes of the 8th FOCAC ministerial conference, which is of great significance. As the first innovative demonstration site of vocational education reform in China, and with the guidance and support of the Ministry of Education, Tianjin has pioneered and promoted the implementation of the Luban Workshop to give young Africans wings to "make their dreams come true through practical work".

Fang Jun gave a keynote speech on "Current Situation and Prospects of China-Africa TVET Cooperation", saying that the hope of China-Africa cooperation lies in youth and the hope of youth lies in education, and it is more important than ever for both sides to strengthen the exchange of experiences in vocational education, enhance cooperation and mutual learning, and cultivate young talents together. In order to implement the "Future of Africa—A project for China-Africa cooperation on vocational education" in the "Nine Programs" issued on FOCAC, the two sides have initially built a cluster of influential cooperation projects, which have become a new model of China-Africa vocational education cooperation. Looking ahead, China is willing to work with African government departments and educational institutions to draw a better blueprint for China-Africa vocational education cooperation by strengthening policy dialogue, deepening the integration of education and industry, improving collaborative development and promoting digital transformation.

Liu Junfeng gave a keynote speech on "Strengthen China and Africa's Development Cooperation in TVET to Contribute to Africa's Sustainable Development". He noted that vocational education is an important part of China's cooperation with Africa, and as the competent department of China's foreign aid and international development cooperation, the Agency will take the implementation of global development initiatives as an opportunity to provide support and assistance to promote the development of Africa within its capacity. He suggested that vocational education cooperation between the two sides should be closely aligned with Africa's development needs, constantly enrich the connotation of development cooperation and deepen the level of international cooperation, and looked forward to more fruitful vocational education cooperation between China and Africa.

During the Forum, Dai Yuwei, Secretary of CPC Committee of Tianjin Light Industry Vocational Technical College, China, released *A Study on China-Africa Vocational Education Cooperation*, the research result of the African Vocational Education Research Center. The research focused on the cases of vocational education cooperation between China and six countries: South Africa, Zambia, Kenya, Uganda, Burkina Faso and Egypt.

The special seminar of the Forum was hosted by He Wenping, Senior Researcher at Institute of West-Asian and African Studies (IWAAS) at Chinese Academy of Social Sciences (CASS) and Dai Yuwei, Secretary of CPC Committee of Tianjin Light Industry Vocational Technical College, China. Jahou Faal, Secretary General of Association of Technical Universities and Polytechnics in Africa (ATUPA), Liu Hongwu, Director of Institute of African Studies at Zhejiang Normal University, China, Lyu Jingquan, Vice President of Tianjin University of Technology and Education, China, Benjamin Moignon, Senior Pedagogical Inspector of Minister of Vocational Training of Gabon, Teshale Berecha, Director General of Federal Technical and Vocational Training Institute of Ethiopia, Liu Jianchao, President of Chengdu Aeronautic Polytechnic, China, Osei Wusu-Achaw, Vice Chancellor of Kumasi Technical University of Ghana and Yi Jun, Secretary of CPC Committee of Chongqing Vocational Institute of Engineering, China, held a seminar on the themes of "TVET—An Impetus to Economic Growth" and "TVET Innovation Empowers Generation Z". They shared the successful practices of vocational education in China and Africa in helping economic and social development, and discussed the effective implementation methods of vocational education in helping economic development and industrial transformation.

The successful holding of the China-Africa TVET Cooperation Forum summed up the experience of China-Africa VET cooperation, further gathered the consensus among China and African countries, coordinated domestic and foreign VET resources, clarified the development direction and added new connotation to China-Africa VET cooperation, which will help promote vocational education to play a more active role in global industrial development and transformation, and jointly build a China-Africa vocational education community.

# (二)

# 欢迎辞

中国教育国际交流协会会长　刘利民

大家好，非常高兴同各位嘉宾、新老朋友在中国天津和云端相聚，共同出席本次中非职业教育合作与发展论坛。在此，我谨代表中国教育国际交流协会向中华人民共和国教育部、国家国际发展合作署及非洲各国合作伙伴对本论坛给予的指导与支持表示衷心的感谢，向积极参与活动的中非院校及行业企业代表致以诚挚的问候和热烈的欢迎！

中国与非洲是老朋友、真朋友、好朋友。长期以来，中国坚持秉持真、实、亲、诚的理念，同非洲各国开展多领域务实合作。从坦赞铁路、蒙内铁路到共建“一带一路”，从“八大行动”到“九项工程”，中非合作的锦绣画卷正以共商共建共享为底色逐笔绘就。在当前世界多极化、经济全球化、文化多样化不断发展的趋势下，中非友好合作关系必将为构建新型国际关系树立光辉典范，注入强劲动能。

随着中非各方关系的深化与交往的推进，中非教育交流合作不断呈现出新亮点、新形式与新突破。作为最大的发展中国家和发展中国家最集中的大陆，中国与非洲在职业教育领域的合作与双方发展战略高度契合，互利共赢、前景广阔。在“一带一路”倡议的框架下，双方已逐步建立起良好的合作机制，大批项目取得实质性进展，中非职业教育合作进入全新的发展时期。

中国教育国际交流协会是中国最早开展中外民间教育合作与交流的全国性组织。多年来，我们一直致力于搭建民间教育国际交流合作的各种平台。在教育部的指导和支持下，中国教育国际交流协会统筹国内资源，积极同非洲国家分享中国职业教育发展经验与优质成果。

2021 年，为落实中非合作论坛成果，推动能力建设工程建设，协会与非洲技术大学和学院协会（ATUPA，读作“阿图帕”）合作，共同实施“未来非洲—中非职业教育合作计划”，并成立“中非职业教育联合会”，搭建中非职业教育务实合作平台。同时，协会积极推进在非鲁班工坊建设，与中国机电产品进出口商会、中航成套设备有限公司等在非中资商会和企业合作实施各种职业教育项目，积极解决当地用工问题，为推动中非经贸合作可持续发展提供技术技能人才支撑。面向未来，我们将继续与非洲朋友一道努力，全力提升中非项目质量，在更高水平上实现共享、共赢、共同发展，使中非合作成果更好惠及双方人民。

各位嘉宾，女士们，先生们！习近平主席在中非合作论坛第八届部长级会议上提出，中非友好合作精神是双方休戚与共、并肩奋斗的真实写照。本次论坛为中非双方职教同仁提供了良好的交流平台，希望各位专家能够借此机会畅所欲言，凝聚共识，积极探索新形势下中非合作创新模式，为构建互利共赢的中非职业教育共同体做出更大贡献。

最后，预祝本次论坛取得圆满成功，愿中非友谊长存！谢谢！

## (三)

# 坦桑尼亚技能教育转型

坦桑尼亚教育、科学和技术部部长　阿道夫·姆肯达

感谢中华人民共和国教育部和中国教育国际交流协会组织这次会议，也要真诚感谢中国在教育领域，特别是职业和技术教育领域向坦桑尼亚提供的各种非常有益的支持。我相信，这次会议将激发中国和坦桑尼亚之间以及非洲和中国之间在技术和职业培训领域更深入的合作。

众所周知，全球范围内普遍呼吁进行重大教育改革。今年 9 月的联合国教育峰会是对这一呼声的恰当回应。新冠病毒疫情对教育系统提出的挑战促使人们深入思考如何管理和提供教育。推动坦桑尼亚和许多其他国家寻求改革的关键问题首先是优质教育本身，其次是所提供的教育的影响力。关于影响力，有人问，我们的教育制度是否让青年充分利用当地的社会经济环境，并且帮助青年做好准备，迎接全球化的挑战，利用全球化提供的大量机会。

在坦桑尼亚，讨论主要集中于技术教育的技能问题，所以坦桑尼亚正在进行的关于教育改革的讨论总是侧重于技能、接受教育、实用知识、就业能力和自营职业。我们正在进行的重大教育改革将重新配置课程，以推动技能发展，必须使我们的青年做好准备，让他们用技能和实践知识谋生。为此，我们希望向其他国家学习合作和交流经验，希望与中国在这方面的合作能进一步扩大。

下面我想单独谈谈坦桑尼亚教育系统在技能方面需要改进的一些领域。以农业部门为例，大多数人仍然从事农业，坦桑尼亚约 2/3 的劳动力从事农业。尽管如此，农业只贡献了我国 1/3 的 GDP，所以 2/3 的劳动力只贡献了 1/3 的 GDP，这意味着农业部门的生产率极低，也解释了农村地区普遍贫困的原因。农业部门劳动力技能的提高，能够提高生产率，增加农民收入，同时提高我国的 GDP。为了达到这一目的，我们需要职业技术学院来培训年轻人如何以提高生产力的方式进行耕

作。再例如，旅游业变得越来越重要，如果在接待、技能和导游方面对年轻人进行更好的培训，可以为年轻人提供更多的就业机会。我们需要在这些领域进行更多投资。

在经济发展相当迅速的行业，如建筑业，存在技术工人短缺的问题，因此教育和职业培训将帮助我们解决这个问题，为青年创造就业机会，满足想为青年创造更多就业机会的人的愿望。

我们进口相当多的商品，但是如果国内的技术工人具备合适的技术技能则可在当地生产这些商品，如服装、汽车零件等，所以提升技能的教育，特别是技术教育和职业教育将帮助我们生产这些商品供自己消费，也尝试满足全球需求、出口到其他国家。具体而言，我们希望与其他国家，特别是中国在以下领域开展合作。

首先，继续培训教师，为职业和技术教育学院服务。我们正在扩大坦桑尼亚的大学、教室和车间等基础设施，因为需要更多的人力资源将知识传授给年轻人，因此非常希望有机会将我们需要培训的年轻教师派往海外进修。同时，我们也需要有一个国内大学和海外大学之间的人员交流计划，这样我们的人员就可以看到其他国家是如何做的，海外人员也可以来看看我们是如何进行培训的，可以交流想法，看看我们如何改进技能培训。

其次，在中国和其他国家，与国内外的跨国公司建立学徒计划。我们的年轻人接受培训后，可以花一些时间在实际工作中，了解实际工作情况，以便为未来的就业或自营职业做好准备。

最后，我们仍然需要投资于基础设施，建设更多的教室和学院来满足我国对技能教育的需求。

我们希望通过所有这些努力，加快其他国家向我国进行技术转让的进程，因此技术和职业培训为培养我们的青年和提高教育系统的影响力提供了巨大机会。在这方面，非洲内部以及中国和非洲之间有很多的合作机会，我们期待着在这一领域扩大合作。

## iii. Skill and Educational Transformation in Tanzania

**Adolf Mkenda, Minister of Education, Science and Technology, Tanzania**

I'd like to thank the Ministry of Education of the People's Republic of China and China Education Association for International Exchange for organizing this conference. Let me also express our sincere thanks to the People's Republic of China for the various and very useful supports that it extended to Tanzania in education in general and in vocational and technical education in particular. I believe this conference will inspire even deeper cooperation between China and Tanzania and between Africa and China on matters of technical and vocational training.

As we all know, there is a general clamor for major education transformation globally. The UN Education Summit in September this year is a fitting response to this clamor. While the challenge that COVID-19 pandemic pose to education system has prompted deep reflection on how education should be managed and delivered. The key issues driving the quest for reform in Tanzania and in many other countries are first quality education itself and second the relevance of education that is delivered. With regards to relevance, questions are being asked whether our education system prepares our youth to make the most out of our local social economic environment, and also prepares youth to face the challenges of globalization and harness the mass opportunities that globalization offers.

In Tanzania, discussions boil down to issues of skills in technical education. That is the reason that the ongoing discussion about education reform in Tanzania invariably focuses on skills, taking education, practical knowledge, employability and self-employment. The major education reforms that we are embarking on will reconfigure curriculum to expand skills development that must prepare our youth to earn their living through their skills and through their practical knowledge. To this end, we hope to learn from others to cooperate and exchange experience with other countries. And we hope our cooperation with China in this regard will be expanded even more.

Let me single out some areas where education system needs to improve with regard to skills in Tanzania. Let's take agriculture sector as an example. Agriculture still employs the majority of people in the country. It employs about two-thirds of the labor force in Tanzania. Nevertheless, agriculture contributes only a third of the GDP of our country, so two-thirds of the labor force contributes only a third of the GDP. That means productivity in the agriculture sector is extremely low. And it explains widespread poverty in rural area. With better skills to the labor force in the agriculture sector, we'll be able to lift the productivity to improve income of our farmers, and at the same time improve the GDP in our country. To reach that end, we need our vocational and technical colleges to train our youth on how to conduct farming in the manner that will improve productivity. We have other examples. For instance, tourism as a sector that is becoming even more important in the country can increase employment opportunities for the youth, if we train them even better in terms of hospitality, skills, and also tour guides. We need to invest more in those areas.

Such sectors that are growing quite fast in our economy such as building which needs skills that are in short supplies locally, so education and vocation training will help us to meet the demand, and at the same time create employment for our youth and actually meet the quest for people that will create more employment for our youth.

We import quite a number of goods that we should be able to produce here with proper skills and technical capabilities, like clothes, parts for cars and so on, so education that will impact skills, particularly technical education and vocation education will help us not only to produce some of these goods for own consumption, but also to try to meet the global demand and export in other countries. Specifically, therefore, we hope to cooperate with other countries, and China in particular in the following areas.

Firstly, we need to continue to train instructors that will man our colleges of vocational and technical education. We are expanding infrastructure in terms of colleges, classrooms, workshops in Tanzania, as we need more human resources to help to teach and impart the knowledge to the youth, and more opportunities to send our young instructors who need training overseas would be highly welcome. But we also need to have a program for stuff exchange between our colleges and overseas colleges so that our stuff can see how it's done in other countries and also stuff from overseas to come and see how we are doing our training, so we can exchange ideas and see how we can improve our skills training.

Secondly, we need to establish apprenticeship schemes with multinational corporations within the country and overseas, in China and in other countries, where our youth after receiving the training, they can go and spend some time in actual work and see how it's done so that they can prepare themselves for future employment or self-employment.

Finally, we still need to invest in infrastructure, building more classrooms and more colleges to meet the demand for technical education in our country.

We hope through all these systems we should be able to hasten the process of technological transfer to our country, so technical and vocational training offers immense opportunities for developing our youth and for increasing the relevance of our education system. There are many opportunities for collaboration within Africa, and between China and Africa in this regard. We look forward to the expanded cooperation in this area.

# （四）

# 中非职业教育合作的探索

非洲技术与应用型大学和学院协会秘书长　扎哈·法勒

我的发言主要围绕职业技术教育与培训对经济增长的推动作用。任何国家经济繁荣的核心在于国家为全体人民创造可持续就业机会的能力。事实证明，职业技术教育与培训是让人们有效参与社会、经济和技术创新进程的关键，这对于任何社会经济结构的发展都至关重要。

非洲大陆可以说是世界上最多样化的地区之一，居住着最多的年轻人。迅速扩大的青年人口凸显了非洲国家的成就。根据亚伯拉罕基金会的数据，2020 年，非洲青年人口将占全球青年人口的 22.7%。在这一新兴发展格局中，职业技术教育与培训长期以来被视为非洲人类和社会经济发展的重要工具。

职业技术教育与培训的主要作用是在就业市场创造就业机会。不过，职业技术教育与培训更大的作用在于促进自营职业，由于就业机会不足，个人不得不自主就业。有了适当的政策，自营职业可以将失业率保持在最低水平，并促进中小企业发展。有了让课程对口劳动力市场的政策以及充足的资源，就业机会就可以增加。

然而，在非洲围绕职业技术教育与培训计划的政策环境表现出不平等和歧视性。无论是在洲、地区还是国家层面，职业技术教育与培训都没有专门针对性别和能力不同的人的综合政策。

非洲联盟的职业技术教育与培训大陆战略强调了政府在减少职业技术教育与培训性别不平等和歧视方面的作用。其主张进行制度转变，以确保女性在各行各业的平等代表性，因为我们需要的是理念的改变。但是，在职业技术教育与培训机构内部和工作场所，当涉及性别和性别角色时，在许多国家还没有任何重大的制度转变，职业技术教育与培训主流政策还没有重大变革。

尽管如此，已经取得的进展表明，若职业技术教育与培训促进性别平等的改革得以实施，将有促进非洲大陆经济发展的巨大潜力。因此确保女性平等和充分参与劳动，特别是像科学、技术、工程和数学这样的非传统部门，不仅对增强女性的经济赋权至关重要，而且对非洲的整体发展和可持续发展也至关重要。

正是在这种背景下，非洲技术与应用型大学与学院协会在努力提高职业技术教育与培训中女性的参与程度，与英联邦学习共同体合作开展了一个项目，以建设和加强整个非洲大陆职业技术教育与培训机构分会和倡导者的能力。

按照非洲联盟的规定，职业技术教育与培训的运行系统能够很好地培训非洲创造财富和摆脱贫困所需的技能和创业劳动力。职业技术教育与培训部门的这一新动态符合非洲联盟的 2063 年议程，该议程设想了一个由非洲人民驱动的一体化、和平与繁荣的非洲，以在全球社会和知识经济中占据其应有的位置。

职业技术教育与培训的作用在每个经济体中都是显而易见的，但与新兴经济体或落后经济体相比，其在发达经济体中的重要性是不同的。一方面，经济规模较大的发展中国家的技能发展有助于维持增长战略；另一方面，经济规模小的发展中国家和欠发达国家需要技能发展，以渗透到新兴产业中。

发展中国家一直强调职业技术教育与培训的需求，并将其纳入国家政策和发展计划。非洲技术与应用型大学和学院协会与中国教育国际交流协会正共同努力，在职业技术教育与培训上建立强有力的中非合作。2019 年，两个协会达成了合作伙伴关系和谅解备忘录。这是为了在中国的职业技术教育与培训机构和非洲的机构之间建立强有力的联系，并在这两个大陆之间建立人民之间的友谊。同年 6 月，首届中非职业技术教育与培训合作会议在内罗毕举行，来自中国的 30 位职业技术教育与培训院校的校长以及来自非洲的 70 多位职业技术教育与培训机构的校长和负责人出席了会议。中方实施的管理人员和教师能力建设项目已经取得了成功，该项目旨在培养能力，增进非洲和中国之间的相互了解和交流。非洲职业技术教育与培训机构的一些学生有机会在中国接受部分培训，受益于先进技术和设备的知识和经验。

人们普遍认为，职业技术教育与培训能够解决非洲技能短缺和技能缺失的问题，也能够衔接培训和年轻人就业。毫无疑问，职业技术教育与培训在增加就业、经济发展以及最终增强非洲年轻人的经济驱动力方面拥有巨大潜力。职业技术教育与培训对经济的可持续性和增长作出了诸多贡献，这可能在世界各国情况有所差异。

技能的不断发展和就业机会的可能性最终促进劳动力的发展。一些人可能选择在就业市场工作，而一些人可能更喜欢自主创业或自由职业，这种决定因各个国家当前的情况而异。但不管怎样，它通过创收和税收来改善国家的经济形势，任何国家的劳动力的力量都可以由其熟练和半熟练劳动力来定义。

许多政府利用职业技术教育与培训来培养各种职业的技能，确保国家获得变化中的经济所需的各个领域的技能。许多由职业技术教育与培训系统驱动工业的社会可以产生世界级的技术劳动力。

总之，职业技术教育与培训将促进未来经济增长，使我们下一代生活得更好。

# iv. Exploration in Promoting China-Africa Vocational Education Cooperation

**Jahou Faal, Secretary General of Association of Technical Universities and Polytechnics in Africa (ATUPA)**

The topic of my discussion is going to be centered around Technical and Vocational Education and Training (TVET) as an impetus to economic growth. The economic prosperity of any nation revolves around the country's ability to create sustainable jobs for all. TVET has been proven as the key for enabling people to effectively participate in social, economic, and technological innovation processes, which is essential for the development of any social economic structure.

The continent of Africa can be said to be one of the most diverse regions in the world and inhabited by the largest number of young people. The achievements of African nations are underscored by a rapidly expanding youth population. According to M.T. Abraham Foundation, Africa's youth population amounts for 22.7% of global youth population in 2020. Within this emergent development landscape, TVET has long been recognized as a vital tool for the human and social economic development of Africa.

TVET primary role stands on employment generation in the job market. However, TVET is regarded more significantly to do more self-employment, where employment opportunities are insufficient and individuals are forced into the informal sector. With suitable policies, self-employment could maintain the unemployment rate at minimum level and promote small and medium enterprises among its population. With policies for the alignment of curricular and the labor market, and adequate resources, employment opportunities could be enhanced.

However, the policy landscape surrounded TVET program in Africa emerges as inequitable and discriminatory. There is no comprehensive policy governing gender and people that are differently able in TVET specifically, whether at the continental, regional, or country level.

The African Union's Continental Strategy for TVET highlights the role of government in reducing gender inequalities and discrimination in TVET. It asserts that a paradigm shift is required to ensure equal representation of women and girls across all sectors, because what is needed is a change in mindset. But within TVET institutions and in the workplace when it comes to gender and gender roles, unfortunately, there has not been any major paradigm shift in many countries and TVET mainstream policies are yet to shift into fundamental changes.

Nonetheless, the progress that has been made highlights the potential that gender responsive TVET reforms have on the ability of the TVET sector to contribute to economic development on the continent. Therefore, ensuring women's equal and full participation in labor force and particularly in nontraditional sectors like STEM are vital for not just women's economy empowerment, but for the overall promotion and sustainable development in Africa.

It is against this background that ATUPA in its drive towards improving female participation in TVET, partnered with the Commonwealth of Learning in a project to strengthen and build capacity of chapters and champions in TVET institutions across the continent.

As defined by the African Union, TVET delivery systems are well placed to train the skill and entrepreneur workforce that Africa needs to create wealth and emerge out of poverty. This emergent development in the sector of TVET program is compatible with the African Union's 2063 Agenda that envisions an integrated peaceful prosperous Africa driven by its own people to take its rightful place in the global community and the knowledge economy.

The role of TVET is visible in each economy, but the importance is different in advanced economies as compared to emerging or poor economies. On one hand, skill development in developing nations with bigger economies assist to maintain growth strategy. While on the other hand, developing nations with small economies and underdeveloped nations require skill development to penetrate into new growing industries.

Developing nations have been emphasizing the need of TVET and including it in the country's policies and development plans. ATUPA and China Education Association for International Exchange are working together to establish strong China-Africa cooperation in TVET. In 2019, these two associations entered into a partnership and Memorandum of Understanding. This was the aim of creating strong ties between TVET institutions in China and those in Africa as well as building people-to-people friendship between the two continents. The first China-Africa TVET Cooperation Conference was held in June of the same year in Nairobi which was attended by 30 principals of TVET institutes, colleges and technical universities in China, and over 70 principals and heads of TVET institutions in Africa. Already success is recorded on the implementation of the capacity building program for administrators and teachers to build up capacities and enhance mutual understanding and exchange between Africa and China. A number of students in TVET institutions in Africa are accorded the opportunities to undertake part of their training in China to benefit from knowledge and experience with the state-of-the-art technology and equipment.

It has been widely accepted that TVET has the answer to the skills shortage and skills missing manage in Africa and the missing link for the training and integration of youth in the labor market. TVET no doubt holds tremendous potential for increasing employment, economic development, and ultimately economic empowerment for young Africans in particular. TVET has numerous contributions to economic sustainability and growth, which may or may not be similar in countries across the world.

The continuous developments of skills and the possibilities of employment opportunities ultimately lead to workforce development. Some individuals may choose to work in the job market, while some may prefer to work on their own and such decisions vary with the country's current situation. But either way, it helps the nation's economic situation through income generation and tax revenues, the strength of work force of any nation can be defined by its skilled and semi-skilled labor forces.

TVET has been used by many governments to produce skills in diverse occupations, ensuring the nation gets skills in all the fields, required within the changing economies. Many societies with industry driven by TVET systems could produce world class technical workforce.

In summary, the future is TVET for improved economic growth, giving the future generations a better life.

## （五）

# 职业教育创新发展　强技赋能 Z 时代

加纳库马西技术大学副校长　奥塞依·乌苏阿齐奥

感谢有机会在这个场合与大家讨论“职业教育创新发展，强技赋能 Z 时代”这个主题。我将着重谈谈非洲的发展动态。职业技术教育与培训在各国社会经济发展中的重要性现已得到公认。职业技术教育与培训提供技能，促进青年就业，提高了国家社会经济发展所需的技能劳动力；通过创业培训，帮助受训者建立自己的企业并独立发展，同时，也有助于降低失业率。因此全球一致努力使各国将职业技术教育与培训纳入教育系统的主流，许多国际宣言和公约证明了这一点。特别是联合国教科文组织于 1999 年在韩国首尔举办的第二届国际职业和技术教育大会，将职业技术教育与培训确定为解决 21 世纪各国面临的就业和其他社会经济挑战的真正工具。2015 年，世界教育论坛在《2030 年教育：仁川宣言和行动框架》中提出了可持续发展目标，并强调了职业技术教育与培训的重要性，并建议各国可持续地增加拥有相关技能的青年和成年人的数量，包括就业、远程工作、创业方面的技术和职业技能。

据联合国教科文组织称，职业技术教育与培训的使命包括通过向广大失学青年和成年人传授适销对路的技能来消除失业；为高质量生活注入充分的职业力量；加强和维持国家经济和技术发展和国家经济繁荣。几个发达国家的职业技术教育与培训数据似乎支持上述观点。根据联合国教科文组织的数据，在经合组织国家，2018 年约有 18% 的 15—24 岁青年人加入了职业技术教育与培训计划和机构。在中国这一数字为 6.2%。这些接受职业技术教育与培训的青年人比例高的国家也是那些在社会经济发展方面取得足够进步的国家。

相比之下，莫·易卜拉欣基金会的数据显示，到 2017 年，撒哈拉以南非洲 15—24 岁年龄组中只有 1% 的年轻人接受职业教育。因此，撒哈拉以南非洲国家在工业、经济和技术发展方面远远落后于欧洲和中国的同行。

非洲国家现在意识到，在寻求实现非洲大陆的社会经济发展时，有必要将职业技术教育与培训纳入其教育系统的主流。例如，寻求在加纳推广职业技术教育与培训的新监管措施于 2006 年颁布，并于 2020 年进行了进一步改革，使职业技术教育与培训从加纳教育系统的边缘进入主流。结果是，加纳第二轮职业技术教育与培训方案中的青年人比例从 2015 年的 5% 跃升至 2021 年的约 15%。在双边伙伴，特别是中国和德国的支持下，对加纳的职业技术教育与培训分部门也进行了大量投资。

类似的变化正在几个撒哈拉以南的非洲国家发生，包括科特迪瓦、贝宁、多哥等。但是，尽管有这种变化，仍有许多挑战阻碍着非洲职业技术教育与培训的发展，包括职业技术教育与培训机构数量不足，缺乏培训设施和材料，技术教师和辅导员不足，大多数非洲国家缺乏农业技术和职业教育与培训，职业技术教育与培训学生的学术发展道路不明确。

为了克服这些挑战，使非洲能够从职业技术教育与培训教育中受益，建议采取以下措施。

非洲必须利用数字技术来解决受训人员缺乏足够培训空间的问题；解决培训材料和设施的缺乏问题；解决项目培训教员不足的问题；并能够在整个非洲大陆开展大量培训。

非洲国家必须利用 Z 时代的特质，即出生于 20 世纪 90 年代中期至 21 世纪 10 年代中期的一代人，他们被视为对新技术的自信用户，他们极其依赖互联网了解世界，习惯了全球互联。这一代人的主要特点是精通数字技术，拥抱多样性，务实，是真正的消费者，是政治进步人士。非洲国家可以利用这一青年群体的特点来提高他们对职业技术教育与培训的兴趣。

最后，非洲必须利用与中国和其他友好国家的双边合作。非洲与中国有着长期且自然有益的合作，必须利用这种合作吸引资源和专业知识到非洲大陆，以促进职业技术教育与培训。最近，加纳在中国政府的支持下，在所有 10 所技术大学和一些技术学院建立了职业技术教育与培训讲习班，这些机构的部分工作人员接受了中国专家的培训，其他非洲国家也可以这样做。

总之，如果非洲能够结合数字技术提供的机会、Z 时代的属性及其与中国等国家的双边关系，为众多的年轻人提供职业技术教育与培训，就可以加速非洲大陆的职业技术教育与培训，从而加速提供非洲大陆支持其社会经济发展所需的熟练劳动力。

## v. TVET Innovation and Development, Strong Technology to Empower Generation Z

**Osei Wusu-Achaw, Vice Chancellor of Kumasi Technical University, Ghana**

Thanks for the opportunity to engage you on this occasion on the topic: TVET Innovation and Development, Strong Technology to Empower Generation Z. I will be focusing on developments in Africa. The relevance of technical and vocational education and training in the socio-economic development of nations is now well established. Technical and Vocational Education and Training (TVET) provides skills that make the youth employable. It raises the skill workforce needed to anchor the social and economic development of nations. It provides entrepreneurial skills to trainees to set up their own businesses and lead independent lives. And it helps reduce unemployment. As such, there are concerted efforts globally to get the nations to mainstream TVET in the educational systems, as evidenced by a number of international declarations and conventions, notably the 2nd International Congress on Vocational and Technical Education in Seoul, ROK, which was organized by UNESCO in 1999, identified TVET as a veritable tool for solving the employment and other social-economic challenges, confronting nations in the 21st century. The World Education Forum in 2015 in the *Education 2030: Incheon Declaration and Framework for Action* proposed the Sustainable Development Goal and emphasized among others the importance of TVET and suggested that nations sustainably increased the number of youths and adults who have relevant skills, including technical and vocational skills for employment, distant jobs and entrepreneurship.

According to UNESCO, the mission of TVET includes the elimination of unemployment through equipping the generality of out-of-school youths and adults with salable skills; infusion into all adequate vocational efficiency for effective living; Enhancement and sustenance of national economic and technological development; and engendering of national economic prosperity.

Data on TVET education in several developed countries appear to support the forgoing observations. According to UNESCO, in the OECD countries, about 18% of the youth in the 15–24-year group in 2018 were enrolled in TVET programs and institutions. In China, the figure was 6.2%. These countries with high proportions of youth in TVET education are also those that have made enormous progress in social economic development.

In contrast, data from the MO Ibrahim Foundation indicate that by 2017, barely 1% of the youth in the 15–24-year group in Sub-Saharan Africa when enrolled in vocational education. Perhaps it is not surprising therefore that countries in Sub-Saharan Africa substantially lag behind their counterparts in Europe and China in industrial, economic and technological development.

African countries are now awakening to the need to mainstream TVET in their educational systems as they seek to engender social-economic development on the continent. For example, a new regulatory environment that seeks to promote TVET in Ghana was enacted in 2006, saw further reforms in 2020 and has brought TVET from the fringes to the mainstream education system in Ghana. The result has been that the percentage of the youth in second-cycle TVET programmes in Ghana jumped from 5% in 2015 to about 15% in 2021. There have also been massive investments in the TVET sub-sector in Ghana with support from bilateral partners, notably China and Germany.

Similar changes are taking place in several Sub-Saharan African countries including Côte d'Ivoire, Benin, Togo, among others. But in spite of this awakening, there are a number of challenges that still mitigate against the growth of TVET education in Africa. This includes inadequate number of TVET training institutions, a lack of training facilities and materials, inadequate technical teachers and facilitators, a lack of TVET agriculture in most African countries, and an ill-defined academic progression path for TVET students.

To surmount these challenges and so Africa can benefit from TVET education, the following are suggested: Africa must leverage digital technology to be able to curb the lack of sufficient training spaces for trainees; to curb the lack of training materials and facilities; to curb the program of inadequate training instructors; and to be able to reach out to a great number of training across the continent.

African countries must leverage the unique attributes of Generation Z, the generation that are people born between the mid-1990s and the mid-2010s. They are seen as confident users of new technology. They do not know the world without the internet, and they are used to global connectivity. The key attributes of note of this generation are: They are digitally savvy; They embrace diversity; They are pragmatic; They are true consumers; And they are political progressives. African countries can leverage these attributes of this group of youth to promote interest in their youth in TVET education.

Finally, Africa must leverage bilateral collaborations with countries such as China and other friendly nations. Africa has had a long-standing and naturally beneficial collaboration with China. It must leverage this collaboration to draw resources and expertise onto the continent to promote TVET education. Recently, Ghana, through the support of the Chinese government, constructed a number of TVET workshops in all the 10 technical universities and a number of technical institutes. Several staff of these institutions have received training from Chinese experts. Other African countries could do the same.

In conclusion, if Africa could integrate the opportunities offered by digital technology, the attributes of its Generation Z and its bilateral relations with countries such as China to provide TVET training to its teeming youth, it can accelerate TVET on the continent and thereby hasting the provision of skilled workforce required by the continent to support its social-economic development.

# （六）

# 中非教育合作现状与展望

中华人民共和国教育部国际合作与交流司副司长　方　军

中非是好朋友、好伙伴、好兄弟。建立外交关系六十余年来，双方休戚与共、并肩奋斗，缔造了历久弥坚的中非友好合作精神。中非合作的希望在青年，青年的希望在教育。2021 年 11 月，习近平主席在出席中非合作论坛第八届部长级会议开幕式时提出，中方同非洲密切配合共同实施“九项工程”，其中包括“未来非洲—中非职业教育合作计划”等多项教育领域重要举措，彰显了教育在中非关系中的重要作用，也为双方未来合作指明了方向。

职业教育是国民教育体系和人力资源开发的重要组成部分，是提升产业发展动力、破解发展难题的重要驱动器。当前，中国和非洲都面临抗击疫情、稳定经济、保障民生的艰巨任务，我们比以往任何时候都需要在职业教育领域加强经验交流，增进合作互鉴，共育青年英才。在此，我愿与各位交流以下三个内容。

### 1. 中国职业教育发展成果

中国政府高度重视职业教育，加大力度推动职业教育改革发展，不断增强职业教育对经济社会发展需求的适应性。目前，中国已建成全世界规模最大的职业教育体系。2021 年，高职学校招生 557 万人，相当于 10 年前的 1.8 倍；中职学校（不含技工学校）招生 489 万人，招生规模企稳回升；中高职学校每年培养 1 000 万左右的高素质技术技能人才，为经济社会发展提供了充足动力。

中国职业教育主动适应经济结构调整和产业变革、服务经济社会发展，推进专业升级和数字化改造。近十年来，教育部淘汰落后专业 108 种，升级和补充专业 1 007 种，更新幅度超过 70%。目前，全中国的职业学校共开设 1 300 余个专业和 12 余万个专业点，基本覆盖了国民经济各领域，使人才培养结构调整与需求结构变迁更好地对接起来，中国成为全世界唯一拥有全部工业门类的国家。

在“一带一路”倡议框架下，中国职业教育在“引进来”和“走出去”中不断实现“再提升”。目前，我们已与 70 多个国家和国际组织建立了稳定联系，400 余所高职院校与国外办学机构开展合作办学，面向“一带一路”沿线发展中国家实施了一系列人才培训、学校援建项目，在互利共赢中为世界各国提供可借鉴可推广的中国方案、中国智慧。

2. 中非职教合作进展

近年来，中国与非洲各国在职业教育领域的合作范围不断扩大，合作内容不断丰富，合作质量不断提高，展现出广阔的合作前景。目前，已有 14 个非洲国家建立 16 所鲁班工坊；在非孔子学院积极适应非洲社会需求，培养“中文 + 职业技能”人才；中国政府在联合国教科文组织设立援非教育信托基金，重点支持非洲国家的高等职业教育发展。与此同时，在非洲的中国企业也积极为当地员工提供培训机会，提升职业技能。

在此，我要特别向大家介绍一下“未来非洲——中非职业教育合作计划”实施进展。该计划在整合优化原有中非职业教育合作的基础上，围绕人才培养、标准建设、能力提升三大核心目标，共同培养服务于先进制造业、数字经济等新兴产业的应用型技能人才。在双方牵头单位，中国教育国际交流协会和非洲技术与应用型大学与学院协会共同推动下，已形成中国与非洲 11 个国家的 13 所院校 15 对合作伙伴关系，招收留学生近 300 人，为 300 余名非洲校长和骨干教师提供培训和实训，完成土木、机电和信息通信三个专业群技能等级证书建设方案和证书标准制定，初步构建了较有影响力的合作项目群，成为中非职业教育合作的新典范。

3. 对于中非职教合作的展望

当前，全球 1/5 的 25 岁以下人口居住在快速发展的撒哈拉以南非洲，人口红利优势凸显。非洲多国政府将职业教育作为社会经济发展和转型的引擎，对职业技术教育与培训的重视程度与日俱增。在昨天举行的大会上，坦桑尼亚、尼日利亚等国教育部长分享了在推进职业教育体系建设方面的成功经验和发展愿景，听后深受启发。

展望未来，我们愿与非洲各国政府部门、教育机构一道，结合各自需求，共同推进中非职业教育合作提质升级。在此，我愿提出以下四点倡议。

一是加强政策对话。发挥政府、院校、行业机构、企业等不同层级主体的作用，建立机制化对话平台，交流职业教育及经济社会发展信息，分享职业教育战略规划、政策制定、制度建设等领域的经验，议定未来合作方向。

二是深化产教融合。鼓励中非职业院校立足地区产业和自身特点，主动对接企业需求，进一步优化人才培养方案和教育教学模式，推进人才培养链与产业链、创新链有效衔接，为区域经济高质量发展提供人才支撑和智力支持。

三是完善协同发展。推动中非职业院校依托“未来非洲”计划、鲁班工坊等平台，共同建设优质教育资源，共同推进人才培养模式改革创新，共同开展学术研究攻关，共同创设具有国际水平的职业教育标准。

四是推进数字转型。顺应世界科技革命和产业革命发展趋势，重塑职业教育生态合作，共同推进职业教育智慧平台建设，分享优质职业教育数字化资源，合作培养具有数字化素养和能力的中高端技术技能人才。

各位同事，“同道而相益，同心而共济”，期待与会各方以今天的论坛为契机，携手同行，共同绘就中非职业教育合作美好蓝图，为构建新时代中非命运共同体贡献力量。

## （七）

# 加强中非职教发展合作，助力非洲可持续发展

中华人民共和国国家国际发展合作署地区二司司长　刘俊峰

中非是风雨同舟、守望相助的好朋友、好伙伴、好兄弟，中非合作是当今“南南合作”的典范。习近平主席在去年中非合作论坛第八届部长级会议上总结提出“真诚友好、平等相待，互利共赢、共同发展，主持公道、捍卫正义，顺应时势、开放包容”的中非友好合作精神。正是在这一精神指引下，中国秉持正确义利观和真实亲诚合作理念，推动中非发展合作取得了大批“看得见、摸得着、惠民生”的成果。

职业教育是中国对非合作的重要组成部分。中国坚持平等互利、形式多样、务求实效、共同发展的原则大力开展对非职业教育援助，为非洲国家可持续发展提供人才支撑发挥了重要作用。六十六年来，中国先后在卢旺达、马拉维、埃及、利比里亚、赤道几内亚等数十个非洲国家援建了综合或专科学校、职业技术学校或职业培训中心；为埃塞俄比亚、马达加斯加、布隆迪等国提供大量职业技术教育物资，帮助提升当地职业教育水平；组织开展农林牧渔、加工制造、建筑工程、科教文卫、手工技艺等各领域培训和技术援助，迄今已为非洲培训各领域的人才近 20 万名。其中，援苏丹恩图曼职业培训中心已经成为苏丹全国职业教育师资培训基地，累积为苏方培训了数千名学员；中国与埃塞开展的农业职业教育培训，向埃方派出 400 余人次中国教师，培养了埃方农技人员数万名；援布基纳法索职业培训中心技术援助成功激活了当地职业教育事业发展。

当前，世界变局和百年疫情交织叠加，新冠病毒疫情影响持续发酵，全球减贫进程严重受挫，联合国 2030 年可持续发展议程落实面临严峻挑战，实现共同发展仍然任重道远。去年 9 月，习近平主席站在全人类福祉的高度，在联合国提出全球发展倡议，以构建全球发展共同体为目标，秉持发展优先、以人民为中心等理

念，推动加快落实联合国 2030 年可持续发展议程，致力实现更加强劲、绿色、健康的全球发展。国家国际发展合署作为中国对外援助和国际发展合作的主管部门，将以落实全球发展倡议为契机，为促进非洲发展提供力所能及的支持和帮助。职业教育是落实全球发展倡议、推动实现 2030 年议程的重要方面。对下一步开展中非职业教育发展合作，我有以下几点建议。

一是紧密对接非洲发展需要。职业教育能够将发展中国家人口资源转化为人口红利，是促进就业和发展的重要途径。中非职业教育将主动融入中非共建“一带一路”合作框架，同非洲联盟《2063 年议程》和非洲各国发展战略紧密对接，充分分享中国的发展经验和实用技术，助力非洲工业化和一体化进程。

二是不断充实发展合作内涵。中方将秉持“授人以渔”的理念，不断提升在职业教育基础设施、物资、技术合作、人员培训等方面的合作力度。今年是中非合作论坛第八届部长级会议成果落实的开局之年，未来三年，国家国际发展合作署将为非洲援助新建或升级 10 所学校，邀请 10 000 名非洲高端人才参加研修研讨活动，并将继续支持同非洲国家合作设立鲁班工坊，进一步增强中非职业教育合作成效。

三是不断深化国际合作水平。中方将继续坚持平等合作、开放包容，不断加强同联合国、非盟等多边组织和机构、发达国家和发展中国家在职业教育方面的交流互鉴，积极探讨三方或多边合作。今年 6 月，在全球发展高层对话会上，习近平主席宣布了落实全球发展倡议的重要举措。其中，国家国际发展合作署将负责升级全球发展和南南合作基金，举办全球共享发展行动论坛，成立全球发展促进中心，设立发展项目库。国家国际发展合作署愿结合上述举措落实，同各方在对非职业教育合作上立项，实施更多务实项目，为加速落实 2030 年可持续发展议程注入强劲动力。

习近平主席指出，青年是中非关系的希望所在。职业教育将为非洲青年提供更多就业机会、更好发展空间。相信在中非双方和国际社会共同努力下，中非职业教育合作定将结出更多硕果，惠及中非和世界人民。

## （八）

# 进一步推进中非职业教育合作与优秀人才培养

浙江师范大学非洲研究院院长　刘鸿武

中国与非洲的教育交流与合作历史悠久，通过互派留学生、互派学者访学、教育代表团互访、职业教育培训等形式促进了双方人文交流、教育国际化以及人力资源发展，是一项惠及广大中非人民的伟大事业。多年来，浙江师范大学（以下简称浙师大）非洲研究院通过平台建设和协同机制促进中非人才培养，用学术成果支撑对非教育合作与培训，取得了丰硕成果，积累了宝贵经验。在推进中非职业教育合作与优秀人才培养方面，浙江师范大学非洲研究院也正在积极探索创新实践路径。

### 1. 浙江师范大学中非教育合作与优秀人才培养成果与经验

第一，浙师大多年来承担国家部委对非培训任务，服务中非高端人才培训。作为教育部“教育援外基地”、商务部“中国基础教育援外研修基地”，孔子学院总部“汉语教学志愿者非洲研修中心”，过去二十多年，浙师大先后承担了相关部委培训项目近 200 期；培训非洲高级政府官员、大中小学校长、专业人才、智库媒体领袖累计达 4 000 多人次；成立浙师大非洲校友会，校友遍布非洲 50 多个国家，成为推进中非合作的高端人才队伍。现任中非共和国总统福斯坦·阿尔尚热·图瓦德拉就曾于 2005 年在浙师大参加培训，在多次外交场合对浙师大的对非教育合作给予高度肯定。

第二，浙师大多年来成为吸收非洲留学生和进修生最多的高校之一。在过去的三十多年中，先后已经有将近 2 万名非洲留学生在浙师大开展研究和学习；近三年，每年在浙师大的非洲留学生都达 1 300 人以上。广大非洲留学生学成回国，成长为非洲各行各业优秀人才，如现任喀麦隆中文教学督导杜迪先生、喀麦隆雅温德第二大学孔子学院的周丽彤（中文名）博士，华大基因援建非洲火眼实验室技术人员秦鹏和（中文名）都是近年浙师大培养的优秀非洲学子。

第三，浙师大多年来输送大批赴非中国留学生和学者，在非洲建立合作教学研究基地。多年来，基于丰富的对非教育合作实践，浙师大已和非洲 17 个国家签订了 37 份教育合作协议。同时，承担了国家留学基金管理委员会非洲学创新人才国际合作培训项目、非洲教育高层次人才联合培训项目。依托这些重要项目，浙师大每年选拔 20 多名师生赴尼日利亚伊巴丹大学、南非纳逊曼德拉大学、坦桑尼亚达累斯萨拉姆大学以及埃及艾孜哈尔大学、开罗大学等开展联合培养。同时，学校自主设立专项基金，资助学校师生赴非洲国家开展调研访问。近年，浙师大非洲研究院已有学生考取国际组织实习生，赴非工作调研。

2018 年，浙师大在南非成立非洲研究院南非分院，聘请了一批在南非的华人学者和南非学者担任兼职研究人员。学者们在南非发声、发言，为中非友好合作积极宣传，产生了极好的影响。2019 年，浙师大与坦桑尼亚达累斯萨拉姆大学联合成立了中非法律研究中心，一大批达大教授成为中心成员，与中国学者成为友好合作伙伴。同时，浙师大已在非洲四个国家建立了孔子学院，先后派遣 4 000 多人次前往非洲孔子学院担任志愿者，培养了一大批非洲的汉语教师，使非洲国家汉语受训学生达到了 10 多万人次。

第四，浙师大多年来广泛搭建中非学术合作网络，为讲好中国故事、推动中非人文交流作出贡献。几十年来，学校先后聘请的非洲籍学者已有 15 位之多，为中非友谊、浙非友谊作出了积极贡献，多人获得了“中国友谊奖”“西湖友谊奖”。他们回国后在非洲国家积极建立各种形式的中非合作学术网络。浙师大非洲研究院高级研究员、非洲博物馆馆长、马里学者约罗参赞回国后，在疫情期间主动推动中马合作，召开了中非合作论坛马里峰会。非洲研究院尼日利亚籍留学生、学者乌比博士回国以后，担任了尼日利亚外交部国际问题研究所的所长和研究部主任，与尼日利亚中国研究中心主任查尔斯博士共同推动中尼学术交往，同时，在尼媒体对中尼关系宣传中起到非常积极的引导作用。浙师大非洲研究院南非分院执行主任、旅居南非的刘钊轶女士近两年内引外联，在中央和地方领导人出访南非期间发挥了重要作用，同时，也为浙师大学生赴南非留学牵线搭桥、提供指导。

**2. 进一步推进中非职业教育合作与优秀人才培养的对策建议**

中非职业教育合作在促进人文交流的同时助力提升人力资源水平，帮助非洲青年提高职业技能从而改善生活，是更加惠及民生、值得我们为之奋斗的事业。

首先，做好中非职业教育合作，需要加强对非洲国家的研究。非洲 54 个国家受自然、历史、文化、宗教、语言等影响各具发展特色和水平，不同国家在经济社会发展过程中对人才需求也呈现不同类型。中国学者首先要扎根非洲，开展对非洲国家客观、全面、深入的研究，打好历史、地理基础，做好基本功，用心、用情、用意坚持扎根于非洲，能坚持，能扎下根来，一直去做，一直行走，就可以了。同时，在研究非洲方面没有谁比非洲人更是我们的老师，要做好非洲研究，非洲学者是我们最好的合作伙伴，我们要以非洲人为师，由他们来带领、培养中国的科研人员。

其次，做好中非职业教育合作，需要加强对非洲职业教育体制政策的研究。以中非产能合作推动对非职业教育合作，我们一定要知道非洲所需、非洲所求和非洲的优势。参与中非职业教育合作的中国职业院校也应发挥学科专业优势，建立非洲区域国别职业教育研究中心，对非洲职业教育政策、法律法规及非洲的工会制度、税收制度和劳工制度等政策进行专门研究，为对非职业教育培训和中非产能合作提供理论指导。

再次，做好中非职业教育合作，需要共建中非职业教育培训体系和知识体系。依托中非职教联盟、鲁班工坊等中非职业教育合作项目，双方需要分享职业教育经验，聚焦如何将中国的优势和非洲国家的需要有效对接，在课程开设、教师培养、学生教育等方面进行创新改造，形成对象化、地域化和全球化的职业教育合作体制。尤其要聚焦当前高科技、信息化、互联网化、绿色发展等经济领域的产能合作需要，通过联合培养人才、共同开发课程、互派师生交换交流等方式，与非洲国家建立起综合全面的深度合作关系，中非双方建构起共享的职业教育与技能培训体系、知识体系，走出一条中非双向、均衡、互利的职业教育国际合作道路。

最后，做好中非职业教育合作，需要大力推广中国发展经验。要把中国过去四十多年改革开放、减贫的经验转化为非洲可以接受的话语体系。在过去的汉语教师和职业教育的基础上开设出更多的“中国发展”专业的职业教育学科。同时，将中国高职院校高端的教育培训基地更多的落地到非洲前线国家，从而使得中非教育合作成为一项百年事业。

总而言之，依据习近平总书记提出的“构建人类命运共同体”理念发展中非友好合作关系，我们就要努力建设“中非命运共同体”。为此，我们必须有能支撑、解释、服务共同体意识和新型国际关系的人类共建共通共享的知识体系、思想理念与行动智慧。今天，包括职业教育在内的中非教育合作正是通过学术合作和知识对话，正在努力建设“中国的非洲学”与“非洲的中国学”，这已不是西式的殖民之学、霸权强权之学，而是融汇人类各区域、各国家、各民族文明成果的人类共建共通共享的知识、思想与文化体系，是“人类命运共同体构建之学”。基于此，世界才能相向而行、相互欣赏、美美与共、合作共赢。

## （九）

# 分享中国职教模式　助力非洲区域经济发展

## ——埃及鲁班工坊建设模式与实践

天津轻工职业技术学院党委书记　戴裕崴

2018年9月，习近平主席在2018年中非合作论坛北京峰会开幕式上提出“八大行动”，其中包括在非洲设立10个鲁班工坊，向非洲青年提供职业技能培训。2019年4月25日，习近平主席会见埃及塞西总统时提出“中方将在埃及设立鲁班工坊，向埃及青年提供职业技能培训”。

天津市委、市政府高度重视埃及鲁班工坊建设，多次召开非洲鲁班工坊建设专题协调推动会，在市委、市政府领导下，按照天津市教委的统一部署，天津轻工职业技术学院与天津交通职业学院在天津市教委指导下，自2018年12月开始筹建埃及鲁班工坊。

2019年1月，天津职业教育代表团出访埃及，先后拜会了中国驻埃大使馆、埃及两个教育部以及埃及的大学和中资企业，进行了广泛调研。

2019年3月，艾因夏姆斯大学代表团、埃及教育与技术教育部副部长带队的埃及教育代表团先后来津，双方举办了中埃职业教育研讨会并沟通鲁班工坊建设事宜，埃方表达了强烈的合作意愿。3月底，天津轻工职业技术学院、天津交通职业学院再次出访埃及，考察鲁班工坊选址工作，最终研究确定在埃及建设两个鲁班工坊，并与艾因夏姆斯大学签署了鲁班工坊合作备忘录，与中非泰达投资股份有限公司、汉能薄膜发电集团及中交一公局集团有限公司签署了埃及鲁班工坊校企合作备忘录。4月1日，代表团访问埃及教育与技术教育部，天津市教委与埃及教育与技术教育部签订开展职业教育合作备忘录。此外，我校和天津交通职业技术学院还先后与埃方签订了《中国天津轻工职业技术学院、天津交通职业学院与埃及基础教育与技术教育部技术教育司、埃及开罗高级维修技术学校建立埃及鲁班工坊合作协议》《中国天津轻工职业技术学院、天津交通职业学院与埃及艾因夏姆斯大学建立埃及鲁班工坊合作协议》以及与两校的师资培训协议和设备捐赠协议。

2019年6月7日至7月10日，中方两校对艾因夏姆斯大学6位专业教师进行了为期5周的鲁班工坊工程实践创新项目教学模式师资培训，涉及新能源技术专业、数控设备应用与维护专业、汽车运用与维修技术专业。2019年9月3日—10月2日，埃及开罗高级维修学校两位教师分别在天津轻工职业技术学院和天津交通职业学院进行为期一个月的鲁班工坊工程实践创新项目教学模式师资培训，培训专业分别为数控加工技术和汽车维修技术。两所中方院校制订了周密、具体的培训方案，配备专业技能精、责任心强的“双师”骨干教师及班主任，聘请企业工程师培训团队并多次召开专题讨论会，针对埃及教师的专业背景与从教经历，分析制订教学内容、设计教学衔接、开发双语培训教材，采用工程实践创新项目教学模式对埃及教师进行定制培养。通过职业教育专家讲座、技能训练、企业实践、文化考察等途径让埃及教师感受中国职业教育，体验工程实践创新项目教学模式，领略中国先进技术和职业教育理念。中方两所院校为埃方提供了适合埃及的国际化专业教学标准，双方共同开发研究了5个专业的双语教材及课程标准。

2019年12月28日，天津轻工职业技术学院、天津交通职业学院专业教师及企业工程师联合团组26人飞赴埃及，完成埃及鲁班工坊捐赠设备的安装与调试、实训室装饰等任务，对埃及鲁班工坊的师生进行现场培训。12月31日，埃及鲁班工坊完成了全部建设任务。埃及教育与技术教育部副部长穆罕默德·穆贾希德教授和埃及高教与科研部副部长穆罕默德·艾曼·埃舒尔博士莅临工坊，对鲁班工坊建设所呈现的中国质量与中国速度给予高度评价。至此，天津在埃及共建成两个鲁班工坊，一个在埃及艾因夏姆斯大学，占地约1 200平方米，建设数控设备应用与维护、新能源应用技术、汽车运用与维修技术三个专业，一个在埃及开罗高级维修技术学校，占地约620平方米，建设数控加工技术和汽车维修技术两个专业。

2020年11月30日，埃及鲁班工坊云揭牌仪式在中埃两国同时举行，分设埃及艾因夏姆斯大学、埃及教育与技术教育部、中国驻埃及大使馆、埃及驻中国大使馆、天津市教委5个线上会场，两国嘉宾在5个分会场共同见证了鲁班工坊启动运营。新华社和人民日报等主流媒体报道了埃及鲁班工坊揭牌启运仪式。12月20

日，廖力强大使在埃及《宪章报》发表署名文章《中埃职业教育牵手联合培养技能人才——写在埃及鲁班工坊启动运营之际》。

天津轻工职业技术学院和天津交通职业学院积极深化埃及鲁班工坊功能，助力中非产教融合。2021 年 2 月 4 日，由天津轻工职业技术学院策划并联合天津交通职业学院主办的埃及鲁班工坊产教融合工作会暨中资企业赴埃及投资推介会在云端举行。中国驻埃及使馆教科处、经商处和天津市教委职教处领导以及中埃·泰达苏伊士经贸合作区执行董事等 23 家企业在线上参加会议。会议旨在以埃及鲁班工坊为平台，进一步深化产教融合、校企合作，为中资企业“走出去”搭建实体桥梁，为已在埃及投资的企业和准备在埃及投资考察的企业建立双向沟通交流的平台和媒介，从而发挥鲁班工坊的更大作用，实现合作共赢。

2021 年 9 月 14 日，非洲职业教育研究中心正式揭牌。按照教育部和天津市人民政府共同制定的《关于深化产教城融合　打造新时代职业教育创新发展标杆的意见》，天津市教育委员会依托天津轻工职业技术学院发起成立了“非洲职业教育研究中心”。中心聚焦非洲各国职业教育的发展历程与实际需求，从推进中非合作与人文交流的视角，深入研究中国职业教育支撑服务非洲产业和社会发展的政策、机制与做法，探索建立中非职业教育论坛对接机制，科研引领创新发展，打造中非国际产教融合的“桥头堡”。

2021 年 10 月 17 日，启动了课题研究发布会，研究成果非常丰富。7 所职业院校针对 6 个典型的非洲国家进行了调研，最后形成了中英文双语版专著《中非职业教育合作研究》，共计 70 余万字。2022 年，非洲职业教育研究中心将以“职业教育合作服务中非产能发展”为主题继续开展六个典型非洲国家调研，将于年后完成第二个研究成果，并正式出版《职业教育合作服务中非产能合作》中英文版专著。

2021 年 12 月 30 日，为贯彻落实习近平主席在中非合作论坛第八届部长级会议上提出的“中国将继续同非洲国家合作设立鲁班工坊，鼓励在非中国企业为当地提供不少于 80 万个就业岗位”的讲话精神，为促进中国和埃及职业教育合作交流，共同培养服务埃及当地经济发展的应用型技术技能人才，由天津轻工职业技术学院、天津交通职业学院、艾因夏姆斯大学、埃及泰达特区开发公司四家单位携手共建的埃及鲁班工坊培训就业基地举行了揭牌仪式。埃及鲁班工坊培训就业基地将就埃及鲁班工坊数控设备应用与维护专业、新能源应用技术专业、汽车运用与维修技术专业开展合作，共同培养鲁班工坊学员，合作四方积极参与人才培养。未来，本着双选的原则，培训基地积极向中埃·泰达苏伊士经贸合作区的园区企业推荐鲁班工坊学员实习、就业，择优录用。

今年，非洲职业教育研究中心扩大了研究团队，还增加了外方院校和在非投资的中资企业，将围绕着服务非洲的国际产能合作进行具体的研究。2022 年的研究重点主要在 5 个方面，即合作伙伴的认可度、需求导向、专业课程标准、师资培训和人才培养质量的评价。

# （十）

# 并肩助力中非职业教育合作 携手共育中非技术技能人才

成都航空职业技术学院校长　刘建超

中非职业教育合作是中非合作关系重要的组成部分，展现着巨大的生命力、凝聚力和创造力。成都航空职业技术学院（以下简称成航）内涵式发展蓄力，外向型服务发力，主动参与中非合作论坛框架下的职业教育领域交流与合作，为中非教育治理发展贡献成航方案、成航智慧。

**1. 内涵式发展蓄力，服务国家对外开放战略**

成航作为一所诞生于三线建设初期的航空院校，在近 60 年的办学历程中，始终不忘航空报国初心和航空强国使命，始终坚持“服务航空、服务国防、服务区域经济”的办学定位。学校是国家“双高”建设单位，是中国航空工业集团、中国国航 Ameco（北京飞机维修工程有限公司）唯一全面战略合作高职院校，也是中国教育国际交流协会职教分会副理事长单位。在国际化的实践探索上，学校聚焦“职业性”资格与能力的流通认可和对国家“走出去”战略的服务支撑，以“一横一纵一点”的战略布局为纲领，横向上巩固拓展与亚洲国家交流网络，纵向上深化与先进职业教育机构合作内涵，重点聚焦服务“一带一路”沿线与非洲国家建设。同时，积极践行优质资源引进、融合创生能力提升、海外职教培训输出“三要素循环”可持续发展路径，形成了国际化建设“引得进、用得上、出得去”的良好局面。当前，学校已与全球 23 个国家和地区的 60 所教育机构建立合作关系，培养了 250 余名留学生，主持并参与 3 项全球无人机标准制订。2018 年，学校荣获“世界职业院校与技术大学联盟卓越奖”。

2. 中非职业教育合作背景下的成航做法

学校从2015年培训首批“援外”非洲学员到2021年在非洲建立首个海外分校，始终坚持“共育非洲技术技能人才、助力非洲工业化发展”的宗旨，着力打造非洲职业教育高地，合力共育中非技术技能人才。

（1）校企协同，行稳致远，共建加蓬海外分校。一是顶层规划，执行有力。搭建“校+企+校”顶层合作模式，学校与同根同源的航空产业头部企业中航国际成套设备有限公司（以下简称中航国际）、非洲加蓬灯塔型职业学校恩考克职业教育中心（以下简称恩考克）建立战略合作关系，建立“高层沟通、中层对接、基层落实”三层贯通的工作机制，形成上传下达、前后协调的良好态势。

二是深入调研，办学有序。三方团队对恩考克办学现状与加蓬职业教育环境进行深刻调研，确立“三阶计划”：第一阶段对恩考克进行师资培训，耕耘本土化人才培育沃土；第二阶段对恩考克实施辅助运营管理，孕育办学内生动力；第三阶段建立加蓬分校，保障恩考克2021年4月正式开门办学，首批招收机械加工、焊接工程、电气与电子工程、汽车维修专业全日制学生达160人，逐渐形成“中文+职业教育”海外可行范式。

三是贴近需求，精准有度。学校秉持“优质、负责、精准”输出的原则，以问题为导向，梳理组织架构、核心能力、专业建设三大发展需求，形成整体服务方案。在组织架构上，构建合乎恩考克自身发展运作的教学治理体系；在核心能力上，以教师教研能力与技术服务能力为中心，构建学校自我造血机能；在专业建设上，围绕教学规范、资源开发、条件建设、过程管理、技术服务五个专题建立“正面清单”。

恩考克项目在全球疫情肆虐的背景下实施，学校先后派出12名中层干部与骨干教师赴加蓬，实施提供师资培训、教学标准、教育教学资源开发、学校治理一体化援助，开发了人才培养方案、课程标准和管理文件50余份，培训加蓬教师29名，海外培训量超5 400人/日。2021年12月，学校联合中航国际、恩考克三方共建的首个海外分校正式落成。

（2）院校结对，深度融合，共育非洲技能人才。学校深入参与教育部“未来非洲—中非职业教育合作计划”，是中非职业教育联合会发起单位之一，承担执行秘书处工作。同时，也是全国首批14所“中非应用型联合人才培养项目”试点单位，与非洲塞内加尔圣路易理工学院结对，开展电气自动化专业人才联合培养项目。通过以下举措，与非洲院校共育技能人才。

一是突出优势资源，共建与服务结合。在中国教育国际交流协会统筹指导下，聚焦标准打造，学校将课程标准共建与输出教育服务相结合，与圣路易理工学院联合开发《机械工程材料》等课程标准，并开展国际职业教育认证标准的研究与对接。

二是强调共育要素，技能与人文结合。学校遴选15名中国学生与15名塞内加尔留学生组建“电气自动化技术专业国际班”，以1+2+1的模式联合培养，定制国际班人才培养方案和专业教学标准，推动中非国际化电气工程师技术技能人才培养与中非青年人文交流互动。

三是重视能力建设，理念与方法结合。在为圣路易理工学院开展管理人员和骨干教师专题培训中，学校将教育理念与方法相结合，以互动研讨、案例分享的形式，凝聚职业教育共识。

**3. 思考启发：推动中非职业教育合作高质量发展**

要持续深入推动中非职业教育合作高质量发展，以下几点尤为重要。

（1）整体规划定基础。一方面将中非合作项目作为学校国际化工作的最重要抓手，纳入学校“十四五”发展规划统筹考虑；另一方面，充分调研论证，对外做好目的国和合作院校国际化背景分析，对内做好自身国际化水平能力和需求评估，在此基础上形成操作性强、灵活度高的整体规划方案。

（2）多方联动聚合力。职业院校要积极将自身办学资源与优势产业资源对接，充分利用政府搭台，建立多方联动的长效协同机制，优势互补，解决职业院校“走出去”所面临的机制、资金、安全等诸多困难。

（3）需求导向立根本。习近平主席强调，中非关系最大的“义”，就是用中国发展助力非洲的发展，实现互利共赢、共同发展。中非职业教育合作的核心在于通过深刻分析非洲发展需求，因地制宜地提供优质职业教育产品与服务，其合作范式实现从“授鱼”到“授渔”转换，形成非洲经济社会发展的内生动力。

（4）和而不同是关键。中非职业教育合作不同于以往西方为主导的知识体系建构，不对非洲大陆自身发展产生制度性干预。面对差异，我们彼此尊重、相互包容，依逻辑而行，循章法而动，务本与布新相结合，通过柔性分享传播中国特色职业教育成功经验与案例，助推中非职业教育合作高质量可持续发展。

中非合作论坛峰会的会徽是“合抱之手”，它寓意着“相拥、相融、相亲”。我相信无论过去、现在还是未来，我们与非洲职教同仁都会勠力同心，同向同行，并肩助力中非职业教育合作，携手共育中非技术技能人才，构建更加紧密的中非职业教育命运共同体！

# （十一）

# 构筑 CEC 产教融合共同体，共育“一带一路”技术技能人才

重庆工程职业技术学院党委书记　易　俊

2014 年，习近平主席在联合国教科文组织总部的演讲强调，文明因交流而多彩，文明因互鉴而丰富。文明交流互鉴，是推动人类文明进步和世界和平发展的重要动力。中国政府倡导建设人类命运共同体，积极推动“一带一路”建设。推动职业教育国际交流合作，对于全球职业教育整体水平提升和“一带一路”建设具有重要意义。举办世界职业技术发展大会，为增进职业教育国际交流合作搭建了有益平台。

我校地处中国中西部的重庆市，有七十多年的办学历史，是国家级示范高职、优质高职和“双高”建设单位。学校开设有覆盖电子信息等 50 多个专科专业，学生规模近 18 000 人。近年来，学校在加强国际交流合作方面迈出了坚实的步伐，探索构建了“文明互鉴、三方共建、双元培养”的高职教育国际合作新路径——CEC 产教融合共同体。

## 1. 主要做法

（1）“搭平台”——打通壁垒，理念创新多级发力。联合国内院校（College）、企业（Enterprise）及国外院校（College）等多主体，通过共建中泰职教联盟、中俄智能制造国际学院、中德莱茵产业创新中心等形式，共同建设国际化人才培养“CEC”平台。优化人才培养标准（Criterion）、评价体系（Evaluation）和课程教学（Curriculum）等要素组合，通过开发国际标准、质量评价、课程资源等形式，构建了国际化人才培养“CEC”要素结构。集合作（Cooperation）、教育（Education）和创新（Creation）等一体化功能，通过国家“未来非洲——中非职

业教育合作计划”项目、重庆市政府外国留学生市长奖学金丝路项目、创新创业大赛等项目，充分发挥“CEC”平台育人功能。

以坦桑尼亚境外办学项目为例。2019 年，学校、联合建设国际有限公司以及坦桑尼亚达累斯萨拉姆大学以 CEC 模式共同开展境外项目。中方学校提供教育标准、人才培养、师资、教学资源、评价和包括“未来非洲”等项目资源。企业提供实训场地和企业导师。外方学校提供教学场地和中国文化、语言类培训。

（2）“定标准”——需求导向，汇聚优势精准定位。研制专业教学标准。参与教育部《职业教育专业目录》和《职业教育专业简介》《职业教育专业教学标准》修订工作；与国际、国内第三方权威认证机构德国莱茵 TÜV 和重庆市教育评估院共同研制了机电一体化技术等 8 个具有国际化特色的专业教学标准。研制人才培养方案。融合华为、西门子等国际领先企业技术，研制了中亚现代移动通信技术等 8 个专业国际化人才培养方案，增设国际通识法规等相关课程，并在人才培养目标和规格方面细化了国际化的要求。研制课程标准。将企业岗位能力、在线课程、技能大赛、“1+X”证书、“中文 + 职业技能”课程等标准融为一体，开发课程标准 172 个。

（3）“育范式”——以生为本，整合资源共建共享。依托教育部中外语言交流合作中心“汉语桥”项目，根据不同专业和课程，结合岗位职业素养和国际规则，挖掘思政内容，与教学内容同步设计、相互融合，并组织 81 个中泰职教联盟成员单位共同开发中英泰多语种国际化在线课程教学资源 102 个，实现资源共建共享。实施分层分段培养。专业群分类、学习进程分段、企业需求分层，制订个性化培养实施方案。针对境内具有行业优势和境内外有成熟的实训基地的，如现代移动通信技术等电子与信息大类相关专业，采用“2+1”（即中国学习 2 年，国外实习 1 年）模式，“引进来”“走出去”双向培养国际人才；针对境内有产能外溢需求和境外有实际项目的，如建筑工程技术等土木建筑大类相关专业，采用境外合作办学“1+2+1”（即国外学习 1 年，中国学习 2 年，国外实习 1 年）模式，走出去协助推进国际学生人才培养；针对境外具有行业标准优势和境内有企业的，如机电一体化技术等装备制造大类相关专业，采用中外合作办学“3+0”（即中国学习实习 3 年）模式，引进融合与本土改造形式推进国内学生人才培养。2022 年，我校与达累斯萨拉姆理工学院签订中非应用型人才培养合作协议，实施“1+2+1”模式人才培养；实施订单式培养，与益海嘉里、潍柴动力、华为等走出去企业开展个性化人才培养，建成“红海 – 华为”等 30 个企业订单班，为企业定制国际化技术技能型人才。教学模式采用国内＋国外、线上＋线下、文化＋技能、理论＋虚拟仿真＋线下实训，师资采用“中外教师＋中资企业导师”双师国际混编师资团队教学。

（4）“见实效”——增值评价，全面发力提质促优。研制国际化项目评价指标体系，研制了包含国际化发展战略、国际化人才培养等 14 项二级指标和 156 项三级指标的事前、事中和事后的全程质量监控评价指标体系。开发的智能评价平台，根据国际化项目需求，动态择优匹配合作单位，确保项目建设质量和可持续发展。研制国际化人才培养评价指标体系，校企共同开发基于学生职业能力的本土化增值评价体系，共同实施评价，企业依据评价结果精准选人用人，学院依据评价结果推行实施教学诊断与改进，实现“多元评价主体、多维评价指标、多样评价形式”提高国际化人才培养质量。

**2. 主要成效**

一是促进了学生发展。试点专业毕业生 16% 进入中冶赛迪、海力士等世界 500 强企业，试点专业机电一体化技术专业群毕业生满意度 98.8%，家长满意度 99.5%，企业满意度 100%。2021 年，学生参加全国职业院校技能大赛一等奖获奖数量位居全国之首；学生获中国国际“互联网＋”大学生创新创业大赛市级银奖以上 34 项，获奖数量位居全国第一。与坦桑尼亚等 17 个国家 66 所院校 20 000 余名师生和 70 个企业开展海外留学生培养和技术服务。培训了来自泰国、坦桑尼亚等国家的企业 1 000 余名中高级管理人员及员工。

二是促进了教师发展。建成国家级职业教育教师教学创新团队 2 个，国家级课程思政教学团队 1 个，获国家级教师教学能力大赛一等奖 2 项。主持高等学校教育教学改革课题 58 项。与企业联合开展技术服务项目 162 项，每年派出 70 名教师深入企业顶岗实践。引进外籍教师近 60 人次，派出近 100 名校内教师赴海外开展 3 个月以上研修和工作，完成 23 门课程的全英语教学。

三是提升了国际影响。在国内外主办、承办国际会议 11 次，共有 25 个国家 1 100 余人次参与讨论分享。受邀在国际会议主题发言 20 次，共有 50 余个国家 300 余所单位 1 500 余人次听取相关报告，泰国东方技术学院等 100 所国内外高职院校借鉴了成果经验。牵头成立中泰职教联盟，成员单位 77 所，其中，国外 37 所；联盟平台连续 4 年被写入重庆市教育发展重点工作，得到重庆市教育委员会国际处的广泛推广。2019 年，学校入选中国—东盟高职院校特色合作项目，在东盟教育部长会议上分享课程建设经验，全球 50 000 余名观众在线观看。2020 年，学校入选“未来非洲—中非职业教育合作计划”子项目，成为鲁班工坊建设联盟副理事长单位，建成坦桑尼亚境外合作办学中心。学校先后获得教育部中德先进职业教育合作项目、法国施耐德电气绿色低碳产教融合项目、中德“工业 4.0”产教融合项目等，泰国教育部主管职业教育的副部长苏拉撤差翁发来亲笔贺信。2019 年，坦桑尼亚驻华大使专程来到我校参加坦桑尼亚建筑高级管理技术技能培训班结业典礼，同年，22 个非洲国家驻华使节团一行来访我院专题交流“一带一路”职业教育成果。2022 年，在坦桑尼亚副总统见证下，与联合建设签约成立我校在坦方第二个境外办学项目，预计未来为中坦工业园培养 10 万本土化人才。与中国教育国际交流协会、坦桑尼亚达累斯萨拉姆大学共同完成了首届中坦职业教育合作论坛。海力士重庆分公司感谢学院为企业个性化培养了留得住、用得好的人才。重庆市教育委员会国际处特别说明学院国际化建设取得显著成绩，具有引领示范作用。中国教育报、新华社、人民日报等 20 余家国内主流媒体宣传报道本成果。2022 年 4 月 23 日，中国教育电视台 CETV4“梦开始的地方”系列栏目对学院国际化人才培养进行专题报道。坦桑尼亚 Daily News、The Guardian、泰国暹罗日报等 12 家国外媒体专题报道本成果。

中非交往源远流长，传统友谊基础深厚。未来，学校将进一步加强与非洲各国的职教合作和人文交流，重点围绕境外办学、中外合作办学等，把握机会、找准定位，为后疫情时代中非职教合作发挥积极作用，为构建更加紧密的新时代中非命运共同体作出新的更大贡献。

# 六
# “一带一路”合作与鲁班工坊建设发展论坛

协助组织单位：天津职业大学

# VI. “The Belt and Road Initiative” and Luban Workshop

Co-organizer: Tianjin Vocational Institute

02
沙赫里约尔·萨杜洛佐达
Shahriyor Sadullozoda

03
索勒赫佐达·乌迈德
Solehzoda umed

04
陈海荣
Chen Hairong

05
于忠武
Yu Zhongwu

06
刘斌
Liu Bin

**分享与交流鲁班工坊建设的理念与行动，遵循“共同建设、共促发展、共享成果”的基本原则，探索深化鲁班工坊发展模式，丰富鲁班工坊内涵和形式。**

In this session, the participants share the notions and activities concerning Luban Workshop, and based on the principle of “working together for common development and shared achievements”, explore the modes and pathways of enhancing the development of Luban Workshop, and enriching its connotation and forms.

## (一)

# “一带一路”合作与鲁班工坊建设发展论坛概述

天津职业大学国际交流处副处长　孟　峥

2022 年 8 月 19—20 日，以“后疫情时代职业技术教育发展：新变化、新方式、新技能”为主题的“世界职业技术教育发展大会”，在天津成功举办。“‘一带一路’合作与鲁班工坊建设发展”论坛作为大会十四个平行论坛之一，由天津职业大学协办并承办。

天津市人民政府副市长李树起、中国教育国际交流协会会长刘利民、中华人民共和国教育部国际合作与交流司副司长方军、天津市人民政府副秘书长王璟、中国教育国际交流协会秘书长王永利、天津市教育委员会一级巡视员孙惠玲、天津市人民政府外事办公室副主任赵剑岭、中国教育国际交流协会副秘书长余有根出席论坛。埃塞俄比亚驻华大使、马达加斯加驻华大使、马里驻华大使，委内瑞拉、阿尔及利亚、日本、南非、津巴布韦、乌兹别克斯坦、斐济、乌干达、蒙古、柬埔寨、巴基斯坦等国驻华使节及亚太空间合作组织、中国工合国际委员会、上海合作组织、德国汉斯·赛德尔基金会、全球化智库等国际组织代表出席论坛，两百余名国内外院校、企业、行业组织和研究机构代表在线上、线下参加论坛。

鲁班工坊是在教育部的大力支持与指导下，天津市主动作为、发挥优势，首创并率先实践职业教育“走出去”的品牌，为合作国家培养熟悉中国技术、了解中国工艺、认知中国产品的技术技能人才，有效服务国家外交大局和“一带一路”高质量发展，带动了中国装备出口，输出了技术和方案，实现了模块化运作和品牌化运营。鲁班工坊致力于培养更多全球工匠，以中国“工匠精神”为依托，承载着中国劳动人民伟大智慧和精湛的创造精神，是中国职业教育走出国门与世界分享的重要平台，是促进“一带一路”人文交流和民心相通的重要载体。2016 年 3 月，在教育部的指导下，天津渤海职业技术学院与泰国大城技术学院基于职业教育交流成果，合作设立了全球首个鲁班工坊。自此，一张职业教育国际合作的亮丽名片应运而生。

2018 年以来，习近平总书记已先后 10 次在重大外交场合对建设鲁班工坊作出重要指示，为鲁班工坊建设指明了方向，提供了根本遵循。鲁班工坊建设服务国家外交大局，在重大外交活动中贡献积极力量，实现了中国标准、中国模式、中国装备与中国方案的整体输出，不断提升影响力，得到党和国家领导人的肯定，广泛得到合作国家欢迎。

在论坛中，李树起副市长致辞，希望以鲁班工坊为平台，增进各国相互了解、促进各国民心相通、推进各国共同发展，把鲁班工坊打造成为“一带一路”的技术驿站。

方军副司长在致辞中表示，以鲁班工坊为代表的诸多海外办学品牌项目，在加强我国与“一带一路”沿线国家政府、企业、院校之间的国际交流与合作，促进中外人文交流，提升中国职业教育国际影响力等方面发挥了重要作用，取得了丰硕成果。

王永利秘书长在致辞中提出，积极做鲁班工坊的建设者、推动者和创新者，共同谱写“一带一路”建设的新篇章，助力鲁班工坊朝着更高水平、更高质量的方向前进。

在本次论坛上，刘利民会长为全国首批鲁班工坊运营项目授牌，天津已建成的20个鲁班工坊及浙江、陕西、四川的5个项目共25所院校代表集体受领了“鲁班工坊运营项目”标牌，鲁班工坊运营项目的授牌标志着由天津原创并率先实践的鲁班工坊项目正式走向全国，成为全国性教育国际合作品牌。

论坛邀请14名来自中外院校、研究机构、政府部门和企业的嘉宾交流发言，围绕“中国的鲁班工坊，世界的鲁班工坊”“服务‘一带一路’的中国职教国际合作”“面向未来的鲁班工坊”等主题进行了高水平交流研讨，互学互鉴、共商共享，探索鲁班工坊建设及职业教育国际合作的新路径、新模式。

泰国鲁班工坊外方建设院校泰国大城技术学院院长玛悠丽介绍了泰国鲁班工坊的建设成果，她表示多年来在泰中双方合作下，尤其是在泰国鲁班工坊项目的合作中，提升了泰国教育国际发展水平，加强了泰中人文交流培训、泰中师生交流互访，增进了泰中两国人民友谊。葡萄牙塞图巴尔理工学院鲁班工坊负责人何塞·卢卡斯以2018年揭牌运行的葡萄牙鲁班工坊为例，分享工坊中所使用的仿真生产线等先进实训设备及其应用，特别是在“工业4.0”的工业自动化技术应用的背景下，鲁班工坊对葡方院校教学理念、实训方式所带来的巨大提升和对人才培养方式的提升作用。埃塞俄比亚职业技术培训学院校长特舍里·博里查指出，埃塞俄比亚职业技术培训学院的职业教育得益于鲁班工坊项目，应用工程实践创新项目教学模式极大地提升了该校职业教育的水平与能力。中国中材国际工程股份有限公司尼日利亚分公司人力总监伊丽莎白·阿得雷蒂就鲁班工坊服务人类减除贫困的作用进行了分享，鲁班工坊为员工技能习得提供了核心要素，提高了员工未来的就业能力、职业发展潜力和收入潜力，改善了人民福利，改善了经济状况，促进了发展中国家的可持续发展，在解决普遍贫困问题方面具有重大影响。塔吉克斯坦工业与新技术部副部长索勒赫佐达·乌迈德指出，职业技术教育与培训体系是有效保持经济快速增长的重要因素。鲁班工坊项目为大量的职业教育学生提供职业技能培训，提高劳动者的技能水平，以满足日益增长的劳动力需求。塔吉克斯坦技术大学副校长沙赫里约尔·萨杜洛佐达认为，塔吉克斯坦鲁班工坊项目提升了塔吉克斯坦大学的科研能力，提升了塔吉克斯坦大学生使用现代化仪器设备技能水平，为塔吉克斯坦市场培养了更多职业人才，为塔吉克斯坦经济发展提供助力。

中国土木工程集团有限公司党委副书记严学斌作为“中资走出去”企业的代表

介绍了中国土木响应国家倡议，参建铁路和铁道交通项目，助力“一带一路”沿线国家经济社会发展，共建吉布提鲁班工坊的情况。体现了鲁班工坊产教融合发展，助力优质中国企业海外发展的独特和突出的作用。在鲁班工坊建设院校的分享中，金华职业技术学院副校长陈海荣、宁波职业技术学院副校长岑咏分别介绍了在卢旺达鲁班工坊“1321 工程”发展计划的愿景——即在“一平台、三联盟、二工坊、一中心”的愿景下实现输出一批专业课程教学标准、建设一个丝路学院、服务一批中资企业“走出去”，以及和贝宁鲁班工坊建设中所采取的“坚持政府、行业、企业、学校协同，聚焦政府援外工程，推动职业教育服务中非命运共同体”的国际项目建设经验。天津铁道职业技术学院校长于忠武介绍了非洲首家鲁班工坊——吉布提鲁班工坊，在建设过程中逐步形成了“一体两翼三维”的工坊建设模式，与企业共同实践“4+2+1+1”新路径。天津中德应用技术大学副校长张巾帼介绍了澜湄职业教育培训中心暨柬埔寨鲁班工坊项目的“三步走”战略，设定了初期（2017—2018 年）、中期（2019—2020 年）、远期（2021—2022 年）逐步实现开展学科研究、留学研究生联合培养、全面开展学历教育、开展应用本科教育、实施市场化运作等办学目标。中方院校的分享展示了全国院校在海外国际职业教育合作项目建设中因地制宜，多样化、灵活性的建设实践和面向未来持续发展建设鲁班工坊的深度思考。

围绕鲁班工坊的标准化建设和持续发展，天津市鲁班工坊研究与推广中心副主任杨延以“天津鲁班工坊建设的探索与创新”为主题，介绍了天津首创的鲁班工坊的五项建设原则、五项核心内涵、五个建设规范和八项指标，详细说明了天津在鲁班工坊建设中对质量与标准的严格要求。鲁班工坊建设联盟理事长刘斌介绍了联盟在推动鲁班工坊建设的协调管理的功能，并就全国鲁班工坊建设标准制定、项目管理、未来鲁班工坊联盟成员的扩大发展、建设工坊智库、汲取全球智慧等后续工作进行了详细介绍。

论坛聚焦“分享与交流鲁班工坊建设的理念与行动，遵循‘共同建设、共促发展、共享成果’的基本原则，探索深化鲁班工坊的发展模式，丰富鲁班工坊内涵和形式的途径”，中外代表开展了深入的交流与研讨，为未来鲁班工坊高质量持续发展提供了经验与借鉴，增强了鲁班工坊的国际影响力。

## i. Overview of the Session on "The Belt and Road Initiative" and Luban Workshop

**Meng Zheng, Deputy Director of International Communication Department, Tianjin Vocational Institute, China**

From 19 to 20 August, 2022, World Vocational and Technical Education Development Conference was successfully held in Tianjin with the theme of "Vocational and Technical Education Development in the Post-pandemic Era—New Changes, New Ways and New Skills". As a parallel session of the Conference, the session of "The Belt and Road Initiative" and Luban Workshop was co-organized and hosted by Tianjin Vocational Institute.

Li Shuqi, Vice Mayor of Tianjin Municipal People's Government, China, Liu Limin, President of China Education Association for International Exchange (CEAIE), Fang Jun, Deputy Director General of Department of International Cooperation and Exchanges of the Ministry of Education of People's Republic of China, Wang Jing, Deputy Secretary-General of Tianjin Municipal People's Government, Wang Yongli, Secretary-General of China Education Association for International Exchange (CEAIE), Sun Huiling, First Class Inspector of Tianjin Municipal Education Commission, Zhao Jianling, Deputy Director of Foreign Affairs Office of Tianjin Municipal People's Government, and Yu Yougen, Deputy Secretary-General of China Education Association for International Exchange (CEAIE) attended the session. Ambassador of Ethiopia to China, Ambassadors of Madagascar to China, Ambassador of Mali to China, officers of foreign affairs of Venezuela, Algeria, Japan, South Africa, Zimbabwe, Uzbekistan, Fiji, Uganda, Mongolia, Cambodia, Pakistan and representatives of international organizations such as Asia-Pacific Space Cooperation Organization, International Committee for the Promotion of Chinese Industrial Cooperatives, Shanghai Cooperation Organization, Hanns Seidel Stiftung, Center for China and Globalization, etc. attended the session. More than two hundred representatives from domestic and foreign universities, enterprises, industrial organizations and research institutions attended online and offline.

With the strong support and guidance from Chinese Ministry of Education,

Tianjin has taken the initiative and given full play to its advantages to create and take the lead in implementing the brand of vocational education "going global"—Luban Workshop, which has cultivated technical skill talents who are familiar with Chinese technology, understand Chinese craftsmanship and recognize Chinese products for the partner countries and effectively served the overall situation of national diplomacy and the high-quality development of the "Belt and Road", driving the export of Chinese equipment, exporting technology and solutions, and realizing the modular management and branding operation. Dedicated to cultivating more global craftsmen, based on Chinese "craftsmanship" and carrying the great wisdom and exquisite creative spirit of Chinese working people, Luban Workshop is an important platform for Chinese vocational education to go abroad and share with the world and a key vehicle to promote people-to-people communication in "the Belt and Road". In March 2016, under the correct guidance of the Ministry of Education, Tianjin Bohai Vocational Technology College, China and Ayutthaya Technical College, Thailand established the world's first Luban Workshop based on the results of vocational education exchange. Since then, a bright name card of international cooperation in vocational education has been created.

Since 2018, General Secretary Xi Jinping has given important instructions on the construction of Luban Workshop for 10 times on major diplomatic occasions, which has pointed out the direction and provided fundamental guidelines for the construction of Luban Workshop. The construction of Luban Workshop has served the overall situation of national diplomacy, contributed positively to many multi-lateral and bilateral major diplomatic activities, realized the overall export of Chinese standards, Chinese models, Chinese equipment and Chinese solutions, and continuously enhanced its influence, which has been affirmed by the Party and State leaders and widely welcomed by the cooperating countries.

During the forum, Li Shuqi delivered a speech, expressing his hope that the Luban Workshop can be used as a platform to enhance mutual understanding, promote people-to-people communication and common development among countries, and make it a technical station of the "Belt and Road".

Fang Jun stated in his speech that many overseas schooling brand projects, represented by the Luban Workshop, have played an important role and gained fruitful results in strengthening international exchanges and cooperation between China and governments, enterprises and institutions along the "Belt and Road", promoting people-to-people exchanges between China and foreign countries, and enhancing the international influence of Chinese vocational education.

In his speech, Wang Yongli stated that we would actively be the builder, promoter and innovator of Luban Workshop, write a new chapter of the "Belt and Road" construction together, and help Luban Workshop advance towards a higher level and higher quality.

In this session, Liu Limin awarded the first number of Luban Workshops operating projects in China, and representatives from 25 institutions, including 20 established Luban Workshops in Tianjin and 5 projects in Zhejiang, Shaanxi and Sichuan, collectively received the "Luban Workshops Operating Projects" plaque. The awarding of the operating projects of Luban Workshops marked that the original Luban Workshops projects, which were practiced by Tianjin, have been formally introduced to the whole country and become a national brand of international cooperation in education.

The session invited 14 guests from Chinese and foreign universities, research institutions, government departments and enterprises to deliver speeches and conduct high-level exchanges and discussions on several themes, such as "China's Luban Workshop Belongs to the World", "International Cooperation of Vocational Education in China to Serve the Belt and Road" and "Luban Workshop for the Future", to share with and learn from each other, and to explore new paths and new models for the construction of Luban Workshop and international cooperation in vocational education.

Mayuree Sriraboot, Director of Ayutthaya Technical College, which co-constructed with China the first Luban Workshop in Thailand and also in the world, introduced the fruits of Luban Workshop. She said that over the years, the cooperation between Thailand and China, especially in the Luban Workshop project in Thailand, has enhanced the international development of Thai education, strengthened the people-to-people communication and training between the two countries, increased the exchange and visits between Thai and Chinese teachers and students, and enhanced the friendship between Thai and Chinese people. José Lucas, Head of Luban Workshop at Polytechnic Institute of Setúbal, Portugal, shared the example of the Portuguese Luban Workshop, which was inaugurated in 2018, and the advanced training equipment used in the workshop such as the simulation production line and their application. He especially highlighted the important role Luban Workshop played in improving the teaching concept, practical training method and talent cultivation of Portuguese institutions, in the context of industrial automation technology application in Industry 4.0. Teshale Berecha, President of Technical and Vocational Training Institute of Ethiopia, noted that the Institute has benefited from the Luban Workshop, in which the level and capacity of vocational education of the Institute has been greatly improved by the application of EPIP (Engineering, Practice, Innovation, Project) teaching method. Elizabeth Adereti, Human Resource Manager of Sinoma International Engineering Co., Ltd., Nigeria, shared her views on the key role of Luban Workshop in poverty reduction, noting that the workshop can provide core elements for employee skill acquisition, enhance future employability, career development potential and income potential of the employees, improve people's welfare and economic conditions, and promote sustainable development in developing countries, all of which have a significant impact in addressing the issue of widespread poverty. Solehzoda Umed, Deputy Minister of Industry and New Technologies of Tajikistan, stated that Technical and Vocational Education and Training (TVET) system is an important factor in effectively maintaining rapid economic growth. The Luban Workshop project can provide vocational skill training for a large number of vocational education students to improve the skills of the workers and to meet the growing demand for labor. Shahriyor Sadullozoda, Vice President of Tajik Technical University named after academician M. S. Osimi, believed that the Tajikistan Luban Workshop project has improved the scientific research capacity of Tajik universities, enhanced the skills of Tajik university students in using modern instruments and equipment, cultivated more professional talents for the Tajik market, and provided a boost to Tajikistan's economic development.

Yan Xuebin, Deputy Secretary of CPC Committee of China Civil Engineering Construction Corperation, a representative of Chinese enterprises going abroad, introduced that China Civil Engineering, responding to the national initiative, has been participating in the construction of railroads and railway transportation projects, helping the economic and social development of countries along the "Belt and Road", and jointly building the Luban Workshop in Djibouti, which reflected the unique and outstanding role of Luban Workshop in integrating the development of industry and education and helping high-quality Chinese enterprises to develop overseas. In the sharing of the construction institutions of Luban Workshop, Chen Hairong, Vice President of Jinhua Polytechnic, China, introduced the vision of the "1321 Project" development scheme of Luban Workshop in Rwanda, which is, with the vision of "one platform, three alliances, two workshops and one center", to export a number of professional curriculum teaching standards, build a Silk Road School and serve a number of Chinese enterprises to "go abroad"; Cen Yong, Vice President of Ningbo Polytechnic, China, introduced the international project constructing method of "adhering to the collaboration among government, industry, enterprises and institutions, focusing on the government's assistance projects abroad and promoting vocational education to serve the China-Africa community with a shared future" adopted in constructing Luban Workshop in Benin. Yu Zhongwu, President of Tianjin Railway Technical and Vocational College, China, introduced that during the construction of Djibouti Luban Workshop, the first Luban Workshop in Africa, a workshop constructing method of "one body, two wings and three dimensions" was gradually formed and the new path of "4+2+1+1" was practiced together with enterprises. Zhang Jinguo, Vice President of Tianjin Sino-German University of Applied Sciences, China, introduced the "three-step" strategy adopted in the construction of the Lancang Mekong Vocational Education Training Center and Cambodian Luban Workshop Project, which set the goals of the initial (2017—2018), mid-term

(2019—2020) and long-term (2021—2022) phases to gradually achieve disciplinary research, joint training of postgraduate students, comprehensive academic education, undergraduate education application and market-oriented operation. The sharing of Chinese institutions demonstrated the localized, diversified and flexible construction practices of national institutions in the construction of overseas international TVET cooperation projects and the in-depth thinking of building Luban Workshops for sustainable development in the future.

Focusing on the standardized construction and sustainable development of Luban Workshop, Yang Yan, Deputy Director of Tianjin Luban Workshop Research and Promotion Center, China, with the theme of "exploration and innovation of Luban Workshop construction in Tianjin", introduced the five construction principles, five core connotations, five construction specifications and eight indicators of the Luban Workshop initiated by Tianjin, detailing Tianjin's strict requirements for quality and standards in the construction of Luban Workshop. Liu Bin, General Director of Luban Workshop Construction Alliance, China, introduced the functions of the Alliance in promoting the coordination and management of the construction of Luban Workshops, and gave a detailed introduction to the follow-up work such as the development of national standards for the construction of Luban Workshops, project management, the future expansion and development of Luban Workshop Alliance, and the construction of a workshop think tank to draw the wisdom around the world.

The session focused on "sharing and exchanging the concept and action of Luban Workshop, following the basic principle of 'jointly building, promoting development and sharing results', exploring and deepening the development mode of Luban Workshop, and enriching the connotation of Luban Workshop". The Chinese and foreign delegates conducted in-depth exchanges and discussions, which provided experience and reference for the future high-quality and sustainable development of Luban Workshops and enhanced the international influence of Luban Workshops.

## （二）

# 中塔合作共建鲁班工坊，促进职业教育合作与友谊的发展

塔吉克斯坦技术大学副校长　沙赫里约尔·萨杜洛佐达

对于就业者来说，提升职业技能是工作中不可或缺的一环，直接影响着劳动者的工作效率。意识到这一点，同时为了完成塔吉克斯坦总统埃莫马利·拉赫蒙赋予的使命，塔吉克斯坦技术大学领导层不断开设不同形式的课程、举办各种活动，以提升大学教职工、国有企业员工、私有制公司人员和全体人民的工作技能。

由于用人单位对不同工种就业人员的能力水平和权威性不断提出更高的要求和更高质量标准，院校的首要目标是不断更新专业技术人员和课程学习者的理论知识和实践水平。此外，一个重要因素是提高就业人员积极性和本国人才的教育水平，以实现本国和上海合作组织各成员国的发展目标。需要强调的是，上海合作组织框架内的培训和进修领域合作潜力巨大，目前众多高校已经积极地参与进来。加强培训和进修领域的联系，有助于满足普遍的技术需求、对合格专业人员的需求以及该教育领域支持计划的实施。特别要指出的是，中国政府提出的“一带一路”倡议作为积极发展技能提升进程的一个要素，非常有效。得益于“一带一路”倡议的理念和中塔两国友好关系，在塔吉克斯坦技术大学建设了中亚地区首家鲁班工坊。

鲁班工坊作为培训的中心，完全能够提供一系列举办培训和进修活动的机会。我们相信，本次鲁班工坊在塔吉克斯坦技术大学的建立将把我校的科研实力提升到一个全新的水平。得益于鲁班工坊项目，塔吉克斯坦技术大学的师生们可以使用现代化仪器和设备，其中大部分仪器和设备还未在中亚地区使用过。在我们的中方合作伙伴——天津城市建设管理职业技术学院同事们的支持下，由世界级专家为塔吉克斯坦技术大学的科研人员和教师开展现代化仪器和设备的正确使用方法培训。同时完善我校教学过程和培养过程以满足劳动市场要求的人才。

在建设鲁班工坊的过程中，我们与天津城市建设管理职业技术学院的同事们和供应商合作伙伴都收获颇丰，正能量满满。鲁班工坊建设是友谊、相互尊重和建立有效伙伴关系的典范。

2021 年 7 月 13 日，时任中华人民共和国国务委员、外交部部长王毅在与塔吉克斯坦外交部部长西罗吉丁・穆赫里季诺维奇进行第三次会晤时宣布，将在塔吉克斯坦建成中亚首家鲁班工坊。

由于塔吉克斯坦技术大学拥有巨大的科研潜力，而且在工程领域处于领先地位，我校被选为拟建工坊的机构。中华人民共和国主席习近平在与塔吉克斯坦总统埃莫马利・拉赫蒙会晤时，表示将加快在塔建成中亚首家鲁班工坊。得益于两国密切友好的合作伙伴关系，2021 年 12 月 24 日，塔吉克斯坦技术大学与天津城市建设管理职业技术学院的领导举行了会议。这次会议开启了基本文件的规划和协商阶段，并于短时间内完成了大量工作。2022 年 1 月 4 日，双方签署了鲁班工坊建设合作备忘录。2022 年 5 月 6 日，在塔吉克斯坦举行了鲁班工坊开工仪式。在塔吉克斯坦技术大学领导、天津城市建设管理职业技术学院领导与中资企业代表的共同见证下，开始了工坊场馆的施工和装修作业。我们在 87 天内建成了所有必要的基础设施，交付了大量设备，并于 2022 年 8 月 1 日启动了鲁班工坊建设项目第二阶段。双方均致力于中亚地区首家鲁班工坊项目的加快落成和投入运转。

今天，我满怀信心地告诉大家：通过双方共同努力，我们将把塔吉克斯坦鲁班工坊建设成为致力于培养国民经济各领域科技人才的先进培训中心。工坊投入使用后，我们计划为当地道路建设公司和能源行业的代表组织培训班，塔吉克斯坦技术大学的学生也将在工坊学习基础课程框架内的实训课程。

## ii. Luban Workshop Co-founded by China and Tajikistan: Promoting Collaboration and Friendship in TVET

Shahriyor Sadullozoda, Vice President of Tajik Technical University named after academician M.S. Osimi, Tajikistan

Повышение квалификации является неотъемлемой частью трудовой деятельности и напрямую влияет на эффективность рабочего персонала. Осозновая это, а также во исполнение поручения основателя мира и национального единства, лидера нации, президента республики Таджикистан уважаемого Эмомали Рахмона (Emomali Rahman). Руководство Таджикского университета имени академика Мухамада Осими, на постоянной основе предпринимает конкретные меры по проведению курсов и мероприятий другого формата с целью повышения квалификации сотрудников университета, а также представители государственных структур компаний, частного сектора и населения в целом.

По причине повышения требований работодателя и стандартов качества к уровню компетентности работников различных профессий, приоритетной целью является обновление практики теоретических знаний специалистов и участников курсов. Кроме того, немаловажным фактором является увеличение мотивации персонала и воспитания собственных кадров для достижения цели развития страны и обширного региона стран ШОС. Хотел бы отметить что сотрудничество в области повышения квалификации в рамках Шанхайской организации сотрудничества имеет огромный потенциал, который уже сейчас активно осваивается Высшими учебными заведениями. Развитие связей в этом направлении способствует общности потребностей, спросу на квалифицированных специалистов и реализации программ для поддержки усилий в данной сфере образования. В особенности хочу отметить эффективность инициативы властей КНР «Один пояс – один пут» как элемент активного развития процесса повышения квалификации. Благодаря концепции данной инициативы и дружеских отношений между республикой Таджикистан и Китайской народной республикой на базе Таджикского университета имени академика Мухамада Осими, было построено первое в центральной Азии мастерская имени Лу Баня.

Мастерская Лу Бань - это центр позволяющий в полной мере обеспечить целый комплекс возможностей для проведения курсов повышения квалификации. Мы уверены, что основание этой мастерской, мы выведем научный потенциал нашего университета на совершенно новый уровень. Благодаря этой мастерской преподавателям и студентам Таджикского университета стали доступны современные приборы и оборудование, большая часть которых ещё не эксплуатировалось в регионе Центральной Азии. При поддержке партнеров из КНР, а именно наших уважаемых коллег из Тянцзинского профессионального технического института градостроительства, специалисты мирового уровня обучают научно-педагогический состав Таджикского университета полноценному использованию современных приборов и оборудования. Одновременно с этим внося вклад в совершенствование учебного процесса университета и подготовки кадров способных удовлетворять требования рынка труда.

На пути возведения Мастерской Лу Баня мы совместно с коллегами с Тянцзинского профессионального технического института градостроительства и партнерами поставщиков получили огромное количество и массу позитивных эмоций. Этот путь стал примером дружбы, взаимоуважения и эффективного партнёрства.

Впервые, 13 июля 2021 года член государственного совета, бывший Министр иностранных дел КНР Ван И, в ходе третьей встречи с Таджикским коллегой Сироджиддином Мухридиммом (Sirojiddin Muhriddinovich) заявил, что первая мастерская Лу Бань в центральной Азии будет построена в Республике Таджикистан.

Учитывая большой научный потенциал и статус передового высшего учебного заведения в области инженерии Таджикский университет имени академика Мухамада Осими, был выбран в качестве учреждения, в котором было запланировали строительство мастерской. В ходе встречи с Основателем мира и национального единства, лидером нации, президентом Республики Таджикистан уважаемого Эмомали Рахмона, председатель КНР уважаемый Си Дзинь Пинь высказался о необходимости усиления процессов строительства мастерской Лу Бань в республике Таджикистан, который является первым объектом такой концепции в Центральной Азии. В результате тесного сотрудничества двух дружественных и братских стран, 24 декабря 2021 года, состоялась встреча руководства Таджикского университета имени М. Осими с руководством Тянцзинского профессионального технического института градостроительства. С этой встречи начался этап планирования и согласования основательно-правовых документов. В короткие сроки был выполнен большой объём работы. Уже 4 января был подписан меморандум о строительстве мастерской. 6 мая 2022 года в Республике Таджикистан состоялась церемония начала строительства мастерской Лу Бань. При участии руководства Таджикского технического университета и представителей Тянцзинского профессионального технического института градостроительства и китайских компаний, на строительной площадке в здании где будет распологаться мастерская начались ремонтные восстановительные работы. Ударными темпами удалось за 87 дней возвести всю необходимую инфраструктуру, доставили широкий перечень оборудования и 1 Августа 2022 года прошла церемония начала второго этапа реализации проекта по строительству мастерской Лу Баня, что является показателем высокой заинтересованности сторон в скорейшем завершении данного проекта и ввода в эксплуатацию первой на территорию Центральной Азии мастерской Лу Баня.

Уже сегодня я хочу с уверенностью утверждать что совместными усилиями мы превратим мастерскую Лу Баня в Таджикистане в ведущий центр подготовки кадров самых разных областях науки и техники экономики народного хозяйства. После введения мастерской в эксплуатацию, мы планируем организацию курсов для повышения квалификации представителей местных компаний по дорожному строительству и промышленности энергетики. А студенты Таджикского технического университета академика имени М. Осими в мастерской будут проходить лабораторные занятия в рамках основного курса.

# （三）

# 后疫情时代职业技术教育的发展

## ——新变化、新途径、新技能

**塔吉克斯坦工业与新技术部副部长　索勒赫佐达·乌迈德**

职业教育被牢牢地纳入世界主要国家社会经济发展的国家纲领。我们都知道，居住人口受到良好的教育是一个国家全球竞争力的主要因素。

要制订职业技术教育指标及对指标进一步的监测，寻找提高其质量和可获得性的机会，就必须了解职业教育的性质、功能、目标和主要特征。

职业技术教育是职业教育的一种形式，目的是为职业技术教育机构的某些经济领域培养拥有知识、技能、本领，且能熟练完成某项特定工作的高水平人才。

继续职业教育（培训）体系的现状和发展取决于以下几个关键因素：相关性、入学率、受教育率、教育质量、教育体系的资金和管理。因此政府和有关人士应该优先考虑前三个因素。

职业技术教育与培训体系是有效保持经济快速增长的重要因素。因此职业技术教育与培训是为大众提供初级培训，以满足日益增长的劳动力需求。同时，培训目的在于提高劳动者的技能水平，减少技术参与者的职能和责任分工，强化他们之间的合作。为此，必须大力改革职业技术教育与培训的结构和战略。现阶段职业技术教育的战略是为需要人才的经济部门提供合格的人才。

由劳动、移民和就业部，科学和教育部，工业和新技术部负责职业技术教育与培训。职业技术教育与培训制度的运作受若干法律法规的制约。

塔吉克斯坦工业和新技术部下辖的教育机构培养专家的主要方向是工业，需要组织合作，对学生进行生产培训，并根据企业的要求培养专家，加强科学与生产的联系。2019 年 10 月 14 日，国家领导人埃莫马利·拉赫蒙在会见本国实业家时指出，“科学和教育部，劳动、移民和就业部，工业和新技术部有必要制定教育机构的教育计划和方案，修订基础教育、中等教育和高职教育计划和方案，使初、中、高级职业教育机构从专业需求的角度，根据行业的优先方向和前景，采取具体措施培养专家。

政府大力支持职业劳动者的技能发展，提高全社会能力水平。国家教育战略和计划包括发展职业生涯技能、发展公民普遍权利技能、扩大社会能力体系和文化、支持职业技术教育体系、促进和加强为公民服务的能力、协调工作和教育以及公众支持。

值得注意的是，《塔吉克斯坦 2030 年国家教育发展战略》规定向双重教育过渡。这种形式指的是在教育机构进行理论培训，在工作场所进行实践培训。

在双重教育体制下，用人单位的作用得到了强化，并发生了质的变化。在企业领域，已经为学生创建了通过虚拟仿真设备进行培训的工作场所，有专业人才都可进行培训。

我们认为，在培养各级专家方面应用世界经验为我国教育的发展提供了动力。毫无疑问，世界主要国家在职业培训、再培训和技能提升领域的经验，特别是对国家实践和世界趋势的研究，将有助于有效落实塔吉克斯坦的国家教育政策，并建立完整的国家级职业技术教育管理体系。

# iii. The Development of Vocational and Technical Education in the Post-pandemic Era

## —New Changes, New Approaches and New Skills

**Solehzoda Umed, Deputy Minister of Industry and New Technologies of Tajikistan**

Тема профессионального образования прочно входит в национальные программы социально-экономического развития ведущих стран мира. Известно, что хорошо образованное население – основной фактор конкурентоспособности страны в глобальном мире.

Разработка показателей технического профессионального образования (далее – ТПО), их дальнейший мониторинг, а также определение возможностей по улучшению его качества и доступности требуют понимания природы профессионального обучения, его функций, целей и основных характеристик.

Профессионально-техническое образование, форма профессионального образования, имеющая целью подготовку квалифицированных рабочих для отраслей экономики в профессонально-технических учебных заведениях; совокупность систематизированных знаний, умений и навыков, позволяющих квалифицированно выполнять работу по определенной рабочей профессии, специальности.

Состояние и развитие системы непрерывного профессионального образования (обучения) определяются степенью реализации следующих ключевых факторов: релевантность, доступ, доля участия населения в образовании, его качество, финансирование и управление системой образования. В связи с этим органы власти и заинтересованные стороны должны оптимально расставить приоритеты, связанные с первыми тремя факторами.

Система профессионального технического образования и подготовки является фактором эффективного поддержания быстрого экономического роста. Следовательно, система профессионального технического образования и подготовки направлена на обеспечение начальной подготовки для больших групп населения для удовлетворения растущего спроса на рабочую силу. При этом, система профессионального технического образования и подготовки должна переориентирована на повышение уровня квалификации работников.

Цель профессионального технического образования и подготовки заключается в уменьшении разделения функций и обязанностей участников технического профессионального образования **(ТПО)** и укреплении между ними сотрудничества. Для этого необходимо предпринят широкомасштабные усилия, направленные на реформирование структуры и стратегии профессионального технического образования и подготовки. Стратегия **ТПО** сегодняшнего этапа состоит в обеспечении квалифицированными кадрами отраслей экономики, которые испытывают спрос в кадрах.

Вопросы профессионального технического образования и подготовки находятся в ведении Министерства труда, миграции и занятости населения, Министерства науки и образования и Министерства промышленности и новых технологий Республики Таджикистан. Функционирование системы профессионального технического образования и подготовки регулируется ряд нормативно-правовыми актами.

Основным направлением подготовки специалистов в образовательных учреждений находящихся в ведении Министерства промышленности и новых технологий Республики Таджикистан является прежде всего промышленность, что обязывает наладить кооперацию для организации производственного обучения студентов, подготовки специалистов согласно требованиям предприятий, усиления связи науки и производства. Лидер нации уважаемый Эмомали Рахмон в ходе встречи с промышленниками страны 14 октября 2019 года отметил, что «Необходимо, чтобы Министерства образования и науки, труда, миграции и занятости совместно с Министерством промышленности и новые технологии, разработать образовательные планы и программы образовательных учреждений, пересмотреть начальные, средние и высшие профессиональные учебные заведения страны с точки зрения потребности в необходимых профессиях, принять конкретные меры по подготовке специалистов с учетом приоритетных направлений и перспективы отрасли».

Правительства страны всяческий поддерживает развитие профессиональных навыков работников, чтобы повысить уровень компетентности общества в целом. Национальные стратегии и программы в области образования подразумевают развитие навыков в течение всей трудовой жизни, развитие навыков как всеобщего права граждан, так и расширения системы и культуры компетентности общества, поддержание системы ТПО, продвижение, укрепление компетенций уже работающих граждан, гармонизацию между работой и образованием, а также поддержку населения.

Следует отметить, что в *Национальном стратегии развития образования Республики Таджикистан на период до 2030 года предусматривается переход к дуальной формы обучения*, при котором теоретическая часть подготовки проходит на базе образовательной организации, а практическая-на рабочем месте.

В дуальной системе обучения усиливается и качественно меняется роль работодателя. На территории предприятия создаются учебные рабочие места для студентов, которые могут отличаться от обычного рабочего места наличием виртуального симуляционного оборудования. Важнейший компонент-наличие подготовленных кадров, которые выступают в качестве наставников.

На наш взгляд, применение мирового опыта по подготовке специалистов различных уровней создает стимул развития образования нашей страны. Бесспорно, что опыт ведущих стран мира в области профессиональной подготовки, переподготовки и повышения квалификации, особенно исследование лучших национальных практик и мировых тенденций, будет полезен для эффективной реализации государственной политики Республики Таджикистан в сфере образования и формирования целостной системы управления процессом профессионального технического образования на национальном уровне.

# （四）

# 政校企协同，推动中卢职教合作走深走实

## ——金华职业技术学院卢旺达办学实践

金华职业技术学院副校长　陈海荣

中非合作论坛为深化中非教育合作提供了机遇，中国高职院校非洲办学也由此踏上发展快车道。金华职业技术学院（以下简称金职院）响应国家“一带一路”倡议和中非命运共同体理念，积极参与中非合作论坛行动计划及能力建设工程，主动对接国家在卢旺达的教育援外工程，与卢旺达穆桑泽职业技术学校开展职业教育国际合作，合作创办国际学院，服务卢方亟须的技能型人才培养。下面从“模式、路径、愿景”三个关键词，介绍金职院在卢旺达的办学情况。

### 1. 模式：政校企协同走出去

穆桑泽职业技术学校是卢旺达理工学院下辖的 8 所院校之一，是卢旺达北方省最大的职业技术教育与培训中心，是我国在卢旺达的教育援外工程。工程 2015 年动工，2017 年完成一期建设，2021 年完成二期建设，可容纳在校生 4 000 人。2017 年，该国际学校正式挂牌，标志着金职院推动职业教育“走出去”，服务非洲技能型人才培养、服务中非命运共同体建设、服务国家战略迈出了坚实步伐。聚焦国家援外教育工程，开展职业教育国际合作，国际学校的建设与发展得到了中卢两国政府的高度重视和支持。同时，学校携手在卢中资企业开展校企合作，既培养了卢方急需人才，又服务了中资企业走稳走好。

与卢旺达的职业教育合作始于 2013 年，金职院与卢旺达教育部签署委托培养留学生的合作备忘录；2014 年，首届四个专业 30 余名留学生正式到校。金职院精心研制人才培养方案，创新实践“1 年学中文、3 年学职业技能”的“1+3”培养模式。合作以来，卢方大使十分关心留学生培养，每年来校考察并看望留学生，

对留学生在HSK考级（汉语水平考试）、技能竞赛、职业能力等方面的培养质量高度认可。几年来，学校面向旅游管理、通信网络、物联网、汽车维修等卢方重点产业，累计培养学历留学生95名。正因为优质的培养质量和多年的良好合作，2016年，金职院与卢旺达劳动部共同签约在穆桑泽职业技术学校合作创办海外分校。2018年，学校选派管理干部和骨干教师赴卢启动学院建设。2020年，金职院又与卢旺达理工学院签署全面合作协议，将合作从穆桑泽职业技术学校辐射到卢旺达理工学院下辖的所有8所院校。国际学校的建设发展，探索了“政校—校企—校校”协同的职业教育国际合作的金职院样本。

2. 路径：需求导向 + 标准引领

在推进国际学校内涵建设中，我们始终坚持“需求导向 + 标准引领”的实践路径。

需求导向：就是面向卢方重点发展的产业布局，培养产业急需技能人才作为内涵建设的逻辑起点。创办初期，金职院选派教师赴卢开展产业发展与劳动力市场调研，了解技能人才需求状况。数字经济是卢旺达政府面向2030经济规划的战略性新兴产业，也是浙江省经济发展的“一号工程”、金华市的“一号产业”。浙江中国小商品城集团在卢旺达设有海外仓、阿里巴巴集团设有跨境电商eWTP（电子世界贸易平台）。所以，选取电子商务、自动化两个专业率先“走出去”合作，在合作领域、功能定位、运行机制和标准输出等方面进行系统规划。

标准引领：就是在需求导向基础上，以专业课程标准输出为引领，推进课程资源、教学团队、实训基地等专业内涵建设。经过近一年时间，牵头完成了《电子商务专业教学标准（6~7级）》《电气自动化技术专业教学标准（6~7级）》的专业教学标准研制。2021年，两项标准通过卢旺达教育部劳动资源发展署和高等教育委员会认证，正式纳入卢旺达教育资格框架体系，真正意义上实现了专业标准“走出去”。

在人才培养方面，国际学校推进信息技术支撑下的“中文 + 职业技能”教学改革，提升学生的中文表达能力和综合职业能力。在创新人才培养模式上，针对政府委托培养的学历留学生，从2013年起采用同地两段“1+3”模式；2022年，国际学校合作的两个专业在基于已通过卢旺达教育部认证的专业标准开展培养的同时，创新实践“中文 + 职业技能”的两地两段“2+1”模式，即前两个学年在卢旺达穆桑泽国际学院学习，最后一个学年在金华职业技术学院学习。两个合作专业的

124 名学生在新的人才培养模式下于 2022 年 3 月正式开学。项目也入选了“未来非洲—中非职业教育合作计划”。

在课程资源开发上，围绕专业教学标准，组织团队开发网络学习平台，完成了一批双语课程、双语教材、技能培训包的开发；同时传承卢方原有体系特点，融入了学校“双高”建设的优质资源，开发系列化教学资源。在实训条件建设上，为服务“走出去”中资企业，培养本土化技能人才，根据专业教学标准，先后携手华为、浙江中国小商品城集团等民族品牌（企业）共建华为信息通信技术认证、自动化、直播电商、中文语言训练等实训室，合作研制系列实训教学标准。疫情发生以来，学校组织专业团队利用现代通信网络技术开发基于远程实景的实验平台。该平台能够实现远程的编程与建模，在我国境内的真实设备上开展在线实景实训，创新了实践教学模式。

在师资队伍建设上，我们秉持“授人以渔”的理念，重视卢方师资能力培养，努力让卢方师资尽快胜任合作专业教学标准的教学组织实施工作。为此我们通过三种方式来培养教师：第一首先通过选派骨干教师赴卢常驻，手把手培养卢方教师；第二每年接收卢方重点培养的专业骨干来华跟岗学习；第三利用网络学习平台开展一对一结对师资培训。通过上述多种形式不断提高卢方师资的执教理念、实践能力和教学水平。

国际学校一直得到了中国驻卢旺达使馆的大力支持和高度赞赏。中国驻卢旺达大使饶宏伟每年莅临海外分校，看望在岗教师，也对双方合作给予很多指导。2019 年 3 月，饶大使在二期工程启动期间来校考察，用四个“Right”（Right time, Right partner, Right person, Right place）高度肯定国际学校的办学成效。时任浙江省省长袁家军于 2019 年访问非洲三国时访问卢旺达，观看了由我校、阿里巴巴集团、浙江省科学技术厅联合举办的援卢成果展览，对我校在卢旺达办学取得成果给予高度评价。通过职业教育国际合作，增进了城市之间的友谊和联系，也推进了中卢友好城市的对接。2019 年，在第三届浙江金华中非文化合作交流周暨中非经贸论坛上，金华市和穆桑泽市签订了友好城市意向书。同年，新任卢旺达驻华大使詹姆斯·基莫尼奥上任刚一个月便马不停蹄地来到金职院看望卢旺达政府委托培养班的学生，对留学生的培养质量给予高度肯定。

### 3. 愿景：“1321 工程”发展计划

为共筑中非命运共同体的美好愿景，未来我校将推进“一平台、三联盟、两工坊、一中心”计划。“一平台”，是指基于2021年升格为国家级论坛的中国（浙江）中非经贸论坛暨中非文化合作交流周，学校将每年在这个平台上承办中非职业教育论坛，分享和借鉴职业教育走进非洲的办学经验。“三联盟”，是指通过加入鲁班工坊联盟、非洲中文教育联盟以及中非数字经济职业教育产教协作联盟，吸收和融入各联盟的优质资源，持续深化中非职业教育合作。“两工坊”，是指借助于入选和建设鲁班工坊和中文工坊，迭代升级“中文+职业技能”的丝路学院。“一中心”，是指借助浙江省现代职业教育研究中心和浙江师范大学非洲研究院的研究力量和研究资源，成立中非职业教育研究中心，聚焦中非产业与职业教育的发展和合作，开展学术研究，深化国际学院建设。

2018年7月21日，国家主席习近平访问卢旺达前夕，在当地主要媒体《新时代报》发表题为《中卢友谊情比山高》的署名文章，文中提到“穆桑泽职业技术学校已成为卢旺达北方省最大的职业技术培训中心”。我们深刻感受到，在习近平主席关心的这个学校开展职业教育海外合作办学、服务中非命运共同体，责任重大，使命光荣！

# （五）

# 和衷共济　和合共生

## ——鲁班工坊助力构建人类命运共同体

天津铁道职业技术学院校长　于忠武

大道之行，天下为公，人类命运共同体汇聚着世界各国人民对和平、发展、繁荣的美好向往。作为共建“一带一路”和构建人类命运共同体的具体实践，鲁班工坊承担着推广中国装备、传播中国技术、推行中国标准、展示中国成果的重要作用，正在助力各国青年梦想起航。

在天津市委市政府的指导下，天津铁道职业技术学院积极拓展与“一带一路”沿线国家的职业教育合作，服务“走出去”企业和合作国经济社会发展，按照“中国铁路修到哪，铁路技术技能人才培养就跟到哪”的建设思路，自2018年起，先后建成3个鲁班工坊，为合作国培养高铁、普铁、城轨建设运营所需的本土化技术技能人才。

### 1. 厘清鲁班工坊建设理路

“根之茂者其实遂，膏之沃者其光晔”。天津铁道职业技术学院始建于1951年，是一所行业特色鲜明、国际交流广泛的公办高等职业院校。自2001年起，先后为坦赞铁路、亚吉铁路等项目培养本土化技术技能人才1 100余名。2017年，学院确定了“建国际品牌，树国内名牌”的办学思路，以鲁班工坊为切入点，全面推进国际化办学进程。

为服务中泰铁路建设、运营，2018年7月，学院建成了我国在境外的第一个高铁类技术技能人才培养中心——泰国鲁班工坊铁院中心。2019年7月，铁院中心入选了“中国—东盟高职院校特色合作项目”。为落实2018年习近平主席在中非合作论坛北京峰会讲话精神，2019年3月，学院建成了非洲第一家鲁班工坊——吉布提鲁班工坊。吉布提总统盖莱、总理卡米勒等 100 余人出席建成仪式。工坊填补了吉布提国民教育的空白，为非洲青年技术技能人才的培养提供了可借鉴、可复制成功范例。2020 年 11 月，学院在非洲第一大经济体——尼日利亚建成鲁班工坊，开创了鲁班工坊“一体两翼”建设定位的新局面。

**2. 形成校企合作典型范式**

“问渠那得清如许，为有源头活水来”。在鲁班工坊建设过程中，逐步形成了“一体两翼三维”的工坊建设模式，与企业共同实践“4+2+1+1”新路径。

校企协同共建专业标准和师资队伍。校企共同按照中国轨道交通标准，运用技术、装备，构建以亚吉铁路、中泰高铁、阿布贾城铁等工程项目为引领，与“走出去”中国企业岗位需求相匹配的国际化专业人才培养体系。目前，（高铁）动车组检修技术、铁道工程技术等 4 个专业已经纳入合作国国民教育体系。授人以鱼不如授人以渔，在师资培养方面，学院采用“四双五能四有”的师资培训模式。

在培养吉布提鲁班工坊教师时，学院教师按照因地制宜的原则，充分调研亚吉铁路线路、道口具体情况。考虑到吉布提终年高温、当地人安全意识亟待增强等情况，学院教师在培训中着重介绍了高温影响下线路维修、道口看守等安全方面的注意事项。再比如，为了让工坊学生更好地服务亚吉铁路，为“一带一路”设施联通提供人才支撑，我们充分调研了国内外企业的需求，在师资培训过程中着重介绍了有缝线路养护、钢轨接头病害整治等相关内容，做到“线路有缝，对接无缝”。

校企协同共建实训基地和装备研发。学院与中国土木工程集团有限公司（以下简称中土集团）共建两个非洲鲁班工坊，中土集团提供 1 600 平方米场地和 110 余万资金用于场地装修、设备购置。此外，学院在中土集团投建营一体化的亚吉铁路那噶得车站、阿布贾城轨车辆段建设鲁班工坊坊外实训基地，充分满足了工坊教学实习、技能实训、岗前培训等需求。学院与合作企业骥腾公司共同研发职业技能大赛装备，获得实用新型专利、发明专利，该装置也成为泰国轨道交通职业技能大赛的指定装备，骥腾公司与 10 余家泰国企业达成销售订单近 4 000 万元。

校企协同拓宽国际人才培养新途径。在学历教育方面，按照“听得懂、用得上、学得会、干得好”的人才培养目标，校企共同建设标准化、规范化、专业化的教学资源。在技能培训方面，为服务亚吉铁路当地员工线上培训项目，制作工务、通信、信号等共 8 个工种全英文录播课，共计 550 余课时。通过“实物实操 + 虚拟仿真”的呈现形式，逐步构建了科学的“三服三化三对接”的人才培养体系。此外，探索中国特色学徒制在鲁班工坊的本土化实践，吉布提鲁班工坊的 24 名学生已全部实现订单式培养，毕业后直接进入亚吉铁路工作。

吉布提鲁班工坊 2019 级学生中，有一个叫奥斯曼的男孩。他原计划到中国留学，没想到设有铁道专业的鲁班工坊开到了吉布提。工坊启动仪式的时候，他激动地拉着我的手说："您知道吗，中国的工程师一直是我的榜样，因为他们有着非常专业的技术。当知道我们国家也有了铁道专业时，我感觉就像做梦一样。谢谢鲁班工坊！谢谢中国！鲁班工坊改变了我的命运，也圆了我的梦。"

3. 承担中国职教时代责任

"谋度于义者必得，事因于民者必成"。学院为三个工坊制定国际化人才培养方案 7 个；校企共同编写双语教材、实训指导书 70 余本，完成在线精品课 11 门；累计培养教师 122 人次，培养工坊学生 185 名，培训员工 95 人；建成坊内教学区 25 个，坊外实训基地 2 个，被人民日报、新华社、中央电视台《新闻联播》等 34 家中外主流媒体报道 90 余次。

当前，鲁班工坊在专业建设、人才培养、师资培训等方面均取得了显著成效，凸显了中国职业教育特色活力，为推动鲁班工坊可持续发展，要继续坚持两个方面。

一是要加强生态建设，营造可持续发展的环境。以鲁班工坊的现状为出发点，借助政策支持与市场需求，发挥校企合作的潜能，实现人才培养、功能实现和社会反响的良性循环，构建鲁班工坊内、外循环生态环境，推动鲁班工坊长效、稳定、持续高质量发展。其中，在外循环方面，要加强顶层设计，争取更多的政策支持；开展风险评估，为鲁班工坊可持续发展提供条件保障；了解各方需求，为鲁班工坊可持续发展提供市场保障；深化国际化校企合作，为鲁班工坊可持续发展提供动力支持。在内循环方面，要加强鲁班工坊的内涵建设，完善其人才培养目标、专业设置、资源建设、师资培养、教学环境和实训基地等方面建设，促进鲁班工坊的内涵式发展。

二是开拓创新发展，提升鲁班工坊服务能力。切实服务合作国经济社会发展和"走出去"中资企业需求，将职业教育发展与生产、经济社会发展相结合，创造更多价值；基于"线上线下、虚实结合"的混合教学模式，开发建设教学资源、实训基地、技能大赛装备、技能等级认定证书，推动技术技能人才培养的数字化转型，彰显鲁班工坊品牌价值；为"走出去"中资企业海外发展提供多形式、多层次人才培养与技术创新等智力支持服务，实现鲁班工坊的造血功能，惠及合作国民生福祉，助力区域经济发展。

故积力之所举，则无不胜也；众智之所为，则无不成也。让我们携起手来，让鲁班工坊成就“一带一路”国家青年的成才梦，为构建更加紧密的人类命运共同体贡献我们职教人的智慧和力量！

# （六）

# 夯实“中国职教品牌”走出去的根基

## ——鲁班工坊建设联盟工作介绍

鲁班工坊建设联盟理事长　刘　斌

鲁班工坊是天津原创并率先实践的中外人文交流品牌项目，是国家现代职业教育改革创新示范区的标志性成果，是职业教育国际化发展的重大创新，已成为促进国际人文交流和民心相通的重要载体。

为共建共享鲁班工坊建设经验和成果，共同打造中国职业教育“走出去”国家品牌，2020 年 11 月，鲁班工坊建设联盟在天津成立。这对于加快鲁班工坊建设速度、保障鲁班工坊建设质量、扩大鲁班工坊影响力具有重要作用和重大意义。

### 1. 联盟成立以来开展的主要工作

（1）搭建平台，集聚资源。搭建鲁班工坊理论研究、项目建设和宣传推广平台，规范全国鲁班工坊建设。目前，共有包括国内高校、“走出去”企业和职业教育研究机构在内的 72 个成员单位，秘书处设在天津职业大学。

建章立制。制定完成《鲁班工坊建设规程》《鲁班工坊建设联盟工作办法》，经联盟成员大会第一次会议审议通过后面向全国发布，首次明确了建设鲁班工坊的程序和条件，约定了联盟运行的基本规范。

调查研究。会同天津市教育科学研究院，先后走访江苏、浙江、福建、重庆、湖南等省市的高校和研究机构，深入了解国内职业教育典型合作项目的主要特色和发展瓶颈，调研成果通过《鲁班工坊建设与发展报告》向社会发布，为制定适用于全国鲁班工坊建设的标准体系奠定良好基础。

（2）标准引领，打造品牌。面对国内职业教育国际合作项目质量参差不齐、“走出去”品牌杂乱繁多等现状，联盟坚持民间属性，基于天津市鲁班工坊建设经验，为携手打造职业教育“走出去”国家品牌开展了一系列实践探索。

顶层规划。在中国教育国际交流协会支持下，统筹推进全国鲁班工坊建设。牵头建立了集项目培育、建设运营、质量评估为一体的鲁班工坊建设质量保障体系，按照“质量优先、分级管理”的原则组织实施。

组建智库。面向全国广泛征集院校、企业和研究机构专家，完成联盟专家库首批专家遴选工作，目前在库专家共 99 人，均为研究或实践经验丰富的行业企业专家、研究机构专家和院校专家，为鲁班工坊项目评审和质量评估提供智力支持。

建立标准。为保障鲁班工坊高质量建设和可持续发展，围绕鲁班工坊的发展定位与核心要素，联合研究机构共同制定了《鲁班工坊运营项目认定标准（试行）》，并应用于全国首批鲁班工坊运行项目遴选和认定工作。

**2. 联盟计划开展的重点工作**

联盟成立以来，始终坚持民间属性，引领全国职业院校以“天津实践”为参考开展多元化办学，共同打造中国职业教育“走出去”国家品牌。联盟理事长受邀参加第二十二届中国国际教育年会并做主旨报告，面向海内外院校、企业全面介绍了联盟运行管理情况和主要成效。鲁班工坊标准化建设、可持续发展、职业教育“走出去”国家品牌打造等理念和实践探索得到了与会单位的一致认可和积极响应。2022 年下半年，联盟计划围绕如下几方面重点发力，搭好平台、做好服务。

项目建设方面。按照分级推进原则，制定培育项目、运营项目、示范项目的建设标准（运营项目标准已制定完成）、申报程序及工作指南。配合交流协会开展鲁班工坊建设项目申报及认定工作。首批运营项目认定中被确定为“有条件运营”的项目，将设置一年的成长期，由联盟组织专家进行“一对一”指导，一年后进行专家复核。

项目管理方面。建立鲁班工坊建设项目档案管理体系，形成三类项目从立项、建设、认证、验收的全部基础档案资料，并做好过程管理和质量监管工作。

联盟纳新方面。制定联盟纳新工作方案，按程序接纳更多有意愿参与鲁班工坊建设的单位加入联盟，共同推动全国范围的鲁班工坊高质量建设，计划将联盟成员单位扩充到 100 家左右。

培训交流方面。根据联盟成员单位及有意愿开展鲁班工坊建设相关单位的实际需求，结合首批运营项目认定工作发现的问题，有针对性地开展鲁班工坊建设专题培训活动；召开联盟第一届年会，同期举办鲁班工坊建设国际研讨会及成果展。

学术研究方面。与研究机构合作组织联盟成员单位开展鲁班工坊建设相关课题研究，夯实鲁班工坊高质量建设的理论基础，丰富鲁班工坊建设成果。

宣传推广方面。建立联盟官方微信公众号和联盟官方网站，搭建鲁班工坊项目管理和建设成果分享的线上平台；建立统一的、安全稳定的对外宣传口径，多渠道开展鲁班工坊建设成果宣传和推广工作，编印《鲁班工坊建设成果集》，形成丰富多样的成果资源。

# 七

# 普通（学术）教育与职业教育协调发展论坛

协助组织单位：北京大学教育经济研究所

# VII. Integration of Academic and Vocational Education

Co-organizer: Institute of Economics of Education, Peking University

01
哈巍
Ha Wei

02
阎凤桥
Yan Fengqiao

03
李善华
Sunhwa Lee

04
玛拉 · 布鲁贾
Mara Brugia

05
托马斯 · F · 雷明顿
Thomas F. Remington

**介绍相关国家资历框架建设案例，分享各国普职协调发展的经验，强调产教融合与产学研协同创新，推动现代职业教育体系构建。**

This session introduces cases of how relevant countries set up their qualifications frameworks. The participants share their experience in the integrated development of academic and vocational education in different countries, highlighting the integration of industry and education, the collaborative innovation of industries, universities and research institutes, in order to improve the modern mechanism for the coordinated development of vocational and technical education.

## （一）

# 普通（学术）教育与职业教育协调发展论坛情况概述

北京大学教育学院　哈　巍
北京大学教育经济研究所　徐万蓉

2022 年 8 月 19—20 日，由中华人民共和国教育部、中国联合国教科文组织全国委员会和天津市人民政府共同主办的首届世界职业技术教育发展大会在津召开。来自 123 个国家（地区）的政府机构、国际组织、行业企业、学校、研究机构代表出席了大会，围绕“后疫情时代职业技术教育发展：新变化、新方式、新技能”的主题进行深入交流、广泛探讨。北京大学教育经济研究所是“普通（学术）教育与职业教育协调发展”论坛的协助组织单位，北京大学教育学院副院长哈巍主持了论坛。

本论坛的宗旨是分享各国普职协调发展的经验，强调产教融合与产学研协同创新，推动现代职业教育体系构建。论坛分为“普通教育与职业教育协调发展的区域治理模式研究”“普职协调发展的国际比较研究”“普职协调下的现代职业教育体系深度优化研究”三大专题。以线上与线下结合的形式，邀请了来自发达国家、新兴工业化国家、新兴经济体和发展中国家的多元背景的 11 位嘉宾进行交流对话。

北京大学教育学院院长、联合国教科文组织亚太地区高等教育讲席阎凤桥线上出席论坛并致欢迎辞。他谈到在“后疫情时代”，世界正面临技能人才短缺与青年失业愈加严重等问题，因此职业教育必须根据经济与就业市场的动态变化进行具有灵活性、适应性的人才培养。为了避免教育制度的社会分层陷阱，我们有必要讨论普通（学术）教育与职业教育的协调发展与融合创新，使用一些系统化的公共政策工具来抵消职业教育与普通教育之间的不平等。

**专题研讨一：普通教育与职业教育协调发展的区域治理模式研究**

这一专题旨在通过分享不同区域普职协调发展的制度治理经验，学习不同区域的实践模式，探索解决普职双轨运行造成的制度隔离与边界鸿沟等问题。

欧洲职业培训发展中心副所长玛拉·布鲁贾聚焦于职业教育与学术教育的界限问题，对此提供了欧洲的解决方案。她认为教育应当以人为单位，关注一个人在其人生与所处社会中共同的发展需求。职业教育要密切对接经济与劳动力市场，并推动政府、市场、院校等多方合作，实现共商共建。

北京大学教育经济研究所管理委员会委员杨钋系统论述了学术教育与职业教育融合的路径与模式，针对融合发生的层次、场域与形式进行了讨论，并总结了影响二者融合发展的关键因素，即技能形成体系与高等教育的扩展，并分别阐述了东亚国家的融合模式。

亚洲基础设施投资银行社会基础设施局局长金宪认为，缺乏一支熟练的劳动力队伍可能成为诸多国家就业市场的一大瓶颈。随着新经济形势的到来，劳动者将持续面临适应性挑战，因此各国政府和国际社会迫切需要组织规模化应对措施，并且应考虑对数字素养技能的提升进行投资。

亚洲开发银行社会部门首席专家李善华围绕南亚国家基础教育薄弱对职业教育

造成的影响应当如何解决提供了经验分享。南亚国家基础教育质量与数量扩展并未同步发展，而基础技能的不足又极大地影响了职业教育的成效。“工业 4.0”的技术变革时代加快了技能升级的步伐，也同时要求学生具备更高的综合素质，因此普通（学术）教育与职业教育协调发展十分必要。

**专题研讨二：普职协调发展的国际比较研究**

世界各国国情相异，但是却面临共同的问题，即如何在教育、经济与社会协调发展的情况下实现普职融合创新，探索出一条可持续的、有效的普职协调发展路径。

同济大学职业技术教育学院副教授谢莉花选取德国作为样本，在统一的分析框架下呈现德、中两国职普教育的协调发展现状，分析两国采取的发展策略，以期相互借鉴与学习。她认为注重普职协调发展应当注重纵向贯通与并重互通，进行横向融通与形式创新，并进行体系统筹与关系塑造，实现结构上的统筹协调发展。

印度尼西亚文化与教育部职业教育与工商业协调合作部门主任李健提出 ABG-CM 模型，即学术界、商界、政府、社区和媒体五个利益相关者的互动模型对中国—印度尼西亚教育外交中的三个支柱具有协调与支撑作用。为应对“工业 4.0”时期的一系列挑战，李健认为世界各国可以在共同价值观、国际条约与宣言的基础上建立共同目标。良好的教育国际合作关系依赖 ABG-CM 多元主体的参与。

亚洲开发银行高级项目官卢兰兰主要分享了亚洲开发银行对中国教育部门提供的支持。例如，湖南职业技术培训示范项目，在课程开发、技术普及、助力高等教育改革与普惠化、开展绿色技能培训、创建包容性的创新生态系统以及创造终身学习的机会等方面，产生了一系列积极影响。

**专题研讨三：普职协调下的现代职业教育体系深度优化研究**

在后疫情时代，“工业 4.0”正在加速技术变革，经济社会对劳动者技能提出更高要求，倒逼职业教育改革。因此，现代职业教育体系应当因时而变，进行体系优化与制度升级，适应现代经济发展需要与学生成长需求。

中国职业技术教育学会副会长、北京外国语大学教授孙善学聚焦中国当前建设职业教育贯通培养体系的具体实践与思考。他指出，应当注重：一是企业的深度参与；二是学生自身在超长的学制中的成长变化；三是参与联合培养的学校彼此之间必须形成良好协同关系；四是对贯通培养过程的关注与对比研究。

美国埃默里大学政治学系古德里奇·C·怀特名誉荣休教授托马斯·F·雷明顿介绍了美国在发展STEM（科学、技术、工程、数学）学习中的措施、困境与反思。美国的体验式学习具有良好的历史基础，但是STEM教育在美国的推广仍存在诸多困境。雷明顿对过去五年美国国家自然基金支持的项目进行了文本分析，得出了STEM体验式学习项目需要各方共同努力、项目有效性难以评估等结论。

哈萨克斯坦教育部技术与职业教育司技能合作办公室主任阿尔加济诺娃·卡拉姆卡斯分享的重点用一个字来概括，即“变”。她强调，在瞬息万变的当下，职业教育体系应当更加灵活，适应经济、科技的快速发展。去年，哈萨克斯坦采用了终身学习（继续教育）概念，注重教育培养的连续性、一致性。为此，哈萨克斯坦正在进行巩固认证系统的立法。

贯彻落实习近平总书记在全国职业教育大会上强调的“推动职普融通”，推进高等教育、职业技术教育与培训更加协调发展，在我国有着深远的现实意义。促进普通高等教育与职业技术教育的协调发展，在国际上已成为中等后教育改革的共同趋势。“普通（学术）教育与职业教育协调发展”论坛的举办正当其时，收获颇丰，对中国推动职普融通发展具有良好借鉴意义。论坛主持人哈巍教授认为，时代呼唤职业技能的提升，在教育发展与经济发展相互协调的基本原则之上，借鉴他国经验也必须要经过本土化论证。在改革过程中，教育经济学学者有责任对改革过程进行评价并对改革成效进行研究。

# i. Overview of the Session on Integration of Academic and Vocational Education

**Ha Wei, Graduate School of Education, Peking University**
**Xu Wanrong, Institute of Economics of Education, Peking University**

The First World Vocational and Technical Education Development Conference, co-hosted by the Ministry of Education of the People's Republic of China, the National Commission of the People's Republic of China for UNESCO and the Tianjin Municipal People's Government, was held in Tianjin from August 19 to 20, 2022. Representatives from government agencies, international organizations, industries, enterprises, colleges and research institutions from 123 countries (regions) attended the conference and had in-depth exchanges and extensive discussions on "Vocational and Technical Education Development in the Post-pandemic Era—New Changes, New Ways and New Skills". As the parallel session of the Conference, the Integration of Academic and Vocational Education Session was co-organized by the Institute of Economics of Education, Peking University, and chaired by Ha Wei, Tenured Associate Professor and Associate Dean of Graduate School of Education, Peking University, China.

The purpose of the session is to share the experience in the coordinated development of academic education and vocational education in different countries, to emphasize the integration of industry and education and collaborative innovation of industries, universities and research institutes, and to promote the construction of modern vocational education system. The session was divided into three topics: "Research on Regional Governance Model of Coordinated Development of Academic Education and Vocational Education", "International Comparative Research on Coordinated Development of Academic Education and Vocational Education" and "Research on Deep Optimization of Modern Vocational Education System under Coordinated Development of Academic Education and Vocational Education", and was held both online and offline, with 11 guests from developed countries, emerging industrial countries, emerging economies and developing countries who discussed and shared opinions with each other.

Yan Fengqiao, Dean of Graduate School of Education, Peking University, China,

UNESCO Chair on Higher Education in Asia and the Pacific attended the session online and delivered a welcome speech. He noted that in the post-pandemic era, the world is facing a shortage of skilled personnel and increasing youth unemployment. Therefore, vocational education must conduct flexible and adaptable talent cultivation based on the dynamic changes in the economy and the job market. In order to prevent the education system from social stratification, it is necessary to discuss the coordinated development, integration and innovation of academic and vocational education, and to use some systematic public policy tools to offset the educational inequality between vocational and academic education.

**Seminar I : Research on Regional Governance Model of Coordinated Development of Academic Education and Vocational Education**

This seminar is to share the experience of institutional governance of the coordinated development of academic and vocational education in different regions, to learn from the practice models of different regions, and to explore solutions to institutional segregation and boundary gaps caused by the dual-track operation of academic and vocational education.

Mara Brugia, Deputy Director of European Centre for the Development of Vocational Training (CEDEFOP), focused on the issue of the boundaries between vocational and academic education and offered the European solution. She believed that education should be people-oriented, focusing on the common development needs of a person in his or her life and in society. Vocational education should be closely connected to economy and the labor market, and promote cooperation among the government, market and institutions to achieve extensive consultation and joint contribution.

Yang Po, Member of the Steering Committee of Institute of Economics of Education, Peking University, China, systematically addressed the paths and models of the integration of academic and vocational education. She discussed the levels, fields and forms of integration, and summarized the key factors affecting the development of the integration, i.e., skill formation system and expansion of higher education, and illustrated the integration models in East Asian countries respectively.

Hun Kim, Director General of Social Infrastructure Department of Asian Infrastructure Investment Bank, observed that the lack of a skilled workforce could become a major bottleneck in many countries' job markets. With the advent of the new economy trend, workers will continue to face adaptability challenges, so there is an urgent need for governments and the international community to organize responses on a scale, and to consider investing in digital literacy skills improvement.

Sunhwa Lee, Principal Social Sector Specialist at Asian Development Bank, shared experiences on how to address the impact of weak primary education on vocational education in South Asian countries. The quality of primary education in South Asian countries has not developed in tandem with its quantitative expansion, while the lack of basic skills has greatly affected the effectiveness of vocational education. Industry 4.0 represents an era of technological change, which has accelerated the pace of skills upgrading and requires students to have higher comprehensive abilities, so it is necessary to coordinate academic and vocational education.

**Seminar II: International Comparative Research on Coordinated Development of Academic Education and Vocational Education**

Despite different conditions, countries around the world are faced with one common problem, that is, how to realize the innovation and integration of academic and vocational education in the context of the coordinated development of education, economy and society, and explore a sustainable and effective path of coordinated development of academic and vocational education.

Xie Lihua, Associate Professor of School of Vocational and Technical Education of Tongji University, China, took Germany as a sample, presented the current status of the coordinated development of vocational and academic education in Germany and China under a unified analysis framework, and analyzed the development strategies adopted by the two countries, with a vision of mutual learning. She believed that the coordinated development of academic and vocational education should focus on vertical connectivity and equal emphasis on interoperability, horizontal integration and form innovation, as well as system planning and relationship shaping, so as to achieve structural coordinated development.

Yudil Chatim, Head of Administration of Directorate of Partnership and Alignment of Vocational Education with Business and Industry, Indonesian Ministry of Culture and Education proposed that the ABG-CM model, an interactive model of five stakeholders—academia, business, government, community and media—had a coordinating and supporting role for the three pillars in China-Indonesia education diplomacy. To address a range of challenges in the Industry 4.0 era, Yudil Chatim believed that countries around the world could establish common goals based on shared values, international treaties and declarations. A good international partnership in education relied on the participation of multiple subjects of ABG-CM.

Lu Lanlan, Senior Project Officer of Asian Development Bank, shared mainly the support provided by ADB to the education sector in China, such as the Hunan Technical and Vocational Education and Training Demonstration Project, which has had a series of positive impacts in terms of curriculum development, technology popularization, assisting higher education reform and universalization, conducting green skills training, creating an inclusive innovation ecosystem, and offering opportunities for lifelong learning.

Seminar Ⅲ: Research on Deep Optimization of Modern Vocational Education System under Coordinated Development of Academic Education and Vocational Education

In the post-pandemic era, Industry 4.0 is accelerating technological changes. The economy and society are putting forward higher requirements for workers' skills, forcing vocational education to reform. Therefore, modern vocational education system should change with the times, optimize and upgrade the system to meet the needs of modern economic development and student growth.

Sun Shanxue, Vice President of the Chinese Society for Technical and Vocational Education and Professor of Beijing Foreign Studies University, China, focused on the specific practice and reflections on the current construction of China's vocational education run-through cultivation system. He pointed out that we should focus on: firstly, the deep involvement of enterprises; secondly, the growth and changes of students themselves in the extra-long education system; thirdly, the schools involved in joint training must form a good cooperative relationship with each other; fourthly, the attention and comparative study of the run-through cultivation process.

Thomas F. Remington, Goodrich C. White Professor (Emeritus) of Political Science at Emory University, US, introduced the measures, dilemmas, and reflections in the development of STEM learning in the United States. Experiential learning in the US has a good historical foundation, but there are still many dilemmas in the promotion of STEM education in the US. Professor Remington conducted a textual analysis of NSF-supported projects over the past five years and concluded that the experiential learning through STEM requires concerted efforts and that program effectiveness is difficult to measure.

Algazinova Kalamkas, Head of Partnership and Skills Department, Department of Technical and Vocational Education of the Ministry of Education of Kazakhstan, gave a presentation that could be summarized in one word: change. She emphasized that vocational education system should be more flexible and adjusted to high-speed economic, technological and scientific development at this time of rapid changes. Last year Kazakhstan adopted the concept of lifelong learning (continuing education), focusing on the continuity and consistency of education and training. To this end, Kazakhstan is working on legislation to consolidate the accreditation system.

The implementation of "promoting the integration of vocational and academic education" as emphasized by General Secretary Xi Jinping at the National Vocational Education Conference and the promotion of more coordinated development of higher education, vocational and technical education and training have far-reaching practical significance in China. Promoting the coordinated development of regular higher education and vocational and technical education has become a common trend in the post-secondary education reform around the world. The Integration of Academic and

Vocational Education Session was held at the right time and was very fruitful, which has good referential significance for China to promote the development of integration of vocational and academic education. According to Ha Wei, the moderator of the parallel session, the era calls for the improvement of vocational skills, and when learning other countries' experiences, while adhering to the basic principle of mutual coordination between educational development and economic development, we must also justify them through localization. During the reform, scholars of the economics of education have the responsibility to evaluate the reform process and to study its effectiveness.

# （二）

# 欢迎辞

北京大学教育学院院长、联合国教科文组织亚太地区高等教育讲席　阎凤桥

非常欢迎各位嘉宾出席本次大会“普通（学术）教育与职业教育协调发展”平行论坛。这个平行论坛的主题是非常切中时代节点的，因为世界正在与年轻人的技能短缺、就业不足和高失业率作斗争。技术和经济结构的快速发展，如“工业4.0”、人工智能、大数据等，对我们的教育体系提出了进一步要求，即培养具有高水平科研能力和实践技能的人才。经济和就业市场的动态状况影响着再就业和多重就业等问题。因此，教育系统必须具有灵活性，为毕业生提供从一个岗位转换到另一个岗位，甚至从一个行业转换到另一个行业的能力。事实上，教育制度随着社会和经济制度的发展而日益分化，从而减少了社会的流动性。在这一过程中，职业技术教育与培训通常被认为是来自弱势背景的学生的一种选择。为了使教育体制更加公平和公正，出于经济和社会目的，提出了学术教育和职业教育融合的需求。

我们迫切需要对职业教育和普通教育进行重塑和转型，以回应时代呼唤。需要采取具体而系统的公共政策和措施，来抵消这些自然出现但不公平的力量。职业技术教育与培训应该和普通教育有机结合，而不应只是后者的补救方案。

今天，我们聚集了来自世界各地的杰出演讲嘉宾，讨论现有模式和新路径，以更好地将职业教育与普通教育结合起来。他们是来自不同的学术背景的教授、政府官员以及国际组织官员，在各自领域有着丰富的教育经验。他们还代表了多元的背景：发达国家、新兴工业化国家、新兴经济体以及发展中国家。希望接下来的讨论能帮助我们更好地理解职业技术教育与培训和普通教育整合的挑战和机遇，并为这一领域未来的改革奠定基础。

## ii. Welcome Remarks

**Yan Fengqiao, Dean of Graduate School of Education, Peking University, UNESCO Chair on Higher Education in Asia and the Pacific**

A warm welcome to all of you who are attending this session on the Integration of Academic and Vocational Education at this conference. This session is very timely as the world struggles with both a shortage of skills and rampant underemployment and unemployment of people, especially among young people. Rapid advancements in technology and economic structure such as Industry 4.0, Artificial Intelligence, and Big Data ask more from our education system to cultivate high-order academic and practical skills. The dynamic situations in the economy and job market address such issues as re-employment and multiple employment. As a result, the education system has to be flexible and provides its graduates with such competence to change from one position to another position, even from one industry to another industry. In reality, our education system, following the footstep of social and economic system, has become increasingly stratified which in turn reduces social mobility. In this process, Technical and Vocational Education and Training (TVET) is often considered an option for those students from disadvantaged background. To make the educational system more equitable and fair, there emerges the need for integration of academic and vocational education for both economic and social purposes.

We urgently need to reshape and transform both TVET and general education to answer this call. Concrete and yet systematic public policies and measures are required to counteract these natural but unfair forces. TVET should be fully integrated with general education, not as an afterthought.

Today, we have gathered a team of distinguished speakers from all over the world to discuss the existing patterns and emerging pathways to better integrate TVET with general education. These prestigious speakers come from different backgrounds—professors, government officials, and officials from international organizations—all have rich experiences in education under their belt. They also represent a diverse set of contexts: developed countries, newly industrialized countries, emerging economies as well as developing countries. I hope the delineation and discussion will help us better understand the challenges and opportunities in integrating TVET with general education and hopefully set the stage for future reforms in this area.

## （三）

# 职业教育的机遇与挑战：南亚的经验

亚洲开发银行社会部门首席专家 李善华

今天和大家分享我在南亚国家工作的经验和心得。首先，我介绍一下这些国家的人口和教育背景。接下来介绍基本技能薄弱所带来的挑战，它制约职业教育的发展，而职业教育正在转型升级，需要扩大教育规模。其次，我再谈一谈职业和技能的发展趋势。最后，我将以印度为例，介绍怎样整合职业教育和学术教育。

在其他东亚或东南亚国家面临比较严重的人口老龄化问题时，南亚国家的青年劳动年龄人口仍在不断增长。学龄人口逐渐减少，而劳动年龄人口在增加。除斯里兰卡外，许多南亚国家的人口年龄中位数低于 30 岁，印度、孟加拉国和尼泊尔为 27 岁至 29 岁。特别是到 2026 年，印度将拥有全球最多的青年劳动力人群，届时，预计 15 岁至 59 岁的人口将达到 9 亿。考虑到如此庞大的劳动力队伍，对于这些国家来讲，拥有受过良好教育且技能熟练的劳动力对于发挥科学技术和知识经济在未来发展中的作用至关重要。这些国家努力扩大教育规模，增加入学机会，取得了重大进展。初等教育基本普及，中等教育的入学率也在稳定增长。大多数南亚国家的中等教育毛入学率为 60% 至 80%。但是 11 年级和 12 年级的净入学率仍然为 50% 至 70%。在这种情况下，最大的问题是教学质量不佳，尤其是学习效果差，这已被这些国家视为学习危机。而新冠病毒疫情导致学校长时间停课，进一步削弱了学习效果。

接下来，我会以印度为例解释前文提到的学习危机。印度一直在定期开展全国性的教育成果调查。根据针对 3 年级学生受访者的调研，约有 1/3 的学生无法阅读简单的课文或完成简单的数学运算，而这些都是该年级的基本教学要求。这些早期的学习差距随着时间的推移在扩大。到 8 年级，几乎一半的学生无法阅读或无法完成该年级教学要求的数学运算。所以，印度的教学侧重针对不同年级提高不同程度的基本识字和算术能力，尤其是3年级学生的阅读能力。众所周知，3年级是小学阶段的转折点，该年级的教学目标是让孩子们学会阅读，以便他们以后可以通过阅读来学习。这种教学侧重点对于提升学生未来的学习能力和技能获取能力至关重要。我们也谈到了技能的转型升级，但是基础知识欠缺导致了学生就业能力或技术技能较弱，这就意味着必须要重视职业技能教育，它是建立在拥有扎实的基础知识上的。

就技术、职业和技能趋势而言，受新冠病毒疫情的影响，技术变革（如工业4.0）在重塑未来的职业，特别是人工智能和自动化技术。低技能工作更容易受到上述趋势的影响，而新兴的工作则需要更高水平的技能。特别是常规工作岗位正在减少，而对工人基本技能水平的要求则越来越高。接受过技能培训的工人的就业机会越来越多，而低薪酬工作机会的增加很有限。社交和情感技能（包括软技能）也越来越重要。事实上，新冠病毒疫情加速了颠覆性技术的应用。对职业技能要求如此迅速的变化表明，无论是对于现在的产业工人，还是新入行者，都需要不断地提升自己的职业技能。

该怎么做呢？必须具备非常扎实的基本技能和软技能，让员工能够学习和重新学习，以应对工作性质和相关技能要求的变化。因此，印度2020年国家教育政策强调职业教育的重要性，但它不建议硬性分离职业和学术教育，而是更注重将职业教育融入普通教育中。那么，具体建议方案是什么呢？6—8年级的学生将开始接触职业指导，提升他们对各种职业技能要求的认识。对于9—10年级的学生，将引入多技能职业和生活技能模块，作为附加科目，以丰富职业教育技能的内容。这在很大程度上取决于当地的实际情况，印度各邦在工业发展程度和就业机会方面存在很大的差异。11—12年级将职业课程作为选修和必修课，让学生至少可以修习某些特定的职业课程。

这是目前国家教育政策的建议方案，但各邦很少切实实施。有的邦开设了多门类似的职业课程，但有的邦还没有真正实施。鉴于新冠病毒疫情带来的学习上的不便，教学侧重于未来技能的准备和习得。亚洲开发银行刚刚批准了一项对印度的贷款项目，在未来技能方面也有所侧重。

对于1—5年级的学生，侧重于基础教育，提升3年级和5年级学生的基础学习能力，目标是100%熟练掌握基础知识。对于6—12年级的学生，引入了STEAM教学方法（STEAM指集科学、技术、工程、艺术、数学多领域融合的综合教育），对传统理科科目形成补充。同时，将批判性思维、沟通和协作能力以及软技能引入到教学体系中。

我给大家举一个简单的例子，关于前一段时间，亚洲开发银行在喀拉拉邦支持实施的，在完成基础教育以后的额外技能习得项目。该项目为 11 年级和 12 年级的高中学生开设了额外的基础和职业课程，以提高青年的就业能力。一方面，这些额外的技能课程并非常规课程，但它作为额外课程，起初在两三千所学校实施，目前正扩大至所有的高中。另一方面，印度有一种叫作工业技术学院的技术学院，它的教学侧重点是贸易技能。但是，此类工业技术学院就业率历来较低，低于 40%，而且这种学院实际上不教授任何学科知识，只教授大量的贸易技能技巧。这些机构专门针对 10 年级的毕业生，有时甚至是 8 年级的毕业生，他们实际上没有掌握牢固的基础知识。

所以，目前的发展趋势是整合一部分软技能课程和语言课程。印度的通识教育和职业技术教育都采用了这种整合的方法，其他的南亚国家也采用了类似的方法。

# iii. Challenges and Opportunities for Vocational Education: Experiences from South Asia

**Sunhwa Lee, Principal Social Sector Specialist, Asian Development Bank**

Let me share the experiences and lessons from the South Asian countries in which I've been working. Let me first share the demographic and educational context in these countries. And then let me describe challenges arising from weak foundational skills, which are posing as a constraint for vocational education, which is really being upgraded, requiring a lot of scaling. Then I will turn to trends in jobs and skills requirements. And finally, I will show you some of the approaches to integrate vocational and academic education with examples from India.

Compared to other East Asian or Southeast Asian countries where population aging is an important issue, South Asian countries still have a growing young working-age population. The school-age population is declining gradually, whereas the working-age population is increasing. The median age for many of the South Asian countries, except Sri Lanka, is below 30, and it is between 27 and 29 in India, Bangladesh, and Nepal. India in particular will have the world's largest youth workforce by 2026, estimated 900 million between the ages of 15 and 59. Given this large workforce, having a well-educated and skilled workforce is essential for these countries in fostering technology adoption and knowledge-based economy for future development. These countries have made tremendous progress in terms of expanding access to schooling. Primary education is almost universal and secondary education also has been increasing quite steadily. For most South Asian countries, the gross enrollment ratio at secondary level is between 60% and 80%. However, the net enrollment rate for grades 11 and 12 is still about 50% to 70%. The big issue in this context has been the inadequate quality of education, especially poor learning outcomes, which has been recognized as a learning crisis in these countries. And the COVID-19 pandemic, which caused the prolonged closure of schools, has aggravated this learning situation.

Next, let me give illustration of what kind of learning crisis we are talking about with an example from India. India has been carrying out national achievement surveys periodically, and according to the survey of grade 3 students, about 1/3 of them cannot read a simple text or do simple maths, which is required at that grade level. And these early learning gaps are becoming amplified over time. By grade 8, almost half of the students cannot read or cannot do maths expected at that grade. So there is a grade emphasis in India, which is improving foundational literacy and numeracy, especially grade 3 reading, which is known to be an inflection point where the children are expected to "learn to read", so that they can "read to learn" afterwards. So this emphasis is essential for future learnability and future skills acquisition. We have also talked about the skills that are being upgraded for more advanced skills and so on. Inadequate foundational skills lead to weak employable or technical skills, meaning that the capacity to observe vocational education is really important, which is based on strong foundational skills.

In terms of the trends in technology, jobs, and skills, under the COVID-19 pandemic, technology changes (such as Industry 4.0) are reshaping the world of work, especially artificial intelligence and automation technologies. And low-skilled jobs are more at risk of these trends while emerging jobs require higher level skills. Especially when the routine jobs are disappearing, the basic skill level requirement is increasing. Job opportunities are increasing for technology-trained workers, whereas there is limited growth for low-wage jobs. And there is a growing importance of social and emotional skills, including soft skills. COVID-19 has accelerated, actually, the pace of adoption of subversive technologies. Such rapid changes in skill requirements in jobs indicate there is a constant need of scaling and rescaling for today's industrial workers as well as new entrants.

So how do you do that? There have to be really solid foundational skills and soft skills for individual workers to be able to learn and relearn in coping with the changes in the nature of jobs and associated skills requirements. So in India, the National Education Policy 2020 is emphasizing vocational education, but it recommends no hard separation between vocational and academic streams, but to integrate vocational education into general education. So what are these recommendations? For grades 6–8, the students are going to be exposed to vocational orientations, raising their awareness of various occupations and skills requirements. For grades 9–10, multi-skill vocational and life skill modules are being introduced to give a flavor of the kind of vocational education skills as additional subjects. This would be very much based on the local context. In India, the states vary widely in terms of industry and development context, as well as employment opportunities. For grades 11–12, vocational courses will be given as elective and compulsory courses, so that the students can at least have some specific vocational courses.

Currently, these are the NEP's recommendations. But there are very limited practices across the states. Some states are actually doing quite a lot of these vocational courses, but some states are not actually implementing this approach yet. Given the

COVID-19 pandemic and the learning issues, additional emphasis has also been placed on future skills readiness and availability. In fact, ADB has just approved a new lending program for India, where we are also emphasizing this aspect.

For grades 1–5, there is a huge emphasis on improving foundational learning with a target of 100% proficiency for grade 3 and grade 5 students. For grades 6–12, the STEAM (Science, Technology, Engineering, Arts and Mathematics) Learning is being introduced to complement traditional science and maths subjects, and also critical thinking, communication skills and collaboration, as well as soft skills.

Let me just give you one brief example of what ADB supported in the state of Kerala recently—additional skills acquisition program in post-basic education. That project created additional foundational and vocational courses in higher secondary grades 11 and 12 to enhance their employability. These additional skills are not a regular curriculum, but as additional courses implemented initially in 2 000 or 3 000 schools, and are now being scaled up to all higher secondary schools. On the other hand, there's a technical institute called the Industrial Technical Institutes in India, which is very much focusing on trade skills. However, in these ITIs, job placement has been very low, below 40%, and these institutes actually do not teach any of the academic subject matters, only trade technical skills. And these institutes are for the graduates of grade 10, and sometimes, even grade 8, who actually do not have sufficient foundational skills.

So now, the trend is actually to incorporate some of the soft skills courses and language courses for this institute. There is this integrated approach coming from the general education as well as the technical education side in India, and a similar approach is also being taken in other South Asian countries.

## （四）

# 全面审视普通教育与职业教育协调发展

欧洲职业培训发展中心副所长　玛拉·布鲁贾

有很长一段时间，我们都趋向于把普通教育和职业教育当成二元对立的教育方式，认为普通教育以理论为基础，教会人们理论的本质是什么；而职业教育则以实践为基础，让人们知道理论在实际生活中要如何应用。但这两者的边界并不是绝对清晰的。我们的工作也证明了这两种教育形式都能达到同样高的水平。

我们在应对当前和今后所面临的挑战时需要从全局视角看待问题。每个人在其人生历程中，都有机会掌握一些自己成功需要的技能或公司成功需要的技能，而获取技能的途径可以是正规的教育培训，也可以是其他一些渠道，获取的技能类型也是多样的。这种全局视角意味着我们要发挥不同类型、不同水平的教育各自的优势，并且各方也要通力合作。

下面将列举一些实例，供大家讨论。这些实例基于我们长久以来对欧盟职业教育的研究，也基于欧盟职业教育与劳动市场的趋势和需求之间发生的相互作用。欧洲职业培训发展中心已成立 45 年有余，目标是制定、推广并落实欧盟在职业教育方面的政策和认证体系。为此，我们和欧盟成员国、企业组织和工会之间开展了积极的合作。

从早期开始，欧盟就采用了一种宏观视角去看待职业教育，认为学生和成年人通过接受职业教育可以获取初级技能认证，并不断更新和精进自己掌握的技能。除了传授职业技能，职业教育也有助于个人发展。但政策往往更注重学徒制或课堂教育，主要面向 16 至 20 岁的年轻人，培养他们成为技术熟练的工人进入劳动力市场，至此，职业教育的阶段就结束了。但有些国家也会提供更高阶的职业教育课程，特别是那些理论和普通教育水平较高的国家。

学术理论教育固然重要，但职业教育也开始向着更高水准不断发展，衍生出了更多可以替代“传统”高等学术教育的形式。我们在发展欧洲未来职业教育的工作中，也会综合这两种教育形式。虽然有些国家在职业教育学术化的过程中更注重课堂理论教学，但更多国家还是更偏向以实践为基础的教学形式，并且重视与劳动力市场的紧密合作。调查显示，在过去 15 年中，欧洲有 60% 的职业教育培训机构都增加了与工作相关的课程内容的比重。这一数据说明与课堂教学相比，人们认为课外实践对就业更有帮助，同时也体现出欧洲职业教育政策的融合与互鉴收获了良好的效果。

与此同时，横向技能与软技能显然也越来越受重视。除了要掌握通用技能，职业教育的学生还要具备创造力和自主应对突发情况的能力，并且能够不断精进自己掌握的技能，这些能力都变得越来越重要。但课堂教学对这些能力的培养是非常有限的，课堂外的实践才是最佳途径。越来越多的国家开始提供不同水平的高级职业教育课程项目，其中还包括博士课程。德国近期就推出了此类本科和研究生项目，不仅印证了这种趋势，也强调了高等教育并非只能被大学所垄断。提供这类课程项目的有公立机构也有私营企业，有正式教育体制内的学校也有非学校类的机构。这一现象反映出劳动力市场对职业教育技能的需求在与日俱增，为双元制学制和高等学徒制文凭的推广奠定了基础。

高等职业教育课程在成人继续教育中也发挥着关键作用。人们在学习这类课程的过程中，可以结合自己在工作中习得的知识和技能，并在此基础上继续深造。除此之外，这类课程还为人们开辟了新的道路，职业教育的学生可以通过这类课程完成理论深造，接受普通教育的学生可以通过这类课程进一步学习具体专业，已经步入职场的人也可以通过这类课程继续学习新的专业知识。总之，职业教育将工作中需要的软技能与实践相结合，帮助人们做出改变、适应改变并创造新的商业模式。这种教育形式需要将强有力的理论和通识与以实践为本的教学模式相结合，并且这种教学模式是与劳动力市场紧密相关的。

在制定欧洲的职业教育政策时，目前的关键问题就是要找到一个恰到好处的平衡，化解各方的矛盾。为了让政策行之有效，政府要加强各个利益相关方之间的合作，重视劳动力市场和技能人才的对接。欧洲职业培训发展中心在其中发挥着重要的作用。人们通过接受职业教育，可以掌握一定的技能组合，拥有积极进取的人生态度，提高工作适应能力和创新能力。这也说明了从各个层面来讲，职业教育在普通教育、研究和创新领域都发挥着重要作用，能为社会做出突出的贡献。从我们近期的工作也可以看出，应对气候危机并加快绿色经济转型也需要从各个层面上充分挖掘人们的潜力。

在整个欧盟范围内，各个职业教育学院、大学、研究中心、企业、行业和其他相关方之间，都建立了形式多样的合作模式。这些合作与国家、地区以及行业背景息息相关。在全球化的大环境下，国际合作与互学互鉴发挥着至关重要的作用。

从今天的这些案例可以看出，国家职业教育认证体系框架、欧洲的职业教育认证体系框架以及世界各地体系框架的制定能够让职业教育与普通教育之间的关系更为清晰，促进国际合作。

# iv. Vocational Education and Training (VET) and Academic Education: A Holistic Perspective

**Mara Brugia, Deputy Director of European Centre for the Development of Vocational Training (CEDEFOP)**

For a long time, there was a tendency to see academic and vocational education as a dichotomy. We might want to say that academic education is more theory-oriented and focuses on the knowing *what*, while vocational educational training or VET as we call it, is more skills/practice-oriented and focuses on knowing *how* to apply the theory. However, things are not as clear cut. And our work has demonstrated that the outcomes of both forms of learning can reach equally high levels.

Today's and tomorrow's challenges require a holistic perspective. Everyone throughout their lives, must have the chance to acquire the skills that they and companies need to succeed, whether through formal education and training or not and whatever the types. This holistic view also means drawing on the strengths of the different types and levels of education, and pooling forces with our partners.

Allow me to share with you some of CEDEFOP's evidence as a frame for your discussions. This evidence is rooted in our long-standing research on VET in the European Union and its interplay with labour market trends and needs. CEDEFOP was set up over 45 years ago. Its task is to help shape, promote and realise EU policy in VET's, skills and qualifications. To this end, we work together with the European Commission, Member States, employer organisations and trade unions.

Since its early days, the EU has had a broad view of VET: enable young people and adult workers to acquire initial qualifications, update their skills or retrain; and besides purely vocational skills, also promote personal development. Nevertheless, the policy focus has often been on apprenticeships or school-based VET of mainly 16 to 20 year-olds, enabling them to enter the labour market as skilled workers. Often this marked the end of their formal education career. But progression to higher levels has also been possible in several countries, particularly from those with a higher share of theory and academic education.

While these types remain important, they have been complemented by a rise of VET offers at higher levels. They are an alternative to what many would consider 'traditional' academic higher education. In our work on the future of VET in Europe, what we see is a mixed picture: while we observe a clear 'academic' drift with priority to theory and classroom-based learning in some countries, more countries put a particular focus on practice-based learning and closer cooperation with the labour market. 60% of the European providers we surveyed stated that the work-related character of VET has increased in the past 15 years. This reflects recognition of the employment premium that work-based learning has over academic education. It also reflects the impact of collaboration on VET policy and mutual learning in Europe.

What has also become evident is an increasing emphasis on transversal or soft skills. Besides their general and technical skills base, the ability of VET learners to operate autonomously, tackle unforeseen problems, be creative and continuously update their skills is becoming more important. But promoting these skills can only to a limited extent happen through classroom lectures. They are best learned in real-life situations. An increasing number of countries now build advanced VET programmes at all levels, including a doctoral level. The recent introduction in Germany of 'Professional Bachelors and Masters' illustrates this tendency, underlying that higher education is not the monopoly of universities. Such programmes are offered by a variety of public and private providers within and outside formal education systems. This reflects the understanding that advanced VET skills are in increasing demand by the labour market. It has, thus, also paved the way towards dual studies and apprenticeship degrees at higher levels.

VET at higher levels can also play a key role in upskilling and reskilling adults: it can help people to build on previous studies and skills acquired at work or elsewhere, it can open up new paths from VET to 'academic' higher education or vice versa, from one form of VET to another, from work to specialised education and back. To conclude, by combining job specific, transversal skills and practice, VET enables people to shape and adapt to change and create new business models. This requires ensuring a strong theory and general knowledge integrated in ways that suit VET learners, and its strong practice-based delivery mode in close cooperation with the labour market.

Finding an appropriate balance and easing the tensions involved are currently the key issues in European VET policies. To be effective, VET policy also need to be underpinned by governance based on partnerships of the key stakeholders and strong labour market and skills intelligence. At EU level, CEDEFOP has a key role in this. Through its combination of skills in line and its 'can-do attitude', VET can be a tool for resilience and a co-driver of innovation, a linchpin of skills ecosystems. This entails understanding VET at all levels as an important partner in the knowledge square of education, research, innovation, and service to society. As our recent work shows, tackling the climate crisis and shifting to greener economies require tapping people's potential at all levels.

Across the EU, various cooperation models are emerging among different VET institutions, universities, research centres, business and industry and other stakeholders. While VET is strongly linked to a given national, regional and sectoral context, in a globalised world, international cooperation and learning from each other is crucial. At EU level the 'centres of vocational excellence' initiative promotes such cross-border collaboration.

As today's examples will demonstrate, the national and European qualifications frameworks and the development of regional frameworks across the globe help us to make the relationship of VET and academic education more visible and foster international corporation.

# （五）

# STEM 教育与职业技术教育

美国埃默里大学政治学系古德里奇·C·怀特名誉荣休教授　托马斯·F·雷明顿

建设一支在科学、技术、工程和数学（STEM）方面具备良好资质的劳动力队伍，以满足不断变化的劳动力市场的需求，这一点的重要性在近年得到了很大关注。人们正在采取多项举措来提高中等和高等教育机构中 STEM 教育的质量，尤其是扩大体验式学习方法的使用这一举措。这些方法试图围绕正式教学与非正式学习的结合来塑造学习环境，将 STEM 内容应用于项目和问题解决中。这些学习方法通常需要学生之间进行合作。这样的体验式学习方法可以被纳入教育课程中，但很多时候，学校会与其他组织形成伙伴关系，包括企业、研究机构、博物馆等。体验式学习方法的倡导者希望通过将学术课程与通过个人经验获得的知识相联系，加强教育成果。体验式学习旨在加强培养高阶思维技能的能力，超越对信息死记硬背或通过多次重复获得成功的方式。现在的雇主们越来越看重高阶的思维能力。因此，体验式学习有助于缩小学术教育，或者称为普通教育，与以职业为导向的职业培训之间的差距。它同时也有助于激励学生在学术方面取得成功。许多实践者发现，对在传统正式教育中感受到沮丧和挫败的年轻人，通过有计划、有组织的体验式方法，成功地将非正式学习与正式学习结合起来，可以激发他们的个人能动性和奋斗意识。

尽管存在一些阻碍，美国还是做出了许多努力，设计了一些基于 STEM 的体验式学习模式。许多地方性的举措试图将非正式和正式学习联系起来，并唤起人们对 STEM 教育和职业的兴趣。例如，更频繁地组织参观科学博物馆，对 STEM 教育进行课程改革，采用新技术，以及鼓励雇主更积极地参与实践培训。美国国家科学基金会资助了其中部分举措。

这些举措通常是针对特定社区的特定教育机构，而不是在全州范围内实施的，反映出美国分散的教育系统和面向地方的劳动力市场等特点。它们还应用了各种标签——综合方法、基于项目的学习等，同时它们所借鉴的教育文献也存在很大差异。通常，这些举措试图通过项目工作促进 STEM 概念的整合和应用，创造结构化的方式来激发学习者对 STEM 内容的兴趣和掌握。这种定义体验式学习的方式将正式和非正式学习尽可能多地联系起来。我所使用的术语“基于 STEM 的体验式学习”，指的是通过围绕正式的 STEM 内容的整合和应用来组织教育，努力塑造学习环境，从而将正式学习和非正式学习联系起来。

体验式学习同时发生在课堂和工作环境中。在后者中，学校与其他组织（通常是企业）合作，提供以实践为导向的机会，以深化知识并将其应用于解决现实世界的问题。这种合作在美国以很多种形式开展，其中学徒制在美国仍然比较少见，而当地的教育活动则广泛而多样。

美国的 STEM 教育越来越强调科学 - 数学 - 技术知识与实际应用的结合。按照一种引用较为广泛的定义，STEM 是“一种跨学科的学习方法，其中严谨的学术概念与现实世界的课程相结合，学生在学校、社区、工作和全球企业相互联系的环境中应用科学、技术、工程和数学，使 STEM 素养得到发展，从而获得在新经济中的竞争力。”

正如这一定义所表明的，STEM 的范围要比科学、技术、工程和数学广泛得多。它指的是跨学科的联系，以及与学生作为社会成员、公民和工人准备进入的世界的联系。以这种方式采用 STEM 意味着向甚至还没有参加职业技术教育课程的学生教授科学、数学和技术科目，以及教授超出学术课程之外的特定学科内容。这意味着展示人们如何使用工具和技术来塑造世界。我们对美国国家科学基金会资助的项目进行了研究并得出结论：受资助的很多项目间有很大的相似之处。通常，它们的目的是培养特定技术和应用技能（如生物医学、无人驾驶航空系统、农业设备），而不是培养某一学科的一般知识（如化学或物理）。这些项目主要服务于在种族、民族、性别、地理、社会经济方面处于弱势的群体，重点帮助在 STEM 领域中长期处于少数的群体扩大机会。

涉及中学的项目通常会强调课堂内外的教学资源，视其为促进 STEM 成功的驱动因素。这些项目倾向于侧重教师发展和课程开发，目的是使学生为 STEM 相关职业做好准备。这些项目通常包括体验式学习机会。大多数项目都希望能够改善劳动力发展和毕业生的工作机会。

社区大学和职业大学提供两年制的教育课程，这一层次的项目也迎合了人们的期待，具备更具体的职业方向。它们倾向于明确地以劳动力发展为框架，旨在为未来的技术工人、工程师和技术人员创造工作机会。为此，这些项目更趋于响应当地行业的需求，并围绕与雇主的合作关系来制定规划。

总体而言，涉及四年制学院和大学的项目较为多样化。它们往往不太直接强调劳动力发展或就业。同样，它们往往不包含基于工作场所的体验式学习，而且通常不针对职业学生。然而，有些项目会面向特定的技术应用（如无人驾驶飞行器、云计算）。

我们还对单个项目的案例研究信息和涵盖 STEM 教育举措的学术文献进行了汇编。这些项目中有许多针对特定人群，特别是妇女、代表性不足的少数民族、残疾学生和经济上处于弱势的学生。

我们同时对作为发起人、主办机构和合作伙伴的组织的身份进行了认定。大多数主办机构都是教育机构，其中中学、两年制和四年制教育机构的数量大致相当。在少数情况下，博物馆、政府机构和商业公司也会担任主办单位。部分中学项目是在校外进行的。政府机构有时充当主办机构。工业公司有时也主办教育活动。

合作组织会提供多种类型的资助：物质（资金、用品、设施）、组织支持（课程开发、教师专业发展、外部评估）和人力资源（包括雇员和志愿者）。许多机构提供财政支持。其他组织提供人力资源作为支持。

案例研究中涉及的基于 STEM 的学习项目范围非常广泛。我们对多种将体验式学习与正式学习相结合的方法进行了观察：课堂内外的项目式学习，社区的服务式学习项目，公司、博物馆和其他组织的实地考察参观，见习工作，夏令营，实习及其他。许多项目涉及合作关系，部分是与多所学校和 / 或外部伙伴合作。我们分析的项目在合作伙伴的贡献方面也有差异。有些项目对学校、公司和社区伙伴的投资需求相对较少，而另一部分项目则需要在时间和组织上的大量投入，如对整个课程进行重组的案例就是如此。

对项目评估不够重视是一个令人不安的问题。只有数量少得惊人的项目和论文对项目实现目标的效果给出了最基本的分析。很少有研究采用了严格的研究设计，如随机治疗研究，甚至是治疗组和对照组的比较都很少见。鉴于政府、教育组织和企业为推动美国 STEM 教育而付出的巨大开支，缺乏对评估的关注是令人担忧的。

根据 2016 年的一项研究，以 STEM 为重点的学校的项目发现 STEM 学校有几个共同特点，一个是将帮助学生通过批判性思维解决现实世界的问题作为其总体目标；另一个是鼓励主动的，而非被动的学习。这些学校通过以下方式达成这些目标：围绕结构化的、严密的问题解决思路来组织学习；不仅注意培养技术技能，而且注意培养职业发展和管理成年人社会生活需求的能力；通过教师的专业发展和所有教学人员之间的广泛沟通，保持良好的校园文化；让家长和其他社区成员参与进来，以提高学校的课程水平。这些技能是取得成功的基础，不仅在 STEM 职业领域中，在任何领域的职业生涯中普遍如此。

从这些我们分析的研究和项目中，可以得出三个结论。

首先，通过 STEM 的体验式学习在教育和经济理论中有着深厚的基础。它可以成为助力先前缺乏机会的人群获取优质工作和职业的一种方式，它能够使所有学生掌握技能，不仅是技术上的技能，还包括社会、行为和认知技能，使他们能够创建成功的事业。

其次，想要通过 STEM 成功实施体验式学习，需要教育者的共同努力，同时需要雇主和社区中其他人的积极参与。要持续成功地建立这种努力合作模式，通常需要对机构进行精心设计，其中也包括中介组织的积极作用。

最后，无论体验式 STEM 学习项目设计得多么精巧，如果不能对实现项目目标的条件进行系统性评估，那么它们取得实质性成果的能力都将会受到限制。对这些项目对学生的成功、就业和社区发展的影响进行严谨的比较研究是有必要的。取得积极的结果多大程度上取决于教师的专业发展、中介组织的参与以及雇主和学校之间的密切联系等问题，都有待于进行系统性的分析。如果基于 STEM 的体验式教育是为了缩小劳动力市场供需之间的差距，扩大学生的机会和流动性，提高国家竞争力，那么我们必须将努力建立在比目前更有力的证据基础之上。

## v. STEM Education and TVET

**Thomas F. Remington, Goodrich C. White Professor (Emeritus) of Political Science, Emory University, US**

In recent years, a great deal of attention has been paid to the importance of building a workforce well-qualified in science, technology, engineering and math to meet the needs of a changing labor market. Many initiatives are being undertaken to improve the quality of STEM education in secondary and higher educational institutions, particularly by expanding the use of experiential learning methods. These methods seek to shape the learning environment around the integration of formal instruction with informal learning, by applying STEM content to projects and problem-solving. They frequently require collaboration among students. Such experiential learning methods may be incorporated in educational curricula, but schools often form partnerships with other organizations, including businesses, research institutions, museums, and the like. Advocates of experiential learning methods aspire to strengthen educational outcomes by linking the academic curriculum to knowledge acquired through personal experience. Experiential learning seeks to strengthen abilities to develop higher-order thinking skills, going beyond rote information memorization or successful performance of repetitive tasks. Employers increasingly demand higher-order thinking skills. Experiential learning, therefore, helps bridge the gap between academic, or general, education and career-oriented vocational training. It also helps motivate students towards academic success. Many practitioners find that successfully integrating informal with formal learning through planned, structured experiential methods can awaken senses of personal agency and striving in young people for whom traditional formal education produces discouragement and failure.

Notwithstanding the obstacles, a number of efforts to design models of experiential learning based on STEM have been undertaken in the United States. Many local initiatives seek to link informal and formal learning and awaken interest in STEM education and careers. Examples include more frequent visits to science museums, curricular reforms of STEM education, adoption of new technologies, and encouragement of greater involvement by employers in practical training. Some of these initiatives are funded by the American National Science Foundation (NSF).

Reflecting the decentralized American educational system and locally-oriented labor markets, these initiatives are usually directed at particular educational institutions in particular communities, rather than implemented state-wide. They also use a variety of labels—integrated methods, project-based learning, and so on—and vary widely in the educational literatures upon which they draw. Commonly, they attempt to create structured ways to awaken interest in and mastery of STEM content by facilitating the integration and application of STEM concepts through project work. This way of defining experiential learning connects formal and informal learning as much as possible. As I employ, the term STEM-based experiential learning refers to deliberate efforts to shape the learning context in order to connect formal and informal learning by organizing education around the integration and application of formal STEM content.

Experiential learning takes place in both classroom- and work-based contexts. In the latter, schools cooperate with other organizations—typically businesses—to provide practice-oriented opportunities for deepening knowledge and applying it to real-world problems. Such cooperation takes many forms in the United States, where apprenticeships are still relatively rare and local educational initiatives widespread and diverse.

STEM education in the United States has increasingly come to emphasize integration of scientific-mathematical-technical knowledge with practical applications. According to one widely-cited definition, STEM is "…an interdisciplinary approach to learning where rigorous academic concepts are coupled with real-world lessons as students apply science, technology, engineering and mathematics in contexts that make connections between school, community, work and the global enterprise enabling the development of STEM literacy and with it the ability to compete in the new economy."

As this definition suggests, STEM is much broader than just science, technology, engineering and math. It refers to connections across academic subjects and with the world students prepare to enter as members of society, citizens and workers. Embracing STEM in this way means teaching science, math, and technical subjects even to students not enrolled in career-technical education programs, and teaching discipline-specific content outside of academic programs. It means demonstrating how people use tools and techniques to shape their world. Our examination of projects funded by the NSF led us to conclude that many of the funded programs have significant similarities. Frequently, they aim to build skills in specific technologies and applications (e.g., biomedicine, unmanned aeronautical systems, farming equipment), rather than to cultivate general knowledge within a discipline (e.g., in chemistry or physics). Programs are predominately designed to serve underprivileged constituencies—racial, ethnic, gender-based, geographic, socioeconomic—indicating emphasis on expanding opportunity for groups historically underrepresented in STEM careers.

Projects involving secondary schools typically emphasize pedagogical resources—both in-class and out-of-school—as drivers of success in STEM. They are likely to focus on teacher development and curriculum development in order to prepare students for STEM-related careers. These projects often incorporate experiential learning opportunities. Most aspire to improve workforce development and job opportunities for graduates.

As would be expected of community colleges and vocational colleges, which offer two-year educational programs, projects at this level have a more specific vocational orientation. They are likely to be framed explicitly in terms of workforce development, and are meant to place prospective skilled workers, engineers, and technicians in jobs. To that end, they are more likely to respond to local industry's needs and to build programming around partnerships with employers.

In general, projects involving four-year colleges and universities are diverse. They tend to place less direct emphasis on workforce development or employment. Likewise, they tend not to incorporate workplace-based experiential learning and do not typically target vocational students. However, some are oriented towards specific technological applications (e.g., unmanned aerial vehicles and cloud computing).

We also compiled information on case studies of individual projects and scholarly literature covering STEM education initiatives. Many of these projects targeted specific populations, in particular women, underrepresented minorities, students with disabilities, and economically disadvantaged students

We also sought to identify organizations serving as initiators, host institutions, and partners. Most of the host institutions were educational institutions, distributed roughly equally across secondary, two-year, and four-year levels. In a few cases, museums, government agencies, and business firms served as hosts. Some secondary programs are held outside the school environment. Government agencies sometimes serve as host institutions. Industrial firms also sometimes host educational initiatives.

Partner organizations provide several types of assistance—material (financing, supplies, facilities), organizational support (curriculum development, professional development for teachers, external assessment), and human resources (both employees and volunteers). Many institutions provide financial support. Other organizations provide human resources as support.

The range of STEM-based learning projects covered in the case studies is extremely wide. We observe a variety of means to integrate experiential with formal learning—project-based learning inside and outside the classroom; service-learning projects in the community; site visits to companies, museums and other organizations; job shadows; summer camps; internships; and the like. Many projects involve partnerships, some with multiple schools and/or outside partners. The projects we reviewed also range in intensity of commitment on the part of partners. Some required relatively low investment by schools, companies, and community partners, while others were time- and organizationally-intensive, as was the case when an entire curriculum was reorganized.

A troubling problem is the lack of attention paid to assessment. Surprisingly few projects and papers reviewed offered even the most elementary analysis of projects' effectiveness in achieving goals. Few studies employed a rigorous research design, such as a randomized treatment study, or even a comparison of treatment and control groups. The lack of attention to evaluation is troubling in view of the enormous expenditures being made to advance STEM education in the United States both by the government and by educational organizations and businesses.

Programs in STEM-focused schools, according to a 2016 study, found that STEM schools share several common features. One was an overall goal of helping students address real-world problems through critical thinking. Another was to encourage active, rather than passive, learning. The schools pursued these goals by organizing learning around structured, rigorous problem-solving; paying attention not only to building technical skills, but also to building abilities to pursue careers and manage the demands of adult community life; maintaining supportive school cultures through professional development for teachers and extensive communication among all instructional staff; and involving parents and other community members to reinforce the school curricula. These skills are fundamental not only to success in STEM careers, but more generally in occupational careers in any field.

We draw three conclusions from these studies and the projects we reviewed.

First, experiential learning through STEM has a deep foundation in educational and economic theory. It can be one way to open good jobs and careers to population groups formerly lacking opportunities to enter them, and it equips all students with the skills—not only technical, but social, behavioral and cognitive skills as well—that allow them to build successful careers.

Second, successful implementation of experiential learning through STEM requires concerted effort by educators, with the active involvement of employers and others in their communities. Sustained success in building such cooperative endeavors usually requires well-designed institutions, including active roles for intermediary organizations.

Finally, however well-designed experiential STEM learning programs may be, their abilities to achieve substantial results are limited by the lack of systematic assessments of conditions enabling projects to meet their goals. Rigorous comparative studies of the impacts of these initiatives on student success, employment, and community development are needed. Questions as to the degree to which positive outcomes rely on professional development for teachers, involvement by intermediary organizations, and close links between employers and schools are required systematic analysis. If STEM-based experiential education is to close the gap between labor market demand and supply, widen opportunity and mobility for students, and raise national competitiveness, we must base our efforts on a far more robust body of evidence than exists at present.

# (六)

# 探索中国特色普职协调之路

北京大学教育学院副院长　哈　巍

非常感谢各位嘉宾的分享！我从五个方面来总结这次分论坛的收获。

世界上的职业教育系统呈现出非常强的多样性，因此我们既要学习与互鉴他人的经验，又要注意不能照搬别人的经验。因为每个国家的经验都根植于自身的文化、政治和经济历史当中。

虽然复制别人的成功经验很难，但是仍然有一些基本的原则可以遵循。其中一个最关键的原则就是教育发展要与经济发展相协调。在这个意义上，中国和其他东亚经济体是非常幸运的，经济起飞对职业教育体系的形成提出了要求，也提供了发展的条件。反过来，职业教育的发展又助力经济的发展和产业的升级，形成了良性循环。

职业教育的举办成本是昂贵的，因此不能仅依靠公共财政投入，企业的参与是必须的，因为职业教育培养的人才最终为企业所雇佣。必须改变教育与企业相割裂的现状，改变校企合作中"企冷校热"的局面。

经济发展和产业革命呼唤技能的提升，无论是职业教育还是普通教育都要面对这个挑战。对于职业教育体系而言，技能的升级意味着职业教育层次的上移。

近年来，国内外在职业教育上的改革举措很多，但是对于其成效却缺少严谨的实证研究。作为教育经济学的学者，我们有责任研究这种改革的成本效益。

# 八
# 技能重塑与终身学习论坛

协助组织单位：国家开放大学

# VIII. Reskilling and Upskilling for Lifelong Learning

Co-organizer: The Open University of China

02
陈善意
Pasupha Chinvarasopak

03
拉明 · B · 曼内
Lamin B. Manneh

04
马尔西奥 · 波赫曼
Marcio Pochmann

05
安德烈 · 布里
André Burri

06
高文兵
Gao Wenbing

07
王飞
Wang Fei

08
林群声
Paul LAM Kwan-sing

09
程洪莉
Cheng Hongli

**交流各国职业技能体系建设经验，以“社会崇尚技能”为价值导向，分析新时期技能型国家、城市和组织建设的途径和策略，推动全民终身学习，共同探讨构建人类技能共同体。**

This session focuses on global experience of developing Vocational skills systems fostering the value of “society advocates skills”. The speakers share their insights into the strategies of building skill-oriented countries, cities and organizations in the new era, promoting “lifelong learning for all” and building a community with shared skills for mankind.

# （一）

# 技能重塑与终身学习论坛情况概述

国家开放大学　张　一、陈　娜

2022 年 8 月 19—20 日，中华人民共和国教育部、中国联合国教科文组织全国委员会和天津市人民政府在天津举办首届世界职业技术教育发展大会（以下简称“大会”）。本届大会以“后疫情时代职业技术教育发展：新变化、新方式、新技能”为主题，形成“会、盟、赛、展”的职业技术教育国际交流崭新平台。其中，十四个平行论坛之一的技能重塑与终身学习论坛由国家开放大学协助组织。论坛按照“内涵丰富、富有新意、影响广泛、意义深远”的要求，圆满完成专题讨论，实现了高质量、高水准的预期目标。

1. 论坛概况

技能重塑与终身学习论坛以“社会崇尚技能”为价值导向，分析新时期技能型国家、城市和组织建设的途径和策略，推动全民终身学习，共同探讨构建人类技能共同体。论坛分为“数字时代下的技能重塑”和“地域与行业视角下的终身学习”两个专题，来自 9 个国家和地区的 12 位专家作主题报告，从不同层面分享了对技能重塑与终身学习的认识与实践，并对如何持续满足技能重塑和提升，进而推进终身学习变革提出了建议。论坛由国家开放大学副校长范贤睿主持，国家开放大学党委书记、校长荆德刚致欢迎辞。

荆德刚表示，习近平主席的贺信为论坛主题指明了方向。进入后疫情时代，全球职业教育发生了格局性变化，以传统校园面授教学为主的职业院校进入大调整、大变革的适应期，疫情期间积累的在线教育经验和做法，很大程度上会成为职业教育的新常态。以在线教学为主的国家开放大学必须适应这种新常态，主动变革、积极作为，提供更加灵活多样、适应终身学习需要的教育和培训机会。荆德刚介绍，近年来，国家开放大学以助力“技能重塑”和“终身学习”为己任，以“互联网 + 大学”为路径，加速数字化转型和智能升级，着力打造终身教育的主要平台、在线教育的主要平台和灵活教育的平台、对外合作的平台。同时，按照中央《关于推动现代职业教育高质量发展的意见》要求，积极建设海外学习中心，努力拓展学历教育、社会培训、老年教育内涵，共同构建人类命运共同体。国家开放大学正在加快推进“四个转变”。启动实施了“教育数字化战略行动”，开通了终身教育平台。今年 6 月 24 日，联合国教科文组织在巴黎总部举行教育信息化颁奖典礼，国家开放大学“一村一名大学生计划”荣获 2020 年度联合国教科文组织信息和通信技术奖——哈马德国王奖，这些都为国家开放大学在“技能重塑”和“终身学习”方面积累了经验。“国家开放大学的实践探索是中国高校在变革中创新、在改革中发展的一个缩影”，荆德刚指出，“期待进一步加强与世界各国和地区机构的交流和合作，共同应对在世界变革中的技能重塑与终身学习变革，积极为全球职业教育改革发展贡献中国智慧”。

联合国教科文组织终身学习研究所所长戴维·阿乔莱纳作了题为“拓展高等教育范围：从学位教育到灵活的技能重塑”的报告，从国际视角和全球视野提出当今教育政策争论的关键在于如何持续满足技能重塑和提升，并就大学向终身学习进行转变提出了意见和建议。中国成人教育协会会长高文兵作了题为“技能教育与培训的新使命——以终身学习助力新时代技能强国战略实施”的报告，提出技能教育与培训要与新业态新产业相向而行，并从更广阔的视野提出重塑技能与生存、生产、生活、生命等的关系。泰王国驻华大使馆科技处公使衔参赞陈善意作了题为“泰国的技能重塑、技能提升及新技能”的报告，分享了泰国运用科学、技术和创新提升本土产品质量、提高人民生活质量、增加收入和降低生活成本的一系列项目和实践。冈比亚国家认证与质量保证委员会质量保证部主任拉明·B·曼内作了题为“技能重塑与终身学习”的报告，提出当传统的职业教育与培训无法满足工人在技术转型时代的职场需求时，要通过终身学习不断重塑和提升技能。英国国际贸易部职业技术教育与培训专家、专业特许协会专家乔纳森·莱杰作了题为“面向未来的职业成功技能”的报告，通过展示成功的技能培训国际合作案例，提出了雇主、政府和教育机构只有通过密切合作，才能为人们提供恰当所需的技能培训的观点。巴西卢拉研究所所长马尔西奥·波赫曼作了题为“数字时代终身教育面临的挑战”的报告，他认为科技的快速发展和疫情的持续影响，使在线教育的灵活性和便捷性更为突出，变得更受欢迎，同时也面临挑战，应考虑对教育系统进行调整更新和优化升级，以实现不同类型知识之间的互通互联，为专业化的发展路径带来突破。中华人民共和国人力资源和社会保障部职业能力建设司技工院校管理处处长王飞作了题为“大力发展技工教育”的报告，从五个方面详细介绍了中国技工院校历经几十年发展形成的办学特色和独特优势。同时提到，中国人力资源和社会保障部计划大力推进工学一体化技能人才培养模式，巩固技工院校学制教育招生和职业培训规模，研究制定支持企业办技工院校支持政策，大力推动技工教育集团（联盟）建设。英国特许证券与投资协会首席执行官西蒙·卡尔亨作了题为“金融行业技能重塑和技能提升的终身学习”的报告，提出英国教育政策一直聚焦成人继续教育和技能培训，并致力于提高人力资源质量目标，英国特许证券与投资协会的“继续专业发展项目”为员工专业能力的持续提升起到了保驾护航的作用。香港都会大学校长林群声作了题为“香港职业专才教育：挑战与策略”的报告，提出职业教育在数字化发展背景下催生出零工经济，这需要职业教育与时俱进，能够提供弹性灵活的课程，面对当下挑战，应大力发展学生的数字素养和能力，增强职业教育的适应性，支持学生攻读职业和专业教育计划。中关村学院院长程洪莉作了题为“新时代城市终身职业技能培训体系的建构”的报告，认为职业技能培训是城市全面提升劳动者就业创业能力、缓解技能人才短缺的结构性矛盾、提高就业质量的根本举措，是城市发展的关键。今后可以加强沟通与合作，共同为构建终身职业技能培训体系、完善终身职业技能培训的政策和组织制度贡献力量。新西兰国立毛利学院教授约翰·克莱顿作了题为“新西兰视角下的终身学习”的报告，提出传统的学历教育无法适应现代产业对技能和能力提出的新要求，而终身学习将成为个人生活、工作和学习方式的常态，只有训练有素的专业人员和商务人员有机会快速获取技能，并且能在各产业间实现跨产业、跨地区以及跨国无缝流动，才会创造出生产力、利润和就业机会。瑞士技能联合会主席安德烈·布里作了题为“通识化与专业化：职业体系中的技能提升与重塑”的报告，分享了瑞士如何在技能培训的专业化和通识化之间找到有效结合点。

**2. 论坛特色和亮点**

一是主题鲜明。论坛以“社会崇尚技能”为价值导向，聚焦“技能重塑”和“终身学习”，设置了“数字时代下的技能重塑”和“地域与行业视角下的终身学习”两个专题，分析新时期技能型国家、城市和组织建设的途径和策略。论坛主题既是国家的战略定位，也是国家开放大学的发展方向，成为大会十四个平行论坛的一大亮点。

二是代表性强。论坛嘉宾既有联合国教科文组织官员，泰国驻华大使馆参赞、冈比亚国家认证与质量保证委员会质量保证部主任等国外政要，也有服务巴西前总统卢拉的著名经济学家、英国国际贸易部职业技术教育与培训专家、新西兰国立毛利学院教授等专家学者，参会嘉宾都是各自领域的权威代表，研究领域广泛，涉及经济、政治、文化、社会、国际关系等领域，这使论坛具有很高的学术水平和实践价值。

三是内容丰富。12 位嘉宾演讲内容涵盖“不同国家和地区之间的技能重塑和终身学习探索、面向未来的职业成功技能、高等教育范围的拓展、技能教育与培训的新使命、数字时代终身教育面临的挑战”等方面，有利于与会嘉宾深入了解国内外职业教育领域发展的先进经验，增进交流学习，对构建现代职业教育体系、推进经济社会高质量发展具有重要意义。

# i. Overview of the Session on Reskilling and Upskilling for Lifelong Learning

**Zhang Yi and Chen Na, the Open University of China**

From August 19 to 20, 2022, the first World Vocational and Technical Education Development Conference (WVTEDC) was held in Tianjin by the Ministry of Education of the People's Republic of China, the National Commission of the People's Republic of China for UNESCO, and Tianjin Municipal People's Government. The WVTEDC, with the theme of "Vocational and Technical Education Development in the Post-pandemic Era—New Changes, New Ways and New Skills", has formed a new platform featured by "conference, league, competition and exhibition" for international exchange of vocational and technical education. The "Reskilling and Upskilling for Lifelong Learning" session, one of the 14 parallel sessions, was co-organized by the Open University of China (OUC). The Session successfully completed the thematic discussion and achieved the high quality and high-level goals as expected, meeting the requirements of carrying "abundant connotation, rich innovation, extensive impact and far-reaching significance".

1. Overview of the Session

The "Reskilling and Upskilling for Lifelong Learning" session, guided by the value of "society advocates skills", analyzed the ways and strategies of building skilled countries and cities in the new era to promote lifelong learning for all and discussed the construction of a community with shared skills for mankind jointly. Focusing on two topics: "Skills Remodeling in the Digital Era" and "Lifelong Learning from the Perspective of Region and Industry", twelve experts, from nine countries and regions, delivered thematic reports, shared their understandings and practices of skills on remodeling and lifelong learning at different levels, and gave advice on how to meet the continuous needs for skills remodeling and upgrading in the reforms of lifelong learning. Fan Xianrui, Vice President of the Open University of China, presided over the forum and Jing Degang, Secretary of CPC Committee and President of the Open University of China, delivered a welcome speech.

Jing Degang said that President Xi Jinping's congratulatory letter pointed out a clear direction for the forum. In the post-pandemic era, global vocational education has undergone structural changes. Vocational colleges dominated by traditional face-to-face campus teaching have entered a period of adaptation to major adjustments and changes. The experience and practices of online education attained during the pandemic will be a new normal for the vocational education. The OUC dominated by online teaching must adapt to this "new normal state", and take the initiative to provide more flexible and diversified education and training opportunities that meet the needs of lifelong learning. Jing Degang introduced that in recent years, the OUC has accelerated digital transformation and intelligent upgrading by taking the mission of assisting "skills remodeling" and "lifelong learning" and following the path of "Internet + University". It has made substantial efforts to build a major platform for lifelong education, while simultaneously a major platform for online education, a platform for flexible education and a platform for international cooperation. Meanwhile, the OUC, implementing the requirements in *Guidelines on Promoting the High-Quality Development of Modern Vocational Education* issued by the CPC Central Committee and the State Council, has been actively building overseas study centers, striving to expand the development of degree education, public training and education for the old for the construction of a human community of a shared future. The OUC is accelerating the implementation of "four transformations". It has initiated the "digital education strategic action" and launched a lifelong education platform. On 24 June 2022, the OUC's "One College Student Per Village" program was awarded the 2020 UNESCO ICT Prize—King Hamad Bin Isa AI-Khalifa Prize at the award ceremony for educational informationization held at the UNESCO headquarters in Paris. All these are experiences for the OUC in terms of "skills remodeling" and "lifelong learning". "The OUC's practices and explorations are the epitome of innovations in the transformation and developments in the reform made by Chinese universities", Jing Degang added. He expected "that international and regional cooperation will help cope with the transformation of skills remodeling and lifelong learning in the global revolutionary context, actively contributing China's wisdom to the reform and development of vocational education around the world".

David Atchoarena, Director of UNESCO Institute for Lifelong Learning, delivered a report entitled "Broadening the Scope of Higher Education: From Degrees to Flexible Reskilling", in which he, from international and global perspectives, proposed that the key to today's education policy debate is how to continuously meet the needs of skills remodeling and upgrading, and gave advice on the transformation to lifelong learning for universities. Gao Wenbing, President of China Adult Education Association, delivered a report entitled "New Mission of Skill Education and Training—Facilitate the Implementation of Powerful Skilled Country Plan in the New Era with

Lifelong Learning", putting forward that skills education and training should be in line with the new businesses and new industries, and that the relationship between skills remodeling and survival, production, life, lives, etc. should be reshaped from a broader perspective. Pasupha Chinvarasopak, Minister Counsellor (Science and Technology) of Royal Thai Embassy, China, made a report entitled "Thailand's Reskill, Upskill, and Newskill", sharing a series of projects and practices about how Thailand uses science, technology and innovation to improve local products quality, raise people's living quality, increase income and reduce living costs. Lamin B. Manneh, Director of Quality Assurance, National Accreditation and Quality Assurance Authority (NAQAA), Gambia, made a report entitled "Reskilling and Upskilling for Lifelong Learning", proposing constantly remodeling and upgrading skills through lifelong learning when traditional vocational education and training cannot meet the job needs of workers in the era of technological transformation. Jonathan Ledger, Technical and Vocational Education and Training (TVET) and Chartered Bodies Specialist, Department for International Trade of UK, made a report entitled "Future Proof Skills for Successful Careers". By showing successful international cooperation cases in skills training, he put forward that employers, governments and educational institutions can provide people with the appropriate skills training only through intensive cooperation. Marcio Pochmann, President of the Institute of Lula, Brazil, gave a report entitled "The Challenge of Lifelong Education in the Digital Age". He believed that online education has become more popular thanks to its outstanding flexibility and convenience, which is influenced by the rapid development of science and technology and the continuous impacts of the epidemic, but meanwhile, it also faces challenges. Therefore, we should consider adjusting, updating, optimizing and upgrading the education system to achieve mutual connectivity between different types of knowledge so as to bring breakthroughs to the specialization development path. Wang Fei, Director of Technical School Administration Division, Department of Vocational Capacity Building, Ministry of Human Resources and Social Security, P.R. China, made a report entitled "Vigorously Advance the Development of Technical Education", which introduced the characteristics and unique advantages of technical schools in China after decades of development from five aspects in detail. At the same time, he mentioned that the Ministry of Human Resources and Social Security of China plans to promote the technical talents training mode integrating working and learning, consolidate the enrollment and vocational training scale of technical schools, study and formulate support policies for enterprises to run technical schools, and vigorously promote the construction of technical education groups (leagues). Simon Culhane, Chief Executive of the Chartered Institute for Securities and Investment, UK, made a report entitled "Reskilling and Upskilling for Lifelong Learning in Financial Industry", in which he proposed that British education policy has always focused on adult further education and skills training, and is committed to improving human resources qualities with the "Further Professional Development" program of British Chartered Institute for Securities and Investment safeguarding the continuous improvement of employees' professional abilities. Paul LAM Kwan-sing, President of Hong Kong Metropolitan University, China, delivered a report entitled "Vocational and Professional Education in Hong Kong: Challenges and Strategies", proposing that vocational education has given birth to the Gig Economy in the context of digital development, which requires vocational education to provide flexible courses to keep pace with the times. Facing current challenges, people should cultivate students' digital qualities and capabilities devotedly, enhance vocational education adaptability, and support students to study for vocational and professional degrees. Cheng Hongli, Principal of Zhongguancun Institute, China, made a report entitled "Construction of Training System for Urban Lifelong Vocational Skills in the New Era". She believed that vocational skills training is the key to urban development because it is the fundamental measure for cities to comprehensively boost the employability and entrepreneurship of workers, alleviate the structural contradiction of skilled personnel shortage, and enhance the quality of employment. She also advocated that we can strengthen communication and cooperation, jointly contributing to building a lifelong vocational skills training system, and perfecting its policies and organizational regulations. John Clayton, Professor of Te Whare Wānanga o Awanuiārangi, New Zealand, gave a report entitled "Lifelong Learning: A New Zealand View", mentioning that traditional academic education cannot adapt to the new requirements of modern industries for skills and abilities, while lifelong learning will become the normal of personal life, work and study. Only if well-trained professionals and business personnel have the opportunity to acquire skills quickly, and achieve seamless flow in all kinds of industries cross industries, regions and even countries, will it create productivity, profits and employment opportunities. André Burri, Director of SwissSkills, Switzerland, gave a report entitled "Generalization and Specialization: Up- and Re-skilling in Occupational Systems", sharing how Switzerland found an effective combination between specialization and generalization of skills training.

2. Features and Highlights of the Forum

First, this forum has a distinctive theme. Guided by the value that "society advocates skills", the forum, focusing on two topics—"Upskilling and Reskilling in the Digital Era" and "Lifelong Learning from the Perspective of Region and Industry", analyzed the ways and strategies of building a skilled country and city in the new era. This theme is not only national strategic positioning, but also OUC development orientation, which has become a highlight of the 14 parallel forums of the WVTEDC.

Second, this forum is highly representative. Its distinguished speakers include not only foreign dignitaries such as officials of UNESCO, Minister Counsellor of Royal Thai

Embassy, China, and the Director of Quality Assurance of NAQAA, Gambia, but also famous economist serving the former Brazil President Lula, Technical and Vocational Education and Training (TVET) and Chartered Bodies Specialist, Department for International Trade of UK and professor of Te Whare Wānanga o Awanuiārangi, New Zealand, etc., all of whom are authoritative representatives in their respective fields with extensive research fields ranging from economy, politics, culture, society, international relations to other ones, therefore this forum features high academic level and practical value.

Third, this forum is informative. The speeches reported by 12 speakers, covered the topics of "reskilling and lifelong learning exploration, future-orientated vocational success skills, higher education scope expansion, new mission of technical education and training, and challenges faced by lifelong education in the digital era among different countries and regions". They are helpful to the speakers' in-depth understanding of the domestic and foreign advanced experience in the development of vocational education, and in enhancing exchange and learning so as to play a significant role in building a modern vocational education system and promoting high-quality economic and social development.

# (二)

# 泰国的技能重塑、技能提升及新技能

泰王国驻华大使馆科技处公使衔参赞　陈善意

今天我和大家分享的主题是泰国高等教育科研与创新部关于技能重塑、技能提升及新技能的政策。主要包括三个方面。

首先，请允许我介绍一下泰国高等教育科研与创新部。它成立于 2019 年，融合了高等教育、科学、技术和研究职能以促进协同合作。这个新的部门旨在促进、支持和指导高等教育、科学、研究和创新，以促进泰国发展，跟上当今世界的飞速变化。目前，泰国共有 175 所大学，其中 155 所隶属于高等教育科研与创新部。泰国的大学可分为以下五个类别：第一类是全球前沿研究型大学，进行世界级的研究，培养高技能人才，以开展满足全球需求的高质量研究。第二类是技术创新型大学，负责开发满足泰国国内需求的新技术，推动创新，特别是在农业、工业和服务领域的创新。第三类是地区性和社区大学，负责传授知识和技能，以促进泰国当地社区的发展。此外，这类大学的目标还包括创造更多的就业机会，提高国内收入，特别是农业领域的收入。第四类是道德和思想培养大学，这类大学将宗教教义纳入大学课程。第五类是专业性大学，培养泰国学生的特定技能，如体育、音乐、戏剧等。

其次，2020 年，泰国高等教育科研与创新部启动了“大学重塑计划”，该计划是泰国首次根据大学的专业领域将其分为不同的类别，旨在提升泰国大学的水平，培养能够满足泰国工业需求的高技能人才。该计划将改革泰国大学的管理体制，改进课程，以满足行业发展对技能的需求，支持和鼓励泰国大学提升国际竞争力，并提升其质量。该计划是泰国政府发展计划和经济模式的重要组成部分。

该计划着重培养 12 个关键行业所需的高技能人才，这些行业将为下一代提供大量的就业机会，包括汽车、智能电子、高端医疗保健、旅游、农业和生物技术、未来食品、自动化和机器人、物流和航空、生物燃料和生物化学、数字工业、医疗服务、国防工业和教育发展。

根据“大学重塑计划”，大学将选择 5 个平台作为重点。第一，人力资源，旨在提高教学质量。第二，智力，包括技能重塑、技能提升和终身学习。第三，全球视角，大学将与国际伙伴建立合作。第四，研究与创新，旨在有效管理研究与创新。第五，参与互动，加强大学与政府部门及非政府组织的国内外合作。

最后，是技能提升和重塑计划。该计划制定了促进技能提升、技能重塑和为劳动力发展传授新技能的措施。目的是让受新冠病毒疫情影响的人和即将毕业的大学生掌握行业所需的技能。该措施还旨在通过非学历课程促进终身学习。

高等教育科研与创新部被委以重任，重组泰国的高等教育。该部门采用协作式职业融合教育方案作为关键框架，在公共部门的激励和配合下，由私营企业承担当地人力资源技能提升和技能重塑的主要工作，以应对不断的变化。

在协作式职业融合教育框架下，泰国高等教育科研与创新部、劳工部、教育部、泰国投资委员会和东部经济走廊等相关机构携手合作，确保国家支持投资人的技能需求，并推进泰国技术型经济的发展。泰国高等教育科研与创新部将采用新的框架确保学生具备全球社会经济发展所需的多种技能和职业适应能力，以及在沟通交流、数字通信和学习方面的全球技能。同时，泰国高等教育科研与创新部将启动更多选择，如增加职业学校学生和大学生提前毕业的灵活性，只要他们的技能和知识能够匹配需求，或者如果他们参加了技能培训课程，可将这些课程的学分转移到适合的课程中。

我相信，中泰两国在职业教育技能提升、技能重塑和新技能发展方面的国际合作潜力巨大。我也相信，随着“一带一路”倡议的不断深入，我们可以携手发展高质量的教育和培训，这将极大地有利于两国实现经济转型和社会发展的共同目标。

## ii. Thailand's Reskill, Upskill, and Newskill

**Pasupha Chinvarasopak, Minister Counsellor (Science and Technology) of Royal Thai Embassy, China**

Today I would like to share Thailand's Reskill, Upskill, and Newskill, which is the policy of the Ministry of Higher Education, Science, Research and Innovation (MHESI). The policy has three points of focus.

First, let me introduce Thailand's Ministry of Higher Education, Science, Research and Innovation which was established in 2019 by merging higher education, science, technology, and research to foster collaboration and synergies. This new ministry aims to promote, support, and direct higher education, science, research, and innovation to develop Thailand so as to keep up with the rapid change in the world today. Presently, there are 155 out of 175 universities in Thailand under the MHESI. Thai universities are classified into the following five strategic groups: The first group is Global and Frontier Research, which is producing world-class research, and building highly-skilled human resources to develop high-quality research that meets the global demand. The second group is Technology and Innovation, which is responsible for developing new technology and innovation to respond to Thailand's demands, especially in agricultural, industrial, and service areas. The third group is the Area-Based and Community, which teaches knowledge and technology to strengthen the development of local Thai communities. It also aims to create more jobs and generate domestic income, particularly in the farming sector. The fourth group is the Moral and Intellectual Cultivation, which incorporates religious teachings into university curricula. The fifth group is the Specialized and Professional, which builds specific capacity of Thai students in areas such as sports, music, drama, etc.

Second, in 2020, the MHESI launched the Reinventing University Initiative. This initiative is the first time that Thailand has categorized its universities into different groups based on their areas of expertise. The initiative's objective is to enhance Thai universities' excellence, and cultivate highly-skilled workers with the capacity to respond to Thailand's industrial needs. The initiative will reform the administrative system of Thai universities, improve the curriculum to match industry skills needs, support and encourage Thai universities to be more globally competitive, and lift their quality, which is a significant component of the Thai Government's development plan and economic model.

The initiative has a particular focus on producing highly-skilled workers in 12 key industries which may create many jobs for the next generation: automotive, smart electronics, affluent medical and wellness, tourism, agriculture and biotechnology, food for the future, automation and robotics, logistics and aviation, biofuels and biochemicals, digital industry, medical services, defense industry, and education development.

Under the Reinventing University Initiative, there are five platforms that universities will choose to focus on. The first is Manpower. This platform is to enhance teaching and learning quality. The second is Brainpower that covers reskilling, upskilling, and lifelong learning. The third is Global Perspective in which universities will work collaboratively with international partners. The fourth is Research and Innovation which aims to manage research and innovation efficiently. The fifth is Engagement, which is a platform for universities to increase domestic and international collaboration with both the government and non-government organizations.

Finally we come to the upskilling and reskilling program. This program formulates measures to promote upskilling, reskilling, and imparting new skills for workforce development. The objective is to equip those affected by COVID-19 and university students, who are soon to graduate with skills required by industry. The measure also aims to promote lifelong learning via non-degree curricula.

The MHESI has been entrusted to reorganize the country's tertiary education. The Ministry uses a Cooperative and Work-Integrated Education (CWIE) program as the key framework in which the private sector plays a big role in upskilling and reskilling the local human resources to cope with constant change, with incentives and collaboration by the public sector.

Under the CWIE framework, there are relevant agencies such as the MHESI, the Ministry of Labour, the Ministry of Education, the Thai Board of Investment, and the Eastern Economic Corridor are collaborating to ensure that the country supports investors' demand for skills, and advance Thailand's technology-orientated economy. The MHESI will adopt a new framework to ensure that students are equipped with multi-skill and multi-career adaptability that is demanded by the global socio-economy, and with global skills in communication, digital communication, and learning. The MHESI will initiate more options, such as increasing flexibility for vocational and university students to graduate ahead of schedule if their skills and knowledge match demand, or transferring credits from relative courses to the appropriate curriculum if they receive skills-building courses.

I believe that there will be great potential for international cooperation in vocational education in upskilling, reskilling, and new-skill development between

China and Thailand. With the continuous expansion of the Belt and Road Initiative, I also believe we can work together in developing high-quality education and training which will greatly benefit our mutual aims for economic transformation and social development.

# (三)

# 技能重塑与终身学习

**冈比亚国家认证与质量保证委员会质量保证部主任　拉明 · B · 曼内**

我演讲的题目是技能重塑与终身学习。简单来说，技能提升是指员工需要获得新的技能来帮助他们在当前的工作中表现得更好，而技能重塑是指员工需要知识和技能来从事不同的或新的工作。就这一点而言，涵盖非正式和正式学习的终身学习对参加职业技术教育与培训的人员至关重要，他们需要不断提升和重塑技能，才能紧跟行业变化和技术进步。

技能发展和终身学习一直是国际劳工组织的核心工作。国际劳工组织关于技能、培训和终身学习的职责依据其章程制定，并在国际劳工标准和其他文件中加以规定，以提高劳动者在自由、平等、安全和具备人性尊严的条件下获得体面工作的机会。因此每个成员国都有责任使其教育和培训政策符合上述要求。

正如我们现在所知，“工业 4.0”正在进行商业革新和数字化，并通过改变世界各地的劳动力和人员流动给全球化带来了强烈的影响。劳动力技能提升和重塑成为全球性问题。虽然许多教育组织和个人可能仍然想知道“工业 4.0”会对教育系统产生怎样的影响，但其中一些如今已经开始实施变革，并为未来做好准备，那时他们的业务将能通过人工智能和网络物理系统实现全球联通。

世界经济论坛在《2020 年就业前景报告》中预测，到 2025 年，全球将有一半的职员需要提升技能以获得新技术所需的技能。专家们还认为，“教育、培训和终身学习对提高个人、企业、经济和社会的整体利益都具有重要意义，特别是考虑到在全球经济中实现充分就业、消除贫困、社会包容和经济持续增长所面临的重大挑战”。

我们注意到一个积极的方面是，世界各国政府都认识到发展人的能力在促进全面就业、提高生产力和减轻贫困方面起着关键作用。我们还意识到，不同国家在经济和受教育与培训程度方面处于不同的水平。因此要确认和预测劳动力市场提供的真实机会种类，以便明确优先群体，找出他们所拥有的技能与雇主要求技能之间的主要差距，确定可采取的实际行动，使现有劳动者重塑和提升技能以满足需要，并弥补技能差距。

我们坚信，数字化和技术创新，如人工智能、自动化和机器人以及我们管理和选择使用它们的方式将对劳动力市场产生重大影响，影响人们的工作方式、从事的工作类型以及他们有效开展新任务所需的技能。现在的问题是，作为机构和政府，我们如何都能有效地为这些变化做好准备。

国际劳工组织认为，就教育与培训的质量和包容性而言，可持续发展目标 4 的具体目标远未实现。世界一半以上的儿童和青少年没有达到阅读方面的最低熟练程度标准，撒哈拉以南非洲地区面临的差距最大，对后续学习和技能发展将构成严重障碍。

2018 年，冈比亚开展了一项劳动力调查，按受教育程度对失业率进行分析，男性失业率为 42.9%，女性失业率为 57.1%。调查还显示，全国 15—64 岁的失业者有 234 725 人（失业率为 35.2%）。

我们强调，技能不匹配是当今劳动力市场上日益严峻的挑战，对工人、企业和未来工作都产生了诸多后果。因此人生各个阶段的技能培训、技能重塑和技能提升是人们获得体面工作机会和顺利过渡到劳动力市场的前提条件和推动力量。

政府和社会伙伴需要共同开发和实施新一代技能和终身学习的生态系统，以确保公平、全面地过渡到有助于经济、社会和环境方面可持续发展的未来工作。该系统应向所有人开放，特别应关注妇女、工作不稳定人群以及所有处于不利情况的群体和弱势群体。

我们呼吁“政府、雇主和工人重申对终身学习的承诺”，必须强调“教育、培训和终身学习是基础，应成为综合经济、财政、社会和劳动力市场政策和计划不可缺少的组成部分，并与之保持一致，这些政策和计划对可持续经济增长、创造就业和社会发展至关重要”。

最后，我想明确一点，技能重塑和技能提升不是一次性举措，应视之为规范。因此，任何希望具有竞争力的国家或组织都必须将技能重塑和技能提升作为其首要考虑事项。

# iii. Reskilling and Upskilling for Lifelong Learning

**Lamin B. Manneh, Director of Quality Assurance, National Accreditation and Quality Assurance Authority (NAQAA), Gambia**

My topic of discussion is upskilling and reskilling for lifelong learning. In simple terms, upskilling means that employees need to gain new skills to help them perform better in their current jobs whereas reskilling refers to the employees' needs for knowledge and skills to take different or new jobs. In this regard, lifelong learning, which covers informal and formal learning, will become essential for TVET learners, who will require continual upskilling and reskilling to keep up with industry changes and technological advances.

Skills development and lifelong learning have long been at the heart of the work of the International Labour Organization (ILO). The ILO's mandate for skills, training and lifelong learning is based on its constitution and has been set out in international labour standards and other instruments that promote opportunities for women and men to obtain decent work in conditions of freedom, equity, security and dignity. Thus, it is the responsibility of every member state to align their education and training policies to the above stated requirements.

As we now know that Industry 4.0 is revolutionizing and digitizing businesses and has a powerful impact on globalization by changing the workforce and the mobility of people around the world. The need for upskilling and reskilling the workforce is a global issue. While many educational organizations and individuals might still wonder how Industry 4.0 could affect the education system, some are implementing changes today and preparing for a future when artificial intelligence (AI) and cyber-physical systems can connect their businesses globally.

The World Economic Forum projected in its *Future of Jobs Report 2020* that half of all employees worldwide would need reskilling by 2025 in order to acquire the skills needs of new technology. Experts have also argued that "education, training and lifelong learning contribute significantly to promoting the interests of individuals, enterprises, the economy and society as a whole, especially considering the critical challenge of attaining full employment, poverty eradication, social inclusion and sustained economic growth in the global economy".

It is positive to note that governments all over the world are aware of the fact that the development of human capacity plays a critical role in overall employment promotion, productivity increase and poverty reduction. We are also aware that different countries are at different levels in terms of economies and attainment of education and training. Therefore, it is important to identify and anticipate the types of real labour market opportunities available in order to identify priority groups, identify the main gaps between the skills they have and those needed by employers, identify practical actions that can be taken to reskill and upskill existing workers to meet these needs, and bridge the skills gaps.

It is strongly believed that digitalization and technological innovations, such as AI, automation and robotics, and the way we manage and choose to use them will have a significant impact on labour markets, influencing how people work, the types of jobs they perform and the skills they need to carry out new tasks effectively. The question now is, how do we all effectively prepare ourselves as institutions and governments for these changes?

According to ILO, the targets of SDG 4 are far from being achieved with respect to the quality and inclusiveness of education and training. More than half of the world's children and adolescents do not meet minimum proficiency standards in reading, with sub-Saharan Africa facing the biggest gap, which is a major impediment to subsequent learning and skills development.

In Gambia, a Labour Force Survey was conducted in 2018 and the analyses of unemployment rates by the level of educational attainment show that unemployment rate is 42.9 percent for males and 57.1 percent for females. The survey further revealed that there are 234 725 unemployed persons aged 15-64 (35.2% unemployment rate) in the country.

It has been emphasized that skills mismatches are a growing challenge in today's labour markets, with many consequences for workers, businesses and the future of work. Thus, skilling, reskilling and upskilling through all stages of life is the precondition and an accelerator for people to access decent work opportunities and enable smooth transitions into labour markets.

A new generation of skills and a lifelong learning ecosystem need to be jointly developed and implemented by governments and social partners to ensure a just and inclusive transition to a future of work that contributes to sustainable development in the economic, social and environmental dimensions. The system should be accessible to all, with a specific focus on women, people in precarious employments and all disadvantaged and vulnerable groups.

There are calls on "governments, employers and workers to renew their commitment to lifelong learning" and it is important to emphasize that "education, training and lifelong learning are fundamental and should form an integral part of, and be consistent with, comprehensive economic, fiscal, social and labour market policies and programmes that are important for sustainable economic growth, employment creation and social development".

In conclusion, I want to make this clear that reskilling and upskilling are not one-off initiatives—they need to be considered as norms. Therefore, any country or organization that wants to be competitive, must consider reskilling and upskilling as a top priority.

## （四）

# 数字时代终身教育面临的挑战

巴西卢拉研究所所长　马尔西奥·波赫曼

数字化时代的到来为全球各个国家的组织在工作岗位提供方面带来了挑战。这种趋势无法扭转，无论是面对教育、科学和技术体系还是职业准备，我们都需要重新思考这种挑战在现在以及未来出现的可能性。

随着社会经济数字化的推进，当前对教育的重新定义有两个方面显得尤为突出。首先是强调有必要对终身教育体系进行重组，其次是让培训内容更能激发人们的好奇心，让人们能够更好地进行跨专业知识整合，这些专业领域与当今的信息系统密切相关。

随着文盲的增加，终身教育的观点应运而生。文盲现象在老一辈人中普遍存在，因为当时的教育比较匮乏，随着时间的推移，这些人将会逐步加入数字时代新的通信和信息交流方式。

对我们来说，至关重要的是应重新构建教育系统，使之能够解释终身的视角。同时，关键在于创造出能激发新一代青年的求知欲和好奇心，并能与现实互动的内容。这是因为一些传统教育方法往往难以激发当代青年的学习动力。

值得注意的是，过去的长期职业教育培训体系亟待做出一些变革。回想早期的农耕社会，我们会发现在农耕社会根本不存在如今所熟知的教育，即正规教育和职业培训。在过去，知识传递大多是通过代代相传实现，长者在农耕社会的威望一般较高，因为他们经历了岁月的洗礼，积累的知识越来越丰富。虽然教育不存在，但随着时间的推移，农业生产知识以及应季而生的行为在某种程度上也成为知识再生产的重要组成部分。这一点在那些人口分散的社会中表现尤为明显，因为在这些社会中，对知识传承的关注是明确的，允许各种不同文明随着时间推移保持其传统，同时结合一些来自与其他民族交往过程中的知识。

随着人类从农耕社会发展到工业社会，尤其是从18世纪工业革命开始，伴随着西方为主导的思潮、文艺复兴、启蒙运动逐步涌现，随着新启蒙教育路径、新型教育体系和职业教育与培训的产生，尤其是当你发现人口从农村迁移到城市时，城市的启蒙教育过程将与过去的农耕社会不同，父母会在居住地工作，子女会外出工作，不会再陪伴父母。通过这种方式建立的教育体系是为了让新一代能够做好准备，在现今的城镇社会中共存，并顺应工业化发展。这种教育体系是专为培养年轻一代设计的，将推动儿童、青少年和青年的培养，尤其是将来要接受高等教育成为医生、工程师等专业人士的青年。

这些启蒙教育体系看起来非常有效，能够与科学技术领域衔接并融合，对推进工业城市社会自身的发展至关重要，因为它通过技术创新解决了在信息与发展中面临的各种挑战。在建设工业化城镇社会的整个时期，东、西方世界在增加知识、扩大入学方面，都展现出了巨大的可能性，尤其是在解决文盲问题上，但直至工业化时期，文盲问题仍然存在。

信息和通信的运用打破了壁垒，让更多的社会阶层有机会获得知识、科学和技术。城镇化工业社会的时代被远远甩在身后，随着新时代的发展，数字化技术、新的信息与通信系统在某种程度上既能与教育和培训体系形成交互，又给其带来了亟待解决的挑战。实际上，我们正在迈向数字时代第一阶段的终点，在这个阶段，我们作为个体接收政府的信息，政府工作人员不断通过电脑、电话、平板电脑等工具将日常信息放到互联网上，诸如日程安排、通讯录、支出决策、视频、音乐等。这就容易引发深度的不平等，这与人们所处的社会阶层有很大关系，特别是在教育、收入等方面，这也加深了源自新数字化社会和经济发展所产生的不平等。确切地说，这就是我们为什么要认识到信息系统需要更好地连通，特别是涉及工作场所的信息系统，而政府和相关机构也正在为此努力，这样才能在面临挑战时更好地调整教育。对我们来说，最重要的是身份认同。我们不能再局限于只为儿童、青少年和年轻人提供教育，成年人和老年人也要和现在这个新的数字化社会连接。为此，新型学校要预先考虑这一新的需求。因此终身学习的理念在世界很多地方都已经确立，甚至是在一些公司里、社区里也是如此。

最后，我们需要认识今天的教育体系，它有着悠久的历史渊源、众所周知的经典理论，在某种程度上，它们很难和新的科技产生关联。今天的教育着眼于未来的视角，因此需要认识到大部分信息和知识都可以从互联网本身获得。我们真正需要的是形成一种新的方法论，它能够激发反思、抽象概念，能够与不同种类的知识互联互通，能为专业化的发展路径带来突破，也使获得越来越多的知识成为可能。因此在科技更新教育的框架下，对职业教育培训体系进行反思尤为必要。特别是当政府、民间团体等意识到在面临新数字时代兴起的时候，我们要做的事情还有很多。

## iv. The Challenge of Lifelong Education in the Digital Age

**Marcio Pochmann, President of the Institute of Lula, Brazil**

The advent of the digital age challenges job production in organizations in different countries of the world. As it could not be reversible, the education, science and technology systems as well as the preparation for work demand a rethink about its possibilities in our time now and the time to come.

Two aspects stand out in the redefinition of education for the present time in the face of the advancing of the social economic digitization. The first aspect to be highlighted is related to the need to reorganize the lifelong education system and the second aspect has to do with the prevalence of training content with greater capacity to awaken the curiosity and integration of knowledge beyond the areas of specialization that the information system today is strongly connected to.

The perspective of a lifelong education results from the increase of illiteracy, a kind of lack of education that is widespread among the older generations. They would join the new ways of communication and information coming from the digital age in the process of time.

Reorganizing the educational system so that it can account for the perspective of a lifetime, seems crucial to us. At the same time, the production of content that interacts with reality and that stimulates thirst for knowledge and curiosity in the new generations becomes essential, since certain traditional educational methods tend to have some difficulties in reaching a higher motivation with the youth of our time.

It is important to note that the long-term education training system for work in the past needs some changes. If we go back in time and remember the period of the early agrarian societies, we will realize that in this period, education as we know today, the formal education and training for work, were practically inexistent in agrarian societies. It was generally done by the passing-on of knowledge from the elders down. In general, the elderly were more recognized within these agrarian societies because they had knowledge accumulated throughout the time. Although education was inexistent, agricultural production knowledge and the behavior corresponding to weather change was somehow an important part of the reproduction of knowledge over time. This is accomplished especially in the sphere of the agglomerated communities that had thinned out throughout the territory in which the concern about the passing-on of knowledge was specific and allowed for different civilizations over time to maintain tradition and at the same time the incorporation of knowledge coming from the relationship with other peoples.

In the industrial societies, which came after the agrarian period, especially from the 18th century on with the Industrial Revolution, with the Western-led thoughts, Renaissance and Illuminism, with a new formative circuit, new educational systems, education and training for work emerging, especially when you start to see the displacement of the population from the countryside to the cities, the formative process will no longer take place in the city as in the agrarian past. Parents will go to work where they live, and their children will not accompany them in the exercise of working outside the home. This way, the educational system is established with the objective of preparing the new generations for co-existence within societies that are now urban, submitted to the industrial dynamics, and the educational systems are specifically conducted for the generations of the younger age group who will constitute the segment conducive to the training of children, adolescents and the youth especially some of whom will pursue higher education to become doctors, engineers and professionals.

These formative systems, seem to be very effective, articulating and integrating into the fields of science and technology, which are crucial to the advancement of industrial urban societies themselves by innovating technologically and addressing the challenges that arise in these societies both in information and development. This entire period of the building of industrial and urban societies that take place in the Western and Eastern worlds demonstrate enormous possibility of the increase of knowledge and schooling, especially addressing illiteracy which was lingering on until then.

Therefore, the exercise of communication and information has been breaking down barriers and allowing for more segments of society to have access to knowledge, education, science and technology. The era of the urban-industrial society is falling more and more behind, as a new era is established. Digitization, the new information and communication system, which in a certain way interacts with and poses challenges which need addressing on the education and training systems. We're practically wrapping up the first phase of the digital age, when we as individuals are stuck in the governments that have been putting their everyday information onto the Internet through computers, telephones, tablets, among others. The information such as agenda, phonebook, payment decisions, videos, music, etc. was actually placed on the Internet. And this generated profound inequalities in relation to the different segments within the societies especially in terms of education and income, etc., which has deepened exactly an inequality generated from these advances concerning the new digitized society and economy. Precisely, that is why it seems important to recognize that the information systems, especially concerning the workplace, require a better connection that is being done by the government and institutions with the objective of better adapting education in the face of the challenges that are being posed. What seems to us is of utmost importance is the aspect of identification. We can no longer be restricted to the education system that only accounts for children, adolescents and young people since the adult and the elderly are supposed to be connected to this new digitized society, and to this end the new school presupposes to account for this new configuration, thus the idea of lifelong education has already been established even among companies and some communities in different parts of the world.

Lastly, we need to identify the formative system that we have today. It has long-standing historical ties and well-known classic methodologies, and in a way struggle to have a connection relationship with new technologies. Today's education is done through the perspective of the future, therefore requires recognizing that much of the stock of information and knowledge is available on the Internet itself. What we certainly need is to move forward in a methodology that stimulates reflection, the abstract, and the ability to interconnect with different kinds of knowledge, bringing a breakthrough to the trajectory of specialization, which allows for acquiring more and more knowledge. Therefore the system of training for work within the framework of a renewal of the education in science and technology seems to be essential to be reflected upon, especially when governments and the civil society realize that there is much to be done in the face of the emergence of the new digital age.

## （五）

# 通识化与专业化：职业体系中的技能提升与重塑

瑞士技能联合会主席　安德烈·布里

在瑞士，职业培训注重在企业中的实践经验，从而确保以市场为导向的培训以及日常的技能重塑和技能提升。这一制度对进入职业教育体系的年轻人很有吸引力。据一项完全基于瑞士的研究，目前，尚存的数百万个工作岗位中，预期未来将对其中约 100 万个岗位不再有任何需求。同时，未来也会再创造约 100 万个新的就业机会。这个数字是否准确并不重要，但它应该能够表明，我们未来将面临具有挑战性的变化。以下简要总结了产生变化的原因——我们也正是从这些要素出发来培养新的能力。

与国际体系不同的是，瑞士进行的是通才教育，人们完成主要培训后，就可以继续专业化培训。而国际体系往往在早期就注重专业化培训，由于缺乏重要的基础知识，开展技能重塑就非常有难度了。

在今年的世界技能大赛上，我们有一些方法想与大家分享。在一定程度上，这些方法已经在瑞士进行了应用。第一个方法我们称为数字徽章或微学分，这意味着小型活动——如学习新的软件、学习商业算术或职业安全再培训——都以小型证书的形式得以确认。这些证书的总和显示了员工所拥有的额外技能。第二个方法是逐步开展技能重塑，瑞士已开展相关工作，它可以很好地记录员工在工作期间的学习成果。这种模式需要与教育机构、行业协会和企业通力合作，使年轻人能在早期就为新的任务做好准备，而现有员工，比如说 50 岁以上的员工，则可以进行适度的培训。这很有挑战性，尤其是对年纪较大的员工来说，因为与职业生涯还很长的年轻人相比，他们接受进一步广泛培训的意愿要低得多。

最后，我们还要问问自己，哪些技能是真正需要再额外获得的，是在将来会有需求的。我认为此处还可另辟新路，那就是让年轻人及时做好准备，加强这些技能，关注这些技能。在瑞士技能联合会，我们试着以 Mission Future（未来使命）软件来做到这一点，向年轻人展示他们所拥有的优势，以便他们能够在日常工作中具体使用这些优势。这些技能将使年轻人重塑或提高自己的技能。这些技能是在工作中无法学到的，但你必须让自己得到提升，因为它们对未来的生存至关重要。我相信到那时，技能重塑和提升是每个人都理所当然要面对的事情，拥有这些技能后就可以更具灵活性地工作了。

## v. Generalization and Specialization: Up- and Re-skilling in Occupational Systems

André Burri, Director of SwissSkills, Switzerland

In Switzerland, we focus on the practical experience in the companies in vocational training. This ensures market-orientated training and daily re-skilling and up-skilling. This system is very attractive for young people entering the vocational education system. According to a study, which is purely related to Switzerland, of the current several millions of jobs, about one million will no longer be needed in the future. On the other hand, about one million new jobs will be created. The accuracy of this number is not crucial, but it should show that we have a challenging change ahead of us. The reasons for the change are briefly summarized as follows, and it is precisely from these elements that we will have to develop new capabilities.

In contrast to the international systems, we in Switzerland work with a generalist education and then specialize further once we finish the main training. International systems tend to focus on specialization at an early stage, which makes re-skilling rather difficult because the basic foundation is not there.

We have some approaches to this at WorldSkills International, which I would like to share with you. To some extent, these have been already applied in Switzerland. The first is what we call digital badging or the idea of micro crediting. This means that small activities, such as learning new software, learning commercial arithmetic or further training in occupational safety, are confirmed in the form of a small certificate. The sum of the certificates shows the additional skills the employee has. The second is re-skilling in small steps. It already takes place in Switzerland and employees' achievements "on the job" can be well documented. This is a kind of cooperation that can be ensured together with educational institutions, with associations and with companies, and thus an ongoing process takes place so that young people are prepared for the new tasks at an early stage and existing employees, let's say over 50, can be gently trained. It is a challenge, especially with older employees, because the willingness for extensive further training is significantly lower than young people, who still have a large part of their working life ahead of them.

Finally, we also have to ask ourselves, which skills are really additionally needed and will be in demand? I think there is a second approach here. And this second approach is to prepare young people in a timely manner to strengthen these skills and to become aware of these skills. We, at SwissSkills, try to do this in the form of the "Mission Future", where we try to show the young people what strengths they have, so that they can use them specifically in their everyday work. These are the skills that will enable young people to re-skill or up-skill themselves. Skills that you can't learn on the job but you have to develop for yourself are extremely important for you to survive in this future environment. I believe that re-skilling and up-skilling will then be a matter of course for everyone, which will enable us to work more flexibly.

# (六)

# 技能教育与培训的新使命

## ——以终身学习助力新时代技能强国战略实施

中国成人教育协会会长　高文兵

中国成人教育协会成立于41年前，是中国组织和推进成年人继续教育和终身学习的非营利性社会组织，是国际成人教育协会单位会员。促进和发展青年与成年人的职业技能教育和培训，是协会的重要任务之一。长期以来，协会努力为构建覆盖人人、开放包容的技能型社会，培养能工巧匠、培养特殊文化艺人、培养乡村致富带头人等工作积极贡献力量。结合本次大会主题和本论坛主题，分享三方面想法。

### 1. 新时代需要重塑技能教育与培训

当前，中国正迈进在全面建设社会主义现代化国家新征程中。中国政府高度重视技能教育与培训，将它作为终身学习体系的重要组成部分，并制定新时代技能强国的战略、策略和途径。习近平主席指出，“职业教育前途广阔、大有可为”“要培养更多高素质技术技能人才、能工巧匠、大国工匠”。2021年，中国政府相继发布了《关于推动现代职业教育高质量发展的意见》《“技能中国行动”实施方案》等政策文件。今年，新修订的《中华人民共和国职业教育法》颁布。这些为中国新时期培养高质量技能人才、构建技能型社会、建设技能强国提供了完整系统的法律和政策保障。

当前，中国经济发展已由高速增长阶段转向高质量发展阶段。从全球看，在科技革命、数字经济迅速发展、产业结构快速变革的同时，又叠加了新冠病毒疫情、经济增长乏力等严峻形势。回应新形势新变化对与日俱增的新型技能人才的需求，我们应大力推进职业技术教育高质量发展，积极推动技能重塑。应在以下方面发力。

构建现代技能形成体系。深化产教融合、校企合作，提升职业教育适应性，着重完善职业技能培训制度，建立灵活包容、面向全民的终身技能开发体系。

完善技能人才发展制度。引导企业提升技术技能人才经济待遇，加大对技术技能人才的认定与奖励力度，健全技术技能人才职业晋升通道与发展机制。

营造崇尚技能社会氛围。加强崇尚职业劳动的舆论引导，通过劳动教育、劳模宣传、技能大赛等形式，大力弘扬劳模精神、劳动精神、工匠精神。

深化技能重塑相关研究。要针对推进高质量发展进程中的重点、难点、痛点、堵点，开展有针对性的研究，使理论创新根植于实践，服务于战略需要。

**2. 新时代的终身学习要求技能重塑**

《中国教育现代化 2035》提出“更加注重终身学习”，并把“建成服务全民终身学习的现代教育体系”确定为 2035 年主要发展目标。建设国家重视技能、社会崇尚技能、人人学习技能、人人拥有技能的技能型社会，要通过社会各界的共同努力，实现技术技能“人人皆学、处处能学、时时可学”。从终身学习视角看:

在学习者的维度上，在数字经济、科技革命、产业变革的背景下，获取新的技能是终身学习的必然要求，技能学习要与新产业、新业态相向而行。技能重塑是人类生存的需求、生产的需求、生活的需求乃至生命意义之所在。这是我们人类共同面临的问题。

在时间维度上，充分发挥职前职后教育一体化的作用。学历职前教育和职后非学历教育，要重塑各自的“教育”“培训”功能，既在思想启蒙、知识积累的基础教育方面，又在新技能培训、获取等实践应用方面。非学历的职业培训与学习适用对象更多元，学习方式更多样，是终身学习体系的关键组成部分。

在空间维度上，覆盖学校、企业、社会培训机构等多元场所。学校具有社会性和公益性，是基础性和通用性教育与培训的主体。企业具有营利性，是专门性和特殊性技能培训的主体。社会培训机构角色多样，可以成为灵活提供个性化和补充性的教育与培训的主体。

在国家资格框架维度上，应实现不同时间和空间学习等值融通，以等级的形式对学习和工作中完成任务、处理问题、研究创新等方面的能力进行描述，推进学习成果互认。尤其还应积极探索面向成年人的先前学习认可机制。

**3. 推进人类技能共同体构建，加快技能重塑**

在经济全球化和数字经济背景下，构建人类技能命运共同体是现实所需，也是历史必然。为此需要开展务实有效的国际合作，我们提出以下建议。

以技能组织机构为载体，建立畅通有效的对话机制。充分发挥专业技能组织的关键作用，将世界各国紧密联系起来，通过畅通有效的对话机制，合力解决在技能建设过程中遇到的共同问题。

以专业技能赛事为抓手，促进技能经验的交流共享。以世界技能大赛等国际专业技能赛事为载体，搭建技能展示和技能教育的交流平台，促进全球对技能问题的关注和技能经验的共享。

以技能交流合作为核心，形成开放包容的技能文化。组织开展专项技能项目交流研讨，选派技能青年开展互访实习交流，组织职业能力建设管理人员出国交流等，促进不同国家间技能重塑经验的传播、开放包容的技能文化的形成。

以职业资格证书为纽带，促进技能人才的合理流动。根据技术技能形成的一般规律，探索职业资格证书国际互认管理办法，推动区域性资历框架建设，促进技术技能人才合理的跨境流动，实现更大范围的技能交流与共享。

中国成人教育协会期望与各位加强交流合作。

## （七）

# 大力发展技工教育

中华人民共和国人力资源和社会保障部职业能力建设司技工院校管理处处长　王　飞

技工教育是国民教育体系和人力资源开发的重要组成部分，承担着为经济社会发展培养高素质技能人才的重要任务，是开展技工教育、职业培训、技能鉴定、竞赛集训、公共实训、就业服务等工作的综合性技工教育培训基地。技工教育源自新中国成立初期的失业工人转业训练，经计划体制“一厂一校”发展到市场经济体制下专门培养技术工人的职业教育类型。习近平总书记指示要大力发展技工教育。李克强总理批示要紧扣需求发展现代职业教育、办好技工院校，发挥全国 2 000 多所技工院校作用，扩大招生规模，纳入各地统一的招生平台，并召开国务院常务会议研究进一步增加技校招生规模。新修订的《中华人民共和国职业教育法》首次对技工教育、技工学校、技师学院作出规定，为技工教育发展奠定了法制基础。截至 2021 年底，全国有技工院校 2 492 所，在校生 426.7 万人；当年招生 167.2 万人，开展职业技能培训 600.7 万人次，各项指标再创新高；毕业生就业率继续保持在 97% 以上，优质技工院校毕业生供不应求。技工院校历经几十年发展形成鲜明办学特色和独特优势，在我国工业化、现代化进程中发挥了不可替代的重要作用。

坚持弘扬工匠精神，大力培养面向生产服务一线的中高级技能人才。技工院校把立德树人作为根本任务，将劳模精神、劳动精神、工匠精神融入人才培养全过程，培养学生养成劳动观念、劳动态度、劳动习惯和劳动情怀。技工院校以培养综合职业能力为核心，以培养输送生产服务一线技能人才为目标，结合产业升级和技术进步规划设置专业、组织实施教学、强化生产实习，逐步发展为产业技术工人的培养摇篮和成长基地。

坚持就业导向，着力强化校企合作。技工院校传承企业办学基因，以校企合作为基本办学制度，长期坚持“校企双制、工学一体”，专业设置对接企业需求、教学内容对接职业标准、教学过程对接生产过程。通过校企共同招生招工、共商专业规划课程开发、共组师资队伍、共建实训基地，将企业典型工作任务转换为教学内容，将学习过程与工作过程融通合一，努力实现技能人才与企业用人无缝衔接，毕业生深受企业欢迎。

坚持全方位服务，系统开展技能人才培养培训、评价选拔、职业指导。技工院校在开展学制教育的同时，注重发挥师资、实训等优势，设立企业培训服务站，积极面向企业职工、农民工等就业重点群体和贫困及脱贫人员开展职业技能培训，每年培训量500余万人次。坚持“双证”并重，为毕业生和培训学员提供职业技能鉴定和等级评价服务，支持帮助他们获得学历证书、培训证书和职业资格证书（职业技能等级证书），提供全流程职业指导和就业服务。

坚持突出重点群体，面向农村和城市新市民生源针对性赋能。技工院校在校生85%以上来自农村户籍家庭，30%以上来自贫困家庭，绝大多数孩子由于传统学历教育升学无望，希望通过就读技工院校掌握一技之长，实现就业。技工院校帮助他们成长成才，成为全面发展的社会主义建设者和新时代产业工人，为农村家庭子女创造人生出彩的机会。

坚持提升人才培养质量，努力代表中国技能走向世界。技工院校长期注重学生技能培养。中国代表团在第44、45届世界技能大赛中荣登金牌榜、奖牌榜，荣获团体总分第一名。金牌选手中，技工院校学生达80%左右；获奖选手中，技工院校学生达60%以上，极大地提升了我国职业技能在世界的影响力。江苏省常州技师学院学生宋彪以全场最高分荣获第44届世界技能大赛参赛选手最高奖项——阿尔伯特·维达大奖。

下一步，我们将深入贯彻落实党中央、国务院决策部署要求，重点做好以下工作：一是加强党建引领，在公办技工院校建立党组织领导的校长负责制；二是统筹推动技工教育“十四五”规划实施，通过任务实施以评促建，加大政策和资金支持力度；三是在全国技工院校大力推进工学一体化技能人才培养模式，力争在“十四五”末期实现“百千万”目标；四是坚持多元办学，巩固技工院校学制教育招生和职业培训规模，组织发动各类技工院校落实职业培训职责，面向企业职工和就业重点群体高质量开展政府补贴性培训和市场化社会培训；五是研究制定支持企业办技工院校支持政策，大力推动技工教育集团（联盟）建设；六是指导技工院校扎实做好学生实习、资助管理、疫情防控等各项基础工作。

# （八）

# 香港职业专才教育：挑战与策略

香港都会大学校长　林群声

我很高兴与各位分享我对大学教育，特别是职业专才教育（以下简称“职专教育”）方面的挑战及策略的看法。

职专教育是政府的一项重要任务。因为职专教育培养出具备合适能力以满足就业市场需求的人才，它提升了社会向上流动的机会，使劳动力技能得以提升和重塑，以应对日新月异的经济形势和大众对终身学习的需求。职专教育在香港特别行政区也扮演着重要的角色。过去几十年，香港已经从一个制造业枢纽发展成为国际金融和服务中心。这种转变也影响职专教育在香港的生态，譬如我们建立了相关的基础架构和模式，即资历架构。

世界各国政府和教育机构也一直在职专教育中发挥着积极作用。然而，职专教育的发展依然存在障碍。我会谈到职专教育面临的三个关键挑战以及相关应对策略，还会举例分享我所任职的香港都会大学是如何推动职专教育发展的。

职专教育面对的第一个主要挑战是数字化。数字技术迅速发展，重新划分了人与机器之间的劳动分工，从而导致全球和当地劳动力格局发生了重大变化。根据世界经济论坛最近的一份报告预测，到 2025 年，将有 8 500 万个工作岗位可能被技术自动化所取代，如数据录入、会计和工厂装配工等相关的岗位。与此同时，将会有 9 700 万个工作岗位顺应数字化应运而生，如人工智能、数字化营销和流程自动化等岗位。这一现象在香港也引起了极大关注。据普华永道最近一项关于就业保障的调查显示，56% 的香港受访者表示他们担心由于技术自动化而失业，而 41% 的人则表示他们的工作将会因为技术的进步而被淘汰。

这些工作不仅对技术的要求越来越高，而且呈现出多样化和短期化的特点。这带来了第二个挑战，即越来越多的公司会通过线上平台来雇用员工从事短期工作。2020—2021 年，美国和欧洲估计分别约有 800 万人和 700 万人从事这种“零工”。同样，在香港估计也有大约 70 万人（占香港总劳动力约 1/5）曾经做过这种工作。由于越来越多的个人和机构面临数字化和“零工”经济带来的数字化转型，劳动力的技能提升和重塑变得至关重要。对教育工作者而言，这意味着需要培养专职技能人才，来服务、领导和推动社会和经济发展。

为了帮助年轻学生或在职人士有效地为香港作出贡献，香港都会大学将适合不同学科的数字技术融入专业课程中，并且在质量保证体系中引进了学术和行业专家，以确保课程符合职业和专业需求。

传统职专教育面对的第三个挑战是缺乏灵活性。我们所录取的学生，尤其是那些在职人士，他们的背景各不相同，有些学生具备一定的学科基础知识，有些累积了较多的技能在身，而有些则完全没有。他们当中有些人可能只需要深化对某一门课程的知识理解，而其他人则需要完成整个学位课程。若一刀切地要求所有学生按照同一种路径学习，则可能会浪费一部分学生的努力，并使得那些需要提升和重塑技能的人望而却步。

为了应对这一挑战，香港都会大学将课程设置得非常灵活，学生可以选择在不同阶段开始或完成某一课程的学习，亦可以选择修读单独的科目。这种灵活的修读模式有效地满足学习者的弹性需求。举个例子，我们的研究生课程由三个部分组成，学生每修读完一个部分都能获得相应的资格证书，若顺利完成所有三个部分的学习，学生便可以获得硕士学位。此外，还设置了灵活的学分机制，学生可以自行决定他们每个学期想要修读的科目数量。当学生可享受更大的学习灵活性和能选择合适的学习模式时，他们不仅会对自己的学习负起责任，而且还会适当地控制自己的学习进度。

这些年来，香港都会大学一直大力支持职专教育在香港的发展，目前是香港提供职专教育的最大规模自资院校，为高中毕业生和在职人士提供约 220 个课程。就全日制课程而言，香港每六名本科生中就有一名就读于香港都会大学。

最后，我想强调，职专教育要克服数字化和“零工”经济带来的挑战，必须确保课程设置符合行业对专业人员的培养、技能提升和技能重塑的需求，而且职专教育也应该灵活满足学习者的不同学习需要。香港都会大学诚挚欢迎与各界同仁合作，共同应对以上挑战。

# viii. Vocational and Professional Education in Hong Kong: Challenges and Strategies

**Paul LAM Kwan-sing, President of Hong Kong Metropolitan University, China**

I am delighted to share my thoughts and observations about the challenges and strategies in relation to university education, especially vocational and professional education, or VPE.

We know that VPE is a priority of governments, because first, it produces talents with the knowledge and skills that meet the needs of industry. Second, it enhances upward social mobility. And third, it upskills and reskills the workforce to meet the needs of the ever-changing economy and to provide lifelong learning. VPE also plays an important role in Hong Kong SAR. Over the past several decades, Hong Kong SAR has evolved from a manufacturing hub into an international financial and service centre. This evolution has influenced the landscape of VPE in Hong Kong SAR, such as the establishment of related infrastructure like the Qualifications Framework.

Governments and educational institutions worldwide have taken an active role in developing and promoting VPE. But there are still barriers to VPE development. I will talk about three key challenges to VPE and some strategies for addressing these challenges. I will also share what my institution, Hong Kong Metropolitan University, or HKMU, has been doing to support VPE.

A predominant challenge in VPE is digitalisation, as data technologies are rapidly reshaping the division of labour between humans and machines, leading to major changes in the landscape of the global and local workforce. According to a recent report by the World Economic Forum, it is estimated that by 2025, 85 million jobs may be displaced by technology automation, such as positions related to data entry, accounting and assembly, while 97 million jobs adapted to digitalisation will emerge, such as positions in AI, digital marketing and process automation. This phenomenon causes great concern to workers in Hong Kong SAR. In a recent Pricewaterhous Coopers (PWC) survey on job security, 56% of Hong Kong workers expressed concern about potentially losing their jobs because of technology and automation, and 41% of respondents expected their jobs to become obsolete owing to technology advances.

Jobs are not only becoming increasingly technologically demanding; they have also grown more diverse and short-term. This poses another challenge in that an increasing number of companies hire staff for short-term tasks through online platforms. It is estimated that from 2020 to 2021, eight million people in the US and seven million people in Europe are engaged in 'gig' work. And in Hong Kong SAR, an estimated one-fifth of the workforce, about 700 000 people, have been involved in this type of work at one time or another. As more and more individuals and organisations undergo digital transformation resulting from digitalisation and the gig economy, the need for upskilling and reskilling the workforce becomes even more critical. This means that it is important for educators to nurture talent that has the vocational and professional competence to serve, lead and ensure the sustainable development of our community and economy.

To help our students who are young or working adults contribute effectively to Hong Kong SAR, HKMU incorporates in the curricula of our qualification programmes suitable types of digital skills by discipline, and builds into our quality assurance system experts from academia and industry to ensure the curricula fit Hong Kong SAR's vocational and professional needs.

The third challenge to conventional VPE is its lack of flexibility. Students admitted to a study programme, especially working adults, may have diverse backgrounds. Some may have a certain basic knowledge of the discipline and some may have already developed greater competence, but some may have none. Also, some may just need to develop an understanding of the knowledge in just one course in a degree programme, while others may need to complete the whole programme. Pushing all students to follow the same pathway could waste the time and effort of some students and drive some of those who need upskilling and reskilling away.

To address this challenge, HKMU has made the programmes more flexible so that students can enter and exit a programme at different levels and select individual courses to meet their needs. Our multiple entry and exit options in study programmes meet learners' needs for flexibility. For example, a postgraduate programme may consist of three parts, each of which leads to a certificate qualification, but by completing all three parts, the students may obtain a master's degree. We also offer a flexible credit system. Students may decide on the number of courses that they wish to take each semester. When students are given greater learning flexibility and suitable study options, they not only take responsibility for their own learning, but also take proper control of their learning pace.

Over the years, HKMU has put great effort into supporting the development of VPE in Hong Kong SAR. We are now the biggest self-financing VPE provider in Hong Kong SAR, with about 220 programmes provided for school leavers and working adults. In full-time programmes, one in every six bachelor degree students in Hong

Kong SAR is studying at HKMU.

To conclude, I have highlighted that VPE should overcome the challenges of digitalisation and gig economy by ensuring that curricula suit the needs of industry for nurturing, upskilling and reskilling professionals, and that VPE should be flexible in meeting the diverse learning needs of our students. HKMU welcomes collaboration to overcome these challenges together.

# （九）

# 新时代城市终身职业技能培训体系的建构

中关村学院院长　程洪莉

随着互联网、人工智能、区块链等新技术的运用，催生了许多新产业和业态，就业创业能力不断增强，引发了人才培养、就业模式等方面的变革。特别是后疫情时代，产业的需求、企业的用工方式、劳动者的就业观念等都发生了变化，至少四类人亟待技能重塑。

一是不断有大批存量劳动力要转岗。这些人包括在产业转型升级过程中被淘汰的劳动力、城市化进程中的农民、复转军人以及城市中自愿尝试新职业的人员，都需要重新参加技能培训来实现自身人力资本的增值。例如，在我校考取 2018 级健康管理专业专科学习的 62 名成年人学员中，就有 2 名留学回国的博士、24 名硕士和 5 名复转军人，他们的目标就是转岗。

二是我国每年大约有 1 500 万新增劳动力要就业。今年我国仅高校毕业生总数就将达到 1 076 万人，但是企业招不到合适的人才，很多毕业生找不到工作，解决人才需求的这种结构性矛盾，就需要岗前最后“一公里”的培训。我们还有大批的初高中毕业生需要进行职业技能学习。

三是要满足战略新兴产业紧缺人才的需求。海淀区战略新兴产业专业技术紧缺人才需求目录显示，紧缺人才主要集中在大数据、智能智造等六大战略新兴产业，高等学校一些传统专业培养的学生需要技能重塑。2020 年，北京人工智能产业急需的技术型人才缺口为 29.94 万人，技能型人才缺口为 16.46 万人，现有劳动力的技术技能储备需要更新与提升。

四是创新创业人员群体的需要。随着产业升级，涌现出一大批创业者。2016 年，中关村科技园区管理委员会与我校联合举办的“中小企业自主创新大讲堂”由原来的每月 1 期增加到后来的每月 2 期，仍是一座难求。

因此解决人才、劳动力和市场需求匹配的问题，需要构建终身职业技能培训体系，进行技能重塑。那么新时代怎样构建城市终身职业技能培训体系，我想有这样四个方面。

一是要建立一个终身职业技能培训系统。首先，这个系统将实现学校、行业、企业、社会等职业技能培训的跨界融合，为每个学习者的个性化培训和学习需求提供基本的服务。实现劳动者、培训机构、企业、人力资源组织、行业协会、社区与政府部门等多主体参与、全方位资源及信息等联通共享。其次，这一系统将满足个人终身的职业素养教育、基本技术技能学习、继续教育等需求，覆盖在校学生、企业职工、转岗人员、创新创业及退休人员等所有群体，同时也满足每个个体在学习形式、内容、时间、结果等全方位的需要。这一系统将以互联网、大数据和人工智能等现代技术为支撑，建设培训就业一体化、服务功能多元化的信息服务平台。

二是要制定一系列终身职业技能培训的国家制度和区域政策。2018 年，国务院印发了《关于推行终身职业技能培训制度的意见》，提出了宏观的政策指导。作为政府各级管理部门，要完善相应政策，围绕终身职业技能培训系统，建立配套的职业技能培训市场准入制度、财政支持政策、组织保障措施、资源分配制度、技能人才评价标准、质量监督管理办法等保障制措施，以促进终身职业技能培训的发展。

三是要建立一个学历教育与技能培训相互衔接的课程运行机制。该机制融合学历教育、短期培训和职业资格（1+X 职业技能等级证书）培训，按照岗位工作过程，在构建职业教育新的课程体系中，将专业课程与职业资格证书标准进行有机融合，实现每一门专业课程既是学历教育的必修课，也是一门独立的职业技能培训课程；一门或几门专业课程同时对应相关职业资格证书或 1+X 职业技能等级证书。实现学习者可自主选择学习方式，既可以按职业学历教育课程体系，从公共基础课到专业核心课再到专业拓展课的系统学习，取得毕业证书后就业，又可以选直接学习相关的专业核心课或专业拓展课，考取相关职业资格证书或 1+X 职业技能等级证书后，直接走向工作岗位或创业。通过这一机制，学生与员工之间身份随意切换，实现“入职即入学、工学交替、校企协同”。我校的科技服务学院与 4 个科技园区孵化器合作的中小企业运营与管理专业采用的就是这个运行机制，非常受欢迎。

四是建立和完善三种高质量终身职业技能培训模式。“工学一体化”培训模式，以产业转型升级、企业用工需求和职业活动需要为导向，以培养高素质技能型人才为核心，通过校企合作、工学交替、产教融合的方式，建立校企人才双向流动机制，形成“政府引导、企业为主、院校参与”的职业技能培训模式，全面提升劳动者职业技能水平。“职业培训包”模式，根据国家职业技能标准或企业岗位技术规范，建立国家通用的“基本职业培训包”和行业“特色职业培训包”，纳入国家职业教育课程体系中。创新创业培训模式，它是城市终身职业技能培训的通用培训。遵循创业逻辑，我校研究出创新创业的“五创理论”，即创意、创新、创造、创业、创富。通过产品创意激发，形成创新方案并设计制作，完成产品试制和用户体验的产品创造，按照一定的业务逻辑和商业模式完成最初的创业，在发展到一定规模后，通过融资路演和资本运作，最终实现创富。通过创新创业能力递进发展路径，帮助不同的培训对象，实现不同的培训目标。2017 年，我校创办该培训模式以来，共孵化了 17 家科技创新企业，帮助 2 家企业融资超过 2 000 万元，其中一家企业在新三板融资平台上市。

新时代构建终身职业技能培训体系是缓解技能人才短缺的结构性矛盾、提升就业质量的根本举措，需要国家制度的支持、个人与组织的终身学习理念支撑，才能实现技能的重塑。

# 九
# 职业教育助推全球减贫进程论坛

协助组织单位：北京师范大学中国扶贫研究院

# IX. Vocational Education for Poverty Reduction and Inclusive Growth

Co-organizer: China Institute for Poverty Reduction, Beijing Normal University

02
克利奥法斯·高井佐
Cleophas Takaiza

03
巴卡图拉·恩祖齐·玛丽·玛德琳
Bakatula Nzuzi Marie Madeleine

04
宁亚宁
Ning Yaning

05
段福生
Duan Fusheng

06
杨天仪
Yang Tianyi

**分享各国技能减贫有效做法，介绍中国职业教育助力脱贫攻坚案例，共同探讨职业教育助推国际减贫行动策略。**

This session introduces effective global practice of reducing poverty through skills, including China's experiences of VTE facilitating poverty alleviation, and explores the strategies of promoting international poverty alleviation through VTE jointly.

## （一）

## 职业教育助推全球减贫进程论坛情况概述

北京师范大学中国扶贫研究院　董　菡、王嘉茜

2022 年 8 月 19—20 日，由中华人民共和国教育部、中国联合国教科文组织全国委员会、天津市人民政府共同主办的首届世界职业技术教育发展大会在天津顺利召开。习近平主席向大会发来贺电，孙春兰副总理向大会致辞。职业教育助推全球减贫进程论坛作为十四个平行论坛之一，旨在从国际视野和国内实践两个切入点出发，深入探讨职业教育在全球减贫中的内在优势和作用路径，总结经验启示并创新职教模式，以实现更好、更精准地服务于中国乡村振兴和全球减贫进程。本论坛

采取线上和线下相结合的方式进行，由中国乡村振兴与发展研究中心主任、北京师范大学中国扶贫研究院院长张琦主持，来自 10 个国家和地区政府部门、高等院校、职业技术学院、社会组织的 22 位专家学者围绕主题作了精彩报告并充分交流。

参会人员共同聆听了习近平主席致世界职业技术教育发展大会贺信，深刻领会习近平主席对职业教育作用的科学评价——“职业教育与经济社会发展紧密相连，对促进就业创业、助力经济社会发展、增进人民福祉具有重要意义”。

张琦在论坛总结时说道，在本次论坛上，国内外专家学者讨论热烈，尤其是就职业教育以职业培训和技能习得方式，促进就业创业和收入增长的“造血式”扶贫功能达成共识，大家普遍认同职业教育对阻断贫困代际传递作出突出贡献，在振兴乡村经济、促进包容性增长方面发挥着不可替代的作用。同时，参会专家还表达了进一步推动全球职业教育，助力全球减贫进程的共同期望，希望通过互学互鉴、共建共享，广泛支持开展国际职业教育促进减贫的国际经验交流，加强职业技术技能培训国际合作，构建职业教育促进全球减贫的合作交流机制，携手推动全球职业教育实现高质量发展、高效率减贫，共建后疫情时代美好世界，推动和加快实现联合国 2030 年可持续发展议程倡导的消除一切形式贫困的目标。此外，围绕职业教育减贫的政策制度、经验模式和实践探索，国内外学者立足国情、各抒己见，分享了各国职业教育体系促进减贫增收与发展的成功案例和有益经验。现将专家观点综述如下。

### 1. 对职业教育扶贫减贫内在优势与行动模式的学理认知探讨

治贫先治愚，扶贫必扶智。北京师范大学中国乡村教育研究中心主任李兴洲从学理上阐释了职业教育扶贫减贫的内在机理，即职业教育与精准扶贫在目标上的一致性、在对象上的重合性、在内容上的兼容性、在方法上的协调性，其行动模式主要包括职业教育政策扶贫减贫、校企合作共同扶贫减贫、送教下乡实地扶贫减贫以及创新创业高效扶贫。北京教育科学研究院终身学习与可持续发展教育研究所所长史枫从贫困的个体归因分析出发，提出技能短缺是个体贫困的关键性归因，而教育与培训则是解决农村个体贫困的关键路径。香港大学亚洲创业及营商价值研究中心副总监陈炳雄认为教育创新是全球减贫的催化剂，但职业教育需要解决学校课程与实际工作之间的转化、学生信心的建立、学生认可度以及培训项目的可及性这四大痛点。

### 2. 对国家职业教育助力就业圆梦和国际职业教育援助的探讨交流

为实现“职教一人，就业一个，脱贫一家”的目标，我国针对职业教育扶贫开发采取了一系列举措。国家乡村振兴局考核评估司副司长延欣详细介绍了我国自 2004 年开始实施的旨在提升农村贫困家庭新成长劳动力技能水平的人力资源开发项目——“雨露计划”。该计划成效显著，已高效带动超过 1 500 万贫困人口脱贫增收，极大改善了脱贫劳动力素质结构。针对数字化贫困成为当代社会一种新型贫困形式这一问题，国家开放大学国家数字化学习资源中心主任单丛凯提出“数字化赋能、扶贫先扶智”的总体思路，通过数字化学习，培养职业技能，并介绍了国家开放大学扶贫项目“智富课堂”。此外，我国还积极开展国际职业教育援助项目。北京外国语大学国际教育学院副院长苑大勇介绍了我国对“一带一路”国家职业教育援助取得的丰硕成果：职业教育援助的理念不断成熟、范围不断扩大、方式更加丰富、资金来源更加多元。刚果（金）外交学院负责人巴卡图拉·恩祖齐·玛丽·玛德琳则从刚方视角，分享了作为中刚合作成果之一的刚果（金）外交学院孔子学院，在刚果（金）职业培训和扶贫中产生了显著降低失业率的积极影响。

### 3. 聚焦职业教育助推精准阻断贫困代际传递的地方实践分享

职业教育扶贫精准阻断贫困代际传递的作用在地方实践上也得到了充分验证。云南省乡村振兴局副局长宁亚宁和贵州省教育厅党组成员、副厅长杨天仪分别以云南、贵州的职业教育减贫实践为案例，讲述了职业教育扶贫在打赢脱贫攻坚战，尤其是攻克深度贫困壁垒中形成的经验模式。宁亚宁总结云南经验，一是构建体系，夯实基础，推动职业教育可持续发展；二是依托联盟，多方协作，推动职业教育再上新台阶；三是政策加持，创新模式，增强职业教育正向激励作用。杨天仪认为贵州经验有四个方面，一是抓好“顶层设计”，搭建职教兴黔富民通道；二是首创“校农结合”模式，开辟群众增收致富渠道；三是落实“四个精准”，构筑脱贫输血造血管道；四是立足“技能贵州”，铺就衔接乡村振兴大道。

### 4. 分享社会力量参与乡村人才振兴的经验和做法

在国家专项计划举措之外，社会组织也在积极参与乡村人才培养，为服务乡村振兴战略注入了来自社会资本和民间力量的新鲜血液。国务院参事、友成基金会副理事长汤敏介绍 2018 年发起的“乡村振兴领头雁计划”，以“互联网 +”模式，对返乡创业青年、大学生村官、农村基层干部合作社、驻村企业负责人等开展系统培训，为乡村振兴大规模、高效率、低成本地培养人才。

5. 职业院校创新探索助力脱贫攻坚经验总结和案例分享

职业院校是推进职业教育的主要阵地和一线战场，在助推职业教育扶贫中肩负着重要的特殊使命。在本次论坛上，多所职业院校代表分享了他们在教学实践中的经验与举措，为深入推进职业教育扶贫提供了有益思路。北京市昌平职业学校校长段福生深耕职教沃土、服务乡村振兴，总结了职业教育减贫的“五子”经验：钉好“长学制”的钉子、挂好“短培训”的牌子、研好“新产业”的点子、系好“东西部”的带子、下好“大数据”的棋子。汉中职业技术学院党委书记余德华扎根秦巴，服务基层，通过实施产教协同育人工程、“65432”重大行动、铸魂强技助困工程、秦巴山区匠师工程，做到专业对接产业、课程对接岗位、服务对接需求。聊城市技师学院党委副书记、院长刘德云坚持立德树人，强调培养“德技并修”高素质技能人才。兴安职业技术学院党委副书记、院长范勇毅践行“扶贫扶志扶技术”教育扶贫理念，坚持“立足兴安、面向兴安、服务兴安”的办学宗旨和发展方向。

6. 职业教育助推全球减贫进程的国际经验分享

职业教育扶贫减贫始终是国际上解决贫困问题的重要制度安排和政策工具。各国参会代表分享了职业教育助推全球减贫进程的国际经验。赞比亚技术教育、职业和创业培训局局长克利奥法斯·高井佐提到，技能与职业培训被广泛认为在解决青年失业问题方面发挥着重要作用，并介绍了旨在为青年创造生产性就业机会的青年技能赋权计划。德国汉斯·赛德尔基金会在华农村发展项目首席代表迈克尔·克劳斯强调，为了充分发挥职业教育在乡村振兴中的作用，应提高政府机构和社会大众对职业教育的认知。

瑞士发展与合作署经济与教育科科长迪帕克·埃尔默认为，职业教育培训是瑞士经济成功的主要支柱，瑞士模式表明成功的职业教育培训不仅是国家的责任，而且还需要政府机构、培训机构和私营企业之间的密切互动与合作，他强调私营企业应在职业教育培训中发挥重要作用。厄瓜多尔大都会设计学院教授达莎·桑切斯·马克西莫娃则基于统计研究视角，以拉丁美洲高等教育变革运动为例，进一步论证私营企业在推动教育创新、提高劳动生产率、促进经济增长方面的显著作用。

马来西亚国际文化交流中心首席顾问、拿督萧进平认为，职业教育以技能习得为目标，可以促进发展中国家的经济发展。此外，荷兰马斯特里赫特大学博士布鲁纳·卡拉多介绍了由教育和社会学家保罗·弗莱雷领导的巴西教育革命，有力推动了针对巴西贫困人口的教育改革，并成功启发了荷兰目前广泛使用的问题导向学习法。以上分享对职业教育促进全球减贫与发展有很好的借鉴价值。

# i. Overview of the Session on Vocational Education for Poverty Reduction and Inclusive Growth

**Dong Han and Wang Jiaqian, China Institute for Poverty Reduction, Beijing Normal University, China**

From August 19 to 20, 2022, the first World Vocational and Technical Education Development Conference, which was co-sponsored by the Ministry of Education of the People's Republic of China, the National Commission of the People's Republic of China for UNESCO and the Tianjin Municipal People's Government, was successfully held in Tianjin. President Xi Jinping sent a congratulatory letter to the conference, and Vice Premier Sun Chunlan delivered a speech at the conference. As one of the fourteen parallel sessions, the session on "Vocational Education for Poverty Reduction and Inclusive Growth" aims to have an in-depth discussion on the inherent advantages and acting paths of vocational education in global poverty reduction from both the international perspective and domestic practice, sum up experience and enlightenment, and innovate vocational education models, so as to better and more accurately serve the rural revitalization in China and the global poverty reduction process. The forum was held both online and offline. It was presided over by Zhang Qi, Director of China Rural Revitalization and Development Research Center and President of China Institute for Poverty Reduction of Beijing Normal University, China. Twenty-two experts and scholars from government departments, universities, vocational and technical colleges and social organizations of 10 countries and regions delivered wonderful speeches and exchanged ideas on the theme.

Participants listened to President Xi Jinping's congratulatory letter to World Vocational and Technical Education Development Conference, and had an in-depth understanding of the scientific evaluation given by President Xi Jinping—"vocational education is closely linked with economic and social development, and has great significance for promoting employment and entrepreneurship, boosting economic and social development, and improving people's well-being".

Zhang Qi concluded that experts and scholars at home and abroad had enthusiastic discussions at the session. In particular, we reached a consensus on the "hematopoiesis" function of vocational education in poverty reduction to promote employment, entrepreneurship and income growth by means of vocational training and skills acquiring. It was generally agreed that vocational education had made outstanding contributions to blocking intergenerational transmission of poverty and played an irreplaceable role in revitalizing rural economy and promoting inclusive growth. At the same time, the participating experts also expressed their common expectation of further promoting global vocational education to advance the global poverty reduction process. They hoped to widely support the exchange of international vocational education experience to promote poverty reduction, strengthen international cooperation in vocational and technical skills training, build a cooperation and exchange mechanism for vocational education to promote global poverty reduction, work together to achieve high-quality development in global vocational education and thus high-efficiency poverty reduction, build a better world in the post-pandemic era, and promote and accelerate the realization of the goal of eliminating all forms of poverty in the UN 2030 Agenda for Sustainable Development. In addition, around the policy system, empirical mode and practical exploration of poverty reduction through vocational education, scholars at home and abroad expressed their opinions based on their national conditions, and shared successful cases and useful experience of vocational education systems in various countries in promoting poverty reduction and income increase and development.

The experts' opinions are summarized as follows:

### 1. Discussion on the Theoretical Cognition of the Internal Advantages and Action Modes of Poverty Alleviation through Vocational Education

We should eliminate ignorance before poverty alleviation, and help increase knowledge before supporting the poor. Li Xingzhou, Director of China Rural Education Research Center of Beijing Normal University, China, explained the internal mechanism of poverty alleviation through vocational education, that is, vocational education and targeted poverty alleviation are consistent in goals, overlapping in objects, compatible in contents and coordinated in methods. Their action modes mainly include poverty alleviation through vocational education policies, school-enterprise cooperation, providing education to the countryside, and efficient poverty alleviation through innovation and entrepreneurship. Shi Feng, Director of the Institute of Lifelong Learning and Education for Sustainable Development of Beijing Academy of Educational Sciences, China, based on the analysis of individual attribution of poverty, proposed that skill shortage is the key attribution of individual poverty, while education and training are key paths to alleviate individual poverty in rural areas. Chen Bingxiong, Associate Director of Centre for Asian Entrepreneurship and Business Values of the University of Hong Kong, China, believed that educational innovation is a catalyst for global poverty reduction, but vocational education needs to meet four major requirements, the transformation between school curriculum and practical work, the building of students' confidence, students' recognition and the accessibility of training programs.

2. Discussion and Exchange on National Vocational Education Assisting Successful Employment and International Vocational Education Assistance

To achieve the goal of "Helping one family out of poverty by obtaining employment through vocational education", the state has taken a series of measures for poverty alleviation and development programs through vocational education. Yan Xin, Deputy Director General of the Assessment and Evaluation Department of the National Rural Revitalization Bureau of China, detailed the "Dewdrop Project", a human resources development project implemented in China since 2004 to improve the skill level of the new labor force of poor rural families. The plan has achieved remarkable results, which has efficiently helped more than 15 million poor people out of poverty and increased their income, and greatly improved the competence structure of the out-of-poverty labor force. In view of the problem that digital poverty has become a new form of poverty in contemporary society, Shan Congkai, Director of the National Digital Learning Resource Center of the Open University of China, put forward the general idea of "helping the poor increase knowledge with digital means before supporting the poor", and cultivating vocational skills through digital tools, and introduced the poverty alleviation project "Zhifu Classroom" of the Open University of China. In addition, China also actively undertaken international vocational education assistance projects. Yuan Dayong, Deputy Dean of Graduate School of Education, Beijing Foreign Studies University, China, introduced the fruitful achievements of China's vocational education assistance to the "Belt and Road" countries: the concept of vocational education assistance continues to mature, and the scope is constantly expanding with more methods and more diversified sources of funds. Bakatula Nzuzi Marie Madeleine, Head of the Congolese Diplomatic Academy, from the perspective of the Democratic Republic of Congo (D. R. Congo), shared the successful case of the Confucius Institute of the Congolese Diplomatic Academy, which is one of the achievements of the cooperation between China and D. R. Congo, and has exerted a positive effect on significantly reducing unemployment rate through vocational training and poverty-alleviation efforts in D. R. Congo.

3. Focus on the Local Practice of Accurately Blocking Intergenerational Transmission of Poverty with the Help of Vocational Education

The role of vocational education in poverty alleviation and accurately blocking intergenerational transmission of poverty has also been fully verified in local practice.

Ning Yaning, Deputy Director of Rural Revitalization Bureau of Yunnan Province, China, and Yang Tianyi, Member of CPC Leadership Group and Deputy Director-General of the Department of Education of Guizhou Province, China, respectively took the cases of poverty alleviation through vocational education in Yunnan and Guizhou, and described the empirical mode formed in winning the battles of eradicating poverty, especially in overcoming the barriers of extreme poverty. Ning Yaning summed up Yunnan's experience in three aspects. First, they build a system and lay a solid foundation to promote the sustainable development of vocational education; Second, they rely on alliances and work collaboratively to promote vocational education to a higher level; Third, they provide policy support and innovate model to enhance the positive incentive of vocational education. Yang Tianyi believed that Guizhou's experience should be concluded in four aspects. First, they pay attention to the "top-level design" and build a channel for vocational education to make Guizhou prosper and enrich people; Second, they create the model of "combining school and agriculture" and open up channels for the masses to increase income and become rich; Third, they implement "Four Accuracies" and build a channel for providing talents to alleviate poverty; Fourth, under the context of "Skilled Guizhou", they pave the way for rural revitalization.

4. Share the Experience and Practice of Social Forces Participating in Rural Talent Revitalization

In addition to the national special plan, social organizations are also actively participating in the training of rural talents, injecting young blood from social capital and non-governmental forces to serve the rural revitalization strategy. Tang Min, Counselor of the State Council and Vice Chairman of Youcheng Foundation, China, introduced the "Bellwethers Program for Rural Revitalization" launched in 2018, which carried out systematic training for returning young entrepreneurs, college-graduate village officials, rural grass-roots cadre cooperatives and heads of resident enterprises in the "Internet plus" mode to train talents for rural revitalization on a large scale, with high efficiency and low cost.

5. Experience Summary and Case Sharing on the Innovation and Exploration of Vocational Colleges in Helping Eradicate Absolute Poverty

Higher vocational colleges are the main battlefields and frontline to promote vocational education, and shoulder important and special missions in boosting poverty alleviation through vocational education. At this session, representatives from many vocational colleges shared their experiences and measures in teaching practice, which provided useful ideas for further promoting poverty alleviation through vocational education. Duan Fusheng, Principal of Beijing Changping Vocational School, China, who cultivated the promising field of vocational education to serve rural revitalization, summed up the "five instruments" experience of poverty reduction through vocational education: stick to the "long-term system", provide "short-term training", study intensively the idea of "new industry", serve as a connection between the "East and West" and arrange "big data" layout. Yu Dehua, Secretary of CPC Committee of Hanzhong Vocational and Technical College, China, took root in Qinba mountain area and served the grass-roots. Through the implementation of the cultivation project of production-education collaboration, the "65432" major action, the poverty-relief project of forging souls and strengthening skills, and the craftsman project in Qinba Mountain area, he successfully matched specialties with industries, curricula with jobs, and service with needs. Liu Deyun, Deputy Secretary of CPC Committee and President of Technician College of Liaocheng City, China, insisted on fostering virtue through education, and emphasized the cultivation of high-quality skilled talents with "good training in morality and skills". Fan Yongyi, Deputy Secretary of CPC Committee and President of Xing'an Vocational and Technical College, China, practiced the educational concept of "supporting the poor, supporting aspirants and providing technical support", and adhered to the school-running purpose and development direction of "Embracing Xing'an and Serving Xing'an by keeping a foothold in Xing'an".

6. International Experience Sharing on "Vocational Education's Role in Boosting Global Poverty Reduction Process"

Poverty reduction through vocational education has always been an important institutional arrangement and policy tool to solve poverty problems in the world. Participants from different countries shared their international experience on vocational education's role in boosting global poverty reduction process. Cleophas Takaiza, Director General of Technical Education, Vocational and Entrepreneurship Training Authority (TEVETA) of Zambia, mentioned that skills and vocational training are widely considered to play an important role in solving the problem of youth unemployment, and introduced the Youth Skills Empowerment Plan which aimed at creating productive employment opportunities for young people. Michael Klaus, Chief Representative of the Hans Seidel Fourdation's Rural Development Projects in China, stressed that in order to give full play to the role of vocational education in rural revitalization, government officials and the society should heighten their recognition of vocational education.

Diepak Elmer, Head of Economy and Education Section of the Swiss Agency for Development and Cooperation, believed that vocational education and training are the main pillars of economic success in Switzerland. The Swiss model shows that successful vocational education and training is not only the responsibility of the state, but also requires close interaction and cooperation among the public sector, training institutions and the private sector. He emphasized that the private sector should play a leading role in vocational education and training. Dasha Sánchez Maximova, a professor at Metropolitan Institute of Design in Quito, Ecuador, further demonstrated the remarkable role of the private sector in promoting educational innovation, improving labor productivity and promoting economic growth from the perspective of statistical research, taking the Latin American higher education reform movement as an example.

Siow Chen Pin, Dato and Chief Advisor of International Cultural Communication Center of Malaysia, believed that vocational education aims at skill acquisition and can promote the economic development of developing countries. In addition, Dr. Bruna Calado of Maastricht University in the Netherlands introduced the Brazilian educational revolution led by Paulo Freire, an educationist and sociologist, who strongly promoted the educational reform for the poor in Brazil and successfully inspired the problem-oriented learning method widely used in the Netherlands. The experience and views shared above have a good reference value for vocational education in promoting global poverty reduction and development.

# （二）

# 通过技术教育、职业和创业培训解决青年失业问题

赞比亚技术教育、职业和创业培训局局长　克利奥法斯·高井佐

和其他许多发展中国家一样，赞比亚的青年失业率居高不下。为了缓解这一情况，赞比亚正在筹划各种方法，帮助青年人就业。《技术教育以及职业和创业培训政策（2020 年）》的主要目标就是通过促进技能发展和创业，解决青年人失业率较高的问题。本文对赞比亚目前正在实施的青年技能赋能项目进行介绍，该项目遵照职业和技能培训政策，同时也与政府的宣言一致，通过权力下放和增加对选区发展项目资金的分配，实现全民发展。

## 1. 青年失业问题

根据赞比亚统计局 2020 年的数据估算，在赞比亚 1 790 万人口中，超过 550 万是青年人。其中，约有 140 万青年人口处于失业状态，缺乏谋生技能。尽管赞比亚已经采取措施增加教育和培训机会并初显成效，但是仍然有很多青年人找不到工作。大量失学和失业的青年人口导致了各类社会性问题的出现。

## 2. 技术、职业培训和就业

目前公认的一点是，技术和职业培训在解决青年失业问题方面发挥着重要作用。技术和职业培训的方向是找到工作和获取就业技能，意味着培训能够很好地解决技能不匹配等问题。而正是技能不匹配等问题阻碍了众多青年顺利完成从学校到职场的过渡。因此，解决青年失业问题的最佳方案就是确保青年可以获得基本技能和相关培训，帮助他们自信地进入职场并能够把握当地的就业机会。

赞比亚已经认识到，要实现联合国 2030 年可持续发展议程的愿景，国家需要

技能人才，尤其是女性、青年和边缘化群体。赞比亚希望在各个层面加强技能发展。此外，赞比亚正在通过权力下放，为人民争取发展机会和更多的资源。因此给选区发展基金会的拨款会增加，尤其是在农村地区，大笔的款项会进入当地社区，帮助他们确定、优先选择和实施发展项目。

推动这类项目可持续性发展的前提是社区有相应的技能人才。这就要求当地人，尤其是当地青年能够掌握技能，推动各自地区的可持续发展。

### 3. 选区一级的技能培训通道

截至 2022 年 6 月 30 日，有大约 311 家培训机构在赞比亚注册，开展技术教育以及职业和创业培训。但是这些培训机构大多数都设立在城市地区。这就意味着一些选区和农村地区可能没有足够的渠道获取技能培训资源。

### 4. 青年技能赋能战略

青年技能赋能战略是一项政府计划，它的首要目标是通过补充赞比亚政府关于就业和财富创造方面的政策承诺，为年轻人提供生产性工作。政府希望以前由中央政府承担的工作开始由地方当局来完成。地方当局通过选区发展基金会与当地社区合作，这就需要更多技术技能人才来支持项目的实施。因此有必要让青年做好准备，承担选区的一线工作。

（1）青年就业能力。技能水平和能力的提升对提高青年人的就业能力至关重要。该战略的重点是提高和发展青年人的技能水平和能力，帮助他们做好准备，积极参加由选区发展基金会资助的项目以及其他项目。

（2）创业。推动创业和商业发展服务能够为青年赋能，帮助他们进入商业领域。创业能够推动非正规部门逐步向正规部门转变，从而为青年人创造更多、更好的工作机会。没有能够独立发展的企业，就没有办法为青年人提供有意义的工作。因此通过制度化、综合化的方法推动创业发展是很有必要的。

### 5. 实施安排

（1）科技部。科技部负责所有技能发展计划的管理。在实施这一战略的过程中，政府通过科技部科学规划、协调和推动所有关于技能培训计划的合作和管理。

（2）地方政府和农村发展部 / 地方当局。地方政府和农村发展部已经发布了关于利用选区发展基金会的指导方针和标准。为了促进青年就业，地方当局需要确保以下几点：优先为具有适当技能的青年人提供就业机会；优先考虑符合标准的本地供应商；将维护工作留给雇用本地青年劳动力的企业；优先考虑青年和女企业家的技能发展；为有技能的青年和女性提供补助或贷款，用于购买设备和工具。

（3）技术教育、职业和创业培训局。在此战略背景下，赞比亚技术教育、职业和创业培训局将通过技术教育、职业和创业培训基金的适当供资窗口，促进技能培训的发展。合作规划和协调技能培训工作。监督和评估技能培训项目，对成功受训的青年进行评估并颁发合格证书。促进与商业发展服务提供者的联系，以促进创业发展。

（4）培训机构。培训机构的作用是提供培训，帮助参加项目的青年掌握核心工作技能和基础知识，更好地进入职场。

（5）选区发展委员会。选区发展委员会在促进和推动选区内青年技术培训、建立和发展青年领导企业 / 合作社方面扮演着重要角色。同时，选区发展委员会还将提供体制框架，为青年企业家创造有利的创业环境。

### 6. 资金

鉴于这些旨在解决青年人失业问题的干预措施涉及多层面、多部门，该项目已经寻求了不同的资金来源。通过技能发展基金会的收益，技术教育、职业和创业培训基金会可以设立推动青年人的技能和创业发展的机制。选区发展基金会也会发放助学金，帮助需要生活补助的学习者接受技能培训。

### 7. 合作

为了确保所推广的技能能够满足需求，培训机构需要提供证明，证实其在确定技能培训计划时，已经与相关部门进行过协商，包括地方当局、民间团体、青年组织等。青年人的参与也有助于明确其在获得技能方面所面临的主要挑战，并加强他们对项目的主人翁意识。

### 8. 成果

该项目于 2022 年 2 月正式启动。87 家培训机构参与了第一期项目，一共招收了来自 131 个选区的 7 665 位受训者。这些受训者将进入由选区发展委员会根据当地优先发展事项选出的 32 个不同的技能领域学习受训。

9. 挑战

赞比亚青年对技能的需求已经超过了注册培训机构的能力。此外，有些农村地区没有培训机构，无法直接提供青年所需的技能培训。

10. 机遇

参与促进和创立青年就业和创业机会的各相关部门，正在以结构化方式协调、推动青年就业计划。政府已将技能发展列为优先事项，我们期待着对技能发展部门进行更多的投资。政府也在鼓励私人投资，以扩大技能发展渠道和提高技能发展质量。

政府已承诺推动电动汽车电池生产行业的技能发展，欢迎该领域的公司加入。

赞比亚已经将技能发展作为解决青年失业问题的关键并将其作为优先考虑事项。高质量且公平的技能发展是实现包容性发展的一个重要组成部分。

## ii. Tackling Youth Unemployment Through Technical Education, Vocational and Entrepreneuship Training (TEVET)

**Cleophas Takaiza, Director General of Technical Education, Vocational and Entrepreneurship Training Authority (TEVETA), Zambia**

The Republic of Zambia, like many other developing countries, is facing high youth unemployment rate. In an effort to mitigate the problem, Zambia is devising ways of helping the youth get a job either in the formal or informal sectors. The main objective of the TEVET Policy of 2020 is to address the problem of high unemployment rate among the youth through promoting skills development and entrepreneurship. This paper presents a Skills for Youth Empowerment Programme that is implemented in Zambia in line with the Policy of Technical and Vocational Training as well as the pronouncements to realize development of all the people through decentralisation and increasing allocation of funds for developmental project in the constituencies.

### 1. The Challenge of Youth Unemployment

The Zambia Statistics Agency (2020) estimates that more than 5.5 million of Zambia's 17.9 million people are the youth. About 1.4 million of the youth were unemployed and lacked skills for self-employment. Despite some gains that Zambia has been making on increasing access to education and training, many young people have remained unemployed. The large number of youth who were out of school and unemployed leads to many social problems.

### 2. Technical and Vocational Training and Employment

Technical and Vocational Training is widely recognised as having an important role to play in tackling youth unemployment. Its orientation lies in the acquisition of jobs and employability skills, which means that it is well placed to address issues such as skills mismatch jobs, which have impeded smooth school-to-work transitions for many young people. The best answer to the unemployment of youth is to ensure that young people acquire the basic skills and relevant training that helps them enter the workplace with confidence and take advantage of local opportunities.

The Zambia has recognised the fact that for the country to attain the vision of UN 2030 Agenda, it needs skilled and competent talents especially women, youths, and marginalised groups. Zambia desires to enhance skills development at all levels. Furthermore, it strives for development opportunities and more resources for people through decentralisation. Consequently, allocations towards Constituency Development Fund (CDF) have been increased, especially in the rural areas where significant amount of money are now getting into communities for them to identify, prioritise and implement development projects.

Sustainable implementation of such projects can only occur when there is availability of appropriate skills in the communities, which demands the locals, especially the youth, to grasp skills to support sustainable development in each constituency.

### 3. Access to Skills Training at Constituency Level

Up to 30 June 2022, there were about 311 training institutions registered to conduct TEVET in Zambia. However, most of these institutions are located in urban areas, which implies that some of the rural districts and constituencies may not have adequate access to skills training.

### 4. The Skills for Youth Empowerment Strategy

The overarching goal of the Skills for Youth Empowerment Strategy, a government programme, is to provide productive jobs for young people by complementing the policy commitments of the Zambian Government on job and wealth creation. It is the desire of the government that jobs that were previously undertaken by the Central Government begin to be performed by local authorities. The local authorities working with the local communities through CDF requires more technical talents to support the implementation of projects, hence there exists the need to prepare youths with skills to take up the jobs at constituency level.

(1) Youth Employability. Skills and competencies are essential to enhance the employability of young people. This strategy focuses on developing and upgrading the skills and competencies among the youth to prepare them to participate actively in the financing projects from CDF as well as other projects.

(2) Entrepreneurship. Entrepreneurship and business development services can help empower the youth and facilitate their entry into business. It has potential to promote gradual transformation from the informal economy to formal sectors which create more and better jobs for young people. Meaningful jobs cannot be created for the youth without viable enterprises. An institutionalized and integrated approach to entrepreneurship development is a necessity to promote entrepreneurship.

## 5. Implementation of Arrangements

(1) Ministry of Technology and Science. The Ministry of Technology and Science is the policy holder for all skills development initiatives. During the implementation of this strategy, the government authorizes the Ministry of Technology and Science to plan, coordinate and promote the cooperation and management of all skills training initiatives.

(2) Ministry of Local Government and Rural Development/Local Authorities. The Ministry of Local Government and Rural Development has issued guidelines and standards for the utilisation of the CDF. To promote youth employment, the local authorities should ensure the following: the youth with appropriate skills have priority to jobs; preference should be given to local suppliers who meet the criteria; maintenance jobs will be reserved for enterprises that employ the local youth; prioritize skills development for young and women entrepreneurs; provide grants or loans to the youth and women with skills for purchasing equipment and tools.

(3) Technical Education, Vocational and Entrepreneurship Training Authority (TEVETA). In the context of this strategy, TEVETA of Zambia will facilitates the development of skills through appropriate funding windows of the TEVET Fund; collaborate planning and coordination of skills training; monitor and evaluates skills training programmes as well as assessing and certifying successful candidates; promote linkages with business development service providers to promote entrepreneurship development.

(4) Training Institutions. The role of training institutions is to deliver training that enables the youth on the programme to acquire core work skills, competencies and the underpinning knowledge that facilitate transition into the workplace.

(5) Constituency Development Committees (CDCs). The CDCs play the role of promoting and facilitating skills training for the youth in the constituencies as well as promoting establishment and development of youth-led enterprises/cooperatives. CDCs also provides the institutional framework to promote a favorable environment for young entrepreneurs.

## 6. Financing

In view of the multidimensional and multisectoral nature of interventions aiming at addressing the youth unemployment, the programme has explored different sources of funding. The TEVET Fund, through proceeds from the Skills Development Fund, provides a mechanism that facilitates skills and entrepreneurship development targeting the youth. The bursary component of the CDF also supports learners that need subsistence allowance to access skills training.

7. Coordination

To ensure the skills being promoted meet needs, training providers are required to show evidence of having consulted with relevant stakeholders in identifying skills training programmes. The consultations include engagements with the local authorities, civil societies, youth organizations, etc. The involvement of young people also helps identify key challenges that the youth face in accessing skills and enhance ownership of the programmes.

8. Achievements

The programme was officially launched in February 2022. 87 training institutions are participating in the first cycle of the programme and have enrolled 7 665 learners from 131 constituencies. The learners are enrolled in 32 different skill areas as prioritised by the CDCs in line with the local development priorities.

9. Challenges

The demand for skills has surpassed the capacity of registered training providers. Furthermore, there are some rural constituencies that do not have training institutions, and such a situation poses challenges to training skills that respond directly to their requirements.

10. Opportunities

The Youth Employment programme is being implemented in a structured and coordinated manner by the various stakeholders involved in the promotion of youth employment and entrepreneurship. More investments are expected to the skills development sector. The government is also encouraging private investment to expand access and improve quality of skills development.

The government has pronounced its commitment to promote the skills development that will support the manufacturing of batteries for electric cars. Corporations in this regard would be welcome.

Zambia has prioritised skills development as the key ingredient for tackling youth unemployment. High-quality and equitable skills development are an important ingredient for inclusive development.

## （三）

# 刚果（金）外交学院孔子学院对刚果（金）职业培训扶贫的影响

刚果（金）外交学院负责人　巴卡图拉·恩祖齐·玛丽·玛德琳

中刚合作拥有数十年历史，刚果民主共和国也是“一带一路”合作伙伴之一。中国企业在刚果民主共和国经济中占有重要地位，不仅数目繁多，而且投资水平以数十亿美元计，其主要经营领域包括采矿业、通信业、建筑业、农业、林业等。

正是在这一背景下，中南大学与刚果（金）外交学院共同设立的孔子学院于2018年在刚果（金）正式揭牌，而本人有幸自学院成立以来担任刚方院长一职。目前，孔子学院成立将满4年，已与3所当地机构建立伙伴关系。

如今，刚果同胞对汉语学习和两国人民跨文化交流的兴趣日渐浓厚。虽然疫情限制了我们的工作条件，但刚果（金）外交学院孔子学院迄今已培养300余名不同性别、不同层次的学员，包括国家政府官员、企业家、大学生、中学生等。

对我国而言，掌握汉语有以下几方面优势：促进在中文环境中的交流；学习采矿、信息技术、建筑、农业等领域的技术；帮助就职于中国企业的代理人提高工作效率和薪资水平。

刚果（金）同胞在刚果（金）外交学院孔子学院接受的培训有以下几方面作用：帮助他们获得中国奖学金，在中国攻读采矿、医学、商业、信息技术、农业等领域的本科、硕士和博士学位，学成归国后将所学知识应用于实践；帮助他们掌握笔译和口译专业技能，提高在就业市场上的竞争力，获得更多工作机会；帮助他们了解中国文化，看到世界的多样性，在未来获得成功。

在全球文化交流、资源共享的前提下，刚果（金）外交学院孔子学院提高了刚果公民的汉语和中国专业知识水平，使其掌握各领域现代技术，这有助于降低失业率，帮助刚果民主共和国实现进一步发展。

## iii. Impact of the Confucius Institute of the Congolese Diplomatic Academy on Poverty Reduction Through Professional Training

**Bakatula Nzuzi Marie Madeleine, Head of the Congolese Diplomatic Academy**

Dans le cadre de la coopération sino-congolaise, qui date de plusieurs décennies, à l'image du projet de la Nouvelle Route de la Soie, les entreprises chinoises occupent une place importante dans l'économie de la République Démocratique du Congo, non seulement en raison de leur nombre, mais aussi leur niveau d'investissement estimé à des milliards de dollars. Elles opèrent principalement dans le secteur minier, la communication, la construction, l'agriculture, la forêt, etc.

C'est dans cette perspective qu'à la suite de l'accord entre l'Université Centrale du Sud de la République Populaire de Chine et l'Académie Diplomatique Congolaise de la République Démocratique du Congo, l'Institut Confucius a ouvert officiellement en République Démocratique du Congo. Je suis Directrice Locale de l'Institut Confucius de l'Académie Diplomatique Congolaise depuis sa création en 2018. Il totalisera bientôt quatre années d'existence et est actuellement en partenariat avec 3 institutions locales.

Aujourd'hui, les compatriotes congolais sont de plus en plus intéressés par l'apprentissage de la langue chinoise et l'échange interculturel entre nos deux peuples. À ce jour, l'Institut Confucius de l'ADC a déjà formé plus de 300 candidats dont: fonctionnaires de l'État, hommes d'affaires, étudiants d'universités, élèves du secondaire, etc.; hommes et femmes, des différents niveaux, malgré la pandémie du COVID-19 qui nous a contraint à travailler dans des conditions difficiles.

La connaissance de la langue chinoise offre plusieurs avantages, notamment:

1. la facilitation de la communication dans un environnement chinois;

2. l'acquisition de la technologie dans les domaines ci-après: minier, informatique, construction, agricole, etc.;

3. l'augmentation du rendement et le niveau de salaire des agents qui travaillent dans les entreprises chinoises; etc.

La formation reçue par les compatriotes congolais à l'Institut Confucius de l'Académie Diplomatique, leur permet:

1. d'accéder aux bourses chinoises, pour y poursuivre leurs études du cycle de licence, master et doctorat, dans différents domaines, je cite: mines, médecine, business, informatique, agriculture... Après leurs études en Chine, ils reviendront au pays pour mettre en application leur connaissance;

2. Cette même formation leur permet aussi d'avoir la maîtrise des métiers de traducteur et d'interprète, qui offre des opportunités d'emploi parce qu'il rend compétitif sur le marché professionnel;

3. Aussi, cette formation leur permet de comprendre la culture chinoise, permettant de voir le monde dans sa diversité, en vue de la réussite à venir.

Le monde étant une communauté d'échange et de partage, l'Institut Confucius de l'Académie Diplomatique Congolaise joue un rôle important au renforcement des connaissances linguistiques et professionnelles chinoises des citoyens congolais, afin d'acquérir les techniques modernes dans différents domaines de la vie, et cela permet de contribuer à la réduction du taux de chômage et ainsi accompagner la République Démocratique du Congo dans sa démarche vers le développement.

# (四)

# 职教一人，脱贫一户

## ——云南职教扶贫精准阻断贫困代际传递

云南省乡村振兴局副局长　宁亚宁

治贫先治愚，扶贫先扶智。如果说教育扶贫是“断穷根”的一把利器，那么职业教育就是教育扶贫中更接地气、更契合农村的“主力军”。2015 年，习近平总书记在中央扶贫开发工作会议上指出，“一个贫困家庭的孩子如果能接受职业教育，掌握一技之长，能就业，这一户脱贫就有希望了。”

近年来，我们在云南减贫实践中充分证明，在打赢脱贫攻坚战中，门槛低、成本小、就业通道直接的职业教育，不仅点亮了贫困家庭子女的人生梦想，也阻断了贫困的代际传递。职业教育扶贫以其“润物细无声”又“平地起惊雷”的特点，在脱贫攻坚战尤其是攻克深度贫困堡垒中，展示出了不可替代的重要作用。

构建体系，夯实基础，推动职业教育可持续发展。滇西边境片区，是我国 14 个集中连片特困地区之一，涉及云南省 10 个州市，集少数民族地区和边境地区于一体，属劳动者智力技能和产业发展不足所致的智力型贫困，贫困面广、程度深。2011 年 11 月，中央扶贫开发工作会议决定，对集中连片特殊困难地区予以重点帮扶，并确定了部委定点联系的工作机制。其中，滇西边境片区由教育部直接牵头定点帮扶，教育部直属大学及其直属单位共同参与，稳定的帮扶架构，为云南开展以职业教育为中心的智力扶贫奠定了坚实基础。

2012 年，为了培养服务滇西特色优势产业的高层次技术技能人才，建设滇西应用技术大学提上日程。随着滇西应用技术大学的建成，以其为中心成功创建了具有滇西边境片区扶贫开发特色的劳动者技能培育和提升机制：第一，创新滇西应用技术大学办学机制，采用本部和分校结构，改变滇西边境片区本科高等职业教育结构；第二，建立东部 10 个职业教育集团对口帮扶滇西边境片区 10 个州市现有中高职业学校办学能力机制；第三，搭建东部 4 个发达省市职业学校定点招收滇西边境片区贫困家庭“两后生”和职教学生到东部发达省市接受教育和就业机制。

涓滴成海，众木成林，在各方倾力支持下，滇西职业教育格局初成。目前，滇西应用技术大学已经全面运行，在滇西边境片区建立起了布局合理、功能齐全的本科职业教育体系，如普洱市的普洱茶学院、西双版纳州的傣医药学院、临沧市的滇西科技师范学院、保山市的珠宝学院。这些高等职业教育平台的建立彻底改变了滇西边境片区本科教育和高等职业教育的布局，为滇西边境片区脱贫和可持续发展提供了源源不断的动力。

依托联盟，多方协作，推动职业教育再上新台阶。回望来时路，职业教育扶贫深刻而温暖。在云南脱贫攻坚战中，贫困人口能够通过职业教育掌握一技之长、拥有安身立命的本领，从根本上拔除“穷根”，离不开聚沙成塔的各方力量，也离不开因脱贫攻坚这个神圣使命凝聚而成的联盟平台。

一座桥梁，带来更多资源。教育部参与扶贫的部属大学均分布在全国经济文化发达地区，38 所大学属于国内重点大学，可以动员的人力和社会资源丰富。这些高校在参与扶贫工作中，充分利用自己的资源优势，做好桥梁作用，让滇西边境片区“人力资源开发扶贫示范区”建设的各种扶贫项目得以顺利进行，中山大学、中国地质大学、浙江大学等知名高校为办学和管理贡献了诸多领域的杰出学者。

一个联盟，带来更多机会。发挥沪滇职教联盟优势，利用上海职业教育的辐射作用，为云南省贫困地区提供更多更好的教育资源和就业机会。自 2017 年以来，上海市 30 多所中职校在沪滇职教联盟统筹协调下，招收云南建档立卡“两后生”7 461 人。通过定期召开校企合作会议、共建校企合作基地、邀请合作企业到云南调研等形式，整合行业协会、合作企业等资源，共同探索人才共育新模式，为云南学生打通职业教育、实习锻炼、上岗就业的通道。

一个平台，带来更多发展。在沪滇协作机制推动下，同济大学在昆明成立中德同济职业学校，并在对口帮扶县开办集“校区、园区、社区”三区合一的高等级职业培训学校。中德职业教育联盟云南示范基地、中德（云南）跨企业培训中心、同济大学巴伐利亚文教部中德职教师资培养云南基地、云南交通职业技术学院中德学院等教研机构相继落地，有力推动了云南职业教育的深化改革和创新发展。

政策加持，创新模式，增强职业教育正向激励作用。2020 年底，云南如期完成了脱贫攻坚的目标任务，千年梦想照进十万大山。脱贫摘帽不是终点，而是新生活、新奋斗的起点。职业教育作为一种类型教育，“就业便利、领域丰富、一技傍身”，这些容易触摸得到的教育边界让贫困家庭的子女看到了希望。我们将进一步补齐职业教育资源短板，打破职业教育上升“天花板”，创新各层次各类型职业教育模式，持续增强职业教育吸引力，推动职业教育进一步发展。

保持帮扶政策总体稳定，严格落实“四个不摘”要求，不断巩固拓展脱贫攻坚成果。2021 年以来，云南省坚持把落实“雨露计划”政策作为防止农民家庭子女因困难失学辍学的重要措施，保持“雨露计划”政策稳定，鼓励和支持脱贫家庭、农村低收入家庭子女接受职业教育。2021 年，全省共发放“雨露计划”补助资金 49 473.06 万元、补助贫困家庭子女 29.013 5 万人次，“雨露计划”收到了明显成效。

探索职业教育教学模式创新，增强主动学习技术技能积极性。在乡村振兴背景下，职业教育更需要探索教育教学模式创新，开发适用、实用的课程，增强适宜人群主动学习技术技能的积极性。随着大数据、物联网、人工智能等的发展，一批新模式、新业态下的岗位需求随之产生，职业教育应充分关注这些就业新变化，在助力“互联网 +”、数字经济、平台经济等行业发挥职业教育吸纳就业的优势。例如，北京商业学校物流专业的 3 名保山学生，毕业后回到家乡创设 4 家快递站点，带动了 20 多人就业，这就是鲜活的成功案例。

授人以鱼，不如授人以渔。云南滇西的脱贫实践告诉我们，敞开职业教育的大门，让一批又一批贫困学子“进得去、上得起、学得好、有出路”，努力推动职业教育高质量发展，培养千千万万拥有一技之长的劳动者，我们将见证更多乡村剧变的精彩故事，书写更多经济社会发展的崭新篇章!

在此，我也代表云南省乡村振兴系统，诚邀各界友人、有志之士来到这片充满生机与活力的云岭大地，与我们一同绘制出乡村振兴更加美好的蓝图!

## （五）

# 精准扶贫中的职教作为

## ——北京市昌平职业学校的思考与实践

北京市昌平职业学校校长　段福生

贫困，是人类社会的顽疾。尽管当今世界科学技术和物质资料发展水平已经很高，但世界仍有 10% 的人口生活在极端贫困中。消除贫困始终是人类发展的共同目标，也是全球发展面临的共同挑战。

减贫的手段有很多种，其中最不应该被忽视的力量，就是教育，特别是职业教育的力量。职业教育在助力减贫中发挥了“鱼渔兼授”“志智双扶”的作用，在对象上实现了各年龄段、各种人群的全覆盖；在过程上实现了“立志—培智—扶技—促业”的全链条；在途径上既有“长学制”，又有“短培训”，长短结合，灵活多样；在机制上，开展“东西协作”，提升了优质职教资源的效能；在效果上，通过职业教育赋能产业，为贫困地区打造优势产业，让人在产业中有业、稳业、乐业，从根本上拔除了穷根。

北京市昌平职业学校在多年实践中，依据区域村镇的情况，积极盘活存量、激活增量、引入流量、应对变量、锚定质量，形成职业教育的“五子联动”乡村振兴模式，为助力精准脱贫、促进乡村振兴做出了一些贡献。

### 1. 钉好“长学制”的钉子

阻断贫困代际传递既是职业教育的重要使命，也是职业教育的优势所在。根据相关调研数据，目前全国中职 70% 以上的学生来自农村或者城市经济困难家庭。从国家层面，中职免学费覆盖超过 90% 学生，国家助学金资助对象达到在校生总数的 40% 左右，解除了贫困学生的后顾之忧，中职毕业生就业率常年保持在 95% 以上，大量贫困家庭学生通过职业教育实现就业，带动了整个家庭脱贫。

从院校实践层面，积极落实《职业教育专业目录（2021 年）》，对接农业新业态，适应农业新业态发展，致力于培养高素质、复合型农业人才。同时积极开展“三五七”多元学制人才培养，通过开展三年职高、五年中高职一体化、七年中高本贯通培养等方式，让更多贫困家庭子女通过职业教育实现拥有第一代大学生的梦想，给他们更高的发展起点和向上流动的机会，从根子上斩断贫困的代际传递。

### 2. 挂好“短培训”的牌子

“育训并举”既是职业教育的法定职责，也是作为类型教育的特色所在。学校提出“五个面向”的培训理念，从镇村干部、乡村振兴人才、农村实用人才、高素质农民和新村民五端发力，年培训 1.2 万人。

学校为农村两委班子的现任干部和后备干部开设学历提升专班，提供能力培养系列培训，提升干部干事创业的理想信念，提高实践能力水平；通过开办益农村校，开展“点餐式”培训，以“线上 + 线下”的方式提升职业农民的技能水平与专业素养；探索区域乡村社区学院建设，创新“订单 + 派单”制培训模式，通过送教入村、送技到户、量身定制，对农民开展数字经济、法治教育、村域文化、生活技能等培训，满足不同群体的培训需求，为乡村振兴提供了有力的人才支撑。

### 3. 研好“新产业”的点子

职业教育一头连着教育，一头连着产业。对于人来讲，短期发展靠打工，长期发展则靠产业。学校充分发挥村镇资源，以“资源变项目，项目促产业，产业留人才”的振兴思路，创新“校镇村”合作模式，成立乡村社区学院，形成“一村一品”的职教精准扶贫品牌，带动农民、农业、农村全面发展。

学校开发出“正德春饼宴”“昌平蝴蝶兰”“真顺苹果酒”“流村黄花酱菜”等 16 个区域特色产业项目，成立“校企农社”产城教联盟，联合昌平区 56 家合作社，策划昌平苹果节、草莓节、西瓜节活动，带动昌平区林果业、民俗旅游业的转型升级，实现农民本地就业 8 000 余人，帮助农民增收 5 500 余万元。

同时，学校也将校企合作中的企业资源引流至乡村建设之中，架起企业与乡村的沟通桥、合作桥、共赢桥；修善农民数字意识与能力的高速路。

发挥龙头企业的品牌辐射效应，建成京东产教融合学院，开发数字农旅服务平台，开设“松兰甄选”电商直播间，直播带货昌平特色农产品，累计培养电商运营、直播营销、电商客服等农业技术人才 400 余人；联合字节跳动成立“振兴乡村产业人才培养联盟”，设立“字节乡村学堂”，开展乡村电商直播培训与认证，提升新农人新媒体运营能力；协同美团帮助农村进行数字化改造，助力农民就近就地就业，将新经济、新模式、新业态、新产业的发展成果下沉到乡村，发展红利惠及更多农民。

**4. 系好“东西部”的带子**

学校通过“校校结对”“东西结对”等形式，积极推动理念、师资、课程、技术等资源向中西部地区流动，形成了多层次、多形式、全方位的扶贫协作和对口支援格局，充分体现了“先富帮后富”，守望相助的中华民族命运共同体理念。

自 2013 年开始，学校与河南栾川、河北尚义、青海玉树、内蒙古太仆寺旗等地密切合作，先后接纳 1 521 名建档立卡户贫困家庭子女来校就读，为他们提供学历教育、实习实训、大赛指导、就业推荐等系列职教服务。学生将学到的知识技能用于支援家乡建设，教育成果转变为实打实的就业成效，帮扶地区全部脱贫摘帽。

学校联合对口帮扶地区所在地政府，探索出“政、校、企、家”四位一体式精准扶贫模式，即政府负责招生并提供项目经费，学校负责进行技能培训，合作企业负责提供就业岗位，招生招工一体，培训就业一体，以技能培训促学员就业，以学员就业促家庭脱贫。这一模式在国家级贫困县巨鹿县得到了很好的应用。

此外，学校通过开设国际技术技能培训驿站，将优质职教资源共享至东帝汶、吉布提、南苏丹等 5 个国家，精准培养当地紧缺的专业技能人才，为各国发展做出中国贡献。

**5. 下好“大数据”的棋子**

学校发挥大数据专业的技术优势，以教育信息化助力乡村数字化，为昌平区打造跨区域、跨产业的农业大数据共享平台，也为昌平区政府提供乡村振兴工作决策参考。自今年 3 月，学校受国家乡村振兴局委托，对全国 460 万“雨露计划”受益学生进行就业情况摸底调研，为精准人岗匹配提供数据支撑。下一步，学校将与相关企业共同开发与职教功能相关的数据标准和数据库，建成集毕业跟踪、培训成果、社会服务等内容为一体的综合职业教育信息平台，促使职业教育进一步发挥类型优势，保障社会稳定和社会民生。

面向未来，学校将进一步发挥职业教育在减贫中的造血能力、内生动力，在人才培养、产业发展、文旅融合、乡村振兴等方面持续发力，为实现巩固脱贫攻坚成果与乡村振兴有效衔接，为减贫事业做出更持久、更突出的贡献！

# （六）

# 贵州省职业教育助推脱贫增收的实践

贵州省教育厅党组成员、副厅长　杨天仪

抓好“顶层设计”，搭建职教兴黔富民通道。贵州省教育厅制定的《贵州省职业教育助力巩固脱贫攻坚成果同乡村振兴有效衔接工作方案》，从建设体系、目标任务、评价考核等方面，为贵州职业教育助力脱贫攻坚完善了政策保障。扎实推进一所高职院校带一所中职学校、围绕一个主导产业、组建一个服务团队的“1+1+1+1”行动计划，着力攻克乡村振兴中有关技术、管理和产品营销问题，解决群众后顾之忧。实施职业教育兴黔富民行动计划，安排省级专项资金 1.7 亿元，立项建设中高职项目 190 个，引领带动职业院校强内涵、助脱贫、兴乡村。

首创“校农结合”，开辟群众增收致富渠道。一是成立专班高位统筹。由省教育厅牵头成立省级专班，设立高等院校、职业院校、营养餐协调和农产品供应协调工作小组，分别负责相关学段“校农结合”工作，形成“贯通省市县、联动农商学、覆盖全学段”的工作合力。二是推动产销精准对接。按照“面上推进、点上突破、点面结合、不断深化”的思路，在铜仁、黔西南、贵阳、黔南地区以及清镇职教城分别抓好各学段“校农结合”集团化试点。形成“定点采购、产业培扶、基地建设、示范引领”发展模式和“贫困户 + 合作社 + 配送中心 + 学校”供销模式，将全省各级各类学校食堂这个稳定而庞大的农产品消费市场让给本地群众、生产大户、家庭农场和农业专业合作社，实现了贫困群众有增收、学校食材质量有提升的“一仗双赢”局面。三是总结经验深化创新。在推进“校农结合”中，我们从关注农产品购买，到助推农业产业结构调整，探索出一条符合贵州实际、具有教育特色、可持续发展的产业扶贫之路。据不完全统计，每年全省各级各类学校食堂累计采购本省农产品 70 万吨左右，采购金额约 50 亿元，有效带动省内 3 980 余个农产品生产基地（合作社）发展，辐射带动近百万群众发展生产，成为贵州群众增收致富的重要渠道。

落实“四个精准”，构筑脱贫输血造血管道。聚焦 14 个深度贫困县、20 个极贫乡镇，以“四个精准”推动实现“职教一人，就业一个，脱贫一家”。一是精准招生。实施政府和学校“双线目标责任制”，精准甄别和引导贫困家庭学生接受职业教育。落实县长、教育局局长、乡镇长、村主任、校长、家长、师长七长责任和义务教育阶段学生整班移交、排查报告、劝返复学三项机制，推动贫困地区学生高中阶段应读尽读。二是精准资助。对农村建档立卡贫困学生，在享受普惠政策基础上，实施“两助三免”。发挥好公益助学项目的同时，开设“绿色通道”，实现贫困学生无障碍入学。三是精准培养。遴选优质职业院校和企业合作，量身定制人才培养方案，丰富工学结合、半工半读内涵和形式，引导贫困学子自立自强、阳光自信，成为德技兼备、人生出彩的技术技能人才。四是精准就业。以订单班形式开办精准脱贫班，通过工学交替确保贫困学生毕业即就业。2015—2018 年，各职业院校完成“精准脱贫班”招生 32 000 余人，每年帮助 4 000 个家庭稳定脱贫。

立足技能贵州，铺就衔接乡村振兴大道。一是实施职业技能学历双提升工程。汇聚公安、人社、统计、商务等部门力量，聚焦 16—59 周岁未上学或低学历劳动者，按照“锁定对象、动员入学、对接产业、分类培养”路径，建立覆盖全省的双提升培训网络。充分考虑受教育者特点，配套编写完成双提升通识文化课程读本和专业技能课程读本，融入种、养殖和农产品加工等 11 个固定专业技能和 4 个地方特色需求专业技能，助其提升文化素养，学习一技之长。通过摸排，已精准锁定 87 万培训对象，已开展培训 7 万人，补齐“人均受教育年限低”短板的同时，让技能贵州建设成果更好地惠及人民。二是实施职业教育“双培养”工程。按照“前置选调、入学跟培、顶岗实习、跟踪管理”思路，每年从新入学中职学生中，择优选拔一批青年骨干进行跟踪培养，作为村级干部后备力量。同时从具备高中及以上学历的在任村党组织书记、村委会主任和优秀有潜力、能长期稳定的村支两委、部分返乡退伍军人中，培养乡村带头人，以人才振兴带动乡村振兴。

世界职业技术教育发展大会
WORLD VOCATIONAL AND TECHNICAL EDUCATION DEVELOPMENT CONFERENCE

# 十 面向未来的职业教育课程变革论坛

协助组织单位：华东师范大学教育学部职业教育与成人教育研究所

# X. Future-oriented Curriculum Reform in Vocational Education

Co-organizer: Institute of Vocational and Adult Education, Faculty of Education, East China Normal University

01
徐国庆
Xu Guoqing

02
克里斯·泽克尔
Chris Zirkle

03
穆罕默德·穆贾希德
Mohamed Megahed

04
王国川
Wang Guochuan

05
徐涵
Xu Han

06
马成荣
Ma Chengrong

**研讨如何围绕未来经济社会发展需求，设计、实施、评估职业教育的课程，分享各国职业教育课程改革的政策与实践经验，并就面向未来的职业教育课程改革方向达成共识。**

This session discusses how to design, implement and evaluate vocational education curriculum in response to the demand of future economic and social development. The participants share the policies and practical experience on curriculum reform in vocational education and try to reach consensus on future direction in this aspect.

## （一）

## 面向未来的职业教育课程变革论坛情况概述

华东师范大学教育学部职业教育与成人教育研究所所长　徐国庆

面向未来的职业教育课程变革论坛宗旨是深入探讨如何围绕未来经济社会发展对技能人才的需求，设计、实施、评估职业教育课程，分享各国职业教育课程改革的政策与实践经验，寻求面向未来职业教育课程改革方向的共识。该论坛由华东师范大学协助组织，教育学部职业教育与成人教育研究所所长徐国庆主持了该论坛。论坛包括两个环节，第一个环节是专家发言，第二个环节是课程理论家与课程实践者对话。共有 13 位专家作了发言，4 位专家参加对话，发言与对话专家分别来自中国、美国、德国、英国、加拿大、澳大利亚和埃及。专家们围绕论坛主题，就各自的研究课题发表见解，精彩纷呈，观点深刻，充满前瞻性。

华东师范大学职业教育与成人教育研究所名誉所长石伟平重点对职业教育教材评价进行了理论反思，从职业教育“好教材”的价值定位、性能分析、水平认证以及质量保障四个方面探讨了什么样的教材是“好教材”。

埃及教育与技术教育部副部长穆罕默德·穆贾希德分享了埃及抗击新冠病毒疫情的对策及面向未来的埃及技术与职业教育课程改革的经验。他认为，后疫情时代的职业教育应该高度重视 ICT（信息与通信技术）和信息化，充分运用虚拟仿真技术、增强现实技术和人工智能技术。目前，埃及主要通过五大支撑政策开启职业与技术教育的改革，例如，建立技术教育质素保障中心与埃及技术质量保证和认证网络等。

中华人民共和国教育部行业职业教育教学指导委员会工作办公室常务副主任王国川主要讨论了职业教育国家专业教学标准的建构逻辑。他认为专业教学标准是在专业层面解决为谁培养人、培养什么人、怎样培养人的问题，并指出专业教学标准的研制应采用需求导向、问题导向的方法论。他倡导根据培养规格要求，进行课程设置，搭建课程体系，并根据课程实施的需要，提出教学条件和师资队伍配置要求的基本逻辑。

沈阳师范大学辽宁省职业教育研究院教授徐涵分析了“工业 4.0”背景下德国职业教育课程改革的基本特征，例如，“工业 4.0”背景下德国职业教育课程改革具有围绕数字能力调整职业特征及资格要求、围绕数字能力调整课程目标，增设了与“数字能力”相关的学习目标等特征，并讨论了这些基本特征对面向未来的职业教育课程改革的启示。

北京师范大学教育学部教授赵志群介绍了 COMET 能力测评（职业能力测评）在职业院校质量评估中的应用。他认为当前我国职业教育质量评价存在内容体系缺失、评估程序专业性不高等一系列现实问题，而解决这些问题的关键在于评价方案的科学化设计。COMET 构建了系统化的评价体系及操作方案，该方案具有高度有效和可靠的测试程序，并以能力轮廓表示能力发展特征，这无疑具有重要意义。试点应用的结果显示，开放式测试任务得到了企业和学生的认可。

澳大利亚莫纳什大学教育、文化与社会学院教授苏珊·韦伯基于其近年来在澳大利亚进行的研究以及所参与的欧洲、北美、南美和南非一些在职业教育环境中提供高等教育的国家的研究（2022 年与简·奈特等人合作），分享了对职业教育与培训及高等教育系统如何响应学生的需求和第四次工业革命挑战的思考，并讨论了这对界限分明的教育系统以及那些意识到利益攸关而变得更加融通的教育系统的启示。

南京工业职业技术大学党委副书记马成荣主要就人本理念与科技范式转型视域下职业本科课程变革的适应性分析进行了阐述。他明确提出了“职业本科课程要回归育人本位，实现社会价值与人本价值的统一”，“以学生的学习、生长和发展为中心”是课程论本真话语的核心理念，科技范式转型为职业本科课程知识创新提供新的契机等观点。

美国俄亥俄州立大学教育与人类生态学院副教授克里斯·泽克尔主要讨论了美国中等学校，社区 / 技术学院、大学和公司在开发就业生涯路径课程中的作用与合作机制。他基于对当前美国存在的技能工人短缺、学生就业生涯规划意识和能力不强、学校和企业之间联系不紧密等问题的分析，提出了当前美国职业教育改革的一个重要方向，即关注学生的就业路径。

德国不来梅大学技术与教育研究所创始所长费利克斯·劳纳非常重视此次论坛，但其已 81 岁高龄，因身体原因，由其学生华东师范大学职业教育与成人教育研究所周瑛仪代为发言。劳纳教授主要就职业技术教育与培训的研究领域和视角展开讨论。他认为工业社会的现代化取决于先进的职业教育体系。职业教育和培训结构的国际化需要深入的相关研究，基于并行的学习路径概念，参与现代职业教育和教育系统的发展。他指出世界比以往任何时候都更需要专业人员和熟练工人的创造力。这种能力的培养需要一种植根于整体问题解决范式的教育理念，且需要建立从新手到专家的并行学习路径。

加拿大阿尔伯塔省劳工与移民部教育评估专员熊杰指出，加拿大是当前世界上国民受教育程度最高的国家，其原因在于加拿大人在高等职业院校获得教育的比例很高，而加拿大的学历职业教育主要为高等职业教育，包括社区、技术学院教育和学徒制教育。她以阿尔伯塔省为例，向我们展示了加拿大的行业如何积极参与高等职业教育课程开发，以确保高等职业教育课程为学生提供胜任未来工作岗位的技能和知识。

澳门科技大学酒店与旅游管理学院院长吴国民指出，中国拥有世界最大的职业教育系统，中国对职业教育的持续推动有助于其工业的进一步发展。他以美国俄克拉荷马州立大学为例，展示了该大学如何为学生的职业教育提供本科学历。

浙江金融职业学院副校长郭福春围绕高职院校数字化教学资源开发与实践，提出“以数字化教学资源推进专业内涵建设”。他认为数字化教学资源是指经过数字化处理，可以在多媒体计算机及网络环境下运行的多媒体教学材料，具有处理技术数字化、处理方式多媒体化、信息传输网络化、学习资源系列化等特征，是现代职业教育高质量发展的现实内在要求。

英国教育部常务秘书长苏珊·阿克兰·胡德分享了对“后疫情时代”英国职业技术教育所面临的主要挑战的思考。她认为在英国，人们已经意识到技术教育的重要性和价值，但近年来的不确定性进一步表明，英国需要面对挑战、克服困难并与其他国家相互学习。她认为职业教育在“后疫情时代”会得到进一步发展，但需要把建立更具弹性的教育和技能体系放在考量的首位。她还阐述了当前英国在职业教育领域面临的三个主要挑战。

在对话环节，南京工业职业技术大学党委书记吴学敏、广州番禺职业技术学院副校长刘佳环、柳州职业技术学院副校长鞠红霞和上海第二工业大学附属浦东振华外经职业技术学校校长董永华，围绕“职业教育课程建设的经验与成果”和“职业教育课程建设过程中面临的问题、挑战及对策”两个主题展开了讨论。

论坛讨论的课题非常广泛，产生了重要学术成果，对引领未来职业教育课程改革具有重要意义。归纳起来，专家们在以下观点上达成共识：（1）世界正处于快速变化中，新技术的涌现，尤其是智能化技术的广泛应用，正在重塑产业形态与工作过程，对技能人才的能力要求发生了深刻变化。职业教育学制体系、课程结构、课程内容、能力评价等均应做出变化，尤其在知识与技能的关系方面，要建立新的平衡模式；（2）职业教育课程设计要充分关注人的生涯发展需求。职业教育不仅要培养学生适应当前岗位的工作能力，更要培养他们在未来生涯发展中的潜力，课程内容要加强基础性；（3）职业教育课程开发要以校企合作为基本方法路径。职业教育课程的目标是培养职业能力，其知识主要存在于工作场所，只有通过深度的校企合作，才能有效开发工作知识，建立符合职业需要的课程内容体系。能力标准开发、证书体系建立、院校课程设计、职业能力评价等环节，均应对这一方法路径有所体现。

# i. Overview of the Session on Future-oriented Curriculum Reform in Vocational Education

**Xu Guoqing, Director of Institute of Vocational and Adult Education, Faculty of Education, East China Normal University, China**

The purpose of the session "Future-oriented Curriculum Reform in Vocational Education" is to discuss in depth how to design, implement and evaluate vocational education courses around the need of future economic and social development for skilled talents, share the policies and practical experiences of vocational education curriculum reform in various countries, and seek a consensus on the direction of future curriculum reform in vocational education. The session was co-organized by East China Normal University and was presided over by Professor Xu Guoqing, Director of the Institute of Vocational and Adult Education of the Faculty of Education. The session consists of two parts, the first part is experts' speeches, and the second part is the dialogue between curriculum theorists and curriculum practitioners. 13 experts made speeches and 4 experts participated in the dialogue. The experts came from China, US, Germany, UK, Canada, Australia and Egypt. Experts expressed their brilliant, profound and forward-looking opinions on their research topics around the theme of the session.

Shi Weiping, Honorary Director of Institute of Vocational and Adult Education, East China Normal University, China, focused on theoretical reflection on the evaluation of vocational education textbooks, and discussed what kind of textbooks could be called "good" from four aspects: value orientation, performance analysis, level certification and quality assurance.

Mohamed Megahed, Deputy Minister for Technical Education of the Ministry of Education and Technical Education, Egypt, shared Egypt's countermeasures against COVID-19 and the experience of future-oriented curriculum reform of technical and vocational education in Egypt. He believed that vocational education in the post-pandemic era should attach great importance to Information and Communications Technology (ICT) and informationization, and make full use of virtual simulation technology, augmented reality technology and artificial intelligence technology. At present, Egypt has started the reform of vocational and technical education mainly through five supporting policies, such as setting up the Technical Education Quality Assurance Center and the Egyptian Technical Quality Assurance and Certification Network.

Wang Guochuan, Executive Deputy Director of the Office of TVET Industry Steering Committee of the Ministry of Education, P.R. China, mainly discussed the construction logic of national professional teaching standards for vocational education. He thought that professional teaching standards could answer questions of for whom we provide the training, what kind of talents we should train and how to train talents at the professional level, and pointed out that the development of professional teaching standards should adopt demand-oriented and problem-oriented perspectives. He proposed setting up curriculum and building curriculum system according to the requirements of training specifications, and put forward the basic logic of teaching conditions and teaching staff allocation requirements according to the needs of curriculum implementation.

Xu Han, Professor of Liaoning Vocational Technical Education Institute, Shenyang Normal University, China, analyzed the basic characteristics of German vocational education curriculum reform under the background of Industry 4.0. For example, under the background of Industry 4.0, the curriculum reform of German vocational education boasts the characteristics of adjusting vocational characteristics and qualification requirements around digital ability, adding learning objectives related to "digital ability" around the curriculum objectives of digital ability adjustment, and he discussed the inspiration of these basic characteristics to future-oriented curriculum reform in vocational education.

Zhao Zhiqun, Professor at Faculty of Education, Beijing Normal University, China, introduced the application of COMET capacity evaluation in the quality evaluation of vocational colleges. He believed that there were a series of practical problems in the quality evaluation of vocational education in China, such as lack of content system and weak expertise in evaluation procedures, but the key to these problems actually lied in the scientific design of evaluation schemes. COMET constructs a systematic evaluation system and operation scheme. Such scheme has a highly effective and reliable test procedure, and it is of great significance to express the characteristics of capability development by capability profile. The results of pilot application have shown that the open test task was well received by enterprises and students.

Susan Webb, Professor at School of Education, Culture & Society, Monash University, Australia, shared her reflection on how vocational education and training and higher education systems respond to the needs of students and the challenges of the fourth industrial revolution based on her research in Australia in recent years, as well as the research on some countries in Europe, North America, South America and South Africa that provide higher education in vocational education environment (with

Jane Knight et al. in 2022), and discussed the inspiration to the well-defined education system and those education systems that have become more flexible when they realized the stakes.

Ma Chengrong, Deputy Secretary of CPC Committee of Nanjing Vocational University of Industry Technology, China, mainly expounded on the adaptability analysis of vocational undergraduate curriculum reform from the perspective of humanistic concept and science and technology paradigm transformation. He put forward the viewpoints that "vocational undergraduate courses should return to people as the center, and realize the unity of social value and humanistic value", "take students' study, growth and development as the center" is the core idea of the true discourse of curriculum theory, and the transformation of science and technology paradigm provides a new opportunity for knowledge innovation of vocational undergraduate courses.

Chris Zirkle, Associate Professor of College of Education and Human Ecology, the Ohio State University, US, mainly discussed the role and cooperation mechanism of American secondary schools, community/technical colleges, universities and companies in developing career pathway courses. Based on the analysis of the shortage of skilled workers, the weak awareness and ability of students' career planning, and the untight link between schools and enterprises in the United States, he gave an important direction of the current vocational education reform in the United States, that is, paying attention to students' career pathways.

Felix Rauner, Founding Director of the Institute of Technology and Education (ITB), University of Bremen, Germany, an internationally renowned vocational education expert, took this forum seriously. However, he asked Dr. Zhou Yingyi, Institute of Vocational and Adult Education, East China Normal University, to speak on his behalf due to health reasons at the age of 81. Professor Rauner mainly discussed the research fields and perspectives of vocational and technical education and training. He believed that the modernization of industrial society depended on advanced vocational education system. Internationalization of vocational education and training structure required thorough research, which was based on the concept of parallel learning path and participates in the development of modern vocational education and education system. He pointed out that the world needed the creativity of professionals and skilled workers more than ever before. The cultivation of this ability required an educational concept rooted in the holistic problem-solving paradigm, and was oriented to the establishment of a parallel learning path from novice to expert.

Xiong Jie, Education Assessor of the Ministry of Labour and Immigration, Government of Alberta, Canada, who has been engaged in higher vocational education research for more than 20 years, pointed out that Canada was a country with the highest education level in the world. The reason lied in a high proportion of Canadians receiving education in higher vocational colleges, while the academic vocational education in Canada was mainly higher vocational education, including community/technical college education and apprenticeship education. She took Alberta as an example, and showed us how Canadian industries actively participated in the development of higher vocational education curriculum to ensure that higher vocational education curriculum provided students with skills and knowledge required for future jobs.

Ben Goh Kok Beng, Dean of Faculty of Hospitality and Tourism Management, Macau University of Science and Technology, China, pointed out that China had the largest vocational education system in the world, and China's continuous promotion of vocational education was conducive to the further development of its industry. He took Oklahoma State University in the US as an example, and showed how the university offered undergraduate degrees for students' vocational education.

Guo Fuchun, Vice President of Zhejiang Financial College, China, put forward "promoting specialty connotation construction with digital teaching resources" around the development and practice of digital teaching resources in higher vocational colleges. He believed that digital teaching resources refered to multimedia teaching materials that had been digitally processed and could run under multimedia computer and network environment. They had the characteristics of digitalization of processing technology, processing in multimedia, networking of information transmission and serialization of learning resources, which was the realistic and inherent requirement for the high-quality development of modern vocational education.

Susan Ackland-Hood, Permanent Secretary at the Department for Education, UK, shared her thoughts on the main challenges facing British vocational and technical education in the post-pandemic era. She believed that people in Britain were aware of the importance and value of technical education, but the uncertainty in recent years further showed that Britain needed to face challenges and learn from other countries. She believed that vocational education was going to be further developed in the post-pandemic era, but it was necessary to put the establishment of a more flexible education and skills system in the first place. She also elaborated on three major challenges facing Britain in vocational education.

In the dialogue session, Wu Xuemin, General Secretary of CPC Committee of Nanjing Vocational University of Industry Technology, China, Liu Jiahuan, Vice President of Guangzhou Panyu Polytechnic, China, Ju Hongxia, Vice President of Liuzhou Vocational and Technical College, China, and Dong Yonghua, Principal of Pudong Zhenhua Foreign Trade Professional School affiliated to Shanghai Polytechnic University, China, discussed "the experience and achievements of vocational education curriculum construction" and "the problems, challenges and countermeasures in the process of vocational education curriculum construction".

The extensive topics discussed on the session produced important academic achievements, which is of great significance for leading the future curriculum reform of vocational education. To sum up, experts have a consensus on the following viewpoints: (1) The world is changing rapidly, and the emergence of new technologies, especially the wide application of intelligent technologies, is reshaping the industrial type and working process, and profoundly changing the capability requirements for skilled talents. The educational system, curriculum structure, curriculum content and ability evaluation of vocational education should change, especially in the relationship between knowledge and skills, and a new balance model should be established. (2) Vocational education curriculum design should pay full attention to career development needs. Vocational education should not only cultivate students' working ability to adapt to current posts but also cultivate their potential in future career development, so the curriculum should strengthen foundation. (3) The curriculum development of vocational education should take school-enterprise cooperation as the basic method and path. The goal of vocational education curriculum is to cultivate vocational ability, and its knowledge mainly exists in the workplace. Only through deep school-enterprise cooperation can we effectively develop working knowledge and establish a curriculum content system that meets vocational needs. The principle of this method should be embodied in the development of ability standard, the establishment of certificate system, the curriculum design of colleges and universities, and the evaluation of vocational ability.

# (二)

# 中等学校、社区 / 技术学院、大学和公司在开发职业 / 就业路径课程中的作用与合作

美国俄亥俄州立大学教育与人类生态学院副教授 克里斯·泽克尔

目前，美国技术工人的短缺促使多部门进行合作，以解决人才重大需求。本报告将探讨这种合作如何助力开发聚焦多个不同职业领域的课程路径，主要是那些与美国高技能、高工资工作相关的职业领域。

目前，由于美国的技术工人短缺，许多技术性专业工作岗位空缺，公司正在努力填补空缺职位。职业教育项目（在美国被称为职业与技术教育）正试图通过开发专注于工作场所需求的新项目来填补这一需求。然而，这些努力受到一些因素的阻碍，包括学生并不是很了解职业机会及许多学生会中途改变教育路径。此外，教育机构和公司在课程开发和职工胜任工作所需的具体技能和知识方面缺乏沟通。

许多年来，美国的职业教育被称为问题学生的“垃圾场”，其特点是学术标准低、课程和设备陈旧、教师准备不充分。但是最近几年这种情况有所改变，已经有许多积极的改进措施，以提高职业教育项目的质量，其中之一便是就业路径的课程创新。

学校用来解决课程开发需求的一个策略是发展就业路径。就业路径是将严谨的高质量教育与培训相结合，其培训重点不是单一的工作，而是特定职业“集群”所需的技能和知识，如制造业、建筑业或健康科学。这些路径还将中等与中等后教育结合起来，为学生创造一个顺畅的学业旅程，以获得行业认可的证书、技术技能和其他教育证书，如副学士和学士学位。根据美国 2014 年《劳动力创新与机会法案》中的定义，就业路径是严谨和高质量的教育、培训和符合以下条件的其他服务的结合：

- 与国家或地区经济中的行业技能需求相一致；

- 为个人在包括注册学徒在内的各类中等教育或中等后教育的选择中取得成功做准备；
- 包括支持个人实现其教育和职业目标的咨询；
- 酌情包括与就业准备活动和特定职业或职业群的培训同时提供的等同的教育；
- 组织教育、培训和其他服务，以满足个人的特殊需要，并在实际可行的范围内促进个人的教育和职业发展；
- 使个人能够获得中等学校文凭或公认的同等学力以及至少一个公认的中等后教育文凭；
- 帮助个人进入特定职业或职业群，或在其中取得进步。(《劳动力创新与机会法案》第3条第7款)

美国教育部设立了16个不同的职业群或就业路径，包括农业、食品和自然资源，建筑与建工，艺术、视听与沟通，商业、管理与行政，教育与培训，金融，政府与公共管理，健康科学，旅店与旅游，公共服务，信息技术，法律、公共安全、惩戒与安保，制造，市场、销售与服务，科学、技术、工程与数学，运输、配送与物流。

学校早在中年级（6年级到8年级）就开始了就业路径课程。这些课程一般是9至18周的短期入门课程，如计算机应用基础和键盘操作，农业简介，卫生、安全与保健，金融素养，工程学基础。

9—10年级的学生需要考虑完成中学教育后的职业方向，许多学校在这些年级开始提供职业咨询。这个年龄段的学生可以考虑大学、大学预科课程或更加聚焦职业的课程。学校会提供更多的路径课程来帮助他们确定学习方向，如健康行业介绍，编程和软件开发基础，农业企业和生产系统的构成，制造业原理。

当学生在11—12年级接近高中毕业时，如果他们选择了更多的聚焦职业和就业的课程，那么课程就开始集中于密集的职业培训以及与职业课程相关的学术准备。例如，如果职业课程属于健康科学领域，学术课程可能包括生物、化学、解剖学和生理学等科目。课程会特别强调技术技能的发展，学生也可以在其学习领域获得行业认可的证书。课程还会注意通过就业技能培训发展学生的软技能，聚焦职业道德、团队合作和人际交往技能等主题。

虽然学生毕业后可能进入劳动力市场，但他们仍有可能在高中毕业后继续在两年制社区或技术学院、大学、学徒制机构或军队接受教育。重要的是要注意，学生并没有被“锁定”在一条道路上——他们可以凭借自己所掌握的技能去工作，或者继续接受更多自己选择的教育。

对继续教育的关注也带来了职业教育课程的更多改进。由于这些就业路径课程的发展，其与中等后教育的联系得到了改善，职业教育现在提供大学预科课程和双学分选择，学生可以同时获得高中和大学的学分，并通过衔接协议将这些学分转移到中等后教育机构，实现从高中到大学的无缝过渡。这些协议还可以缩短获得副学士学位或额外行业认证的时间。

如果一个学生希望继续接受正规教育，他们中有相当一部分人会选择通过社区学院或技术学院接受专业培训。在这些学院中，学生可以获得副学士学位（比学士学位低一级），也可以在副学士学位期间同时获得（或继续获得，如果他们从高中就开始学习）行业认可的证书。这些两年的教育和培训包含高度集中的技术教育和辅助性的普通教育、学术教育。一些课程提供实习或其他类型的基于工作的学习机会。学院可提供的学位包括：建筑管理、紧急医疗技术员、消防员、牙科卫生、游戏开发师等。

以前，雇主和公司没有在员工培训课程开发方面发挥重要作用。然而，最近的劳动力短缺使他们认识到必须参与解决这个问题。因此，在过去几年中，教育机构（高中、社区 / 技术学院和大学）和公司之间建立了更多的伙伴关系，雇主参与课程开发，提供基于工作的学习机会，一般会在教育过程中更多地成为学校的合作伙伴。这些雇主还通过参与咨询委员会向职业教育项目提供建议和咨询，这是项目获得联邦资助的要求。根据其职能，咨询委员会可以在以下领域开展活动：课程和教学、项目审查、招聘和就业安置、学生组织、员工发展、社区关系与公共关系、资源和立法。他们的参与为职业教育项目带来了宝贵的洞察力，并有助于减少学校和雇主之间的脱节。

如前所述，在过去几年中，在就业路径中将基于工作的学习作为职业生涯路径课程一部分的做法已经有了很大的发展。基于工作的学习是一种教学策略，它通过将课堂学习与工作场所联系起来以加强课堂学习效果。过去，围绕职业教育的批评之一是在为学生提供“真实的”工作经验方面缺乏企业和行业的参与，他们本应成为关键合作伙伴。但今天，更多的雇主愿意通过为学生提供机会来支持这些活动。

广义而言，基于工作的学习经验范围很广，可能包括以下活动：（1）合作教育，工作经历是职业课程的一部分，并获得学分；（2）影子实习，学校安排的对工作场所的观察访问；（3）社区服务，由学校安排的支持当地社区的志愿者工作；

（4）实习，职业课程以外的工作经历；（5）辅导，由学校安排一位特定职业领域的成年人进行对接；（6）校办企业，在由学生或教师经营的校内企业工作；（7）职业聚焦，完成单一职业领域的一系列职业课程作业。这些经验旨在“促进对特定职业领域所需任务的深入、亲身参与”（《加强 21 世纪职业与技术教育法案》，2018 年）。

就业路径课程的发展为职业学生、职业教育项目和寻求合格雇员的雇主带来了诸多益处。中等教育和中等后教育机构之间的合作以及与公司和组织的合作，进一步加持了这些益处。就美国职业教育的改进而言，就业路径在课程方面已取得显著积极的发展。

## ii. Roles and Cooperation Between Secondary Schools, Community/Technical Colleges, Universities and Companies in the Development of Vocational/Career Pathway Curriculum

**Chris Zirkle, Associate Professor of College of Education and Human Ecology, the Ohio State University, US**

The present shortage of skilled labor in the United States has prompted cooperation between multiple partners to address this significant need. The presentation will examine how collaboration has helped to develop curricular pathways focused on several different career areas, primarily those associated with high-skill, high-wage jobs in the United States.

At the present time, there is a shortage of skilled labor in the US. Many jobs in the technical disciplines are vacant, and companies are struggling to fill open positions. Vocational education programs (known in the US as career and technical education) are trying to fill this need by developing new programs focused on the needs of the workplace. However, these efforts are hampered by several different variables including students who are not always aware of career opportunities, and many students who start one educational path and then change their mind. In addition, educational institutions and companies have not always communicated with each other in terms of curricular development and what specific skills and knowledge are needed to be successful in the workplace.

For many decades, the vocational education discipline in the United States had a reputation as a "dumping ground" for troubled students, and was characterized by low academic standards, outdated curricula and facilities, and poorly prepared teachers. However, things has changed in recent years, and many positive changes have been implemented to improve the quality of vocational education programs. One of these improvements is the focus on the curriculum innovation of career pathways.

One strategy schools are using to address the curricular development needs is the development of career pathways. A career pathway is a combination of rigorous and high-quality education, with training focused not on a single job, but on the skills and knowledge needed in a specific career "cluster" such as manufacturing, construction or the health sciences. These pathways also combine secondary and postsecondary education to create a smooth journey for students to earn industry-recognized credentials, technical skills and other educational credentials such as associate and bachelor's degrees. As defined by the Workforce Innovation and Opportunity Act (WIOA) in 2014, a career pathway is a combination of rigorous and high quality education, training, and other services that:

• aligns with the skill needs of industries in the economy of the State or regional economy involved;

• prepares an individual for the success in any secondary or postsecondary education options, including registered apprenticeships;

• includes counseling to support an individual in achieving their education and career goals;

• includes, as appropriate, education offered concurrently in the same context as workforce preparation activities and training for a specific occupation or career cluster;

• organizes education, training, and other services to meet particular needs of an individual in a manner that accelerates the educational and career advancement of the individual to the practicable extent;

• enables an individual to attain a secondary school diploma or its recognized equivalent, and at least one recognized postsecondary credential;

• helps an individual enter or advance within a specific occupation or career cluster. [Section 3(7) of WIOA]

There are 16 different career clusters or pathways that have been created by the United States Department of Education including: Agriculture, Food, and Natural Resources; Architecture and Construction; Arts, A/V and Communications; Business, Management and Administration; Education and Training; Finance; Government and Public Administration; Health Science; Hotels and Tourism; Human Services; Information Technology; Law, Public Safety, Corrections, and Security; Manufacturing; Marketing, Sales and Service; Science, Technology, Engineering and Mathematics; Transportation, Distribution and Logistics.

Schools are beginning career pathways as early as the middle grades (from 6th grade to 8th grade). These are generally short-term introductory courses over 9 to 18 weeks and some course examples include: Basic Computer Applications and Keyboarding; Introduction to Agriculture; Health, Safety and Wellness; Financial Literacy; Basics of Engineering.

In grades 9-10, students need to think about a career direction after they complete secondary education, and many schools begin to provide career advising at these grade levels. Students of this age may consider college/university preparatory courses or a more vocational focus. Schools try to offer more pathway courses to help them determine a direction for their studies. Sample courses at this grade level can include: Introduction to Health Careers; Basics of Programming and Software Development; Components of Agribusiness & Production Systems; Manufacturing Principles.

As students approach high school graduation in grades 11–12, if they have chosen a course which focuses more on vocation and career, courses begin to focus on intensive vocational training, with academic preparation related to vocational program. For example, if a vocational program belongs to the health sciences, academic courses may include subjects such as biology, chemistry and anatomy and physiology. There is a specific emphasis on technical skill development, and students can also earn industry-recognized certificates in their area of study. Attention is also given to the development of soft skills through employability skills training, focusing on topics such as work ethic, teamwork and interpersonal skills.

While students may graduate and enter the workforce, there is still an assumption that students may continue education at a 2-year community or technical college, a university, in an apprenticeship or military after they graduated from high schools. It is important to note that students are not "locked in" a path at this point—they can go to work with the skills they have or pursue more education by choice.

The focus on further education also has led to more curricular improvements in vocational education. Ties to postsecondary education have been improved because of the development of these career pathways and vocational education now offers college preparatory courses and dual credit options in which students can earn both high school and college credit simultaneously and transfer these credits to postsecondary institutions via articulation agreements to provide for a seamless transition from high school to college. These agreements can also shorten the time it takes to earn an associate degree or additional industry certification.

If a student wishes to continue their formal education, a significant percentage of them opt for specialized training through a community college or a technical college. In these institutions, a student can earn an associate degree (lower than a bachelor's degree) and can also begin to earn (or continue to earn, if they started in high schools) industry-recognized certificates during their associate degree. The two years of education and training at these institutions contain highly focused technical education with supporting general/academic education. Some programs offer internships or other types of work-based learning opportunities. Sample degrees from these institutions include: Construction Management; Emergency Medical Technician; Firefighter; Dental Hygiene; Game Developer.

Historically, employers and companies have not played significant roles in the development of curriculum for the workplace. However, the recent labor shortage has caused employers to recognize they must be part of the solution to the problem. As a result, more partnerships between educational institutions (high schools, community/

technical colleges and universities) and companies have been developed in the past few years, with employer involvement in curriculum development, participation in work-based learning opportunities, and in general, becoming more of a partner with schools in the educational process. These employers also provide advice and counsel to vocational education programs via participation in advisory committees, a requirement for programs to receive federal funding. Depending on their function, advisory committees may conduct activities in the following areas: curriculum and instruction, program review, recruitment and job placement, student organizations, staff development, community/public relations, resources, and legislation. Their participation brings valuable insight into vocational education programs and helps reduce the disconnection between schools and employers.

As mentioned, the use of work-based learning as part of the curriculum in career pathways has developed considerably in the past few years. Work-based learning is an instructional strategy that enhances classroom learning by connecting it to the workplace. In the past, one of the criticisms surrounding vocational education was the lack of business and industry which should be key partners to provide "real-world" work experiences for students. But today, more employers are willing to support these activities by providing opportunities for students.

Broadly speaking, work-based learning experiences are wide-ranging and may include the following activities: (1) Cooperative Education, a work experience that is part of a vocational class for which credit is earned; (2) Job Shadowing, a school-arranged visit to a workplace for observational purposes; (3) Community Service, volunteer work arranged by the school to support the local community; (4) Internships, work experience that is not necessarily part of a vocational class; (5) Mentoring, a school-arranged match with an adult in an identified career area; (6) School-Based Enterprise, work with a business run by students or teachers within the school; and (7) Occupational Concentration, completion of a sequence of career-coursework in a single occupational field. These experiences are designed to "foster in-depth, firsthand engagement with the tasks required in a given career field" (Strengthening Career and Technical Education for the 21st Century Act, 2018).

The development of career pathways has led to many benefits for vocational students, vocational education programs, and for employers seeking to find qualified employees. The collaborations between secondary and postsecondary education institutions, along with partnerships with companies and organizations have strengthened these benefits even further. Career pathways have been a significantly positive curricular development for the improvement of vocational education in the US.

# （三）

# 埃及抗击新型冠状病毒的对策及面向未来的埃及技术与职业教育课程改革

埃及教育与技术教育部副部长　穆罕默德·穆贾希德

埃及与天津已有建设性的合作经历，埃及已经有两个鲁班工坊，其中一个设立于开罗的一所高级技术学校内。这两个工坊在汽车和数控机床方面开展了建模活动项目。说到埃及技术教育的规模，实际上，埃及拥有中东和北非地区最大的职业技术教育与培训体系。埃及教育和技术教育部（以下简称教育部）建立了一个正规的职业技术教育与培训体系，其中有超过 220 万名活跃学员、约 17 万名教师、3 000 所学校以及 120 多个技术教育项目。另外还有大约 50 万名学员参加了非正式的职业技术教育与培训。最近，我们还创设了新的技术教育学校品牌——应用技术学校。此外，还有一项正在进行的改革战略，叫作“技术教育 2.0”。2020 年 3 月 15 日之后，所有学校都因疫情而暂时关闭。针对这种情况，教育部立刻组建了一个特别工作组，并采取了一系列的应对措施。

在新冠病毒疫情的初期，我们广泛采用了线上会议的形式，创建了线上课堂。所有教师都接受了教育部及其他平台上开展的培训。一些教师接受了电子内容设计的培训，还有一些教师接受了专业视频制作的培训。同时，我们还应用了多元的教学评估手段。例如，在 2020 年，我们记录了所有学生第一学期的学习成绩，第二学期我们要求学生自主提交成绩并申请研究项目。此外，我们还要求学生在第二学年提前 3 周到校，在车间进行实训。这些项目的参与者总数接近 100 万人，其中有 3/4 是学生群体，1/4 是监考教师。当然，政府也必须为此提供有力的财政支持。

从 2020 年年底，我们开始大量使用信息与通信技术及数字化技术来提供混合式学习，运用了模拟器、增强现实、虚拟现实以及人工智能等多种技术。我们还对教师和学生的反馈进行了分析，总结经验教训。

与此同时，我们也正在实施一项技术教育改革的转型战略——技术教育 2.0。这一战略拥有五大核心理念作为其运行基础。第一个理念是提高技术教育的质量，我们马上会建立一个更加优秀的、独立的职业技术教育与培训质量保障部门。第二个理念是用以能力为基础的课程取代以内容为基础的课程，提高技术教育课程的相关性。第三个理念是通过培训和资格认证来实现教师队伍的转型。第四个理念是通过用人单位的参与助力学校转型，应用技术学校和双元制体系就是很好的例子。第五个理念是通过上述所有行动，转变技术教育的形象。

我们成立应用技术学校的核心思路是在 2018 年形成应用技术学校网络。这是一个新的双元制教育体系，以教育部为代表的政府部门、私营企业和国际质量保障机构之间的合作为基础。这实际上保证了应用技术学校能够发挥最大的潜力，其最终目的是让学校和课程能够获得国际认可。

事实上，我们有很多合作方可以作为范例，如东芝、夏普、IBM、大众汽车以及中埃联合控股公司——HST、大型黄金开采制造公司——埃及黄金和大型移动通信公司——VE。

应用技术学校的主要特点是通过建立合作伙伴关系，培养世界一流水平的劳动力。毕业生将会极具竞争力，性格沉稳、技能扎实，并能保持终身学习的习惯。企业参与学校管理，确保应用技术学校能符合当地及全球市场的发展趋势。学校管理人员由私营企业代表主导的董事会领导。当然，课程设置会完全以培育能力为基础，我们也会打造最好的师资力量。此类学校是免费的，学习环境体面舒适，对学生有非常大的吸引力。这些学校形成的专业化、品牌化网络可以提升技术教育的形象。应用技术学校可以发展成为行业能力中心，它不仅是为大型企业服务，而且还为一群小规模的中小企业联合体服务。这是继应用技术学校之后的又一次创新。

我们制订了应用技术学校和能力中心的未来发展计划。我们设立了一个专门的管理部门来管理这些新学校，与时俱进修订了管理规则，还拥有强大的政治决心。埃及总统塞西 2018 年出席了第一所学校的建校典礼。我们在选择合作伙伴时非常细心谨慎。它们必须具备两个条件。首先是企业须承担社会责任，但这还远远不够。它们还需要对高技能型人才求贤若渴，并有明确的发展规划。在这方面，我们有一些国际参与者，如美国和欧盟。各个专业岗位的未来发展是一大关键点。要想建设新的专业，也要借助外部培训师和专家的力量。这些培训师和专家是由行业伙伴提供的，在建成自己的专家人才库之前，我们需要这些帮助。

应用技术学校未来的可持续发展主要基于如下理念。首先，我们允许学校建立收费的职业培训中心，也可以建立服务或生产单位，为周边社区服务。这一构想实际上是可行的，尤其适用于汽车行业。而且，学校也可以为其他机构提供培训服务。现在，在联合国开发计划署发布的全球知识指数中，我们的排名上升了33位。这些都是振奋人心的好消息，必将有助于提高技术教育的社会认可度。

## iii. Egypt's Response to Combating COVID-19 Consequences & Future-Oriented Curriculum Reform in Technical & Vocational Education in Egypt

**Mohamed Megahed, Deputy Minister for Technical Education of the Ministry of Education and Technical Education, Egypt**

We have positive experiences with Tianjin in Egypt since we already have two Luban workshops in Egypt. One of them is located in an advanced technical school in Cairo. And the two workshops run modeling activities programs in automobiles and CNC machines. About the size of the technical education in Egypt, Egypt actually has the largest TVET system in the Middle East and North Africa region. The Ministry of Education and Technical Education (MOETE) provides a formal TVET system, with more than 2.2 million active learners, about 170 000 teachers, 3 000 schools, and more than 120 technical education programs. In the non-formal TVET, we have about 0.5 million learners. Recently, we have a new brand of technical education schools called the Applied Technology Schools. We also have an ongoing reform strategy called Technical Education 2.0. Starting from March 15, 2020, all schools were closed due to the Pandemic, and immediately a task force was started by MoETE, and we started implementing a number of actions.

During the early days of Covid-19, virtual meetings were used extensively. We used it in MoETE portal to create virtual classes. All teachers were trained on the MoETE as well as other platforms. Some teachers were trained to design electronic content, and some other teachers were trained to produce professional videos. We make sure that there is a mix of assessment techniques. For example, in the year 2020, we recorded results of the first semester for all students. And we ask the student to submit results and apply for the research project in the second semester. And also we asked the students to come earlier the next year, to conduct the practical training in the workshops. These items were provided to almost 1 million individuals, of which 3/4 were students and 1/4 were teachers who supervised the exam. Of course, the government has to allocate a lot of financial resources to serve these purposes.

Toward the end of 2020, we started using ICT and digitalization heavily in providing blended learning. We used simulators, augmented and virtual reality and Artificial Intelligence. Teachers' and students' feedback was analyzed to come up with the lessons learned.

At the same time, we were in the middle of implementing a transformation strategy for technical education reform that we call TE 2.0. This strategy actually is based upon five pillars. Pillar number one is transforming quality of technical education. Actually, we are about to establish a finer and independent quality assurance authority for TVET. Pillar number two deals with transforming the relevance of technical education programs through adopting competency-based curricula in place of content-based curricula. Pillar three is transforming teachers through training and qualification. Pillar four is transforming schools through employer engagement, like the example of Applied Technology Schools and the dual system. Pillar five is changing the image of technical education through all the above actions.

In the Applied Technology Schools, the main idea we started with is establishing a network of these schools in 2018. It's the new system of dual technical education based on the partnership between the government, as represented by MoETE, and the private sector plus an international quality assurance agency. This actually ensures that the Applied Technical School reaches its highest possible potential with the final aim of getting international accreditation for the school and the programs.

In fact, we have many examples of partners, including TOSHIBA, SHARP, IBM, VOLKSWAGEN, HST, which is a joint Chinese Egyptian holding company, Egypt Gold, which is a gold manufacturing company, and VE, which is a mobile communication company.

The main feature of the Applied Technology Schools is to establish and develop world-class workforce through partnerships. Competitive graduates with a balanced character and skill foundation will be capable of lifelong learning. The school is co-managed with employers to ensure that the Applied Technology Schools are meeting the local and global market trends. The management is led by a board headed by private sector representatives. Of course, the curricula are totally competency-based. We would prepare the best teachers and mentors. It's the non-fee-based school providing a decent and inviting learning environment. The professionally branded network of school enhances the image of technical education. The Applied Technology Schools can evolve into what we call sectoral centers of competencies that will serve not only big companies, but a group of small and medium enterprises in a consortium as well. This is the next wave of innovation following Applied Technology Schools.

We made future plans for Applied Technology Schools and centers of competencies. We established a dedicated management unit to run these new schools. We changed the regulation where necessary. There is high political commitment. President El-Sisi inaugurated the first school in 2018. We are very careful in selecting the partners. They must have two things. One is corporate social responsibility, but that's not enough. They must actually need skilled workers and have clear expansion plans. We have support from international development partners like the USA and the EU in this regard. The future of jobs is key. To introduce new specialization means also using external trainers and experts that are provided by the industrial partners until MoETE actually develops its own staff.

The future sustainability of Applied Technology Schools is based upon a number of concepts. First of all, we allow the schools to establish fee-based vocational training centers to serve the surrounding community. They can also establish service or production units to actually serve the surrounding community. This is actually applicable, particularly to automotive companies. These schools also provide training or trainer services for other institutions. Now, in the UNDP issues of global knowledge index, we actually make a significant rise of 33 positions. These are good news that will surely serve to enhance the social perception of technical education.

# （四）

# 职业教育国家专业教学标准的建构逻辑

中华人民共和国教育部行业职业教育教学指导委员会工作办公室常务副主任　王国川

进入新时代，党中央国务院高度重视职业教育，加大力度推动职业教育改革发展，不断增强职业教育对经济社会发展需求的适应性。职业教育从体制、机制和保障上加强和完善体系建设，不断巩固类型特征，补短板、强弱项、扬优势，加强内涵建设，对接经济社会改革发展新要求，适应新经济、新业态、新技术、新职业需求，调整专业设置，修订专业教学标准，推进专业升级和数字化改造，切实推动人才培养质量提升。

没有标准就没有质量，专业教学标准是在专业层面解决为谁培养人、培养什么人、怎样培养人的问题，也是职业院校制订人才培养方案、组织专业教学、引导专业建设、开展专业质量评价的基本依据。

制定国家层面的专业教学标准，首先，应该明确用什么理论基础作为指导。经过几十年实践探索，中国职业教育走过了沿袭普通教育模式、借鉴发达国家模式、通过借鉴消化吸收改革形成中国特色的自主模式几个阶段，这一过程中，逐步确立了马克思主义关于人的全面发展学说、教育本质的理论、行动导向教学理论、系统论作为指导专业教学标准建设的理论基础。其次，应明确采用什么方法论实施教学标准研制。鉴于职业教育的类型特征和根本任务，职业教育是以就业为导向的教育，所以职业教育的专业要对接职业，专业内涵要反映职业需求，也就是专业要搞清楚为什么职业领域培养人，培养具备什么素质、拥有什么知识能力结构和处于什么层次的人，专业培养目标反映的是职业需求而不是学科需求，这是职业教育与普通教育的本质区别。依据这样的理念，职业教育国家专业教学标准研制的方法论应该是需求导向、问题导向。再有，应明晰建构逻辑和实现路径。按照需求导向、问题导向的方法论，依据关键要素的相关性，专业教学标准的建构逻辑应该将需求作为逻辑起点，根据需求确定培养目标与规格，根据培养目标与规格搭建课程体系，根据课程体系安排师资队伍和教学条件，根据培养过程和培养规格提出质量保障和毕业要求。具体讲，需求就是专业人才的职业需求，也就是胜任职业领域工作需要的“德”和“技”，“德”就是党和国家对专业人才德智体美劳方面的总体要求，也是对做人的要求，“技”就是技术技能，即学生应具备哪些技术技能，也是对做事的要求。

那么需求从哪里找？怎么找？一是从专业对应的职业标准中找，二是从专业对应的职业领域、技术领域的实际工作任务中找，这需要通过文献调研和实际工作岗位调研获得。实现路径和方法是，选准专业对应的职业、岗位群或技术领域，先调研职业标准，再调研实际工作任务，根据这两方面的调研结果，作职业分析和梳理归纳，形成若干典型工作任务，结合党和国家对人才培养的总体要求，按照素质、知识、能力三个维度进行解构分析，依据系统论原理，采用一定的逻辑编排，形成专业人才培养目标和培养规格要求。培养规格要求确定后，按照前后对应关系搭建课程体系，课程体系按照公共基础课、公共拓展课、专业基础课、专业核心课、专业拓展课属性分类设置课程，需要注意的是，课程设置的依据是培养规格要求，也就是课程是承载培养规格要求的载体单元，培养规格要求条目和课程之间是一对一、一对多或多对一关系。另外，一般情况下，一门专业核心课程会对应一项典型工作任务。课程体系搭建完成后，依据课程实施需要的师资、教学环境和条件，提出师资队伍和教学条件要求，师资队伍、教学条件要体现职业教育特征，强化理实一体化教学理念和校企合作、工学结合、学训结合要求。为了保证人才培养质量，国家专业教学标准对质量保障和毕业要求应该统一，要以提高和保障教学质量为目标，运用系统方法，依靠必要的组织机构，把学校各部门、各环节的教学质量管理活动严密组织起来，将教学和信息反馈的整个过程中影响教学质量的一切因素控制起来，形成一个有明确任务、职责、权限的相互协调、相互促进的质量管理有机整体。为了统一毕业生的层次和规格，国家从宏观上提出德智体美劳要求和最低毕业学分要求是必要的。

综上，职业教育国家专业教学标准的建构逻辑是：落实党和国家对人才培养的总体要求，选准专业对应的职业领域，根据职业、岗位群或技术领域的实际工作内容，进行职业分析，获得典型工作任务，再对典型工作任务按照素质、知识、能力三个维度解构，形成培养规格要求，根据培养规格要求，进行课程设置，搭建课程体系，根据课程实施的需要，提出师资队伍配置和教学条件要求，根据培养过程和培养规格，提出质量保障和毕业要求。这条逻辑线是连续的、递进因果的。

## （五）

# 工业 4.0 背景下德国职业教育课程改革的基本特征及启示

沈阳师范大学辽宁省职业教育研究院教授　徐　涵

数字化和网络化是“工业 4.0”最基本的特征。“工业 4.0”背景下的制造业，物理世界与数字世界联系在一起，形成完全网络化的制造过程。数字素养已经成为数字化工作世界最基本的职业行动能力。

德国联邦职业教育研究所的克雷默与媒体和能力研究所的卢茨在“企业和职业学校的数字能力教育目标”报告（2015）中，采用企业实地调研的方式，对培训师进行深度访谈，并依据访谈结果归纳出以下 8 项具体的数字能力：能够熟练使用本专业的软件；能够借助数字媒体与他人进行有效沟通；自主解决工作过程中出现的问题；对于数字媒体相关的法律法规具有清晰的认识；能够借助数字媒体积极持续地参与专业交流；能够判断新的媒体是否对于自己的专业有用；能够使用普通办公软件；能够自主开发媒体应用。

为了应对经济界对技术技能人才的数字能力的新要求，2016 年，在德国联邦职业教育研究所的支持下，德国金属及电气行业雇主协会、德国机械设备制造业联合会、德国电气和电子制造商协会和德国金属行业工会决定联合修订工业金属和电气行业的《职业教育条例》。《职业教育条例》是德国双元制职业教育的法律依据，既是制订企业一元的职业培训计划的基本依据，也是制订学校一元的框架教学计划的基本依据。2018 年 8 月 1 日，金属和电气行业领域中机电一体工等 11 个教育职业的《职业教育条例》修订完成并正式启用，开启了德国新一轮的职业教育课程改革，此轮改革呈现出以下基本特征。

**1. 围绕数字能力调整教育职业特征及资格要求**

在德国金属和电气行业领域新修订的《职业教育条例》中，一是增设了一个新的教育职业特征“工作数字化、数据保护和信息安全”。要求金属和电气行业领域中的所有教育职业要聚焦工作数字化转型，传授“工作数字化、数据保护和信息安全”内容；二是对现有其他教育职业特征及资格要求进行了调整，增加数字能力方面的要求，例如，教育职业特征“企业和技术交流”中重点要求学生“能够使用互联网技术处理系统，能够在虚拟空间中进行数据交流”；三是新修订的《职业教育条例》增设“数字化网络”“编程”“互联网技术安全”“增材制造工艺”等与数字能力相关的附加资格模块。

**2. 围绕数字能力调整课程目标，增设了与“数字能力”相关的学习目标**

根据《职业教育条例》的变化，修订职业学校一元的框架教学计划，将数字能力融入课程目标。例如，机电一体工的框架教学计划中，学习领域 2“使用机器加工零件”的学习目标中强调，“能够借助应用程序来创建和更改零件图以及制订相应的工作计划”，并补充“利用计算机辅助制图”；学习领域 4“技术系统的维护”中添加“学生使用数字信息，进行技术系统的维护”等。

**3. 课程内容上采取“技术开放”策略**

此次课程改革强调“技术开放”，即对特定的技术、设备或工艺等学习内容不做过于明确细致的要求，技术开放策略为不断快速迭代的数字化、网络化新技术融入课程内容提供了基本的方法与路径。

**4. 课程实施强调数字能力的“横向融入”与“早期培养”**

“横向融入”是强调将数字能力相关学习内容融入相关的“行动领域”和“学习领域”中展开教学，强调在完成典型职业任务的过程中，即在学生独立制订计划、实施任务和检查任务等一系列行动过程中渗透式培养数字能力。“早期培养”强调数字能力的培养要贯穿于学习者教育的全过程，在职业教育的初始阶段就加强对学生的数字能力的培养，旨在学生尽早认识与理解数字化相关内容，以便未来能够应对复杂的数字化、网络化工作世界。

随着我国产业结构的转型与升级，智能制造与数字产业的发展同样对技术技能人才的数字能力提出了新要求，我们可以借鉴德国课程改革的经验，尽快将数字能力的培养作为下一步课程改革的聚焦点。

首先，面向智能制造，明确新的技术技能人才培养目标。加快与智能制造相关专业的数字化改造，通过广泛深入的社会需求调研，细化数字化工作领域的具体数字能力要求，并将这些要求融入相关专业的人才培养目标和培养规格，为培养技术技能人才的数字化能力提供明确的目标指向。

其次，加强与行业企业等利益相关方的协作，尽快修订国家专业教学标准，将数字能力、数字化学习内容融入专业教学标准之中，为职业院校开发、修订体现数字能力的人才培养方案提供基本依据。

最后，构建“融合、可扩展”的课程体系。一是将相关数字化学习内容融入现有相关专业课程内容之中；二是根据职业岗位对数字能力的具体要求设计独立的数字化课程模块。

# (六)

## 人本理念与科技范式转型视域下职业本科课程变革的适应性分析

南京工业职业技术大学党委副书记　马成荣

中国职业本科教育是新生事物，而决定其类型与层次特征的核心和命脉在课程。下面，我从人本理念与科技范式转型两个视角，就职业本科课程变革的适应性这一话题，分享六个观点。

观点一，职业本科课程要回归育人本位，实现社会价值与人本价值的统一。人才培养目标定位是课程变革的前提和基础。职业本科人才培养目标，既要满足技术迭代和产业升级对高级技术型人才的需求，又要体现本科层次对受教育者应达成的素质和能力要求，更要着眼于人的全面发展和社会全面进步，体现德智体美劳全面优培，更好地服务国家经济、政治、文化、社会和生态文明建设。

观点二，“以学生的学习、成长和发展为中心”是课程论本真话语的核心理念。我讲四个“主”：课程的“主语”是学生，课程是学生生活和未来职业经验历程的教育总和，不是知识或学科，课程的完整意义包括目标、内容、组织和评价；教学的“主体”是学生，好的教学应该是让学生“动起来、活起来、笑起来”；学习的“主人”是学生，学习是学生在信息、知识、理解力、态度、价值观、技能、胜任力或者行为方面的改变，在成事中成人，以成人促成事；教材是学生学习的“主料”，这个“主料”来自课程、行业专家和一线教师对课程的开发，更来自广大教师基于国家专业教学标准的开发。

观点三，科技范式从技术驱动向重大场景驱动转型为职业本科课程知识创新提供新的契机。当下科技范式的转型，特别是重大工程、民生和科学等场景，是职业实践、工程实践和科技成果转化实践等知识的生产场域，它为职业本科的知识生产提供了源头活水。知识图谱是知识生产的重要工具，专业教学资源库、慕课、小规模限制性在线课程（SPOC）、微课等是推动课程与课堂变革的重要引擎。

观点四，实践导向课程是职业本科课程的主要形态。我借用亚里士多德对实践作的表述，“一种有目的、有价值导向、致力于问题解决的活动。它在理论与实际操作之间来回修正二者，具有反思性、反身性，要求实践者深思熟虑，在恰当的时机做出适宜的行动。”实践导向的课程，与中国“做”字的内涵要义是相通的，体现和践行了陶行知先生提出的“以做定学、以学定教”和黄炎培先生提出的“手脑并用、双手万能”的教学理想。课程开发重点需要破解知识的结构化、情境化和条件化等技术问题。

观点五，课程与毕业要求的矩阵分析是课程质量建设的有效工具。新修订的《中华人民共和国职业教育法》提出“职业综合素质和行动能力”，而行业企业等用户对毕业生提出的感性诉求是：“来了就能干”“即刻创造效益”。在人才培养上，借鉴工程教育专业认证的经验，以职业本科毕业要求为支点，通过建立课程对毕业要求支撑强度的矩阵分析这一杠杆，以此检验课程建设及人才培养的质量水平。

观点六，教育评价是实现课程变革的“牛鼻子”。在评价理念上，从工具理性向人本立场转变，更加注重评价育人；在评价内容上，从以知识、技能为主向以德为先、能力为重、挖潜为要转变，更加注重德技兼修、全面发展；在评价方式上，从结果性评价向过程性和结果性评价结合转变，更加注重表现性评价和基于大数据的循证评价；在评价主体上，从单一的学校评价向校、企和第三方参与的多元评价转变，更加注重用户评价。

# 十一
# 职业教育与产业转型发展论坛

协助组织单位：中华人民共和国工业和信息化部教育与考试中心

# XI. Vocational Education and Industrial Restructuring

Co-organizer: Education and Examination Center of Ministry of Industry and Information Technology (CEIAEC) of the People's Republic of China

02
科菲·恩盖桑
Koffi N'Guessan

03
年温丹
Nyan Win Than

04
孙卫平
Sun Weiping

05
关志伟
Guan Zhiwei

06
卢小平
Lu Xiaoping

07
陶炜
Tao Wei

08
安晖
An Hui

09
何新飞
He Xinfei

10
郝钊
Hao Zhao

**研讨产业转型发展，包括产业结构、产业组织、产业规模、产业技术对于职业教育发展的影响，职业教育如何在院校设立、专业设置以及教师发展等各方面改革创新，以适应并促进产业转型发展。**

This session discusses the impact of industrial restructuring (including industrial structure, industrial organization, industrial scale and industrial technologies) on vocational education development. The participants also share their ideas on vocational education reform and innovation, including college setup, specialty setting and teacher development to adapt to and further promote industrial restructuring.

## （一）

# 职业教育与产业转型发展论坛情况概述

中华人民共和国工业和信息化部教育与考试中心人才评价处处长　姚　明

当今世界正经历百年未有之大变局，国家间竞争对抗日益激烈，经济社会发展面临各种危机，人民就业和生活面临多重挑战。在此背景下，2022 年 8 月 19—20 日，以“后疫情时代职业技术教育发展：新变化、新方式、新技能”为主题的“世界职业技术教育发展大会”（以下简称大会）在天津成功举办。孙春兰副总理宣读习近平主席贺信并发表视频致辞。“职业教育与产业转型发展”论坛（以下简称论坛）作为十四个平行论坛之一，由中华人民共和国工业和信息化部教育与考试中心组织，天津渤海职业技术学院承办。论坛围绕“面向产业转型的职业教育”“职业教育人才培养模式”“现代职业教育高质量发展”三个专题，探讨人才培养新路径、产教融合新方法、工学结合新思路。

来自科特迪瓦、缅甸、柬埔寨、英国等 9 个国家的 18 名高级官员、院校领导、著名学者和企业家参加论坛。中华人民共和国工业和信息化部教育与考试中心副主任左仁贵主持论坛并致辞。

**1. 职业教育与产业转型发展的时代背景和重大意义**

中国高度重视职业教育。在 2021 年 4 月召开的全国职业教育大会上，习近平总书记指出:“在全面建设社会主义现代化国家新征程中，职业教育前途广阔，大有可为。”在致大会的贺信中，习近平总书记强调:“中国积极推动职业教育高质量发展，支持中外职业教育交流合作。中方愿同世界各国一道，加强互学互鉴、共建共享，携手落实全球发展倡议，为加快落实联合国 2030 年可持续发展议程贡献力量。”

技能人才是支撑中国制造、中国创造的重要力量。中国有世界上最大规模的职业教育体系，现有职业学校 1.12 万所，开设 1 300 余个专业和 12 余万个专业点，在校生 2 915 万人，全国技能人才总量超过 2 亿人，职业教育吸引力、影响力、竞争力不断增强。但同时也存在技术技能人才结构矛盾突出、高技能人才总量不足等问题。我国的高级技工占产业工人的比例只有 6%，西方发达国家的占比超过 35%，日本的占比高达 40%。2022 年 10 月，中办、国办印发的《关于加强新时代高技能人才队伍建设的意见》中明确提出，到“十四五”时期末，技能人才占就业人员的比例达到 30% 以上，高技能人才占技能人才的比例达到 1/3。

产业转型发展，一靠投入，二靠人才。职业教育为产业发展服务，必须紧密围绕产业变革的需要，瞄准技术变革和产业升级的方向，从产业中来，到产业中去，建设高水平、高层次技术技能人才培养体系。

**2. 面向产业转型的职业教育人才培养体系建设**

（1）聚焦产业需求，明确培养方向。产教融合是职业教育的本质特征，也是基本路径。论坛上，多国教育部门负责人阐述了本国在培养适应产业发展需要的技术技能人才方面的理念和做法。

科特迪瓦技术教育、职业培训与学习部部长科菲 · 恩盖桑总结了科特迪瓦政府在构建产教融合的职业教育体系方面的战略部署。一是实施“第二次机会学校”计划，针对有发展前景的行业、产业领域，制订周期短、规模大的培训计划以帮助无学历人员实现长期、稳定就业；二是实施“人才学院”计划，通过更新和丰富基本学历包含的培训课程，提升技能，提高就业率，使受训人员满足企业在技能方面的需求。

柬埔寨劳动与职业培训部职业技术教育与培训司副司长通萨摩介绍了柬埔寨的职业教育培训体系。柬埔寨职业技术培训的宗旨之一就是要响应劳动力市场需求，提升人民生活水平。为此，柬埔寨制定了国家职业技术教育与培训政策（2017—2025）、劳动与职业培训部战略发展计划（2019—2023）等一系列政策标准，设立了国家培训委员会和职业技术工作组，负责职业技术培训相关工作的监督管理。

缅甸科技部职业技术教育与培训司副司长年温丹表示，缅甸职业院校通过组织职业技术教师和行政人员参加面向“工业 4.0”的信息与通信技术技能培训，提升教师专业技能。

（2）强化双向互动，优化办学模式。发展适应产业和社会需要的职业教育，需要动员社会各界，特别是行业企业参与其中。论坛上，学者与企业家们分享了在加强校企合作协同育人方面的关键举措。

英国国际贸易部职业技术教育与培训专家乔纳森·莱杰分享了用人单位深度参与的英国职业教育培养模式。用人单位在培养过程中要进行劳动力市场信息分享、制定标准、开发相关课程、提升员工能力、提供资金支持、评估技能水平、跟进项目情况、加强影响力和价值激励等工作。

新加坡南洋理工学院国际合作与交流机构主任蔡锦平表示，南洋理工学院的核心办学理念是“教学工厂”。学校各部门均设有创新平台，如工程系设有技术创新中心，包括增材制造技术中心、机器人和自动化创新中心等。各中心自成一个创新生态圈，核心是工程系的师资团队，合作伙伴包括政府机构和技术公司，为企业客户服务、开发项目并提供问题解决方案的同时，也为教师能力提升提供了重要平台。

重庆电子工程职业学院党委书记孙卫平介绍了学校“匠师协同·能工巧匠”的培养模式。学校通过聘请大量企业高水平工程师担任实践教学指导，形成了一支知识与技能并重的高水平混编教学双师队伍。近 3 年聘请行业企业领军人才等兼职教师 2 770 余人，培育国家级人才 10 人，建成国家级教师团队 3 个。

天津中德应用技术大学副校长关志伟表示，学校注重培养学生的实践能力，构建了“基本技能 + 综合技能 + 创新项目”的实践体系，本科 4 年实践不断线。学校在 2016 年建设了基础实验实训中心，建立企业生产环境、开展企业安全教育，还与大众、博世等 229 家企业深度合作开展“双元”培养，与企业联合制定培养方案、评价培养质量，将行业标准纳入课程大纲，共同编写教材、指导毕业设计。

奇安信科技集团股份有限公司副总裁何新飞提出“教师 + 教练”的“双教育人”模式。教师指院校教师，他们通过标准化、系统化的教法开展教学活动；教练指企业中销售、运维、安服等岗位的从业人员，通过因岗培养的模式对学生的工作技能、方法、流程等进行专门训练。

（3）推动数字化转型，赋能高质量发展。2022 年，全国教育工作会议提出实施教育数字化战略行动，并提出要大力发展适应新技术和产业变革需要的职业教育。论坛上，专家学者们分享了用数字化思维推动职业教育高质量发展取得的成果。

通萨摩系统总结了柬埔寨职业教育数字化战略部署。柬埔寨已建立了国家职业技术培训数字学习平台，由认证的教师通过视频、电子书等方式远程辅导学生，学生通过自我检测、组团测试、手机软件检测等方式进行测试，测试合格的学生可以获得官方认证学位。

国家工业信息安全发展研究中心系统所所长陶炜提出，要借助数字化思维和方法，推动数字技术与职业教育深度融合。国家工业信息安全发展研究中心已建成多个涉及安全、数字化和软件领域的国家级质检中心和省部级重点实验室，并会同企业在多地建设了数字化转型、工业互联网等体验推广中心，充分运用已有资源，加强跟踪研判，推进资源共享共用。

**3. 职业教育与产业转型的发展趋势**

当前，世界新一轮科技革命和产业变革迅猛发展，职业教育高质量发展要紧紧抓住历史机遇，主动融入经济社会发展格局。举办此论坛是加快构建现代职业教育体系，培养更多高素质技术技能人才的关键途径，是完整、准确、全面贯彻新发展理念，主动服务和融入新发展格局的重要举措。论坛上，各国专家学者从产业发展、人才培养机制等方面提出了未来规划与设想。

（1）瞄准产业转型重点领域。中国电子信息产业发展研究院副总工程师安晖认为，新时期产业转型可以总结为“创新化、数字化、链条化、绿色化”四个方向和“需求牵引、融合创新”两个特点。未来，中国产业转型的重点方向将体现在重点领域加快创新发展、各行业推进数字化转型、产业链供应链韧性增强、产业绿色低碳发展加快四个方面。

北京信息职业技术学院校长卢小平表示，数字产业化催生了经济增长新动能，将对技能劳动者产生不同影响。一是数字经济对高技能劳动力具有补偿效应，增加了高技术技能工人的就业；二是数字经济对低技能劳动力具有替代效应，对劳动密集型产业的就业人员产生了较大的负面冲击。职业教育必须主动迎接数字经济的挑战，在数字产业化、产业数字化领域，走产学研用的新路。

（2）深化产教融合人才培养机制。科菲·恩盖桑提出，各国应共同制定一项将数字技术发展、技术创新和人力资本培训结合起来的技术教育与职业培训行动计划。

马来西亚拉曼理工大学校长李仕伟认为，我们正在经历第四次工业革命，对技能的需求更加多元，职业教育必须主动融入技术变革的浪潮中，重视和行业企业的合作，根据企业对技能的要求更新学校课程，让学生与时俱进。

在人才培养谱系中，职业教育是重要方面和基础力量，是培养高素质技术技能人才、能工巧匠、大国工匠的基础性工程。以此论坛的成功举办为契机，贯彻落实习近平主席贺信的精神，深入研究与会专家学者对所在国家、行业企业推动职业教育与产业转型发展深度融合的模式和经验，为推动中国职业教育高质量发展输送更多高素质技术技能人才，为建设制造强国、网络强国贡献更多力量。

# i. Overview of the Session on Vocational Education and Industrial Restructuring

**Yao Ming, Education and Examination Center of Ministry of Industry and Information Technology (CEIAEC) of the People's Republic of China**

Nowadays, the world is undergoing profound changes unseen in a century. Competition between countries is becoming increasingly fierce, economic and social development is facing various crises, and people's employment and life are amid multiple challenges. With this background, the World Vocational and Technical Education Development Conference (hereinafter referred to as the Conference) with the theme of "Vocational and Technical Education Development in the Post-pandemic Era: New Changes, New Ways and New Skills" was successfully held in Tianjin from 19 to 20 August, 2022. Vice Premier Sun Chunlan read the congratulatory letter from President Xi Jinping and delivered a video speech. As one of the 14 sessions, the Session on "Vocational Education and Industrial Restructuring" (hereinafter referred to as the Session) is organized by the Education and Examination Center of Ministry of Industry and Information Technology (CEIAEC) of the People's Republic of China, and is undertaken by Tianjin Bohai Vocational Technology College. Focusing on three special topics, "Vocational Education Facing Industrial Restructuring", "Vocational Education Talent Training Mode" and "High-quality Development of Modern Vocational Education", the speakers discussed new paths of talent training, new methods of integration between industry and education, and new ideas of work-study combination.

18 senior officials, university leaders, distinguished scholars and entrepreneurs from 9 countries including Côte d'Ivoire, Myanmar, Cambodia and the UK attended the Session. Zuo Rengui, Deputy Director of Education and Examination Center of Ministry of Industry and Information Technology (CEIAEC), P.R. China, presided over the Session and delivered a speech.

### 1. The Historical Backdrop and Significance of Vocational Education and Industrial Restructuring

China attaches great importance to vocational education. At the National

Vocational Education Conference held in April 2021, General Secretary Xi Jinping pointed out that "in the new journey to build China into a modern socialist country in all respects, vocational education has a promising future and great potential". In his congratulatory letter to the Conference, President Xi Jinping emphasized that "China actively pushes forward the high-quality development of vocational education, and supports exchanges and cooperation in vocational education with other countries. The Chinese side stands ready to work with other countries in the world to strengthen mutual learning, joint construction and shared benefits, join hands to implement the Global Development Initiative, and contribute to accelerating the implementation of the UN 2030 Agenda for Sustainable Development".

Skilled talents are an important force supporting "Made in China" and "Created in China". China has the largest vocational education system in the world. There are about 11 200 vocational schools offering more than 1 300 specialties in more than 120 000 course providing stations, with 29.15 million students at school and more than 200 million skilled talents in China. The attractiveness, influence and competitiveness of vocational education are constantly increasing. But at the same time, there are problems such as prominent contradiction in the structure of technical and skilled talents and insufficient total number of highly-skilled talents. Senior artisans account for only 6% of industrial workers in China, but the proportion exceeds 35% in Western developed countries and reaches 40% in Japan. In October, 2022, the *Opinions on Strengthening the Construction of Highly-skilled Talents in the New Era* issued by the General Office of the Communist Party of China Central Committee and the General Office of the State Council of the People's Republic of China clearly stated that by the end of the 14th Five-Year Plan period, the proportion of skilled talents in employed persons will exceed 30%, and the proportion of highly-skilled talents in skilled talents will reach 1/3.

Industrial restructuring depends on investment and talents. To serve industrial development, vocational education must closely focus on the needs of industrial transformation, aim at the direction of technological transformation and industrial upgrading, and build a high-level and highly-skilled technical talent training system based on the principle of "from the industry, to the industry".

### 2. Construction of Vocational Education Talent Training System Facing Industrial Restructuring

(1) Focus on industrial needs and determine the training direction. The integration of industry and education is the essential feature and basic path of vocational education. At the Session, the heads of education departments in many countries expounded their ideas and practices in training technical talents to meet the needs of industrial development.

Koffi N'Guessan, Minister of Côte d'Ivoire Ministry of Technical Education, Vocational Training and Apprenticeship (METFPA), summarized the strategic deployment of Côte d'Ivoire government in building a vocational education system integrating industry and education. First is to implement the "Second Chance School" (E2C) program. Formulate short-term and large-scale training programs for promising trades and industrial fields to help personnel without diploma seek long-term and stable occupations. Second is to implement the "Academy of Talent" (ADT) program. By updating and enriching the training courses offered by the basic diploma, improving skills, and increasing employment rate, the program helps the trainees meet the skills requirements of enterprises.

Thorng Samon, Deputy Director-General of Department of Technical Vocational Education and Training Management, Ministry of Labour and Vocational Training, Cambodia, introduced Cambodia's vocational education and training system. One of the purposes of vocational and technical training in Cambodia is to respond to the needs of the labor market and improve people's living standards. For these purposes, Cambodia has formulated a series of policy standards such as the National TVET Policy 2017—2025, MLVT's Strategic Development Plan 2019—2023, and established the National Training Board (NTB) and Technical Working Group (TWG) to supervise and manage vocational and technical training.

Nyn Win Than, Deputy Director General of the Department of Technical and Vocational Education and Training (DTVET), Ministry of Science and Technology, Myanmar, said that their vocational colleges improved teachers' professional skills by organizing vocational and technical teachers and administrative personnel to participate in information and communication technology skills training applicable to Industry 4.0.

(2) Strengthen two-way interaction and optimize school-running mode. To develop vocational education that meet the needs of the industry and the society, it is necessary to mobilize all sectors of the society, especially industrial enterprises. At the Session, scholars and entrepreneurs shared the key measures in strengthening school-enterprise collaborative education.

Jonathan Ledger, Specialist of Technical and Vocational Education and Training (TVET), Department for International Trade, UK, shared the British vocational education training model with deep involvement of employers. Employers should share labor market information, set standards, develop related courses, improve employees' abilities, provide financial support, evaluate skill level, follow up projects, and strengthen influence and value incentives, etc.

Chua Gim Peng, Senior Manager of Nanyang Polytechnic International, Singapore, said that the core idea of Nanyang Polytechnic was "teaching factory". All departments of the university have innovation platforms. For example, the Engineering Department has the technology innovation center, including the additive manufacturing technology center, robotics and automation innovation center, etc. Each center is an innovation ecosystem, the core of which is the faculty team of the Engineering Department. Its partners include government agencies and technology companies. These centers serve enterprise customers, develop projects and provide problem solutions, and also provide an important platform for teachers to improve their abilities.

Sun Weiping, Secretary of CPC Committee of Chongqing College of Electronic Engineering, China, introduced the college's training mode of "collaboration between best craftsmen and teachers". The college has built a high-level mixed team of double qualified teachers with equal emphasis on knowledge and skills by hiring a large number of high-level engineers from enterprises as practical teaching guides. In the past three years, the college has hired more than 2 770 part-time teachers, such as leading talents from industry and enterprises, cultivated 10 state-level talents, and built 3 state-level teacher teams.

Guan Zhiwei, Vice President of Tianjin Sino-German University of Applied Sciences, China, said that the university paid attention to cultivating students' practical ability. It has built a practical system of "basic skills + comprehensive skills + innovative projects", which provides continuous practice during the 4-year undergraduate program. In 2016, the university built a basic experimental training center, established an enterprise production environment, and carried out enterprise safety education. It also cooperated deeply with 229 enterprises such as Volkswagen and Bosch to carry out "Dual" training, jointly formulated training programs and evaluated training quality, incorporated enterprise (industry) standards into the course syllabus, compiled textbooks and guided graduation design with enterprises.

He Xinfei, Vice President of QI-ANXIN Technology Group Inc., China, proposed the "Dual Education" mode of "Teachers + Coaches". Teachers refer to campus-based teachers who carry out teaching activities through standardized and systematic teaching methods; Coaches refer to company-based employees in sales, operation and maintenance, safety service and other positions, who train students on work skills, methods and processes through work-based training.

(3) Promote digital transformation and empower high-quality development. In 2022, the National Education Work Conference proposed to implement the education digitalization strategy, and to vigorously develop vocational education to meet the needs of new technologies and industrial changes. At the Session, experts and scholars shared the achievements of promoting the high-quality development of vocational education with digital thinking.

Thorng Samon systematically summarized the strategic deployment of vocational education digitalization in Cambodia. Cambodia has established a national E-Learning platform for vocational and technical training, on which certified teachers can tutor students remotely through video and e-books, and students are tested through self-testing, group testing and APP testing, etc. Students who pass the tests can obtain official degrees.

Tao Wei, Director of Institute of Systems of CIC, China, proposed to promote the deep integration of digital technology and vocational education with the help of digitalized thinking and methods. CIC has built a number of national quality inspection centers and provincial and ministerial key laboratories in security, digitalization and software. It has also built experience promotion centers of digital transformation and industrial Internet in many places together with enterprises, making full use of existing resources, strengthening tracking and evaluating, and promoting resource sharing.

### 3. Development Trend of Vocational Education and Industrial Restructuring

At present, a new round of global scientific and technological revolution and industrial transformation is developing rapidly. The high-quality development of vocational education should seize the historical opportunity and actively integrate into the economic and social development pattern. Holding this Session is a critical path to speed up the construction of modern vocational education system and train more high-quality technical talents. It is also an important measure to implement the new development concept completely, accurately and comprehensively, to actively serve and integrate into the new development pattern. At the Session, experts and scholars from all over the world put forward future plans and assumptions from the aspects of industrial development and talent cultivation mechanism.

(1) Aim at key areas of industrial restructuring. An Hui, Assistant Chief Engineer of China Center for Information Industry Development (CCID), believed that the industrial transformation in the new era could be summarized into four directions of "innovation, digitalization, forming chains and going green" and two characteristics of "demand-driven and integration & innovation". In the future, the key direction of China's industrial restructuring will be reflected in accelerating innovation and development in key areas, promoting digital transformation in various industries, enhancing the resilience of industrial chain and supply chain, and expediting the green and low-carbon development of industries.

Lu Xiaoping, Principal of Beijing Information Technology College, China, said that digital industrialization had given birth to new drivers of economic growth, which would have different impacts on skilled workers. First, digital economy has a compensation effect on highly-skilled labor and increases the employment of highly-skilled workers; Second, digital economy has a substitution effect on low-skilled labor, and has a great negative impact on employed people in labor-intensive industries. Vocational education must take the initiative to meet the challenge of digital economy, and take a new path of bringing enterprises, schools, research institutes and end-users together in the field of digital industrialization and industrial digitalization.

(2) Deepen the talent training mechanism of integration of Industry and education. Koffi N'Guessan proposed that all countries should jointly formulate an action plan for technical education and vocational training that combines digital technology development, technological innovation and human capital training.

Lee Sze Wei, President of Tunku Abdul Rahman University of Management and Technology, Malaysia, believed that we were experiencing the fourth industrial revolution, and the demand for skills was more diversified. Vocational education must actively integrate into the surging tide of technological change, attach importance to cooperation with industrial enterprises, and update the school curriculum according to the requirements of enterprises for skills, and enable students keep pace with the times.

In the talent training system, vocational education is an important aspect and a basic force. It is also the basic project for training high-quality technical talents, skilled craftsmen and master craftsmen. Taking the success of this Session as an opportunity, we should implement the spirit of President Xi Jinping's congratulatory letter, have an in-depth study of the modes and experiences of experts and scholars attending the meeting in promoting the deep integration of vocational education and industrial restructuring in their countries and industrial enterprises, so as to provide more high-quality technical talents to promote the high-quality development of China's vocational education and contribute more strength to building China into a country strong in manufacturing and cyberspace.

## （二）

# 科特迪瓦工业转型背景下的技术教育和职业培训构想

科特迪瓦技术教育、职业培训与学习部部长　科菲·恩盖桑

通过全球范围内的经验交流与分享，本次论坛将有利于勾画后疫情时代职业教育的发展趋势。

感谢天津市政府在 2019—2020 年期间资助天津理工大学参建位于亚穆苏克罗的费利克斯·乌弗埃–博瓦尼国立理工学院鲁班工坊工程项目，当时我正担任该院院长。

新冠病毒疫情的暴发对我们日常生活的方方面面都产生了深远的影响。在卫生方面，非洲国家，特别是科特迪瓦，不得不通过寻求国际援助，以弥补防护口罩和疫苗的供应不足。在教育方面，我们见证了众多教育机构的关闭。面对疫情，技术教育和职业培训部门通过为学生提供在线教育材料及对远程教育者的技术培训，来保证教育的连续性，并确保对使用信息通信技术工具学习的学生进行远程辅助和指导。然而就目前的技术而言，这些举措还不够。

综上所述，我们意识到各国必须协同努力，共同制定一项将数字技术发展、技术创新和人力资本培训结合起来的技术教育与职业培训行动计划。这一行动计划不仅可以缓解后疫情时代教育问题，更为重要的是，它还可以更好地应对可能发生的新的危机所带来的冲击。这一计划应积极吸纳全球各国在应对新冠病毒疫情中的成功经验。

在此讨论的众多主题，无一不是在向教育与经济战线的每一位工作者和每一个机构提出问题。不可否认，由于培训与就业之间关系密切，此次疫情导致的产业结构调整必然意味着进行技术教育与职业培训的新方式。

新变化号召公共部门及私有企业的所有人员的积极参与，通过促进教育学习领

域的协同合作，发挥学校和企业这两个系统互补的作用。

就科特迪瓦而言，只有通过结合可预见的事态发展趋势而调整相应课程才能保证其适当性。在技术培训和管理方面，我们认为基于技能培养的教育方案更适合管理技术和职业培训的发展。此外，公共机构的管理也应得到相应的改善。显然，流程规划与管理、教师的培训和培训设备都成问题。因此技术教育和职业培训的数字化转型是必要的，这一转型不仅可以打造更有效的辅导和学习生态系统，还可以培养学生未来职业生涯所必需的数字技能。

这些更好地接受培训的青年将是我国未来复兴的关键。因此在科特迪瓦创造有利于他们发展的环境，向他们传授基本知识和技能来激发他们的创造力就显得尤为重要。

当然这一切需要在更健康平稳的社会经济背景下，通过制定并实施相应的优先重点教育培训计划，并号召不同领域的精英和工匠的参与才能实现。

以此为出发点，科特迪瓦政府采取了两大战略：第一是“第二次机会学校”，指针对有前景的、符合生产部门需要的领域开发周期短、规模大的培训项目，以帮助大量无学历人员实现长期、稳定就业；第二是“人才学院”，旨在通过更新和丰富基本学历包含的培训课程来提高就业率，以此满足受训人群和企业的需求。

技术教育、职业培训与学习部还致力于支持各专业领域逐步实现分支构建，以便更好地通过“领域描绘”，勾勒各领域的清晰愿景及培训规划。我们必定会关注研讨会交流的结论，以便改进我们自己的定位、规划及实施策略。

## ii. Vision of the METFPA Within the Framework of the Industrial Transformation of Côte d'Ivoire

**Koffi N'Guessan, Minister of Côte d'Ivoire Ministry of Technical Education, Vocational Training and Apprenticeship (METFPA)**

Ces réflexions à l'échelle mondiale, contribueront à décrire l'évolution post-pandémique de l'enseignement professionnel, notamment grâce au partage d'expériences.

Je saisis l'occasion qui m'est offerte pour adresser mes compliments au gouvernement chinois ainsi que mes remerciements à la municipalité de Tianjin qui, à travers l'Université de Technologie de Tianjin, a financé en 2019—2020 le projet d'installation d'un Atelier LU BAN à l'Institut National Polytechnique Félix HOUPHOUËT-BOIGNY de Yamoussoukro, lorsque j'occupais la fonction de Directeur Général.

La pandémie du COVID-19 a profondément affecté notre vie dans toutes ses composantes. Au plan sanitaire, les pays africains, et particulièrement la Côte d'Ivoire, ont dû solliciter l'aide internationale pour pallier l'insuffisance des masque de protection et de vaccins. Au plan éducatif, nous avons assisté à la fermeture des établissements. La réponse apportée par l'Enseignement Technique et la Formation Professionnelle (ETFP) a été la mise en ligne de supports pédagogiques à l'attention des élèves pour assurer la continuité pédagogique et la formation de techno-pédagogues pour accompagner les apprenants de notre système de formation à l'utilisation des outils de TIC pour l'apprentissage. Elle demeure insuffisante, au regard des technologies actuelles.

Il apparait donc plus qu'indispensable aux différents pays d'élaborer un plan d'actions de développement de l'ETFP intégrant le développement du numérique, l'innovation technologique et la formation du capital humain. Ce plan d'actions permettra de pallier les problèmes post-pandémie, mais surtout, de pouvoir anticiper de nouveaux chocs. Il devra s'inspirer des expériences réussies de résilience vécues dans les autres pays.

Les thématiques sont nombreuses au cours de ces débats, et elles nous interpellent toutes, nous, institutions et acteurs de la formation et de l'économie. Il est indéniable que la restructuration industrielle qui résultera de cette pandémie, du fait du triptyque adéquation formation-emploi, impliquera nécessairement de nouvelles manières d'aborder l'enseignement et la formation techniques et professionnels.

Les évolutions recommandent aujourd'hui la participation de tous, pouvoirs publics et acteurs du secteur privé, en favorisant les synergies avec le monde de l'apprentissage pour que les deux systèmes, scolaire et entreprise, jouent la carte de la complémentarité.

En ce qui nous concerne en Côte d'Ivoire, nous pensons qu'on ne pourra assurer la pertinence qu'à travers des curricula adaptés, qui tiennent compte des évolutions prévisibles. En la matière, l'Approche par les compétences nous semble mieux indiquée pour gérer le développement de la formation technique et professionnelle, en termes d'ingénierie de formation et de gouvernance. L'amélioration de la gouvernance des institutions publiques devrait être également envisagée. Évidemment, il va se poser le problème de la maîtrise du processus, la formation des formateurs et l'équipement adéquat des structures de formation. La transformation digitale de l'ETFP apparaît donc comme une nécessité afin de non seulement créer un écosystème d'encadrement et d'apprentissage plus efficient mais aussi de fournir des compétences numériques indispensables pour la carrière future des apprenants.

Cette jeunesse mieux formée pourrait être la clé pour la résilience future de nos pays. Il importe donc de stimuler leur créativité en leur fournissant les savoirs et savoir-faire de base et en créant un environnement propice à leur épanouissement dans nos pays.

Tout cela suppose évidemment, que des actions prioritaires soient identifiées et développées dans un contexte socioéconomique assaini et apaisé, avec la participation de tous les acteurs et artisans des différents environnements respectifs.

Dans ce sens, le gouvernement ivoirien a adopté deux stratégies majeures: « l'École de la $2^{\text{ème}}$ chance » (E2C) qui consiste à développer un programme de formation de masse de courte durée sur des métiers porteurs répondant aux besoins du secteur productif afin d'absorber l'important stock de personnes non qualifiées en quête d'insertion professionnelle décente et durable. « l'Académie des Talents » (ADT) qui vise à rénover et diversifier l'offre de formation diplômante initiale afin d'accroître le taux d'insertion professionnelle des apprenants en répondant à la fois aux besoins des populations en formation et à ceux des entreprises en compétences.

Le METFPA travaille également, à accompagner les secteurs professionnels à se structurer, branche par branche, en vue de mieux adresser les besoins en termes de lisibilité et de formation à travers ce que nous avons appelé « Portrait de secteur ». Nous serons évidemment attentifs aux conclusions des échanges dans les ateliers, pour nous permettre d'améliorer nos propres orientations et nos stratégies de planification et de mise en œuvre.

# （三）

# 增强职业教育适应性，加快构建现代职业教育体系

缅甸科技部职业技术教育与培训司副司长　年温丹

我的发言主要包括三部分：一是缅甸关键产业领域与职业技术教育培训情况简介；二是职业技术教育培训体系的数字化转型；三是加速建立现代职业教育培训体系。

首先，简要介绍缅甸几大关键产业：教育、医疗、农牧渔业、制造业及中小企业、技术领域及初创生态、数字化贸易、金融服务、旅游业及餐饮业、交通及物流。

我司所辖职业技术教育培训机构主要包括两个部分：一是高等教育层次，公立职业技术学院提供四年制的技术类本科学位，公立工业技术学院提供三年制的工程类本科文凭；二是中等教育层次，公立职业技术高中提供三年制的技术类中专证书。

缅甸职业技术教育与培训的数字化转型主要有六个方面：一是让学生参与在线学习这一重要的学习过程；二是讲师、实训师和职业技术教育与培训的教师要实现系统性的职业发展；三是要紧跟技术发展脚步并在职业技术教育与培训中妥善应用技术；四是要根据线上平台特点重新开发、更新职业技术教育与培训课程及培训计划；五是鼓励行业的组织机构参与制定课程大纲并提供顶岗实习项目；六是确保线上教学或数字设备中的内容能存储在数字教育平台中，从而让学生便于再次使用。

在职业技术教育与培训中，我们推出了“工业 4.0”战略。主要是支持缅甸职业技术教育与培训向全民开放，通过数字学习中心向学生提供资源，特别是对那些拥有较少机会的弱势群体和残疾人；同时要利用高科技学习与高触感学习手段为职业技术教育与培训开发新的课程，推行数字化学习管理系统。我们还组织了以下活

动：帮助职业技术教育与培训教师和管理人员实现技能提升与技能重塑，助其习得“工业 4.0”时代至关重要的信息通信技术，为职业技术教育与培训机构预先建立小规模的数字学习试点项目，以便其开展数字教学工作；与区域国家或组织合作，向职业技术教育与培训的管理者与教师提供“工业 4.0”领导力与管理培训、课程开发培训和教学教法培训；我们正在工业培训与教育学校等职业技术教育与培训机构中提供现代工业相关的技术培训，还与国内外组织机构合作，设立了有关自动化、物联网、3D 打印、无人机技术等技能建设项目。

关于职业教育教师的未来计划：一是要开发、更新公立职业技术高中、职业技术学院和工业技术学院课程，对接“工业 4.0”所需的知识和技能；二是要开展调查和研究，了解现阶段职业技术教育与培训师生对于“工业 4.0”的认知程度、持有观点和相关准备；三是要提升或重塑职业技术教育与培训教师和管理人员的技能，发展“工业 4.0”时代至关重要的信息与通信技术；四是要提供新的建议，开展区域和国际合作，为职业技术教育与培训教师提供“工业 4.0”知识和技能升级项目。我们正在职业技术教育与培训领域采取创新的手段和措施，落实职业技术教育与培训司提出的“加快建立现代职业教育体系”，以适应“工业 4.0”战略。我们还会推进服务现代职业教育体系的优质人力资源培养，包括教师、管理者和校长等，推动人才技能提升和劳动力发展，满足当地和地区工业发展的需求。

## iii. Making Vocational Education More Adaptable and Accelerate the Establishment of Modern Vocational Education System

**Nyan Win Than, Deputy Director General of the Department of Technical and Vocational Education and Training (DTVET), Ministry of Science and Technology, Myanmar**

My speech includes three parts: First, brief information of prioritized industry sectors and TVET in Myanmar. Second, an innovative digital approach for the TVET System. Third, accelerating the establishment of modern vocational education system.

First of all, I would like to introduce the prioritized industry sectors in Myanmar: Education, Healthcare, Agriculture, Fishery and Livestock, Manufacturing and SME, Technology Sector and Startup Ecosystem, Digital Trade, Financial Services, Tourism and Hospitality, Transportation and Logistics.

The major TVET institutions under DTVET include: Post-secondary level: Government Technological College (GTC), which offers 4-year technology bachelor programmes, and Government Technical Institute (GTI), which offers 3-year engineering diploma programmes; Upper-secondary level: Government Technical High School (GTHS), which offers 3-year certificate in technology programmes.

Our TVET System has 6 innovative digital approaches: To engage students with online education which is a significant learning process; To achieve systematic professional development of instructors, trainers and TVET teachers; To keep pace with technological advancements and use technology appropriately in TVET; To re-develop and upgrade most TVET's curriculum and training programmes in accordance with online platform; To encourage industrial organizations to participate in the formulation of the curricula and provide on-the-job training programmes; To make sure online teaching or contents on digital devices can be saved on e-platform and reused in future for students.

Our Industry 4.0 Strategies for TVET include: Supporting access to TVET education for all, especially, disadvantaged students with less opportunities and for persons with disabilities through digital learning centres; Developing new curriculum for TVET through high-tech learning and high-touch learning; Implementing the TVET digital learning management system. We also implement some activities: Upskilling and re-skilling TVET teachers and administration staffs for ICT skill which is essential in Industry 4.0 age; Preparation of small-scale E-learning pilot projects for digitalizing teaching and learning process in TVET institutions; Providing Industry 4.0 leadership and management training, curriculum development training and teaching pedagogy training to TVET managers and teachers by collaborating with regional countries and organizations; In TVET intuitions, like School of Industrial Training and Education (SITE), trainings of modern industry related technology are currently being provided and conducting capacity building programs for automation, Internet of Things, 3D printing and drone technology in collaboration with both national and international organizations.

Next, I will introduce the future plans for our teachers: First, to develop and update GTHS, GTI/GTC curricula in line with required knowledge and skills in Industry 4.0 age; Second, to conduct survey and research for exploring current awareness, perspectives and preparation of TVET teachers and students for Industry 4.0; Third, to upskill and re-skill TVET teachers and administration staffs for ICT skill which is essential in Industry 4.0 age; Forth, to develop and submit proposals for Industry 4.0 knowledge and skill upgrading programs for TVET teachers in collaboration with regional and international countries. We are taking the innovative approaches to our TVET to accelerate the establishment of Modern Vocational Education System in line with the Industry 4.0 strategies set by DTVET. We are promoting the competent human resources (teachers, managers, principals, etc.) for Modern Vocational Education System to enhance the skills development and the workforce development to meet the local and regional industry needs in the country.

## （四）

# 匠师协同·双能支撑·孵扶联动：创新能工巧匠培育模式助推产业提档升级

重庆电子工程职业学院党委书记　孙卫平

重庆电子工程职业学院（以下简称重电）创建于1965年，学校现在占地2 606亩，学生人数25 000余人，是56所中国特色双高建设的学校之一。重电目前正奋力向应用技术研发引领、电子信息特色鲜明、国际一流的中国特色高水平应用型高等院校迈进。

党的十九届五中全会指出：发展数字经济，推进数字产业化和产业数字化，推动数字经济和实体经济深度融合，打造具有国际竞争力的数字产业集群。针对数字产业技术快速迭代升级，对知识型、技能型、创新型、高素质技术技能人才的需求，学校紧密对接新一代信息技术等战略新兴产业和重庆支柱产业，14个专业群全部实现"智能化"升级，专业对接地方重点产业率达97.14%，系统构建匠师协同·双能支撑·孵扶联动的能工巧匠培养新模式，助推产业提档升级。下面从三个方面进行分析。

### 1. 创新能工巧匠培养模式，人才培养支撑产业发展

构建双能支撑课程体系，夯实学生职业发展基础。从行业调研开始，基于行业、岗位、职业能力分析与专业学科知识梳理，按照整体性原则，将职业道德、科学文化、专业基础和技术技能四类知识，在"平台+模块"课程体系中重组与序化。平台课程重点培养学生基础能力，模块课程培养学生的拓展能力，培育数字化人才30 000余人，学生获得国家级技能竞赛奖项298项。

打造匠师协同教学团队，校企共建卓越师资团队。创新实施人才强校工程，通过持续顶岗实践和技术培训，提升教师工程实践能力。同时我们大量聘请企业高水

平工程师担任实践教学指导和技术创新工作，形成一支知识与技能并重的高水平混编教学双师队伍。近三年聘请行业企业领军人才等兼职教师 2 770 余人，培育国家级人才 10 人，建成国家级教师团队 3 个。

创新孵扶联动培养平台，提升学生后续发展能力。打造校内项目孵化平台与校外发展扶持平台，实施毕业生后续扶持工程，延长了培养链条，实施能工巧匠人才培养模式改革，培养了第 11 届全国大学生十大年度人物杨成兴、长安集团全国技术能手田钭等一大批能工巧匠，有力支撑了地方经济的发展。

**2. 打造数智重电科研平台，技术攻坚服务产业升级**

以数字化赋能传统产业布局科研平台，提升供给保障能力，精准定位传统产业数字化转型的新问题新方向，围绕智慧城市、智慧健康等方向，布局智能建筑工程技术研究中心、智能机器人技术研究中心等 21 个科研平台，实现二级学院“一院一平台”，提高专业群集聚度。近三年技术服务到账经费近 1 亿元，为重庆打造智慧名城、制造重镇，构建技能强市提供了人才支撑，提升了配套供给服务能力。

打造国家级团队引领科研方向，助力地方产业升级。引进杨新民院士等高端专家 4 人，与重庆国家应用数学中心等高端科研机构合作，成立大数据与最优化研究所。围绕产业数字化转型，开展关键核心技术攻关，解决大数据智能化等领域的关键技术问题，助力地方产业升级。

建设环重电创新生态圈，激发动能，助推产业提档升级。校地共建“环重电”创新生态圈，探索相互需求、产权介入、要素融入、效益分享建设模式，营造创新生态，聚集创新要素。近三年获国家级纵向项目 10 项，获重庆市科技进步奖 8 项，助推产业提档转型。

**3. 集聚资源开展海外办学，国际人才助推产业拓展**

培养重电精英学子，服务中国企业“走出去”。先后与澳大利亚、德国、英国等国教育机构在师资培训、境外实习等方面开展合作，助力企业海外业务的发展。牵头组建中非职业教育联盟等平台，为坦桑尼亚等国开发标准，输出中国职业教育体系，打造国际化品牌特色。

培养海外本土数字人才，助力当地数字经济发展。依托重电专业优势与特色，建成中泰国际学院、中欧信息与通信技术鲁班工坊。在印尼、缅甸建立信息与通信技术海外实践实习及就业平台，开展订单式国际化人才培养，扩大中国数字经济在

“一带一路”沿线国家的影响和发展。

开展海外高级研修培训，提升数字经济技术技能。针对海外高级管理人员和工程师组织开展专项人员研修项目、培训，如英国信息与通信技术高级管理人才研究，提升海外人员信息通信技术水平。

学校将继续坚持“人才强校、文化兴校、特色立校”的发展理念，持续强化“智联六合、信安九州”的办学特色，主动服务国家战略，服务区域经济社会发展。

## （五）

# 制造业转型发展背景下应用技术型本科院校人才培养模式研究

天津中德应用技术大学副校长　关志伟

天津中德应用技术大学是从职业教育体系中培养起来的，是全国第一所应用技术大学，肇始于中国、德国、日本、西班牙四国政府在职业教育领域最大的一个合作项目。2015 年 11 月，由教育部正式批复成立中德应用技术大学，学校逐步形成以一流应用技术大学建设为引擎，以国际合作、校企合作、创新创业为支柱的发展格局。学校 2016 年列入天津市双一流建设高校，2020 年获批国务院学位办新增硕士学位授予单位。如今，学校基本上构建了高职、应用本科、专业硕士现代职教体系。下面从以下三个方面进行报告。

**1. 制造业转型升级发展趋势**

《“十四五”智能制造发展规划》中提出“到 2035 年，规模以上制造业企业全面普及数字化网络化，重点行业骨干企业基本实现智能化”。从国际上看，美国的“先进制造领导力战略”、德国的“国家工业战略 2030”、日本的“社会 5.0”等以重振制造业为核心的发展战略，均以智能制造为抓手，抢占全球制造业的新一轮竞争制高点。推动制造业向数字化、网络化、智能化方向发展已经成为共识。

“软硬共生”是制造业数字化转型变革的一个重点。软件就是工业软件，工业互联网实现制造的“换脑”。硬件是基于边缘智能的高端复合加工中心。新的生态是虚拟制造、数字孪生技术促进数字化转型。

“边—网—云协同”是数字化转型的底层逻辑。单一的网络化设备升级，即企业上云转变为面向整线、整厂、整个供应链的系统的解决方案。比如说现在汽车的智能化，由单车的智能，向智能网联和车路协同的发展转变。而新一代的工业网络通信技术构成智能制造底层的连接底座，实现了复杂工业场景的高速低延时、高损耗安全的互联互通。

“工管智融”是数字化转型发展的突破点。工艺是制造的核心，是企业的看家本领和“护城河”。我校去年获批新增硕士受理单位专业为机械专业，以装备加工工艺融合的方向，下设四个方向进行申报。管理方向为企业工艺智能化、管理智能化，将先进的工艺技术和管理理念融合发展是企业数字化转型发展突破的关键。

人才升级是智能制造的根基工程。角色转化即由服务者、操作者转变成规划者、协调者、评估者和决策者。技术升级则要更加注重人才技术性、专业性和能动性。模式再造主要集中在生产设备、框架结构、规章条款方面的改造。

### 2. 制造业产业转型发展对应用型人才的需求

在制造业转型的大背景下，制造业人才的缺口巨大。人社部数据显示，预计到2025年，我国制造业十大重点领域，人才总量将接近6 200万人，而缺口率却达到48%。

从人才层次的结构来看，对高层次应用型人才需求更加迫切；从用人单位的角度看，高层次应用型人才能更好服务客户；从企业运行的技术复杂程度来看，高层次应用型人才能更好更快解决复杂的工程问题和应用问题；从技术升级的适应性来看，高层次应用型人才的创新能力和专业核心能力能更好满足企业的需求。

在人才的规格上，要求的知识基础要宽、能力要多元、素质要综合。除了理论基础外，对实践能力的综合性要求也越来越高，如对数字化能力、编程维修专业能力、解决问题的能力、逻辑思维能力等的要求。

### 3. 学校的一些做法和实践

人才培养布局。我校的定位实际上是为区域经济和社会发展培养政治过硬、技能精湛、诚实守信、理性平和的应用型、技术技能型人才。我校的人才培养布局是专业组群，主要面向天津市“1+3+4”产业和12条产业链，实现专业链、人才链、产业链和创新链的有机衔接。在人才培养的实践当中形成“154”的人才培养模式：“‘1’聚焦是聚焦立德树人的根本任务；‘5’协同是人才培养重实践、强基础、校企化、国际化和综合型的基本原则；‘4’保障是师资队伍保障、校园条件保障、制度保障和校园文化保障”。在人才培养方案里，我们有九大原则：坚持立德树人、突出成果导向、优化课程体系、坚持实践导向、夯实知识技能、探索产教融合、深化国际合作、强化复合能力、坚持五育并举。

人才培养实践。在重实践方面，实践体系涵盖“基本技能+综合技能+创新项目”，实践模式是本科4年培养企业实践不断线。应用本科70%的毕业设计项目来自企业，30%来自科技创新学科竞赛项目。在强基础方面，我校突出理论基础和技能基础并重。学校在2016年建设了基础实验实训中心，大一学生就要开展基础的技能训练，除工科学生须进行训练外，文科、管科、艺术类学生也开展少量的工程训练，以培养学生的实践精神。在校企结合方面，我校和企业进行深度的产教融合，现今我校有现代产业学院、示范性软件学院、会展学院等，学校的重点项目为信创类的产业学院、现代示范性软件学院和服务双碳产业学院。在国际化方面，因我校的起源就是国际合作，所以我校现在与德国10所应用技术类大学开展合作，有10名德国专家长期在各个专业指导专业建设。近几年，学校支持126名教师团组到国外进行培训，目前我校来华留学生有102名。在复合型人才方面，我校主要聚焦于培养学生解决工程复杂问题的能力。当下我校的目标是培养一线工程师具有解决复杂工程问题的能力，每做一个项目都有不确定性，如某工程师做完一个项目，在做下一个项目时，由于边界条件、判决树条件发生了变化，虽然所使用的技术和工具软件是相同的，但仍要重新进行标定计算，这就体现了不确定性。因此我校在课程里融入了云计算、物联网、大数据和人工智能的导论课程来培养学生的复合能力。

# （六）

# 数字经济崛起与职业教育变革

北京信息职业技术学院校长　卢小平

## 1. 数字经济正在迅猛发展

21 世纪以来，新一轮科技革命和产业变革迅猛发展。特别是新一代信息技术、人工智能、生物技术、新能源技术等快速发展，数据已经成为推动经济发展的重要驱动力。

数字经济是以使用数字化的知识和信息作为关键生产要素、以现代信息网络作为重要载体、以信息通信技术的有效使用作为效率提升和经济结构优化重要推动力的一系列经济活动。数字经济的基本特征就是数字要素作为关键生产要素，其创造的价值在国民经济中所占的比重不断扩大。

2020 年，全球数字经济规模达到 32.6 万亿美元，占全球 GDP 比重的 43.7%。我国数字经济规模 5.4 万亿美元，位居全球第二。数字经济沿着数字产业化和产业数字化两条主线迅猛发展。在数字产业化领域，伴随国家“新基建”的全面实施，预计今年我国 5G 产业规模将突破 2 万亿元，大数据产业将突破 1 万亿元，人工智能将突破 1 000 亿元。在产业数字化领域，伴随数字技术的深度渗透，推动传统产业实现升级换代。2020 年，北京的数字经济规模达到 2 万亿元，增速达到 9.2%，GDP 占比达到 55.9%，位列全国第一。其中，数字产业化规模为 6 808 亿元，GDP 占比为 18.9%。产业数字化规模达到 13 371 亿元，GDP 占比为 37%。

## 2. 数字经济既带来机遇，也带来挑战

数字产业化催生了经济增长新动能，因而创造了大量就业机会，有数据显示，数字经济带来的新增岗位，年增速达到 11%。同时，也催生了新的企业生产组织方式，深刻改变了就业形态，如外卖骑手，这才有了曹德旺的焦虑：“半年 60 万工

人跑去送外卖了，制造业怎么办？”对于职业教育而言，我们需要重点关注以下变化。

第一，数字经济对于从业人员的需求正在发生变化。有关调查显示，数字经济从业人员的受教育程度普遍高于非数字经济部门，其中专科占比 22.77%、本科占比 28.71%、研究生占比达到 4.95%。数字经济就业呈现年轻化趋势，京津冀、长三角和粤港澳，数字经济部门 30 岁以下从业人员占比为 44% 至 48%。

第二，数字经济将对不同技能的劳动者产生不同的影响。一方面，数字经济对高技能劳动力具有补偿效应。数字经济增加了高技术、高技能工人的就业。另一方面，数字经济对低技能劳动力具有替代效应，减少了低技能劳动力的需求，对劳动密集型产业的就业人员产生较大的负面冲击。国际经合组织相关研究预测，未来 20 年，在国际经合组织国家，57% 的工作将被人工智能替代。

中国社会科学院大学高文书教授的研究表明：数字经济部门的教育型人力资本水平、技能型人力资本水平等明显高于非数字经济部门。教育年限有正向工资回报，每增加一年教育年限，小时工资增长 6.35%。技能培训有正向工资回报，每增加一年培训经历，小时工资增长 8.2%。但工作年限的回报率，在数字与非数字经济部门基本上没有差别。研究结论为：数字经济对于教育型人力资本和技能型人力资本有更高需求，而对于经验型人力资本的需求呈“中性”。

**3. 职业教育必须主动变革去迎接数字经济的挑战**

一是加强技能型人力资本建设。数字经济呼唤适应数字技术革命与数字产业发展的高技能人才，这就给职业教育提供了更加广阔的舞台。我们要抓住机遇，乘势而上，推动职业教育大发展。

二是加强教育型人力资本建设。近半个世纪以来，发达国家和主要经济体都经历了教育高移，其背后的根本动因，就是日益深刻的科技革命与产业变革。数字经济呼唤教育高移，尤其是职业教育的重心高移。刚刚颁布的新职教法，也为职业教育的重心高移指明了方向。

三是加强人才培养模式的变革。针对数字技术和数字产业新特点，大力推动“产学研”等培养模式和人才培养途径创新。

为主动适应北京发展数字经济、打造全球数字经济标杆城市战略需要，北京信息职业技术学院在推动教育变革方面，研究并形成了自身的战略构想与改革举措。一是超前布局，优化整合二级学院办学资源，成立产业互联网学院、人工智能学院、电子信息学院、数字商务学院、数字艺术学院、教育与健康学院，完成了学科专业的顶层设计。二是围绕数字产业化主线，重点打造软件、大数据、云计算、信息安全、人工智能、产业互联网等专业集群；围绕产业数字化主线，重点建设集成电路、智能网联汽车、数字贸易、商业互联网、智慧健康、文化创意等专业集群，打造“十四五”专业发展新的增长极。三是深化教育教学改革，推动“产学研用”人才培养模式变革，从全球视角看，数字技术和数字产业的人才培养，主流模式就是采用“产学研用”的模式，单靠学校教育是不行的，甚至只提产学结合也不够，在数字产业化、产业数字化领域，必须走“产学研用”的新路子。

## （七）

# 数字化转型升级背景下关于职业教育提质增效的思考

国家工业信息安全发展研究中心系统所所长　陶　炜

当前，以互联网、大数据、云计算为代表的新一代信息技术快速发展及其与经济社会各领域的加速渗透融合，正在深刻影响世界经济的发展方向。主动拥抱数字技术，加速数字化转型，全面提升数字化管理能力势成必然。党中央、国务院高度重视数字化转型，《中华人民共和国国民经济和社会发展第十四个五年规划和 2035 年远景目标纲要》开辟“加快数字化发展 建设数字中国”专篇，要求以数字化转型整体驱动生产方式、生活方式和治理方式变革。

在数字化转型时代背景下，教育数字化也需要加速推进，充分发挥数字技术对教育高质量发展的放大、叠加、倍增作用。职业教育与产业距离最近，在数字时代受到的冲击最大，亟待把握时势，在新时期正确认识和判断发展局势，准确把握党的事业所处的时代坐标和党中央关于经济发展的重大决策部署，深刻认识职业教育与数字化转型相融合的必要性和紧迫性。

当前，我国职业教育正进入提质增效的机遇期和改革攻坚的关键期，需要科学应变、主动求变，坚持问题导向，以需求为牵引，以提升就业为目标，借助数字化思维和方法，推动数字技术与职业教育深度融合，增强职业技术教育的适应性，打造职业教育新生态、新模式。结合从事数字化转型相关工作的经验，下面就数字时代如何促进职业教育提质增效谈三个方面的思考和体会。

一是要积极创新管理模式。应对数字经济大潮，职业教育从管理模式上要不断推陈出新，以适应新的发展趋势格局。各地政府部门可以结合区域实际，组织地方大专院校、龙头企业等，共建共投以物联网、工业互联网、人工智能、大数据、区块链等新工科专业群为基础的现代产业学院，通过政府引导的校企合作，联合开发共建课程和培养模式，针对企业典型岗位的数字技能需求，创新数字人才培养，提升本地院校专业建设的质量和就业的适应性。职业教育要大胆突破“封闭”模式，应给予各地方更多自主权去布局和发展职业教育，支持有意愿、有条件的地方稳步发展职业本科教育、多样化发展中等职业教育。广大职业院校要加快职业教育信息化、数字化建设，结合实际积极出台数字校园规范，逐步对信息化、数字化基础设施建设标准及要求作出明确规定。要加快建设职业院校人才培养工作状态数据采集与管理系统等网络信息系统，通过数字化转型升级，推动实现学生学习行为全数据采集分析，加大数据分析应用的力度，努力实现个性化、精准化资源信息的智能推荐和服务。要加快建设数字化评价技术和手段，着力构建以提升学生数字化素养为导向的教育测量与评价体系。

二是要充分统筹利用各种有效资源。数字技术能促进区域之间、城乡之间、学校之间、师生之间优质职业教育资源的共享和均衡。职业教育要逐步突破传统的工作资源限制，以建设教学形式载体更丰富、教学内容更精准匹配需求、教学时间更富有弹性的专业技能技术学习中心为导向，为学生提供更加智能开放的学习及实习实训环境。要加强职业教育数字化资源建设，健全完善政府引导、市场参与的职业教育数字化职教资源共建共享机制，激发政府、行业、企业、高校、科研院所等多元主体开发资源和持续更新的内在动力，促进资源融通和要素流动，不断增加资源总量、提高资源质量。要积极搭建支撑学生学习、教师教育、学校管理和面向社会提供优质资源的公共平台，以大量的省级、市级、企业级数字课程，积累海量的信息化资源，推进职业教育加快迈向智慧教育，推进生态协同。要及时了解社会需求，同广大企业建立信息沟通渠道，准确掌握企业的人才需求，聚焦从大规模标准化培养向大规模个性化培养的能力跃升，着重培养具有数字化思维和能力的技术技能人才，促进高质量就业。

三是要着力构建新的服务机制。职业教育与数字化的融合过程不能急功近利，要在探索中稳步推进。可以在特定行业、区域推进职业院校数字化改革试点工作，通过纠偏试错、总结试点经验，进而以点带面推进全局。要坚持服务为先，积极建设职业教育数字化资源管理和服务平台，鼓励企业将数字教学资源作为继续教育和培训平台，认可员工通过平台学习取得的成果。要探索与区域重点企业共建学生定向培养体系，针对企业的用工要求针对性设计课程和培养模式，让企业能够通过相关平台及时关注学生学习动向、课程考核等，为就业匹配提供更便捷渠道。要积极建立和完善产业兼职教师的引进、认证与聘用机制，丰富师资力量，推进理论和实践相融合。此外，还可以会同有关社会资源开展职业院校教学能力技能大赛等比赛，总结好的典型示范项目并积极推广应用；可以联合高校、科研院所、企业等共建虚拟仿真实训基地，或依托区域优势产业集聚区或产业园区，打造一批线下实训基地，推进职业教育场景化、生动化；可以充分运用企业、科研院所已经建设或建成的一些数字化体验中心等项目成果，联合签署合作协议，既能充分利用有效资源丰富教育模式，又能把企事业单位已有成果效益最大化。

作为国家级研究咨询机构，国家工业信息安全发展研究中心长期从事两化融合、数字化转型、工业互联网、工业信息安全、开源软件等领域的政策规划、行业研究、标准研制、公共服务平台建设、测试评估诊断、生态构建等工作，已建成多个涉及安全、数字化和软件领域的国家级质检中心和省部级重点实验室，并会同企业在多地建设了数字化转型、工业互联网等体验推广中心。在推进制造业数字化转型进程中，我们同步支撑各地积极开展智慧园区、智慧文旅、智慧乡村等工作。在职业教育与数字化融合进程中，我们将积极与职业院校开展合作，充分运用已有资源，加强跟踪研判，推进资源共享共用，努力为职业教育数字化改革贡献应有力量。

## （八）

# 新时期产业转型现状与发展动向

中国电子信息产业发展研究院副总工程师　安　晖

演化经济理论认为，经济发展是创新和选择两种动力机制不断相互作用的过程。“创新”和“选择”中都蕴含着“转型”的概念。从这个角度看，产业转型是经济发展的必然走向，也是经济发展的突出体现。不同时期的产业转型有不同的重点和特征。近年来，习近平总书记在多次论述中指出了新时期产业转型的方向。从实际情况和主要态势看，可以将新时期产业转型总结为“新、数、链、绿”四个方向和“需、融”两个特点。

“新”即创新化。当前，全球科技创新进入空前密集活跃期。创新化的产业转型，就是选择具有重大战略意义、广阔发展前景、良好技术基础的领域，谋划发展一批前沿科技、新兴产业和未来变革领域。中国正深入实施创新驱动战略，创新能力大幅攀升，产业新动能成长壮大。航空、航天、海洋等领域的重大工程捷报频传，推动产业创新能力加快从量的积累走向质的飞跃、从点的突破走向系统能力提升，促进新能源汽车、机器人等新兴产业培育发展，产业结构持续优化。近年来，中国战略性新兴产业多个细分领域都保持两位数增长。

“数”即数字化。数字技术不断取得突破和加速普及应用，使得推进产业数字化和数字产业化成为顺应世界经济数字化发展大势、催生产业发展新动能的必然选择。近年来，中国数字产业活力十足，5G、人工智能等新兴产业蓬勃发展，集成电路、新型显示等产业迅速崛起，带动了电子信息制造、软件和信息服务、电信等产业的整体快速增长。与此同时，产业数字化步伐不断加快，加速推进农业、工业、服务业向数字化、网络化、智能化深度转型，不断激发传统产业的新活力。协同研发设计、无人智能巡检、数字工厂、智慧矿山等新场景、新模式、新业态密集涌现，重点行业先进产能比例显著提高。

“链”即链条化。推动产业链优化升级是促进现代产业体系建设发展的必由之路。尤其面对近几年复杂交织的多种内外部因素，更须以链条化思维，凝聚产业发展新动能，构建产业发展新优势。中国高度重视产业链供应链建设，已有 29 个省市提出建立产业链“链长制”或开展“链长制”研究；工业和信息化部认定了 25 个先进制造业集群，引导推动经济和产业发展进入“产业链”新时代。

“绿”即绿色化。绿色、生态、环保成为经济社会发展的关键词，新兴绿色低碳技术加速迭代，传统产业绿色化转型步伐加快。中国坚持绿色发展理念，大力推进节能降耗，推动形成绿色生产生活方式，产业绿色低碳水平持续提升，绿色化改造和绿色化转型扎实推进。2012—2021 年，中国单位 GDP 的能耗强度下降了 26.2%。同时新能源产品需求进一步扩大，绿色生态相关产业蓬勃发展，锌铁新能源汽车、太阳能电池等产量增速较高，中国新能源汽车产销量也连续 7 年位居世界榜首。今年 1—7 月份的新能源汽车产、销量双双超过了 300 万辆，同比均增长 1.2 倍。

“需”即需求牵引。消费需求升级是推动产业高质量发展的强大动力。以新需求为牵引，以新技术为依托，能够创造发展新动力、拓展产业发展新空间。近年来，中国坚定实施扩大内需战略，内需继续成为经济增长的“压舱石”。新兴家电、高端电视机、高端自行车、高端旅游用品等需求旺盛，驱动了产业加速创新与供给结构升级。

“融”即融合创新。技术创新、产业创新的集成化特征更趋突出，以交叉融合为特征的集成化创新渐成主流，以渗透辐射为特征的跨领域创新日益凸显。例如，信息技术与制造、材料、能源、生物等技术的交叉渗透日益深化，在推动传统产业升级的同时，培育出工业机器人、智能网联汽车、能源互联网等新模式、新业态。中国把握此机遇，在相关领域已处于全球领先地位。

未来，在提高产业整体素质、推动高质量发展等内在需求驱动下，在新一代科技产业变革、创新驱动发展、“双碳”战略实施、新型城镇化和消费品质升级以及新冠病毒疫情“倒逼作用”等因素的共同驱动下，全球和中国的产业转型仍将是大势所趋。其重点方向将继续体现在四个方面，即重点领域创新发展加快推进、各行业数字化转型纵深推进、产业链供应链韧性持续增强、产业绿色低碳发展稳步推动。同时，需求牵引和融合创新仍将继续发挥强有力的引领与支撑作用。

产业转型需要高质量的人才支撑，需要“塔尖”领军大师和“塔基”技能人才以及创新型和高素质技能型人才。这为人才发展提供更多新的岗位，也给新时期职业教育提出了新目标、新要求。衷心期待职业教育把握产业转型的趋势与要求，加速改革创新，加强人才供给，实现教育发展与产业发展的共同迈进。

## (九)

# “双教”变革，探索网络安全技能人才培养新模式

奇安信科技集团股份有限公司副总裁　何新飞

奇安信科技集团股份有限公司是中国电子信息产业集团有限公司旗下企业，主要为政府、企业和各级社会组织提供网络安全保障和应急服务。我公司目前在国内市场规模第一，在全球市场位列第九。今天分享的题目是:“双教”变革，探索网络安全技能人才培养新模式。

我国的职业教育以《国家职业教育改革实施方案》为阶段性标志。近年来，我国职业教育获得了高速发展，国家也出台了很多保证职业教育发展的配套政策，职业教育也通过“三教”改革为抓手，不断落地教材、教师、教法的改革。我公司深感国家对职业教育的大力投入和支持，并积极响应时代号召，进行很多相关建议工作。在“三教”改革方面，我公司在双师型服务体系建设上，培养了近 70 名工程师作为“教师”参与教学，出版了一整套网络安全专业的优质教材，针对这些教材，考虑到它的实际应用性，我公司主要从实战的角度按照行指委、教指委的要求来编写。为了更好地推动应用型人才培养，我公司在四川绵阳建设了网络安全人才培养基地，进行各类教材、教法、教学实践，不断推动网络安全实战型人才培养。

通过这 3—4 年的努力，我公司在职业教育领域取得了一定成效，同时和高校合作建设了一批网络空间安全产业学院，包括北京电子科技职业学院、合肥职业技术学院、上海电子信息职业技术学院、福建信息职业技术学院等。我公司在产业学院和专业建设方面推出了 15 个细分的方案，对不同场景或者人才培养品类也进行了细分。从实际工作情况来看，我公司三年来合作了几十所全国的“双高”院校，包括一些应用型大学，但在职业教育方面仍有许多不足。

我们提出“双教”育人模式的定义，过去讲“双师型”是指教师和工程师，现

在讲的“双教”则是指学校教师还有企业的教练，即企业的工程师用教练的方法理念来确保学生的应用和技能能够符合现在的岗位需求。我公司在全国各省的办事处至少都在 100 人以上的规模，在办事处里我们有做销售的教练、售前的教练、售后的教练、攻防的教练、交付的教练，甚至包括人力的教练，这样就解决了企业出足够数量和能力的“教师”问题。我公司认为“双教”模式的关键是学校教师和企业教练一起来实施技能和应用型人才的培养。这里就需要企业把实际的岗位职责及其对应能力以及能力所对应教练的要求进行明确并形成实战化的教学内容，从而推动整个“双教”模式的变革。为了保证教学，我公司将进行以下工作：一是把校园网改造成“攻防对抗实战训练”的靶场，学生在学校里就可以做到网络安全的攻防对抗、应急演练。二是要成立“学生攻击队”，通过教练带着学生打比赛、做对抗、做执法检查、做各种实战性演练演习，让学生具备熟练应用网络安全实践技能。三是建立基于云和虚拟化的在线教育平台及网络空间仿真实验室，实现教学资源云共享，从而降低学校的投入。

与此同时，我公司还将把 1+X、注册信息安全渗透测试工程师、信息系统安全专业认证等证书通过“云安”学院的方式进行能力验证类培训和考核，确保毕业生和实际的就业需求对接。

这是一种系统性的工程，需要政府机构、学校、企业以及社会组织形成系统化的建设内容，确保实现“双教”模式。通过企业工程师的“教练型”教法，教会学生在应聘一个岗位时，应该掌握什么样的能力。而学校里各项学习、实战、实训都是围绕着培养能力来进行的，所以学生能够非常清楚地知道毕业之后，是来应聘销售岗位、售前岗位、技术岗位、渗透岗位，还是服务岗位的。

## （十）

# 助力产业数字化转型、赋能复合型技术技能人才

**中兴通讯政企中国营销事业部副总裁　郝　钊**

在我国数字经济相关政策指引下，5G新基建和数字化应用正在持续推进中。目前，我国已建成了全球最大规模的5G网络，截至2022年7月底，全国累计建成了5G基站196.8万个，完成所有城区及96%以上乡镇覆盖。行业数字化应用创新蓬勃开展，部分典型应用场景开始逐步进行规模化推广。去年，国家发布了《5G应用“扬帆”行动计划（2021—2023）》《工业互联网创新发展行动计划（2021—2023）》等一系列具体举措，将进一步推动新型数字技术与各行业的深入融合，驱动产业升级和变革。当前以及未来的两三年，将会是产业数字化全面加速推进的重要时机，也是数字新基建深化创新，打造新引擎的关键阶段。

中兴通讯作为5G龙头企业，一直致力于5G技术创新和行业赋能，与国家新基建战略同频共进、心跳一致。在数字建设的新征程上，中兴通讯的定位是数字经济的筑路者。我们致力于5G为主的新型信息基础设施建设，助力运营商建设性能极致、效率极致的云网底座以及开放灵活的混合平台。加强绿色创新，推动向零碳能源网络远景目标演进，聚焦芯片、操作系统、数据库等底层技术创新，支撑各行业数字化转型和高质量稳固发展。同时我公司也积极推进5G行业应用探索，围绕15个重点行业开展了100多个创新示范应用。

中兴通讯携手全球110多家运营商，500多家合作伙伴，开展了广泛的5G创新应用探索，形成了大量的行业创新应用案例，同时我公司也积极推进自身的数字化转型。在南京的滨江基地，我们用5G制造提升生产效率、降低生产成本。5G商用三年来，在业界各方的凝心聚力下，我们已经看到了5G联合新技术正在逐步渗透至千行百业，为传统行业赋能、赋智、赋值，实现从生产方式到管理理念变

革，并带来了实实在在的经济价值和社会价值。

同时，我们也看到了，在产业数字化和数字产业化的加速推进的背后，多个行业正在或者即将面临大量的复合型技术技能人才的需求缺口。新一轮科技革命和产业革命更加强调人才制造工艺和服务技术能力的迭代，更加突出技能型人才的引领性作用。

职业教育是打造技能型人才的主要通道，是国际新背景下，高层次技能人才培养的主要阵地。在不同的历史阶段，职业教育在不同国家肩负的历史使命也是不一样的。当前，我国的职业教育正处在提质培优、增值赋能、改革攻坚和爬坡过坎的关键节点上，职业教育在我国现阶段最重要的两大使命就是支撑高质量发展和促进高质量就业。基于这两大使命，我们当前最主要的就是要增强职业教育的适应性，在产业数字化的大背景下，用数字化思维系统谋划和推动职业教育发展，使之成为产业进步的参与主体，技术变革的重要力量，实现从大规模标准化培养向大规模个性化培养的系统性变革，以数字化为契机，打出重构现代职业教育高质量发展体系的关键一招。

中兴通讯坚持数字经济筑路者的定位，充分发挥我们在信息与通信技术领域的技术积累，聚焦数字产业化中高效的“数字基础设施”和产业数字化中“可交易的数字能力”，与产业和生态伙伴一起向阳生长，共同加强技术和产品创新。结合目前我国职业教育发展的态势，围绕产业链，强健人才链是中兴通讯正在践行的人才培养之路。

近年来，中兴通讯不断的探索“岗课赛证”融通育人的模式，依托数字化产业学院的建设，通过产教融合、现代学徒制、校企合作、工学结合等多种形式与职业院校一同培养了大批优质的技术技能人才。并结合中兴通讯“5G+ 行业应用”的领先技术和行业经验，通过人工智能、大数据、虚拟仿真等信息技术手段，帮助师生加深对通信行业的理解，加强数字化素养的提升。

对于职业教育来讲，传统的“以就业为导向”和“单一职业为依据”的发展定位已不适应当下的时代需要。中兴通讯作为一家有 37 年历史的通讯领域的龙头民族企业，结合当今数字化转型下社会发展的需求，培养一批具有数字化素养能力的中高端复合型技术型的人才，服务产业数字化是中兴通讯义不容辞的责任与义务。

在如今职业教育发展中，师资队伍的教学能力和实践能力很大程度上影响着学校人才培养质量。中兴通讯在职业院校人才培养的过程中，打造了实战化的培养模式，依托中兴通讯强大的技术力量，组建了一支具备专业技能的高素质讲师队伍。

讲师队伍由 150 名专职的讲师和超过 300 名经过认证的中高层管理人员、研发专家、工程维护专家、兼职讲师组成，并引进企业的骨干人才参与到教学实践中。我们尊重和借鉴行业专家的意见，并在人才培养中发挥专家的主导作用。

在课程方面，中兴通讯形成了一系列标准化赋能课程，已面向全球客户提供了超过 70 万人次的各类系统培训、维护专题培训和管理素质培训。同时，我们在全国打造了多个场景化的实训基地，使学生能够参与到实战中来，在学习过程中掌握未来工作中遇到的操作场景，掌握工作技能。对于通过中兴通讯数字化转型培训课程的在校生和应届毕业生，在符合中兴通讯及中兴通讯生态招聘要求的情况下，我们将会推荐更多的岗位实习和就业机会。

职业教育是推动社会有序发展的重要动力，也是构建人类命运共同体的重要载体。中兴通讯希望与各国职业院校代表充分开展对话交流，共谋职业教育的未来大发展。

# 十二

# 职业教育校企协同育人模式创新论坛

协助组织单位：南京工业职业技术大学

# XII. Innovation in Modes of Education Delivered Through Academia-Industry Collaboration

Co-organizer: Nanjing Vocational University of Industry Technology

01
吴学敏
Wu Xuemin

02
柯马凯
Michael Crook

03
阿卜杜霍里克佐达 · 鲁特菲亚
Abdulkholiqzoda Lutfiya

04
周琳
Zhou Lin

05
马克 · 奥尔德肖
Mark Oldershaw

06
傅睿楠
Thomas Florian Mack

07
赛觉奈乌
Sai Kyaw Naing Oo

08
郑棉发
Te Meang Huot

09
林宇
Lin Yu

10
方乃纯
Fang Naichun

11
张保全
Zhang Baoquan

12
谢永华
Xie Yonghua

13
邢晖
Xing Hui

**分享各国校企协同育人的最新政策与最佳实践，探讨如何融合学校与企业的资源、文化以及管理优势，促进职业教育的创新发展。回应新时代职业教育高质量发展要求，探索各国职业教育人才培养模式，加强产教融合、校企合作。**

This session discusses the latest policies and best practices of academia-industry collaborative education in different countries, and explores how to integrate the advantages on resources, culture and management from both schools and enterprises to promote the innovative development of VTE. In response to the requirement for high-quality development of VTE in the new era, the participants explore the mode of talent training for global VTE, strengthen the ties and coordination between VTE and industries, and between colleges and enterprises.

# （一）

# 职业教育校企协同育人模式创新论坛情况概述

南京工业职业技术大学党委书记　吴学敏

为加强职业教育国际交流和合作，推动职业教育高质量发展，2022 年 8 月 19—20 日，中华人民共和国教育部、中国联合国教科文组织全国委员会和天津市人民政府共同举办了首届世界职业技术教育发展大会，大会主题为“后疫情时代职业技术教育发展：新变化、新方式、新技能”。大会同期举办了十四场平行论坛，由南京工业职业技术大学承办的职业教育校企协同育人模式创新论坛于 8 月 20 日下午成功举办。本次论坛旨在分享各国校企协同育人的最新政策与最佳实践，探讨如何融合学校与企业的资源、文化以及管理优势，促进职业教育创新发展。

论坛由南京工业职业技术大学党委书记吴学敏主持，来自德国、美国、英国、新加坡、塔吉克斯坦、柬埔寨、缅甸、赞比亚、新西兰等20余个国家的200余名中外嘉宾参加了论坛。中华人民共和国教育部职业教育与成人教育司副司长林宇，中国工合国际委员会主席、北京培黎职业学院理事柯马凯，中华职业教育社党组书记、总干事方乃纯，新加坡教育部高教规划司司长陈理圣，空中客车（天津）总装有限公司总经理傅睿楠，国家教育行政学院学术委员会主任邢晖，德国汉斯·赛德尔基金会上海代表处首席代表施泰德，华为技术有限公司人才发展部教育业务总经理党张波，南京工业职业技术大学校长谢永华等20余位政、校、行、企代表围绕主题进行了交流发言。各位嘉宾发言观点精彩纷呈，互动交流坦诚深入，论坛取得了显著成效，结出了累累硕果。

首先，林宇副司长对本次论坛的举办表示热烈祝贺。他指出，职业教育在促进就业、保证供应链的稳定以及提升人民的福祉、支撑实体经济等意义重大、作用明显，正受到社会越来越多的关注。职业院校在实践的过程当中，逐步凝练形成了工学结合、校企合作、产教融合的办学理念。纵观世界各国的职业教育，特别是发达国家的职业教育各具特色、形式多样，但校企合作、协同育人是共识、是方向。他希望，通过论坛的举办，搭建一个交流经验、凝聚共识、孕育成果的平台，通过相互学习、加强交流，共同推动职业教育更好地服务于经济社会的发展，也更好地服务于人的全面发展。

在主旨发言环节，与会嘉宾认为，国内外发展经验均表明，职业院校须走产教融合、校企合作发展之路，才能更好地适应国家发展战略和地方经济社会发展需求，培养高素质技术技能人才。柯马凯表示，习近平总书记在给中国工合国际委员会、北京培黎职业学院的重要回信中指出，要“积极开展国际文化交流，谱写国际友谊新篇章，为促进世界和平与发展、构建人类命运共同体作出新的贡献。”陈理圣探讨了新加坡对产学研合作教育模式创新的看法。方乃纯介绍了中国特色学徒制的实践与探索。英国皇家航空学会中国代表处荣誉主席李安表示，应该大力推动中国航天制造业劳动力转型。北京精雕科技集团有限公司执行总裁张保全指出，精雕细琢分层孕育工匠人才对后疫情时代的职业技术教育至关重要。傅睿楠介绍了空客与各大高校的校企合作创新模式。缅甸科技部职业技术教育与培训司司长赛觉奈乌介绍了缅甸职业技术教育与培训的转型与发展方向。

在专题研讨环节，专家们指出学校的人才培养需要与经济社会的用人需求相适应。当前，培养理论功底扎实、能解决实际问题的高层次技术技能人才是产业转型升级发展的时代需求，也是职业院校的人才培养目标与方向。谢永华探讨了职业本科“三型协同”跨境校企合作平台打造，提出集聚各方优势，培养复合性、精深性、创新性“三性一体化”高层次技术技能人才路径。随后，邢晖，施泰德，党张波以及柬华理事总会常务副会长郑棉发，美国贝茨技术学院校长、首席执行官周琳等分别介绍了校企合作协同育人的政策与实践，指出了校企合作协同育人的重要时代意义，分析了当前校企合作育人中的问题和难题，探讨了问题产生的原因，提出了创新发展的路径，展示了中国、德国、美国、柬埔寨等不同国家在校企合作育人模式创新、平台打造和国际化人才培养的特色与趋势。

在对话环节，专家们继续围绕校企合作育人的机制与实践展开探讨。有色金属工业人才中心副主任宋凯、中国—赞比亚职业技术学院赞方校长乔里克·亚姆夫瓦、武汉铁路职业技术学院校长程时兴、用友集团新道科技股份有限公司董事长陈强兵、博世汽车部件（苏州）有限公司执行总裁安德睿、黄河水利职业技术学院党委书记周保平、惠灵顿联合理工学院首席执行官马克·奥尔德肖进行了分享和交流。专家们从政府、行业企业和院校的角度，分享了各自领域中校企合作育人的典型案例，探讨了校企合作协同育人创新发展路径。

会上举行了《本科职业教育办学的思考与探索》新书发布与赠书仪式。该书以南京工业职业技术大学为范例，对本科职业教育办学进行深入思考和剖析，就如何发挥企业办学主体作用，创新校企协同育人机制等问题进行回应，是本科职业教育办学实践的阶段性成果。江苏省教育厅副厅长曹玉梅向国家教育行政学院、武汉铁路职业技术学院等代表赠书。

吴学敏在论坛总结中指出，为行业企业培养高素质技术技能人才是职业院校的使命和责任。南京工业职业技术大学创始人黄炎培先生 100 年前提出“大职业教育观”，指出“只从职业学校做功夫，不能发达职业教育；只从教育界做功夫，不能发达职业教育；只从农工商职业界做功夫，不能发达职业教育”。学校只有与社会、产业和企业充分沟通与合作，才能办好职业教育。职业教育是与经济社会发展对接最紧密的教育类型，从各国举办职业教育的经验来看，产教融合、校企合作是办好职业教育的必由之路。综合各位发言嘉宾的论述，职业院校要深化产教融合、校企合作，需从以下三个方面着力。

一是练好内功，增强校企合作的主导性。当前，职业院校开展校企合作积极性高，但合作过程中往往处于弱势地位，主要是学校自身对相关技术领域积累不够，不能对企业的技术难题提出可行性技术改进方案，导致合作过程的话语权不足。职业院校须在提升自身技术能力上下功夫，在优势专业领域强化应用研发、注重技能积累，打造技术优势，提升校企合作的主导性。围绕自身办学需求和发展要求，设计符合企业效益的合作方案，提高校企合作协同育人、协同创新的实际成效。校企合作、工学结合是职业教育人才培养模式改革的关键，不能仅停留在浅层合作层面，避免校企合作中“一头热”和人才培养中“两张皮”的现象，需要适应更高层次、更高水平的创新型技术技能人才培养需求，向更深度的校企融合型转变提升。职业院校通过创新合作体制和机制，确保校企合作融入学校治理、院系办学、专业建设、人才培养和社会服务全过程，构建校企协同育人的生态体系。

二是找好基点，扩大校企合作的共赢区。企业和学校之所以能合作，是因为在合作中各自能够达成相关诉求，实现利益共赢。而且，这个共赢的范围越大，合作关系越稳固。因此要在校企合作中找准合作共赢的基点，并在良好合作基础上，不断扩大共赢范围。从学校角度来看，我们不能仅仅想到自身能在合作中得到什么，也要想到合作企业能够在合作中能够得到什么，在不损害自身利益基础上，充分考虑合作企业的利益诉求，从而建立更加稳定的合作关系。目前看来，激励企业成为育人主体的举措尚不完善，企业也无动力参与学校人才培养过程。企业是追求效益的主体，在校企合作过程中如果长时间看不到收益，其参与合作的积极性必然会大打折扣。

三是建好机制，激发校企合作的内生力。校企合作的深入开展，需要学校方方面面的协同配合、共同推进。这就需要学校建立激发各方积极性的评价机制，引导广大教职工通过校企合作提升人才培养质量、提高应用技术研发水平，从而激发出源源不断的内生动力，形成个人与学校相互促进、共同成长的良性循环。当前，校企协同育人评价机制亟待健全，学校层面应完善保障和激励政策，保护激发相关方活力，健全标准体系，加强校企协同育人规范化建设。学校应积极探索校企协同育人创新理念，提出创新举措，开展创新实践，为职业教育高质量发展打开新思路、开拓新视野。

每个国家的职业教育校企合作育人模式都应契合各自国情、融入当地产业发展，彰显不同优势与特色。作为已建成世界上最大职业教育体系的中国，更要加快探索体现中国特色、具有世界水平的职业教育校企合作模式，形成校企合作育人的新局面。本次论坛的成功举办，将有利于我们把握后疫情时代校企协同育人的发展方向，推动职业教育与经济社会发展紧密相连，促进职业教育高质量发展。

# i. Overview of the Session on Innovation in Modes of Education Delivered Through Academia-Industry Collaboration

**Wu Xuemin, Secretary of CPC Committee of Nanjing Vocational University of Industry Technology, China**

To strengthen international exchange and cooperation in vocational education and promote high-quality development of vocational education, the Ministry of Education of People's Republic of China, the China National Commission for UNESCO and the Tianjin Municipal People's Government jointly organized the first World Vocational and Technical Education Development Conference from August 19 to 20, 2022, with the theme of "Vocational and Technical Education Development in the Post-pandemic Era—New Changes, New Ways and New Skills". At the same time, 14 parallel sessions were held at the conference. The Session on Innovation in Modes of Education Delivered through Academia-Industry Collaboration hosted by Nanjing Vocational University of Industry Technology was successfully held in the afternoon of August 20. The Session aimed to share the latest policies and best practices of academia-industry collaborative education in participating countries, and discuss how to integrate the advantages of schools and enterprises in resources, culture and management to promote the innovative development of vocational education.

The Session was chaired by Wu Xuemin, Secretary of CPC Committee of Nanjing Vocational University of Industry Technology, China and attended by more than 200 guests from about 20 countries including Germany, the United States, the United Kingdom, Singapore, Tajikistan, Cambodia, Myanmar, Zambia, and New Zealand. More than 20 representatives from governments, schools, industries and enterprises made speeches around the theme, including Lin Yu, Deputy Director of Department of Vocational and Adult Education of the Ministry of Education, P.R. China, Michael Crook, Chairman of International Committee for the Promotion of Chinese Industrial Cooperatives and Member of the Board of Beijing Bailie University, Fang Naichun, Secretary of CPC Leading Group and Director General of China Vocational Education

Association, China, Tan Li Sheng, Director of the Higher Education Planning Office of Ministry of Education, Singapore, Thomas Florian Mack, General Manager of Airbus (Tianjin) Final Assembly Co., Ltd., Xing Hui, Director of Academic Committee of National Academy of Education Administration, China, Georg Stadler, Chief Representative of Shanghai Office, Hanns Seidel Foundation, Germany, Dang Zhangbo, General Manager of Education Business of Talent Development Department of Huawei Technologies Co., Ltd., China, and Xie Yonghua, President of Nanjing Vocational University of Industry Technology, China. The brilliant speeches of the guests and the frank and in-depth communication yielded remarkable and fruitful results.

First of all, Deputy Director Lin Yu expressed his hearty congratulations on the Session. He pointed out that vocational education is of great significance and plays a prominent role in promoting employment, ensuring the stability of supply chains, enhancing people's welfare and supporting the real economy. Therefore, it is drawing increasing attention from the society. In the process of their practice, vocational schools have gradually formed the idea of work-study combination, academia-industry cooperation and production-education integration. Vocational education throughout the world, especially in developed countries, is organized in various forms with distinct characteristics, while academia-industry collaborative education has become the consensus and direction of all. He hoped that the session would become a platform to exchange experiences, establish consensus and foster achievements, and through mutual learning and communication, we would jointly promote vocational education to better serve the development of economy and society, as well as the overall development of human beings.

In the keynote speech session, the participants believed that both domestic and foreign development experiences have demonstrated that vocational schools should take the path of production-education integration and academia-industry cooperation in order to better adapt to national development strategies and local economic and social development needs, and to cultivate high-quality technical and skilled talents. Michael Crook said that President Xi Jinping pointed out in his important reply to the International Committee for the Promotion of Chinese Industrial Cooperatives and Beijing Bailie University that "we shall actively carry out international cultural exchanges to write a new chapter of international friendship, and to make new contributions to promoting world peace and development and building a community with a shared future for mankind". Tan Li Sheng shared Singapore's perspective on the innovation of the academia-industry collaborative education model. Fang Naichun introduced the practice and exploration of the apprenticeship system with Chinese characteristics. Julian McCormack, Honorary President of the Royal Aeronautical Society in China, UK, said that the transformation of China's aerospace manufacturing workforce should be vigorously promoted. Zhang Baoquan, Chief Executive Officer of Beijing Jingdiao

Group Co., Ltd., China, pointed out that the layered cultivation of craftsmen is crucial to vocational and technical education in the post-pandemic era. Thomas Florian Mack introduced the innovative model of academia-industry cooperation between Airbus and major universities. Sai Kyaw Naing Oo, Director General of the Department of Technical and Vocational Education and Training of the Ministry of Science and Technology, Myanmar, introduced the transformation and development direction of vocational and technical education and training in Myanmar.

In the discussion session, the experts pointed out that the talent training of the schools needs to be adapted to the requirements of employers in the economy and society. At present, it is the demand of the times to cultivate high-level technical and skilled talents with solid theoretical foundation and problem-solving ability for industrial transformation and upgrading, and it is also the goal and direction of talent training in vocational schools. Xie Yonghua discussed the establishment of a cross-border academia-industry cooperation platform for the cultivation of vocational innovative, interdisciplinary and applied undergraduates, and proposed a path to gather the advantages of all parties to cultivate high-level technical and skilled talents with interdisciplinary background, profound knowledge and innovative creativity. Afterwards, Xing Hui, Georg Stadler, Dang Zhangbo, as well as Te Meang Huot, Executive Vice President of Federation of Khmer Chinese in Cambodia, and Zhou Lin, President and Chief Executive Officer of Bates Technical College, US, introduced the policies and practices of academia-industry collaborative education, pointed out the significance of academia-industry collaborative education in this era, analyzed the problems and difficulties in the current academia-industry collaborative education, discussed the causes of the problems, proposed the path of innovation and development, and presented the characteristics and trends of different countries such as China, Germany, US and Cambodia in the academia-industry collaborative education models innovating, platform building and international talent training.

In the dialogue session, the experts continued to discuss the mechanism and practice of academia-industry cooperative education. Song Kai, Deputy Director of China Nonferrous Metal Industry Human Resource Center, China, Jorick Yamvwa, Principal of Local Affairs for Sino-Zam Vocational College of Science and Technology, Zambia, Cheng Shixing, President of Wuhan Railway Vocational College of Technology, China, Chen Qiangbing, Chairman of Yonyou Group Seentao Technology Co., Ltd., China, Georges Andary, General Manager of Bosch Automotive Products (Suzhou) Co., Ltd., Zhou Baoping, Secretary of CPC Committee of Yellow River Conservancy Technical Institute, China, and Mark Oldershaw, Chief Executive of Whitireia and WelTec Polytechnic, New Zealand, shared typical cases of academia-industry collaborative education in their respective fields from the perspectives of government, industry, enterprises and universities, and exchanged views on the innovation and development path of academia-industry collaborative education.

A book release and donation ceremony was held at the meeting. Taking Nanjing Vocational University of Industry Technology as an example, the book, *Reflections and Explorations on Undergraduate Vocational Education* through in-depth thinking and analysis on the operation of undergraduate vocational education, responds to issues such as how to play the primary role of enterprises in running schools and innovate the mechanism of academia-industry collaborative education. It is a milestone of the practice of undergraduate vocational education. Cao Yumei, Deputy Director of the Jiangsu Education Department, China, presented books to representatives of the National Academy of Education Administration and Wuhan Railway Vocational College of Technology.

In the summary of the Session, Wu Xuemin pointed out that it was the mission and responsibility of vocational schools to cultivate high-quality technical skilled talents for industry enterprises. Mr. Huang Yanpei, founder of Nanjing Vocational University of Industry Technology, put forward the "Great Vocational Education Concept" 100 years ago, and pointed out that "vocational education cannot be developed by vocational schools or enterprises only from one end." It means that only by fully communicating and cooperating with the society, industry and enterprises, can schools carry forward vocational education. Vocational education is the type of education that is most closely related to economic and social development. Judging from the experience of various countries in running vocational education, production-education integration and academia-industry cooperation are the only and final path. Based on the discussions of the speakers, vocational colleges need to make efforts in the following aspects to deepen the production-education integration and academia-industry cooperation:

Firstly, we should enhance internal strength and increase the dominance in academia-industry cooperation. At present, vocational schools are highly motivated to carry out academia-industry cooperation, but they are often in an inferior position in the cooperation process, mainly because the schools themselves have not accumulated enough technical know-how and cannot propose feasible improvement solutions for the technical problems of enterprises, resulting in a lack of discourse power. Vocational schools must make serious efforts to improve their own technical capabilities, strengthen application R&D in advantageous professional fields, focus on accumulation of skills, create technical advantages, and enhance the dominance in academia-industry cooperation. Based on our operational needs and development requirements, we should design cooperation programs that are in line with the benefits of enterprises and improve the actual effect of academia-industry collaborative education and innovation. Academia-industry cooperation and work-study combination is the key to the reform of talent training mode in vocational education, and should not stay at the surface but be transformed and upgraded to a deeper level and a greater height through close communication and coordination while adapting to the demand of cultivating innovative technical and skilled talents. Vocational schools, through innovative cooperation systems and mechanisms, can ensure that academia-industry cooperation is integrated into the whole process of school governance, faculty operation, discipline construction, talent training and social services, and build an ecosystem of academia-industry collaborative education.

Secondly, we should find a proper base and expand the win-win zone of academia-industry cooperation. The reason why enterprises and schools can cooperate is that each party can achieve their goals and receive benefits in a win-win situation. Moreover, the larger the range of this win-win zone, the steadier the cooperative relationship. Therefore, it is important to find the base of the win-win cooperation in academia-industry cooperation and to expand the range around such basis. From the schools' point of view, we should consider not only what we can receive from the cooperation, but also what cooperative enterprises can get, which means that we should fully consider the interests of cooperative enterprises without damaging our own interests, to establish more stable partnerships. At present, it seems that the programs to motivate enterprises to become a pillar of education are not yet perfect, and enterprises have not enough incentive to participate in the training of talents in schools. Enterprises are established to pursue benefits. If they cannot see benefits for a long time in the process of school-enterprise cooperation, their enthusiasm will inevitably be greatly reduced.

Thirdly, we should establish a mechanism to stimulate the endogenous force of academia-industry cooperation. The in-depth development of academia-industry cooperation cannot be carried forward without the concerted cooperation and joint promotion from all aspects of schools. This requires schools to establish an evaluation mechanism to stimulate the enthusiasm of all parties, and to guide the majority of faculty and staff to improve the quality of talent training and the R&D level of applied technology through academia-industry cooperation. Thus, the endogenous power can be released constantly, and a virtuous cycle that individuals and schools promote each other and grow together can be formed. At present, the evaluation mechanism for academia-industry collaborative education needs to be improved. Schools should improve the guarantee and incentive policies, protect and stimulate the vitality of related parties, upgrade the standard system, and strengthen the standardization of academia-industry collaborative education. Schools need to actively explore innovative ideas of academia-industry collaborative education, put forward innovative measures, carry out innovative practices, and extend new visions and new horizons for the high-quality development of vocational education.

Each country should develop their academia-industry collaborative vocational education models that fit their national conditions and can demonstrate different advantages and characteristics, and integrate them into the development of local industries. As China has built the largest vocational education system in the world, we should accelerate the exploration of world-class academia-industry collaborative vocational education models with Chinese characteristics, and form a new situation of academia-industry cooperative education. The success of this session has initiated a useful exploration to identify the development direction of academia-industry collaborative education in the post-pandemic era, tighten the connection between vocational education and economic and social development, and promote the high-quality development of vocational education.

# （二）

# “手脑并用、创造分析”的培黎职业教育

中国工合国际委员会主席、北京培黎职业学院理事　柯马凯

## 1. 工合、培黎与职业教育

工合运动是来自新西兰的斯诺夫妇、路易·艾黎等国际友人会同宋庆龄等中国爱国人士组织的一场支持中国抗战的运动，是国际合作的一个典范。“工合”是“工业合作”的简称。工合运动鼓励大家联合起来，“努力干、一起干”，以实体经济支持革命。工合运动发展之初，路易·艾黎就认识到，当时中国急需职业教育，特别是要对难民和农民进行职业教育，让他们掌握生存技能。从1940年起，路易·艾黎开始在全国各地试办培黎学校，接收普通的合作社徒工和逃难的工农子弟入学，有目标、有组织、有计划地进行技术培训。第一所培黎学校在江西赣县创办，随后在陕西、广西等地相继开办了十余所培黎学校。培黎学校是艾黎和何克在抗战后期创办并坚持办下来的半工半读的职业学校，是工合运动的继续。

学生要把学到的知识和技能用于实际操作，在实践中学习，求知与行合一。从1942年工合山丹培黎工艺学校创立，到新中国成立后的1952年，工合国际委员会协助学校筹集机器设备，从世界各国聘请有志于帮助中国的教师，讲授适合工合特点、世界比较先进的科学知识和技能，选派学生到外国去学习，培养出了一批批各方面的人才。

培黎学校是一个融合国际合作、贫困救济、乡村建设和职业教育为一体的创造性综合型组织。培黎学校也是一所具有光荣传统的学校，为国家建设培养了大批人才，经过八十年的探索和实践，已成为中国职业教育和改革历史中一道独特的风景。培黎秉承艾黎和何克倡导的“手脑并用、创造分析”的职业教育思想、校训和优良传统，是国际职业教育长期在中国实践的宝贵财富，是中西方交流和国际职业教育合作的重要成果。

2. 牢记总书记嘱托，弘扬工合精神，传承和践行路易·艾黎职业教育思想

抗战时期，老培黎为中国培养纺织、汽修、石油开采等人才，为支援中国革命贡献了培黎力量；新中国建设时期，培黎响应国家建设需要，为学生提供接受高等教育的平台，培养了大量服务社会主义现代化建设人才。

2017 年 4 月 20 日，习近平总书记给中国工合国际委员会、北京培黎职业学院回信，嘱托“希望你们发扬传承艾老‘努力干，一起干’的工合精神，积极开展国际文化交流，谱写国际友谊新篇章，为促进世界和平与发展、构建人类命运共同体作出新的贡献。”习近平总书记的回信给中国工合国际委员会、北京培黎职业学院指明了新时期建设发展方向。

北京培黎职业学院具有红色基因、优良传统和历史传承。学院传承和创新“手脑并用，创造分析”为核心的艾黎职业教育思想，主动适应国际化发展需求，努力探索发展适合中国国情的新型职业教育，为国家培养了大批技术技能型人才。

（1）创新国际化技能型人才培养，发挥“人才供给”作用。学院将国际化与技能型人才培养有机结合，在全院 5 个专业群 22 个专业实施人才培养方案改革。构建了“德技并修、国际素养、适合教育”的课程体系。建设了“通用能力 + 综合素养”“职业能力 + 职业素养”“国际竞争力 + 国际素养”“个性发展 + 职业发展”4 个课程群，延展国际素养课程。实施学校 + 企业双育人，国内 + 国际双培养；打造国际英才班项目，实践培养国际英才 125 人，已毕业 55 人，其中 10 人取得本科学位，45 人取得硕士学位。学生就业率、升本率、留学率均位于北京市同类院校前列，为北京市乃至全国企业输送大量人才。推进产教融合，建设产业学院、产学工作室，大数据财贸专业群、曙光瑞翼全媒体数字营销师学院获批北京市特色高水平建设项目。

（2）创新德育育人体系，发挥“示范引领”作用。从培黎特有的红色基因、国际主义精神视角切入，以党建为引领，课程为基石，将培黎校史文化和路易·艾黎国际主义精神融入教学，增强了学生的归属感、荣誉感和爱校爱国情怀，学生的人格素养日益健全。

（3）创新育人模式，实施适合学生个体差异的教育。推行学分制改革，设置个性化课程模块，建设课程群，为工学交替、弹性学习以及学分银行的实施提供支撑。推行“爱的教育”，从 2001 年举办全国首个“春蕾计划”大专班开始，在全国妇联、中国儿童少年基金会的大力支持下，已连续举办七届“春蕾班”，累计出资近千万元，资助来自偏远地区、山区的 267 名贫困女生圆了大学梦。

（4）搭建国际交流交往平台，发挥“民间友谊”作用。以习近平总书记回信为引领，深入挖掘路易·艾黎跨越国界、超越民族的国际主义精神，充分发挥海内外资源优势，国际、政府、行业企业、社会团体、学校五方协作建设民间国际交流交往平台。2017 年 4 月，中国工合国际委员会“国际主义教育基地”、北京培黎职业学院“路易·艾黎国际交流中心”相继在培黎成立；2019 年，在日本设立培黎日本东京事务所，同年赴西班牙筹备欧洲办事处，参与新西兰培黎实训基地项目落地。近年来，接待世界各地友好组织来访团组数量和规模不断扩大，接待英中了解协会、新中友好协会、国际合作社联盟组织等来访，应邀组团访问新西兰、加拿大、英国、印度等国家，弘扬中华文化，拓展和巩固国际民间友谊。

开展中国学生出国学习和外国学生来华培训，组织实施不同类型、多种形式的文化交流。推进 20 个专业与西班牙、日本、英国等国家的大学课程对接。2018 年，获批招收外国学生资质，招收来自俄罗斯、印度、哥伦比亚等 40 多个国家，近 300 名留学生就读培黎，留学生的培养对传播中华文化，推动北京职业教育走向国际具有重要意义。培训 30 位“中文＋职业技能”教师，打造了一支“双语＋双师”的国际化职教教师团队。

（5）深化产教融合，培养手脑并用的高素质技术技能型人才。学院认真落实“校企主导、政府推动、行业指导、学校企业双主体实施”的要求，积极探索建立与政府部门、企业在招生、培养、就业等方面的联动机制，与东升镇政府、中关村软件园、金蝶集团、中国汽车流通协会、利星行汽车集团公司等签订了战略合作协议。

2012 年，利星行汽车集团公司与我院签订校企合作协议，设立利星行汽车订单班，在学院建立汽车实训室，捐赠总价值 60 多万元的奔驰发动机和变速箱各一台作为教学设备，为学生实训提供实训条件；委派技术骨干兼任专业课教师，或接受学生去企业实习或上专业课，以企业为课堂，实现校企合作育人。先后有 57 名学生毕业后留在利星行工作。2016 年以来，企业累计出资 50 万元在学院设立奖学金，奖励品学兼优的学生。

充分发挥学院大数据与会计专业特色和优势，北京知诚社会组织众扶发展促进会捐资 50 余万元与学院合作共建“社会组织财税工作室”，将首都地区社会组织发展建设项目融入大数据与会计专业的高素质职业人才培养过程中，实现了职业教育依托社会又反哺社会的效果。

与沃尔玛、明经堂中医馆等签订校企合作协议，接收顶岗实习学生 400 余人，接收就业学生近百人。

学院携手北京大陆航星质量认证中心股份有限公司，举行“访企拓岗促就业，互利共赢向未来”校企合作签约仪式，为学生实习和就业拓宽渠道。

学院高度重视学生就业创业与发展，通过建立和实施学生职业生涯导师计划等举措，为学生学习、成长和发展提供优质服务指导。到2021年，连续14年学生专升本率高于北京市平均录取率，且稳居同类高校前列。连续多年毕业生就业率在同类院校中处于靠前位置。

**3. 促进职业教育国际交流合作，为共同构建人类命运共同体注入“技能力量”**

习近平总书记在许多重要国际会议上多次提出职业教育国际合作新举措。工合和培黎将继续践行习近平总书记回信精神，以培养具有家国情怀兼具国际视野的高素质技能型人才为目标，传承和创新艾黎职业教育思想，积极为国际化技能型人才培养提供更多培黎方案。

（1）建设多角度、宽领域、共发展的民间国际交流交往平台。联合一些国外、境外优质职业教育机构和高新技术企业，建设培黎海内外实训基地和海外办事处，形成集科技合作、人文交流、人才储备、国际培训、数字技术赋能等多功能为一体的民间国际交流交往平台。特别是与“一带一路”沿线国家的职业教育国际合作搭建工作载体。持续开展培训“中文＋职业技能”教师，用数字技术赋能中国文化，助力“一带一路”沿线国家的技术交流、文化交流、职业教育交流，打造国际人才培养基地。

（2）深化产教融合，强化数字技术赋能，服务数字经济发展。围绕数字中国建设，数字经济催生的新产业、新业态、新模式、新场景、新职业，推进与产业深度融合，打造“当地离不开，业内都认可，国际可交流”的特色品牌专业，培养技术技能型人才。

工合国际和北京培黎职业学院一直在为国家建设和发展贡献力量。国际性是工合国际和北京培黎职业学院特有的优势。让我们大家发扬工合精神，“努力干、一起干”，积极开展国际民间友好往来，积极参与推进“一带一路”建设，为践行构建人类命运共同体历史使命作出新的贡献。

# ii. "Mind and Hand, Creation and Analysis"
## —The Bailie Model of Vocational Education

**Michael Crook, Chairman of International Committee for the Promotion of Chinese Industrial Cooperatives, Member of the Board of Beijing Bailie University**

1. Industrial Cooperatives, Bailie and Vocational Education

The Industrial Cooperatives Movement was a movement organized by American friends Helen and Edgar Snow, Rewi Alley from New Zealand and other foreign friends in conjunction with Chinese patriots like Mdm. Soong Ching Ling to support China's War of Resistance Against Japanese Aggression, and is a model of international cooperation. "IC" is the abbreviation for "Industrial Cooperatives". The Industrial Cooperatives Movement encourages everyone to unite and "work hard and work together" to support the revolution with the real economy. Early in the Industrial Cooperatives Movement, Rewi Alley recognized that China was in urgent need of vocational education, especially for war refugees and farmers, so that they could master survival skills. From 1940 onwards, Rewi Alley began to run Bailie schools throughout the country, accepting ordinary cooperative apprentices and children of refugee workers and peasants, and conducting targeted, organized and planned technical training. The first Bailie school was founded in Ganxian County, Jiangxi, then more than ten Bailie schools were opened in Shanxi, Guangxi and other places. The Bailie School was a work-study vocational school founded by Rewi Alley and George Hogg in the late period of the War of Resistance against Japanese Aggression, and was a continuation of the Industrial Cooperatives Movement.

Students should apply the knowledge and skills they have acquired to practical operation, combining knowledge with practice. From the establishment of the Industrial Cooperatives Shandan Bailie Technical School in 1942 until 1952 after the founding of the People's Republic of China, the ICCIC assisted the school in raising machinery and equipment, hired teachers from all over the world who were interested in helping China, taught advanced scientific knowledge and skills suited to the needs of Industrial Cooperatives, sent students to study in foreign countries, and cultivated a batch of talents in all aspects.

The Bailie School is an innovative and integrated organization that integrates international cooperation, poverty relief, rural construction and vocational education. Bailie School is also a school with a glorious tradition, which has cultivated a large number of talents for China's construction, and after eighty years of exploration and practice, it has become a unique feature in the history of China's vocational education and reform. Adhering to the vocational education ideas, school motto and fine traditions of "Mind and Hand, Creation and Analysis" advocated by Rewi Alley and George Hogg, Bailie School is a valuable asset of international vocational education practice in China, and an important achievement of Sino-Western exchanges and international vocational education cooperation.

**2. Bearing in mind the instructions from General Secretary Xi Jinping, carrying forward the spirit of Industrial Cooperatives, inheriting and practicing Rewi Alley's thoughts on vocational education**

During the China's War of Resistance against Japanese Aggression, the Bailie Schools trained talents in textiles, automobile repair, oil exploration and other fields for China, and made great contributions to support the Chinese revolution. During the construction period of new China, in response to the needs of national construction, Bailie provided a platform for students to receive higher education, and cultivated a large number of talents to serve socialist modernization.

On April 20, 2017, General Secretary Xi Jinping wrote to the International Committee for the Promotion of Chinese Industrial Cooperatives and Beijing Bailie University, exhorting us to "carry forward the spirit of 'working hard and working together' of the former president Rewi Alley, carry out international cultural exchanges actively, and write a new chapter of international friendship, to make new contributions to promoting world peace and development and building a community with a shared future for mankind." The reply from General Secretary Xi Jinping pointed the way for our development in the new era.

With "unique genes", fine traditions and historical heritage, Beijing Bailie University inherits and innovates the Rewi Alley's thoughts on vocational education centering on "Mind and Hand, Creation and Analysis", adapts to the needs of international development actively, strives to explore and develop a new type of vocational education suitable for China's conditions, and cultivates a large number of technical and skilled talents for the country.

(1) Innovating the cultivation of international skilled talents and playing a role of "talent supply"

Combining internationalization with skill-based talent training organically, the University implements the reform of talent training programs in 22 majors of 5 specialty groups of the University. It has built a curriculum system of "combining moral and technical training, international literacy, and appropriate education". It has built four course groups of "general ability + comprehensive quality", "vocational ability + professional quality", "international competitiveness + international literacy", "personality development + career development" to extend the international literacy curriculum. It cultivates talents by the University + enterprise jointly, domestically + internationally; it builds an international talent class program, and has trained 125 international talents, among whom 55 have graduated, 10 have obtained undergraduate degree and 45 have obtained master's degree. The student employment rate, the undergraduate rate and the studying-abroad rate are all in the front rank when compared with similar colleges and universities in Beijing, cultivating a large number of talents for enterprises in Beijing and the whole country. We promote the integration of industry and education, build an industrial college, an industry-university studio. The specialty group of Big Data and Shuguang Ruiyi All-media Digital Marketing College have been listed as high-level characteristic construction projects in Beijing.

(2) Innovating the moral education system and playing a "leading" role

Starting from the perspective of Bailie's unique "gene" and internationalist spirit, with party building as the guide and the curriculum as the cornerstone, the great heritage of Bailie School and the spirit of Rewi Alley's internationalism are integrated into teaching, which enhances students' sense of belonging, honor and love for the school and patriotism, and personal quality.

(3) Innovating the modes of education and implementing individualized education

a. We implements the reform of the credit system, set up personalized course modules, and build course groups to provide support for sandwich course, flexible learning, and school credit bank.

b. The University implements "education of love". Since the first "Spring Bud Program" college class in China in 2001, with the strong support of the All-China Women's Federation and the China Youth Foundation, it has held seven "Spring Bud Class" in a row, with a total investment of nearly 10 million *yuan*, and funding 267 poor girls from remote areas and mountainous areas to realize their college dreams.

(4) Building a platform for international exchanges and giving play to "people-to-people communication"

Inspired by General Secretary Xi Jinping's reply, we dig deep into the internationalist spirit of Rewi Alley across national borders and beyond nationalities, give full play to the advantages of resources at home and abroad, and cooperate with international organizations, government, enterprises and NGOs to build a non-governmental international exchange platform. In April 2017, the Beijing Bailie University was designated as a "Site for Education in Internationalism" by the ICCIC, and the "Rewi Alley International Exchange Center" of Beijing Bailie University was established in Bailie. In 2019, the Tokyo Office of Bailie was established in

Japan, and in the same year, a European office was prepared in Spain, and the Bailie Training Base was established in New Zealand. In recent years, we have received many visiting delegations from all over the world, such as the Society for Anglo-Chinese Understanding (SACU), the New-Zealand-China Friendship Society, and the International Cooperative Alliance. We have visited New Zealand, Canada, the United Kingdom, India and other countries, spreading Chinese culture and building and consolidating international people-to-people friendship.

We have sent Chinese students abroad to study, organized foreign students' training in China, carried out cultural exchanges of different types in different forms, promoted the matchmaking of 20 majors with university curricula in Spain, Japan, the United Kingdom and other countries. In 2018, we were approved to recruit international students, with nearly 300 international students from more than 40 countries such as Russia, India, Colombia and so on studying in Bailie. The training of international students is of great significance to spread Chinese culture and push vocational education in Beijing to go global. We have trained 30 "Chinese language + vocational skills" teachers, and constructed an international vocational education team of "bilingual + double-professionally-titled" teachers.

(5) Deepening the integration of industry and education, and cultivating high-quality technical and skilled talents

Implementing the requirements of "joint leadership by university and enterprise, government pushing, industrial guidance, and implementation by double subjects" conscientiously, the University actively explores the establishment of a linkage mechanism with government departments and enterprises in recruitment, training, employment, etc., and has signed strategic cooperation agreements with Dongsheng Town Government, Zhongguancun Software Park, Kingdee Group, China Automobile Circulation Association, Lei Shing Hong Auto Group (LSH) Corporation, etc.

In 2012, LSH Auto Group Co., Ltd. signed a university-enterprise cooperation agreement with us, established a LSH order training class, built an auto training room, and donated a Mercedes-Benz engine and a gearbox worth more than 600 000 *yuan* as teaching equipment to provide practical training for students. It dispatches technical backbones to serve as teachers of specialized courses, and allows students to go there for internship or professional courses. 57 students have been employed by LSH after their graduation. Since 2016, the Company has invested a total of 500 000 *yuan* to set up a scholarship to reward top students.

The Beijing Zhicheng Society for the Promotion of Zhongfu donated more than 500 000 *yuan* to build the "Social Organization Finance and Taxation Studio" in conjunction with the University, integrating the social organization development and construction project in the capital into the process of cultivating high-quality professional talents in big data and accounting, and achieving the effect of vocational education relying on the society and repaying the society in return.

Bailie has signed university-enterprise cooperation agreements with Wal-Mart and Mingjingtang Traditional Chinese Medicine Clinic, etc. to accept more than 400 students for post practice, and recruit nearly 100 students.

The University signed a university-enterprise cooperation agreement with Beijing Continental Hangxing Quality Certification Center Co., Ltd. to create more channels for students' internship and employment.

The University attaches great importance to student employment, entrepreneurship and development, and provides high-quality service and guidance for students' learning, growth and development through the establishment and implementation of student career coach program and other initiatives. By 2021, the students' upgrading rate has been higher than the average admission rate in Beijing for 14 years in a row, and has always been in the front rank of similar universities. For many years, the employment rate of our graduates has been at the forefront of similar institutions.

### 3. Promoting international exchanges and cooperation in vocational education, and injecting "skill power" into the joint construction of a community with a shared future for mankind

General Secretary Xi Jinping has repeatedly proposed new measures for international cooperation in vocational education at many important international conferences. Continuing to practice the spirit of General Secretary Xi Jinping's reply, with the goal of cultivating high-quality skilled talents with both patriotism and international vision, ICCIC and Bailie inherits and innovates Rewi Alley's thoughts on vocational education, and provides more Bailie solutions to the cultivation of international skilled talents actively.

(1) Building multi-dimension and wide-ranging platforms for non-governmental international exchanges with common development

In conjunction with some foreign high-quality vocational education institutions and high-tech enterprises, we build training bases and overseas offices at home and abroad, to form a non-governmental international exchange platform integrating scientific and technological cooperation, people-to-people exchange, talent reserve, international training, digital technology empowerment and other multi-functions, particularly to build a working platform for international cooperation in vocational education with countries along the "Belt and Road". We continue to train "Chinese language + vocational skills" teachers, empower Chinese culture with digital technology, boost technical exchange, cultural exchange and vocational education exchange between countries along the "Belt and Road", and build an international talent training base.

(2) Deepening the industry-education integration, strengthening the empowerment of digital technology, and serving the development of digital economy

Focusing on the construction of Digital China, new industries, new business forms, new models, new scenarios, and new occupations spawned by the digital economy, we promote deep integration with the industry, and create characteristic brand majors that are "locally inseparable, recognized by the industry and internationally", to cultivate technical and skilled talents.

The ICCIC and Beijing Bailie University have been contributing to the national construction and development. Internationalism is a unique advantage of ICCIC and Beijing Bailie University. Let us all carry forward the spirit of "working hard, and working together", carry out international people-to-people friendly exchanges, participate in the construction of the "Belt and Road" initiative actively, and make new contributions to the historic mission of building a community with a shared future for mankind!

## （三）

# 后疫情时代塔吉克斯坦职业教育的发展

塔吉克斯坦教育和科学部副部长　阿卜杜霍里克佐达·鲁特菲亚

初级职业教育是职业教育培训的重要基础之一，在我国发挥着特殊作用。我国共有初级职业教育机构 62 所，其中职业技术学院 55 所，包含农业行业职业学院 7 所，服装行业职业学院 2 所，旅游行业职业学院 1 所，用于培训技术、农业、矿业、服务、经济、旅游等 106 个专业的从业人员。在上述专业技术学院中共有 1 773 名教师（708 名女性）工作，其中，高等职业教育教师 1 448 人（82%），中等职业教育教师 289 人（16%），初级职业教育教师 36 人（2%）。此外，共计 993 人（298 名女性）为职业教育实践教师，其中，460 人具有高等职业教育经历，405 人具有中等职业教育经历，123 人具有初级职业教育经历。目前，初级职业教育机构中缺少 83 名，即 3% 的职业教育教师及技师人才。需要指出的是，今后将增加具有高等专业教育的专业学科教师和工业技师的数量，并提高其资质水平，定期安排他们在国内外接受专业培训。

为了将初级职业教育的全部机构纳入统一的系统，塔吉克斯坦教育和科学部理事会基于与本部及其他部委和部门合作，始终致力于在部门内制定和通过各项法规文件、塔吉克斯坦教育和科学部理事会决议、教育及科学部部长令，并提供给教育机构。

塔吉克斯坦教育和科学部与塔吉克斯坦劳动、移民及居民就业部基于对国内劳动力市场以及哈萨克斯坦、白俄罗斯、俄罗斯联邦、波罗的海地区共和国和中欧劳动力市场的研究，制定了塔吉克斯坦就业专业、雇员职位及关税的国家分类。该分类于 2013 年 3 月 2 日由第 86 号政府法令批准，并已面向初级职业教育机构出版发行 200 册。

目前，在初级职业教育领域，已制定和批准了 200 多项规范性法律文件，成为有助于精简这些机构活动的主要因素。塔吉克斯坦教育和科学部与塔吉克斯坦劳动、移民及居民就业部共同制定了 10 项初级职业教育资格标准，并批准了塔吉克斯坦教育和科学部的合议决定。建立符合现代要求的物质和技术基础，也是培养高素质人才的主要有利因素之一。有关这方面，在合作伙伴、国际和公共组织的支持下，初级职业教育机构正利用预算及预算外资金，进行教育大厦、教室、生产及培训讲习班、厨房与宿舍的修复和重建，并为其配备必要的设备。

值得注意的是，在亚洲开发银行“强化职业教育与培训”的项目框架下，已经对 21 所初级职业教育机构、5 所塔吉克斯坦成人教育中心分校和 2 所职业创业教育中心分校的 17 个专业进行了教室、工作室及车间改造，并配备了现代化设备和教育用品。

在国家教育机构“莱瓦肯特市化工专业学校”及教育部和哈特隆地区国家执政机构里，已经完成对 1 个博物馆、1—3 号教学大楼、宿舍、培训车间、1 个食堂、1 个健身房与 1 个运动场、1 个配备现代设备会议厅的大规模装修。该学院在 2021 年 10 月重建后投入使用，塔吉克斯坦总统埃莫马利・拉赫蒙参与了重建工作。与此同时，通过与塔吉克斯坦总统直属禁毒署署长合作，阿什特区职业技术学院进行了全面翻新，配备了必要的设备，此外，在世界银行、塔吉克斯坦国家社会融资基金资助的“加强社会经济可持续性”项目的支持下，在哈马多尼各区的专业技术学院和库利亚布市的农业和工业学院中修建了一座现代化教学大楼。库利亚布市专业技术学院的部分教学楼在上述项目框架内施工翻新。

关于扩展下级教育机构职业选择的职业指导服务范围，大部分城市及地区的教育机构都开设了“所有职业都是好的”“我的职业我骄傲”“职业世界”等主题讲座。此外，还对 15 517 名失业公民、农民工、家庭主妇及女孩进行了专业培训。

塔吉克斯坦 2021—2025 年公民职业培训计划是根据总统埃莫马利・拉赫蒙的指示和措施制定的。该计划起源于 2019 年 12 月 26 日总统在塔吉克斯坦最高议会发表的国情咨文，由塔吉克斯坦 2021 年 12 月 31 日第 703 号政府令制定和批准，以吸引 18 岁以下无职业公民在未来五年内参加职业培训为宗旨。

为重建初级职业教育机构的教育体系，根据国际劳工组织标准（18CO—2008）对 17 个目标专业进行编码，并根据这些要求制定能力（专业）标准、课程和方案。这一创新举措将使初级职业教育院校毕业生的专业水平有可能在国外劳动力市场上得到认可。为改进和提高初级职业教育机构在培训与创新活动过程中的创新及信息教育，分析了现有有助于接入互联网的多媒体设备的状态，包括投影仪、电子屏、计算机等。

2021—2022 学年，29 名初级职业教育院校产业培训教师和技师在高等职业教育院校教师高级研修所进行了高级培训。在本年度，为了提高培训质量，并为职业教育从业人员、教师和教员提供方法上的帮助，已多次举办了进修课程和培训研讨会。

2021 年，全国 65 个专业的各类职业技术教育合格人数达 11 150 人，其中，女性 2 757 人。众所周知，青少年的主要目标是在初级职业教育机构接受初级职业教育，并在中等和高等职业教育机构接受普通中等教育和继续教育，最终找到一份体面的工作。2021 年，全国中等、高等职业教育机构继续学习的毕业生人数达 2 686 人。分析表明，2021 年全体毕业生就业人数为 3 742 人，占 33.6%。

初等职业教育机构毕业生没有长期就业的主要原因在于国家生产企业和中小民营企业产能不足，初等职业教育机构与生产、服务、商业企业及农场和私营经济等提供就业的单位缺乏良性合作。

有鉴于此，根据 2020 年 9 月 29 日塔吉克斯坦第 526 号政府令批准的《2030 年塔吉克斯坦共和国教育发展国家战略 2021—2023 年中期行动计划》的相关条款，塔吉克斯坦教育和科学部正在采取必要措施。

# iii. Development of Professional and Vocational Education in Post Pandemic Period in Tajikistan

Abdulkholiqzoda Lutfiya, Deputy Minister of Education and Science of Tajikistan

Яке аз зинаҳои муҳим ва асосии таҳсилот ва тайёр кардани касбҳои коргарӣ зинаи таҳсилоти ибтидоии касбӣ ба шумор меравад ва он дар давраи соҳибистиқлолии ҷумҳурӣ нақши хоса дорад. Дар ҷумҳурӣ 62 муассисаи таҳсилоти ибтидоии касбӣ, аз ҷумла 55 литсейҳои касбии техникӣ, 7 литсейҳои касбии саноати кишоварзӣ, 2 литсейи касбии саноати дӯзандагӣ, 1 литсейи кабии соҳаи туризм фаъолият намуда, мутахассисони касбҳои коргариро аз рӯйи самтҳои техникӣ, кишоварзӣ, кӯҳӣ, хизматрасонӣ, иқтисодӣ, сайёҳӣ ва 106 ихтисос омода менмояд. Дар литсейҳои касбии техникии ҷумҳурӣ 1 ҳазору 773 нафар омӯзгор (708 нафар зан) фаъолият доранд. Аз инҳо 1448 (82%) бо таҳсилоти олии касбӣ, 289 нафар (16%) бо таҳсилоти миёнаи касбӣ ва 36 нафар (2%) бо таҳсилоти ибтидоии касбӣ фаъолият доранд. ҳамчунин, 993 нафар (298 зан) устоҳои таълими истеҳсолӣ фаъолият доранд, ки аз инҳо 460 нафар бо таҳсилоти олии касбӣ, 405 нафар бо таҳсилоти миёнаи касбй ва 123 нафар бо таҳсилоти ибтидоии касбӣ фаъолият карда истодаанд. Айни ҳол дар муассисаҳои таҳсилоти ибтидоии касбӣ 83 нафар ё 3% омӯзгорону устоҳои таълими истехсолӣ намерасанд. Бояд тазаккур дод, ки вобаста ба ин, минбаъд теъдоди омӯзгорони фанҳои тахассусӣ ва устоҳои таълими истеҳсолии дорои таҳсилоти олии касбӣ зиёд карда шуда, дараҷаи тахассуснокии онҳо баланд бардошта мешавад ва давра ба давра дар дохил ва хориҷи кишвар, онҳо аз курси такмили ихтисос гузаронида мешаванд.

Ҷиҳати ба низоми муайян даромадани ҳамаи паҳлуҳои зинаи таҳсилоти ибтидоии касбӣ таҳияи ҳуҷҷатҳои меъёрӣ ва қабули онҳотариқи мушовараи Вазорати маориф ва илми Ҷумҳурии Тоҷикистон доимӣ идома дошта, дар ҳамкорӣ бо сохторҳои вазорат ва дигар вазорату идораҳо як қаттор ҳуҷҷатҳо бо қарорҳои мушовараи Вазорати маориф ва илми Ҷумҳурии Тоҷикистон ва фармоишҳои вазири маориф ва илм тасдиқ гардида, ба муассисаҳои таълимӣ дастрас карда шудаанд.

Вазорати маориф ва илм дар ҳамкорӣ бо Вазорати меҳнат, муҳоҷират ва шуғли аҳолии Ҷумҳурии Тоҷикистон дар асоси омӯзиши бозори меҳнати дохилӣ, бозори меҳнати Ќазоқистон, Белорус, Федератсияи Россия, ҷумҳуриҳои соҳили баҳри Балтика ва Аврупои марказӣ Таснифоти давлатии касбҳои коргарӣ, вазифаҳои хизматчиён ва дараҷаҳои тарифӣ дар Ҷумҳурии Тоҷикистонро таҳия намуд. Таснифоти мазкур бо қарори ҳукумати Ҷумҳурии Тоҷикистон 2 марти соли 2013, №86 тасдиқ гардид. Таснифоти мазкур 200 нусха чоп шуда, дастраси муассисаҳои таҳсилоти ибтидоии касбӣ гардонида шуд.

Таҳия ва тасдиқи зиёда аз 200 адад ҳуҷҷатҳои меъёрии ҳуқуқии соҳаи таҳсилоти ибтидоии касбӣ омилҳои аввалиндараҷаи ба низом даровардани фаъолияти муассисаҳои мазкур гаштанд. Вазорати маориф ва илми Ҷумҳурии Тоҷикистон дар ҳамкорӣ боВазорати мехнат, мухочират ва шугли ахолии Ч, умхурии 10 стандарти тахассусии таҳсилоти ибтидоии касбиро таҳия ва бо қарорҳои мушовараи Вазорати маориф ва илми Ҷумҳурии Тоҷикистон тасдиқ намуд.

Яке аз омилхои асосии мусоидаткунанда барои омода кардани кадрхои баландихтисос ин фарохам овардани заминаи моддию техникии ба талаботи муосир чавобгуй мебошад. Вобаста ба ин, дар муассисаҳои таҳсилоти ибтидоии касбӣ бо истифода аз маблағҳои буҷетию ғайрибуҷетӣ ва бо дастгирии шарикони рушд, ташкилотҳои байналмилаливу ҷамъиятӣ корҳои таъмирию азнавсозии биноҳои таълимӣ, синфхонаҳо, устохонаҳои таълимӣ- истеҳсолӣ, ошхона ва хобгоҳҳо, инчунин, чиҳозонидани онҳо бо таҷҳизоти лозимӣ рохандозӣ гардида истодааст. Бояд тазаккур дод, ки дар доираи лоиҳаи Бонки Осиёии Рушд “Тақвияти таҳсилоти касбӣ-техникӣ ва омӯзиш” 21 муассисаи таҳсилоти ибтидоии касбӣ, 5 филиали Маркази таълими калонсолони Тоҷикистон ва 2 филиали Маркази касбомузӣ ва соҳибкорӣ аз рӯйи 17 ихтисос синфхонаҳо, кабинетҳои махсусгардонидашудаи таълимӣ, устохонаҳо таъмир карда шуда, онҳо бо таҷҳизоти замонавӣ, ашёву аёниятҳои таълимӣ муҷаҳҳаз гардонида шуданд.

Дар Муассисаи давлатии таълимии “Литсейи касбии саноати кимиёи шаҳри Левакант” аз ҷониби сарпарастон дар якҷояги бо вазорат ва Макомоти иҷроияи ҳокимияти давлатии вилояти Хатлон Осорхона, биноҳои таълимии №1,2,3, биноҳои хобгоҳ, устохонаҳои таълимӣ, ошхона, толор ва майдончаи варзишӣ, толори маҷлисгоҳ аз таъмири асосӣ бароварда шуда, бо таҷҳизотҳои замонавӣ муҷаҳҳаз гардонида шуданд. Литсейи мазкур баъди азнавсозӣ моҳи октябри соли 2021 бо иштироки Асосгузори сулҳу ваҳдати миллӣ - Пешвои миллат, Президенти Ҷумҳурии Тоҷикистон, муҳтарам Эмомалӣ Раҳмон мавриди истифода қарор дода шуд. Ҳамзамон, дар хамкорӣ бо сарпараст - директори Агентии назорати маводи нашъаовари назди Президенти Ҷумҳурии Тоҷикистон хобгоҳи Литсейи касбии техникии нохияи Ашт пурра таъмир гардида, бо таҷҳизотҳои лозима муҷаҳҳаз гардонида шуд. Илова бар ин, бо дастгирии Лоиҳаи таҳкими устувории иҷтимоӣ-иқтисодӣ бо маблағгузории Бонки умумиҷаҳонӣ аз ҷониби Бунёди миллии иҷтимоии маблағгузории Тоҷикистон дар литсейҳои касбии техникии ноҳияҳои Фархор, ҳамадонӣ ва саноати кишоварзии шаҳри Кӯлоб бинои таълимӣ ба таври замонавӣ сохта шудґ бо таҷҳизотҳои таълимӣ таъмин гардиданд. Аз ҷониби Лоиҳаи мазкур як қисмати бинои таълимии Литсейи касбии техникии сохтмони шаҳри Кӯлоб аз таъмири асосӣ бароварда шуд.

Доир ба васеъ намудани доираи хизматрасониҳои роҳнамоии касбӣ барои интихоби касб барои хамткунандагони муассисаҳои таълимии таҳсилоти умумӣ дар аксарияти муассисаҳои таҳсилоти миёнаи умумии шаҳру ноҳияҳои ҷумҳурӣ гушаҳои касбинтихобкунӣ дар мавзуҳои «ҳамаи касбҳо хубанд», «Касби ман-ифтихори ман», «Олами касбҳо» ва ғайраҳо насб карда шудаанд. Илова бар ин, бо 15 517 нафар шаҳрванди бешуғл, муҳоҷири меҳнатӣ, зану духтар ва ғайра чорабиниҳои роҳнамоии касбӣ анҷом дода шуд.

Барномаи касбомӯзии шаҳрвандони Ҷумҳурии Тоҷикистон барои солҳои 2021–2025 дар асоси дастуру ҳидоятҳои Асосгузори сулҳу ваҳдати миллӣ - Пешвои миллат, Президенти Ҷумҳурии Тоҷикистон муҳтарам Эмомалӣ Раҳмон, ки аз Паёмашон ба Маҷлиси Олии Ҷумҳурии Тоҷикистон аз 26 декабри соли 2019 бармеоянд, бо мақсади дар муддати панҷ соли оянда ба касбу ҳунаромузӣ ҷалб намудани шаҳрвандони аз 18 сола боло, ки касбу ҳунар надоранд, таҳия шуда, бо қарори ҳукумати Ҷумҳурии Тоҷикистон аз 31 декабри соли 2021, №703 тасдиқ гардидааст.

Бо мақсади азнавсозии низоми таълим дар муассисаҳои таҳсилоти ибтидоии касбӣ рамзгузории 17 ихтисоси ҳадафӣ аз рӯйи стандарти Ташкилоти Байналмилалии Меҳнат (18СО-2008) амалӣ карда мешавад ва бо ин талабот стандарти салохият (касбӣ), накшаю барномаҳои таълимӣ коркард шуда истодаанд. Ин навоварӣ имкон медиҳад, ки ихтисосҳои омухтаи хатмкардагони муассисаҳои таҳсилоти ибтидоии касбӣ дар бозори меҳнати хориҷи кишвар эътироф карда шаванд. Бо максади таквият бахшидан ва такмил додани таълими инноватсионӣ - иттилоотӣ дар раванди таълим ва фаъолияти инноватсионӣ дар муассисаҳои таҳсилоти ибтидоии касбӣ, таҳлили вазъи таҷҳизотҳои мултимедӣ аз ҷумла, проектор, тахтаи электронӣ, компютерҳоро нишон медихад, ки барои пайваст намудани онҳо ба шабакаи Интернет мусоидат менамояд.

Дар соли таҳсили 2021–2022 29 нафар омӯзгор ва устои таълими истеҳсолии муассисаҳои таҳсилоти ибтидоии касбӣ дар Донишкадаи такмили ихтисоси омӯзгорони муассисаҳои таҳсилоти олии касбӣ бо аз такмили ихтисос гузаштанд. Давоми соли равон, бахри баланд бардоштани сатхи сифати таълим ва расонидани кӯмакҳои методӣ ба кормандон, омӯзгорону устоҳои таълими истеҳсолӣ якчанд курсхои такмили ихтисос ва семинарҳои омӯзишӣ ба роҳ монда шуданд.

Соли 2021 литсейҳои касбии техникии кишварро 11 ҳазору 150 нафар аз рӯйи 65 ихтисос хатм намуданд, ки 2 ҳазору 757 нафари онҳоро духтарон ташкил медиҳанд. Маълум аст, ки ҳадафҳои асосии ҷавонон аз таҳсил дармуассисаҳои таҳсилоти ибтидоии касбӣ, дар баробари таҳсилоти ибтидоии касбӣ, гирифтани таҳсилоти миёнаи умумӣ ва минбаъд идома додани таҳсил дар муассисаҳои таҳсилоти миёна ва олии касбӣ, инчунин пайдо намудани шуғли арзанда мебошад. Теъдоди хатмкардагони барои идома додани таҳсил ба муассисаҳои таҳсилоти миёна ва олии касбӣ дохилгардида дар соли 2021 ба 2 хазору 686 нафар баробар аст. Таҳлилҳо нишон медиҳанд, ки аз теъдоди умумии хатмкардагони соли 2021-ум 3 ҳазору 742 нафари онҳо (33,6 фоиз) бо ҷойи кори доимӣ таъмин карда шудаанд.

Сабаби асосии бо ҷойи кори доимӣ соҳиб нагардиданди хатмкардагони муассисаҳои таҳсилоти ибтидоии касбӣ ин, бо иқтидори пурра фаъолият накардани корхонаҳои истеҳсолӣ ва корхонаҳои хурду миёнаи хусусии кишвар, мавҷуд набудани ҳамкории судманд байнимуассисаҳои таҳсилоти ибтидоии касбӣ ва корхонаю муассисаҳои истехсолӣ, хизматрасонӣӣ, тиҷоратӣ, новобаста ба шакли моликияташон, инчунин, хоҷагиҳои деҳқонӣ ва бахши хусусии иқтисод дар самти бокортаъминкунии хатмкунандагон аст.

Вобаста ба ин, ќайд менамоям, ки Вазорати маориф ва илми ҷумҳурии Тоҷикистои љињати иҷрои бандҳои дахлдори Нақшаи миёнамуҳлати амал барои солҳои 2021–2023 Стратегияи миллии рушди маорифи Љумҳурии Тоҷикистои барои давраи то соли 2030, ки бо қарори Њукумати Љумҳурии Тоҷикистон аз 29 сентябри соли 2020, №526 тасдиқ гардидааст, чораҳои заруриро роҳандозӣ менамояд.

# （四）

# 加强校企合作　加速学生成功

美国贝茨技术学院校长、首席执行官　周　琳

贝茨技术学院位于华盛顿州，在西雅图南面，距西雅图仅 40 分钟车程。我们是华盛顿州 34 所州立的社区和技术学院之一，这些学院培养了华盛顿州近 40% 工作岗位的员工。贝茨技术学院有 3 个独特的校区，是该州历史最悠久的公立技术学院。

在全美国，有近 950 所公立或州立社区学院和技术学院以及 770 所私立两年制学院。社区学院和技术学院提供相关的学位、学历、认证和证书。社区学院和技术学院的主要区别之一是技术学院是提供就业培训、开始职业生涯的地方，而社区学院大多教授升级课程，为学生继续进入四年制高等教育机构做准备，有些也提供就业相关课程。

当人们提到华盛顿州时，会想到什么？首先就是著名的企业，如微软、亚马逊、星巴克和波音等。在贝茨，我们很荣幸拥有这些行业合作伙伴，我们重视并培养与波音等大型国际公司及医疗保健和制造领域的区域公司和组织的联系。今天，我想谈谈这些合作伙伴如何使用以下策略帮助我们打造育人模式：工作本位学习和学徒制项目、项目咨询委员会、合同和企业培训、先前学习和能力本位学习以及传统的合作伙伴关系。

工作本位学习是一种教育策略，它为学生提供了一个机会来巩固在他们课堂上学到的知识，探索所选择的职业领域，并在真实的现实环境中展示技能。参加工作本位学习的学生有机会在实习或学徒工作中应用自己的技术技能。例如，我们与 8 个学徒制项目（主要在航空航天、建筑和制造领域）合作。学徒制是一种集中的职业培训，有偿在职培训和实操性课堂教学同时进行。随着学徒在项目中不断取得进步，他们也会定期获得加薪。学徒期为 2—5 年，在完成项目后，学生将获得华盛

顿州颁发的州级结业证书。

我们的每个职业培训项目都有一个由行业、企业和劳工代表组成的咨询委员会。咨询委员会定期开会，并向教职员工和学院院长提供意见、反馈和课程建议，帮助塑造学生的教学内容和方式。其目的是确保项目与行业相关，学生可以在毕业后立即进入劳动力市场。通常，这些重要的委员会成员会捐赠设备、提供奖学金，并为学生提供工作机会。

我们还为本地的企业和组织提供合同和企业培训机会，这样就能够为他们的员工提供独特的学习体验，缩小技能和知识之间的差距，并提高个人、团队或部门在工作上取得成功所需的特定的工作技能和能力。

我们确保课程与行业相关的另一种方法是利用先前学习带来的好处。通常，学生来到这里学习，都带着从以前的专业或学术经验中获得的知识和技能，他们因已经拥有的技能和能力获得称赞，我们也支持他们努力尽快实现自己的职业目标。

贝茨以制造和建设项目以及医疗保健项目而闻名。社会对医疗保健专业人员的需求很大。我们与行业合作，为学生开发了一条职业路径，他们首先通过各个医疗机构的招聘流程，然后参加全日制或认证护理课程，由他们的雇主支付学杂费。在完成项目后，学生会被分配到长期的全职职位，并享有福利。这是我们与行业合作来满足需求的一个典型例子。贝茨为医疗机构提供想要进入该行业的合格候选人，帮助解决人才短缺的问题。这些合作努力让我们建立了伙伴关系，支持了学生发展，调整了课程以满足现有的行业需求，为地区创造了一个稳健光明的经济前景，特别是在当前经济不确定的时期，技术教育对我们的经济至关重要。我们的毕业生有医疗工作者、建筑和制造业人才、消防员、信息技术专家、网络安全和工程技术人员以及商业专家，毕业生将帮助地区、企业和行业渡过难关，并带来希望。

## iv. Foster Education-Industry Partnership to Accelerate Student Success

**Zhou Lin, President and Chief Executive Officer of Bates Technical College, US**

Bates Technical College is located in south of Seattle, Washington State, and it's just 40 minutes' journey from Seattle. We are one of 34 state-funded community and technical colleges that trained for nearly 40 percent of Washington's jobs. At Bates, we have 3 unique campuses, and we are the oldest public technical college in the state.

Across the United States, there are nearly 950 public or state-run community and technical colleges, and 770 privately owned 2-year institutions. Community and technical colleges offer associated degrees, diplomas, certifications, and certificates. One of the main differences between a community college and a technical college is that technical colleges are places to train workforce and start one's career, while community colleges are mostly places to offer transformed curriculum which help students to prepare for 4-year higher education, and some also offers workforce programs.

When people think about Washington State, what comes into mind? Famous businesses, such as Microsoft, Amazon, Starbucks and Boeing. At Bates, we're very proud of our industrial partners. We value and cultivate our connections with large international companies like Boeing, and with regional companies and organizations in healthcare and manufacturing fields. Today I'll talk about how these partners help shape models of instruction using the following strategies: work-based learning and apprenticeship programs, program advisory committees, contract and corporate training, prior learning and competency-based learning, and traditional partnership collaboration.

Work-based learning is an educational strategy that offers students an opportunity to reinforce what they have learned in the classroom, explore their chose career fields, and demonstrate their skills in an authentic real-world environment. Students who participate in work-based learning have an opportunity to apply their technical skills, while working as an intern or apprentice. For example, we partner with 8 apprenticeships, primarily in aerospace, construction and manufacturing fields.

Apprenticeships are intensive career training experiences that use both paid on-the-job training and hands-on classroom intellectual education methodologies. As our student apprentice progress through the program, they receive regular salary increases. Apprenticeships last from 2 to 5 years, and upon completing the program, students receive a state-level certificate of completion from Washington State.

Each of our career training programs has an advisory committee that is made up of industry, business and labor representatives. These individuals meet regularly and provide input, feedback and curriculum recommendations to faculty and college deans that help shape what and how we teach our students. The purpose is to ensure our programs are industry-relevant and our graduates are ready to enter the labour market upon graduation. Usually these valuable meeting members offer equipment donations, scholarships, and job opportunities for students.

We also offer contract and corporate training opportunities to businesses and organizations within our community. This allows us to provide their employees unique learning experiences that close gaps between skill and knowledge, and improve job-specific skills and competences required for success in the job of an individual, team or department.

Another way we ensure our curriculum being industry-relevant is to offer benefits like prior learning credit. Usually all students come to us with knowledge and skills from previous professional or academic experience, they are praised for skills and competences they already have, and we can support their effort to reach their career goals as quickly as possible.

At Bates, we're well known for manufacturing and construction programs, and healthcare programs. There is a huge need for healthcare professionals. In partnership with industry, we develop a pathway for students to first go through the hiring process at each medical facility, then, they take full-time or certified nursing courses, and their employer pays tuition and fees. Upon completion of our program, students are placed into permanent full-time positions with benefits. It is a typical case of how we collaborate with industry to fulfill our need. Bates helps to provide our medical facilities with qualified candidates who want to get into the profession and helps to address the shortage of workers. All these efforts to collaborate create partnerships, support students and align our curriculum to meet the existing industry needs, and create a robust and bright economic future for our region, especially during the period of economic uncertainty. Technical education is vital to our economy. Our graduates are healthcare workers, construction and manufacturing professionals, fire fighters, information technicists, cyber security and engineering technicians, and business specialists, and our graduates will help our regions, businesses and industries come through and they can bring hope.

## （五）

# 教产合作——新西兰的经验分享

惠灵顿联合理工学院首席执行官　马克·奥尔德肖

大家都知道，过去两年我们一直都在与新冠病毒疫情抗争，由此引起的封控及无法前往主要市场的情形促使我们近期彻底重新思考学院提供教学的方式，多方面思考我们的整体教学模式，为学术机构和行业之间开展更多合作创造机会。

混合式教学模式已成为课程教学和专业发展的重要组成部分。在国际上，课程内容和教学方式与教学地点是密切相关的。我在新西兰的工作很可能面临新的挑战，例如，需要适应在中文语言环境下工作，还要考虑语言能力和技术问题。我想着重谈谈一个使用模拟技术的新课程。模拟技术使用高科技人体模型来模拟现实生活中的患者情况，用以培训操作人员。护理培训课程越来越多地转向即时护理模拟，这是课程中不可或缺的一部分。现在，这种模拟已经占到护理实践场景的20%。使用模拟技术可以让学生在不危及真实患者的情况下进行护理实践。这样，他们就可以树立信心，并能够在多种场景下进行实践。

为了在中国有效地实现此种课程培训，维特利亚国立理工学院创建了一系列新的培训场景，这些场景设置在文化上与中国社会环境密切相关，从而确保课程易于理解。这些课程已被翻译成中文。我们还创建了一系列“培训师培训”课程，可以进行在线和面对面授课。我们正在与医学模拟公司建立密切的行业合作伙伴关系，该公司可以支持中国的理工类大学和维特利亚国立理工学院。有了这种支持，院校就能够将我们创建的模拟库中的场景集成到模拟设备中，立即投入使用。

在这个案例中，新西兰院校三方合作伙伴关系的三方分别是维特利亚国立理工学院、中国院校和行业合作伙伴，三者共同创建了可以无缝对接的创新型高效培训包。学成的学生和教师将获得该课程各个等级的一系列微型证书。总而言之，我们已经开发了一套不断发展的系统，该系统将有益于国家的卫生系统，减少对患者的潜在伤害，在无需面对面操作和提供所有设备支持的情况下提高护理标准。维特利亚国立理工学院期待着在未来进行更多探索。

# v. Academia-Industry Collaboration
## —A New Zealand Experience

**Mark Oldershaw, Chief Executive of Whitireia and WelTec Polytechnic, New Zealand**

The last two years of dealing with COVID-19, the associated lockdowns and the following lack of ability to travel to key markets have caused a dramatic rethink of the way we are delivering teaching and learning and our general delivery models, and the way to create opportunities for greater collaboration between academic institutions such as ours and industry.

The blended learning mode has become an essential component of delivering courses and professional development. Internationally, it is vital that the course content and delivery are contextually relevant to the location of delivery. My work in New Zealand is likely to meet new challenges. To work in Chinese setting is an example. There are additional considerations in language capability and technology. I would like to focus on one of the new programs using simulation. The simulation uses high-tech mannequins to simulate real-life patient situations for training users. Increasingly, nursing training programs are moving to immediate nursing simulation, an integral part of the curriculum. The simulation can now make up as much as 20% of the nursing practical scenarios, which allows students to practice nursing scenarios without the risk of endangering real patients. They build confidence and allow a wide range of scenarios to be practiced.

To deliver this effectively in China, the Whitireia Community Polytechnic created a series of new scenarios which are culturally relevant for the Chinese community setting to ensure that the lessons are accessible. They have been translated into Chinese. A range of "train-the-trainer" courses have also been created that can be delivered both online and face-to-face. A strong industry partnership is being formed with the medical simulation company which supports both the Chinese universities in polytechnics as well as Whitireia Community Polytechnic. The support enables institutions to fully integrate the scenarios from the simulation library that we created to an immediate use within the simulation equipment.

The three-way partnership between the New Zealand institutions in this case is Whitireia Community Polytechnic, the Chinese institutions and industry partners, which have created seamless delivery of innovative cost-effective training packages. Successful students and trainers will receive a range of micro-credentials from the various levels of this program. In summary, we have developed an ongoing system that will benefit the health system of a country and reduce potential harm to patients, raising the standard of care without the need for face-to-face and country delivery of all components. Whitireia Community Polytechnic will be looking forward to exploring this opportunity at many more stages.

# （六）

# 空中客车与高校的校企合作

空中客车（天津）总装有限公司总经理　傅睿楠

我们面临着相当多的挑战，但都是非常积极的挑战，因为我们处于一个不断成长的环境中。

首先，我简要介绍空客（天津）总装有限公司的情况。在天津，我们实际上有两家公司，一家是合资企业，专注于空客产品的组装、喷漆和最终定型，生产从单通道到宽体飞机的所有空客产品，约有 900 名员工；另一家公司是空客全资子公司——交付中心，总装线把飞机移交给交付中心，交付中心再把飞机移交给客户。交付中心也具有一些生产功能，以满足总装线的需要，如工程功能、适航性测试和飞行测试团队，团队里约有 200 名员工。

天津工厂的占地面积约有 80 万平方米，分成了两个区域。工厂主要是由产品驱动的。从 2008 年开始，我们在此进行所有单通道飞机的全组装过程。2017 年，扩建了新的厂房生产宽体飞机，同年，A330 机型首次交付。2021 年，总装线增加了世界上最现代化的机型——A350，为此我们感到非常荣幸和自豪，现在我们也在中国进行 A350 的客舱安装和飞机喷漆工作。

如今，我们的大部分员工都来自专科院校，但也有相当比例的员工拥有学士学位和硕士学位。我们与天津中德职业技术学院、天津大学、天津理工大学、南开大学等多所当地大学建立了合作关系。当然，还有著名的中国民航大学。

公司提供两种职业发展路径，一种是以技术为方向的职业发展，员工首先从基础培训开始，然后可以在职业培训、技术培训、素质培训中成长和发展。员工素质和资质在这个行业是至关重要的，而取得资质的过程是相当漫长的，需要 12 个月以上。我们的员工在这个过程中不断进步成长，达到不同的质量保证等，首先是获得工作许可，然后获得自检许可，最后获得最高级别的许可——DE 许可，至此，员工就可以完成该类型工作的全流程。另一种是以管理为方向的职业发展路径，通过领导力培训和专业技能培训促进员工的成长。需要说明的是，这两条路径之间没有界限，很多技术人员经过中长期的培训后，也可以在管理岗位上不断发展进步。

在德国，公司会设置两种教育培训模式，首先是传统的学徒制，员工一般从 16 岁开始工作，从事飞机电子产品、机械、微电子生产和涂装等工作。随着新技术的发展，员工在工厂内也会从事其他复合型的工作。而且我们的工作环境不是一成不变的，公司会基于技术趋势和行业趋势不断开发工作环境。所以对我们来说，自动化、计算机科学、人工智能都是越来越热门的话题。但公司更多的是通过双元制来关注这些问题。通过双元制培训模式，学生可以将实际操作经验和课堂所学知识相结合，在这样的环境中成长。一般来说，双元制工程学士的教学模式是让学生在大学课堂学习一段时间，与此同时也会花相当长的时间深入工厂车间进行实践操作。这样一来，他们既可以帮助公司解决一些实际问题，又能将相关话题和实践经验写进学士论文和硕士论文中。在这里，我们甚至可以进一步促进他们的发展，使他们可以继续完成博士论文。我们在德国的职业培训已形成固定的结构，这一点非常重要，因为我们现在越来越多地思考如何在中国的环境中套用这种模式。在中国，学生要先完成学业，从学校毕业后才进入工厂开始工作，这和我们在德国采用的模式有些不同。在德国，学生在第一年开始接受基础培训，学习传统的飞机基础知识及公司相关的知识，然后就开始进入某一个领域，在总装线的结构装配、系统安装的环境中工作。虽然他们会参加短期培训，但也会接受一定时间的课堂授课。一年半之后，他们会参加期中考试，这已是他们职业生涯中非常重要的一步。之后，我们开始给这些未来的员工量身定制发展路径，按照他们各自的兴趣规划路径。在毕业的前一年，他们就已经在之后要从事的领域里工作了。这样，员工经过三年半的学习并通过期末考试之后，就顺利完成了学业，此时他们也已经获得了从事飞机制造工作的首个资质认证。这是我们希望在中国实施的做法。总结来说，员工有 60 周的时间在车间接受培训，有 44 周的时间参加空客培训课程，还有 39 周的时间在学校上课。所以员工的学习重点还是在车间。

在中国，实习生的水平很高，平均每年会招收 100 个实习生。但我们也希望进一步扩大合作范围，不仅能够为实习生提供论文和实验的课题，还希望能够和当地的合作伙伴和职业学校一起推出更多的教育项目。我们想建立一个和德国汉堡公司类似的培训模式，当然，我们也希望延续之前的合作模式，比如在大学里发表演讲、向当地大学展示我们的工作，以吸引更多的人关注我们。现在，我们的主要挑战之一是吸引更多的女性。遗憾的是，今天在我们的一处工厂里，只有 5% 的员工是女性。所以我们的目标之一是让员工更加多元化。

我们能从行业的发展中看出，这个行业还有很大的潜力。总装线对每个人来说都是一个具有吸引力的工作环境，期待着这股发展势头能进一步丰富我们的多样性。

## vi. School-Enterprise Cooperation Between Airbus and Universities

**Thomas Florian Mack, General Manager of Airbus (Tianjin) Final Assembly Co., Ltd.**

We have some challenges ahead of us, but very positive ones, because we are in a growing environment.

Let's start first with an overview of our activities. At Airbus in Tianjin, we have actually two companies. We have, on the one hand, a joint venture, which is focused on the assembly, the paint, and the finalization of our Airbus products. Here we produce all Airbus products from the single-aisle to the wide-body. We have roughly 900 employees. On the other hand, we have a 100% Airbus subsidy, which is the Delivery Center, where the final assembly line hands over the aircraft to the Delivery Center, and Delivery Center hands over the aircraft to the customer. But in this Delivery Center, we also have certain functions allocated, which we need in the final assembly line to be supported, like engineering functions, airworthiness test, and the flight test team, which have roughly 200 people.

Our Campus in Tianjin covers about 800 000 square meters, which is divided into two areas. Here is mainly driven by our products. We started our business in 2008, and we do the full assembly process of all single-aisle aircraft in this area. In 2017, we extended the site with wide-body activities, where we introduced A330 in 2017. We are very honored and proud that we added in 2021 the A350, currently one of the most modern aircraft in the world to our assembly factory. And we are now also doing the cabin completion and the painting of the A350 here in China.

Today, the majority of our people come from vocational colleges. However, we also have a decent share of bachelor's degrees as well as master's degrees. We've cooperated with many local universities, like Tianjin Sino-German Vocational School, Tianjin University as well as Tianjin University of Technology and Nankai University. Last but not least, the famous Aerospace University of China.

Our development paths in the company can be divided into two pieces. On the one hand, we have the technical direction for our workers who start with basic training, and then they can grow and develop through vocational training, technical training, and quality training. Quality and qualification are of utmost importance in our industry, and the qualification in our industry can take quite a long time. It's well beyond 12 months. Our people can grow, getting different quality assurance levels, which start with workforce approval. Then they have self-inspection approval. And then the highest degree is the so-called DE approval where the worker can really finalize the full spectrum of job. On the other hand, we have the management direction where we support the growth of our people with leadership training and professional skills training. And to be clear, there's no boundary between the two paths. We have a lot of technical people who can also grow in management roles in the mid-to-long term.

In Germany, we have two schemes established in the company. First is a classical apprenticeship, where our people start normally at 16 years old, then they do the classical jobs of aircraft electronics, mechanics, microtronics, and coating. With the new technologies, we also do a lot more on the composite. And also, this environment is not static. We continuously develop our environment based on technology and industry trends. So for us, automation, computer science, and artificial intelligence are topics that are coming more and more. But these topics we address more on our Dual-study system, where we support young people to grow in an environment where they combine practical work with university attendance. So, normally, in our Dual-study of bachelor of engineering, they go a certain period of time to university, but they also spend a decent amount of time on the shop floor or in our company environment, contributing to topics we need to solve in the company, and they can do this with the bachelor thesis and master thesis. We even promote them further so that they can also continue with their PhD thesis. Our vocational training is structured in Germany, and that's something that is very important because we are now more and more thinking about how we can share this practice in our Chinese environment. In China, it normally starts with people coming from college and then they go through our environment. In Germany, we do it a little bit differently. The people start in the first year with basic training where they learn the classical aircraft basic knowledge and some company knowledge, and then they start to go in a field for core competence, so they work in an environment of the structure assembly or system installation on the final assembly line. Though they do short training, they go for a dedicated period of time to the school. After 1.5 years, they have the first half of the examination, which is already a very important step in their career. Afterward, we start customizing our future colleagues. We put them in individual planning path according to the interest. In the last year, they are already in the area where they will later work. Then they finish the education of 3.5 years with the final examination. By then they already have the first qualification to work on the aircraft by themselves. And this is something we want to start here in China. In summary, we have 60 weeks for people to have training at the shop floor, 44 weeks for courses for Airbus or Airbus training, and 39 weeks at school.

So these people are very focused on the shop floor.

Today we have a high degree of interns. On average, every year we have even 100 interns here in the company supporting us. But we also want to extend with further collaborations that we can gain and offer the theses and essays. We also push more education programs together with our local partners, together with local vocational schools. We would like to establish a scheme similar to Hamburg. And for sure we want to continue our collaboration, like giving speeches at university, and also hosting local universities to show what we do and to attract people. One of our major challenges is also to attract much more women. Today we have, unfortunately, only a share of 5% females in one of our work environment. This is also a target for us to be more diversified.

The growth, as it was shown in our industry, shows that there's a lot of potential. The final assembly line is an attractive working environment for everybody, and I'm looking forward to that we can use this growth to diversify more.

# （七）

# 缅甸职业技术教育与培训的转型

缅甸科技部职业技术教育与培训司司长　赛觉奈乌

今天，我将以校企协同育人模式创新为主题，就缅甸职业技术教育与培训的情况发表演讲。我的演讲涵盖三点内容：第一点是教育创新，第二点是缅甸目前的职业技术教育与培训，第三点是未来趋势。

我想回顾一下当我们将教育视为一种服务时，创新是如何定义的。教育创新主要与过程创新（方法、实践和组织）相关，包括全新的或显著改进的基于课堂的教学、学习和评估方法以及系统的组织或治理上的变化。因此创新有四种不同的类别：产品创新、过程创新、组织创新以及教学、学习和评估的营销创新。产品创新可以是课程升级、新的教育项目开发、新课程开发或教育软件开发。过程创新可以是新的或改进的技术、信息通信技术应用和教学过程。组织创新可以是管理方面的组织变革或社交通信接口的开发。营销创新可以是价格促销和准入策略。

第二点是缅甸目前的职业技术教育与培训。目前，我们正在升级现有课程并为证书项目、学历项目和技术学士学位项目开发新课程，以符合“工业 4.0”所需的技能。此外，目前我们正在一些职业技术教育与培训机构准备混合式学习项目，教学过程也正在转变为以学生为中心的模式。我们还有翻转课堂，我国的教师一直在一些职业技术教育与培训机构实践这种方法。在组织创新方面，我们正在提供信息通信技术设施，并提升管理人员的信息通信技术技能，以提高使用在线学习管理系统的能力。在营销创新方面，我们引入了在线申请系统和基于媒体的社交联动。

缅甸的教育系统已经启动了产品创新、过程创新和组织创新。未来，我们要基于两个理念，在职业技术教育与培训教育方面进行更多的创新。第一个理念是将工作场所转变为学习环境。今天，不断地接触科技对所有利益相关者来说都非常重要，因为不同行业的技术发展非常迅速，学生需要与工作场所保持联系，未来学校和行业需要更紧密、更和谐地一起合作。第二个理念是在工作中学习。如果不持续学习新知识，我们就无法提升自己的职业技能，所以我们需要进行终身学习（持续学习）来提升职业技能，因此我们必须在工作中学习。未来，通过校企协同，我们将专注于这一方面的创新，在产品创新方面推行实习项目、学徒项目、勤工俭学项目、电子学习项目，在过程创新方面推行混合式学习、翻转课堂、增强现实 / 虚拟现实 / 混合现实教学，以更具交流性和信息性的方式，利用信息通信技术进行组织创新。

# vii. Transformation of TVET Education in Myanmar

Sai Kyaw Naing Oo, Director General of the Department of Technical and Vocational Education and Training of the Ministry of Science and Technology, Myanmar

Today I'm going to deliver a speech related to information on TVET education in Myanmar under the themes of innovation in modes of education delivered through academia-industry collaboration. In this speech, I will cover three points. The first is innovation in education, the second is current TVET education in Myanmar, and the third is the future trends.

I would like to recall how innovation is defined when we consider education as a service. Innovation in education is mainly related to innovation in processes (methods, practices, and organization) and includes new or significantly improved approaches to classroom-based teaching, learning, and assessment, as well as changes in the organization or governance of systems. Therefore, there can be four different categories of innovation: product innovation, process innovation, organization innovation and marketing innovation for teaching, learning, and assessment. Product innovation can be curriculum upgrading or the development of new education programs, or the development of new curricula or educational software. Process innovation can be new or improved technology or ICT use and teaching and learning process. Organization innovation can be organizational changes in administration or the development of ICT interfaces for social communication. Marketing innovation can be price promotion and admission strategies.

The second is the current TVET education in Myanmar. Currently, we are upgrading existing curricula and developing new curricula for certificate program, diploma program and Bachelor of Technology program to be in line with the skills required for Industry 4.0. Also currently, we are preparing blended learning program at some TVET institutions, and our teaching process is being changed to student-centered learning. Then we have the flipped classrooms. Teachers have been practicing in some TVET institutions in our country. For organization innovation, we are providing ICT facilities and scaling ICT skills of our administration staff to handle the online learning management system. For marketing innovation, we have introduced an online application system and media-based society linkage.

So in Myanmar, education has initiated product, process, and organizational innovation. In the future, we have to develop more innovation in TVET education based on two concepts. The first one is the workplace as a learning environment. Today, constant exposure to technologies is very important for all stakeholders because technologies in different industry sectors are changing very fast. So students need to keep in touch with the workplace. Schools and industries need to work more closely and harmonically in the future. The second one is learning in working. Without continuous learning of new things, we cannot upgrade our profession. So we need to do lifelong learning (continuous learning) to upgrade our profession. Thus we have to do learning in working. In the future, through academia-industry collaboration, we are going to focus on internship programs, apprenticeship programs, work-study programs, and e-learning programs for product innovation; blended learning, flipped classroom, teaching with AR/VR/MR for process innovation; and working in a more communicative and informative way using ICT for organizational innovation.

## （八）

# 中文 + 职业教育在柬埔寨的实施

柬华理事总会常务副会长　郑棉发

国家发展靠人才！培养人才、发展教育已成为世界各国重视的工作。就柬埔寨而言，教育是政府鼓励投资的领域，不仅政府加大投资，私人也可以开办学校。

柬埔寨近年来的经济发展形势良好，被誉为“亚洲新虎”，成为全球投资焦点，吸引大量来自中国及世界各地的外来直接投资，推动柬埔寨经济结构转型。目前，柬埔寨正在推行“2015—2025 年工业发展计划”，该计划提出优先发展高附加值、创新型和具有竞争力的新兴工业和制造业，如机械装配、电气设备组装、运输工具装配和自然资源加工；全产业链特别经济区；供出口和国内市场的农产品加工业；农业、旅游业、服装加工业配套产业；对未来产业提供战略支持的支柱产业，如信息通信技术、能源、重工业、文化 / 历史 / 传统工艺产业及绿色技术产业等。以上政策，促使柬埔寨不得不重视人才的培养，而职业技术教育是工业发展的重要基础，也深刻影响着人才培养的质量与人口的结构。

柬埔寨教育部为了平衡国内人力资源供应与人才市场需求，正努力推广专业知识和职业技术教育，以确保高校毕业生的专业技能与职业需求对接，确保初入工作岗位的高校毕业生符合相关职业所具备的技能要求，从而为国家经济发展做贡献。事实上，柬埔寨教育部已经在鼓励各校和国际层面上开展交流合作，把部分先进职场所需的新技能列入高中的教材里，以符合当前人才市场的需求，有效配合工业领域的发展。

据柬埔寨劳工与职业培训部统计，目前，全柬埔寨共有 199 个职业技术学校，其中 39 个是国立，160 个是私立，在校培训学生 50 000 余人。学习的技能主要是建筑、电气、维修汽车、缝纫等职业技能，但与劳动市场的需求远远不匹配。随着科技的发展，疫情期间网络技术的广泛运用，可以说明人工智能、计算机编程语言、搜索引擎优化、网络安全等先进科技也正在成为职业技术教育中的重要专业课程。未来，这方面的人才需求将会更多。同时，我们也非常清楚，当今的中国已是世界第二大经济体，中国的生产技术将走向世界，而中文的使用也会从普通的商务交流扩展到专业技术的交流，因此职业技术教育应该加上中文这门语言，这将是未来发展的时代要求。

柬埔寨与中国可以说是关系牢固和紧密的兄弟国家，中国多年以来一直是柬埔寨最大的贸易伙伴、外来直接投资、外国游客和发展援助的来源地。同时，柬埔寨是中国推动“一带一路”建设的重要节点国家，柬埔寨“四角战略”与中国“一带一路”倡议高度契合。随着《中华人民共和国政府和柬埔寨王国政府自由贸易协定》《区域全面经济伙伴关系协定》的生效，共建“一带一路”倡议加快推进，中柬两国在各个领域合作不断深化，中国在柬埔寨的路桥、水利、电网、港口、码头、机场等基础设施方面注入了大量的投资。可想而知，懂中文的人才需求在增加。为此，柬华理事总会成立 30 多年以来就一直推广中文教育，全柬有 58 家华文学校，学生约 50 000 余人，为柬中合作培养了众多的中柬双语人才。随着时代的进一步要求，我们正在开办柬华理工大学，并与南京工业职业技术大学合作，共建职业教育孔子学院，以“中文 + 职业技术教育”，为柬埔寨培养实用人才。

总之，“职业技术教育”和“中文 + 职业教育”是柬埔寨培养人才的需要，因此我们愿与中国和世界各地的院校、教育机构加强合作，为职业技术教育朝着新时代科技行业的发展作出自己应有的贡献。

# （九）

# 交流发言

中华人民共和国教育部职业教育与成人教育司副司长　林　宇

当今世界百年变局加速演进，世纪疫情改变着我们的生活。职业教育对于促进就业、保证供应链稳定以及提升人民福祉、支撑实体经济，意义重大、作用明显，正受到各国政府和全社会越来越多的关注。中国拥有世界上规模最大、层级明确的职业教育体系。特别是进入 21 世纪以来，中国职业教育进入了快速发展阶段，高等职业教育在规模上已经占到了整个高等教育的半壁江山，中等职业教育和高等职业教育一道，每年为社会输送超过 1 000 万的技术技能人才，极大地支撑了经济社会发展。

在实践过程中，我们逐步地凝练形成了工学结合、校企合作、产教融合的办学理念。在办学理念的引领下，我们修订了职业教育法，大力推动校企合作、产教融合；我们探索了中国特色的学徒制，力争在中国现行体制和制度之下，实现学校和企业双主体育人；我们培育了一批产教融合型企业，试点了一批产教融合型城市；我们推出了包括双高校建设这样的国家级大型项目和改革举措。在这些工作的推动之下，职业教育的质量和形象都得到了极大的改善。我们有一大批的专科层次的职业院校通过高考录取的分数超过本科线；现代制造业新增劳动力中，70% 是职业学校的毕业生。

纵观世界各国的职业教育，特别是职业教育发达国家的职业教育，应该说是各具特色、形式多样，但有一点，那就是校企合作、协同育人是共识、是方向。我想，今天这个论坛就是要提供一个平台，希望通过这个平台，我们可以交流经验、凝聚共识、孕育成果。希望这个平台的交流能够促进我们相互学习，加强交流，共同推动职业教育更好地服务于经济社会发展，更好地服务于人的全面发展。

# (十)

# 中国特色学徒制的实践与探索

**中华职业教育社党组书记、总干事　方乃纯**

中华职业教育社（以下简称中华职教社）成立于1917年，是中国最早的职业教育团体。105年来，中华职教社始终不渝倡导、研究和推行职业教育，提出了一系列符合中国实际的职业教育理念，既是中国近代职业教育的引领者，也是现代职业教育的助推者。近年来，中华职教社始终加强与国内外职业教育界的交流和合作，成为具有联合国咨商地位和联系地位双重身份的非政府组织成员。中华职教社100多年的努力和成绩获得了中国职业教育界的高度认可，并作为助推中国职业教育发展的重要成员，写入新修订的《中华人民共和国职业教育法》。

学徒制是人类传承知识和技能的基本形式，也是职业教育校企协同育人的基本手段。世界上职业教育发达的国家都根据本国实际开展了多种形式的学徒制探索，如德国的双元制、英国的现代学徒制、澳大利亚的新学徒制、美国的注册学徒制等。其他一些经济发达国家也相继结合自身情况开展各具特色的学徒制，但无论怎么做，都从教学组织与管理上将企业本位培训和学校本位教育结合起来，从制度上把劳动用工制度和职业教育制度结合起来，具有“校企双元育人、学徒双重身份”的共性特征。

2014年以来，中国相继启动现代学徒制、企业新型学徒制两种技术技能人才培养模式的试点探索。现代学徒制由教育部门主导，从发展现代职业教育角度，促进职业教育与产业需求对接、与生产过程对接、与职业标准对接，目的是提高学校职业教育人才培养质量。目前，已经开展了三批试点，遴选了558家试点单位，包含地方政府、行业协会、企业、职业院校等四种类型，共有1 000多个学徒制专业点，惠及学生（学徒）10万余名。

企业新型学徒制由人力资源和社会保障部门主导，从加强企业技术技能人才队伍建设角度，强调以企业主导开展职业培训工作，目的在于提升企业员工职业技能的同时提升职业素养，共开展两批试点，参加试点企业 158 家，培养新型学徒制职工 20 000 人。自 2018 年起，人力资源和社会保障部、财政部两部门在全国 30 个省市区全面推行企业新型学徒制。2019 年，国务院办公厅印发的《职业技能提升行动方案（2019—2021 年）》明确要求三年培训 100 万新型学徒。在全面推行后，近三年来共培养新型学徒 100 多万人。

两类学徒制在试点及推广工作中，在校企协同育人机制、招生招工一体化、人才培养制度和标准、校企互聘共用的师资队伍、管理制度等方面均做了大量有益的尝试，形成了以校企协同育人为核心的中国特色学徒制基本内涵，即“双元育人、双重身份，交互训教、工学交替，岗位培养、在岗成才”。目前，现代学徒制和企业新型学徒制正在全国进一步推广，成为中国职业教育的重要育人模式之一。

实践经验表明，中国特色学徒制最大限度地发挥了企业育人主体作用，形成了校企紧密合作的育人新机制，真正实现了产教深度融合，有效解决了参与企业对人才的“选、用、育、留”问题。

相比较职业教育发达国家的现代学徒制，中国特色学徒制还处于探索阶段，也存在一些问题，面临诸多难点，具体为：一是国家层面缺乏学徒制的顶层设计和统筹管理，配套的政策和制度尚不完善，地方政府的学徒制支持政策不到位等问题。二是行业企业参与职业教育的积极性不高，对行业企业参与的激励、保障、约束机制欠缺，尤其是学徒培养成本分担机制不健全。三是修订后的《中华人民共和国职业教育法》明确要求企业须与参与学徒制培养的学生签订学徒培养协议，这明确了企业作为育人主体的地位，但学校、企业、学徒个体之间的责权利有待进一步厘清。四是学徒培养质量监控与评价机制亟待健全。

为了完善中国特色学徒制制度体系，中华职教社今年启动了“中国特色学徒制关键问题研究”课题。根据初步研究成果，我们认为应该：

增加制度供给、完善制度保障。通过完善法律制度，对推行中国特色学徒制给予明确规定和法律保障，尤其是明确学徒与企业之间的法律关系；明确学徒具备学生和员工的双重身份，享受双重保障；明确学徒享受统一的国民教育体系学历保障；明确学徒享受企业员工劳动保护、劳动条件和劳动报酬等权益保障；明确学徒享受统一的国家补贴；明确学徒统一注册标准、教学标准、评价标准等，确保各项法律的一致性和可操作性。

加快构建国家资历框架，探索学位学徒制。建立学徒学历上升通道，打破学徒学历“天花板”，源头上解决知识与技能、学历文凭与资格证书、教育与产业难以互联互通的问题。

完善保障激励政策，保护激发相关方活力。需要明确企业、学校、学生三方的责权利，建立科学合理的成本分担机制，努力调动各方积极性；以政府购买服务的形式引导行业企业和职业院校积极参与，将开展学徒制工作作为产教融合型企业建设和评价的重要内容，推动更多企业积极参与到现代学徒制工作中。

健全标准体系，加强学徒制规范化建设。一是不断完善学徒制专业选拔标准、教学标准、课程标准、企业标准、导师标准、评价标准，建立行业企业导师库。二是基于标准构建政府、行业企业、学校、社会等参与的多元学徒制评价体系。三是要依据学徒制相关标准，加强对学徒制校企协同机制、教育教学质量的全方位监管；探索建立学徒制注册认证制度，强化对参与学校、企业培养资格和培养过程的综合监管。

世界职业教育是一家。100 多年来，中华职教社一直为实现“使无业者有业、使有业者乐业”的职业教育理想而努力奋斗。我们也愿意加强与国内外职业教育界的交流与合作，共同探究职业教育的发展规律，为实现“各美其美，美美与共”的人类命运共同体而做出自己的贡献。

# （十一）

# 精雕细琢分层育匠才

北京精雕科技集团有限公司执行总裁　张保全

很荣幸参加世界职业教育大会职业教育校企协同育人新模式创新论坛，我今天演讲的题目是“精雕细琢分层次育匠才”，主要探讨的话题是高端制造业领域的人才培养的问题，主要想和大家分享两个观点：第一个观点是，中国正在从制造业大国走向制造业强国，高端制造业的蓬勃发展，需要引入高端的制造装备和制造工艺，同时也需要大量的工匠型的技术人才；第二个观点是，培养工匠型的技术人才，要从校企协同，然后采用分段培养的方式进行培养。

制造业强国的标志是高端制造业。在今天的中国，高端制造业已经蓬勃发展起来了，包括航空航天、医疗装备、工程机械，等等。高端制造业不同于传统制造业的地方，不仅在于制造工艺的复杂性，而且在于制造业组织模式的变革。高端制造业的生产组织模式都是以数字化制造体系为支撑，而数字化制造体系的典型特点就是将制造过程分割为以软件体系支撑的信息制造和以设备体系支撑的物理制造。数字化制造体系不仅改变了制造结构，同时也改变了人才结构。数字化制造体系将人工岗位也分解为两类集群，一类是从事信息制造的岗位群，包括产品设计、工艺设计和规划；另一类是从事物理制造的岗位群，包括物流管理、设备操作维护等。不论从事哪个岗位，在数字化制造体系的岗位能力竟然出现了同质化，每个岗位的人要理解工业知识、工业软件、生产设备，并能形成系统性的认识，能成为工匠型的人才。

人才需求的变化，倒逼我们人才培养模式的转变。这种转变体现在三个方面。第一个就是培养内容，从培养操作设备的人才向培养使用软件技术的人才转变。第二个是技能范围，从培养单一技能向培养复合能力转变。第三个是培养途径，从注重知识教育向注重创新思想转变。要落实这三个转变，对一个单纯的学校而言，那是一个非常大的挑战，只有充分利用社会资源，主要是企业资源，实现校企合作培养人才是更佳的途径。考虑改变过程的复杂性，在推进校企协同培养模式时，要优先采用分段培养出工匠型人才的培养思路。这种培养思路的要点就是一种双师合作制的，学校和企业共同出人才，然后进行优势互补，校企各方面把自己的人才培养能力能发挥出来，最后有逐渐的优势，由点到线、由线到面形成一些复合型人才供应的培养计划。

基于校企合作、分段育人思想，北京精雕科技集团有限公司和南京工业职业技术大学共同以产业学院的形式落实校企合作育人的新模式，取得了非常好的效果。产业学院具有教学实战化、教科研一体化、团队融合化的思想。产业学院在学生培养方面的特色是，注重学生对系统知识的理解，同时注重对学生进行分层次培养。强化对系统制造理解的手段，就是在产业学院建设了一套数字化制造系统的实训平台，该平台有信息化制造系统的实训，有物理制造系统的实训，最后通过实践，让学生了解数字化制造体系下如何进行精密零件加工。通过这种实战训练，让学生在学生阶段就能建立一个完整的数字化制造体系的概念，也就是说，学生对以后的工业职业方向有非常清晰地认同。考虑数字化制造体系的复杂性，在培养过程中采用分层次分阶段培养的理念，形成了普通班、卓越班和精英班，既能满足工匠型人才的数量，同时也发掘一些高端领军型的人才。

总的来说，我们采用了兴趣向导、分段培养的理念，促进了职业院校培养高端制造业急需的人才，同时也能助力我国高端制造业和制造装备业的蓬勃发展，对于北京精雕科技集团有限公司这样从事高端数控机床制造的企业来说，也是非常愿意支持该项目的。目前，北京精雕科技集团有限公司已经和国内的多所学校合作，推广应用产业学院的育人模式，每年能够为 4 500 人次提供一些实验平台。

# （十二）

# “三型协同”跨境校企合作培养人才探索

南京工业职业技术大学校长　谢永华

下面我就南京工业职业技术大学“三型协同”跨境校企合作培养人才的思路与探索与大家分享交流。教育部党组书记、部长怀进鹏在《人民日报》撰文指出，加大创新实践能力培养力度，强化科教协同和产教融合育人，加快培养急需紧缺人才，着重培养创新型、复合型、应用型人才。积极发展职业教育，增强职业教育适应性，加快构建现代职业教育体系。校企协同育人是贯彻落实国家产教融合发展战略的需要，也是深化职业教育人才培养模式改革的需要。

## 1. 校企协同育人整体思路

（1）校企协同育人产教融合存在的问题。职业院校在开展校企合作的过程当中面临的问题总结起来就是“三热三不热”的现象，一是官热民不热，二是上热下不热，三是校热企不热。产生问题的主要原因有以下几个方面：第一是产教分离的体制问题尚待解决；第二是政府部门间缺乏相互主动协调；第三是企业主体参与职业教育内驱力不够；第四是学校自身内功不强。校企合作正从原先的初步基础阶段，向深度全方位校企命运共同体阶段过渡。

职业教育作为一种类型教育，具有跨界的天然属性，需要从“校企利益融合”“校企制度融合”“校企资源融合”“校企人员融合”“校企技术融合”“校企文化融合”等方面推进产教融合、协同育人。

（2）职业本科人才培养定位。校企协同育人中，企业更关注培养具有“精深性”岗位能力、有潜力成为“能工巧匠”“大国工匠”的卓越人才，学校则侧重培养具有“创新性”“复合性”的岗位拓展能力的现场工程师、卓越工程师。在职业本科办学中，我们将人才培养定位为：通过育人与育才的统一、教育与教学的结合，培养具有“精深性、复合型、创新性”高素质技术技能人才。学生的能力包括要具备知识的复合性、技能的精深性、自我学习能力的创新性。精深性是企业提出的要求，因为培养的人才是为企业服务的。作为学校，为了满足企业对于精深性人才的需求，必须在知识能力的复合性方面，在学生的创新素养、创新能力方面着力。

（3）产教融合协同育人模式。学校通过与知名企业、地方政府和产业园区合作，打造了四类协同育人平台。一是技术联盟型，与精雕集团等技术上游企业以“技术”纽带构建联盟，主要面向技术下游企业实施现代学徒制培养。二是协同服务型，与地方政府、产业园区和华为培训中心等企业合作，发挥专业与地域优势，建设研发中心。三是双创孵化型，与地方政府和头部企业共建大学科技园，建设创新企业“孵化平台”，成为学生创新实践重要基地。四是国际伴随型，伴随中国有色矿业集团等大型企业走出国门，校企共建境外办学机构，培养当地亟须技术技能人才。

**2. 校企协同育人实践探索**

我们在国际合作中校企协同育人的探索体系分为五个维度进行：一是围绕产业发展和升级，创新培养机制；二是引进国际标准、资源、模式实施“引进来”战略；三是加强援外培训，开展“走出去”境外办学；四是参与国际校企合作体系建设，搭建合作“平台”；五是拓展国际校企合作渠道，强化“项目”实战。

（1）创新人才培养机制。实践国际化校企合作育人目标愿景，从“引进来”和“走出去”两方面推进，以培养具有纵向职业“精深性”技术技能人才基础、多技术“复合型”现场（卓越）工程师为定位，以学校主导、学院主体、师生主角、专业载体、平台支撑、项目牵引，最终实现从“独舞”到“领舞”到“伴舞”。

（2）校企协同育人“引进来”。一是引进来，引进国外优质教育资源，深化教育教学改革。将国际化人才培养目标内涵纳入学校人才培养方案的总体框架；通过合作办学项目引进外方优质教育资源、课程标准和优质教材；通过教育部海外培训项目，引进国外专业标准及内容；通过与国际企业的合作，将企业的人才标准纳入教学内容；开展国际合作科研项目，获得财政资助。二是推动专业对接国际通用职业资格证书。在人才培养方案修订中，把国际通用职业资格证书作为必备内容；国际合作办学形成职业教育范式，获国家教学成果奖一等奖。

（3）校企协同育人“走出去”。一是走出去，服务国家“一带一路”倡议，培养具有国际视野、合理知识结构和应变能力，即“全球能力”的应用型人才；二是参加教育部在有色金属行业试点的首个职业教育“走出去”项目，是首批“走出去”的职业院校，成立中国 – 赞比亚职业技术学院机电分院，培养“一带一路”沿线国家留学生，把中国的职业教育、标准体系推介至赞比亚，成为赞比亚国民教育体系重要组成部分；三是学校研发“中文 + 职业教育”立体化教材和教学资源库，选择柬埔寨王国急需急用的专业进行开发，初级、中级和高级共六套教材计划于年底正式出版。

（4）校企协同育人“平台支撑”。大力构筑学校国际化发展平台。与海外职业教育组织和机构建立起稳固的合作关系，积极打造全国职业院校国际化发展平台，牵头中国教育国际交流协会职教分会、中非职业院校联盟、江苏美国高职院校联盟等高级别平台，2020 年成为全国首家“中文 + 职业技能国际推广基地”。2021 年，学校与柬埔寨柬华理事总会、柬华理工大学合作建设全国首家职业教育特色孔子学院。今年预计招生 9 个专业，采用“1+2+1”模式，第一年教授中文，第二年和第三年教授专业知识，第四年到企业去实践，与在柬中国企业进行合作，学生将来可以获得柬埔寨学历证书，也可以获得我校的学历证书和学位证书，成为校企合作的一个典型案例。

（5）校企协同育人“项目实战”。通过项目载体，校企双方共同培养专业核心技术，通过项目在技术型企业培养学生职业素养和岗位能力，培养出“敢为人先”的创新精神、“艺精技巧”的专业技能、“制造强国”的家国情怀、“敬业乐群”的职业素养、“精益求精”的工匠精神。一是建设产业技术研究院。通过立地科研解决企业生产经营的实际问题，提高教师科研实践能力反哺人才培养。二是大力推动中外合作人才培养“转型提升”。从规模导向转变为质量导向，通过中外合作办学开发专业教学标准和课程标准。三是积极开展留学生企业实习。确保学生有 6 个月时间在企业进行生产实习，在实践中获得专业技能的提升。四是面向赞比亚当地员工开展技能培训。了解企业的培训需求，共同研究制订培训方案和培训计划。

## (十三)

# 中国职业教育校企双元育人的政策与实践

国家教育行政学院学术委员会主任　邢　晖

今年颁布的《中华人民共和国职业教育法》在5月1日正式实施，其中非常明确地提出了“二十四字”的中国职业教育治理模式，即“政府统筹、分级管理、地方为主、行业指导、校企合作、社会参与”，这二十四个字将我国职业教育的五大办学主体明确了，而且将学校和企业的“鱼和水”的关系也清楚了。在涉及管理体制的中央和地方关系中，强调了以地方为主的特点。

我国职业教育政策法规框架，可以概括为三个层面。第一个层面是法律，目前，我国有8部教育法律，其中有两部法律在颁布以来有过大修，一个是《中华人民共和国义务教育法》，一个就是《中华人民共和国职业教育法》，这是最高的规范，它是最高的准绳，是定海神针。第二个层面是国家的顶层设计，主要是中共中央国务院颁发的相关文件，如《国家职业教育改革实施方案》，还包括党和国家领导人的重要指示和讲话精神。第三个层面是分两条线贯彻，一个是条条落实中共中央国务院及各大部委颁布的文件，如《关于职业教育提质培优行动计划》；另一个是块块落实地方省委省政府的文件，如省级、地市、县市级出台的相关的文件。因为职业教育主要是地方的事业，目前9 000多所中职学校、1 518所高职院校、32所职业本科，都是由地方投入和主办主管的，地方政策也就至关重要了。

产教融合、校企合作是我国职业教育公共治理和政策制定的重点之一。从法律规定方面可概括成五个角度。第一，坚持产教融合、校企合作，这是基本制度、基本原则，明确规定企业是职业教育重要的办学主体，要求所有的企业都要支持和参与职业教育，这些是国家意志，总体规范。第二，法律规定企业可以直接举办学校，举办培训机构。第三，没有能力或者说没有举办机构的企业，也必须支持和参与职业教育。参与职业教育，主要是导向高质量发展的内涵建设中的诸多要素，如实施中国特色的学徒制、产教融合实训基地的建设、专业设置的规划、教材的开发、教师的授课和培养培训、教学方法教学手段的改进等。《中华人民共和国职业教育法》在多处提到产教融合、校企合作的问题，把企业作为主语约有 20 多次。第四，国家规定企业要支持参与职业教育，这是社会责任、社会义务，但是也要考虑他们的利益，因为要把责权利统一起来，给企业的优惠一个是奖励，对产教融合、校企合作做得好的，对培养人才有贡献的，对于职校学生就业发挥了企业主体作用的这三个条件就给予奖励；对于产教融合型企业，将其上升到法律高度固化下来的一个专有的中国化表达的概念，对这样的企业给予组合性的政策激励，如金融、土地、税收等政策优惠。第五，学校办学要高质量发展，一定要在产教融合、校企合作上下功夫。主要从四个方面规范：一是用什么形式，如职教集团、共办机构、订单式培养等途径；二是在哪些方面开展校企合作，提出了 15 项内容，这 15 项内容也是随着新形势、新模式、新方法、新理念、新材料等变化，校企合作不断深化，学校对产业企业的支撑力和贡献度要求不断提升；三是校企合作不能停留在口头上，要有契约精神，要有合同，要有协议；四是学校通过社会服务、社会培训所得的收入应该怎么办？可以扩大再生产，改善学校的条件，也可以对教师的收入进行重新分配，这样能够大大的调动学校和教师的积极性。这些是从新修订的《中华人民共和国职业教育法》中所反映出来的一些政府的政策信号和价值导向。

这些年来特别是党的十九大之后，国家高度重视产教融合、校企合作的深化，相关法律也是汲取了 2017—2021 年以来关于产教融合、校企合作的精华成分的。改革开放四十多年来，职业院校没有停止过对产教融合、校企合作的探索，大概的模式仅从动力要素看，分为政府引导型、行业牵引型、企业主动型、学校主导型、校企互动型、多方联动型。但问题和困难还很多，如少动力、少契合、少支持、少保障，有顾虑、有风险、有障碍，不对等、不匹配、不稳定等，需要解决和改善。

关于校企双元育人的实践，中国改革开放这四十多年，特别是近些年来，从没有停止过探索和创新，我国也有丰富多彩的实践，比如四种精神：劳模精神、劳动精神、工匠精神、职业精神。这是国家正在倡导和形成的社会文化风尚；中国特色学徒制，包括教育部门的现代学徒制和人社部门的新型学徒制；职教集团，校企协作体；订单式培养；产教融合型企业；股份制、混合所有制；全国职业技能大赛；技能大师工作室、工程师学院、产业学院；企业举办的学校和培训机构；“1+X”证书试点、国家职业技能证书的实施；行业指导委员会、专业和教学指导委员会；校企双向兼职；鲁班工坊，校企合作请进来、走出去，等等，这些改革创新形式都体现了校企双元育人实践的多样化。

总之，我国职业教育的产教融合、校企合作在不断深化，既要学习借鉴国外先进的经验，又要具有中国特色。中央政府政策的引导，地方主权主责的发挥，企业的支持和参与，学校能动性和适应性的提升，协同才能多赢，要不断探索更加多样实用的校企双元育人模式。产教融合、校企合作，依然在路上。

# 十三
# 职业院校科学教育发展论坛

协助组织单位：天津中德应用技术大学

# XIII. Science Education Development in Vocational Education Institutions

Co-organizer: Tianjin Sino-German University of Applied Sciences, China

01
张兴会
Zhang Xinghui

02
埃贡·米勒
Egon Mueller

03
马姆达利·巴克提耶
Mahmadali Bakhtiyor

04
陈文莉
Chen Wenli

05
潘海生
Pan Haisheng

**探讨科学教育在职业教育高质量发展中的重要作用，探究在职业院校人才培养中融入科学教育、科学方法和科学精神的模式与路径，研讨如何激发学生创新意识，拓展创新思维，培养动手能力和创新能力，促进职业教育高质量创新发展。**

This session explores the importance of science education to the high-quality development of vocational education, and the modes of integrating science education, scientific method, and scientific spirit in talent cultivation of vocational education institutions. The participants also discuss how to raise students' innovation consciousness, develop their innovative thinking skills, and improve their hands-on skills and innovation skills with the purpose of promoting innovative and high-quality development of vocational education.

# （一）

# 职业院校科学教育发展论坛情况概述

天津中德应用技术大学党委书记　张兴会

### 1. 论坛概况

加强职业教育国际交流与合作，推动我国职业教育高质量发展，增强我国在国际职业教育领域的话语权、主动权和影响力，是我国职业教育迈向国际化的重要战略举措。基于此，2022 年 8 月 19—20 日，以“后疫情时代职业技术教育发展：新变化、新方式、新技能”为主题的世界职业技术教育发展大会在天津成功举办。“职业院校科学教育发展论坛”是十四个平行论坛之一，由天津中德应用技术大学协办并承办，论坛嘉宾来自4个国家，覆盖科技界、产业界、教育界和科研院所等领域。

论坛由天津中德应用技术大学党委书记张兴会主持，共分为致辞、主旨报告和发起倡议三个阶段。论坛第一阶段由中国科学院院士、西北工业大学副校长张卫红致辞。论坛第二阶段为主旨报告，共有来自中国、德国、新加坡、塔吉克斯坦4个国家的13位嘉宾围绕科学素质、科学知识、科学方法、人文精神、科学精神、科学思想融入职业教育的方式方法交流思想、碰撞智慧，既有理论探索，又有实践经验分享，为职业教育高质量发展提供了新视角、新思路。论坛第三阶段为发起倡议，张兴会宣读了“职业院校科学教育发展论坛倡议书”，呼吁各级教育行政管理部门积极探索构建大中小一体化科学教育体系；职业院校加大科学教育实践，提升教师教学与科研能力；社会科学界联合会、中国科学技术协会等群团组织和行业企业广泛参与科学教育活动，加强科学普及；社会、政府、学校、家庭合力推进科学教育，为促进科学教育融入职业院校人才培养贡献力量。

**2. 科学教育的内涵**

学者们对“什么是科学”“什么是科学教育”及“科学教育的特点”进行了深入解读。

中国科学院高能物理研究所研究员张双南认为科学的三要素包括科学目的、科学精神和科学方法。科学目的旨在发现各种规律；科学精神体现为质疑、独立和唯一；科学方法表现为逻辑化、定量化和实证化，逻辑化指要符合逻辑论证，定量化指必须能够进行演绎，即推导和计算，实证化指推导和计算出的结论和结果必须被实验或者观测所证实，一方面需要符合已有的实验和观测结果，另一方面也需要做出能够被验证的定量预言。依据这一内涵，他认为科学教育应是科学史、科学方法与科学知识三位一体的教育。

天津市科学技术协会副主席卢双盈认为科学是可以得到实际验证的知识，是按照一定规则和方法认识和解决问题的系统知识；科学教育是现代教育遵循的原则，旨在构建年轻一代求真务实的思维模式，重在培养科学知识、科学方法、科学思想和科学精神。

金华职业技术学院副校长成军认为科学教育是一种通过现代科技知识及其社会价值的教学让学生掌握科学概念，学会科学方法，培养科学态度，且懂得如何面对现实中的科学与社会有关问题，并做出明智抉择，以培养科技专门人才，提高全民科学素养为目的的教育活动，并且从教育目标、教育内容和教育方法三个方面概括了科学教育的特点。

### 3. 科学教育融入职业教育的必要性

（1）高素质技术技能人才培养需要科学教育。中国科学院院士、深圳华大基因理事长杨焕明认为职业院校在人才培养中必须要强调和重视科学教育，包括培养学生科学的精神与态度，获得科学的方法和知识，增强科学的意识与能力。天津大学教育质量管理处副处长潘海生认为新一轮产业革命改变了工作世界的面貌，而工作世界的变化对技术技能人才提出了新要求，面对这一现状，职业教育应当培养适应工作机器智能化的人机协作技能、适应工作活动智慧化的软技能、适应工作关系协作化的在线协作技能，更加注重学生的跨知识、跨岗位、跨能力、跨职业的复合发展能力以及理实结合的融合能力培养，塑就其更加深厚的知识体系和更加综合的技术技能。

（2）社会创新发展需要科学教育。杨焕明认为职业教育培养的人首先应是“社会人”，其次才是“职业人”，要服务社会创新需要，坚持走将科学教育融于职业教育之路。中国科学院院士、南开大学副校长陈军深入分析了科学和技术的关系，认为职业院校在日常教学中应该正确认识科学内涵、提升创新能力，注重人才链、产业链和创新链的有机衔接。百度集团副总裁璩静围绕“人工智能时代需要什么样的人才”，论述了百度在人工智能人才培养上以人工智能赋能职业教育，培养出专业技能超群、具有工匠精神、掌握人工智能技术的复合型技术人才。

（3）职业教育高质量发展需要科学教育。推动职业教育高质量发展是我国经济社会今后一个时期的主题。杨焕明认为职业院校要开展教育教学改革，提倡科学教育，培养出具有科学精神和创新意识的学生，教师要崇尚科学精神、能从整体上把握科学知识体系、具备开拓进取的创新意识；学生要培养科学兴趣、掌握科学知识、运用科学方法和树立科学精神。潘海生认为技术创新形塑了高职教育新内涵，为此，职业教育不能仅停留在技术教育，而应走向科学教育，培养学生的逻辑思维能力和演绎推理能力，帮助学生独立思考职业教育的基本理论，形成科学的逻辑体系。成军认为科学教育对职业教育的作用为坚守人才培养的政治方向、坚守科学研究的学术取向、坚守社会服务的价值导向、坚守文化传承创新的文化自信、坚守国际交流合作的中国立场。

4. **科学教育融入职业教育的路径**

（1）科学教育融入学生全过程培养。杨焕明分别论述了科学教育融入职业教育的路径与模式，路径主要体现为将弘扬科学精神贯穿于育人全链条、开设科学教育相关课程或模块、提升教师科学素质、开展职业科普四个方面；融入模式为树立创新教育理念，推动学生参与、推动开展与专业相关的科普活动；改革课堂教学方法，改变满堂灌的教学方法，倡导教师主导、学生主体的引导式教学方法；鼓励学生社会实践，确认适合的职业，增强就业竞争优势，激活创新思维意识；创新学生评价制度，充分重视职业院校学生的个性和差异性，建立与之相适应的学生评价内容、标准、方法和模式。

（2）科学教育融入科学创新和科研活动。成都航空职业技术学院副校长熊熙以该校航空类专业为例，分析了该校在航空专业领域实施的科普、科创和科研三位一体的育人实践，充分肯定了航空科创活动在专业教育中的促进作用，通过大学生科技协会营造科学教育氛围、大学生创新创业项目深化科学教育内涵、大学生航空科技竞赛打造科学教育品牌，提升了科研项目数量、促进了企业科研发展和科技扶贫助振兴。中国科学技术大学教授、安徽信息工程学院校长吴敏以安徽信息工程学院为例，论述了该校实施科学教育的路径与取得的育人成效。将科学教育理念融入学校的九条教育原则中，形成了创意创新教育、创新创业培养和创业产业孵化逐层递进的“金字塔式”创新创业教育体系。

（3）科学教育与专业教育相结合。广东科学技术职业学院党委书记黄仕初认为随着数字经济的发展，如何提升学生的科技素养，实现学生自身高质量发展是需要面临的一项重要课题。为此，需要创新科学教育融入职业教育的模式，并且贯穿人才培养的全过程。他以广东科学技术职业学院为例，分析了该校的实践探索，一是将科学教育与专业教育融合，将科学思想、科学方法及科学精神融入专业教育中，在全校各专业均开设了人工智能导论课程。二是实施第一课堂与第二课堂的融合。三是注重科学精神与人文精神的融合。成军以金华职业技术学院为例，分析在实施科学教育中的实践探索，具体体现为高规格打造科研服务平台体系，为科技教育夯实基础，高标准创立育人新载体，实现科技教育与人才培养紧密融合。

# i. Overview of the Session on Science Education Development in Vocational Education Institutions

**Zhang Xinghui, Secretary of CPC Committee of Tianjin Sino-German University of Applied Sciences, China**

## 1. Overview of the Session

Strengthening international exchange and cooperation in vocational education, promoting the high-quality development of vocational education in China, and demonstrating China's best practice in vocational education on the global stage are important measures for China's vocational education to go global. As part of this effort, the World Vocational and Technical Education Development Conference with the theme of "Vocational and Technical Education Development in the Post-pandemic Era—New Changes, New Ways and New Skills" was successfully held in Tianjin from 19 to 20 August, 2022. As one of the 14 parallel sessions, Science Education Development in Vocational Education Institutions was co-organized and undertaken by Tianjin Sino-German University of Applied Sciences (TSGUAS), China and attended by guests from four countries in academia, industry, and the education sector.

Chaired by Zhang Xinghui, Secretary of CPC Committee of Tianjin Sino-German University of Applied Sciences, China, the session was divided into three parts: the welcome speech, the keynote speeches, and the release of the initiative of the session. In the first part, Zhang Weihong, Academician of the Chinese Academy of Sciences and Vice President of Northwestern Polytechnical University, China, delivered a speech. In the second stage, 13 speakers from China, Germany, Singapore, and Tajikistan shared their insights on the ways of integrating the knowledge, the method, the spirit, and the thinking of science as well as the humanistic spirit into vocational education. Their theoretical exploration and first-hand experience provided new perspectives and ideas for the high-quality development of vocational education. In the third part, Zhang Xinghui read out the *Initiative of the Session on Science Education Development in Vocational Education Institutions*, calling on education departments at different levels to explore ways to build a science education system covering all levels of education; on vocational schools to practice science education more actively and to improve their teachers' related teaching and research ability; and on non-governmental organizations, such as Social Science Federations, Science and Technology Associations, and the business sector to participate more in science education activities to contribute to the popularization of science. The initiative also calls on society, government, schools, and families to jointly promote science education and to contribute to the effort of integrating science education into vocational education.

### 2. The Essence of Science Education

During the session, the speakers gave an in-depth interpretation of "what science is", "what science education is", and "what the characteristics of science education are".

Zhang Shuangnan, Researcher at the Institute of High Energy Physics of Chinese Academy of Sciences, China, summarized the three elements of science as its purpose, spirit, and method. The purpose of science is to discover the laws of nature and human society. The spirit of science is reflected in the ability to ask good questions and to deliver reproducible results. The method of science is logical, quantitative, and empirical. Being logical means following the laws of logic; being quantitative means being applicable to mathematical deduction; and being empirical means a theory must be verifiable by means of experiments or observations. Based on this understanding, he considered science education as the combined teaching of science history, scientific method, and scientific knowledge.

In the opinion of Lu Shuangying, Vice Chairman of Tianjin Association for Science and Technology, China, "science is a system of knowledge that can be verified in practice and be used to understand and solve problems according to certain rules and methods". Science education is a basic element of modern education. Its aim is to establish a truth-seeking and empirical mindset in young people. The focus of science education is passing on the knowledge, the method, the thinking, and the spirit of science.

Cheng Jun, Vice President of Jinhua Polytechnic, China, described science education as a type of education that enables students to master scientific concepts and method, to have scientific attitudes, and to know how to face scientific and social problems in real life and make wise decisions. Science education provides students with scientific and technological knowledge and helps them to understand its social value. It can not only be used to train Specialists in science and technology, but also be used to improve the science literacy of the general population. He summarized the characteristics of science education from its goals, its content, and its methods.

### 3. The Necessity of Integrating Science Education into Vocational Education

(1) The training of skilled high-quality technical talents requires scientific

education. Yang Huanming, Academician of the Chinese Academy of Sciences and Chairman of BGI Group, China, pointed out that vocational schools must put emphasis on science education in talent training to cultivate the students' scientific spirit and attitude, to help students master scientific method and knowledge, and to enhance their scientific awareness and the ability to practice science. Pan Haisheng, Deputy Director of Education Quality Management Office of Tianjin University, China, pointed out that the new round of industrial revolution has changed the world of work and such changes have put forward new requirements for technical workers Facing this reality, vocational education institutions should develop their students' human-machine collaboration skills, soft skills, and online collaboration skills to help them adapt to an ever smarter and more collaborative work environment. They should also focus more on their students' self-development skills as well as their ability to apply theory to practice.

(2) The innovative development of the society requires science education. Yang Huanming stressed that vocational education graduates should be responsible citizens as well as specialists. Vocational schools must align their education with the needs of innovative social development and adhere to the path of integrating science education into vocational education. Chen Jun, Academician of the Chinese Academy of Sciences and Vice President of Nankai University, China, made an in-depth analysis of the relationship between science and technology. He pointed out that vocational schools should correctly understand what science is, enhance their students' ability to innovate, and pay attention to connecting their education with industry and innovations. Qu Jing, Vice President of Baidu Co., Ltd., China, explained what kind of talents are needed in the era of artificial intelligence and talked about how Baidu empowers vocational education with artificial intelligence in the training of artificial intelligence specialists so that they can have excellent professional skills, craftsmanship, and artificial intelligence know-how.

(3) The high-quality development of vocational education requires science education. Promoting the high-quality development of vocational education is and will be an important matter for China. According to Yang Huanming, vocational institutions should reform what they teach and how they teach, advocate science education, and equip students with scientific spirit and innovation consciousness. Teachers should have scientific spirit and a general understanding of science and are willing to innovate. Students should develop interest in science, master scientific knowledge, have the ability to apply scientific method, and establish scientific spirit. Pan Haisheng noted that technological innovation has reshaped higher vocational education. Therefore, vocational education should go beyond technical education to science education, give their students the ability of logical thinking and deductive reasoning, and help them think independently about the basics of vocational education and form a scientific

logical system. Cheng Jun observed that integrating science education can help vocational institutions to adhere to the correct political position in talent training, to make their scientific research correctly oriented, to fulfill their social responsibilities, to be confident about passing on and building on cultural traditions, and to assert a firm standpoint in international exchanges and cooperation.

### 4. The Pathways of Integrating Science Education into Vocational Education

(1) Integrating science education into the whole process of student training. Yang Huanming discussed the pathways and modes of integrating science education into vocational education. The pathways include emphasizing the spirit of science in every aspect of education, offering science education courses or modules, improving teachers' science literacy, and carrying out vocation-specific science popularization. The integration modes include establishing innovative educational concepts, encouraging students' participation, and promoting the development of science popularization activities based on majors. Schools should reform their way of teaching, moving from teacher-centered instruction to a teacher-led and student-centered approach. They should encourage students to practice in society, to identify suitable occupations, and to enhance their competitive advantage in job hunting and activate their willingness to innovate. The schools' evaluation mechanism should be improved to respect their students individualities and the evaluation content, standards, methods, and models should be developed accordingly.

(2) Integrating science education into scientific innovation and research activities. Taking the aviation major as an example, Xiong Xi, Vice President of Chengdu Aeronautic Polytechnic, China, analyzed the school's practice of combining science popularization, technological innovation, and scientific research. He spoke positively about the role that aviation science and innovation activities have played in promoting professional education. The school set up a students' science and technology association to create an atmosphere of science education, launched students' innovation and entrepreneurship projects to expand the connotation of science education, and held students' aviation science and technology competition to create a well-known event of science education. As a result of such efforts, the number of scientific research projects has been increased, the research and development in enterprises has been fostered, and poverty alleviation by technological means has been promoted. Wu Min, Professor of University of Science and Technology of China, President of Anhui Institute of Information Technology (AIIT), China, took AIIT as an example to discuss the pathway and achievements of the school's science education practice. They added science education to the school's education principles and formed a layered system of innovation and entrepreneurship education and incubator services.

(3) Combining science education with professional education. Huang Shichu,

Secretary of CPC Committee of Guangdong Polytechnic of Science and Technology, China, expressed that with the development of the digital economy, how to enhance students' science and technology literacy and achieve students' high-quality development has become an important issue. He believes it is necessary to embrace a new mode to integrate science education into vocational education and to apply it to the whole process of talent training. He took the practice of Guangdong Polytechnic of Science and Technology as an example. Firstly, the school added science education to its curriculum, integrating scientific thinking, scientific method, and scientific spirit into professional education. For example, the course Introduction to Artificial Intelligence is required for students of all majors. Secondly, it combined classroom teaching with extracurricular activities. Thirdly, it emphasized the integration of scientific spirit and humanistic spirit. Cheng Jun analyzed Jinhua Polytechnic's implementation of science education. Their practices include the establishment of a high-quality scientific research service platform to consolidate the foundation for science and technology education and the building of a high-standard medium to closely integrating science education into student training.

## (二)

# 未来科学教育与职业教育高水平发展面临的挑战和实现方法

德国开姆尼茨工业大学教授　埃贡·米勒

此次发言将围绕在未来的高等教育[①]中我们要做什么、期待什么、所面对的挑战和解决方法有哪些等问题来展开。未来的大趋势包含许多领域，新材料与新技术正实现全球化。我们面临新资源问题、可持续发展问题、信息技术的影响、人口增长、生活方式和价值观的改变。这意味着我们要基于自然科学全面地看待不同事物。学生应在自然科学方面打下良好基础，将其应用到不同领域，并能够将不同领域有机结合起来，这非常重要。在材料和技术、可持续发展、资源使用、信息技术以及社会科学的各个领域，都要有相关的专业人士。我们必须具备整体观。

如何应对这些挑战和问题？答案是必须审视创新的作用。当我们认真审视创新的作用时，不难发现如果想要有竞争力，想要增强在全球范围的经济实力，就必须要引入创新。通过应用实现从发明到创新的转变，创新能带来新的产品或实现现有产品、工艺和环境的提升，从而能够提供新的服务，获取新的客户。当然还有其他能够改善工艺流程的创新应用，比如在制造领域或生产领域存在较多这类应用，如果应用创新性的工艺，就能够确保有竞争力的生产周期和价格。当然，创新需要具备一些特定的条件和要求，其中最重要的就是要拥有能力强并具有创造力的员工。针对这一情况，我们要给高等教育把脉开方。我们的教育要赋予学生进行专业性工作的能力和经验，以应对未来发展的要求。

下面来谈一谈制造业领域的创新。制造业的重要性不言而喻，因为世界是由物质实体构成的。物质实体不可或缺。例如，当我们想要从 $a$ 点移动到 $b$ 点，我们可

① 在德国，高等教育包含高等职业教育。

以坐火车、汽车或乘飞机，可以有不同的交通工具，只是必须为我们所用。人才和知识是制造业未来发展的关键，智能化生产、智能化设备和数字化生产须能够应对我谈到的那些问题。这其中，人才是重中之重，相关的实践和研究也做了很多。这就涉及了“高级学习工厂”这一概念。因为未来各种要求和需求不仅仅是来自市场，还会来自社会和外部环境，因此需要有灵活柔性的能力框架，可以对市场及其他领域的影响作出快速反应，可以更快地应对和解决问题，新的知识可以推动工艺创新、技术创新和可持续性发展。因涉及不同的领域，所以我们必须学会从全局的视角来思考并找到结合点。那么很重要的一点就是，在现在这个数字化的大环境中，人才始终是技术创新、“工业 4.0”等领域的关键，人才和人才潜力是未来发展中最为重要的资源。这意味着需要拓展知识并让人们学会应用这些知识。对于中小企业来说，相关技能应该得到拓展，当我们关注制造工程的时候会发现，中小企业往往不能单独解决这个问题。在制造工程领域，中小企业需要雇佣专业人士解决问题。因此“现有学习环境是否适宜”“课堂中的应用是否足以处理不同问题，还是需要我们建立其他的应用”，这都是亟待解决的问题。

我们需要基于学习环境构建全新的模型，它被称为“高级学习工厂”。在这背后有一个学习环境的设计模型。如何建立这个模型，使之应用于自然科学以获取经验？我们称之为学习环境设计模型，该模型基于能力框架、目标与应用要求设立。第一步，对现存学习环境进行概述。第二步，从行为领域的应用案例找出源头，即未来的要求是什么，其他因素学习模型的来源是什么。第三步，我们要创建学习模型并应用于实践。第四步，与学习环境能力框架相适应，因为这两者间还有一段距离，我们需要弥合这一差距，需要对这一模型的内容进行拓展。第五步，分析是对此类现存环境进行整合还是开发全新学习环境，学习环境的设计依赖于与自然科学应用、制造业、生产工程等领域紧密相关的内容。第六步，对此学习模型进行配置和参数设置，可以将之放在一些学习课程中试用。最后，按照以上步骤进行实践。

这些独立的需求导向知识结构如何形成、如何模块化，又是如何基于用户需求组合到一起的？我们要创建、嵌入哪些实体内容和数字化内容？如何在“高级学习工厂”中实现它们？哪些教学对象和方法适合将新知识有效融入用户环境，我们又该如何去修正？人的哪些属性需要解决，如何将“高级学习工厂”分级对应到学习的全过程中？完整的“高级学习工厂”应该包含哪些流程才算完成了所有的学习课程？我们生活在知识社会和职业高要求的大趋势中，因此当开发这样的学习环境时，可以将其应用于不同的阶段和不同的水平。接下来的问题就是如何实现可持续发展的目标。面对数字化，另一种方法就是“学习创新工程模块”。还有很多模块也同样需要处理，比如创新的技术支持应用程序、视觉应用程序、教与学的形式、翻转课堂模式、同伴指导等，可以用不同的形式去应用。还有一个问题是关于数字化考试的：当在这样的数字化环境中应用它时，其背后的法则是什么，其结构化教学条件的规则是什么。路有千万条，在未来，我们的课程面临着挑战，在更高的自然科学水平上面临各种问题。这需要我们提高竞争力，保持沟通对话，交流经验，相互学习。如何实现科学知识转移的有效赋能，进而实现全球经济的可持续发展，这是今后要面临的挑战。

## ii. Challenges and Solutions for the Future High-level Development of Science Education and Vocational Education

**Egon Mueller, Professor of Chemnitz University of Technology, Germany**

I would like to explain something about my experience related to the challenges and approaches—what we have to do, what we have to expect in the near future and how we have to deal with these questions related to the higher education. Megatrends can be seen in many different fields. We have the new materials and technology that have been globalizing. We have new resources, the sustainability issue, the influence of information technology, the demographic development, and also the lifestyle and value changes. It means that we must have a holistic view to the different things based on natural science. It's very important that the students have very good base in natural science to apply it in the different fields and also to get impression and the possibility to deal with links between these different fields. We must have specialists in materials and technology. We must have specialists in sustainability, in consumption of resources, in information technology and all the other fields in social science. We must have a holistic view.

How can we deal with these challenges and questions? That means we must have a look at the role of innovations. When we have a look at the role of innovations, it means if we want to be competitive and would like to strengthen our economy in the global world, we have to introduce innovations. That means the transition from inventions to innovations by application. Innovations generate new products or improve existing products, processes and environment, so that we deal with new services and new customers. There are also other implications of innovations to improve process, for example related to the manufacturing field and the production field in most cases. If we use innovative processes, we have a competitive lead time and prices. Innovations need special conditions and requirements, among which the most important thing is the competent and creative employees. That means we must develop solutions for higher education. We must give students, when they start professional work, the competency and the experience to deal with the requirements related to their future development.

Now we have a look at the innovation in the field of manufacturing. Manufacturing is very important, because our world exist from physical things. We must have physical objects. When we want to move from point *a* to point *b*, we can take train, we can take a car, we can take a plane, we can take different things, but we must put them in use. Humans and knowledge are the key factors of the future in manufacturing, and intelligent production, intelligent equipment and digitalization of the production must be able to deal with this field. The humans are the most important thing in all processes, and we have done a lot of research related to this. It's called Advanced Learning Factory (ALF). That means the requirements are not only from market, but also from society and the environment. Flexible competence profiles can react quickly not only to market influences, but also to other fields. Problems can be solved faster, and new knowledge creates new process, innovation and sustainability. With all these related fields, we have to think and connect with a holistic view. The very important point is that the humans are always interface to new technologies, Industry 4.0 and other fields in this digitalization environment. Humans and the potential of the humans are the most important resources for the future. We have to develop knowledge and we have to train people to apply this knowledge. That means skills must be expanded, for example, for SMEs. When we look to the production engineering, we can see that SMEs cannot deal with this question alone. They need to hire the professionals in these fields. Then we have to ask, "Is the existing learning environment OK? Is it OK to have only a few applications in the classroom to deal with different questions here or do we have to create other applications?"

We need to construct a different model and need to base on learning environment and we call it ALF. Behind this, we have a design model of learning environment. How to create this to apply natural science to collect experiences? We call it the model for the design of the learning environment on the basis of the competence profiles, objectives and application requirements. In the first step we have to do a profiling of the existing learning environment. The second step is the derivation of the use cases from the fields of action: What are the requirements of the future and the derivation of the learning modules? The third step is we have to create a learning model and deliver it to the applicants. Step four is matching what we have to do with the competence profile of the learning environment, where there is a gap, and what we have to do is to fill in this gap and we must develop the content of this model. The fifth step is the integration in such kind of the existing environment or to develop a completely new learning environment. The design of the learning environment depends on the needed contents related to all the natural science applications or different fields of manufacturing, production engineering or others. Step six is the configuration and parameterization of this learning model set that we can put it together in some study courses, and at the end we have finished the whole process in this way.

How are the individual knowledge-components for need-oriented formation derived, modularized and integrated on user-base? What physical and digital objects we have to create and install there and how can we deal this at ALF? What didactic objects and methods are suitable for the effective transfer of new knowledge into the user environment? How can we deal with the correction? What human attributes need to be addressed and how is ALF classified into the overall learning process? What is the whole process of ALF to complete study courses? We live in the trend of knowledge society and high-professional-demand! When we develop such a learning environment, we can apply it in different stages and different levels. And the question is how we get the goal of being sustainable. Another approach with the digitalization is Learning Innovation Engineering Modules as a further approach. There are many different bricks we have to deal with. There are innovation level technical support apps, visual apps, teaching and learning formats, inverted classroom models, peer instructions and you can apply them differently. Another question is about the digital examination: what are the law rules behind this when we apply it in such digitalization environment, what's the law for structural didactic conditions? There are a lot of approaches and we have challenges in our courses in the future, and we have these questions on a high natural science level. It needs competence development to exchange experience in the community and learn from each other. How to achieve efficient empowerment of scientific knowledge transfer for a sustainable global economy? This is the challenge for us in the future.

# （三）

# 塔吉克斯坦职业技能教育现状与发展

塔吉克斯坦矿业冶金学院校长　马姆达利 · 巴克提耶

塔吉克斯坦共和国普通教育体系目前正在发生着变化，包括延长国家中等义务教育的学习年限、增加人均助学金等，这些变化将进一步增加我国对开展职业技术教育和职业培训的需求。

正如塔吉克斯坦共和国总统埃莫马利 · 拉赫蒙在对塔吉克斯坦共和国最高委员会的讲话中指出的："分析表明，造成（塔吉克斯坦）劳动力市场和社会保障等领域普遍不理想的主要原因是，（塔吉克斯坦的）劳动力资源质量与劳动力市场需求存在很大差距。"

许多亚洲高经济水平国家的经验表明，重视人力资源的发展和成长是促进社会经济发展和保障社会公平的最重要途径之一。此外，完善职业教育和专家人才培训体系也发挥着关键的作用。我国科研人员的首批提案之一就是制订适配市场需求的人才培训计划，有必要让企业和行业的专业人士参与该类培训计划的制订工作。

融资在职业教育体系的深化中发挥着相当重要的作用。我们认为有必要吸引更多的社会投资，而不只是依赖国家补贴或学生的学费。国际组织的相关项目不仅为我国提供了必要的财力资源支持，同时也使我们从中借鉴了国际经验和改革措施，改善了发展环境。

众所周知，近年来，塔吉克斯坦共和国与中华人民共和国的合作已迈上新台阶，已经有数十家中国企业和中塔合资企业开始在我国索格特州地区开展业务。目前，已在运作的企业包括：扎勒尼索尔镇的塔中矿业有限公司、伊斯提克罗尔市的中塔工业园区和塔中矿业冶炼厂、彭吉肯特市的中塔泽拉夫尚有限责任公司（紫金矿业）、华新水泥等大型企业。

鉴于此，在塔吉克斯坦矿业冶金学院开设孔子学院是时代的必然趋势，且这个倡议正是由塔吉克斯坦共和国政府官方发起的。塔中两国的友好关系和互利合作在包括科学和教育在内的各个领域都在逐年深入。2014 年 9 月，上合组织成员国元首理事会第十四次会议在杜尚别举行，并于会议期间签署了一项在塔吉克斯坦冶金学院建立孔子学院的协议。

为确保与当地工业企业保持互动、增进合作，塔吉克斯坦矿业冶金学院和塔吉克斯坦矿业冶金学院孔子学院在相关政府部门的协助下，为增进两国知识、技能、经验和信息的交流创造了条件。未来，孔子学院将持续进行中文教学、矿业和冶金行业人才的培养，这在一定程度上填补了该地区工业企业对高素质人才的需求。合作方向还包括：建立合作实验室、由企业为学院教师组织实习和进修等。

塔吉克斯坦总统埃莫马利·拉赫蒙在给国家议会的信中表达了对本国缺乏各领域高素质专家、发明家和科学家的担忧。总统表示，有关负责人和相关机构要加强对青少年自我认知的疏导，激发他们阅读文学和科学文献的兴趣，同时要更加重视对自然科学和数学的教学。为此，总统提议设立了“2020—2040 年自然科学和数学科学的年度教育发展规划”。不可否认，教育是提高整个国家和个人综合竞争力的最主要工具之一。

为提高教育水平，国家政府和有关部委采取了具体措施，将教师工资提高数倍，重视专业人才的招聘，留住人才，提高教师教学水平，完善培训体系和学生知识评价体系。国家开设 96 个专业方向，除了几乎完全由国家资助的常规文凭课程外，大多数学校还提供收费的短期培训课程。短期培训课程的主要授课对象为需要证明自身实践技能的外来务工人员等。

高等教育机构分为三种类型：大学、研究所和学院。目前，大学和研究所（院）提供学士、硕士和专科学位，而学院只提供学士和专科学位。塔吉克斯坦现有 39 所高等教育机构，这其中包括位于彭吉肯特的塔吉克斯坦国家师范学院和中亚大学。涵盖 15 所大学、16 个研究所和 7 个分支机构以及国家音乐学院。

通过上述途径，（我国的）职业教育促进了社会的公平与包容，实现了可持续的经济增长，并不断向绿色经济和数字经济过渡。

## iii. Current Situation and Development of Vocational and Technical Education in Tajikistan

**Mahmadali Bakhtiyor, President of Mining and Metallurgical Institute of Tajikistan**

Перемены, которые происходят в настоящее время, в общей системе образования Республики Таджикистан (увеличение обязательного срока обучения для получения обязательного среднего образования, переход на подушевое финансирование), еще больше повысят спрос на профессионально-техническое образование и профессиональную подготовку кадров.

Как отметил Президент Республики Таджикистан Эмомали Рахмон в своем Послании Маджлиси Оли Республики Таджикистан: «Как показывает анализ, одной из основных причин неблагоприятного положения на рынке труда и в целом в области социальной защиты является несоответствие качества трудовых ресурсов к требованиям рынка труда».

Как показывает опыт многих развитых азиатских стран, ставка на развитие и наращивание человеческого капитала является одной из важнейших на пути построения сильной экономики и укрепления социальной справедливости. Также система профессионального образования и подготовки специалистов может сыграть ключевую роль.

Одним из первых предложений от лица исследователей стоит соответствие обучаемых программ рыночному спросу. Для продуктивного обучения необходимо привлекать предприятия и профессионалов из индустрий к разработке программ обучения.

Большую роль в развитии и укреплении системы профессионального образования играет финансирование. Необходимо привлекать больше инвестиций, а не рассчитывать на государство или платных студентов.

Проекты международных организаций не только предоставляют необходимые финансовые ресурсы, но также привлекают международный опыт и меры по реформированию для улучшения среды развития.

Известно, что в последнее время сотрудничество между Республикой Таджикистан и Китайской Народной Республикой поднялся на новый уровень, и на территории Согдийской области начали функционировать десятки предприятий с участием китайских компаний. Уже функционируют такие предприятия, как: Таджикско-Китайская горно-промышленная компания в Зарнисоре; Китайско-Таджикская промышленная зона и металлургический завод в городе Истиклоле; золотодобывающая компания «Заравшон»; крупное предприятие по выпуску строительных материалов «Хуаксин-Гаюр цемент» и многое другое.

В связи с этим, возникла идея открытия института по изучению китайского языка и культуры на базе Горно-металлургического института Таджикистан и этот вопрос был инициирован со стороны Правительства Республики Таджикистан, который являлся не случайным решением, а велением времени. Потому что дружеские отношения и взаимовыгодное сотрудничество между РТ и КНР с каждым годом развивается по всем направлениям, в том числе по вопросам науки и образования. Соглашение о создании Института Конфуций при ГМИТ с Штаб-квартирой институтов Конфуция было подписано в сентябре 2014 года в г. Душанбе во время встреч глав государств-участников ШОС.

Для обеспечения поддержания и дальнейшего развития взаимодействий с промышленными предприятиями региона, ГМИТ и ИК при ГМИТ с помощью структурных подразделений будет создавать условия для обмена знаниями, навыками, опытом информаций. Подготовка будущих кадров для горно-металлургической отрасли а также обучение китайскому языку в ИК при ГМИТ будет удовлетворять потребности в высококвалифицированных кадрах промышленных предприятий региона. Создание совместных лабораторий, содействие предприятий в организации стажировок для преподавательского состава института также будет приоритетным направлением для сотрудничества.

Президент Таджикистана Эмомали Рахмон в своем послании к парламенту выразил обеспокоенность тем, что в республике не хватает высококвалифицированных специалистов, изобретателей, ученых во всех областях. Президент заявил, что ответственные лица и соответствующие структуры должны усилить контроль над самопознанием подростков и молодежи, пробудить в них интерес к чтению художественной и научной литературы, уделив при этом больше внимания преподаванию естественных наук и математики. В связи с этим президент предложил объявить 2020–2040 годы-Годами образования и развития естественных и математических наук. Таким образом, образование выступает одним из основных инструментов повышения конкурентоспособности как страны в целом, так и каждого человека в отдельности.

Для повышения уровня образования, Правительство страны и профильные министерства должны принять конкретные меры, а именно, в разы поднять заработную плату педагогических кадров с целью улучшения найма и удержания талантливых кадров в их профессии, улучшить систему подготовки педагогов, улучшить систему оценки знаний учащихся. Профессиональные направления разделены на 96 рабочих специальностей. В дополнение к обычным дипломным курсам, почти полностью финансируемые государством, большинство лицеев предлагают краткосрочные курсы на платной основе. Краткосрочные курсы в первую очередь привлекают таких лиц, как возвращающиеся трудовые мигранты, которым требуется сертификат, подтверждающий их практические навыки.

Существует три типа высших учебных заведений: университеты, академии и институты. В настоящее время университеты и академии предлагают степени бакалавра, магистра и специалиста, тогда как институты предлагают только степени бакалавра и специалиста. В Таджикистане функционирует 39 высших учебных заведений, в том числе частный Таджикский государственный педагогический институт в Пенджикенте и Университет Центральной Азии. В состав вузов входят 15 университетов и 16 институтов с 7 филиалами, а также Национальная консерватория.

Таким образом, профессионального образования способствует справедливому, всеобъемлющему и устойчивому экономическому росту и поддерживает переход к экономике зеленого и цифрового масштаба.

# （四）

# 科技与教学法支持的协作科学论证

新加坡南洋理工大学教授　陈文莉

近年来，在科学教育理论与实践中有一个明显的转变趋势——从专注于探索与实验转向注重科学论证、解释与推理。文献告诉我们，科学论证与解释推理有助于学习者对相关科学理念的理解，更好地理解科学的本质，更深入地学习科学内容，并且进行知识建构。协作论证可以使科学论证进行得更为深入，一方面是学习者可以更好地从不同角度探究科学知识，另一方面也有助于培养学习者的 21 世纪技能。有效的协作科学论证并不是自然而然发生的，需要在科技与教学法方面进行设计与支持。第三个方面是论证协作，目前，我们的研究团队开发了一个叫作 AppleTree（苹果树）的系统支持学习者的协作科学论证。这个系统采用图形化论证的方式，确保学习者可以更多地关注论证的大框架，而不是在细枝末节上进行过于深入的论证。在图形化论证方面，一个椭圆形就是一个论点或者一个假设；长方形是与这个论点或假设有关的论据，每个连接论点与论据的箭头的颜色也表示一定的功能，绿色的箭头表示支持这个论点的论据，红色的箭头是反对这个论点的论据。我们是通过图形化论证确保每一位学习者心中都有论证的大的结构。

在支持协作方面，系统里嵌入了协作知识建构的逻辑模型，这个模型确保学习者在进行协作的时候，不是为协作而协作，而是确保观点观念和科学知识都有一定的提升。一开始，学习者先进行个人知识建构；第二个阶段，在小组内部进行讨论，然后集思广益，生成一个小组论证成果；然后，学习者去其他小组学习，在同伴互评方面，学习者可以方便地对其他小组整体论证成果进行评价，也可以选取论证的某一环节进行互评；下一个阶段，学习者基于其他小组的评价和他们在其他小组学到的知识，进一步精进小组论证结果，这就是相得益彰阶段；最后，又回到个人精益求精阶段，每个学习者内化在协作知识建构中学到的知识，实现个人知识和探究能力的提升。

除此之外，这个系统支持实时学习分析与评测。我们基于文献和教学需求，设计出了一个评测模型框架，这是要实现为学习而进行的测评，而不是给学习进行测评，因此我们计划在社会协作和认知学习上面实现自动测评。

在社会协作方面，主要关注学习者的参与贡献及互动协作。在认知学习方面，我们通过学习分析技术来对论证结构的完整度进行自动测评，然后使用可视化的方法把测评结果实时呈现给教师和学习者。例如，在学习者贡献度方面，我们通过柱状图呈现这个小组是比较倾向于给论点还是给论据以及它的贡献度有多大。我们也通过社会网络分析来确定这个小组在互动上是否平衡与和谐，分析学习者是基于别人的想法共同建构知识与进行科学探究论证，还是更倾向于自己做自己的。

在论证结构的完整度上面，我们通过苹果的颜色来呈现。如果它只有一个论点，而没有论据，系统页面上会出现一个绿苹果（有点酸）；如果学习者加入了一个支持这个论点的论据，那么苹果会变成红色的（甜度增加）；如果学习者再加入一个反对的论据，苹果颜色会变成黄色的（更甜）。随着他加入了更多不同的角度来分析这一段科学现象，那么它会变成一个金苹果（最甜最好的）。

我们在新加坡的科学课堂进行了大量实证研究，结果发现，学习者在科学内容知识的提升以及论证技能的提升方面都有非常大的进步。从一开始的学习者有一些比较零散的想法，通过协作知识建构，小组内各种各样的知识与想法渐渐整合，到最后变成一个系统的论证，所以通过协作论证可以实现非常大的提升。那么在21世纪技能的培养方面，我们发现学习者对知识建构的参与度与投入度越高，也就更有助于培养他们的协作与沟通技能和告诫批判性思维。

# （五）

# 打造技术创新服务平台　助力区域经济高质量发展

天津大学教育质量管理处副处长　潘海生

《中华人民共和国国民经济和社会发展第十四个五年规划和 2035 年远景目标纲要》提出，“坚持创新在我国现代化建设全局中的核心地位”“深入实施科教兴国战略、人才强国战略、创新驱动发展战略”，强调了技术创新在经济高质量发展中的重要作用。习近平总书记指出，职业教育前途广阔、大有可为。要不断增强其适应性，适应性不仅体现在适配的技术技能人才培养，更应通过技术技能人才与技术创新有机互动的技术技能积累能力演化提升科创人才培养质量，成为有效促进区域经济高质量发展的必然需要。

### 1. 技术创新形塑高职教育新内涵

随着新一轮产业革命与技术变革的纵深发展，以“云物大智”为代表的新型技术在发展速度、作用范围、影响程度等方面远超过去，深刻改变着工作世界样貌。一是工作种类和数量的变化。麦肯锡全球研究院的一份数据显示，未来 5% 的职业将被机器完全取代，49% 的工作内容面临被机器取代的风险。二是工作任务和过程的变化。新技术发展导致工作边界逐渐模糊，使工作过程柔性化、工作任务多样化。然而，这种变化对技术技能人才提出了更高要求。由于工作知识深度和强度不断增强，技术技能人才工作模式逐渐向工作过程去分工化、人才结构去分层化、技能操作高端化、工作方式研究化及服务与生产一体化转变，进而使他们的能力从面向工作任务转向面向工作过程乃至工作对象，对其能力结构要求呈现出实践技能与理论知识并重的发展趋势。

面对工作世界的变化，职业教育应当注重学生跨知识、跨岗位、跨能力、跨职业的复合发展能力及理实结合的融合能力培养，塑就其更加深厚的知识体系和更加综合的技术技能。2019 年，《教育部 财政部关于实施中国特色高水平高职学校和专业建设计划的意见》提出建设技术技能创新服务平台。2021 年，《关于推动现代职业教育高质量发展的意见》着重强调了校企应开展双边或多边的技术服务。可见，除人才培养外，技术创新服务已然成为高职院校另一项重要职能。同时，教育科学化是未来教育发展的主要方向，职业教育不能仅停留于技术教育，更应培养学生的逻辑思维能力和演绎推理能力，帮助学生独立思考职业教育的基本理论，形成科学的逻辑体系。基于此，增强高职院校技术技能积累能力成为提升技术技能人才培养质量的关键。

**2. 技术创新能力提升是高职教育高质量发展的必然要求**

所谓高职教育技术技能积累能力实质上是其技术技能人才培养和技术创新服务相互作用的结果，这一作用过程将有效提升学生的技术技能与技术创新能力。技术创新能力提升是高职教育技术技能积累能力形成的关键所在。与普通高校“顶天”研究相比，高职院校因其自身科研能力、团队建设以及科技成果转化不足而导致技术创新能力匮乏，需借助平台优势，深化产教融合、校企合作，整合科技研发资源，服务中小企业技术集成以提升技术创新能力，促进技术技能积累能力演进。

技术创新平台是技术创新能力提升的重要载体。相比普通高校的理论创新而言，高职院校的技术创新服务更接地气、更重实效，立足区域经济需求，以新标准、新工艺、新技术解决生产线上难题，以“立地式”研发引领区域产业、行业发展。高职院校应发挥其与企业联系的优势，以院校的工程技术中心、产品工艺开发中心与成果转化中心为载体，以项目为基础整合行业企业技术专家、科研人员、教师和学生等技术研发资源，深度参与企业技术开发与革新，主动服务于企业工艺改造和管理水平提升，主动提升自身的技术研发和实践能力，并通过反哺教学，加强学生科学素养和培养学生问题解决能力，推动高职院校基本能力建设和专业建设，引领高职教育高质量发展。

产教深度融合是技术创新能力提升的重要保障。技术创新服务平台通过联结行业企业技术创新活动，以共享机制为核心，搭建“产学研创赛”多组织合作创新网络，推动高职院校教研团队专业化发展并促进特定领域技术技能知识积累，支撑企业技术创新与区域产业发展。因此借助技术创新平台能够深化产教融合、校企合作，打破高职院校传统上单一薄弱的技术服务能力和点对点式的产教融合、校企合作，完善和健全高职院校技术协同创新机制，提供系统的、复杂的、持续的技术服务，有效融入区域创新体系，使高职教育成为区域创新体系的黏合剂和催化剂，促进其技术技能积累能力的加速形成。

由此可见，高职院校技术技能积累能力的形成已不仅仅是企业领域向职业教育领域单向技术转移的过程。伴随着高职院校技术创新能力的提升，技术创新服务平台成为技术技能积累的重要来源，最终反哺为高职院校自身的技术技能人才培养能力。

**3. 推动高职院校技术创新服务能力提升策略**

实际上，技术创新服务平台是以高质量发展为目的的一系列共有性结构与制度安排，从资源汇集、机制完善和核心能力建设等方面系统推进平台建设，有助于促进高职院校技术技能积累能力的形成，实现科学教育与技术教育的有机融合。

（1）立足区域创新发展，统筹建设技术创新服务平台。首先，政府应将平台建设纳入区域产业创新发展规划，完善制度政策体系，推进技术创新服务平台将教育链、人才链与产业链、创新链深入融合。其次，要立足区域发展实际与地方资源特色，统筹协调技术创新服务平台建设与发展工作，科学规划其布局与发展模式，形成分工明确、科学的平台体系。最后，各级政府应将其建设融入区域创新体系中，使其成为区域创新体系的重要组成部分，着力培养学生求实、创新、严谨的科学精神和科学发现的方法。在温州，依托温州轻工机械创新技术服务平台、温州服装产业技术创新服务平台、浙南轻工装备智能技术协同创新中心与温州市中小企业公共服务平台，聚焦轻工装备数字化虚拟化设计开发、关键零部件制造新工艺开发与应用、轻工装备控制系统集成技术三大主攻技术研发方向，整合多方技术创新与服务资源，以“立地式”研发推动温州产业转型与升级。

（2）建立实体化运作机制，推动技术创新服务平台良性运作。技术创新服务平台建设的关键在于解决运行问题。一套健全的运行机制不仅有助于维系合作共同体内部结构稳定，更能促进技术创新服务平台科学健康发展。其一要建立以质量为主的评价机制，真实反映技术创新服务平台整体运行情况。其二要建立共建共享的利益联合机制，通过实质性整合、混合制投入、实体化运营，建立企业运行制度，明确政、行、企等主体参与技术创新服务平台建设的职责。其三要建立创新激励机制，对深度参与合作并在提升人才培养与技术创新服务方面有显著成就的合作共同体，探索新型人才培养与技术创新模式，激发各主体创新活力，培育科学价值观和科学精神。例如，重庆电子工程职业学院建立“双循环三融合”治理模式，从科技创新供给与需求两个端口、内外部环境两个维度出发，坚持“全局、全域、全要素”的“大科研”定位，将机构—制度—文化、“政行企校”、平台—项目—成果有机结合。

（3）聚焦核心能力提升，促进技术创新服务平台提质增效。技术创新服务平台建立的目的在于促进新技术、新工艺、新规范向教育教学转化，确保教师所教与学生所学贴近生产实际，提升高职院校服务产业转型升级能力，培养学生适应工作场景变化的创新能力与可持续发展能力。首先，应统筹企业运作与人才培养，将企业真实岗位能力需求转化为人才培养目标，将企业的生产任务转化为教学内容载体。其次，应建立以创新为抓手、项目为手段、团队为载体、转化应用为目的的技术创新体系，挖掘转化前沿技术知识，融入科学教育与人文教育，将产业科技资源转化为教学资源。例如，深圳职业技术学院人工智能学院计算机基础教学部团队坚持以人工智能应用为核心，注重学生综合职业能力培养，融通专业和职业岗位需求，形成了“以人工智能应用为核心”的课程标准、教材体系和课程体系。

# 十四
# 职业院校工程教育发展论坛

协助组织单位：中国工程院二局　上海工程技术大学

# XIN. Engineering Education Development in Vocational Education Institutions

Co-organizers: Bureau II of Chinese Academy of Engineering, Shanghai University of Engineering Science, China

02
金子元久
Kaneko Motohisa

03
尤哈·豪塔宁
Juha Hautanen

04
丁荣军
Ding Rongjun

05
孙建安
Sun Jian'an

06
陈吉红
Chen Jihong

07
谢永华
Xie Yonghua

08
陈晓明
Chen Xiaoming

09
吴新林
Wu Xinlin

10
徐国胜
Xu Guosheng

11
尹万建
Yin Wanjian

12
刘永亮
Liu Yongliang

13
耿洁
Geng Jie

14
龚方红
Gong Fanghong

**审视职业教育中工程教育发展现状与挑战，分享和交流国内外前沿动态与经验。围绕职业院校大国工匠、能工巧匠和高技能人才培养目标，探讨职业院校学生应用能力、实践能力和创新能力发展路径，推动职业教育改革，提升人才培养质量，为社会经济发展提供人才保障。**

This session discusses the current situation of and the challenges for engineering education development in vocational education institutions and shares the latest development and experience in this area across the world. In accordance with the objective of vocational education which is to provide society with consummate craftsmen and skilled professionals, the participants explore the pathways of developing students' ability to apply and practice what they have learned and to innovate. The aim is to foster vocational education reform, to improve the quality of vocational training, and to ensure the adequate supply of skilled professionals for economic and social development.

## （一）

## 职业院校工程教育发展论坛情况概述

上海工程技术大学工程教育发展研究中心高级工程师　王　迪

职业院校工程教育发展论坛由中国工程院二局、上海工程技术大学协助组织，天津职业技术师范大学承办。论坛的成功召开吸引了中外职业教育和工程教育领域的研究者、政策制定者和院校实践者的广泛关注，扩大了业界对职业院校中的工程教育的影响力和关注度，带来了国内外专家多元思想的碰撞和交流，同时也宣传了中国职业教育和工程教育两大教育体系的发展成就、对国家经济发展做出的重大贡献。论坛嘉宾的真知灼见也点出了若干职业教育发展过程中的不足及问题。

1. 论坛背景

2022年3月16日，怀进鹏部长在教育部与中国工程院的会商会上指出："职业学校是开展工程教育的重要阵地。工程教育要培养一大批的工程师、技术人员和大国工匠，这就需要工程教育与职业教育更好的结合"，并确定了本论坛的主题"职业院校工程教育发展"。职业院校中的工程教育，一般意义上指代工科类职业教育，重视工科类职业教育有两方面的背景：一是职业教育人才培养与制造强国战略紧密相关，肩负着培养产业人才、传承技术技能的重要使命，是支撑和实现制造强国战略的重要力量。我国是全世界唯一拥有联合国产业分类中所列全部工业门类的国家，但从推动高质量发展、构建新发展格局的需求来看，我国技术技能人才总量和质量仍然不足，技能劳动者占就业人口总量的比重仅为26%，高技能人才仅占技能人才总量的28%；中华人民共和国人力资源和社会保障部发布的2021年第四季度全国招聘大于求职"最缺工"的100个职业排行中，近一半属于生产制造及有关人员。培养复合型技术技能人才是现代职业教育的紧迫任务和严峻挑战，高等工程教育在培养学生的创新意识和发现问题的能力、加强跨学科知识的学习和创新人才培养模式上拥有深厚的经验，可以为职业教育在技术技能型人才的培养和发展上提供借鉴。二是高等工程教育和职业教育两大教育体系应互相借鉴。我国建成了世界上最大规模的高等工程教育体系，也已形成了世界上规模最大的职业教育体系，工程教育和职业教育均是国民教育体系和人力资源开发的重要组成部分，为国民经济发展发挥了重要的推动作用，为可持续发展打下了坚实的基础。为更好地服务区域经济高质量发展，新时代职业教育与工程教育一样，必须自觉围绕产业人才需要而"转"、随着经济增长方式转变而"动"、适应社会和市场需求而"变"、跟着产业结构调整升级而"走"。从人力资本产出类型看，教育部印发的《职业教育专业目录（2021年版）》中，其97个专业大类全面覆盖了联合国三次产业分类中所列全部41个工业大类，工程教育与职业教育两者培养的工程科技人才、工程应用人才、技术技能人才、产业工人等共同组成和丰富了我国社会经济发展所需要的人力资源立体结构，高等工程教育高质量发展与重塑现代化职业教育体系的过程可以互相借鉴、协同发展。

2. 组织情况

中国高等工程教育研究会副秘书长、联合国教科文组织国际工程教育中心副主任、清华大学教授王孙禺认为，工程教育注重在“研发、设计、小样、生产制造、市场、售后服务和回收（工程退役）”等全工程链上所有要素的教育过程，注重“理论与实践”的结合，与职业教育相比，后者更贴近实践和技艺传承，两者都依托技术来实现目标和推进发展。从现实层面来看，工程教育更多的是面向研发和生产过程的工程设计与技术革新，而职业教育则更偏向于生产过程中技术应用与技能、工法的改进，因此高等工程教育与工科类职业教育应互相借鉴、协同发展。王孙禺邀请了日本国立筑波大学教授金子元久、德国施特拉尔松德孔子学院院长孙建安、芬兰于韦斯屈莱应用科技大学专业教师教育学院院长尤哈·豪塔宁等资深专家。国内方面则邀请了中国工程院院士、浙江大学教授谭建荣，中国工程院院士、中国中车首席科学家丁荣军与会。中华人民共和国教育部职业教育与成人教育司邀请了 4 位来自职业院校的校长，分别是无锡职业技术学院院长龚方红、南京工业职业技术大学校长谢永华、湖南汽车工程职业学院院长尹万建、陕西工业职业技术学院院长刘永亮。来自产业界的武汉华中数控股份有限公司董事长陈吉红与会。演讲嘉宾还包括了天津市教育科学研究院专家及来自中国机械工业联合会的行业组织代表。来自企业行业组织、职业院校和研究机构等不同领域的十余位知名学者线上线下、济济一堂，作了主旨发言和专题研讨，通过审视职业教育中工程教育发展现状与挑战，分享和交流了国内外前沿动态与经验，同时围绕职业院校大国工匠、能工巧匠和高技能人才培养目标，探讨职业院校学生应用能力、实践能力和创新能力发展路径。天津市人民政府副市长朱鹏致辞。

3. 发言概要及结论

论坛主要分为主旨发言和专题研讨两部分。在主旨发言阶段，谭建荣以“建设一流工程学科，培养一流技术人才”为题，论述了职业教育人才培养对我国经济和社会发展的重要性，结合浙江大学工程学科建设和工程技术人才培养提出自己的见解。他同时指出，在人才培养工作中，应认清科学、工程和技术的异同，三者既有密切联系又有本质区别，工程教育并不是单纯的科学应用或技术应用教育，也不是相关技术的简单堆砌和剪贴拼凑，而是科学要素、技术要素、经济要素、管理要素、社会要素、文化要素、制度要素、环境要素等多要素的集成、选择和优化。金子元久从大学改革视角出发，思考工程教育的基本特征，探讨了工程教育的基本问题。他提出随着社会职业的多样化，学习阶段的专业知识和技能培训非常容易过时，这带来教育与产业匹配的不稳定性、复杂性和不明确性，因此特别强调在信息社会中教育的即时改变之重要，这不仅在通识教育，专业教育的变化和变通也尤为重要。同时，他也强调了理论与实践的关系，这是工程教育和职业教育的灵魂所在，以日本经验为例，他认为大学教育改革传统以政府为中心的模式并不怎么成功，应建立以教育学习为基础的改革，这需要教师和学生的共同参与。他也呼应了谭建荣院士对工程、科学与技术关系的论述。丁荣军以高铁工匠培养为例，分享了如何打造具有全球竞争力的高技能人才培养基地，强调了“理论—实践—理论—实践”的螺旋上升关系，认为在本质上工科类职业教育与高等工程教育并没有特别显著的区别。孙建安介绍了德国双元制高等教育的相关情况，强调德国社会产业与教育紧密结合的传统是其制造业成功发展的秘诀之一，高等教育机构和实践伙伴将科学理论知识与实际专业职业技能结合起来，使学生和毕业生达到特别职业技术技能的要求，即将职业教育和高等教育结合起来（职业教育嵌入高等教育的双元制教育专业中），将较长的实践阶段和高等教育结合起来（实践教育嵌入高等教育的双元制教育专业中）。陈吉红向与会者分享了智能制造人才培养与实训教学创新的前沿研究。尤哈·豪塔宁则重点关注教师发展和评价领域，提出工程职业教育教师在持续学习中的问题和挑战。

在专题研讨阶段，与会嘉宾代表就职业技术技能人才培养模式、职业院校工程教育要素、产教融合、工程实践创新等主题进行了深入交流和经验共享。职业院校的校长们认为，高等工程教育与工科类职业教育协同发展有充分的必要性，两大教育体系基于工程和技术各自的特点，应取长补短、协同一致地完成培养高质量社会主义劳动者的目标。

### 4. 问题与挑战

总体上，通过举办本论坛，国内外与会院士、专家和学者分享了智慧，凝聚了共识，论坛的成功召开对于深入借鉴国内外职业技术教育先进经验、建立职业教育国际交流合作的有效机制和途径、构建中国特色现代职业教育体系、培育高素质技术技能人才、推进经济社会高质量发展具有重要意义。但也凸显了工作中的一些问题，一是部分国外学者没有进行工程教育和职业教育的分野，认为各种教育类型都是职业导向的，并基于职业属性来探寻问题、分析问题和解决问题，由于历史原因，我国不少名词和术语内涵范畴界定尚不明确，尚未形成共识。二是在现实层面，对职业教育歧视性的认知与当下全力推进职业教育的氛围不相称，一些偏见难以消除，本次论坛体现出的“职热本冷”现象较为突出，普通本科院校参与率有待提升，关于职业本科与应用型本科区别的探讨有待加强和深化，科学教育、工程教育与职业教育之思辨等主题需要更多专家、学者关注。三是职业院校对工科类职业教育的认知有待提升，部分专家仍停留在微观工作和实践操作层面，国家宏观政策与中、微观工作需进一步匹配贯通，以期推动核心问题的解决，提出符合未来教育发展、符合产业需求的、有突破性创新的中国方案和真切实践。以上三个问题值得深思，也是未来工作的主要挑战。

# i. Overview of the Session on Engineering Education Development in Vocational Education Institutions

**Wang Di, Senior Engineer of Engineering Education Development Research Center of Shanghai University of Engineering Science, China**

The parallel session on Engineering Education Development in Vocational Education Institutions was co-organized by Bureau II of Chinese Academy of Engineering and Shanghai University of Engineering Science, China. The even was undertaken by Tianjin University of Technology and Education. The success of the session has gained attention of researchers, policy makers, and institutional practitioners in vocational education and engineering education in China and abroad and has expanded the influence and awareness of engineering education in vocational education institutions. It also brought about the exchange of diversified ideas among domestic and foreign experts and demonstrated the achievements of China's vocational education and engineering education as well as their significant contribution to the national economic development. The speakers also pointed out some deficiencies and problems in the development of vocational education. The session is summarized hereafter in four parts: its background, its organization, a review of the speeches and conclusion, and problems and challenges.

## 1. Background of the Session

At a meeting held on March 16, 2022 between the Chinese Ministry of Education and the Chinese Academy of Engineering, Minister Huai Jinpeng pointed out that "vocational education institutions are important venues for implementing engineering education. Engineering education aims at providing society with a large number of engineers, technicians, and craftsmen, which requires a better integration of engineering education and vocational education." The meeting set the theme of this session as Engineering Education Development in Vocational Education Institutions. Engineering education in vocational education institutions refers to vocation-oriented engineering education. The reasons for attaching importance to vocation-oriented engineering education are twofold. First, the vocational education is closely related to the strategy of building China into a country with strong manufacturing power. Vocational education serves the important mission of training industrial specialist and imparting techniques and skills and is an important force to support the implementation of the aforementioned strategy. China is the only country in the world that has all the industrial categories listed in the *UN's International Standard Industrial Classification of All Economic Activities*. However, from the perspective of promoting high-quality development and forming a new development pattern, the total number and quality of technical and skilled workers in China are still insufficient: the proportion of skilled workers to the total employed population is only 26%, while highly skilled workers only account for 28% of the skilled workers; the Ministry of Human Resources and Social Security of the People's Republic of China released a ranking of the top 100 occupations with the biggest openings-to-candidates ratio in the fourth quarter of 2021 in which nearly half of the occupations were manufacturing-related. Providing skilled high-quality technical workers is an urgent task and a big challenge for today's vocational education. Higher engineering education institutions have profound experience in raising students' innovative awareness, developing their ability to identify problems, strengthening their study of interdisciplinary knowledge, and innovating talent training models. They can be a reference for vocational education institutions in terms of the training of technical and skilled workers. Second, higher engineering education and vocational education should draw experience from each other. China has the largest higher engineering education system and the largest vocational education system in the world. Both of them are important components of the national education system and human resource development. They have played an important role in promoting the development of the nation's economy and laid a solid foundation for sustainable development. In order to better serve the high-quality development of regional economy, vocational education in the new era must, like engineering education, actively meet the changing requirements for industrial talents, follow the transformation of economic growth mode, adapt to social and market demand, and catch up with the adjustment and upgrading of the industrial structure. From the viewpoint of human capital output types, the *Occupation Catalogue of Vocational Education (2021)* issued by the Ministry of Education includes 97 occupation categories which fully cover all of the UN's 41 industrial categories. The engineering researchers, applied engineering specialists, skilled technical workers, and industrial workers trained by engineering education institutions and vocational education institutions form the multi-leveled human resource structure supporting China's socio-economic development. The high-quality development of higher engineering education and the reshaping of modern vocational education system can provide experience for each other and progress synergistically.

2. Organization of the Session

According to Wang Sunyu, Deputy Secretary General of China Higher Engineering Education Research Association, Deputy Director of UNESCO International Centre for Engineering Education, and Professor of Tsinghua University, engineering education focuses on all the elements in the whole engineering chain, i.e. R&D, designing, prototyping, manufacturing, marketing, after-sales service, and recycling, and on connecting theory to practice, while vocational education stresses hands-on practices and the impartment of skills, both of which rely on technical means to achieve goals and to develop. On practice level, engineering education focuses more on engineering design and technical innovation in R&D and production, while vocational education focuses more on the improvement of technology application and the skills and techniques in the production process. Therefore, higher engineering education and vocational engineering education should seek mutual enrichment and collaborative development. Experts from outside China invited by Wang Sunyu to attend the session included Kaneko Motohisa, Professor of Tsukuba University, Japan, Sun Jian'an, Director of Confucius Institute at Stralsund University of Applied Sciences, Germany and Juha Hautanen, Head of Department at the School of Professional Teacher Education, JAMK University of Applied Sciences, Finland. Domestic experts invited by Mr. Wang included Tan Jianrong, Academician of the Chinese Academy of Engineering and Professor of Zhejiang University, China, Ding Rongjun, Academician of the Chinese Academy of Engineering and Chief Scientist of CRRC Corporation Limited, China. The Department of Vocational and Adult Education of the Ministry of Education, P.R. China invited four senior officials from Chinese vocational schools (Gong Fanghong, President of Wuxi Institute of Technology, Xie Yonghua, President of Nanjing Vocational University of Industry Technology, Yin Wanjian, President of Hunan Automotive Engineering Vocational College, and Liu Yongliang, President of Shaanxi Polytechnic Institute). Chen Jihong, Chairman of Wuhan Huazhong Numerical Control Co., Ltd., China attended the Session as a representative of the corporate sector. Other speakers included experts from Tianjin Academy of Educational Science and China Machinery Industry Federation. Thus, more than ten well-known Chinese and foreign scholars from the Chinese Academy of Engineering, the corporate sector, industry organizations, vocational schools, and research institutions delivered keynote speeches and conducted thematic discussions either in-person or via virtual means. They shared most current practices and experience in the world by examining the status and challenges in the development of engineering education in vocational education and discussed the pathways of developing vocational school student's ability to apply and practice what they have learned and to innovate in accordance with the objective of vocational education which is to provide society with consummate craftsmen, skilled professionals, and highly skilled workers. Zhu Peng, Vice Mayor of Tianjin Municipal People's Government, delivered welcome remarks to the Session.

### 3. Review of the Speeches and Conclusion

The Session consists of two parts: the keynote speeches and the thematic discussion.

The first keynote speaker, Tan Jianrong discussed the importance of vocational education to China's economic and social development, and put forward his insights based on the development of engineering disciplines and the training of engineering and technical specialists at Zhejiang University. He also pointed out that we should distinguish science, engineering, and technology in the process of training. The three are closely related yet essentially different. Engineering is not as simple as applying scientific knowledge and technologies or as creating a college of related technologies. It is about the integration, selection and optimization of scientific elements, technical elements, economic elements, management elements, social elements, cultural elements, institutional elements, environmental elements, etc. Kaneko Motohisa examined the basic characteristics of engineering education from the perspective of university reform and discussed the basic issues in engineering education. He stated that with the diversification of occupations in society, professional knowledge and skills acquired in the learning stage are easily outdated, which brings instability, complexity, and uncertainty to the alignment of education and industry. Therefore, he emphasized that, in the information society, prompt changes and adaptations are important not only to the general education, but also to vocational education. He also emphasized the relationship between theory and practice, which he considered the core of engineering and vocational education. Based on Japan's experience, he argued that the traditional government-led university education reform has not been very successful, and that a reform based on teaching and learning should be established, which requires the joint effort of teachers and students. He also echoed Tan Jianrong's explanation of the relationship between engineering, science, and technology. Taking the training of high-speed railway technicians as an example, Ding Rongjun shared his thoughts about how to build a globally competitive entity for training highly-skilled workers. He emphasized that theoretical researches and applicational practices are mutually reinforcing activities and argued that, in essence, there is no significant difference between vocational engineering education and higher engineering education. Sun Jian'an introduced the Dual Higher Education (DHE) system implemented in Germany and emphasized that the close link between industry and education has been one of the key factors behind the success of the country's manufacturing industry. Higher education institutions and their corporate partners work together to impart theoretical knowledge as well as practical vocational skills, enabling students to meet specific vocational and technical skill requirements. The system combines vocational education and higher education and integrates the long period of internship into the process of higher education. Chen Jihong shared with the attendants some leading researches on the training of smart manufacturing specialists and innovating practical training modes. Juha Hautanen focused on teacher education and evaluation and talked about the challenges faced by vocational engineering education teachers as to continuous learning.

During the discussion, the representatives of the guests exchanged ideas and shared their experience on topics such as the training mode of vocational and technical students, the key components of engineering education in vocational schools, the integration of industry and education, and innovations in engineering practice. The presidents of the vocational schools agreed that the coordinated development of higher engineering education and vocational engineering education is necessary. The two education systems should draw experience from each other, so that they can fulfill the goal of providing high-quality workers to society in a synergistic and consistent manner.

### 4. Problems and Challenges

In general, by holding this Session, the experts and scholars in and outside China shared their thinking and developed consensus. The Session is of great significance for learning from the successful practices in the field of vocational and technical education at home and abroad, establishing a mechanism for the international cooperation of vocational education, building a modern vocational education system suitable for China, training high-quality skilled technical workers, and promoting high-quality economic and social development. The Session also helped us identify some issues. Firstly, some of the foreign scholars make no distinction between engineering education and vocational education. They regard all types of education as occupation-oriented, and tend to explore, analyze and solve problems based on occupational attributes. Due to historical reasons, many terms and wordings used by Chinese scholars and practitioners are in need of definition, and it is difficult to reach a consensus about them yet. Secondly, the general bias against vocational education is incompatible with the current policy of vigorously promoting vocational education, and some prejudices are rather difficult to overcome. The number of non-vocational higher education institutions participating in this session was less than expected. Therefore, the discussion on topics such as the differentiation between vocational undergraduate education and applied undergraduate education and the relationship among science education, engineering education, and vocational education still needs to be conducted more broadly and more thoroughly. Thirdly, vocational schools must establish a comprehensive view of vocational engineering education. Some experts focus primarily on issues at the operational level. National policies and the practice at lower levels need to be effectively integrated so that the core issues can be addressed. In this way, we can deliver innovative solutions and exemplary practices which are suitable for China and are able to meet the future demand of education and industry. The above issues constitute the main challenge for our future endeavor and deserve our serious reflection.

## (二)

# 工程教育的基本问题

日本国立筑波大学教授　金子元久

本次演讲的主要内容是以大学教育改革的视角，梳理工程教育的根本问题。在梳理工程教育的特点之前，我想先对大学教育的方法和工程教育的历史背景加以说明。

首先，我想对工程教育特点的梳理方法进行分析。大学的教育方法基本上是讲课，讲解基本知识和理论及如何掌握这些知识。然后是实验和实训，将通过实验、测量习得的知识加以理论化，并在理解的基础上掌握。此外，还有参与实验室的研究项目，执行指定的研究任务以及教师的指导和学生之间的合作。

从历史上看，工程教育最初是在综合性大学中进行的，特别是 19 世纪德国大学在化学实验室进行的教育。还有一种是理工专科学校的专业工程教育。可以说，现代工程教育继承了这两种趋势。

相较于大学教育，工程教育具有 3 个特点。首先，在授课方面有专业领域的对应关系。另外，一般来说，中国和日本大学的课程都非常多，实验和实训需要大量的时间。在许多情况下，学生被分到实验室进行培训，在研究内容细分之后，导师会给他们提供研究课题，然后让学生研究特定的课题，从而掌握工程教育思维方式及任务的推进方式。此外，也有通过让教师和学生组成小组，来激发学习热情的方式。这一点应该是中日共通的。

由此也会产生一些问题，其中之一便是专业领域过于多样化。在学生们还不了解究竟该如何学习的时候，就让他们学习过于细分的内容。课程的数量随着学科的发展不断增加，因此也产生了学生无法完全吸收课堂内容的问题。再者，在实验室教育中，学生作为教师研究的辅助人员，得到的课题都是经过高度专业化细分之后的产物，虽然也可以成为学生的经验，但也会让学生不知应该如何获取知识。

另一方面，学生正在发生重大变化。一个主要问题是被录取的学生的基础知识水平不一定高，尤其缺少自然科学科目的基础知识，特别是缺乏关于数学等学科的基本知识。由于智能手机和电脑游戏的影响，学生冷静思考的习惯正在逐渐消失。同时，产业结构的多样化增加了就业的机会，但另一方面，这也使得学生更难以具体思考自己的未来，我认为这也是一个重要的事实。

整个社会也在发生着变化。首先，职业正变得更加多样化且更具有流动性。一方面，这意味着社会在进步，但另一方面，专业知识和技能有一种强烈的易过时趋势。因此大学之间很容易在系统的专业知识和职业需求方面出现分歧。目前虽然比较稳定，但是潜在的不稳定因素也在增加，社会局势不稳定、不确定、复杂且不清晰。此外，信息化社会导致个人信息被社会获取及强化，因此个人独立思考变得越来越困难。个人难以独立思考、建立社会观和价值观。正因如此，个人独立思考反而变得更加重要。在大学教育中，无论是哪个专业，都要注重培养学生独立自主的思维方式。为了培养这一点，所谓的通识和素质教育很重要，但同时，专业教育也很重要，也有越来越多的学校重视在专业教育中培养学生独立自主的思考习惯。

那么，工程教育面临什么样的课题呢？从根本上说，自然是要获得基本的工程基础知识和能力，这是一般能力和专业技能。除了听说读写能力以外，学习这样的思维方式也是必要的，不仅是作为知识进行了解，而是需要让学生将之转化为自己的东西。为此需要激发学生对学习的动力。所以如何整理课题，如何引导学生学习是一个很重要的问题。另外，我们有必要建立一个系统来评估学习效果，并将其与学习动机联系起来。 至于实现这一目标还需要做哪些事情，这需要我们重新审视教育方法。

我认为我们既要重新审视授课方法，也要重新审视研究室活动，特别是有必要对授课的性质进行反思。随着知识的进步，越来越多的专业内容被加入课程。教授所有必要的知识会变得越来越困难。我们应当立志于传授基本的专业技能，而不是以教授一切为目标。这就意味着，我们更应该注重学生对作为专业基础的思考方式和知识的掌握。

同时，有必要对学习成果进行评估，并对教学进行反馈。例如，有必要拥有涵盖所有需要教授的不同类型知识的教材，还需要知道如何通过这些教材培养所需的基本技能。日本东京工业大学的岸本教授团队做了一项调查，开发出与基础能力有关的试题库。我想介绍一下，在我刚才提到的这个项目的组织定位方面，在日本发生了什么样的变化。我们分别在 2010 年和 2019 年对大学教员做了两次调查，以了解他们在大学课程中重视哪些内容。调查对象为日本大学教师，涉及工程领域、人文社科及其他领域。结果中值得注意的是，对于“是否会梳理教学内容，让学生上课更加集中这一问题”，回答“稍有梳理”“精心梳理”的比例非常高，而且这一比例正在大幅度提升。特别是在工程领域的比例上升更高，工程领域需要教授的内容增加很多，但没办法全部在课上讲完，所以教师整理了需要掌握的内容，然后让学生们专注于课堂，随后自学。我认为教师在思想上已经有了很大的转变，重要的不是把内容塞进课堂，而是让学生消化课堂内容，使之成为自己的东西。这只是一个例子，但对于工程教育来说非常重要。我们还可以看到其他领域也有相应的趋势，人文社科及其他领域都存在这一趋势。教学的内容在多样化和广泛化的同时，所教内容反而是精选的，重点是主动甄选、汇总介绍并领会。我们应关注到，虽然这是一个普遍强调的趋势，但在工程领域尤其如此。

到目前为止，大学教育的改革一直由政府主导。然而，正如我所说，重要的是学生能够掌握该学科的基础性知识。虽然不同领域教学方法会有差别，但获得工程基础知识和能力已成为必要。为此虽然各方已投入诸多努力并带来了一些变化，然而我认为现在比以往任何时候都更需要教师与学生一起努力来推进改革。

## ii. Fundamental Problems in Engineering Education

Kaneko Motohisa, Professor of Tsukuba University, Japan

本発表の主な内容は大学教育改革の視点から工学教育の基本的な問題点を整理して行くことです。工学教育の特徴を整理する前に、大学教育の方法と工学教育の歴史的な背景を説明したいと思います。

まず最初に工学教育の特徴をどのように整理するかということについて考えてみたいと思います。大学教育の方法というのは、基本的には講義、基本的な知識と理論の ... 説明を修得します。それから、実験と実習です。実験・計測の経験で得し修た知識の理論化をちゃんと理解して身につけます。そして研究室での研究プロジェクトの参加、参加の上で、与えられた与えられた研究課題の実施、そして教員の指導と学生同士の協力ところになるわけです。

歴史的まず工学教育というのは、総合大学で行われたものです。特に 19 世紀のドイツの大学で行われた化学の研究室での教育です。それからもう一つ、ポリテクニックと言われる専門的な工学教育があります。現代の工学教育というのは、この二つの潮流を受け継いでいるということはできると思います。

大学教育に比べて、工学教育には 3 つの特徴があります。一つは講義に関して専門領域が対応であると言うことです。それから、一般的に、中国の大学と日本の大学でも講義の数が非常に多いということです。実験・実習に時間がかかります。研究室に分かれて稽古する場合が多いわけですが、研究内容に迎えてから専門化して、教育員がその研究テーマを与えるということです。そして、特定のテーマを学生に具体的に研究することによって、工学的な考え方、仕事の進め方を体得するという式が取られていることです。それから、教員とほかの学生と構成する集団によって、学修へのモチベーションをあげるというこちらが取られています。これは、日本と中国でもある共通だと思うんです。

そこにどういう問題が生じているかということなんですけれども、一つは分野自体が多様化しているということです。学生はどのように自分が本当に勉強していることがよくわからないうちに、細かいことを学習させられます。講義科目の数が上手く模索されるに従って、拡大して行く、それによって、学生は充分に講義の内容は吸収できないという問題も生じています。それから研究室教育を行う時の大きな問題は教員の研究の補助として高度に専門化して細分化されたテーマを教員が与える場合は確かに学生にとっては経験になるのですけれども、学生自身がどのような知識を獲得しているかというのはあまり把握できないような状況を受けるということです。

もう一方で、学生の大きな変化が起こっています。その基礎学力が必ずしも高くない学生が入学しているということは一つの大きな問題です。特に自然科学系の科目の基礎が不足しています。特に数学などについての基礎的な知識があまりないです。もう一方で、スマホとコンピューターゲームが拡大していることによって、学生の落ち着いて考えるという習慣はなくなっているというふうにも言われています。同時に産業構造が多様化することによって、就業機会のチャンスが増えているわけでありますけれども、逆にそれは自分の将来を具体的に考えることが学生にとっては難しくなっていると言うことを大事にしてるという側面もあるというのは重要な事実だと思います。

社会全体も変化しています。まず第一に職業は多様化、流動化しているということです。これはある意味で社会の進歩しているということでありますけれども、もう一方で、その専門的な知識技能は陳腐化しやすいという傾向は非常に強くなっているわけです。したがって、大学同士より体系的な専門知識と職業上の必要性が乖離しやすいという点があります。上手くやれていますが、潜在的に不安性が増しているということもあり、不安定的で、非確定的、複雑かつ曖昧な社会状況が進んでいると思います。それから情報化社会になっているわけですけれども、社会によって個人情報が獲得され、返して強化されて、したがって、個人が主体的に考えるということはなかなか難しくなっているということです。個人が主体的に考える社会観とか、価値意識を作るということを難しくして、逆にそれが重要になっているということを示していると思います。大学教育はこれはどこの専門でもそうですけれども、主体的に生きて行くための個人としての考え方が重要になっています。それはですね、それを養成するために、いわゆる通識、教養教育が重要でありますけれども、同時に専門教育も重要です。専門教育の中で個人の主体性というものを養成していくということが求められるようになっております。

工学教育はどのような課題があるかということですけれども、基本的には、当然ですけれども、工学的な基礎知識・能力の取得が必要です。これは一般的な汎用能力とコンピテンスといわれるんですけど。例えばコミュニケーション能力とか、よく聞いたり書いたり読んだりする能力だけではなくて、こういう考え方があるということを修得することが必要であります。ただ知識として知っているだけではなくて、自分のものとして修得しているということが必要になっているのではないかと思います。そのためには、学習への動機づけが必要です。そのためにはその学習課題を整理して、学習にどのように誘導して行くのかということが大きな問題であります。さらに、その学習の達成度を評価する仕組みを作り、学習動機につなげていくということが必要になると思います。そのために何が必要なのかということですけれども、その教育方法の見直しが必要になります。

授業のあり方についての見直しも必要ですし、研究室での活動についての見直しも必要になってくると思います。特に授業のあり方についても反省が必要ではないでしょうか。必要になりそうなことをすべて教えるということはだんだん難しくなってきているわけです。その知識が進むに連れて、専門的なものがどんどん増えていきます。それをすべて教えるということを目指すのではなくて、専門的な基礎能力をつくるということは必要になります。それはどういうふうにするかというと、専門の基礎となる考え方や知識を修得するということに焦点を置くべきであり、そういうことになると思います。

それと同時に、学習成果の評価と教育へのフィードバックということが必要になります。例えば、さまざまな必要となる教えるべき知識を全てカバーした教材も必要ですが、それだけじゃなくて、それを通じて必要とされるその基礎能力をどう図るかということも必要になってくると思います。例えば日本の東京工業大学の岸本先生がそのチームで行った調査の結果から出てきたものですけれども、それを通じた基礎能力に関するテストバンクというものを開発されて使われています。今申し上げたこの事業の組織的な位置づけということについて、日本でどういうふうな変化が起こったかということをご紹介したいと思いますけれども。大学先生に大学の授業でどういったことを重視しているかというと、2010年と2019年の二回に調査しました。これは日本の大学の先生に対して調査した結果です。これは工学もありますけれども、人文社会あるいはほかの領域でも行っています。その結果の中で注目されるのは、授業を整理して、学生が個々の授業に集中できるようにするというふうにしていることをやっているか否かということに対して、その回答ですけれども、ある程度行っていると力を入れているという回答の割合が高いです。非常に大幅に増加しています。特に工学分野で増加しています。工学分野で教えるべき内容は非常に増加していますけれども、それを全部教えようとするのではなくて、教えるべき内容を整理し、そして、学生が個々の授業に集中して自分で勉強します。ただ単に授業に内容を詰め込むのではなくて、そこで語れている授業内容を自分でもってよく消化して、自分のものにするということが重要だと言う考え方に大きく変化しているのだと思います。これは一つの例でありますけれども、工学教育などについて、特にそれが重要であります。これは他の分野に行ってもある程度見えるわけです。人文社会と他領域についても、そういった結果が詰まってるわけです。教育内容が多様化、広がると同時にむしろ教えることについては精選すると言います。積極選別して、むしろそれを集中して紹介して、体得するということを重視します。一般的に強調されるようになっているわけですけれども、特に工学分野でそういった傾向が著しいということは注目するべきことだと思います。

これまでの大学教育改革というのは、政府が中心になって推進してきました。ただ、やはり今申し上げたように重要なのは、学生がその基礎的な学習をすると言うことであります。そのための方法は分野によって違うと思いますけれども、工学的な基礎知識や能力を体得するということは必要になってきています。そのためにも、工夫や変化になっているわけでありますけれども、そのためには、今申し上げた変化を学生と共に教師が協力して、その改革していくということがこれまでもなく望まれていると思うわけであります。

## （三）

# VET 教师在持续学习中的挑战

芬兰于韦斯屈莱应用科技大学专业教师教育学院院长　尤哈·豪塔宁

今天，我演讲的主题是关于职业教育及其变化，其中的关键挑战是持续学习。我的灵感来源于几周前参加的一场研讨会，在会上，职业学校的老师正在教驾驶员们操作一款大型林木采伐机。这款机具对林业非常重要，它们可以砍伐并收集木材，完工后再由卡车将木材运送给工厂和最终购买者。其中一位来自这款机器生产商的参会者提出，教师应该忘记他们教给学生的一切，因为这些设备已经发生了很大的变化。技术一直在不断改变着行业。对于刚入行的驾驶员而言，这些过时的知识和技能已经变得毫无用处。也许这位参会者的建议稍显过激，毕竟旧机器也还能使用。但这个故事说明了教师，特别是工程专业的教师在职业教育和应用科学高等教育方面所面临的一些挑战。

前段时间，我正在阅读亚当·格兰特的一本著作——《重新思考》。在这本书的介绍中，作者写道，“智慧通常被视为思考和学习的能力，但在瞬息万变的世界中，还有另一套认知技能可能更重要：重新思考和知识清零能力。”这意味着，我们知道的越多，就越愿意了解和理解我们所学到的东西。现在，我们必须对自己的想法和事物的规律持批判性态度。我们必须学习和理解新事物，同时必须学会忘记之前的做法。

我刚才提到技术正在发生变化，新的发明每时每刻都在涌现。社会在不断变化，如出现人口老龄化，创新动力和时尚风潮在不断变化；环境在不断变化，如出现全球变暖、环境污染、气候变化和自然灾害；法律法规也在不断变化，如关于可回收和可持续发展的法律。我们的竞争对手也在做出改变，我们必须要密切关注他们的一举一动，并做出回应。

课堂上发生了哪些改变？我们作为教师曾经是教室的管理者，我们给学生教授同样的内容，要求他们做同样的事情，他们朝着相同的方向发展，习得了相同的技能和能力。从中世纪开始，课堂就是这种形式，现在的教师还在沿袭着同样的模式。这是一种以管理为基础的教育模式。这种模式的顶层有一个管理者，它规定了教师要教授哪些课程，学生要学习课程设置中描述的那些技能和能力，并在步入职场之后将所学的知识和信息应用到工作当中。同时也会有相应的政策指南来保障整个组织的有序运作。但当环境发生变化时，管理者知道新的环境需要什么样的能力吗？他们知道课程中应该增加什么样的新技能吗？教师能否知道行业真正的需求是什么？他们是否知道如何培养行业需要的未来劳动力？因此我们应该重新思考，认识到教育应该是基于服务的。

在基于服务的教育模式当中，我们要从行业入手，去思考行业真正需要什么样的能力。学生要学习这些行业重视的能力，教师要为学生提供相应的指导，管理者要给教师提供合适的工具和技能培训，并给予充足的时间，同时还要有相应的政策指导。首先，我们如何弄清楚行业需要哪些能力？我们可以直接和行业对话，让他们指出行业需要什么样的能力。调研清楚之后，我们对课程内容作出更新。课程以能力为本位，包含了学生需要学习的各种技能与知识。除了教授知识和技能，教学内容还包括让学生树立正确的态度、积累适当的经验，从而在工作中应用这些知识和技能，这也是训练的一部分内容。还有就是面向未来的能力。目前，我们还不清楚未来具体需要哪些能力。回首十年前，不知道如今会出现哪些职业，不知道有哪些特殊职业会出现，也不知道这些职业需要哪些相应的技能。既然我们不知道技能是什么，又怎么去传授给学生呢？

关键就在于，我们必须紧紧追随世界正在发生的变化——在工作、行业、市场和社会当中所发生的变化。我们必须要时刻了解正在发生的重大事件，比如“黑天鹅事件”这种能引起翻天覆地变化的事件。创造力、创业精神和创新能力，这些积极主动式的能力是学生应该掌握的未来技能。

在价值链或技能需求链中，某些技能需求在下降。通过以服务为基础的教育模式，我们可以积极回应行业产生的需求。价值的传递顺序是由管理层传递给行业，由教师传递给学生。这意味着教师在未来的教育模式中应该承担起新的角色。我们应该把学生当成顾客，教学应该以学生为中心，而学生也可以发挥出更多能动作用，根据自己的意愿决定自己的未来。

在组织内部发生转型的过程中，管理者发挥着重要的领导作用。管理者要做出调整，因为即使学习本身没有发生变化，我们的教学也要做出改进。学习已经不再仅仅是一个传递知识和信息的过程，也不再是一个填鸭式的模式。事实、数据这类信息虽然很重要，但它们并不是知识的全部。学习过程需要学生发挥积极性与能动性。学习者要乐于探寻某个知识点背后的重要意义，要弄清楚自己为什么要去学习这个知识。在了解学习的意义时，反思会起到重要的作用。自我反思，可以了解学习对个人的意义；学生和教师一同反思，可以了解学习对群体的意义以及学习对地区、政府、社会和国家的意义。

学习是一项需要反复练习的活动。我们也须认识到，学习不仅仅会发生在校园里，也会在其他地点以其他形式进行，比如通过爱好来学习知识、在家和朋友一起学习或者通过实地培训学习。这就意味着个人在学习过程中可以充分发挥能动性。而身为教师，我认为教师应该兼备两种不同的身份，一个身份是专家，教师应该掌握所有知识内容并且要把这些知识都传授给学生，这个身份并没有过时。以前，教师要将技能、知识和信息都分享给学生，给学生布置作业，为学生答疑解惑，评估学生的学习情况。但现在面临的挑战是，教师如何通过教育教学来回应技术、行业和市场中所发生的变化，如何帮助学生为未来的职业做好准备。

教师的另一个身份是终身学习者，并且要持续学习。教师要引导学生获取知识、技能和信息，但是他们不必讲出所有知识内容。教师必须要有好奇心、对各种事物有强烈的兴趣。教师给学生布置的作业有开放性答案，而不是只让学生去回答对错。那么这其中遇到的挑战是什么呢？挑战之一就是如何充分信任学生的自身能力，让他们对自己的人生负责；如何确保学生已经学到了足够的知识并掌握了目标技能。这是一个至关重要的问题。如果一位教师在过去 20 年里一直使用一种教学模式，但现在突然要学习新的方法去做这件事，这种转变对教师来说是非常困难的。一方面，我们要思考如何去传授知识与信息，另一方面，我们要研究如何开发面向未来的教育和教学模式。

对于教育机构而言，这意味着什么？我们要和行业展开密切合作，了解真实的工作环境和他们的能力需求。这是管理者应该做出的改变，也是应该肩负的责任。学位课程项目必须有足够的自由度让每个学员制定属于自己的学习路径。教育机构也需要形成一种正确的生态结构，才能与业内的各家企业展开密切合作。这是一种文化上的改变，教师、管理者和学生都要接受培训。在这个改变过程中，教师和管理者发挥着重要作用。此外，管理者要允许不同方式或内容的存在。

## iii. VET Teachers Challenge of Continuous Learning

**Juha Hautanen, Head of Department at the School of Professional Teacher Education, JAMK University of Applied Sciences, Finland**

My presentation is mainly about vocational education and those changes that have happened. I will also try to explain what kind of challenges are regarding continuous learning. About this presentation, my idea came from a couple of weeks ago when I was participating one seminar of vocational teachers who are teaching drivers to operate forest harvesters. Those machines are very important for the forest industry. hey cut the timber and pick them. After that, lorries and trucks transport timbers to factories and end-users.

There was one representative from the company which makes those machines. He told the teachers that they should forget everything what they have have learned and taught how to operate them since the operating system has changed totally. Technology is changing the industry all the time, continuously. Old knowledge and skills are not any more useful and usable for the new drivers of those forest machines. Well, perhaps what the company representative said is a little bit too radical. The old machines still can be used in the future. But this story tells something about the challenge that teachers, especially engineering teachers are facing in vocational and applied science higher educations.

I was reading a book written by Adam Grant. In the introduction of this book, he was saying that intelligence was usually seen as the ability to think and learn, but in a rapidly changing world, there is another set of cognitive skills that matter more: the ability to rethink and unlearn. This means, when we are more intelligent, we are more willing to know and understand what we have learned. Now we have to be critical about what we are thinking and how things have changed. We have to learn new things, meanwhile to unlearn the way how we have done earlier.

Well, as I mentioned before technology is changing, and new inventions come all the time. Society is changing, for example population aging. Motivations and fashion are changing. Environment is changing, for example global warming, pollution, climate change and nature disasters. Law changes, and policy changes, for example, new law on recycling and sustainable development. Competitors are making changes too, so we have to follow what they have done and response to that.

What is happening in the classroom? We, as teachers, used to be as a captain in the classroom. We were telling the same things to our students and asked them to do the same things, the result is they were growing towards the same direction to acquire the same skills and competencies. It looks like this in the classroom and it has been the same from the middle age, and nowadays we are still repeating same model in our education pretty much. So this is a management-based education. There is a management on top of this organization. The management defines the curriculum, which teachers are following. Students are learning those competencies and skills which are described in curricula and then students go to industry and apply those knowledge and information what they have got. And there are policy and guidance to keep the whole organization organized. But when the environment is changing, does the management know what kind competencies are needed, what new skills and competencies should put to the curricula? Are the teachers able to know the needs of industries and how to educate the future workforce the industry need? I could say we should rethink our education more like a service-based education.

So in the service-based education, we start from the industry. What kind of competencies they need? Students learn those competencies, which are important for the industry. Teachers guide students to get the needed competencies and managers support the teachers and give right kind of tools, skills and time. And again, there are policy and guidance. First of all, how can we know what competencies the industries need? We can make an inquiry to examine them tell us what they need. By asking the industries, we are able to have a defined competencies for updating the curriculum. The curriculum is competence-based, it contains different set s of skills and knowledge student need to learn. Besides knowledge and skill, an attitude and experiences that students are able to use those skills and knowledge is also part of training. There is also another set of competencies, which called future competences. What are they? We don't know yet. If you look back ten years, at that time we didn't know much about the professions which exist at the moment. Special professions and those skills what nowadays workers need. It comes to the questions, how we are able to teach those things we don't know yet.

That is we must be able to follow the changes of the world, changes in the world of work, in business, in the market and in society. We have to be able to follow different kind of disruptions and all the radical changes like black swans. The set of creativity, entrepreneurship and innovation are competences which support proactive future skills of students.

In the picture demand of working life goes downwards. Through the service-based education, we are able to respond to those demands. The value chain is from the management to the industry, through the teachers to the students. This means that teachers should have a new role in the future. We should see students as customers, so that our teaching should be student-centered and students are active players with free will about their future.

Management has a very important role to lead this change and transformation inside the organization. The management needs to change. Learning itself hasn't changed but teaching should. We must be able to follow this change. Learning is not only the knowledge and information transforming process from teacher to students, who learn and be able to apply what s/he has learned. Facts, figures and similar kind of information have important roles, but they are not all. Learning needs the motivation. They need to actively explore the meaning and significance of a certain piece of knowledge, what does it mean for me and understand why it's important. Reflection plays an important role in learning process for understand meaning and significance. Reflect alone, what does it mean to me; reflect with the group of students and the teacher, what does this mean for us, what does it mean for our region, for our government, for our society and for our country.

Learning needs work and rehearsal. And learning is not happening only at school. It's happening also outside school, in informal places for example in hobbies, at home with friends, or work places in practical training. This means individuals have an active role in the learning process. As to the teachers, I see that teachers should have two different kinds of identities. We used to have an identity as specialist which represent that the teacher knows everything of content and teach it to students. This identity is still needed. Teacher shares the skills, knowledge and information, gives assignments, gets right and wrong answers from students and measures how they have learned. But now the challenge is how education and teaching to respond to the changes in technology, industry and markets, and how to teach the students to the future professions.

Another identity of teacher is to identity continuous learner. Teacher guides students to get the information, knowledge and skills but they don't have to tell everything. Teachers must have curiosity and interest in different kind of things. They give open assignments to students, so the students' answers are not like right or wrong. There are also some challenges. One challenge is how to trust the students' ability and let them be in charge of their own life? How to assure that students have heard enough content so that they have the right kind of skills? This can be an essential issue. If a teacher has done his teaching one way more than twenty years the change can be very difficult. Role of management is support the change. Nevertheless, I can see that on the left hand is how to deliver the information, on the right hand is how to develop the education and learning for the future.

What does this mean for educational organizations? We need to have close cooperation with the industry to understand the world of work and its need for competencies. This is change management and this is a job of the leaders. Curriculum of a degree program must have enough space or freedom to make the own learning paths of each learner. Educational organizations have to have a right kind learning eco-system and structure to to have for example close industrial cooperation. This is about cultural change, where training to the teachers and the leaders are needed, as well as training for the students. In this cultural change teachers and leaders are in very important roles. Besides, we need permission to act differently.

# （四）

# 高铁工匠培养之道

## ——打造具有全球竞争力的高技能人才培养基地

中国工程院院士、中国中车首席科学家　丁荣军

### 1. 产业发展现状趋势

首先，我认为职业技术教育应该与人才的市场需求相结合，院校培养一定要有好的方向。今天我主要从轨道交通这几年的发展来看技能人才的培养。

就轨道交通装备而言，我国已形成自主创新、配套完整、设备先进、规模经营的集研发、设计、制造、试验和服务于一体的轨道交通装备制造体系，成为世界轨道交通装备制造大国，正朝着轨道交通装备制造强国迈进，我们基本上在全球处在领先或者先进水平。在路网规模方面，截至 2021 年年底，我国铁路网规模达到 15 万千米，特别是高铁营业里程达到 4 万千米，全球第一；城市轨道交通规模达 9 207 千米。在装备容量方面，城市群建设对未来轨道交通产品需求也在增速。未来的路网车需求还在进一步增加，对人才的需求也在不断增加。

我国高速列车有九大关键技术和十大配套技术，不管是关键技术还是配套技术，都必须达到一个完整的、很高的标准才能满足用户需求，涉及电、控制、机械和材料等。随着轨道交通装备正在朝着安全、绿色、智能、高速、重载和互联互通方向发展，对高技能人才的培养提出了更高的要求，未来如何培养多技能、多专业，满足不同产业需要的人才队伍是非常关键的。

### 2. 技能人才发展需求

习近平总书记强调：“劳模精神、劳动精神、工匠精神是以爱国主义为核心的民族精神和以改革创新为核心的时代精神的生动体现，是鼓舞全党全国各族人民风雨无阻、勇敢前进的强大精神动力”。

我国是轨道交通装备制造业大国，依托产业优势，培养了很多能工巧匠和大国工匠，产业人才需求依然旺盛，产业高精尖人才短缺问题日益凸显。据预测，到2025年，中国制造业技术人才缺口达3 000万，先进轨道交通装备人才缺口将高达10.6万人。一列“复兴号”中国标准动车组，由7 100余种共计55万多个零部件组成，需要14 000余名专业技术人才合作完成。可以说，从“中国制造”到“中国创造”，“复兴号”中国标准动车组奔驰在祖国广袤的大地上，实现了由“追赶者”到“领跑者”的伟大跨越，而在这场跨越中，技术工人是当仁不让的创新主角，他们对产品精雕细琢、精益求精，身体力行地践行了工匠精神。轨道交通专业具有接口复杂、与现场环境紧密结合等特点，从人才需求的角度主要分为土建、设备和运营三个大类，培养对象包括设计、施工、监理、装备研发制造、质检、调度、检修、运营管理等。人才培养的主要目标是为轨道交通的制造、运营、维护等岗位培养高素质一线技术技能型人才。用工匠精神引领和培育高技能人才，使之成为能工巧匠乃至大国工匠，是当前轨道交通类高职院校的主要任务。

3. 工匠人才培养新模式

我在湖南铁路科技职业技术学院任专家委员会主任期间，基本上每年都开设讲座，与师生也都有交流。我经常讲人才的培养一定要尽快适应中国高速铁路、中国城际化和城市轨道交通产业需求，形成自己的特色。这几年，湖南铁路科技职业技术学院建立了由院士、行业科学家、职业教育专家和大国工匠组成的跨界专家智库，通过专家智库深度参与学校文化铸魂、人才培养强基、课程体系重构、工匠之师锤炼、校企协同育人、双创素养提升等“六大工程”建设，走出了一条培养高素质技术技能人才、能工巧匠、大国工匠的特色之路。

（1）文化铸魂工程。构建了学校“铁肩担道、路远行德”文化，培养学生“执着专注、精益求精、一丝不苟、追求卓越”的品质，为培养轨道交通行业高素质技术技能人才和高铁工匠补足职业精神之“钙”。秉持“火车头精神”和“育大国工匠”教育理念，强化思政教育，推进“课程思政”，打造大学生时政学习社等思政教育品牌，实施副科级及以上干部兼任班主任、学生“半军事化管理”等制度。立项教育部课程思政示范项目1个、省大学生思想道德素质提升工程项目6个、高校思想政治工作质量提升工程项目2个，获评全省思想政治工作优秀创新案例1个。

（2）人才强基工程。依托轨道交通行业专家和职业教育专家组成的师资体系，践行“1333”人才培养模式。“1条主线”：将思想政治教育贯穿人才培养全过程。

“3 个对接”：教学内容对接岗位标准、教学过程对接运输生产、素质教育对接铁路文化。“3 个融合”：人文素质教育、职业能力培养、创新创业教育相融。“3 类证书”：职业技能等级证书 + 学历证书 + 工作经历证书。学校连续多年“两抽查”合格率为 100%，学生订单培养率位居全省同类院校前列，毕业生就业率始终保持在 95% 以上，入选“全国高职院校学生发展指数 100 所优秀院校”。

（3）课程重构工程。紧密对接轨道交通产业链，推进“四新四融”课程体系重构与升级，增强高技能人才培养的适应性。“四新”：新技术、新工艺、新材料、新设备；“四融”：“岗位、课程、竞赛、证书”融通。学校主持完成两门国家级专业教学资源库课程建设，1 本教材获全国教材建设奖二等奖，立项教师教学创新团队、精品在线开放课程等多个国家级项目。

（4）匠师培育工程。一是提升教师的科研能力，获取高层次科研项目，产出高质量科研成果，逐步成长为“科研名师”。二是提升专业综合技能，具备解决生产技术问题和技艺革新攻关能力，逐步打造为“技能大师”。三是提升教师整合资源、开发资源、升级课程的能力，逐步成长为“教学名师”。学校打造国家级教师教学创新团队 1 个，全国优秀教师 1 人，黄炎培职业教育杰出校长 1 人，全国轨道交通运输行业教育教学名师 3 人，“芙蓉学者”1 人、芙蓉教学名师 2 人，学校入选“全国高职院校教师发展指数 100 所优秀院校”。

（5）协同育人工程。院士、行业科学家、职业教育专家、大国工匠深度合作，通过“校企双主体、育训结合”的途径，依据企业需求，针对不同层次的培养对象，分层分类订单式培养，打通高铁工匠人才成长渠道，打造具有国际竞争力的技能人才培养基地。培养的毕业生中，涌现出黄海涛、彭志强、何益文、谭祥、张峰嘉等一大批“全国技术能手”“全国五一劳动奖章”“全国青年岗位能手”“全路技术能手”“全国铁路劳动模范”“中华全国铁路总工会火车头奖章”“高铁工匠”等优秀人物。

（6）素养提升工程。实施“一引、两驱、三融合”双创素养提升工程，增强了学生的创新意识，提高了创新能力，提升了创新素养。“一引”：课程引领；“两驱”：项目驱动，载体驱动；“三融合”：双创教育与专业教育融合、学校培养与企业培养融合，领导体制与管理机制融合。近几年，学生参加省级、国家级职业院校技能竞赛，“互联网 +”“黄炎培”“挑战杯”创新创业大赛成绩斐然，获得国家级竞赛奖项 27 项，省级竞赛奖项 253 项。

最后，借这个机会，我还想提三方面的建议：第一，怎么样可以推进新的职业教育法的落地。一定需要国家政策的支持，社会一直对职业技术人才不太重视，怎么从政策这个角度来提高这些技术技能人才的社会影响力和价值的认同度。第二，推进本科层次职业教育，让职业教育真正成为一种类型教育，也可以适当借鉴国外的一些做法。第三，怎么把技术教育和技能教育相结合，希望职业院校培养出来的学生不仅会动手，也要有一定的基本技能和技术理论知识，这样既有利于自己能够成长成才，也有利于他在未来的工作中，怎么去为设计人员提出更好的想法，重要的是怎么把两者能够互相促进、互相融合。

# （五）

# 协同培养高素质技能人才
## ——德国双元制高等教育

德国施特拉尔松德孔子学院院长　孙建安

德国的职业教育在全球非常著名。在德国，职业教育和工程教育是紧密相关的。德国职业院校的教师在培养过程中，特别是工程职业的教师首先要获得一个工程的学位，才能成为从事职业教育的教师。可以说，工程教育是贯穿在工程职业教育教师培养过程中的。今天我主要介绍的是德国高等教育的另一个方面——双元制是如何延伸到高等教育。

双元制高等教育具有两个主要特征：第一，具有二元性，涉及两个学习场所，就是企业和学校。第二，双元制高等教育要求学生在学习过程中或者教育的过程中，掌握科学理论要求的一种教育形式。按照德国科学委员会对双元制高等教育的定义，所谓双元制高等教育是高等教育机构和实践伙伴通过建立一种特殊的人才培养模式，即双元制高等教育专业设立，将科学理论知识与实际专业技术技能结合起来，从而使得学生或者毕业生能够达到特别的职业技术技能要求。所以在组织和教学的过程中分别由两个地点来实施，主要采用的模式有两种：第一种是将职业教育和高等教育相结合，把它称为职业教育嵌入高等教育的一种双元制高等教育专业。第二种是将一段实践或者较长的实践阶段和高等教育相结合的形式，把它称为实践教育嵌入高等教育的双元制高等教育专业。整个发展过程中，借鉴了德国传统的职业教育体系的法规和经验，建立起一个高等教育机构与实践伙伴（企业或者其他实践机构）合作培养技术技能人才机制。近年来，随着双元制高等教育在高等院校的不断发展，把这两种形式混合来组织高等双元制高等教育，因此我们把这第三种模式称为混合式双元制高等教育。2019 年，混合式双元制高等教育学士学位专业占比为 14.6%（2016 年为 13.9%）。

双元制高等教育的三种模式是如何在各类不同高等院校实施呢？德国的双元制高等教育最早发源于50年前的德国高等教育改革，产生了一种称为职业学院的教育机构，这种学院最早是产生在德国的巴登－符腾堡州，那里聚集了大量工业企业，如奔驰公司、博世公司，等等。巴登－符腾堡州职业学院到今天已经发展为双元制大学，而在两德统一以后，在新的联邦州又引入了巴登－符腾堡州职业学院这种高等双元制教育模式。这种职业学院的模式，一般学习时间为3年，共6个学期。在6个学期里，以12周在企业、12周在学校来组织教学，形成了一个理论→实践→理论相互交替的教学模式。这种模式从入校开始一直持续到毕业，学生在一个企业里完成整个实践学习。这是一种最传统最早的双元制的高等教育模式。

随着应用科学大学迅速发展，在20世纪70—80年代以来，应用科学大学也引入了双元制的教育模式，这种模式与职业学院模式不太一样，它把职业教育的培养模式与高等教育的培养模式结合起来，换句话说，学生在高等教育学习前已经开展了两个学期的职业教育，在第5学期，要对学生进行职业技能考核，通常职业技能考核是由工商协会来组织的，是7个学期再加上2个学期职业教育的双元制高等教育形式。在欧洲高等教育一体化时期，欧盟对高等教育的时间有要求，在应用科学大学里开设的双元制高等教育专业的学习时间要比普通高等教育专业的时间长一点，这里是以埃姆登－里尔应用科学大学为例。

近期，以一种在传统大学采用混合式双元制高等教育模式的发展非常迅速。特别是一些传统的工科院校，如在一些工业大学，都采用这种混合式的模式。主要形式有两种：第一种形式是把实践教育和高等教育相结合，学习时间一般是4年，由企业实践和高校学习相互交替，组成前6个学期的学习，第7个学期进行学士学位的论文撰写或设计。这是实践嵌入式的双元制高等教育。第二种形式是把职业教育嵌入高等教育。以传统大学科特布斯－森夫滕贝格－勃兰登堡工业大学为例，这一形式的学习时间较长，为期5年，学生用1年时间在企业和职业学校完成职业教育，第2年参加由工商会举行的职业教育中期考核，第5年参加工商会举行的职业教育结业考核。在培养过程中，对企业和学校都提出了不同的要求，首先要建立一个教学场所间的关系，对科学知识提出要求，对实践进行设计。按照“博洛尼亚协议”规定，学士学位每个学期一般是30学分，在企业里如果是一个完整的学习，也含有一定的学分，而且学分获得并不是依据在企业的时间长短来确定的，而是以企业所要求掌握的知识面来确定的。同时，实践机构也要承担一定的任务，学生到企业去并不是简单的认知过程。另外，在德国，高校开设的所有专业都要进行第三方专业认证，高校要按照学士学位教育的相关要求明确自身所承担的任务。最后，双元制高等教育专业还要考虑成本经费的问题，根据德国法律规定，企业需要支付学生在企业实践过程中的基本生活费。

无论是对学生，还是对企业，双元制高等教育都有着明显的优势。首先，对于学生来说，可以有更多的接触实践的机会，学生学习时间相对较短，毕业率较高，学生在学习期间还能获得一定的生活费。另外，学生还会获得较好的学习条件和就业机会。对于企业来说，通过这种教育模式能够获得更高素质的员工，因为在整个过程中企业可以不断地发掘人力资源。其次，建立了学生与企业之间的密切联系。最后，为企业为未来人力资源的发展节约了成本。同时，因为学生加入企业，又为企业增添了活力。最重要的一点，通过这种模式，企业和高校建立了紧密的合作方式，使得企业不但能够与高校联合培养人才，也可以把一些技术、科研难题交给高校来完成。

欧洲高校在签订“博洛尼亚协议”以后，都建立了高等教育质量保证体系。同样，双元制高等教育也建立相应质量保证体系，这一质量保证体系强调所有的专业都要经过第三方的专业认证，在教学场所关系上需要合理分配理论与实践之间的关系；在科学理论要求方面，强调高校学习时间的要求及教学人员的资质保障；在实践教育要求方面，对实践指导人员和实践内容的制定都有严格的要求。最为突出的是双元制学士学位获得者，也就是本科毕业生的学生还有进入普通硕士专业学习的机会。

全球化对工程教育提出了新的要求，最早的双元制高等教育大部分是工程专业，因此全球化对双元制高等工程教育也提出了一个新的要求，主要表现在跨文化能力、外语能力和国际化企业实践能力上。德国很多院校在双元制高等教育国际合作中，建立了所谓的国际双元制高等教育专业，由第三方进行专业认证，如 2016 年，合肥学院、世界 500 强企业德国大陆集团（中国公司轮胎工厂）和德国埃姆登 - 里尔应用科学大学共同合作开设的双元制高等教育合作班（大陆班）——生产工程专业，完全借鉴德国双元制的教育模式开展高等教育。学生前两年在合肥学院学习，第三年，一部分学生接受大陆集团中国公司合肥工厂的实践教育，按照教学计划实习一年并获得相应的学分；另外一部分通过德语考试的学生，到德国大陆集团总部的汉诺威工厂接受职业培训及到埃姆登 - 里尔应用科学大学的生产工程专业学习，第四年回到中国，合肥学院和大陆集团联合培养一年，完成毕业论文，获得合肥学院的毕业证书和学位证书以及德国埃姆登 - 里尔应用科学大学成绩证书和在大陆集团的实践证明。由于这种模式还未与德国的埃姆登－里尔应用科技大学实现学习内容的相互认可，要进一步完善中德的双元制高等教育，要建立一个真正的国际双元制高等教育。未来，设想以中国和德国合作的“2+3”模式（2 年在中国学习，3 年在德国学习）为基准，最终让学生通过这种模式既获得企业的认可，也获得中方和德方的双学位、双毕业证。这是建立国际双元制高等教育的典型案例。

双元制高等教育在德国的发展越来越迅速，主要是两类高等教育机构实施，一类是应用科技大学，一类是职业学院。目前，71% 的双元制高等教育专业在应用科学大学，而 9.1% 在职业院校，14.5% 在双元制大学里。应用科学大学是全德国都有的院校，而职业学院并不是德国每个州都有的院校模式。在 3% 的传统大学里现在也开始采用校企相结合的人才培养模式，既双元制的模式。双元制高等教育专业的开设也在不断发展，如从最早的工程类专业发展到经济类专业、信息类专业及健康、教育等其他专业。如果把工程类、信息类专业比例合二为一，可以看到双元制高等教育专业主要是在工程信息技术领域开设的；同时在分布方面，截止到 2018 年，德国的 16 个联邦州都有这种新型的校企联合培养高技能、高素质人才培养模式。

德国高等教育界和企业界对双元制高等教育的展望：首先，进一步拓展新的专业和职业领域；其次，实践场所经费支持和承担任务更加明确；再次，德国的双元制高等教育模式不断向海外输出；最后，面向各类不同形式的高等教育类型，即在传统大学里也开展这种模式。

# （六）

# 智能制造人才培养与实训教学创新

武汉华中数控股份有限公司董事长　陈吉红

制造强国战略正在加速推动中国制造业优化升级，数字化、网络化、智能化是传统制造向智能制造转型、生产型制造向服务型制造转型的重要技术支撑，中国将智能制造作为制造强国战略的主攻方向。由于这类新技术的应用，制造业缺乏大量的智能制造人才，这样的人才应该怎么培养呢？我从以下两方面汇报我们所做的探索和取得的成效。

## 1. 智能制造技术发展趋势及人才培养方案探索

根据国家发展战略目标及自身产业发展和技术优势，围绕着高端化、自动化、网络化和智能化，我们开创性提出现代大学生智能制造复合型人才培养的“三门课一中心”模式，即“多轴及高速高精加工”“工业机器人应用技术”“智能制造应用技术”三门课程，同时将原来的金工实训中心升级成为面向智能制造的工程训练中心。为什么要增加“三门课一中心”呢？第一是高端化趋势。从高端化来看，数控机床是“工业母机”，代表国家制造业的核心竞争力，可以制造各种工业产品。未来数控技术需要向着高速、高精、多轴复合方向发展。

高速加工技术应用方面。目前，在3C行业高速加工技术应用非常普遍，机床快移速度达 60 m/min，加速度达 1 $g$，主轴转速超过 20 000 r/min。不但可以成倍地提高生产效率、改善零件的加工精度和表面质量，而且有效地解决了常规加工中难以解决的问题，如超薄零件的加工问题、某些特殊材料（钛合金、纤维增强塑料等）的高效加工问题。

高精、多轴复合方面。目前，航空航天、汽车制造领域的企业大量应用五轴联动的数控机床，这些机床不仅可以用于金属切削，在复合材料加工等领域也在广泛应用。配置直线电机的五轴机床在实现高速加工的同时，还有一个特点，就是机床加工精度在不断提升，我们完全可以做到定位精度达到 1 μm 以内的高精度机床，并应用此高精度的机床成功加工出零件达到镜面。因此我国机加工的精度正在实现“由丝入微”的升级。

高端化涉及多轴加工技术、复合加工技术、高速高精加工技术，而掌握这些技术，不可能看一看就可以学会的，必须动手实训才能掌握。据此，我们设计了“多轴及高速高精加工”课程，并设计了一系列实训案例，学生可以通过五轴机床加工出各种非常复杂的零件，增强实践动手能力，从而真正掌握多轴加工技术。华中数控股份有限公司与沈阳工学院共建的智能高速五轴加工实训基地就是很好的应用案例。

第二是自动化趋势。工业机器人已经广泛应用到各个制造行业，不仅可以应用到机械加工、电器装配、新能源汽车电池组装，还可以应用于食品的加工生产，甚至可以制造鞋子等产品。这些原来都是依靠人力制造，而现在则利用机器代替人力，由原来需要 60 多人的生产线，变成现在只需要 5~6 人管理的自动化生产线。根据岗位需求，我们梳理了机器人的岗位能力矩阵。在自动化领域，工业机器人的装配维护与生产线集成是一个重要的技术岗位。我们还分别设计了制造专业和非制造类专业的课程，增加了工业机器人关键核心部件的认知实训内容，包括各种典型结构的工业机器人认知内容。我们还希望非工科的学生也能够学习与机器人有关的课程，通过学生自己设计的一些机器人创新应用，如机器人绘画、机器人下五子棋等，让更多学生了解先进制造模式。此外，我们把“工业机器人机电装调与维护”也作为一个重要内容，设计了工业机器人的机电装调与维护、机械本体结构装调、电气原理与装调等课程。以前，在机械设计的教学中，有一个拆装变速箱的实训项目，而现在可以通过机器人拆装来替代传统的人工拆装变速箱。目前，我们已经在国内建设完成 100 多个工业机器人实训中心，每年培养超过 10 万人。

第三是网络化和智能化趋势。在航空航天、汽车等重点制造领域，目前已经大量应用了各种各样的智能生产线与柔性生产线，同时建立了相应的大数据中心，将所有的设备都实现互联互通。借助数据中心，可以进行生产统计、远程运维，实现从设备到车间的数字孪生。应用新一代信息技术，未来的智能机床，还能够实现自主感知、自主学习并产生和积累知识，自主决策，自主执行，实现高效、优质、可靠、低耗的加工过程。为此，我们研制了华中九型新一代智能数控系统，该数控系统内部装载了高性能的人工智能芯片，不仅可以实现数控的所有基本操作，还可以实现各种各样的智能化功能，这些功能涉及网络化技术、智能化技术、传感器技术、物联网技术、机器视觉、智能设备 / 车间、数字孪生、云计算、工业大数据、信息物理融合系统、新一代人工智能技术等智能化技术。基于以上技术，我们设计了“智能制造应用技术”这门课，把机床、机器人、清洗机、打标机以及数字化立库等做成了智能制造单元，这些智能单元通过自动导引运输车和立体仓库联调在一起，构成一条智能制造生产线，帮助学校开展智能制造实训。我们在山东劳动职业技术学院、湖南工业职业技术学院、唐山工业职业技术学院等打造了一批智能制造实训中心。

围绕上述三门课程，我们撰写了若干教材，特别是周济院士牵头编写的《智能制造导论》以及本人牵头编写的《新一代智能化数控系统》。此外，我们还开设了若干师资培训课程，进行师资培训。这三门课程不仅可以加入机械设计与制造专业、数控专业以及其他的机械类或机电类专业中，增加智能制造内涵，升级传统专业，还可以面向全校打造智能制造的公共实训实践平台，提高面向新时代的工程实践水平。

**2. 华中科技大学智能制造工程实践创新中心建设**

华中科技大学的机械学科是学校的特色学科，一直以来对金工实习（金属加工工艺实习）非常重视。2000 年，学校将数控机床引入金工实习。但随着《中国制造 2025》的推进，工程训练实践课程内容陈旧、新技术和新工艺缺少、与工业企业智能化生产新模式脱节等问题日益突出，亟待把与第四次工业革命相关的一些新知识、新应用、新技术、新理念、新模式运用到工程实践教学中来。

2018 年 12 月，华中科技大学确立“建设世界一流工程实践创新中心”的目标，与工程训练课程建设相配套，立项建设智能制造工程训练创新中心，就是以智能制造为引领，全面升级原来的金工实训中心。中心服务构建新发展格局，加强数控实践板块，将原来的普通车床升级为数控车床，普通铣床升级为数控铣床，普通磨床升级为数控磨床，原来的两轴、三轴机床升级成四轴、五轴机床。

目前，华中科技大学智能制造工程训练创新中心已购置了十多台五轴机床。今年年初，中心开设了冬奥会吉祥物冰墩墩加工实践课程，学生积极参与，饱怀热情地创新制作了属于自己的个性化的冰墩墩。中心贯彻新发展理念，充实工业机器人实践板块，将机器人的核心零部件认知、典型工业机器人应用、机器人的离线编程与仿真、机器人应用编程、机器人机械装调等引入教学。同时，中心立足新发展阶段，将智能制造也引入教学内容中，在智能制造工程训练创新中心可以看到由数控机床、机器人、清洗烘干单元、检测单元、打标单元、装配单元、立体仓库、自动导引运输车配送系统、总控系统等组成的智能制造生产线，学生可以利用数据中心和总控中心自主设计定制化零件并下发到生产线完成从设计到生产制造的全过程。原来需要手工制作的锤子，现在不仅可以用数控机床来做，也可以用智能生产线来定制个性化的锤子。

该中心目前已经基本实现理工医文管全校专业全覆盖，工程实践大学四年不断线；按院系设置“工程训练”课程教学方案，实现了“一院一方案，一生一课表”；同时中心还把企业技师请进实训课堂，把学生带到真正的智能制造生产企业，真正感悟实际工厂生产模式；中心提出“保障生均耗材经费投入”的实践教学理念，将生均耗材经费纳入实践教学是否得到保障的重要衡量指标中；中心秉承中国制造，以国产装备深化思政教育，99.6% 的设备是中国制造，68.6% 的设备是华中科技大学的科研技术成果产业转化。中心自投入教学运行以来，平均每年承担超 80 万人 / 时的教学实践，智能制造工程实践平台得到了许多学生的认可，很多兄弟院校都来这里参观交流。

在此基础上，我们也与其他的本科院校，包括西安交通大学、华南理工大学、武汉首义学院、哈尔滨剑桥学院等共同建设了新的工程训练中心，还与武汉文华学院共建了智能制造工程实践创新中心，另外还与其他职业院校共建了诸多类似的工程实践创新中心。

“与智能制造同频共振，助中国制造开道超车”，华中数控股份有限公司希望与更多的学校合作，共同实现“智能制造”启智润心，“中国制造”培根铸魂。

# （七）

# 职业本科“三性一体化”人才培养模式与工程教育实践

南京工业职业技术大学校长　谢永华

今天，基于 2019 年以来职业本科教育探索实践，我将以“职业本科‘三性一体化’人才培养模式与工程教育实践”为题向各位作报告，主要有五个方面。

## 1. 坚定“三性”培养定位

职业本科教育与职业专科教育相比，其专业对接的职业岗位和岗位群发生了上移，因此其培养定位也要相应改变。基于办学实践分析研判，我们认为职业本科教育应坚定“三性”培养定位，即掌握多项技术技能的“复合性”、通晓基础理论和核心技术技能的“精深性”、适应和推动技术变革的“创新性”。具体到每个专业的人才培养定位应在技术技能的复合性、精深性、创新性三个方面找到各自的侧重，形成更为精准的人才培养定位，进而确定具体的培养目标。例如，本科职业教育机械电子工程技术专业对比专科层次的机电一体化技术专业，对接技术岗位从一线维修人员变为现场工程师，要具备懂数字化设计、会集成控制、技术改进等能力。因此在培养定位上要重点强调提升“复合性”，突出了技术领域的“创新性”，同时在核心技术技能的“精深性”上也提出了明确要求，这就形成了这个专业培养定位“三性”个性化组合。

## 2. 建设“三并组合”课程体系

一是建设“德技并修”通识课程。落实立德树人根本任务，开设人文社科、艺术与美育、自然科技等 6 大类通识课程，开发通识类新课 20 余门。二是强化“理实并举”基础课程。强化大学数学、大学物理等基础理论课程学习，夯实学生学科和专业基础，对比专科同类专业，以上课程课时增加超 50%。增加基础实训课程的深度和比重，强化实训室建设和实训教学改革，通过理实结合提升基础理论的掌握深度。三是开发“三跨并行”专业课程。综合分析产业多岗位能力需求，跨岗位提取公共技术技能开发建设专业平台课程 30 余门、提取专项技术技能开发专业方向课程 40 余门；基于工作过程系统化逻辑，跨专业打破学科、院系限制整合专业教学资源、师资团队等，学生跨专业选课比例达到 20% 以上；基于典型工作任务需求，跨平台整合实习实训资源，开展系列化综合项目训练，占实践总课时比例 30% 左右。

3. 推进“三阶递进”创新教育

一是普及“创新初识”。坚持价值导向，面向所有学生开设“创新思维与创新方法”“创新思维与创业基础”等创新必修课程两门、“TRIZ 创新方法”“创意与创新：文化产业概论”等创新选修课程 24 门，全面提高学生创新思维与意识和基本创新素质。二是深化“专创融合”。坚持问题导向，面向有专业基础的学生开设“专创融合”课 35 门，引入最新专业创新实践成果构建典型教学案例，推进大学生创新创业训练计划，重点教会学生将创新方法运用到专业技术开发领域，着力提升专业创新能力。三是推动“创新实践”。坚持需求导向，面向准毕业生开发创新实践项目，依托专业社团，聘任指导教师，以五级竞赛体系为辅助，实现“赛中创”；引导支持学生在相关创新型企业进行顶岗实习，以专利形式开展毕业设计，实现“学中创”；组建 51 个师生创新工作室，开放实验实训平台，遴选优秀学生参与教师科研课题，实现“研中创”。

4. 打造“三师融合”师资队伍

坚持把教师作为职业本科教育发展的第一资源。推进校内教师、企业工程师、领军技能大师融合发展。一是做强校内专任教师队伍。推进骨干教师“专家化”，引进培训国家级高层次人才 21 人，专业型博士 293 人；推进博士教师“双师化”，新进博士须在企业实践，并跟岗校内导师研修一年，经考核合格才能上课堂；获评全国“黄大年式”教师团队 1 个、教育部教师教学创新团队 2 个；推进专业教师“国际化”，近年来，开展专题式、项目制等专业教师海外培训近 50 批次、150 余人次。二是做实校外企业兼职教师队伍。合作企业长期派驻校内的工程师 50 余人，聘任企业工程师 90 余人，全程参与人才培养方案制定与实施，重点指导学生实习实训。三是做特领军技能大师队伍。建立技能大师工作室 12 个，引进培训全国技术能手 9 人、省技术能手 20 人，重点参与指导学生综合实训、各类技能和创新竞赛，推进技术革新、工艺改造，并一对一帮扶青年博士教师成长、着力提升技能水平。

### 5. 构筑四类协同育人平台

一是技术联盟型，与精雕集团、西门子等技术上游企业以“技术”纽带构建联盟，主要面向技术下游企业实施现代学徒制培养。二是协同服务型，与地方政府、产业园区和华为培训中心等企业合作，发挥专业与地域优势，建设 5 个省级研发中心，聚焦企业一线技术难题，师生共同参与企业技术难题攻关 519 项。三是双创孵化型，依托国家双创示范基地，与南京秦淮区政府和金蝶集团共建省级大学科技园、建设校内大学生创业园、孵化创新企业 100 余个，成为学生创新实践重要基地。四是国际伴随型，伴随中国有色矿业集团等大型企业走出国门，校企共建境外办学机构，培养当地亟须技术技能人才。

南京工业职业技术大学职业本科教育的办学实践充分证明，职业本科教育具有良好的发展前景和旺盛的生命力，是与普通教育同等重要的教育类型，既满足了经济社会发展对高层次技术技能人才的需要，又回应了广大人民群众对高质量就业和教育的需求，为人才多元化发展提供了多样化途径，在全国职教战线发挥了示范带动作用，引领了中国职业教育高质量发展。

# （八）

# 中国先进制造业发展中的职业院校工程教育要素浅析

中国机械工业联合会教育培训部主任　陈晓明

基于机械行业人才培养工作经验，聚焦“职业院校工程教育”主题，探讨以下三个话题：第一是“先进制造业发展与人才需求变化”，明确职业教育支撑制造业发展的重要意义及开展工程教育的现实价值。第二是“职业技术教育的工程要素及体系”，探讨面向高质量发展，职业院校实施工程教育需要融入哪些关键要素，明确职业院校开展工程教育的聚力点和特色。第三是“职业院校工程教育实施策略和建议”，从行业视角为职业院校实施工程教育提出若干建议。

## 1. 先进制造业发展与人才需求变化

进入新时代以来，在全球回归实体经济、回归制造业，特别是在新一轮科技革命背景下，我国立足工业现代化发展实际，以实现制造强国为目标，聚力推动制造业转型升级。这一时期的发展，具有重要时代意义的关键节点有三个：一是2015年5月，国务院印发《中国制造2025》，其作为实施制造强国战略的第一个十年行动纲领，吹响了中国制造强国建设的集结号；二是2019年《政府工作报告》明确提出要构建现代产业体系，推进制造业向高质量发展，为产业变革赋予新的使命；三是2020年国家“十四五”规划强调推进产业基础高级化、产业链供应链现代化，坚定不移建设制造强国、质量强国、网络强国、数字中国。

从推动制造业高质量发展的角度看，今后5～10年，制造业发展的核心任务与战略措施主要是贯彻新发展理念，加快发展先进制造业、推进工业强基、实现产业链供应链安全可控、增强制造业竞争优势等方面，落脚点是“碳达峰、碳中和”战略目标的实现。

从产业政策、产业体系、产业技术、产业生态等方面观测，近十年来，中国先进制造业变革体现出“创新驱动、融合赋能、聚合优化和要素提升”的主要趋势。推动高质量发展，行业企业更加重视价值链提升，更多关注生产力要素配置上移的影响，特别是数据成为生产力新要素的驱动效应。从技术变革上看，一是产业新技术、新业态、新场景、新职业的变化十分迅猛；二是产业基础高级化、产业链现代化具有鲜明的技术高端化特征；三是发展服务型制造，推动网络协同制造、个性化定制等技术的创新应用；四是大型成套装备制造、微纳精密制造呈现出技术集成应用的极致化特征；最后，数字化技术是先进制造技发展的显著特征。

基于对产业和人才发展的长期研究，“十四五”期间，预测机械行业对技术技能人才的需求将达到 280 万。观察行业人才需求及变化，需要着重关注产业基础、智能制造、服务型制造、绿色制造和工业数字化、人工智能、新能源汽车、智能装备、精密检测、新材料成型与控制、工业工程等重点技术领域，并对产业链、技术链、价值链和新技术应用场景、生产组织方式、工作岗位及岗位能力 6 个方面作系统分析，其中，“技术革命→新技术应用场景→生产组织方式变化→岗位和岗位能力要求变化”是高质量育人的关键链节。机械行业对基础型、复合型、知识型、创新型、应用型等各类技术技能人才的岗位需求旺盛，基础性技能工作岗位是企业发展的重要支撑，专项技能培养是造就大批能工巧匠、大国工匠的重要基础，更加体现出对职业人才工程素养的普遍性要求。

**2. 职业技术教育的工程要素及体系**

回顾中国工业发展史不难看出，职业技术教育、工程教育在行业人才培养中始终呈现出共生共融的基本特征，并成为支撑产业变革优化的重要基础。习近平主席在给本届大会的贺信中提出“互学互建、共建共享”的理念，对建设高质量工程教育具有重要的指导和实践意义。面向工程教育领域，2017 年，教育部提出关于“新工科”建设的“5 个新”：工程教育的新理念、学科专业的新结构、人才培养的新模式、教育教学的新质量、分类发展的新体系，值得职业院校研究借鉴。

当前及未来一定时期，制造业“智改数转”成为技术变革的核心任务，先进制造技术（“本体”技术）实施创新工程，数字化、网络化、智能化技术（“赋能”技术）实施应用工程，加快推进二者的深度融合和创新升级，围绕“细分行业和场景应用”，形成鲜明的新技术“赋能”路径。在此进程的不同阶段，分布着诸多工程和工程教育要素。

职业院校需要立足我国高质量发展新阶段，走出一条具有职业教育特色的工程教育之路。在此提供以下参考思路：积极回答未来产业、未来技术、未来人才需要何种工程素养的问题；进而考虑未来专业、未来资源、未来优势以及未来生态的打造，确立职业院校开展工程教育的逻辑起点；再则是如何针对制造业“本体”技术与“赋能”技术融合创新及其细分应用，将先进制造的工程要素有机融入职业教育人才培养全过程。因此教育过程本身就具有工程属性。

职业院校开展面向未来的工程教育，建议注重探究工程教育的系统性、专业性、应用性、创造性、科学性等要素，构建要素逻辑体系；从新职业岗位需求、岗位工程要素、工程教育专业架构入手，再到工程教育课程体系、工程实践能力育成、工程教育人才评价进行系统性探索和规划；在把握先进制造领域工程要素、工程需求、工程岗位的基础上，聚焦培养学生的工程意识、工程思维、工程体验、工程规范，形成职业院校开展工程教育的有效路径和人才培养体系。

### 3. 职业院校工程教育实施策略和建议

首先，以创新引领构建高质量发展的战略理念，以辩证扬弃界定高质量发展的根本基点，以优化服务找准高质量发展的实现路径，以营造生态打造高质量发展的标志成果明确实施工程教育的总体设计思路和发展目标。值得关注的是，2022年6月6日，教育部部长怀进鹏在第二届亚太教育部长视频会上提出，“建设更具韧性更加包容公平的高质量教育体系……推动产教融合、科教融合……把学校和教师作为发展高质量教育的关键基础”，这为职业院校开展工程教育提供了重要导向。

在产教融合与校企合作的辩证作用关系中，产教融合是校企合作的前提、目标和动力，校企合作是产教融合的具体行动、价值体现和生命力所在；在产教融合与校企合作的聚力方向上，产教融合更聚焦国家战略、产业政策、行业发展和产业价值链，校企合作则更聚焦区域政策、区域产业集群、区域龙头企业及其发展战略。明晰二者交互协同的动力机制，才可以最终实现人才培养与产业需求的良性互动、精准对接。

探讨产教科融合发展理念下的工程教育，必须遵循产业发展和人才发展的基本规律。需要结合“专业—专业群—课程—模块化课程体系”构建，建设“产学研用创评”融合共进的工程教育平台，形成具有工程特色、体现工程教育创造力的人才培养体系。

基于产教融合、科教融合的根本逻辑和关键路径，推进职业院校工程教育体系建设，行业层面更关注工程教育的契合度、贡献度和影响力，学校方面则应更好地体现工程教育的针对性、协同性和持续力。职业院校应在人才培养目标中与时俱进地融入工程要素，更加注重人才工程素质的培养和锻炼。这需要政校行企多元协同，共创职业教育高质量发展新生态。

# （九）

# 中国中车产教融合育人之道

中国中车集团有限公司人力资源中心副主任　吴新林

在去年召开的中央人才工作会议上，习近平总书记对工程科技创新和工程师队伍建设作出重要指示，为深化我国工程教育改革、加快建设具有中国特色世界水平的工程师培养体系提供了根本遵循。面对百年未有之大变局和新冠病毒疫情的影响，工程教育对经济社会发展和产业升级的“发动机”作用日益凸显，培养造就更多卓越工程师和高质量技术技能人才，对建设教育强国、服务现代化建设，具有重大战略意义。中国中车集团是全球规模领先、品种齐全、技术一流的轨道交通装备供应商，是以研制“复兴号”高速动车组为产品谱系的我国轨道交通装备行业唯一一家产业化集团，服务于全球 109 个国家和地区。作为一家有着百余年历史的制造企业，自诞生以来，一直把工程教育作为工作中的重中之重来部署、推进、落实。近年来，我们把工程教育的侧重点放在产融结合上，取得了新突破。下面，我从“过去、现在、未来”三个纬度谈一下中国中车集团在工程教育方面的探索与实践。

回望过去，我们以产业报国为宗旨，推动人才育成。中国中车集团第一家铁路工厂诞生于 1881 年，并制造了中国第一台蒸汽机车——“龙号”机车，这是中国人积极学习西方先进工程技术以求自强的缩影。

中华人民共和国成立后，中国中车集团肩负着“共和国长子”的神圣职责，创办了全国最早的技工学校。20 世纪，中国中车集团曾创办了 20 余所职业学校（目前仍在办常州铁道高等职业技术学校、大连机车技师学院），为行业和社会培养了大批工程技术和技能人才，在践行实业兴邦、产业报国的初心使命中发挥了中流砥柱作用。

进入新时代，中车人认真贯彻习近平总书记三次视察中车重要指示批示精神，一手抓科技创新，一手抓人才育成，在建设中国特色社会主义伟大事业中铸就一批“大国重器”：从“和谐号”创造世界铁路运营试验最高速，到“复兴号”树立世界高铁运营新标杆，再到“绿巨人”进藏入疆，近 4 000 列高铁列车奔驰在祖国广袤的大地上，实现从追赶到领跑的伟大跨越，成为中国递向世界的一张亮丽名片。

立足当下，我们以制造强国为使命，推动人才育成。2012 年以来，特别是《国家职业教育改革实施方案》出台后，中国中车集团先行一步，敢闯敢试，统筹规划、顶层设计中国中车集团职业教育改革、建设国家产教融合型企业等实施方案，积极探索技术技能人才队伍培养的新路径、新举措。把握新发展阶段、新发展理念、新发展格局，明确提出“成为央企职业教育产教融合典范”目标，并列入中国中车集团“十四五”发展纲要。按照“两一体、两统筹”总体思路（即企业办学校，突出校企一体；依托职业学校办中车培训中心，职业教育与培训一体；统筹专业规划建设，打造高水平轨道交通装备制造专业群；统筹校企实训基地布局与建设，打造高水平实训基地群），稳步推进职教改革和产教融合，在人才育成方面结出了新的硕果。目前，中国中车集团拥有国家高速列车技术创新中心以及 13 个国家级研发机构、21 个国家级企业技术中心，并在全球建立了 15 个海外研发中心。拥有中华技能大奖获得者 9 人，全国技术能手 123 人，享受国务院政府特殊津贴 94 人，中车首席技能专家 64 人，资深技能专家 277 人，技能专家 777 人。一大批“大国工匠”“高铁工匠”的不断涌现，为我国走向制造强国、装备强国提供了强大支撑。我们的主要做法有六项。

一是发挥管理优势，丰富工程教育学科体系。满足“一带一路”建设和国际化战略的需要，按照 6 大职类、26 个职群、130 个职种，建立职位体系和人才标准体系，针对工程技术、制造技术等领域，构建了 7 个一级学科、64 个二级学科和 416 个三级学科组成的学科体系，形成了包括工程技术人才在内的中车全球一体化人力资本管理体系，为产业链、创新链与人才链、教育链有机衔接提供了罗盘和标尺。

二是发挥校企一体优势，构建工程教育创新平台。以中车培训中心为引领，以常州铁道高等职业技术学校为主体，整合中车人才、技术、实训等资源，建立教育培训、师资人才、课程体系、实训基地、业务运营等五个“一体化”管理机制。充分发挥现代产业链“链长”作用，与江苏常州共建“三位一体”产教融合基地，有效贯通职业教育与职业培训。

三是发挥人才优势，培育“双师型”创新团队。充分发挥卓越工程师队伍和高铁工匠人才优势，成立中车高铁工匠协同创新中心，实施工程教育师资校企混编，建立企业培训师与院校教师交流机制，让技术专家、技能大师进校园参与职业教育，将企业培训技术、培训课程移植学校、移植课堂，有力推进“三教”改革，促进职业教育高质量发展。

四是发挥技术优势，支撑专业群建设优化升级。围绕先进轨道交通装备九大关键技术和十项配套技术，形成轨道交通装备职业教育专业群建设规划框架，开发轨道交通装备职业教育专业地图，成立由校企专家共同参与的专业建设委员会，校企合作开发新形态教材，有力推进产业链、创新链与人才链、教育链的深度融合。

五是发挥资源优势，打造工程教育实训基地群。整合中车34个国家级技能大师工作室、12个全国示范性劳模创新工作室、68个省部级技能大师工作室以及138个职业技能实训基地资源，健全校企实训资源共享机制。以轨道交通装备智能制造技术为基础，建设国家级公共实训基地。

六是发挥创新优势，放大产学研用合作效能。加强与高等学校、职业院校、科研院所开展战略合作，在人才培养、人才评价、科技创新、成果转化和研发平台建设等方面开展产学研用深度合作，推动组建近百家单位参与的先进轨道交通职教集团（联盟），营造多元开放融合的工程教育共同体。

展望未来，我们以建设现代化强国为目标，推动人才育成。当前和今后一个时期，是加快建设社会主义现代化强国的重要时期，不仅需要大批卓越工程师，也需要大量具有专业知识和较强技术背景的能工巧匠。实现工程教育的改革与创新，是中央企业义不容辞的使命、责任和担当。下一步，我们将深入贯彻习近平总书记重要指示批示精神，深入实施“五个对接”，即学校建设规划与中车战略对接，专业设置与轨道交通装备制造产业对接，课程内容与职业技能标准对接，教学过程与生产过程对接，学生与学徒对接，培养具有“产业报国、勇于创新、为中国梦提速”的高铁工人精神，掌握高端装备制造技术技能，具备职业化道德修养、行为规范的新时代“大国工匠”“高铁工匠”，创新实施“校企融为一体、产教充分融合、职培相互融通、育训有机结合、校企协同育人”的人才培养新模式，努力造就一批引领产业变革、铸就大国重器的优秀工程人才，为践行“交通强国、装备支撑”提供中车方案，贡献中车力量。

# (十)

# 工程化在职业技术技能人才培养中的实践与探索

世界技能大赛中国（天津）研究中心主任、天津职业技术师范大学工程实训中心主任
徐国胜

工程是一种有组织的造物活动。工程实践创新能力是人生价值的助推器和倍增器。“工程化”是借真实工程教、依真实工程学，在真实工程做，用真实工程考。“工程化”的目标是使学生在真实世界、现实生活中能得心应手的工作、生活。

## 1. 工程化的人才培养理论依据

工程实践创新项目教学模式是现代产业转型视野下探索出的一种教育界与产业界互动，以实际工程项目为导引，以实践应用为导向，以创新能力培养为目标，以项目实践为统领的应用型技术技能型人才培养新途径。工程实践创新项目模式遵循了工程的规律，用工程方法培养学生，是“做中学”在经济社会新常态下具化的教学模式。工程实践创新项目教学模式的核心内涵是工程化、实践性、创新型、项目式。

## 2. 工程化的专业标准设计

现代职业技术技能人才培养需要依靠工程化专业标准。为探索工程化专业标准设计，我校在工程实训中心开设了机械设计制造及其自动化专业卓越班——工程实践教育实验班。该班旨在协同普通高校、企业和职业院校进行人才培养，探索工程实践创新应用型人才培养模式。实践过程，构建以工程实践教学体系为主体，以“工程实践创新能力”和“工程实践教学能力”为核心的“一体两翼”培养体系。“一侧翼”以知行合一的核心课程提升理论认知水平，“另一侧翼”以实践、反思、

再实践的方式强化教育教学能力，使学生的理论学习、实践学习与现场体验不脱节。以学期为单元，以连续的工程实践创新能力训练为主体，使学生的动手体验、技能习惯形成和创新实践过程不间断。教学理念为知行合一。培养体系为一体两翼。知识是通过思维获得的，能力是通过行动养成的，思维会对行动产生影响，行动也会对思维形成支撑，思维与行动相互作用才能获得真知。

### 3. 工程化的教学团队建设

现代职业技术技能人才培养需要一支工程化教学团队。根据工程实践教育实验班的需求，我们建立了一支理论基础扎实、实践经验丰富、特色鲜明的工程化教学团队，成员包括教授、教学名师、技能大师、世界技能大赛技术指导专家、全国技能大赛专家、全国技能大赛冠军、全国技术能手、企业一线操作人员及工艺师和产品研发人员。

### 4. 工程化的教学环境建设

为了满足“知行合一、理实一体”的教学要求，在校内、校外教学环境建设方面，强化企业真实环境、现场工艺流程的模拟与再现。满足工程实践创新项目专业建设的“创新型”能力培养需求，寓专业能力、职业素质、工程素养于实训实习中。一是在校内教学环境的建设方面，探索校内实训基地与生产性实训协同实施，探索校企合作、产教融合。注重设备的先进性，加强创新工作室的建设，突出工程实践创新项目专业建设的“创新型”。二是在校外教学环境建设方面，要适度前移核心技术和技能培养，使学生在参与顶岗实习时已基本掌握专业技术技能，提升学生实习的服务性、参与性，使企业受益。为企业提供技术服务，探索“双赢”模式下的校外实训基地建设，强化工程实践创新项目专业建设的“创新型”。

### 5. 工程化的项目式建设

工程实践创新项目模式要求建立一个个从简单工程到复杂工程的情境和载体。工程化教学项目要能真实、完整地培养学生的自主学习能力、观察问题能力、分析问题能力和解决问题能力。为实现以工程项目为线索，对教学内容的知识结构体系和内容进行更新与完善，使课堂传授知识与机械真实工程项目同步，突出“以学生为中心”的理念，发挥教师引导作用，提高学生综合工程实践能力和创新能力。设计了相应的工程化的教学项目作为载体，通过“一主线六互通”的教学设计，以学生行动为主线，实现课上与课下互通、线上与线下互通、理论与实践互通、教室与现场互通、校内与校外互通、本门课程与其他课程互通，提高学生的实践能力，培养学生的创新思维。

**6. 工程化的考核方案实施**

“工程化”的核心是“真实”。工程要真实，实践要真实，创新要真实，项目要真实，考核要真实，教育学的整体要真实。工程化考核方案旨在培养学生问题意识、创新意识，构建多种解题思路，锤炼学生的批判性思维。课程考核环节要求学生寻找在工程训练课程中遇到的实际工程问题，用课程中相应的理论知识进行分析，制订解决方案并动手实践。具体采取实际问题解决、方法总结提炼和答辩相结合的方式进行。通过这种与实践紧密结合的工程化考核，激发学生学习动机和兴趣，真正实现了理论与实践的无缝衔接，培养学生发现问题、分析问题、解决问题的能力和协作意识。

高端技术技能人才必须增强工程实践能力，提升创新精神和创新能力，提高综合素质，实现五个“真实”结合，即动脑与动手真实结合，理论与实践真实结合，学校与企业真实结合，职业教育与经济社会真实结合，教育与人的全面发展真实结合，将个人的潜力健康地发挥到极致，为中华民族伟大复兴贡献最大的力量。

# （十一）

# 开窗破壁，创新赋能高职院校汽车工程人才培养

湖南汽车工程职业学院院长　尹万建

在世界百年未有之大变局和新冠病毒疫情叠加冲击之下，职业技术教育推动经济社会有序发展的作用日益显著。“新工科”建设背景下，为适应新经济、新产业发展需要，处于工程教育中实践应用型职业院校必然要做出相应的行动。

## 1. 工程教育发展的时代必然

（1）重新认识工程教育。在职业教育新的历史发展期，中国需要大量的现场工程师和卓越工程师，而工程教育恰恰是解决这个问题的关键所在。工程师通过开发制造产品而服务社会，大多数工程设计是通过应用和改进现有技术来满足社会的变化需求，而好的工程师通常会采用最先进的技术来推动新的前沿并开拓创新，即开创性的工作和突破性的创新。工程师所需要的理想特质包括但不限于以下：一是很好地理解工程科学基础，包括数学、物理、化学、生命科学和信息技术等；二是很好地理解设计和制造的过程，了解设计理念和制造过程所需要的知识和技能；三是具有多学科复合性和系统性思维和视角，能够综合考虑产品的各个环节和过程；四是了解工程实践的背景环境，了解企业状况、社会经济、历史、当地环境及顾客和社会需求；五是有良好的沟通交流能力，可书写报告、具有口头表达能力、熟悉图表、有聆听能力等；六是具备良好的职业素养和职业道德；七是具备批判性和创造性思维；八是快速适应重大变化的能力和自信；九是好奇心和终身学习的能力；十是懂得团队合作的重要性和具备团队协调能力。

目前，工程教育就是要让工程师领导或参与产品、过程和系统全生命周期的各个阶段，通过构思、设计、实施和运行四个步骤完成产品的设计制作使用等环节。

而培养工程师的工程教育改革需要做到：第一，做好调研，在调研基础上做好教学标准，在教学标准基础上形成自己的人才培养方案；第二，做好课程标准，要解释清楚需要教什么及在哪里教的问题；第三，贯彻实施课程标准，在实施中要进行过程控制；第四，评价和改进预期目标；第五，做好工作学习场地和设备配备，也就是教学硬件的准备。这些内容都要贯彻构思→设计→实施→运行的理念。

（2）“新工科”建设背景下，产业的转型升级使工程教育的舞台日益宽广。工程科技、工程教育对经济社会发展和产业升级的“发动机”作用日益凸显，培养造就更多现场工程师和高质量技术技能人才，是推进我国科技自立自强、加快建设世界重要人才中心和创新高地的必然选择，对于建设教育强国、服务现代化建设，具有重大战略意义。

数学是科学的基础，科学是技术的基础，技术是工程的基础，产业的转型升级要求职业教育构建起数学、科学、技术和工程四位一体的教育体系。而工程教育就是通过传授数学、科学和技术的知识技能，培养学生解决问题的综合能力，以培养能将科学技术转化为生产力的工程师的专门教育，其舞台将日益宽广。

### 2. 高职汽车工程人才培养存在的问题

从现实来看，汽车工程人才培养上出现了两个明显的倾向：一是重专业、轻复合，随着科技的发展，要求多专业融合，复合型专业越来越多，而往往对一个专业的研究实践较深，对复合型专业研究实践较少较浅；二是重眼前就业，轻后续发展，职业院校专业的划分越来越细，学生学习的操作技能面越来越窄，导致职业院校毕业生职场成长能力脆弱，后续发展乏力，甚至被边缘化。职业院校工程人才的培养必须坚持复合性、创新性、工程性、发展性等逻辑要素，这是目前高职汽车工程人才培养亟待解决的问题。

### 3. 湖南汽车工程职业学院培养汽车工程人才的探索实践

湖南汽车工程职业学院作为一所对接服务汽车产业的专门院校，坚持“立足汽车行业、服务汽车产业、培养汽车人才、打造汽车品牌”办学思路，在培育汽车产业需要的高素质技术技能人才方面做了一些有益的探索。

（1）师资保障为汽车工程人才培养保驾护航。在汽车产业由传统能源向新能源、由人工驾驶向智能驾驶的转型升级阶段，学院率先签约湖南省首个高职院校“院士工作站”——李德毅院士湖南汽车工程职业学院工作站推进智能驾驶技术、

“驾驶小脑”方面理论和应用研究。在李德毅院士精心指导下，工作站师生专注于无人驾驶汽车的产业化研究，致力于无人驾驶汽车底盘线控技术研究与应用。基于师生汽车底盘线控化改造及汽车嵌入式系统设计方面的大量实践和研究基础，汽车专业学生在解决汽车线控底盘控制程序的调试、试验、优化方面，线控底盘制动、转向系统的平滑控制等方面取得了突破性进展。

2019 年，汽车运用与维修技术专业教学团队成功立项为首批国家职业教育教师教学创新团队；2021 年，智能网联汽车技术专业教学团队立项为第二批国家职业教育教师教学创新团队。国家级教师教学创新团队助力学校“双高计划”智能网联汽车技术、汽车智能技术等双高 A 类专业群的专业骨干教师培育、专业教学改革和人才培养模式改革。

凝聚人才力量，形成人才智库。学院自 2022 年起开始组建校级科研创新团队，到 2026 年，力争打造 30 个左右高水平科研创新团队。为产出一批高水平科技成果提供智力支持，同时也为学生成长提供强力支撑。

（2）实践竞赛使汽车工程人才成长笃学精技。秉持“厚德精技、笃学致用”宗旨，学院以技能大赛为抓手，不断推动岗课赛证融通综合育人，提升学生职业技能水平。2015 年，作为湖南省唯一代表，学院汽车制造与装配技术专业师生首探巴哈汽车大赛赛场，通过对车辆的设计、制造、装配到调试全过程的真实体验，师生完成了一次破冰之旅。从 2015 年前往山东潍坊荣和国际赛车场的参与体验，到 2017 年内蒙古乌兰布察站获得二等奖；从燃油越野车设计获不俗成绩到携独立自主设计的电动赛车参赛收获一等奖。在带队教师精心指导下，参赛选手们顽强拼搏、团结协作，一路过关斩将，出色地完成了一次次车检、赛车设计、引力测试、操控性测试、耐力测试等多个环节的赛项考验。更难得可贵的是，赛车的整体设计、动态测试和焊接总装全过程参与，培养了学生分工合作、通力协作的团队精神；磨炼了夜以继日、为梦想而奋斗的吃苦耐劳意志；更是积累了经验，提升了学生的工程实践能力。

比赛是最好的成长，实践是最好的学习。师生同心、团队互助，相互切磋、相观而善，从理论研究到实践操作，从技术设想到产品孵化全过程参与汽车制造服务的成长路径，助推了湖南汽车工程职业学院汽车工程人才的技能提升。

（3）创新创业教育为汽车工程人才培养增智长能。创新是一个民族进步的灵魂，是一个国家兴旺发达的不竭动力。高等学校作为培养人才的重要基地，责无旁贷地担负着培养创新人才的神圣使命。湖南汽车工程职业学院高度重视学生创新意识培养，出台了《湖南汽车工程职业学院大学生创新创业孵化基地入驻项目评估办法》等制度，筹建“梦工坊（创新创业中心）”，聘请行业专家进行指导，极大提高了师生参与创新创业工作的能力和水平。

近两年，学院双创工作成效明显，2021 年共获得 11 个国家级奖项，22 个省级奖项。其中，在第 5 届中华职业教育创新创业大赛全国总决赛中，参赛项目“车路云互联视域下的智能行车诱导系统”，与来自全国 122 所院校的 135 个项目展开激烈角逐，斩获国赛一等奖，成为湖南省唯一一所荣获一等奖的高职院校。用创新来激发学生思维，促进他们对事物全面深刻的理解，同时也是鼓励学生获得追求卓越和“再学习”能力，激励高职汽车专业人才迈向更广阔的天地。

职业教育和工程教育都有工程和实践的元素，在目前职业本科发展的前提下，汽车工程教育值得研究探索。汽车工程人才的培养，需要高等院校打破常规，明确复合是前提，创新是关键、工程是主旨、智能是趋势。从师资保障到平台搭建，从跨界培养到创新实践，我院目前还只是做了一些初步尝试，还需要下大力气研究职业教育，创新办学理念，改革体制机制，构建更加完善人才培养体系。

# （十二）

# 服务制造强国战略　职业教育大有可为

陕西工业职业技术学院院长　刘永亮

职业教育能不能培养出一线高素质工程技术人才？这是每一个职教人需要思考的严肃话题。当国人在为神舟遨游蓝天欢呼雀跃的时候，有谁可曾想到，在全国唯一的液体发动机制造厂商航天六院，在其梦之队团队成员中，有320多名工程技术人员毕业于同一个职业专科学校，何小虎就是其中的一个代表，他工作12年，解决了高尖技术75项，其中6项技术被称为国宝。邢小颖，清华大学基础工业训练中心实践课教师，她的“铸造”课程获得了2亿的播放量和百万点赞，连续7年荣获清华大学基础工业训练中心实践教学特等奖和一等奖，成为一名职业院校毕业后在顶尖的本科院校任教的优秀教师。这两位是我们学校17万毕业生中代表。下面给大家汇报三个问题。

## 1. 职业教育给工程教育提供新模式

工程教育是一种专业技术教育，培养的是从事产业化工作的科技人才。职业教育属于类型教育，培养适应生产一线的高素质技术技能人才。从现行的教育体系框架看，属于两种不同类型的教育，但从教育的本质、过程、内涵、目标和方式等因素来看，它们是同质同源、同向同生、相融共长、互为促进。我国的职业教育经过二十多年的快速发展，类型教育的理论模型基本成型，现代职业教育体系构建正在加快推进。职业教育的办学方针、目标定位、培养模式、教学原则等或者借鉴了工程教育的理念和做法，或者为工程教育提供了可参考的样本和案例。主要表现：在理论基础上，注重“做中学”的教育原则，以能力为导向；在人才培养目标上，强调技术技能，以应用为导向；在课程内容上，力求引入生产中的典型案例，使用活页式教材，以问题为导向；在教学方式上，推崇因材施教，“授人以鱼不如授人以渔”，以学生为中心；在教学过程中，注重教学情境化，把生产性实训基地建设作为重点，强调学生真学、真做、出真成果；在培养模式上，注重产教融合、校企合作，把产学研结合放在重中之重，强调专业与产业（岗位）对接、课程内容与职业资格证书对接、教学过程与生产过程对接、学历证书与资格证书对接；在师资队伍建设上，凸显“双师型”特征，强调立德树人，注重师德师风，按照“双师”标准去招、聘、引、培、管、评，培养工匠之师。同时，工程教育实践中的CDIO模式、课程开发模式、专业认证等特色，也被职业教育以工作过程导向的教学方法、“1+X”证书制度等广为借鉴。

2. 高职院校开展工程教育的新问题

我们以制造业为例。制造业是立国之本、兴国之器、强国之基，而人才的供给现状却不尽人意。从“量”上来看，2021年，我国制造业增加值总量为31.4万亿元，连续12年位居世界首位，占全球比重近1/3。产值与人才呈很强的正相关增长态势。据统计，在全国超2亿的技能劳动者中，高技能人才仅有5 000多万人，高级技工缺口高达2 200万人。人社部发布的今年第三季度全国“最缺工”的100个职业中，有58个属于“生产制造及有关人员”。一线制造企业高技能人才缺乏已经成为制约“中国制造”迈向“中国创造”的重要障碍。中国智能制造行业的“企业招工难”“人才培养难”“产业支撑难”三难问题将更加凸显。

从“质”上来看，随着制造业产业迭代升级，设备更新换代，新职业和新业态不断催生，传统制造业完成数字化转型最终实现智能制造，对从业人员的岗位能力要求也将提质升级。与之相对应，高职院校人才培养三大“不适应”则显得越来越明显。一是人才培养方案适应性不足，培养目标与产业数字化升级改造所需人才规格不适应；二是人才培养模式相对滞后，课程体系与先进制造产业所需岗位人才能力标准不适应；三是人才培养的关键要素缺乏活力，包括双师型队伍、生产性实训基地、数字化教学资源、项目化活页式教材等与智能制造新业态、新场景适应性不足。因此直面问题、精准施策则成了高职院校高质量发展的关键。

3. 职业院校工程教育的新路径

陕西工业职业技术学院是一所立足陕西、面向西部，扎根装备制造业，为服务制造强国战略培养时代工匠的特色鲜明的国家示范高职院校。建校72年来，始终致力于育训并举，培养德技并修的高素质技术技能人才，为装备制造业累计输送了近 17 万名合格毕业生。2019 年，被教育部、财政部确定为“双高计划”A 档建设院校。孙春兰副总理称赞是一所“有历史、有精神、有伙伴、有口碑”的优质高职院校。

近年来，学院积极对接先进制造产业发展，与行业企业深度合作，聚焦新岗位职业能力要求，扎实开展专业人才培养，通过营造新场景、构建新模式、建立新机制、开拓新视野，取得工程技术人才培养新成效。

一是适应产业新业态，营造工程教育新场景。立足新技术给制造业从以产品为中心转向以用户为中心、从单个企业竞争转向数据平台和企业集群竞争、从批量生产转向少量多样制造、从人工操作管理转向智能产线管理等新业态特征，学校与北京精雕、宁夏共享、西安航天发动机有限公司等行业龙头企业合作，将学校原有的机加工技术训练中心升级改造为先进制造技术工程中心，新建“5G+ 智能材料成型”实训基地，完成了包括数字化制造虚拟仿真中心等 16 个校内实训基地的数字化、智能化升级，在校内营造包含数字化设计、数字化工业、数字化检测的先进制造企业生产实境，展现新职场、新业态、新岗位、新工种，让学生在教学实践中切身体会数字化升级后带来的新体验，更直接了解先进制造的新特征，营造职前新氛围。

二是适应企业新需求，构建人才培养新模式。紧密对接先进制造产业岗位迁移带来的能力需求变化，立足教学规律和学生成长规律，将学生的理论学习、技能训练、创新创业能力培养有机结合，形成“学做创”一体化人才培养新模式。一是抓好“学”，强根基。立足新岗位工作标准，整合重构包括“基础课程、核心课程、通识课程”专业课程体系，在专业核心课程中增加数字化设计、数字化工艺、智能制造与数字化工厂等；在通识课程中增加人工智能、关键节能环保技术、未来通信技术等，凸显课程的“新”和“实”，确保培养目标实现由“传统”到“高端”、由“单项”到“复合”、由“动手”到“手脑并用”的提档升级。二是求真“做”，强实操。引入企业真实案例和项目，重新设计实践教学内容和形式，让学生通过仿做案例、参与项目、带团队做项目的递进式训练，实现在实战中演练和提升。三是立足“创”，强孵化。学校成立创新创业学院，建立创新创业课题体系，依托 13 个国家级生产性实训基地、协同创新中心以及众创空间、创业平台等，设立全天开放式“秦工坊”，通过导师领创、企业参与、社团组队、学生试水，把科技创新、成果转化、智力扶贫等与专业教学有机结合，让学生在课堂上头脑风暴、拓展思维，在项目中加以验证、不断完善，培养学生的创新意识和创业能力。

三是推进产教深度融合，建立共建共享新机制。按照“平台共建、成果共享、利益共赢、资源共用”的思路，通过校企“七联合”，积极推进技术、资源、人员、利益、制度、文化等产教“六维融合”。一是强化平台建设。学校牵头组建陕西装备制造业职教集团、机械行业材料成型与控制技术职业教育集团、陕西工匠学院、校企协同育人战略联盟等平台，在二级学院建设 6 个产业学院，在专业群建设 4 个协同创新中心、10 个技术研发中心。年均设立服务地方专项项目 21 项。针对企业在装备制造、新材料等领域的“卡脖子”环节开展研究，累计服务区域内中小微企业及科研院所 138 家，社会培训人数年增长 300%，为企业创造经济效益 2.56 亿元。二是搭建优质团队。针对工程教育对教师工程和科学素养、实践能力要求高等特点，坚持“内培”与“外引”相结合，打造“院士领衔、梯队合理、专兼结合”的“双师”队伍。建立从初级、中级、高级、工匠型四级递进的双师认定机制，建设院士工作站（室）2 个，全国高校黄大年式教师团队、国家级职业教育教师教学创新团队等国家级团队 10 个，引进大国工匠、产业教授、技能大师 38 人，校企协同建设技能大师工作室 4 个。三是加强项目带动。采取“走进企业征集问题、归纳梳理形成课题、面向教师发布项目、组建团队揭榜挂帅、合同管理绩效考核、评优晋级挂钩联动”的方式，推进教科研一体化发展，提升社会服务能力。

四是强化对外交流合作，拓宽国际合作新路径。学校对接国际工程教育发展，持续完善国际化管理服务机制和保障体系，着力提升师生对工程教育的国际视野。一是大力开展国际合作。牵头成立中德高等职业教育合作联盟（陕西—柏林），建立中国—新西兰职业教育教师培训基地；成为世界职教院校联盟会员单位，设有 61 个师生交流项目，派出 687 名师生赴国（境）外交流学习。二是积极拓展海外办学。成立陕西工院赞比亚分院、印尼秦工苑，培训外籍员工 1.9 万余人，培养学历教育学生 306 人；学校与印尼曼达拉经济学院设立本科生联合培养项目，首批 14 名学生开始线上教学。招收海外学历留学生 176 人、短缺交流生 400 多人。三是主动服务中国企业“走出去”。学校紧随产业“走出去”，与中国有色矿业集团公司、陕鼓集团等合作，在国外开展技术技能人才培养，开发“双语”活页式教材 6 本、“双语”在线课程 7 门，培训认证“双语”教师 36 人。四是强化职业标准输出。学校利用 70 余年厚重的职业教育文化积淀及国家示范、国家“双高”计划建设等机遇，总结梳理学校职业教育新制度、新经验、新成果，对接外海需求，面向赞比亚全境、尼日利亚 7 所院校输出软件技术等 16 个专业标准、182 门课程标准，为中国职业教育走出国门、中国文化发扬光大做出了积极探索。学校荣获世界职业院校联盟“教育可持续发展卓越奖”金奖。

学校建校 70 多年来，坚持扎根西部，服务装备制造产业。毕业生中，有的扎根制造行业，有的服务西部区域发展，有的在国家制造大类骨干企业就业。每年开设中国特色学徒制、企业订单班 66 个，49% 的毕业生实现了提前预订、合作培养、定向就业，毕业生受到社会高度认可。学校近三年共取得引领职业教育改革发展的重大成果 27 项，取得支撑国家战略、陕西区域经济发展的高品质建设成果 262 项，取得支撑职业教育高质量发展的政策、制度、标准类成果 269 项。获评全国机械行业骨干职业院校、全国机械行业校企合作与人才培养优秀职业院校、中国工业优秀单位等国家级荣誉 128 项，彰显了高职院校引领改革、支撑发展的新作为。

未来，学校将继续深化工程教育与职业教育的融合培养探索，抢抓机遇，锐意改革，强化内涵，提高质量，培养更多服务“制造强国”战略的工程技术人才，为我国职业教育迈向现代化贡献最优方案。

# （十三）

# 工程实践创新项目（EPIP）教学模式应用与推广研究

工程实践创新项目（EPIP）国际教育联盟顾问、天津市教育科学研究院职业教育研究中心主任
耿　洁

在世界职业教育领域，教学模式作为一种理论话语的表现形式和表达方式，影响和引导着职业教育教学的发展，如德国的“双元制”、澳大利亚的职业技术教育学院（TAFE）等。在中国天津，从近代工业的发端开始，实业教育、职业教育的教学模式探索未曾停止，与时俱进，持续创新，形成了以工程实践创新项目教学模式为代表的、具有中国特色的职业教育教学模式话语体系。接下来将从工程实践创新项目教学模式话语构建的历史逻辑、理论逻辑、实践逻辑三个方面，对工程实践创新项目教学模式产生背景的内涵逻辑及未来面向进行分析。

## 1. 工程实践创新项目教学模式话语构建的历史逻辑

职业教育教学模式话语构建与社会发展直接关联，以天津为代表的中国职业教育在不同历史时期，构建了与时代相适应的模式话语。

天津在近代工业文明的摇篮中创立了“工学并举”。近代中国的天津由于独特的区位优势，形成了以工业为主体，商业贸易、金融、交通、通信共同发展的格局，成为北方最早的通商口岸，向世界开放的前沿和窗口，直接带动近代实业学堂的产生，形成校企天然一体的行业办学模式。周学熙等创办了直隶工艺总局及一批实业学堂，探索“工学并举”教学模式。

天津在中华人民共和国成立初的工业建设中创立了“半工半读”。1958 年 5 月，刘少奇在天津视察时指示试办半工半读学校，同年 5 月 27 日，全国第一所厂办半工半读学校在天津国棉一厂开学，《人民日报》发表社论《举办半工半读的工人学

校》。此后，以天津为试点的“半工半读”在全国展开，建立了“两种劳动制度，两种教育制度”。

天津在改革开放后至新世纪第一个十年的工业东移战略中确立了“工学结合”。天津职业教育伴工业发展而生，随产业发展而变。天津从 1985 年到 2010 年基本完成工业战略东移目标，天津职业教育形成了行业办学为主的办学特色，确立了培养过程灵活性的“工学结合”模式。2005 年，教育部在天津召开职业教育工学结合座谈会，同年，天津市人民政府与教育部于共同签订了《关于共建国家职业教育改革试验区的意见》。

天津在新世纪第二个十年的现代工业体系建设中创立了“五业联动”。党的十八大以来，天津围绕“一基地三区”定位，加快产业调结构、换动能、促转型，以智能科技产业为引领的“1+3+4”现代工业产业体系基本建立。天津职业教育接连探索 2011—2015 年“示范区”建设，推进形成了“五业联动”，创立工程实践创新项目教学模式。

**2. 工程实践创新项目教学模式话语构建的理论逻辑**

中国职业教育思想从古代的墨子、鲁班到近代陶行知、黄炎培，再到新时代中国特色社会主义教育思想，诠释了各时代“教什么、怎样教”“学什么、怎样学”。

工程实践创新项目教学模式传承中国古代教育思想。工程实践创新项目教学模式吸纳墨子著名的“素丝说”“兼士”“扣则鸣，不扣则必鸣”“士虽有学，而行为本”等教育思想，确立环境育人、实践育人等模式内涵。探索建立工程实践创新项目视域下的产教融合、专业建设路径，回答了职业学校如何真实地融入经济社会发展；建立工程实践创新项目视域下的教学团队、赛教互动路径，回答了教师如何在真实完整的环境中成长、如何做到以赛促教。

工程实践创新项目教学模式坚守中国近代教育思想。工程实践创新项目教学模式把黄炎培、陶行知的教育思想发展为宇观的办学思想、宏观的教育论和教学论、中观的专业建设、微观的课程改革和纳观的知技素思想。五观论回答了职业学校从课程、专业到办学的“依据是什么”的问题，即让职业院校教师真教真做，职业院校学生真学真练，让整个职业院校因为“真实”和“完整”焕发新的活力。创新性地提出专业“核心技术一体化”概念、“四层两段一贯穿”课程结构体系。

工程实践创新项目教学模式坚定中国当代教育思想。吕景泉教授带领教学团队用 20 余年教学实践和理论研究创立的工程实践创新项目教学模式，将产教融合、校企合作、工学结合、知行合一创造性转化和创新性发展，概括为“12345”，即一宗“知行合一”，二核“真空和完整”，三谛“实谛、名谛、合谛”，四元“工程化、实践性、创新型、项目式”，五观“宇观的办学思想、宏观的教育论和教学论、中观的专业建设、微观的课程改革和纳观的知技素思想”，构建了基于“真实 / 完整”的职业教育教学理论。

### 3. 工程实践创新项目教学模式话语构建的实践逻辑

工程实践创新项目源于工矿企业实践和教学实践。工程实践创新项目源于真实生活，源自工矿企业实践和教学实践，是建立在企业技术服务之上的教学实践探索和研究的成果。吕景泉教授用 17 年时间形成基于工厂 / 企业技术改造的教学实践研究成果，在 1990—2006 年，探索产学合作专业建设、开发自动化类专业领域实训基地、实训项目与设备配置，推进天津市职业教育区域综合性实训基地建设。用 13 年时间构建工程实践创新项目职业教育教学模式并取得重大成效，2007 年，先后开发专业教学标准、核心课程建设标准、机电专业类师资知技素框架标准并付诸推广；2008 年，开发首届全国职业院校技能大赛“自动线安装与调试赛项”和教学资源。成功开展一系列教学改革，取得重大成果，获得职业教育国家级教学成果奖特等奖、一等奖等多项殊荣。

作为鲁班工坊核心的工程实践创新项目融入世界。2016 年，基于工程实践创新项目教学模式的鲁班工坊走向世界。鲁班工坊以中国原创首创的“工程实践创新项目”为教学模式、以教育部主导开发国际化专业教育标准为基本依据、以全国职业院校技能大赛（国赛）优秀赛项装备为主要载体、以师资培训先行及教材教学资源开发为必要保障，依靠合作国本土化院校和合作国本土化教师，走进了合作国国民教育体系和合作国教学标准认定，有效地服务了合作国经济社会和合作国青年就业创业。

截至 2022 年 3 月，海外鲁班工坊已建成 20 个，覆盖亚洲、非洲和欧洲三大洲，47 个中外合作建设的专业，很好地回答了中国职业教育如何整体走出去、走进去。工程实践创新项目教学模式是鲁班工坊建设的重要内涵，先后在中国天津渤海职业技术学院、泰国大城技术学院、葡萄牙塞图巴尔理工学院建立“工程实践创新项目体验中心”“工程实践创新项目研究中心”等中外工程实践创新项目教学研究的集散地。

#### 4. 工程实践创新项目教学模式的未来面向

“教”与“学”新生态的建立。工程实践创新项目教学模式把真实工程、真实世界、现实生活、实际问题迁移到职业学校，融入专业，延伸到课程，解决了教学做一体化的工程化精度、实践性深度、创新型宽度、项目式整度问题，解决了产教真融合、校企真合作的内生内审标度问题，将构建一个“真实”“完整”的教育教学新生态。在近十年的教育教学实践中，以《工程实践创新项目教程》为代表的一批教材及其他教学资源，激活了职业院校现有的教学理念、教学团队、教学设施、教学方案、教学管理、教学环境、教学考评等各种教育教学环节和要素。形成了一批电气自动化技术、机电一体化技术、光伏工程技术、智能制造装备技术等专业和智能电梯、风光互补发电系统安装与调试、数控加工技术等课程应用工程实践创新项目教学案例。

教师职业成长与发展的融入路径。2022 年 5 月，教育部办公厅发布《关于开展职业教育教师队伍能力提升行动的通知》，再一次对职业教育教师成长与发展提出新要求。新入职的职业院校教师应该经过入岗训练、适岗锻炼、胜岗历练三个阶段成长为“双师型”素质教师。用工程实践创新项目理念和思想，设计新教师的职业规划，让教师在真实中掌握基于实际工程导向的课程设计，成为具备实施专业情境式工程实践课程能力和可持续发展能力的高素质教师，这是时代的需求。

推广工程实践创新项目教学模式应用已经纳入《教育部天津市人民政府关于深化产教城融合打造新时代职业教育创新发展标杆的意见》，已经写入天津市教育现代化“十四五”规划，已经成为中国职业教育同世界分享的国际话语。

# （十四）

# 技术引领、四方协同，服务技能型社会建设

无锡职业技术学院院长　龚方红

无锡职业学院是 1959 年成立的原无锡农业机械制造学校，1999 年升级为无锡职业技术学院，2019 年，学校入选国家“双高”A 类校建设单位。建校 63 年来，始终扎根机械行业，致力于服务装备制造业，打造了以“技术引领、并跑产业”为特征的高质量发展之路，实现从机电类专业“单打冠军”到领军全国智能制造特色校的转型升级。无论是当时的农业机械，还是到后来的机械工程、机电一体化、机电两化融合、智能制造，应该说是一脉相承，随着产业的需求升级，不断提升办学的水平。下面从三个方面进行交流，第一遵循技术技能人才成长规律，推进岗课赛证研融合育人；第二坚持产学研用深度融合，推进专业集群数字化转型升级；第三借鉴工程教育专业认证理念，健全教学诊断与改进体系。

## 1. 遵循技术技能人才成长规律，推进岗课赛证研融合育人

工程类职业院校应结合地方产业发展，加强产教融合，提高工程技术人才的培养质量，积极探索现场工程师和高技能人才培养的方法与路径，推进“课岗赛证研”融合育人，在教学内容、教学模式、教学方法等方面适应产业转型升级的需要。

按照“培养基本科学素养、掌握特定专业知识、侧重工程技术应用、强化实际操作技能”的原则，大力开展工程教育教学改革和创新，服务制造业转型升级，这是学校在教学改革过程当中一个重要的抓手。

通过对接产业岗位需求研制职业图谱，实现人才培养快速响应产业转型发展；通过构建学分制框架下的柔性课程体系实现教学内容快速对接产业最新技术；通过专业方向选学、证书选考、大赛选拔等方式实现学生成长成才的多通道；通过学生

参与教师的研究项目，提升研究能力，有效探索了“岗课赛证研”相融合的基于职业能力培养的教学模式改革，而改革的核心引领是在“研”字上面。为了应对职业教育多样化的生源，我校坚持以“三教”改革为引领，探索“C-C-I”模式：第一个“C”是双证实用型（Certified），覆盖 100% 的学生，要获得一张证书；第二个“C”是专业复合型（Compound），根据产业的需求，覆盖 70% 的学生；第三个“I”是创新创业型（Innovative）技术技能人才培养，通过创新创业学院来培养，覆盖 15% 的学生。这种培养起到了比较好的效果，为 20 年以后拥有一批杰出校友打下了一定基础。

### 2. 坚持产学研用深度融合，推进专业集群数字化转型升级

装备制造业原来被誉为经典长线专业，但是在制造业数字升级化的过程中受到冲击最大的可能就是经典长线产业，装备制造业需要的新技术、新工艺、新规范倒逼着专业的升级改造。新版专业目录修订过程中，装备制造类专业目录实际上变动较大。在如何实现数字化升级方面，学校的经验是根据地方制造类企业“智改数转”的痛点难点，以智能制造设计、生产、物流、销售和服务等全生命周期为主线，与行业龙头企业深度合作，推进平台建设，依托平台开展人才培养、技术研发、生产示范和社会服务，通过平台把四大功能串联起来，通过这样的一条线串起来。引导教师依托平台开展技术研究，掌握核心技术，通过教师掌握核心技术，再推进专业的数字化的升级改造。以智能制造全产业链的需求，把全校 85% 以上的专业通过一条主线串联起来，组成智能制造专业集群，当然这条线就是智能制造的全生命周期技术要点，学校也形成了特色鲜明的智能制造专业集群。坚持技术引领、并跑产业，形成了专业技术标准研发与教学标准优化同步的专业建设模式。探索“人工智能 +”的新型教学模式，开展“课堂即工厂”“课堂即赛场”“课堂即项目”等活动，着力推进“教法”的改革。

### 3. 借鉴工程教育专业认证的理念，健全教学诊断与改进体系

最后环节就是如何保障质量的实施与达成，我校借鉴了工程教育专业认证的理念，健全了教学诊断与改进体系。工程类职业教育面临着“提高质量、提升形象”的难题。应充分借鉴工程教育专业认证理念，构建完善的内部教学质量保证体系，建立职业院校教学质量诊断与改进体系，利用配套的信息化平台精准地保障质量保障体系的实施。这个信息化平台根据学校的工作流程，坚持以学生为中心，以成果

为导向，构建持续改进、循环提升的教学质量保证体系。依托信息化平台，实现教学过程和教学管理透明化，实现“常态纠偏”和“阶段改进”，不断提升人才培养质量。通过平台的即时反馈，实现常态纠偏，通过数据的积累，实现阶段改进。该平台要依托“五全”智慧校园，建设学习中心、服务大厅、质量保证体系、内部控制系统和决策咨询系统，支撑学校的高质量发展。其中“五全”就是全师生覆盖，构建新型教育教学生态；全业务上网，推进服务供给模式升级；全数据交互，助力内部治理水平提升；全系统安全，保障智慧校园健康运行；全方位决策支持，大数据智能化分析。信息化应用从教育教学向学校治理水平的提升全面扩展，依托智慧校园保障学校的办学理念实施和教学质量的达成。

## 郑重声明



读者意见反馈

为收集对教材的意见建议，进一步完善教材编写并做好服务工作，读者可将对本教材的意见建议通过如下渠道反馈至我社。

咨询电话 400-810-0598

反馈邮箱 zz_dzyj@pub.hep.cn

通信地址 北京市朝阳区惠新东街 4 号富盛大厦 1 座

高等教育出版社总编辑办公室

邮政编码 100029

世界职业技术教育发展大会
WORLD VOCATIONAL AND TECHNICAL EDUCATION DEVELOPMENT CONFERENCE

# 2022年世界职业技术教育发展大会成果汇编

（下册）

世界职业技术教育发展大会组委会

# Compilation of Achievements of World Vocational and Technical Education Development Conference 2022

（Volume III）

Organizing Committee of World Vocational and Technical Education Development Conference

中国教育出版传媒集团
高等教育出版社·北京

**图书在版编目（C I P）数据**

2022年世界职业技术教育发展大会成果汇编 ：全3册/世界职业技术教育发展大会组委会编. -- 北京 ：高等教育出版社，2023.6
ISBN 978-7-04-060676-8

Ⅰ. ①2… Ⅱ. ①世… Ⅲ. ①职业技术教育－世界－文集 Ⅳ. ①G71-53

中国国家版本馆CIP数据核字(2023)第104511号

策划编辑 贾瑞武　　责任编辑 董梦也　于海宁　　封面设计 赵　阳　　责任绘图 邓　超
版式设计 赵　阳　　责任校对 刘娟娟　　责任印制 赵义民

| | | | |
|---|---|---|---|
| 出版发行 | 高等教育出版社 | 网　　址 | http://www.hep.edu.cn |
| 社　　址 | 北京市西城区德外大街4号 | | http://www.hep.com.cn |
| 邮政编码 | 100120 | 网上订购 | http://www.hepmall.com.cn |
| 印　　刷 | 北京盛通印刷股份有限公司 | | http://www.hepmall.com |
| 开　　本 | 787mm × 1092mm　1/16 | | http://www.hepmall.cn |
| 本册印张 | 10.5 | | |
| 本册字数 | 190千字 | 版　　次 | 2023年6月第1版 |
| 购书热线 | 010-58581118 | 印　　次 | 2023年6月第1次印刷 |
| 咨询电话 | 400-810-0598 | 总 定 价 | 260.00元 |

本书如有缺页、倒页、脱页等质量问题，请到所购图书销售部门联系调换

物 料 号　60676-002

# 目录

## 大会、大赛、博览会综述及新闻报道



## 国际视野与中国国情
### ——2022 年世界职业技术教育发展报告

# Contents

## Introduction to the Conference, the Competition, the Expo and Media Digests



## Global Vision and China's Reality
### ——World Vocational and Technical Education Development Report 2022

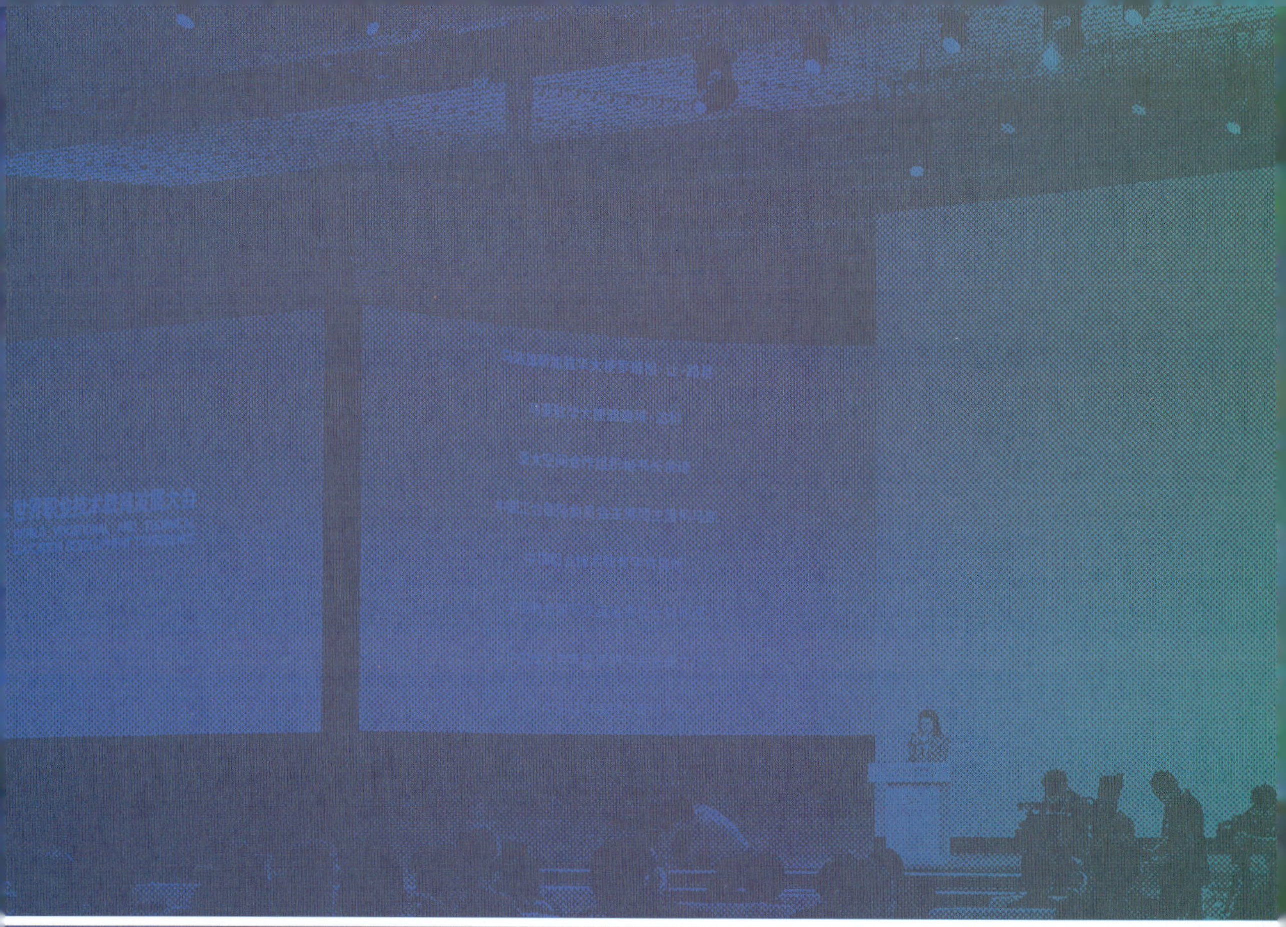

# 大会、大赛、博览会综述及新闻报道

# Introduction to the Conference, the Competition, the Expo and Media Digests

# 一

# 世界职业技术教育发展大会综述

世界职业技术教育发展大会组织委员会办公室主任、
中华人民共和国教育部职业教育与成人教育司司长　陈子季
Chen Ziji, Director of the Organizing Committee Office of World Vocational and Technical Education Development Conference, Director of the Department of Vocational and Adult Education of the Ministry of Education, the People's Republic of China

为落实习近平总书记2021年9月21日在第76届联合国大会上提出的全球发展倡议，扩大职业教育国际合作与交流，经国务院批准，教育部、中国联合国教科文组织全国委员会和天津市人民政府共同举办了首届世界职业技术教育发展大会（以下简称“大会”）。大会以“后疫情时代职业技术教育发展：新变化、新方式、新技能”为主题。习近平总书记专门为大会致贺信，孙春兰副总理宣读贺信并发表视频致辞。在外交部、发改委、商务部、国合署等部门大力支持和天津市委、市政府通力合作下，大会按照“富有新意、特色明显、影响深远”的要求，克服疫情反复和国际形势复杂变化带来的不确定性，圆满完成各项议程，实现了国际化、高标准、高质量的预期目标。

### 1. 大会概况

大会包含开幕式、主论坛、十四个平行论坛和闭幕式，并同期举办了首届世界职业院校技能大赛、世界职业教育产教融合博览会。大会期间，我们与有关国家开展了双边会谈，提出了筹建世界职业技术教育发展联盟和创设国际职业教育大奖的倡议，发布了《中国职业教育发展报告（2012—2022 年）》和大会共识性文件《天津倡议》，形成了职业教育国际交流合作崭新平台和范式。

（1）各国政府高度重视，各方代表共襄盛会。来自 123 个国家和地区的 196 名国际代表和 500 余名国内代表，以线上线下相结合的方式参加会议。国外共有 25 位部长级别官员、17 个国际组织负责人（代表）以及 11 位驻华大使出席。工信部、农业农村部、税务总局、国资委、乡村振兴局等部门负责人，天津、黑龙江、山东、广西壮族自治区等省（自治区、直辖市）政府负责人，8 位两院院士，中国银行、中车集团、格力公司、东软集团董事长等知名企业家，国内外专家学者，行业组织、高等院校、研究机构代表，各省区市教育部门负责同志，齐聚天津、共襄盛会。

中央政治局委员、天津市委书记李鸿忠出席大会开幕式及主论坛，并致欢迎辞。开幕式和主论坛共有中国、阿根廷、巴西、英国、埃塞俄比亚、马来西亚、蒙古、新西兰、尼日利亚、巴基斯坦、俄罗斯、新加坡、瑞士、委内瑞拉、韩国等 15 国教育部长级代表，加纳、爱尔兰等国驻华大使和联合国教科文组织执行委员会主席、联合国儿童基金会教育及青少年发展全球负责人等国际组织代表以及国际电信联盟、国际汽车工程师学会联合会等国际行业组织和知名企业、院校等多位代表分别致辞和发表演讲。闭幕式由联合国教科文组织驻华代表处主任致辞，天津市市长张工宣读《天津倡议》，教育部部长怀进鹏作会议总结并宣布闭幕。十四个平行论坛内容涵盖数字化赋能、产教融合、绿色技术、技能与减贫、促进公平、终身学习、科学与工程教育等世界职业教育发展的热点重点问题，来自 53 个国家的 230 名中外知名专家学者进行了充分而有效的讨论，分享了各国的实践经验，增进了彼此间的相互了解。

（2）大会活动精彩纷呈，促进各国交流合作。举办世界职业院校技能大赛，世界各国职业院校师生在大会期间同台竞技，展现了新技术和产教融合新成果。大赛共设 23 个赛项，分竞赛类 15 个赛项和展演类 8 个赛项。来自全球 107 个国家和地区的 293 所院校 988 名选手、489 名指导教师，共 207 个团队参加大赛，有效搭建起中外职教师生增进友谊、切磋技能、展示风采的国际平台。

举办世界职业教育产教融合博览会，博览会以“大力发展适应新技术和产业变革需要的职业教育”为主题，以线上线下相结合的形式召开。线下展设立两个展区，集中展示鲁班工坊建设和天津市职业教育发展成果。线上展为“云上博览会”，设置了云展馆等 8 大版块和工程教育展等 9 个专题展，306 家单位通过云上博览会展示了各国、各行业职业教育与经济产业融合发展的新成果、新方法，吸引超过 2 000 万人次“云上逛展”。

（3）发布倡议达成共识，协力推动世界职教发展。发布《天津倡议》，反映了世界各国教育发展的共同关切与中国职业教育改革发展重点，明确了后疫情时代职业教育功能定位、职责使命和发展方向，提出了世界职业教育高质量发展的行动纲领。

发布创设国际职业教育大奖的倡议，通过在全球选树一批为职业教育作出突出贡献、取得重大研究和实践成果的组织或个人，激励社会各界积极支持和推动职业教育发展。欢迎各国广泛加入、行业企业大力支持，共同研究设立、实施职教大奖。

发布筹建世界职教发展联盟的倡议，按照“全球性、非政府、非营利”的原则，呼吁全球教育界、产业界和其他社会组织、个人共同参与，协商组建世界职业技术教育发展联合体。会议期间，已有 36 个国家的 148 家高校、企业及行业组织参与联盟发起工作。

发布白皮书《中国职业教育发展报告（2012—2022 年）》，系统梳理总结了中国职业教育发展成绩和经验，与国际社会分享中国职业教育创新举措，发出职业教育合作邀约。

（4）社会反响普遍较好，中外媒体广泛关注。会议期间，百余个网站平台账号参与大会主论坛网络直播，各国院校、企业和机构通过视频会议系统参会 2.2 万人，各类媒体报道覆盖人群超过 6.73 亿，直播浏览量达 9.2 亿，成功打造“百网同播、万人同屏、亿人同观”的盛况。

大会引起了中外媒体广泛关注。《人民日报》、新华社、中央广播电视总台、《光明日报》、《经济日报》、《中国日报》等中央主要媒体及所属新媒体，在重要版面位置、重点新闻节目中连续报道这一盛会，深入广泛介绍我国职业教育改革创新发展成效和天津职业教育发展特色。央视《新闻联播》对国家主席习近平向世界职业技术教育发展大会致贺信进行报道，并推出“职业教育为产业强国夯实技术技能基础”报道，对大会召开及我国职业教育发展进行深入报道。《人民日报》先后刊发《习近平向世界职业技术教育发展大会致贺信》《世界职业技术教育发展大会召开》，推出大会综合报道《助力职业教育高质量发展》。海内外媒体原创报道 664 篇，媒体转载量超过 1.3 万余篇。微博、抖音等新媒体对大会有关内容进行实时直播报道，大会期间微博话题总阅读量超过5.5亿。美通社、雅虎财经等10余家外国主流媒体发布或转载约67篇相关报道，推特等海外社交媒体发布大会相关信息超过4 000条。

2. 会议成果

（1）习近平总书记贺信引起热烈反响。习近平总书记的贺信充分体现了党中央对职业教育的高度重视和办好职业教育的坚强决心，深刻阐述了职业教育对促进就业创业、助力经济社会发展、增进人民福祉的重要意义，充分展现了中国愿同世界各国一道加强互学互鉴、共建共享，携手落实全球发展倡议的愿望，体现了为落实联合国2030年可持续发展议程贡献力量的担当，为深化职业教育国际交流与合作提供了根本遵循和努力方向。习近平总书记的贺信得到与会嘉宾、国内教育系统广大干部和师生、国际社会的高度评价，引起热烈反响。这是继2021年全国职业教育大会后，习近平总书记再次对职业教育作出的重要指示，贺信极大鼓舞和增强了教育系统做好职业教育工作的信心和决心。

广大干部和师生纷纷表示，习近平总书记的贺信充分体现了党中央对职业教育的高度重视，明确了新时代职业教育改革发展的目标与任务，为我国职业教育高质量发展指明了方向。国际人士表示，习近平总书记的贺信体现出中国政府对促进职业教育高质量发展的高度重视和坚定决心，期望中国在促进全球职业教育高质量发展中发挥更大作用。各国教育部长和国际组织负责人普遍希望与中方进一步加强务实合作，共同推进联合国2030年可持续发展议程的落实，为推动构建人类命运共同体注入“技能力量”。

（2）孙春兰副总理视频致辞获得广泛赞誉。孙春兰副总理的致辞分享了中国政府大力推动职业教育改革发展的做法与经验，发起了各国共同应对挑战、共创职业教育繁荣发展新局面的倡议，得到各国与会嘉宾的高度评价和积极响应。

国内教育系统广大干部和师生纷纷表示，孙春兰副总理的视频致辞精辟阐述了职业教育的发展定位，指明了职业教育发展的本质规律，大家深受感动、倍感鼓舞。致辞充分展示了我国职业教育发展成就，彰显了中国特色社会主义发展道路的优势，有力提升了国际影响力和国家软实力，极大鼓舞和增强了职教战线做好职业教育工作的信心和决心，为深化职业教育国际交流与合作增添了动力和干劲。国际人士还纷纷表示，孙春兰副总理的致辞体现了中国携手各国推动全球发展倡议的深刻认识和坚定决心，使他们深感振奋，特别是一些亚非国家，对中国的治理能力越来越认同，愿与中国合作，携手共进、共促发展。

(3) 搭建了国际职业教育交流合作崭新平台和机制。大会以《天津倡议》提出发展职业教育的价值理念，以联盟构建国际职业教育交流合作运行机制，以大奖激励职业教育创新发展，以大赛增进各国互学互鉴和技能切磋，以展会彰显产教融合新成果新亮点，以发展报告向世界展示我国职业教育发展成就与模式经验。各国各界代表高度赞赏中国为推动世界职业教育发展作出的努力和贡献，认为大会搭建了职业教育国际交流合作的有效平台，为进一步开展职业教育务实合作奠定了坚实基础。

(4) 达成了后疫情时代全球职业教育发展普遍共识。与会各方普遍认为，本届大会的宗旨与全球经济社会发展和职业教育重点，特别是联合国倡导可持续发展议程高度契合、紧密相关。教育与产业界、企业界和经济社会深度交融，是这次大会的最大特色和基本共识。

联合国教科文组织执行委员会主席塔玛拉女士表示，此次大会主题既关乎职业教育改革和人类发展的重要方面，也关乎联合国教科文组织的核心使命。联合国教科文组织驻华代表处主任夏泽翰表示，职业技术教育与培训是联合国教科文组织的首要战略重点，中国作为一个负责任大国，发起此次大会，供各国与会者齐心协力，共同审视、研究后疫情时代全球职业技术教育与培训新问题、新方法，是了不起的成果。联合国儿童基金会教育及青少年发展全球负责人詹金斯表示，此次大会表明中国将职业教育摆在了国民经济社会发展中前所未有的重要战略位置，以实际行动走出了一条具有中国特色的职业教育发展道路。多位外国发言嘉宾在致辞中一致肯定中国职业教育发展成就，与会各国部长均提出加强职业教育国际合作交流的意愿和建议，达成了全球职业教育发展普遍共识，为进一步合作奠定了坚实基础。多所职业院校在平行论坛框架下，与企业在人才培养、技术研发等方面达成合作协议。在部分平行论坛，完成了首批鲁班工坊运营项目授牌，发布了《中非职业教育合作发展研究》专著成果以及我国职教办学成果等。

此次大会的成功举办充分说明，当前和今后一个时期，虽然人类社会仍然面临各种严峻挑战，只要我们积极顺应世界各国人民对和平发展更加殷切的期盼、对公平正义更加强烈的呼声、对合作共赢更加坚定的追求，坚决落实习近平总书记代表党和政府发出的全球发展倡议和全球安全倡议，努力把准各领域交流的共识点、找准各方面合作的突破口，就一定能够用造福世界、惠及人民的实际成果，不断巩固人类命运共同体这个汇聚着各国人民对和平、发展、繁荣向往的最大公约数。

### 3. 落实大会成果

将以此次大会成功举办为契机，坚决贯彻落实习近平总书记贺信精神，加快构建现代职教体系。重点做好以下工作。

（1）深入贯彻落实习近平总书记“促进就业创业、助力经济社会发展、增进人民福祉”“积极推动职业教育高质量发展”的重要指示，推进大会系列成果落地落实，深化现代职业教育体系建设改革。

系统总结梳理发展职业教育的国际经验，密切跟踪全球发展趋势，以全球视野谋划、推动教育和创新。对与会嘉宾介绍的所在国家、行业企业和国际组织推动职业教育发展的战略、政策、项目、平台以及先进经验和典型做法等开展持续深入研究，结合我国职业教育的现实样态和中国特色国情，博采众长、学习借鉴，更好地在时代前进的潮流中把握我国职业教育发展的大势和比较优势，实现自身的提质增效。全面梳理大会形成的共识事项、创新机制、实践路径等成果，制定大会成果转化工作落实清单，切实把大会成功举办的势能转化为事业源源不断持续发展的动能，着力把职业教育摆在教育改革创新和经济社会发展中更加突出的位置，以建设国家现代职业教育示范合作区为主体，以打造区域产教联合体和行业产教融合联合体为两翼，通过“一体两翼”深化现代职业教育体系建设改革，提升职业院校核心办学能力，深化产教融合，推动普职融通，更好服务学生的全面发展和经济社会的高质量发展，加快构建现代职业教育体系，奋力把习近平总书记对职业教育“大有可为”的殷切期待转变为“大有作为”的生动实践。

（2）深入贯彻落实习近平总书记贺信的重要精神，深入交流、增进共识、加强合作，让职业教育发展成果惠及世界各国人民，充分发挥职业教育服务国家外交大局、教育对外开放等方面的独特优势，落实全球发展倡议，创新国际交流与合作机制，推进职业教育国际务实合作。

深化与各国政府、国际组织间、院校间、校企间的务实合作。立足我国职业教育新的发展阶段和形势，扩大职业教育对外开放，深度参与职业教育全球治理。在持续办好世界职业技术教育发展大会、成立世界职业技术教育发展联盟、设立国际职业教育大奖的同时，一是围绕区域优势、发展战略和支柱产业，面向“一带一路”倡议、东盟、金砖国家等，打造一批职业教育国际合作平台；二是建设一批高水平国际化的职业学校，推出一批具有国际影响力的专业标准、课程标准，开发一批教学资源、教学设备；三是推进鲁班工坊专业化、模块化发展，健全标准规范、创新运维机制，打造职业教育国际品牌；四是推广“中文＋职业技能”项目，为中国企业“走出去”培养国际化人才，提升中国职业教育的国际影响力和引领力。

# I. Introduction to World Vocational and Technical Education Development Conference

To implement the Global Development Initiative proposed by General Secretary Xi Jinping at the 76th United Nations General Assembly on September 21, 2021 and expand international cooperation and exchanges in vocational education, the Ministry of Education, the Chinese National Commission for UNESCO and the Tianjin Municipal People's Government jointly organized the first World Vocational and Technical Education Development Conference (hereinafter referred to as WVTEDC or the Conference) with the approval of the State Council. The theme of WVTEDC is "Vocational and Technical Education Development in the Post-pandemic Era — New Changes, New Ways and New Skills". General Secretary Xi Jinping sent a congratulatory letter to the Conference, and Vice Premier Sun Chunlan read out the letter and delivered a video speech. With strong support of the Ministry of Foreign Affairs, the National Development and Reform Commission, the Ministry of Commerce, China International Development Cooperation Agency and other departments, as well as full cooperation of the Tianjin Municipal Committee of the CPC and Tianjin Municipal People's Government, the agenda has been successfully completed in accordance with the requirement of "holding an innovative and distinctive event with far-reaching influence", and the expected goals of internationalization, high standard and quality have been achieved, overcoming the uncertainties brought about by the recurrence of the epidemic and the complex changes in the international situation.

## 1. Overview of WVTEDC

WVTEDC consists of the opening ceremony, the keynote session, 14 parallel sessions and the closing ceremony, and the first World Vocational College Skills Competition and the World Expo on the Integration of Vocational Education with Industry were held at the same time. During the Conference, we held bilateral talks with relevant countries, put forward the initiative to establish the World TVET League and the International TVET Prize, released the *"Report on the Development of Vocational Education in China (2012–2022)"* and the "Tianjin Initiative", a consensus document of WVTEDC, and formed a new platform and paradigm for international exchanges and cooperation in vocational education.

(1) Governments of various countries attached great importance and sent representatives to attend the event

The Conference was attended by 196 international delegates from 123 countries and regions and more than 500 domestic delegates in a hybrid offline/online manner. A total of 25 foreign officials at the ministerial level, 17 heads (representatives) of international organizations, and 11 ambassadors to China attended the event. The heads of the Ministry of Industry and Information Technology, the Ministry of Agriculture and Rural Affairs, the State Taxation Administration, the State-owned Assets Supervision and Administration Commission of the State Council, the National Rural Revitalization Administration and other departments, the heads of provincial (regional and municipal) governments such as Tianjin, Heilongjiang, Shandong, and Guangxi, 8 academicians of the Chinese Academy of Sciences and Chinese Academy of Engineering, well-known entrepreneurs such as the chairmen of Bank of China, CRRC, Gree, and Neusoft Group, experts and scholars at home and abroad, representatives of industry organizations, colleges and universities, and research institutions, and the heads of education departments of provinces, autonomous regions and municipalities gathered in Tianjin to participate in the grand event.

Li Hongzhong, member of the Political Bureau of the CPC Central Committee and Secretary of the CPC Tianjin Municipal Committee, attended the opening ceremony and the keynote session and delivered welcome remarks. Ministerial representatives from 15 countries (China, Argentina, Brazil, the UK, Ethiopia, Malaysia, Mongolia, New Zealand, Nigeria, Pakistan, Russia Singapore, Switzerland, Venezuela and ROK), ambassadors of Ghana, Ireland and other countries to China, representatives of international organizations such as the Chairperson of the Executive Board of UNESCO and the Director of Education and Adolescent Development of UNICEF, and representatives of international industry organizations such as the International Telecommunication Union, FISITA, and well-known enterprises and colleges attended the opening ceremony and the keynote session and delivered speeches respectively. At the closing ceremony, the Director of the UNESCO Beijing office delivered a speech, Zhang Gong, the Mayor of Tianjin, read out the "Tianjin Initiative", and Huai Jinpeng, Chinese Minister of Education, made a summary of WVTEDC and announced its closing. The 14 parallel sessions covered popular topics in the development of vocational education in the world, such as digital empowerment, integration of industry and education, green technology, skills and poverty reduction, promotion of equity, lifelong learning, science and engineering education, etc. 230 Chinese and foreign experts and scholars from 53 countries had full and effective discussions, sharing the practical experience of various countries and enhancing mutual understanding.

(2) Splendid activities were held to promote exchanges and cooperation among countries

The World Vocational College Skills Competition was held. Teachers and students of vocational colleges around the world competed on the same stage during the Conference, showing new techniques and new achievements in the industry-education integration. There were 23 events arranged: 15 for competition and 8 for exhibition and performance. With a total of 207 teams composed of 988 contestants and 489 instructors from 293 institutions in 107 countries and regions around the world participating in the competition, an international platform for Chinese and foreign vocational teachers and students to enhance friendship, exchange skills, and exhibit talents has been effectively built.

The World Expo on the Integration of Vocational Education with Industry was held. With the theme of "vigorously developing vocational education to meet the needs of new technology and industrial transformation", the expo was also held both online and offline. Two offline exhibition areas were set up to show the construction of Luban Workshop and the achievements of vocational education development in Tianjin. The online expo was carried out on the "cloud", with 8 sections including the Cloud Exhibition Hall and 9 special exhibitions including the Engineering Education Exhibition. Through the cloud expo, 306 exhibitors showcased their new achievements and new methods of integrated development of vocational education and economic industry in various countries and industries, attracting more than 20 million online visitors.

(3) With consensus reached, an initiative was released to jointly promote the development of worldwide vocational education

The "Tianjin Initiative" reflects the common concerns about education development in the world and the focus of China's vocational education reform and development, clarifies the functional positioning, responsibilities, missions and development direction of vocational education in the post-pandemic era, and proposes an action plan for the high-quality development of vocational education in the world.

The proposal to set up the International TVET Prize was released to motivate all walks of society to actively support and promote the development of vocational education by recognizing a group of organizations or individuals worldwide who have made outstanding contributions to vocational education and achieved significant results in research and practice. We welcome the participation of all countries and substantial support from industries and enterprises to jointly study the establishment and implementation of the Prize.

The proposal to establish the World TVET League was released in accordance with the principle of "global, non-government, and non-profit", calling on the global education community, industries and other social organizations and individuals to negotiate the establishment of the League. During the Conference, 148 universities, enterprises and industrial organizations from 36 countries participated in the proposal.

The White Paper *Report on the Development of Vocational Education in China* was released, in which the host systematically summarized the achievements and experience of China's vocational education development, shared China's innovative initiatives in vocational education with the international community, and sent out invitations for vocational education cooperation.

(4) The event aroused favorable social response and extensive attention from Chinese and foreign media

During the Conference, more than 100 website platform accounts participated in the live webcast of the keynote session, 22 000 people attended through the video conference system, and more than 673 million people were covered by various media reports. With 920 million live views, WVTEDC successfully became a grand event watched by an audience of millions of people simultaneously through various online platforms.

WVTEDC attracted extensive attention from Chinese and foreign media. *People's Daily*, Xinhua News Agency, China Media Group, *Guangming Daily*, *Economic Daily*, *China Daily* and other major central media and their affiliated new media continuously reported the event in important pages and key news programs, introducing the effectiveness of China's vocational education reform and innovation development and the characteristics of Tianjin's vocational education development in depth and extensively. CCTV's "Xinwen Lianbo" reported on President Xi Jinping's congratulatory letter to WVTEDC, and launched a thematic program "Vocational Education Consolidates the Foundation of Technical Skills for a Powerful Industrial Country", providing in-depth coverage of the conference and the development of vocational education in China. *People's Daily* published "Xi Jinping Extends Congratulations to World Vocational and Technical Education Development Conference" and "World Vocational and Technical Education Development Conference Opening", and presented a comprehensive report "Boosting the High-Quality Development of Vocational Education". Domestic and overseas media produced 664 original articles, leading to more than 13 000 media reprints. WVTEDC streamed live on new media such as Weibo and Douyin, and the total number of readers of Weibo topics exceeded 550 million during the Conference. More than 10 foreign mainstream media, such as PR Newswire and Yahoo Finance, published or reprinted about 67 related reports, and more than 4 000 posts of information about WVTEDC were released on Twitter and other overseas social media.

## 2. Achievements of the Conference

(1) General Secretary Xi Jinping's congratulatory letter aroused enthusiastic reactions

The congratulatory letter from General Secretary Xi Jinping fully reflects the great importance the CPC Central Committee attaches to vocational education and its strong determination to improve vocational education, profoundly elaborates on the importance of vocational education in promoting employment and entrepreneurship, boosting economic and social development and enhancing people's welfare, demonstrates China's willingness to join hands with other countries to strengthen mutual enrichment and sharing and to implement global development initiatives, represents China's commitment to contribute to the implementation of the United Nations 2030 Agenda for Sustainable Development, and provides a fundamental guideline and direction for deepening international exchanges and cooperation in vocational education. General Secretary Xi Jinping's congratulatory letter was highly appreciated and enthusiastically responded by the guests, cadres, teachers and students of the domestic education system, and the international community. This is another important instruction given by General Secretary Xi Jinping on vocational education after the National Vocational Education Conference in 2021. The letter greatly enhanced the confidence and determination of the education system to fulfill their duties in vocational education.

The cadres, teachers and students all expressed that the congratulatory letter from General Secretary Xi Jinping fully reflects the great importance attached by the CPC Central Committee to vocational education, clarifies the goals and tasks of the reform and development of vocational education in the new era, and points out the direction for the high-quality development of vocational education in China. The international attendants said that the letter reflects the considerable attention paid by the Chinese government to the high-quality development of vocational education and its firm determination, and they expressed the hope that China will play a greater role in promoting the high-quality development of global vocational education. Ministers of education and heads of international organizations generally showed interests in further strengthening practical cooperation with China, jointly promoting the implementation of the United Nations 2030 Agenda for Sustainable Development, and injecting the "skill power" in building a community with shared future for mankind.

(2) Vice Premier Sun Chunlan's video speech received widespread acclaim

In her speech, Vice Premier Sun Chunlan shared the practices and experiences of the Chinese government in vigorously promoting the reform and development of vocational education, and initiated the proposal for all countries to jointly respond to the challenges and create a new situation for the prosperity and development of vocational education, which was highly appreciated and positively responded by the guests from various countries.

The cadres, teachers and students of the domestic education system were deeply inspired as Vice Premier Sun Chunlan's video message incisively exposits the development orientation of vocational education and points out the essential law of vocational education development. The speech fully demonstrates the development achievements of vocational education in China, highlights the advantages of the socialist development path with Chinese characteristics, effectively enhances the international influence and national soft power of China, greatly encourages and strengthens the confidence and determination of the vocational education faculty to fulfill their duties, and boosts the enthusiasm and motivation to deepen international exchanges and cooperation in vocational education. International guests also said that they were greatly encouraged by Vice Premier Sun Chunlan's speech which reflects China's profound understanding and firm determination to join hands with other countries to promote global development initiatives, especially some Asian and African countries, who have increasingly recognized China's governance ability and are willing to cooperate with China to promote common development.

(3) A brand-new platform and mechanism for international exchange and cooperation in vocational education was built

The Conference put forward the value concept of developing vocational education with the "Tianjin Initiative" , built an international vocational education exchange and cooperation mechanism through the League, stimulated the innovation and development of vocational education with the Prize, promoted mutual enrichment and skills exchange among countries with the Competition, demonstrated the new achievements and highlights of the integration of industry and education with the Expo, and showed China's vocational education development achievements and model experience to the world with the Report. Representatives of all communities from various countries highly appreciated China's efforts and contributions to promoting the global development of vocational education, and believed that WVTEDC had built an effective platform for international exchanges and cooperation in vocational education and laid a solid foundation for further practical cooperation.

(4) A general consensus on the development of global vocational education in the post-epidemic era was reached

It was generally agreed that the purpose of this Conference is highly compatible and closely related to global economic and social development and vocational education priorities, especially the sustainable development agenda advocated by the UN. The deep integration of education with industry, business and economic society is the most brilliant feature and basic consensus of the Conference.

Ms. Tamara, Chairperson of the Executive Board of UNESCO, said that the theme of WVTEDC not only embodied an important aspect of vocational education reform and human development, but also represented one of the core missions of UNESCO. Shahbaz khan, Director of UNESCO Beijing Office, said that TVET was the top strategic priority of UNESCO. It was a great achievement for China, as a responsible great nation, to initiate this Conference for participants from various countries to work together to review and look into new issues and approaches concerning global vocational and technical education and training in the post-pandemic era. Mr. Jenkins, Director of Education and Adolescent Development of UNICEF, said that WVTEDC showed that China had raised vocational education to an unprecedented strategic height in the development of the national economy and society, and had taken practical measures to embark on a vocational education development path with Chinese characteristics. The foreign speakers unanimously affirmed the achievements of China's vocational education development in their speeches, and the ministers of the participating countries all expressed their willingness to strengthen international cooperation and exchange in vocational education and offered relevant suggestions. A general consensus on the development of global vocational education has been reached, laying a solid foundation for further cooperation. Under the framework of parallel sessions, a number of vocational institutions reached cooperation agreements with enterprises in personnel training, technology research and development, etc. In some parallel sessions, the licenses for the first batch of Luban Workshop operation projects were awarded, and the report *A Study on China-Africa Vocational Education Cooperation* and the results of China's vocational education were released.

The success of the event fully illustrates that, although human society is facing and will still face various serious challenges at present and in the near future, as long as we actively respond to the more ardent expectations of the people around the world for peaceful development, the stronger calls for fairness and justice, and the more determined pursuit of win-win cooperation, and resolutely implement the global development initiatives and global security initiatives proposed by General Secretary Xi Jinping on behalf of the CPC and Chinese government, make efforts to identify the consensus of exchanges and the sally port in cooperation in various areas, we will be able to use the practical results that benefit the world and the people to continuously consolidate the community with a shared future for mankind, which represents the largest possible agreement that brings together the aspirations of all peoples for peace, development and prosperity.

### 3. Implementation of the Achievements

We will take the success of WVTEDC as an opportunity to resolutely implement the spirit of the congratulatory letter from General Secretary Xi Jinping, and speed up the construction of a modern vocational education system. The following work are listed as priorities.

(1) We will implement the important instructions of General Secretary Xi Jinping to "promote employment and entrepreneurship, support economic and social development and enhance people's welfare" and "actively advance the high-quality development of vocational education", facilitate the implementation of a series of achievements of the Conference, and deepen the construction and reform of the

modern vocational education system.

We will systematically summarize and sort out the international experience in the development of vocational education, closely follow the global development trend, and plan and promote education and innovation with a global vision. We will conduct continuous and in-depth research on the strategies, policies, projects and platforms of countries, industry enterprises and international organizations that promote the development of vocational education, as well as advanced experiences and typical practices introduced by the guests, while taking into account the reality of vocational education in China and the national conditions with Chinese characteristics, to better grasp the general trend and comparative advantages of China's vocational education development in the trend of the era, and raise its quality and efficiency. We will comprehensively sort out the consensus items, innovative mechanisms, practical paths and other achievements produced during the Conference, make a list for the transformation of such achievements, effectively transform the potential energy of the success of the Conference into the driving force for the continuous development of the cause, and raise vocational education to a more prominent height in education reform and innovation and economic and social development. With the construction of the national modern vocational education demonstration cooperation zone as the body, and the industry-education integration alliances on regional level and industrial level as two wings, we will deepen the reform of modern vocational education system, enhance the core capacity of vocational institutions, deepen the integration of industry and education, promote the connection of general education and vocational education, better serve the all-round development of students and high-quality economic and social development, accelerate the construction of a modern vocational education system, and strive to transform General Secretary Xi Jinping's ardent expectation for vocational education to be tangible achievements.

(2) We will implement the important instructions of General Secretary Xi Jinping in his congratulatory letter, deepen exchanges, enhance consensus, and strengthen cooperation to let the fruits of vocational education development benefit people around the world, and give full play to the unique advantages of vocational education in serving the overall national diplomatic strategy and the opening of education to the world, implement global development initiatives, innovate international exchanges and cooperation mechanisms, and promote international practical cooperation in vocational education.

We will further pragmatic cooperation with governments of various countries, as well as among international organizations, institutions, schools and enterprises. In the new development stage and based on the status quo of vocational education in China, we will expand the opening of TVET to the world and intensively participate in the global governance of TVET. While continuing to organize the World Vocational and

Technical Education Development Conference, establishing the World TVET League, and setting up the International TVET Prize, we will (1) build a number of international cooperation platforms for vocational education based on our regional advantages, development strategies and pillar industries to increase connection with the "Belt and Road", ASEAN and BRICS countries; (2) build a number of high-level international vocational schools, issue a series of professional standards and curriculum standards of international influence, and develop various teaching resources and teaching equipment; (3) promote the professional and modular development of Luban Workshop, improve the standards and norms, innovate the operation and maintenance mechanism, and establish an international brand of vocational education; and (4) advocate the "Chinese+Vocational Skills" programs to train international talents for Chinese enterprises to "go global", and enhance the international influence and competitiveness of China's vocational education.

# 二

# 世界职业院校技能大赛综述

首届世界职业院校技能大赛（以下简称世校赛）于8月9—20日在中国天津、江西两个赛区及世界相关院校赛点成功举办。教育部部长怀进鹏、副部长孙尧出席世校赛开幕式、闭幕式活动，巡查赛场并为获奖团队颁奖。本次大赛共设置23个赛项，来自亚洲、非洲、欧洲、南美洲、北美洲等五大洲107个国家和地区的293所院校，207个团队的988名选手及489名指导教师参加比赛。比赛共产生15枚金牌、15枚银牌、15枚铜牌、56枚优胜奖牌，合计101枚。世校赛以“技炫青春、能创未来”为主题，走出了职业教育国际赛事新路子，受到世界各国职业院校师生广泛关注和好评，总体圆满顺利，达到预期目标。

**1. 主要举措及成效**

按照办好一届“富有新意、影响深远”的大赛总体思路，首届世校赛在目标定位、形式内容等方面进行了有益探索和创新，为各国参赛选手搭建了切磋技能、互学互鉴、友好交流的平台。

（1）依托中国技能赛事基础，构建世界职业院校技能大赛新格局。一是充分用好国内技能竞赛基础和经验，助力打造大赛新体系。首届世校赛是全国职业院校技能大赛的国际赛，开设的依据是《全国职业院校技能大赛章程》。全国职业院校技能大赛是由教育部发起并牵头、35家部委及行业组织等联合举办的公益性职业院校师生综合技能竞赛活动，自2008年起已成功举办14届，建立了学校、省（市）、国家三级竞赛体系。首届世校赛的举办，依托全国职业院校技能大赛的基础和经验，助力构建中外联通、多元融合的大赛新体系，拓展了各国职业院校师生参与世界级技能竞赛通道，意义重大。二是充分利用职业教育“走出去”的经验和成果，扩大参赛选手覆盖面。发挥鲁班工坊等各地职业教育国际合作项目的桥梁作用和“走出去”企业力量，挖掘职业院校国际合作资源和潜能，广泛邀请世界各国师生积极参与，使首届世校赛成为参与国家和院校数量最多的国际技能赛事。三是充分发挥世校赛品牌效应，助力世界职业技术教育发展大会平台建设。世校赛围绕大会“后疫情时代职业技术教育发展：新变化、新方式、新技能”主题，遵循“简约绿色共享”原则，以大赛形式展示各国职业院校师生风采和教学成果，传递关注青年、重视技能、崇尚劳动的理念，让与会各国代表了解世界职业教育尤其是中国职业教育发展水平，激发各国关注、投身职业教育和技能提升的热情，促进落实世界职业技术教育发展大会精神。

（2）创新理念和办赛方式，打造世界级技能赛事新范式。一是育人为主，包容并举。世校赛的定位是引领世界职业教育发展，核心是培养国际视野强、文化素养好、技能水平高的综合型技术技能人才，淡化锦标主义，突出国际交流，除设置竞赛类赛项，还设置中国制造与传统文化、能工巧匠、中华非遗文化等展演类赛项，有效传承和弘扬中华优秀文化，促进中外人文交流，以更加开放、更加包容的姿态，将技能比拼、展示体验、思想交流融为一体，打造了集聚才、识才、育才于一体的世界职业教育嘉年华。二是中外合作，促进交流。在比赛方式上，创造性地推出中外选手“手拉手”组队参赛模式，分成中外联合组队（中方与外方选手各自在本国参赛）和中外混合编队（中方与外方选手混合在中国比赛）两种，以队为单位报名、比赛和获奖，创造了更多国内外师生深入学习交流、合作共进的机会。三是紧跟前沿，彰显特色。顺应科技发展趋势，紧跟新产业、新业态、新工艺发展，突出数字技能、绿色技能，聚焦装备制造、电子与信息、交通运输、财经商贸、能源动力与材料等领域设置竞赛类 5 个竞赛单元、15 个赛项。增材制造技术、碳中和可再生能源工程技术等赛项，有效对接现代技术革新，充分彰显时代特色，顺应世界产业发展潮流。

（3）广泛开展宣传引导，营造关注技能、崇尚技能新氛围。一是以文化产品设计助力大赛预热。首届世校赛开展主题词、标识、吉祥物等征集活动，得到全社会广泛响应。共征集到主题词作品 174 个，标识作品 103 个，吉祥物作品 26 个，经组织评审，最终确定世校赛主题词为“技炫青春，能创未来”，标识为以汉字书法“世”之笔意为基础，融入世界五大洲元素进行的变形设计，吉祥物为以“中华龙”“能工巧匠”等元素设计的“技宝”，助力弘扬“劳动光荣、技能宝贵、创造伟大”的时代风尚，吸引青年一代参与大赛、投身技能。二是以双重奖励增强赛事吸引力。首届世校赛设置双重“国际大奖”，既有代表世界顶级荣誉的奖牌和证书，也有助力职业教育发展的丰厚奖金，为每个金牌队奖励人民币 50 万元、银牌队 30 万元、铜牌队 20 万元、优胜队 10 万元，引起强烈反响。通过大奖的“聚变”效应，吸引世界优秀技能学子汇聚赛事，世界头部企业融入赛事，各国专家热情参与赛事，不断提升世校赛办赛水平，助力世界职业教育融合发展。三是以多维宣传拓展大赛影响力。首届世校赛得到各国媒体界高度关注，全球融媒体聚焦报道，国内外主流媒体广泛宣传。百度中文搜索条目达 4 160 万条，百度英文搜索条目达 497 000 条。国内主流媒体中央电视台报道 292 条，学习强国报道 57 条。抖音、快手等新媒体现场直播、微视频达到 270 万条。美联社、《欧洲时报》、德国 Archyde 等外国媒体以及新华网英文版、《人民日报》英文版、《中国日报》、中国网等主流外宣媒体相关报道 39 200 条。海量宣传引发全球关注，助力中国职业教育模式和标准走向世界。

### 2. 工作打算

下一步，我们将认真学习贯彻习近平总书记致世界职业技术教育发展大会的贺信精神，坚决落实教育部领导对大赛的指示要求，以将大赛打造成世界知名职业技能大赛为目标，总结经验，反思不足，前瞻谋划，不断推进世校赛专业化、规范化、制度化建设。

第一，着力提升赛事质量。加强顶层设计和统筹谋划，完善健全世校赛体制机制。密切关注科技变革和产业发展动向，对接行业企业职业技能国际标准，紧贴生产实际和企业真实环境，专业论证、科学设置赛项和规程赛题，提高先进制造业、战略性新兴产业和现代服务业等领域相关赛项占比，推动世界教育链、人才链、产业链、创新链深度融合，为后疫情时代经济发展提供有力人才和技术技能保障。

第二，稳步扩大赛事规模。逐步扩大世校赛覆盖面，包括赛区布局、赛项数量、参赛队伍数量、参与院校数量等。充分挖掘国际化资源，依托世界职业技术教育发展联盟、中国—东盟职业教育联合会等平台吸引更多国家、更多院校参赛。进一步深化产教融合、校企合作，吸引更多跨国企业、龙头企业参与办赛，提升经费、技术、资源支持保障能力。

第三，持续深化队伍建设。优化专家队伍结构，面向社会广泛征集、扩充世校赛专家队伍，重点针对专业性强、技术领域新的赛项，增加行业、企业专家队伍数量。逐步扩充具有国际化背景的专家，建设国际专家库。健全专家队伍管理机制，加强专业培训，完善准入和退出机制，打造一支具备国际视野、世界水平的高素质、高技能专家队伍。

第四，深入研究资源转化应用。坚持创新引领，结合科技革命、世界经济发展趋势，开展世校赛理论研究，尤其是世校赛资源转化研究。坚持以我为主，借助大赛推动中国职业教育教学标准、设备平台、课程教材走向世界。坚持应用为王，推动产教融合、校企合作，通过世校赛“练兵场”检验新技术、新技能在生产一线实际应用效能，促进产业发展和技术提升。

# II. Introduction to World Vocational College Skills Competition

The first World Vocational College Skills Competition (hereinafter referred to as the WVCSC) was successfully held from August 9 to 20, 2022 in Tianjin and Jiangxi in China, as well as in relevant colleges and universities around the world. Huai Jinpeng, Minister of Education and Sun Yao, Vice Minister of Education, attended the opening and closing ceremonies of the WVCSC, inspected the venues and awarded prizes to the winning teams. There were 23 events in this competition, including 988 competitors and 489 instructors forming 207 teams, from 293 colleges and universities in 107 countries and regions in five continents, including Asia, Africa, Europe, South America and North America. The competition presented 15 gold medals, 15 silver medals, 15 bronze medals and 56 winning medals, totaling 101 awards. With the theme of "Skilled Youth, Shining Future", the WVCSC has paved a new way for international vocational education competitions, and has received extensive attention and praise from vocational colleges and students all over the world. It is generally successful and achieves the expected goals.

## 1. Main Measures and Results

In accordance with the general idea of successfully running an "innovative competition of far-reaching influence" , the first WVCSC has made beneficial exploration and innovation in terms of target orientation, form and content, building a platform for participants from all countries to compete with each other, learn from each other, and communicate in a friendly way.

(1) Based on China's skills competition, build a new pattern of world vocational college skills competition

First, make full use of the foundation and experience of domestic skills competition, so as to build a new system of WVCSC. The first WVCSC was held as the international track of the National Vocational Students Skills Competition on the basis of its Constitution. The National Vocational Students Skills Competition is a non-profit comprehensive skills competition for vocational college teachers and students, initiated and led by the Ministry of Education and jointly organized by 35 ministries, commissions and industry organizations. Since 2008, it has been successfully held for 14 sessions, establishing a three-level competition system: school level, provincial (municipal) level and national level. Based on such foundation and experience, the first WVCSC has built a new system of the international skills competition for vocational colleges, with mutual exchanges, communication and integration as its characteristics. It has expanded the channels for TVET teachers and students from all countries to participate in a world-class skills competition, which is of great significance.

Second, make full use of the experience and achievements of China's vocational education "going global", so as to expand the coverage of competitors. WVCSC could give play to the role of international vocational education cooperation projects in various regions such as Luban Workshop, and the strength of enterprises "going global", tap the resources and potential of international cooperation in vocational colleges, and invite teachers and students from all over the world to participate actively. The first WVCSC has become the international skills competition with the largest number of participating countries and colleges.

Third, give full play to the brand effect of the WVCSC to help build the platform of the World Vocational and Technical Education Development Conference. Under WVTEDC's theme of "Vocational and Technical Education Development in the Post-pandemic Era—New Changes, New Ways and New Skills," and following the principle of simplicity, green, and sharing, WVCSC displays the talents and skills of teachers and students in vocational colleges in various countries through competitions, passes on the concept of paying attention to youth, attaching importance to skills, and advocating labour, helps the representatives of participating countries understand the development level of world vocational education, especially China's, stimulates enthusiasm for paying attention to and devoting to vocational education and skills improvement, and promotes the implementation of the spirit of World Vocational and Technical Education Development Conference.

(2) Innovate ideas and ways of holding events, and create a new paradigm for world-class skills competitions

First, focus on educating people and being inclusive. WVCSC is positioned to lead the development of vocational education in the world. Its core is to cultivate comprehensive technical and skilled talents with strong international vision, good cultural literacy and high skill level, weaken the championship doctrine, and highlight international exchanges. In addition to setting up competing events, it also sets up exhibition and performance events such as Chinese Manufacturing and Traditional Culture, Craftsman, and Chinese Intangible Cultural Heritage, effectively inheriting and carrying forward excellent traditional Chinese culture, promoting cultural exchanges between China and foreign countries. With a more open and inclusive gesture, it has integrated skills competition, experience and exhibition as well as thought exchange, creating a world vocational education "carnival", where talents are gathered, cultivated and recognized.

Second, cooperate with foreign countries and promote exchanges. In terms of the forms of competition, WVCSC has creatively adopted the "hand-in-hand" team formation mode, containing two types, namely Chinese-Foreign Joint Team (Chinese and foreign competitors compete in their own countries) and Chinese-Foreign Mixed Team (Chinese and foreign competitors compete in China together). Competitors shall register, compete, and receive awards as a team, creating more opportunities for teachers and students at home and abroad regarding in-depth study, exchange and cooperation.

Third, keep up with the forefront and highlight its own characteristics. Complying with the development trend of science and technology, it closely follows the development of new industries, new formats and new techniques, highlights digital skills and green skills, and sets up 5 competition units and 15 events with the focus on equipment manufacturing, electronics and information, transportation, finance and commerce, energy power and materials and other fields. Additive manufacturing technology, carbon neutral renewable energy engineering technology and other events closely connected with modern technological innovation, fully demonstrating the characteristics of the time, and conforming to the trend of world industrial development.

(3) Carry out extensive publicity and guidance, and create a new atmosphere of focusing on skills and advocating skills

First, use cultural product design to warm up the atmosphere of the competition. The first WVCSC publicly collected theme words, logos, and mascots, which attracted extensive participation. A total of 174 theme works, 103 logo works and 26 mascot works were collected. After the review and examination, the slogan of the first WVCSC was "Skilled Youth, Shining Future". The logo was a variant design of calligraphy style of the Chinese character " 世 " (means "the world"), combined with the elements of the five continents of the world. The mascot "Jibao" (means a person with skills) integrates the elements such as "Chinese dragon" and "skilled craftsman". These help promote the culture of "labor is glorious, skills are precious, and they can create greatness", and attract the young generation to participate in competitions and devote themselves to the improvement of skills.

Second, use double rewards to enhance the attraction of the event. The first WVCSC set up double "international awards", including not only medals and certificates that represent the world's top honors, but also rich bonuses that help the development of vocational education. Each gold-medal team was awarded 500 000 RMB, silver-medal team 300 000 RMB, bronze-medal team 200 000 RMB, and other winning team 100 000 RMB, which stimulated a strong response. Through the "fusion" effect of the grand prize, the event attracts excellent skilled students, leading enterprises and experts from all over the world to participate in the competition enthusiastically, constantly improving the operation level of the WVCSC, and enabling the integrated development of world vocational education.

Third, expand the influence of the competition with multi-dimensional publicity. The first WVCSC has received high attention from the media of all countries, focused reporting from the global media, and wide publicity of mainstream media at home and abroad. There were 41.6 million Chinese search items about WVCSC and 497 000 English items on Baidu. CCTV, the mainstream media in China, has reported 292 related articles and the platform of "Xue Xi Qiang Guo" has posted 57 articles. Douyin, Kuaishou and other new media have 2.7 million live broadcasts and short videos. There were 39 200 relevant reports from foreign media such as the Associated Press, Nouvelles D'Europe, Germany's Archyde, and English version of mainstream media such as Xinhua. net, People's Daily, China Daily, and China.org.cn. Massive publicity has attracted global attention and helped China's vocational education mode and standards go global.

### 2. Plan for the Future

Next, we will earnestly study and implement the spirit of the congratulatory letter from the General Secretary Xi Jinping to the World Vocational and Technical Education Development Conference, resolutely implement the instructions and requirements of the Ministry of Education leaders for the competition, and aim at making the competition a world-famous vocational skills competition. We will learn from the experience, reflect on deficiencies, and make forward-looking plans, so as to constantly promote the professionalization, standardization and institutionalization of the WVCSC.

First, focus on improving the quality of the competition. We will keep working on top-level design and overall planning, and improve the system and mechanisms for the WVCSC. We will keep close watch on scientific and technological changes and industrial development trends, connect with the international standards of professional skills of industry and enterprises, stay close to the actual production and real environment of enterprises, conduct a professional demonstration, set up events and tasks scientifically. We will increase the proportion of events in such fields as advanced manufacturing, strategic emerging industries and modern service industries, and promote the deep integration of the world education chain, talent chain, industry chain and innovation chain, so as to provide powerful talents and technical skills for economic development in the post-pandemic era.

Second, steadily expand the scale of the event. We shall gradually expand the coverage of the WVCSC, including the layout of the competition areas, the number of events, the number of participating teams, and the number of participating institutions. We will fully tap international resources, and attract more countries and colleges to participate through the platforms of the World TVET League and the China-ASEAN TVET Consortium. We will further deepen the integration of industry and education as well as school-enterprise cooperation, attract more multinational enterprises and leading enterprises to participate in the event, and improve the ability to support funds, technology and resources.

Third, continue to deepen team building. We will optimize the structure of the expert team, recruit and expand the expert team of the WVCSC from society, and increase the number of experts from the industry and enterprises for new events in the technical fields with strong professionalism. We will gradually increase the number of experts with international backgrounds and build a foreign expert database. We will improve the management mechanism of the expert team, strengthen professional training, improve the access and exit mechanisms, and build a high-quality and highly skilled expert team with international vision and world level.

Fourth, conduct in-depth research on resource transformation and application. We will adhere to the guidance of innovation, combine the scientific and technological revolution and the development trend of world economy, and carry out theoretical research of the WVCSC, especially the research on the transformation of resources of the competition; Adhere to the principle of "gathering resources for our development", and introduce China's vocational education teaching standards, equipment platforms, and curriculum materials to the world with the help of the competition; Adhere to the principle of "application is the core", facilitate the integration of industry and education, school-enterprise cooperation, test the actual application efficiency of new technologies and new skills in the production line through the "training ground" of the WVCSC, and promote industrial development and technology upgrading.

智能停车库
智能交通灯标志物

Chinese Manufacturing and Traditional Culture

世界职业院校技能大赛
World Vocational College
Skills Competition
中国·天津 TIANJIN·CHINA

世界职业技术教育发展大会
WORLD VOCATIONAL AND TECHNICAL EDUCATION DEVELOPMENT CONFERENCE
世界职业院校技能大赛
世界职业院校技能大赛闭幕式
Closing Ceremony of the
World Vocational College Skills Competition
中国·天津 2022年8月20日
TIANJIN·CHINA AUGUST 20th 2022

2022年世界职业院校技能大赛
信息技术应用创新赛项
信息技术应用创新赛项
参赛代表队
攻击态势
高危攻击
中危攻击
低危攻击
172
42
4
活跃攻击源
设备运行状态
评分排名

八段锦
CHINESE QIGONG

ompetition Unit on Equipment Manufacturing 装备制造
世界职业院校技能大赛
Skilled Youth, Shining Future
中国 · 天津 TIANJIN · CHINA
2022.08
增材制造技术赛项
W04
南非鲁班工坊项目

# 三

# 世界职业教育产教融合博览会综述

2022 年 8 月 19 日，世界职业教育产教融合博览会（以下简称博览会）线上线下同时开展。与会者紧扣世界职业技术教育发展大会（以下简称大会）主题，较为全面地展示了适应新技术和产业变革需要的职业教育在产教融合、深度互动方面取得的成效。

### 1. 博览会的重大意义

落实全球发展高层对话会的一项重要成果共识。2022 年 6 月 24 日，中国国家主席习近平主持召开全球发展高层对话会，与会国家领导人共同讨论了全球发展问题，达成了一系列重要成果共识，将举办世界职业技术教育发展大会列入了成果清单。博览会作为大会的重要组成部分，旨在推动中国职业教育走向世界，加快落实全球职业教育发展倡议，面向世界各国、国际合作伙伴开展职业教育交流互鉴、资源共享、合作发展。

促进职业教育高质量发展的迫切需要。职业教育作为与经济发展、产业变革、劳动就业结合最为紧密的教育类型，在数字经济时代，要很好地适应新技术和产业变革，就必须进行升级改造、提升内涵、提高质量，切实发挥好职业教育服务国家发展战略、服务地方区域经济发展的作用。

世界职业教育领域交流合作共享发展的共同意愿。面对后疫情时代职业教育新格局，世界各国对职业教育的需要比以往任何时候都更加迫切，对高素质技术技能人才的需求比以往任何时候都更加强烈。世界职业教育发展呼唤搭建职业教育“国际舞台”，共同构建全球职业教育发展共同体、命运共同体，按下全球职业教育产教融合进程“快进键”。

### 2. 博览会筹办过程

从筹办“中国职业教育博览会”到筹办以线上为主的国际展会，博览会前后历经三年，经历了三个阶段。

填补历史空白。党的十八大以来，我国职业教育取得格局性变化，成为最有希望领跑世界的教育类型。数字经济的发展催生着生产方式、生活方式和治理方式的变革，对教育方式和服务方式也提出新的要求。为充分展示职业教育发展成就、提升职业教育地位、改善职业教育形象，经教育部办公厅批准，中国职业技术教育学会自 2020 年 10 月开始筹办中国职业教育博览会，经过近一年的努力，博览会筹备工作基本就绪。这一举措填补了中国职业教育领域没有博览会的历史空白。

走向世界舞台。2022 年 3 月，按教育部党组要求，中国职业教育博览会调整为世界职业教育产教融合博览会。世界职业技术教育发展大会的举办意义重大，博览会作为世界职业技术教育发展大会的重要组成部分，承载着推动中国职业教育走向世界舞台、实现领跑职业教育发展的重要使命。

跃上数字平台。2022 年 5 月 25 日，由于疫情形势变化，大会组委会决定将博览会调整为以线上为主、线上线下结合的方式举行。为落实大会组委会的决策和教育部党组“加快实施教育数字化战略行动”的重要部署，博览会运用数字技术进行筹备，推动产教科融合结构性、数字化改造，为职业院校及有关企业、科研单位提供分享资源、交流经验的数字平台。

### 3. 博览会展出情况

2022 年 8 月 19 日上午 9 时 30 分，博览会在线上线下同时启幕。截至 8 月 20 日 18 时，全国省（市、区）教育行政部门、近 10 000 家国内外知名企业、近 10 000 所职业学校组织观看了博览会开展仪式并开展“云上逛展”，观众达 2 100 万人次。有 120 余万人参与“凝星聚力、职通未来”云接力活动。

博览会线上展会设置“云展馆、云场景、云视界、云服务、云学会、云学校、云风采、云互动”八大板块和“数字经济、智能制造、专精特新、前沿科技、绿色经济、省市区、工程教育、数字教育、国际教育”九大专题展。汇聚百余家企业、组织以及200余所学校、机构，展示新技术应用场景，展示数字化转型整体驱动生产方式、生活方式、治理方式变革成果，展示职业教育应对数字化变革、产教科融合发展的成效。

一是“云展馆”。分为三个部分和九个专题展，有百余家企业和二十余个省市区：数字经济展重点展示数字经济领域的创新成果、核心技术以及先进应用场景（如用友新道的精智工业互联网平台、360的本地安全大脑与天相系统等）；智能制造与高端装备展重点展示智能制造业的新技术、新产品（如华为的5G Star智能制造专网训练系统、优比选的智能机器人、东软的高端医疗设备、大族激光的生产制造设备、科大讯飞的城市超脑等）；专精特新展展示专业化、精细化、特色化、新颖化的技术创新与应用（如越疆科技的人工智能机器人）；元宇宙前沿科技展重点展示前沿技术（如微软、深圳中电港等企业）；绿色经济“碳达峰”“碳中和”展重点展示行业领域数字化、绿色化改造与发展（如施耐德电气的全球能源管理和工业自动化管理）；省市区展重点展示职业教育服务当地产业、科技、经济发展的成果（如上海市、浙江省、辽宁省等）；工程教育展重点展示职业教育在培养学生创新能力、解决复杂现场问题能力等方面的经验与成果（如深圳职业技术学院、天津中德应用技术大学、浙江机电职业技术学院等）；数字教育展重点展示新技术在职业教育治理模式、教学模式、评价模式等方面变革的应用成果（如广联达、高等教育出版社、国家职业教育平台等）；国际教育展聚焦职业教育互学互鉴、共商共建共享等国际交流合作成果（如德国GIZ）。

二是“云场景”。有近400个新场景，分为三个方面：生产方式方面展示人工智能、量子信息、集成电路等新技术，展示灯塔工厂、熄灯工厂、低碳工场生产运营数字化和智能化场景（如5G十大应用案例、数字化车间、工业机器人、人工智能产业等）；生活方式方面展示新技术在生命科学领域以及在生活、学习、工作中的应用场景（如智慧城市、智慧医疗、医护机器人、共享出行、智能网联汽车等）；治理模式方面展示新一代信息技术在社会治理、组织治理中的应用（如智慧司法、智慧城市等）。

三是“云视界”。搭建信息即时交互平台，远程如当面。在博览会展览期间，有科大讯飞、网易有道等企业在云端面向全球“直播”，内容以产业前沿、技术创新、产教融合等为主。

四是“云服务”。构建校企互通、双向融合的平台，分为四个部分：“政策动态”宣传关于职业教育的重要政策资讯（如《关于加快发展现代职业教育的决定》

《国家职业教育改革实施方案》《中华人民共和国职业教育法》等）；“企业服务”发布岗位需求、教育教学产品、实践实习岗位、技术服务等（如科大讯飞的人才培养、人工智能实验室以及博导的实习就业服务、职业技能鉴定服务、专业建设策划等）；“学校服务”发布培训项目、技术研发与成果转化等信息；“合作共享”展示校企合作、师资互通成果，包括“企业人才培养基地”“校内实训基地”，合作开发课程、共建专业等。

五是“云学会”。介绍中国职业技术教育学会的历史沿革与第五届理事会成立以来的工作成果以及学会围绕“十大工作载体”在政治站位、研究水平、服务能力、发展合力等方面开展工作取得的成果（如“说专业 · 说课程 · 说专业群”活动风采、建党百年系列课程、新版专业目录解读动态、新型智库建设成果等）。

六是“云学校”。分为高等职业教育与初、中等职业教育，共有 200 余所职业学校。以“校企合作、产教融合、立德树人”为主线，设“学校简介、治理模式、教师发展、学生发展、教育教学、社会服务、国际交流合作”等模块，展示办学理念、治理架构、专业设置、招生就业、队伍建设等（如浙江机电职业技术学院、天津中德应用技术大学、湖南铁道职业技术学院等）。

七是“云风采”。分为“工、匠、人、才”四个部分，讲述上万名现场工程师、大国工匠、新产业工人以及专业技术人才的事迹，展示职业技术人才在推动中国经济高速发展和产业奇迹中发挥的重要作用（如大国工匠年度人物、国家级 / 省级技术能手、全国职业院校技能大赛获奖选手等）。

八是“云互动”。分为云接力与云交流，微信打卡吸引社会关注职业教育，同时针对职业教育热点事件设置话题。截至 8 月 22 日，有 110 余万人参与“云接力”活动，“博览会开展”话题下有近 400 条留言，来自社会各界的人士留下了对职业教育的祝福。

博览会线下展分为三个区域。一是线下微展，其中包含 9 个微展台与 200 个展板，汇聚行业龙头企业、高新技术企业、高科技产业中心与科研院所以及高水平职业学校，对新技术发展应用场景、产教科融合成果、办学成果进行展示。二是天津市展区，展示天津优势产业，突出产教融合特色。三是鲁班工坊展厅，呈现中国职业教育走出去办学，服务“一带一路”建设，助力国际产能合作、促进中外人文交流的丰硕成果。

#### 4. 博览会亮点

聚焦新技术。展示职业教育利用 5G、大数据、云计算、区块链、数字孪生及人工智能等前沿科技融合发展及其应用场景，引导职业教育加速适用新技术、应用新技术。

聚焦产业变革。展示职业教育在应对数字化变革转型和推进产教科融合发展方面的实际成效，展示产业转型升级整体驱动生产方式、生活方式、治理方式变革成果，携手共同打造多元融合、灵活开放的职业教育产教科融合新生态，增强职业教育吸引力。

聚焦新生态。通过线上线下展会板块、主题展区、应用场景的成果推介展示职业教育发展成就，通过探讨职业教育改革及产教融合发展的新内涵、新模式、新产品、新成果、新趋势和新进展，通过受邀院士、青年科学家、大国工匠、企业家、国家英雄航天员的访谈、主旨演讲，通过发起“云接力”活动，发动吸引全社会和全行业关注、支持、参与职业教育，使得职业教育“有学头、有盼头、有奔头”。

聚焦“永不落幕”。“云上博览会”致力于全球化、综合性、高水平的数字化服务平台，展会后将落实跟踪链条，“八朵云”继续发挥产教融合成果推介、科研成果转化、技术服务等功能，驱动职业教育适用新技术和产业变革，实现博览会“永不落幕”。

聚焦高质量发展。博览会汇聚来自全球海量级的学校、企业、科研单位、国际组织等职业教育资源要素，形成教育教学、产业发展、生产经营、科技研发等新技术应用场景，集展示、主旨论坛、交流、研讨、交易、互动于一体，从而推动职业教育高质量发展和全球行业整体发展。

#### 5. 博览会成效

聚焦新兴技术，瞄准技术变革和产业优化升级。聚焦人工智能、量子信息、集成电路等新技术，展示 5G、大数据、云计算等技术的创新应用。

搭建数字平台，着力推动职业教育高质量发展。汇聚百余家企业、机构与 200 余家学校、单位，推动职业教育适用新技术，促进产教融合成果推介，实现高质量发展。

展示成果风采，致力重塑职教发展良好生态。讲述上千个现场工程师、大国工匠、新产业工人、专业技术人才、“黄大年式”教师团队、职业学校优秀教师、职业学校学生的事迹，营造良好生态。

烘托热烈氛围，博览会开展仪式吸引了2 100万人次观看，汇聚了科技界、产业界、教育界等社会各界广泛关注并参与职业教育，为世界职业技术教育发展大会的成功开幕烘托了气氛，营造了氛围，凝聚了力量。

# Ⅲ. Introduction to World Expo on the Integration of Vocational Education with Industry

On August 19, 2022, the World Expo on the Integration of Vocational Education with Industry (hereinafter referred to as the Expo) was held both online and offline. The attendants closely followed the theme of the World Vocational and Technical Education Development Conference (hereinafter referred to as the Conference), and comprehensively demonstrated the achievements of vocational education that adapts to the needs of new technology and industrial change in terms of the integration of industry and education and in-depth interaction.

1. Significance of the Expo

The Expo is part of an important consensus reached at the High-level Dialogue on Global Development. On June 24, 2022, Chinese President Xi Jinping chaired the High-level Dialogue on Global Development. The leaders of the participating countries jointly discussed global development issues, reached a series of important consensus, and added the World Vocational and Technical Education Development Conference to the list of achievements. As an important part of the Conference, the Expo aims to promote China's vocational education to reach out the world, accelerate the implementation of the global vocational education development initiative, and carry out vocational education exchanges and mutual learning, resource sharing, and cooperative development for countries around the world and international partners.

The Expo meets the urgent need to promote the high-quality development of vocational education. Vocational education is the type of education most closely integrated with economic development, industrial change, and employment. In the digital economy era, in order to adapt to new technology and industrial change, we must upgrade vocational education, elevate its connotation, improve its quality, and effectively play the role of vocational education in serving the national development strategy and local regional economic development.

The Expo is held according to the common will of exchange, cooperation and development in the world vocational education field. In the face of the new development pattern of vocational education in the post-pandemic era, countries around the world need vocational education more urgently than ever before, and the demand for high-quality technical and skilled personnel is stronger than ever before. The development of world vocational education calls for jointly building an "international stage" and a global vocational education development community with a shared future by pressing the "fast forward key" in the process of the integration of industry and education of global vocational education.

### 2. Preparation of the Expo

Starting from the preparation of the "China Vocational Education Expo" to the preparation of online oriented International exhibitions, the Expo has experienced three years and three stages.

The Expo is the first of its kind in history. Since the 18th National Congress of the Communist Party of China, China's vocational education has made structural changes and become the most promising type of education to lead the world. The development of digital economy promotes the transformation of production mode, lifestyle, and governance mode, and also puts forward new requirements for education mode and service mode. In order to fully demonstrate the development achievements of vocational education, raise the status of vocational education and improve the image of vocational education, with the approval of the General Office of the Ministry of Education, the Chinese Society for Technical and Vocational Education has been preparing for the China Vocational Education Expo since October 2020. After nearly a year's efforts, the preparations for the Expo are mostly completed. This rewrites the history that there was no exposition in the field of vocational education in China.

The Expo goes on the world stage. In March 2022, according to the requirements of the MOE leading Party group, China Vocational Education Expo should be expanded to the World Expo on the Integration of Vocational Education with Industry. The holding of the World Expo on the Integration of Vocational Education with Industry is of great significance. As an important part of the World Vocational and Technical Education Development Conference, the Expo carries the important mission of promoting China's vocational education to step on the world stage and leading the development of world vocational education.

The Expo uses a digital platform. On May 25, 2022, due to the change of epidemic situation, the organizing committee of the Conference decided that the Expo will be held mainly online, as well as offline. In order to implement the decision of the organizing committee of the conference and the important deployment of the ministerial Party group to "accelerate the implementation of the strategic action of digital education", the Expo uses digital technology to make preparations, promoting the structural and digital transformation of the integration of industry, education and science, and providing a digital platform for vocational colleges, relevant enterprises and scientific research institutions to share resources and exchange experience.

### 3. Exhibition of the Expo

At 9:30 on August 19, 2022, the Expo opened online and offline at the same time. Till 18:00 on August 20, audience from provincial (municipal, district) education administrative departments, nearly 10 000 well-known enterprises at home and abroad, and nearly 10 000 vocational schools watched the opening ceremony of the Expo, and "enjoyed the exhibition online", with 21 million visitors. More than 1.2 million people participated in the cloud relay activity of "Gathering for the Future of Vocational Education".

The online exhibition of the Expo has eight sections, including "Cloud Pavilion, Cloud Scenario, Cloud Vision, Cloud Service, Cloud Society, Cloud School, Cloud Charm and Cloud Interaction", along with nine special exhibitions, including "Digital Economy; Intelligent Manufacturing; Professionalization, Refinement, Specialization and Novelty; Advanced Science and Technology; Green Economy; Provincial, Municipal and Autonomous Regional Exhibition; Engineering Education; Digital Education; and International Education". It gathered more than 100 enterprises and organizations, as well as more than 200 schools and institutions, so as to show the application scenario of new technology, the results of the overall digital transformation driving the transformation of production mode, lifestyle and governance mode, and the effectiveness of vocational education in responding to digital change and the integration of industry, education and science.

The "Cloud Pavilion" has been divided into three parts and nine special exhibitions, with more than 100 enterprises and more than 20 provinces, municipalities and autonomous regions. The "Digital Economy" Exhibition focuses on displaying innovative achievements, core technologies and advanced application scenarios in the field of digital economy (such as Seentao's industrial internet platform, 360's local safe brain and sky system, etc.); The "Intelligent Manufacturing and High-end Equipment" Exhibition focuses on new technologies and products of intelligent manufacturing (such as 5G Star intelligent manufacturing private network training system of Huawei, intelligent robots of UB Selection, high-end medical equipment of Neusoft, production and manufacturing equipment of Han's Laser, urban super brain of iFlytek, etc.); The "Professionalization, Refinement, Specialization and Novelty" Exhibition displays professional, refined, special, and novel technology innovation and application (such as the artificial intelligence robot of DOBOT); The "Advanced Technology" Exhibition of the Metaverse displays cutting-edge technologies (such as in Microsoft, Shenzhen CECport and other enterprises); the Green Economy "Carbon Peak" and "Carbon Neutral" Exhibition displays the digitalization, green transformation and development of the industry (such as global energy management and industrial automation management of Schneider Electric); the "Provincial, Municipal and Autonomous Regional" Exhibition displays the achievements of vocational education in serving local industry, technology and economic development (e.g. Shanghai, Zhejiang, Liaoning, etc.); the "Engineering Education" Exhibition displays the experience and achievements of vocational education in cultivating students' innovation ability and the ability to solve complex field problems (such as Shenzhen Polytechnic, Tianjin Sino-German University of Applied Sciences, Zhejiang Institute of Mechanical & Electrical Engineering, etc.); the "Digital Education" Exhibition focuses on the application results of new technologies in the reform of vocational education governance mode, teaching mode, evaluation mode and other aspects (such as Glodon, Higher Education Press, National Vocational Education platform, etc.); the "International Education" Exhibition focuses on the achievements of international exchanges and cooperation such as mutual learning, consultation, joint construction and sharing in vocational education (such as GIZ in Germany).

The "Cloud Scenario" has nearly 400 new scenarios divided into three aspects. The aspect of the production mode displays new technologies such as artificial intelligence, quantum information, and integrated circuit, as well as the intelligent and digital scenarios of production and operation of lighthouse factories, lights-out factory, and low carbon factory (such as ten application cases of 5G, digital workshop, industrial robots, artificial intelligence, etc.). The aspect of lifestyle displays the application scenarios of new technologies in the field of life sciences, as well as in life, study and work (such as smart city, smart healthcare, medical robot, shared mobility, intelligent connected vehicle, etc.). The aspect of governance mode shows the application of the new generation of information technology in social and organizational governance (such as smart justice, smart city, etc.).

The "Cloud Vision" builds an instant information exchange platform, making remote communication similar to face-to-face communication. During the Expo, some companies, such as iFlytek and NetEase Youdao, delivered "live broadcasts" on the cloud to the world, focusing on the forefront of industry, technological innovation and the integration of industry and education.

The "Cloud Service" builds a platform of mutual communication and two-way integration between schools and enterprises. It is divided into four parts: "Policy Dynamic Publicity Services" release important policy information about vocational education (such as "Decision on Accelerating the Development of Modern Vocational Education", "National Vocational Education Reform Implementation Plan", "Vocational Education Law of the People's Republic of China"); "Enterprise Services" release job demand, education and teaching products, practical internship positions, technical services, etc. (such as iFlytek's talent training, artificial intelligence laboratory, and doctoral tutors' internship and employment services, vocational skills identification services, professional construction planning); "School Services" release information on training projects, technology research, and development and achievement transformation; "Cooperation and Sharing Services" show the achievements of school-enterprise cooperation and teacher exchange, including "enterprise talent training base", "campus training base", co-development of courses, co-construction of majors, etc.

The "Cloud Society" introduces the historical evolution of the Chinese Society for Technical and Vocational Education and the achievements of the fifth Council since its establishment, as well as the achievements of the work on the "Ten Work Carriers" in terms of political position, research level, service ability, development force, etc. (such as the activities of "Talk about majors, Talk about courses, Talk about major groups", the series of courses for the centenary of the founding of the Party, the interpretation of the new version of the major catalog, the construction of new think tanks).

The "Cloud School" has been divided into higher vocational education and primary and secondary vocational education, with more than 200 vocational schools. Centered around the theme of "school-enterprise cooperation, industry-education integration, and moral education", there are modules like "school profile, governance mode, teacher development, student development, education and teaching, social services, international exchange and cooperation", so as to show the school philosophy, governance structure, specialty setting, enrollment and employment, team building, etc. (such as Zhejiang Institute of Mechanical & Electrical Engineering, Tianjin Sino-German University of Applied Sciences, Hunan Railway Professional Technology College).

The "Cloud Charm" is divided into four parts, namely "Workers, Craftsmen, People, and Talents". It narrates the stories of tens of thousands of field engineers, national craftsmen, workers from new industries, and professional and technical personnel, showing the important role of professional and technical talents in promoting China's rapid economic development and industrial miracle (such as National Craftsman of the Year, national/provincial technical experts, winners of the National Vocational College Skills Competition).

The "Cloud Interaction" is divided into cloud relay and cloud communication. WeChat punch attracts social attention to vocational education, and sets topics for hotspot events of vocational education. By the end of August 22, more than 1.1 million people had participated in the "Cloud Relay" activity, and nearly 400 messages had been left under the topic of "the Expo opens", with people from all walks of life leaving wishes for vocational education.

The offline exhibition of the Expo is divided into three areas. The first is the offline micro exhibition. It contains 9 micro booths and 200 exhibition boards, gathering leading enterprises in the industry, high-tech enterprises, high-tech industry centers and scientific research institutes, as well as high-level vocational schools, so as to display the development and application scenarios of new technologies, the integration results of industry, education and science, and the educational achievements. The second is the Tianjin exhibition area. It showcases Tianjin's dominant industries, highlighting the integration of industry and education. The third is Luban Workshop exhibition hall. It shows the fruitful results of China's vocational education going global, serving the Belt and Road Initiative, helping international production capacity cooperation and promoting cultural exchanges between China and foreign countries.

**4. Highlights of the Expo**

It focuses on new technologies. It shows the integrated development and application scenarios of vocational education using cutting-edge technologies such as 5G, big data, cloud computing, blockchain, digital twin and artificial intelligence, and guides vocational education to accelerate its adaptation to and application of new technologies.

It focuses on industrial change. It shows the practical achievements of vocational education in addressing digital transformation and promoting the integration of industry, education and science, as well as the achievements of industrial transformation and upgrading in driving the transformation of production mode, lifestyle and governance mode, working together to create a diversified and integrated, flexible and opening new ecology for the integration of industry, education and science of vocational education, and to enhance the attractiveness of vocational education.

It focuses on new ecology. The achievements of vocational education development are demonstrated through the promotion of the achievements of online and offline exhibition sectors, theme exhibition areas and application scenarios. By discussing the new connotation, new modes, new products, new achievements, new trends and new progress of vocational education reform and integrated development of industry and education, and by inviting academicians, young scientists, national craftsmen, entrepreneurs and national heroes to participate in interviews and deliver keynote speeches, the "Cloud Relay" activity has been launched, attracting the whole society and industry to pay attention to, support and participate in vocational education, so as to make vocational education have "something to learn, something to look forward to, something to run for".

It focuses on "never ending" exhibition. The "Cloud Expo" has been committed to the development of a globalized and comprehensive platform with high-level service. After the exhibition, the track chain would be implemented, and the "eight clouds" should continue to serve the functions of the achievement promotion of the integration of industry and education, transformation of scientific research achievements, and technical services. Vocational education would also be promoted to apply new technology and industrial change, realizing the "never ending" exhibition of the Expo.

It focuses on high-quality development. The Expo gathers vocational education resource elements from a large number of schools, enterprises, scientific research institutions, and international organizations, forms new technology application scenarios for education and teaching, industrial development, production and operation, scientific and technological research and development, and integrates exhibition, keynote forum, exchange, discussion, transaction and interaction, thus promoting the high-quality development of vocational education and the overall development of the global industry.

### 5. Effects and Achievements of the Expo

It focuses on emerging technologies and aims at technological change and industrial optimization and upgrading. It focuses on new technologies such as artificial intelligence, quantum information and integrated circuits, and showcases innovative applications of technologies such as 5G, big data and cloud computing.

It builds digital platforms to promote high-quality development of vocational education. It has brought together more than 100 enterprises, institutions and more than 200 schools and units, so as to promote vocational education to apply new technology, and to promote the achievements of the integration of industry and education, achieving high-quality development.

It displays the achievements and strive to reshape the sound ecology of vocational education development. It narrates the stories of tens of thousands of field engineers, national craftsmen, workers from new industries, and professional and technical personnel, "Huang Danian" Style Teachers Team, excellent teachers from vocational schools, and students of vocational schools, so as to create a good ecology.

It creates a warm atmosphere. The opening ceremony of the Expo attracted 21 million people from scientific and technological circles, industrial circles, educational circles and other social sectors to pay attention to and participate in vocational education, creating the atmosphere and gathering forces for the successful opening of the World Vocational and Technical Education Development Conference.

校园简介
WEIVEI
校园文化

世界职业教育产教融合博览会
习近平总书记关于
职业教育的重要论述和要求
WEIVEI 2022

# 四

# 主要媒体报道摘要

## 首届世界职业技术教育发展大会8月19日至20日在天津举办　助力职业教育高质量发展

8月19日至20日，首届世界职业技术教育发展大会在天津举办。8月19日，国家主席习近平向世界职业技术教育发展大会致贺信。

大会以“后疫情时代职业技术教育发展：新变化、新方式、新技能”为主题，来自全球123个国家约700名代表，通过线上线下结合方式“会聚”渤海之滨，凝聚共识力量，共话推动职业教育高质量发展大计。大会发布《中国职业教育发展报告》白皮书，向世界介绍中国职业教育发展经验，提出中国方案、贡献中国智慧；大会主论坛和14个平行论坛围绕当前全球关心的热点问题展开，分享经验做法，指出面向未来的职业教育发展方向，发布了《天津倡议》。

与会代表表示，我国发起并举办首届世界职业技术教育发展大会，对搭建各国职业教育界深化交流合作的有效机制和平台具有重要的现实意义，是推动我国职业教育高质量发展的重要途径。

**我国职业教育进入提质培优、增值赋能新阶段**

记者从大会了解到，我国职业教育进入提质培优、增值赋能新阶段。

教育部部长怀进鹏在大会主论坛发表主旨演讲时表示，我国始终高度重视职业教育，在有效支撑国家经济社会高质量发展、不断满足人民群众对美好生活的需要、持续畅通学生多样化成长成才的渠道等方面取得了历史性成就，建成世界上最大规模的职业教育体系，构建了职业教育与普通教育协调发展的教育格局，实现了从学校为主举办到多元参与办学、从规模扩张发展到高质量内涵发展的转变。

“大会落户天津，将为全市职业教育改革发展注入新的强大动力。”天津市委教育工委常务副书记、市教委主任荆洪阳介绍，天津持续在职业教育领域强化政策支持、保障投入力度、营造创新发展氛围。截至 2021 年底，天津共有职业教育类大学 2 所；独立设置公办高职院校 25 所、民办高职院校 1 所；全市 70% 左右的高职院校和 50% 左右的中职学校由行业企业举办，形成了产业、行业、企业、职业、专业“五业联动”的办学模式。政府统筹、行业主办、教育管理、企业参与的办学体制机制成为天津职业教育的鲜明特色。

天津职业技术师范大学党委书记张金刚表示，近年来，天津职业技术师范大学致力于服务国家职业教育和天津经济社会发展需求，积极推进教育教学改革，“《天津倡议》秉持公平全纳、有教无类，面向人人、质量优先的理念，彰显了推动职业教育创新、共建美好生活的坚定信心。”今后，学校将继续深入开展新时代职业院校教师专业发展研究、职业院校师德师风建设研究，为新时代职业教育教师发展提供支持。

### 持续推进职业教育与经济社会发展紧密相连

职业教育与经济社会发展紧密相连，对促进就业创业、助力经济社会发展、增进人民福祉具有重要意义。

在大会同期举办的世界职业院校技能大赛展示区，时代楷模、国网天津市电力公司工程师张黎明带领团队展演的人工智能配网带电作业机器人项目引来许多人驻足。“我毕业于职业学校，现在还在两所天津本地职业院校兼任教师。我深切感受到，职业教育的变迁与经济社会的发展密不可分，我们大有可为！”张黎明说，希望能激励更多的青年人走技能成才、技能报国之路，为高质量发展贡献自己的一分力量。

中国职业技术教育学会常务副会长兼秘书长刘建同表示，近年来，我国大力发展适应新技术和产业变革需要的职业教育，着力促进教育链、人才链与产业链、创新链有效衔接，深化产教融合，推进职业教育高质量发展。

作为从职业学校发展起来的应用技术大学，近年来，天津中德应用技术大学持续推进产教融合、校企合作，聚焦工业发展需求，向社会输送了大量实用型人才。“本次大会突出强调教育与产业的融合发展，让我们坚定了办好职业本科教育的信心。”学校党委书记张兴会表示，今后，天津中德应用技术大学将持续推动产业链、创新链、教育链的有效衔接，开展与制造业头部企业的深度合作，不断改进教学水平。

**加强互学互鉴、共建共享**

煮水、沏茶、倒茶……全部动作由机器人臂完成，我国传统茶艺与现代工业技术完美结合。这是发生在大会展览区的一幕。“葡萄牙师生制作了倒红酒的机械手臂；我国师生制作了能沏茶的机械手臂。这样的互动促进了交流，增进了友谊。”天津机电职业技术学院副校长王维园说，“机械臂”在不同场景的应用，正是学校与葡萄牙塞图巴尔理工学院合作建立的葡萄牙鲁班工坊的教学成果之一。

“英国鲁班工坊开发的国际化教学标准经核准认证纳入英格兰国家普通和职业学历框架，实现了中国职业教育标准进入英国职业教育体系的新突破。”天津市经济贸易学校校长刘恩丽介绍，英国鲁班工坊是天津在欧洲建立的首个鲁班工坊，由天津市经济贸易学校（原天津市第二商业学校）与英国奇切斯特学院合作共建，开展中餐烹饪专业人才培养。未来，英国鲁班工坊将继续探索学历教育的持续进阶，为在世界推广标准化的中餐烹饪技艺发挥积极的作用。

天津市教育科学研究院终身教育研究所所长、天津鲁班工坊研推中心副主任杨延介绍，天津已在 19 个国家建成 20 个鲁班工坊，对 3 000 余人开展了学历教育，并在海外建立起从中职到高职再到本科、从技术技能培训到学历教育全覆盖的职业教育体系。

加强互学互鉴、共建共享。“我将与团队共同编写配网带电作业机器人培训课程，希望借助鲁班工坊，将技术推广到‘一带一路’沿线国家，为电网安全和供电质量提升出一份力。”张黎明说。

本报记者：武少民、李家鼎

来源:《人民日报》2022 年 8 月 21 日

## 一场高规格高水平高质量的大会
### ——与会代表高度赞赏世界职业技术教育发展大会成果

本报天津 8 月 20 日讯　经过两天紧张而高效的交流和研讨，首届世界职业技术教育发展大会取得了丰硕成果，发布《天津倡议》，于今天落下帷幕。

大会期间，各国部长、国际组织负责人、驻华使节、行业企业和院校代表们以世界眼光和专业视角，围绕职业教育展开了广泛而深入的研讨，为推动全球职业教育高质量发展积极建言献策。与会代表纷纷表示，《天津倡议》提出了共同的价值认识、行业自律和努力方向，聚焦世界发展面临的重要课题，深化了对职业教育重大意义和功能定位的思想认识。

多位与会嘉宾表示，大家在大会上结合各自实际，深刻分析了相关领域的发展现状，探讨了面临的问题和挑战，增进了彼此的了解，为进一步合作奠定了坚实基础。各国代表详细介绍了所在国家或行业领域推动职业教育及技能培训的战略设计、项目实施等最新实践，对推动全球职业教育高质量发展具有积极的启发和助益。

与会代表认为，在联合国教科文组织《技术和职业教育培训战略》指引下，大家围绕数字化转型、可持续发展、终身学习等新议题贡献了新观点，世界各国职业院校师生在大会期间同台竞技，展现了新技术。本次大会聚焦“产教融合”，与会嘉宾不仅有教育界和院校代表，更有各国政府机构、国际组织、行业企业、科研院所等社会各界代表，设置的议题不仅涉及职业教育自身，还更多地体现了职业教育与产业变革、技术革命、绿色发展、扶贫减贫之间的紧密互动，是一场高规格、高水平、高质量的大会。

大会期间，中国教育部发布中国职业教育发展白皮书（《中国职业教育发展报告（2012—2022）》），同样引起各国代表关注。各国各界代表高度赞赏中国为推动世界职业教育发展作出的努力和贡献，表示中国颁布了新修订的职业教育法，为构建现代职业教育体系夯实了法治基础，期待中国职业教育迎来新的更大发展，为构建人类命运共同体，促进全球经济社会可持续发展作出新的更大贡献。

本报记者：高毅哲、陈欣然　见习记者：程　旭

来源：《中国教育报》2022 年 8 月 21 日第 1 版　版名：要闻

# 职业教育为全球产业升级赋能
## ——首届世界职业技术教育发展大会平行论坛侧记

产业转型发展对职业教育产生了哪些影响？职业教育青年教师专业化能力体系怎样建设？如何通过中外职业教育合作构建人类技能共同体？ 8月20日，首届世界职业技术教育发展大会上，十四个平行论坛同时举行，来自全球职业教育领域的专家学者对职业教育相关主题进行了深入研讨。

### 产业转型对职业教育提出新要求

“我们所处的时代，科技和信息技术不断更迭，因此我们的专业设置必须与时俱进，确保教学适应企业的发展需求……”在大会平行论坛——职业教育与产业转型发展论坛上，新加坡南洋理工学院国际部主任蔡锦平介绍了该校应对产业转型进行的探索。

在职业教育与产业转型发展论坛、职业教育数字化转型发展论坛、人工智能+职业教育创新发展论坛等论坛上，与会专家普遍认为，近年来随着全球产业转型的迅猛发展，产业结构、产业组织、产业规模、产业技术的升级对职业教育产生深远影响。职业教育必须在院校治理、专业建设和教师发展等各方面进行改革创新，以适应并促进产业转型发展。

蔡锦平介绍，新加坡南洋理工学院工程系设有许多技术创新中心，其核心是工程系的师资团队，合作伙伴包括政府机构和技术公司，为企业客户服务开发项目来提供问题解决方案。“这些技术创新中心为我们提供了教师能力提升的重要平台，促进了我们的技术和教学内容更新，也带动了课程改革和创新。”

在职业教育数字化转型发展论坛上，深圳职业技术学院校长许建领认为，高职院校在数字经济社会中肩负着不可替代的数字化技能人才供给使命。当前，我国已经有不少高职院校加快数字化转型步伐，紧盯数字经济发展趋势，与行业龙头联合组建了人工智能、大数据、云计算等学院，与时俱进地进行数字化产业及产业数字化专业群布局，新开设了市场紧缺的数字技术技能人才培养专业，数字化职业教育育人生态初步成型。

**推动职业教育育人模式创新**

全球职业教育青年教师发展论坛、职业院校科学教育发展论坛、职业教育校企协同育人模式创新论坛、职业院校工程教育发展论坛……首届世界职业技术教育发展大会上，探讨职业院校改革的平行论坛占据半壁江山。很多院校正在进行的改革实践，也成为其他兄弟院校的他山之石。

中华职教社党组书记、总干事方乃纯在职业教育校企协同育人模式创新论坛上谈及中国特色学徒制的实践与探索时表示，中国特色学徒制最大限度地发挥了企业育人主体的作用，形成了校企紧密合作的育人新机制，真正实现了产教深度融合，有效解决了参与企业对人才的选用预留问题，增强了职业教育的适应性。同时他也指出，中国特色学徒制还处于探索阶段，也存在一些问题，面临诸多难点，比如行业企业参与职业教育的积极性不是特别高，对行业企业参与的激励保障约束机制欠缺等，还需要不断改进与完善。

应对数字化转型，职业院校教师是关键。在全球职业教育青年教师发展论坛上，中国科学院院士、西北工业大学学术委员会主任黄维认为，培养职业教育教师的数字素养，将成为职教教师教育的新趋势："我们要按照数字化要求，完善人才培养方案，搭建学科专业平台，健全课程教学体系，构建数字技术加教师教育的职业教育教师职前培养体系和在职培养培训体系。还要加强数字化环境建设，打造师生互动的云端数字化学习平台，建设融线上线下教学为一体的智慧教室和实训基地。"

**构建人类技能共同体**

在全球一体化背景下，构建人类技能共同体已成为大势所趋。我国近年来进行了积极探索，如在"一带一路"沿线国家开设鲁班工坊、大力开展中非职业教育合作等。"一带一路"合作倡议与鲁班工坊建设发展论坛、中非职业教育合作与发展论坛总结了相关工作取得的成果，对构建人类技能共同体进行了展望。

泰国鲁班工坊是世界第一家鲁班工坊。在"一带一路"合作倡议与鲁班工坊建设发展论坛上，泰国大城技术学院院长玛悠丽介绍，天津渤海职业技术学院与大城技术学院共同建立鲁班工坊，在中国院校的帮助下，泰国学生掌握了先进的制造业技术。截至目前，泰国鲁班工坊学历教育培养 1 125 人，技能培训交流师生 8 000 余人次。学生分别获得泰国首届"职业教育宝石王杯"大赛金牌冠军、泰国首届铁道运输系统邀请赛冠军奖等 9 项荣誉。此外，招收泰国学生 200 多人，已毕业的

66 名泰国学生，27 人前往本科院校深造，其余均已就业，就业率达 100%。

记者从中非职业教育合作与发展论坛上获悉，截至目前，天津已在 19 个国家建成 20 个鲁班工坊，其中在 10 个非洲国家建立了 11 个鲁班工坊，为非洲青年插上成就梦想的翅膀。

由天津职业技术师范大学与埃塞俄比亚技术大学共同建设的埃塞俄比亚鲁班工坊，建成 1 年来运行顺利。埃塞俄比亚技术大学校长特舍里 · 博里查说："我们的鲁班工坊将成为非洲职业技术教育领域的典范。"

《中非职业教育合作发展研究》一书也在这次论坛首次亮相。该研究报告从中非职业教育合作的时代背景、实践与创新、问题与挑战、对策与建议等维度展开，为中非职业教育合作提供决策建议和实践指导。

本报天津 8 月 20 日电

本报记者：陈欣然　见习记者：程　旭

来源：《中国教育报》2022 年 8 月 21 日第 1 版　版名：要闻

# 职业教育为产业强国夯实技术技能基础

习近平总书记指出，在全面建设社会主义现代化国家新征程中，职业教育前途广阔、大有可为。党的十八大以来，我国积极推进职业教育高质量发展，支持中外职业教育交流合作。十年来，通过提质培优、产教深度融合，我国已建成世界上规模最大、质量较高的职业教育体系，为促进经济社会发展和提高国家竞争力提供了有力支撑。

在首届世界职业技术教育发展大会上，世界职业院校技能大赛备受关注。增材制造是一种新兴技术，如今正在被应用于大火箭、大飞机等先进制造业。在这一赛项中，来自天津职业大学的周雅婷团队夺得冠军。工业部件的增材制造考验的是对力学结构、设计建模、精确制造的全方位把握。

面对国际赛场强手如云，周雅婷和队友们沉着应对，不断尝试创新突破。周雅婷说，这其实和他们日常学校的实训项目很像，企业出题，学校作答，他们面临的都是真实的科研任务。

像周雅婷一样，而今，越来越多的职教生有了更宽广的梦想舞台，这份底气和自信源于国家对职业教育的大力发展。习近平总书记指出，实体经济是我国经济的重要支撑，做强实体经济需要大量技能型人才，需要大力弘扬工匠精神，发展职业教育前景广阔、大有可为。他强调，要加快构建现代职业教育体系，培养更多高素质技术技能人才、能工巧匠、大国工匠。党的十八大以来，我国职业教育实现新的历史跨越，“中职—高职专科—职业本科”一体化的职业学校体系基本建成。尤其是近年来，职业教育产教融合底色更鲜明，走上了提质培优、增值赋能的快车道。

党的十八大以来，职业教育主动调整院校专业布局，对接新经济、新业态、新职业发展。2021 年，新版职业教育专业目录发布，共设立 19 个专业大类、97 个专业类、1 349 个专业，更新幅度超过 60%。仅在西部的成渝地区，近 3 年就新增云计算、工业机器人、智能网联汽车技术等 1 000 多个专业点。这几天，三星堆博物馆新馆建设迎来新的节点，整个工期比预期提前了 40 天，在高效率建设的背后，幕后英雄正是一支来自“智能建造技术”新专业的职业院校毕业生团队。

目前，我国已建成世界上规模最大的职业教育体系，每年培养的高素质技术技能人才超过 1 000 万。在先进制造业、战略性新兴产业和现代服务业等领域，一线新增从业人员 70% 以上是职业院校的毕业生。我国职业学校开设专业基本覆盖了国民经济各领域，有力支撑了我国成为全世界唯一拥有全部工业门类的国家和世界第二大经济体，为全面建设社会主义现代化国家提供有力人才和技术技能保障。

来源：央视网 2022 年 8 月 23 日

## 世界职业院校技能大赛开幕式举行
## 100 多个国家和地区 1 000 多位选手参赛

本报天津 8 月 19 日讯　世界职业院校技能大赛开幕式今天在天津举行。教育部副部长孙尧出席开幕式并致辞。

此次世校赛与世界职业技术教育发展大会同期举行，是中国教育部发起，联合相关部门、行业组织和地方共同举办的一项公益性、国际性职业院校师生综合技能竞赛活动。本届世校赛共有来自亚洲、欧洲、非洲、南美洲、北美洲五大洲 100 多个国家和地区、近 300 所学校的 1 000 多位选手参赛，成为目前参赛国家数量最多的世界职业院校技能大赛。

世校赛分别在天津赛区和江西赛区两个赛区举办，8 月陆续进入线上线下比赛进程。世校赛共设 23 个赛项，聚焦高端制造类、数字经济、新产业、新业态、新技术等，开设涉及装备制造、电子与信息、交通运输、财经商贸、能源动力与材料等领域的竞赛类赛项，还特别设置中国制造与传统文化、能工巧匠、中华非遗文化等展演类单元赛项，有效传承和弘扬中华优秀文化，促进中外人文交流。

本报记者：高毅哲、陈欣然

来源:《中国教育报》2022 年 8 月 20 日

## 大力发展适应新技术和产业变革需要的职业教育
## 世界职业教育产教融合博览会开展

本报天津8月19日讯　世界职业教育产教融合博览会开展仪式今天在天津举行。教育部副部长孙尧、中国职业技术教育学会会长鲁昕出席仪式并致辞。

博览会以“大力发展适应新技术和产业变革需要的职业教育”为主题，以线上为主、线上线下结合的形式举办。线上展以“云展馆”“云场景”“云视界”“云服务”“云学会”“云学校”“云风采”“云互动”的“八朵云”方式呈现，展示新技术应用场景，展示数字化转型整体驱动生产方式、生活方式、治理方式变革成果，展示职业教育应对数字化变革、产教科融合发展的成效。共有百余家头部企业、200余家职业学校、20余个省（市、区）参加线上博览会。线下展分为线下微展、天津市展区、鲁班工坊展厅三个区域。

据悉，博览会有三大特点。一是聚焦新兴技术，瞄准技术变革和产业优化升级。聚焦人工智能、量子信息、集成电路等新技术，展示5G、大数据、云计算等技术的创新应用。二是搭建数字平台，着力推动职业教育高质量发展。汇聚百余家企业、机构与200余家学校、单位，推动职业教育适用新技术，促进产教融合成果推介，实现高质量发展。三是展示成果风采，致力重塑职教发展良好生态。讲述上千名现场工程师、大国工匠、新产业工人、专业技术人才、黄大年式教师团队、职业学校优秀教师、职业学校学生的事迹，营造良好生态。

本报记者：高毅哲、陈欣然

来源:《中国教育报》2022年8月20日第1版　版名：要闻

## 这条路前景广阔
## ——来自世界职业技术教育发展大会的观察

新华社天津8月20日电　8月19日至20日，由我国政府首次发起并主办的世界职业技术教育发展大会在天津举办，120多个国家和地区的代表注册参会。

党的十八大以来，在习近平总书记的关心、关怀下，我国职业教育被摆在经济社会发展全局中更加突出的战略位置，不仅规模居世界首位，而且实现了从规模扩张发展到高质量内涵发展的重要转变。

最近这十年来，我国职业教育面貌发生哪些历史性、格局性变化？此次大会提供了重要的观察窗口，记者走进大会寻找答案。

**打破学历衔接“天花板”，现代职业教育“香起来”**

重重叠叠的迷宫里，机器人快速穿梭，短短几秒就成功走出。这是大会中世界职业院校技能大赛展示赛的精彩一幕。

“三百六十行，行行出状元。进入职业院校，也可以有出彩机会。”操控机器人的于欣令一脸笑意。他刚从天津渤海职业技术学院毕业，即将保送进入本科院校深造。

“这得益于天津建立起完整的‘中高本硕博’职业教育培养体系。”天津渤海职业技术学院机电工程学院副院长吉红说，她所在学院每年都有几十名学生升入本科。

大赛上，天津轻工职业技术学院毕业生刘华庚参与设计搭建的风光互补项目表现同样抢眼。今年9月，他将进入天津中德应用技术大学学习，与他同宿舍的4位同学也都顺利升本。

“观念变了，职业教育正逐渐‘香起来’。”天津轻工职业技术学院副院长李云梅说。

来自大会主办方的信息显示：2022年，全国职业本科专业点数备案936个，其中四年制专业备案点数比2021年增加了44%。“中职、高职专科、职业本科”

一体化的职业学校体系基本建成。

打破止步专科的学历“天花板”，只是我国职业教育历史性、格局性变化的一个侧面。

大会上，“重视程度前所未有”被与会职业院校负责人频频提及。

从《国家职业教育改革实施方案》启动“中国特色高水平高职学校和专业建设计划”到《关于推动现代职业教育高质量发展的意见》等为职业教育发展指明路径，再到新修订的职业教育法明确“职业教育是与普通教育具有同等重要地位的教育类型”，近年来密集出台的法律制度和政策举措，有力促进了我国职业教育从规模发展到高质量内涵发展的重要转变。

截至目前，我国现有职业院校超过 1 万所，设置 1 300 余种专业和 12 万多个专业点，近 10 年来累计培养输送 6 100 万高素质劳动者和技术技能人才。

教育部部长怀进鹏表示，我国职业教育在有效支撑国家经济社会高质量发展、不断满足人民群众对美好生活的追求、持续畅通学生多样化成长成才的渠道、积极服务构建全面开放新格局方面取得了历史性成就。

这一点也得到与会外国嘉宾“点赞”。

“中国职业教育发展迅猛，积累了诸多可供借鉴的宝贵经验。”联合国儿童基金会教育和青少年发展全球负责人罗伯特·詹金斯说。

**打造产教融合“立交桥” 技术技能人才“强起来”**

走进大会展区，天津职业大学机械工程实训中心主任李建国正在讲解一套“叶片振动、间隙测量系统”。

“长期以来，转子叶片加工动平衡是精密加工中的一道难题。”李建国解释，一旦处理不好，高速运转中可能发生事故。

这套装置是在产教融合引领下，天津职业大学与企业联合攻关的成果，运用于我国航空发动机、燃气轮机等重要装备上。参与研发的学生们就业十分抢手。

离李建国所在展台不远处，一台填补空白的手表机芯零件高速精密级进冲模，为“国货之光”海鸥表插上了“翅膀”。

天津轻工职业技术学院教师周京说，学院与天津海鸥表业集团有限公司等企业成立了“中国轻工业精密模具工程技术研究中心”，共研手表机芯零件高速精密级系列级进模具项目 35 项，为企业创造经济价值 2 000 余万元。

作为大会重要组成部分，世界职业教育产教融合博览会吸引着职教人的目光。

参加博览会的浙江机电职业技术学院校长贺星岳说：“职业院校要通过产教融合，增强专业设置上的前瞻性。”

与浪潮集团合作共建浪潮产业学院、与京东教育共建跨境电商产业学院、与飞腾信息技术有限公司校企深度融合……展区内，一个个校企合作的鲜活案例体现着产教融合的丰硕成果。

目前，全国组建了 1 500 多个职业教育集团（联盟），涵盖了企业、学校、行业、科研机构在内的 4.5 万余家成员单位，形成了资源共享、责任共担、合作发展的具有中国特色的职业教育办学模式。

“我们成立中车高铁工匠学院，让企业技术人才、技能大师进校园，让企业培训技术、培训课程进课堂。”中国中车集团有限公司董事长孙永才会上介绍道。

供需适配，离不开专业设置优化、课程不断迭代。2021 年，新版职业教育专业目录发布，首次一体化设计中职、高职专科、高职本科专业体系，更新幅度超过 60%。

10 年来，职业教育对接重点产业，强化工学结合、更加注重实训、推广模块化教学，广泛采用学徒制培养、订单制培养，职业学校毕业生年终就业率总体保持在 95% 以上。

“学校围绕战略新兴产业等优化专业布局，就业率始终保持在 98% 以上，每年 16% 的毕业生入职 500 强企业。”深圳职业技术学院党委书记杨欣斌说。

**打开国际合作“出海口”，中国职教名片“亮起来”**

在大会鲁班工坊建设 · 成果展现场，来自泰国的黄可莹操纵机械臂，轻巧地抓起一把鲁班锁。

黄可莹 2013 年从泰国到天津深造，毕业后加入天津渤海职业技术学院，深度参与了首个鲁班工坊在泰国的筹建。

展览现场的屏幕上，清晰地显示着鲁班工坊的发展脉络。

2015 年，教育部与天津市签署协议，共建国家现代职业教育改革创新示范区，其中任务之一便是创建职业教育国际化新窗口。天津原创并率先实践鲁班工坊由此起航。

参与泰国鲁班工坊建设的天津渤海职业技术学院院长于兰平，这样阐释鲁班工坊内核：“带去的不仅有先进的专业教学标准、教学装备，还有先进的教育理念、教育模式，为合作国家培养急需的技术技能人才和能工巧匠。”

如今，鲁班工坊这一我国职业教育对外交流的知名品牌，已在泰国、印度、英国、葡萄牙等 19 个国家落地。

继英国后，葡萄牙 2018 年底成为天津在欧洲第二家鲁班工坊的签约落地国。这一由天津机电职业技术学院和塞图巴尔理工学院建立的鲁班工坊已显现出深远影响。

“鲁班工坊人才培养标准和专业建设质量被合作国广泛认同。”天津机电职业技术学院校长张维津在展会上介绍说。

目前，鲁班工坊有 11 个国际化专业教学标准获得合作国教育部认证，开设了工业机器人、新能源、动车组检修等 49 个专业，合作的学历教育包括中职、高职、应用本科、研究生四个层次。

“天津职业技术师范大学在埃塞俄比亚开设的鲁班工坊，帮助学生满足全球新兴市场技能要求。”埃塞俄比亚劳动与技能部部长穆费里亚特·卡米勒·艾哈迈德对鲁班工坊表达了赞赏。

在天津职业技术师范大学党委书记张金刚看来，这一鲁班工坊承担重要使命，面向非洲国家培养高端技术技能人才，为东非国家培养高水平职教师资。

多位与会外国嘉宾认为，鲁班工坊正为世界职业教育发展贡献中国智慧和力量。

“鲁班工坊是两国合作的典范，在人工智能、网络安全以及智能技术等方面，巴基斯坦都有可以向中国学习的地方。我们需要大量技能人才实现巴基斯坦的工业化，希望有更多合作。”巴基斯坦驻华使馆教育专员阿菲法·沙吉娅说。

透过大会，中国职业教育以实践作答：职业教育前景广阔、大有可为。

记者：刘元旭、邵香云、白佳丽、张建新、刘惟真

来源：新华网 2022 年 8 月 21 日

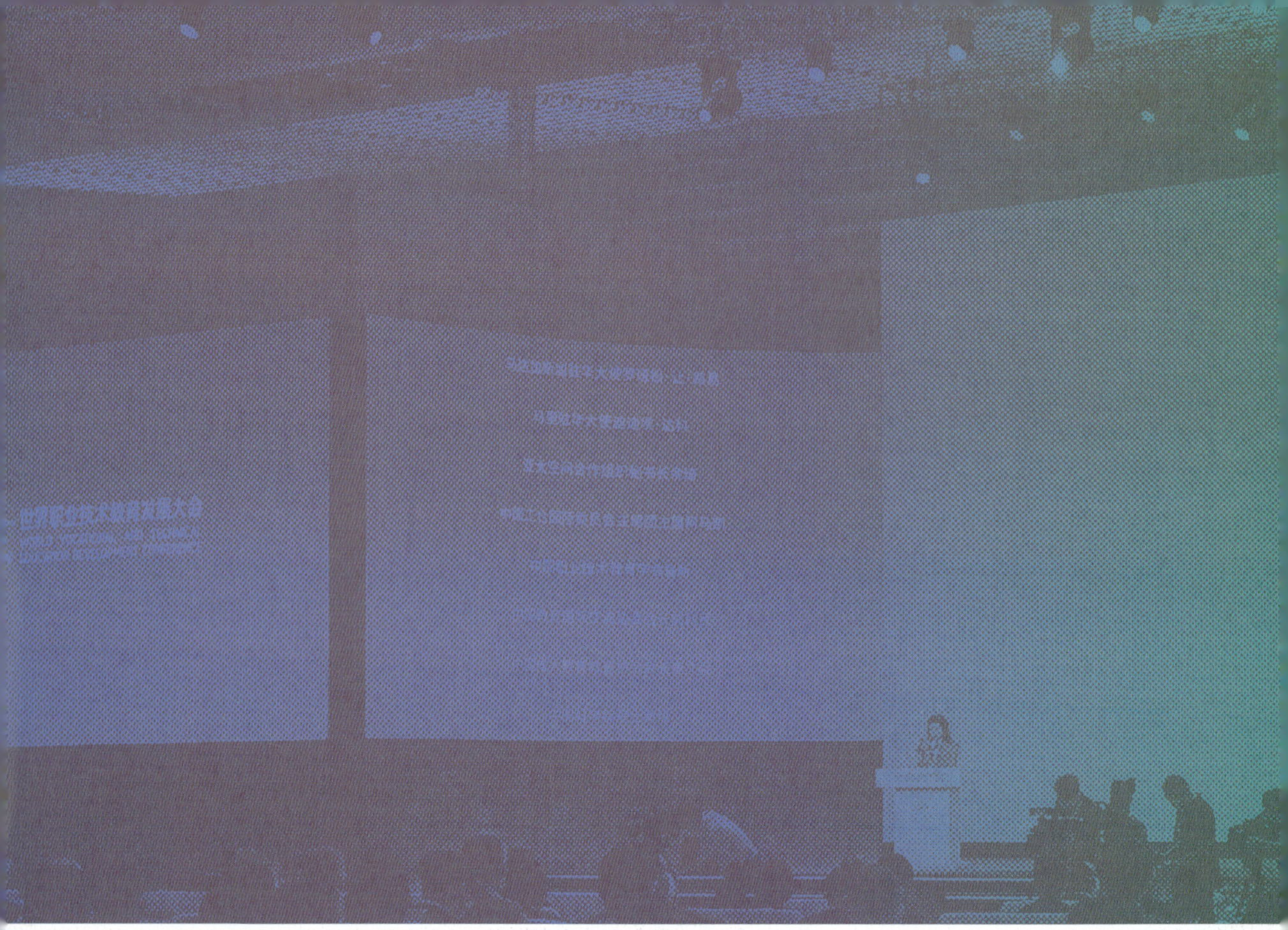

# 国际视野与中国国情

——2022年世界职业技术教育发展报告

# Global Vision and China's Reality

—World Vocational and Technical Education Development Report 2022

德国“工业 4.0”战略、“中国制造 2025”规划以及其他西方发达国家的工业化路径表明：全球新一轮科技和产业革命已经来临。“工业 4.0”对传统工业的生产模式、生产方式、技术应用以及工作组织形式等多方面产生深刻变革。随着“工业 4.0”时代制造业新技术、新模式、新业态的不断出现，技术技能人才的需求结构正在发生改变，社会需要发展创新性和复合型人才。职业技术教育人才结构也将发生变化，技术发展尖端化、集成化，更新速度加快，对技术技能人才的知识结构和层次需求有所提高。职业技术教育人才的类型需求也处于变革之中。在“工业 4.0”智能制造的背景下，企业由生产型制造向服务型制造转变，生产制造环节的价值比重下降，设计、安装、维护等服务环节的价值比重提升。未来将衍生出大量服务型人才，这些服务型人才属于既懂专业技术，又懂营销、管理的高端复合型人才。“工业 4.0”对人才观、教育观具有革命性的冲击，尤其是对直接培养高技术技能人才的职业技术教育提出了更大的挑战。

新冠病毒疫情的出现加剧了技术冲击和社会环境变化对职业技术教育带来的挑战。首先，突如其来的疫情加剧了劳动力市场的结构化不平衡。一方面，失业率显著上升，非正规就业岗位对青少年、低技能群体的就业吸纳能力下降；另一方面，技能人才短缺情况加剧，制造业和服务业领域自动化、智能化程度进一步提升，对技能劳动力的需求难以得到满足，这进一步加剧了机器换人的速度，加速了中等技能岗位的消失。其次，为了解决疫情带来的青少年失业等问题，各国继续采用高等教育规模扩张政策，进一步压缩了职业技术教育发展的空间。最后，多数国家经济增长停滞，政府通过财政性教育投入支持职业技术教育发展的能力下降。

与此同时，后疫情时代也出现了职业技术教育发展的新机遇。首先，中低收入国家重新意识到职业技术教育在促进经济增长和抑制收入不平等方面的重要贡献，在国际组织的支持下加大了对其的重视和投入。其次，科技创新需要通过知识扩散进入企业生产过程，技术技能型人才在知识溢出、工艺和产品创新方面的价值日益凸显。更加值得注意的是，不同行业的数字化转型加大了对高技术技能人才的需求，高低技能互补性和高技能人才的消费溢出都增加了对中低技能人才的需求，提高了各类人才的技能回报。

为了更好地把握后疫情时代职业技术教育的发展方向，有必要对全球职业技术教育发展模式进行归纳、对各国职业技术教育发展新趋势进行预测、对我国职业技术教育的特色与挑战进行分析，并在此基础上对世界职业技术教育发展方向进行判断。本报告将基于上述四个方面的讨论，回答“后疫情时代职业技术教育应该如何高质量创新发展”的问题。

本报告主要基于对学术文献、政策文件、各国职业技术教育前沿趋势报告和部分政策咨询报告的综述，并适当引用对国内和国际职业教育发展统计数据的分析。报告分为四个部分：国家职业技术教育发展模式，国际职业技术教育发展趋势，我国职业技术教育发展的经验、特色与挑战和结论与讨论。

# 一

# 国家职业技术教育发展模式

在全球范围内，发达国家和发展中国家采用了多元化的国家职业技术教育发展模式。职业技术教育是人力资本投资的重要组成部分，也是技能形成的主要载体。技能形成是一个复合型概念，是以学校为基础的技能学习和以工作场所为基础的技能实践的统一。

## （一）国家技能形成体制的内涵和划分

马克思主义劳动过程理论详细分析了工业革命进程中的技能形成，提出技能及其形成是生产控制权问题。该理论关注的是劳动过程中的劳资冲突，而不是国家技能形成的模式。20 世纪中期产生的人力资本理论强调，通过普通教育和职业技术教育培训可以提升个体的通适性和专用性技能，从而促进个体收入提升和国家经济增长。该理论聚焦于教育的经济社会后果，而不关注国家间教育制度的差异。以阿马蒂亚 · 森为代表的发展型社会政策理论认为，以劳动技能培训为载体的人力资本投资有助于提高经济竞争力、促进社会融入和整合。劳动者技能培训是推动社会政策从再分配功能转向作为一种生产要素发挥作用的基本路径[1]。发展型社会政策理论关注职业技术教育的社会功能，而非其制度安排。

进入 21 世纪，资本主义多样性文献首次从资本主义国家经济治理机制的高度，强调不同国家的经济治理机制对企业技能形成方式的选择产生重要影响，由此形成了不同的技能形成制度安排。学者认为，广义上的技能形成体制是指一国在技能形成方面的一整套制度安排，即所谓的“制度包”，涉及培训风险承担、技能标准化和认证制度、职业学位体系的分层和差异化、培训主体的角色安排以及与其他社会经济制度的关联等方面。由于各个国家在这些方面的制度安排不同，造就了不同的国家技能形成体制[2][3]。也有学者提出，国家技能形成体系在狭义上包括财政制度、职业培训认证制度和劳动过程制度三大部分[1]。

目前，学术界普遍采用两个维度对国家技能形成体制进行划分：一是企业技能形成的卷入程度，即企业对技能形成的投资行为和意愿；二是国家对技能形成的卷入程度，包括国家对职业技术教育与培训的补贴、制定职业资格证书制度和构建职业资格框架等。基于这两个维度，可以将发达工业化国家的技能形成体制分为四种类型（见表 1）。四种类型分别是以美国和英国为代表的自由主义技能形成体制（国家和企业卷入程度都低）、以日本和韩国为代表的分割主义技能形成体制（国家卷入程度低，企业卷入程度高）、以瑞典和法国为代表的国家主义技能形成体制（国家卷入程度高，企业卷入程度低）、以德国和瑞士为代表的集体主义技能形成体制（国家和企业卷入程度都高）。

**表 1　发达工业国家技能形成体制的类型**

| | | 企业对技能形成的卷入程度 | |
|---|---|---|---|
| | | 低 | 高 |
| 国家对技能形成的卷入程度 | 低 | 自由主义技能形成体制（美国、英国） | 分割主义技能形成体制（日本、韩国） |
| | 高 | 国家主义技能形成体制（瑞典、法国） | 集体主义技能形成体制（德国、瑞士） |

各个国家采用何种技能形成体制主要取决于历史和文化因素。历史制度主义的分析表明，英国自由主义技能形成体制的形成与中世纪行会的衰落和工业化进程加速密切相关，而德国集体主义技能形成体制的维系与其特定的政治经济发展历史高度一致[4]。国家的技能形成体制深深嵌入企业生产体制、劳资关系、企业治理、跨企业关系、金融市场、社会保障形成的社会经济制度网络中，需要这些配套性制度安排的支持。因此，一个国家的技能形成体制具有一定的稳定性。

学者也对东亚发展中国家的技能形成体制进行了分析，提出东亚国家存在一种发展主义技能形成体制。该体制的特征是国家卷入程度高，由强有力的经济部门控制集权化的职业技术教育系统，并用产业政策协调职业技术教育体系与行业企业合作，满足共性技能需求[5]。有研究采用资本主义多样性的分析模式提出，中国在计划经济体制时期采用了类似于集体主义技能形成体制的模式，即国家和企业卷入程度都高，但是企业自主性低，受到强有力的国家计划和劳动部门的协调；中国在市场经济转型时期采用了具备国家主义技能形成体制特征的模式，国家卷入程度高，企业被边缘化，职业技术教育由企业内部转移到学校，教育、人社、发改、工信等多个国家部委参与职业技术教育的发展[3]。

### （二）不同国家技能形成体制的特征

不同国家技能形成体制在技能形成主体、技能培训成本的分担、技能类型、体制开放程度方面具有不同的特征（见表 2）。

表 2 不同国家技能形成体制的特征

| 体制类型 | 技能形成主体 | 技能培训成本的分担 | 技能类型 | 体制开放程度 |
|---|---|---|---|---|
| 国家主义技能形成体制 | 各类职业院校提供；企业被边缘化，参与度和积极性均较低 | 主要由公共财政承担 | 通适性技能，职业院校课程标准化 | 强调流动性和开放性，职业技术教育与学术教育融合程度高 |
| 自由主义技能形成体制 | 典型的以职业院校为基础的供给体系，各类职业学校和社区学院是技能培训的主体 | 国家投入少、受训者和企业是主要承担者 | 通适性技能，培训市场应用导向强，会根据“市场热度”及时调整课程内容 | 技能劳动力就业竞争激烈；职业教育社会地位较低；职业技术教育和学术教育融合程度低 |
| 集体主义技能形成体制 | 双轨技能培训体系是主要的技能供给方式；职业院校与车间培训被整合为一体且分工明确 | 国家和企业分担技能培训成本 | 技能培训标准化，以企业专用和行业专用技能为主，但是由于企业卷入程度比较高，较好地回应企业专用技能偏好 | 中介组织作用巨大；限制技能劳动力在不同教育体系之间的流动 |
| 分割主义技能形成体制 | 以企业内部技能养成为主；国家提供少量在职培训 | 企业是主要承担者，受训者分担部分成本 | 以企业专用技能为主 | 职业技术教育和学术教育融合程度低 |

国家主义技能形成体制强调以各级各类职业院校为技能形成主体，由公共财政承担技能培训的主要成本，以通适性技能为主，以职业院校提供的标准化课程为载体进行培训。此体制强调流动性和开放性，鼓励普职融通。与此相反，集体主义技能形成体制是以工作场所为主体的技能形成体制，采用双元师徒制培训，国家和企业共同分担培训成本。技能培训同时包括行业和企业专用技能，同时限制劳动力在不同教育体系之间的流动。自由主义技能形成体制以职业院校培训为主，受训者和企业分担成本，强调通适性技能培养，普职融合程度低。分割主义技能形成体制以企业为主，企业为了培养企业专用技能而承担主要成本，普职融合程度极低。

中国在计划经济和市场经济转型时期采用了不同的技能形成体制，特征差异明显（见表3）。在计划经济时期，技能形成的主体是企业，通过师徒制和企业办学来提供，国家和企业卷入程度都很高，公共财政支持企业行业专用技能培养，职业教育与普通教育部门之间难以流动。在市场经济转型时期，职业院校成为技能形成的主体，企业被边缘化，国家和受教育者分担成本，职业院校教育以通适性技能和行业专用技能为主，职业技术教育与学术教育逐步融合。

表3　中国在不同时期技能形成体制的特征

| | 技能形成主体 | 技能培训成本的分担 | 技能类型 | 体制开放程度 |
|---|---|---|---|---|
| 计划经济时期 | 结合企业双元学徒制和中等职业教育的技能供给体系 | 企业和国家卷入程度高，培训成本主要由公共财政承担 | 以企业专用技能和行业专用技能为主；能较好回应企业的技能偏好 | 限制劳动力在不同企业和不同教育体系间流动 |
| 市场经济转型时期 | 典型的以职业院校为基础的供给体系；企业被边缘化，参与度较低 | 企业投入少，国家和受训者是主要承担者 | 以通适性技能和行业专用技能为主；职业院校课程标准化 | 职业技术教育与学术教育逐步融合；劳动力自由流动 |

## （三）不同国家职业技术教育发展模式的特征

在这四种国家技能形成体制之下，各个国家形成了差异化的职业技术教育体系。在自由主义技能形成体制和国家主义技能形成体制下，企业卷入程度比较低，一般采用以学校为基础的企业外部技能形成方式，这是以政府为主导的职业技术教育体系。相比之下，在分割主义技能形成体制和集体主义技能形成体制国家中，企业卷入程度高，一般采用以工作场所为基础的企业内部技能形成方式，通过师徒制或者厂办技校等方式提供技能教育与培训，即以企业为主导的职业技术教育体系。

各国差异化的职业技术教育体系在职业技术教育体系化程度、国家资历框架、成本分担和产教融合制度化程度方面各具特色（见表 4）。在职业技术教育体系化程度方面，实施国家主义技能形成体制和集体主义技能形成体制的国家，均采用了双轨制模式，有平等且不同的职业技术教育体系；同时，国家开始构建职业技术教育贯通培养模式，将中等职业教育与不同形式的高等教育衔接，形成了各种形式的中等和高等教育、职业和普通教育的纵向混合模式。而实施自由主义技能形成体制的国家，中等教育阶段实施包含学术轨道和职业轨道的综合高中制度，进行横向整合，并开始将高等职业教育提升到本科层次。在国家资历框架方面，同属于欧洲的实施国家主义和集体主义技能形成体制的国家多数采用了国家资格框架，且与欧盟一致。中国在 1995 年采用了国家职业资格框架，但是尚未形成统一的普通教育和职业技术教育的国家资格框架。在成本分担方面，中国与北欧的国家主义技能形成体制国家类似，采用国家财政性投入为主要模式，企业与个人也参与成本分担。在产教融合制度化方面，集体主义和分割主义等以企业为主导的技能形成体制产教融合制度化程度较高，国家主义和自由主义等技能形成体制产教融合制度化程度较低。中国正在逐步提高产教融合制度化程度，以现代产业学院等为抓手构建校企合作机制。

表 4　不同国家职业技术教育发展模式的特征

| | 国家主义技能形成体制国家 | 自由主义技能形成体制国家 | 集体主义技能形成体制国家 | 分割主义技能形成体制国家 | 市场经济转型时期中国 |
|---|---|---|---|---|---|
| 职业技术教育体系化程度 | 双轨制；纵向整合体系；职业技术教育贯通培养 | 横向整合体系；职业技术教育学历层次提升 | 双轨制；混合体系（中等职业教育加高等教育） | 分化程度低；职业技术教育边缘化 | 双轨制；纵向整合体系；职业技术教育贯通培养 |

续表

| | 国家主义技能形成体制国家 | 自由主义技能形成体制国家 | 集体主义技能形成体制国家 | 分割主义技能形成体制国家 | 市场经济转型时期中国 |
|---|---|---|---|---|---|
| 国家资历框架 | 有国家资格框架；与国际框架一致 | 有国家资格框架 | 有国家资格框架；与国际框架一致 | 国家资格框架发展中 | 有职业资格框架，无统一职业与学术教育国家资格框架 |
| 成本分担 | 国家投入为主 | 个人投入为主 | 企业和国家分担成本 | 企业投入为主 | 国家投入为主，个人和企业参与成本分担 |
| 产教融合制度化程度 | 产教融合制度化程度低，企业被边缘化 | 产教融合制度化程度低 | 产教融合制度化程度高，企业为主体协调 | 产教融合制度化程度高，企业内部协调 | 产教融合逐步制度化 |

## （四）不同国家职业技术教育发展模式的优势和局限

不同国家职业技术教育发展模式对技能供给与需求、技能供给效率和质量、职业技术教育投入和社会接纳程度产生了不同的影响（见表5）。在技能供给与需求方面，北欧和中欧国家技能级差工资低，收入较为平等；中国技能溢价不高，长期存在技能劳动力供给不足现象。从技能供给效率和质量来看，德国、瑞士、奥地利等实施集体主义技能形成体制国家的企业专业技能供给效率和质量高，北欧等实施国家主义技能形成体制国家以通适性技能培训为主，企业专业技能供给质量和效率比较低。中国与之类似，通适性技能培训供给质量和效率比较高，企业专业技能供给效率和质量低。在职业技术教育投入方面，各个国家投入主体差异较大，水平差异也较大。从社会接纳程度来看，在实施国家主义技能形成体制的北欧国家，应用技术大学等职业技术教育机构具有与研究型大学平等但不同的社会地位，在德国等实施集体主义技能形成体制国家双元制的社会接纳程度也很高。中国于2022年修订了《中华人民共和国职业教育法》，明确将职业教育定位为类型教育，其社会接纳程度有待进一步提高。

表 5　不同国家职业技术教育发展模式的优势和局限

| | 国家主义技能形成体制国家 | 自由主义技能形成体制国家 | 集体主义技能形成体制国家 | 分割主义技能形成体制国家 | 市场经济转型时期中国 |
|---|---|---|---|---|---|
| 技能供给与需求 | 技能级差工资低，青少年就业机会少 | 技能级差工资高，技能供给不足，劳动力流动性高 | 技能级差工资低，有利于青少年就业 | 终身雇佣保障高，技能供给旺盛 | 技能级差工资低，技能供给长期不足 |
| 技能供给效率和质量 | 通适性技能培训，企业专用技能供给质量和效率比较低 | 技能更新快，热门专业供给多，制造业等技能短缺 | 企业专用技能供给质量和效率比较高 | 企业专用技能供给质量和效率高 | 通适性技能培训供给质量和效率比较高，企业专业技能供给效率和质量低 |
| 职业技术教育投入 | 政府投入水平较高，保障充足 | 政府投入水平低 | 政府和企业合作投入水平高 | 企业投入水平高 | 政府投入水平较高，企业投入少 |
| 社会接纳程度 | 平等但不同的社会地位 | 社会接纳程度较低 | 社会接纳程度较高 | 社会接纳程度一般 | 职业教育作为类型教育，接纳程度有待提高 |

综上所述，在历史发展过程中，不同国家依据历史和文化传统采用了不同的国家技能形成体制和相应的职业技术教育体系。中国在不同历史时期先后发展了具有集体主义和国家主义技能形成体制特征的体制，因而在职业技术教育体系化程度、国家资历框架、成本分担和产教融合制度化程度方面，更接近集体主义技能形成体制国家。当前，各国的职业技术教育发展模式对技能劳动力供给规模、效率和质量产生了多元化的影响，国家和社会对职业技术教育的投入水平和接纳程度也有很大差异。这些差异表明职业技术教育领域不存在国际的“最佳模式”，各个国家在配套性制度安排的支持下，形成了本国当前的职业技术教育发展模式。

# 二

# 国际职业技术教育发展趋势

“工业 4.0”智能化时代浪潮席卷全球，云计算、大数据、人工智能和区块链等数字技术不断涌现，生物技术、新材料技术、新能源技术交叉融合，推动全球新一轮科技革命和工业革命加速前进[6]。数字化和可持续发展构成科技革命的两大主题。

“工业 4.0”将改变对劳动者的技能需求和产生新的业态。2009 年，欧盟定义先进制造、生命科学技术、微 / 纳米电子和光子学、人工智能、安全与互联互通为关键促成技术，与其他“工业 4.0”技术结合，形成一系列新产品和新工艺在制造业中使用的基础。2020 年，世界经济论坛指出，未来五年内目前在职劳动者所掌握的核心技能将有 44% 发生变化，将有 8 500 万个工作岗位被取代，机器人革命将创造 9 700 万个新岗位，到 2025 年，全球预计有 50% 的劳动者需要接受再培训以适应新的岗位需求[7]。人工智能改变了劳动的性质，程序性体力类和程序性认知类劳动者率先受到冲击，非程序性认知类劳动者和体力劳动者则得到发展[8]。未来的工作更多地需要信息技术、编程、数字处理技能以及复杂信息处理、创新等能力，对基础数据处理、读写算和普通设备操作技能的需求将大幅下降[9]。

2019 年以来，新冠病毒疫情导致全球经济和劳动力市场低迷，与数字化转型为科技革命下的劳动力技能转型带来了双重挑战。通过何种教育、如何通过教育实现劳动者技能转型，成为应对科技革命的关键问题。2016 年，德国率先提出《“职业教育 4.0”框架倡议（2016—2018)》，提出培养面向未来的数字化人才、一揽子项目资助计划、发展中小企业的“新入职者”计划、职业教育实践能力测评等战略要点。此后，以欧盟国家为主的世界各国出台各项战略，探索发挥职业技术教育在完成劳动者技能转型中的作用。本部分将从职业技术教育规模、投入、产教融合、数字化、绿色发展和国际合作六个方面展开国际比较。

## （一）更加注重融合渗透（普遍特征），形成混合式培养模式

全球技术变革背景下，职业技术教育层级上移，继续职业教育规模扩大。教育可以增加受教育者的人力资本，进而提升受教育者的就业收入。人力资本可以分为通用性人力资本和专用性人力资本，前者在大部分岗位中都能发挥作用，后者只在与特定的岗位匹配时才能发挥作用[10]。普通教育主要是培养人的通用性人力资本，注重学习能力和基础知识；职业技术教育主要是培养专用性人力资本，培养周期短、就业岗位明确。技术变革时代，工作岗位和技术需求快速变化，通用性人力资本较专用性人力资本更能带来长期、稳定的收益[11][12]。一方面，技术变革需要职业技术教育层级上移，让受教育者获得更多的一般性人力资本和通用性人力资本，使得职业技术教育毕业生不仅能与当下工作岗位匹配，还能应对不断变化的劳动技能需求；另一方面，技术变革使得大量成年劳动力面临职业变更和技能转变，这需要大力发展继续职业技术教育，建设职业技术教育终身发展体系。

### 1. 职业技术教育规模与结构变化趋势

（1）职业技术教育规模扩大，层级上移。从 40 个经济合作与发展组织国家来看，初中和高中阶段的职业技术教育规模基本保持不变，但短期本科教育阶段和本科阶段的职业技术教育规模在 2013—2019 年间增加了 58.5%，职业技术教育层级呈现出上移趋势（如图 1 所示）。

（2）高中阶段职业技术教育比例下降。图 2 展示了中国和 7 个主要经济体的高中阶段职业技术教育比例的变化趋势。其中，中国的职业技术教育比例从 2000 年至 2019 年经历了先下降、后上升、再下降的变化过程；俄罗斯的职业技术教育比例在 2004—2016 年间持续上升，只有 2017 年后略微有所下降；日本、韩国、法国和德国从 2000 年开始均呈现下降的趋势，其中德国的职业技术教育比例从 2000 年的 63.2% 下降到 2019 年的 48.1%，奥地利的职业技术教育比例在 2004 年和 2013 年分别经历了一升一降，其他年份基本保持稳定；只有瑞士的职业技术教育比例一直保持在 63% 左右。

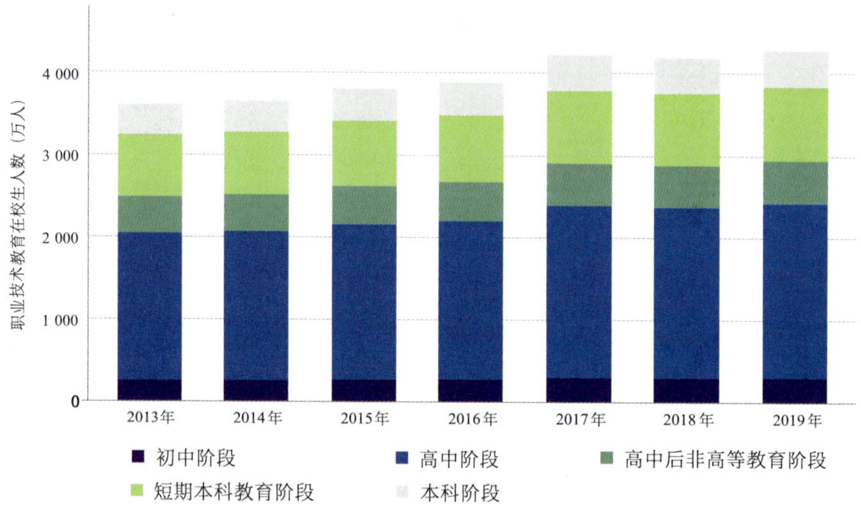


**图 1　2013—2019 年经济合作与发展组织国家职业技术教育规模与结构变化趋势**

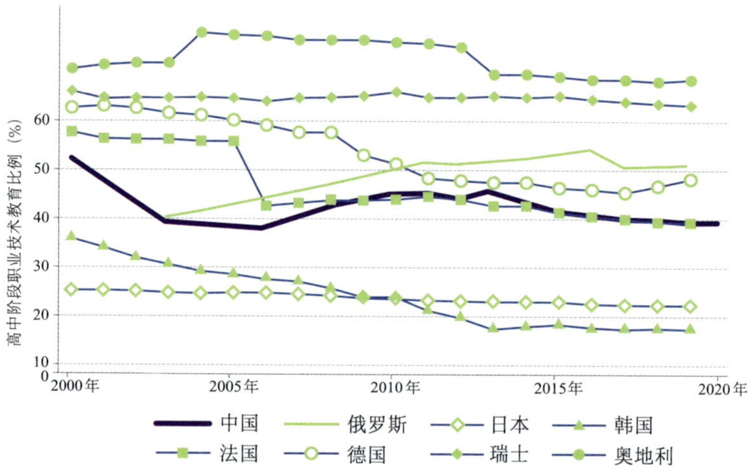


**图 2　2000—2020 年主要经济体高中阶段职业技术教育比例变化趋势**

注：数据来源于 The UNESCO Institute for Statistics. http://data.uis.unesco.org/.

### 2. 职业技术教育纵向贯通

职业技术教育层级上移需要其有清晰的纵向贯通体系，以促进青少年的全面发展，适应社会的变革。具体而言，构建中职—高职—应用本科—专业学位硕士应用型人才培养体系是各国职业技术教育发展的重要议题。一方面，不断完善职业技术教育体系，增加职业技术教育专业学士和专业硕士学位；另一方面，提倡两级职业技术教育贯通培养，特别是中高职，以统筹设置职业技术教育培养方案。以 2014 年起连续 7 年蝉联“全球人才竞争指数”第一名的瑞士为例[13]，其职业技术教育有着明确的发展路径，已经实现了基础职业技术教育到本科、硕士等高等职业技术教育的贯通（如图 3 所示）。另外，德国普通高校新生中，有 1/3 毕业于职业技术教育，其中应用科技大学中超过九成的学生毕业于职业技术教育。

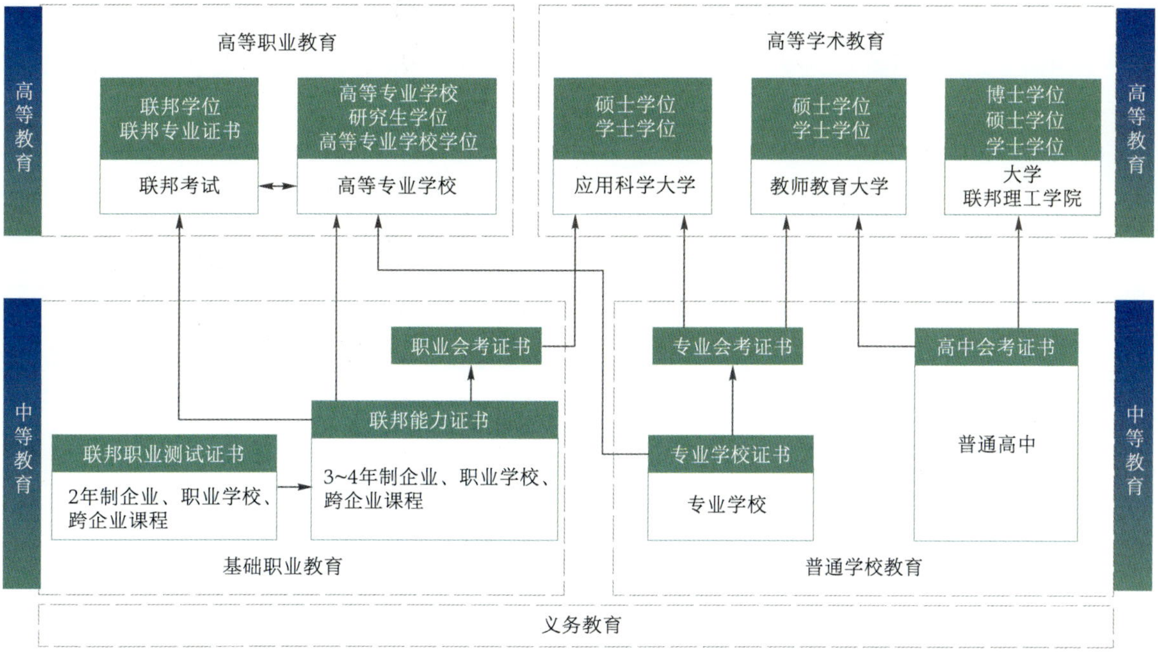


图 3　瑞士的职业技术教育体系 [14]

### 3. 职业技术教育与普通教育横向融通

职业技术教育层级上移需要职业技术教育与普通教育的横向融通，以保障青少年自由发展。横向融通包括：构建职业技术教育与普通教育之间互相转换和衔接的通道；交叉结合职业技术教育与普通教育教学要素，或开发跨类型的教育项目，让学生同时接受不同类型的教育，获取不同类型的证书；职普融通需要政府出台统一两类教育的资格框架 [15]。

以德国联邦教育与科研部 2013 年开创的跨类型项目“IT 专家”（如图 4 所示）为例，职业技术教育和普通高等教育中均有与信息技术相关的专业项目，前者培养信息技术专员，后者培养信息科学学士、硕士和博士；该项目将这些专业项目融合在一起，学习者从该项目毕业后，即可获得“IT 行家”证书，然后可继续修读职业技术教育体系的“IT 操作专家”；或者攻读普通教育中的信息科学学士学位，并且“IT 专家”项目累计的学分可以转为高校学习时的学分 [16]。该项目得以实施，有赖于德国政府出台的“国家资质框架”，它使得两类教育的知识和能力更加透明更可比 [17]。

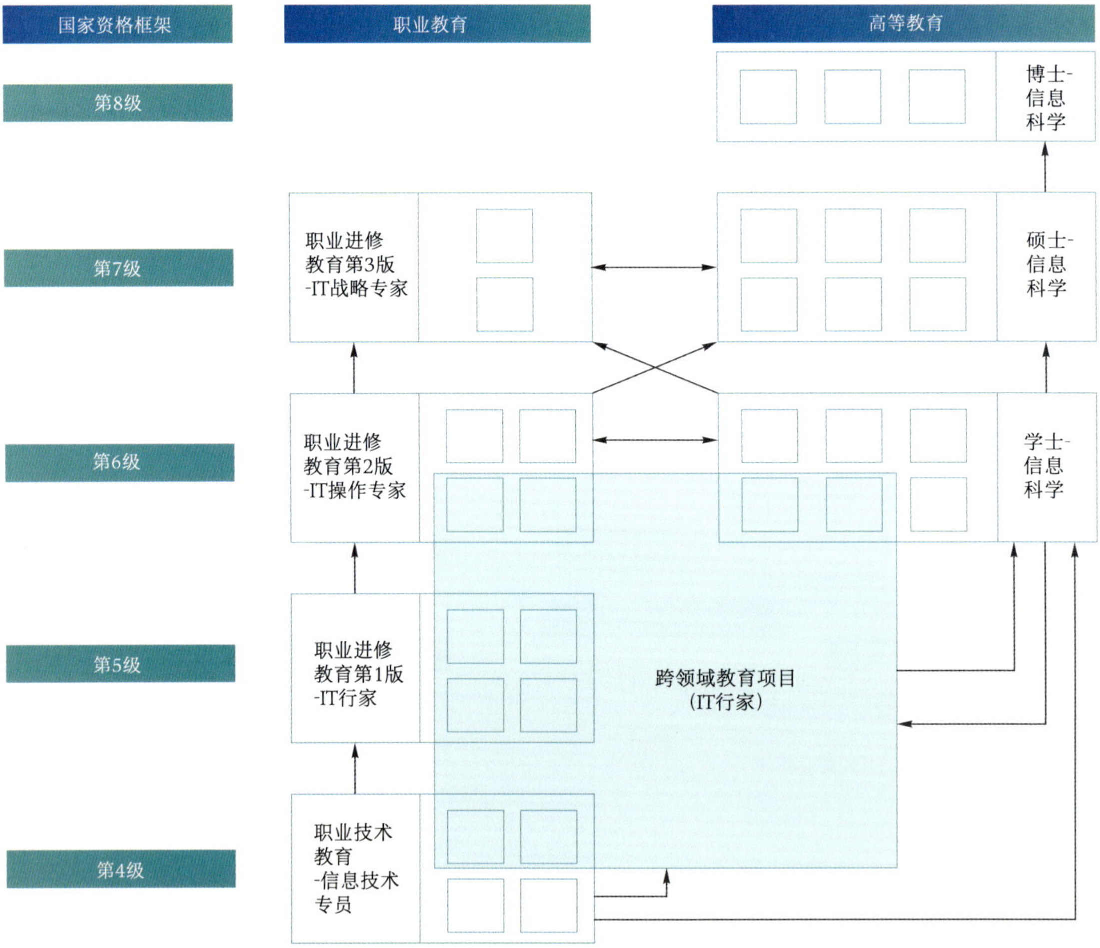


**图 4　德国“IT 专家”项目示意图**[14][15]

#### 4. 构建灵活的职业技术教育终身学习体系

发展继续职业教育需要构建灵活的终身职业技术教育体系，学历与非学历之间、正式与非正式之间、课程与证书之间需要有机结合。

学历与非学历教育融合，打通从业者与职业技术教育的通道。例如，2020 年，瑞典推行高职“快速通道”，帮助从业者快速获得高职学历。再如瑞士的联邦考试制度，为社会人士进入职业技术教育提供了机会，并将职业培训纳入学位制度中，是构建终身职业技术教育体系的成功案例[14]。社会人士可以通过联邦考试获得与高等专业学校学位处于同一层次的联邦专业证书，或者与高等专业学校研究生学位处于同一层次的联邦学位。如图 5 所示，近 20 年来，通过联邦考试获得高等职业技术教育学位的人数呈上升趋势，得到了瑞士公民的认可。

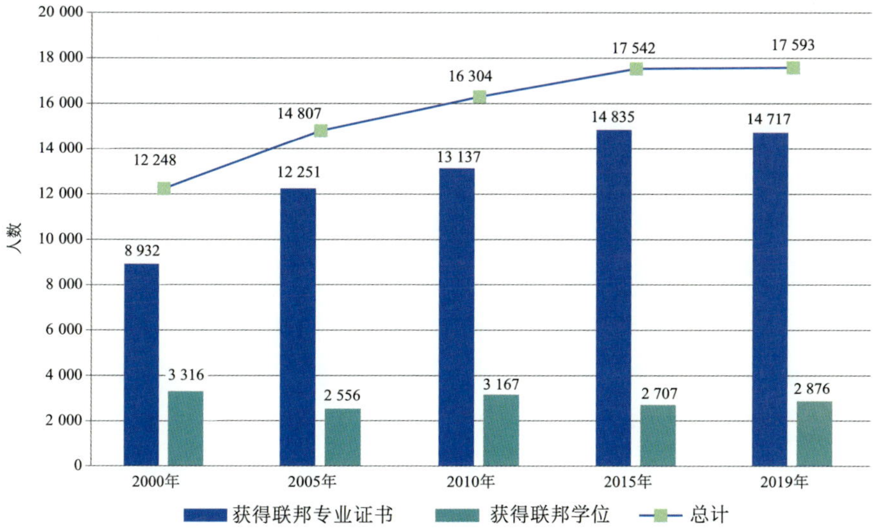


**图 5　2000—2019 年瑞士通过联邦考试获得高等职业技术教育学位的人数** [14]

正式与非正式、课程与证书结合，推动职业技术教育非全日制学习常态化。微课程是继续职业教育的主要形式；学分银行或学习账户是将微课程与证书相结合、正式教育与非正式教育相结合的制度保障。如欧盟在“博洛尼亚进程”下，形成独具特色的工程教育认证体系及记录学习成果和能力的“都柏林指标”，并开发了“欧洲通行证”和“欧洲职业技术教育与培训学分转换制度”。在这些体系下，通过设立个人学习账户、微证书，加强短期技能培训结果认可度。这些举措增加了职业资格证书的透明度、比较度、认可度和转化度，进而激励在职劳动者参与继续教育。

## （二）开发绿色技能，促进可持续发展

世纪之交以来，为应对气候变化、能源短缺、技术创新与市场转型等严峻挑战，绿色可持续发展理念逐渐为国际社会所广泛接受，绿色技能开发也日益成为职业技术教育与培训（TVET）领域的重要议题之一，世界各个组织、国家和地区都积极将绿色技能开发纳入职业技术教育与培训发展政策之中并予以实践，努力推动社会经济的可持续性发展。

### 1. 绿色技能开发的理念

绿色技能开发的理念起源较早。20 世纪 80 年代初，世界银行就提出了“绿色

GDP”核算指标。1987 年，联合国提出“可持续发展”理念，得到国际社会广泛响应。1989 年，英国政府报告《绿色经济蓝图》首次提出“绿色经济”概念，提倡以可持续发展为目标，以高效、公平、低碳的形式发展经济。

迈入 21 世纪后，绿色经济理念在职业技术教育与培训领域不断渗透，绿色技能概念逐渐形成。绿色技能又称可持续发展技能，是指劳动力支持并促进资源节约、经济社会可持续发展所需的技术、知识、价值和态度[18]。2002 年，世界可持续发展峰会积极倡导职业技术教育课程融入绿色发展理念。2005 年，“联合国可持续发展教育十年（2005—2014 年）”行动强调了职业技术教育与培训对可持续发展的关键性作用。2007 年，第四届国际环境教育大会强调了在职业技术教育与培训中开发绿色技能的重要意义。2012 年，第三届世界职业技术教育大会明确了职业技术教育与培训对绿色经济发展的关键作用。2016 年，联合国教科文组织提出职业技术教育与培训“促进向绿色经济和可持续社会转变”的总体目标[19]，联合国教科文职教中心强调了绿色技能开发对绿色经济发展的重要战略意义[20]。

**2. 绿色技能开发的政策**

目前，绿色技能开发的政策推广范围广泛，涵盖不同国家及地区。2010 年之前，各国政府相继出台政策，如澳大利亚的《绿色技能协议》、德国的《可持续发展教育国家行动计划》，基于开发国家培训包、构建特定领域职业可持续性能力、创设绿色职教学习基地等形式，将绿色技能开发纳入职业技术教育与培训建设体系[18]。2020 年，英国提出“绿色工业革命十点计划”[21]，采取“终身技能保障”改革举措，拟从国家技能基金中划拨专项财政，创建约 25 万个绿色学徒岗位及技能中心网络[22]，为就业者提供绿色技能培训服务与资格证书[23]。同时成立绿色工作特别小组，负责绿色技能开发、长期计划设计、绿色工作与劳动力开发、传统行业工人接受绿色技术培训等方面工作[23]。2020 年，德国通过在“教育职业 / 培训职业”规章中设置“标准培训元素”，构建包括“环保和可持续”在内的“四项职业资质”体系，提供就业者在经济、生态、社会各方面所需绿色技能[18]。

绿色技能政策推广与当地社会经济发展需求紧密结合。面对日益多样化、不可预测和迅速变化的经济社会发展需求，各国政府越来越重视职业技术教育与培训发展与当地需求相结合，拓展职业技术教育与培训体系发展活力，促进绿色经济转型。2010 年，德国在职业教育专业目录修订中，结合国家汽车工业、电子电气工业、可再生能源等行业绿色发展需要，新增 82 个专业，增添环境保护与低碳经济专业课程内容。美国通过绿色职业资格证书开发，培养具备资源保护、新能源材料、绿色建筑等方面知识与技能的“绿色工人”，同时大力资助高中、社区学院开展“绿领工人”培训项目，对职业教育教师开展“可持续产业”知识与技能培训。例如，2013 年，美国密歇根州根据区域能源发展需要，开设社区学院“风力涡轮技师”培训项目，对地区新兴产业发展产生重要影响[25]。加拿大在明确绿色职业或工作的具体职责及需要获得资格的基础上，基于社区学院开设绿色技能课程、“绿化”原有职业技术教育课程内容，助推职业教育促进地区经济发展可持续化进程[18]。

### 3. 绿色技能开发的实践

为实现向绿色经济过渡，促进社会公平与繁荣的可持续，绿色技能融入职业技术教育与培训体系推动劳动力市场绿色转型，已成为各国职业技术教育与培训实践中的核心议题。国际劳工组织预测，到 2030 年，绿色经济转型会创造约 2 400 万个岗位，绿色技能将会融入约 12 亿个传统岗位之中。全球绿色技能需求正快速增长，并已形成完善的绿色技能理念框架与宏观政策。然而，职业技术教育与培训绿色技能开发在院校实践层面仍处于起步探索阶段，难以应对产业实践需要。鉴于此，有必要梳理现行绿色技能开发实践案例，为绿色技能开发纳入职业技术教育与培训体系改革，促进传统行业向绿色行业过渡、填补新兴产业发展与职工绿色技能之间的鸿沟提供核心发展框架。

（1）“绿色车轮”项目：新能源汽车行业绿色技能开发案例。新能源汽车行业作为新兴绿色行业，其职业技术教育培训体系严重滞后于产业发展对技术工人的需求。为针对产业需求开展职业技术教育实践，匈牙利现代教育中心协同捷克、斯洛伐克、英国，于 2016 年开发“绿色车轮”项目，面向职业院校学员提供新能源汽车维修、保养、服务开放学习课程体系，满足汽车培训领域对绿色技能开发的新需求[26]。该项目侧重开发适切性学习材料，并在课程教学体系中嵌入批判性思维等通用性绿色技能，基于探究式协作学习、翻转课堂与同伴教学等前沿教学方法，实现汽车行业高职学员绿色技能培育。“绿色车轮”项目的实施弥补了职业技术教育与培训与行业之间的差距，在新能源汽车领域建立起完善且具有可迁移性的课程体系，为汽车行业职业技术教育与培训课程教学体系创新提供了参照。

（2）NIB-Scout 项目：面包烘焙行业转型的绿色技能开发案例。面对德国传统烘焙行业熟练工人短缺、行业吸引力不足、学徒离职率高等转型问题，ADB Nord

公司于 2018 年开发 NIB-Scout 培训项目，为烘焙行业职业学院学员创建全新绿色教育培训体系[27]。该项目通过在烘焙行业职业技术教育与培训课程体系中融入废物处理、电力节约、有机产品等方面的绿色知识、观念与技能，促进烘焙行业高职学员可持续观念与绿色技能水平提升[28]。NIB-Scout 项目基于构建交互式、过程性教学方法，模拟现实工作场景开展教学，帮助学员将绿色技能融入日常工作之中，并推动其绿色发展与可持续意识提升。NIB-Scout 项目被德国教科文组织和德国联邦教育研究部认定为“可持续学习基地”，并推动烘焙行业职业教育国家标准更新，在促进德国烘焙业高职学员绿色技能提升、职业资格认定与应对烘焙行业向绿色经济转型方面发挥了重要功用[27]。

（3）FOENAKO 项目：零售业转型的绿色技能开发案例。为推动传统零售业绿色转型与可持续发展，德国 BKAL 职业学院于 2016 年开设 FOENAKO 项目，旨在基于数字化“工具包”创建学习情境，促进零售业职业技术教育与培训学员应对行业转型的绿色技能开发[29]。FOENAKO 项目创建的数字化“工具包”涵盖网络社区、线上频道、工作坊与文件库等，能够满足高职学员在移动学习环境中获取绿色知识和技能的需求。该项目构建的学习情境包括课程介绍、教学安排与目标、学习成果和能力评估三个部分，融入环境标准、公平贸易、定价、商品采购和企业目标等方面所需的绿色技能，开发出销售过程中的环境使用标准、有机产品标签、绿色商品销售、有机食品价格计算等多套具体化绿色技能学习情境，以帮助高职学员迅速响应零售业绿色发展需求。

### （三）构建多元化产教融合模式，增强职业技术教育的适应能力

发达国家在长期历史发展过程中形成了不同的市场经济体制，由此发展出了职业技术教育的多种模式。其中许多模式在吸引企业参与、增强校企合作等方面总结出了成熟的经验，如德国双元制、英国“三明治”模式、澳大利亚 TAFE 学院等。值得指出的是，在这些模式中政府的投入和企业的参与程度都有很大的差异，背后反映的是这些模式植根于发达国家特定时期的政治经济环境和文化背景。在发展援助的背景下，由发达国家主导的多边国际机构在发展中国家推行职业技术教育的援助项目，有意识地推广发达国家的经验和模式，使得发展中国家的职业技术教育未能与本国经济发展水平相契合，进而难以培养出与市场相适应的技能人才，也无法解决职业技术教育中校企合作困境的难题。

**1. 发达国家职业技术教育校企合作模式**

（1）德国“双元制”。德国作为职业技术教育探索较为成功的国家之一，其“双元制”是校企合作的典型模式。“双元制”产生于20世纪初，形成于20世纪中叶，是脱胎于12世纪手工业行会中的学徒式职业教育[30]。“双元制”是传统学徒制与现代学校教育制度的结合，整个职业技术教育过程在企业和职业院校交替进行（见表6）。职业院校是“双元制”的一元主体，主要任务是传授普通文化知识和职能专业知识；企业是“双元制”的另一元主体，主要职能是为学生提供学徒合同和相应的学习条件[31]。具有职业技术教育资质的企业根据自身需要制订年度学徒培养计划，向学生提供学徒岗位。企业与学生签订职业技术教育合同，为学生提供导师、培训车间、设备和原材料等学习资源，支付生活津贴，学生在对应的专业职业技术学院学习理论知识[32]。这种双向培养机制能保证学生具备企业学徒与专业院校学生的叠加身份，也保证企业和学校共同完成对学生的理论知识和实践技能的培训[33]。从效果来看，德国“双元制”的完成率很高，一般在90%以上，对保持较低的青年失业率有重要作用。但是，“双元制”也受到德国经济发展的影响，企业抱怨行业场所短缺、工资成本增加、休息时间增加，等等[34]。

**表6　德国“双元制”职业技术教育基本情况一览表**[30]

| | 企业/跨企业培训中心 | 职业院校 |
|---|---|---|
| 学习地点 | 实训车间与工作岗位 | 教室与实验室 |
| 师资 | 企业培训师或师傅 | 理论教师和实训教师 |
| 学习者身份 | 学徒 | 学生 |
| 法律基础 | 联邦职业教育法 | 各州的学校法 |
| 监督管理机构 | 行业协会 | 各州教育部 |
| 经费来源 | 企业 | 公共基金 |
| 课程标准 | 培训框架计划 | 框架教学计划 |
| 课程内容 | 实践技能 | 理论知识 |
| 时间安排 | 每周3~4天 | 每周1~2天 |
| 培养目标 | 生产一线的熟练技术工人 | |

（2）英国“三明治”教育模式。“三明治”教育模式是对半工半读、工学交替职业技术教育模式的一种形象比喻，是一种“理论—实践—理论”或“实践—理论—实践”交替进行的教育模式[35]。早在 20 世纪初，英国部分技术学院就开始尝试“三明治”教育模式，到 20 世纪 50 年代获得了政府认可，“三明治”教育模式被列为技术学位文凭教育[36]。根据在生产现场工作实践的时间长短，“三明治”教育分“厚”和“薄”两种。“厚三明治”教育模式的一般学制为 4 年，第三年安排在生产现场工作实习，最后一年返回学校修满学业；“薄三明治”教育模式则将前往生产现场的工作和实习分解为 2~5 个时间较短的阶段，根据课程的具体情况在不同时间安排[37]。“三明治”教育模式采用包括企业评估、指导教师评价以及学生自我评价等方面的全过程考核体系（见表 7），注重对学生学习过程的考核监督[38]。在“三明治”教育模式下，企业和学校之间对实践场所、岗位设置、劳动报酬、学生工作质量的监督及学习效果的考核等都形成了一套灵活的运行机制，实现了企业和学校的双赢。

**表 7　英国“三明治”教育模式的全过程考核体系[35]**

<table>
<tr><th colspan="2">考核构成</th><th>考核材料</th><th>操作执行</th></tr>
<tr><td colspan="2">企业评估</td><td>实习情况评价</td><td>依据实习表现及工作报告给出评价</td></tr>
<tr><td rowspan="3">指导教师评价</td><td>实习前指导</td><td rowspan="3">学生个人实习发展规划、实习日记和企业反馈</td><td>指导、督促</td></tr>
<tr><td>实习中监督</td><td>电话、邮件咨询</td></tr>
<tr><td>实习后总结</td><td>实习企业实地座谈调查</td></tr>
<tr><td colspan="2">学生自我评价</td><td>工作日记、报告</td><td>每月给学院交实习报告，最后报告涵盖整个学期情况</td></tr>
</table>

（3）澳大利亚 TAFE 模式。TAFE（Technical and Further Education）学院是澳大利亚职业技术教育与培训的主要模式。澳大利亚大力构建大学教育、TAFE 与中学教育之间的“立交桥”，使得受教育者在高中、中职与高职院校、大学和在职培训机构之间自由流动，在全国形成了以 TAFE 为主体的完整的终身教育体系和职业技术教育网络[39]。TAFE 学院始于 1974 年澳大利亚政府颁布的《坎甘报告》。当时，澳大利亚产业结构发生改变，通信、金融等新兴行业的不断发展催生了大量职业技术教育需求，因此这份报告提出建立新型的技术和继续教育学院，将技术教育与继续教育、学历教育与岗位培训结合到一起[40]。TAFE 学院在 20 世纪 80 年代迅

速发展，其数量远超过大学和高等教育学院的总和。企业参与职业技术教育与培训主要表现在参与政策制定和参与 TAFE 学院办学两个方面。企业通过行业技能委员会、行业培训咨询委员会等在培训政策制定、培训重点确定、培训包的开发与修订等方面发挥着核心作用[41]。企业还参与 TAFE 学院的课程开发，把 TAFE 学院的课程设置、能力标准、教学模式等方面纳入行业需求的轨道。企业还通过以专家身份加入学院董事会的方式直接参与学校管理，鼓励和安排专业技术人员到学校做兼职教师，同时接受学校教师到企业实践锻炼。

从这些模式中可以提炼出企业参与职业技术教育的几种方式。一是企业参与制订课程和技能需求的框架，二是企业成立行业技能协会之类的协调机构，三是企业为学生提供实习和就业机会，提供师资培训或者派出兼职教师。但是，这些模式本身都是带有多种配套措施的整体项目，如果将从中抽离出的片面的方式移植到发展中国家，就难免出现水土不服的情况。

**2. 发展中国家职业技术教育校企合作模式**

发展中国家在职业技术教育中从两个方面吸纳了发达国家的经验，一是建立国际职业资格框架，二是建立行业技能委员会。

国家职业资格框架在 20 世纪 90 年代中期被澳大利亚、英国、新西兰等发达国家提出，是一整套有关职业技术教育结果的标准。许多国家在制定职业技术教育技能体系的过程中邀请私人部门参与，对各个行业中劳动力需要掌握的技能做出规定。非洲教育发展协会在 2012 年提出，要推动非洲各国建立国家性的职业资格框架，包括关键能力的鉴定、学习成果考核、教学质量保证体系、学分转移系统等[42]。南亚国家也有推行类似的政策。由加拿大政府资助、国际劳工组织实施的孟加拉国就业和生产力技能项目通过建立先前学习认定系统，使培训者获得了国家职业资格框架的证书。其他国家，如印度于 2012 年出台的“国家职业教育资格框架”主要包含制定“国家职业标准”、实施“先前学习认定”等内容，马来西亚政府制定了国家职业技能标准，尼泊尔政府的国家技能测试理事会广泛邀请行业专家，共同商定职业技能标准[43]。

行业技能委员会也是一种校企合作模式，一般由政府控制，但是由企业领导的机构来监督特定行业的培训和职业资格认定，目的就是增强职业技术教育中技能匹配度。国际上有行业技能委员会的全球网络，包括澳大利亚、加拿大、英国、印度等国家，旨在提升行业技能委员会在职业技术教育发展中的重要性[44]。许多南亚国家也引入了这种方式，如印度引入行业技能委员会来提供职业技术培训，它是行业领导的培训机构，由来自行业、政府、学界的代表组成，全国共有38个行业技能委员会；斯里兰卡也采用行业技能委员会的模式，作为相关产业和培训部门的平台，截至2018年，建筑、信息、旅游、照明工程、养老五个行业成立了相应的行业技能委员会。2022年，埃及在欧洲复兴开发银行的援助下成立旅游业的行业技能委员会，旨在通过定制的培训项目来重振新冠病毒疫情冲击下的埃及旅游业。

发达国家关于职业技术教育的发展援助并非单纯地提供资金，填补受援国教育经费的缺口，更重要的是通过资金流动来引导发展中国家的教育政策，改革其教育体制。发展中国家也会在本国教育的目标设定和改革措施上向援助国或国际机构看齐。德国主要通过德国复兴信贷银行和德国技术合作公司两个执行机构来实施教育援助。自20世纪90年代开始，德国技术合作公司支持了55个国家的职业技术教育合作项目，其中16个项目是为了开展或巩固双元制培训学徒服务的[42]。与德国不同的是，法国在非洲的职业技术教育援助优先支持正规的职业技术教育和培训，这折射出法国作为国家主义技能形成体系的代表，强调职业技术教育的公共财政承担，企业的参与程度更低。

## （四）职业技术教育投入的多元化

### 1. 各国职业技术教育财政体系回顾

高效的财政体系是保障公共服务供给效率和公平的重要因素[45]。从人力资本理论视角看，由于参与或受益于职业技术教育的利益主体数量众多，职业技术教育投资对于投资者和受益者双方的作用机制较复杂。尽管职业技术教育经费的重要性毋庸置疑，但目前还没有一种方法能够较完善地解决各国职业技术教育财政体系和经费体制面临的问题[45]。同时，不同主体的统计口径也有所差异，企业及其他机构在职业技术教育或培训方面的投入数据无法纳入统一的国家预算体系，一定程度上造成了各国职业技术教育经费相关数据统计的困难和影响相应指标体系的构建。

整体而言，各国职业技术教育经费的来源主要包括政府拨款、企业投资、个人学费和学校创收等，然而由于职业技术教育实操、设备、培训和实践等成本相对较高，职业技术教育经费的充足性难以保障。因此，有必要建立更有效的职业技术教育经费筹措体系和统筹制度[46]。纵观世界，以政府投入为主体、不断减轻个体负担、增强校企合作、促进企业经费投入和发展学徒制等是多国职业技术教育经费体系的相似之处，职业技术教育经费来源的多样化和主体多元化成为各国共同的发展趋势[47]。以部分国家为例，英国政府向职业技术教育基金会的拨款为职业技术教育学校经费的主要来源，占其经费支出的 75%[48]；美国中等职业教育经费中联邦政府、州政府、地方政府拨款和学生学费的比例约为 10%、20%、45% 和 10%，相关法律和政策对各级政府拨款额度及比例有明确的规定[49]；澳大利亚的职业技术教育经费亦大部分由州政府和联邦政府承担，学生承担学费的比例不到 10%[50]。而在职业技术教育发展中处于世界领先地位、长期实行“双轨制”的德国，企业为职业技术教育经费的主要承担者，其负担的技能培训、企业培训等经费占德国总体职业技术教育经费的 60%~70%，政府承担的职业学校日常经费仅占 30%左右[51]。许多发展中国家，如埃塞俄比亚、阿尔及利亚、墨西哥、沙特阿拉伯，都在政府财政预算中明确规定分配给职业技术教育经费的资金比例（如埃塞俄比亚明确规定职业技术教育经费投入不低于总教育经费投入的 4.2%），并鼓励多元化、多渠道的职业技术教育经费筹集方法[52]。

近年来，各国职业技术教育经费筹集体系的发展主要有以下五个方向：第一，通过向企业征收培训税来促进公私成本分担；第二，增加职业技术教育培训的学费；第三，通过奖励机制鼓励企业提供更多、更高质量的职业技术教育培训；第四，提高职业技术教育培训机构所提供服务的有效性，包括发展私人培训市场和增加公私培训机构之间的竞争；第五，建立一种较新的筹资机制——国家培训基金，在许多国家，此类基金作为职业技术教育与培训的主体在职业技术教育与培训中起到主导作用[46]，如英国的职业教育基金会。此外，传统企业的职业技术教育培训仍然与市场技能需求密切相关，在此过程中缺少政策性的约束和干预。故职业技术教育财政体系的发展重点不仅在于寻求额外的资金来源，还在于加强国家对培训市场的干预，以及在政策法规层面对企业及其他机构实施约束，尽可能在促进企业投入的同时更好地管理经费去向[45]。

2. 学徒制财政支持

学徒制是英、美、德等国家职业技术教育发展过程中多元主体参与、政府与企业多方合作、通过培训和实践助力学校职业技术教育发展和技能型人才培养的重要体现。学徒制主要体现为在国家相应政策下，让职业学校的学生进入企业、工厂，在相关产业和职业领域中进行有资质的、官方认可的员工培训，从而实现技能落地，促进学生实践能力和综合素质的提升，以更好地与人力资本市场对接，在扩大就业的同时增强企业竞争力，支持制造业发展。

国家对学徒制的政策保障和财政支持是其顺利发展的重要原因。1937 年，美国颁布了《国家学徒制法案》。进入 21 世纪以来，美国学徒制进入改革发展阶段。面对产业转型、人才需求结构变化以及智能化、数字化先进制造业转变，美国于 2014 年建立了“注册学徒制与院校联盟”，强化行业企业与学校之间的联系，拓宽学徒升学渠道。2017 年美国提出“扩张学徒制”计划，培养智能制造产业及行业急需的学徒；2019 年美国劳工部推出“行业认可学徒计划”，提出行业认可的学徒制 6 个方面的核心要素。2021 年美国新修订的《国家学徒制法案》中提出：5 年内投资 35 亿美元用于扩大注册学徒制、青年学徒制等，打造企业与社区学院和高等教育机构合作联合体。

英国规定学徒可以获得工资，并享有其他福利待遇，如搬迁津贴和公共交通折扣、带薪假期至少每年 20 天、享有银行假期，等等。为激励企业提供学徒的动机，英国还实施了学徒税政策。学徒税是指那些年度工资总额超过 300 万英镑的雇主（英国约 2% 的企业）缴纳的用于学徒制培训和评估的税种，税率为须缴学徒税企业年度工资总额的 0.5%。缴纳这一税种的雇主每月能够获得政府提供的 1 250 英镑的补贴以及政府 10% 的配套经费。

法国教育部和劳动部于 2018 年采取相应政策和措施，为雇用学徒的企业提供约三年学徒工资的 2/3 的资助，改造职业技术教育体系，加强职业技术教育内部学制贯通和类别转换，打破全日制职业技术教育与学徒制教育的对立，增加职高内学徒制学部的数量。各级接受学徒制教育的总人数在 2019—2020 年度为 47.9 万，较上年增加 6.3%。

## （五）重视数字化转型，提升职业技术教育质量

### 1. 职业技术教育政策的数字化转型

近些年来，世界多国陆续推出针对产业数字化升级的战略，如德国的“工业 4.0”战略、美国的先进制造计划、欧盟的数字化欧洲工业计划等。在此背景下，多国职业技术教育战略普遍呈现出重视数字化转型的趋势。德国于 2016 年出台的《“职业教育 4.0”框架倡议（2016—2018）》将数字化建设与发展作为核心内容，提出要加快在职业技术教育中使用和普及数字媒体，将数字化对行业与职业的影响列为三大研究重点之一[53]。其他国家也纷纷提出职业技术教育的数字化战略。

从联合国教科文组织和欧盟[54]的相关文件来看，职业技术教育中的数字化转型主要包含两重含义：

第一，教学方式上，注重依托数字化资源开展教学，加强在线学习工具、技能认证工具和新型教学媒体应用。欧盟关注职业技术教育培训证书的数字化认证

体系，建立新型终身学习文化[55]。德国提出依靠数据和软件驱动开展数字化教育，构建数字化教育网络平台，劳动者获得参与数字化进程、使用数字媒体开展自主学习的机会，以全面提升劳动者的职业素养，推进德国的职业技术教育现代化改革。俄罗斯工匠计划强调加强数字化资源在职业技术教育中的应用。

第二，教学内容上，注重培养数字化技能，专业设置、课程设计要面向“工业4.0”的未来发展方向，符合通信技术、生物、人工智能等新兴产业人才需求。德国将数字化教育作为德国中长期（至2030年）教育改革的重点内容[56]。澳大利亚提出推动国家各行各业工作进行数字化转型[57]。日本设置专门职大学院，开设与新型产业界关系紧密的实践课程。瑞士强调培养青年学习者的数字化能力和跨专业领域所需的关键能力[58]。

### 2. 教学方式转型升级，加强数字化资源建设

（1）打造在线微课教学与认证平台，助力完善国家职业技术教育资历框架。大数据时代，完善国家职业技术教育资历框架需要成熟的信息技术，存储、更新受教育者的微课学习与证书信息。目前，在线教育平台主要针对K12（学前教育至高中教育）、本科和研究生教育，提供丰富的数字化技术课程内容，为发展职业技术教育在线教学提供基础条件。国际上主流的在线教育平台梳理见表8。

表8 国际主流在线教育平台

| 平台 | 国家 | 面向人群 | 规模 | 技能课程 | 资质认证 |
|---|---|---|---|---|---|
| 可汗学院（Khan Academy） | 美国 | 本科生、计算机专业人员 | 9 000万 | 计算机编程、经济学、考试辅导 | |
| Coursera | 美国 | 本科生、研究生 | 8 700万 | 数据科学、商务、计算机科学、物理科学与工程、语言学习、信息技术 | 与美国多所大学合作，课程可以抵项目要求学分 |
| Codecademy | 美国 | 计算机专业人员 | 4 000万 | 交互式、自定进度的课程和实践学习，涵盖应用程序开发、数据科学、云和网络安全等多个领域的14种编程语言 | |

区块链技术具有数据难以篡改和去中心化的特点，因此能够建立真实可信的职业教育学历认证信息系统。2017 年，马耳他教育与就业部与一家公司签署协议，开展利用区块链技术存储数字证书信息的项目，其中包括人们的职业技术教育与培训受教育信息。项目参与者的职业技术教育学历信息将通过区块链技术存储在网络上，方便雇主进行查询和查伪。截至 2019 年 2 月，马耳他所有的教育证书都将存储在区块链上。

（2）借助数字化工具提高教学效率。“工业 4.0”时代，应用 5G、AI 和 VR 等新型数字化工具，能提高职业技术教育的教学效率。人工智能、虚拟现实工具能够帮助学生进行沉浸式技能学习，打造 AI/VR/AR 虚拟仿真实训基地，能够提高教学效率。互联网为世界不同地区的职业技能经验交流提供了工具。

2017 年，德国和欧洲社会基金共同开展针对残疾人的“在职业教育中通过数字媒体实现包容性”项目，应用数字媒体挖掘残疾人的教育潜力，进一步满足劳动力市场的要求。同时项目也对非残疾人开放。以其中的“VR 支持的机电一体化培训项目”为例，该项目旨在通过基于 VR 技术的数字化学习，使目标群体能胜任汽车机电一体化技术员 [59]。

**3. 改革教学内容，打造数字化课程体系**

“工业 4.0”时代是一场前所未有的“人工智能革命”，在未来，信息技术知识、数据处理分析与统计等知识和能力将成为劳动者必备的技术技能 [60]。这就要求职业教育的技能框架、知识体系和课程设计做出应对和改变。

案例一：2016 年，德国文教部长联席会提出“面向数字世界”的课程与能力框架。该课程计划以面向“数字世界”的劳动能力框架为核心，涉及专业能力、方法论能力、沟通能力、判断和决策能力。其中，专业能力指了解并恰当运用经济学、技术学等领域专业知识的能力，可以对应于劳动者能力结构中全面的工艺知识，如数字媒体（云存储技术、大数据统计与分析技术）、数字制造（3D 打印、激光切割机、智能机器人）、数字生活（智慧家居、智能手机、智能手表）、数字科研（卫星图像提取、机器学习）、项目管理（在线交流与合作、市场分析、广告制作）[61]。

德国巴登-符腾堡州经济部推出“学习工厂 4.0”计划，自 2016 年起，该州斥资 680 万欧元建设了 16 个“学习工厂 4.0”，自 2018 年底又增资 480 万欧元新建 21 个同类机构，在此类创新机构中配备智能机器和数控生产模块，开发相应的教学方案和师资培训方案，为培训生创造贴近“工业 4.0”工作实践的学习环境[53]。

案例二：澳大利亚 TAFE 学院联合政府和企业等利益主体为学生提供长期连续性的、实践应用性的数字技能指导。在西澳大利亚州，当地政府和 TAFE 学院联合开发了专业化的数字技能培训项目及相配套的课程培训包。新南威尔士州的 TAFE 学院数字实验室与企业合作，共同开发学生在机器学习、人工智能、机器人自动化、移动应用开发等领域的数字能力。学校不但开设前沿的数字化新兴课程，还在校内建设数字实验室，满足学生动手实践操作的需求，培养应用型数字技能人才[62]。

案例三：荷兰“让 IT 工作”项目旨在为学生提供高质量的、最新的、能够直接应用于工作中的信息技术技能。在该项目中，学生首先接受为期 4 个月的高强度培训，随后在公司中工作 6 个月，课程改为每周一天。政府和雇主将共同承担学生的培训费用。项目吸引了 200 余名学生参与，其中 97% 的学生留在了项目中工作的公司。

## （六）加强职业技术教育国际合作

### 1. 相关国际组织在职业技术教育方面的政策变迁

通过对联合国教科文组织在 1962 年、1974 年、2001 年和 2015 年提出的职业技术教育与培训建议的研究，我们可以深入了解关于职业技术教育与培训多边共识的演变过程。1962 年提出的最初建议是相对不完善的，而且通常是一些现在看来相对不透明的描述。在这些建议中，对标西方主要国家的做法占有相当重要的地位，因此可能被视为职业技术教育与培训发展方案拟订的一个基本方面。1974 年的建议大大扩展了 1962 年的建议，进一步强调终身学习、有关的经济预测和对职业技术教育与培训政策的国家系统研究。2001 年的建议似乎与 1974 年的建议没有太大的不同，这可能是建议重点转向通识教育的结果。2015 年，联合国教科文组织建议的基调发生了最显著的转变，摒弃了 1974 年和 2001 年的结构，更多地考虑职业技术教育与培训发展的其他路径，并在公共话语中提升对职业技术教育与培训的尊重。与 2001 年相比，对职业技术教育与培训路径的重视和对通识教育“职业化”的相对缺乏是 2015 年建议再次重点关注职业技术教育与培训的证据。有趣的是，这份文件提出了“根据具体条件、治理结构和规定”考虑政策的建议，建议支持更具体的国家做法。此外，本文件似乎不太强调有关国际交流的建议，先前提到的“国际规范”也全部删除。然而，这些建议在联合国教科文组织的实践范围内得到了多大程度的落实仍然是个问题。例如，2018 年，联合国教科文组织制定了职业技术教育与培训的 10 个基本基石（见表 9）。尽管 2015 年的建议包含了一些要素（如对职业技术教育与培训的尊重），但一种普遍的、规定的“基本要素”方法似乎与让国家能够根据其自身环境的具体需要制定职业技术教育与培训体系的概念相违背。

表 9　TVET 的 10 个基本基石和建议 [63]

| TVET 的 10 个基本基石 | TVET 建议 |
|---|---|
| 1. 跨政策领域的领导力和目标明确性 | 1. 国家资格框架 |
| 2. 劳动力市场相关性和需求驱动的供给 | 2. 融合、阶段课程 |
| 3. 运作良好的伙伴关系和网络，促进可获得性和公平、拥有充分代表多方利益的合作伙伴 | 3. 学徒制、实习、在岗学习 |
| 4. 高绩效、高质量的培训机构 | 4. 终身学习、成人和继续教育 |
| 5. 标准化的质量保证机制和资格的可转移性 | 5. 与产业和私人部门的伙伴关系 |
| 6. 稳定持续的融资 | 6. 职业技术教育与股权融资混合 |
| 7. 运作良好的机构、激励机制和问责机制 | 7. 职业技术教育机构与高等教育机构对接 |
| 8. 公众的尊重，高毕业率和就业率 | |
| 9. 准确数据和信息的可获得性，包括劳动力管理信息系统 | |
| 10. 政策学习和持续改善的文化 | |

注：TVET= 职业技术教育与培训。TVET 的 10 个基本基石来自 UNESCO 和 ILO（2018），TVET 的建议来自 Fawcett、El Sawi 和 Allison（2014），略有修订。构成部分 7 和 8 都与高等教育有关，因此合并。

来源：UNESCO and ILO. 2018. Taking a Whole of Government Approach to Skills Development. Geneva: United Nations Educational, Scientific and Cultural Organization and International Labour Organization; C. Fawcett, G. El Sawi, and C. Allison. 2014. TVET Models, Structures, and Policy Reform: Evidence from the Europe and Eurasia Region. Washington, DC: United States Agency for International Development.

### 2. 职业技术教育的国际化

发达国家国际留学程度总体来说较高，他们注重本国职业技术教育体系的形成与向外输出，如澳大利亚和德国等国家就非常重视教育和职业技术教育的国际化问题。2019 年，澳大利亚发布了《职业教育和培训国际参与战略 2025》，2017 年，德国发布了《教育与科研国际化战略》。2019 新冠病毒疫情后，澳大利亚和德国更新了相关内容，加大了政府对职业教育国际化的支持力度。

2019 年，澳大利亚政府发布了《职业教育与培训国际参与战略 2025》。这一战略旨在发挥澳大利亚职业技术教育与培训部门的国际潜力，发挥其在满足全球企业、员工、学生和各国迅速变化的技能需求方面的重要作用。该战略提出了如下目标：一是澳大利亚被认为是提供有质量的 VET 的首选国家；二是澳大利亚被视为帮助各国满足本国技能开发需要的首选战略伙伴；三是澳大利亚具有有质量的 VET 框架，产品和服务在主要国际市场上受到高度追捧；四是澳大利亚被公认为培养全球技术工人的国际领先者。这一战略提出了十大行动：确保澳大利亚政府宣传、品牌和信息的一致性；鼓励对在岸国际 VET 学生提供更多的社区支持；与双边伙伴、多边论坛和负责技能发展的国际机构建立战略联系；增加海外市场准入机会；鼓励和推广更开放的培训模式和交付产品模式；在国际上推广澳大利亚的 VET 框架和系统，为澳大利亚 VET 提供者创造机会；促进国际合作，改善劳动力市场数据收集，确定和应对国际技能需求的变化；鼓励更多的商业对商业的参与，包括利用澳大利亚贸易委员会网络和聘用澳大利亚 VET 校友；加强国际 VET 培训的基础，以适当地培养全球劳动力；为 VET 学生、毕业生和员工提供在全球经济中发展的机会。新冠病毒疫情使去澳留学生下降了 70%, 为促进澳大利亚国际教育的迅速恢复，澳大利亚政府发布了《澳大利亚国际教育战略 2021—2030》。2021 年 4 月，澳大利亚政府宣布投入 5 360 万澳元支持国际教育恢复。澳大利亚政府还发布了对留学生在签证、就业、疫苗等方面的优惠或有限政策[64]。

2017 年，德国发布了《教育与科研国际化战略》，在“互联与创新的国际合作”主题下，确定了五个目标领域和相应措施，其中特别强调了进一步加强职业技术教育国际合作，深入推进职业技术教育国际化。一是加强顶层设计，将国际能力作为普通教育和职业技术教育的关键能力；加强外语教育，出台职业技术教育外语教学标准；出台职业技术教育国际化战略，建立跨部门的职业技术教育合作圆桌会议机制，整合合作资源，加强沟通协调，形成合力。二是大力推进职业技术教育师生国际流动，积极参与欧盟“伊拉斯默计划”，并实施“面向世界的职业教育”资助计划，支持职业技术教育学校、机构及组织建立广泛的国际合作网络。三是积极推广德国经验，坚持将职业技术教育国际合作与发展援助紧密结合并作为发展援助政策的重点，向发展中国家推广德国经验；实施“iMOVE”（职业技术教育国际推广）资助计划，支持企业和教育机构开展国际合作，推广德国经验。

**3. 国际职业技术教育大会**

国际职业技术教育大会是联合国教科文组织在职业技术教育领域最重要的机制性会议，每 10 年左右召开一次。2012 年，第 3 届国际职业技术教育大会在中国上海举办，并设置了 8 个议题，包括青年人工作技能的培养、提升职业技术教育与培训体系的适应性、经费投入与提高职业技术教育与培训效率、职业技术教育的社会不公平与排斥、改革管理和加强利益相关方对职业技术教育与培训的参与、通过职业技术教育与培训促进创新与可持续发展、提高教育教学质量、构建提高技能与终身学习相联系的资历认证制度。大会还专设中国职业技术教育专题会议，举办中国 – 联合国教科文组织职业技术教育展及专场演出，通过多种形式向世界全面介绍中国职业技术教育改革发展的成就与经验[65]。

时隔 5 年，中华人民共和国教育部、河北省人民政府、中华职业教育社与联合国教科文组织、德国教育部首次合作召开国际职业技术教育大会中期推进会。会议主题为“不断变化的技能：全球趋势与本土实践”。当前，世界正处在一个大发展大变革大调整时代，许多国家都充分认识到职业技术教育的重要意义，把发展职业技术教育作为应对危机、促进就业、迎接新技术革命挑战的重要举措。中国将促进职业技术教育发展与转变经济发展方式紧密结合，与教育改革发展紧密结合，与每个人的终身教育学习和发展紧密结合，不断提高职业技术教育质量。中国愿意与各国加强职业技术教育合作办学，为经济全球化和国际产能合作服务。中国也愿意积极推进职业技术教育服务“一带一路”国家之间的合作，继续探索发展中国家更高水平的职业技术教育模式与经验，分享发展成果与理念，为世界各国职业技术教育迈向更高水平做出新的贡献[66]。

# 三

# 我国职业技术教育发展的基本经验、特色与挑战

## （一）我国职业技术教育发展的基本经验

经过几十年的探索，尤其是改革开放 40 余年来的发展和积累，我国已经建成了全球规模最大的职业技术教育体系。2021 年，我国中等职业学校 7 294 所，在校生 1 312 万人；本科层次职业学校 32 所，高职（专科）学校 1 486 所，职业本科在校生 12.9 万人，高职（专科）在校生 1 590 万人[67]。在长时期的发展过程中，我国职业技术教育领域形成了一些基本发展经验。

### 1. 通过“摸着石头过河”，逐步形成了具有中国特色的职业技术教育发展模式

我国在职业技术教育探索过程中，经历了向他国学习和自主探索的阶段。中华人民共和国成立初期，为了实现加速工业化的目标，全面采用了苏联的计划经济体制，单位制逐步形成。单位制是一系列制度的组合，包括统一的工资制度、计划性用工制度、单位福利主义和双重领导架构[68]。为了满足加速工业化的人才需求，我国同时借鉴了苏联职业技术教育模式，形成了以学徒制为主体、厂办技校为补充、内外部结合的技能养成体系。在计划经济时期，我国的技能形成体制有两个特点：一是企业内部技能养成为主体的技能培训体系；二是以企业专用和行业专用技能为主的技能培养模式。在这段时期，双元学徒制和中等职业教育是产业工人技能积累的主要方式，国家和企业卷入程度都比较高。

改革开放以后，随着我国企业用工制度的变革、国有企业市场化改革和单位制的解体，企业内部技能养成体系逐步衰落，以职业院校为主的外部养成方式成为

产业工人技能的主要来源，公共财政加大了对以学校为基础的职业技术教育的支持。1980 年到 20 世纪 90 年代中后期，我国先后尝试引入德国的“双元制”和英国的“国家资格框架”。“双元制”在多个地区进行了试点，进行了相关的教师培训和课程开发工作。1995 年，国务院出台相关政策，由劳动部门主导制定国家职业资格框架，建立了国家职业分类大典，形成了兼具苏联模式和英国模式特点的技能资格认证体系。

中国加入世界贸易组织以来，随着高等教育规模的扩大和经济全球化，中等职业教育的吸引力下降，高等职业教育大规模发展，占据高等教育的半壁江山。为了提升教育质量，国家加强了中等和高等职业教育的质量建设工作，同时通过大量专项性投入建设了一批具有示范引领作用的高水平职业院校。在此期间，国际组织加大了对中国职业技术教育的技术和资金支持。总体上，中国并没有全盘采纳“国际最佳实践”——如行业技能委员会、国家职业资格框架、劳动力信息系统等，而是发展出适合本国国情的校企合作、产教融合的职业技术教育模式。

在试错的过程中不断调整，吸纳国际经验以发展本土实践，是中国职业技术教育发展的基本经验之一。

### 2. 国家主导，强调顶层设计

国家在职业技术教育发展过程中发挥了积极的领导力，将技能形成与产业政策在国家发展战略和部门策略中紧密结合，形成了具有中国特色的职业技术教育战略和政策体系。

在计划经济时期，职业技术教育是国家五年计划等重要经济发展战略的有机组成部分。为了支持“赶超战略”，我国为 684 个国家重点工业建设项目配套建设了职业院校，优先满足重点工程、重点项目对技能人才的需求。1978 年以来，形成了从国家战略到国家发展规划，再到教育部门发展战略的顶层设计流程[69]。从 20 世纪 80 年代到 90 年代末期（如图 6 所示），我国改革开放和市场经济转型两大国家战略落地实施，形成了国家经济和教育发展战略的基础，并通过一系列教育改革和职业技术教育改革方案转化为职业技术教育发展政策。

国家主导将职业技术教育发展与国家发展战略紧密联系起来，形成教育部门相关职业技术教育政策，是我国发展的另一基本经验。国家主导有利于在技能形成领域形成可信承诺，形成对地方政府发展职业技术教育强有力的激励。我国政府通过三种相辅相成的政策工具，即事权与支出责任调整、财政投入和项目制激励地方政府进行技能人力资本投资[70]。

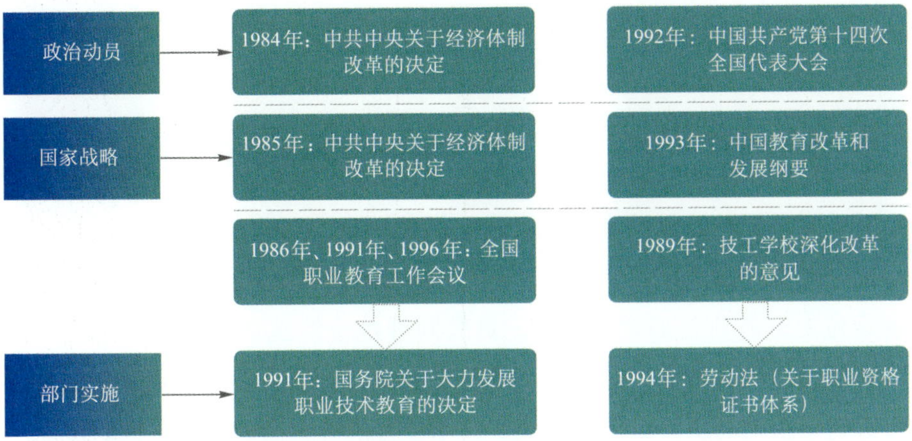


**图 6　职业技术教育与国家发展战略整合**

### 3. 地方政府支持校企合作的多元化实践，以地方创新推动产教融合发展

自 2007 年以来，全球出现了六大类提升职业技术教育地位和重要性的“国际最佳实践”，包括校企合作和雇主参与、发展国家培训体系、发展国家和区域资格框架、引入质量保障机制、实施多元筹资机制和提升民办教育培训参与度。但是这些“国际最佳实践”在包括中国在内的发展中国家出现了“水土不服”的现象。

在中国的实践中，职业技术教育高质量发展依赖于地方政府提供的地方化产权保护。企业在人力资本投资中面临种种风险，不愿意参与技能合作。我国地方政府发挥中介组织的作用，通过认可、激励、协调和参与的方式促成了职业技术教育领域的校企合作。在给定的激励机制和约束条件下，地方政府可以通过提供公共产品（如优惠信贷、优惠合同、财政投入、优惠土地、税收优惠）等支持企业与职业院校合作。地方政府提供的各种公共产品和采取的促进政策形成了对校企合作的地方化产权保护。2019 年，国务院印发的《国家职业教育改革实施方案》就提出，鼓励地方政府通过组合式激励促进产教融合，降低企业面临的各种不确定性，提高企业参与技能投资的收益，从而将企业重新变为职业技术教育的合作供给主体。

以地方创新推动产教融合发展是我国职业技术教育发展的基本经验的核心。在缺乏成熟的中介组织条件下，地方政府可以发挥中介组织角色，促进校企形成长期合作，为产业发展构建“技能人力资本的公地”。

## （二）我国职业技术教育发展的特色

### 1. 定位和构建现代职业技术教育体系

我国存在学术和职业双轨制教育体系。近年来，我国职业教育已经成为与普通教育不同、但是具有同等重要地位的教育类型。与北欧国家类似，职业教育平等但不同的类型定位在《国家职业教育改革实施方案》中得到了确立。该方案提出把职业教育定位为一种与普通教育平行，具有同等地位的教育类型，构建普职纵向贯通、横向融通的教育体系。对职业技术教育的这一定位，把国家对此类型教育的重视程度提到了新的高度，对于提升职业技术教育的教育属性，促进普职协调、健康发展具有深远意义。

为了实现这一定位，我国自 2014 年开始进行现代职业技术教育体系构建，强调职业技术教育纵向贯通培养、横向与普通教育融合，开放了学术和职业技术教育之间的流动机会。在此战略指导下，我国形成了较为完备的职业技术教育体系。首先，在学历层次上，包括中等职业教育、职业专科教育和职业本科教育。其次，在专业方面，教育部对《职业教育专业目录》再次进行修订，同意了中高等职业教育专业分类，形成了一体化规划的三级职业教育专业设置，将现代职业技术教育体系建设落实到专业层面。再次，在招生录取制度方面，除了提供中高职衔接、中高本衔接、专本衔接、专本硕衔接等项目外，还建设了与普通高考平行的职教高考和各种衔接录取制度，形成了较为完善的流动通道。这一体系的建立，使得我国职业技术教育与欧洲哥本哈根议程倡导的职业技术教育贯通培养体系具备了相同的功能，为职业技术教育毕业生提供了多种选择机会和支持，实现了教育机会平等。

### 2. 加强职业技术教育质量体系建设

近年来，我国职业技术教育质量保障工作不断加强，取得了一系列重要进展。在质量工作方面，各级政府开展了一系列卓有成效的工作[3]。我国已经建立和完善了常规性质量标准和内外部质量保障体系。在投入质量保障方面，职业技术教育质量保障的常规性工作分为准入认证和教学标准、过程质量建设和结果性质量评估，政府颁布了六大类职业技术教育标准。

为提升职业技术教育过程质量，政府开展了以提升教学质量为目标的教学改革、以内部质量保障体系建设为目标的教学工作诊断和改进和以职业院校内涵发展为目标的职业院校管理水平提升改革。例如，教学工作诊断与改进制度是教育过程质量建设最主要的载体之一。在“管办评分离”背景下，国家教育主管部门提出以教学工作诊断与改进工作为突破口，建立我国职业院校常态化的、自主的人才培养质量保障机制，即职业技术教育内部质量保障体系。2015 年，教育部办公厅颁布《关于建立职业院校教学工作诊断与改进制度的通知》。2016 年，《中等职业学校教学工作诊断与改进指导方案（试行）》提出，教学工作诊断与改进工作的首要目标是构建中等职业学校教学工作自主诊断、持续改进的工作制度和运行机制；搭建中等职业学校人才培养工作状态数据管理系统。2015 年发布的《高等职业院校内部质量保证体系诊断与改进指导方案（试行）》提出采用“自主诊改、抽样复核”的工作机制。

在结果质量保障方面，各级政府开展了对职业技术教育机构和人才培养过程的外部评估和监测，其内容包括职业教育人才培养工作评估、职业教育质量年报、职业教育督导评估以及职业教育工作状态数据的常态监测。以高等职业教育为例，我国高等职业教育评估经历了三个发展阶段，即 2004—2008 年的高职高专院校人才培养工作水平评估、2008—2016 年的高等职业院校人才培养工作评估、2016 年以后的高等职业院校适应社会需求能力评估。《国家中长期教育改革和发展规划纲要（2010—2020 年）》明确提出要建立高校质量年报发布制度。教育部在 2011 年颁布的《关于推进高等职业教育改革创新引领职业教育科学发展的若干意见》中，倡导各地要建立质量年报发布制度。

除了常规性质量保障工作外，国家教育行政部门先后采用了多种项目性政策工具来实现“点穴似的”干预，促进特定领域职业技术教育结构性质量、过程性质量和结果性质量的提升。我国政府在“十一五”和“十二五”期间，开展了一系列中央财政支持的专项工程，有力地提升了中等和高等职业教育质量。“十一五”期间，中央和地方加大了职业技术教育基础能力建设的力度，中等职业学校的办学条件有了明显的改善。中央财政对职业技术教育投入 100 亿元，重点支持职业技术教育实训基地建设、充实教学设备，实施“国家技能型人才培养培训工程”等“四大工程”和“国家示范性高等职业院校建设计划”等“四大计划”。

我国职业技术教育质量工作取得显著成效。具体表现在：一是我国初步建立了中央教育行政部门、地方教育行政部门、企业、行业、院校和相关社会组织等多元主体共同参与，以专业化的监测数据平台为支撑，内部质量保证和外部质量评价机制共同运作的职业技术教育质量保障体系；二是学校专业设置、教学和实习实训、师资等国家标准的建立和更新，带动职业技术教育结构性质量的普遍改善；三是以人才培养常态监测、教学诊断与改进工作、质量年报发布为主要内容的内部质量保证工作卓有成效，为过程性和结果性质量的改善带来了积极影响；四是通过示范校引领、教师发展等项目，建立了一批高水平的职业院校和专业，推动了师资等核心质量要素的改善；五是学徒制、职教集团、教学成果奖、技能大赛等项目性努力成效显著，为职业技术教育过程性质量的改善提供了模式探索。

### 3. 理清职业技术教育投入责任，加大职业技术教育投入

党的十八届三中全会提出“事权与支出责任相适应”的原则。根据此原则，《中华人民共和国职业教育法》对中央政府、地方政府、职业学校举办者、企业和公民的投入责任进行了规定。2022 年的修订版进一步对各级政府相关的财政支出责任进行了规定，如“各级人民政府应当按照事权和支出责任相适应的原则，根据职业教育办学规模、培养成本和办学质量等落实职业教育经费，并加强预算绩效管理，提高资金使用效益”。2019 年，国务院印发《教育领域中央与地方财政事权与支出责任划分改革方案》，将中等职业教育免学费补助、国家助学金和国家奖学金纳入中央与地方共同事权范畴，职业教育总体为中央和地方共同事权，所需财政补助经费主要按照隶属关系等由中央和地方财政分别承担。

近年来，我国完善了职业技术教育财政政策体系，建立了职业技术教育财政的制度基础，形成了包括学生资助、生均拨款标准、职业技术教育基础能力建设、示范引领建设四大类投入机制（见表 10）。

**表 10　我国职业技术教育财政政策体系**

| 时间 | 发文部门 | 文件名称 | 文件号 | 涉及领域 |
|---|---|---|---|---|
| | | 学生资助 | | |
| 2007 年 | 国务院 | 关于建立健全普通本科高校、高等职业学校和中等职业学校家庭经济困难学生资助政策体系的意见 | 国发〔2007〕13 号 | 学生资助 |
| 2009 年 | 财政部、国家发展改革委、教育部、人力资源和社会保障部 | 关于中等职业学校家庭经济困难学生和涉农专业学生免学费工作的意见 | 财教〔2009〕442 号 | 学生资助 |

续表

| 时间 | 发文部门 | 文件名称 | 文件号 | 涉及领域 |
|---|---|---|---|---|
| 2010 年 | 财政部、教育部、人力资源和社会保障部 | 关于印发中等职业学校免学费补助资金管理暂行办法的通知 | 财教〔2010〕3 号 | 学生资助 |
| 2010 年 | 财政部、国家发展改革委、教育部、人力资源和社会保障部 | 关于扩大中等职业学校免学费政策覆盖范围的通知 | 财教〔2010〕345 号 | 学生资助 |
| 2012 年 | 财政部、国家发展改革委、教育部、人力资源和社会保障部 | 关于扩大中等职业教育免学费政策范围 进一步完善国家助学金制度的意见 | 财教〔2012〕376 号 | 学生资助 |
| | | 生均拨款标准 | | |
| 2014 年 | 财政部、教育部 | 关于建立完善以改革和绩效为导向的生均拨款制度 加快发展现代高等职业教育的意见 | 财教〔2014〕352 号 | 生均拨款标准 |
| 2015 年 | 财政部、教育部、人力资源和社会保障部 | 关于建立完善中等职业学校生均拨款制度的指导意见 | 财教〔2015〕448 号 | 生均拨款标准 |
| | | 职业教育基础能力建设 | | |
| 2004 年 | 教育部、国家发展改革委、财政部、人事部、劳动和保障部、农业部（今农业农村部）、国务院扶贫办 | 关于进一步加强职业教育工作的若干意见 | 教职成〔2004〕12 号 | 职业教育实训基地建设 |
| 2004 年 | 国家发展和改革委员会、教育部、劳动和社会保障部 | 关于组织制订推进职业教育发展专项建设计划的指导意见 | 发改社会〔2004〕2073 号 | 职业教育实训基地建设 |
| 2006 年 | 教育部、财政部 | 关于实施中等职业学校教师素质提高计划的意见 | 教职成〔2006〕13 号 | 中等职业教育师资培训 |
| 2011 年 | 教育部、财政部 | 关于实施职业院校教师素质提高计划的意见 | 教职成〔2011〕14 号 | 职业院校师资培训 |
| 2013 年 | 教育部办公厅、财政部办公厅 | 职业院校教师素质提高计划中等职业学校专业骨干教师培训项目管理办法 | 教师厅〔2013〕3 号 | 职业院校师资培训 |

续表

| 时间 | 发文部门 | 文件名称 | 文件号 | 涉及领域 |
| --- | --- | --- | --- | --- |
| | | 示范引领建设 | | |
| 2006 年 | 教育部、财政部 | 关于实施国家示范性高等职业院校建设计划、加快高等职业教育改革与发展的意见 | 教高〔2006〕14 号 | 示范性高等职业院校建设 |
| 2010 年 | 教育部、财政部 | 关于进一步推进“国家示范高等职业院校建设计划”实施工作的通知 | 教高〔2010〕8 号 | 骨干高等职业院校建设 |
| 2010 年 | 教育部、人力资源和社会保障部、财政部 | 关于实施国家中等职业教育改革发展示范学校建设计划的意见 | 教职成〔2010〕9 号 | 中等职业教育示范学校建设 |
| 2011 年 | 教育部、人力资源和社会保障部、财政部 | 国家中等职业教育改革发展示范学校建设计划项目管理暂行办法 | 教职成〔2011〕7 号 | 中等职业教育示范学校建设 |

注：笔者根据王蓉、田志磊（2018）和田志磊（2018）整理，有增减。

在这些政策的指引下，各级政府加大了职业技术教育财政性经费投入。2019 年，全国普通高职高专学校总投入为 2 404.1 亿元，比上年增长 11.34%。其中，国家财政性教育经费为 1 592.56 亿元，比上年增长 12.95%。一般公共预算教育经费为 1 514.24 亿元，比上年增长 11.17%。全国普通高职高专学校教育经费收入构成中，国家财政性教育经费占 66.24%，事业收入经费占 30.39%，其他教育经费占 2.73%，民办学校举办者投入经费占 0.53%，捐赠收入经费占 0.11%。

#### 4. 形成具有中国特色的产教融合制度

校企合作、产教融合是我国职业技术教育的办学理念，也是一种育人方式和办学模式，是我国职业技术教育的基本形态。首先，作为办学理念，校企合作满足技能形成的基本规律，将以学校为基础的技能知识学习和以工作场所为基础的技能习得结合起来。其次，作为育人方式，产教融合将企业专用技能内容、技能实践方式、技能评价标准和技能认证引入学校职业技术教育体系的课程设置、教学实践和学生评价过程，实现了通适性技能和专用性技能的整合，提高了职业技术教育人才培养效果。最后，作为办学模式，校企合作一直是我国职业院校办学的重要方式。21 世纪早期，我国出现了职业院校内的校企订单班、二级学院、顶岗实习等模式，此后出现了校企合作共建的实习实训基地、厂中校、校中厂等模式，近年来，出现了校企双主体办学的职教集团、现代产业学院等新模式。

产教融合实质上已经成为地方职业技术教育发展的主要载体，出现了政府多部门联合推动的校企自主合作机制，形成了多样的技能合作伙伴关系。按照合作伙伴投资成本高低和合作伙伴之间合作范围的宽窄，我国不同地区出现了四种技能合作伙伴关系模式（如图 7 所示）。例如，在湖南株洲，中车集团与湖南铁路职业技术学院、湖南铁路科技职业技术学院合作，形成了家长制模式。在广东省中山市的专业特色小镇中，古镇镇与中山职业技术学院合作形成了灯饰学院，为本地灯饰产业提供技能人才培养和在职培训。地方政府在此类产教融合模式发展中充当了中介角色，形成了共同体模式，提供了地方化的产权保护。

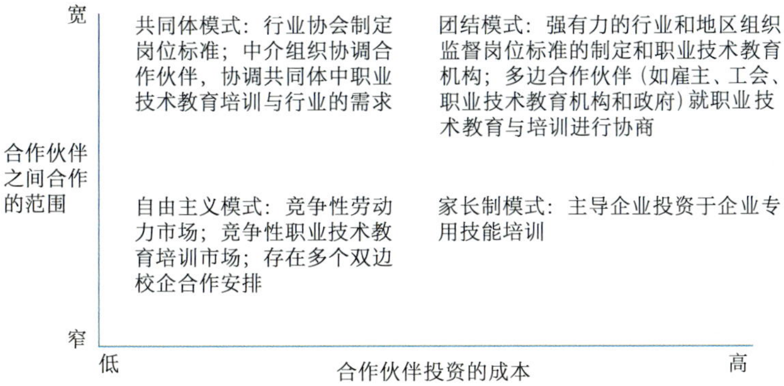


**图 7　四种技能合作伙伴关系模式**

### 5. 支持双师型教师队伍建设和数字化资源建设

发展高水平的双师型教师队伍是我国职业技术教育的重要策略。2006 年以来，中央出台了一系列政策支持中职和高职教师发展。2011 年，教育部、财政部《关于实施职业院校教师素质提高计划的意见》设定目标任务，计划支持 2 万名中等职业学校青年教师到企业实践，提高教师的产业文化素养和专业技能水平。2016 年，教育部、财政部《关于实施职业院校教师素质提高计划（2017—2020 年）的意见》明确提出，2017—2020 年，组织职业院校教师、校长分层分类参加国家级培训，带动地方有计划、分步骤实施五年一周期的教师全员培训，提高教师“双师”素质和校长办学治校能力。2016 年，教育部等七部门印发《职业学校教师企业实践规定》，进一步加强职业学校“双师型”教师队伍建设，促进职业学校教师专业发展。与此同时，一批技能大师工作室在职业院校落户。按照《国家职业教育改革实施方案》提出的要求，到 2022 年，“双师型”教师占专业课教师总数要超过 1/2。这一目标实现后，我国职业教育师资队伍将再上一个台阶。

职业技术教育数字化资源建设取得突出成绩。2010 年印发的《中等职业学校专业设置管理办法（试行）》提出了中等职业学校专业设置的四项条件，将具备数字化教学资源作为基本办学条件。2012 年，教育部《关于加快推进职业教育信息化发展的意见》要求加快开发职业教育数字化优质信息资源，开发包括网络课程、虚拟仿真实训平台、工作过程模拟软件、通用主题素材库（包括行业标准库、实训项目库、教学案例库、考核试题库、技能竞赛库等）、名师名课音像以及专业群落网站等多种形式的职业教育数字化信息资源。目前，我国已建立了国家、省、校三级的职业技术教育专业教学资源库，其中国家级资源库 203 个，覆盖高职的 19 个专业大类，形成了丰富的数字化教育资源供给。

## （三）我国职业技术教育发展面临的挑战

当前，我国职业技术教育发展面临几个关键挑战。首先，我国经济社会发展进入新阶段，经济增速放缓，国家发展重点从增长转向均衡，致力于在全面建成小康社会的基础上实现共同富裕。实现共同富裕的关键是“提低、扩中”，扩中的重点群体包括高校毕业生、技术工人、农民工、国有单位基层职工等。职业技术教育可以为这些重点群体提供技术技能培训，提升其收入潜力，帮助他们实现收入组的跨越，进入中等收入群体。职业技术教育如何在我国向高收入国家转型过程中支持中等收入群体的扩大、促进收入格局的优化，是当前职业技术教育面临的最大挑战。

其次，人口老龄化、少子化等人口趋势有可能降低适龄人口规模，如何在新的人口形势下建设富有吸引力和活力的职业技术教育体系是我国面临的又一个挑战。

再次，我国当前的普职分流、职业技术教育贯通培养等政策的目标是提升职业技术教育人才培养质量，并促进中高本衔接，从而促进职普融通。如何设计合理的贯通培养体系以适应劳动力市场和家庭的双重需求是新发展阶段职业技术教育急需解决的难题。

最后，当前我国中等和高等职业教育以政府财政性投入为主，家庭和企业适度分担教育成本。随着我国经济增速放缓，财政收支紧缩，以政府投入为主的局面难以持续，需要进一步深化职业技术教育领域的成本分担，实施多元化筹资机制。如何为家庭、企业与社会资本投资职业教育创造更好的政策环境，是摆在政策制定者面前的新挑战。

# 四

# 结论与讨论

## （一）职业技术教育发展的最佳实践溯源

实际上，不存在职业技术教育发展的最佳实践，而是要发展适合本国国情的国家职业技术教育体系。作为工业革命的发源地和率先开展工业革命的西方发达国家，在各自迥然不同的政治、经济和文化传统基础上生发出了形式多样的技能形成体制，如前述的四种类型。各国的技能形成体制深深嵌入企业生产体制、劳资关系、企业治理、跨企业关系、金融市场、社会保障形成的社会经济制度网络当中。因此，不存在职业教育的“最佳模式”，需要发展适合中国国情的职业技术教育体系。

## （二）世界职业技术教育发展趋势

技术冲击和外部环境变化对职业技术教育发展提出新挑战。21 世纪以来，以“工业 4.0”、云计算、大数据、人工智能和区块链为代表的新一轮科技革命对劳动者的技能提出了新的需求，程序性体力类劳动者（如机器操作工、物流分拣员）和程序性认知类劳动者（如会计、翻译）等因可替代性高而率先受到冲击，非程序性认知类劳动者（如研究人员、数据科学家、算法工程师）和体力劳动者（如手工业者、理发师）将得到发展。2020 年召开的世界经济论坛预计，到 2025 年，全球将有 50% 的劳动者需要接受再培训以适应新的岗位需求。这对各国的技能形成系统提出了新的挑战，要求职业技术教育系统不仅对于已就业者提供再培训，还要将一代代年轻人培养成为能适应新技术革命需求的技术技能人才。在此背景下，各国的技能形成体制做出了许多调整。

各国职业技术教育在平稳发展过程中，出现层级上移趋势。首先，通过对联合国教科文统计局和经合组织的数据的综合研判发现，近年来主要发达国家的职业技术教育在总体规模平稳的情况下，出现了层级上移的趋势。高中阶段的职业技术教育占比有所下降，高职和本科阶段的职业技术教育规模上升。这种职业技术教育层级上移需要具有清晰的纵向贯通体系，具体而言，构建中职—高职—应用本科—专业学位硕士应用型人才培养体系是各国职业技术教育发展的重要议题。同时，在国家资质框架下实现职业技术教育与普通教育的横向融通也是应有之义。一方面，构建职业技术教育与普通教育之间互相转换和衔接的通道；另一方面，交叉结合职业技术教育与普通教育的教学要素，或开发跨类型的教育项目，让学生同时接受不同类型的教育，获取不同类型的证书。各国也试图打破传统职业技术教育体系的边界，构建灵活的终身职业技术教育体系，实现学历与非学历之间、正式与非正式之间、课程与证书之间的有机结合。在此背景下，中国可以在高职连续三年扩招的基础上，适度提前布局应用本科转型。

其次，在新一轮工业革命蓬勃发展和可持续发展理念深入人心等大趋势下，职业技能绿色化和职业教育数字化的理念与实践方兴未艾。一方面，它带来了建立新型职业课程、新兴专业的需求；另一方面，它对现有职业技术教育课程体系、师资力量的绿色化和数字化提出了要求，提供了机遇，但是具体实施的模式还在探索之中，相关创新案例的成效还有待进一步评估。中国的职业技术教育应该抓住这个历史机遇，深入落实习近平总书记 2015 年 12 月在第二届世界互联网大会开幕式上提出的“推进‘数字中国’建设”的要求和 2020 年 9 月在第七十五届联合国大会上宣布的“双碳”目标，争取实现这两个领域的弯道超车。

上述职业技术教育的转型需要各国职业技术教育财政体系提供支持。虽然以政府投入为主体、不断减轻学生负担、增强校企合作、促进企业经费投入和发展学徒制等是多国职业技术教育经费体系的相似之处和共同的发展趋势，但是，由于职业技术教育投资对于投资者和受益者双方的作用机制比较复杂，目前还没有一种方法能够较完善地解决当前面临的问题。尽管如此，我们发现在职业技术教育财政上，有的国家尝试利用市场化手段来提高财政资金的使用效率，如从生均成本拨款向以学业或者就业结果为导向拨款转变，或者让公立职业技术教育机构与民办机构在项目招标上进行竞争。另一个与我国不同之处是很多国家都建立了国家技能发展基金，将国家职业技术教育财政拨款、对企业征收的职工培训费和捐赠资金进行统筹。我国除了职业技术教育财政拨款外，规定地方教育附加费用中不少于 30% 用于职业技术教育发展，同时允许企业发生的职工教育经费支出中不超过工资薪金总额 8% 的部分税前扣除，用来激励企业增加对员工的培训。进入新发展阶段，党中央把实现全体人民共同富裕摆在更加重要的位置上。我们可以在职业技术教育领域推动建立我国的国家技能发展基金，鼓励高新技术企业和大型国企以无偿捐赠的形式投入国家技能发展基金中，并辅之以财政配套资金，模仿国家自然科学基金的运作方式进行科学化、透明化、分权式、参与式管理，促进我国职业技术教育模式的创新与发展。

### （三）我国职业技术教育发展的启示

历史上，主要西方发达国家都在通过国际交流、国际援助向发展中国家“推销”自己的职业技术教育模式，忽视了发展中国家的国情，极大干扰了发展中国家关于职业技术教育的决策，导致了职业技术教育政策的摇摆。在试错的过程中不断调整，吸纳国际经验以发展本土实践，是中国职业技术教育发展的基本经验之一，也是可供发展中国家借鉴之处。根据国情，我国职业技术教育体制经历了两次大的转型。首先是中华人民共和国成立初期借鉴苏联职业技术教育模式，形成了以学徒制为主体、厂办技校为补充、内外部结合的技能形成体制。后来，伴随着由计划经济向市场经济转型，在充分借鉴世界职业技术教育发展经验的基础上，扎根中国国情，本着“摸着石头过河”的改革精神，探索出具有中国特色的工学结合、校企合作、产教融合的职业技术教育模式，建立了全球规模最大的职业教育体系。但是，很多发展中国家一方面在宏观政策上被发达国家牵制，教育发展的重点在职业教育与普通教育之间大幅摇摆；另一方面在操作层面上又脱离本国经济发展阶段和工业基础，全盘照搬国际组织所谓的职业技术教育“最佳实践”——如行业技能委员会、国家职业资格框架、劳动力信息系统、引入质量保障机制、实施多元筹资机制等，导致其技能体制的建设出现了严重“水土不服”的问题。

我国一方面可以讲好中国职业技术教育发展的故事，积极参与并影响国际组织的日程设定，另一方面要适时呼吁职业技术教育领域有更多的南南合作或者南南合作与南北合作，助力我国的教育对外开放政策和“一带一路”倡议。

最后，职业技术教育作为教育的一种类型，需要一个独特的生态系统。与普通教育相比，如果没有很好地解决校企合作、产教融合模式问题，职业技术教育与社会需求脱节的问题会更加突出，职业技术教育的社会地位将难以提高，新一轮的读书（职业技术教育）无用论可能又会甚嚣尘上。构建具有活力、生命力和可持续性的职业技术教育生态系统仍然任重道远。要创建一个教育协同创新的共同体，关键是要有一套明确的激励机制，并且需要建立更加全面的职业技术教育评价体系，明确每一个个体（学生或者企业、机构、政府）占有的公共职业技术教育资源和应承担的教育责任以破解教育协同创新的难题[70]。

哈　巍、杨　钋、林　璐、曹宇莲、肖　烨
张文杰、陈思源、徐万蓉、王　瑶
北京大学教育经济研究所　2022 年 3 月

## 参考文献

[1] 王星．技能形成、技能形成体制及其经济社会学的研究展望[J]．学术月刊，2021，53(07): 132-143.

[2] Blossfeld, H. -P. Is the German dual system a model for a modern vocational training system?[J]. International Journal of Comparative Sociology, 1992, 33(3): 168.

[3] 杨钋．技能形成与区域创新：职业教育校企合作的功能分析[C] // 北京大学中国教育财政科学研究所．中国教育财政政策咨询报告（2019−2021）．[出版者不详]，2022：284-288.

[4] Busemeyer, M. R. & Trampusch, C. (eds.). The political economy of collective skill formation [M]. Oxford: Oxford University Press, 2012.

[5] Green, A. Education and globalization in Europe and East Asia: convergent and divergent trends [J]. Journal of education policy, 1999, 14(1): 55-71.

[6] 中国教育科学研究院国际与比较教育研究所．新科技革命：全球数字化教育在行动[M]．北京：科学出版社，2020.

[7] Centre for the New Economy and Society. The future of jobs report 2018 [R]. Geneva: World Economic Forum, 2018.

[8] 任平，贺阳．德国工业 4.0 背景下学校劳动课程改革新举措[J]．劳动教育评论，2020(04): 76-91.

[9] Bughin, J., Hazan, E., Lund, S., et al. Skill shift: automation and the future of the workforce [J]. McKinsey Global Institute, 2018, (1): 3-84.

[10] Becker, G. S. Investment in human capital: a theoretical analysis [J]. Journal of political economy, 1962, 70 (5, Part 2): 9-49.

[11] Goldin, C. The human-capital century and American leadership: virtues of the past [J]. The Journal of Economic History, 2001, 61(2): 263-292.

[12] Krueger, D. & Kumar, K. B. Skill-specific rather than general education: a reason for US–Europe growth differences?[J]. Journal of economic growth, 2004, 9(2): 167-207.

[13] INSEAD. The Global Talent Competitiveness Index 2014-2021[EB/OL]. [2022-4-12]. https://www.insead.edu/faculty-research/research/gtci.

[14] 孙凤敏，邵建东，王亚南．瑞士高等职业教育学位制度的现状、特征及发展趋向[J]．外国教育研究，2021，48(08): 97-112.

[15] 孙进，郭荣梅．双向贯通 交叉结合 趋同融合——德国职业教育与学术教育融通的三种模式[J]．中国高教研究，2022, (02), 76-82.

[16] Hemkes, B., Wllbers, K., Zinke, G. Brücken zwischen hochschule und berufsbildung durchbereichsübergreifende bildungsgänge (aus) bauen [J]. Berufsbildung in wissenschaft und praxis, 2015, 44(3), 35-39.

[17] Hemkes, B., Wllbers, K., Zinke, G. Bereichsübergreifende bildungsmaßnahmen als brücke zwischen hochschule und berufsbildung [J]. Hochschule und weiterbildung, 2015 (1), 27-31.

[18] 刘育锋．高职院校应关注和开发“绿色技能”[J]．中国高等教育，2014(01): 35-37.

[19] UNESCO. Strategy for Technical and Vocational Education and Training (TVET) (2016-2021) [EB/OL]. [2022-04-12]. https://en.unesco.org/sites/default/files/tvet.pdf.

[20] UNESCO. International conference on transforming technical and vocational education and training for successful and just transitions[EB/OL]. (2021-12-08) [2022-04-12]. https://events.unesco.org/event?id=1304288987 & lang=1033.

[21] Department for Business, Energy & Industrial Strategy (UK).The Ten Point Plan for a Green Industrial Revolution [EB/OL]. (2020-11-18)[2022-04-12]. https://www.gov.uk/government/publications/the-ten-point-plan-for-a-green-industrial-revolution/title.

[22] Department for Education, Department for Work and Pensions, The Rt Hon Thérèse

Coffey MP, The Rt Hon Boris Johnson MP, and The Rt Hon Sir Gavin Williamson CBE MP(UK). Hundreds of Free Qualifications on Offer to Boost Skills and Jobs [EB/OL]. (2021-01-01)[2022-04-12]. https://www.gov.uk/government/news/hundreds-of-free-qualifications-on-offer-to-boost-skills-and-jobs.

[23] Department for Business, Energy & Industrial Strategy, Department for Education, The Rt Hon Gillian Keegan MP, and The Rt Hon Kwasi Kwarteng MP (UK). UK government launches taskforce to support drive for 2 million green jobs by 2030[EB/OL]. (2020-11-12) [2022-04-12]. https://www.gov.uk/government/news/uk-government-launches-taskforce-to-support-drive-for-2-million-green-jobs-by-2030.

[24] 杜明明. 英国绿色 TVET 发展路径探析[J]. 职业技术教育，2021，42(22)：72-79.

[25] 谢良才，孙玲. 美国绿色职业教育运动进展与经验[J]. 比较教育研究，2017，39(07)：71-78.

[26] CFME, Hungary. Green Wheels[EB/OL]. (2019-10)[2022-04-12]. https://unevoc.unesco.org/pub/greening_cfme_green_wheels.pdf.

[27] ADB Nord gGmbH, Germany. Bridging Innovation and Learning in TEVT. NiB-Scout: Sustainability in the Bakery Trade[EB/OL]. (2021-04)[2022-04-12]. https://unevoc.unesco.org/pub/greening_adb_nord_ggmbh__nib-scout.pdf.

[28] Apelojg Benjamin, Hochmuth Jörg, Röhrig Anne. NiB-Scout-Lernarrangements im bäckerhandwerk zur förderung nachhaltigkeitsorientierter beruflicher handlungskompetenzen[J]. HiBiFo-Haushalt in bildung und forschung. 2020, 9(3).

[29] BKAL, Germany. FOENAKO[EB/OL]. (2019)[2022-04-12]. https://unevoc.unesco.org/pub/greening_bkal_foenako.pdf.

[30] 李继延等. 中外职业教育体系建设与制度改革比较研究[M]. 上海：复旦大学出版社，2014.

[31] 贾文胜，何兴国，梁宁森. 职业教育校企合作机制及政策保障研究[M]. 北京：中国商务出版社，2019.

[32] 姜大源. 德国“双元制”职业教育再解读[J]. 中国职业技术教育，2013(33)：5-14.

[33] 刘勇. 职业教育发达国家校企合作模式及经验借鉴[J]. 改革与开放，2018(20)：9-11.

[34] 杰克·基廷，艾略特·梅德奇，维罗妮卡·沃尔科夫，等. 变革的影响：九国职业教育与培训体系比较研究[M]. 杨蕊竹，译. 北京：首都经济贸易大学出版社，2018.

[35] 陈鹏磊，李郡. 英国职业教育协同育人模式的经验借鉴——基于“三明治”教育模式与现代学徒制模式[J]. 职业教育研究，2015(07)：84-87.

[36] 刘娟，张炼. 英国三明治教育发展历程及其政策举措分析[J]. 现代教育科学，2012(01)：35-39.

[37] 刘洪一，李建求，卿中全. 产学研作协同育人的理念与实践[M]. 北京：商务印书馆，2013.

[38] 郑红梅. “Sandwich Courses”英国职业教育发展新阶段[J]. 教育与职业，2006(04)：90-92.

[39] 杨一琼. 澳大利亚 TAFE 模式对我国职业教育的启示[J]. 职教通讯，2016(12)：77-80.

[40] 冯梅. 澳大利亚 TAFE 学院校企合作实践的研究[D]. 重庆：西南大学，2011.

[41] 张基宏. 澳大利亚职业教育与培训模式成功的密码——赴澳大利亚研修报告[J]. 世界教育信息，2012，25(08)：47-52.

[42] 陈明昆. 非洲职业教育发展与援助研究[M]，北京：北京大学出版社，2020.

[43] 王为民. 印度“国家职业教育资格框架”设计理念探析[J]. 外国教育研究，2014，41(02)：120-128.

[44] Maclean R., Jagannathan S., Sarvi J. Skills development issues, challenges, and strategies in Asia and the Pacific[M] // Maclean R., Jagannathan S., Sarvi J. Skills development for inclusive and sustainable growth in developing Asia-Pacific. Technical and vocational education and training: issues, concerns and prospects, vol

19. Springer, Dordrecht. 2013.
[45] European Training Foundation. Financing vocational education and skills development: a policy area for ETF support[R]. EU: ETF, 2018.
[46] Ziderman, A. Funding mechanisms for financing vocational training: an analytical framework[J]. Education finance, equality, and equity, 2018: 135-164.
[47] The UNESCO-UNEVOC International Centre for Technical and Vocational Education and Training. Revisiting global trends in TVET: reflections on theory and practice [R]. Bonn: UNEVOC, 2013.
[48] 邓志军，黄日强．英国职业教育的经费[J]．荆门职业技术学院学报，2007(04): 93-96.
[49] 年艳，潘建林．美、德、日三国职业教育经费筹措机制比较及启示[J]．职业技术教育，2019，40(12): 67-73.
[50] 张晶晶．美国职业教育经费投入与来源分析[J]．职教论坛，2016 (28): 75-80.
[51] 杨红荃，夏雪薇．比较视野中的高等职业教育经费投入研究[J]．职教论坛，2017(34): 65-73.
[52] 宋吉华，许祥鹏．国外职业教育经费投入保障的比较研究[J]．中国管理信息化，2015，18(04): 236-237.
[53] 伍慧萍．德国职业教育的数字化转型：战略规划、项目布局与效果评估[J]．外国教育研究，2021，48(04): 76-88.
[54] European Commission. Digital Education Action Plan (2021-2027) [R]. Brussels: European Commission, 2020.
[55] European Commission. Osnabruck Declaration 2020 on vocational education and training as an enabler of recovery and just transitions to digital and green economies[R]. Brussels: European Commission, 2020.
[56] 德国联邦政府．面向数字化知识社会的教育行动 [R]．柏林：德国联邦政府，2016.
[57] 澳大利亚政府．数字化转型战略：2018—2025 [R]．悉尼：澳大利亚政府，2018.
[58] 瑞士政府．职业教育发展使命宣言[R]．伯尔尼：瑞士政府，2018.
[59] 张栋科，王泽，吴婷婷．以数字媒体实现职业教育包容性的德国路径探析——基于“包容性数字职业教育行动”的解读[J]．职教论坛，2021，37(11): 152-161.
[60] International Labor Organization. The digitization of TVET and skills systems [R]. Geneva: International Labor Organization, 2020.
[61] 任平，贺阳．德国工业 4.0 背景下学校劳动课程改革新举措[J]．劳动教育评论，2020(04): 76-91.
[62] 翟俊卿，石明慧．提升数字技能：澳大利亚职业教育人才培养的新动向[J]．职业技术教育，2021，42(19): 73-79.
[63] Asian Development Bank (ADB). Crossing the river by touching the stones: alternative approaches in technical and vocational education and training in the People’s Republic of China and the Republic of Korea [M]. Manila: Asian Development Bank, 2022.
[64] 马娜，董丽丽．澳大利亚国际教育战略及其启示——基于对《2025 年国际教育国家战略》的探析[J]．世界教育信息，2020，33: 29-33+42.
[65] 新华社．第三届国际职业技术教育大会将在上海市召开[EB/OL]. (2012-05-02) [2022-11-01]. http://www.gov.cn/jrzg/2012-05/02/content_2128128.htm.
[66] 中国教育报．国际职业技术教育大会召开[EB/OL]. (2017-07-05)[2022-11-01]. http://www.moe.gov.cn/jyb_xwfb/gzdt_gzdt/moe_1485/201707/t20170705_308674.html.
[67] 中华人民共和国教育部．2021 年《教育部公报》[EB/OL]. (2021-12-20)[2022-11-01]. http://www.moe.gov.cn/jyb_xxgk/gk_gbgg/moe_0/gb_2021/.
[68] 王星．1978 年以来中国“国”与“民”关系之历史演进——立足于国家自主性理论的思考[J]．人文杂志，2011(02): 58-70.
[69] Lieberthal, K. & Oksenberg, M. Policy making in China: leaders, structures, and processes[M]. Princeton: Princeton University Press, 1988.
[70] 哈巍，范皑皑，李孟泽，等．从全球到中国：社会与学校的教育协调创新[J]．华东师范大学学报（教育科学版）．2022，40(12): 110-126.

## 附表 1　参会国家（地区）

## Appendix 1　Countries and Regions Participated

| 序号 | 参会国家（地区） | Countries and Regions Participated |
|---|---|---|
| 1 | 阿尔巴尼亚 | Albania |
| 2 | 阿尔及利亚 | Algeria |
| 3 | 阿根廷 | Argentina |
| 4 | 厄立特里亚 | Eritrea |
| 5 | 埃及 | Egypt |
| 6 | 埃塞俄比亚 | Ethiopia |
| 7 | 爱尔兰 | Ireland |
| 8 | 安哥拉 | Angola |
| 9 | 安提瓜和巴布达 | Antigua and Barbuda |
| 10 | 奥地利 | Austria |
| 11 | 澳大利亚 | Australia |
| 12 | 巴基斯坦 | Pakistan |
| 13 | 巴拉圭 | Paraguay |
| 14 | 巴勒斯坦 | Palestine |
| 15 | 巴西 | Brazil |
| 16 | 白俄罗斯 | Belarus |
| 17 | 贝宁 | Benin |
| 18 | 比利时 | Belgium |
| 19 | 波兰 | Poland |
| 20 | 巴哈马 | Bahamas |
| 21 | 布基纳法索 | Burkina Faso |
| 22 | 布隆迪 | Burundi |
| 23 | 朝鲜 | DPRK |
| 24 | 赤道几内亚 | Equatorial Guinea |
| 25 | 丹麦 | Denmark |
| 26 | 德国 | Germany |
| 27 | 俄罗斯 | Russia |
| 28 | 厄瓜多尔 | Ecuador |
| 29 | 法国 | France |
| 30 | 菲律宾 | Philippines |
| 31 | 斐济 | Fiji |
| 32 | 芬兰 | Finland |
| 33 | 佛得角 | Cape Verde |
| 34 | 冈比亚 | Gambia |
| 35 | 刚果（布） | Congo |
| 36 | 刚果（金） | Congo (Kinshasa) |
| 37 | 哥伦比亚 | Colombia |
| 38 | 格林纳达 | Grenada |
| 39 | 哈萨克斯坦 | Kazakhstan |
| 40 | 韩国 | ROK |
| 41 | 荷兰 | Netherlands |
| 42 | 吉布提 | Djibouti |
| 43 | 几内亚比绍 | Guinea-Bissau |
| 44 | 加拿大 | Canada |

续表

| 序号 | 参会国家（地区） | Countries and Regions Participated |
|---|---|---|
| 45 | 加纳 | Ghana |
| 46 | 加蓬 | Gabon |
| 47 | 柬埔寨 | Cambodia |
| 48 | 捷克 | Czech Republic |
| 49 | 津巴布韦 | Zimbabwe |
| 50 | 喀麦隆 | Cameroon |
| 51 | 卡塔尔 | Qatar |
| 52 | 科特迪瓦 | Côte d'Ivoire |
| 53 | 肯尼亚 | Kenya |
| 54 | 老挝 | Laos |
| 55 | 利比里亚 | Liberia |
| 56 | 卢森堡 | Luxembourg |
| 57 | 卢旺达 | Rwanda |
| 58 | 罗马尼亚 | Romania |
| 59 | 马达加斯加 | Madagascar |
| 60 | 马拉维 | Malawi |
| 61 | 马来西亚 | Malaysia |
| 62 | 马里 | Mali |
| 63 | 毛里塔尼亚 | Mauritania |
| 64 | 美国 | US |
| 65 | 蒙古 | Mongolia |
| 66 | 孟加拉国 | Bangladesh |
| 67 | 秘鲁 | Peru |
| 68 | 牙买加 | Jamaica |
| 69 | 缅甸 | Myanmar |
| 70 | 摩洛哥 | Morocco |
| 71 | 摩纳哥 | Monaco |
| 72 | 墨西哥 | Mexico |
| 73 | 纳米比亚 | Namibia |
| 74 | 南非 | South Africa |
| 75 | 尼泊尔 | Nepal |
| 76 | 尼日利亚 | Nigeria |
| 77 | 葡萄牙 | Portugal |
| 78 | 日本 | Japan |
| 79 | 瑞士 | Switzerland |
| 80 | 萨尔瓦多 | El Salvador |
| 81 | 塞尔维亚 | Serbia |
| 82 | 塞拉利昂 | Sierra Leone |
| 83 | 塞内加尔 | Senegal |
| 84 | 沙特阿拉伯 | Saudi Arabia |
| 85 | 圣多美和普林西比 | Sao Tome and Principe |
| 86 | 斯里兰卡 | Sri Lanka |
| 87 | 苏丹 | Sudan |
| 88 | 苏格兰 | Scotland |

续表

| 序号 | 参会国家（地区） | Countries and Regions Participated |
|---|---|---|
| 89 | 所罗门群岛 | Solomon Islands |
| 90 | 索马里 | Somalia |
| 91 | 塔吉克斯坦 | Tajikistan |
| 92 | 泰国 | Thailand |
| 93 | 坦桑尼亚 | Tanzania |
| 94 | 突尼斯 | Tunisia |
| 95 | 土耳其 | Türkiye |
| 96 | 东帝汶 | Timor-Leste |
| 97 | 瓦努阿图 | Vanuatu |
| 98 | 委内瑞拉 | Venezuela |
| 99 | 文莱 | Brunei |
| 100 | 乌干达 | Uganda |
| 101 | 乌克兰 | Ukraine |
| 102 | 乌拉圭 | Uruguay |
| 103 | 乌兹别克斯坦 | Uzbekistan |
| 104 | 西班牙 | Spain |
| 105 | 新加坡 | Singapore |
| 106 | 新西兰 | New Zealand |

| 序号 | 参会国家（地区） | Countries and Regions Participated |
|---|---|---|
| 107 | 匈牙利 | Hungary |
| 108 | 叙利亚 | Syria |
| 109 | 也门 | Yemen |
| 110 | 伊拉克 | Iraq |
| 111 | 吉尔吉斯斯坦 | Kyrgyzstan |
| 112 | 以色列 | Israel |
| 113 | 意大利 | Italy |
| 114 | 印度 | India |
| 115 | 印度尼西亚 | Indonesia |
| 116 | 英国 | UK |
| 117 | 越南 | Vietnam |
| 118 | 赞比亚 | Zambia |
| 119 | 智利 | Chile |
| 120 | 中非共和国 | Central African Republic |
| 121 | 中国台湾 | Taiwan, China |
| 122 | 中国香港 | Hong Kong, China |
| 123 | 中国 | China |

## 附表 2　十四个平行论坛发言嘉宾名单

| 论坛一　人工智能 + 职业教育创新发展 | | | |
|---|---|---|---|
| 主持人：北京师范大学教育学部教授　赵志群 | | | |
| 排序 | 发言嘉宾姓名 | 发言嘉宾单位 / 职务 | 发言嘉宾题目 |
| 1 | 罗方述 | 中华人民共和国教育部高等学校科学研究发展中心主任 | 欢迎辞 |
| 2 | 龚克 | 中国新一代人工智能发展战略研究院执行院长 | 职业教育数字化转型：为什么，是什么，怎么做 |
| 3 | 展涛 | 联合国教科文组织教育信息技术研究所所长 | 联合国教科文组织视角下的人工智能与职业技术教育 |
| 4 | 富强 | 新加坡工艺教育局商业及服务业学院副署长 | 应用人工智能改善和加强教学——新加坡视角 |
| 5 | 菲利普·波伦茨 | 德国马格德堡大学人文社会科学与教育学院副院长 | 变是唯一的不变：人工智能时代对高等职业教育的新要求——教育研究与发展的回应 |
| 6 | 王福岗 | 德国克诺尔轨道车辆系统有限公司工程与创新主管 | 克诺尔铁路车辆系统——智能技术和技术人员的强化培训 |
| 7 | 本杰明·因登 | 德国北黑森应用技术大学技术工程学院副院长 | 利用变换网络改进远程教育 |
| 8 | 田敏 | 南京信息职业技术学院校长 | 高职人工智能专业群建设的思考与实践 |
| 9 | 马艳军 | 百度集团 AI 技术生态总经理 | 产教融合培育人工智能技术技能人才 |
| 10 | 克里斯蒂安·李贝特 | 德国巴登-符腾堡双元制大学教授 | 人工智能对职业教育和培训的影响 |
| 11 | 保罗·多伊尔 | 爱尔兰都柏林理工大学计算机科学学院院长 | 关于未来人工智能和数字强化教育的思考 |
| 12 | 项顺 | 国家职业教育虚拟仿真示范实训基地总经理 | 人工智能在职业教育实训的应用与发展 |
| 13 | 郑文先 | 深圳云天励飞技术股份有限公司副总裁 | 开源 AI 算法训练　推动 AI 职教新突破 |

**论坛二　职业教育数字化转型发展**

**主持人：中国电子学会副秘书长　王天虹**

**中国职业技术教育学会常务副会长兼秘书长　刘建同**

| 排序 | 发言嘉宾姓名 | 发言嘉宾单位 / 职务 | 发言嘉宾题目 |
|---|---|---|---|
| 1 | 鲁昕 | 中国职业技术教育学会会长 | 欢迎辞 |
| 2 | 黄维 | 中国科学院院士、西北工业大学学术委员会主任 | 面向颠覆性技术创新体系　构建开创新时期职业教育国际合作新格局 |
| 3 | 葛道凯 | 江苏省教育厅厅长 | 全力探索职业教育数字化转型的“江苏之路” |
| 4 | 胡思莹 | 东南亚教育部长组织职业技术教育与培训区域中心电子学习教学设计和内容编辑师 | 疫情后技术职业培训与教育中的数字化学习 |
| 5 | 许建领 | 深圳职业技术学院校长 | 数字化时代高职院校人才培养模式转型 |
| 6 | 伊克萨卡·埃古尔比德 | 西班牙机床技术学院董事 | 技术学院的数字化转型战略与支持 |
| 7 | 汤兆武 | 浙江机电职业技术学院党委书记 | 职业教育数字化转型与智能制造 |
| 8 | 扬·海因策 | 德国海因策学院董事 | 职业培训的数字化转型 |
| 9 | 卢坤建 | 广东轻工职业技术学院校长 | 互联网 + 教育的变革：我们的实践探索 |
| 10 | 蔡元文 | 特许公认会计师公会中国教育事务总监 | 数字赋能未来专业会计师培养 |
| 11 | 王丹中 | 南京信息职业技术学院党委书记 | 职业院校专业数字化转型的“南信实践” |

续表

| 排序 | 发言嘉宾姓名 | 发言嘉宾单位 / 职务 | 发言嘉宾题目 |
|---|---|---|---|
| 12 | 王晖 | 深圳信息职业技术学院校长 | 产教融合，分层分类推动专业建设改革创新 |
| 13 | 陈达 | 浙江省教育厅职业教育与成人教育处处长 | 数字化转型与浙江职业教育模式变革 |
| 14 | 刘积仁 | 东软集团股份有限公司董事长 | 数字经济与职业教育 |
| 15 | 陈涛 | 科大讯飞股份有限公司联合创始人、安徽信息工程学院董事长 | 项目化教学在数字技能人才培养方面的思考与实践 |
| 16 | 冯马丁 | 深圳职业技术学院荣誉教授 | 工业 4.0 背景下的职教 4.0 转型 |
| 17 | 钟美华 | 华为技术有限公司培训服务专家委员会主任 | 5G 时代呼唤泛行业数字化人才生态繁荣 |
| 18 | 迈克尔·布拉基斯 | 克兰菲尔德商学院物流采购供应链管理中心主任、英国教育科技协会专家 | 商业和物流新技能 |
| 19 | 沈毅伟 | 马来西亚奎斯特国际大学计算机和工程学院院长 | 第四次工业革命背景下的教育改革 |
| 20 | 韦青 | 微软（中国）有限公司首席技术官 | 数智时代的职业教育 |
| 21 | 张晓蕾 | 北京信息职业技术学院副校长 | 数字化时代教师职业能力提升 |
| 22 | 刘谦 | 广联达科技股份有限公司党委书记、董事、高级副总裁 | 人才为本　建筑人才培养数字化转型正当时 |

| 论坛三　可持续发展背景下的全球绿色技能战略 | | | |
|---|---|---|---|
| 主持人：中华人民共和国教育部职业教育发展中心研究员、联合国教科文组织高级项目专家　刘育锋 | | | |
| 排序 | 发言嘉宾姓名 | 发言嘉宾单位 / 职务 | 发言嘉宾题目 |
| 1 | 彭斌柏 | 中华人民共和国教育部职业教育发展中心主任 | 欢迎辞 |
| 2 | 李昌徽 | 国际劳工组织中国和蒙古国局局长 | 可持续发展的绿色技能战略 |
| 3 | 乔展 | 联合国开发计划署驻华代表处常驻副代表 | 绿色技能和可持续发展 |
| 4 | 博仁・沙克龙 | 联合国教科文组织总部政策与终身学习系统部主任 | 联合国教科文组织职业技术教育与培训战略（2022—2029 年）：绿色和可持续经济转型 |
| 5 | 夏泽翰 | 联合国教科文组织驻华代表处主任 | 促进职业技术教育可持续发展技能 |
| 6 | 肖丽萍 | 世界银行驻华代表处高级教育专家 | 世界银行在疫情期间及之后推动技能开发的 GRID 模式 |
| 7 | 菲尔・洛夫德 | 澳大利亚国家职业教育研究中心执行经理 | 绿色创新所需的技能 |
| 8 | 孔海德 | 欧盟商会东北分会主席、基艾弗姆（辽宁）教育科技有限公司董事长 | 德国双元制及绿色技能促进职业教育转型 |
| 9 | 阿斯丽汗・阿利坎 | 土耳其包装制造商协会秘书长 | 为环境可持续发展而制造 |
| 10 | 赫伯特・朗斯代尔 | 英国汽车工业协会全球技能大使 | 新能源汽车技术 |
| 11 | 曾天山 | 中华人民共和国教育部职业教育发展中心副主任 | 绿色技能开发的全球使命与中国方案 |

续表

| 排序 | 发言嘉宾姓名 | 发言嘉宾单位 / 职务 | 发言嘉宾题目 |
|---|---|---|---|
| 12 | 玛格丽塔 · 帕夫洛娃 | 联合国教科文组织职业技术教育中心（香港）主任 | 面向未来的职业教育：可持续发展的绿色技能 |
| 13 | 辛秀兰 | 北京电子科技职业学院副院长 | 高职院校绿色技能的实践探索——以北京电子科技职业学院为例 |
| 14 | 梁克东 | 金华职业技术学院校长 | 金华职院“三融三式”绿色教育的探索与实践 |
| 15 | 张萨萨 | 海南省技师学院副院长 | 积极探索绿色技能培养　助力自贸港可持续发展 |
| 16 | 贾科莫 · 博西奥 | 联合国教科文组织国际职业技术教育培训中心绿色技能开发项目助理 | 可持续发展目标和绿化职教与培训 |
| 17 | 刘宝民 | 中华人民共和国教育部职业教育发展中心副主任 | 总结词（摘录） |

| 论坛四　全球职业教育青年教师发展 | | | |
|---|---|---|---|
| 主持人：天津职业技术师范大学副校长　吕景泉 | | | |
| 排序 | 发言嘉宾姓名 | 发言嘉宾单位 / 职务 | 发言嘉宾题目 |
| 1 | 任友群 | 中华人民共和国教育部教师工作司司长 | 中国职业教育教师队伍建设的经验与展望 |
| 2 | 张金刚 | 天津职业技术师范大学党委书记 | 后疫情时代中国职教教师教育体系的创新发展 |

续表

| 排序 | 发言嘉宾姓名 | 发言嘉宾单位 / 职务 | 发言嘉宾题目 |
|---|---|---|---|
| 3 | 朱旭东 | 北京师范大学教育学部部长 | 世界百年未有之大变局中的中国职业教育 |
| 4 | 袁振国 | 华东师范大学教育学部主任 | 职业教师队伍建设的全球议题 |
| 5 | 阿米娅·鲍米克 | 马来西亚林肯大学学院校长 | 教师塑造人品 |
| 6 | 哲仁 | 泰国央拷镇行政管理机构理事会主席 | 中国教学模式在泰国鲁班工坊的运用与推广 |
| 7 | 黄维 | 中国科学院院士、西北工业大学学术委员会主任 | 数字化与职业教育教师发展 |
| 8 | 韩士兰 | 天津职业技术师范大学鲁班工坊国际发展研究中心外籍专家、埃塞俄比亚联邦职业技术培训学院机器人研发工程师 | 工程实践创新项目（EPIP）教学模式在职业教育领域的实施与应用 |
| 9 | 张建军 | 唐山工业职业技术学院党委副书记、院长 | 数字化背景下职教青年教师专业化发展的院校实践 |
| 10 | 明竺 | 全球化智库研究员 | 教育的影响：技术培训和技能培养项目如何促进“一带一路”合作 |
| 11 | 于立国 | 河北石油职业技术大学校长 | 产教融合背景下的职业教育“双师”队伍建设 |
| 12 | 史蒂文·罗兹 | 英国尼斯港塔尔伯特学院全球营运副校长 | 职业教育教师培训 |
| 13 | 何辉 | 浙江建设职业技术学院校长 | 高等职业院校促进青年教师全面发展的实践与创新 |
| 14 | 埃里克·斯沃斯 | 瑞士联邦职业教育与培训学院国际事务部主任 | 职业教育与培训的创新教学——以瑞士为例 |
| 15 | 米靖 | 天津职业技术师范大学职业教育学院院长 | 职业教育青年教师培养的中国模式——以天津职业技术师范大学为例 |

| 论坛五　中非职业教育合作与发展 | | | |
|---|---|---|---|
| 主持人：中国教育国际交流协会秘书长　王永利<br>中国教育国际交流协会职业教育与培训部主任　何　培 | | | |
| 排序 | 发言嘉宾姓名 | 发言嘉宾单位 / 职务 | 发言嘉宾题目 |
| 1 | 杨兵 | 天津市人民政府副市长 | 欢迎辞 |
| 2 | 阿道夫 · 姆肯达 | 坦桑尼亚教育、科学和技术部部长 | 坦桑尼亚技能教育转型 |
| 3 | 刘利民 | 中国教育国际交流协会会长 | 欢迎辞 |
| 4 | 方军 | 中华人民共和国教育部国际合作与交流司副司长 | 中非教育合作现状与展望 |
| 5 | 刘俊峰 | 中华人民共和国国家国际发展合作署地区二司司长 | 加强中非职教发展合作，助力非洲可持续发展 |
| 6 | 贺文萍 | 中国社会科学院西亚非洲研究所高级研究员 | 教育扶贫：如何破解制约非洲发展的三大短板之一 |
| 7 | 扎哈 · 法勒 | 非洲技术与应用型大学和学院协会秘书长 | 中非职业教育合作的探索 |
| 8 | 刘鸿武 | 浙江师范大学非洲研究院院长 | 进一步推进中非职业教育合作与优秀人才培养 |
| 9 | 吕景泉 | 天津职业技术师范大学副校长 | “一带一路”与“非洲 2063 愿景”对接，职业技能人才培养互鉴共享的机制建设 |
| 10 | 邦雅曼 · 穆瓦尼翁 | 加蓬职业教育部总学监 | 加蓬的职业培训改革 |
| 11 | 戴裕崴 | 天津轻工职业技术学院党委书记 | 分享中国职教模式　助力非洲区域经济发展——埃及鲁班工坊建设模式与实践 |

续表

| 排序 | 发言嘉宾姓名 | 发言嘉宾单位 / 职务 | 发言嘉宾题目 |
|---|---|---|---|
| 12 | 特舍里 · 博里查 | 埃塞俄比亚职业技术培训学院校长 | EPIP 模式在埃塞俄比亚职业教育中的实际应用 |
| 13 | 刘建超 | 成都航空职业技术学院校长 | 并肩助力中非职业教育合作　携手共育中非技术技能人才 |
| 14 | 奥塞依 · 乌苏阿齐奥 | 加纳库马西技术大学副校长 | 职业教育创新发展　强技赋能 Z 时代 |
| 15 | 易俊 | 重庆工程职业技术学院党委书记 | 构筑 CEC 产教融合共同体，共育“一带一路”技术技能人才 |
| 16 | 余有根 | 中国教育国际交流协会副秘书长 | 总结词 |

| 论坛六　“一带一路”合作与鲁班工坊建设发展 | | | |
|---|---|---|---|
| 主持人：天津职业大学党委副书记　王海龙 | | | |
| 排序 | 发言嘉宾姓名 | 发言嘉宾单位 / 职务 | 发言嘉宾题目 |
| 1 | 杨延 | 天津市鲁班工坊研究与推广中心副主任 | 天津鲁班工坊建设的探索与创新 |
| 2 | 玛悠丽 | 泰国大城技术学院院长 | 全球第一所鲁班工坊 |

续表

| 排序 | 发言嘉宾姓名 | 发言嘉宾单位 / 职务 | 发言嘉宾题目 |
|---|---|---|---|
| 3 | 何塞·卢卡斯 | 葡萄牙塞图巴尔理工学院鲁班工坊负责人 | 葡萄牙鲁班工坊和工业 4.0 |
| 4 | 于忠武 | 天津铁道职业技术学院校长 | 和衷共济　和合共生——鲁班工坊助力构建人类命运共同体 |
| 5 | 陈海荣 | 金华职业技术学院副校长 | 政校企协同，推动中卢职教合作走深走实——金华职业技术学院卢旺达办学实践 |
| 6 | 索勒赫佐达·乌迈德 | 塔吉克斯坦工业与新技术部副部长 | 后疫情时代职业技术教育的发展——新变化、新途径、新技能 |
| 7 | 严学斌 | 中国土木工程集团有限公司党委副书记 | 协同推动鲁班工坊走向世界　着力构建“一带一路”人才培养生态雨林 |
| 8 | 伊丽莎白·阿得雷蒂 | 中国中材国际工程股份有限公司尼日利亚分公司人力总监 | 职业教育促进减除贫困和包容性增长的作用 |
| 9 | 岑咏 | 宁波职业技术学院副校长 | 政行企校四方联动　打造海外办学多元育人平台 |
| 10 | 艾哈迈德·埃尔萨巴格 | 埃及艾因夏姆斯大学工程学院副院长 | 埃及职业培训战略的发展 |
| 11 | 刘斌 | 鲁班工坊建设联盟理事长 | 夯实“中国职教品牌”走出去的根基——鲁班工坊建设联盟工作介绍 |
| 12 | 特舍里·博里查 | 埃塞俄比亚职业技术培训学院校长 | EPIP 教学法在埃塞俄比亚鲁班工坊的应用 |
| 13 | 张巾帼 | 天津中德应用技术大学副校长 | 聚焦人才培养，坚持“六化并举”探索应用技术大学鲁班工坊建设新模式 |
| 14 | 沙赫里约尔·萨杜洛佐达 | 塔吉克斯坦技术大学副校长 | 中塔合作共建鲁班工坊，促进职业教育合作与友谊的发展 |

| 论坛七　普通（学术）教育与职业教育协调发展 | | | |
|---|---|---|---|
| 主持人：北京大学教育学院副院长　哈　巍 | | | |
| 排序 | 发言嘉宾姓名 | 发言嘉宾单位 / 职务 | 发言嘉宾题目 |
| 1 | 阎凤桥 | 北京大学教育学院院长、联合国教科文组织亚太地区高等教育讲席 | 欢迎辞 |
| 2 | 玛拉 · 布鲁贾 | 欧洲职业培训发展中心副所长 | 全面审视普通教育与职业教育协调发展 |
| 3 | 杨钋 | 北京大学教育经济研究所管理委员会委员 | 亚洲职业教育与普通教育协调发展经验 |
| 4 | 金宪 | 亚洲基础设施投资银行社会基础设施局局长 | 后疫情时代技能发展的挑战 |
| 5 | 李善华 | 亚洲开发银行社会部门首席专家 | 职业教育的机遇与挑战：南亚的经验 |
| 6 | 谢莉花 | 同济大学职业技术教育学院副教授 | 普职协调发展：中德比较与互鉴 |
| 7 | 李健 | 印度尼西亚文化与教育部职业教育与工商业协调合作部门主任 | ABG-CM 在加强职业教育中的角色 |
| 8 | 卢兰兰 | 亚洲开发银行高级项目官 | 亚洲开发银行支持中国 TVET 的项目经验 |
| 9 | 孙善学 | 中国职业技术教育学会副会长、北京外国语大学教授 | 中国职业教育贯通培养体系 |
| 10 | 托马斯 · F · 雷明顿 | 美国埃默里大学政治学系古德里奇 · C · 怀特名誉荣休教授 | STEM 教育与职业技术教育 |
| 11 | 阿尔加济诺娃 · 卡拉姆卡斯 | 哈萨克斯坦教育部技术与职业教育司技能合作办公室主任 | 在普通（学术）教育与职业教育协调发展论坛上的发言 |

| 论坛八　技能重塑与终身学习 | | | |
|---|---|---|---|
| 主持人：国家开放大学副校长　范贤睿 | | | |
| 排序 | 发言嘉宾姓名 | 发言嘉宾单位 / 职务 | 发言嘉宾题目 |
| 1 | 荆德刚 | 国家开放大学党委书记、校长 | 欢迎辞 |
| 2 | 戴维·阿乔莱纳 | 联合国教科文组织终身学习研究所所长 | 拓展高等教育范围：从学位教育到灵活的技能重塑 |
| 3 | 高文兵 | 中国成人教育协会会长 | 技能教育与培训的新使命——以终身学习助力新时代技能强国战略实施 |
| 4 | 陈善意 | 泰王国驻华大使馆科技处公使衔参赞 | 泰国的技能重塑、技能提升及新技能 |
| 5 | 拉明·B·曼内 | 冈比亚国家认证与质量保证委员会质量保证部主任 | 技能重塑与终身学习 |
| 6 | 乔纳森·莱杰 | 英国国际贸易部职业技术教育与培训专家、专业特许协会专家 | 面向未来的职业成功技能 |
| 7 | 马尔西奥·波赫曼 | 巴西卢拉研究所所长 | 数字时代终身教育面临的挑战 |
| 8 | 王飞 | 中华人民共和国人力资源和社会保障部职业能力建设司技工院校管理处处长 | 大力发展技工教育 |
| 9 | 西蒙·卡尔亨 | 英国特许证券与投资协会首席执行官 | 金融行业技能重塑和技能提升的终身学习 |
| 10 | 林群声 | 香港都会大学校长 | 香港职业专才教育：挑战与策略 |
| 11 | 程洪莉 | 中关村学院院长 | 新时代城市终身职业技能培训体系的建构 |
| 12 | 约翰·克莱顿 | 新西兰国立毛利学院教授 | 新西兰视角下的终身学习 |
| 13 | 安德烈·布里 | 瑞士技能联合会主席 | 通识化与专业化：职业体系中的技能提升与重塑 |

| 论坛九　职业教育助推全球减贫进程 | | | |
|---|---|---|---|
| 主持人：中国乡村振兴与发展研究中心主任　北京师范大学中国扶贫研究院院长　张　琦 | | | |
| 排序 | 发言嘉宾姓名 | 发言嘉宾单位 / 职务 | 发言嘉宾题目 |
| 1 | 延欣 | 国家乡村振兴局考核评估司副司长 | 雨露计划：职教赋能就业增收 |
| 2 | 汤敏 | 国务院参事、友成基金会副理事长 | 如何大规模、低成本、高效率地培养乡村振兴人才 |
| 3 | 布鲁纳·卡拉多 | 荷兰马斯特里赫特大学博士 | 教育在消除贫穷方面的角色 |
| 4 | 萧进平 | 马来西亚国际文化交流中心首席顾问、拿督 | 减贫与包容性增长 |
| 5 | 迪帕克·埃尔默 | 瑞士发展与合作署经济与教育科科长 | 瑞士发展合作组织中的职业技能发展 |
| 6 | 陈炳雄 | 香港大学亚洲创业及营商价值研究中心副总监 | 教育创新为全球减贫之催化剂 |
| 7 | 克利奥法斯·高井佐 | 赞比亚技术教育、职业和创业培训局局长 | 通过技术教育、职业和创业培训解决青年失业问题 |
| 8 | 孔智博 | 乌干达鲁扬子理工学院院长 | 将学术和职业教育纳入乌干达教育体系 |
| 9 | 巴卡图拉·恩祖齐·玛丽·玛德琳 | 刚果（金）外交学院负责人 | 刚果（金）外交学院孔子学院对刚果（金）职业培训扶贫的影响 |
| 10 | 迈克尔·克劳斯 | 德国汉斯·赛德尔基金会在华农村发展项目首席代表 | 职业教育对乡村振兴的贡献：总体构想与特定情形 |

续表

| 排序 | 发言嘉宾姓名 | 发言嘉宾单位 / 职务 | 发言嘉宾题目 |
|---|---|---|---|
| 11 | 卡洛斯·欣里希森 | 智利圣塞瓦斯蒂安大学数字设计与创意产业学院院长 | 值得进行的对话：使学习计划与社会和行业需求保持一致 |
| 12 | 宁亚宁 | 云南省乡村振兴局副局长 | 职教一人，脱贫一户——云南职教扶贫精准阻断贫困代际传递 |
| 13 | 杨天仪 | 贵州省教育厅党组成员、副厅长 | 贵州省职业教育助推脱贫增收的实践 |
| 14 | 段福生 | 北京市昌平职业学校校长 | 精准扶贫中的职教作为——北京市昌平职业学校的思考与实践 |
| 15 | 李兴洲 | 北京师范大学中国乡村教育研究中心主任 | 职业教育扶贫减贫的内在优势与行动机理 |
| 16 | 单从凯 | 国家开放大学国家数字化学习资源中心主任 | 数字化学习助力乡村减贫 |
| 17 | 史枫 | 北京教育科学研究院终身学习与可持续发展教育研究所所长 | 贫困的个体归因与职业教育终身化应对策略 |
| 18 | 余德华 | 汉中职业技术学院党委书记 | 发挥职业教育优势，助力秦巴山区乡村振兴 |
| 19 | 苑大勇 | 北京外国语大学国际教育学院副院长 | “一带一路”职业教育合作与教育援助 |
| 20 | 范勇毅 | 兴安职业技术学院党委副书记、院长 | 多措并举助力乡村人才振兴 |
| 21 | 刘德云 | 聊城市技师学院党委副书记、院长 | 践行孔繁森精神“雨露计划”赋技减贫 |
| 22 | 达莎·桑切斯·马克西莫娃 | 厄瓜多尔大都会设计学院教授 | 拉丁美洲的贫困与高等教育：一个统计方法 |

| 论坛十　面向未来的职业教育课程变革 | | | |
|---|---|---|---|
| 主持人：华东师范大学教育学部职业教育与成人教育研究所所长　徐国庆 | | | |
| 排序 | 发言嘉宾姓名 | 发言嘉宾单位 / 职务 | 发言嘉宾题目 |
| 1 | 石伟平 | 华东师范大学职业教育与成人教育研究所名誉所长 | 什么样的教材是“好教材”？——职业教育教材评价的理论反思 |
| 2 | 穆罕默德·穆贾希德 | 埃及教育与技术教育部副部长 | 埃及抗击新型冠状病毒的对策及面向未来的埃及技术与职业教育课程改革 |
| 3 | 王国川 | 中华人民共和国教育部行业职业教育教学指导委员会工作办公室常务副主任 | 职业教育国家专业教学标准的建构逻辑 |
| 4 | 徐涵 | 沈阳师范大学辽宁省职业教育研究院教授 | 工业 4.0 背景下德国职业教育课程改革的基本特征及启示 |
| 5 | 赵志群 | 北京师范大学教育学部教授 | 职业能力评价研究 |
| 6 | 苏珊·韦伯 | 澳大利亚莫纳什大学教育、文化与社会学院教授 | 天壤之别抑或利益攸关：对职业教育、成人教育和高等教育界限的再思考 |
| 7 | 马成荣 | 南京工业职业技术大学党委副书记 | 人本理念与科技范式转型视域下职业本科课程变革的适应性分析 |
| 8 | 克里斯·泽克尔 | 美国俄亥俄州立大学教育与人类生态学院副教授 | 中等学校、社区 / 技术学院、大学和公司在开发职业 / 就业路径课程中的作用与合作 |
| 9 | 费利克斯·劳纳 | 德国不来梅大学技术与教育研究所创始所长 | 评价职业知识：什么样的知识是职业能力的基础 |
| 10 | 熊杰 | 加拿大阿尔伯塔省劳工与移民部教育评估专员 | 行业积极参与的加拿大高等职业教育课程：以阿尔伯塔省为例 |
| 11 | 吴国民 | 澳门科技大学酒店与旅游管理学院院长 | 职业教育四年制学位的选择 |
| 12 | 郭福春 | 浙江金融职业学院副校长 | 高职院校数字化教学资源开发与实践 |

续表

| 排序 | 发言嘉宾姓名 | 发言嘉宾单位 / 职务 | 发言嘉宾题目 |
|---|---|---|---|
| 13 | 苏珊·阿克兰·胡德 | 英国教育部常务秘书长 | 交流发言 |
| 14 | 吴学敏 | 南京工业职业技术大学党委书记 | 课程理论家与课程实践者对话 |
| 15 | 刘佳环 | 广州番禺职业技术学院副校长 | 课程理论家与课程实践者对话 |
| 16 | 鞠红霞 | 柳州职业技术学院副校长 | 课程理论家与课程实践者对话 |
| 17 | 董永华 | 上海第二工业大学附属浦东振华外经职业技术学校校长 | 课程理论家与课程实践者对话 |

| 论坛十一　职业教育与产业转型发展 | | | |
|---|---|---|---|
| 主持人：中华人民共和国工业和信息化部教育与考试中心副主任　左仁贵 | | | |
| 排序 | 发言嘉宾姓名 | 发言嘉宾单位 / 职务 | 发言嘉宾题目 |
| 1 | 科菲·恩盖桑 | 科特迪瓦技术教育、职业培训与学习部部长 | 科特迪瓦工业转型背景下的技术教育和职业培训构想 |
| 2 | 孙卫平 | 重庆电子工程职业学院党委书记 | 匠师协同·双能支撑·孵扶联动：创新能工巧匠培育模式助推产业提档升级 |
| 3 | 年温丹 | 缅甸科技部职业技术教育与培训司副司长 | 增强职业教育适应性，加快构建现代职业教育体系 |

续表

| 排序 | 发言嘉宾姓名 | 发言嘉宾单位 / 职务 | 发言嘉宾题目 |
|---|---|---|---|
| 4 | 乔纳森·莱杰 | 英国国际贸易部职业技术教育与培训专家 | 技能协作助力创新 |
| 5 | 岗川雄健 | 日本 SKO 株式会社社长 | 增强职业教育适应性，加快构建现代职业教育体系 |
| 6 | 蔡锦平 | 新加坡南洋理工学院国际合作与交流机构主任 | 适应型职教系统和校企合作——南洋理工学院经验 |
| 7 | 索克·钱里西 | 柬埔寨劳动与职业培训部职业技术教育与培训司特聘职业技术教育研究顾问、职业技术培训智库成员 | 柬埔寨的职业技术教育与培训体系和产业转型发展 |
| 8 | 易卜拉欣·穆罕默德·法里斯 | 埃中应用技术学院院长 | 埃及职业技术教育——以埃中应用技术学院（ECCAT）为例 |
| 9 | 李仕伟 | 马来西亚拉曼理工大学校长 | 职业教育与产业转型发展 |
| 10 | 孟山恩 | 柬埔寨工业技术学院院长 | 职业教育与产业转型发展 |
| 11 | 何新飞 | 奇安信科技集团股份有限公司副总裁 | “双教”变革，探索网络安全技能人才培养新模式 |
| 12 | 郝钊 | 中兴通讯政企中国营销事业部副总裁 | 助力产业数字化转型、赋能复合型技术技能人才 |
| 13 | 关志伟 | 天津中德应用技术大学副校长 | 制造业转型发展背景下应用技术型本科院校人才培养模式研究 |
| 14 | 通萨摩 | 柬埔寨劳动与职业培训部职业技术教育与培训司副司长 | 柬埔寨职业技术教育与培训的数字化 |
| 15 | 孟繁锡 | 英国教育科技协会专家 | 职业技术教育在现代农业发展中的角色与作用 |
| 16 | 安晖 | 中国电子信息产业发展研究院副总工程师 | 新时期产业转型现状与发展动向 |
| 17 | 陶炜 | 国家工业信息安全发展研究中心系统所所长 | 数字化转型升级背景下关于职业教育提质增效的思考 |
| 18 | 卢小平 | 北京信息职业技术学院校长 | 数字经济崛起与职业教育变革 |

## 论坛十二　职业教育校企协同育人模式创新

主持人：南京工业职业技术大学党委书记　吴学敏

| 排序 | 发言嘉宾姓名 | 发言嘉宾单位 / 职务 | 发言嘉宾题目 |
|---|---|---|---|
| 1 | 林宇 | 中华人民共和国教育部职业教育与成人教育司副司长 | 交流发言 |
| 2 | 柯马凯 | 中国工合国际委员会主席、北京培黎职业学院理事 | “手脑并用、创造分析”的培黎职业教育 |
| 3 | 阿卜杜霍里克佐达·鲁特菲亚 | 塔吉克斯坦教育和科学部副部长 | 后疫情时代塔吉克斯坦职业教育的发展 |
| 4 | 陈理圣 | 新加坡教育部高教规划司司长 | 新加坡对产学研合作教育模式创新的看法 |
| 5 | 方乃纯 | 中华职业教育社党组书记、总干事 | 中国特色学徒制的实践与探索 |
| 6 | 李安 | 英国皇家航空学会中国代表处荣誉主席 | 推动中国航天制造业劳动力转型 |
| 7 | 张保全 | 北京精雕科技集团有限公司执行总裁 | 精雕细琢分层育匠才 |
| 8 | 傅睿楠 | 空中客车（天津）总装有限公司总经理 | 空中客车与高校的校企合作 |
| 9 | 赛觉奈乌 | 缅甸科技部职业技术教育与培训司司长 | 缅甸职业技术教育与培训的转型 |
| 10 | 谢永华 | 南京工业职业技术大学校长 | “三型协同”跨境校企合作培养人才探索 |
| 11 | 郑棉发 | 柬华理事总会常务副会长 | 中文 + 职业教育在柬埔寨的实施 |

续表

| 排序 | 发言嘉宾姓名 | 发言嘉宾单位 / 职务 | 发言嘉宾题目 |
|---|---|---|---|
| 12 | 邢晖 | 国家教育行政学院学术委员会主任 | 中国职业教育校企双元育人的政策与实践 |
| 13 | 施泰德 | 德国汉斯·赛德尔基金会上海代表处首席代表 | 学习德国职业教育校企合作新思考 |
| 14 | 党张波 | 华为技术有限公司人才发展部教育业务总经理 | 校企协同育人：华为 ICT 数字化人才培养实践 |
| 15 | 周琳 | 美国贝茨技术学院校长、首席执行官 | 加强校企合作 加速学生成功 |
| 16 | 宋凯 | 有色金属工业人才中心副主任 | 发挥企业办学主体作用，创新校企联合育人机制 |
| 17 | 乔里克·亚姆夫瓦 | 中国—赞比亚职业技术学院赞方校长 | 校企合作，为赞比亚培养高技能人才而努力 |
| 18 | 程时兴 | 武汉铁路职业技术学院校长 | 校企“双主体”育人，提高人才培养适应性 |
| 19 | 陈强兵 | 用友集团新道科技股份有限公司董事长 | 用中国实践，育数智新人——用友产教融合最佳实践分享 |
| 20 | 安德睿 | 博世汽车部件（苏州）有限公司执行总裁 | 博世学徒制和一线人才发展 |
| 21 | 周保平 | 黄河水利职业技术学院党委书记 | 连接黄河与赞比西河的人才培养驿站—校企协同培养水利国际化技能人才模式探索与实践 |
| 22 | 马克·奥尔德肖 | 惠灵顿联合理工学院首席执行官 | 教产合作——新西兰的经验分享 |

| 论坛十三　职业院校科学教育发展 | | | |
|---|---|---|---|
| 主持人：天津中德应用技术大学党委书记　张兴会 | | | |
| 排序 | 发言嘉宾姓名 | 发言嘉宾单位 / 职务 | 发言嘉宾题目 |
| 1 | 张卫红 | 中国科学院院士、西北工业大学副校长 | 欢迎辞 |
| 2 | 陈军 | 中国科学院院士、南开大学副校长 | 加快职业技术教育，服务国家“双碳”战略 |
| 3 | 杨焕明 | 中国科学院院士、深圳华大基因理事长 | 有机融入科学教育　助推职业教育高质量创新发展 |
| 4 | 张双南 | 中国科学院高能物理研究所研究员 | 科学教育的三位一体：科学史、科学方法与科学知识 |
| 5 | 卢双盈 | 天津市科学技术协会副主席 | 科学教育在职业教育“一体化”教学改革中的作用 |
| 6 | 璩静 | 百度集团副总裁 | 共育 AI 沃土，人人皆可成才——人工智能时代的人才培养理念与实践 |
| 7 | 陈文莉 | 新加坡南洋理工大学教授 | 科技与教学法支持的协作科学论证 |
| 8 | 吴敏 | 中国科学技术大学教授、安徽信息工程学院校长 | 构建学科和专利竞赛体系　培养学生实践和创新能力 |
| 9 | 潘海生 | 天津大学教育质量管理处副处长 | 打造技术创新服务平台　助力区域经济高质量发展 |
| 10 | 熊熙 | 成都航空职业技术学院副校长 | “科普—科创—科研”三位一体的航空科教融合育人实践 |
| 11 | 黄仕初 | 广东科学技术职业学院党委书记 | 创新科学教育模式，立足提高科学素养 |
| 12 | 成军 | 金华职业技术学院副校长 | 做强平台、创新载体，科学教育助力高职教育高质量发展 |
| 13 | 马姆达利·巴克提耶 | 塔吉克斯坦矿业冶金学院校长 | 塔吉克斯坦职业技能教育现状与发展 |
| 14 | 埃贡·米勒 | 德国开姆尼茨工业大学教授 | 未来科学教育与职业教育高水平发展面临的挑战和实现方法 |

| 论坛十四　职业院校工程教育发展 | | | |
|---|---|---|---|
| 主持人：天津职业技术师范大学副校长　阎　兵 | | | |
| 排序 | 发言嘉宾姓名 | 发言嘉宾单位 / 职务 | 发言嘉宾题目 |
| 1 | 谭建荣 | 中国工程院院士、浙江大学教授 | 建设一流工程学科，培养一流技术人才 |
| 2 | 金子元久 | 日本国立筑波大学教授 | 工程教育的基本问题 |
| 3 | 丁荣军 | 中国工程院院士、中国中车首席科学家 | 高铁工匠培养之道——打造具有全球竞争力的高技能人才培养基地 |
| 4 | 孙建安 | 德国施特拉尔松德孔子学院院长 | 协同培养高素质技能人才——德国双元制高等教育 |
| 5 | 陈吉红 | 武汉华中数控股份有限公司董事长 | 智能制造人才培养与实训教学创新 |
| 6 | 尤哈 · 豪塔宁 | 芬兰于韦斯屈莱应用科技大学专业教师教育学院院长 | VET 教师在持续学习中的挑战 |
| 7 | 谢永华 | 南京工业职业技术大学校长 | 职业本科“三性一体化”人才培养模式与工程教育实践 |
| 8 | 陈晓明 | 中国机械工业联合会教育培训部主任 | 中国先进制造业发展中的职业院校工程教育要素浅析 |
| 9 | 吴新林 | 中国中车集团有限公司人力资源中心副主任 | 中国中车产教融合育人之道 |
| 10 | 徐国胜 | 世界技能大赛中国（天津）研究中心主任、天津职业技术师范大学工程实训中心主任 | 工程化在职业技术技能人才培养中的实践与探索 |
| 11 | 尹万建 | 湖南汽车工程职业学院院长 | 开窗破壁，创新赋能高职院校汽车工程人才培养 |
| 12 | 刘永亮 | 陕西工业职业技术学院院长 | 服务制造强国战略　职业教育大有可为 |
| 13 | 耿洁 | 工程实践创新项目（EPIP）国际教育联盟顾问、天津市教育科学研究院职业教育研究中心主任 | 工程实践创新项目（EPIP）教学模式应用与推广研究 |
| 14 | 龚方红 | 无锡职业技术学院院长 | 技术引领、四方协同，服务技能型社会建设 |

# Appendix 2 List of Speakers of 14 Parallel Sessions

| Parallel Session 1 Artificial Intelligence Impacts on Innovation in Vocational Education | | | |
|---|---|---|---|
| Moderator: Zhao Zhiqun, Professor of Faculty of Education, Beijing Normal University, P. R. China | | | |
| Order | Name | Institution and Position | Title |
| 1 | Luo Fangshu | Director of Center for Scientific Research and Development in Higher Education Institutes, Ministry of Education, P.R.China (CSRD) | Welcome Remarks |
| 2 | Gong Ke | Executive Director of the Chinese Institute of New Generation Artificial Intelligence Development Strategies (CINGAI) | Digital Transformation in Vocational Education: Why, What, How |
| 3 | Zhan Tao | Director of UNESCO Institute for Information Technologies in Education (IITE) | Artificial Intelligence (AI) in TVET: UNESCO's Perspective |
| 4 | Fu Qiang | Deputy Director of the School of Business & Services, Institute of Technical Education, Singapore | Using AI Applications to Improve and Enhance Teaching & Learning—A Singapore Perspective |
| 5 | Philipp Pohlenz | Vice President of the Faculty of Humanities, Social Sciences and Education, Otto von Guericke University Magdeburg (OVGU), Germany | Change Is the Only Constant: New Demands Towards Higher and Vocational Education in an Era of Artificial Intelligence—Responses of Educational Research and Development |
| 6 | Wolfgang Paul Straube | Head of Engineering & Innovation, Knorr-Bremse Railway Vehicle Systems Co., Ltd., Germany | Knorr-Bremse Systems for Railway Vehicles—Intelligent Technology & Enhancing Training of Technical Personnel |
| 7 | Benjamin Inden | Deputy Director of Technology Engineering Department, DIPLOMA University of Applied Sciences North Hesse, Germany | Improvement of Distance Education by Transformer Networks |
| 8 | Tian Min | President of Nanjing Vocational College of Information Technology, China | Thinking and Practice on the Construction of Artificial Intelligence Major Group in Higher Vocational Education |

Continued

| Order | Name | Institution and Position | Title |
|---|---|---|---|
| 9 | Ma Yanjun | General Manager, Baidu AI Platform & Ecosystem, Baidu Inc., China | Integration of Industry and Education to Cultivate Talents with AI Technology and Skills |
| 10 | Christian Liebelt | Professor of Baden-Wuerttemberg Cooperative State University, Germany | Impacts of Artificial Intelligence on Vocational Education and Training |
| 11 | Paul Doyle | Head of the School of Computer Science, Technological University Dublin, Ireland | Future Thoughts on AI and Digital Enhanced Education |
| 12 | Xiang Shun | General Manager of National Vocational Education Virtual Simulation Demonstration Training Base, China | Application and Development of Artificial Intelligence in Vocational Education and Training |
| 13 | Zheng Wenxian | Vice President of Shenzhen Intellifusion Technologies Co., Ltd., China | Open Source AI Algorithm Training Paradigm Is Triggering the Breakthrough of AI Vocational and Technical Education |

| Parallel Session 2 Digital Transformation of Vocational Education | | | |
|---|---|---|---|
| Moderators: Wang Tianhong, Executive Vice President and Secretary-General of the Chinese Society for Technical and Vocational Education (CSTVE), China<br>Liu Jiantong, Deputy Secretary-General of the Chinese Institute of Electronics (CIE), China | | | |
| Order | Name | Institution and Position | Title |
| 1 | Lu Xin | President of the Chinese Society for Technical and Vocational Education (CSTVE) | Welcome Remarks |

Continued

| Order | Name | Institution and Position | Title |
|---|---|---|---|
| 2 | Huang Wei | Academician of Chinese Academy of Sciences, Director of Academic Committee of Northwestern Polytechnical University, China | Facing the Subversive System of Technology Innovation, Building a New Pattern for TVET International Collaboration in the New Era |
| 3 | Ge Daokai | Head of Jiangsu Education Department, China | Exploration on "Jiangsu-Style" of TVET Digitel Transformetion |
| 4 | Foo Sze-yeng | E-Learning Instructional Designer and Content Editor of Sontheast Asian Ministers of Education Organization Regional Centre for Vocational and Technical Education and Training (SEAMEO VOCTECH) | Digital Learning in Post-Pandemic Technical Vocational Training and Education (TVET) |
| 5 | Xu Jianling | President of Shenzhen Polytechnic, China | Transformation of Talent Cultivation Mode in Higher Vocational Institutions in the Digital Era |
| 6 | Ixaka Egurbide | Managing Director of Machine Tool Institute, Spain | Institutional Strategy for Digital Transition Support |
| 7 | Tang Zhaowu | Secretary of CPC Committee of Zhejiang Institute of Mechanical and Electrical Engineering, China | Digital Transformation of Vocational Education and Intelligent Manufacturing |
| 8 | Jan Heinze | Managing Director of Heinze Akademie, Germany | Digital Transformation in Vocational Training |
| 9 | Lu Kunjian | President of Guangdong Industry Polytechnic, China | Internet + Education Reform: Our Practical Exploration |
| 10 | Aileen Cai | Regional Head of Education of Association of Chartered Certified Accountants (ACCA) | Digitization Empowering the Cultivation of Professional Accountants for Future |
| 11 | Wang Danzhong | Secretary of CPC Committee of Nanjing Vocational College of Information Technology, China | Practice of Nanjing Vocational College of Information Technology: Digital Transformation of Vocational Colleges |
| 12 | Wang Hui | President of Shenzhen Institute of Information Technology, China | Stratify and Categorize Industry-Education Integration to Promote Innovation and Reform of Education |

Continued

| Order | Name | Institution and Position | Title |
|---|---|---|---|
| 13 | Chen Da | Director of Vocational and Adult Education Division of Zhejiang Provincial Education Department, China | Digital Transformation and the Reform of Zhejiang Vocational Education Model |
| 14 | Liu Jiren | Chairman of Neusoft Corporation, China | Digital Economy and Vocational Education |
| 15 | Chen Tao | Co-founder of iFlytek Co., Ltd. and President of Anhui Institute of Information Technology, China | Thinking and Practices about Project-Based Teaching in Digital Talents Training |
| 16 | Martin Fleischer | Honorary Professor of Shenzhen Polytechnic, China | From Industry 4.0 to VE 4.0 |
| 17 | Zhong Meihua | Director of Learning Service Expert Committee, Huawei Technologies Co., Ltd., China | The 5G Era Calls for a Prosperous Pan-Industry Digital Talent Ecosystem |
| 18 | Michael Bourlakis | Director of the Center of Logistics, Procurement and Supply Chain Management of Cranfield School of Management, Expert of the Association of Education and Technology (AET),UK | New Skills in Business and Log |
| 19 | Yee Wai Sim | Dean of the Faculty of Computing and Engineering of Quest International University, Malaysia | Transformation of Education in the Context of Fourth Industrial Revolution |
| 20 | Wei Qing | Chief Technology Officer of Microsoft (China) Co., Ltd. | Vocational Education in the Digital Intelligence Era |
| 21 | Zhang Xiaolei | Vice President of Beijing Information Technology College, China | Improving Teachers' Professional Ability in the Digital Era |
| 22 | Liu Qian | Secretary of CPC Committee, Director and Senior Vice President of Glodon Co., Ltd., China | Talent – Oriented — the Right Time for the Digital Transformation of Construction Talent Cultivation |

| Parallel Session 3 Green Skill Strategy for Sustainable Development | | | |
|---|---|---|---|
| Moderator: Liu Yufeng, Researcher of Center for Vocational Education Development, Ministry of Education, P. R. China (CVED), Senior Programme Specialist UNESCO | | | |
| Order | Name | Institution and Position | Title |
| 1 | Peng Binbai | General Director of Center for Vocational Education Development, Ministry of Education, P.R. China (CVED) | Welcome Remarks |
| 2 | Changhee Lee | Director of International Labour Organization (ILO) Country Office for China and Mongolia | Green Skill Strategy for Sustainable Development |
| 3 | James George | United Nations Development Programme (UNDP) Deputy Resident Representative in China | Green Skills and Sustainable Development |
| 4 | Borhene Chakroun | Director of the Division of Policies and Lifelong Learning Systems at UNESCO Headquarters | UNESCO's Global Strategy for TVET 2022–2029, with Highlight on Green and Sustainable Economic Transition |
| 5 | Shahbaz Khan | Director of the UNESCO Beijing Office | ESD+TVET Promoting Skills for Sustainable Development |
| 6 | Xiao Liping | Senior Education Specialist of the World Bank Office, Beijing | World Bank's GRID Approach for Skills Development During and After Pandemic Period |
| 7 | Phil Loveder | Executive Manager of National Centre for Vocational Education Research (NCVER), Australia | Skills for Green Innovation |
| 8 | Harald Kumpfert | Chairman of Northeast Branch of European Chamber, General Manager of GfM (Liaoning) Education Technology Ltd., Co. | German Dual-System and Promoting the Transformation of Vocational Education with the Green Technologies |
| 9 | Aslihan Arikan | General Secretary of Turkish Packaging Manufacturers Association (ASD), Türkiye | Manufacturing for Environmental Sustainability |

Continued

| Order | Name | Institution and Position | Title |
|---|---|---|---|
| 10 | Herbert Lonsdale | Global Skills Ambassador for the Institute of the Motor Industry (IMI) , UK | New Energy Automotive Skills |
| 11 | Zeng Tianshan | Vice Director of Center for Vocational Education Development, Ministry of Education, P.R.China (CVED) | Global Mission for Green Skills Development and the Chinese Path |
| 12 | Margarita Pavlova | Director of the UNESCO-UNEVOC Centre (Hong Kong) | Future Ready VTE: Green Skills for Sustainable Development |
| 13 | Xin Xiulan | Vice President of Beijing Polytechnic, China | Practical Exploration of Green Skills in Higher Vocational Colleges—Taking Beijing Polytechnic as an Example |
| 14 | Liang Kedong | President of Jinhua Polytechnic, China | Exploration and Practice of Jinhua Polytechnic on "Green Skills" Strategy Implementation: Three Integrations and Three Types |
| 15 | Zhang Sasa | Vice President of Hainan Technician College, China | Green Skills for Sustainable Development in FTP |
| 16 | Giacomo Bosio | Assistant of Green Skills Project of UNEVOC | SDGs and Greening TVET |
| 17 | Liu Baomin | Vice Director of Center for Vocational Education Development, Ministry of Education, P.R.China (CVED) | Summary |

| Parallel Session 4 Teacher Professional Development in Vocational Education | | | |
|---|---|---|---|
| Moderator: Lyu Jingquan, Vice President of Tianjin University of Technology and Education, China | | | |
| Order | Name | Institution and Position | Title |
| 1 | Ren Youqun | Director of the Department of Teacher Education, Ministry of Education, P.R. China | Experience and Prospects of the Construction of Vocational Education Teachers in China |
| 2 | Zhang Jingang | Secretary of CPC Committee, Tianjin University of Technology and Education, China | The Innovative Development of China's Vocational Teacher Education System in the Post-pandemic Era |
| 3 | Zhu Xudong | Director of the Faculty of Education, Beijing Normal University, China | Vocational Education in China Under the Great Changes Unseen in the World in a Century |
| 4 | Yuan Zhenguo | Director of the Faculty of Education, East China Normal University, China | Global Issues of Vocational Teacher Team Construction |
| 5 | Amiya Bhaumik | President of Lincoln University College, Malaysia | Teacher Builds Human Character |
| 6 | Jarun Youbrum | Chairman of Yangkhao Subdistrict Administrative Organization Council, Thailand | Application and Promotion of Chinese Teaching Model in Thailand Luban Workshop |
| 7 | Huang Wei | Academician of Chinese Academy of Sciences, Director of Academic Committee of Northwestern Polytechnical University, China | Digitization and Vocational Education Teacher Development |
| 8 | Handiso Selamu Yisihak | Researcher of Luban Workshop International Development Research Center of Tianjin University of Technology and Education, Robot R&D Engineer from Federal Democratic Republic of Ethiopia Technical and Vocational Training Institute | Engineering Practice Innovation Project (EPIP) Teaching Model Implementation and Application in Technical and Vocational Education and Training (TVET) Sector |

Continued

| Order | Name | Institution and Position | Title |
|---|---|---|---|
| 9 | Zhang Jianjun | Deputy Secretary of CPC Committee and President of Tangshan Polytechnic College, China | College Practice for Professional Development of Young Teachers in Digital Background |
| 10 | Zoon Ahmed Khan | Research Fellow at the Center for China and Globalization (CCG) | Impact Through Education: How Technical Training and Skills Development Programs Are Facilitating the "Belt and Road" Cooperation |
| 11 | Yu Liguo | President of Hebei Petroleum University of Technology, China | "Dual Certified" TVET Team Construction Under the Background of Integration of Production and Education |
| 12 | Steven Rhodes | Assistant Principal Worldwide Operations, Neath Port Talbot College and Coleg Powys (NPTC) Group of Colleges, UK | Vocational Teacher Training |
| 13 | He Hui | President of Zhejiang College of Construction, China | Practice and Innovation of Promoting the All-Round Development of Young Teachers in Higher Vocational Colleges |
| 14 | Eric Swars | Head of International Affairs of the Swiss Federal University for Vocational Education and Training (SFUVET) | Innovative Teaching and Training in VET—The Swiss Case |
| 15 | Mi Jing | Dean of School of Vocational Education in Tianjin University of Technology and Education, China | China Model of the Development of Young Faculty in Vocational Education—The Case of Tianjin University of Technology and Education |

Parallel Session 5 China-Africa TVET Cooperation Forum

Moderator: Wang Yongli, Secretary-General of China Education Association for International Exchange (CEAIE)
He Pei, Director of Department of TVET and Professional Training of China Education Association for International Exchange (CEAIE)

| Order | Name | Institution and Position | Title |
|---|---|---|---|
| 1 | Yang Bing | Vice Mayor of Tianjin Municipal People's Government, China | Opening Remarks |
| 2 | Adolf Mkenda | Minister of Education, Science and Technology, Tanzania | Skill and Educational Transformation in Tanzania |
| 3 | Liu Limin | President of China Education Association for International Exchange (CEAIE) | Opening Remarks |
| 4 | Fang Jun | Deputy Director General, Department of International Cooperation and Exchanges, Ministry of Education, P.R. China | Current Situation and Prospects of China-Africa TVET Cooperation |
| 5 | Liu Junfeng | Director General, Second Department of Regional Affairs, China International Development Cooperation Agency | Strengthen China and Africa's Development Cooperation in TVET to Contribute to Africa's Sustainable Development |
| 6 | He Wenping | Senior Researcher at Institute of West-Asian and African Studies (IWAAS), Chinese Academy of Social Sciences (CASS) | Poverty Alleviation Through Education: How to Crack One of the Three Shortcomings Constraining Africa's Development |
| 7 | Jahou Faal | Secretary General of Association of Technical Universities and Polytechnics in Africa (ATUPA) | Exploration in Promoting China-Africa Vocational Education Cooperation |
| 8 | Liu Hongwu | Director of Institute of African Studies, Zhejiang Normal University, China | Enhancing Cooperation Between China and Africa to Cultivate Vocational and Technical Talents |

Continued

| Order | Name | Institution and Position | Title |
|---|---|---|---|
| 9 | Lyu Jingquan | Vice President of Tianjin University of Technology and Education, China | The "Belt and Road" Meets the "Agenda 2063"—Mechanism Construction of Mutual Learning and Sharing of Cultivating Vocational and Technical Talents |
| 10 | Benjamin Moignon | Senior Pedagogical Inspector of Minister of Vocational Training, Gabon | Vocational Training in Gabon |
| 11 | Dai Yuwei | Secretary of CPC Committee of Tianjin Light Industry Vocational Technical College, China | Sharing Chinese Vocational Education Mode and Promoting Regional Economic Development in Africa—Construction Mode and Practice of Egypt Luban Workshops |
| 12 | Teshale Berecha | Director General of Federal Technical and Vocational Training Institute, Ethiopia | Practical Application of EPIP Model in Vocational Education of Ethiopia |
| 13 | Liu Jianchao | President of Chengdu Aeronautic Polytechnic, China | To Boost China-Africa TVET Cooperation Side by Side, to Foster Chinese and African Skilled Talents Hand in Hand |
| 14 | Osei Wusu-Achaw | Vice Chancellor of Kumasi Technical University, Ghana | TVET Innovation and Development, Strong Technology to Empower Generation Z |
| 15 | Yi Jun | Secretary of CPC Committee of Chongqing Vocational Institute of Engineering, China | Build a CEC Industry-Education Integration Community, and Jointly Educate Skilled and Technical Talents of the "Belt and Road" |
| 16 | Yu Yougen | Deputy Secretary-General of China Education Association for International Exchange (CEAIE) | Closing for China-Africa TVET Cooperation Forum |

| Parallel Session 6 "The Belt and Road Initiative" and Luban Workshop | | | |
|---|---|---|---|
| Moderator: Wang Hailong, Deputy Secretary of CPC Committee of Tianjin Vocational Institute, China | | | |
| **Order** | **Name** | **Institution and Position** | **Title** |
| 1 | Yang Yan | Deputy Director of Tianjin Luban Workshop Research and Promotion Center, China | Exploration and Innovation of Luban Workshop Construction in Tianjin |
| 2 | Mayuree Sriraboot | Director of Ayutthaya Technical College, Thailand | The First Luban Workshop in the Globe |
| 3 | José Lucas | Head of Luban Workshop at Polytechnic Institute of Setúbal, Portugal | Portuguese Luban Workshop and Industry 4.0 |
| 4 | Yu Zhongwu | President of Tianjin Railway Technical and Vocational College, China | Luban Workshop Helps Build a Community with a Shared Future for Mankind |
| 5 | Chen Hairong | Vice President of Jinhua Polytechnic, China | Government-School-Enterprise Collaboration to Promote the Concrete China-Rwanda Vocational Education Cooperation—The Practice of Jinhua Polytechnic in Rwanda |
| 6 | Solehzoda Umed | Deputy Minister of Industry and New Technologies of Tajikistan | The Development of Vocational and Technical Education in the Post-pandemic Era—New Changes, New Approaches and New Skills |
| 7 | Yan Xuebin | Deputy Secretary of CPC Committee of China Civil Engineering Construction Corporation | Working Together to Build Up a Global Luban Workshop and an Ecosystem for "Belt and Road Initiative" Talents |
| 8 | Elizabeth Adereti | Human Resource Manager of Sinoma International Engineering Co., Ltd, Nigeria | Vocational Education for Poverty Reduction and Inclusive Growth |
| 9 | Cen Yong | Vice President of Ningbo Polytechnic, China | Developing an Inclusive International Education Platform Through Government-Industry-Corporate-School Cooperation |
| 10 | Ahmed Elsabbagh | Deputy Dean of Faculty of Engineering, Ain Shams University, Egypt | Development of Vocational Training Strategy in Egypt |

Continued

| Order | Name | Institution and Position | Title |
|---|---|---|---|
| 11 | Liu Bin | General Director of Luban Workshop Construction Alliance, China | Strengthen the Foundation of "China's TVET Brand Going Global"—Introduction of Luban Workshop Construction Alliance |
| 12 | Teshale Berecha | President of Technical and Vocational Training Institute, Ethiopia | Application of EPIP Model in Ethiopian Luban Workshop |
| 13 | Zhang Jinguo | Vice President of Tianjin Sino-German University of Applied Sciences, China | Focus on Talents Cultivation, Keep "Six Integrations" to Explore a New Model of Luban Workshop Construction Based on University of Applied Sciences |
| 14 | Shahriyor Sadullozoda | Vice President of Tajik Technical University named after academician M.S. Osimi, Tajikistan | Luban Workshop Co-founded by China and Tajikistan: Promoting Collaboration and Friendship in TVET |

| Parallel Session 7 Integration of Academic and Vocational Education | | | |
|---|---|---|---|
| Moderator: Ha Wei, Associate Dean of Graduate School of Education, Peking University, China | | | |
| Order | Name | Institution and Position | Title |
| 1 | Yan Fengqiao | Dean of Graduate School of Education, Peking University, China, UNESCO Chair on Higher Education in Asia and the Pacific | Welcome Remarks |
| 2 | Mara Brugia | Deputy Director of European Centre for the Development of Vocational Training (CEDEFOP) | Vocational Education and Training (VET) and Academic Education: A Holistic Perspective |

Continued

| Order | Name | Institution and Position | Title |
|---|---|---|---|
| 3 | Yang Po | Member of the Steering Committee of Institute of Economics of Education, Peking University, China | Integrating Vocational and General Education in Asian Economies |
| 4 | Hun Kim | Director General of Social Infrastructure Department, Asian Infrastructure Investment Bank | Challenges to Skills Development in the Post Pandemic Era |
| 5 | Sunhwa Lee | Principal Social Sector Specialist, Asian Development Bank | Challenges and Opportunities for Vocational Education: Experiences from South Asia |
| 6 | Xie Lihua | Associate Professor of School of Vocational and Technical Education, Tongji University, China | Coordinated Development of General Education and Vocational Education: Comparison and Mutual Learning Between China and Germany |
| 7 | Yudil Chatim | Head of Administration of Directorate of Partnership and Alignment of Vocational Education with Business and Industry, Indonesian Ministry of Culture and Education, Indonesia | The Role of ABG-CM in Strengthening Vocational Education |
| 8 | Lu Lanlan | Senior Project Officer, Asian Development Bank | ADB Project Experiences to Support TVET Sector Development in the PRC |
| 9 | Sun Shanxue | Vice President of the Chinese Society for Technical and Vocational Education, Professor of Beijing Foreign Studies University, China | Vocational Education Run-through Training System |
| 10 | Thomas F. Remington | Goodrich C. White Professor (Emeritus) of Political Science, Emory University, US | STEM Education and TVET |
| 11 | Algazinova Kalamkas | Head of Partnership and Skills Department, Department of Technical and Vocational Education of the Ministry of Education of Kazakhstan | Speech on Integration of Academic and Vocational Education |

| Parallel Session 8　Reskilling and Upskilling for Lifelong Learning | | | |
|---|---|---|---|
| Moderator: Fan Xianrui, Vice President of the Open University of China | | | |
| Order | Name | Institution and Position | Title |
| 1 | Jing Degang | Secretary of CPC Committee and President of the Open University of China | Welcome Remarks |
| 2 | David Atchoarena | Director of UNESCO Institute for Lifelong Learning | Broadening the Scope of Higher Education: From Degrees to Flexible Reskilling |
| 3 | Gao Wenbing | President of China Adult Education Association | New Mission of Skill Education and Training—Facilitate the Implemetation of Powerful Skilled Country Plan in the New Era with Lifelong Learning |
| 4 | Pasupha Chinvarasopak | Minister Counsellor (Science and Technology) of Royal Thai Embassy, China | Thailand's Reskill, Upskill, and Newskill |
| 5 | Lamin B. Manneh | Director of Quality Assurance, National Accreditation and Quality Assurance Authority (NAQAA), Gambia | Reskilling and Upskilling for Lifelong Learning |
| 6 | Jonathan Ledger | Technical and Vocational Education and Training (TVET) and Chartered Bodies Specialist, Department for International Trade, UK | Future Proof Skills for Successful Careers |
| 7 | Marcio Pochmann | President of the Institute of Lula, Brazil | The Challenge of Lifelong Education in the Digital Age |
| 8 | Wang Fei | Director of Technical School Administration Division, Department of Vocational Capacity Building, Ministry of Human Resources and Social Security, P.R. China | Vigorously Advance the Development of Technical Education |
| 9 | Simon Culhane | Chief Executive of the Chartered Institute for Securities and Investment, UK | Reskilling and Upskilling for Lifelong Learning in Financial Industry |
| 10 | Paul LAM Kwan-sing | President of Hong Kong Metropolitan University, China | Vocational and Professional Education in Hong Kong: Challenges and Strategies |

Continued

| Order | Name | Institution and Position | Title |
|---|---|---|---|
| 11 | Cheng Hongli | Principal of Zhongguancun Institute, China | Construction of Training System for Urban Lifelong Vocational Skills in the New Era |
| 12 | John Clayton | Professor of Te Whare Wānanga o Awanuiārangi, New Zealand | Lifelong Learning: A New Zealand View |
| 13 | André Burri | Director of SwissSkills, Switzerland | Generalization and Specialization: Up- and Re-skilling in Occupational Systems |

| Parallel Session 9 Vocational Education for Poverty Reduction and Inclusive Growth | | | |
|---|---|---|---|
| Moderator: Zhang Qi, Director of China Rural Revitalization and Development Research Center, President of China Institute for Poverty Reduction, Beijing Normal University, China | | | |
| Order | Name | Institution and Position | Title |
| 1 | Yan Xin | Deputy Director General of the Assessment and Evaluation Department of the National Rural Revitalization Bureau, China | Dewdrop Project: Vocational Education Promotes Employment and an Increase in Income |
| 2 | Tang Min | Counselor of the State Council, Vice Chairman of Youcheng Foundation, China | How to Train Rural Revitalization Talents on a Large Scale, at Low Cost and with High Efficiency? |
| 3 | Bruna Calado | Ph.D. of Maastricht University, the Netherlands | The Role of Professional Education in Poverty Reduction |
| 4 | Siow Chen Pin | Dato, Chief Advisor of International Cultural Communication Center, Malaysia | Poverty Reduction and Inclusive Growth |

Continued

| Order | Name | Institution and Position | Title |
|---|---|---|---|
| 5 | Diepak Elmer | Head of Economy and Education Section of the Swiss Agency for Development and Cooperation | Vocational Skills Development in Swiss Development Cooperation Organization |
| 6 | Chen Bingxiong | Associate Director of Centre for Asian Entrepreneurship and Business Values, the University of Hong Kong, China | Education Innovation as a Catalyst for Poverty Alleviation |
| 7 | Cleophas Takaiza | Director General of Technical Education, Vocational and Entrepreneurship Training Authority (TEVETA), Zambia | Tackling Youth Unemployment Through Technical Education, Vocational and Enterpreneurship Training (TEVET) |
| 8 | Oswald Ndoleriire | Principal of Luyanzi Institute of Technology, Uganda | Integration of Academic and Vocational Education in the Uganda Education System |
| 9 | Bakatula Nzuzi Marie Madeleine | Head of the Congolese Diplomatic Academy | Impact of the Confucius Institute of the Congolese Diplomatic Academy on Poverty Reduction Through Professional Training |
| 10 | Michael Klaus | Chief Representative of the Hans Seidel Foundation's Rural Development Projects in China | Contribution of Vocational Education to Rural Revitalization: General Thoughts and Situation Adaptions in China |
| 11 | Carlos Hinrichsen | Director of School of Digital Design and Creative Industries at the San Sebastián University, Chile | Dialogues Worth Having: Aligning Study Programs with Society and Industry Needs |
| 12 | Ning Yaning | Deputy Director of Rural Revitalization Bureau of Yunnan Province, China | One Person Engages in Vocational Education Means That One Household Is Lifted out of Poverty—Yunnan Implements Targeted Poverty Alleviation Through Vocational Education to Prevent the Intergenerational Transmission of Poverty |
| 13 | Yang Tianyi | Member of CPC Leadership Group and Deputy Director-General of the Department of Education of Guizhou Province, China | The Practice of Vocational Education in Guizhou Province to Promote Poverty Alleviation and Income Increase |

Continued

| Order | Name | Institution and Position | Title |
|---|---|---|---|
| 14 | Duan Fusheng | Principal of Beijing Changping Vocational School, China | The Contribution of Vocational Education in Precision Poverty Alleviation—The Thinking and Practice of Beijing Changping Vocational School |
| 15 | Li Xingzhou | Director of China Rural Education Research Center, Beijing Normal University, China | Internal Advantages and Action Mechanism of Poverty Reduction by Vocational Education |
| 16 | Shan Congkai | Director of the National Digital Learning Resource Center, the Open University of China | Digital Learning Helps Rural Poverty Alleviation |
| 17 | Shi Feng | Director of the Institute of Lifelong Learning and Education for Sustainable Development, Beijing Academy of Educational Sciences, China | Individual Attribution of Poverty and Coping Strategies of Lifelong Vocational Education |
| 18 | Yu Dehua | Secretary of CPC Committee of Hanzhong Vocational and Technical College, China | Exertion of Advantages of Vocational Education and Helping Rural Revitalization in Qinba Mountain Area |
| 19 | Yuan Dayong | Deputy Dean of Graduate School of Education, Beijing Foreign Studies University, China | Vocational Education Cooperation and Aid to Educational Development Under the Framework of the "Belt and Road" |
| 20 | Fan Yongyi | Deputy Secretary of CPC Committee and President of Xing'an Vocational and Technical College, China | The College Takes Multiple Measures to Help Rural Talents Revitalize |
| 21 | Liu Deyun | Deputy Secretary of CPC Committee and President of Technician College of Liaocheng City, China | Uphold the Kong Fansen Spirit and Achieve Poverty Alleviation by Teaching Skills Under the Framework of Dewdrop Project |
| 22 | Dasha Sánchez Maximova | Professor of Metropolitan Institute of Design, Ecuador | Poverty and Higher Education in Latin-America: A Statistical Approach |

| Parallel Session 10 Future-oriented Curriculum Reform in Vocational Education | | | |
|---|---|---|---|
| Moderator: Xu Guoqing, Director of Institute of Vocational and Adult Education, Faculty of Education, East China Normal University, China | | | |
| Order | Name | Institution and Position | Title |
| 1 | Shi Weiping | Honorary Director of Institute of Vocational and Adult Education, East China Normal University, China | What Kind of Textbook Is a "Good Textbook"?—A Theoretical Reflection on the Evaluation of Vocational Education Textbooks |
| 2 | Mohamed Megahed | Deputy Minister for Technical Education of the Ministry of Education and Technical Education, Egypt | Egypt's Response to Combatting COVID-19 Consequences & Future-Oriented Curriculum Reform in Technical & Vocational Education in Egypt |
| 3 | Wang Guochuan | Executive Deputy Director of the Office of TVET Industry Steering Committee of the Ministry of Education, P.R. China | The Logic of Constructing National Professional Teaching Standards for Vocational Education |
| 4 | Xu Han | Professor of Liaoning Vocational Technical Education Institute, Shenyang Normal University, China | Basic Characteristics and Enlightenment for Germany Vocational Education Curriculum Reformation Under Industry 4.0 Background |
| 5 | Zhao Zhiqun | Professor at Faculty of Education, Beijing Normal University, China | Research on Evaluation Methods of Professional Competence |
| 6 | Susan Webb | Professor at School of Education, Culture & Society, Monash University, Australia | Worlds Apart or Shared Interests: Rethinking the Divisions Between Vocational, Adult and Higher Education |
| 7 | Ma Chengrong | Deputy Secretary of CPC Committee of Nanjing Vocational University of Industry Technology, China | Adaptation Analysis of Vocational Undergraduate Curriculum Change in the Perspective of Humanistic Concept and Technology Paradigm Transformation |
| 8 | Chris Zirkle | Associate Professor of College of Education and Human Ecology, the Ohio State University, US | Roles and Cooperation Between Secondary Schools, Community/Technical Colleges, Universities and Companies in the Development of Vocational/Career Pathway Curriculum |

Continued

| Order | Name | Institution and Position | Title |
|---|---|---|---|
| 9 | Felix Rauner | Founding Director of the Institute for Technology and Education (ITB), University of Bremen, Germany | Assessment of Vocational Knowledge: What Kind of Knowledge Contributes to the Foundation of Vocational Competence |
| 10 | Xiong Jie | Education Assessor of the Ministry of Labour and Immigration, Government of Alberta, Canada | Industry Engagement in Postsecondary-Vocational-Education Curricula in Canada: The Case of Alberta |
| 11 | Ben Goh Kok Beng | Dean of Faculty of Hospitality and Tourism Management, Macau University of Science and Technology, China | Options of a 4 Year Degree for Vocational Education |
| 12 | Guo Fuchun | Vice President of Zhejiang Financial College, China | Development and Practice of Digital Teaching Resources in Higher Vocational Institutions |
| 13 | Susan Ackland-Hood | Permanent Secretary at the Department for Education, UK | Presentation |
| 14 | Wu Xuemin | General Secretary of CPC Committee of Nanjing Vocational University of Industry Technology, China | Dialogue Between Curriculum Theorists and Practitioners |
| 15 | Liu Jiahuan | Vice President of Guangzhou Panyu Polytechnic, China | Dialogue Between Curriculum Theorists and Practitioners |
| 16 | Ju Hongxia | Vice President of Liuzhou Vocational and Technical College, China | Dialogue Between Curriculum Theorists and Practitioners |
| 17 | Dong Yonghua | Principal of Pudong Zhenhua Foreign Trade Professional School affiliated to Shanghai Polytechnic University, China | Dialogue Between Curriculum Theorists and Practitioners |

| Parallel Session 11 Vocational Education and Industrial Restructuring | | | |
|---|---|---|---|
| Moderator: Zuo Rengui, Deputy Director of Education and Examination Center of Ministry of Industry and Information Technology (CEIAEC), P.R. China | | | |
| Order | Name | Institution and Position | Title |
| 1 | Koffi N'Guessan | Minister of Côte d'Ivoire Ministry of Technical Education, Vocational Training and Apprenticeship (METFPA) | Vision of the METFPA Within the Framework of the Industrial Transformation of Côte d'Ivoire |
| 2 | Sun Weiping | Secretary of CPC Committee of Chongqing College of Electronic Engineering, China | Integration of Craftsmen and Instructors · Dual Capabilities · Coordination of Cultivation and Support: Innovate the Craftsmen Cultivation Mode to Help Upgrade Industries |
| 3 | Nyan Win Than | Deputy Director General of the Department of Technical and Vocational Education and Training (DTVET), Ministry of Science and Technology, Myanmar | Making Vocational Education More Adaptable and Accelerate the Establishment of Modern Vocational Education System |
| 4 | Jonathan Ledger | Specialist of Technical and Vocational Education and Training (TVET), Department for International Trade, UK | Driving Innovation Through Skills Collaboration |
| 5 | Okagawa Yuken | President of SKO Corporation of Japan | Enhancing the Adaptability of Vocational Education and Accelerating the Construction of a Modern Vocational Education System |
| 6 | Chua Gim Peng | Senior Manager of Nanyang Polytechnic International, Singapore | Adaptive TVET System and Industry Collaboration—The NYP's Experience |
| 7 | SOK Chanrithy | TVET and Education Consultant and Member of TVET Thinktank of Directorate General of TVET of Ministry of Labour and Vocational Training, Cambodia | TVET System and Industrial Restructuring in Cambodia |
| 8 | Ibrahim Mohamed Fares | Dean of Egyptian Chinese College for Applied Technology, Egypt | Vocational and Technical Education in Egypt with Reference to the Egyptian-Chinese College for Applied Technology (ECCAT) |

Continued

| Order | Name | Institution and Position | Title |
|---|---|---|---|
| 9 | Lee Sze Wei | President of Tunku Abdul Rahman University of Management and Technology, Malaysia | Vocational Education and Industrial Restructuring |
| 10 | Moan Sam Oeurn | President of Advanced Institute of Technology, Cambodia | Vocational Education and Industrial Restructuring |
| 11 | He Xinfei | Vice President of QI-ANXIN Technology Group Inc., China | "Double Educators" Reform, Exploring a New Mode of Training Network Security Skills Talents |
| 12 | Hao Zhao | Vice President of Sales Department of Government-Enterprise, ZTE, China | Fuel Industrial Digitalization and Empower Compound Technical Talents |
| 13 | Guan Zhiwei | Vice President of Tianjin Sino-German University of Applied Sciences, China | Research on Talent Cultivation Mode in Application-Oriented Undergraduate Universities Under the Background of Transformation and Development of Manufacturing Industry |
| 14 | Thorng Samon | Deputy Director-General of Department of Technical Vocational Education and Training Management, Ministry of Labour and Vocational Training, Cambodia | Digitalization of TVET in Cambodia |
| 15 | Meng Fanxi | Expert of the Association of Education and Technology, UK | Role and Function of Vocational Education in the Development of Modern Agriculture |
| 16 | An Hui | Assistant Chief Engineer of China Center for Information Industry Development (CCID) | The Situation and Development of Industrial Restructuring in the New Era |
| 17 | Tao Wei | Director of Institute of Systems of CIC, China | Thoughts on Advancing Quality and Efficiency for Vocational Education Under the Background of Digital Transformation and Upgrading |
| 18 | Lu Xiaoping | Principal of Beijing Information Technology College, China | The Rise of Digital Economy and the Vocational Education Reform |

| Parallel Session 12 Innovation in Modes of Education Delivered Through Academia-Industry Collaboration | | | |
|---|---|---|---|
| Moderator: Wu Xuemin, Secretary of CPC Committee of Nanjing Vocational University of Industry Technology, China | | | |
| Order | Name | Institution and Position | Title |
| 1 | Lin Yu | Deputy Director of Department of Vocational and Adult Education of the Ministry of Education, P.R. China | Speech |
| 2 | Michael Crook | Chairman of International Committee for the Promotion of Chinese Industrial Cooperatives, Member of the Board of Beijing Bailie University | "Mind and Hand, Creation and Analysis"—The Bailie Model of Vocational Education |
| 3 | Abdulkholiqzoda Lutfiya | Deputy Minister of Education and Science of Tajikistan | Development of Professional and Vocational Education in Post Pandemic Period in Tajikistan |
| 4 | Tan Li Sheng | Director of Higher Education Planning Office of Ministry of Education, Singapore | Singapore's Perspective on Innovation in Modes of Education Delivered Through Academia-Industry Collaboration |
| 5 | Fang Naichun | Secretary of CPC Leading Group and Director General of China Vocational Education Association, China | Exploration and Practice of Apprenticeship with Chinese Characteristics |
| 6 | Julian McCormack | Honorary President of the Royal Aeronautical Society in China, UK | Enabling the Workforce Transformation in China Aerospace Manufacturing Industry |
| 7 | Zhang Baoquan | Chief Executive Officer of Beijing Jingdiao Group Co., Ltd., China | Cultivating Talents Through Innovative Dual Education Mode |
| 8 | Thomas Florian Mack | General Manager of Airbus (Tianjin) Final Assembly Co., Ltd. | School-Enterprise Cooperation Between Airbus and Universities |
| 9 | Sai Kyaw Naing Oo | Director General of the Department of Technical and Vocational Education and Training of the Ministry of Science and Technology, Myanmar | Transformation of TVET Education in Myanmar |

Continued

| Order | Name | Institution and Position | Title |
|---|---|---|---|
| 10 | Xie Yonghua | President of Nanjing Vocational University of Industry Technology, China | Exploration of Cultivating Innovative, Interdisciplinary and Applied Talents Through Cross-Border University-Enterprise Cooperation |
| 11 | Te Meang Huot | Executive Vice President of Federation of Khmer Chinese in Cambodia | Implementation of Chinese+Vocational Education in Cambodia |
| 12 | Xing Hui | Director of Academic Committee of National Academy of Education Administration, China | Policy and Practice on School-Enterprise Dual Education for Vocational Education in China |
| 13 | Georg Stadler | Chief Representative of Shanghai Office, Hanns Seidel Foundation, Germany | New Considerations About Learning from Cooperation Between Industry and Education on Vocational Training in Germany |
| 14 | Dang Zhangbo | General Manager of Education Business of Talent Development Department of Huawei Technologies Co., Ltd., China | School-Enterprise Collaborative Education: Huawei Practice of ICT Digital Talent Training |
| 15 | Zhou Lin | President and Chief Executive Officer of Bates Technical College, US | Foster Education-Industry Partnership to Accelerate Student Success |
| 16 | Song Kai | Deputy Director of China Nonferrous Metal Industry Human Resource Center, China | Innovation in Mechanisms of Education Delivered Through Academia-Industry Collaboration by Giving Full Play to the Main Role of Enterprises in Running Schools |
| 17 | Jorick Yamvwa | Principal of Local Affairs for Sino-Zam Vocational College of Science and Technology, Zambia | School-Enterprise Cooperation, and Strive to Cultivate Highly Skilled Talents for Zambia |
| 18 | Cheng Shixing | President of Wuhan Railway Vocational College of Technology, China | School and Enterprise Dual System Education, Enhance the Adaptability of Talent Cultivation |

Continued

| Order | Name | Institution and Position | Title |
| --- | --- | --- | --- |
| 19 | Chen Qiangbing | Chairman of Yonyou Group Seentao Technology Co., Ltd., China | Cultivate Intellectualized & Digitalized Talents with China's Practices—The Best Business Practice of Industry-Education Integration from Yonyou |
| 20 | Georges Andary | General Manager of Bosch Automotive Products (Suzhou) Co., Ltd. | Bosch Apprenticeship and Shop-Floor Talent Development |
| 21 | Zhou Baoping | Secretary of CPC Committee of Yellow River Conservancy Technical Institute, China | Talent Training Center Connecting the Yellow River and the Zambezi River—Exploration of School-Enterprise Joint Training of International Talents in Water Conservancy |
| 22 | Mark Oldershaw | Chief Executive of Whitireia and WelTel Polytechnic, New Zealand | Academia-Industry Collaboration—A New Zealand Experience |

| Parallel Session 13 Science Education Development in Vocational Education Institutions | | | |
| --- | --- | --- | --- |
| Moderator: Zhang Xinghui, Secretary of CPC Committee of Tianjin Sino-German University of Applied Sciences, China | | | |
| Order | Name | Institution and Position | Title |
| 1 | Zhang Weihong | Academician of the Chinese Academy of Sciences, Vice President of Northwestern Polytechnical University, China | Welcome Speech |
| 2 | Chen Jun | Academician of the Chinese Academy of Sciences, Vice President of Nankai University, China | Accelerating Vocational and Technical Education to Serve the National Carbon Peaking and Carbon Neutrality Goals |

Continued

| Order | Name | Institution and Position | Title |
|---|---|---|---|
| 3 | Yang Huanming | Academician of the Chinese Academy of Sciences, Chairman of BGI Group, China | Scientific Education Promotes the High-quality and Innovative Development of Vocational Education |
| 4 | Zhang Shuangnan | Researcher at the Institute of High Energy Physics of Chinese Academy of Sciences, China | Trinity of Science Education: History of Science, Scientific Methods and Scientific Knowledge |
| 5 | Lu Shuangying | Vice Chairman of Tianjin Association for Science and Technology, China | Role of Science Education in the Integrated Teaching Reform of Vocational Education |
| 6 | Qu Jing | Vice President of Baidu Co., Ltd., China | Co-cultivation of AI Fertile Soil, Everyone Can Become a Talent—Talent Training Concept and Practice in the Era of Artificial Intelligence |
| 7 | Chen Wenli | Professor of Nanyang Technological University, Singapore | Technological and Pedagogical Design for Computer-Supported Collaborative Argumentation in Science Learning |
| 8 | Wu Min | Professor of University of Science and Technology of China, President of Anhui Institute of Information Technology (AIIT), China | Building Discipline and Patent Competition System to Cultivate Students' Practical and Innovative Abilities |
| 9 | Pan Haisheng | Deputy Director of Education Quality Management Office of Tianjin University, China | Build Technical Skill Innovation Service Platform to Promote the High-quality Development of the Regional Economy |
| 10 | Xiong Xi | Vice President of Chengdu Aeronautic Polytechnic, China | Aviation Education Practice from the Perspective of Science Popularization, Innovation and Research |
| 11 | Huang Shichu | Secretary of CPC Committee of Guangdong Polytechnic of Science and Technology, China | Innovating the Mode of Science Education for Improving Scientific Literacy |

Continued

| Order | Name | Institution and Position | Title |
|---|---|---|---|
| 12 | Cheng Jun | Vice President of Jinhua Polytechnic, China | Strengthen Platform as Innovation Carrier, Driving the Quality Development with Mutually Motivated Scientific Education and Vocational Education |
| 13 | Mahmadali Bakhtiyor | President of Mining and Metallurgical Institute of Tajikistan | Current Situation and Development of Vocational and Technical Education in Tajikistan |
| 14 | Egon Mueller | Professor of Chemnitz University of Technology, Germany | Challenges and Solutions for the Future High-level Development of Science Education and Vocational Education |

| Parallel Session14 Engineering Education Development in Vocational Education Institutions | | | |
|---|---|---|---|
| Moderator: Yan Bing, Vice President of Tianjin University of Technology and Education, China | | | |
| Order | Name | Institution and Position | Title |
| 1 | Tan Jianrong | Academician of the Chinese Academy of Engineering, Professor of Zhejiang University, China | To Build a First-class Engineering Discipline and Train First-class Technical Personnel |
| 2 | Kaneko Motohisa | Professor of Tsukuba University, Japan | Fundamental Problems in Engineering Education |
| 3 | Ding Rongjun | Academician of the Chinese Academy of Engineering, Chief Scientist of CRRC Corporation Limited, China | Growth Path of High-speed Rail Artisans: Build a Globally Competitive Training Base for Highly Skilled Talents |
| 4 | Sun Jian'an | Director of Confucius Institute at Stralsund University of Applied Sciences, Germany | Collaborative Cultivation of High-quality Technical and Skilled Talents—German "Dual System" Higher Education |

Continued

| Order | Name | Institution and Position | Title |
|---|---|---|---|
| 5 | Chen Jihong | Chairman of Wuhan Huazhong Numerical Control Co., Ltd., China | Intelligent Manufacturing Talent Training and Practical Teaching Innovation |
| 6 | Juha Hautanen | Head of Department at the School of Professional Teacher Education, JAMK University of Applied Sciences, Finland | VET Teachers Challenge of Continuous Learning |
| 7 | Xie Yonghua | President of Nanjing Vocational University of Industry Technology, China | "Three-Features-in-One" Talents Training Model for Vocational Education and Engineering Education Practice |
| 8 | Chen Xiaoming | Director of Education and Training Department of China Machinery Industry Federation | Analysis of Engineering Education Elements in Vocational College with China's Advanced Manufacturing Development |
| 9 | Wu Xinlin | Deputy Director of Human Resources Center, CRRC Corporation Limited, China | The Way of Integrated Education of CRRC |
| 10 | Xu Guosheng | Director of Worldskills Competition China Research Center (Tianjin), Director of Engineering Training Center of Tianjin University of Technology and Education, China | Practice and Exploration of Engineering in the Training of Vocational and Technical Talents |
| 11 | Yin Wanjian | President of Hunan Automotive Engineering Vocational College, China | Innovation and Enabling Vocational College Automotive Engineering Talent Training |
| 12 | Liu Yongliang | President of Shaanxi Polytechnic Institute, China | Servicing the Country's Manufacturing Power Strategy, Vocational Education Has a Great Potential |
| 13 | Geng Jie | Consultant of Alliance of Engineering Practice Innovation Project (EPIP) International Education, Director of Vocational Education Research Center of Tianjin Academy of Educational Science, China | Research on the Application and Popularization of Engineering Practice Innovation Project (EPIP) Teaching Mode |
| 14 | Gong Fanghong | President of Wuxi Institute of Technology, China | Technology-lead, Four-parts Collaboration, Serve the Construction of a Skilled Society |